lonely pl

Central America

Mexico's Yucatán & Chiapas p48

Belize p232

Guatemala p104

Honduras p357

El Salvador p292

Nicaragua p429

Costa Rica p514

Panama p623

Ashley Harrell, Isabel Albiston, Ray Bartlett, Celeste Brash, Paul Clammer, Steve Fallon, Bridget Gleeson, Paul Harding, John Hecht, Brian Kluepfel, Tom Masters, Carolyn McCarthy, Re

PLAN YOUR TRIP

ON THE ROAD

MARK READ/LONELY PLANET ©

PARQUE NACIONAL SOBERANÍA, PANAMA P645

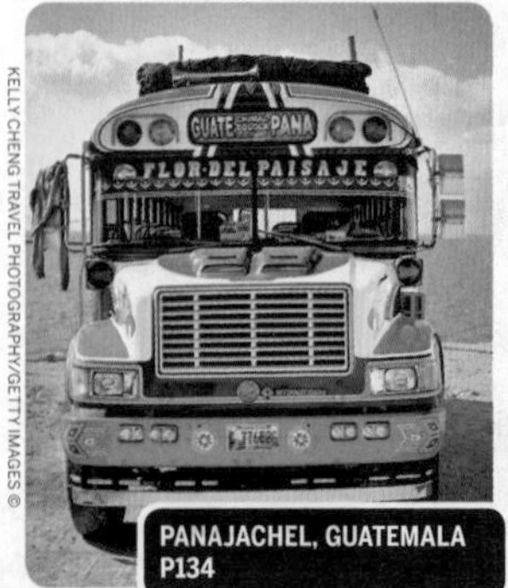

KELLY CHENG TRAVEL PHOTOGRAPHY/GETTY IMAGES ©

PANAJACHEL, GUATEMALA P134

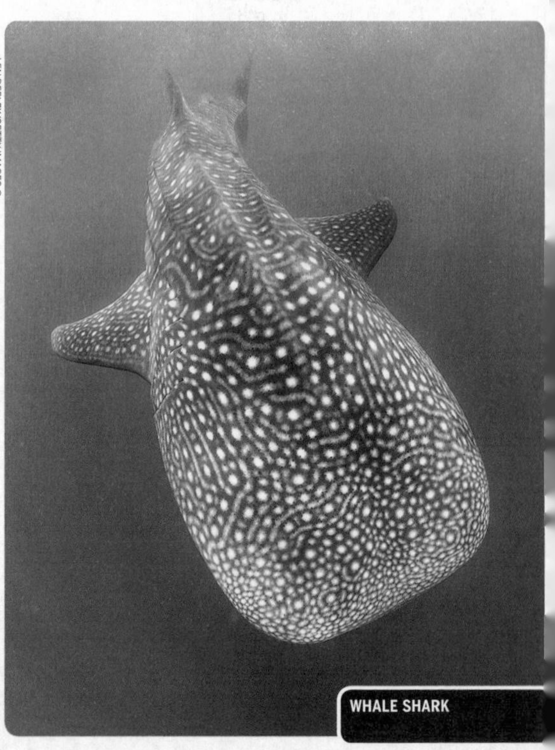

LEN DEELEY/GETTY IMAGES ©

WHALE SHARK

Contents

ON THE ROAD

MORGAN ARNOLD/GETTY IMAGES ©

NICARAGUA P429

RIDERFOOT/SHUTTERSTOCK ©

ISLA DE OMETEPE, NICARAGUA P455

Contents

Welcome to Central America

With cerulean seas and verdant forests, magnificent Maya ruins and smoking volcanoes, Central America is like a tropical fairy tale – except all of it is real.

Outdoor Adventures

Central America's seven countries plus Mexico's Yucatán and Chiapas states equal 300-plus volcanoes, two expansive coasts and one giant playground. Paddle deep into indigenous territories in a dugout canoe, or explore the remains of Spanish forts. Zip through rainforest canopies, swim alongside sea turtles or trek to cloud-forest vistas. Everywhere you go, you'll be accompanied by a wild cast of characters: a resplendent quetzal on the highland trail; a troop of swinging monkeys; and a breaching whale beside the ferry. Your adventures are limited only by your will.

Maya Ruins

The Maya civilizations sprawled from Mexico to Honduras, leaving behind ruins in five present-day countries where visitors can still step back into an ancient, mysterious past. Explore the lost temples of Tikal, soaring above the Guatemalan jungle canopy. Investigate otherworldly Palenque and Tulum, perched above the surf. See jaguars carved to life at Copán, and find out why Chichén Itzá is one of the new Seven Wonders of the World. Discover a culture that harks back 4000 years, and persists today.

Diverse Cultures

Central America may take up less space than Texas, but its rich mix of people has created a dynamic society. With more than 20 Maya languages, Guatemala is the region's indigenous heartland. The Spanish left their mark with colonial plazas and siestas. African culture permeates the Caribbean, from the Congo rebel traditions to lip-smacking *rondón* (spicy seafood gumbo). And the last century brought the rest of the world – Asians, Europeans, North Americans – along with Panama City's transformation into a contemporary capital.

Sun & Sea

With chilled-out Caribbean vibes on one side and monster Pacific swells on the other, Central America is perched between the best of both beach worlds. From deserted *playas* (beaches) to full-moon parties, this region can deliver any sun-soaked experience your inner beach bum desires. What's more, there's that magnificent, mysterious world that begins at the water's edge. Seize it by scuba diving with whale sharks in Honduras, snorkeling the world's second-largest coral reef in Belize, getting stoked on Costa Rica's world-class surf breaks, or setting sail among Panama's virgin isles. Hello, paradise.

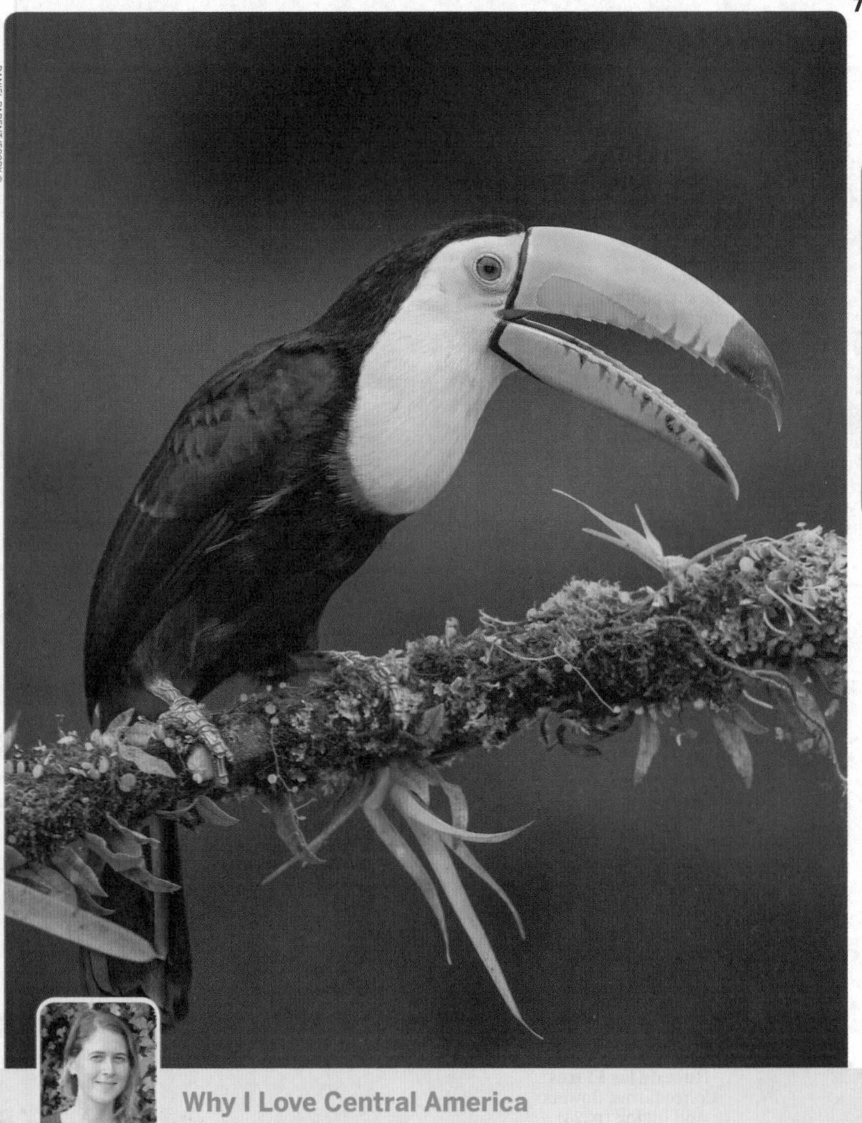

DANIEL PARENT/500PX ©

Why I Love Central America

By Ashley Harrell, Writer

When I was 12, my dad took me on a medical mission to Nicaragua, where I vividly remember diving into a murky swimming hole, devouring my first whole fried fish – eyeballs included – and drinking a Toña, my first beer (thanks Dad!). Twenty years and countless beers later, I wanted more of those raw, unpackaged travel experiences, so I moved to Central America and stayed three years. The highlights include sledding down an active volcano, dancing wildly to Garifuna drumming and diving with hammerhead sharks. Oh, and learning that you can even eat fried fishtail, which tastes like a potato chip.

For more about our writers, see p768

Above: Toucan, Costa Rica (p514)

Central America

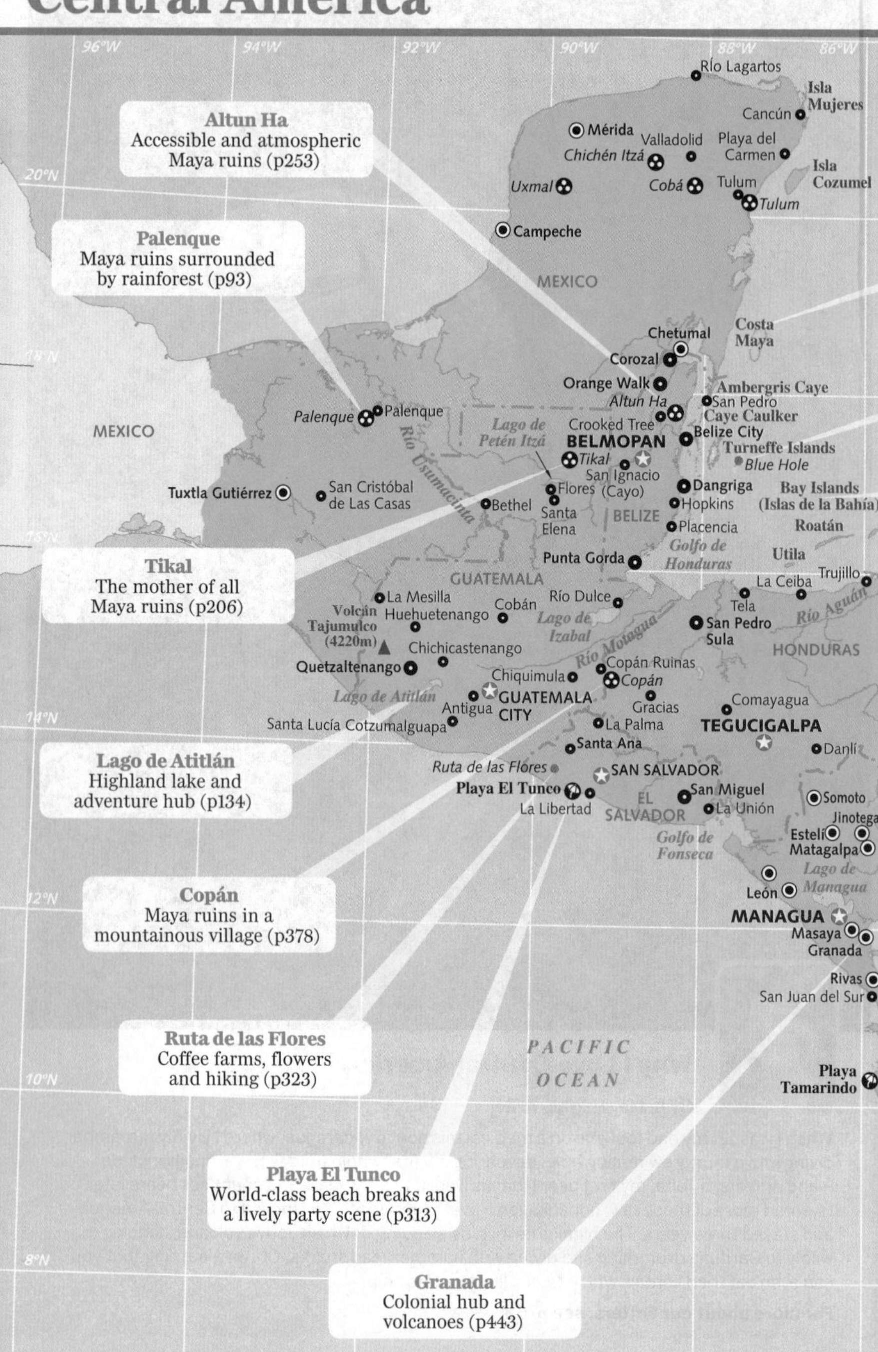

Altun Ha
Accessible and atmospheric Maya ruins (p253)
Palenque
Maya ruins surrounded by rainforest (p93)
Tikal
The mother of all Maya ruins (p206)
Lago de Atitlán
Highland lake and adventure hub (p134)
Copán
Maya ruins in a mountainous village (p378)
Ruta de las Flores
Coffee farms, flowers and hiking (p323)
Playa El Tunco
World-class beach breaks and a lively party scene (p313)
Granada
Colonial hub and volcanoes (p443)
96°W
94°W
92°W
90°W
88°W
86°W
20°N
18°N
16°N
14°N
12°N
10°N
8°N
Río Lagartos
Isla Mujeres
Cancún
Mérida
Valladolid
Playa del Carmen
Chichén Itzá
Isla Cozumel
Uxmal
Cobá
Tulum
Tulum
Campeche
MEXICO
Chetumal
Costa Maya
Corozal
Orange Walk
Ambergris Caye
Altun Ha
San Pedro
Caye Caulker
Palenque
Palenque
Lago de Petén Itzá
Crooked Tree
Belize City
MEXICO
Río Usumacinta
BELMOPAN
Turneffe Islands
Tikal
Blue Hole
San Ignacio (Cayo)
Tuxtla Gutiérrez
San Cristóbal de Las Casas
Flores
Dangriga
Bay Islands (Islas de la Bahía)
Bethel
Santa Elena
Hopkins
BELIZE
Placencia
Roatán
Golfo de Honduras
Punta Gorda
Utila
GUATEMALA
Trujillo
La Ceiba
La Mesilla
Río Dulce
Tela
Volcán Tajumulco (4220m)
Huehuetenango
Cobán
Lago de Izabal
San Pedro Sula
Río Aguán
Río Motagua
Chichicastenango
HONDURAS
Quetzaltenango
Copán Ruinas
Chiquimula
Copán
Lago de Atitlán
GUATEMALA CITY
Comayagua
Antigua
Gracias
Santa Lucía Cotzumalguapa
La Palma
TEGUCIGALPA
Santa Ana
Danlí
Ruta de las Flores
SAN SALVADOR
Playa El Tunco
San Miguel
Somoto
La Libertad
EL SALVADOR
La Unión
Jinotega
Estelí
Matagalpa
Golfo de Fonseca
Lago de Managua
León
MANAGUA
Masaya
Granada
Rivas
San Juan del Sur
PACIFIC OCEAN
Playa Tamarindo

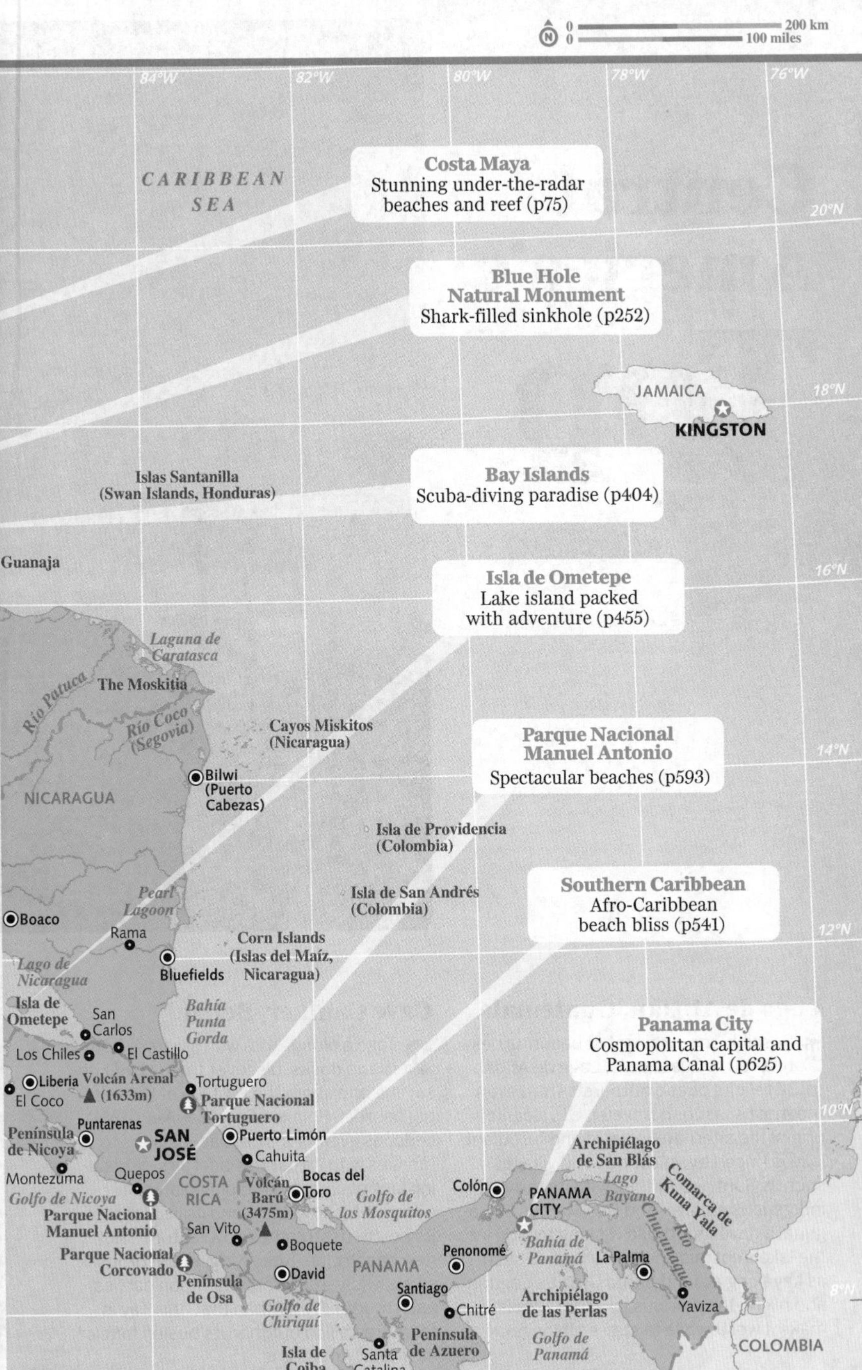

0 200 km
0 100 miles
CARIBBEAN SEA
Costa Maya
Stunning under-the-radar beaches and reef (p75)
Blue Hole Natural Monument
Shark-filled sinkhole (p252)
JAMAICA
KINGSTON
Islas Santanilla (Swan Islands, Honduras)
Bay Islands
Scuba-diving paradise (p404)
Guanaja
Isla de Ometepe
Lake island packed with adventure (p455)
Laguna de Caratasca
The Moskitia
Río Patuca
Río Coco (Segovia)
Cayos Miskitos (Nicaragua)
Parque Nacional Manuel Antonio
Spectacular beaches (p593)
Bilwi (Puerto Cabezas)
NICARAGUA
Isla de Providencia (Colombia)
Southern Caribbean
Afro-Caribbean beach bliss (p541)
Pearl Lagoon
Isla de San Andrés (Colombia)
Boaco
Rama
Bluefields
Corn Islands (Islas del Maíz, Nicaragua)
Lago de Nicaragua
Isla de Ometepe
San Carlos
Bahía Punta Gorda
Panama City
Cosmopolitan capital and Panama Canal (p625)
Los Chiles
El Castillo
Liberia
Volcán Arenal (1633m)
El Coco
Tortuguero
Parque Nacional Tortuguero
Península de Nicoya
Puntarenas
SAN JOSÉ
Puerto Limón
Cahuita
Archipiélago de San Blás
Montezuma
Quepos
COSTA RICA
Volcán Barú (3475m)
Bocas del Toro
Golfo de Nicoya
Parque Nacional Manuel Antonio
Golfo de los Mosquitos
Colón
PANAMA CITY
Lago Bayano
Comarca de Kuna Yala
Río Chucunaque
San Vito
Boquete
Bahía de Panamá
Parque Nacional Corcovado
Península de Osa
David
PANAMA
Penonomé
La Palma
Santiago
Chitré
Golfo de Chiriquí
Archipiélago de las Perlas
Yaviza
Isla de Coiba
Santa Catalina
Península de Azuero
Golfo de Panamá
COLOMBIA
84°W
82°W
80°W
78°W
76°W
20°N
18°N
16°N
14°N
12°N
10°N
8°N

Central America's Top 17

Lago de Atitlán, Guatemala

1 Possibly the single most beautiful destination in Guatemala, Lage de Atitlán (p134) elicits poetic outbursts from even the most seasoned traveler. Of volcanic origin, the alternately placid and turbulent lake is ringed by volcanoes and villages such as Santiago Atitlán, with its thriving indigenous culture, and San Marcos La Laguna, a haven for those wishing to plug into the lake's cosmic energy. Activities such as kayaking around Santa Cruz La Laguna and hiking the glorious lakeshore trails make it worthwhile to stay a bit longer.

Caye Caulker, Belize

2 Take a plunge into warm waters from island docks, discover the rush of kitesurfing or explore the big blue of Belize's barrier reef. Relaxed Caye Caulker (p241) seduces everyone from backpackers to families with its paradisiacal airs, refreshing lack of cars and heaping plates of coconut-fused kebabs and grilled lobster. Its northern stretches now feature a hot new beach club, Koko King, which drops some wildly exuberant full-moon parties each month. Other than that, this cay is far more chilled out than its busier, fancier neighbor, Ambergris.

1

CULTURA RM EXCLUSIVE/BEN PIPE PHOTOGRAPHY/GETTY IMAGES ©

2

SIMON VELAZQUEZ/500PX ©

Bocas del Toro, Panama

3 No wonder this Caribbean island chain (p667) is Panama's number-one vacation spot. 'It's all good,' say the relaxed locals. Pedal to the beach on a cruiser bike, hum to improvised calypso on Isla Bastimentos and laze over dinner in a thatched hut on the waterfront. Accommodation options include cheap digs, stunning jungle lodges and luxury resorts on outer islands. Surfers hit the breaks, but there's also snorkeling among dazzling corals and oversized starfish, or volunteering opportunities to help nesting sea turtles.

Bay Islands, Honduras

4 Imagine living the Caribbean dream – swimming in balmy, turquoise waters off a white-sand beach, then sipping a sundowner – but on a backpacking budget. Well, Honduras' Bay Islands (p404) offer that opportunity. Blessed with a fascinating British and buccaneering heritage, today these islands are renowned for their fabled coral reefs and terrific scuba diving. Search for the world's biggest fish, the whale shark, off the island of Utila, or explore shipwrecks in Roatán. Then feast on surf-fresh seafood and investigate the islands' surprisingly lively bar scenes. Scuba diving, Roatán (p404)

3

DAMSEA/SHUTTERSTOCK ©

4

J.T. LEWIS/500PX ©

CALAVERAPHOTOGRAPHY/500PX ©

MAREK KUBINEK/500PX ©

ADRIANNA WILLIAMS/GETTY IMAGES ©

Copán, Honduras

5 There may be hundreds of Maya sites dotted around Central America, but few can rival the beauty of Copán. Its location in an idyllic river valley, home to scarlet macaws and other birdlife and surrounded by pine-forested hills, is simply sublime. The site itself (p384) is also very special, with a towering hieroglyphic stairway and a great plaza dotted with imposing, fabulously carved stelae (standing stone monuments) and altars. When you've had your fill of exploring Maya temples, you'll find the charming little neighboring town of Copán Ruinas (p378) a delightful base.

Detail, Gran Plaza (p386)

Granada, Nicaragua

6 Granada (p443) is a town of immense and palpable magnetism. At the heart of the city's charms are the picture-perfect cobblestone streets, polychromatic colonial homes (pictured) and churches, and a lilting air that brings the city's spirited past into present-day focus. Most trips here begin and end on foot; simply dawdling from gallery to restaurant to colonial church can take up the better part of a day. Nearby, myriad wild areas, islands, volcanoes and artisan villages await further exploration of their treasures.

Costa Maya, Mexico

7 Do yourself a favor and get to this region while the going's still good. Unlike in overdeveloped Cancún and Riviera Maya, you can still find quiet fishing villages on the Costa Maya that put a premium on sustainable development, such as charming Mahahual (p75). This is the place to slow down, lounge on luxurious powder-sand beaches (pictured), kayak in the crystal-clear Laguna Bacalar and feast on the freshest of seafood. Offshore, divers and snorkelers can explore Banco Chinchorro – the largest coral atoll in the northern hemisphere.

PHILIP LEE HARVEY/LONELY PLANET ©

JUSTIN FOULKES/LONELY PLANET ©

MAISANT LUDOVIC / HEMIS.FR ©

Isla de Ometepe, Nicaragua

8 This laid-back island (p455), Lago de Nicaragua's beloved centerpiece, is home to archaeological remains, waterfalls, monkeys and birdlife, as well as lapping waves. Activity-seekers can take to the twin volcanoes, zip lines and lush hillsides cut by walking tracks, or kayak, bike and climb their way through this lost paradise. At the heart of the island's charms are the cool hostels, camping areas and peaced-out traveler scenes. Customize your experience, from high-end luxury lodges to groovy-groupie hippie huts: Ometepe is big enough for all kinds. Ojo de Agua (p459)

Tikal, Guatemala

9 The remarkably restored temples (p206) that stand in this partially cleared corner of the jungle still astonish, with both their monumental size and architectural brilliance, as an early-morning arrival at the Gran Plaza proves. It's a testament to the cultural and artistic heights scaled by this jungle civilization, which thrived for some 16 centuries. A highlight is the sky-high vantage provided by towering Temple IV, on the west edge of the precinct. Equally compelling is the abundance of wildlife, which you'll see while strolling ancient causeways between ceremonial centers. Templo I, Gran Plaza (p207)

Panama City, Panama

10 Panama City (p625) is high-octane Latin America: think crowds, casinos and a stacked skyline of shimmering glass and steel towers that calls Miami to mind. This city of nearly a million people both sits within striking distance of one of the world's great marvels of engineering, the Panama Canal, and features the atmospheric colonial architecture of Casco Viejo and the romantic ruins of Panamá Viejo. It's incongruous, yet appealing – and undeniably authentic. Oh, and the lush rainforest and sandy beaches are just a short day trip away.

Playa El Tunco, El Salvador

11 Playa El Tunco (p313) is the most famous beach in El Salvador. Known for its throbbing weekend party scene, world-class beach breaks and relatively large international crowd, El Tunco delivers in black-sandy spades. But if you'd rather chill out than party down, many surrounding beach hamlets are far less hectic. At the western reaches, Barrio de Santiago is wild and windswept and sea turtles hatch along its shores. Plug further east and find blissful beaches you can have all to yourself.

Palenque, Mexico

12 Get ready for these impressive ruins (p93), some of the Maya world's finest. Here pyramids rise above jungle treetops and howler monkeys sound off like monsters in the dense canopy. Wander the maze-like Palacio, gazing up at its unique and iconic tower. Scale the stone staircase of the Templo de las Inscripciones, the lavish mausoleum of Pakal (Palenque's mightiest ruler), and survey the sprawling ruins from atop. Then head downhill, following the Otulum River and its pretty waterfalls, and finish by visiting Palenque's excellent museum.

JOHN COLETTI/GETTY IMAGES ©

BOHEMIA8/GETTY IMAGES ©

Blue Hole Natural Monument, Belize

13 The famed Blue Hole Natural Monument (pictured; p252) is a brilliant sinkhole that divers can't help but plunge into. The sheer walls of the hole drop more than 400ft into the ocean, and although it is half filled with silt, the depth still creates a perfect circle of startling azure that is visible from above. The wall of the Blue Hole is decorated with a dense forest of stalactites from times past, and a school of reef sharks sometimes keeps divers company as they descend into the mysterious ocean depths.

Ruta de las Flores, El Salvador

14 Driving through coffee plantations and mountain villages may seem like a sedate affair, but don't be fooled. Traversing the volcanic Apeneca Range, the Flower Route (p323) is packed with waterfalls, food fairs and hiking trails. At the northern end of the 60km highway ascent is Tacuba, a gateway town to the spectacular Parque Nacional El Imposible on the Guatemalan border. Near the southern tip is Lago de Coatepeque, a pristine volcanic lake where the ancients used to swim, and Volcán Santa Ana, which makes for a great day hike (pictured).

13

MATTEO COLOMBO/GETTY IMAGES ©

14

HUGO BRIZARD - YOUGOPHOTO/SHUTTERSTOCK ©

FRANCIS WONG/500PX ©

SIMONDANNHAUER/GETTY IMAGES ©

DAINEKO NATALIA/SHUTTERSTOCK ©

Parque Nacional Manuel Antonio, Costa Rica

15 It's easy to understand why Parque Nacional Manuel Antonio (p593) is Costa Rica's most popular national park: this gem is blessed with stunning beaches, accessible trails and bountiful wildlife. A perfect day here entails a leisurely morning of navigating the trails and scanning the canopy for wildlife (such as iguanas, pictured), and an even more leisurely afternoon of picnicking under swaying beach palms and swimming in the turquoise Pacific. At day's end, dinner is served at a cliffside restaurant as the sun sets the horizon ablaze. *Pura vida*, indeed.

Southern Caribbean, Costa Rica

16 By day, lounge in a hammock, cruise by bike to snorkel off uncrowded beaches, hike to waterfall-fed pools and visit the remote indigenous territories of the Bribrí and Kéköldi. By night, dip into zesty Caribbean cooking and sway to reggaetón at open-air bars cooled by ocean breezes. The villages of Cahuita, Puerto Viejo de Talamanca and Manzanillo, all outposts of this unique mix of Afro-Caribbean, Tico and indigenous culture, are perfect bases for adventures on the Caribbean's southern coast (p541). Playa Cocles (p549)

Altun Ha, Belize

17 Though not the largest Maya site in Belize, Altun Ha (p253) is definitely the country's best known. An easy trip from Belize City, the 607-hectare site contains a central ceremonial precinct of two plazas surrounded by two temples, including the Temple of the Green Tomb and the Temple of the Masonry Altars (pictured, and it's the one you'll recognize from both the Belikin Beer label and Belizean banknote). After a day of exploring, have your weary muscles pampered at the Belize Boutique Resort & Spa, 24km north of the site.

Need to Know

For more information, see Survival Guide (p729)

Languages

Spanish, English

Visas

Generally not required for under 90 days. Belize issues 30-day visas. The Centro America 4 (CA-4) (p738) agreement allows 90 days in Guatemala, Nicaragua, Honduras and El Salvador.

Money

ATMs are widespread, except for in remote areas. Credit cards are accepted by midrange and high-end hotels, restaurants and tour operators. Bargaining is OK for informal transactions.

Cell Phones

Cell phones are widely used. You can purchase a local cell phone in a kiosk for as little as US$20, or a prepaid SIM card for around US$5 (the cell phone you use it with must be GSM-compatible and SIM-unlocked).

Time

Central Standard Time (GMT/UTC minus six hours)

When to Go

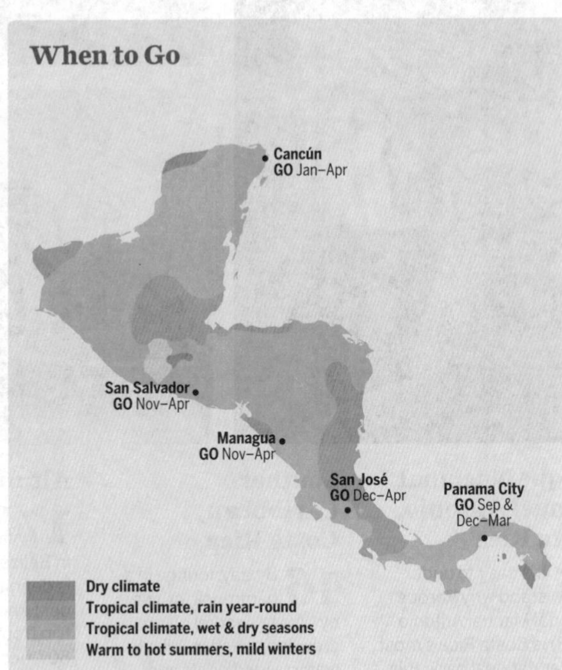

High Season (mid-Dec–mid-Apr)

- Dry season throughout most of the region.
- Higher demand for hotels; rates increase by 25% to 50%.
- Significantly more tourists in the most popular destinations.

High Season Peak (holidays)

- Includes Christmas, New Year and Easter week.
- Hotel rates may be up to double the normal rates.
- Resorts, festival towns and beaches are crowded with national vacationers.

Low Season (mid-Apr–early Dec)

- Rainy season in most of the region; hurricane season between June and November.
- Many destinations can still be enjoyed – check regional climates.
- Accommodations and resorts are better priced.

Useful Websites

Planeta (www.planeta.com) Regional articles, events, reference material and links, with an emphasis on sustainable travel.

The Tico Times (www.ticotimes.net) Based in Costa Rica, a long-standing online newspaper covering Central America news and culture.

Lonely Planet (www.lonelyplanet.com/central-america) Destination information, hotel bookings, traveler forum and more.

Tourist Information

Travelers will find a tourist office in the capital city of each country; some countries have them in outlying towns as well. If you're a student, look for student travel agencies in the capital cities of Costa Rica and Panama and in Cancún, Mexico.

Check www.visitcentroamerica.com, which has standard tourist-board coverage of all countries.

Responsible Travel

Go overland Take buses, not planes.

Give right Handouts to kids encourage begging; give directly to schools or clinics.

Buy local Eat and stay at family-owned places and use community-owned services.

Volunteer Make a difference by preserving turtle-nesting sights, teaching English or working with reputable nonprofits.

Reduce waste Bring or buy a refillable water bottle.

Respect local traditions Dress appropriately when visiting local churches or traditional communities.

Daily Costs

Budget: Less than US$50

- Dorm bed: from US$10–15
- Set meals or street food: US$4–8
- Public transport: US$5–15

Midrange: US$50–180

- Double room in a midrange hotel: from US$30–60
- Restaurant meals: US$8–20
- Park fees or surf lessons: US$8–25

Top End: More than US$180

- Double room in a high-end hotel, resort or lodge: from US$60–140
- Guided hikes and tours: US$30–60

Arriving in Central America

Cancún International Airport (Mexico; p102) Airport shuttles cost around M$160 per person; taxis cost up to M$500.

Aeropuerto Internacional La Aurora (Guatemala City; p117) Authorized taxis wait out the front of departures.

Philip Goldson International Airport (Belize City; p240) Taxis into town start at BZ$50.

Monseñor Óscar Arnulfo Romero International Airport (San Salvador, El Salvador; p308) Buses run to the city center every hour. Taxis cost about US$30 to US$35 (45 minutes).

Toncontín International Airport (Tegucigalpa, Honduras; p367) Arrange for a transfer (L200 to L300).

Managua International Airport (Nicaragua; p440) Official taxis inside the airport charge around US$20 to US$25.

Aeropuerto Internacional Juan Santamaría (San José, Costa Rica; p529) Buses (about US$1.50) run to central San José. Taxis charge from US$30.

Tocumen International Airport (Panama City; p640) Catch taxis (from US$30) at the transport desk near baggage claim.

Getting Around

Buses are the cheapest and most accessible way to get around, particularly along the Pan-American Hwy (also called the Panamericana or Interamericana), which runs through all the countries except Belize.

Air Because of the region's skinny stature, a flight can save several hours of backtracking. Each country has at least one international airport, as well as regional and charter flights via national airlines.

Boat Various types of boat serve islands and some borders.

Bus The main form of regional transport, from comfortable, air-conditioned, long-haul buses to run-down former school buses.

Car & Motorcycle Rentals are usually not allowed to cross international borders.

Train Limited to the Panama City–Colón route in Panama, and a basic commuter service in Costa Rica's Central Valley.

For much more on **getting around**, see p742

First Time Central America

For more information, see Survival Guide (p729)

Checklist

➡ Make sure your passport is valid for at least six months past your arrival date.

➡ Check the visa situation and government travel advisories.

➡ Organize travel insurance.

➡ Check flight restrictions on luggage and camping or outdoors equipment.

➡ Check your immunization history.

➡ Contact your credit card company to see if your card includes car rental insurance.

What to Pack

➡ Phrasebook

➡ Flip-flops or sandals

➡ Hiking shoes

➡ Poncho or rain jacket

➡ Binoculars

➡ Bug repellent with DEET

➡ Refillable water bottle

➡ Driver's license (if you plan to rent a car)

➡ Field guide of local fauna and/or flora

➡ Batteries and chargers

➡ Flashlight or headlamp

Top Tips for Your Trip

➡ Learn as much Spanish as you can – even just basic phrases. It can't hurt, and it might very well help you bond with the locals.

➡ Pack half the clothes that you think you'll need: laundry service is cheap in the region.

➡ Visit local *mercados* (markets) – not just to eat fresh food cheaply, but also to sample a lively slice of local life.

➡ Be aware that Belize, Costa Rica and Mexico are more expensive than other countries. The cheapest are Guatemala, Honduras, El Salvador and Nicaragua.

➡ Relax and bring a good book everywhere; Central Americans are rarely in a hurry and it helps to go with the flow.

What to Wear

Locals rarely wear shorts when they're not at the beach. Bring lightweight pants or skirts and short sleeve tops. Dining and nightlife can be formal in bigger cities. Bring dress shoes (or sandals for women), and pants and a dress shirt for men or a skirt or dress for women. A fleece and lightweight shell are necessary for the highlands.

Sleeping

Booking ahead is rarely necessary except in peak seasons.

Hotels Come in every stripe; save money with private doubles in hostels.

Camping Campgrounds are uncommon, but do exist in national parks and reserves (particularly in Costa Rica).

Guesthouses/B&Bs A good midrange option; usually family-run and small.

Hostels Not just for the young, hostels range from quiet digs to party central.

Lodges Ranging from rustic to high-end; good places to commune with nature.

Homestays Private quarters in a home, with shared bathrooms and meals.

Safe Travel

- Parts of Honduras, El Salvador and Guatemala are plagued by high crime rates and gang activity. Visitors are rarely affected, but some have been victims of grab-and-run theft, assault, rape, carjacking and murder.
- Capital cities tend to have the highest rates of crime.
- Many sexual assaults occur on isolated beaches.
- Avoid night buses (with the possible exception of Mexico and Panama), as highway robberies often happen at night.
- Avoid drug use entirely.
- Seek out updates from other travelers, tourist offices, police, guesthouse owners and Lonely Planet's Thorn Tree (www.lonelyplanet.com/thorntree).

Bargaining

It's OK to bargain in markets and at street stalls, but educate yourself first by asking around to get an idea of the pricing of different items and the specific factors that contribute to the quality of what you're bargaining for.

Tipping

Restaurants Tip 10% (but check first to see if it's included in the bill).

Taxis Tipping is optional but you can round up to leave extra, especially at night.

Guides Tip US$1 to US$2 per person for day tours, with more substantial tips for specialized guides.

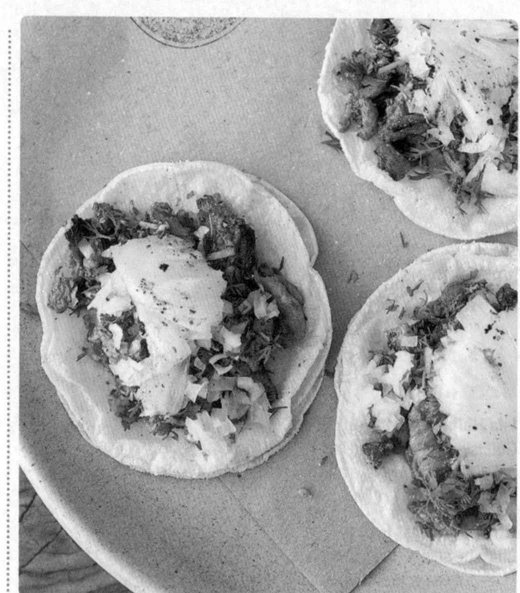

Pork tacos, Mexico

Etiquette

Asking for help Say *disculpe* to get someone's attention; *perdón* to apologize.

Personal space Be aware that Central Americans often have fewer boundaries about personal space than is customary in Western countries.

Indigenous communities Ask permission to take photos and dress modestly. Bargain for crafts, but not for lodgings or food.

Eating

Central America is not a culinary destination, with beans and rice tending to dominate the plate. But an amalgam of cultures, fertile soils, varied climates and expansive shorelines have resulted in some seriously delicious dishes. The Caribbean side of the isthmus tends to work with more spice and coconut milk, with excellent results, but those looking for a true foodie's paradise should make for Mexico.

Language

Beyond English-speaking Belize, Spanish is the primary language of Central America. Knowing some very basic Spanish phrases is not only courteous but also essential. Parts of the Caribbean coast speak English.

If you visit indigenous communities, pick up a few words in the local language beforehand – it's the best way to warm relations.

If You Like...

Snorkeling

Isla Holbox, Mexico An offbeat Gulf island surrounded by sea turtles, manta rays and barracuda. (p61)

Utila, Honduras For the ultimate snorkeling experience seek out the gargantuan whale shark in the big blue. (p410)

Belize Mile upon mile of the Western hemisphere's finest reef makes Belize a snorkeling paradise. (p232)

Parque Nacional Coiba, Panama It's not easy to get here, but this marine park offers pristine conditions. (p654)

Hiking

Volcán Mombacho, Nicaragua Accessible cloud forest with great hiking and even better birdwatching. (p448)

Parque Internacional La Amistad, Panama True wilderness hiking, accessible via the highlands or Caribbean coast. (p667)

Parque Nacional Cusuco, Honduras Dramatic and mountainous: trails are laced with giant ferns, dwarf forest and hidden quetzals. (p376)

Parque Nacional Chirripó, Costa Rica Climbing to the top of Cerro Chirripó is a thrilling, chilling adventure. (p605)

Volcán Tajumulco, Guatemala Central America's highest point is a relatively easy climb (especially if you camp overnight). (p156)

Wildlife Watching

Peninsula de Osa, Costa Rica Monkeys and macaws, sloths and snakes – wildlife is prolific around the Osa. (p607)

Isla Bastimentos, Panama From July to August, loggerhead, hawksbill, green and leatherback turtles hatch on the north shore. (p676)

The Moskitia, Honduras Wetlands, savanna and tropical forest – the best place for searching for jaguar and tapir. (p414)

Monterrico, Guatemala Save a turtle, spot a whale or go birdwatching from this Pacific village. (p174)

Parque Nacional Tortuguero, Costa Rica On late-night tours, watch turtles lay eggs in the sands of this wildlife-rich park. (p541)

Scuba Diving

Roatán, Honduras Outstanding wall dives at the Cayman trench edge feature corals and prolific sea life. (p404)

The Blue Hole, Belize This deep blue sinkhole has you swimming under stalactites with bull sharks and hammerheads. (p252)

Isla Cozumel, Mexico The famed reefs, particularly Palancar Shallows and El Cielo, beckon diving aficionados. (p67)

Isla del Caño, Costa Rica Sea turtles and humpback whales make this a popular destination for dive trips. (p604)

Corn Islands, Nicaragua Excellent cave and reef dives in crystal-clear Caribbean waters. (p493)

Parque Dos Ojos, Mexico One of the best cenotes around Tulum for underwater exploration. (p70)

Off the Beaten Track

Pearl Keys, Nicaragua Live out your shipwreck fantasies beneath coconut palms on these tiny, idyllic Caribbean islands. (p492)

Bahía de Jiquilisco, El Salvador Pounding surf, lush mangroves, fishing villages and an unspoiled biosphere offer *Survivor*-style wonder. (p333)

The Darién, Panama Steeped in indigenous culture and exotic wildlife, this remote province is wild and pristine. (p688)

DANNYBREG/GETTY IMAGES ©

SHELLYGRAPHY/SHUTTERSTOCK ©

Top: Resplendent quetzal (p41)

Bottom: Yoga practice, Costa Rica (p514)

La Campa, Honduras A lovely heartland *pueblo* (village); zip-line over canyons, find authentic ceramics and hike the highlands. (p390)

Crooked Tree Wildlife Sanctuary, Belize A real gem for nature lovers and seekers of a peaceful rural community in a beautiful setting. (p256)

Calakmul, Mexico Remote Maya ruins are surrounded by lush rainforest in Campeche. (p86)

Colonial Cities

Antigua, Guatemala A riot of cobblestone streetscapes, crumbling ruins and noble churches. (p120)

Granada, Nicaragua This wonderfully preserved colonial showpiece lays on the charm from the moment you arrive. (p443)

Suchitoto, El Salvador A picture-book, historic town littered with art galleries. Festivals reign most weekends. (p341)

Casco Viejo, Panama City Great for night owls: underground bars, brew pubs, wine bars and live-music venues. (p625)

Comayagua, Honduras Relaxed and prosperous, with a historic core of elegant churches and buildings. (p369)

Surfing

Dominical, Costa Rica Bring your board: you may never want to leave this easygoing hippie haunt. (p596)

Santa Catalina, Panama No souvenir shops in this dusty village – it's all about world-class waves. (p655)

Pavones, Costa Rica Surfers flock here to catch one of the longest left breaks on Earth. (p609)

Las Flores, El Salvador Tucked into the untrodden east and as good as anywhere in Latin America. (p337)

Puerto Viejo, Costa Rica Ride the legendary Salsa Brava wave; in December it gets up to 7m. (p549)

Punta Mango, El Salvador Access the famed break by boat from Las Flores or El Cuco. (p337)

Playa Maderas, Nicaragua This prime surf hangout offers one of the country's best beach breaks. (p463)

Ruins

Tikal, Guatemala This regional superstar is totally worth a visit for its soaring, jungle-shrouded temples. (p206)

Chichén Itzá, Mexico The massive El Castilo pyramid will wow you, especially during equinox. (p77)

Copán, Honduras An exquisite temple acropolis with some of the most intricate Maya carvings anywhere. (p378)

Tulum, Mexico Maya ruins perched atop a cliff offer jaw-dropping views of the Caribbean down below. (p69)

Tazumal, El Salvador The country's most impressive Maya ruins were once the site of human sacrifices. (p320)

Altun Ha, Belize The Maya ruins that inspired Belikin Beer labels and the nation's banknotes. (p253)

Palenque, Mexico Surrounded by lush jungle, these ruins are among Mexico's most impressive. (p93)

Volcanoes

Volcán Masaya, Nicaragua Watching red lava bubble in the crater at night. (p451)

Volcán Barú, Panama Steep, foggy and muddy – but the top lets you view both oceans at once. (p664)

Parque Nacional Los Volcanes, El Salvador The land of volcanoes: Santa Ana is the largest; and conical-shaped Izalco the most dramatic. (p318)

Volcán Arenal, Costa Rica The fireworks show is no longer, but Arenal still boasts a gorgeous cone and myriad hot springs. (p554)

Beaches

Guna Yala, Panama Known for perfect – and plentiful – postage-stamp islets with turquoise waters. (p685)

Playa Norte, Mexico This gorgeous, swimmable, fine-sand jewel is sometimes called Mexico's most beautiful beach. (p57)

West Bay, Honduras A classic, white-sand Caribbean beach with the added bounty of a coral reef offshore. (p410)

Little Corn Island, Nicaragua Brilliant turquoise waters meet snow-white sand in secluded coves on this enchanted isle. (p495)

Placencia, Belize A popular and beautiful 16-mile (26km) stretch of Caribbean sand. (p277)

Playa El Tunco, El Salvador Chill out on black-sand beaches with pro surfers and local revelers. (p313)

Yoga

Science & Soul Wellness, Belize The only antigravity studio in the country, set in a soothing space run by real professionals. (p247)

Danyasa Yoga Arts School, Costa Rica Classes for all levels, including dance-yoga-flow hybrid styles and ecstatic moon dance. (p597)

RandOM Yoga, Belize Donation-based, open-air rooftop yoga with a fabulous teacher in Caye Caulker. (p241)

Lago de Atitlán, Guatemala A lovely setting in which to practice, and the Yoga Forest studio offers truly spectacular views. (p134)

Month by Month

TOP EVENTS

Carnaval, February or March

Semana Santa, March or April

Bolas de Fuego, August

Día de los Muertos, November

Garifuna Settlement Day, November

January

The dry season and tourist season are both at their peaks, with great kitesurfing and swimming available in warm Pacific waters. Quetzal-viewing season begins in Costa Rica's Monteverde (through July).

Sound Tulum, Mexico

A music festival drawing in top international artists in the underground electronic scene, held over two weeks at multiple venues in and around magical Tulum. (p70)

Panama Jazz Festival

The weeklong jazz festival is one of the biggest musical events in Panama, drawing top-caliber international musicians from jazz, blues, salsa and other genres. Held around Panama City; the open-air events are usually free. (p634)

February

It's prime time for surfing both on Pacific and Caribbean swells. Carnaval, a feature of all Central American countries, takes place in February or March.

Carnaval, Mexico

A big street bash preceding the 40-day penance of Lent, Carnaval is exuberantly cele-brated in Mérida, Campeche and Isla Cozumel with parades, music, dancing and lots o' fun.

Festival de Diablos y Congos, Panama

Held two weeks after Carnaval (either in February or March), this festival in Portobelo celebrates rebellious slave ancestors with spirited public dancing, cheeky role-playing and beautiful masks and costumes. (p682)

March

Easter celebrations may take place in March or April. Semana Santa (Holy Week) offers reenactments of the crucifixion and resurrection of Christ. On Good Friday, religious processions are held across Central America.

Envision, Costa Rica

Costa Rica's version of Burning Man festival, with four days of spoken word, music, yoga, performance art, permaculture and DJs in Uvita in early March (or late February). (p598)

Desfile de Bufos, Guatemala

Guatemala City university students take to the streets during the Parade of Fools (held on the Friday before Good Friday) to mock the government and make other political statements.

April

The tail end of the dry season. In the jungle lowlands of Guatemala, March and April are scorchers; it's the best time to see whale sharks off Honduras or Belize.

Día de Juan Santamaría, Costa Rica

April 11 commemorates Costa Rica's national hero, who died driving failed US conqueror William Walker out of Costa Rica in 1856. The weeklong national holiday features parades, parties and other celebrations, especially in Santamaría's hometown of Alajuela.

May

The rainy season is upon the isthmus. May begins a five- to six-month nesting season for both loggerhead and green sea turtles in the Caribbean.

Chocolate Festival, Belize

This festival in mid-May in the southernmost region of Belize brings together folks who grow chocolate, sell chocolate and just plain *love* chocolate. Also showcases the Toledo district's history and culture.

La Feria de San Isidro, Honduras

Honduras' largest fiesta takes place in the streets and clubs of La Ceiba, culminating in late May with hundreds of thousands of people attending parades. Costumed dancers and revelers fill the city to bursting.

June

June to November is hurricane season, though big weather events are sporadic and hard to predict. Forty days after Easter, Corpus Christi features colorful celebrations throughout the region in May or June.

Festival Corpus Christi, Panama

One of the most popular and elaborate of the region's Corpus Christi celebrations takes place in La Villa de Los Santos and lasts two weeks. Highlights include costume parades, fabulous drag queens and dancers in devil costumes.

Lobsterfest, Belize

A celebration (www.belize.com/lobsterfest-in-belize) of the world's favorite crustacean, along with libations galore. Takes place in San Pedro in mid-June, in Placencia in the last week of June, and then Caye Caulker in early July.

July

Though it's the middle of rainy season, the weather is relatively dry on the Caribbean side; Belize can be uncomfortably hot. It's off-peak for visitors and hotels offer better rates.

Rabin Ajau, Guatemala

Guatemala's most impressive indigenous festival, this folkloric gathering takes place in Cobán in late July or early August. (p177)

August

Breeding humpback whales can be observed in the Pacific. And though rainy season continues, in between showers there's still plenty of sunshine to be had.

Festival del Invierno, El Salvador

For the Winter Festival, hip, lefty students flood the small mountain town of Perquín and party like the war has just ended.

Costa Maya Festival, Belize

This massive festival (www.internationalcostamayafestival.com) may be held in San Pedro, Belize, but it draws participants from all over Central America. The streets come alive with music, parades, dancing and drinking. The bodybuilding contest is a bonus.

Bolas de Fuego, El Salvador

To commemorate an eruption of Volcán San Salvador that destroyed their original town, local scallywags paint their faces like devils and throw fireballs at each other – just a bit of (potentially harmful) fun. Held on August 31 in Nejapa.

September

Though it's peak hurricane season further north, rains let up around Panama City and Costa Rica's Caribbean side is less wet than the Pacific. Flooding in Honduras is possible through February.

September Celebrations, Belize

Two weeks of patriotic celebrations across Belize City include the Belize Carnaval, where Belizeans don colorful costumes and dance to Caribbean beats. The party begins on the country's National Day and culminates on Independence Day.

Costa Rican Independence

Action centers on a relay race that passes a 'Freedom Torch' from Guatemala to Costa Rica. The torch arrives at Cartago in the evening of September 14, when the nation breaks into the national anthem.

Festival de la Mejorana, Panama

Panama's largest folk festival, held in Guararé, showcases music and dance by the country's many indigenous and ethnic groups, along with visiting performers from around Latin America.

October

In most of the region, October 12 is Día de la Raza (Columbus Day) – a dubious legacy nonetheless celebrated by every high-school brass band. Loggerhead turtles nest on the Pacific coast from now through March.

Feria de Isla Tigre, Panama

Indigenous Guna people converge on Isla Tigre for three days of tireless traditional dancing. It's visually engaging and fully authentic. Held in mid-October, with a three-day fair featuring art shows and canoe races.

Noche de Agüizotes, Nicaragua

This spooky festival, held on the last Friday in October in Masaya, brings to life characters from horror stories of the colonial period with elaborate costumes. Keep an eye out for the headless priest.

November

Seasonal rains have tapered off in most of the region, except for Honduras' north coast, where flooding can occur through February. In Panama, the whole country celebrates multiple independence-related holidays.

Día de Todos los Santos, Guatemala

In Santiago Sacatepéquez and Sumpango, just outside Antigua, celebrations marking All Saints' Day include the flying of huge kites, while in the tiny highlands town of Todos Santos Cuchumatán, November 1 is celebrated with drunken horse races through town. (p169)

Día de los Muertos, Mexico

On November 1 and 2, families build altars in their homes and visit graveyards to commune with their beloved dead, taking garlands and gifts. Theme park Xcaret in the Riviera Maya arranges beautiful altars.

Garifuna Settlement Day, Belize

On November 19, this holiday celebrates the arrival of the first Garifuna people to Belize by boat. The best spots to partake in the three Ds – dancing, drinking and drumming – are Dangriga and Hopkins. (p273)

December

December and January are the coolest months on the Pacific coast, from Nicaragua to the jungle lowlands of Guatemala. The Christmas holidays disrupt the region's work schedule – cities empty out and beaches are full.

Las Fiestas de Zapote, Costa Rica

For one week, this celebration embraces all things Costa Rican – from rodeos to fried food, bullfights to carnival rides, and a whole lot of drinking. It takes place in Zapote, southeast of San José.

Itineraries

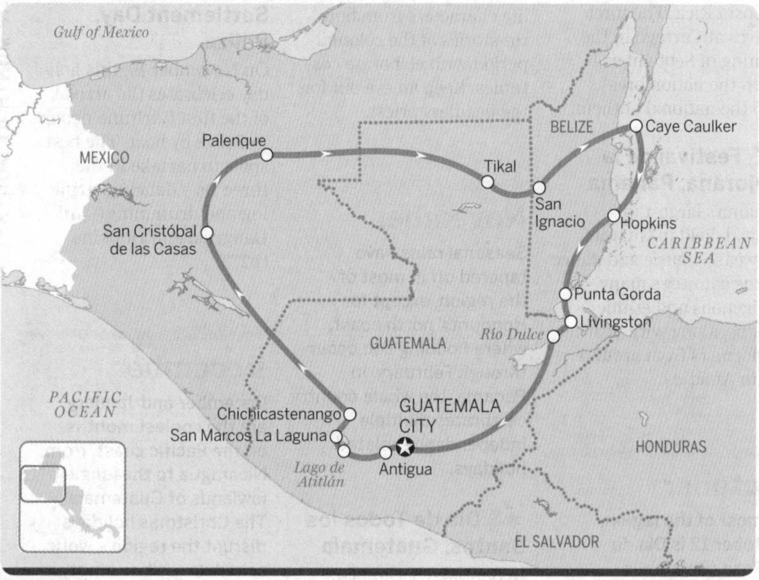

Northern Loop: Guatemala, Mexico & Belize

Rich in culture and coastline, this route loops through many of the region's northern highlights, including Maya ruins, reef snorkeling and jungle cruising.

From **Guatemala City**, head straight to colonial **Antigua**, fitting in a volcano climb and perhaps a crash course in Spanish. At **Lago de Atitlán** go for a few days of hiking and swimming in the new-age magnet **San Marcos La Laguna**. Then continue on to **Chichicastenango** to see the famous Maya market.

Venture north to Mexico on a Chiapas loop, exploring the colonial city of **San Cristóbal de las Casas** and nearby Maya villages, as well as the jungle-set Maya ruins at **Palenque**. Make your way back to Guatemala and **Tikal**, the mother of all Maya sites.

Bus east to Belize, stopping to go river tubing or caving outside hilly **San Ignacio**, before splashing into the Caribbean – and the barrier reef near either **Hopkins** or **Caye Caulker**. From **Punta Gorda**, catch a *lancha* (small motorboat) to **Lívingston**, starting point for a serious jungle river cruise to **Río Dulce**. From there, hop one of the frequent buses back to Guatemala City.

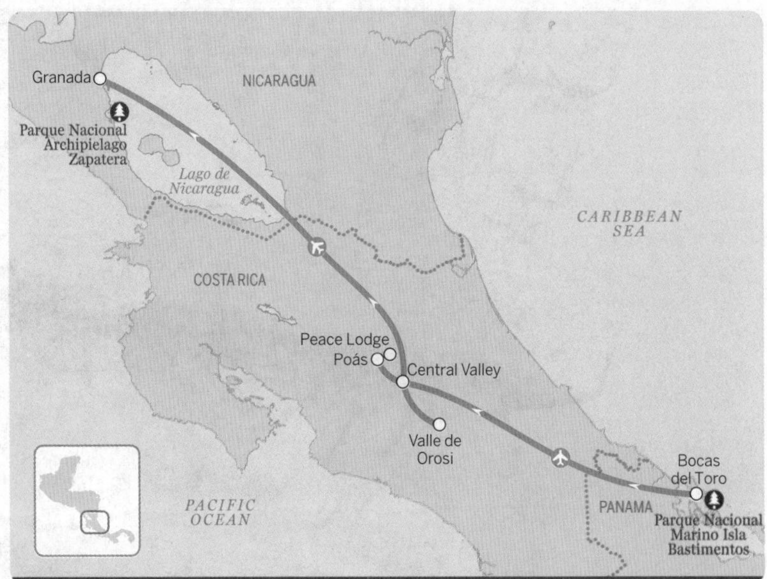

Southern Sampler: Sea, City & Countryside

Not everybody gets ample vacation time, and Central America is tough to squeeze into a week. But for those hungry for a three-in-one trip involving some beach bumming, countryside and a splash of colonial character, here's one way it can be done.

Touch down into Panama's top tourist draw, the **Bocas del Toro** archipelago, where you can shimmy through the emerald-green Caribbean, spying on sea life and communing with coral, and then stalk monkeys and sloths in Parque Nacional Marino Isla Bastimentos or chill on the vanilla sands of Red Frog Beach. In the evening, you'll devour fresh seafood by candlelight before sucking down potent cocktails and partying the night away in Bocas Town or on Isla Carenero. After a couple of days of snorkeling and island exploration, hop a plane to Costa Rica's lush and undulating **Central Valley**.

Forget the gritty capital and instead point those wheels for the verdant highlands that surround it, opting either for the storybook **Valle de Orosi** and its well-paved 32km loop through rolling hills, terraced coffee plantations and pastoral villages, or the strawberry-studded hills of **Poás** and its fussy, namesake volcano (best visited early in the morning). A stay at **Peace Lodge**, with its wonderful animal rescue project, will introduce you to the country's fauna and some epic waterfalls. Save time for relaxing in the cave-like showers (with a waterfall option!) and the bubbling hot tubs.

Another short plane ride away is Nicaragua's capital city (skip this too), which is just an hour from the colonial gem of **Granada**. Here you can stroll down postcard-perfect cobblestone streets lined with magnificent churches, or cruise around Lake Nicaragua's islets, which were formed thousands of years ago by the erupting Mombacho Volcano. You can also help support locals by visiting a nearby community-tourism project, or check out an impressive collection of petroglyphs and statues in Parque Nacional Archipiélago Zapatera.

Top: Detail, Tulum Ruins (p70), Mexico

Bottom: Reserva Biológica Bosque Nuboso Monteverde (p562), Costa Rica

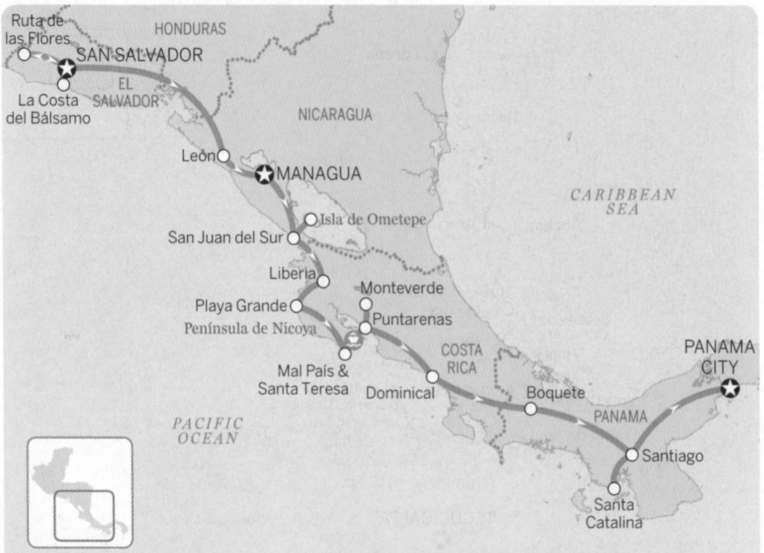

Pacific Coast: El Salvador to Panama

This sinuous coastline has something to suit everyone, from insatiable surfers to dedicated beach bums. Inland there are coffee farms, cloud forests and even more diverse landscapes. Let your spirit soar on this itinerary that takes in four countries, countless monster curls and infinite adventure. In El Salvador and Nicaragua, peak surf season is March to December, while further south it's February to March.

Arrive in San Salvador and beam to **La Costa del Bálsamo**, home to world-class surf breaks; Playas El Zonte and Sunzal offer reasonable seaside digs and lessons for budding boarders. Take a detour to the **Ruta de las Flores**, where you can hike to hidden waterfalls and discover the region's culinary delights.

Moving east, cross the border(s) to Nicaragua. Stop in offbeat **León** for a dose of art and eclecticism. From **Managua**, catch a shuttle to **San Juan del Sur**, a chilled-out town ringed by beaches with big waves. You're also within striking distance of **Isla de Ometepe**, an island packed with opportunities for adventure.

Continue south to **Liberia**, Costa Rica and veer west to hit some surf spots on the Península de Nicoya. **Playa Grande** is a long, pristine stretch of sand, where you can catch waves by day and spy on nesting turtles at night. Hardy souls should brave the bumpy ride to the southern tip of the peninsula, where **Mal País and Santa Teresa** offer some of the best breaks in the region. The gorgeous beach and easygoing vibe are beacons for surfers, yogis and free spirits of all types. Nearby Cabo Blanco was Costa Rica's first nationally protected nature reserve – it's still worth a day trip.

Take a shortcut to the mainland with a ferry to **Puntarenas**. Hardcore surfers should continue south to the waves of **Dominical**. Alternatively, an inland jaunt to **Monteverde** offers cooler temperatures, canopy tours and magical cloud forest. From there head east to Panama. If you missed Monteverde, take a detour to **Boquete**, another mountain town with cool air and strong coffee. Otherwise, make for **Santa Catalina** and its Hawaii-style waves. From **Santiago**, bus it to **Panama City** or David.

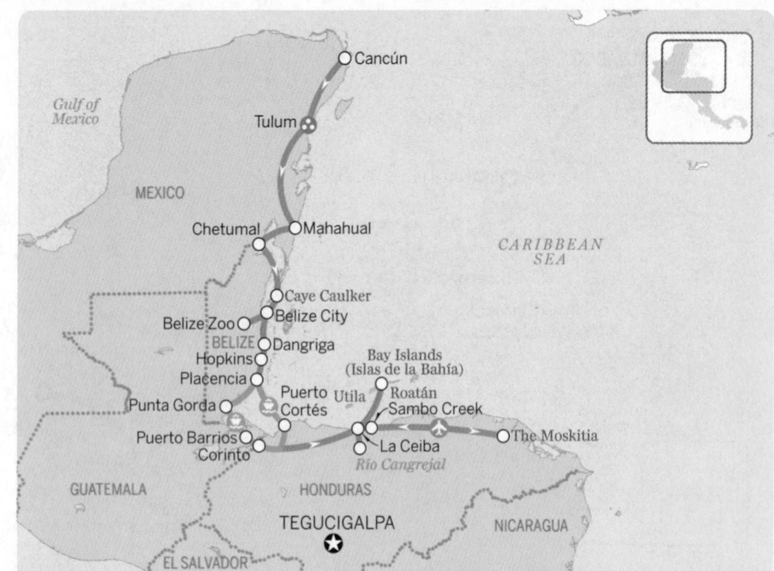

Caribbean Coast: Mexico to Nicaragua

Explore the 'other side' of Central America – where Spanish is heard less than English or Kriol, and Latin beats give way to reggae rhythms and Garifuna drumming. This east-coast route shows off the rich cultural blend and wild natural scenery that make the Caribbean unique.

Fly into **Cancún**, maybe hit up a salsa club, and start working your way south. Your first stop is **Tulum**, an impressive Maya ruin set on prime beachfront property. Next, head south to **Mahahual** to snorkel the largest coral atoll in the northern hemisphere.

From **Chetumal**, catch a boat to chilled-out, budget-friendly **Caye Caulker**, Belize for some days of sunning, swimming and snorkeling. Return to the mainland via **Belize City**, perhaps sneaking in a side-trip to the **Belize Zoo**. If you're up for some more island-hopping, catch the bus to **Dangriga**, from where you can get a boat to Tobacco Caye. Here you can snorkel right off the shore, and there are plenty of hammocks to go around afterward. **Hopkins** is also a laid-back Garifuna town with a beach, if you prefer to stay on the mainland.

You'll save yourself some time and hassle if you can catch the weekly boat from **Placencia** direct to **Puerto Cortés**, Honduras. Otherwise, continue south through Toledo to Punta Gorda to catch a more frequent boat to **Puerto Barrios**, Guatemala. Then take a minibus to the Honduras border at **Corinto**.

Buses run to **La Ceiba**, via San Pedro Sula. Along this coastline, there are countless attractions that are unique to this region, including river-rafting on the **Río Cangrejal** and visiting the Garifuna village of **Sambo Creek**. The **Bay Islands** are an absolute must for divers (or would-be divers).

And now, you have reached the final frontier: **The Moskitia**. This huge expanse of untamed wilderness is inhabited in only a few isolated places. If you're curious, consider signing up for a tour to the Moskitia (available in La Ceiba) – there are few roads there and plenty of crime.

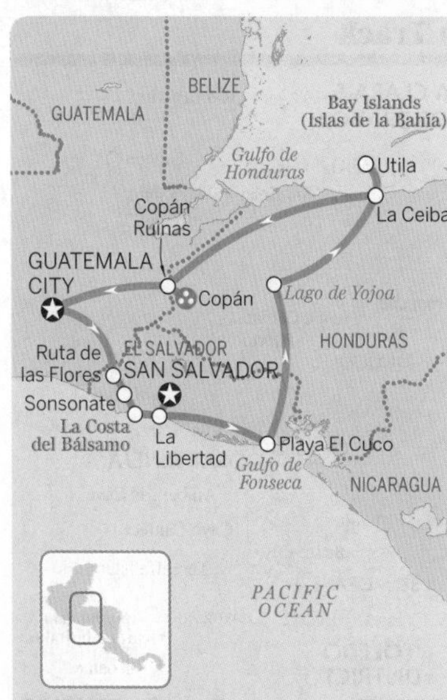

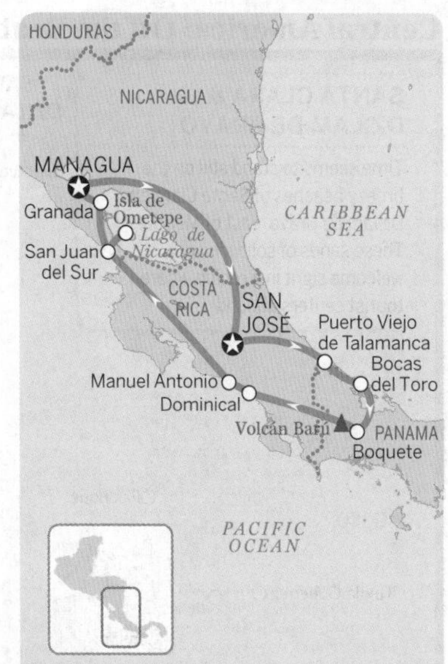

2 WEEKS The Center of Central America

This route explores the less-traveled, less-costly and lesser-known countries of Central America, taking in two coastlines and all the spectacular scenery in between.

From **Guatemala City**, journey east over the El Salvador border to Tacuba, start of the **Ruta de las Flores**, replete with hiking trails and food festivals. From **Sonsonate**, turn south toward **La Costa del Bálsamo** for a few days of riding waves and catching rays in **La Libertad**. Stop in **San Salvador** to sample the country's best nightlife, before heading east to **Playa El Cuco** for a quirky (and eco-conscious) stay at La Tortuga Verde.

Turn north and cross into Honduras, heading toward **Lago de Yojoa** to search for quetzals in the cloud forest. Continue north to **La Ceiba**, the jumping-off point for the region's star diving destination – the **Bay Islands**. **Utila** offers the chance to spot enormous whale sharks suspended in the big blue.

Head back to Guatemala, but not before a stop in the cobblestone town of **Copán Ruinas**, which offers river-tubing, mountain horseback rides and namesake ruins.

2 WEEKS Southern Loop

From volcano climbs to barefoot beach towns, southern Central America offers equal parts adventure and R&R. The green giant, Costa Rica, is flanked by two vibrant countries with colonial character and off-the-beaten-path allure.

Starting in **San José**, Costa Rica journey to hippie haven **Puerto Viejo de Talamanca** for good food, surf and rainforest rich in wildlife. Cross the Panamanian border and hop on a boat to the sugar-sand beaches of **Bocas del Toro**. From here turn south to **Boquete** and slog up **Volcán Barú** for 360-degree views.

Back in Costa Rica, stop off in free-wheeling **Dominical** for a surf and a yoga session, then cut over to the Pacific coast to explore the monkey-crowded trails and picture-perfect beaches in **Manuel Antonio**. Continue up the Interamericana and into Nicaragua. Test the surf and swing in a hammock in laid-back **San Juan del Sur**, then rest up for an adventure on **Isla de Ometepe**, a volcanic island in a sea-sized lake. Follow up with a trip to admire the colonial architecture in **Granada**, before heading on to **Managua** to grab a direct bus back to San José.

Central America: Off the Beaten Track

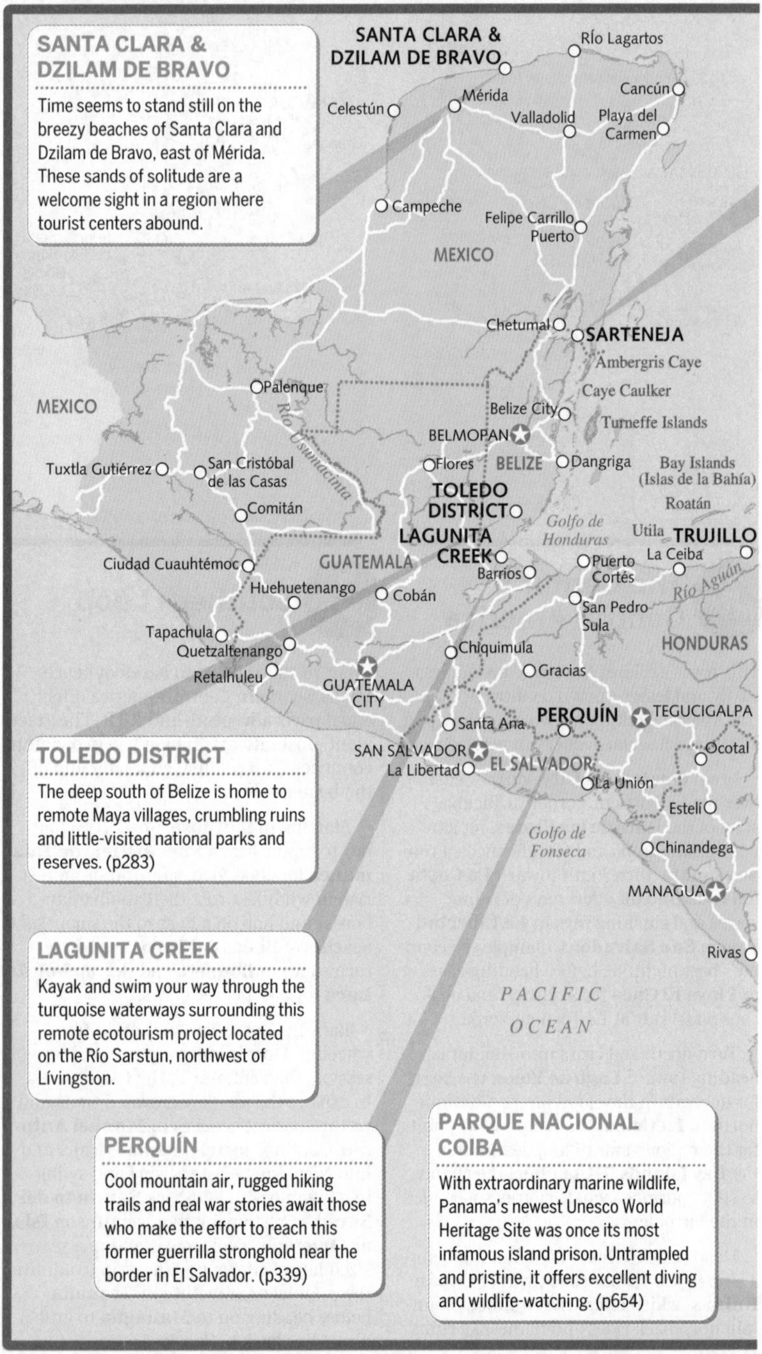

SANTA CLARA & DZILAM DE BRAVO

Time seems to stand still on the breezy beaches of Santa Clara and Dzilam de Bravo, east of Mérida. These sands of solitude are a welcome sight in a region where tourist centers abound.

TOLEDO DISTRICT

The deep south of Belize is home to remote Maya villages, crumbling ruins and little-visited national parks and reserves. (p283)

LAGUNITA CREEK

Kayak and swim your way through the turquoise waterways surrounding this remote ecotourism project located on the Río Sarstun, northwest of Lívingston.

PERQUÍN

Cool mountain air, rugged hiking trails and real war stories await those who make the effort to reach this former guerrilla stronghold near the border in El Salvador. (p339)

PARQUE NACIONAL COIBA

With extraordinary marine wildlife, Panama's newest Unesco World Heritage Site was once its most infamous island prison. Untrampled and pristine, it offers excellent diving and wildlife-watching. (p654)

SARTENEJA

Stroll the shoreline to admire the wooden sailboats still constructed here and explore the nearby Shipstern Nature Reserve, a hub of birding, fishing and wildlife-watching. (p259)

TRUJILLO

The best slice of Honduras' Caribbean coastline is a gorgeous place, with lots of history, a delightful end-of-the-road feel, and some of the mainland's best beaches nearby. (p402)

PEARL KEYS

Lush and mostly uninhabited, these coconut islands offer snorkeling in crystalline waters. It's a boat ride away from Bluefields and well worth the splurge. (p492)

CAÑO NEGRO

Not many travelers make it to the far reaches of Costa Rica's northern lowlands. This network of languid lagoons is a birding wonderland, home to some 365 species of birds. (p560)

SAMBÚ

This jungle hub makes a good base for Darién adventures. Guides take visitors up the Río Sambú and its tributaries to Emberá and Wounaan villages, or in search of harpy eagles and petroglyphs. (p694)

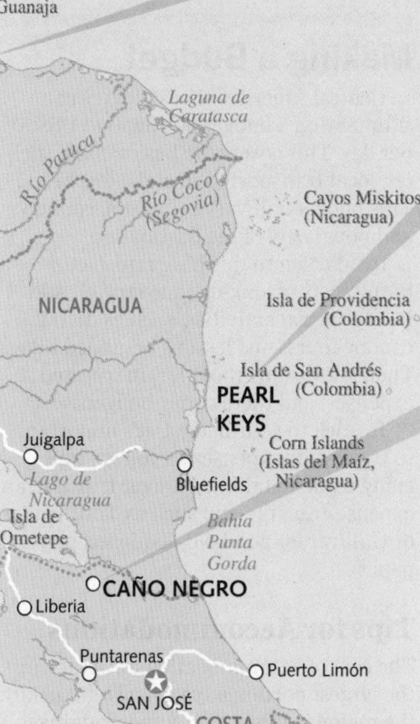

Plan Your Trip

Big Adventures, Small Budgets

The best things in life are free – certainly in Central America, where you don't pay a cent for sand, surf and sun, gorgeous scenery and prolific wildlife. Of course, you have to eat... But you can do a lot with a little if you plan wisely and watch your spending.

Sticking to Your Budget

- Consider traveling in low season.
- Opt for lower-budget destinations.
- Avoid package deals.
- Shop online for airfares.
- Stay in hostels or rooms with shared bathrooms.
- Travel by public transportation.
- Eat street food and cook where you can.
- Snorkel instead of dive.
- Get around by bicycle.
- Take self-guided hikes and tours.
- Consider WWOOF-ing, volunteer programs (p739) and Spanish programs that include a room.

Making a Budget

In Central America, shoestringers can skimp by on a budget of US$30 to US$50 per day. This covers the basics: food, shelter, local transportation and a few beers. This budget will vary by season, country and popularity of the destination.

In addition to this base rate, factor in the costs of long-distance travel. Add in any special activities, such as diving, canopy tours, surf lessons or guided hikes. Then allow some room for unexpected expenses, and there's your budget.

To stick to your budget, it's important to track your expenses as you go, especially if you're taking a longer trip. Use an expense-tracking app such as Trail Wallet or Gulliver (or good old-fashioned pen and paper).

Tips for Accommodations

The cost of accommodations will take up the largest portion of your budget. Luckily, the region is filled with simple lodgings that charge simple prices. The more creature comforts (air-con, hot water, private bathroom) you can forsake, the more money you'll save. Here are some tips for keeping this line item lean.

- The cheapest accommodations around are often in campgrounds. Of course, camping equipment requires an initial investment and a fair amount of lugging. But if you're prepared to do that, it's often free (or nearly free) to pitch a tent.

- Hostels are also great options for budget accommodations – and you don't have to bring your own bed. Many hostels offer communal kitchens and low-priced outings catering to their budget clientele..
- If you prefer a bit more privacy, most hostels and many guesthouses offer lower-priced private rooms with shared bathrooms.
- If the price is too high, ask if the hotel or guesthouse has anything cheaper. Independent businesses sometimes alter their prices.
- It is easier to negotiate rates in low season.
- Pay per day rather than all at once. This gives you the option of changing hotels if the conditions are unsuitable or if you change plans.

When to Go

Tourist Seasons

Generally speaking, the high tourist season in Central America goes from mid-December to mid-April, while the low tourist season goes from mid-April to mid-December. There are mini peak seasons (higher than high) around major holidays, including the last two weeks of December and the week before Easter.

High season means higher prices for accommodations and for some activities; peak season means *really* high – sometimes double. High season also brings more tourists.

Low season means that prices may be lower – sometimes 25% to 40% – and crowds are thinner. Traveling during low season is an excellent, easy way to make your money go further.

HOW MUCH DOES IT COST?

- Bottle of beer: US$2–5
- Domestic bus ticket: US$5–15
- Fixed-price meal: US$5–8
- Hostel bed: US$10–20
- Domestic flight: US$80–150
- National park admission: US$8–15
- Canopy tour: US$40–60
- Snorkel tour: US$35–55

Meteorological Seasons

Central America has two meteorological seasons: dry and rainy (or 'green,' as some marketers have tried to rebrand it).

Not surprisingly, the high tourist season corresponds roughly with the dry season, which is from January to March or April in most of the region. Likewise, the rainy season generally runs from May to December, with hurricane season making matters worse between June and November.

It should be noted that there are several places where it's pretty rainy all the time, namely the rainforest. This doesn't have to spoil your fun, and it doesn't usually rain all day every day, but travelers should be prepared for wet weather.

Where to Go

While Central America generally enjoys a lower cost of living than North America or Europe, there are discrepancies within the region: Belize, Costa Rica and Panama are significantly more expensive than the other countries here. Shoestring travelers will find that their money will last longest in Guatemala, Honduras and Nicaragua. Of course, these are more impoverished countries with less tourist infrastructure, so there's a trade-off.

Generally speaking, there's a sort of dual economy everywhere in Central America, where services catering to tourists are more expensive than those used by locals. Tourist towns are more expensive than towns that revolve around agriculture, industry or some other business. Fortunately, travelers are not restricted to upscale restaurants, private shuttles and guided tours (or tourist towns, for that matter). The more you can live like the locals (self-catering, local restaurants, public transportation etc), the more you will save. Knowing a bit of Spanish can go a long way toward getting good information in this regard.

Destination Tips

The following are the cheapest places to have the best time across Central America.

Mexico The Costa Maya (specifically Mahahual and Laguna Bacalar) offers affordable lodging and eats, as well as plenty of low-cost activities, such as swimming in cenotes, snorkeling at Banco Chinchorro and beach-bumming.

Guatemala San Pedro La Laguna is a perfect budget destination: cheap hotels, cheap food and cheap drinks, set against the impossibly pretty volcano-fringed Lago de Atitlán.

Belize The central cays are the best bet for budget travelers. Tobacco Caye is right on the reef, so if you bring your own gear you can snorkel for free just off the island. San Ignacio has the country's best offerings of budget accommodations (including camping).

El Salvador Pitch your tent in Parque Nacional El Imposible and spend your days hiking through the forests (for free). The eastern beaches of Las Flores, El Cuco and Esteron are less developed than those on La Costa Bálsamo, but better value, more beautiful and worth your time.

Honduras The whole country is a great bargain at the moment: the US dollar goes a long way and the trickle of visitors means that competition between agencies and hostels is fierce. Utila remains the biggest backpacker destination, beloved for its cheap diving. Lago de Yojoa has a brewery, a great hostel and all manner of affordable activities.

Nicaragua San Juan del Sur and the nearby beach towns are prime budget destinations. The outdoor attractions are free of course, and there are plenty of hostels, cheap places to eat, and services that cater to budget travelers. If you need a guide, they are also inexpensive (just be sure to tip).

Costa Rica The Caribbean coast is the most affordable part of the country. Puerto Viejo de Talamanca has some great budget lodging. It's free to go to the beach – and you can rent a bicycle to get there. You can also hike for free in the nearby Gandoca-Manzanillo National Wildlife Refuge.

Panama Bocas del Toro and (especially) Boquete offer some excellent budget accommodations – and there's plenty of adventure right on the doorstep.

Packing

Believe it or not, how you pack will have an impact on your budget. Or rather, your budget should decide how you pack.

If you're a shoestring traveler and you're on the move, you'll have to carry your bag everywhere. Make your life simpler by keeping things compact. A smaller bag will better fit into the limited storage area on buses and boats, as well as making it easier for you to climb on and off said buses and boats. Additionally, a smaller bag will make it easier to walk through villages in search of the best hostel. And – most importantly – you'll be less of a target for touts and troublemakers.

Also, it's cheap to do laundry in Central America. Bring less, wash more.

Gadgets

It's tempting to bring gadgets on your trip – phones, tablets, laptops, cameras – but there are several reasons to limit your electronics: first, they take up space; second, the risk of theft or damage is high. Central America is wet and muddy, bags get dropped and tossed, thieves and pickpockets want what you have, and it only takes a short rainstorm to short-circuit your device.

Here are some tips for traveling smartly with technology.

- Limit yourself to one or two versatile devices: a tablet with which you can read books and check emails or a smartphone that can do it all.
- Store your electronics in dry packs and separate the batteries in case of rain.
- Use a voltage converter, as some destinations have power surges that can fry sensitive equipment.
- USB roaming sticks, available through local cell-phone providers, enable near-universal internet access from your computer.
- Look into the international plans offered by your cell-phone provider to avoid expensive roaming charges.
- Get a travel insurance policy that covers theft of or damage to your equipment.

Plan Your Trip

Outdoor Activities

Offering two dramatic and diverse coastlines, Central America lures all types of water lovers with its Pacific swells and Caribbean reef. Meanwhile, the inland terrain is studded with mountains and volcanoes begging for exploration, the tropical rainforests are rich with birds and wildlife, and raging rivers crisscross the region. Adventure awaits!

Hiking

Central America's dense forests, steaming volcanoes and abundant wildlife make for great hiking. The terrain ranges from cloud forests and rainforests to tropical dry forest, including river trails and palm-lined beaches.

Most tourist-oriented parks and reserves offer ample trails that are well maintained and well marked, most of which do not require a guide. Longer-distance hikers can take their pick from several popular, multiday treks. If you really want to get off the beaten track, you can do that too (though you'll definitely want to hire a guide).

When to Go

In the rainforest (and the cloud forest, for that matter), hiking trails can be muddy. Throughout the region, trails are maintained to varying degrees. They may be reinforced with concrete blocks or wooden supports, but the mud prevails. Trails are obviously firmer and easier to navigate during the dry season, which is when travelers should plan their hiking trips (late December to April).

Best Footwear for Hiking

Some suggestions for sturdier tropical-hiking footwear to supplement the flip-flops:

Rubber boots

Pick these up at any hardware store (approximately US$10). They're indestructible, protect you from creepy-crawlies and can be hosed off at day's end. Downsides: they're not super-comfortable, and if they fill up with water or mud, your feet are wet for the rest of the day.

Sport sandals

Great for rafting and river crossings, though they offer minimal foot protection. Closed toes are recommended.

Waterproof hiking boots

If you are planning a serious trek in the mountains, it's best to invest in a pair of solid, waterproof hiking boots.

Where to Go

Guatemala The most popular hiking destinations are the volcanoes around Antigua (p120). The ultimate is the 60km hike into the Petén jungle to El Mirador (p215), a sprawling, largely unexcavated Maya city.

Belize The jungly terrain and low-lying mountains are studded with Maya ruins. The best places to hike include Cockscomb Basin Wildlife Sanctuary (p274) (aka the 'jaguar reserve') and Mountain Pine Ridge (p269).

El Salvador Explore the tropical mountain forests of Parque Nacional El Imposible (p329).

Honduras Spot a quetzal in the cloud forests around Lago de Yojoa (p373) or near the peak of Montaña de Santa Bárbara (p374).

Nicaragua Hike to prehistoric petroglyphs on Nicaragua's Isla de Ometepe (p455), or climb a volcano, such as Volcán Mombacho (p448) or the volcanoes near León (p467).

Costa Rica Hike to waterfalls near Arenal (p554), and lose yourself in the clouds at Monteverde (p562). It takes two days to summit Cerro Chirripó (p605), the country's highest peak.

Panama Roam the coffee-scented hills around Volcán Barú (p664) in the Chiriquí highlands.

Wildlife-Watching

The unexpected appearance of a toucan, howler monkey or sloth will surely be a highlight of your trip. Central America is rife with opportunities to spot these kinds of creatures in the wild, thanks to an extensive system of protected areas throughout the region. Often the best sightings occur when you're not really looking – perhaps in your hotel's garden or on the roadside in a remote area. In short: keep your eyes peeled.

Early morning and late afternoon are the best times to watch for wildlife activity anywhere.

> **TURTLE TOURS**
>
> Sea turtles nest on both the Caribbean and Pacific coasts of Central America. During the nesting seasons, travelers can witness various species of turtle returning to their natal beaches to lay their eggs, sometimes in great numbers. It's a truly awe-inspiring experience to watch something that feels at once grandly cosmic and incredibly intimate. Top spots for turtles include Playa Ostional, near Sámara (p581), and Tortuguero (p541) in Costa Rica, Isla Cañas (p651) in Panama and La Flor (p454) in Nicaragua.

Where to Go

Mexico Howlers are commonly sighted along the Mexico–Guatemala border.

Guatemala You can go whale-watching in Monterrico (p174). There's also a slim chance of seeing manatees (and a very good chance of seeing other wildlife) around Refugio Bocas del Plochic (p190). An early-morning bird hike at Tikal (p212) enhances the magic of that place.

Belize The black howler monkey lives only in Belize and is practically guaranteed to be seen at the Community Baboon Sanctuary (p253). Go to Cockscomb Basin Wildlife Sanctuary (p274) for possible jaguar sightings, as well as for tapirs, black howlers and 290 species of bird.

Honduras Montaña de Celaque (p392) and Cusuco (p376) are great birding destinations, though mammals are somewhat harder to spot. If you're really up for adventure, venture into the Moskitia (p414).

Nicaragua Take a boat down the jungly Río San Juan (p501) to spot sneaky monkeys, sunbathing caimans and prolific birdlife.

Costa Rica Corcovado (p607) is the ultimate wildlife-watching destination, where you can spot four species of New World monkeys, the endangered Baird's tapir, kinkajous, sloths and more. The canals of Tortuguero (p541) and the lazy rivers around Puerto Viejo de Sarapiquí (p559) are also teeming with animals.

Panama Sign up for a boat tour to see some of the 381 bird species and 120 mammal species on Isla Barro Colorado (p646). Alternatively, visit the rainforest of Parque Nacional Soberanía (p645), which is easy to access and brimming with wildlife.

Surfing

Surf's up, all across Central America. This sport's popularity is on the rise, with many places offering weeklong surf camps, hourly lessons and board rentals.

Costa Rica has the most developed scene and, arguably, the most and biggest waves. But El Salvador, Nicaragua, Panama and even Guatemala have up-and-coming surfing scenes. The waves might not be 'world-class' – at least not all of them – but they're pretty darn good. Plus, there are fewer surfers in these lesser-known spots, so you may have the breaks all to yourself.

When to Go

The surf season varies throughout the region – but there's always a wave to ride somewhere.

El Salvador Along the south-facing coastline, the months from May to August bring the biggest swells, but they also bring massive amounts of rain. Seasoned surfers claim that the tail end of the dry season (late March and early April) offers the best of both worlds, with still-glorious weather and the first southern swells.

Nicaragua The Pacific coast here sees the biggest waves from April to June, thanks to southern swells and offshore winds. The surf is dependable anytime between March and November, though. Again, the rain starts in May, so be prepared.

Costa Rica and Panama These two countries are among a select group of destinations where you can surf two oceans in one day. In both countries, the Caribbean surf season lasts from November to April, with an additional mini season in June and July. You can't really escape the rain on this coast.

On the Pacific side, in Costa Rica, the most consistent surf comes from the southwest between late May and August. Panama's Pacific coast peaks from April to June, with offshore winds and consistent southwesterly swells. In both cases, the surfing is reliably good anytime between February and August. Again, expect more rain (but fewer crowds) starting in May.

Where to Go

Guatemala Surfing is not as big here as it is further south, but there is a scene growing up near El Paredón (p172), with dedicated surf lodges, classes and board rentals.

El Salvador There is great surfing all along La Costa del Bálsamo (p312). La Libertad is a shady port town, but the right-hand break at Punta Roca, La Libertad (p311) is tops.

Nicaragua The beaches north and south of San Juan del Sur (p460) are the main surf destinations. Find your own private wave at Las Peñitas (p473) or the Tola beaches (p465).

Costa Rica Famous for Salsa Brava at Puerto Viejo de Talamanca (p549) and the three-minute left at Pavones (p609) (for experts only!). But the surf is also phenomenal up and down the Pacific coast, including Playa Grande – and all the beaches around Tamarindo (p576) – Santa Teresa and Mal País (p583), and further south at Dominical (p596).

Panama Surfing on both coasts! The waves at Santa Catalina (p655) are among the biggest in the region, while the Bocas del Toro (p667) has mostly reef breaks (ouch!).

THE BIG FIVE FOR BIRDERS

The birdlife is rich all around the region, but of course species vary widely depending on the habitat. Some highlights and where to spot them:

Scarlet macaw Ubiquitous around Corcovado (p607) and Carara (Costa Rica; p588)

Great green macaw Valle de Sarapiquí (Costa Rica; p559)

Resplendent quetzal Monteverde (Costa Rica; p562), Lago de Yojoa (Honduras; p373) and Volcán Barú (Panama; p664)

Jabiru stork Crooked Tree (Belize; p256) and Caño Negro (Costa Rica; p560)

Harpy eagle Nests around the Reserva Natural Punta Patiño in the Darién (Panama; p688)

Snorkeling & Diving

The Caribbean coast of Central America includes miles and miles of nearly unbroken barrier reef, making this one of the world's superlative spots for diving and snorkeling. Life under the sea is dramatic and diverse, from the fantastic coral formations and the kaleidoscopic fish that feed there to the massive (and sometimes menacing) creatures lurking in deeper waters. Mexico, Belize and Honduras offer world-class underwater viewing, but there are also snorkeling and diving opportunities further south.

Top: Cenote, Parque Dos Ojos (p70), Mexico

Bottom: Scarlet macaw

The Pacific coast is also rich with life. There is no reef, but there's still plenty to see, especially from October to February when conditions are normally clearer. There are recommended dive sites near San Juan del Sur (p460), Nicaragua, as well as Playa del Coco (p573), Quepos (p591) and Bahía Drake (p603) in Costa Rica.

Aside from the two great bodies of blue, Central America has some intriguing opportunities for inland diving. Mexico offers otherworldly dives in cenotes (freshwater limestone sinkholes); check out some options reachable from Tulum (p69). How about diving in a crater lake? You can do it at the Laguna de Apoyo (p449) in Nicaragua. In Guatemala, you can go high-altitude diving at Lago de Atitlán (p134).

Where to Go

Mexico There is a slew of well-trafficked dive and snorkel sites around Isla Cozumel (p67), while Banco Chinchorro, near Mahahual (p75), is a lesser-known gem.

Belize The dive-snorkel hub is the Northern Cays (p241), from where you can access the Blue Hole and the barrier reef. The reef is protected here, so even snorkeling requires a licensed guide. Hopkins (p275) or Placencia (p277) are bases for the central reef. Snorkel off the beach at Tobacco Caye (p274).

Honduras The Bay Islands (p404) are known for the low cost of open-water certification and Roatán's diving is pretty spectacular. It's only off Utila that you can see whale sharks though.

Nicaragua Little Corn Island (p495) offers an atmospheric location and varied dive sites, including underwater caves and the occasional hammerhead shark.

Costa Rica It doesn't really compare to the sites further north, but you can snorkel or dive all along the southern Caribbean coast (p541) in Costa Rica. Conditions are highly variable.

Panama There is plenty of sea life around Bocas del Toro (p667) and Comarca de Guna Yala (p685), but murky conditions make it difficult to see.

White-Water Rafting

Central America offers some of the best white-water rafting in the tropics, including in Guatemala, Honduras, Panama and especially Costa Rica. The Central American rivers offer everything from frothing Class IV white water to easy Class II floats. Most rivers can be run year-round, though more rain brings higher waters.

Where to Go

Guatemala The Río Cahabón in Las Verapaces is equal parts adrenaline rush and luscious nature, with excellent trips offered by ADETES (p181).

Honduras Sublime scenery and prolific birdlife along Class III rapids will give you a charge on the Río Cangrejal, near La Ceiba (p395).

Costa Rica Thrilling white water on two rivers near Turrialba (p539), especially the Río Paquare. The Río Sarapiquí (p559) will also get your heart beating fast.

Panama Cruise through narrow canyons and past hidden waterfalls on the Ríos Chiriquí and Chiriquí Viejo, near Boquete (p660).

Cycling

Many shops rent out bicycles for casual local exploration, but there are only a few options for cycling tours or other long-distance riding or mountain biking in the region.

Mexico In San Cristóbal de las Casas, sign up for **Jaguar Adventours** (Map p90; ☎967-631-50-62; www.adventours.mx; Belisario Domínguez 8A; bicycle rental per hour/day M$50/250; ⏰9am-2pm & 4-8pm) bicycle tours to nearby Maya villages and other intriguing destinations.

Guatemala Several outfits in Antigua (p120) offer mountain-biking trips in the surrounding hills, from half-day to weeklong tours.

Nicaragua Local operator Nica on Pedals (p435) offers challenging mountain-biking routes and adrenaline-packed day trips from Managua and beyond.

Costa Rica The Arenal area is a mountain-biking hot spot, with a wide variety of tours and rental offered by Bike Arenal (p555). If you can bring your own bike, **Vuelta al Lago** (www.vueltaallago arenal.com; ⏰Mar) is an awesome annual two-day ride around Lago de Arenal.

Countries at a Glance

The green link between North and South America, the seven compact countries that make up Central America, plus the southern strip of Mexico, are a true backpackers' paradise: a complex web of cultures, ancient ruins, tropical wildlife and adventure. In the region's northern stretches, where the Maya once reigned supreme, you can traipse through jungle to jaw-dropping pyramids and bask in ancient traditions. Along the vast stretches of Caribbean and Pacific coastline, you can curl up with a Spanish phrasebook, learn to dive dirt-cheap or surf waves crashing over swaths of multicolored sand. Wherever you land in the isthmus, there are opportunities to summit volcanoes, spy on wildlife, sample the cuisine and visit colonial towns and traditional villages.

Top: Iglesia de la Recolección (p470), León, Nicaragua
Centre: Red-eyed tree frog, Costa Rica (p514)
Bottom: Comarca de Guna Yala (p685), Panama

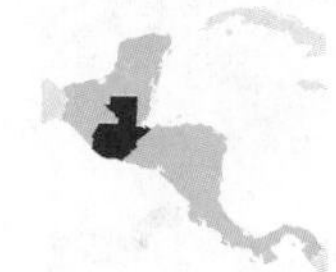

Mexico's Yucatán & Chiapas

Archaeology
Outdoor Activities
Food

Ruin-Hopping

There are so many Maya ruins. World-famous Chichén Itzá is a must-see, but do yourself a favor and get there early, before the tour buses arrive.

Adventure Awaits

Swim with 15-ton whale sharks, explore some of the world's best coral reefs, spot crocs and flamingos by motorboat, or swim in astonishing cenotes (limestone sinkholes).

Cocina Yucateca

Food experts say the Yucatán is one of Mexico's finest culinary destinations. Sure, you can try classic *yucateco* fare such as *sopa de lima* elsewhere, but it won't taste the same.

p48

Guatemala

Archaeology
Nature
History

Maya Mysteries

With a multitude of sites sprinkled across the jungle lowlands, you can delve deeply into the mysteries of Classic Maya civilization, from the temples of Tikal to the seldom-seen astronomical observatory of Uaxactún.

Natural Marvels

Lush cloud forests, Caribbean beaches, steamy jungles, dramatic volcanic landscapes and breathtaking freshwater lakes define Guatemala's often untamed countryside.

Colonial Cities

Whether the architecture crumbles gracefully in places such as Guatemala City and Quetzaltenango, or has been renovated like much of Antigua, the Spanish legacy offers postcard-perfect views – and a chance to scramble through history.

p104

Belize

Outdoor Activities
Archaeology
Relaxation

Aquatic Adventures

With miles of coastline, uncountable islands and the Western Hemisphere's most spectacular reef, Belize offers endless opportunity for fun, from sailing to kitesurfing.

Maya Past & Present

This tiny country is packed with Maya archaeological sites: major ruins such as Caracol and Lamanai, and smaller sites around San Ignacio (Cayo) and Toledo. For modern Maya culture, take a week to explore the villages of the deep south.

Take a Break

'Slow Down' reads the sole traffic sign on chilled-out Caye Caulker. Revel in your R&R while swinging in a hammock in a country that prides itself on taking it easy.

p232

El Salvador

Landscapes
History
Surfing

Small Packages

The fast track to your Central American fix, El Salvador has black-sand beaches, volcanic lakes, Maya ruins, hip coffee towns and cranking nightlife, all of it within 100km of the capital.

Civil War Stories

See the tide of history turning in remote mountain villages, where the civil war was most fiercely fought. To fill in the blanks, visit excellent regional museums and the galleries of San Salvador.

Wicked Waves

Surf the smoothest and most uncrowded waves in Latin America, from the international flavor of Costa del Bálsamo to the more remote eastern breaks. (The secret may be out, but most folks just don't listen.)

p292

Honduras

Diving & Snorkeling
National Parks
Outdoor Activities

Go Deep for Cheap

Few places are as inexpensive for learning how to dive as the Bay Islands. Boasting outstanding reefs, famous wrecks and bountiful sea life, Utila and Roatán offer memorable marine time.

Call of the Wild

Honduras' national parks are fantastic places to spot elusive wildlife. Look for the resplendent quetzal in the cloud forests of Parque Nacional Cusuco; crocodiles in the wetlands near Tela; and birds and monkeys in the Moskitia.

Endless Adventure

Seek out adventure in the great outdoors of Honduras. The magical Lago de Yojoa features waterfall hikes, birdwatching boat trips, caves and ruins.

p357

Nicaragua

Surfing
History
Outdoor Activities

Surf Scene

It's hard to beat Nicaragua for surf. After you hit dawn patrol at legendary spots such as Playas Hermosa and Maderas, you can chill out with breakfast, cool tunes and friendly companionship in a beachfront hammock paradise.

Colonial Charms

Experience complex and nuanced history in nearly every corner of intact colonial cities such as Granada and León, and in the festivals, art and living culture.

Offbeat Adventures

Isla de Ometepe and Nicaragua's Caribbean coast exemplify the country's nature and offbeat culture. Discover petroglyphs, climb volcanoes, kayak to lost coves and chill out in travelers' enclaves.

p429

Costa Rica

Surfing
Wildlife
Nature

Year-Round Waves

Point and beach breaks, lefts and rights, reefs and river mouths – the warm water and waves available year-round make Costa Rica a legendary surfing destination, where parts of *The Endless Summer II* were filmed.

Amazing Animals

The biodiversity astounds: more than 800 species of birds, almost 400 kinds of reptiles and amphibians, six species of wild cat, four types of monkey and the one and only Baird's tapir. Wowza!

Cloud Forest

Covering only 0.25% of the planet's land surface, the cloud forest is a mysterious Neverland, dripping with mist and mossy vines, sprouting with ferns and bromeliads.

p514

Panama

Design
Wildlife
Islands

Engineering Marvel

The enlarged locks at the Panama Canal offers even more reasons to see this 80km cross-continental cut. There's also fishing, kayaking and wildlife-watching off the shipping lanes.

Jungle Love

It seems counter-intuitive, but some of the region's best wildlife-watching happens just outside Panama City (such as the Darién or Parque Nacional Coiba). Think canopy towers, rainforest resorts and birding hot spots.

Tropical Paradise

The hundreds of idyllic San Blas resort islands comprise little more than thatched huts and a few hammocks surrounded by turquoise waters – but what more do you need?

p623

On the Road

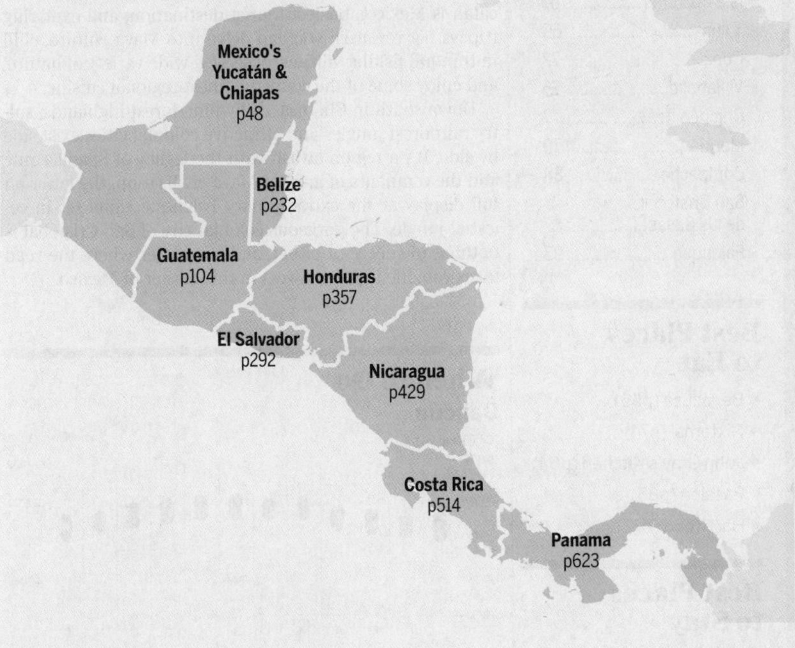

Mexico's Yucatán & Chiapas
p48

Belize
p232

Guatemala
p104

Honduras
p357

El Salvador
p292

Nicaragua
p429

Costa Rica
p514

Panama
p623

Mexico's Yucatán & Chiapas

☎52 / POP 127.9 MILLION

Includes ➡

Best Places to Eat

- ➡ Benazuza (p55)
- ➡ Nixtamal (p74)
- ➡ John Gray's Kitchen (p64)
- ➡ Passion (p65)
- ➡ Hartwood (p72)

Best Places to Stay

- ➡ Hotel El Rey del Caribe (p53)
- ➡ Casa Sirena (p57)
- ➡ La Posada del Sol (p71)
- ➡ Rancho Encantado (p74)

Why Go?

Flanked by the turquoise waters of the Caribbean and the wildlife-rich Gulf coast, the Yucatán Peninsula wows visitors with its Maya ruins, limestone swimming holes, colorful coral reefs and soulful colonial cities. Unsurprisingly the Yucatán is Mexico's busiest tourist destination, and exploring it pays big rewards: you can delve into Maya culture, chill in tranquil fishing villages, observe a wide variety of nature, and enjoy some of the country's finest regional cuisine.

Down south in Chiapas, chilly pine-forest highlands, sultry rainforest jungles and attractive colonial cities exist side by side. It's a region awash with the legacy of Spanish rule and the remnants of ancient Maya civilization, the latter on full display at the extraordinary Palenque ruins set in celestial jungle. The gorgeous colonial city of San Cristóbal is nothing to sneeze at either, and no matter where the road takes you, life is pretty sweet in this corner of Mexico.

When to Go

Cancún

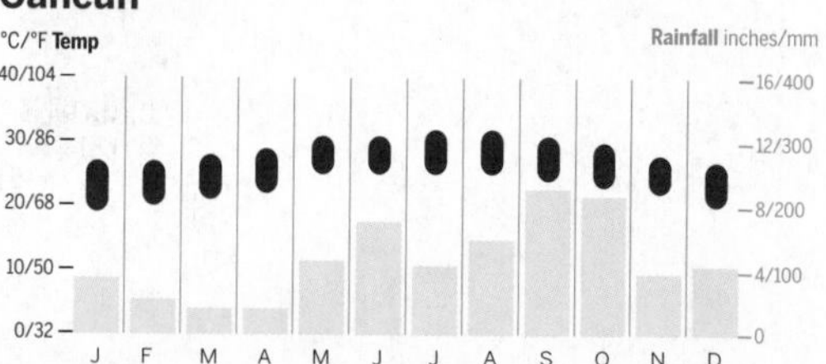

Jan Cultural capital Mérida hosts a month-long festival featuring concerts, art and dance.

Jun–Sep Swim with ginormous whale sharks near Isla Holbox.

Oct–Nov Cooler climes and cheaper accommodations make low season an ideal time to visit.

Entering the Country

As well as flying in, you can enter Mexico by car or bus from Guatemala or Belize and take a boat from the Belizian coast to Quintana Roo. Mexico's road borders with Guatemala include Ciudad Cuauhtémoc–La Mesilla, Ciudad Hidalgo–Ciudad Tecún Umán and Talismán–El Carmen, all of which are linked to nearby Mexican cities via plentiful buses and/or combis. We recommend crossing at Talismán–El Carmen. For those traveling from Belize, frequent buses run from Chetumal's Nuevo Mercado Lázaro Cárdenas to various destinations in Mexico.

TWO-WEEK ITINERARY

Greet the first day with a splash in the turquoise waters of Cancún's **Zona Hotelera**, then hit downtown for affordable eats and some nocturnal mischief. Visit nearby gorgeous beaches on **Isla Mujeres** and **Isla Blanca**, then return to the mainland and head south for **Playa del Carmen**. Catch a ferry to **Isla Cozumel**, a world-famous diving destination. Next, head on down to **Tulum**, known for its spectacular oceanfront Maya ruins, and further south to **Mahahual**, a laid-back fishing and diving village.

At the start of week two, return north to catch the turnoff to **Valladolid**, a colonial city with a small-town feel. West of Valladolid awaits **Chichén Itzá**, the mother of all Maya ruins. Continue on to the peninsula's cultural capital, **Mérida**, and indulge in Yucatecan cuisine. From there go south to the immaculately preserved walled city of **Campeche**. Stop at the archaeological sites of **Edzná** and **Calakmul** as you make your way down to the southern state of Chiapas. Drop by **Palenque**, where unforgettable Maya structures sit pretty in a dreamlike forest. For the last hurrah, hit **San Cristóbal de las Casas**, a highland colonial town surrounded by Maya villages.

Essential Food & Drink

Cochinita pibil Slow-cooked pork marinated in citrus juices and annatto seed spice.

Panuchos Fried tortilla filled with beans and topped with chicken, lettuce and pickled red onion.

Mezcal An alcoholic agave drink that packs a punch.

Sopa de lima Turkey, lime and tortilla-strip soup.

Top Tips

- For beaches and scuba diving, visit the Caribbean side. For culture, ruins and nature experiences, head west and south.
- Visiting Maya communities brings money into local economies.
- Driving at night can be dangerous, mainly due to unexpected livestock or potholes in the road.

FAST FACTS

Currency Mexican peso (M$)

Visas Tourist permit required; some nationalities also need visas (see p101).

Money ATMs are widely available in medium-size and large cities.

Emergency ☎911

Languages Spanish, Maya

Exchange Rates

Australia	A$1	M$13.69
Belize	BZ$1	M$9.51
Canada	C$1	M$14.57
Euro zone	€1	M$21.80
Guatemala	Q1	M$2.48
Japan	¥100	M$17.28
New Zealand	NZ$1	M$13.12
UK	UK£1	M$25.50
USA	US$1	M$19.17

Daily Costs

- Double room in a budget hotel: M$400–800; in a comfortable hotel: M$600–1500
- Street eats or economical set menu: M$20–80; lunch or dinner in a restaurant: M$80–240

Resources

Lonely Planet (www.lonelyplanet.com/mexico)

Yucatán Today (www.yucatantoday.com)

Yucatán Travel (www.yucatan.travel)

Turismo Chiapas (www.turismochiapas.gob.mx)

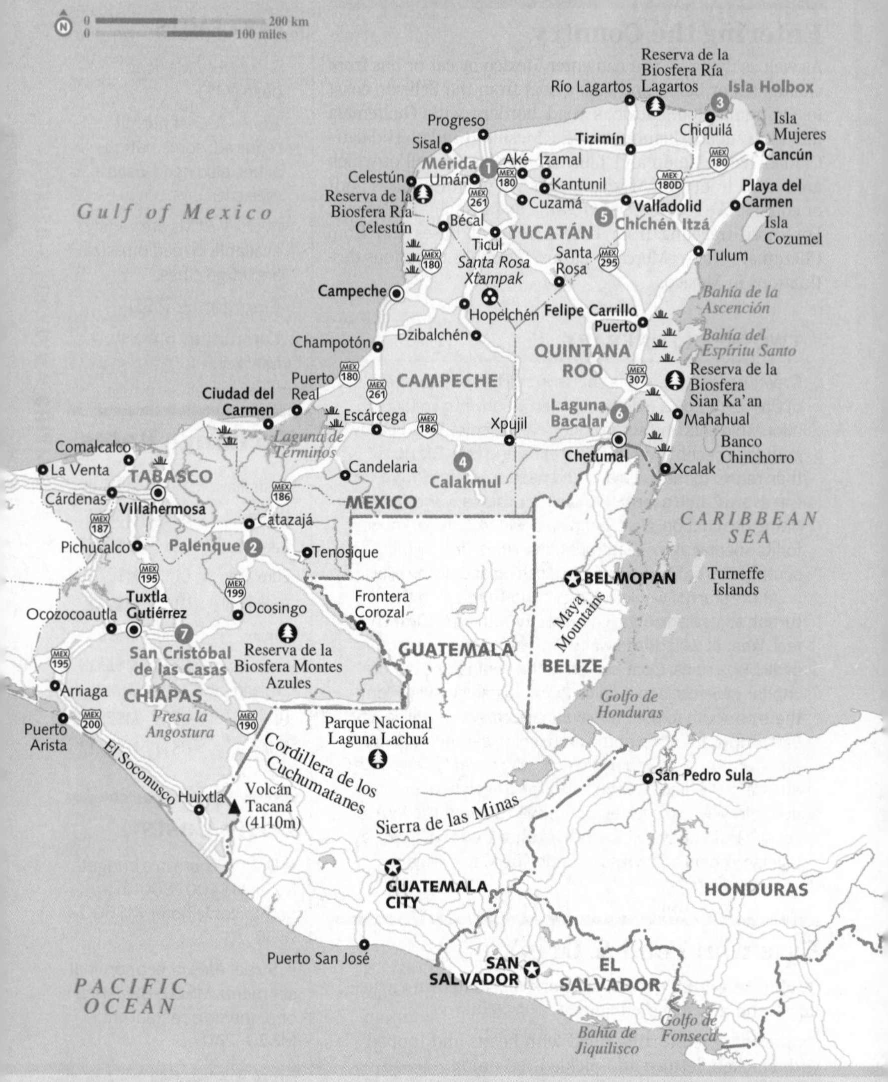

Mexico's Yucatán & Chiapas Highlights

1. **Mérida** (p79) Wandering this magnificent colonial capital and feasting on local treats.

2. **Palenque** (p93) Scaling the jungly hills and soaring Maya temples.

3. **Isla Holbox** (p61) Snorkeling with 15-ton whale sharks or spotting rare birds in nearby islands.

4. **Calakmul** (p86) Exploring and climbing some of the Maya's largest and tallest pyramids, with awesome views of the surrounding jungle.

5. **Chichén Itzá** (p77) Staring in awe at the massive El Castillo pyramid and learning about Maya culture.

6. **Laguna Bacalar** (p73) Plunging into the 90m-deep Cenote Azul and delighting at the lake of seven colors.

7. **San Cristóbal de las Casas** (p87) Strolling the high-altitude cobblestone streets.

THE YUCATÁN

Chock-full of fun and thrilling surprises, the Yucatán is brimming with Maya ruins, Caribbean beaches, old-world colonial cities, famed diving destinations and a host of natural wonders.

Cancún

998 / POP 628,000

Cancun is a tale of two cities, with the Zona Hotelera offering majestic Caribbean beaches and Maya culture, and Cancún Centro providing the local flavor.

One look at Cancún's aquamarine Caribbean waters and it makes perfect sense why planners back in the 1970s were so eager to develop the area as Mexico's next big resort destination. With about 19km of powdery white-sand beaches in the Zona Hotelera and a quieter 15km stretch of coast north of downtown, Cancún is a beach-bum's haven.

Certainly when most people think of Cancún, 'wild party town' comes to mind. But you can also soak up some Maya culture in between the fiestas, and feast on everything from Yucatecan comfort food and to haute cuisine. Moreover, outdoorsy types and children will truly appreciate the nearby diving and snorkeling sites, underwater cave systems and myriad water activities.

Sights & Activities

Most of Cancún's star attractions – namely its beaches, museum, ruins and water-related activities – are in the Zona Hotelera. If you're staying in Cancún Centro, any 'R-1,' 'R-2,' or 'Zona Hotelera' bus will drop you off at any point along the coast.

Most of Cancun's activities involve water-related fun in the great outdoors. Among the many things to do are snorkeling at a unique underwater sculpture museum; swimming with enormous whales sharks off the coast of Isla Contoy; ocean and cenote diving; birdwatching and hiking on an uninhabited island; and boat tours through mangroves.

★Museo Maya de Cancún MUSEUM

(Maya Museum; 998-885-38-43; www.facebook.com/museomayacancun; Blvd Kukulcán Km 16.5; adult/child under 13yr M$70/free; 9am-6pm Tue-Sun; R-1) Holding one of the Yucatán's most important collections of Maya artifacts, this modern museum is a welcome sight in a city known more for its party scene than cultural attractions. On display are some 400 pieces found at key sites in and around the peninsula, ranging from sculptures to ceramics and jewelry. One of the three halls shows temporary Maya-themed exhibits.

★Museo Subacuático de Arte SNORKELING

(MUSA Underwater Museum; 998-849-52-26; www.musamexico.org; snorkeling tour US$42, 1-tank dive US$65) Built to divert divers away from deteriorating coral reefs, this aquatic museum features hundreds of life-size sculptures in the waters of Cancún and Isla Mujeres. Only snorkeling is allowed at the 4m-deep artificial reef at Cancún's Punta Nizuc gallery, while the deeper Isla Mujeres' gallery is ideal for first-time divers. Organize outings through dive shops; Scuba Cancún is recommended.

Scuba Cancún DIVING

(998-849-52-25; www.scubacancun.com.mx; Blvd Kukulcán Km 5.2; 1-/2-tank dive US$62/77; 7am-8pm, from 8am Sun) A family-owned and PADI-certified dive operation with many years of experience, Scuba Cancún was the city's first dive shop. It offers a variety of snorkeling, fishing and diving expeditions (including cenote and night dives). It also runs snorkeling and diving trips to the underwater sculpture museum, aka MUSA (p51), as well as whale shark outings.

Asterix TOURS

(998-886-42-70; www.contoytours.com; Calle Vialidad s/n, V&V Marina; adult/child 5-12yr US$117/102; tours 9am-5:30pm Tue-Sun) Boats to Isla Contoy depart from the V&V Marina (aka La Amada), just north of the Punta Sam car ferry terminal. The tours include guide, breakfast, lunch at Isla Mujeres, open bar and snorkeling gear. Hotel pick-up costs an additional US$17 per person.

Sleeping

Mayan Monkey HOSTEL $

(Map p54; 998-217-53-32; www.mayanmonkey.com; Av Náder 32; dm/r incl breakfast & dinner from US$17/83; ; R-1) This monkey-themed hostel is as clean and comfortable as they come, and it's a hell of a deal with two free meals included. The rooftop pool and bar area provide sweeping city views and fun-filled nights with free activities like salsa classes. There are female-only and mixed dorms, and modern private rooms adorned with hipster monkey art.

The Yucatán

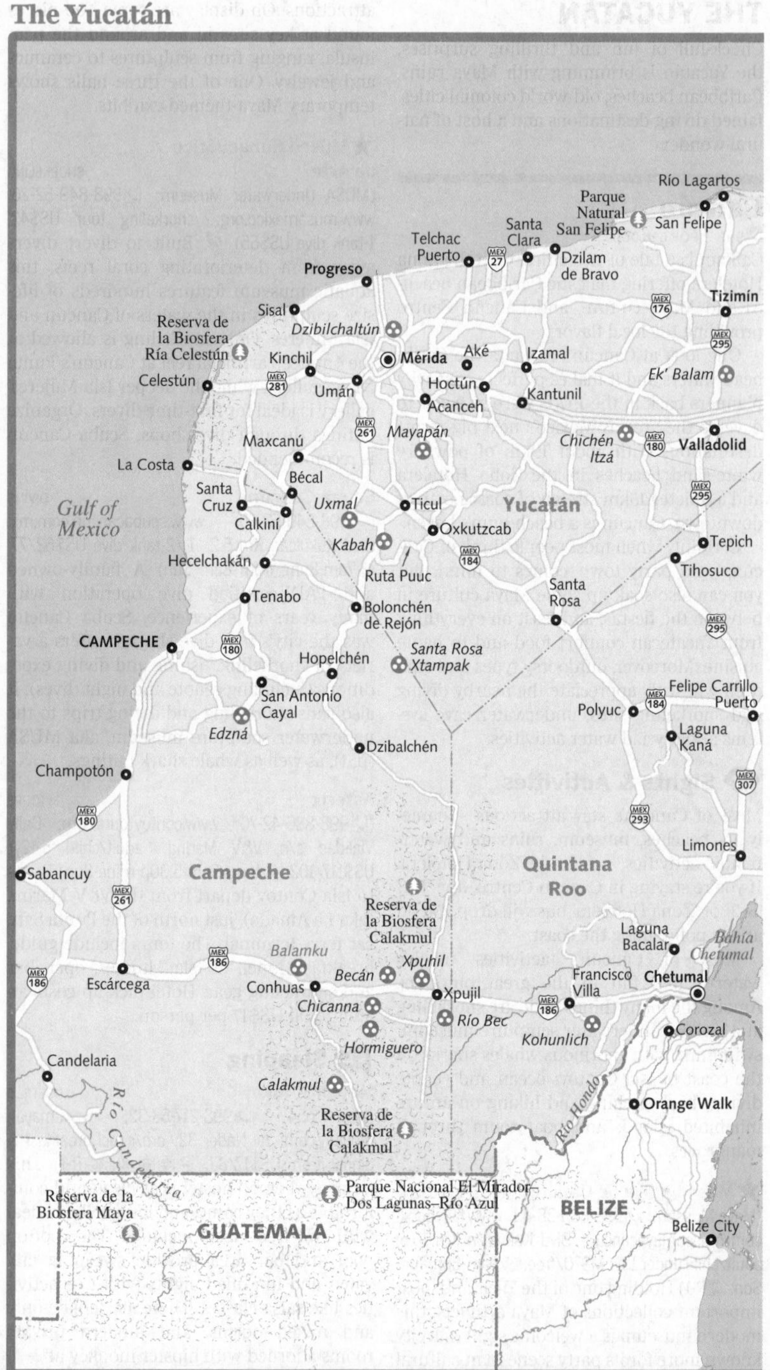

Río Lagartos
Parque Natural San Felipe
San Felipe
Santa Clara
Telchac Puerto
Dzilam de Bravo
Progreso
Tizimín
Sisal
Reserva de la Biosfera Ría Celestún
Dzibilchaltún
Mérida
Aké
Izamal
Kinchil
Celestún
Umán
Hoctún
Kantunil
Ek' Balam
Acanceh
Mayapán
Chichén Itzá
Valladolid
Maxcanú
La Costa
Bécal
Santa Cruz
Calkiní
Uxmal
Ticul
Yucatán
Gulf of Mexico
Oxkutzcab
Kabah
Tepich
Hecelchakán
Tihosuco
Ruta Puuc
Tenabo
Bolonchén de Rejón
Santa Rosa
CAMPECHE
Hopelchén
Santa Rosa Xtampak
San Antonio Cayal
Felipe Carrillo Puerto
Polyuc
Edzná
Laguna Kaná
Dzibalchén
Champotón
Limones
Sabancuy
Campeche
Quintana Roo
Reserva de la Biosfera Calakmul
Laguna Bacalar
Bahía Chetumal
Balamku
Xpuhil
Francisco Villa
Chetumal
Escárcega
Becán
Conhuas
Xpujil
Chicanna
Río Bec
Corozal
Kohunlich
Hormiguero
Candelaria
Calakmul
Río Hondo
Orange Walk
Río Candelaria
Reserva de la Biosfera Calakmul
Reserva de la Biosfera Maya
Parque Nacional El Mirador–Dos Lagunas–Río Azul
BELIZE
GUATEMALA
Belize City

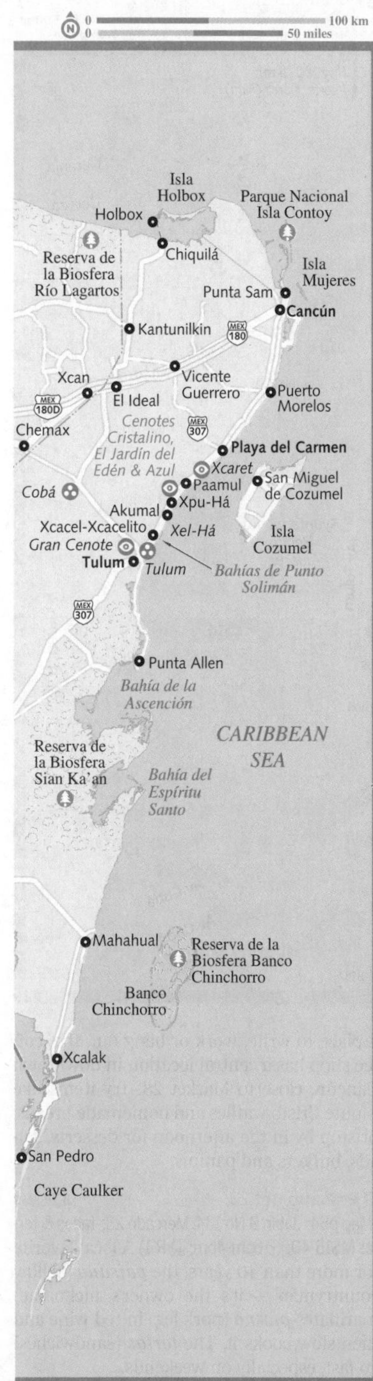

Mezcal Hostel HOSTEL $

(Map p54; ☎998-255-28-44; www.mezcalhostel.com; Mero 12; dm/r incl breakfast & dinner from US$14/65; ; R-1) If getting a made-to-order omelet in the morning doesn't grab you, perhaps the swimming pool, the bar, the numerous activities or the nightly excursions to the clubs will. Mezcal Hostel occupies a beautiful two-story house in a quiet residential area. Smoke can be thick in the common areas, but the dorms are smoke-free.

Hostel Natura HOSTEL $$

(☎998-883-08-87; www.facebook.com/hostelcancunnatura; Blvd Kukulcán Km 9.5; dm US$30, r without/with bathroom US$65/75; ; R-1) Up above a health-food restaurant of the same name, this fun, vibrant Zona Hotelera hostel offers private rooms with lagoon views and somewhat cramped dorms, offset by the airy rooftop terrace and a nice common kitchen area. The party zone is just a stumble away, and the staff are helpful and friendly.

★**Hotel El Rey del Caribe** HOTEL $$$

(Map p54; ☎998-884-20-28; www.elreydelcaribe.com; Av Uxmal 24; r incl breakfast from US$90; ; R-1) El Rey is a true ecotel – it recycles, employs solar collectors and cisterns, uses gray water on the gardens, and has some rooms with composting toilets. This beautiful spot has a swimming pool and Jacuzzi in a jungly courtyard that's home to a small family of *tlacuaches* (opossums). All rooms have a fully equipped kitchenette, comfortable beds and fridges.

★**Le Blanc** RESORT $$$

(☎998-881-47-48, 800-462-07-92, US 800-986-5632; www.leblancsparesort.com; Blvd Kukulcán Km 10; d/ste all-inclusive from US$793/868; P; R-1, R-2) You can't miss the glaring white exterior of the aptly named Le Blanc, arguably Cancún's most sophisticated resort. This adults-only retreat comes with all the amenities you'd expect in this category: gorgeous infinity pool, cold welcome drink on check-in, coconut-scented hand towels – the works. There's even butler service should life in Cancún become too complicated. Discounts for multiple-night stays.

Eating

Eating options in Cancún Centro range from your standard taco joints to upscale seafood restaurants. You'll find many restaurants clustered around Parque de las Palapas and lining nearby Avenida Yaxchilán. Trendy new

Cancún Centro

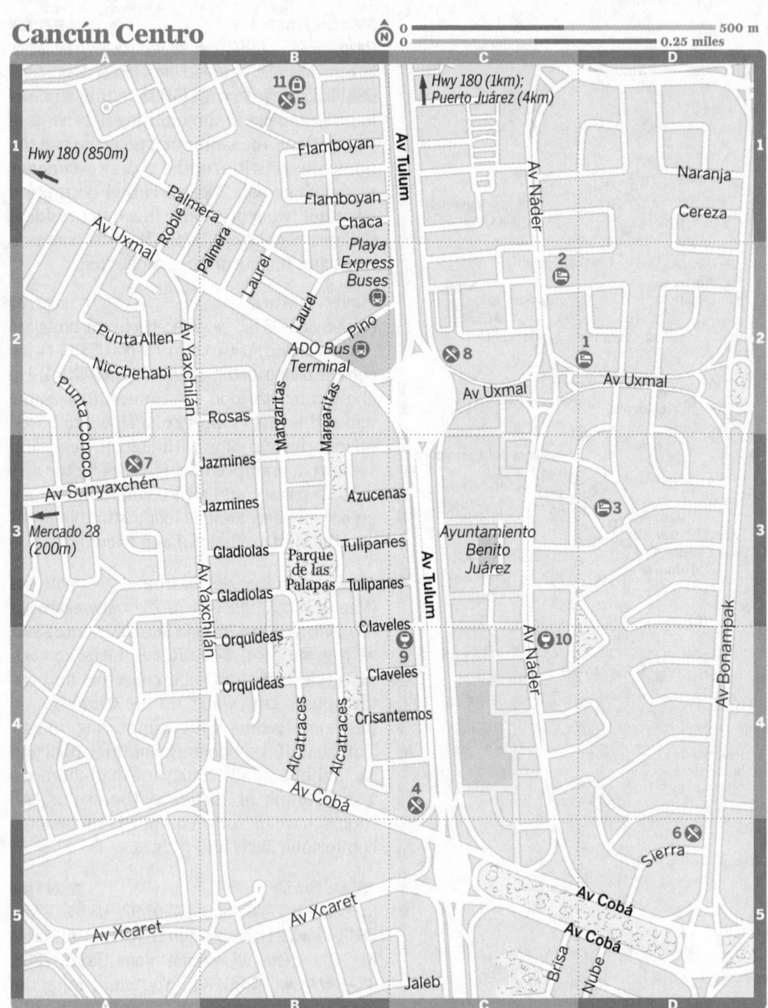

spots are popping up on or around Avenida Náder, between Avenidas Uxmal and Cobá. Mercados 23 (p55) and **28** (Mercado Veintiocho; 998-892-43-03; www.facebook.com/mercado28cancunmexico; cnr Avs Xel-Há & Sunyaxchén; 8am-7pm) serve up good market food, and for groceries, try 24/7 **Soriana** (Map p54; cnr Avs Tulum & Uxmal; 24hr), close to the bus station, or **Chedraui Supermarket** (Map p54; cnr Avs Tulum & Cobá; 7am-11pm; P; R-1).

Rooster Café Sunyaxchen CAFE $

(Map p54; 998-310-46-92; Av Sunyaxchen s/n, Plaza Sunyaxchen; mains M$75-160; 7am-11pm;) A main go-to cafe for locals in search of a place to write, work or hang out, this coffee shop has a central location in downtown Cancún, close to Market 28. Try items like Monte Cristo waffles and homemade breads, or stop by in the afternoon for desserts, salads, burgers and paninis.

El Paisano del 23 MEXICAN $

(Map p54; Jabín 9 No 134, Mercado 23; tacos & tortas M$15-40; 6am-4pm; R-1) A local favorite for more than 40 years, the *paisano* ('fellow countryman' – it's the owner's nickname) marinates *pierna* (pork leg) in red wine and then slow cooks it. The *tortas* (sandwiches) go fast, especially on weekends.

Cancún Centro

Sleeping

1 Hotel El Rey del Caribe........................D2
2 Mayan Monkey........................C2
3 Mezcal Hostel........................D3

Eating

4 Chedraui Supermarket........................C4
5 El Paisano del 23........................B1
6 Peter's Restaurante........................D5
7 Rooster Café Sunyaxchen........................A3
8 Soriana........................C2

Drinking & Nightlife

9 11:11........................C4
10 Amarula con Acento Tropical........................C4

Shopping

11 Mercado 23........................B1

El Galeón del Caribe SEAFOOD $$
(cell 998-2148175; www.facebook.com/elgaleondelcaribe; Blvd Kukulcán Km 19.4; pescadillas M$16, mains M$140-190; noon-7pm; R-1, R-2) Famed for its *pescadillas* (fried tortillas stuffed with fish), this low-key seafood *palapa* has an outdoor kitchen and lagoonside setting. It's near the southern end of the Hotel Zone and easy for in-the-know tourists to access, but its out-of-the-way location and authentic Mexican seafood make it a favorite Sunday afternoon hangout for Cancún locals too.

Kiosco Verde SEAFOOD $$
(cell 998-1988402; www.facebook.com/kioscoverdemarisqueria; Av López Portillo 570, Puerto Juárez; mains M$120-273; 12:30-8pm Wed-Mon; P; R-1) The Green Kiosk just might be the most underrated seafood restaurant in all of Cancún. It began in 1974 as a small grocery store and now it excels in well-prepared seafood dishes like grilled octopus and hogfish. The Kiosko also has a new cantina that stays open until 11pm.

★ **Peter's Restaurante** INTERNATIONAL $$$
(Map p54; 998-251-93-10; www.facebook.com/peterscancun; Av Bonampak 71, btwn Calles Sierra & Robalo; dinner M$375-655; 6-10pm Tue-Sat) Set on one of downtown Cancún's busiest avenues, Peter's Restaurante has a homey charm and some of the best cooking in the city. Dutch Chef Peter Houben has blended European, Mexican and international cuisine, with beautifully prepared dishes like the mushroom ravioli appetizer and fresh salmon fillet in lemon sauce with a spicy hint of *chile de àrbol* (tree chili).

★ **Benazuza** MEXICAN $$$
(998-891-50-00; www.facebook.com/restaurantebenazuza; Blvd Kukulcan Km 19.5, Grand Oasis Sens Resort; per person M$1376; 7-10pm Mon-Sat; R-1) Up to 30 courses of surprising molecular cuisine. The dining experience at contemporary restaurant Benazuza incorporates traditional Mexican-inspired dishes like tacos and chilies that have been transformed into new shapes, flavors and textures using cutting-edge cooking technology. The price here includes molecular cocktails at the bar, all dinner courses, and desserts unlike any you've ever tried.

Drinking & Nightlife

★ **Amarula con Acento Tropical** COCKTAIL BAR
(Map p54; cell 998-3325680; www.facebook.com/amarulaconacentotropical; Av Náder 104; 9pm-3:30am Wed-Sat; R-1) Identified from the street only by a doorway and neon sign, Amarula blends dark, sultry style with the architectural details of an old Cancún house. The cocktail menu far outshines the food here: signature drinks use classic Mexican ingredients like *jamaica* (hibiscus flower), regional fruits and chili peppers.

The City CLUB
(998-883-33-33; www.thecitycancun.com; Blvd Kukulcán Km 9; open bar US$65; 10:30pm-4am Fri; R-1) The largest nightclub in Latin America still manages to fill up every Friday night. Frequently hosting world-famous DJs and musicians, this massive place offers wild nightlife, whether you're dancing on top of the central stage or watching it all from the stadium-style side levels. Due to the large crowds and 'party hearty' atmosphere, it can feel overwhelming at times.

11:11 GAY
(Once Once; Map p54; cell 998-1352243; www.1111gayclubcancun.com; Claveles s/n; 10pm-6am Fri-Sun; R-1) The main room in this large house stages drag shows, go-go dancers and the like, while DJs in smaller rooms spin electronica and pop tunes till the sun comes up. Look for the black and rainbow design outside.

Shopping

Mercado 23 MARKET
(Map p54; www.facebook.com/mercado23cancun; Jabín 9; 8am-7pm; R-1) This market is a nice reality check if you're tired of seeing the same old tourist knickknacks elsewhere.

Getting There & Away

AIR

Aeropuerto Internacional de Cancún (p102) is the busiest airport in southeast Mexico. It has all the services you would expect from a major international airport: ATMs, money exchange and car-rental agencies. It's served by many direct international flights and by connecting flights from Mexico City, including by low-cost Mexican carriers VivaAerobus, Interjet and Volaris.

There are flights to Cancún from Guatemala City and Flores (Guatemala), Havana (Cuba), Panama City and São Paulo (Brazil). Some Havana–Cancún flights continue to Mérida.

BOAT

There are several ferry departure points for Isla Mujeres from Cancún. From the Zona Hotelera, you can depart from **El Embarcadero** (Blvd Kukulcán Km 4), **Playa Caracol** (Blvd Kukulcán Km 9.5; parking per day M$100) or **Playa Tortugas** (Blvd Kukulcán Km 6.5). From Cancún Centro, there are two passenger ferry terminals in Puerto Juárez: **Ultramar** (www.ultramarferry.com) and a less popular dock about 500m north shared by Marinsa (www.marinsaturismo.com) and Naveganto (www.naveganto.com). From Puerto Juárez, the one-way fare is M$140 to M$160, while leaving from the Zona Hotelera runs about M$270.

For Isla Contoy, boats (p51) depart from the **V&V Marina**, just north of the Punta Sam car ferry terminal.

BUS

Cancún's modern bus terminal **ADO** (Map p54; www.ado.com.mx) occupies the wedge formed where Avenidas Uxmal and Tulum meet. It's a relatively safe area, but be aware of your bags and make sure to establish the fare before getting into a taxi.

Across Pino from the bus terminal, a few doors from Avenida Tulum, is the ticket office and mini-terminal of **Playa Express** (Map p54; Pino s/n, cnr Av Tulum), which runs air-conditioned buses down the coast to Playa del Carmen every 10 minutes until early evening, stopping at major towns and points of interest. ADO covers the same ground and beyond with its 1st-class and 2nd-class lines. To reach Isla Holbox up north, take a bus to Chiquilá.

ADO sets the 1st-class standard. Mayab provides good 'intermediate class' (tending to make more stops than 1st class) to many points.

Isla Mujeres

998 / POP 12,600

Isla Mujeres generally has a quieter and more relaxing vibe than what you'll find across the bay in Cancún, and there's just

BUSES FROM CANCÚN

DESTINATION	COST (M$)	DURATION (HR)	FREQUENCY (DAILY)
Bacalar	276-424	5-5½	frequent
Cancún airport	78	½	frequent
Chetumal	308-546	5½-6	frequent
Chichén Itzá	163-316	3-4	hourly
Chiquilá	180-244	3-3½	4
Felipe Carrillo Puerto	200-222	3½-3¾	6
Mahahual	230	5½-5¾	2; 6:45am & 4:45pm
Mérida	384-698	4-5	frequent
Mexico City	1200	27¼	1 to Terminal Norte; 6:30pm
Mexico City (TAPO)	1200-1387	25-26½	4
Palenque	760-1398	13-13¼	5
Playa del Carmen	36-74	1½	frequent ADO & Playa Express
Puerto Morelos	25-32	½-¾	frequent ADO & Playa Express
Ticul	296	8	frequent
Tizimín	140	6	4
Tulum	148-172	2¼-2¾	frequent
Valladolid	140-228	2-2¼	frequent
Villahermosa	656-1350	12¾-14¾	frequent

enough here to keep you entertained: scuba-diving and snorkeling, visiting a turtle farm, or simply swimming and lazing around on the island's gorgeous north shore.

Sure, there are quite a few ticky-tacky tourist shops, but folks still get around by golf cart and the crushed-coral beaches are undeniably lovely. As for the calm turquoise water of Isla Mujeres, well, you really just have to see it for yourself.

Come sunset, there are plenty of dining options, and the nightlife scene moves at a carefree pace.

Some people plan their vacation around Cancún and pencil in Isla Mujeres as a side trip, but the island is truly a destination in its own right, and a surprisingly affordable one at that.

Sights & Activities

★Playa Garrafón BEACH

Head to this beach for excellent snorkeling. It's 6.5km from the tourist center. A cab costs M$100.

Playa Norte BEACH

Once you reach Playa Norte, the island's main beach, you won't want to leave. Its warm, shallow waters are the color of blue raspberry syrup and the beach is crushed coral. Unlike most of the island's east coast, Playa Norte is safe for swimming and the water is only chest deep, even far from shore.

Isla Mujeres Turtle Farm FARM

(Isla Mujeres Tortugranja; 998-888-07-05; www.facebook.com/tortugranja.mx; Carretera Sac Bajo Km 5; M$30; 9am-5pm;) Although they're endangered, sea turtles are still killed throughout Latin America for their eggs and meat. In the 1980s, efforts by a local fisherman led to the founding of this *tortugranja* (turtle farm), 5km south of town, which safeguards breeding grounds and protects eggs. It's a small spot, with a number of sizes of turtles and a few different species. The farm is easily reached from town by taxi (M$75) or golf cart.

★Hotel Garrafón de Castilla SNORKELING

(998-877-01-07; Carretera Punta Sur Km 6; admission M$70, snorkel-gear rental M$80; 10am-6pm) Avoid the overpriced Playa Garrafón Reef Park and instead visit Hotel Garrafón de Castilla's beach club for a day of snorkeling in translucent waters. A taxi from town costs M$100.

DON'T MISS

PARQUE NACIONAL ISLA CONTOY

Spectacular **Isla Contoy National Park** (998-887-19-97; contoy@conanp.gob.mx) is a bird-lover's delight: an uninhabited national park and sanctuary that is an easy day trip from Cancún or Isla Mujeres. About 800m at its widest point and more than 8.5km long, it has dense foliage that provides ideal shelter for more than 170 bird species, including brown pelicans, olive cormorants, turkey birds, brown boobies and frigates, and is also a good place to see red flamingos, snowy egrets and white herons.

MUSA Isla Mujeres DIVING, SNORKELING

(Museo Subacuático de Arte; 998-877-12-33; www.musamexico.org; Manchones reef; 1-tank dive US$70) An amazing gallery with hundreds of life-sized sculptures submerged in the waters on the island's south side. At 8m deep, the Isla Mujeres Manchones gallery is ideal for first-time divers, though snorkelers are welcome as well. Organize outings through dive shops; Sea Hawk is recommended.

Sea Hawk Divers DIVING

(998-877-12-33; www.seahawkislamujeres.com; Carlos Lazo s/n; 1-/2-tank dive incl equipment US$80/90, intro course US$115, whale shark tour US$125; 8am-6pm) Offers reef dives, intro courses, fishing trips and whale shark snorkeling tours. Sea Hawk also goes to the Isla Mujeres site of underwater sculpture museum MUSA, on the island's south side. Rents rooms, too, for US$85 to US$115.

Sleeping & Eating

Apartments Trinchan APARTMENT $

(cell 998-1666967; atrinchan@prodigy.net.mx; Carlos Lazo 46; r/apt M$700/800;) Since it has no website, you'll have to take our word for it when we say this is one of the best budget deals in town – and the beach is right around the corner. Opt for one of the large apartments with full kitchen, but avoid No 8, which catches noise from a nearby hostel's late-night beach parties.

★Casa Sirena B&B $$$

(cell 998-2425906; www.casasirenamexico.com; Hidalgo s/n; r incl breakfast from US$208;) Get the full-fledged B&B treatment in this lovingly restored historic house, where guests get excellent breakfast served

YVONNE M. CORNELL/SHUTTERSTOCK ©

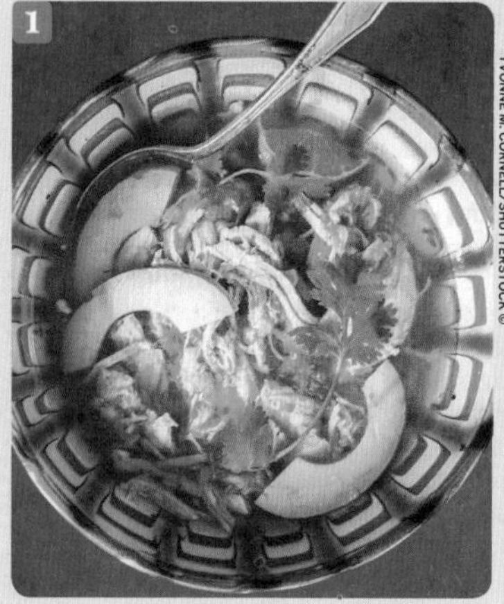

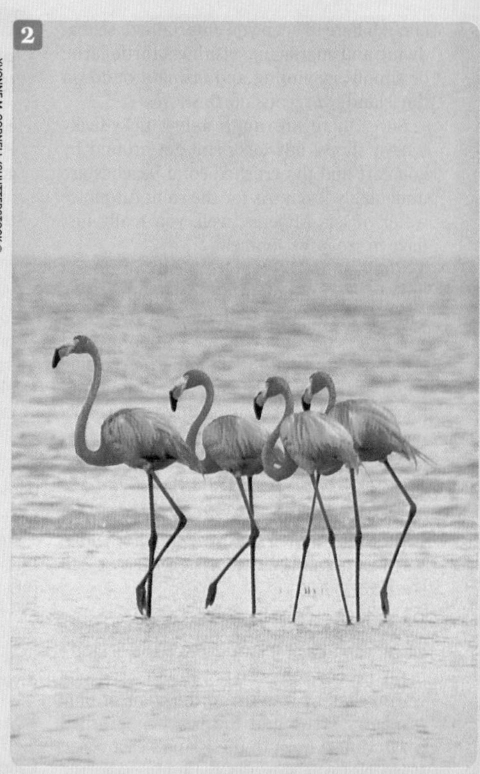

1. Sopa de lima (p49)
A classic Mexican soup made with turkey, lime and tortilla strips.

2. Isla Holbox (p61)
Flamingos are among the more than 150 bird species found on Holbox.

3. Cenote X'Kekén (p76)
A popular cenote for swimming in Valladolid.

4. Calakmul (p86)
The ancient Mayan city of Calakmul was once home to over 50,000 people.

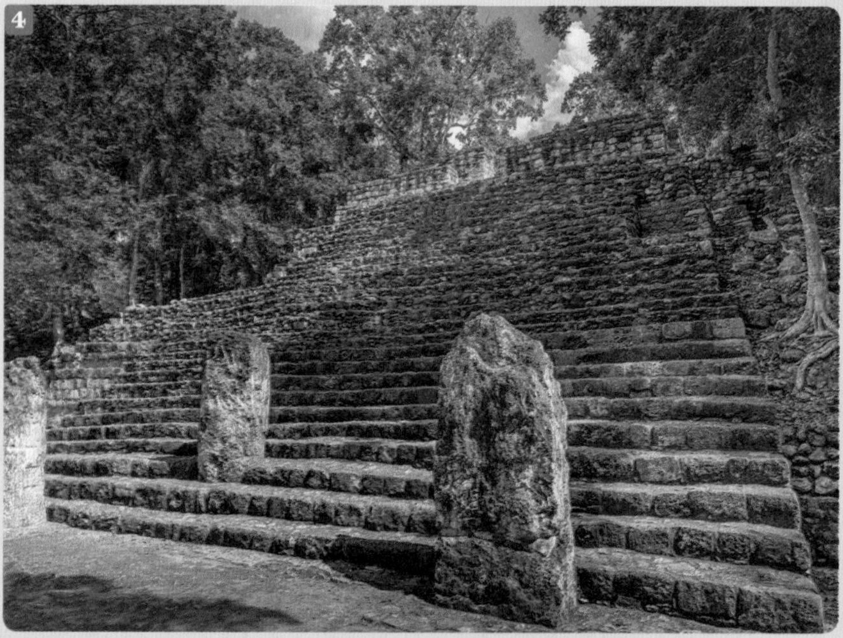

3

JOSE IGNACIO SOTO/SHUTTERSTOCK ©

in a shady courtyard along with a complimentary happy hour on a rooftop bar area featuring a plunge pool and sunny deck overlooking the ocean. The adults-only *casa* houses six elegant rooms, including one with a sea view balcony. Two-night minimum stay required.

Bobo's FISH & CHIPS **$$**
(www.facebook.com/bobosfishchips; Matamoros 14; mains M$95-115; ⊙3-11pm) This bar and grill fries up excellent locally caught triggerfish for its popular fish and chips, and there's malt vinegar to go along with it (a rare find in Mexico). Bobo's is also known for its burgers and convivial streetside bar.

Mango Café BREAKFAST **$$**
(☎998-400-19-04; www.facebook.com/mangocafeisla; Payo Obispo 101, Colonia Meterológico; mains M$100-170; ⊙7am-3pm Tue & Wed, to 9pm Thu-Mon;) See the south side of town and drop by Mango Café for some self-serve coffee and a hearty Caribbean-inspired breakfast. The hot items here are coconut French toast and eggs Benedict in a curry hollandaise sauce. It's a short bike or cab ride away, about 3km south of the ferry terminal.

★**Javi's Cantina** SEAFOOD **$$$**
(www.javiscantina.com; Juárez 12; mains M$225-550; ⊙5-10:30pm;) More like a restaurant than a cantina, but Javi's does have happy hour and live music. The menu consists of seafood, choice beef cuts, chicken and various salad and veggie options. A house specialty is the fresh-caught parmesan-crusted fish fillet with tamarind sauce. Dine in the front room or sit back in the rear courtyard with a pleasant terrace.

Lola Valentina FUSION **$$$**
(☎998-315-94-79; www.facebook.com/lolavalentinaislamujeres; Hidalgo s/n; mains M$145-410; ⊙8am-11pm;) Overlooking the quieter north side of the restaurant strip, Lola does excellent Mexican fusion with dishes like coconut shrimp with a mango-Sriracha-soy dipping sauce. Also on the menu are several vegan, gluten-free items, and the decidedly non-vegan, non-GF Latin Surf n' Turf. Its added swings at the bar (fun!) and redone its tasty cocktail menu (yum!). Cash only.

Drinking & Nightlife

★**La Tablita** BAR
(Av Guerrero s/n; ⊙noon-8pm Mon-Sat) For a little local flavor, spend a lazy afternoon over cold drinks and free snacks in this atmospheric, fan-cooled Caribbean house. The jukebox selection of Spanish-language tracks is *muy buena*.

Poc-Na Hostel BAR
(☎998-877-00-90; www.pocna.com; Matamoros 26; ⊙7pm-3am;) Has a lobby bar with nightly live music and a beachfront bar with thumping music and more hippies than all the magic buses in the world. It's a scene, and an entertaining one at that. Drinks aren't expensive, but aren't magically good either.

Getting There & Away

There are several points of embarkation from Cancún to reach Isla Mujeres. Most people cross on Ultramar passenger ferries. The R-1 'Puerto Juárez' city bus in Cancún serves all Zona Hotelera departure points and Puerto Juárez, in Ciudad Cancún. If you arrive by car, daily parking fees in and around the terminals cost between M$100 and M$150, but it can be as low as M$50 if you go further from the terminal.

Puerto Morelos

☎998 / POP 9200

Halfway between Cancún and Playa del Carmen, Puerto Morelos retains its quiet, small-town feel despite the encroaching building boom north and south of town. While it offers enough restaurants and bars to keep you entertained by night, it's really the shallow Caribbean waters that draw visitors here. Brilliantly contrasted stripes of bright green and dark blue separate the shore from the barrier reef – a tantalizing sight for divers and snorkelers – while inland a series of excellent cenotes beckon the adventurous. There's a nice market just south of the plaza with a good selection of crafts and handmade hammocks that are much higher quality than ones you'll find in Cancún or Playa.

Sights & Activities

Jardín Botánico Dr Alfredo Barrera Marín GARDENS
(Jardín Botánico Yaax Che; ☎998-206-92-33; www.facebook.com/jbpuertomorelos; Hwy 307 Km 320; adult/child 3-10yr M$120/50; ⊙8am-4pm;) One of the largest botanical gardens in Mexico, this 65-hectare reserve has about 2km of trails and sections dedicated to epiphytes (orchids and bromeliads), palms, ferns, succulents (cacti and their relatives) and plants used in traditional Maya medicine. The garden also holds a large animal population,

WORTH A TRIP

ISLA HOLBOX

Isla Holbox (hol-bosh) has sandy streets, colorful Caribbean buildings, lazing, sun-drunk dogs, and sand so fine its texture is nearly clay. The greenish waters are a unique color from the mixing of ocean currents, and on land there's a mixing too: of locals and tourists, the latter hoping to escape the hubbub of Cancún.

'Hoping' is the operative word, because while there are no throbbing nightclubs here, and while it's beautiful, it's not exactly peaceful (what with the throngs of people and constant buzzing of noisy gasoline-powered golf carts), unless you really do get away from it all: to the more remote beaches either by golf cart or boat.

It's a fantastic spot for wildlife. Lying within the Yum Balam reserve, Holbox is home to more than 150 bird species, including roseate spoonbills, pelicans, herons, ibis and flamingos. In summer, whale sharks congregate nearby.

Not surprisingly, *cabañas* (cabins) and bungalows are everywhere along the beach. Some of the most upscale places can be found east of town, out along the island's northern shore in what locals call the Zona Hotelera. Most budget and midrange accommodations are clustered within several blocks of the plaza.

Ferries (Chiquilá dock; one way M$150; 6am-9:30pm) run to Holbox from the port town of Chiquilá, usually from 6am to 9:30pm. It takes about 25 minutes to reach the island. Smaller, faster and wetter *lanchas* (motorboats) make the crossing after dark for M$1200. **Rentadora El Brother** (984-875-20-18; Tiburón Ballena s/n; cart per hour/day M$200/1000; 9am-8pm) rents out golf carts.

including the only coastal troops of spider monkeys left in the region.

Crococun Zoo ZOO
(998-850-37-19; www.crococunzoo.com; Hwy 307 Km 31; adult/child 6-12yr US$32/22; 9am-5pm) About 23km south of the Cancún airport, this former crocodile farm now calls itself a conservationist zoo that protects some of the area's endangered species and rescue animals. The price of admission includes a guided tour in which visitors are allowed to interact with some of the animals, such as white-tailed deer, boa constrictors, macaws, crocs and spider monkeys.

Aquanauts DIVING
(998-206-93-65; www.aquanautsdiveadventures.com; Av Melgar s/n, Hotel Hacienda Morelos; 1-/2-tank reef dive US$70/90, 2-tank cenote dive US$165-190, snorkeling US$30-80; 8am-4pm Mon-Sat) Runs many interesting tours, including drift diving, cenote and shipwreck dives, and lionfish hunting. The dive shop is one block south of the plaza.

Sleeping & Eating

Casitas Kinsol GUESTHOUSE $$
(998-206-91-52; www.casitas-kinsol.com; Av Zetina Gazca 18; r US$49;) Great for people who want to see what life's like on the other side of town (yes, there are signs of life west of the highway!), Kinsol offers fan-cooled *palapa*-style huts with beautiful design details such as Talavera tile sinks and handcrafted furnishings. It's a peaceful spot where even the dogs and cats get along. It's 3km west of town.

★ **Posada El Moro** HOTEL $$$
(998-871-01-59; www.hotelelmoro.mx; Av Rojo Gómez s/n; r/ste incl breakfast from M$1548/1890; P) A pretty property, with cheery geraniums in the halls and courtyard. Some rooms have kitchenettes, most have couches that fold out into futons, and there's a small pool in a tropical garden. Prices drop substantially in low season or via their webpage (not the booking sites). It's northwest of the plaza.

Mangata BREAKFAST $$
(cell 998-2015624; www.facebook.com/mangatapuertomorelos; Av Niños Héroes 15; mains M$90-125; 8am-4pm Tue-Sat, 9am-3pm Sun;) If you like eggs Benedict you're gonna love the 'Mangata Benedictin' (poached eggs with slow-cooked roast beef smothered in a rich hollandaise sauce). Strong coffee and a good selection of vegetarian and vegan options are also available at this pleasant open-air cafe with mismatched furniture.

El Pesquero SEAFOOD $$
(998-206-91-29; www.facebook.com/elpesqueropuertomorelos; Av Melgar 4C; mains M$110-270; 1-7:30pm) OK, so it's not right on the

Chichén Itzá

A DAY TOUR

It doesn't take long to realize why the Maya site of Chichén Itzá is one of Mexico's most popular tourist draws. Approaching the grounds from the main entrance, the striking castle pyramid 1 **El Castillo** jumps right out at you – and the wow factor never lets up.

It's easy to tackle Chichén Itzá in one day. Within a stone's throw of the castle, you'll find the Maya world's largest 2 **ball court** alongside eerie carvings of skulls and heart-devouring eagles at the Temple of Jaguars and the Platform of Skulls. On the other (eastern) side are the highly adorned 3 **Group of a Thousand Columns** and the 4 **Temple of Warriors**. A short walk north of the castle leads to the gaping 5 **Sacred Cenote**, an important pilgrimage site. On the other side of El Castillo, you'll find giant stone serpents watching over the High Priest's Grave, aka El Osario. Further south, marvel at the spiral-domed 6 **Observatory**, the imposing Nunnery and Akab-Dzib, one of the oldest ruins.

Roaming the 47-hectare site, it's fun to consider that at its height Chichén Itzá was home to an estimated 90,000 inhabitants and spanned approximately 30 sq km. So essentially you're looking at just a small part of a once-great city.

TOP TIPS

➡ Arrive at 8am and you'll have a good three hours or so before the tour-bus madness begins. Early birds escape the merchants, too.

➡ Remember that Chichén Itzá is the name of the site; the actual town where it's located is called Pisté.

El Caracol
Observatory
Today they'd probably just use a website, but back in the day priests would announce the latest rituals and celebrations from the dome of the circular observatory.

Grupo de las Mil Columnas
Group of a Thousand Columns
Not unlike a hall of fame exhibit, the pillars surrounding the temple reveal carvings of gods, dignitaries and celebrated warriors.

El Castillo

The Castle

Even this mighty pyramid can't bear the stress of a million visitors ascending its stairs each year. No climbing allowed, but the ground-level view doesn't disappoint.

YIMING CHEN/GETTY IMAGES ©

Gran Juego de Pelota

Great Ball Court

How is it possible to hear someone talk from one end of this long, open-air court to the other? To this day, the acoustics remain a mystery.

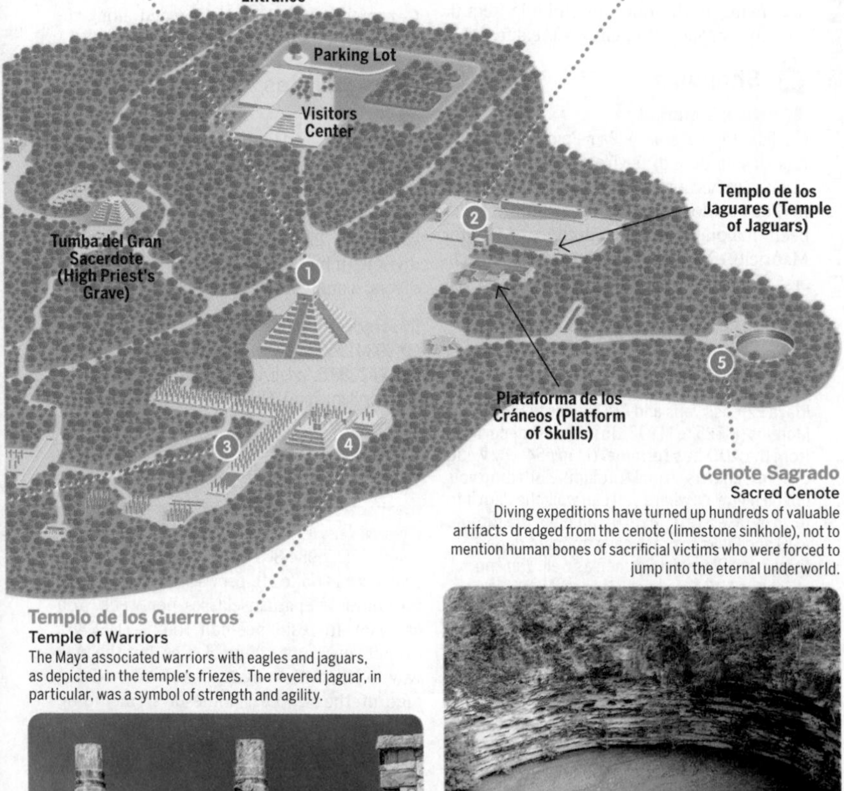

IRINA KLYUCHNIKOVA/SHUTTERSTOCK ©

Entrance

Parking Lot

Visitors Center

Tumba del Gran Sacerdote (High Priest's Grave)

1

2

Templo de los Jaguares (Temple of Jaguars)

Plataforma de los Cráneos (Platform of Skulls)

3

4

5

Cenote Sagrado

Sacred Cenote

Diving expeditions have turned up hundreds of valuable artifacts dredged from the cenote (limestone sinkhole), not to mention human bones of sacrificial victims who were forced to jump into the eternal underworld.

MATYAS REHAK/SHUTTERSTOCK ©

Templo de los Guerreros

Temple of Warriors

The Maya associated warriors with eagles and jaguars, as depicted in the temple's friezes. The revered jaguar, in particular, was a symbol of strength and agility.

KIEVVICTOR/SHUTTERSTOCK ©

beach, but the sand floor, *palapa* roof, fan-cooled dining area and fresh fish sure make you feel like you're there. Start with a tuna tostada, then go with the excellent *pescado frito* (fried whole fish), which can be cooked 'natural' style or *al ajillo* (in chili-garlic sauce). If available, try the *boquinete* (hogfish).

★**John Gray's Kitchen** INTERNATIONAL **$$$**
(998-871-06-65; www.facebook.com/johngrayskitchen; Av Niños Héroes 6; breakfast M$60-100, dinner M$270-450; 8am-10pm Tue-Sat, from 5pm Mon) One block west and two blocks north of the plaza, this 'kitchen' turns out some truly fabulous food. The chef's specialty, though not listed on the regularly changing menu, is the duck in chipotle, tequila and honey sauce. It opens for breakfast too.

Shopping

★**Artisans Market** ARTS & CRAFTS
(Av Rojo Gómez s/n; 9am-8pm) The hammocks sold here differ from what you'll find elsewhere because they're created right here in Puerto Morelos by a local family that's been making them for decades. (Ask for Mauricio!) You can also buy dream catchers, *alebrijes* (colorful wooden animal figures from San Martín Tilcajete), handbags, masks, jewelry and more.

Getting There & Away

Playa Express vans and ADO buses to Puerto Morelos (M$25 to M$32, 35 minutes) depart from the **ADO bus terminal** (Map p54; www.ado.com.mx; cnr Avs Uxmal & Tulum). Both drop you on the highway, where you can walk the 2km into town or take a taxi (M$30) waiting at the turnoff. ADO and Playa Express have frequent departures from Playa del Carmen as well. You can purchase ADO tickets at a **bus station** (www.ado.com.mx; Hwy 307, cnr Morelos) next to the highway turnoff.

From Cancún airport (p102), buses depart frequently to Puerto Morelos for M$110. They usually run from 7am to 10pm.

Cabs parked at the town plaza will take you back to the highway. Some drivers will tell you the fare is per person or overcharge in some other manner; strive for M$30 for as many people as you can stuff in.

Playa del Carmen

984 / POP 150,000

Playa del Carmen, now one of Quintana Roo's largest cities, ranks right up there with Tulum as one of the Riviera's trendiest spots. Sitting coolly on the lee side of Cozumel, the town's beaches are jammed with super-fit Europeans. The waters aren't as clear as those of Cancún or Cozumel, and the sand isn't quite as powder-perfect as they are further north, but still Playa grows and grows.

The town is ideally located: close to Cancún's international airport, but far enough south to allow easy access to Cozumel, Tulum, Cobá and other worthy destinations. The reefs here are excellent and offer diving and snorkeling close by. Look for rays, moray eels, sea turtles and a huge variety of corals. The lavender sea fans make for very picturesque vistas.

With cruise ship passengers visiting from Cozumel, Playa can feel crowded along the first several blocks of the tourist center.

Activities

★**Phocea Mexico** DIVING
(Map p66; 984-873-12-10; www.phocea-mexico.com; Calle 10 Norte s/n; 2-tank dive incl gear US$104, cenote dives incl gear US$150; 7:30am-8pm;) French, English and Spanish are spoken at Phocea Mexico. The shop does dives with bull sharks (US$90) for advanced divers, usually from November to March.

Río Secreto ADVENTURE
(998-113-19-05; www.riosecreto.com; Carretera 307 Km 283.5; adult/child 4-12yr from US$79/40; tours 8am-2pm) Hike and swim through a 1km-long underground cavern 5km south of Playa del Carmen. Some aspects are hyped, but there is a lot that is just plain awesome.

International House Riviera Maya LANGUAGE
(Map p66; 984-803-33-88; www.ihrivieramaya.com; Calle 14 Norte 141; per week US$230) Offers 20 hours of Spanish classes per week. You can stay in residence-hall rooms (US$36), even if you're not taking classes, but the best way to learn the language is to take advantage of the school's homestays (including breakfast, US$33 to US$39) with Mexican host families.

Sleeping & Eating

The Yak Hostel HOSTEL **$**
(Map p66; 984-148-09-25; www.yakhostel.com; Calle 10 bis s/n; dm/r incl breakfast from M$280/800;) One of the cleanest and most comfortable hostels in town, this well-run property offers a variety of lodging options ranging from air-conditioned mixed

dorms to 'deluxe' private digs with dining rooms and kitchens. Common areas include a rooftop terrace and a gravel courtyard with a fun bar scene.

★Hotel Playa del Karma BOUTIQUE HOTEL **$$**
(Map p66; ☎984-803-02-72; www.hotelplayadelkarma.com; 15 Av Norte, btwn Calles 12 & 14; d from M$1100;) The closest you're going to get to the jungle in this town; rooms here face a lush courtyard with a small – no, make that tiny – pool. All rooms have air-con and TV, and some come with kitchenette, sitting area and sweet little porches with hammocks. The hotel arranges tours to nearby ruins and diving sites.

Hotel Barrio Latino HOTEL **$$**
(Map p66; ☎984-873-23-84; www.hotelbarriolatino.com; Calle 4 Norte 153; r incl breakfast M$1200;) Offers 18 clean rooms with warm, rustic decor, good ventilation, ceiling fans or air-con, tiled floors and hammocks (in addition to beds). The place is often full and the front gate often locked. Discounted rates are available for extended stays, and the prices drop precipitously in low season. Guests get to make free international calls.

Chez Céline BREAKFAST **$**
(☎984-803-34-80; www.chezceline.com.mx; cnr 5 Av Norte & Calle 34 Norte; breakfast M$72-129; 7:30am-11pm;) Good, healthy breakfasts and a range of yummy baked goods are what keeps this French-run bakery-cafe busy.

La Cueva del Chango MEXICAN **$$**
(☎984-147-02-71; www.lacuevadelchango.com; Calle 38 Norte s/n, btwn Av 5 Norte & beach; breakfast M$90-114, lunch & dinner M$168-198; 8am-10:30pm, to 2pm Sun;) The 'Monkey's Cave,' known for its fresh and natural ingredients, has seating in a jungly *palapa* setting or a verdant garden out back. Service is friendly, but the kitchen can be slow. The food is delicious; try the stuffed ancho chili peppers and *chilaquiles* (fried tortillas bathed in sauce).

★Passion BASQUE **$$$**
(☎984-877-39-00; www.passionbymb.com; 5 Av Norte, Paradisus Hotel; mains M$600-1100, tasting menu M$1950; 6pm-9:30pm Mon-Sat;) With a French-Basque-inspired menu created by Michelin-starred chef Martin Berasteguí, this is unquestionably one of Playa's finest restaurants. Diners can order from the à la carte menu or opt for the exquisite seven-course tasting menu. Reserve ahead and dress appropriately for a meal served in an elegant dining room at the Paradisus Hotel.

Drinking & Nightlife

★Dirty Martini Lounge BAR
(Map p66; www.facebook.com/dirtymartinilounge; 1 Av Norte 234; noon-2am, to 3am Fri & Sat) The Dirty Martini Lounge doesn't have a foam machine, there's no mechanical bull and there's minimal nudity – a refreshing change for crazy Playa. The decor is something you'd find in the American West, with comfy cowhide upholstery and brown wood panels, and it's a place where you can sip something tasty while actually hearing yourself think.

Playa 69 GAY
(Map p66; www.facebook.com/sesentaynueveplaya; off 5 Av Norte, btwn Calles 4 & 6; cover after 10pm M$60; 9pm-4am Wed-Sun) This popular gay dance club proudly features foreign strippers from such far-flung places as Australia and Brazil, and it stages weekend drag-queen shows. It may also open Tuesdays at key vacation times. Find it at the end of the narrow alley.

★Fusion LIVE MUSIC
(Map p66; ☎cell 984-8797174; www.facebook.com/fusionbeachbarcuisine; Calle 6 Norte s/n; 8am-1am) This beachside bar and grill stages live music, along with a fun belly-dancing and fire-dancing show. The fire-dancing comes later in the evening (around 11pm). From 6pm and on, it's just a cool spot to have a beer or cocktail and listen to rock, reggae and Latin sounds.

Getting There & Away

BOAT

Passenger ferries depart frequently to Cozumel from Calle 1 Sur, where you'll find two companies with **ticket booths** (Map p66; Av 1 Sur s/n, cnr Calle 1 Sur). Prices are subject to change. The **Calica-Punta Venado terminal** (Terminal Marítima Punta Venado; www.calica.com.mx/terminal-maritima-punta-venado; Hwy 307 Km 282) south of Playa operates car ferries to Cozumel.

Mexico Waterjets (Map p66; ☎984-872-15-88; www.winjet.mx; Av 1 Sur s/n; one-way fare adult/child 6-11yr M$175/90; 8am-10pm) Online promotions can bring fares down by about 20% for all travelers.

Playa del Carmen

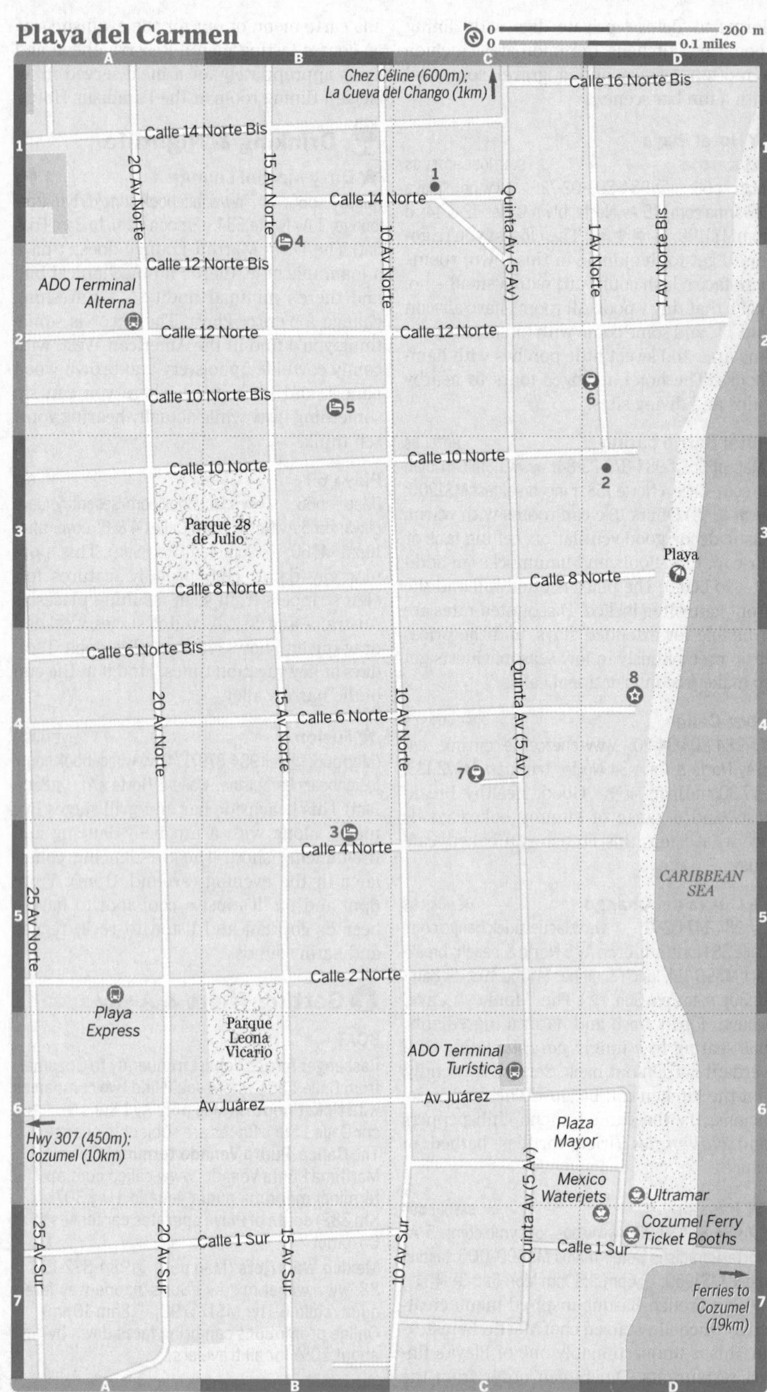

0 200 m
0 0.1 miles
Chez Céline (600m);
La Cueva del Chango (1km)
Calle 16 Norte Bis
Calle 14 Norte Bis
Calle 14 Norte
Calle 12 Norte Bis
Calle 12 Norte
Calle 10 Norte Bis
Calle 10 Norte
Calle 8 Norte
Calle 6 Norte Bis
Calle 6 Norte
Calle 4 Norte
Calle 2 Norte
Av Juárez
Calle 1 Sur
25 Av Norte
20 Av Norte
15 Av Norte
10 Av Norte
Quinta Av (5 Av)
1 Av Norte
1 Av Norte Bis
25 Av Sur
20 Av Sur
15 Av Sur
10 Av Sur
ADO Terminal Alterna
ADO Terminal Turística
Parque 28 de Julio
Parque Leona Vicario
Playa Express
Playa
CARIBBEAN SEA
Plaza Mayor
Mexico Waterjets
Ultramar
Cozumel Ferry Ticket Booths
Hwy 307 (450m);
Cozumel (10km)
Ferries to Cozumel (19km)

Playa del Carmen

Activities, Courses & Tours
1 International House Riviera Maya...... C1
2 Phocea Mexico.................................D3

Sleeping
3 Hotel Barrio Latino.............................B5
4 Hotel Playa del Karma.........................B1
5 The Yak Hostel....................................B2

Drinking & Nightlife
6 Dirty Martini Lounge............................D2
7 Playa 69...C4

Entertainment
8 Fusion..D4

Transcaribe (987-872-76-71; www.transcaribe.net; Hwy 307 Km 282, Calica-Punta Venado; one-way fare M$500) Daily car ferries to Cozumel. One-way fare includes passengers. The ferry terminal is 8km south of Playa del Carmen.

Ultramar (Map p66; 998-881-58-90, 998-293-90-92; www.ultramarferry.com/en; Av 1 Sur s/n; one-way fare adult/child 6-11yr M$200/130, one-way car ferry M$400; 7am-11pm) The most spiffy of the ferries, and claims to be the least prone to seasickness. Offers a 1st-class option with a lounge, more room, priority boarding and leather seats. Operates car ferries from the Calica-Punta Venado terminal.

BUS

Playa has two bus terminals; each sells tickets and provides information for at least some of the other's departures. You can save money by buying a 2nd-class bus ticket, but remember that it's often stop-and-go along the way.

The **ADO Terminal Alterna** (Map p66; www.ado.com.mx; 20 Av Norte s/n, cnr Calle 12) is where most long-distance bus lines arrive and depart. Buses heading to destinations within the state of Quintana Roo leave from the **ADO Terminal Turística** (Terminal del Centro; Map p66; www.ado.com.mx; 5 Av Norte s/n, cnr Av Juárez).

Playa Express (Map p66; Calle 2 Norte s/n) shuttle buses are a much quicker way to get around the Riviera Maya between Playa del Carmen and Cancún. It has frequent service to Puerto Morelos (M$25, 40 minutes) and downtown Cancún (M$38, 1¼ hours).

COLECTIVO

Colectivos (Calle 2 Norte s/n, cnr 20 Av; 5am-11:30pm) are a great option for cheap travel southward to Tulum and north to Cancún. They depart as soon as they fill (about every 15 minutes) and will stop anywhere along the highway between Playa and Tulum. Luggage space is somewhat limited, but they're great for day trips. From the same spot, you can grab a *colectivo* to Cancún (M$40). There are also daily departures to Isla Holbox (M$250) at 11:30am and 6:30pm.

Isla Cozumel

987 / POP 79,500

Fascinating for its dual personality, Cozumel offers an odd mix – quietly authentic neighborhoods existing alongside tourist-friendly playgrounds. Leaving the tourist area behind, you'll find garages that still have shrines to the Virgin and a spirited Caribbean energy in the air. And, of course, there are epic experiences to be had, such as diving at some of the best reefs in the world.

While diving and snorkeling are the main draws, the town square is a pleasant place to spend the afternoon, and it's highly gratifying to explore the less-visited parts of the island on a rented scooter or in a convertible car. The coastal road leads to small Maya ruins, a marine park and cliffside bars, passing captivating scenery along the unforgettable windswept shore. And while the nightlife has nothing on Playa del Carmen's or Cancún's, there's plenty to do after the sun goes down.

Sights & Activities

Most people, understandably, visit Cozumel for its famed diving and snorkeling, but you'll find plenty of other things to do, including cycling along the island's scenic coast road, horseback riding on the beach or hitting the surf on the island's east side. You can even go spearfishing for lionfish.

★El Cielo BEACH

Living up to its heavenly name, El Cielo's shallow turquoise waters are ideal for snorkeling and swimming among starfish, stingrays and small fish. Located on the island's southwest side, it's only accessible by boat but all the dive shops make trips there.

Sea Walls PUBLIC ART

(Map p69; www.pangeaseed.foundation/cozumel-mexico; San Miguel de Cozumel) Local and international artists backed by the PangeaSeed foundation created 36 large-scale public murals in 2015 to raise awareness about ocean conversation and responsible coastal development. A DIY walking tour reveals cool downtown works like a towering sea monster mural on Calle 1 Sur and

Avenida 20 Sur. Ask the **tourist office** (Map p69; ☎987-869-02-12; www.cozumel.travel; Av 5 Sur s/n, Plaza del Sol, 2nd fl; 8am-3pm Mon-Fri) for a printed map of the murals.

Aldora Divers DIVING

(Map p69; ☎987-872-33-97; www.aldora.com; Calle 5 Sur 37; 1-/2-tank dive incl equipment US$66/113, 3-tank shark-cave dive US$232; 7am-3pm & 6-8pm) One of the best dive shops in Cozumel, Aldora will take divers to the windward side of the island when weather is bad on the western side. It also offers full-day excursions to caves with sleeping sharks; these trips include a stop at a lagoon with Maya ruins.

Cozumel Surfing School & Rental SURFING

(☎US 612-287-5549, cell 987-1119290; www.cozumelsurfing.com; Carretera Coastal Oriente Km 42.9, Playa Chen Río; surfboard per day US$30-40, surfing class US$110, spear-fishing US$80) Hit the surf with Nacho Gutierrez (who is rocking the Johnny Depp look in a serious way). You'll find Nacho at **El Pescador** restaurant (Km 42.9) on Playa Chen Río. He usually holds surfing classes at Punta Chiqueros, where you can rent boards at **Playa Bonita** restaurant (Km 37). Reserve ahead for surfing lessons. Nacho also runs spear-fishing outings.

Sleeping & Eating

Casa del Solar GUESTHOUSE $

(Map p69; ☎987-869-30-77, cell 987-5648680; teresagonzalez230172@gmail.com; Av 5 Norte 280; d US$35-40;) Six rooms, all with comfortable beds and some with the old house's original tile floors, overlook a sunny courtyard with a large *mamey* (sapote) tree. Coffee is made each morning in a common kitchen. Like many budget guesthouses, this one has its quirks: at last visit, wi-fi was spotty and one room's electric water heater delivered harmless but eye-opening shocks.

Hotel Mary Carmen HOTEL $$

(Map p69; ☎987-872-05-81; www.hotelmarycarmen.com.mx; Av 5 Sur 132; d M$900;) Clean, colorful rooms overlook a central courtyard where the owner keeps more than a dozen tortoises, so watch your step, especially at night. It's just a short walk from the ferry terminal before you reach the hotel's airy lobby, full of antique furnishings. Discounted rates offered throughout most of the year.

★**Hotel B Cozumel** BOUTIQUE HOTEL $$$

(☎987-872-03-00; www.hotelbcozumel.com; Carretera San Juan Km 2.5; d/ste incl breakfast from US$124/196;) This hip hotel on the north shore may not have that sand beach you're after, but just wait till you get a look at the crystalline saltwater pool and oceanfront hot tub. Rooms are fitted with handmade furnishings, there's weekly live jazz, and free bikes are available. Rates quoted are for jungle-view rooms; ocean views cost extra.

Camarón Dorado SEAFOOD $

(☎987-872-72-87, cell 987-1181281; www.facebook.com/camaron.dorado; cnr Av Juárez & Calle 105 Sur; tortas M$29-55, tacos M$18-35; 7am-1:30pm Tue-Sun;) If you're headed to the windward side of the island or just want to see a different aspect of Cozumel, drop by the Camarón Dorado for a bite, assuming you're early enough. Be warned: the *camarón empanizado* (breaded shrimp) *tortas* and tacos are highly addictive. It's 2.5km southeast of the passenger ferry terminal.

Jeanie's MEXICAN $$

(Map p69; ☎987-878-46-47; www.jeaniescozumel.com; Av Melgar 790; breakfasts M$79-125, mains M$110-230; 7am-10pm;) The views of the water are great from the outdoor patio here. Jeanie's serves waffles, plus hash browns, eggs, sandwiches and other tidbits including vegetarian fajitas. Frozen coffees beat the midday heat. Between 5pm and 7pm they do a lovely happy hour too.

★**Kinta** CONTEMPORARY MEXICAN $$$

(Map p69; ☎987-869-05-44; www.kintarestaurante.com; Av 5 Norte 148; mains M$260-340; 5-11pm;) Putting a gourmet twist on Mexican classics, this chic bistro is one of the best restaurants on the island. The Midnight Pork Ribs are a tried-and-true favorite, while the wood-fired oven turns out spectacular oven-baked fish. For dessert treat yourself to a *budín de la abuelita,* aka 'granny's pudding.'

Drinking & Nightlife

★**Turquoise Beach Bar** LIVE MUSIC

(☎cell 987-1155057; www.facebook.com/turquoisecozumelbeachclub; Av Melgar Km 2.8; 9am-8pm Mon-Sat, 10am-11pm Sun) Rock cover bands, some surprisingly good, play fun sunset shows several times a week. If you get tired of the beer routine, order a cocktail or potent mezcal. A festively plump pet pig named Taluhla roams the beach here

San Miguel de Cozumel

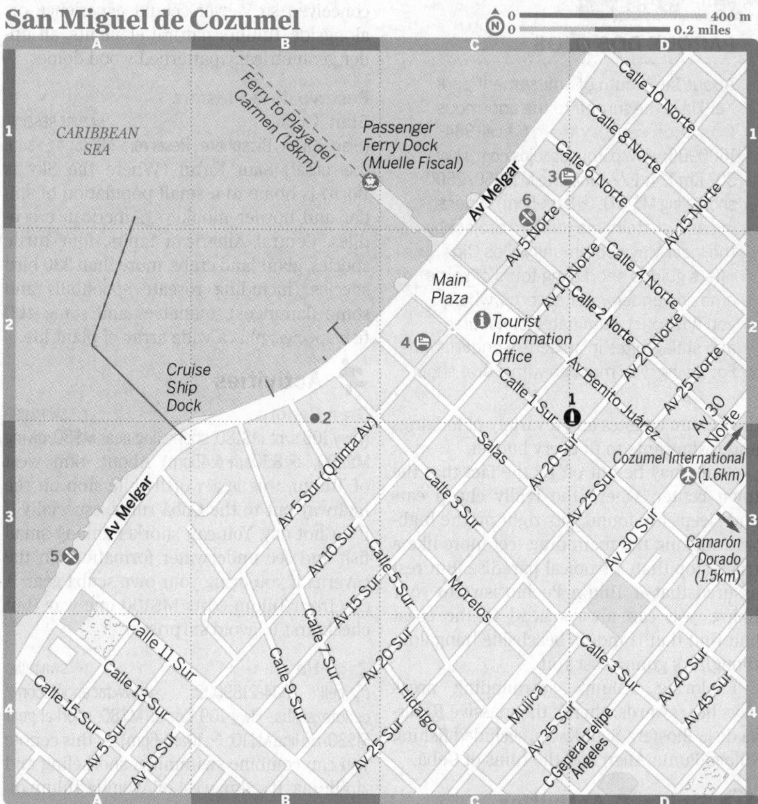

San Miguel de Cozumel

Sights
1 Sea Walls D2

Activities, Courses & Tours
2 Aldora Divers B2

Sleeping
3 Casa del Solar C1
4 Hotel Mary Carmen C2

Eating
5 Jeanie's A3
6 Kinta C1

for table scraps and she seems to be making out quite well. It's about 1km south of the car ferry dock.

Getting There & Around

Most people arrive by ferry, but there's a small airport as well. Bus tickets for onward travel in the Yucatán can be purchased in Cozumel, but you actually board the bus in Playa del Carmen and continue from there.

Passenger ferries operated by Ultramar (p67) and Mexico Waterjets (p65) run frequently to Cozumel from Playa del Carmen from 7am to 11pm (one way M$175 to M$200), leaving from and arriving at the **Passenger Ferry Dock** (Map p69; Isla Cozumel).

In order to see most of the island you will need to rent a vehicle or take a taxi (M$1500 to M$2000 for a day trip); cyclists should be prepared to brave the regular strong winds.

Tulum

984 / POP 18,200

Tulum's spectacular coastline – with all its confectioner-sugar sands, cobalt water and balmy breezes – makes it one of the top beaches in Mexico. Where else can you get all that *and* a dramatically situated Maya ruin? There's also excellent cave and cavern

DON'T MISS

PARQUE DOS OJOS

About 1km south of amusement park Xel-Há is the turnoff to the enormous **Dos Ojos cave system** (cell 984-1600906; www.parquedosojos.com; Hwy 307 Km 124; 1-/2-tank dive M$1850/2600, snorkeling M$470; 8am-5pm). Operating as a sustainable tourism project by the local Maya community, Dos Ojos offers guided snorkeling tours of some amazing underwater caverns, where you float past illuminated stalactites and stalagmites in an eerie wonderland. For diving, you must go with a dive shop.

diving, fun cenotes and a variety of lodgings and restaurants to fit every budget.

Some may be put off by the fact that the town center, where the really cheap eats and sleeps are found, sits right on the highway, making the main drag feel more like a truck stop than a tropical paradise. But rest assured that if Tulum Pueblo isn't to your liking, you can always head to the coast and find that tranquil, beachside bungalow, though it's gonna cost you.

Exploring Tulum's surrounding areas pays big rewards: there's the massive Reserva de la Biosfera Sian Ka'an, secluded fishing village Punta Allen and the ruins of Cobá.

Sights & Activities

★Tulum Ruins ARCHAEOLOGICAL SITE
(www.inah.gob.mx; Hwy 307 Km 230; M$70, parking M$180, tours from M$560; 8am-5pm; P) The ruins of Tulum preside over a rugged coastline, a strip of brilliant beach and green-and-turquoise waters that'll leave you floored. It's true the extents and structures are of a modest scale and the late-post-Classic design is inferior to those of earlier, more grandiose projects – but, wow! Those Maya occupants must have felt pretty smug each sunrise.

★IK Lab GALLERY
(984-980-06-40; www.iklab.art; Carretera Tulum-Boca Paila Km 5; 10am-noon) FREE In this mind-bending contemporary art gallery at Azulik resort, guests enter barefoot to interact with floors of polished concrete and *bejuco* (vine-like wood) as living organisms. Opened by the great-grandson of art collector Peggy Guggenheim, the dreamlike exhibition space of meandering expanses was conceived so viewers could experience art alongside Tulum's natural elements, all under geometrically patterned wood domes.

Reserva de la Biosfera Sian Ka'an NATURE RESERVE
(Sian Ka'an Biosphere Reserve; M$35; sunrise-sunset) Sian Ka'an (Where the Sky is Born) is home to a small population of spider and howler monkeys, American crocodiles, Central American tapirs, four turtle species, giant land crabs, more than 330 bird species (including roseate spoonbills and some flamingos), manatees and some 400 fish species, plus a wide array of plant life.

Activities

Gran Cenote SWIMMING
(Hwy 109 s/n; M$180, snorkeling gear M$80, diving M$200; 8:10am-4:45pm) About 4km west of Tulum, this is a worthwhile stop on the highway out to the Cobá ruins, especially if it's a hot day. You can snorkel among small fish and see underwater formations in the caverns if you bring your own scuba gear. A cab from Tulum costs M$100 one way (but check first to avoid surprises).

Zacil-Ha SWIMMING
(cell 984-2189029; www.facebook.com/cenotezacilha; Hwy 109 Km 8; M$80, snorkel gear M$30, zip line M$10; 10am-6pm) At this cenote you can combine swimming, snorkeling and zip-lining. It's 8km west of Avenida Tulum on the road to Cobá. There's even a bar too!

Xibalba Dive Center DIVING
(984-871-29-53; www.xibalbadivecenter.com; Andromeda Oriente 7, btwn Libra Sur & Geminis Sur; 1-/2-cavern dive incl gear US$90/150) One of the best dive shops in Tulum, Xibalba is known for its safety-first approach to diving. The center specializes in cave and cavern diving, visiting sites such as Dos Ojos and the spooky **Cenote Angelita** (Hwy 307 Km 213; cenote dives M$300, snorkeling M$200; 7am-5pm). Xibalba doubles as a hotel (rooms from US$100) and offers attractive packages combining lodging, diving trips and courses.

Festivals & Events

Sound Tulum MUSIC
(www.soundtulum.com; late Dec & early Jan) A two-week-long music festival drawing top international names in the underground electronic music scene. Events take place in Tulum. See website for lineup, venues and tickets.

Sleeping & Eating

Cenote Encantado CAMPGROUND $

(WhatsApp only 55-3028-2253; www.cenoteencantado.com; Carretera Tulum-Boca Paila Km 10.5; tents per person M$500;) A rare budget option near the beach, this new-agey spot gets its name from a pretty cenote right in the campground's backyard. Guests stay in large tents with beds, rugs and nightstands, and there's a yoga/meditation room here too. It's not on the beach, but you can walk there. Rates increase in December and January, sometimes significantly.

Lum Hostal HOSTEL $

(984-160-04-21; www.facebook.com/lumhostal; Alfa Norte, cnr Sagitario Poniente; dm/d M$500/1500;) This spiffy, clean, well-run hostel in the town center offers modern rooms and six-bed dorms with polished concrete floors, air-con, common kitchen and bar areas, and, best of all, free bikes to get to the beach and ruins.

Mango Tulum HOTEL $$

(55-1204-0339; www.mangotulum.com; Polar Poniente, cnr Av Cobá; r from US$55;) A quiet, comfortable and relaxing midrange stay with minimalist rooms overlooking a swimming pool and lush garden fitted with picnic benches. Ruins, cenotes and a supermarket are all nearby, and it lies just a block from the beach access road. Do not confuse it with Casa Mango, on the road to Cobá.

★ **La Posada del Sol** BOUTIQUE HOTEL $$$

(cell 984-1348874; www.laposadadelsol.com; Carretera Tulum-Boca Paila Km 3.5; r incl breakfast US$100-190;) Using recycled objects found on the property after a hurricane, Posada del Sol stands out for its natural design details and creative architecture. All 11 rooms have air-con, but the pricier ones on the beach side of the road usually catch a nice ocean breeze. The solar- and wind-powered hotel has a sweet beach and a great crafts store too.

★ **Taquería Honorio** TACOS $

(984-134-87-31; www.facebook.com/taqueriahonorio; Satélite Sur; tacos M$16-22, tortas M$35-40; 6am-2pm) It began as a street stall and became such a hit that it's now a taco place with a proper roof overhead. Most folks go here for the *cochinita* (pulled pork in annatto marinade) served on handmade tortillas or *tortas* (sandwiches). Also well worth seeking out here are Yucatecan classics like *relleno negro* (shredded turkey in a chili-based dark sauce).

Azafran BREAKFAST $$

(cell 984-1296130; Av Satélite s/n, cnr Calle 2 Poniente; mains M$75-125; 8am-3pm Wed-Mon;) A great little German-owned breakfast spot in a shady rear garden, the favorite dish here is the 'hangover breakfast,' a hearty portion of homemade sausage, mashed potatoes, eggs, rye toast and bacon – you might even have a lettuce sighting. There are lighter items on the menu too, such as freshly baked bagels topped with brined salmon. Cash only.

La Gloria de Don Pepe TAPAS $$

(cell 984-1524471; www.facebook.com/lagloriadedonpepe; Orión Sur, cnr Andromeda Oriente;

BUSES FROM TULUM

DESTINATION	COST (M$)	DURATION (HR)	FREQUENCY (DAILY)
Belize City	675	6	2; 12:45am & 10am
Cancún	148-218	2-2½	frequent
Cancún airport	242	2	5
Chetumal	258-378	3¼-4	frequent
Chichén Itzá	232	2½-2¾	2; 9am & 2:45pm
Chiquilá (for Isla Holbox)	334	3½	1; 8:10am
Cobá	55	1	10:11am
Felipe Carrillo Puerto	65-104	1¼	4; consider taking a frequent *colectivo*
Laguna Bacalar	222-252	3	frequent
Mahahual	296	3-3½	2; 9:10am & 7:05pm
Mérida	356-500	4-4½	9
Playa del Carmen	49-108	1	frequent
Valladolid	110-134	1½-1¾	frequent

tapas M$60-195; ⏲1:30-10:30pm Tue-Sun) With its 'A meal without wine is called breakfast' sign, this spot tickles the taste buds with delicious tapas plates and fine seafood paella. And wine – did we mention there's wine? A perfect place to come to talk to a friend for a couple of hours without being drowned out by noise. Alfresco seating is also possible.

★**Hartwood** FUSION **$$$**
(www.hartwoodtulum.com; Carretera Tulum-Boca Paila Km 7.5; mains M$380-500; ⏲5:30-10pm Wed-Sun) Assuming you can get in (it accepts walk-ins and online reservations made one month in advance), this sweet 'n' simple nouvelle cuisine restaurant down on the beach road will definitely impress. Ingredients are fresh and local; flavors and techniques are international. The chalkboard menu changes daily, and the solar-powered open kitchen and wood-burning oven serve to accentuate the delicious dishes.

Getting There & Away

The 24-hour **ADO bus terminal** (☎984-871-21-22; www.ado.com.mx; Av Tulum, btwn Calles Alfa Norte & Jupiter Norte; ⏲24hr) is simple but adequate, with some chairs for waiting, but not much else.

Colectivos leave from Avenida Tulum for Playa del Carmen. Colectivos to Felipe Carrillo Puerto depart from a block south of the bus terminal. Colectivos to Cobá depart every two hours or so from 9am to 6pm (M$70).

Cobá

☎984 / POP 1300

Cobá's ruins are a treat and exploring them is a big part of the reason for coming here: the state's tallest pyramid, a beautiful ball court and a variety of other structures make for a fun few hours. The village is quiet and cute, with a croc-filled lagoon, a series of cenotes, and a growing number of hotels and restaurants…but people mostly come for the ruins. In droves. By the busload. In fact, that's its biggest problem: arrive after 11am and you'll be one of literally hundreds of other people coming in from Cancún, Playa and Tulum.

From a sustainable-tourism perspective, it's great to stay the night in small communities like Cobá, but don't plan on staying up late.

Sights

★**Cobá Ruins** ARCHAEOLOGICAL SITE
(www.inah.gob.mx; M$70, guides M$600-650; ⏲8am-4:30pm; P) Cobá's ruins include the tallest pyramid in Quintana Roo (the second tallest in all of Yucatán) and the thick jungle setting makes you feel like you're in an Indiana Jones flick. Many of the ruins are yet to be excavated, just mysterious piles of root- and vine-covered rubble. Walk along ancient *sacbés* (ceremonial limestone avenues or paths between great Maya cities), climb up ancient mounds, and ascend Nohoch Mul for a spectacular view of the surrounding jungle.

➡ **Grupo Cobá**
(Cobá Ruins) The most prominent structure in the Grupo Cobá is **La Iglesia** (the Church). It's an enormous pyramid; if you were allowed to climb it, you could see the surrounding lakes (which look lovely on a clear day) and the Nohoch Mul pyramid. To reach it walk just under 100m along the main path from the entrance and turn right.

Take the time to explore Grupo Cobá; it has a couple of corbeled-vault passages you can walk through. Near its northern edge, on the way back to the main path and the bicycle concession, is a very well-restored **juego de pelota** (ball court).

➡ **Grupo Macanxoc**
(Cobá Ruins) Grupo Macanxoc is notable for its numerous restored stelae, some of which are believed to depict reliefs of royal women who are thought to have come from Tikal. Though many are worn down by the elements, a number of them are still in good condition and are worth a detour.

➡ **Grupo de las Pinturas**
(Cobá Ruins) The temple at Grupo de las Pinturas (Paintings Group) bears traces of glyphs and frescoes above its door and remnants of richly colored plaster inside. You approach the temple from the southeast. Leave by the trail at the northwest (opposite the temple steps) to see two stelae. The first of these is 20m along, beneath a *palapa*. Here a regal figure stands over two others, one of them kneeling with his hands bound behind him.

➡ **Grupo Nohoch Mul**
(Cobá Ruins) Nohoch Mul (Big Mound) is also known as the Great Pyramid (which sounds a lot better than Big Mound). It reaches a height of 42m, making it the second-tallest Maya structure on the Yucatán Peninsula

(Calakmul's Estructura II, at 45m, is the tallest). Climbing the old steps can be scary for some. Two diving gods are carved over the doorway of the temple at the top (built in the post-Classic period, AD 1100–1450), similar to sculptures at Tulum.

Activities

In addition to the ruins, the area has several cenotes south of town. If you **rent a bike** (near ruins bus stop; bikes per day M$50; ⏲10am-5pm) it makes a nice ride. Otherwise, you'll need to find your own way to get there.

Cenotes Choo-Ha, Tamcach-Ha & Multún-Ha SWIMMING
(☎cell 984-1338561; per cenote M$55; ⏲8am-6pm) About 6km south of the town of Cobá, on the road to Chan Chen, you'll find a series of three locally administered cenotes: Choo-Ha, Tamcach-Ha and Multún-Ha. These cavern-like cenotes are nice spots to cool off with a swim, or a snorkel if you bring your own gear. Children under 10 enter free.

Sleeping & Eating

Hotel Maya HOTEL $$
(☎cell 984-1443006; www.facebook.com/hotelsacbecoba; Av Principal s/n; d M$800-1000;) The best deal in town. Clean, colorful and comfortable rooms (some with cable TV) await upstairs behind wooden doors designed with Maya god carvings, while downstairs there's an inviting blue-tiled swimming pool. It's on the main avenue and just a short walk to the ruins.

★**Aldea Cobá** RESORT $$$
(☎cell 998-3420198, cell 998-1476623; www.aldeacoba.com; Av Principal 1; M$1760-2900;) A lovingly designed jungle-set resort with cool, comfortable rooms featuring furnishings crafted by local artisans. Bungalows and the larger villas overlook an inviting pool surrounded by vegetation. On-site restaurant Pischán, which specializes in Yucatecan cuisine, welcomes nonguests and is worth visiting. It's 2.5km from the ruins, so you'll need a car or have to hoof it into town.

Restaurant La Pirámide MEXICAN $$
(☎984-206-71-75, 984-206-70-18; Av Principal s/n; mains M$105-170, buffet M$180; ⏲8am-5pm;) At the end of the town's main drag, by the lake, this restaurant is pretty touristy but does decent Yucatecan fare like *cochinita* or *pollo pibil* (achiote-flavored pork or chicken), or you can opt for the lunch buffet between noon and 3pm. The open-air setup allows for nice lagoon views.

Getting There & Away

Most buses serving Cobá swing down to the ruins to drop off passengers at a small **bus stop**; but you can also get off in town.

Buses run eight times daily between Tulum and Cobá (M$50 to M$55, one hour) and there are about five daily departures to Playa del Carmen (M$94 to M$142, two hours). Buses also go eight times daily to Valladolid (M$52, one hour), where you'll find frequent bus services (p77) to Chichén Itza and Mérida. For Cancún (M$174, 3½ hours), a bus leaves Cobá at 3:10pm.

Day-trippers from Tulum can reach Cobá by taking colectivos (p72; M$70) that depart every two hours or so from Calle Osiris Norte and Avenida Tulum.

The road from Cobá to Chemax is arrow-straight and in good shape. If you're driving to Valladolid or Chichén Itzá, this is the way to go.

Cobá-based taxis charge M$450 to Tulum and M$650 to Valladolid.

Laguna Bacalar

☎983 / POP 11,000

Laguna Bacalar, the peninsula's largest lagoon, comes as a surprise in this region of scrubby jungle. More than 60km long with a bottom of sparkling white sand, this crystal-clear lake offers opportunities for camping, swimming, kayaking and simply lazing around, amid a color palette of blues, greens and shimmering whites that seems more out of Photoshop than anything real life could hold.

Some would say this area is the 'new' Tulum. Small and sleepy, yet with enough tourism to have things to do and places to eat, the lakeside town of Bacalar lies east of the highway, 115km south of Felipe Carrillo Puerto. It's noted mostly for its old Spanish fortress and popular *balnearios* (swimming grounds). There's not much else going on, but that's why people like it. Around the town plaza, you'll find ATMs, a money exchange office, a small grocery store, a taxi stand and tourist information office.

Sights & Activities

Fortress FORTRESS
(☎cell 983-8361065; cnr Av 3 & Calle 22; adult/child 9-17yr M$100/25; ⏲9am-7pm Tue-Sun) The fortress above the lagoon was built in 1733 to protect Spanish colonists from pirate attacks and rebellions by local indigenous people. It also served as an important outpost for the

Spanish in the War of the Castes. In 1859 it was seized by Maya rebels, who held the fort until Quintana Roo was conquered by Mexican troops in 1901.

★Los Rápidos KAYAKING

(☎cell 983-1205920; www.facebook.com/losrapidosbacalar; off Hwy 307 Km 8; adult/child 2-12yr M$50/25, kayak per hour M$150; ⏲10am-7pm) A gorgeous spot for kayaking and birdwatching, here you can paddle up a slow-flowing, crystalline stream brimming with large underwater stromatolites (live ancient rock-like structures formed by cyanobacteria). Some are believed to be billions of years old! Beat the crowds with a midweek morning visit and try to avoid stepping on the exceedingly rare stromatolites.

Balneario SWIMMING

(Av Costera s/n, cnr Calle 14; ⏲9am-6pm) FREE This beautiful public swimming spot lies several blocks south of the fort, along Avenida Costera. Admission is free, but parking costs M$10.

Cenote Azul SWIMMING

(☎983-130-65-69; Hwy 307 Km 34; adult/child under 11yr M$25/free; ⏲10am-6pm) Just shy of the south end of the *costera* (coast highway) and about 3km south of Bacalar's town center is this cenote, a 90m-deep natural pool with an on-site bar and restaurant. It's 200m east of Hwy 307, so many buses will drop you nearby. Taxis to the cenote from the main square cost M$50.

Sleeping & Eating

Yak Lake House HOSTEL $

(☎983-834-31-75; www.yakbacalar.com; Av 1 s/n, btwn Calles 24 & 26; dm M$330-400, r M$1600; P⊖❄☎) If lounging around all day in your bikini is your idea of fun, then Yak House won't disappoint. It's steps away from Laguna Bacalar and there are ample chairs, docks and decks on which to soak up the sun. Free breakfast, friendly staff, clean rooms and comfy mixed dorms make this a sweet spot to park yourself for several days.

★Hotel Maria Maria HOTEL $$

(☎983-834-21-16; www.facebook.com/hotelmariamaria; Av 3 No 600, cnr Calle 14; r M$950-1050, ste M$1150; P⊖❄☎) Just a block away from a lovely swimming spot and a short walk from the town square, this well-run little hotel offers tastefully designed suites with lagoon views and two slightly more affordable rooms on the ground floor. Guests have use of a kitchen upstairs and the host, Maria, is very accommodating.

★Rancho Encantado CABAÑAS $$$

(☎998-884-20-71; www.encantado.com; Hwy 307 Km 24; d/ste incl breakfast from M$2637/3007; P⊖❄☎≋) Laguna Bacalar is absolutely beautiful in its own right, so imagine staying at one of the most striking locations along the shore. A typical day on the *rancho* (ranch) goes something like this: wake up in comfy cabin or room, have breakfast with lagoon view, kayak or swim in calm, translucent waters and unwind in a Jacuzzi.

Christian's Tacos TACOS $

(☎cell 983-1149094; www.facebook.com/taqueriachristiansbacalar; Calle 18 s/n, btwn Avs 7 & 9; tacos M$12-29, nachos M$65-120; ⏲6pm-1am) If Christian's were in Mexico City – the *al pastor* (spit-roasted marinated pork) capital – it would compete with the best of them. The popular, yet artery-choking, *pastor nachos* are topped with slices of pork, beans and cheese. The new bar means you can wash down your food with your favorite alcoholic libations as well.

Los Aluxes MEXICAN $$

(☎983-834-28-17; www.losaluxesbacalar.com; Av Costera 69; mains M$120-270; ⏲7am-9pm; P☎) An open-air *palapa* restaurant serving regional and fusion dishes, this waterfront restaurant prepares interesting creations such as *pechuga sikil pak* (Yucatecan-style chicken and pasta dish). A life-sized Al Capone statue lurks in the bathroom, gun drawn. It's 1km south of town.

★Nixtamal GRILL $$$

(☎cell 983-1347651; www.facebook.com/nixtamalcocinaafuegoyceniza; López Mateos 525, cnr Calle 12; mains M$120-280, lobster M$1500; ⏲7pm-11pm Wed-Mon; ☎) The *slooow*-food experience here pushes your patience to the limit, but grill master Rodrigo Estrada makes it well worth the wait. Exquisite dishes such as marinated rib eye and whole grilled lobster are cooked over a wood-and-charcoal grill and finished in a wood-fired oven (no gas or electrical appliances are used). The candlelit open-air restaurant stages live music on weekends.

Getting There & Away

Buses don't enter town, but taxis and some *colectivos* will drop you at the town square. Buses arrive at Bacalar's **ADO station** (☎983-833-31-63; www.ado.com.mx; Hwy 307 s/n, btwn Calles 28 & 30) on Hwy 307, near Calle 30. From there it's about a 10-block walk southeast to the main square, or you can grab a local taxi for M$20.

If you're driving from the north and want to reach the town and fort, take the first Bacalar exit and continue several blocks before turning left (east) down the hill. From Chetumal, head west to catch Hwy 307 north; after 25km on the highway you'll reach the signed right turn for Cenote Azul (p74) and Avenida Costera, aka Avenida 1.

Mahahual

☎983 / POP 920

Mahahual changed forever when the cruise ship dock was completed, and it grows larger every year. Despite the (literally) boatloads of tourists, there's a lovely, relaxed, Caribbean vibe that you won't find further north, and once the passengers have returned to their ships, a quiet calm settles over the town. Mahahual is the only spot in the Costa Maya that's large enough to support a diversity of sleeping and eating options, while still being right on the beach.

Sights & Activities

★Banco Chinchorro DIVE SITE

Divers won't want to miss the reefs and underwater fantasy worlds of the Banco Chinchorro, the largest coral atoll in the northern hemisphere and known for its shipwreck sites, coral walls and canyons. Some 45km long and up to 14km wide, Chinchorro's western edge lies about 30km off the coast, and dozens of ships have fallen victim to its barely submerged ring of coral.

★Amigos del Mar DIVING

(☎984-132-79-75, cell 984-1516758; www.amigosdelmar.net; Malecón s/n, cnr Coronado; 2-tank dive incl equipment US$150, snorkeling US$100; ⏲9am-6pm) One of the few dive shops in town authorized to visit the spectacular Banco Chinchorro.

Sleeping & Eating

★Posada Pachamama HOTEL $$

(☎983-834-57-62; www.posadapachamama.net; Huachinango s/n, btwn Coronado & Martillo; d M$1000-1300, q M$1800; P⊖❄📶🐾) Rooms at the Pachamama (which means Mother Earth in Inca) range from small interior singles and doubles with ocean views to more ample digs that sleep four. The staff are very knowledgeable about local activities and the accommodations are fairly priced by Mahahual standards.

Palmeras de Mahahual Cabañas CABAÑAS $$$

(☎cell 983-1377949; www.facebook.com/palmerasdemahahual; Atún s/n, btwn Malecón & Sardina; d M$2400; P⊖❄📶) Just four air-conditioned, wood cabin rooms are on offer at this pleasant, laid-back hotel. All have comfortable beds, mini-fridges and terraces with an ocean view. At last visit, construction was going on next door but you could still catch a good eight hours of shut-eye. Prices drop considerably during low season. Rents out bikes too.

★Nohoch Kay SEAFOOD $$

(Big Fish; ☎983-834-59-81; miplayanohochkay@outlook.com; cnr Malecón & Cazón; mains M$145-240; ⏲12:30pm-9pm; 📶) Nohoch Kay, aka the Big Fish, definitely lives up to its name. Don't miss this beachfront Mexican-owned restaurant, where they prepare succulent whole fish in a garlic and white-wine sauce, and seafood paella for two (M$350), which includes mussels, clams, shrimp, calamari and octopus.

Getting There & Around

There's no official bus terminal in Mahahual. Liquor store Solo Chelas doubles as an ADO bus stop and sells tickets for a twice-daily northbound bus, which departs Mahahual at 10:30am and 5:30pm for Felipe Carrillo Puerto (M$166, 1¾ hours), Tulum (M$296, three hours), Playa del Carmen (M$378, four hours) and Cancún (M$450, 5½ hours). A Xcalak-bound Caribe bus (M$52, 40 minutes) stops here as well, usually around 8:10am and 6:40pm. Westbound buses to Laguna Bacalar (M$80 to M$90, 1½ hours) and Chetumal (M$90 to M$236, 2½ hours) leave frequently from 6:30am to 7:30pm.

Shuttle vans leave hourly from 5:20am to 8:20pm to Chetumal (M$90, 2½ hours), Laguna Bacalar (M$75, two hours) and Limones (M$50, one hour), where you can catch frequent northbound buses. The terminal is on the corner of Calles Sardina and Cherna, on the soccer field's north end.

Valladolid

☎985 / POP 52,000

Once known as the Sultana of the East, Yucatán's third-largest city is famed for its quiet streets and sun-splashed pastel walls. It's worth staying here for a few days or longer, as the provincial town makes a great hub for visits to Río Lagartos, Chichén Itzá, Ek' Balam and a number of nearby cenotes. The city resides at that magic point where there's plenty to do, yet it still feels small, manageable and affordable.

Sights & Activities

★Casa de los Venados MUSEUM
(☎985-856-22-89; www.casadelosvenados.com; Calle 40 No 204, btwn Calles 41 & 43; M$100; ⏰tours 10am or by appointment) Featuring over 3000 pieces of museum-quality Mexican folk art, this private collection is interesting in that objects are presented in an actual private house, in the context that they were originally designed for, instead of being displayed in glass cases. The tour (in English or Spanish) touches on the origins of some of the more important pieces and the story of the award-winning restored colonial mansion that houses them.

Templo de San Bernardino CHURCH
(Convento de Sisal; cnr Calles 49 & 51; Mon-Sat M$30, Sun free; ⏰9am-7pm) The Templo de San Bernardino and the adjacent Convento de Sisal are about 700m southwest of the plaza. They were constructed between 1552–60 to serve the dual functions of fortress and church. The church's charming decoration includes beautiful rose-colored walls, arches, some recently uncovered 16th-century frescoes and a small image of the Virgin on the altar. These are about the only original items remaining; the grand wooden *retablo* (altarpiece) dates from the 19th century.

★Hacienda San Lorenzo Oxman SWIMMING
(off Calle 54; cenote M$70, cenote & pool M$100, open bar M$50; ⏰9am-6pm) Once a *henequén* plantation and a refuge for War of the Castes insurgents in the mid-19th century, today the hacienda's main draw is a gorgeous cenote that's far less crowded than other sinkholes in and around Valladolid, especially if you visit Monday through Thursday. If you buy the entry to both, you have a M$50 credit to use at the cafe.

★Yucatán Jay Expeditions & Tours BIRDWATCHING, CULTURAL
(☎cell 999-2805117; www.yucatanjay.com; ⏰8am-8pm) This cooperative, run by five informative and enthusiastic individuals from the Xocén community, 14km south of Valladolid, offers a fabulous array of tours, from birdwatching to tours based on Maya culture and gastronomy. They can take you to cenotes and other locations, providing excellent insights into their culture.

Cenote X'Kekén y Samulá SWIMMING
(Cenote Dzitnup & Samulá; 1/2 cenotes M$80/125; ⏰8:30am-6:30pm) One of two cenotes at Dzitnup (also known as X'Kekén Jungle Park), X'Kekén is popular with tour groups. A massive limestone formation with stalactites hangs from its ceiling. The pool is artificially lit and very swimmable. Here you can also take a dip in cenote Samulá, a lovely cavern pool with *álamo* roots stretching down many meters. You can also rent horses (M$225 per 30 minutes), ATVs (M$275 per 30 minutes) or bikes (M$100 per hour).

Sleeping & Eating

★Hostel La Candelaria HOSTEL $
(☎985-856-22-67; www.hostelvalladolidyucatan.com; Calle 35 No 201F; dm/r incl breakfast from M$265/575;) A friendly place right on a quiet little square, this hostel can get a little cramped and hot (but some dorms have air-con). The kitchen, a gorgeous elongated garden complete with hammocks, a gals-only dorm and plenty of hangout space make it one of the best hostels in town. The hostel also rents out bikes for M$20 per hour.

Hotel Tunich-Beh B&B $$
(☎985-856-22-22; www.tunichbeh.com; Calle 41A, btwn Calles 46 & 48; d incl breakfast from M$1200;) In a lovely historic street, this old house with a bright-blue facade has been converted into a hotel. It features well-equipped rooms around a swimming pool, plus some nice *palapa*-shaded common areas for kicking back. The staff are very helpful and there are bikes available for rent to ride to nearby cenotes (M$25 per hour).

Casa Marlene BOUTIQUE HOTEL $$$
(☎985-856-04-99; www.casatimicha.com; Calle 39 No 193; r incl breakfast M$1700-2100;) A sister property of boutique hotel **Casa Tía Micha** (Calle 39 No 197; r incl breakfast M$1700-2100;), and right on the same block, the Marlene house is a lovely 19th-century building with six rooms surrounding a pretty courtyard garden with an attractive little Jacuzzi.

★La Palapita de los Tamales MEXICAN $
(☎998-106-34-72; Calle 42 s/n, cnr Calle 33; tamales M$40; ⏰8-10pm Mon-Sat;) The menu changes daily here, but you'll always find a welcome *tamal* to snack on. Sweetcorn and

pork was on the menu recently, as was excellent *pozole* (a pork and hominy soup). There's casual indoor or patio seating, and takeout is popular.

★ Yerba Buena del Sisal MEXICAN $

(☎985-856-14-06; www.yerbabuenadelsisal.com; Calle 54A No 217; mains M$85-140; ⏲8am-5pm Tue-Sun;) Wonderfully healthy and delicious dishes are served in a peaceful garden. Tortilla chips and three delectable salsas come to the table while you look over the menu, which offers many great vegetarian and mostly organic dishes, such as the delightful *tacos maculum* (with handmade corn tortillas, beans, cheese and aromatic Mexican pepper leaf).

Getting There & Away

Valladolid's main bus terminal is the convenient **ADO bus terminal** (☎985-856-34-48; www.ado.com.mx; cnr Calles 39 & 46; ⏲24hr). The main 1st-class services are by ADO, ADO GL and OCC; Oriente and Mayab run 2nd-class buses.

Buses to Chichén Itzá/Pisté stop near the ruins during opening hours (but double-check).

Chichén Itzá

☎985 / POP 5500 (PISTÉ)

The most famous and best restored of the Yucatán Maya sites, Chichén Itzá, while tremendously overcrowded – every gawker and his or her grandmother is trying to check off the new seven wonders of the world – will still impress even the most jaded visitor. Yes, it's goosebump material. Many mysteries of the Maya astronomical calendar are made clear when one understands the design of the 'time temples' here. Other than a few minor passageways, climbing on the structures is not allowed.

The heat, humidity and crowds in Chichén Itzá can be fierce, as can competition between the craft sellers who line the paths (not to mention the irritating habit of hordes clapping to illustrate the pyramid acoustics). To avoid this, try to explore the site either early in the morning or late in the afternoon.

A nightly sound and light show gets some people fired up; others less so.

Sights

Chichén Itzá ARCHAEOLOGICAL SITE

(Mouth of the Well of the Itzáes; http://chichenitza.inah.gob.mx; off Hwy 180, Pisté; adult/child under 13yr M$254/70, guided tours M$1200; ⏲8am-5pm; P) Certainly on the top of many visitors' 'must see' lists, Chichén Itzá is a stunning ruin and (despite the crowds) well worth visiting for its spectacular, iconic structures, and the historical importance. It is even visible from far-away Ek' Balam. To fully take in the details you should hire a guide, but if that's not in your budget, just walking around offers insight into one of the greatest cities of the Maya world. Due to tourist injuries, climbing structures is prohibited.

➡ **El Castillo**

Upon entering Chichén Itzá, El Castillo (aka the Pyramid of Kukulcán) rises before you in all its grandeur. The first temple here was pre-Toltec, built around AD 800, but the present 25m-high structure, built over the old one, has the plumed serpent sculpted along the stairways and Toltec warriors represented in the doorway carvings at the top of the temple. You won't see the carvings, however, as ascending the pyramid was prohibited after a woman fell to her death in 2006.

➡ **Gran Juego de Pelota**

The great ball court, the largest and most impressive in Mexico, is only one of the city's eight courts, indicative of the importance the games held here. The court, to the left of the visitors center, is flanked by temples at either end and is bounded by towering parallel walls with stone rings cemented up high. Along the walls of the ball court are stone reliefs, including scenes of decapitations of players.

➡ **Templo del Barbado**

The structure at the ball court's north end, called the Temple of the Bearded Man after a carving inside it, has finely sculpted pillars and reliefs of flowers, birds and trees.

➡ **Plataforma de los Cráneos**

The Platform of Skulls (Tzompantli in Náhuatl, a Maya dialect) is between the Templo de los Jaguares y Escudos and El Castillo. You can't mistake it, because the T-shaped platform is festooned with carved skulls and eagles tearing open the chests of men to eat their hearts. In ancient days this platform was used to display the heads of sacrificial victims.

➡ **Plataforma de las Águilas y los Jaguares**

Adjacent to the Plataforma de los Cráneos, the carvings on the Platform of the Eagles and Jaguars depict those animals

WORTH A TRIP

BREAD & BONES IN POMUCH

Quiet and dusty, Pomuch may not even warrant a stop unless one of two things is true: if you're hungry, the bread shops here are so famous that people detour up to an hour to snack on the rolls, sweets and loaves. Denser, chewier and (sorry to be harsh, Mexico) fresher than the Mexican norm, the breads here hit the spot, and they travel well – grab one or two for the road.

The other reason to stop by is for its unique, somewhat macabre *Dia de los Muertos* (Day of the Dead) display. Unlike the typical Mexican *ofrendas* (altars), residents here actually disinter and clean the real bones of their ancestors and display them in special boxes. While it may seem gruesome, it's perhaps one tradition that has its origins in the ancient Maya, a culture where death, life and sacrifice were interlinked.

Pomuch is served by ATS as a stop between Mérida and Campeche. You can also get here from Hecelchakán in a quick M$8 combi ride.

gruesomely grabbing human hearts in their claws. It is thought that this platform was part of a temple dedicated to the military legions responsible for capturing sacrificial victims.

➡ Cenote Sagrado

From the Plataforma de los Cráneos (p77), a 400m rough stone *sacbé* (path) runs north (a five-minute walk) to the huge sunken well that gave this city its name. The Sacred Cenote is an awesome natural well, some 60m in diameter and 35m deep. The walls between the summit and the water's surface are ensnared in tangled vines and other vegetation.

➡ Grupo de las Mil Columnas

This group east of El Castillo (p77) pyramid takes its name – which means 'Group of the Thousand Columns' – from the forest of pillars stretching south and east. The star attraction here is the **Templo de los Guerreros** (Temple of the Warriors), adorned with stucco and stone-carved animal deities. At the top of its steps is a classic reclining chac-mool figure, but ascending to it is no longer allowed.

➡ El Osario

The Ossuary, otherwise known as the Bonehouse or the Tumba del Gran Sacerdote (High Priest's Grave), is a ruined pyramid to the southwest of El Castillo. As with most of the buildings in this southern section, the architecture is more Puuc than Toltec. It's notable for the beautiful serpent heads at the base of its staircases.

➡ El Caracol

Called El Caracol (the Snail) by the Spaniards for its interior spiral staircase, this observatory, to the south of the El Osario, is one of the most fascinating and important of all Chichén Itzá's buildings (but, alas, you can't enter it). Its circular design resembles some central highlands structures, although, surprisingly, not those of Toltec Tula.

Sleeping & Eating

Doralba Inn Chichen Itzá HOTEL $$

(985-858-15-55; www.doloresalba.com; Hwy 180 Km 122; r incl breakfast from M$1000;) This is a good midrange option with substantial online discounts, and kids will dig the hotel's two pools (one has a rock bottom). The 32 semi-rustic rooms won't wow you, but they're comfy enough. Dolores Alba offers transport to Chichén Itzá at 8am, but you're on your own getting back. It's opposite the Ik Kil Parque Eco-Arqueológico, 5km from Chichén Itzá's entrance.

★Hacienda Chichén RESORT $$$

(999-920-84-07, US 877-631-0045; www.haciendachichen.com; Zona Hotelera Km 120; d from US$268;) About 300m from the Chichén Itzá entrance, this resort sits on the well-manicured grounds of a 16th-century hacienda with an elegant main house and towering ceiba trees. The archaeologists who excavated Chichén during the 1920s lived here in bungalows, which have been refurbished and augmented with new ones. Monthly activities on offer include Maya cooking classes and birdwatching.

Las Mestizas MEXICAN $$

(985-851-0069; Calle 15 s/n; mains M$90-115; 9am-10pm;) *The* place to go in town if you're craving decent Yucatecan fare (photos of each dish help you decide). There's indoor and outdoor seating – depending on the time of day, an outdoor table may mean you'll be getting tour-bus fumes (and lines of people) to go along with that *poc chuk* (pork marinated in orange juice and garlic and grilled M$115).

Restaurant Hacienda Xaybe'h d'Camara MEXICAN $$

(985-851-00-00; Calle 15A No 42; buffet lunches M$140; 9am-5pm; P) Set a block back from the highway opposite Hotel Chichén Itzá, this is a large place with attractive grounds. It's popular with tours and the food is a bit overpriced, but the selection of salads makes it a good option for vegetarians. Diners can use the swimming pool for free.

Getting There & Away

Oriente has ticket offices near the east and west sides of Pisté, and 2nd-class buses passing through town stop almost anywhere along the way.

Many 1st-class buses arrive and depart from the ruins only. These also head to Mérida and Valladolid, as well as to coastal locations in Quintana Roo: Playa del Carmen, Tulum and Cancún. If you plan to see the ruins and then head directly to another city by 1st-class bus, to secure your seat, buy your bus ticket at the visitors center before hitting the ruins.

Colectivos (shared vans) to Valladolid (M$35, 40 minutes) enter the car park.

Mérida

999 / POP 800,000

Since the Spanish conquest, Mérida has been the cultural capital of the entire Yucatán Peninsula. A delightful blend of provincial and cosmopolitan, it is a town steeped in colonial history. It's a great place to explore, with narrow streets, broad central plazas and the region's best museums. It's also a perfect place from which to kick off your adventure into the rest of Yucatán state. It has excellent cuisine and accommodations, thriving markets, and events happening just about every night.

Long popular with European travelers looking to go beyond the hubbub of Quintana Roo's resort towns, Mérida is a tourist town, but a tourist town too big to feel like a tourist trap. And as the capital of Yucatán state, Mérida is also the cultural crossroads of the region. There's something just a smidge elitist about Mérida: locals have a beautiful town, and they know it.

Sights & Activities

★Gran Museo del Mundo Maya MUSEUM

(999-341-04-30; www.granmuseodelmundomaya.com.mx; Calle 60 Norte 299E; adult/child under 13yr M$150/75; 8am-5pm Wed-Mon; P) A world-class museum celebrating Maya culture, the Gran Museo houses a permanent collection of more than 1100 remarkably well-preserved artifacts, including a reclining chac-mool sculpture from Chichén Itzá and a cool underworld figure unearthed at Ek' Balam (check out homeboy's punk-rock skull belt and reptile headdress). If you're planning on visiting the area's ruins, drop by here first for some context and an up-close look at some of the fascinating pieces found at the sites.

★Parque Santa Lucía PARK

(Map p80; cnr Calles 60 & 55) The pretty little Parque Santa Lucía has arcades on the north and west sides; this was where travelers would get on or off the stagecoaches that linked towns and villages with the provincial capital. Today it's a popular restaurant area and venue for **Serenatas Yucatecas**, a free weekly concert on Thursday at 9pm.

★Casa de Montejo MUSEUM

(Museo Casa Montejo; Map p80; 999-253-67-39; www.casasdeculturabanamex.com/museocasamontejo; Calle 63 No 506, Palacio de Montejo; 10am-7pm Tue-Sat, to 2pm Sun) FREE Casa de Montejo is on the south side of Plaza Grande and dates from 1540. It originally housed soldiers, but was soon converted into a mansion that served members of the Montejo family until the 1800s. Today it houses a bank and museum with a permanent exhibition of renovated Victorian, neo-rococo and neo-renaissance furnishings of the historic building.

Museo Fernando García Ponce-Macay MUSEUM

(Museo de Arte Contemporáneo; Map p80; 999-928-32-36; www.macay.org; Pasaje de la Revolución s/n, btwn Calles 58 & 60; 10am-5:15pm Wed-Mon) FREE Housed in the former archbishop's palace, the attractive museum's impressive collection holds permanent exhibitions of three of Yucatán's most famous painters of the Realist and Ruptura periods (Fernando Castro Pacheco, Fernando García Ponce and Gabriel Ramírez Aznar), as well as rotating exhibitions of contemporary art from Mexico and abroad.

Mérida

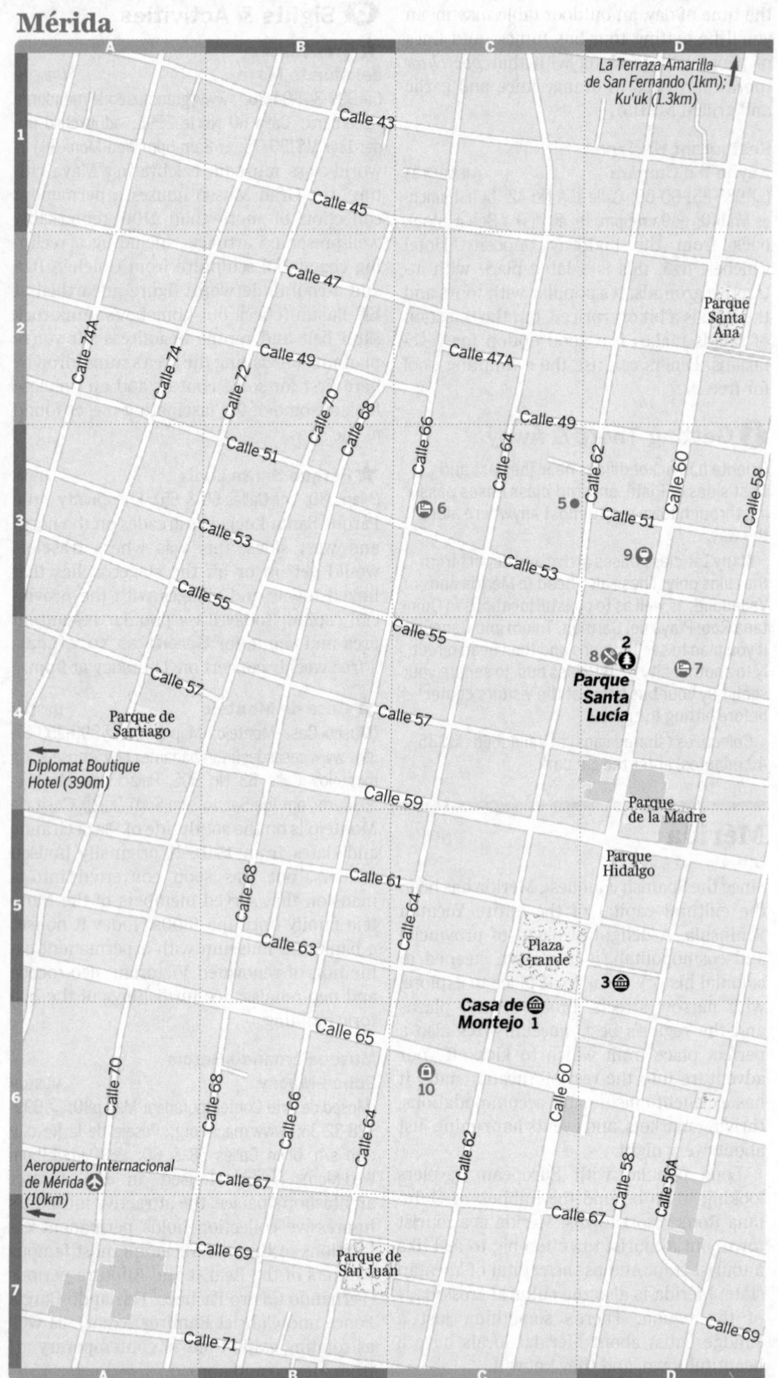

La Terraza Amarilla de San Fernando (1km); Ku'uk (1.3km)
Calle 43
Calle 45
Calle 47
Calle 47A
Calle 49
Calle 51
Calle 53
Calle 55
Calle 57
Calle 59
Calle 61
Calle 63
Calle 65
Calle 67
Calle 69
Calle 71
Calle 74A
Calle 74
Calle 72
Calle 70
Calle 68
Calle 66
Calle 64
Calle 62
Calle 60
Calle 58
Calle 56A
Parque Santa Ana
Parque Santa Lucía
Parque de Santiago
Diplomat Boutique Hotel (390m)
Parque de la Madre
Parque Hidalgo
Plaza Grande
Casa de Montejo
Aeropuerto Internacional de Mérida (10km)
Parque de San Juan

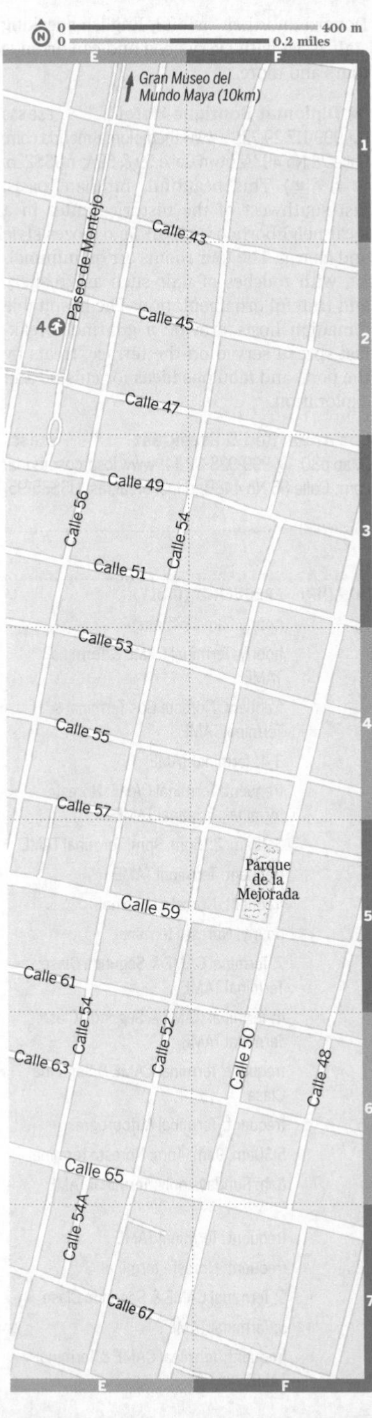

Mérida

Top Sights
1 Casa de Montejo ... C6
2 Parque Santa Lucía ... D4

Sights
3 Museo Fernando García Ponce-Macay ... D5

Activities, Courses & Tours
4 Bici Mérida ... E2
5 Nómadas Hostel ... C3

Sleeping
6 Los Arcos Bed & Breakfast ... C3
7 Luz en Yucatán ... D4
Nómadas Hostel ... (see 5)

Eating
8 Apoala ... D4

Drinking & Nightlife
9 Mercado 60 ... D3

Shopping
10 Hamacas Mérida ... C6

Nómadas Hostel TOURS
(Map p80; ☎999-924-52-23; www.nomadastravel.com; Calle 62 No 433; tours from M$665) Nómadas arranges a variety of tours, such as day trips including transportation and guide to the ecological reserve of Celestún (M$900) and outings to the Maya ruins of Chichén Itzá (M$665) and Uxmal and Kabah (M$665). The hostel also provides informative DIY sheets with written instructions detailing costs and transportation tips for more than a dozen destinations in the region.

Bici Mérida CYCLING
(Map p80; ☎999-287-35-38; Paseo de Montejo s/n, btwn Calles 45 & 47; per hour M$30; ⏲8am-10pm Mon-Fri, to 5pm Sat, to 3pm Sun) Rents out mountain bikes, tandems, bicycles for kids and other cool rides.

Festivals

Mérida Fest CULTURAL
(www.merida.gob.mx; ⏲Jan) This cultural event held throughout most of January celebrates the founding of the city with art exhibits, concerts, theater and book presentations at various venues.

Sleeping

★**Nómadas Hostel** HOSTEL $
(Map p80; ☎999-924-52-23; www.nomadashostel.mx; Calle 62 No 433; dm from M$229, d

M$600, without bathroom M$500, incl breakfast;) One of Mérida's best hostels, it has mixed and women's dorms as well as private rooms. Guests have use of a fully equipped kitchen with fridge, as well as showers and hand-laundry facilities. It even has free salsa, yoga, *trova,* and cooking classes, and an amazing pool out back. See the hostel's website for various tours available to nearby ruins.

★Luz en Yucatán HOTEL **$$**
(Map p80; ☎999-924-00-35; www.luzenyucatan.com; Calle 55 No 499; r US$58-100;) While many much blander hotels are loudly claiming to be 'boutique,' this one is quietly ticking all the boxes while creating its own guesthouse niche – individually decorated rooms, fabulous common areas and a wonderful pool-patio area out back. Knowledgeable and enthusiastic owners Tom and Donard and their helpful, English-speaking staff assist with every need and can arrange tours and more.

★Diplomat Boutique Hotel B&B **$$$**
(☎999-117-29-72; www.thediplomatmerida.com; Calle 78 No 493A, btwn Calle 59 & 59A; r US$225;) This beautiful, intimate oasis, just southwest of the historic center in a local neighborhood of Santiago, oozes style and charm. The four rooms err on minimalist, with touches of flair such as greenery and tasteful ornamentation. The hospitable Canadian hosts provide a gourmet breakfast spread served on the terrace, treats by the pool, and fabulous ideas for cuisine and exploration.

Los Arcos Bed & Breakfast B&B **$$$**
(Map p80; ☎999-928-02-14; www.losarcosmerida.com; Calle 66 No 448B; d incl breakfast US$85-95;

BUSES FROM MÉRIDA

DESTINATION	FARE (M$)	DURATION (HR)	FREQUENCY (DAILY)
Campeche	240	2½-3	hourly 6am-11:45pm
Cancún	280-460	4½-6½	hourly; Terminal CAME & Terminal TAME
Celestún	58	2½	frequent; Noreste Bus Terminal & Terminal TAME
Chetumal	339-446	5½-6	3-4; Terminal TAME
Chichén Itzá	99-180	1½-2	frequent; Terminal CAME; Noreste terminal; Terminal TAME
Escárcega	306-430	4-4½	8:30am, 2:15pm, 9pm; Terminal TAME
Felipe Carrillo Puerto	234	6	frequent; Terminal TAME
Izamal	31	1½	frequent; Noreste terminal
Mayapán	37	1½	hourly; Noreste terminal
Mexico City	999-1900	20	7; Terminal CAME & Segunda Clase; Terminal TAME
Palenque	662-680	7½-10	4; Terminal CAME & Segunda Clase; Terminal TAME
Playa del Carmen	280-498	4-6	frequent; Terminal CAME & Segunda Clase
Progreso	21	1	frequent; Terminal Autoprogreso
Río Lagartos/San Felipe	170-250	3½	5:30am, 9am, 4pm; Noreste terminal
Ruta Puuc (round-trip; 30min at each site)	166	8-8½	8am Sundays only; Terminal TAME
Ticul	57	1¾	frequent; Terminal TAME
Tizimín	125-190	4-5	frequent; Noreste terminal
Tulum	205-356	4-4½	5; Terminal CAME & Segunda Clase
Uxmal	68	1½	5; Terminal TAME
Valladolid	125-216	2½-3	frequent; Terminal CAME & Terminal TAME

P ⊖ ❄ ᯤ ≋) Certainly not for minimalists – there's art on every wall and knickknacks filling every space – Los Arcos is a lovely, gay-friendly ('everyone-friendly') B&B with two guestrooms at the end of a drop-dead-gorgeous garden and pool area. Rooms have an eclectic assortment of art and antiques, plus excellent beds and bathrooms. No pets.

Eating

★La Terraza Amarilla de San Fernando MEXICAN **$**

(☎999-189-62-10; Av Cupules 503D; tacos & tortas M$15-24; ⏲7am-3pm) Mouthwatering cheap eats well worth detouring for, La Terraza Amarilla is a gem: you choose between four styles of mains (tacos, tortas etc) and one of seven different fillings and in seconds your plastic plate arrives. Each menu item is the recipe of the chef-owner and his wife, who will lovingly detail each option for you given the chance.

Nectar YUCATECAN **$$**

(☎999-938-08-38; www.nectarmerida.mx; Av A García Lavín 32; mains M$115-320; ⏲1:30-midnight Tue-Sat, 2pm-6pm Sun; ❄) Inventive and delicious takes on traditional Yucatecan cuisine, a setting that would win design awards, and super-friendly and helpful staff make for a winning combination at this north Mérida (take a taxi) destination restaurant. The *cebollas negras* (blackened onions; M$150) might look unappealing but the taste soon dispels any doubts. And you can't go wrong with the meat and fish mains.

★Apoala MEXICAN **$$$**

(Map p80; ☎999-923-19-79; www.apoala.mx; Calle 60 No 471, Parque Santa Lucía; mains M$130-300; ⏲1pm-midnight Mon-Sat, 2-10pm Sun; ᯤ) With influences of dishes from Oaxaca, which like the Yucatán is known for its extraordinary regional cuisine, Apoala reinvents popular dishes such as *enmoladas* (stuffed tortillas in a rich *mole* sauce) and *tlayudas* (a large tortilla with sliced beef, black beans and Oaxaca cheese). It's in a lovely spot on Parque Santa Lucia (p79) and rubs shoulders with some other great eateries.

★Ku'uk INTERNATIONAL **$$$**

(☎999-944-33-77; www.kuukrestaurant.com; Av Rómulo Rozo No 488, cnr Calle 27; mains M$290-550, tasting menu M$1600; ⏲1:30-11pm Tue-Sat, to 5pm Sun) The stunning historic home, at the end of Paseo Montejo, sets the scene for what's to come: a high-end, high-gourmet meal that will end up setting a very high benchmark for Mexican cuisine. You can dine in a number of elegant, if slightly bare, rooms. The cuisine gives a nod to Yucatecan cuisine with contemporary preparation and flavor twists.

Drinking & Nightlife

Mercado 60 COCKTAIL BAR

(Map p80; www.mercado60.com; Calle 60, btwn Calles 51 & 53; ⏲6pm-late) For a fun night of booze and cheap(ish) international eats, head to this atmospheric, lively and diverse culinary market, where the margaritas (or fine wines) will have you dancing alongside trendy locals to live salsa music. This modern concept is a cocktail bar meets beer hall, with different businesses serving up different concoctions.

Shopping

Hamacas Mérida ARTS & CRAFTS

(Map p80; ☎999-924-04-40; www.hamacasmerida.com.mx; Calle 65 No 510, btwn Calles 62 & 64; ⏲9am-7pm Mon-Fri, to 1pm Sat) Has a large catalog with all kinds of sizes, shapes and colors of hammocks (and chairs), plus it ships worldwide.

Getting There & Away

AIR

Mérida's **Aeropuerto Internacional de Mérida** (Mérida International Airport; ☎999-940-60-90; www.asur.com.mx; Hwy 180 Km 4.5; 🚌R-79) is a 10km, 20-minute ride southwest of Plaza Grande off Hwy 180 (Avenida de los Itzáes). It has car-rental desks, several ATMs, currency-exchange services and an information desk for assisting you to find transport into town.

BUS

Mérida is the bus transportation hub of the Yucatán Peninsula. Take care with your bags on night buses and those serving popular tourist destinations (especially 2nd-class buses); there have been reports of theft on some routes.

There are a number of bus terminals, and some lines operate from (and stop at) more than one terminal. Tickets for departure from one terminal can often be bought at another, and destinations overlap greatly among bus lines. Check out www.ado.com.mx for ticket info on some of the lines.

Campeche

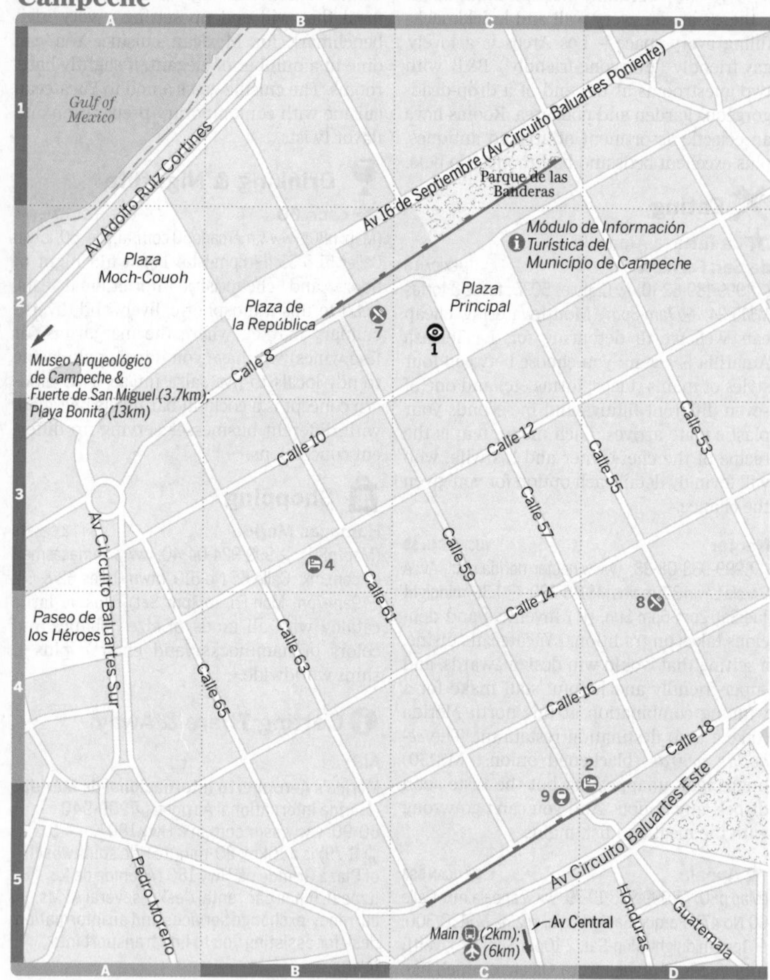

Campeche

981 / POP 250,000

Tucked into the southwestern corner of the Yucatán Peninsula, Campeche state is home to low-key villages, vast stretches of tangled jungle, bird-dotted mangroves and lagoons, and some of the region's most imposing Maya ruins – many of which you might have all to yourself. On deserted beaches endangered turtles lay their eggs, while offshore playful dolphins frolic in the surf. The walled capital city of Campeche is the region's cultural epicenter, providing a great jumping-off point for your adventures into this offbeat hinterland.

Campeche is the least visited of the Yucatán's states, laced through with lonely back roads, friendly people, quiet coastlines and a provincial, lost-land charm. It makes a welcome break from the tourist hordes that descend on the peninsula's more popular destinations; here you'll find peace, surprising attractions and very genuine, local experiences.

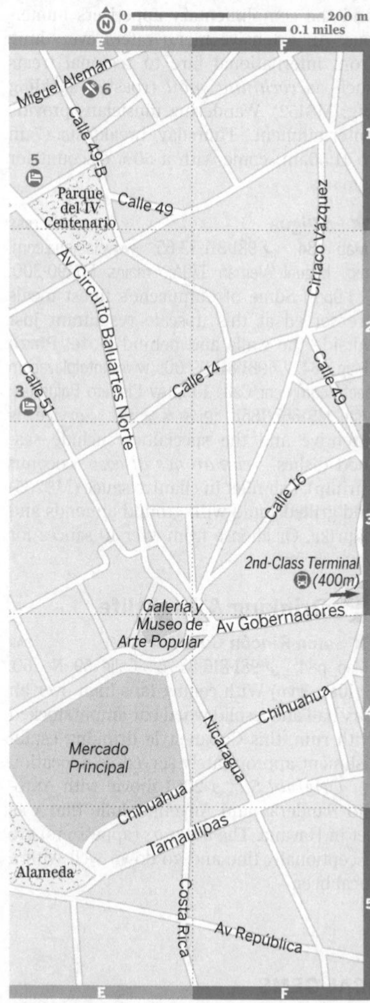

Campeche

Sights

1 Centro Cultural Casa Número 6 .... C2

Sleeping

2 Hacienda Puerta Campeche D4
3 Hostal Viatger E2
4 Hotel López B3
5 Hotel Plaza Campeche E1

Eating

6 La Pigua E1
7 Marganzo B2
8 Sotavento Café D4

Drinking & Nightlife

9 Salón Rincón Colonial C5

Sights

★Museo Arqueológico de Campeche & Fuerte de San Miguel MUSEUM, FORT

(Campeche Archaeological Museum; Av Escénica s/n; M$55; ⏲8:30am-5pm Tue-Sun; P) Campeche's largest colonial fort, facing the Gulf of Mexico some 4km southwest of the city center, is now home to the most important of Maya museums, the excellent Museo Arqueológico de Campeche, the city's one must-see museum. Here you can admire emblematic pieces from the sites of Calakmul and Edzná, and from Isla de Jaina, an island north of town once used as a burial site for Maya aristocracy. Much of the info is in English.

Centro Cultural Casa Número 6 CULTURAL CENTER

(Map p84; Calle 57 No 6; M$20; ⏲8am-9pm Mon-Fri, 9am-9pm Sat & Sun) During the prerevolutionary era, when this mansion was occupied by an upper-class *campechano* family, Número 6 was a prestigious plaza address. Wandering the premises, you'll get an idea of how the city's high society lived back then. The front sitting room is furnished with Cuban-style pieces of the period. Inside are exhibition spaces, a pleasant back patio and a gift shop.

Sleeping & Eating

★Hostal Viatger HOSTEL $

(Map p84; ☎981-811-4500; Calle 51 No 28, btwn Calles 12 & 14; dm/d/tr incl breakfast M$250/790/830; P ⊖ ❄ ☜) Of the plethora of hostels that have popped up in the last few years, we like this one for its location in the historic center (but away from the crowds), plus its friendly ambience. Dorms are nothing fancy, but women can enjoy their own space and there's the option of private doubles and triples, some with TVs and air-con. Bike rentals are M$15 per hour.

★Hotel López HOTEL $$

(Map p84; ☎981-816-33-44; www.hotellopezcampeche.com.mx; Calle 12 No 189; s/d/ste M$950/1080/1250; ⊖ ❄ ☜ ≋) This business hotel is one of Campeche's best midrange options. Modern, comfortably appointed rooms open on to art deco–styled balconies around oval courtyards and pleasant greenery. Bring your swimsuit for the lovely pool out back. Prices are considerably lower outside high season.

★Hacienda Puerta Campeche BOUTIQUE HOTEL $$$
(Map p84; ☎981-816-75-08; www.luxurycollection.com; Calle 59 No 71; r from US$443; ❄📶🏊) This beautiful boutique hotel has 15 suites with high ceilings and separate lounges. Perfectly manicured gardens and grassy lawns offer peace, while the partly covered pool has nearby hammocks that are fit for a Maya king. There's an on-site spa, restaurant and bar in case you really don't want to leave the premises. It also runs a restored luxury hacienda 26km outside the city, on the way to the Edzná ruins.

Sotavento Café CAFE $
(Map p84; ☎981-811-38-92; www.facebook.com/CafeteriaSotavento; Calle 55 No 20, btwn Calles 14 & 16; coffee M$26-55, lunch mains M$69-169; ⏰7am-11pm; 📶) Nice, clean and quirky, with interesting art and curios around the multicolored walls, this cafe-gallery has tasty espresso drinks, plus a variety of sandwiches, burgers, pastas and veggie options. Those staying within the old city walls will find it's in a convenient central location too.

★Marganzo MEXICAN $$
(Map p84; ☎981-811-38-98; Calle 8 No 267; mains M$158-322; ⏰7am-10:45pm; 📶) Marganzo is popular with tourists and locals for good reason – the food is great, the portions large and the complimentary appetizers numerous. An extensive menu offers everything from international fare to regional treats such as *cochinita pibil* (roasted suckling pig; M$152). Wandering musicians provide entertainment. Thursday breakfasts (7am to 11:30am) come with a 50% discount for females.

★La Pigua SEAFOOD $$$
(Map p84; ☎981-811-33-65; www.lapigua.com.mx; Miguel Alemán 179A; mains M$190-300; ⏰1-9pm) Some of Campeche's finest meals are served at this upscale restaurant just outside the walls and behind **Hotel Plaza** (Map p84; ☎981-811-99-00; www.hotelplazacampeche.com; cnr Calle 10 & Av Circuito Baluartes; r/ste M$1667/1851; P⊖❄📶🏊). Service is attentive and the specialties include seafood dishes – *camarones al coco* (coconut shrimp), fish fillet in cilantro sauce (M$235) and grilled squid with ground almonds and paprika. Or choose from over 10 sauces for your shrimp.

Drinking & Nightlife

★Salón Rincón Colonial BAR
(Map p84; ☎981-816-83-76; Calle 59 No 60; ⏰10am-9pm) With ceiling fans high over an airy hall and a solid wood bar amply stocked with rum, this Cuban-style drinking establishment appropriately served as a location for *Original Sin,* a 2001 movie with Antonio Banderas and Angelina Jolie that was set in Havana. The *botanas* (appetizers) are exceptionally fine and go down well with a local beer.

DON'T MISS

CAMPECHE STATE'S ARCHAEOLOGICAL GEMS

Edzná (M$60, guide M$400; ⏰8am-5pm) Edzná's massive complexes, that once covered more than 17 sq km, were built by a highly stratified society that flourished from about 600 BC to the 15th century AD. During that period the people of Edzná built more than 20 complexes in a melange of architectural styles, installing an ingenious network of water-collection and irrigation systems. (Though it's a long way from such Puuc Hills sites as Uxmal and Kabah, some of the architecture here has elements of the Puuc style.)

Calakmul (combined admission M$198; ⏰8am-5pm) Possibly the largest city during Maya times, Calakmul was 'discovered' in 1931 by American botanist Cyrus Lundell. The site bears comparison in size and historical significance to Tikal in Guatemala, its chief rival for hegemony over the southern lowlands during the Classic Maya era. It boasts the largest and tallest known pyramid in Mexico's Yucatán, and was once home to over 50,000 people. At the time of research, you pay three different fees: the community entrance (M$50), biosphere entrance (M$78) and the site entrance M$70. This combination seems subject to change. Note too that the outer gates close for entry at 2:30pm.

Information

Hospital Dr Manuel Campos (981-811-17-09; Av Circuito Baluartes Norte, btwn Calles 14 & 16)

Módulo de Información Turística del Municipio de Campeche (Map p84; 981-811-39-89; Plaza Central; 8am-9pm Mon-Fri, 9am-9pm Sat & Sun) Basic information on Campeche city.

Getting There & Away

Campeche's **main bus terminal** (981-811-99-10; Av Patricio Trueba 237), usually called the ADO or 1st-class terminal, is about 2.5km south of Plaza Principal via Av Central. Buses provide 1st-class and deluxe service to Mérida, Cancún, Chetumal (via Xpujil), Palenque, Veracruz and Mexico City, along with 2nd-class services to Sabancuy (M$142, two hours), Hecelchakán (M$48, one hour) and Candelaria (M$215, four hours).

CHIAPAS

Chilly pine-forest highlands, sultry rainforest jungles and attractive colonial cities exist side by side within Mexico's southernmost states, a region awash with the legacy of Spanish rule and the remnants of ancient Maya civilization.

San Cristóbal de las Casas

967 / POP 185,000

Set in a gorgeous highland valley surrounded by pine forest, the colonial city of San Cristóbal (cris-*toh*-bal) has been a popular travelers' destination for decades. It's a pleasure to explore San Cristóbal's cobbled streets and markets, soaking up the unique ambience and the wonderfully clear highland light. This medium-sized city also boasts a comfortable blend of city and countryside, with restored century-old houses giving way to grazing animals and fields of corn.

Surrounded by dozens of traditional Tzotzil and Tzeltal villages, San Cristóbal is at the heart of one of the most deeply rooted indigenous areas in Mexico. A great base for local and regional exploration, it's a place where ancient customs coexist with modern luxuries.

The city shook violently during the September 2017 Chiapas earthquake; though some buildings were damaged or collapsed, in general the town escaped serious damage.

Sights & Activities

★Na Bolom HISTORIC BUILDING
(Map p90; 967-678-14-18; www.nabolom.org; Guerrero 33; M$60, incl tour M$70; 9am-7pm) An atmospheric museum-research center, Na Bolom for many years was the home of Swiss anthropologist and photographer Gertrude Duby-Blom (Trudy Blom; 1901–93) and her Danish archaeologist husband Frans Blom (1893–1963). Na Bolom means 'Jaguar House' in the Tzotzil language (as well as being a play on its former owners' name). It's full of photographs, archaeological and anthropological relics, and books.

★Templo & Ex-Convento de Santo Domingo de Guzmán CHURCH
(Map p90; Av 20 de Noviembre; 6:30am-1:45pm & 4-8pm Mon-Sat, 7am-9pm Sun) FREE Located just north of the center of town, this imposing 16th-century church is San Cristóbal's most beautiful, especially when its facade catches the late-afternoon sun. This baroque frontage, with outstanding filigree stucco work, was added in the 17th century and includes the double-headed Hapsburg eagle, then the symbol of the Spanish monarchy. The interior is lavishly gilded, especially the ornate pulpit.

Centro de Textiles del Mundo Maya MUSEUM
(Map p90; www.fomentoculturalbanamex.org/ctmm; Calz Lázaro Cárdenas; M$46; 9am-5:45pm Tue-Sun) Upstairs inside the Ex-Convento de Santo Domingo, this excellent museum showcases over 500 examples of handwoven textiles. Two permanent exhibition rooms display *huipiles* (sleeveless tunics) – including a 1000-year-old relic fashioned from tree bark. Videos show how materials and clothes are created, and there are some explanations in English. Admission is bundled with the **Museo de los Altos de Chiapas**.

Natutours OUTDOORS
(967-706-41-80; www.natutours.com.mx) Specializes in ecotourism (including intriguing tree-climbing outings), jungle treks and cultural tourism, and also holds workshops to promote sustainable practices and recycling in the region – although hopefully you're already doing that!

Sleeping & Eating

★Puerta Vieja Hostel HOSTEL $
(Map p90; 967-631-43-35; www.puertaviejahostel.com; Mazariegos 23; dm incl breakfast M$160,

Chiapas

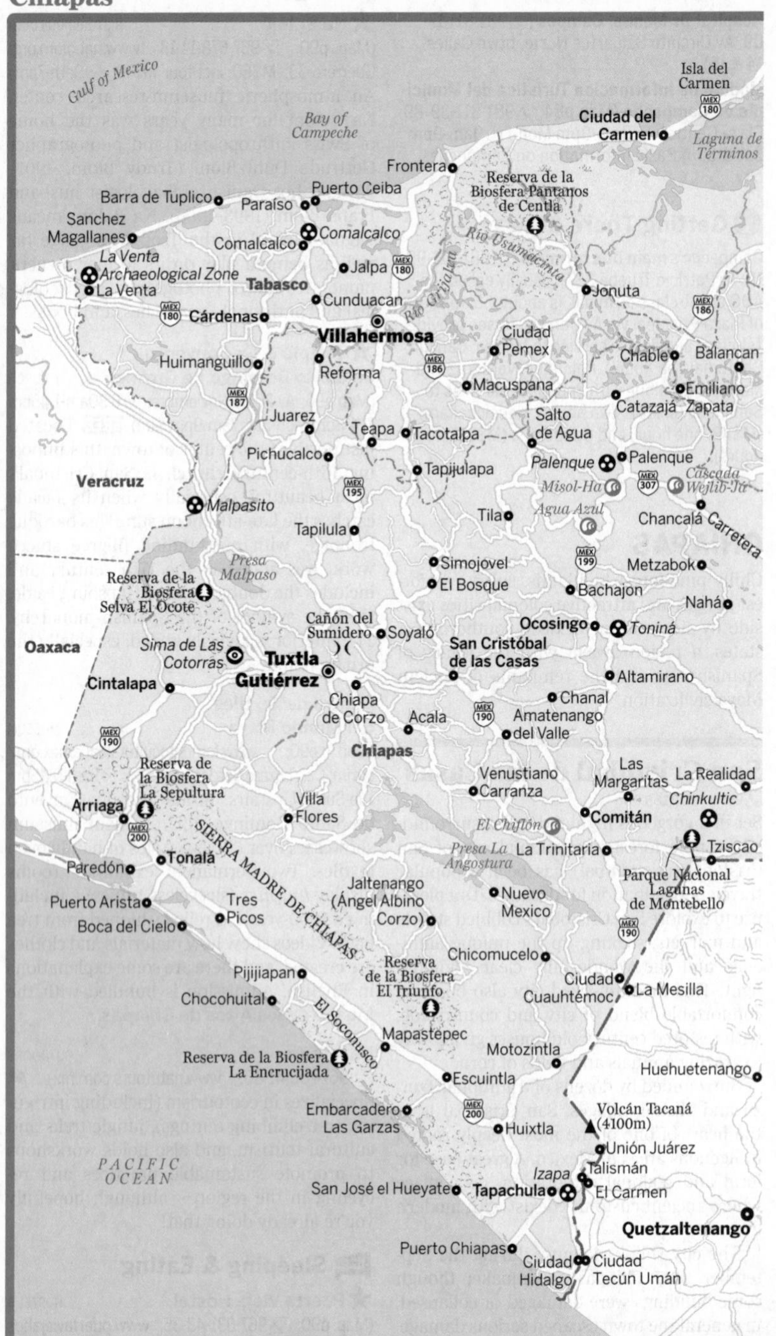
Gulf of Mexico
Bay of Campeche
Isla del Carmen
Ciudad del Carmen
Laguna de Términos
Frontera
Reserva de la Biosfera Pantanos de Centla
Puerto Ceiba
Barra de Tuplico
Paraíso
Sanchez Magallanes
Comalcalco
Comalcalco
La Venta Archaeological Zone
La Venta
Jalpa
Tabasco
Río Usumacinta
Río Grijalva
Jonuta
Cunduacan
Cárdenas
Villahermosa
Ciudad Pemex
Chable
Balancan
Huimanguillo
Reforma
Macuspana
Emiliano Zapata
Catazajá
Juarez
Salto de Agua
Teapa
Tacotalpa
Pichucalco
Palenque
Palenque
Tapijulapa
Misol-Ha
Cascada Wejlib-Já
Veracruz
Malpasito
Agua Azul
Tila
Chancalá
Carretera
Tapilula
Presa Malpaso
Simojovel
Metzabok
Reserva de la Biosfera Selva El Ocote
El Bosque
Bachajon
Nahá
Cañón del Sumidero
Soyaló
Ocosingo
Toniná
Oaxaca
Sima de Las Cotorras
Tuxtla Gutiérrez
San Cristóbal de las Casas
Altamirano
Cintalapa
Chiapa de Corzo
Chanal
Acala
Amatenango del Valle
Chiapas
Reserva de la Biosfera La Sepultura
Venustiano Carranza
Las Margaritas
La Realidad
Arriaga
Villa Flores
Chinkultic
Comitán
El Chiflón
SIERRA MADRE DE CHIAPAS
Tonalá
Presa La Angostura
La Trinitaria
Tziscao
Paredón
Parque Nacional Lagunas de Montebello
Jaltenango (Ángel Albino Corzo)
Puerto Arista
Tres Picos
Nuevo Mexico
Boca del Cielo
Chicomucelo
Reserva de la Biosfera El Triunfo
Pijijiapan
Ciudad Cuauhtémoc
La Mesilla
Chocohuital
El Soconusco
Mapastepec
Motozintla
Reserva de la Biosfera La Encrucijada
Escuintla
Huehuetenango
Embarcadero Las Garzas
Volcán Tacaná (4100m)
Huixtla
Unión Juárez
PACIFIC OCEAN
Izapa
Talismán
San José el Hueyate
Tapachula
El Carmen
Quetzaltenango
Puerto Chiapas
Ciudad Hidalgo
Ciudad Tecún Umán
MEX 180
MEX 186
MEX 187
MEX 195
MEX 199
MEX 307
MEX 190
MEX 200

r with/without bathroom M$440/370;) A spacious, modern, traveler-savvy hostel in a high-ceilinged colonial building with a large garden strung with hammocks, kitchen, temascal (pre-Hispanic steam bath) and sheltered interior courtyard. Its dorms (one for women only) are a good size, and the rooftop ones have fab views. Private rooms have one queen and a bunk bed. There's occasional karaoke in the garden.

Hostal Akumal HOSTEL $
(Map p90; cell 967-1161120; www.hostalakumal.com; Av 16 de Sepiembre 33; dm/d incl breakfast M$140/400;) Friendly, live-in owners and a big cooked breakfast that changes daily (a prominent sign quite rightly states 'Continental breakfast is not real breakfast') are some of the winning points at this centrally located hostel. There's a roaring fireplace in the lounge for chilly nights, a funky courtyard hangout area, and the rooms and dorms are adequate, if nothing exciting.

Rossco Backpackers HOSTEL $
(Map p90; 967-674-05-25; www.backpackershostel.com.mx; Real de Mexicanos 16; dm from M$139, d with/without bathroom M$550/400;) Rossco Backpackers is a friendly, sociable and well-run hostel with good dorm rooms (one for women only), a guest kitchen, a movie-watching loft and a grassy garden. Private upstairs rooms have nice skylights. A free night's stay if you arrive by bicycle or motorcycle!

La Tertulia San Cris CAFE $
(Map p90; 967-116-11-45; Cuathémoc 2; mains M$40-80; 8am-11pm) This small, theatrical, boho cafe does great breakfasts, yummy salads and a passable pizza, all served up in a paintbox of colors. A little on-site gift store selling local produce and souvenirs rounds out the picture.

Comida Thai THAI $
(Map p90; 967-133-74-48; Paniagua 2B; mains M$50-90; 12:30-8:30pm Thu-Mon) For a little extra spice pop by this very simple Thai place. The family who runs it make just three or four different dishes a day, but they're all made with extreme care (as the sign says, this is 'Very, very slow food').

★Santo Nahual FUSION $$
(Map p90; 967-678-15-47; www.santonahual.com; Hidalgo 3; mains M$130-240; 9am-11pm;) This new venture impresses with its glass-roofed courtyard dining area filled with

San Cristóbal de las Casas

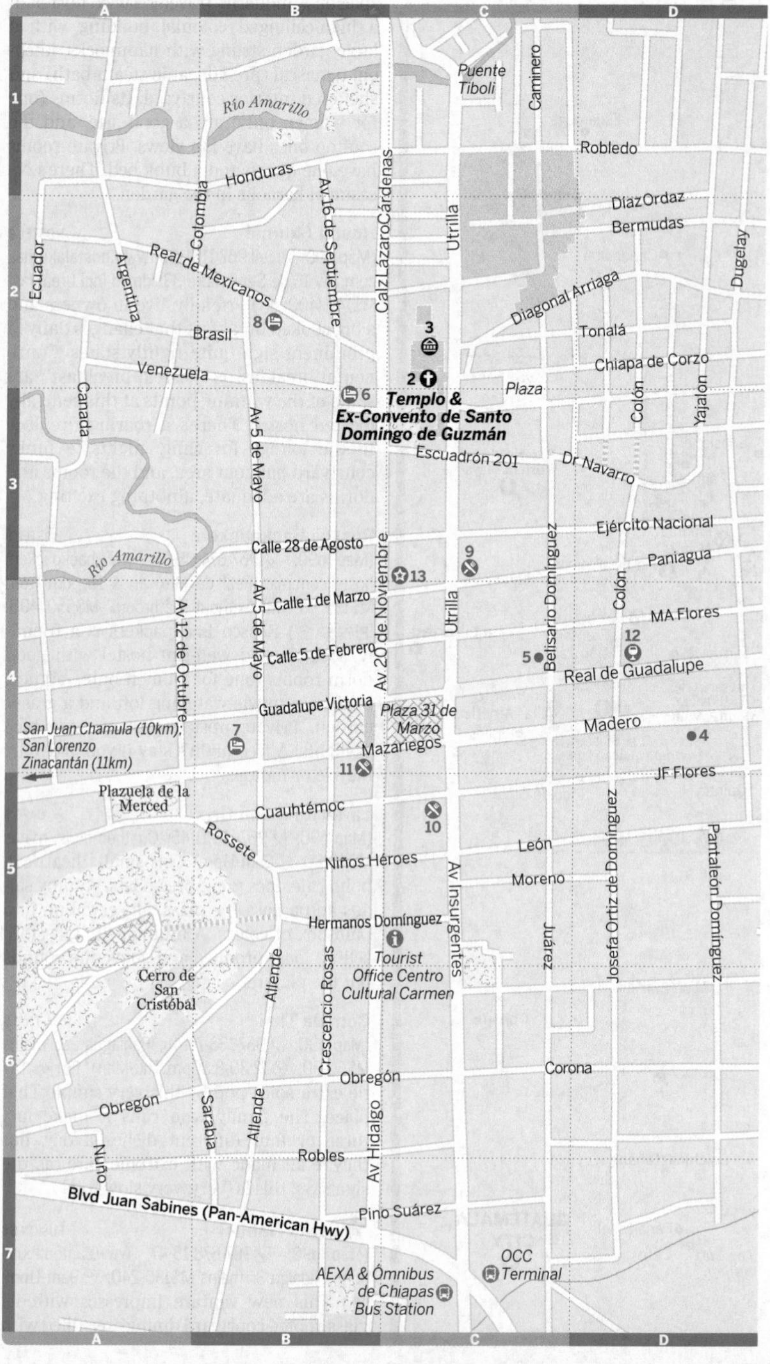

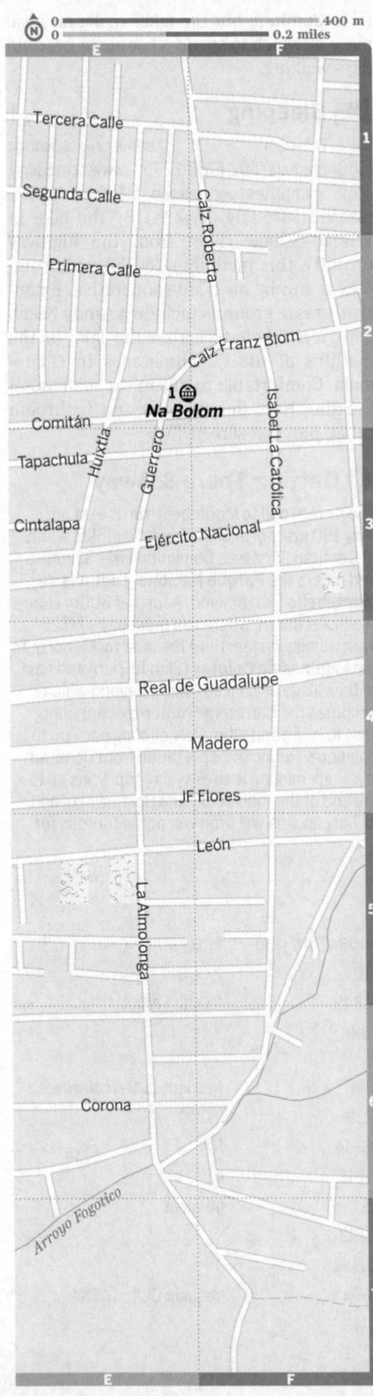

San Cristóbal de las Casas

Top Sights
1 Na Bolom E2
2 Templo & Ex-Convento de Santo Domingo de Guzmán C2

Sights
3 Centro de Textiles del Mundo Maya C2
Museo de los Altos de Chiapas .... (see 3)

Activities, Courses & Tours
4 Instituto Jovel D4
5 Jaguar Adventours C4

Sleeping
6 Hostal Akumal B3
7 Puerta Vieja Hostel B4
8 Rossco Backpackers B2

Eating
9 Comida Thai C3
10 La Tertulia San Cris C5
11 Santo Nahual B4

Drinking & Nightlife
12 Cocoliche D4

Entertainment
13 Cafe Bar Revolución C3

worn timbers, smooth pebbles, glossy-leafed banana plants and even a day-glo piano. And when the food, which is best described as modern fusion Mexican, does come you'll find it every bit as imaginative as the decor.

Drinking & Entertainment

Cocoliche COCKTAIL BAR
(Map p90; 967-631-46-21; Colón 3; mains M$60-210; 1pm-midnight;) By day Cocoliche is a bohemian restaurant with lots of Asian dishes, but in the evening its vintage lanterns and wall of funky posters set the scene for drinking boozy or virgin cocktails with friends. Jostle for spot near the fireplace on chilly evenings, and check out the nightly jazz, funk and swing music.

★**Cafe Bar Revolución** LIVE MUSIC
(Map p90; 967-678-66-64; www.facebook.com/elrevomx; Calle 1 de Marzo 11; 11am-3am) There's always something fun at Revolución, with two live bands nightly and an eclectic line up of salsa, rock, blues, jazz and reggae. Dance downstairs or order a mojito or caipirinha and chat in the quieter upstairs *tapanco* (attic).

Information

Tourist Office Centro Cultural Carmen (Map p90; Av Hidalgo 15; ⌚9am-8pm) Tourist information is available inside this cultural center.

Getting There & Away

The main 1st-class **OCC terminal** (Map p90; cnr Pan-American Hwy & Av Insurgentes) is also used by ADO and UNO 1st-class and deluxe buses, plus some 2nd-class buses. AEXA buses and Ómnibus de Chiapas minibuses share a **terminal** (Map p90) across the street from the OCC terminal. All *colectivo* vans (combis) and taxis have depots on the Pan-American Hwy a block or so from the OCC terminal.

For Guatemala, most agencies offer a daily van service to Quetzaltenango (M$350, eight hours), Panajachel (M$350, 10 hours) and Antigua (M$450, 12 hours); Viajes Chincultik is slightly cheaper, and also has van service to Guatemala City and Chichicastenango. Otherwise go to Ciudad Cuauhtémoc and pick up onward transportation from the Guatemala side.

Lagos de Montebello

The temperate pine and oak forest along the Guatemalan border east of Chinkultic is dotted with more than 50 small lakes of varied hues, known as the Lagos (or Lagunas) de Montebello. The area is very picturesque, peaceful and, after the steamy heat of the nearby jungles, beautifully cool and refreshing. Most people just come on a day trip from Comitán, but the lakes make an ideal place at which to spend a couple of peaceful days walking.

Sleeping

Villa Tziscao CABAÑAS, CAMPGROUND **$$**
(Guatemala 502-5780-27-75; www.ecotziscao.com; campsites per person M$80, d M$845, cabaña M$845-1314; P) By the lake in Tziscao village (2km from the highway turnoff), this medium-sized lakeside complex is run by an *ejido* cooperative. Extensive, grassy grounds include a sandy beach with terrific views across the lake to the foothills of the Cuchumatanes in Guatemala. Comfortable rooms in the main hotel building have decent beds and bathroom tiling, plus flat-screen TVs.

Getting There & Away

The paved road to Montebello turns east off Hwy 190 just north of La Trinitaria, 16km south of Comitán. It passes Chinkultic after 32km, and enters the **Parque Nacional Lagunas de Montebello** 5km beyond. A further 800m along is a ticket booth, where you must pay a M$25 park-admission fee. Here the road forks: north to the **Lagunas de Colores** (2km to 3km) and east to the village of Tziscao (9km), beyond which it becomes the Carretera Fronteriza, continuing east to Ixcán and ultimately circling back up to Palenque. Public transportation from Comitán is a snap, making it an easy day trip. Vans go to the end of the road at Laguna Bosque Azul and to Tziscao, and will drop you at the turnoffs for

BUSES FROM SAN CRISTÓBAL

DESTINATION	FARE (M$)	DURATION (HR)	FREQUENCY (DAILY)
Campeche	408-680	10	2 OCC
Cancún	1024-1422	18-19	3 OCC; 1 AEXA
Ciudad Cuauhtémoc (Guatemalan border)	100-170	3¼	3
Comitán	88-100	1¾	frequent OCC & *colectivos*
Mérida	564-789	12¾	2 OCC
Mexico City (TAPO & Norte)	808-1494	13-14	10
Oaxaca	404-740	11-12	4
Palenque	184-332	5	frequent
Pochutla	403-740	11-12	3
Puerto Escondido	446-810	12½-13	3
Tuxtla Gutiérrez	58-86	1-1¼	frequent OCC; 4 AEXA
Tuxtla Gutiérrez airport (Ángel Albino Corzo)	242	1½	9
Villahermosa	254-514	5½-7	5 OCC

WORTH A TRIP

MADRE SAL

Drift to sleep pondering the waves crashing onto the black-sand beach at **Madre Sal** (☎ USA 966-666-6147, USA 966-100-7296; www.elmadresal.com; Manuel Ávila Camacho; cabañas M$950; P), an ecotourism project 25km south of Puerto Arista. Named for a mangrove species, its restaurant (meals from M$100) and thatched two-bed en suite *cabañas* sit astride a skinny bar of pristine land between a lagoon and the Pacific that's reached via *lancha* (M$25) through mangroves.

Guests use candles after the 11pm power shutoff, and crabs skitter along the sand when stars fill the night sky. In season, sea turtles come ashore to lay eggs, and the night watchman can wake you if you want to watch or help collect the eggs for the Boca del Cielo hatchery.

From Tonalá, take a taxi (M$50 shared, M$500 private) or combi (M$40) to Manuel Ávila Camacho; combis charge an extra M$5 to the *embarcadero*, or you can walk five minutes or ride on the back of a motorbike (M$10).

Museo Parador Santa María, Chinkultic and the other lakes. The last vehicles back to Comitán leave Tziscao and Laguna Bosque Azul in the early evening.

Yaxchilán

Jungle-shrouded **Yaxchilán** (M$70; ⊙8am-5pm, last entry 4pm) has a terrific setting above a horseshoe loop in the Río Usumacinta. The control this location gave it over river commerce, along with a series of successful alliances and conquests, made Yaxchilán one of the most important Classic Maya cities in the Usumacinta region. Archaeologically, Yaxchilán is famed for its ornamented facades and roofcombs, and its impressive stone lintels carved with conquest and ceremonial scenes. A flashlight is helpful for exploring some parts of the site.

Getting There & Away

To reach Yaxchilán from Palenque, first head to Frontera Corozal. Autotransporte Chamoán runs vans run to Frontera Corozal (M$130, 2½ to three hours, every 40 minutes from 4am to 5pm), leaving from the outdoor *colectivo* terminal near the Maya head statue and south of the bus station.

Lanchas (motorboats) take 40 minutes running downstream from Frontera Corozal, and one hour to return. The boat companies are in a thatched building near the Frontera Corozal *embarcadero* (jetty), and all charge about the same price for trips. The return journey with 2½ hours at the ruins for one to three people costs M$800, four people M$1050, five to seven people M$1450 or eight to 10 people M$1800. *Lanchas* normally leave frequently until 1:30pm or so; try to hook up with other travelers or a tour group to share costs.

Palenque

☎916 / POP 43,000

Swathed in morning jungle mists and echoing to a dawn chorus of howler monkeys and parrots, the mighty Maya temples of Palenque are deservedly one of the top destinations of Chiapas and one of the best examples of Maya architecture in all of Mexico. By contrast, modern Palenque town, a few kilometers to the east, is a sweaty, humdrum place without much appeal except as a jumping-off point for the ruins and a place to find internet access. Many prefer to base themselves at one of the forest hideouts along the road between the town and the ruins, including the funky travelers' hangout of El Panchán.

Sights & Activities

Combis to the ruins (M$24 each way) run about every 10 minutes during daylight hours. In town, look for 'Ruinas' combis anywhere on Juárez west of Allende. They will also pick you up or drop you off anywhere along the town–ruins road.

★**Palenque Ruins** ARCHAEOLOGICAL SITE

(M$48 plus M$22 national park entry fee; ⊙8am-5pm, last entry 4:30pm) Ancient Palenque stands at the precise point where the first hills rise out of the Gulf coast plain, and the dense jungle covering these hills forms an evocative backdrop to Palenque's exquisite Maya architecture. Hundreds of ruined buildings are spread over 15 sq km, but only a fairly compact central area has been excavated. Everything you see here was built without metal tools, pack animals or the wheel.

Palenque Ruins

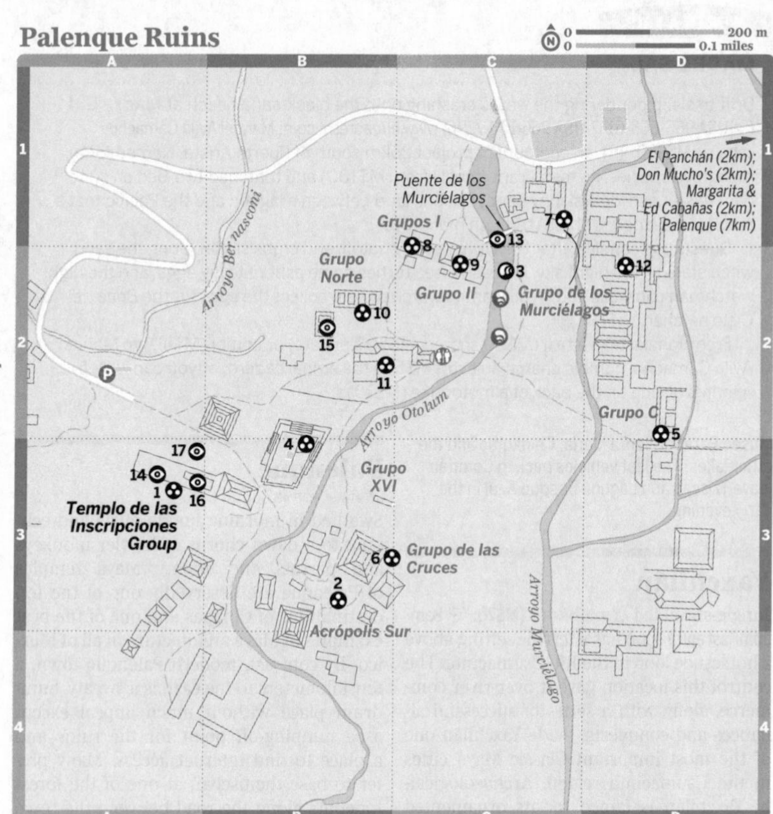

➡ Templo de las Inscripciones Group

As you walk in from the entrance the vegetation suddenly peels away to reveal many of Palenque's most magnificent buildings in one sublime vista. A line of temples rises in front of the jungle on your right, culminating in the Templo de las Inscripciones about 100m ahead; El Palacio, with its trademark tower, stands to the left of the Templo de las Inscripciones; and the Grupo de las Cruces rises in the distance beneath a thick jungle backdrop.

The first temple on your right is Templo XII, called the **Templo de la Calavera** (Temple of the Skull) for the relief sculpture of a rabbit or deer skull at the foot of one of its pillars. The second temple has little interest. Third is **Templo XIII**, containing a tomb of a female dignitary, whose remains were found colored red (as a result of treatment with cinnabar) when unearthed in 1994. You can look into the **Tumba de la Reina Roja** (Tomb of the Red Queen) and see her sarcophagus. With the skeleton were found a malachite mask and about 1000 pieces of jade. Based on DNA tests and resemblances to Pakal's tomb next door, the theory is that the 'queen' buried here was his wife Tz'ak-b'u Ajaw. The **tomb of Alberto Ruz Lhuillier**, who discovered Pakal's tomb in 1952, lies under the trees in front of Templo XIII.

The **Templo de las Inscripciones** (Temple of the Inscriptions), perhaps the most celebrated burial monument in the Americas, is the tallest and most stately of Palenque's buildings. Constructed on eight levels, the Templo de las Inscripciones has a central front staircase rising 25m to a series of small rooms. The tall roofcomb that once crowned it is long gone, but between the front doorways are stucco panels with reliefs of noble figures. On the interior rear wall are three panels with the long Maya

Palenque Ruins

Top Sights

1 Templo de las Inscripciones Group....A3

Sights

2 Acrópolis Sur....B3
3 Baño de la Reina....C2
4 El Palacio....B3
5 Grupo C....D2
6 Grupo de las Cruces....B3
7 Grupo de los Murciélagos....C1
8 Grupo I....C1
9 Grupo II....C2
10 Grupo Norte....B2
11 Juego de Pelota....B2
12 Palenque Northeastern Groups....D2
13 Puente de los Murciélagos....C1
14 Templo de la Calavera....A3
15 Templo del Conde....B2
16 Templo XIII....A3
17 Tomb of Alberto Ruz Lhuillier....A3

inscription, recounting the history of Palenque and this building, for which Mexican archaeologist Alberto Ruz Lhuillier named the temple. From the top, interior stairs lead down into the **tomb of Pakal** (now closed to visitors indefinitely to avoid further damage to its murals from the humidity inevitably exuded by visitors). Pakal's jewel-bedecked skeleton and jade mosaic death mask were removed from the tomb to Mexico City, and the tomb was re-created in the Museo Nacional de Antropología. The priceless death mask was stolen in an elaborate heist in 1985 (though recovered a few years afterward), but the carved stone sarcophagus lid remains in the closed tomb – you can see a replica in the site museum.

➡ El Palacio

(The Palace) Diagonally opposite the Templo de las Inscripciones is El Palacio, a large structure divided into four main courtyards, with a maze of corridors and rooms. Built and modified piecemeal over 400 years from the 5th century on, it was probably the residence of Palenque's rulers.

➡ Acrópolis Sur

In the jungle south of the Grupo de las Cruces is the Southern Acropolis, where archaeologists have made some terrific finds in recent excavations. You may find part of the area roped off. The Acrópolis Sur appears to have been constructed as an extension of the Grupo de las Cruces, with both groups set around what was probably a single long open space.

➡ Grupo de las Cruces

(Group of the Crosses) Pakal's son, Kan B'alam II, was a prolific builder, and soon after the death of his father started designing the temples of the Grupo de las Cruces (Group of the Crosses). All three main pyramid-shaped structures surround a plaza southeast of the Templo de las Inscripciones. They were all dedicated in AD 692 as a spiritual focal point for Palenque's triad of patron deities.

➡ Grupo Norte

(Northern Group) North of El Palacio is a **Juego de Pelota** (Ball Court) and the handsome buildings of the Northern Group. Crazy Count de Waldeck lived in the so-called **Templo del Conde** (Temple of the Count), constructed in AD 647.

➡ Palenque Northeastern Groups

East of the Grupo Norte, the main path crosses Arroyo Otolum. Some 70m beyond the stream, a right fork will take you to **Grupo C**, a set of jungle-covered buildings and plazas thought to have been lived in from about AD 750 to 800.

If you stay on the main path, you'll descend some steep steps to a group of low, elongated buildings, probably occupied residentially from around AD 770 to 850. The path goes alongside the Arroyo Otolum, which here tumbles down a series of small falls forming natural bathing pools known as the **Baño de la Reina** (Queen's Bath). Unfortunately, you can't bathe here anymore.

The path then continues to another residential quarter, the **Grupo de los Murciélagos** (Bat Group), and then crosses the **Puente de los Murciélagos**, a footbridge across Arroyo Otolum.

Across the bridge and a bit further downstream, a path goes west to **Grupo I** and **Grupo II**, a short walk uphill. These ruins, only partly uncovered, are in a beautiful jungle setting. The main path continues downriver to the road, where the museum is a short distance along to the right.

El Panchán AREA

(Carretera Palenque-Ruinas Km 4.5) Just off the road to the ruins, El Panchán is a legendary travelers' hangout set in a patch of dense rainforest. It's the epicenter of Palenque's alternative scene and home to a bohemian bunch of Mexican and foreign residents and wanderers.

Once ranchland, the area has been reforested by the remarkable Morales family, some of whom are among the leading archaeological experts on Palenque. Today El Panchán has several (mostly rustic) places to stay, a couple of restaurants, a set of sinuous streams rippling their way through every part of the property, nightly entertainment (and daily drumming practice), a meditation temple, a temascal (pre-Hispanic steam bath) and a constant stream of interesting visitors from all over the world.

Viajes Kukulcán TOURS
(WhatsApp only 967-158-36-74; www.kukulcantravel.com; Av Juárez 8) Based in Palenque, this reliable agency offers transportation packages to Agua Azul and Misol-Ha, to Bonampak, Yaxchilán and Lacanjá Chansayab, and to Flores, Guatemala.

Sleeping

★Yaxkin HOSTEL $
(916-345-01-02; www.hostalyaxkin.com; Prolongación Hidalgo 1; dm M$120, d without bathroom M$280, d with air-con & bathroom M$650; P) Channeling laid-back El Panchán from pretty La Cañada, this former disco has been revamped into a modern hostel with a guest kitchen, a ping-pong table, multiple lounges and a swanky restaurant-bar and cafe. Rooms without air-con are monastic but funky. The fan-cooled dorms (one for women only) and private rooms with air-con feel more pleasant and comfortable.

Cabaña Safari CABAÑAS $
(916-345-00-26; Carretera Palenque-Ruinas Km 1; r from M$711; P) Enjoyable, jungly *palapa*-roofed *cabañas* with air-con, private porches and flat-screen TV (just in case you get bored absorbing the jungle atmosphere from your terrace!). Rocks, tree branches and wall murals give personality to the spacious (including some two-level) rooms. There's a plunge pool, temascal and full restaurant. Music from the restaurant can be a bit loud at night.

Margarita & Ed Cabañas GUESTHOUSE $
(916-348-69-90; www.margaritaandedcabanas.blogspot.com; Carreterra Palenque-Ruinas Km 4.5, El Panchán; cabañas M$285, r with fan M$320-410, s/d with air-con M$480/570; P) With the most spotless digs in the jungle, Margarita has welcomed travelers to her exceptionally homey place for decades. Bright, clean and cheerful rooms have good mosquito netting, and the more rustic screened *cabañas* are well kept too, with reading lights and private bathrooms. There's free drinking water, a book exchange, and a lovely newer building with super-spacious rooms.

Hotel Chablis Palenque HOTEL $$
(916-142-03-77, 916-345-08-70; www.hotelchablis.com; Merle Green, 7; r from M$1095;) With sunny colors, high-quality, thick mattresses, neatly tiled (if small) bathrooms, a decent restaurant and an attractive flora-filled courtyard with a pristine pool, this appealing little hotel is hard to beat. Although it's in the center of town, it's set a little way back from the road, which keeps things fairly quiet.

Eating

★Café Jade MEXICAN, CHIAPANECO $
(916-688-00-15; Prolongación Hidalgo 1; breakfast M$50-100, mains M$60-120; 7am-11pm;) This very cool bamboo construction has indoor and outdoor seating and is one of the most popular places in town. Its growing fame hasn't led to a reduction in quality though, and it serves good breakfasts, some

BUSES FROM PALENQUE

DESTINATION	FARE (M$)	DURATION (HR)	FREQUENCY (DAILY)
Campeche	437-470	5-5½	5 ADO
Cancún	740-1458	12-13½	4 ADO
Mérida	387-688	8	5 ADO
Mexico City (1 TAPO & 1 Norte)	1200	13½	2 ADO
Oaxaca	511	15	ADO at 5:30pm
San Cristóbal de las Casas	188-384	8-9	9 ADO, 4 AEXA
Tulum	476-1074	10-11	4 ADO
Tuxtla Gutiérrez	191-394	6½	8 ADO, 5 AEXA
Villahermosa	95-226	2½	frequent ADO & AEXA
Villahermosa airport	350	2¼	4 ADO

Chiapan specialties and international traveler classics such as burgers. Has a reasonable number of vegetarian options and really good fresh juices too.

Don Mucho's MEXICAN, INTERNATIONAL **$**

(☎916-112-83-38; Carretera Palenque-Ruinas Km 4.5, El Panchán; mains M$60-150; ⏰7am-1am Tue-Thu, to 2am Fri, to 3am Sat, to midnight Sun & Mon) In El Panchán, popular Don Mucho's provides great-value meals in a jungly setting, with a candlelit ambience at night. Busy waiters bring pasta, fish, meat, plenty of *antojitos* (typical Mexican snacks), and pizzas (cooked in a purpose-built Italian-designed wood-fired oven) that are some of the finest this side of Naples.

★El Huachinango Feliz SEAFOOD **$$**

(☎916-129-82-31; Hidalgo s/n; mains M$90-160; ⏰8am-11pm) A popular, atmospheric restaurant in the leafy La Cañada neighborhood. It has an attractive front patio with tables and umbrellas, and there's also an upstairs covered terrace. Seafood is the specialty here: order seafood soup, seafood cocktails, grilled fish that's beautifully crunchy on the outside and soft on the inside, or shrimp served 10 different ways. The service is slooow but the food is worth the wait.

Monte Verde ITALIAN **$$**

(☎916-119-17-87; mains M$100-180; ⏰2-10:30pm Sun-Tue, Thu & Fri, to 11pm Sat) There's a real Mediterranean vibe to this Italian restaurant tucked away in the forest (do a bit of bird- and monkey-watching while waiting for your lunch!) and though most people go for the delicious thin-crust pizzas, the meat and pasta dishes are worthy of your time. Try the seafood tagliatelle piled high with giant prawns and you'll leave happy.

ℹ Getting There & Away

Whichever direction you come from it's safer to travel to Palenque in daylight hours as armed hold-ups along roads leading to Palenque are not unheard of. For the moment it's best not to travel directly from Ocosingo to Palenque, and at the time of research most transportation was taking alternative and much longer, but safer, routes. There have also been recent reports of thefts on the night bus from Mérida. When taking buses along these routes, consider stowing valuables in the checked luggage compartment.

BUS

ADO Bus terminal (www.ado.com.mx) ADO has the main bus terminal in town, with deluxe and 1st-class services, an ATM and left-luggage facilities; it's also used by OCC (1st class).

Agua Azul & Misol-Ha

These spectacular water attractions – the thundering cascades of Agua Azul and the 35m jungle waterfall of Misol-Ha – are both short detours off the Ocosingo–Palenque road. During the rainy season they lose part of their beauty as the water gets murky, though the power of the waterfalls is magnified. Both are most easily visited on an organized day tour from Palenque.

Sights

Agua Azul WATERFALL

(M$40) Agua Azul is a breathtaking sight, with its powerful and dazzling white waterfalls thundering into turquoise (outside rainy season) pools surrounded by verdant jungle. On holidays and weekends the place is packed; at other times you'll have few companions. The temptation to swim is great, but take extreme care, as people do drown here. The current is deceptively fast, the power of the falls obvious, and there are many submerged hazards like rocks and dead trees.

Misol-Ha WATERFALL

(total M$30) Just 20km south of Palenque, spectacular Misol-Ha cascades approximately 35m into a wonderful wide pool surrounded by lush tropical vegetation. It's a sublime place for a dip when the fall is not excessively pumped up by wet-season rains. A path behind the main fall leads into a cave, which allows you to experience the power of the water close up. Misol-Ha is 1.5km off Hwy 199 and the turnoff is signposted, and two separate *ejidos* (communal landholdings) charge admission.

Sleeping

Centro Turístico Ejidal Cascada de Misol-Ha CABIN **$**

(☎916-345-12-10; www.misol-ha.com; cabin M$290; ⏰restaurant 7am-7pm; P⊖☎) Has atmospheric wooden cabins among the trees near the waterfall, with fans, hot-water bathrooms and mosquito netting, plus a good open-air restaurant (mains M$80 to M$160). Nighttime swims are dreamy.

UNDERSTAND MEXICO'S YUCATÁN & CHIAPAS

Mexico's Yucatán & Chiapas Today

Tourism is one of the driving forces behind life in the Yucatán, Mexico's most-visited destination. For better or worse, the industry helps shape politics, economics and many of the region's important social and environmental issues. There have been some high-profile closings of popular clubs in Cancún and Playa del Carmen, but the area remains one of the safest and most visitor-friendly places in all of Mexico – the tourism economy is thriving like never before.

Yet despite the tourism boom, a broad segment of the population continues to live in poverty and rapid development is causing long-lasting environmental and cultural degradation. A big cause for concern is the gradual disappearance of indigenous languages as more and more hotels and restaurants seek English speakers.

History

The Maya created many city-states across southern Mexico, but the population began falling into decline before the Spanish arrived, resulting in the deaths of 90% of the remaining inhabitants. A couple of Spaniards – Diego de Mazariegos in present-day Chiapas, and Francisco de Montejo in the Yucatán – had the area under Spanish control by the mid-16th century. Then in 1821, Mexico won independence from Spain and 1824 the country pulled in Chiapas from the United Provinces of Central America.

Long oppressed by Spaniards and *criollos* (Latin Americans of Spanish lineage), the Maya minority rose in the War of the Castes in 1847, which saw bloody massacres and the destruction of churches. And while the war ostensibly ended in 1901, social inequality still festered. As the North American Free Trade Agreement (NAFTA) kicked into effect in 1994, the mainly Maya Zapatistas stormed San Cristóbal de las Casas. Their struggle has since quieted down now that they run autonomous zones (called *caracoles,* literally 'snails') outside San Cristóbal.

Culture

Travelers often comment on the open, gentle and gregarious nature of the people of the Yucatán, especially the Maya. Here more than elsewhere in Mexico, it seems, you find a willingness to converse and a genuine interest in outsiders. This openness is all the more remarkable when you consider that the people of the Yucatán Peninsula have fended off domination by outsiders for so long. The situation persists today – much of the land is foreign-owned and the Maya generally have no say in the big infrastructure decisions.

Landscape & Wildlife

Separated from the bulk of Mexico by the Gulf of Mexico, and from the Greater Antilles by the Caribbean Sea, the Yucatán Peninsula is a vast, low limestone shelf extending under the sea for more than 100km to the north and west. The eastern (Caribbean) side drops off much more precipitously. This underwater shelf keeps Yucatán's coastline waters warm and the marine life abundant.

The isolation of the Yucatán Peninsula and its array of ecosystems results in an extraordinary variety of plant and animal life, including a number of species that are unique to the region. Whether you like watching birds, following the progress of sea turtles as they nest on the beach, swimming next to manta rays and schools of iridescent fish, or spying wildcats through your binoculars, you'll have plenty of nature activities to do here.

SURVIVAL GUIDE

Directory A–Z

ACCESSIBLE TRAVEL

Lodgings on the Yucatán Peninsula and in Chiapas generally don't cater for travelers with mobility issues, though some hotels and restaurants (mostly toward the top end of the market) and some public buildings now provide wheelchair access. The absence of institutionalized facilities, however, is largely compensated for by Mexicans' accommodating attitudes toward others, and special arrangements are gladly improvised.

Mobility is easiest in the major tourist resorts. Bus transportation can be difficult; flying or taking a taxi is easier.

Society for Accessible Travel (www.sath.org)
Mobility International USA (www.miusa.org)

ACCOMMODATIONS

The Yucatán and Chiapas offer an assortment of affordable sleeping options, including hostels, *cabañas* (cabins), campgrounds, guesthouses and economical hotels. Rooms in this category are assumed to have bathrooms, unless otherwise stated. Recommended accommodations in this range will be simple and without frills, but generally clean.

Hostels exist in nearly all the region's most popular tourist destinations. They provide dorm accommodations (for about M$200 to M$300 per person), plus communal kitchens, bathrooms and living space, and often more expensive private rooms. Standards of hygiene and security vary. Always ask if the dorms come with air-con – you might need it on a hot day.

CLIMATE

Hot, sunny and humid days are the norm for much of the year, although the season of *nortes* (storms bringing wind and rain from the north) lowers temperatures a bit from November through February or March. During the rainy season, which runs from May through October, you can expect heavy rains for an hour or two most afternoons, but generally clear weather otherwise. The hurricane season lasts from June to November, with most of the activity from mid-August to mid-September.

CUSTOMS REGULATIONS

Visitors are allowed to bring the following items into Mexico duty-free:

- two cameras
- 10 packs of cigarettes
- 3L of alcohol
- medicine for personal use, with prescription in the case of psychotropic drugs
- one laptop computer
- one digital music player
- cell phone

You cannot carry more than US$10,000 in cash without declaring it.

See www.sat.gob.mx for more details.

After handing in your customs declaration form, an automated system will determine whether your luggage will be inspected. A green light means pass; a red light means your bags will be searched.

EMBASSIES & CONSULATES

It's important to understand what your own embassy can and can't do to help you if you get into trouble. Generally speaking, it won't be much help in emergencies if the trouble you're in is remotely your own fault. Remember that you are bound by the laws of the country you are in. In genuine emergencies you might get some assistance, such as a list of lawyers, but only if other channels have been exhausted.

Embassy details can be found at Secretaría de Relaciones Exteriores (www.sre.gob.mx) and Embassyworld (www.embassyworld.org).

Many embassies or their consular agencies are in Mexico City (including Australia, Ireland and New Zealand); Cancún is home to several consulates, and there are some diplomatic outposts elsewhere in the region as well.

Canadian Consulate Cancún (998-883-33-60; www.mexico.gc.ca; Blvd Kukulcán Km 12.5, Centro Empresarial Oficina LE7; 9am-1pm Mon-Fri); Playa del Carmen (984-803-24-11; www.canadainternational.gc.ca; 3rd fl, Av 10 Sur s/n, btwn Calles 3 & 5 Sur, in Plaza Paraíso Caribe; 9am-1pm Mon-Fri)

Dutch Consulate Mérida (999-924-31-22; http://mexico.nlambassade.org; Calle 64 No 418; 8:30am-5:30pm Mon-Fri)

French Consulate Mérida (999-930-15-42, 999-930-15-00; merida.chfrance@gmail.com; Calle 60 No 385, btwn 41 and 43; 9am-5pm Mon-Fri)

German Consulate Cancún (998-884-15-98; www.mexiko.diplo.de; Punta Conoco SM24; 9am-3pm Mon-Fri); Mérida (999-944-32-52; merida@hk-diplo.de; Calle 51 No 329 btwn, Calles 52 & 54, Fracc Francisco de Montejo; by appt only)

Guatemalan Consulate Comitán (963-110-68-16; www.minex.gob.gt; 1a Calle Sur Poniente 35, Int 3 4th fl, Comitán; 9am-1pm & 2-5pm Mon-Fri); Tapachula (962-626-12-52; www.minex.gob.gt; Central Poniente s/n, 1st fl; 9am-5pm Mon-Fri)

UK Consulate Cancún (Mexico City 55-1670-3200; www.gov.uk/world/mexico; Torre la Europea 202, Blvd Kukulcán Km 12.6; 8am-1pm Mon-Fri)

US Consulate Cancún (999-316-71-68, 998-883-02-72; https://mx.usembassy.gov; Torre La Europea 301, Blvd Kukulcán Km 12.6; 8:30am-1:30pm Mon-Fri); Mérida (999-942-57-00; https://mx.usembassy.gov/embassy-consulates/merida; Calle 60 No 338K; by appointment only)

SLEEPING PRICE RANGES

The following price ranges refer to accommodations for two people in high season, including any taxes charged.

$ less than M$800

$$ M$800–1600

$$$ more than M$1600

EMERGENCY & IMPORTANT NUMBERS

Country code	52
Directory assistance	040
Emergencies	911, 066
International access code	00; 011 from USA and Canada
Roadside assistance	078
Domestic/international operator	020/090

Mexican toll-free numbers start with 800, followed by seven digits; they always require the 01 long-distance prefix.

INTERNET ACCESS

Internet cafes (which charge about M$10 to M$15 per hour) still exist in the Yucatán and Chiapas, but are going the way of the dodo; increasingly, there's free wi-fi in public plazas, and often it's available in restaurants and shops as well. It's the same for hotels with a computer for guests: here and there, they're available (and big hotels always have a business center), but mostly it's just wi-fi.

Many places (hotels, bars and restaurants) have wi-fi, but in some hotels the signal only reaches the lobby. We use the wi-fi icon in our reviews if the signal reaches at least some part of the premises; an internet icon refers to establishments with internet-ready computers for guests.

LGBTIQ+ TRAVELERS

Mexico is more broad-minded about sexuality than many might expect. LGBTIQ+ travelers rarely attract open discrimination or violence, though it's still uncommon to see open same-sex affection in the smaller rural towns. PDAs even between heterosexual couples are uncommon in countryside Yucatán, so same-sex affection may raise an eyebrow.

Discrimination based on sexual orientation has been illegal since 1999 and can be punished with up to three years in prison. Gay men have a more public profile than lesbians. Cancún has a small gay scene, and there are a number of gay-friendly establishments in Mérida listed at www.gaymexicomap.com.

Gay Mexico (www.gaymexico.com.mx) Useful online guide for gay tourism in Mexico.

International Gay & Lesbian Travel Association (www.iglta.org) Provides information on the major travel providers in the gay sector.

Out Traveler (www.outtraveler.com) Helpful general resource.

MONEY

Mexico's currency is the peso, usually denoted by the 'M$' sign.

International credit cards are accepted for payment by most airlines, car-rental agencies, many midrange and upscale hotels, and some restaurants, gas stations and shops; they can also be used to withdraw cash from ATMs. Many businesses take debit cards as well, but you'll usually wind up paying the card issuer a 3% international transaction fee.

As a backup to credit or debit cards, always carry cash, especially when visiting remote towns with few or no ATMs available.

Bargaining

Most stores have set prices. You can do some friendly haggling in some arts and crafts markets, but don't get carried away – most of the artisans are just trying to make a living. Some hotels are willing to negotiate rates with walk-ins, especially during low season.

Tipping

Hotels About 5% to 10% of room costs for staff.

Restaurants 15% if service is not included in check.

Supermarket baggers/gas-station attendants Usually around M$5.

Porters M$25 per bag.

Taxis Drivers don't expect tips unless they provide an extra service.

Bars Bartenders usually don't get tipped so anything is appreciated.

OPENING HOURS

Hours at some places may decrease during shoulder and low seasons. Some shops, restaurants and hotels may close for several weeks – or several months – during low season.

Archaeological sites 8am–5pm

Banks 9am–5pm Monday to Friday; some open 10am–2pm Saturday (hours may vary)

Cafes 8am–9pm

Cenotes 9am–5pm

Museums 9am–5pm Tuesday to Sunday

PUBLIC HOLIDAYS

Banks, post offices, government offices and many shops throughout Mexico are closed on the following national holidays.

Año Nuevo (New Year's Day) January 1

Día de la Constitución (Constitution Day) February 5

Día del Nacimiento de Benito Juárez (Anniversary of Benito Juárez' birth) March 21

Día del Trabajo (Labor Day) May 1

Día de la Independencia (Independence Day) September 16

Día de la Revolución (Revolution Day) November 20

Día de Navidad (Christmas Day) December 25

In addition, many offices and businesses close on the following optional holidays:

Día de la Bandera (National Flag Day) February 24

Viernes Santo (Good Friday) Two days before Easter Sunday

Cinco de Mayo (Commemorates Mexico's victory over French forces in Puebla) May 5

Día de la Raza (Columbus' 'discovery' of the New World) October 12

Día de Muertos (Day of the Dead) November 1 and 2

Día de Nuestra Señora de Guadalupe (Day of Our Lady of Guadalupe) December 12

SAFE TRAVEL

Despite all the grim news about Mexico's drug-related violence, the Yucatán Peninsula and Chiapas remain relatively safe for those not engaged in illegal activities. Most of the killings you hear about happen between rival drug gangs, so tourists are rarely caught up in the disputes – especially in the Yucatán, which keeps a safe distance from the turf wars occurring elsewhere in Mexico. Cancún, Playa del Carmen and Tulum have all seen a gradual rise in drug violence, but major US cities such as New York and Chicago have higher murder rates than the entire state of Yucatán.

That said, purchasing recreational drugs or even engaging pushers in conversation can mark you as a target for interrogation or worse by police or gangs. You are best off avoiding this entirely.

TELEPHONE

Many US cell-phone companies offer Mexico roaming deals. Local SIM cards can only be used on phones that have been unlocked.

VISAS

Every tourist must have a Mexican government tourist permit, which is easily obtainable. Some nationalities also need to obtain visas.

- Citizens of the US, Canada, EU countries, Australia, New Zealand, Iceland, Israel, Japan, Norway and Switzerland are among the dozens of countries whose citizens do not require visas to enter Mexico as tourists.
- The website of the **Instituto Nacional de Migración** (☎ toll-free 800-004-62-64; www.inm.gob.mx; Calle Homero 1832, Polanco, Mexico City) lists countries that must obtain a visa to travel to Mexico. If the purpose of your visit is to work (even as a volunteer), to report, to study, or to participate in humanitarian aid or human-rights observation, you may well need a visa whatever your nationality. Visa procedures can take several weeks and you may need to apply in your country of citizenship or residence.
- US citizens traveling by land or sea can enter Mexico and return to the USA with a passport card, but if traveling by air will need a passport. Non-US citizens passing (even in transit) through the USA on the way to or from Mexico should check well in advance on the US's complicated visa rules. Consult a US consulate, the US State Department (www.travel.state.gov) or US Customs and Border Protection (www.cbp.gov) websites.
- The regulations sometimes change. It's wise to confirm them with a Mexican embassy or consulate. Good sources for information on visa and similar matters are the London consulate (https://consulmex.sre.gob.mx/reinounido) and the Washington consulate (https://consulmex.sre.gob.mx/washington).

Tourist Permit & Fee

The Mexican tourist permit (tourist card; officially the *forma migratoria multiple* or FMM) is a brief paper document that you must fill out and get stamped by Mexican immigration when you enter Mexico and keep till you leave. It's available at official border crossings, international airports, ports and often from airlines. It's also available online. Important: at land borders you won't usually be given one automatically (eg if crossing by car) – you have to ask for it; ensure you do.

A tourist permit only permits you to engage in what are considered to be tourist activities (including sports, health, artistic and cultural activities).

- The maximum possible stay is 180 days for most nationalities, but immigration officers will sometimes put a lower number unless you tell them specifically what you need.
- The fee for the tourist permit, called the *derecho de no residente* (DNR; non-resident fee), is M$533 (or US$27 equivalent), but it's free for people entering by land who stay less than seven days. If you enter Mexico by air, however, the fee is usually included in your airfare.
- If you enter by land, you must pay the fee at a bank in Mexico at any time before you reenter the frontier zone on your way out of Mexico (or before you check in at an airport to fly out of Mexico). Most Mexican border posts have on-the-spot bank offices where you can pay the DNR fee. When you pay at a bank, your tourist

EATING PRICE RANGES

The following price ranges refer to the cost of a main dish for lunch or dinner.

$ less than M$100

$$ M$100–200

$$$ more than M$200

permit will be stamped to prove that you have paid.

➡ Look after your tourist permit because it may be checked when you leave the country. You can be fined for not having it.

VOLUNTEERING

Volunteering is a great way of giving back to local communities. In the Yucatán there are various organizations that welcome any help they can get, from environmental and wild-life-conservation NGOs to social programs. You can always look for opportunities at your local hostel or language school, some of which offer part-time volunteering opportunities. Most programs require a minimum commitment of at least a month, and some charge fees for room and board.

WEIGHTS & MEASURES

Mexico uses the metric system.

Getting There & Away

AIR

The majority of flights into the peninsula arrive in Cancún or Mérida. The Yucatán's major airports are as follows.

Aeropuerto Ángel Albino Corzo (aka Tuxtla Gutiérrez; ☎961-153-60-68; www.chiapasaero.com; Sarabia s/n) serves San Cristóbal de las Casas in Chiapas.

Aeropuerto Internacional de Cancún (Cancún International Airport; ☎998-848-72-00; www.asur.com.mx; Hwy 307 Km 22)

Aeropuerto Internacional de Mérida (p83)

Cozumel Airport (☎987-872-20-81; www.asur.com.mx; Blvd Aeropuerto Cozumel s/n)

Other cities with airports include Campeche, Chetumal, Ciudad del Carmen, Palenque and Villahermosa.

BOAT

Water taxis depart from Chetumal's *muelle fiscal* (dock) on Blvd Bahía to San Pedro (Belize). Between the two companies operating water taxis, there's daily service to the island. See www.sanpedrowatertaxi.com and www.belizewatertaxi.com for more information.

Mahahual, Puerto Chiapas, Progreso and Isla Cozumel are ports of call for cruise ships. Many cruise-ship lines serve these ports.

Carnival Cruise Lines (☎toll-free USA 800-764-7419; www.carnival.com)

Crystal Cruises (☎toll-free USA 888-722-0021; www.crystalcruises.com)

Norwegian Cruise Lines (☎toll-free USA 866-234-7350; www.ncl.com)

P&O Cruises (☎UK 0344-338-8003; www.pocruises.com)

Princess Cruises (☎toll-free USA 800-774-6237; www.princess.com)

Royal Caribbean International (☎Mexico 55-877-3492, toll-free USA 866-562-7625; www.royalcaribbean.com)

BORDER CROSSINGS

Belize

➡ Crossing from Mexico into Belize, at the southern tip of Quintana Roo, is easy for most tourists.

➡ Each person leaving Belize for Mexico needs to pay a US$15 exit fee for visits less than 24 hours and US$20 for longer stays. All fees must be paid in cash, in Belizean or US currency – officials usually won't have change for US currency.

➡ Frequent buses run from Chetumal to the Belizean towns of Corozal (around M$50, one hour) and Orange Walk. The buses depart from the old ADO bus station and some continue on to Belize City.

➡ A boat departs from Chetumal to San Pedro; this is an easier, if more expensive route than taking a bus to Belize City and then taking a local boat.

➡ Car-rental companies do not allow you to cross the Mexico–Belize border with their vehicles.

Guatemala

➡ The borders at La Mesilla/Ciudad Cuauhtémoc, Ciudad Tecún Umán/Ciudad Hidalgo and El Carmen/Talismán are all linked to Guatemala City, and nearby cities within Guatemala and Mexico, by plentiful buses and/or combis (minibuses).

➡ Agencies in San Cristóbal de las Casas offer daily van service to the Guatemalan cities of Quetzaltenango, Panajachel and Antigua.

➡ Additionally, several buses depart from the San Cristóbal de las Casas bus station that goes to the Ciudad Cuauhtémoc border, where you can catch Guatemalan buses on the other side in the border town of La Mesilla.

➡ **Transportes Palenque** (☎Guatemala 01-91-6345-2430; www.transportespalenque.com/home/; Calle Allende, enter Av 20 de Noviembre y Corregidora, Col Centro, Palenque Chiapas) runs vans out of Palenque to Tenosique (Tabasco), where you'll find onward connections to Guatemala.

➡ Travelers with their own vehicles can travel by road between Tenosique and Flores (Guatemala), via the border at El Ceibo.

➡ Car-rental companies do not allow you to cross the Mexico–Guatemala border with their vehicles.

Getting Around

BOAT

Frequent ferries depart from Playa del Carmen to Isla Cozumel, Cancún to Isla Mujeres and Chiquilá to Isla Holbox. The following prices are one-way fares.

Isla Holbox M$150

Isla Cozumel M$175 to M$200

Isla Mujeres M$160 from Puerto Juárez; about US$14 from Zona Hotelera

Cancún and Chiquilá have long-term parking available near the terminals. For more information about schedules, points of departure and car ferries, see www.granpuerto.com.mx and www.transcaribe.net. The Holbox ferries do not have websites.

To reach the uninhabited island of Isla Contoy, you can hook up with tour operators with boats departing from Cancún (p51) and **Isla Mujeres** (☎ cell 998-2570100, cell 998-1436758; cnr Av Rueda Medina & Morelos; snorkeling from US$35, whale shark tour US$100, Isla Contoy US$75; ⏰7am-6pm).

BUS

The Yucatán Peninsula has a good road and bus network, and comfortable, frequent, reasonably priced bus services connect all cities. Most cities and towns have one main bus terminal where all long-distance buses arrive and depart. It may be called the Terminal de Autobuses, Central de Autobuses, Central Camionera or simply La Central (not to be confused with *el centro*, the city center). If there is no single main bus terminal, different bus companies will have separate terminals scattered around town. **Grupo ADO** (☎ Mexico City 55-5784-4652; www.ado.com.mx) operates many of the bus lines that you'll be using.

COLECTIVOS & COMBIS

On much of the peninsula, a variety of vehicles – often Volkswagen, Ford or Chevrolet vans – operate shared transportation services between towns or nearby neighborhoods. These vehicles usually leave whenever they are full. Fares are typically less than those of 1st-class buses. Combi is a term often used for the Volkswagen variety; *colectivo* refers to any van type. *Taxi colectivo* may mean either public or private transport, depending on the location.

HITCHHIKING

Hitchhiking is never entirely safe in any country and even in Mexico's relatively safe Yucatán region it's best avoided. Travelers who decide to hitch should understand that they are taking a potentially serious risk. Keep in mind that kidnappings for ransom can – and do – still happen in Mexico.

Guatemala

POP 17.3 MILLION

Includes ➡

Why Go?

Central America's most diverse country captivates travelers with its amazing landscapes and a civilization-spanning culture that reaches back centuries. If you're into the Maya, the mountains, the markets, kicking back lakeside or exploring atmospheric pre-Columbian ruins and gorgeous colonial villages, you're bound to be entranced.

The dizzying pyramids of Tikal are Guatemala's most famous tourist drawcard, and the Maya culture continues to evolve to this day. The Spanish also left behind plenty of footprints from their colonial conquest of Guatemala, with the best dotted around Antigua, the old capital, with its neat plazas and crumbling ruins.

The natural beauty of the volcano-ringed Lago de Atitlán has been enthralling travelers for centuries. The swimming hole that launched a thousand postcards, Semuc Champey, has to be seen to be believed, and you can dip your toes in both the Pacific Ocean and the Caribbean Sea.

Best Places to Eat

- ➡ Ambia (p113)
- ➡ La Cocina de Señora Pu (p112)
- ➡ Kacao (p113)
- ➡ Café El Artesano (p144)

Best Places to Stay

- ➡ Casa Tenango (p178)
- ➡ Casa Nostra (p193)
- ➡ Dai Nonni Hotel (p112)
- ➡ Earth Lodge (p129)

When to Go

Guatemala City

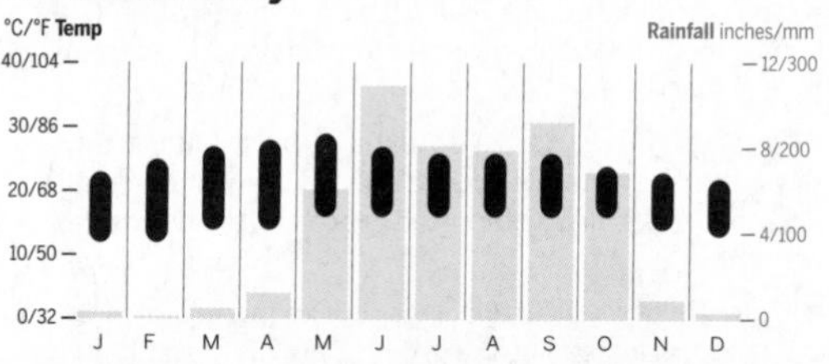

Dec–May Festivities such as Christmas and Easter are celebrated with gusto.

Apr–Sep Prices drop and crowds thin out as the rainy season starts in earnest.

Oct–Nov Rains begin to ease, making for good hiking weather.

Entering the Country

With land borders on three sides, river- and sea-port entries and two international airports, it's not hard to get into or out of Guatemala.

TWO-WEEK ITINERARY

With a week up your sleeve you won't see it all, but you can at least catch the Big Three. Make a beeline for **Antigua** and spend a couple of days wallowing in colonial glory and climbing volcanoes before heading off to **Lago de Atitlán**. Choose which village suits you, from bustling Panajachel to laid-back San Marcos, and explore the lake and its surrounds by boat, kayak, horseback, bike or whatever else takes your fancy. From there, head back to Guatemala City and catch a bus or plane to Flores, your stepping-off point for the mother of all Maya ruins, **Tikal**.

Add another week and you'll have time for a quick dip in the lovely limestone pools at **Semuc Champey** and a boat ride down the lush **Río Dulce**. Try to set a day aside for **Guatemala City's** fantastic collection of museums and galleries.

Essential Food & Drink

Frijoles Beans, served refried or whole.

Tortillas A Guatemalan meal is naked without a serving of corn tortillas.

Tamal Steamed corn dough served a dozen ways with a dozen names.

Rellenitos Fried plantain meal served sweet as a finger-licking dessert.

Top Tips

- If possible, learn some Spanish before you arrive and some more when you get here – Guatemalans are extremely patient and will love you for just giving it a go.
- Pack as lightly as possible. Anything that locals use on a day-to-day basis can be bought cheaply. Anything remotely luxurious (electronics, imported goods etc) will be cheaper at home.
- Be aware of your surroundings (but not paranoid). If your gut tells you something is not right, it probably isn't.
- Be realistic in your planning. Sure you'd like to see everything, but it's better to focus on quality time in a few places rather than rushing from place to place and spending most of your time on a bus.

FAST FACTS

Currency Quetzal (Q)

Visas Many nationalities do not require tourist visas and will be given a 90-day stay upon entry; citizens of some countries do need visas.

Money ATMs widely available.

Capital Guatemala City

Emergency ☎120

Languages Spanish (official), Maya languages, Garifuna

Exchange Rates

Australia	A$1	Q5.05
Canada	C$1	Q5.86
Euro zone	€1	Q8.77
Japan	¥100	Q6.70
New Zealand	NZ$1	Q5.27
UK	UK£1	Q10.26
USA	US$1	Q7.71

Daily Costs

- Double room in a budget hotel: Q130–180; in a midrange hotel: Q200–550
- Set meal in a *comedor* (cheap eatery): Q30–45; à la carte meal in a local restaurant: Q100–130

Resources

Lonely Planet (www.lonelyplanet.com/guatemala)

Entre Mundos (www.entremundos.org)

Xela Pages (www.xelapages.com)

Pacunam (www.pacunam.org)

Guatemala Highlights

❶ **Tikal** (p206) Sidestepping the tour groups to find out for yourself why this is Guatemala's number-one tourist attraction.

❷ **Antigua** (p120) Eating, drinking and sleeping well, studying Spanish and climbing volcanoes in this cosmopolitan and picturesque town.

❸ **Lívingston** (p192) Seeing another side of Guatemala in this Garifuna enclave.

❹ **Chichicastenango** (p149) Shopping for souvenirs in the coutry's largest traditional Maya market.

❺ **Semuc Champey** (p182) Discovering why people call this the most beautiful place in the country.

❻ **Río Dulce boat tour** (p189) Taking a spectacular boat ride through a jungle-walled canyon on the Río Dulce between Río Dulce town and Lívingston.

❼ **San Marcos La Laguna** (p146) Exploring Lake Atitlán's prettiest and most laid-back village.

❽ **El Paredón** (p172) Catching the Pacific waves at Guatemala's growing surf hub.

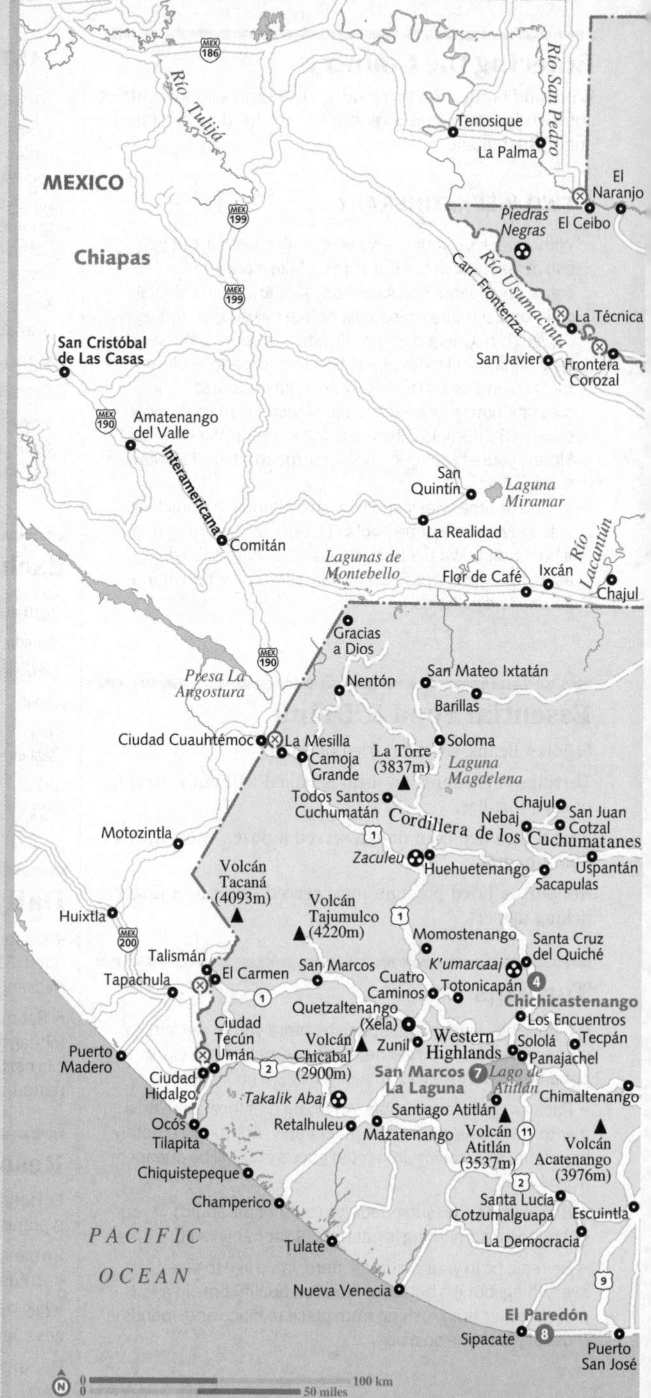

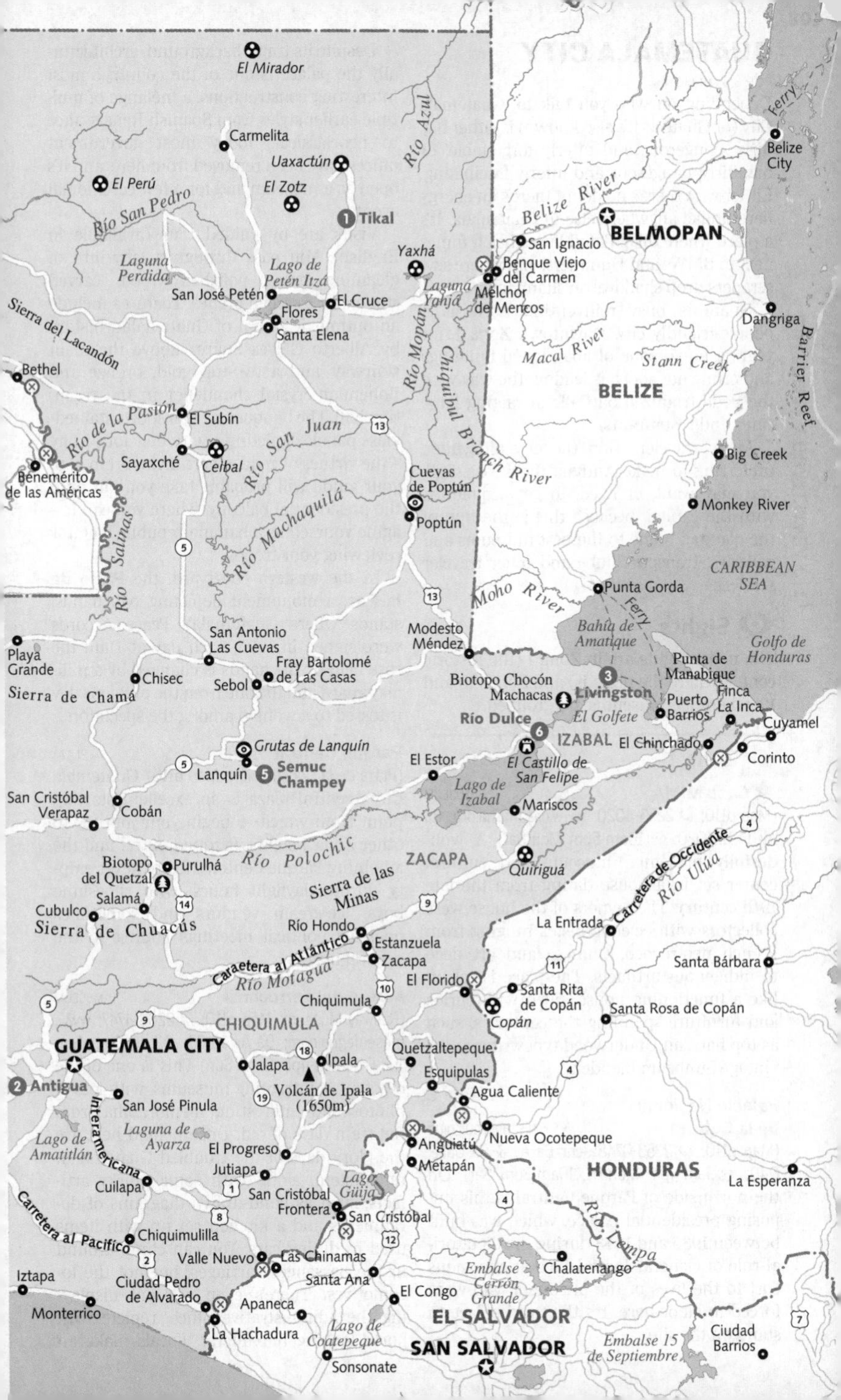

El Mirador
Carmelita
Uaxactún
El Perú
El Zotz
Río San Pedro
Río Azul
1 Tikal
Laguna Perdida
Lago de Petén Itzá
Yaxhá
San José Petén
El Cruce
Flores
Santa Elena
Laguna Yahjá
Melchor de Mencos
Benque Viejo del Carmen
San Ignacio
Belize River
BELMOPAN
Belize City
Ferry
Dangriga
Barrier Reef
Macal River
Stann Creek
BELIZE
Sierra del Lacandón
Bethel
Río de la Pasión
El Subín
Río San Juan
Río Mopán
Chiquibul Branch River
Sayaxché
Ceibal
Benemérito de las Américas
Río Salinas
Río Machaquilá
Cuevas de Poptún
Poptún
Big Creek
Monkey River
CARIBBEAN SEA
Punta Gorda
Moho River
Modesto Méndez
Bahía de Amatique
Golfo de Honduras
Playa Grande
San Antonio Las Cuevas
Fray Bartolomé de Las Casas
Chisec
Sebol
Sierra de Chamá
Biotopo Chocón Machacas
3 Livingston
Punta de Manabique
Puerto Barrios
Finca La Inca
Cuyamel
Río Dulce
El Golfete
6
IZABAL
El Chinchado
Corinto
Grutas de Lanquín
Lanquín
5 Semuc Champey
El Estor
El Castillo de San Felipe
Lago de Izabal
Mariscos
San Cristóbal Verapaz
Cobán
Río Polochic
ZACAPA
Quiriguá
Carretera de Occidente
Río Ulúa
Biotopo del Quetzal
Purulhá
Sierra de las Minas
Salamá
Cubulco
Sierra de Chuacús
Río Hondo
Estanzuela
Zacapa
La Entrada
Santa Bárbara
Caraetera al Atlántico
Río Motagua
El Florido
Santa Rita de Copán
Copán
Chiquimula
Santa Rosa de Copán
CHIQUIMULA
GUATEMALA CITY
Quetzaltepeque
Jalapa
Ipala
Esquipulas
2 Antigua
Volcán de Ipala (1650m)
Agua Caliente
Interamericana
San José Pinula
Laguna de Ayarza
Lago de Amatitlán
El Progreso
Anguiatú
Nueva Ocotepeque
Jutiapa
Metapán
HONDURAS
La Esperanza
Lago Güija
Cuilapa
San Cristóbal Frontera
San Cristóbal
Carretera al Pacífico
Chiquimulilla
Río Lempa
Valle Nuevo
Las Chinamas
Embalse Cerrón Grande
Chalatenango
Iztapa
Ciudad Pedro de Alvarado
Santa Ana
El Congo
Monterrico
Apaneca
EL SALVADOR
La Hachadura
Lago de Coatepeque
SAN SALVADOR
Embalse 15 de Septiembre
Ciudad Barrios
Sonsonate

GUATEMALA CITY

POP 3.5 MILLION

Depending on who you talk to, Guatemala City (or Guate as it's also known) is either big, dirty, dangerous and utterly forgettable, or big, dirty, dangerous and utterly fascinating. Either way, there's no doubt there's an energy here unlike anywhere else in Guatemala. It's a place where dilapidated buses belch fumes next to BMWs and Hummers, and where skyscrapers drop shadows on shantytowns.

Guate is busy reinventing itself as a people-friendly city. Downtown Zona 1, for years a no-go zone of abandoned buildings and crime hot spots, is leading the way with the pedestrianized 6a Calle attracting bars, cafes and restaurants.

Many travelers skip the city altogether, preferring to make Antigua their base. Still, you may want, or need, to get acquainted with the capital, because this is the hub of the country, home to the best museums and galleries, transport hubs and other traveler services.

Sights

The major sights are in Zona 1 (the historic center, where the plaza is) and Zonas 10 and 13, where the museums are grouped.

Zona 1

★Casa MIMA MUSEUM

(Map p110; ☎2253-4020; www.casamima.org; 8a Av 14-12; Q20; ⊙10am-5pm Mon-Sat) A wonderfully presented museum and cultural center set in a house dating from the late 19th century. The owners of the house were collectors with eclectic tastes ranging from French neo-rococo, Chinese and art deco to indigenous artifacts. The place is set up like a functioning house, filled with curios and furniture spanning the centuries, such as top hats, an Underwood typewriter and a vintage Sunbeam blender.

Palacio Nacional de la Cultura HISTORIC BUILDING

(Map p110; ☎2253-0748; cnr 6a Av & 6a Calle; Q40; ⊙9am-4pm Mon-Fri, 10am-3pm Sat) On the north side of Parque Central is this imposing presidential palace, which was built between 1936 and 1943 during the dictatorial rule of General Jorge Ubico at enormous cost to the lives of the prisoners who were forced to labor here. It's the third palace to stand on the site.

Despite its tragic background, architecturally the palace is one of the country's most interesting constructions, a mélange of multiple earlier styles from Spanish Renaissance to neoclassical. Today most government offices have been removed from here, and it's open as a museum and for a few ceremonial events.

Visits are by guided tour (available in English). You pass through a labyrinth of gleaming brass, polished wood, carved stone and frescoed arches. Features include an optimistic mural of Guatemalan history by Alberto Gálvez Suárez above the main stairway, and a two-ton gold, bronze and Bohemian-crystal chandelier in the reception hall. The banqueting hall sports stained-glass panels depicting – with delicious irony – the virtues of good government. From here your guide will probably take you out onto the presidential balcony, where you can imagine yourself as a banana-republic dictator reviewing your troops.

In the western courtyard, the **Patio de la Paz**, a monument depicting two hands, stands where Guatemala's Peace Accords were signed in 1996; each day at 11am the rose held by the hands is changed by a military guard and the one from the previous day is tossed to a woman among the spectators.

Parque Central PLAZA

(Plaza de la Constitución; Map p110) Guatemala City's central plaza is an excellent starting point from which to begin your journey to other Zona 1 sights. Parque Central and the adjoining Parque Centenario are never empty during daylight hours, with shoeshine boys, ice-cream vendors and sometimes open-air political meetings adding to the general bustle.

Museo del Ferrocarril MUSEUM

(Railway Museum; Map p110; ☎2208-4747; www.museofegua.com; 9a Av 18-03; Q2; ⊙9am-4pm Tue-Fri, 10am-4pm Sat & Sun) This is one of the city's more intriguing museums, with lots of photos and interesting memorabilia from the train days of old. Documented here are the glory days of the troubled Guatemalan rail system, along with some quirky artifacts, such as hand-drawn diagrams of derailments and a kitchen set up with items used in dining cars. You can climb around in the passenger carriages, but not the locomotives. There's even a room displaying the administrative office, replete with bored-looking bureaucrat. Locals make an afternoon out of it by bringing along a picnic lunch to eat inside the train cars.

Museo Nacional de Historia MUSEUM

(Map p110; ☎2253-6149; 9a Calle 9-70; Q50; ⏰9am-5pm Mon-Fri, to noon & 1-4pm Sat & Sun) This museum hosts a jumble of historical relics with an emphasis on photography and portraits. Check out the carefully coiffed hairstyles of the 19th-century generals and politicos.

Zona 2

Mapa en Relieve MONUMENT

(Relief Map; ☎3525-0397; www.mapaenrelieve.org; Av Simeón Cañas Final; Q25; ⏰9am-5pm) North of Zona 1, Zona 2 is mostly a middle-class residential district, but it's worth venturing along to Parque Minerva to see this huge open-air map of Guatemala showing the country at a scale of 1:10,000. The vertical scale is exaggerated to 1:2000 to make the volcanoes and mountains appear dramatically higher and steeper than they really are.

Constructed in 1905 under the direction of Francisco Vela, it was fully restored and repainted in 1999. Viewing towers afford a panoramic view. This is an odd but fun place, and it's curious to observe that Belize is still represented as part of Guatemala. It's an easy walk (or short cab ride) from Parque Central.

Parque Minerva PARK

(Av Simeón Cañas Final) Minerva, the Roman goddess of wisdom, technical skill and invention, was a favorite of President Manuel Estrada Cabrera. Her park is a placid place, good for walking among the eucalyptus trees and sipping a cool drink. Watch out, however, for pickpockets and purse-snatchers.

Zonas 10 & 11

Museo Ixchel MUSEUM

(Map p114; ☎2361-8081; www.museoixchel.org; 6a Calle Final, Zona 10; Q45; ⏰9am-5pm Mon-Fri, to 1pm Sat) This museum is named for the Maya goddess of the moon, women, reproduction and textiles. Photographs and exhibits of indigenous costumes and other crafts show the incredible richness of traditional arts in Guatemala's highland towns. Guided tours are available in English (with prior reservation) or Spanish.

If you enjoy Guatemalan textiles at all, you must visit this museum. It has access for travelers with disabilities, a section for children, a cafe, a shop and a library.

Museo Popol Vuh MUSEUM

(Map p114; ☎2338-7896; www.popolvuh.ufm.edu; 6a Calle Final, Zona 10; adult/child Q45/15; ⏰9am-5pm Mon-Fri, to 1pm Sat) Inside Museo Popol Vuh you'll find well-displayed pre-Hispanic figurines, incense burners and burial urns, plus carved wooden masks and traditional textiles filling several rooms of this museum. Other rooms hold colonial paintings and gilded wood and silver artifacts. A faithful copy of the *Dresden Codex,* one of the precious 'painted books' of the Maya, is among the most interesting pieces. Also here is a colorful display of animals in Maya art.

Museo Miraflores MUSEUM

(☎2208-0550; www.museomiraflores.org.gt; 7a Calle 21-55, Zona 11; Q25; ⏰9am-7pm Tue-Sun) This excellent modern museum is inauspiciously jammed between two shopping malls a few kilometers out of town. Downstairs focuses on objects found at **Kaminaljuyú** (11a Calle 25-50 & 24a Av, Zona 7; Q50; ⏰8am-4pm), with fascinating trade-route maps showing the site's importance. Upstairs there are displays on textiles and indigenous clothing, separated by region, from around the country.

Signs are in Spanish and (for the most part) English. Out back is a pleasant grassy area with paths and seating – a good place to take a breather.

To get here, catch any bus from the center going to Centro Comercial Tikal Futura. The museum is 250m down the road between it and the Miraflores shopping center.

Zona 13 & Around

The attractions here in the city's southern reaches are all ranged along 5a Calle in the Finca Aurora area, northwest of the airport. While here you can also drop into the **Mercado de Artesanías** (Crafts Market; Map p114; ☎2475-5915; cnr 5a Calle & 11a Av, Zona 13; ⏰9am-6pm).

Museo Nacional de Arqueología y Etnología MUSEUM

(Map p114; ☎2475-4399, 2475-7010; www.munae.gob.gt; 6a Calle, Sala 5, Finca La Aurora, Zona 13; Q60; ⏰9am-4pm Tue-Fri, to noon & 1:30-4pm Sat & Sun) This museum has the country's biggest collection of ancient Maya artifacts, but explanatory information is very sparse. There's a great wealth of monumental stone sculpture, including Classic-period stelae from Tikal, Uaxactún and Piedras Negras; a superb

Guatemala City North

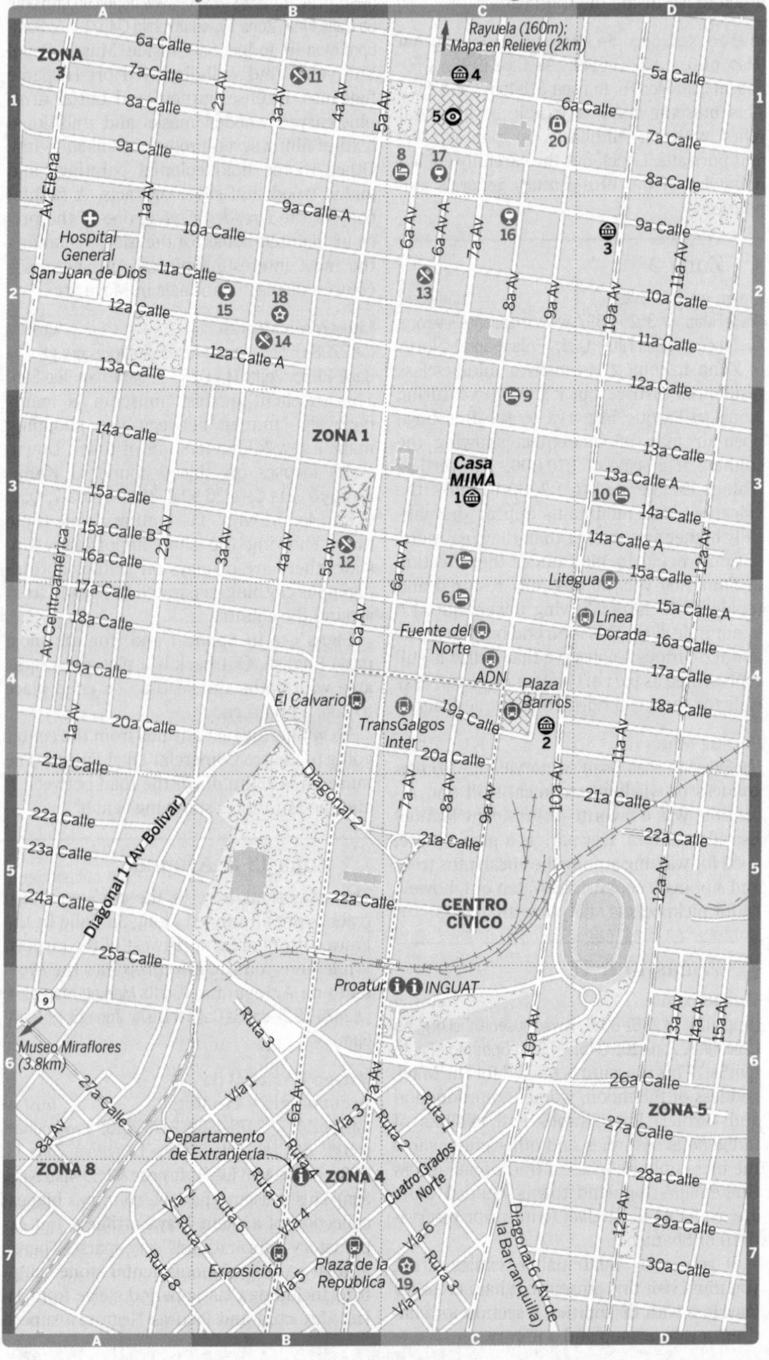

0 400 m
0 0.2 miles

Rayuela (160m); Mapa en Relieve (2km)

ZONA 3
ZONA 1
ZONA 4
ZONA 5
ZONA 8
CENTRO CÍVICO

Casa MIMA 1
2
3
4
5
6
7
8
9
10
11
12
13
14
15
16
17
18
19
20

Hospital General San Juan de Dios
Litegua
Línea Dorada
Fuente del Norte
ADN
Plaza Barrios
El Calvario
TransGalgos Inter
Proatur
INGUAT
Departamento de Extranjería
Exposición
Plaza de la Republica
Museo Miraflores (3.8km)

Av Elena
Av Centroamérica
Diagonal 1 (Av Bolívar)
Diagonal 2
Diagonal 6 (Av de la Barranquilla)
Cuatro Grados Norte

1a Av
2a Av
3a Av
4a Av
5a Av
6a Av
6a Av A
7a Av
8a Av
9a Av
10a Av
11a Av
12a Av
13a Av
14a Av
15a Av

5a Calle
6a Calle
7a Calle
8a Calle
9a Calle
9a Calle A
10a Calle
11a Calle
12a Calle
12a Calle A
13a Calle
13a Calle A
14a Calle
14a Calle A
15a Calle
15a Calle A
15a Calle B
16a Calle
17a Calle
18a Calle
19a Calle
20a Calle
21a Calle
22a Calle
23a Calle
24a Calle
25a Calle
26a Calle
27a Calle
28a Calle
29a Calle
30a Calle

Ruta 1
Ruta 2
Ruta 3
Ruta 4
Ruta 5
Ruta 6
Ruta 7
Ruta 8
Vía 1
Vía 2
Vía 3
Vía 4
Vía 5
Vía 6
Vía 7

9

Guatemala City North

Top Sights
1 Casa MIMA....C3

Sights
2 Museo del Ferrocarril....C4
3 Museo Nacional de Historia....D2
4 Palacio Nacional de la Cultura....C1
5 Parque Central....C1

Sleeping
6 Hotel Ajau....C4
7 Hotel Clariss....C3
8 Hotel Pan American....C1
9 Hotel Spring....C3
10 Posada Belen....D3

Eating
11 Café de Imeri....B1
12 Café-Restaurante Hamburgo....B3
13 La Cocina de Señora Pu....C2
14 La Majo....B2

Drinking & Nightlife
15 Black....B2
16 El Gran Hotel....C2
17 Las Cien Puertas....C1

Entertainment
18 La Bodeguita del Centro....B2
19 TrovaJazz....C7

Shopping
20 Mercado Central....C1

throne from Piedras Negras; and animal representations from Preclassic Kaminaljuyú.

Also here are rare wooden lintels from temples at Tikal and El Zotz, and a room with beautiful jade necklaces and masks. Don't miss the large-scale model of Tikal. The ethnology section has displays on the languages, costumes, dances, masks and homes of Guatemala's indigenous peoples.

Museo Nacional de Arte Moderno GALLERY
(Map p114; 2472-0467; 6a Calle, Sala 6, Finca La Aurora, Zona 13; Q50; 9am-4pm Tue-Fri, 9am-noon & 1:30-4pm Sat & Sun) Here you'll find a collection of 20th-century Guatemalan art including works by well-known Guatemalan artists such as Carlos Mérida, Carlos Valente and Humberto Gavarito.

Activities

Asociación Ak' Tenamit VOLUNTEERING
(2254-3346; www.aktenamit.org; 11a Av A 9-39, Zona 2; 9am-4pm Mon-Fri) A grassroots NGO focusing on development in indigenous communities.

Pasos y Pedales WALKING
(Map p114; 10am-2pm Sun) If you're here on a Sunday, check out a wonderful municipal initiative that sees the Av de las Americas in Zona 10, and its continuation, Av La Reforma in Zona 13, blocked off to traffic for 3km and taken over by jugglers, clowns, in-line skaters, dog walkers, food vendors, tai chi classes, skate parks and playgrounds for kids.

It's a great place to go for a walk (or you can hire bikes or in-line skates on the street) and check out a very relaxed, sociable side of the city that otherwise is rarely seen.

Sleeping

For budget and many midrange hotels, make a beeline for Zona 1. If you have just flown in or are about to fly out, there are a number of convenient guesthouses near the airport. Top-end hotels are mostly located around Zona 10.

Zona 1

★ **Posada Belen** BOUTIQUE HOTEL $$
(Map p110; 2253-4530; www.posadabelen.com; 13a Calle A 10-30; s/d Q322/411;) One of Zona 1's most stylish options, this boutique hotel has just 10 rooms, arranged around a couple of lush patios. Rooms are well decorated with *típico* (traditional) furnishings and there's a good restaurant on-site (reservations required).

Hotel Spring HOTEL $$
(Map p110; 2230-2858; www.hotelspring.com; 8a Av 12-65; s/d from Q200/250, without bathroom Q150/195; P@) With a beautiful courtyard setting, the Spring has a lot more style than other Zona 1 joints. It has central but quiet sunny patios. The 43 rooms vary greatly, but most are spacious and clean with high ceilings. Have a look around if you can. All rooms have cable TV; some of the more expensive ones are wheelchair accessible.

It's worth booking ahead. A cafeteria serves meals from 6:30am to 11:30am. Rooms have neither a fan nor air-con.

Hotel Clariss HOTEL $$
(Map p110; 2232-1113; 8a Av 15-14; dm/s/d Q100/250/355; P) This friendly place is set in a modern building with some good-sized rooms (and other, smaller ones). Those at the front get more air and light, but also the bulk of the street noise.

Hotel Ajau HOTEL $$
(Map p110; ☎2232-0488; www.hotelajau.net; 8a Av 15-62; s/d Q190/265, without bathroom Q110/180; P ⊖ @ ☎) One of the few cheaper hotels in Guate with any tangible sense of style, the Ajau is a pretty good deal, with lovely polished floor tiles and cool, clean rooms. Room sizes vary, and those at the front can get very noisy. Fans only here – no air-con.

Hotel Pan American HOTEL $$$
(Map p110; ☎2244-0850; www.hotelpanamerican.com.gt; 9a Calle 5-63; s/d Q700/760; P ⊖ ☎) Guatemala City's only luxury hotel before WWII, the Pan American is one of the few hotels in the city with any air of history. There's a fine, art deco lobby that's filled with plants and a not-too-shabby restaurant. Rooms are simple but large, often with three or more beds. The bathrooms are stylish and modern, with good-sized tubs. Avoid rooms facing the noisy street.

Zonas 10 & 13

Quetzalroo HOSTEL $
(Map p114; ☎5746-0830; www.quetzalroo.com; 6a Av 7-84, Zona 10; dm/s/d without bathroom Q147/275/360; P ⊖ @ ☎) Guatemala City's best downtown hostel has nine private rooms and 14 beds in four different dorms, a cramped kitchen area and a great rooftop terrace. The location's handy for the Zona Viva eating and nightlife scene. Simple breakfast is included and it sells craft beers well into the night. Call for free pick-up from the airport or bus terminal.

Hostal Los Lagos HOSTEL $
(☎2261-2809; www.loslagoshostal.com; 8a Av 15-85 Aurora 1, Zona 13; dm/s/d Q140/243/372; P ⊖ ☎) This is the most hostel-like of the near-the-airport options. Rooms are mostly set aside for dorms, which are airy and spacious, but there are a couple of reasonable-value private rooms. The whole place is extremely comfortable, with big indoor and outdoor sitting areas.

★**Eco Suites Uxlabil** APARTMENT $$
(Map p114; ☎2366-9555; www.uxlabil.com; 11a Calle 12-53, Zona 10; s/d incl breakfast Q389/479; ⊖ ❄ ☎) If you're planning on being in town for a while (or even if you're not), you could do a lot worse than these sweet little apartments decked out in indigenous motifs and tucked away in a leafy corner of Zona 10. Weekly discounts apply.

★**Dai Nonni Hotel** HOTEL $$
(☎2362-5458; www.dainonnihotel.com; 15 Av A 5-30, Zona 13; s/d/tr incl breakfast Q456/522/608; P ⊖ @ ☎) Just south of the Zona 10 action, this small hotel wins points for its eclectic decorations, backyard hangout areas and big rooms. Discounts are available for cash payments and longer stays.

Eating

For cheap eats head to Zona 1 – there are little *comedores* around the Mercado Central, and the cheapest of all are inside the market, on the lower floor. Zonas 10 and 14 have the lion's share of upscale restaurants, with a good selection of international cuisines. American fast-food chains are sprinkled liberally throughout Zona 1 and across the city. Pollo Campero is Guatemala's KFC clone.

Zona 1

★**Café de Imeri** CAFE $
(Map p110; ☎2232-3722; 6a Calle 3-34; mains Q40-70; ⏲7am-7pm Mon-Fri, to 6:30pm Sat; ☎) Interesting breakfasts, soups and pastas. The list of sandwiches is impressive and there's a beautiful little courtyard area out the back.

Café-Restaurante Hamburgo GUATEMALAN $
(Delicadezas Guatemaltecas; Map p110; ☎2238-4029; 15a Calle 5-34; mains Q22-44; ⏲7:30am-9:15pm Mon-Sat, to 8:30pm Sun) This bustling spot facing the south side of Parque Concordia serves good Guatemalan food, with chefs at work along one side and aproned waitstaff scurrying about. At weekends a marimba band adds atmosphere.

★**La Cocina de Señora Pu** GUATEMALAN $$
(Map p110; ☎5055-6480; www.senorapu.com; 6a Av A 10-16, Zona 1; mains Q75-125; ⏲noon-3pm & 6-9pm Mon-Fri, noon-9pm Sat) This tiny hole-in-the-wall eatery serves up excellent 'modernized' versions of classic Maya dishes. The menu is impressively wide – featuring beef, chicken, pork, duck, turkey, pigeon, rabbit, fish and shrimp – considering it's all done on a four-burner stove in front of your eyes. The flavors are delicious and sometimes surprising. Sit at the counter or in the new expanded dining area.

La Majo GUATEMALAN $$
(Map p110; 12a Calle 3-08, Zona 1; mains Q50-80; ⏲2-11:30pm Wed-Sat; ✎) Downtown Guatemala

City's cultural renaissance continues in this pleasing little boho cafe set in a crumbling colonial house. There's some OK food on offer and a couple of vegetarian and vegan dishes, but the big draw is the events calendar, featuring live music, theater and other local acts.

Zonas 10 & 14

Arbol de la Vida VEGETARIAN $

(2368-2124; 17 Calle A 19-60, Zona 10; mains Q35-60; 7am-6pm Mon-Fri, 7:30am-4pm Sat & Sun; P) Zona 10's best vegetarian restaurant opens up for early breakfasts and offers a wide menu with tasty soups and mains featuring veg-friendly goodies such as tofu and quinoa.

San Martín & Company CAFE, BAKERY $

(Map p114; 2420-9916; 13a Calle 1-62, Zona 10; light meals Q40-60; 6am-10pm Mon-Sat, 7am-8pm Sun;) Cool and clean, with ceiling fans inside and a small terrace outside, this Zona Viva cafe and bakery is great at any time of the day. For breakfast try a scrumptious omelet and croissant (the former arrives inside the latter); later there are tempting and original sandwiches, soups and salads.

★**Kacao** GUATEMALAN $$

(Map p114; 2337-4188; 2a Av 13-44, Zona 10; mains Q90-160; noon-10:30pm Mon-Sat, to 9:30pm Sun) Set under a thatched *palapa* roof with a soft marimba soundtrack, this is Zona 10's best *comida típica* (regional food) restaurant. The atmosphere and food are both outstanding.

★**Ambia** FUSION $$$

(2312-4666; http://ambia.com.gt; 10a Av 5-49, Zona 14; mains Q115-510; noon-midnight Mon-Sat, to 3:30pm Sun) As the prices may suggest, this is some of the city's finest dining, with a wide-ranging menu offering some good fusion dishes, leaning heavily on influences as far ranging as Asia and Peru. The presentation is fantastic and the ambience superb. On balmy nights, the outdoor courtyard-lounge area is the place to be.

★**Bistro Tamarindos** FUSION $$$

(Map p114; 2336-7364; Plaza Fontabella, 2F, Zona 10; mains Q130-300; 7am-10:30pm Mon-Thu & Sat, to 11pm Fri, to 5pm Sun;) This upscale bistro is in one of Guate's ritziest shopping malls. It has an inspiring range of salads on offer and some very good Japanese and Thai-inspired dishes. The decor is stylish and the service prompt but friendly.

Drinking & Nightlife

Zona 1 has a clutch of good drinking places, including some Latin music and dance venues, all advantageously within half a block of each other just south of Parque Central.

Zona 10 has a few electronic dance clubs, but many of these have now moved further south to the outskirts of town. Check flyers around town for special nights.

★**Rayuela** BAR

(2221-2453; www.facebook.com/rayuelagt; 6a Av 3-61, Zona 1; 11am-1am) This small spot for craft beers and cocktails is dedicated to the author Julio Cortázar, as aficionados will know from the name *Rayuela* (one of the author's novels). Inside, you'll find a red-walled montage of photos, quotes and trivia all connected somehow to one of Latin America's greatest literary minds, with friendly 20- and 30-somethings and decent food as well.

El Gran Hotel PUB

(Map p110; www.facebook.com/ElGranhotel; 9a Calle 7-64, Zona 1; 6pm-1am Tue-Sun) You can't actually stay here, but the downmarket renovated lobby of this classic hotel is one of Zona 1's better-looking bars. It also hosts one of the area's more reliable dance floors, alternating between Latin and electronic music.

Las Cien Puertas BAR

(Map p110; 9a Calle 6-45, Pasaje Aycinena 8-44, Zona 1; 4pm-1am Mon-Sat) This superhip (but not studiously so) little watering hole is set in a colonial arcade that's said to have a hundred doors (hence the name) and is sometimes closed off for live bands. Bring a Sharpie (or ask them to lend you one!) and scribble a note.

The bar and the alley are both called Las Cien Puertas. Little bars spring up in this area all the time – it's one of the few places in Zona 1 you can really go bar-hopping, with dozens to choose from in this alley alone.

Black GAY

(Map p110; 5904-1758; www.blackclubgt.com; 11a Calle 2-54, Zona 1; 7pm-1am Thu-Sat) A well-established gay disco-bar in a former private house near the city center with drag shows and theme parties most weekends. Once called Black & White Bar, it's now known as Black.

Entertainment

Guatemala City is home to nearly half the country's population, so it's no surprise that

Guatemala City South

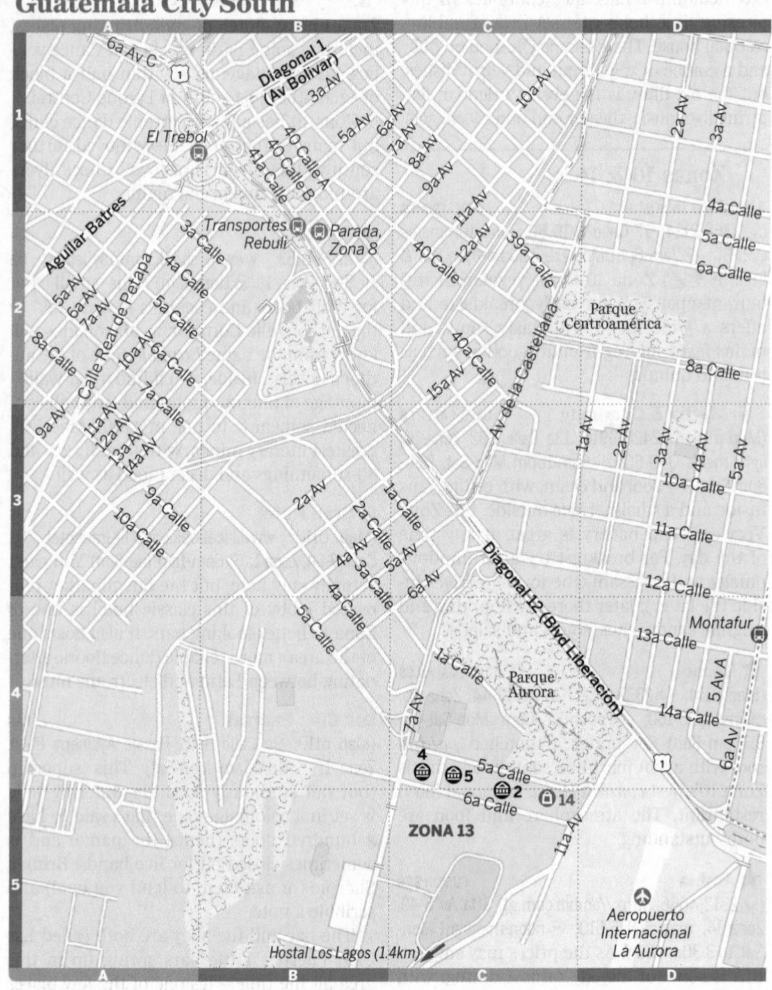

Guatemala City South

Sights

1 Museo de Historia Natural F1
2 Museo de los Niños C5
3 Museo Ixchel G2
4 Museo Nacional de Arqueología y Etnología C4
5 Museo Nacional de Arte Moderno C4
6 Museo Popol Vuh H2

Activities, Courses & Tours

7 Pasos y Pedales E2

Sleeping

8 Eco Suites Uxlabil H4
9 Quetzalroo F2

Eating

10 Bistro Tamarindos F4
11 Kacao F4
12 San Martín & Company F4

Shopping

13 Centro Comercial Los Próceres E5
14 Mercado de Artesanías C5
15 Oakland Mall G4
16 Sophos F4

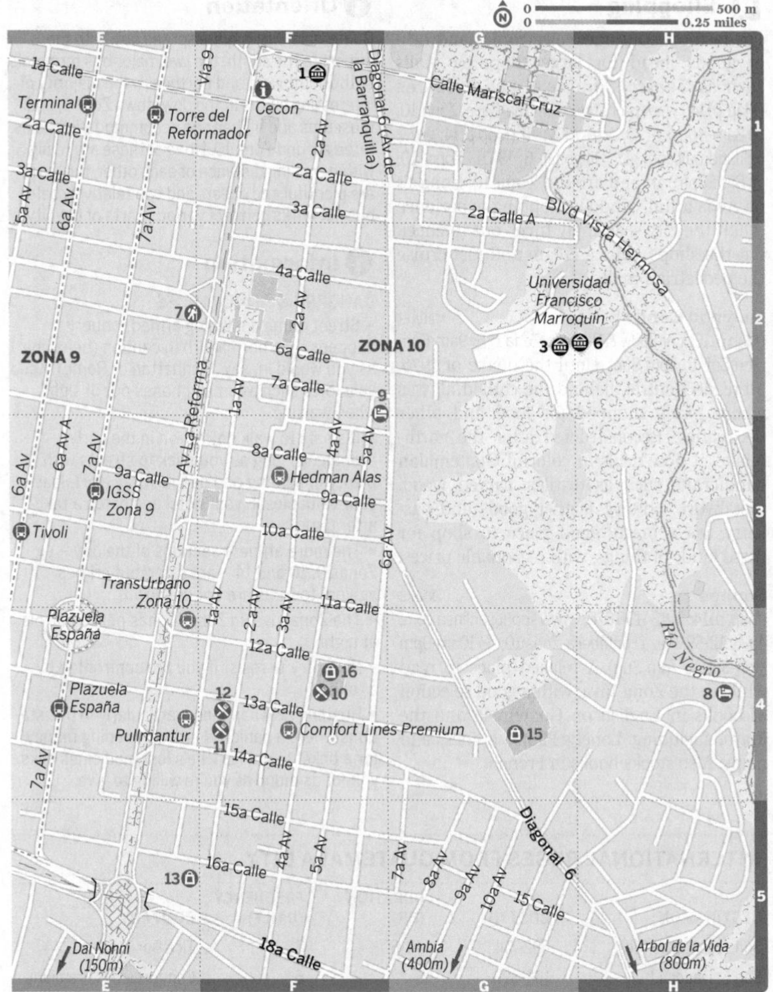

there are entertainment options to spare. The city's various cultural centers are the place to catch music and art shows, and there's live music most nights in the bars around Parque Central, and in the park itself most Sundays.

★La Bodeguita del Centro LIVE MUSIC
(Map p110; ☎2230-2976; 12a Calle 3-55, Zona 1; ⊙9pm-1am Tue-Sat) There's a hopping, creative local scene in Guatemala City, and this large, bohemian hangout is one of the best places to connect with it. There's live music of some kind almost every night from Thursday to Saturday, usually starting at 9pm, plus occasional poetry readings, films or forums.

Posters featuring the likes of Che, Marley, Lennon, Victor Jara, Van Gogh and Pablo Neruda cover the walls from floor to ceiling. Entry is usually free Tuesday to Thursday, with a charge of Q25 to Q60 on Friday and Saturday nights; food and drinks are served.

TrovaJazz LIVE MUSIC
(Map p110; ☎2267-9388; www.trovajazz.com; Vía 6 3-55, Zona 4; ⊙noon-6pm Mon-Wed, to 1am Thu-Sat) Jazz, blues and folk fans should look into what's happening here.

Shopping

For fashion boutiques, electronics and other goods, head for large shopping malls such as **Centro Comercial Los Próceres** (Map p114; www.proceres.com; 16a Calle, Zona 10; ⌚8am-8pm) or **Oakland Mall** (Map p114; www.oaklandmall.com.gt; Diagonal 6 13-01, Zona 10; ⌚8am-8pm) in and around Zona 10. Zona 1's 6a Av is a fun window-shopping experience – half the city seemingly turns out to check out the shops, eat ice cream and just cruise the pedestrian mall.

Mercado Central MARKET
(Map p110; cnr 8a Av & 8a Calle, Zona 1; ⌚9am-6pm Mon-Sat, to 2pm Sun) Until the quake of 1976, Mercado Central, behind the cathedral, was where locals shopped for food and other necessities. Reconstructed after the earthquake, it now deals in colorful Guatemalan handicrafts such as textiles, carved wood, metalwork, pottery, leather goods and basketry. It's a pretty good place to shop for these kinds of things, with reasonable prices.

Sophos BOOKS
(Map p114; ☎2419-7070; www.sophosenlinea.com; 4a Av 12-59, Plaza Fontabella, Zona 10; ⌚10am-9pm Mon-Sat, to 7pm Sun) A relaxed place to read while in the Zona Viva, with a good selection of books in English on Guatemala and the Maya, including Lonely Planet guides, and maps. Also stocks books in French.

Orientation

Guatemala City is quite spread out, with the airport to the south, the two major bus terminals to the southwest and northeast, the majority of interesting sights in the downtown Zona 1, and museums and higher-end accommodations clustered around Zona 10. None of these are really within walking distance of each other, but taxis are plentiful and cheap, and two relatively safe bus networks connect various parts of the city.

Information

DANGERS & ANNOYANCES

- Street crime, including armed robbery, happens. Use normal urban caution (behaving as you would in, say, Manhattan or Rome). Keep valuables such as smartphones out of sight when walking.
- It's safe to walk downtown in the early evening, as long as you stick to streets with plenty of lighting and people. Stay alert, leave your valuables in your hotel and catch a taxi after dark.
- The more affluent sections of the city – eg Zonas 9, 10 and 14 – are safer, but crimes against tourists are not unknown.
- The Zona Viva, in Zona 10, has police patrols at night.
- Never try to resist if you are confronted by a robber.
- Hustling also happens, particularly in bus stations where a panicked 'priest' needing money for a ticket to get his wife's lost medicines bilks you for as much as you're willing to give.

INTERNATIONAL BUSES FROM GUATEMALA CITY

DESTINATION	COST (Q)	DURATION (HR)	FREQUENCY (DAILY)	COMPANY
San José, Costa Rica	692-714	40-60	3	Tica Bus
San Salvador, El Salvador	168-390	5	6	Comfort Lines Premium, Pullmantur, Tica Bus
Copán, Honduras	278-520	5	1	Hedman Alas
La Ceiba, Honduras	442-690	12	1	Hedman Alas
San Pedro Sula, Honduras	405-645	8	1	Comfort Lines Premium, Hedman Alas
Tegucigalpa, Honduras	336-697	10-35	6	Hedman Alas, Comfort Lines Premium, Pullmantur, Tica Bus
Tapachula, Mexico	175-228	5-7	2	Tica Bus, Transportes Galgos Inter, Línea Dorada
Managua, Nicaragua	462-545	16-35	2	Comfort Lines Premium, Tica Bus
Panama City, Panama	1034-1176	76	2	Tica Bus

EMERGENCY

Guatemala City (and, in fact, all of Guatemala) has no area codes – just dial the number as you see it.

INGUAT Tourist Information	2421-2854
Tourist Police Liaison (24hr)	1500

MEDICAL SERVICES

Guatemala City has many private hospitals and clinics. Public hospitals and clinics provide free consultations but can be busy; to reduce waiting time, get there before 7am.

Hospital Centro Médico (2279-4949; 6a Av 3-47, Zona 10; 24hr) Recommended. This private hospital has some English-speaking doctors.

Hospital General San Juan de Dios (Map p110; 2321-9191; 1a Av 10-50, Zona 1; 24hr) One of the city's best public hospitals.

MONEY

Card skimming is rife in Guatemala City – try to use ATMs that are under some sort of watch at all times, such as those inside stores or shopping malls, rather than those accessible 24 hours on the street.

American Express (2331-7422; 12a Calle 0-93, Centro Comercial Montufar, Zona 9; 8am-5pm Mon-Fri, to noon Sat) In an office of Clark Tours.

Banco Agromercantil (7a Av 9-11, Zona 1; 9am-7pm Mon-Fri, to 1pm Sat) Changes US dollars (cash, not traveler's checks).

Banrural (Aeropuerto Internacional La Aurora; 7am-6pm) Located on the airport departures level, this bank offers currency-exchange services. You can also purchase tickets for ruins such as Tikal, but it's not generally set up for tourist transactions.

Visa/MasterCard ATMs (16a Calle, Zona 10; 10am-8pm Mon-Sat, to 7pm Sun) Inside Los Próceres Mall.

TOURIST INFORMATION

Cecon (Centro de Estudios Conservacionistas de la Universidad de San Carlos; Map p114; 2334-7662; www.cecon.usac.edu.gt; Av La Reforma 0-63, Zona 10; 7:30am-3:30pm Mon-Fri) Administers several protected areas and can arrange stays in them.

Disetur (Tourist Police; 3033-7759, 4063-9567; 11a Calle 16-53, Zona 1; 24hr) Guatemala's tourist police; travelers are advised to contact its liaison, **Proatur** (Map p110; toll-free, in English 1500; 7a Av 1-17, Zona 4; 24hr).

Fundación Defensores de la Naturaleza (2310-2929; www.defensores.org.gt; 4a Av 23-01, Zona 14; 7:30am-4:30pm Mon-Thu, to noon Fri) Administers several protected areas and can arrange stays in them.

INGUAT (Map p110; 2290-2800; www.visitguatemala.com; 7a Av 1-17, Zona 4; 8am-4pm Mon-Fri) Main office of the Guatemalan tourism department; has limited handout material, but staff are extremely helpful. There's also a branch (3128-6900 6am-9pm) at the airport.

Getting There & Away

AIR

Guatemala City's **Aeropuerto Internacional La Aurora** (GUA; Guatemala City; Map p114; 2260-6257) is the country's major airport. All international flights to Guatemala City land and take off here. The arrivals hall has a sometimes-working ATM, sometimes-attended tourist information booth nd currency-exchange desks. Travelers have complained about the rates given at the exchange booth inside arrivals. There is also a reliable ATM in the departures hall, helpfully hidden behind the stairs leading up to the mezzanine.

At the time of writing, the country's only *scheduled* domestic flights were between Guatemala City and Santa Elena with **Avianca** (2279-8222; www.avianca.com), leaving Guatemala City at 6am and 7:30pm, and **TAG** (2380-9494; http://tag.com.gt; Aeropuerto Internacional La Aurora; 7am-7pm), which depart at 6:30am and 5:15pm. Domestic flights *may* leave from the domestic terminal, a 15-minute cab ride from the international terminal.

Tickets to Flores cost around Q900 one way with either Avianca or TAG, but some travel agents, especially in Antigua, offer large discounts on these prices.

Fourteen international airlines also serve Guatemala, flying direct from North, Central and South America and Europe.

BUS

Buses from Guatemala City run all over Guatemala and into Mexico, Belize, Honduras, El Salvador and beyond. Many bus companies have their own terminals, some of which are in Zona 1. The city council has been on a campaign to get long-distance bus companies out of the city center, so it may be wise to double-check with INGUAT or staff at your hotel about the office location before heading out.

Buses for the Pacific coast mostly leave from the **CentraSur** (Zona 12) terminal in the southern outskirts of town. Departures for Central and Eastern Guatemala and El Petén mostly leave from **CentraNorte** (2500-9800; http://centranorte.com.gt; Carretera 9; 6am-8pm), Zona 8 in the city's northeast. Second-class buses for the Western Highlands leave from a series of roadside paradas (Map p114), El Trebol (Map p114), or bus stops, on 41a Calle between 6a and 7a Avs in Zona 8.

International Buses

The following companies offer 1st-class bus services to international destinations.

Hedman Alas (Map p114; ☎2362-5072; www.hedmanalas.com; 2a Av 8-73, Zona 10) Serves multiple destinations in Honduras.

Comfort Lines Premium (Map p114; ☎2501-1000; www.king-qualityca.com; 4a Av 13-60, Zona 10) Serves most Central American capitals.

Línea Dorada (Map p110; ☎2415-8900; www.lineadorada.com.gt; cnr 10a Av & 16a Calle, Zona 1; ⏲5:30am-10pm) Has a service to Tapachula, Mexico.

Pullmantur (Map p114; ☎2495-7000; www.pullmantur.com; 1a Av 13-22, Holiday Inn, Zona 10) Covers El Salvador and Honduras.

Tica Bus (☎2473-3737; www.ticabus.com; Calz Aguilar Batres 18-35, Zona 12; ⏲5am-6pm) Covers all of Central America and Mexico.

TransGalgos Inter (Map p110; ☎2230-5058, 2232-3661; www.transgalgosintergt.com; 7a Av 19-44, Zona 1; ⏲5am-5pm) Can book connections to Tapachula, Mexico. Also goes to El Salvador.

National Pullman Buses

The following bus companies have services to Guatemalan destinations.

ADN (Map p110; ☎2251-0610; www.adnautobusesdelnorte.com; 8a Av 16-41, Zona 1) Connects Guatemala City to Flores, Santa Elena, and points in between.

Fortaleza del Sur (☎2230-3390; CentraSur, Zona 12) Covers the Pacific coast.

Fuente del Norte (Map p110; ☎2251-3817; 17a Calle 8-46, Zona 1) Covers the whole country.

Hedman Alas (p118) Daily departures between Guatemala City and Antigua.

Línea Dorada (p118) Luxury buses to El Petén, Quetzaltenango, Huehuetenango etc.

Litegua (Map p110; ☎2220-8840; www.litegua.com; 15a Calle 10-40, Zona 1; ⏲3:30am-7pm) Covers the east and Antigua.

Los Halcones (☎2439-4911; Calz Roosevelt 37-47, Zona 11) For Huehuetenango.

Monja Blanca (CentraNorte, Zona 18; ⏲3am-6pm) For Cobán and points in between.

Rapidos del Sur (☎2232-7025; CentraSur, Zona 12) For the Pacific coast.

Rutas Orientales (☎2503-3100; CentraNorte, Zona 18) Covers the east.

Transportes Álamo (☎2471-8646; 12a Av A 0-65, Zona 7) For Quetzaltenango.

Transportes Rebuli (Map p114; ☎2230-2748; 41a Calle, btwn 6a & 7a Av, Zona 8) For Panajachel.

SHUTTLE MINIBUS

Shuttle services from Guatemala City to popular destinations such as Panajachel and Chichicastenango (via Antigua; both around Q260) are offered by travel agencies in Antigua. Quetzaltenango-based travel agents also have shuttles to and from Guatemala City.

NATIONAL PULLMAN BUSES FROM GUATEMALA CITY

DESTINATION	COST (Q)	DURATION (HR)	FREQUENCY	COMPANY
Antigua	50-70	1	7 daily	Hedman Alas, Litegua
Chiquimula	40-50	3-4	half-hourly, 5am-6:30pm	Rutas Orientales
Cobán	50-80	5	hourly, 4am-5pm	Monja Blanca
El Carmen	90	7	hourly, 4am-5pm	Fortaleza del Sur
Esquipulas	65-75	4-5	half-hourly, 4:30am-7pm	Rutas Orientales
Flores & Santa Elena	130-205	8-10	6-8 daily	ADN, Fuente del Norte, Línea Dorada
Huehuetenango	90-100	5	4 daily	Línea Dorada, Los Halcones
Poptún	120-200	8	3 daily	Línea Dorada, Fuente del Norte
Puerto Barrios	100-150	5-6	hourly, 3:45am-7pm	Litegua
Quetzaltenango	70	4	10 daily	Álamo, Fuente del Norte, Línea Dorada
Retalhuleu	85	3	5 daily	Fuente del Norte
Río Dulce	80-100	5	hourly, 5:30am-5pm	Litegua
Tecún Umán	75	6	4 daily	Fortaleza del Sur

Getting Around

ARRIVING IN GUATEMALA CITY

Aeropuerto Internacional La Aurora (p117) Guatemala City's international airport is in Zona 13, a Q80 taxi ride from Zona 1 and Q70 from Zona 10 or 13. If you're arriving late at night, a popular option is to spend the night in one of the guesthouses close to the airport and get a fresh start the next day.

Bus Arriving from other parts of the country, you'll most likely be coming in on a bus. Guatemala City's bus stations are scattered all over town. Wherever you're going, if it's more than a few blocks away it's a good idea to grab a taxi. Taxis are plentiful (especially around bus stations) and a whole lot cheaper than getting mugged while lugging your backpack around.

BUS

Due to an increase in (sometimes violent) crime on Guatemala City's red city buses, it is pretty much universally accepted that tourists should only use them in case of dire emergency. The major exceptions are the TransMetro and TransUrbano buses, which are most useful for getting to the CentraSur and CentraNorte bus terminals, respectively.

For the thrillseekers out there, we've listed the most useful red-bus routes. Buses will stop anywhere they see a passenger, but street corners and traffic lights are your best bet for hailing them – just hold out your hand. Buses should cost Q1 per ride in the daytime (but this can as much as quadruple on public holidays or at the driver's whim). You pay the driver or the driver's helper as you get on. Don't catch these buses at night.

Airport to Zona 1 (Bus 82) Travels via Zonas 9 and 4.

Zona 1 to Airport (Bus 82) Travels via 10a Av in Zona 1 then down 6a Av in Zonas 4 and 9.

Zona 1 to Zona 10 (Bus 82 or 101) Travels via 10a Av, Zona 1, then 6a Av and Ruta 6 in Zona 4 and Av La Reforma.

Zona 10 to Zona 1 (Bus 82 or 101) Travels via Av La Reforma then 7a Av in Zona 4 and 9a Av, Zona 1.

Trans Metro

In early 2007, in answer to growing concerns about traffic congestion and security on urban buses, Guatemala City inaugurated the TransMetro system (www.muniguate.com/muni/transmetro). TransMetro buses differ from regular old, red urban buses because they are prepaid (the driver carries no money, thus reducing the risk of robberies), travel in their

2ND-CLASS BUSES FROM GUATEMALA CITY

These services are all 2nd-class bus ('chicken bus') services.

DESTINATION	COST (Q)	DURATION (HR)	FREQUENCY	DEPARTS
Amatitlán	5	30min	every 4-10min, 7am-8:45pm	CentraSur, Zona 12
Antigua	10	1	every 5min, 7am-8pm	El Trebol
Chichicastenango	30	3	hourly, 5am-6pm	Parada, 41a Calle, Zona 8
Ciudad Pedro de Alvarado	50	2½-3	15min, 4am-5pm	CentraSur, Zona 12
Esquintla	10-15	1	half-hourly, 3:30am-7:30pm	CentraSur, Zona 12
Huehuetenango	70	5	half-hourly, 7am-5pm	Parada, 41a Calle, Zona 8
La Democracia	30	2	half-hourly, 6am-4:30pm	CentraSur, Zona 12
La Mesilla	100	8	hourly, 8am-4pm	Parada, 41a Calle, Zona 8
Monterrico	60	3	3 daily	CentraSur, Zona 12
Panajachel	60-80	3	half-hourly, 7am-5pm	El Trebol
Puerto San José	25	2	every 30min, 5am-5pm	CentraSur, Zona 12
Salamá	35-50	3	half-hourly, 5am-5pm	17a Calle 11-32, Zona 1
San Pedro La Laguna	60	4	few, 2am-2pm	Parada, 41a Calle, Zona 8
Santa Cruz del Quiché	35	4	every 10min, 5am-5pm	Parada, 41a Calle, Zona 8
Santiago Atitlán	45	4	half-hourly, 4am-5pm	CentraSur, Zona 12
Tecpán	15	2	every 15min, 5:30am-7pm	El Trebol

own lanes (not getting caught in traffic jams), only stop at designated stops and are new, comfortable and bright green.

There are currently seven routes in operation, each named for the zone they reach: thus, Línea 13 takes you out to Zona 13. Among the routes, one connects Zona 1's Plaza Barrios with the CentraSur bus terminal, from where the majority of buses for the Pacific coast now depart. Another runs south from Plaza Barrios through Zonas 9 and 10.

Crime has increased so much on Guate's regular red buses that travelers are advised not to use them, but TransMetro buses are safe, fast and comfortable. All rides cost Q1, payable with a Q1 coin at the bus stop before boarding.

Trans Urbano

A more recent improvement to Guatemala City's bus scene is TransUrbano, a much wider network of buses that aren't quite as slick as TransMetro but are still safe, reliable and comfortable. They're slower because they don't have a dedicated lane, but safer than the old red buses because to board you need a magnetic rechargeable card (card and first ride free), which can only be obtained by showing your passport or Guatemalan ID card. The rechargeable cards are available from special booths, the most useful for travelers being in Zona 1's Plaza Barrios, the CentraNorte bus terminal and the **Zona 10 TransUrbano office** (Map p114; cnr Av Reforma & 12a Calle, Zona 10).

TAXI

Plenty of taxis cruise most parts of the city. Fares are negotiable; always establish your destination and fare before getting in. Zona 1 to Zona 10, or vice-versa, costs around Q50. If you want to phone for a taxi, **Taxi Amarillo Express** (☎1766) has metered cabs (figure on Q5 per kilometer) that often work out cheaper than others, although true *capitaleños* (capital city residents) will tell you that taxi meters are all rigged and you get a better deal bargaining for a flat price.

ANTIGUA

POP 46,700

Antigua's beguiling beauty starts to seduce the moment you arrive. Once capital of Guatemala, its streetscapes of pastel facades unfold beneath the gaze of three volcanoes, and beautifully restored colonial buildings sit next to picturesque ruins in park-like surroundings. The city's World Heritage–listed status means that even fast-food chains have to hide themselves behind traditional building facades.

While Antigua's churches, plazas and markets throb with activity, the town is also a global hot spot with a laid-back vibe, thanks to the dozens of Spanish-language schools that operate here. Outside the city, Maya communities, coffee plantations and volcanoes offer ample opportunities for exploration.

Through the course of its history, this city has suffered earthquakes, floods, volcanic eruptions and virtual abandonment. But in recent decades it has re-emerged with a vengeance, buoyed by the pride of its inhabitants. It's no wonder Antigua remains Guatemala's most visited destination.

History

Founded in 1543, Antigua served as the Spanish colonial capital of Guatemala for 233 years. The capital was transferred to Guatemala City in 1776 after the devastating earthquake of 1773.

The town was slowly rebuilt, retaining much of its traditional character. In 1944 the Legislative Assembly declared Antigua a national monument and in 1979 Unesco declared it a World Heritage Site.

Most of Antigua's buildings were constructed during the 17th and 18th centuries when the city was a rich Spanish colonial outpost and the Catholic church was ascending to power. Many handsome, sturdy colonial buildings remain, and several impressive ruins have been preserved and are open to the public.

Sights

Echoes of Antigua's former grandeur are everywhere, rewarding a stroll in any direction. Begin exploring at Parque Central, the city's verdant heart, surrounded by superb colonial administrative buildings. Dotted around town are dozens of ecclesiastical complexes established by the myriad Catholic orders in the city's heyday, now in various states of decay. Once glorious in their gilded baroque finery, Antigua's churches and monasteries have suffered indignities from both nature and humankind. Rebuilding after earthquakes gave the churches thicker walls, lower towers and belfries, and unembellished interiors. Aside from their architectural interest, most of the complexes feature tranquil cloisters and gardens, and a few contain museums, notably the Convento de Santo Domingo.

Parque Central

Surrounded by superb colonial structures, this broad and beautiful **plaza** (Map p124; btwn 4a Calle & 5a Calle) is the gathering place for *antigüeños* and visitors alike – a fine, verdant place to sit or stroll and observe the goings-on, from hawkers and shoeshiners to school kids and groups of tourists. The buxom mermaids in the central fountain are a reconstruction of the original 1738 version, which was trashed early in the 20th century.

Catedral de Santiago CATHEDRAL
(Map p124; cnr 4a Av Norte & 5a Calle Oriente; ruins Q8; ruins 9am-5pm, parish 6:30am-noon & 3-6:30pm Mon, Tue, Thu & Fri, 8am-noon & 3-7pm Sat, 5:30am-1pm & 3-7:30pm Sun) Antigua's cathedral was begun in 1545, wrecked by the quake of 1773, and only partially rebuilt over the next century. The present sliver of a church – the parish of San José – occupies only the entrance hall of the original edifice. Behind it are the roofless **ruins** of the main part of the cathedral, which are entered from 5a Calle Oriente.

The ruin is a haunting place, with massive chunks of pillars strewn beneath sweeping brick archways and vegetation sprouting from cracks in the walls. Reproductions of the intricate plasterwork figures and moldings between the arches seem all that more impressive against the ruined backdrop. Behind the main altar, steps lead down to a former crypt, now serving as a chapel, with a smoke-blackened Christ.

The main part of the cathedral was built in the 17th century by Joseph de Porres, an architect of African-Maya descent.

Antiguo Colegio de la Compañía de Jesús HISTORIC BUILDING
(Map p124; 7932-3838; www.aecid-cf.org.gt; 6a Av Norte; 9am-6pm) FREE Established in 1626, the Jesuit monastery and college was a vital component of Antigua life until the order was expelled in 1767; just six years later, the great earthquake left it in ruins. Rescued from the rubble by the Spanish government, the complex has been reborn as a cultural center, the Centro de Formación de la Cooperación Española.

Palacio de los Capitanes Generales HISTORIC BUILDING
(Palace of the Captains General; Map p124; 7832-2868; www.centroculturalrealpalacio.org.gt; 5a Calle Poniente; 9am-4:30pm Wed-Sun) FREE Dating from 1549, the palace was colonial headquarters for all of Central America, from Chiapas to Costa Rica, until the capital was relocated in 1776. The stately double-arcaded facade that anchors the south side of the plaza is all that remains of the original complex. Following extensive renovations, the palace now hosts occasional art exhibits and performances.

> **GETTING TO ANTIGUA**
>
> The classic exit strategy on arrival at the airport is to make a beeline for elsewhere, usually Antigua. Door-to-door minibuses run to any address in Antigua (usually Q80 per person, one hour). Look for signs in the airport exit hall or for people holding up 'Antigua Shuttle' signs. The first shuttle leaves for Antigua at about 7am and the last around 8pm or 9pm, although there's often one hanging around to meet the last flight (around midnight). For groups, the other option is a taxi (around Q200), but if there is only one or two of you, shuttle minibuses are more economical (if a bit slower and less comfortable).

Palacio del Ayuntamiento HISTORIC BUILDING
(City Hall Palace; Map p124; 4a Calle Poniente) This double-decker structure on the north side of the park dates from the 18th century. Besides town offices, the palace houses the Museo del Libro Antiguo (p122), showcasing the early days of Guatemalan printing. The stone benches looking over to the park from beneath the lower arcade make a fine people-watching perch.

West of Parque Central

★**Arco de Santa Catalina** ARCHITECTURE
(Map p124; 5a Av Norte) The Arco de Santa Catalina is Antigua's most iconic monument, and an early-morning or late-afternoon photo opportunity framing Volcán Agua through its arch is an essential part of any visit to the town. It was built in 1694 to enable nuns from the Santa Catalina convent to cross the street without being seen; the clock tower is a 19th-century add-on.

★**Iglesia Merced** CHURCH, MONASTERY
(Iglesia y Convento de Nuestra Señora de la Merced; Map p124; cnr 1a Calle Poniente & 6a Av Norte;

monastery ruins Q15; ⌚church 6am-noon & 3-8pm, ruins 8:30am-5:30pm) At the northern end of 5a Av is La Merced – a striking yellow building trimmed with white plaster filigree. Its facade is one of the most beautiful in Guatemala The thick-walled structure was built to withstand earthquakes, and three centuries after its construction it remains in good shape. Only the church is still in use; a candlelit procession, accompanied by bell ringing and firecrackers, starts and ends here on the last Thursday evening of each month.

East of Parque Central

★Iglesia y Convento de Santo Domingo — MONASTERY

(Map p124; ☎7820-1220; 3a Calle Oriente 28; Q42; ⌚9am-6pm Mon-Sat, 11:45am-6pm Sun) Founded by Dominican friars in 1542, Santo Domingo became the biggest and richest monastery in Antigua. Following three 18th-century earthquakes, the buildings were pillaged for construction material. The site was acquired as a private residence in 1970 by a North American archaeologist, who performed extensive excavations before it was taken over by the Casa Santo Domingo Hotel (p128). The archaeological zone has been innovatively restored as a 'cultural route.'

The zone includes the picturesque ruined monastery church, the adjacent cloister with a replica of the original fountain, workshops for candle and pottery makers, and two underground crypts that were discovered during the church excavations. One of these, the **Calvary Crypt**, contains a well-preserved mural of the Crucifixion dating from 1683.

Also part of the archaeological zone are six museums, with extraordinarily rich collections presented in top-class exhibitions. All can be visited with one admission ticket. This museum route may be entered either through the hotel or the Universidad de San Carlos extension on 1a Av Norte. Starting from the hotel side, the route includes the following museums: the **Museo de la Platería**, with silverwork masterpieces including incense burners, candelabras and crowns; the **Museo Colonial**, with canvases and wooden sculpture on religious themes from the 16th to 18th centuries; the **Museo Arqueológico**, with ceramic and stone objects from the Maya Classic period; the cleverly curated **Museo de Arte Precolombino y Vidrio Moderno**, with Maya sculpture and ceramics shown as art pieces alongside glass works by modern artists; the **Museo de Artes y Artesanías Populares de Sacatepéquez**, with exhibits on traditional handicrafts from the Antigua region; and the **Museo de la Farmacia**, a restored version of a 19th-century apothecary's shop from Guatemala City.

Iglesia y Convento de la Recolección — RUINS

(Map p124; Av de la Recolección; Q40; ⌚9am-5pm) A serene air pervades the remains of the monastery of La Recolección, which stands well west of the center. Erected in the early 18th century by the Récollets (a French branch of the Franciscan order), its church was one of the largest in Antigua at the time. The earthquake of 1773 toppled the structure, of which only the great arched doorway remains intact.

La Antigua Galería de Arte — GALLERY

(Map p124; ☎7832-2124; www.facebook.com/LaAntiguaGaleria; 5a Avenida Norte 29; ⌚10am-7pm Mon-Sat, noon-6pm Sun) FREE Displaying works by more than 70 Guatemalan artists in the halls and patio of a colonial mansion, Antigua's premier art gallery merits an extended visit. There are regular expositions of new and old artists.

Museo del Libro Antiguo — MUSEUM

(Old Book Museum; Map p124; ☎7832-5511; 4a Calle Poniente, Palacio del Ayuntamiento; Q30; ⌚9am-4pm Tue-Fri, 9am-noon & 2-4pm Sat & Sun) The fascinating Museo del Libro Antiguo showcases the greatest hits of the early days of Guatemalan printing, plus a replica of Guatemala's first printing press, which began work here in the 1660s. One of its earliest products is prominently displayed: a first edition of *Don Quixote de la Mancha (Part II)*.

Activities

★La Tortilla — COOKING

(Map p124; ☎4181-8227; www.latortillacookingschools.com; 3 Calle Poniente 25; lessons Q225-375 (2-6 dishes)) This excellent cooking school runs classes twice a day at 10:30am and 4:30pm. The personable instructors guide you through classes from a 90-minute one covering two dishes, to a three-hour lesson with six dishes from mains and sides to dessert (and unlimited wine).

★De la Gente — TOUR

(☎5585-4450; www.dlgcoffee.org; tour per person (min 2 people) Q200) This NGO, based in San Miguel Escobar, works toward improving the lot of local farmers and artisans through sustainable economic development and direct trade. Tours, led by growers themselves (with translator if needed), focus on coffee growing and processing. At the end participants are guided through traditional roasting methods and share a cup with the family.

Old Town Outfitters ADVENTURE SPORTS
(Map p124; ☎5399-0440; www.adventureguatemala.com; 5a Av Sur 12C) Mountain biking, rock climbing, kayaking and trekking are among the high-energy activities offered by this respected and highly responsible operator, which works with guides from local communities.

New Sensation Salsa Studio DANCING
(Map p124; ☎5033-0921; www.facebook.com/salseandosevivemejor; 7a Av Norte 78; private classes per hour Q85) If you want to get your dancing shoes on, try the free salsa group classes every Monday and Tuesday from 5pm to 6pm. New Sensation also offers one-on-one instruction in salsa and *bachata* – either by the hour or in extended packages.

Courses

Antigua's Spanish-language schools attract students from around the world. There are dozens of schools to choose from. The **INGUAT tourist office** (Map p124; ☎7832-0787; info-antigua@inguat.gob.gt; 5a Calle Oriente 11; 8am-4pm Mon-Fri, 9am-5pm Sat & Sun) has a list of authorized schools, but price, teaching quality and student satisfaction can vary greatly. The most popular classes are for conversational Spanish, but if you want to focus on your grammar, or learn for a specific purpose (such as for medicine, business or law), you'll find the class to suit you in Antigua.

Classes start every Monday at most schools, though you can usually be placed with a teacher any day of the week. Most schools cater for all levels and allow you to stay as long as you like. Three or four weeks is typical, though it's OK to do just one week. The busiest seasons are during January and from April to August, and some schools request advance reservations for these times.

Instruction is nearly always one-on-one and costs Q900 to Q1200 per week for four hours of classes daily, five days a week. Most schools offer to arrange room and board with local families, usually with your own room and three meals daily (except Sunday), for around Q850 per week (a bit more with private bathroom). Most schools also offer lessons by Skype if you want to continue your study or start lessons before you arrive.

Homestays are meant to promote the total immersion concept of language learning, but this becomes tricky where there are several foreigners staying with one family or separate mealtimes for students and the family. Indeed, there are so many foreigners about Antigua, it can take discipline to converse in Spanish rather than your native tongue. Many enjoy this social scene, but if you think it may deter you, consider studying in Quetzaltenango, El Petén or elsewhere, where there are fewer foreign students.

Cambio Spanish School LANGUAGE
(Map p124; ☎7832-8033; www.cambiolanguageschool.com; 4a Calle Oriente 28) All profits from this school support Niños de Guatemala, a local educational program for underprivileged kids. Teachers use the curriculum devised by the Spanish Instituto Cervantes.

Proyecto Lingüístico Francisco Marroquín LANGUAGE
(Map p124; ☎7832-1422; www.spanishschoolplfm.com; 6a Av Norte 43) Antigua's oldest Spanish school, founded in 1969, is run by a nonprofit foundation to preserve indigenous languages and culture, with capacity to teach K'iche', Mam, Kaqchiquel and other Maya tongues (advance booking needed to arrange local teachers).

Antigüeña Spanish Academy LANGUAGE
(Map p124; ☎5735-4638; www.spanishacademyantiguena.com; 1a Calle Poniente 10) Regularly recommended school, and authorized by the Ministry of Education. Lessons take place in a leafy hacienda, and the school has two student apartments as well as homestay options.

Academia de Español Sevilla LANGUAGE
(Map p124; ☎7832-5101; www.facebook.com/SpanishSchoolAntigua; 1a Av Sur 17C) This well-managed institute offers plenty of free activities, and it can arrange volunteer work in local community projects. One-on-one classes are conducted amid the remnants of a colonial monastery. Shared student housing is offered as an accommodations option alongside homestays.

Spanish School San José el Viejo LANGUAGE
(Map p124; ☎7832-3028; www.sanjoseelviejo.com; 5a Av Sur 34) Long-standing school with parklike study environment, complete with

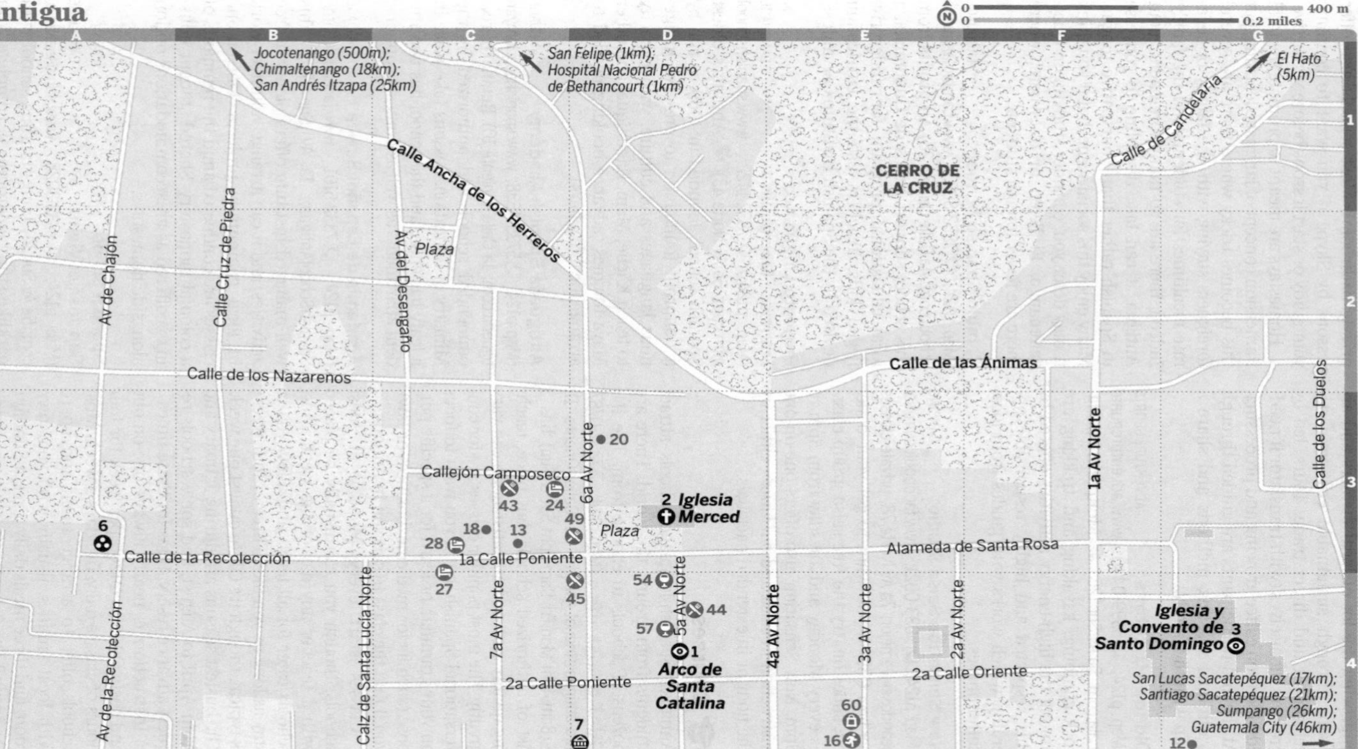

Antigua
0 — 400 m
0 — 0.2 miles
Jocotenango (500m); Chimaltenango (18km); San Andrés Itzapa (25km)
San Felipe (1km); Hospital Nacional Pedro de Bethancourt (1km)
El Hato (5km)
Calle de Candelaria
CERRO DE LA CRUZ
Calle Ancha de los Herreros
Plaza
Av de Chajón
Calle Cruz de Piedra
Av del Desengaño
Calle de los Nazarenos
Calle de las Ánimas
Calle de los Duelos
1a Av Norte
20
Callejón Camposeco
6a Av Norte
43
24
49
2 Iglesia Merced
Plaza
18
13
28
6
Calle de la Recolección
1a Calle Poniente
Alameda de Santa Rosa
27
45
54
57
5a Av Norte
44
1
Arco de Santa Catalina
Av de la Recolección
Calz de Santa Lucía Norte
7a Av Norte
4a Av Norte
3a Av Norte
2a Av Norte
2a Calle Poniente
2a Calle Oriente
7
60
16
Iglesia y Convento de Santo Domingo 3
San Lucas Sacatepéquez (17km); Santiago Sacatepéquez (21km); Sumpango (26km); Guatemala City (46km)
12

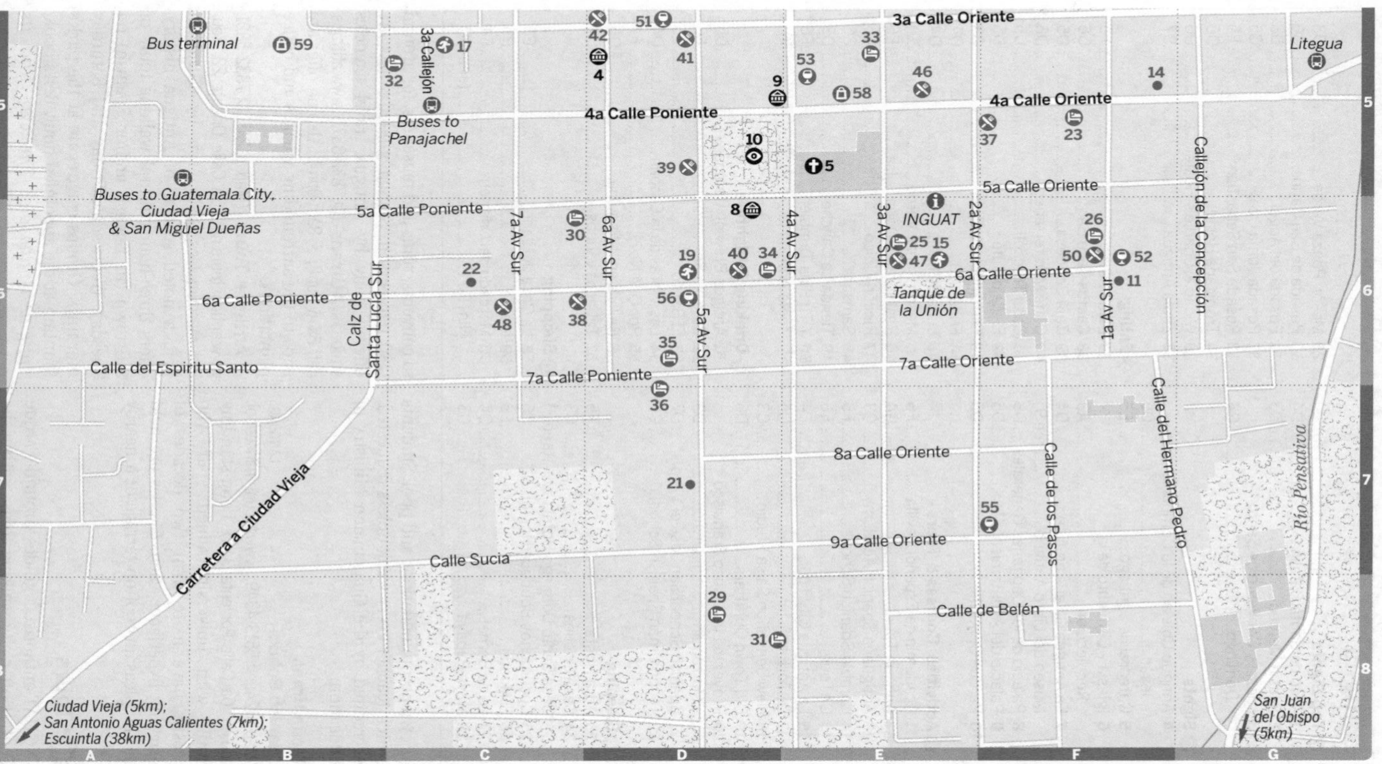
Bus terminal
59
3a Callejón
17
32
Buses to Panajachel
Buses to Guatemala City, Ciudad Vieja & San Miguel Dueñas
42
4
51
41
3a Calle Oriente
33
53
9
58
46
4a Calle Poniente
4a Calle Oriente
14
Litegua
37
23
10
39
5
5a Calle Poniente
5a Calle Oriente
8
INGUAT
30
7a Av Sur
6a Av Sur
19
40
34
4a Av Sur
3a Av Sur
25
15
47
2a Av Sur
26
50
52
11
Callejón de la Concepción
22
6a Calle Poniente
6a Calle Oriente
56
Tanque de la Unión
1a Av Sur
48
38
Calz de Santa Lucía Sur
35
5a Av Sur
Calle del Espíritu Santo
7a Calle Poniente
7a Calle Oriente
36
Calle del Hermano Pedro
8a Calle Oriente
Calle de los Pasos
Carretera a Ciudad Vieja
21
55
Río Pensativo
9a Calle Oriente
Calle Sucia
29
Calle de Belén
31
Ciudad Vieja (5km); San Antonio Aguas Calientes (7km); Escuintla (38km)
San Juan del Obispo (5km)
A
B
C
D
E
F
G
5
6
7
8

GUATEMALA

Antigua

Top Sights

1 Arco de Santa Catalina D4
2 Iglesia Merced D3
3 Iglesia y Convento de Santo Domingo G4

Sights

4 Antiguo Colegio de la Compañía de Jesús D5
5 Catedral de Santiago E5
6 Iglesia y Convento de la Recolección A3
7 La Antigua Galería de Arte D4
Museo del Libro Antiguo .... (see 9)
8 Palacio de los Capitanes Generales D6
9 Palacio del Ayuntamiento D5
10 Parque Central D5

Activities, Courses & Tours

11 Academia de Español Sevilla F6
12 Antigua Tours G4
13 Antigüeña Spanish Academy C3
14 Cambio Spanish School F5
15 CATours E6
16 La Antigua City Tour E4
17 La Tortilla C5
18 New Sensation Salsa Studio C3
19 Old Town Outfitters D6
20 Proyecto Lingüístico Francisco Marroquín D3
21 Spanish School San José el Viejo D7
22 Tecún Umán Spanish School C6

Sleeping

23 Adra Hostel F5
24 Casa Cristina C3
Casa Santo Domingo Hotel .... (see 3)
25 Cucuruchos Boutique Hostel E6
26 El Hostal F6
27 Lo de Bernal C4
28 Maya Papaya C3
29 Mesón Panza Verde D8
30 Posada de San Carlos C6
31 Posada del Ángel D8
32 Posada Juma Ocag C5
33 Posada San Sebastián E5
34 Tropicana Hostel D6
35 Wicho & Charlie's Hostel D6
36 Zoola Antigua D7

Eating

37 Bistrot Cinq F5
38 Cactus Taco Bar C6
39 Café Condesa D5
40 Caffé Mediterráneo D6
41 Casa Troccoli D5
42 El Viejo Café D5
43 Fernando's Kaffee C3
44 Fridas D4
45 Luna de Miel D4
Mesón Panza Verde .... (see 29)
46 Restaurante Doña Luisa E5
47 Rincón Típico E6
48 Samsara C6
49 Tienda La Canche D3
50 Y Tu Piña También F6
Zoola Antigua .... (see 36)

Drinking & Nightlife

51 Antigua Brewing Company D5
52 Café No Sé F6
53 El Barrio E5
54 Las Vibras de la Casbah D4
55 Por Qué No? F7
56 Reilly's en la Esquina D6
57 Tabacos y Vinos D4

Shopping

58 La Casa del Jade E5
59 Market B5
60 Mercado del Carmen E4
Nim Po't .... (see 44)

its own accommodations and pool. Students switch teacher every week unless requested. Accredited by the Guatemalan Ministry of Education.

Tecún Umán Spanish School LANGUAGE
(Map p124; ☎5513-4349; www.tecunumanschool.edu.gt; 6a Calle Poniente 34A) Long-standing outfit with university-trained staff who mostly have more than two decades of teaching experience each. Classes are held on the pleasant rooftop terrace of a nearby cafe.

Tours

INGUAT-authorized guides around Parque Central offer city walking tours, with visits to convents, ruins and museums, for around Q80 per person. Similar guided walks are offered daily by Antigua travel agencies such as **Atitrans** (☎7832-3371; www.atitrans.net; 6a Av Sur 8; ⏲8am-9pm). Also on offer are trips to the surrounding villages and coffee plantations.

Antigua Tours (Map p124; ☎7832-5821; www.antiguatours.net; 3a Calle Oriente 22; tour incl museum fees Q190), run by Elizabeth Bell, a noted scholar of Antigua history, offers three-hour cultural walking tours of the town (in English and/or Spanish) on Tuesday, Wednesday, Friday and Saturday mornings. Groups congregate at the park's fountain at the appointed hour. Bell's book, *Antigua Guatemala: The City and its*

Heritage, is well worth picking up. It has extensive descriptions of all the monuments, and neatly encapsulates the city's history and fiestas. Bell and company also offer tours to the nearby villages of San Antonio Aguas Calientes and San Andrés Itzapa to investigate weaving workshops and Maya shrines, respectively.

La Antigua City Tour (Map p124; 7832-6151; www.antiguacitytour.com; 2½hr tour Q200; 9am-5pm) runs a little bus around town, hitting all the key sites from Cerro de la Cruz to Parque Central.

De la Gente (p122) offers tours of coffee plantations around San Miguel Escobar, a suburb of Ciudad Vieja, with local growers demonstrating cultivation, harvesting and processing techniques. At the end, participants are guided through traditional roasting methods and share a cup with the family. Tours (three to five hours) depart at 9am or 1pm and should be booked at least a day in advance.

Art Tours Antigua (4149-4663; http://artintheamericas.net/art-tours-antigua-guatemala/; Q375) offers specialized gallery tours to learn more about contemporary Guatemalan art.

CATours (Map p124; 7832-9638; www.catours.co.uk; 6a Calle Oriente 14; 9am-5pm Tue-Sun) offers motorbike day tours around Volcán Agua, as well two-day trips to Lago de Atitlán or Monterrico from Q1400.

Festivals & Events

★Semana Santa RELIGIOUS

(Holy Week; Easter week) In the week leading up to Easter, hundreds of devotees garbed in deep purple and white robes bear revered icons from their churches in daily street processions in remembrance of Christ's crucifixion. It's one of the biggest commemorations of its kind in Latin America – Antigua is fit to bursting during Semana Santa and accommodations book out far in advance.

Celebrations start on Palm Sunday and run through to Good Friday, when congregants reenact the Stations of the Cross. The largest of the icons, from Iglesia Merced, weighs several tons and requires 80 men to carry it, all the time wreathed in incense and accompanied by brass bands. Maps of the processional routes – covered with elaborately patterned carpets of technicolor sawdust – are available during the fiesta from the tourist office and hotels.

Sleeping

★Cucuruchos Boutique Hostel HOSTEL $

(Map p124; 7832-1479; www.facebook.com/hostelcucuruchos; 3a Ave Sur 1A; d Q100-125, r Q435;) This hostel hits stylish heights without the need to break the budget. Bunk-bed dorms are spacious and very well appointed, sleeping four, six and 12 people (prices vary according to which place you take) with excellent bathrooms. There's a cute courtyard and a roof terrace and one of the nicest communal kitchens we've ever seen.

★Maya Papaya HOSTEL $

(Map p124; 7832-2837; www.mayapapayaantigua.com; 1a Calle Poniente 20; dm Q100, r with/without bathroom Q460/370;) Modern and well-designed, Maya Papaya knows its flashpacker market well. The hostel opens onto a modest bar area, where breakfasts are also taken, while at the rear (where it is quieter) are airy spacious dorms (one mixed, one women only) with all mod cons.

★Adra Hostel HOSTEL $

(Map p124; www.adrahostel.com; 4a Calle Oriente 15; dm Q165, incl breakfast dm/r Q165/860;) The Adra is one of several upscale hostels that have sprung up in Antigua recently. It's a gorgeous affair – Scandi-style dorms with impressively structured bunks fitted with generously sized beds, lights and power, great communal facilities and a pretty courtyard garden festooned with fairy lights. The bar shuts early so everyone sleeps well, and the cafe-restaurant serves clever French food. The private rooms sleep eight.

Tropicana Hostel HOSTEL $

(Map p124; 7832-0462; www.tropicanahostel.com; 6a Calle Poniente 2; dm Q80, r with/without bathroom Q300/200;) Check in any time you like to this party hostel and join the flock of global youth sunning by the poolside bar or soaking in the hot tub against a backdrop of bright murals. Mixed-gender dorms feature triple-decker bunks each with built-in lockers, curtains and power outlets. Don't be surprised if you're checked in by a receptionist in a rainbow unicorn onesie.

El Hostal HOSTEL $

(Map p124; 7832-0442; www.elhostalbnb.com; 1a Av Sur 8; incl breakfast dm/s/d/tr without bathroom Q85/200/280/380;) Within stumbling distance of plenty of cafes and restaurants, El Hostal is a super-relaxed budget option with a hint of colonial style. Set around a cheery little patio-cafe are half a dozen neatly kept private rooms and dorms with sturdy single beds or well-spaced bunks, a few sticks of furniture and creatively painted walls. There's a sparkling guest kitchen and good gas-heated showers.

Wicho & Charlie's Hostel HOSTEL $
(Map p124; ☎7832-1215; www.facebook.com/wichoandcharlies; dm Q75-120) This is a quiet hostel for outdoorsy types, particularly as it specializes in its own volcano hiking trips. It's a cute but modest place, with capsule-hotel style boxed-in bunks (each with its own light and fan), and some with double beds. There's a hot tub and a terrace, a kitchen and a mostly friendly cat and dog to welcome guests.

Zoola Antigua HOSTEL $
(Map p124; ☎7832-0364; www.zoolaantigua.wix.com/zoola; 7a Calle Poniente 15; dm/r incl breakfast Q75/200; 📶) The Antigua branch of the Israeli-run hostel on Lago de Atitlán translates well to Antigua's colonial setting: sparsely furnished dorms surround an open courtyard where travelers chill and nosh on healthy Middle Eastern snacks from its restaurant (p129) beneath a rainbow canopy. A spectacular roof-terrace bar has a hot tub with volcano views. There's a moderate party scene, but we were still surprised to see bouncers on the door.

★ **Lo de Bernal** B&B $$
(Map p124; ☎7832-3242; www.lodebernal.com; 1a Calle Poniente 23; r Q530; 📶) Don't be intimidated by the full suit of armour at this small new bed and breakfast; service here comes with a warm and personal touch. Rooms are comfortable with lovely bedsteads, and breakfast is taken in a cozy lounge area near a rippling fountain.

Posada de San Carlos HOTEL $$
(Map p124; ☎7832-4698; www.posadadesancarlos.com; 5a Calle Poniente 11; dm/s/d Q70/400/500; 📶🐾) A global inn with an emphasis on comfort, the San Carlos features spacious rooms along a corridor that opens onto a neat patio with fountain. Both private rooms and the seven-bed dorm have colonial flair, with carved wood beds and chests. The front cafe whips up tasty natural fare and there are bikes available for exploring.

Posada San Sebastián GUESTHOUSE $$
(Map p124; ☎7832-2621; www.posadasansebastian.com; 3a Av Norte 4; s/d Q490/570; 📶) What do you show for a lifetime of collecting? San Sebastián's auteur-owner has the answer – a guesthouse packed to the gunwales with curios and museum pieces, from old phones and abandoned statues of saints to restored antique furniture. Each of the nine rooms is like a gallery, with big bathrooms including tub a bonus, along with the roof terrace and pretty little courtyard garden. If you can bear to tear yourself away, it's all close to the action around the Parque Central.

Casa Cristina HOTEL $$
(Map p124; ☎7832-0623; www.casa-cristina.com; Callejón Camposeco 3A; s/d Q300/400; 📶) There are just a dozen rooms at this hotel on a pretty backstreet near La Merced. Though compact, all are quaintly appointed with *típico* (traditional) bedspreads, brushed-on pastels and wood-stained furniture, and the plant-laden roof terrace makes a nice retreat. Discounts are sometime available for the downstairs rooms with internal windows only. *Muy tranquilo.*

Posada Juma Ocag HOTEL $$
(Map p124; ☎7832-3109; www.posadajumaocag.com; Calz Santa Lucia Norte 13; r Q180-200; 📶) Juma Ocag's seven spotless, comfortable rooms have quality mattresses and traditional appointments including wrought-iron bedsteads, armoires and mirrors crafted in-house, and there's a kitchen for guests. Despite the hectic location opposite the market, it remains peaceful – especially the upstairs rooms – with a rooftop patio and well-tended little garden.

★ **Posada del Ángel** BOUTIQUE HOTEL $$$
(Map p124; ☎7832-0260; www.posadadelangel.com; 4a Av Sur 24A; r/ste from Q1600/2400; P📶🏊) Hidden behind a very unassuming door, the luxury at this *posada* just keeps unfolding. The five rooms and two suites all have fireplaces, fresh flowers, four-poster beds and highly polished tile floors. There's a hint of the Marrakesh town house happening here, including the utterly delightful minipool.

Casa Santo Domingo Hotel HOTEL $$$
(Map p124; ☎7820-1220; www.casasantodomingo.com.gt; 3a Calle Oriente 28A; r from Q1400; P@📶🏊) 🍃 Innovatively created from the remains of the sprawling Santo Domingo monastery, this is Antigua's premier lodging. The 128 rooms and suites are of an international five-star standard, while the grounds retain their colonial splendor, dotted with

WORTH A TRIP

A TREE HOUSE NEAR ANTIGUA?

High in the hills above Jocotenango, this extraordinary 16-hectare spread is set around a working avocado farm, and the views of the Panchoy valley and volcanoes are truly mesmerizing. Developed and overseen by an affable North American couple, the ecofriendly retreat **Earth Lodge** (5664-0713; www.earthlodgeguatemala.com; dm Q65, s/d cabin Q200/280;) offers plenty to do: hiking trails, birdwatching, yoga sessions, a chuj (Maya sauna) or just hanging in a hammock.

Accommodations are in lovely A-frame cabins, an eight-bed dorm and a couple of fabulous tree houses (which book up well in advance). Lip-smacking food is served with a view, and a portion of the profits buys supplies for the village school.

To get here, your best bet is to call at least a day in advance to see if the lodge can pick you up from Antigua (Q30 per person with two passengers). Otherwise, an 'El Hato' bus leaves from behind the market in Antigua at least six times Monday, Thursday and Saturday, and less often the rest of the week. From there it's a 25-minute walk downhill – any villager can give you directions – just ask for 'los gringos.' Note that it's a 10-minute walk down to the lodge even from the shuttle drop-off point (and twice that uphill with luggage).

archaeological relics and featuring a large swimming pool, several fine restaurants, five museums and lots of art. The Dominican friars never had it so good.

Free shuttles from the hotel take you to Santo Domingo del Cerro, a recently developed component of the complex atop a hill to the south, with a fine restaurant, an art and sculpture garden and stunning views.

Eating

★Luna de Miel — CRÊPES $

(Map p124; 7882-4559; www.lunademielantigua.com; 6a Av Norte 40; crepes Q34-55; 10am-9:30pm Mon & Tue, 9am-9:30pm Wed-Sun;) Loungey Luna de Miel offers dozens of savory and sweet variations on the classic crepe – try the *chapín* version stuffed with avocado, cheese and fried tomatoes – plus fabulous tropical smoothies. Eat on the roof deck, amid murals depicting Marilyn Monroe, Yoda and Maradona all enjoying the same fare. Be prepared for long queues on weekends.

Samsara — VEGETARIAN $

(Map p124; 7832-2200; 6a Calle Poniente 33; breakfast Q26-38, salads around Q40; 7am-10pm;) At this small veggie cafe fresh organic ingredients are excitingly combined in soups, salads and drinks. How about a kale, peanut butter and avocado smoothie? For breakfast there's quinoa porridge or banana and amaranth-seed pancakes, along with French-press coffee and numerous tea blends.

Zoola Antigua — ISRAELI $

(Map p124; 7a Calle Poniente 15; salads Q45, sandwiches Q35-50; 8am-10pm;) The restaurant in this popular hostel whips up authentic Israeli fare. Nosh on falafel, kebabs or *sabich* – a wrap stuffed with hummus, eggplant and salad. Seating is at low coffee tables surrounded by pillows. On Friday evenings Zoola offers a buffet-style spread of salads. The bar upstairs has great rooftop volcano views.

Tienda La Canche — GUATEMALAN $

(Map p124; 6a Av Norte 42; set lunch Q25; 7am-8pm) A hole in the wall if there ever was one, this eatery behind a 'mom and pop' store consists of two tables and a dining room behind the counter. Just a couple of traditional options are prepared daily, such as *pepián de pollo* (a hearty chicken stew), accompanied by thick tortillas. *Frescos,* home-squeezed fruit beverages, are served alongside.

Y Tu Piña También — SANDWICHES $

(Map p124; 1a Av Sur 10B; sandwiches & salads Q40-50; 7am-7pm;) An international crossroads, this natural-foods cafe does healthy fare for foreign students on the go. There's a tempting array of sandwiches (served on whole wheat, pita or bagel) and salads. It opens early and makes a good breakfast stop, with omelets, abundant fruit salads and banana pancakes, plus excellent coffee.

Café Condesa — CAFE $

(Map p124; 7832-0038; www.cafecondesa.com.gt; Portal del Comercio 4; cakes & pies Q20-26; 7am-8pm Sun-Thu, to 9pm Fri & Sat;) Baked goods – pies, cakes, quiches and house-baked whole-wheat sandwich bread – are the strong suit at this grand old cafe set around the patio of a 16th-century mansion off the main square. You can also enjoy big healthy salads or just a cold beer in the courtyard. The lavish Sunday buffet (Q85), from 9am to 1pm, is an Antigua institution.

Fernando's Kaffee CAFE $
(Map p124; ☎7832-6953; www.fernandoskaffee.com; cnr 7a Av Norte & Callejón Camposeco; cinnamon rolls Q10, empanadas Q40; ⏰7am-7pm Mon-Sat, noon-7pm Sun; 📶) Long a draw for coffee and chocolate mavens, this friendly corner cafe also bakes an array of fine pastries, including some delightfully gooey cinnamon rolls. Beyond the counter is an inviting patio courtyard ideal for a low-key lazy breakfast. We're not sure if the house cat ever moves from the counter, but it's good at collecting tips and cuddles.

Restaurante Doña Luisa CAFE $
(Map p124; ☎7832-2578; 4a Calle Oriente 12; sandwiches & breakfast mains Q20-45; ⏰7am-9:30pm) Refreshingly local in character, this cafe is a place to enjoy the colonial patio ambience over breakfast or a light meal. It's hard to beat the selection of pastries from the attached bakery; banana bread comes hot from the oven around 2pm daily.

★**Casa Troccoli** INTERNATIONAL $$
(Map p124; ☎7832-0516; cnr 3a Calle Poniente & 5a Av Norte; mains Q90-175; ⏰11:45am-10pm) Front of house at this restaurant looks just like the early-20th-century general store it once was, but with the walls racked with a rather more impressive collection of wine bottles. Amid the period photos and bistro furniture, enjoy superior seafood and meat dishes, including good racks of lamb and local rabbit stew – all washed down with a good glass, of course.

The clientele is well heeled, but the extensive kitchen behind also served as a base for an NGO feeding program after the 2018 eruption of nearby Volcán Fuego, helping to feed over 10,000 displaced locals daily.

★**Cactus Taco Bar** MEXICAN $$
(Map p124; ☎7832-2163; 6a Calle Poniente 21; tacos Q45-60; ⏰11am-11pm) The bright 'Andy Warhol does Zapata' wall mural at Cactus gives an idea of how it mixes up traditional and new-wave Mexican food, with superb salsas served in clay bowls. The shrimp and bacon tacos are heartily recommended. It's along the nightlife corridor; start the evening with a chili-fringed margarita or a bottle of good craft beer.

★**Rincón Típico** GUATEMALAN $$
(Map p124; 3a Av Sur 3; breakfast Q20, mains Q30; ⏰7am-8pm) This courtyard restaurant is always packed with locals who know a good thing when they see it. If you don't come for the huge Guatemalan breakfast, make it for the chicken cooked over coals with garlicky potatoes or pork *adobado* (pork marinated with paprika and pepper), served up at simple bench tables by never-stopping waitstaff.

★**Fridas** MEXICAN $$
(Map p124; ☎7832-1296; 5a Av Norte 29; mains Q75-140; ⏰noon-midnight) Dedicated to the eponymous artist, this brightly colored and ever-busy bar-restaurant has an enormous range of tasty Mexican fare, including some of the best soups and tacos in town. There's live music on Thursday and Friday evenings, and a lively, queer-friendly bar upstairs. The restaurant's Frida Kahl-meets-Patti Smith poster art is inspired.

El Viejo Café CAFE $$
(Map p124; ☎7832-1576; www.elviejocafe.com; 3a Calle Poniente 12; breakfasts from Q25, mains from Q50; ⏰7am-9pm; 📶🐾) Popular with tourists and *chapínes* (Guatemalans) alike, this atmospheric cafe strewn with antique curios makes an ideal breakfast stop. Choose from an array of fresh-baked croissants and well-roasted Guatemalan coffees and settle into a window nook to start your day.

Caffé Mediterráneo ITALIAN $$
(Map p124; ☎7882-7180; 6a Calle Poniente 6A; mains Q90-140; ⏰noon-3pm & 6-10pm Wed-Sat & Mon, noon-4:30pm & 7-9pm Sun) Here you'll find the finest, most authentic Italian food

LGBTIQ+ ANTIGUA

Antigua has a veneer of cosmopolitanism and tolerance beyond that of other similar-size Guatemalan cities. There are Pride events here every June, and the nightlife scene embraces every persuasion. Particularly queer-friendly spaces include the restaurant-bar Fridas, which hosts a queer dance party with DJs on the final Saturday of each month (upstairs), and the dance club **Las Vibras de la Casbah** (Map p124; ☎3141-5311; www.lasvibrasantigua.com; 5a Av Norte 30; ⏰5pm-1am Wed-Sat).

in Antigua, plus superb service, in a lovely candlelit setting. The chef does a tantalizing array of salads, homemade pasta and delicately prepared carpaccio, using seasonally available ingredients.

★ **Mesón Panza Verde** FUSION $$$
(Map p124; ☎7832-2925; www.panzaverde.com; 5a Av Sur 19; mains Q150-200; ⏰6-10pm Mon, noon-3pm & 6-10pm Tue-Sun) The restaurant of the exclusive B&B **Mesón Panza Verde** (r/ste from Q950/1700; P@🛜☒) dishes up divine continental cuisine in an appealing Antiguan atmosphere. The menu features an eclectic global lineup, with the French-trained chef putting an emphasis on fresh seafood and organic ingredients. Live music (jazz, Cuban) enhances the ambience Wednesday to Saturday nights, while locals turn out for the popular Sunday brunch buffet (10am to 2pm).

Bistrot Cinq FRENCH $$$
(Map p124; ☎7832-5510; www.bistrotcinq.com; 4a Calle Oriente 7; mains Q140-220; ⏰noon-10:30pm) Popular among the mature expat crowd, the Cinq is a faithful replica of its Parisian counterparts, offering zesty salads and classic entrees such as escargots and filet mignon. Check the blackboard for nightly specials. Be sure to make it down for the excellent Sunday brunch spread (served from noon to 5pm).

Drinking & Nightlife

The bar scene jumps, especially on Friday and Saturday evenings when the hordes roll in from Guatemala City for some Antigua-style revelry. Besides the watering holes, the restaurants Fridas and Bistrot Cinq are at least as popular for the cocktails as the cuisine. Start drinking early and save: *cuba libres* and mojitos are half price between 5pm and 8pm at many bars.

★ **Antigua Brewing Company** BAR
(Map p124; 3a Calle Poniente 4; ⏰11am-10pm Sun-Thu, 11am-1am Fri & Sat) Put your Gallo beer down for one moment and get to the forefront of Guatemala's craft-brewing revolution at the Antigua Brewing Company. Sup its signature Fuego IPA while looking out to Volcán Agua from the roof terrace, or try a flight of beers (Q75) ranging from Belgian blondes to rich coffee stouts.

Other Guatemalan craft brewers are also represented, plus imported ales and plenty of non-beer drink options, as well as bar food and DJs spinning tunes in the evenings.

Tabacos y Vinos WINE BAR
(Map p124; 5a Av Norte 28B; ⏰10am-11pm) Tucked right next to the Santa Catalina arch is this small but perfectly formed wine bar with an extensively sourced cellar. Wine by the glass starts at Q35, but if you keep with the same bottle it gets cheaper with each refill. The bar is no smoking but it also has a wide selection of cigars, as well as local chocolates and coffee.

Por Qué No? PUB
(Map p124; ☎4324-5407; www.porquenocafe.com; cnr 2a Av Sur & 9a Calle Oriente; ⏰6-10pm Mon-Sat) This alternative cafe is a vertically oriented space that takes up an absurdly narrow corner of an old building (grab the rope to reach the upper level). Vintage bric-a-brac hangs from the rafters and every surface is scrawled with guest-generated graffiti. The vibe is relaxed and conversational and a crowd spills out the door each evening. If you fancy a bite, the short menu is scrumptious; the musical mix is similarly splendid.

El Barrio PUB
(Map p124; ☎5658-9028; 4a Av Norte 3; ⏰4:30pm-1am) Just off Parque Central, this sprawling bar tavern has wall-length sofas, murals of literary and sports heroes, and board games. Upstairs is a popular and lively rooftop bar. Round up a gang for the trivia nights, but take care if you overindulge: we're never too sure about a bar that has its own tattoo parlour at the back.

Café No Sé BAR
(Map p124; www.cafenose.com; 1a Av Sur 11C; ⏰2pm-1am) Something of a local institution, this downbeat little bar is a point of reference for Antigua's budding young Burroughses and Kerouacs. It's also the core of a lively music scene, with players wailing from a corner of the room most evenings. Be sure to try its home-brand legal Mezcal.

Reilly's en la Esquina IRISH PUB
(Map p124; ☎7832-6251; 6a Calle Poniente 7; ⏰noon-12:30am) Holding a key corner of Antigua's nightlife corridor, Reilly's packs in both Guatemalans and gringos on weekends. The sprawling pub has several bars, but most of the action focuses on the central patio. Midweek it's mellower, with the billiards table, pub grub and Guinness on tap pulling in a faithful following. Particularly good when there's a big sporting event.

Shopping

Woven and leather goods, ironwork, paintings and jade jewelry are some of the items to look for in Antigua's various shops and markets. For beautiful *típico* fabrics, first get educated at the **Casa del Tejido Antiguo** (☎7832-3169; www.casadeltejido.org; 0 Av 4-16, San Antonio Aguas Calientes; Q15; ⏲9am-5pm Mon-Fri, to 4pm Sat), then have a look around **Nim Po't** (Map p124; ☎7832-2681; www.nimpotexport.com; 5a Av Norte 29; ⏲9am-9pm Sun-Thu, to 10pm Fri & Sat) or the big handicrafts markets near the bus terminal and next to Iglesia El Carmen.

Mercado del Carmen ARTS & CRAFTS

(Map p124; cnr 3a Calle Oriente & 3a Av Norte; ⏲9am-6pm) Next to the ruins of the Iglesia El Carmen, this excellent market is a good place to browse for textiles, pottery and jade, particularly on weekends, when activity spills out onto 3a Av Norte. The inside is a warren of individual stalls, so take your time to find the treasure you're after.

Market MARKET

(Map p124; Calz de Santa Lucía Sur; ⏲6am-6pm Mon, Thu & Sat, 7am-6pm Tue, Wed & Fri, 7am-1pm Sun) Antigua's market – chaotic, colorful and always busy – sprawls north of 4a Calle Poniente. The best days are the official market days (Monday, Thursday and especially Saturday) when villagers from the vicinity roll in and spread their wares north and west of the main market building.

The entrance to the market is dominated by tourist goods, so make sure you continue past to get to the heart of the everyday commerce.

La Casa del Jade JEWELRY

(Map p124; www.lacasadeljade.com; 4a Calle Oriente 10; ⏲9am-6pm) More than just a jewelry shop, the Casa has a small museum displaying dozens of pre-Hispanic jade pieces and an open workshop where you can admire the work of contemporary craftspeople. It's inside the Casa Antigua El Jaulón shopping arcade.

Orientation

Antigua's focal point is the broad Parque Central (p119); few places in town are more than 15 minutes' walk from here. Compass points are added to the numbered Calles and Avs, indicating whether an address is *norte* (north), *sur* (south), *poniente* (west) or *oriente* (east) of Parque Central.

Three volcanoes provide easy reference points: Volcán Agua is south of the city and visible from most points within it; Volcán Fuego and Volcán Acatenango rise to the southwest (Acatenango is the more northerly of the two).

Another useful Antigua landmark is the Arco de Santa Catalina (p121), an arch spanning 5a Av Norte, 2½ blocks north of Parque Central, on the way to La Merced church.

Information

DANGERS & ANNOYANCES

- Antigua generally feels safe to walk around, but street crime does occur, so don't let your guard down completely or flash wads of cash or smartphones. This holds doubly true after the bars close at 1am; after 10pm, consider taking a taxi back to your accommodations.
- Pickpockets work the busy market, doing overtime on paydays at the middle and end of the month. December (bonus time) brings a renewed wave of robberies.
- Some of the more remote hiking trails have seen muggings, though stepped-up police patrols have reduced the likelihood of such incidents. If you're planning on hiking independently, check with **Proatur** (☎5578-9835; operacionesproatur@inguat.gob.gt; 6a Calle Poniente Final; ⏲24hr) about the current situation.

EMERGENCY

Ambulance	☎125
Fire (Bomberos Voluntarios)	☎7832-0234
Police	☎120
Tourist Police	☎1500 or ☎2421-2810

MEDIA

The free English-language *Revue Magazine* (www.revuemag.com) has reasonable information about cultural events; it's available everywhere.

MEDICAL SERVICES

Farmacia Cruz Verde Ivori (☎7832-8318; 7a Av Norte; ⏲24hr) Convenient pharmacy with some English spoken.

Hospital Nacional Pedro de Bethancourt (☎7831-1319; ⏲24hr) Public hospital in San Felipe, 2km north of the center, with emergency service.

Hospital Privado Hermano Pedro (☎7790-2000; www.hospitalhermanopedro.net; Av de la Recolección 4; ⏲24hr) Private hospital that offers 24-hour emergency service and accepts foreign insurance.

MONEY

The following banks around Parque Central all change US dollars and euros, and have Visa/MasterCard ATMs:

Bac Credomatic (Portal del Comercio, facing Parque Central)

Banco Agromercantil (4a Calle Poniente 8; ⌚9am-7pm Mon-Fri, to 5pm Sat & Sun)

Banco Industrial (5a Av Sur 4; ⌚9am-7pm Mon-Fri, to 1pm Sat)

Citibank (cnr 4a Calle Oriente & 4a Av Norte; ⌚9am-4:30pm Mon-Fri, 9:30am-1pm Sat)

TOURIST INFORMATION

INGUAT The tourist office has free city maps, bus information and helpful, bilingual staff.

Proatur The tourism assistance agency has its headquarters on the west side of town, three blocks south of the market. If you're the victim of a crime, the staff will accompany you to the national police and assist with the formalities, including any translating that's needed. Given advance notice, Proatur can provide an escort for drivers heading out on potentially risky roads.

Getting There & Around

BUS

Buses (Map p124; cnr 5a Calle Poniente & Calle de Recoletos) from Guatemala City, Ciudad Vieja and San Miguel Dueñas arrive and depart from a street just south of the market, across from the Mercado de Artesanías.

Antigua is off the major highways, so for most onward travel you'll need to head to the nearby junction towns of Chimaltenango or Escuintla and change there. Buses for these depart from the main **bus terminal** (Map p124; Av de la Recolección).

For the Highlands (including Chichicastenango, Quetzaltenango and Huehuetenango) take one of the many buses to Chimaltenango, on the Interamericana Hwy, then catch an onward connection. The same station has buses to Escuintla, where you should change for all destinations along the Carretera al Pacifico Hwy.

If you're heading out to local villages, go early in the morning and return by mid-afternoon, as bus services decrease dramatically as evening approaches.

SHUTTLE MINIBUS

Antigua's many travel agencies (and every hotel and hostel) sell tickets for tourist shuttles. They cost more than buses, but are comfortable and convenient, with door-to-door pick-up and drop-off. Bear in mind that if you're leaving town, shuttles can sometimes spend an hour driving around Antigua collecting passengers.

Every conceivable traveler destination is served, but some typical one-way prices include: Guatemala City (Q80, one hour), Panajachel (Q80, two hours), Quetzaltenango (Q175, four hours), San Pedro La Laguna (Q80, two hours), El Paredón (Q100, two hours), Monterrico (Q100, two hours) and Cobán (Q125, three hours), as well as to the airport (Q80, one hour).

Cross-border shuttles include those to Copán (Honduras), San Cristóbal de Las Casas (Mexico) and Belize City.

TAXI & TUK-TUK

Taxis wait where the Guatemala City buses stop and on the east side of Parque Central. An in-town taxi ride costs Q25 to Q30. *Tuk-tuks* are Q5 to Q15. Note that *tuk-tuks* are not allowed in the center of town, so you'll have to hike a few blocks out to find one; they do not operate after 8pm.

BUSES FROM ANTIGUA

DESTINATION	COST (Q)	DURATION (HR)	FREQUENCY	SERVICE
Chimaltenango	5	30min	every 10min	
Ciudad Vieja	5	15min	every 15min	Take a San Miguel Dueñas bus.
Escuintla	10	1	every 20min	
Guatemala City	10	1	every 15min from 7am to 8pm	A Pullman service (Q60; 9:30am and 4pm) by **Litegua** (Map p133; ☎7832-9850; www.litegua.com; 4a Calle Oriente 48) also runs from its office at the east end of (p124)
Panajachel	45	2½	one bus daily at 7am	**Transportes Rebulli service** (Map p133), departing from Panadería Colombia on 4a Calle Poniente, half a block east of the (p124)
San Antonio Aguas Calientes	5	20min	every 10min	

THE HIGHLANDS

The highlands – El Altiplano – stretch from Antigua to the Mexican border; they comprise Guatemala's most breathtaking region by some degree. Maya identity is stronger here than anywhere in the country and over a dozen distinct groups dwell within the region, each with its own language and clothing. Indigenous tradition blends most tantalizingly with Spanish, and it is common to see Maya rituals taking place in front of and inside colonial churches.

Most travelers spend a spell at the dizzyingly beautiful Lago de Atitlán, an azure lake dramatically ringed by volcanoes. From here it's easy to strike out to the exuberant spectacle of the weekly market at Chichicastenango. Head west to Quetzaltenango, Guatemala's laid-back second city. Northward spread the Cuchumatanes mountains, where Maya life follows its own rhythms amid picturesque villages and fantastic mountain landscapes. For hikers, this is the promised land.

Lago de Atitlán

Nineteenth-century traveler/chronicler John L Stephens, writing in *Incidents of Travel in Central America*, called Lago de Atitlán 'the most magnificent spectacle we ever saw,' and he had been around a bit. Today even seasoned travelers marvel at this incredible environment. Fishers in rustic crafts ply the lake's aquamarine surface. Fertile hills dot the landscape, and over everything looms the volcanoes, permeating the entire area with a mysterious beauty. It never looks the same twice. No wonder many outsiders have fallen in love with the place and made their homes here.

The main lakeside town is Panajachel and most people initially head here to launch their Atitlán explorations. Working around the lake, Santiago Atitlán has a strong indigenous identity, San Pedro La Laguna has a reputation as a backpacker party haven, and San Marcos La Laguna is a refuge for newagers. Santa Cruz La Laguna and Jaibalito, nearer to Panajachel, are among the lake's most idyllic, picturesque locales.

Getting There & Away

Panajachel is the gateway to Lago de Atitlán and is easily accessed by bus and shuttle from the Interamericana, either directly or by changing at La Cuchilla junction just west of Los Encuentros. Shuttles also serve San Pedro La Laguna from Antigua and El Paredón, as well as direct buses from Quetzaltenango to San Pedro La Laguna.

Getting around the lake is most rapidly and easily accomplished by frequent *lancha* (motorboat) service, though some towns are linked by road as well.

Panajachel

POP 14,950 / ELEV 1584M

The busiest and most built-up lakeside town, Panajachel ('Pana') is the gateway to Lago de Atitlán for most travelers. Strolling the main street, Calle Santander – crammed with travel agencies, handicraft hawkers and rowdy bars, dodging noisy *tuk-tuks* all the way – you may be forgiven for supposing this paradise lost.

Heading to the lake, though, gives a better idea of why Pana attracts so many visitors. Aside from the astounding volcano panorama, the town's excellent transportation connections, copious accommodations, varied restaurants and thumping nightlife make it a favorite destination for weekending Guatemalans.

Pana is an unexpectedly cosmopolitan crossroads in an otherwise remote and rural vicinity. This makes for a convenient transition into the Atitlán universe – but to truly experience the beauty of the lake, most travelers venture onward soon after arrival.

Sights & Activities

Lago de Atitlán is a cycling and hiking wonderland, spreading across hill and dale. But before setting out for any hike or ride, make inquiries about safety with Proatur (p141), and keep asking as you go. Volcán San Pedro climbs with numerous operators in town cost around Q700 per person, including boat transportation, taxi to the trailhead, entry fees and guide. Paddleboards are available for rent from **Pana Surf** (Map p138; per hour Q100).

★ **Reserva Natural Atitlán** PARK
(☎7762-2565; www.atitlanreserva.com; adult/child Q50/25; ⊙8am-5pm) A former coffee plantation being reclaimed by natural vegetation, this reserve is 200m past the Hotel Atitlán on the northern outskirts of town. It makes a good outing on foot or bicycle. You can leisurely walk the main trail in an hour: it leads up over swing bridges to a waterfall, then down to a platform for viewing local spider monkeys.

Lago de Atitlán

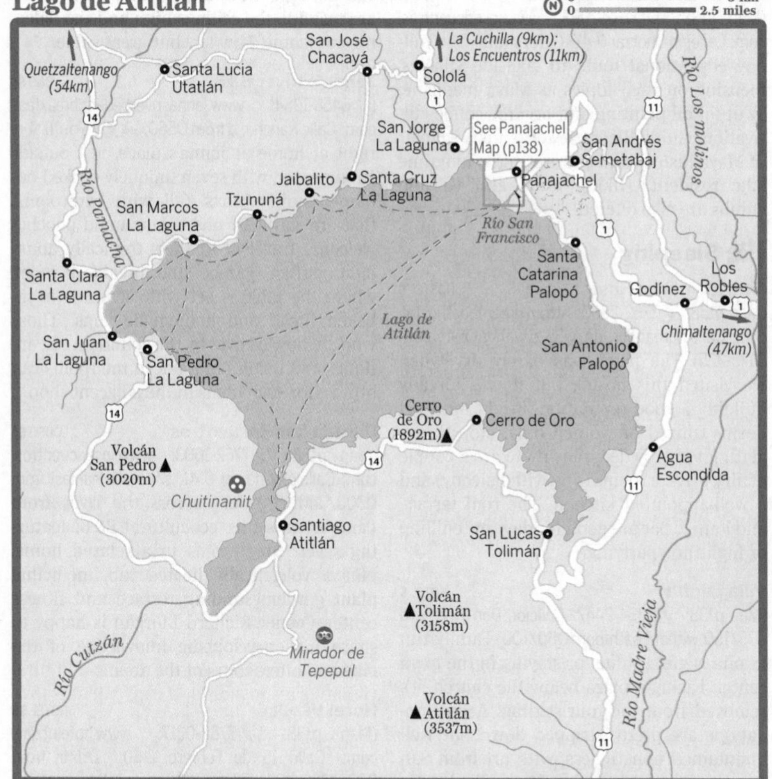

You should also see pisotes (coatis), relatives of the raccoon with long snouts and furry tails. The reserve includes a butterfly enclosure and herb garden, an interpretive center, a small coffee plantation and an aviary. For more extreme thrills, there are various zip lines spanning canyons and forest, the longest of which extends nearly a kilometer.

RealWorld Paragliding GLIDING
(Map p138; ☎5634-5699; www.realworldparagliding.jimdo.com; Calle Santander, Centro Comercial San Rafael; tandem flights Q700) The lake has become a center for paragliding enthusiasts and RealWorld Paragliding provides tandem flights, with passengers seated in a canvas chair attached to the flier's harness so you're free to take photos or simply gaze in amazement at the panorama below.

Roger's Tours ADVENTURE SPORTS
(Map p138; ☎7762-6060; www.rogerstours.com; Calle Santander; bike rental per hour/day Q35/170) This outfit rents out quality mountain bikes and leads a variety of cycling tours (Q450 per person including helmet, guide and lunch). One tour travels by boat from Panajachel to Tzununá, then by bike west via dirt trail to San Marcos La Laguna and road to San Pedro La Laguna, finally returning to Pana by boat. Roger's Tours also arranges volcano hikes, horseback riding and kayak tours on the lake.

Courses & Tours

Panajachel has a niche in the language-school scene. Two well-set-up schools are **Jardín de América** (Map p138; ☎7762-2637; www.jardindeamerica.com; Calle del Chalí) and **Jabel Tinamit** (Map p138; ☎7762-6056; www.jabeltinamit.com; cnr Avenida de Los Árboles & Callejón Las Armonías; per week Q980, homestay per week additional Q650). The former is set amid ample gardens, while the latter is in the center of town. Four hours of one-on-one study five days per week, including a homestay with a local family, will cost around Q1600 per week.

Posada Los Encuentros TOURS
(Map p138; ☎7762-2093; www.losencuentros.com; Callejón Chotzar 0-41) Offers half- and full-day educational tours to lakeside villages, focusing on such topics as Maya medicine, Tz'utujil oil painting and organic coffee cultivation. Guide Richard Morgan is a scholar of Maya history and culture, and a longtime lake resident. Hiking tours and volcano climbs are also offered.

Sleeping

★Dreamboat Hostel HOSTEL $
(Map p138; ☎7762-2530; http://dreamboathostel.com; Calle Santander; dm Q65, d without bathroom Q175-225) The paint was barely dry when we visited this hostel, but it was already building a good reputation. Bright four-bed dorms (mixed or women only) stop things getting too crowded, plus there are a couple of airy private rooms (one with balcony) and a well-appointed kitchen. The roof terrace and lounge bar are good for daytime chilling or nighttime partying.

Villa Lupita HOTEL $
(Map p138; ☎5054-2447; Callejón Don Tino; s/d Q75/150, without bathroom Q50/100) Family-run Lupita is great value for staying in the town center. Facing a plaza below the church, it's removed from the tourist drag. Accommodations are pretty stripped down but well maintained nonetheless, with art from San Juan wrapping around a flower-filled patio with a broken-tile mosaic.

Mario's Rooms HOTEL $
(Map p138; ☎7762-1313; Calle Santander; s/d incl breakfast Q150/230; ᯤ) On Pana's main drag, Mario's rooms are arranged on two floors facing a plant-filled courtyard. Despite being in the middle of everything, it somehow remains low-key, with helpful staff.

Hospedaje Sueño Real HOTEL $
(Map p138; ☎7762-0608; hotelsuenorealpana@hotmail.com; Calle Ramos; s/d from Q150/180; P@ᯤ) A good budget option close to the Playa Pública, the Sueño Real has cheerfully decorated, if smallish, rooms with TV and fan. The best are the upstairs triples, opening on a plant-covered terrace with lake views.

Hotel Larry's Place HOTEL $
(Map p138; ☎7762-0767; www.hotellarrysplace.com; Calle 14 de Febrero; s/d/tr Q125/150/200; P) Centrally located but set back from the road behind a wall of vegetation, Larry's Place offers good-sized, cool rooms in a sylvan setting. Traditional fabric furnishings are tasteful, the ceilings high and the balconies welcome. Low key but great value.

Jenna's River B&B B&B $$
(☎5458-1984; www.jennasriverbedandbreakfast.com; Calle Rancho; d from Q560; ᯤ) You'll feel right at home at Jenna's place, just outside Pana proper, with seven uniquely decked-out hard-standing 'yurts' (all with bathrooms) that are starlit by night. Jenna and pooches welcome travelers to their tropically abundant garden, gazebo and breakfast room, where the table is set with her own fresh-baked bread and homemade jams. Those who are bowled over by the abundant art, antiques and textiles that adorn the rooms can browse for such items in the adjacent shop.

Posada Los Encuentros LODGE $$
(Map p138; ☎7762-1603; www.losencuentros.com; Callejón Chotzar 0-41; s/d incl breakfast from Q300/340; ᯤ) Just across the river from Pana town is this 'ecocultural B&B,' featuring seven cozy rooms in a relaxed home, plus a volcanically heated tub, medicinal plant garden, sunning terrace and fitness center. Owner Richard Morgan is happy to share his encyclopedic knowledge of the lake and offers tours of the area.

Hotel Utz-Jay HOTEL $$
(Map p138; ☎7762-0217; www.hotelutzjay.com; Calle 15 de Febrero 2-50; s/d/tr from Q225/360/495; Pᯤ) These eight cottages stand amid lush gardens bursting with heliconia, orange trumpet and ferns where no fewer than 46 types of birds have been spotted. Rooms are decorated with traditional fabrics and have cozy porches out front. Good breakfasts are available and there's a *chuj* (traditional Maya sauna).

Hotel Montana HOTEL $$
(Map p138; ☎7762-0326; atitlanhotelmontana@hotmail.com; Callejón Don Tino; s/d Q180/300; Pᯤ) Down a narrow street near the church, the Montana is an old-fashioned establishment with simple rooms and wonderful plant-laden balconies fronted by pot-bellied railings. Choose a room on the upper level for brilliant views of the mountainside to enjoy the greenery inside and out.

Posada de los Volcanes HOTEL $$
(Map p138; ☎7762-0244; www.posadadelosvolcanes.com; Calle Santander 5-51; s/d from Q380/450; ᯤ) This chalet-style lodging has lovely pine-paneled rooms. On the 4th

floor, you'll be rewarded with your own private terrace, suitable for kicking back with cocktails and surveying the lake. Breakfast is included: the freshly squeezed juice and homemade jams are a nice touch.

★Hotel Atitlán HERITAGE HOTEL **$$$**
(Map p138; ☎7762-1441; www.hotelatitlan.com; Finca San Buenaventura; r incl breakfast from Q1400; P@☎≋) A coffee plantation for much of the 20th century, this estate was remade as Pana's loveliest hotel in the 1970s. Located on the lakeshore 1.5km northwest of the town center, it's a rambling, semicolonial affair surrounded by manicured tropical gardens.

The 60 rooms all have lake-facing balconies; decor goes heavy on religious imagery, wood carvings and wrought iron. A restaurant, bar and lakefront pool with killer volcano views ensure you'll never want to leave the premises, except perhaps on one of the hotel's kayaks.

Casa Texel HOTEL **$$$**
(Map p138; ☎7762-2076; www.casatexel.com; Calle Rancho Grande; s/d/tr incl breakfast Q480/850/1250; P☎) This pristine hotel a block from the lakefront is a swish spread with a proper dose of indigenous style. Rooms on three levels line up along brick balconies with terraces at the end and plenty of lake views. Decor is modern with colorful bedspreads, pretty tiles, cast-iron fixtures and vintage photos. Borrow a bike to explore, or relax in the spa.

Eating

There are plenty of restaurants lining Calle Santander, which swell in the late afternoon and evening with taco stalls and other cheap street eats. Near the south end of Calle del Lago, thatched-roof restaurants crowd the lakefront. All serve the local specialties of lake mojarra and black bass.

★Circus Bar ITALIAN
(Map p138; ☎7762-2056; Av Los Árboles; ⊙noon-midnight) Behind the swinging doors, Circus Bar has a cabaret atmosphere, with live music nightly from 7:30pm to 10:30pm. There is good pizza and even better pasta, plus a respectable wine list and imported liquors. Flamenco, folk or marimbas nicely complement the cozy atmosphere.

★El Patio GUATEMALAN **$$**
(Map p138; ☎7762-2041; Plaza Los Patios, Calle Santander; mains Q30-60; ⊙7am-9:30pm) This is a locally popular joint for lunch; the front terrace makes an obvious meeting place. Try to make it for Monday lunch when everyone chows down on *caldo de res* (chunky broth), served with all the trimmings.

Chero's Bar SALVADORAN **$**
(Map p138; Av Los Árboles; pupusas Q10; ⊙12:30pm-1am Tue-Sat) Usefully located in the nightlife zone, Chero's can get pretty lively, with beer-drinking patrons gathering around simple wood tables as *tuk-tuks* zip by. Salvadoran staff slap out *pupusas,* either straight up or filled with such items as *güicoy* (a kind of squash) or the spinach-like herb *chipilín,* and served with the customary pickled cabbage and salsa.

Fuentes de Vida GUATEMALAN **$**
(Map p138; Market; lunch Q20; ⊙7:30am-4pm) This is the largest of a group of rather rustic cooking stalls at the rear of the market building, near the pork vendors. It offers half a dozen menu options daily, all of which come with beans, tortillas and a fiery salsa made from dried red chilies.

Mister Jon's AMERICAN **$$**
(Map p138; ☎4710-8697; www.mister-jon.com; Calle Santander; breakfast Q35-50; ⊙7am-10pm Tue-Sun; ☎) All the perks of a US diner are here in abundance, including buttermilk pancakes, great omelets with hash browns or country biscuits on the side, and free coffee refills (of Guatemala's finest). But it's no gringo ghetto – *chapínes* (Guatemalans) who've been up north like it too. Mister John's also has more power sockets than anywhere we've been in Guatemala – perfect if you need to catch up with your laptop.

Restaurante Hana JAPANESE **$$**
(Map p138; ☎4298-1415; www.restaurantehana.com; Calle 14 de Febrero; mains Q65-85; ⊙noon-9pm Tue-Sun) Serving authentic Japanese cuisine, Hana is ensconced in the serene courtyard of the **Casa Cakchiquel** (☎7762-0969; ⊙7am-8pm), graced by hanging plants and a gallery of photos of old Pana. Besides preparing such classics as sushi and tempura, Chef Mihoko does uramaki ('inside-out' sushi), donburi and cold udon noodles just as they're done in her native Japan.

Guajimbo's STEAK **$$**
(Map p138; ☎7762-0063; Calle Santander; mains Q55-100; ⊙7:30am-9:30pm Fri-Wed) This Uruguayan grill serves up generous helpings of steak, sausage and chicken dishes with

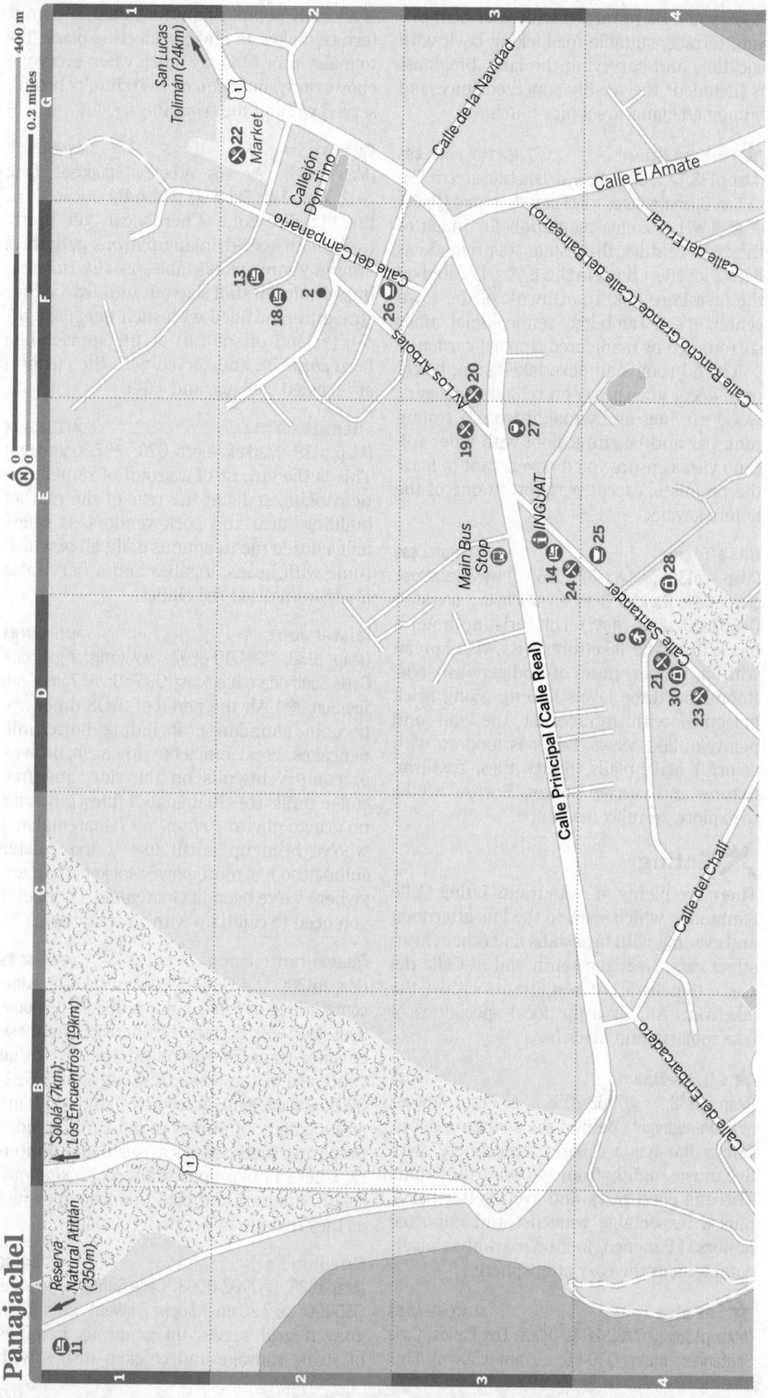

Panajachel

0 400 m
0 0.2 miles

11
Reserva Natural Atitlán (350m)
Sololá (7km); Los Encuentros (19km)
San Lucas Tolimán (24km)
22 Market
13
18
2
Callejón Don Tino
Calle del Campanario
26
Av Los Árboles
Calle de la Navidad
19
20
Main Bus Stop
27
INGUAT
14
24
25
Calle Principal (Calle Real)
6
21
30
23
Calle Santander
28
Calle Rancho Grande (Calle del Balneario)
Calle El Amate
Calle del Frutal
Calle del Embarcadero
Calle del Chalí

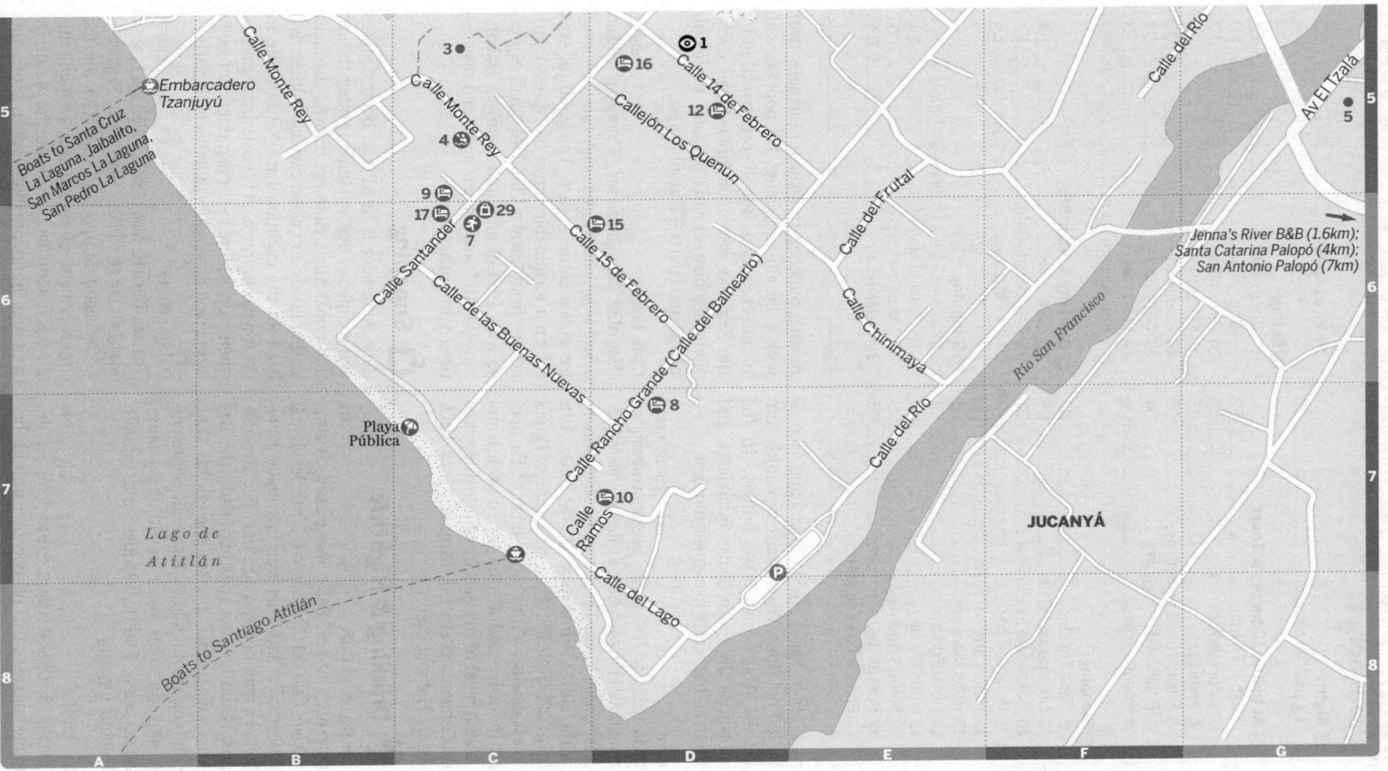

Embarcadero Tzanjuyú
Boats to Santa Cruz La Laguna, Jaibalito, San Marcos La Laguna, San Pedro La Laguna
Calle Monte Rey
Calle Monte Rey
Calle 14 de Febrero
Callejón Los Quenun
Calle Santander
Calle 15 de Febrero
Calle de las Buenas Nuevas
Calle Rancho Grande (Calle del Balneario)
Calle del Frutal
Calle Chinimaya
Calle del Río
Calle del Río
Av El Tzala
Jenna's River B&B (1.6km); Santa Catarina Palopó (4km); San Antonio Palopó (7km)
Río San Francisco
Playa Pública
Calle Ramos
Calle del Lago
JUCANYÁ
Lago de Atitlán
Boats to Santiago Atitlán
1
3
4
5
7
8
9
10
12
15
16
17
29
A
B
C
D
E
F
G
5
6
7
8

Panajachel

Sights
1 Casa Cakchiquel D5

Activities, Courses & Tours
2 Jabel Tinamit F2
3 Jardín de América C5
4 Pana Surf C5
5 Posada Los Encuentros G5
6 RealWorld Paragliding D4
7 Roger's Tours C6

Sleeping
8 Casa Texel D7
9 Dreamboat Hostel C5
10 Hospedaje Sueño Real D7
11 Hotel Atitlán A1
12 Hotel Larry's Place D5
13 Hotel Montana F2
14 Hotel Primavera E3
15 Hotel Utz-Jay D6
16 Mario's Rooms D5
17 Posada de los Volcanes C6
Posada Los Encuentros .... (see 5)
18 Villa Lupita F2

Eating
19 Chero's Bar E3
Chez Alex .... (see 14)
20 Circus Bar F3
21 El Patio D4
22 Fuentes de Vida G2
23 Guajimbo's D4
24 Mister Jon's E3
Restaurante Hana .... (see 1)

Drinking & Nightlife
25 Café Loco E4
26 Crossroads Café F2
27 La Palapa E3

Shopping
28 Comerciales de Artesanías Típicas Tinamit Maya E4
29 Libros del Lago C6
30 Oxlajuj B'atz' D4

vegetables, salad, garlic bread and rice or boiled potatoes. Vegetarians can enjoy tofu kebabs. You won't leave hungry. In the mornings there are hearty breakfasts, and there is frequently live music at night.

Chez Alex EUROPEAN **$$$**
(Map p138; ☎7762-0172; www.primaveraatitlan.com; Hotel Primavera, Calle Santander; mains Q95-180; ⊙noon-10pm) The restaurant component of the **Hotel Primavera** (☎7762-2052; s/d/tr from Q225/300/375;) serves some of Pana's finest cuisine, with a hefty dash of European influence and a wine list to back it up. After a meal of mussels in white-wine sauce or Camembert-stuffed schnitzel, kick back with a Habana cigar.

Drinking & Nightlife

Crossroads Café CAFE
(Map p138; ☎5292-8439; www.crossroadscafepana.com; Calle del Campanario 0-27; ⊙9am-1pm & 2:30-6pm Tue-Sat) This cafe has made Panajachel a major crossroads for coffee aficionados. When he's not roasting beans, the Bay Area owner/head barista spends his time combing the highlands for small estate coffees to add to his roster, including the tangy Acatenango Eighth Wonder and smooth Huehue Organic.

La Palapa PUB
(Map p138; Calle Principal; ⊙9am-1am) As the name suggests, this party center unfolds beneath a thatched-roof shelter (actually two), with a beachy ambience. It's popular with volunteer gringos, but all sorts crowd in for the Saturday afternoon BBQ. Other diversions include weekend live music, trivia quiz nights and sports TV at all times.

Café Loco COFFEE
(Map p138; Calle Santander; ⊙9am-8pm Tue-Sun, 3-8pm Mon) This Korean-run cafe is heaven for coffee connoisseurs. The youthful staff set up a formidable range of espresso variations, from 'Brown Cloud' (a small espresso with a bit of milk and foam) to 'Habana Blues,' with brown sugar sprinkled over espresso grounds.

Shopping

Calle Santander is lined with booths, stores and complexes that sell (among other things) traditional Maya clothing, colorful blankets, leather goods and wood carvings. Otherwise, head for the traditional market building in the town center, which is busiest on Sundays when every square meter of ground alongside is occupied by vendors in indigenous garb.

Oxlajuj B'atz' ARTS & CRAFTS
(Thirteen Threads; Map p138; ☎7762-2921; www.oxlajujbatz.org.gt; Plaza Hotel Real Santander; ⊙10am-6pm) Supporting an NGO for the empowerment of indigenous women, this fair-trade shop features beautiful naturally dyed rugs, handbags, handwoven goods and

beaded jewelry. Pick up a bar of locally made chocolate while you're there.

Libros del Lago BOOKS
(Map p138; Calle Santander; ⏲10am-6:30pm) Has a refreshingly good stock of books in English and Spanish on Guatemala, the Maya and Mesoamerica, plus maps and Latin American literature in English.

Comerciales de Artesanías Típicas Tinamit Maya ARTS & CRAFTS
(Map p138; ⏲8am-7pm) Be sure to browse the many stalls of this extensive handicrafts market, which has an impressive variety of bags, clothing, blankets, belts and hammocks. More booths line up along the beach end of Calle Santander.

ℹ Information

EMERGENCY

Proatur (Programa de Asistencia al Turista; ☎5874-9450; proatur.solola@gmail.com; Calle Rancho Grande; ⏲9am-5pm)

MEDICAL SERVICES

PanaMed (☎4224-2648; Callejon Juzgado, Zona 2) The nearest hospital is in Sololá.

Pana Medic (☎4892-3499; drzulmashalom@hotmail.com; Calle Principal 0-72) Clinic run by an English-speaking doctor.

MONEY

Banco de América Central (Calle Santander, Centro Comercial San Rafael; ⏲9am-5pm Mon-Fri, 9am-1pm Sat) ATM; Visa, American Express and MasterCard cash advances; US dollars exchanged.

Banco Industrial (Calle Santander, Comercial Los Pinos; ⏲9am-4pm Mon-Fri, 9am-1pm Sat) Visa/MasterCard ATM.

5B ATM Visa/MasterCard ATM.

TOURIST INFORMATION

INGUAT (Map p138; ☎2421-2953; info-pana@inguat.gob.gt; Calle Principal 1-47; ⏲9am-5pm)

ℹ Getting There & Away

BOAT

There are two docks for passengers boats.

Boats for Santiago Atitlán (30 minutes) depart from the **Playa Pública** (Map p138) at the foot of Calle Rancho Grande. All other departures leave from the **Embarcadero Tzanjuyú** (Map p138), at the foot of Calle del Embarcadero. From here, *lanchas* (small motorboats) go counterclockwise around the lake, with direct and local service to San Pedro La Laguna (Q25, 25 minutes). The local services stop in Santa Cruz La Laguna (15 minutes), Jaibalito, Tzununá, San Marcos La Laguna (30 minutes), San Juan La Laguna and San Pedro La Laguna (45 minutes). The first boat to San Pedro departs at 7am; the last around 5pm.

BUSES FROM PANAJACHEL

DESTINATION	COST (Q)	DURATION (HR)	FREQUENCY	ALTERNATIVE
Antigua	45	2½	11am Mon-to Sat	Guatemala City bus; change at Chimaltenango
Chichicastenango	20	1½	5 services 6:45am-6pm	Any bus heading to Los Encuentros (via Sololá); change buses there
Ciudad Tecún Umán (Mexican border)				By the Pacific route (via Mazatenango), bus to Cocales and change there; by the Highland route, transfer at Quetzaltenango
Guatemala City	60	3½	5 services 4:30am-3pm	Bus to Los Encuentros (via Sololá); change there
Huehuetenango		3½		Bus to Los Encuentros (via Sololá), then Huehue- or La Mesilla–bound bus. Or Quetzaltenango service, change at Cuatro Caminos
Los Encuentros	10	40min		Bus to Sololá; change there
Quetzaltenango	25	2	4 services 5am-1pm	Bus to Los Encuentros (via Sololá); change there
Sololá	5	15min	Every 10min 7am-7pm	

One-way passage to San Pedro, Santiago or San Lucas costs Q25. Closer destinations like Santa Cruz shouldn't top Q10.

Lanchas are also available for private hire from the Playa Pública or Embarcadero Tzanjuyú: expect to pay around Q400 to San Pedro La Laguna.

BUS

Panajachel's **main bus stop** (Map p138; Calle Real) is at the junction of Calles Santander and Principal, immediately west of the Centro Comercial El Dorado.

SHUTTLE MINIBUS

Pretty much every tourist destination you could think of is served by a shuttle minibus. You can book at a number of travel agencies on Calle Santander.

Typical one-way fares include Antigua (Q80), Chichicastenango (round-trip Thursday and Sunday Q120), Guatemala City (Q160), Quetzaltenango (Q125) and San Cristóbal de Las Casas, Mexico (Q280).

Santiago Atitlán

POP 53,200

Santiago Atitlán is the largest of the lake communities, with a strong indigenous identity. Many *atitecos* (as its people are known) proudly adhere to a traditional Tz'utujil Maya lifestyle. Women wear purple-striped skirts and *huipiles* embroidered with colored birds and flowers, while older men still wear lavender or maroon striped embroidered pants. The town's *cofradías* (brotherhoods) maintain the syncretic traditions and rituals of Maya Catholicism. There's a large arts and crafts scene here too. Boatbuilding is a local industry, and rows of rough-hewn *cayucos* (dugout canoes) are lined up along the shore. The liveliest days to visit are Friday and Sunday, the main market days, but any day will do.

Santiago is worth a trip to visit the home of the Maya spirit Maximón (mah-shee-*mohn*). He changes house every year, but he's easy enough to find by asking around (would-be guides will approach you at the dock).

Sights

★Cofradía Maximón RELIGIOUS SITE

(donation requested) Maximón is a traditional Maya deity who resides in Santiago Atitlán. He appears as a life-sized but broken-legged effigy in a hat, dark suit and glasses, surrounded by candles, flowers and the scent of burning incense. His *cofradía* (brotherhood) looks after him, and receives visitors who give offerings. In the syncretic way of much tradtional Maya belief, he is also associated with Judas Iscariot.

Maximón ceremonially moves to a new home every year on May 8 (after Semana Santa).

Cojolya Association of Maya Women Weavers MUSEUM

(☎7721-7268; www.cojolya.org; Calle Real, Comercial Las Máscaras, 2nd fl; donation requested; ⌚9am-5pm Mon-Fri, 9am-2pm Sat) This small museum and showroom is devoted to the art of backstrap loom weaving. Well-designed exhibits show the history of the craft and the process from spinning the cotton fibers to the finished textile. There's a shop, daily demonstrations of backstrap loom techniques and, if you want to really learn more, weaving lessons (Q150; book ahead).

Tours

There are several rewarding **day hikes** around Santiago. Most enticing of all are the three volcanoes in the vicinity: Tolimán, Atitlán and San Pedro. Before attempting a climb, inquire about the current security situation. It's best to go with a guide; the Posada de Santiago can set up a reliable one. Guided volcano climbs cost about Q450 for two to five people.

Less daunting a challenge than the massive volcanoes in the vicinity, **Cerro de Oro** (1892m) still yields great views and features several Maya ceremonial sites. It's some 8km northeast, about halfway between Santiago and San Lucas Tolimán.

Milpas Tours (☎5450-2381; milpastours@yahoo.es) leads a variety of fascinating tours in and around Santiago Atitlán. It can take you to the Tz'utujil community of Chuk Muk on the slopes of Volcán Tolimán, with an unexcavated archaeological site; show you the temporary shrine devoted to locally worshiped saint Maximón (Q170); or visit the workshops of local weavers, painters, sculptors and chefs.

Another worthy destination is the **Mirador de Tepepul**, about 4km south of Santiago, near where the inlet ends (four to five hours round-trip, Q250 per person). The hike goes through cloud forest populated with many birds, including parakeets, curassows, swifts, boat-tailed grackles and tucanets, and on to a lookout point with views all the way to the coast.

The pre-Hispanic Tz'utujil capital of **Chuitinamit** is across the inlet from Santiago.

The hilltop archaeological site features some carved petroglyphs as well as some fanciful painted carvings of more recent vintage. From the dock, it's a 20-minute hike to the top, where there are good views of Santiago. Milpas Tours can take you across the inlet by *cayuco* and accompany you up the tenuous trail to the site.

Dolores Ratzan Pablo CULTURAL
(☎5730-4570; dolores_ratzan@yahoo.com) This English-speaking Tz'utujil woman can introduce you to the wonders of Maya birthing and healing, point out examples of Maya-Catholic syncretism at the church and *cofradías,* and describe the incidents that led to the massacre at the Parque de Paz in 1990. Tours typically last two hours and cost Q300 per person.

Sleeping & Eating

Hotel La Estrella HOTEL $$
(☎7721-7814; www.hotel-laestrella.blogspot.com; Calle Campo; s/d/tr Q180/320/450; P 📶) This good-value option is a short walk north of the ferry dock along the San Lucas road. It has modern, comfortable units with handsome wood ceilings and locally woven bedspreads. Room 13, adjacent to the top terrace, takes best advantage of the hotel's lakeside position, looking straight across the inlet at Volcán San Pedro. There's a small restaurant too.

Posada de Santiago LODGE $$$
(☎7721-7366; www.posadadesantiago.com; s/d Q300/400, cottages Q500-1200; P @ 📶 🏊) Somewhere between rustic and luxurious, this North American–owned *posada* makes a great retreat. Seven cottages (some sleeping six) and five suites, all with stone walls, fireplaces, porches, hammocks and folk art, are set amid rambling gardens. Across the road stretches a lakeside resort with pool and bar. The restaurant is celebrated locally for its eggs Benedict with blue corn tortillas.

The *posada* is 1.5km from the town dock. Catch a *tuk-tuk* (Q10) or hire a *lancha* over to the hotel's own dock.

Comedor Santa Rita GUATEMALAN $
(Calle de Santa Rita 88; lunch Q25-30; ⊙7am-9pm Mon-Fri) The latest incarnation of a generations-old dining hall, this is a good place to try such Maya specialties as *pulique* (a veggie-rich stew) and *patín* (an Atitlán fish stew) served with a stack of tortillas. Half a block east of the Parque Central.

Restaurant El Gran Sol GUATEMALAN $$
(☎4271-4642; Cantón Tzanjuyú; mains Q55; ⊙8am-7pm Mon-Sat) One block up from the dock on the left, this highly popular family-run establishment is a great bet for breakfast, lunch or snacks, with a spiffy kitchen and breezy deck over a busy junction. Thelma and clan love to cook; try the soups, pancakes or quesadillas (with homemade cheese).

Information

G&T Continental (⊙8:30am-5pm Mon-Fri, 9am-1pm Sat) There's a Cajero 5B ATM at G&T Continental, on the south side of the Parque Central.

Getting There & Away

Boats leave hourly from Santiago's **dock** for San Pedro La Laguna (Q25, 30 minutes) and slightly more frequently to Panajachel (Q25, 30 minutes). Pickups to Cerro de Oro and San Lucas Tolimán depart from in front of the market. Buses to Guatemala City (Q40, 3½ hours) leave every half -our from 3am to 6am, then hourly until 3pm, from the main plaza.

There is a weekday tourist shuttle (Q150, three hours) to El Paredón, operated by **Pacifico Surf Transport** (www.facebook.com/pacificsurfgt).

San Pedro La Laguna

POP 12,300 / ELEV 1592M

Spreading onto a peninsula at the base of the volcano of the same name, San Pedro remains among the most visited of the lakeside villages – due as much to its reasonably priced accommodations and global social scene as to its spectacular setting. It's a backpacker haven – travelers tend to dig in here for a spell, in pursuit of (in no particular order) drinking, fire-twirling, African drumming, Spanish classes, volcano hiking, hot-tub soaking, partying and hammock swinging.

While this scene unfolds around the lakefront, up the hill San Pedro follows more traditional rhythms. Clad in indigenous outfits, the predominantly Tz'utujil *pedranos* (as the locals are called) congregate around the market zone. You'll see coffee being picked on the volcano's slopes and spread out to dry on wide platforms at the beginning of the dry season.

Activities

Looming above the village, Volcán San Pedro (3020m) almost demands to be climbed by anyone with an adventurous spirit and

DON'T MISS

CHEESE AND WINE ON THE LAKE

Café El Artesano (☎4555-4773; Salida a Guatemala; cheese or smoked meat platter Q125, sharing platters per person Q110; ⊙noon-4pm Mon-Fri) offers one of Guatemala's best dining experiences. Let the staff guide you around the platter of two dozen cheeses (all produced in Guatemala and aged in-house), from creamy goat through blue to hard pecorino, served with fruits, nuts, jams, pickles and artisanal breads. The same is on offer for some extraordinary home-smoked meats.

Everything is served under a delightful rustic arbor, with perfectly matched wines. When the food is this good, you'll understand why reservations are essential.

a reasonable level of fitness. It is the most accessible of the three volcanoes in the zone and, classified as a municipal ecological park, it's regularly patrolled by tourism police.

Guides (required) take you up from San Pedro for around Q130, including entrance fee. Start your climb at dawn.

The ascent is through fields of maize, beans and squash, followed by primary cloud forest. It's a three- to -four-hour climb and two hours back down; take water, snacks, a hat and sunblock.

Another popular hike goes up the hill referred to as **Indian Nose** – its skyline resembles the profile of an ancient Maya dignitary. **Asoantur** (☎4379-4545; www.facebook.com/asoantur; 4a Av A 3-60; ⊙7am-7pm), an association made up of 16 INGUAT-authorized guides from the local community, leads expeditions to the peak for Q100 per person. It also offers cultural tours of San Pedro and nearby coffee plantations, horseback-riding tours, and kayak, bicycle and motorbike rentals. It operates from a hut on the lane up from the Pana dock.

Courses

San Pedro is making a name for itself in the language game with ultra-economical rates at its various Spanish institutes. The standard price for four hours of one-on-one classes, five days a week, is Q900. Accommodations with a local family, with three meals daily (except Sunday), typically cost Q50. Volcano hikes, Maya culture seminars and dance classes are among the extracurricular activities offered.

Community Spanish School LANGUAGE
(☎5466-7177; www.communityspanishschool.com) A professionally managed school staffed by accredited local instructors, who lead one-on-one classes in thatched huts along a strip of garden running down to the lakefront.

San Pedro Spanish School LANGUAGE
(☎5715-4604; www.sanpedrospanishschool.org; 7a Av 2-20) A well-organized school on the street between the two docks, with consistently good reviews. Classes are held under thatched-roof huts amid an attractive garden setting. The school supports Niños del Lago, an organization that provides education, health care and nutrition for local Tz'utujil children. It has a sister school in San Marcos using the same curriculum.

Celas Maya LANGUAGE
(☎5933-1450; www.spanishschool.com.gt) The lake branch of the prestigious Quetzaltenango institute uses documentaries, TV reports and storytelling as the basis for one-on-one classes aimed at building speaking and listening skills. Classes in Tz'utujil are also offered. It's at the end of the lakefront trail from the Pana dock.

Sleeping

Mr Mullet's Hostel HOSTEL $
(☎4419-0566; www.mrmullets.com; incl breakfast dm Q60, r with/without bathroom Q140/95;) This party point in lakeside San Pedro overflows with fun seekers who pile into the four-bed dorms and cell-like private rooms on two levels or crowd the hammocks in the patio/bar at rear, which shuts at 11pm for those who actually want to sleep. From the Pana dock, it's a five-minute walk to the left.

Hostel Fe HOSTEL $
(☎3486-7027; www.hostelfe.com; incl breakfast dm/r Q75/200;) Fe's flag-draped front is unmissable if you arrive in San Pedro by boat. It's a massive concrete block 100m south of the Pana dock. It's a destination of choice for global youth, who come more for the lively waterfront cafe and sundeck bar (with waterslide) than the sparsely furnished steel-doored rooms and dorms.

Zoola HOSTEL $
(☎5847-4857; dm Q60, r with/without bathroom Q170/140;) 'Ultra-laid-back' best describes this Israeli-run establishment. It's reached down a long, jungly boardwalk opposite the Museo Tz'unun 'Ya. Behind the cafe/chill-out lounge, low adobe blocks of dorms extend to the lake, where a canopied swimming pool is the focus of nightly parties. Two-night minimum stay.

Hotel Sak'cari El Amanecer HOTEL $$
(☎7721-8096; www.hotel-sakcari.com; 7a Av 2-12, Zona 2; s/d/tr Q275/305/385;) About midway along the trail between the two docks, the Sak'cari (Tz'utujil for 'sunrise') has 20 clean wood-paneled rooms with lots of shelves. Rooms at the rear are best (and priciest), with big balconies overlooking the lake past a landscaped lawn that's a splendid place for hammock swinging. More active guests can grab a kayak and navigate the lake.

Hotel Mikaso HOTEL $$
(☎7721-8232; www.mikasohotel.com; 4a Callejon A-88; dm Q60, s/d/tr from Q150/180/300;) The Mikaso stands proudly at Atitlán's shores, surrounded by local kitchen gardens. Big rooms with carved wood furniture and ceiling fans ring a garden bursting with birds of paradise; a few have private patios. The rooftop bar/restaurant has fantastic lake views and a baby grand piano, plus there's a deck/lounge that features a Jacuzzi and pool table.

Eating

Blue Parrot BURGERS $
(7a Avenida; burgers from Q50) An airy sports bar that does a wicked line in over two dozen different gourmet burgers, plus chili dogs and seriously filled sandwiches to go down with its extensive range of craft beers. Friday night is seafood night, and there's always a scene when there's a big match on.

Shanti Shanti ISRAELI $
(6a Av; mains Q20-30; 7am-11pm;) With terraced seating cascading down to the lakeside, this makes a pleasant perch for Mideast staples such as falafel, baba ghanoush and hummus, plus hearty soups.

Hummus-Ya MIDDLE EASTERN $$
(6 Av A, Zona 2; platters Q25-50; 11am-10pm Mon-Sun) *Sabich,* an Israeli sandwich lovingly stuffed with hard-boiled eggs, hummus and fried eggplant, is just one highlight on the menu at this cheerful Mideast eatery upstairs, midway between the Pana and Santiago docks. Order rounds of hummus, baba ghanoush, Moroccan lentils and Iraqi filo pastry rolls stuffed with ground beef and feta.

Drinking & Nightlife

D'Juice Girls JUICE BAR
(juices from Q20; 7am-11pm) D'Juice Girls are young Hebrew-speaking Tz'utujil women who squeeze the tropical fruits of Guatemala into supernutritious combos, such as carrot-ginger-beet. This popular stand is a five-minute walk east of the Pana dock.

Café Las Cristalinas CAFE
(7am-9pm;) To savor a shot of the coffee grown on the surrounding slopes (and roasted here), head for this thatched-roof structure on the way up from the Pana dock to the center of town. Come for breakfast and be sure to also try the excellent banana bread, which you may enjoy on various inviting terraces.

Bar Sublime BAR
(noon-1am) Bar Sublime is the current epicenter of San Pedro's party scene. During the day its lakefront terraces are pretty relaxed and you can enjoy good sandwiches, pasta and salads, but things ramp up as the sun starts to dip. Expect cheap mixers, thumping music and crowds of the young, the beautiful and the slightly disheveled.

El Barrio PUB
(7a Av 2-07, Zona 2; 5pm-1am) This boisterous pub on the path between the two docks has one of the most happening happy hours in town (5pm to 8pm). Every night has a different theme; we particularly liked the curry night on Saturdays.

Information

ATM There's a Cajero 5B ATM just up from the Panajachel dock on the left.

Banrural (8:30am-5pm Mon-Fri, 9am-1pm Sat) You can change cash US dollars and euros here, two blocks east of the market in the town center; has a Visa ATM.

Clínica Los Volcanes (☎7823-7656; www.clinicalosvolcanes.com) A private clinic providing medical and dental services, with English-speaking staff. It's near the Pana dock.

Getting There & Away

San Pedro has two docks: one for Panajachel and villages on the northern shore, and another for Santiago Atitlán.

From **Pana Dock**, boats to Panajachel (Q25) run every half-hour or so from 6am to 5pm. Some go direct; others make stops at San Juan (though it's quicker to take a *tuk-tuk* direct), San Marcos (Q10) and Jaibalito/Santa Cruz (Q20) en route.

From **Santiago Dock**, boats to Santiago (Q25, 25 minutes) run hourly from 6am to 4pm.

San Pedro's main **bus stop** is outside the Catholic church. Buses leave hourly from 3am to 2pm for Guatemala City (Q60, four hours) and seven buses leave for Quetzaltenango (Q40, three hours) between 4:45am and 1:30pm Monday to Saturday. Buses to both destinations travel via Santiago, and have reduced services on Sunday.

San Pedro's myriad travel agencies can sell tickets for the twice-daily tourist shuttle to Antigua (Q80, two hours) and onward connections.

San Marcos La Laguna

POP 5800 / ELEV 1580M

One of the prettiest of the lakeside villages, San Marcos La Laguna lives a double life. The mostly Maya community occupies the higher ground, while expats and visitors cover a flat jungly patch toward the shoreline with paths snaking through banana, coffee and avocado trees. The two converge under the spreading *matapalo* (strangler fig) tree of the central plaza.

San Marcos has become a magnet for global seekers, who believe the place has a spiritual energy that's conducive to learning and practicing meditation, holistic therapies, massage, Reiki and other spiritually oriented activities. It's an outlandish mélange of cultures – evangelical Christians, self-styled shamans, Kaqchiquel farmers and visionary artists – against a backdrop of incredible natural beauty.

Whatever you're into, it's a great spot to kick back and distance the everyday world for a spell. Lago de Atitlán is beautiful and clean here, and you can swim off the rocks.

Sights & Activities

Cerro Tzankujil NATURE RESERVE
(Q15; 8am-6pm) This nature reserve is on a sacred hill west of San Marcos village. Well-maintained pebbly trails lead to swimming areas with shelters by the bank and a diving platform. The water is crystal clear here. A branch off the main trail ascends to a Maya altar on the summit, while a lower spur reaches a volcano lookout.

Yoga Forest YOGA
(3301-1835; www.theyogaforest.org; yoga classes Q50) Up in the hills north of town amid lush forest, this is a blissfully secluded perch to learn and practice shamanic healing and other esoteric arts, with a magnificent yoga platform built into the hillside. A cafe prepares vegetarian food and accommodations are available in shared adobe *cabañas* with thatched roofs and magnificent lake views.

Fé Cookery Classes COOKING
(3009-5537; pcsa1521@gmail.com; classes Q225) Restaurant Fé has two branches on opposite sides of the street – the one on the right as you walk up from the dock hosts cookery classes. With advance notice you can learn to cook almost anything you like over three hours, but most people start with the Guatemalan basics, from tortillas and tamales to rich stews like *pepián* and *jocón*.

Las Pirámides Meditation Center MEDITATION
(5205-7302; www.laspiramidesdelka.com; 75min yoga & meditation sessions Q50) This retreat by the lake has been providing spiritual guidance for more than two decades. Most structures on the property are pyramidal in shape and oriented to the four cardinal points, including the two temples where sessions are held. A one-month personal development course begins every full moon, with three sessions daily (Q6000).

There's also a three-month solar course running from each equinox to the following solstice (the moon course is a prerequisite). Nonguests can come for the morning meditation or Hatha yoga sessions. Accommodations are available to course participants in pyramid-shaped houses, including use of the sauna and access to the esoteric library. The center also has a vegetarian restaurant and room to wander about in the medicinal herb garden.

Festivals

Festival of Consciousness CULTURAL
(www.festivalofconsciousness.weebly.com; festival pass Q475; Mar) Held around the spring equinox, this weekend festival is devoted to expansion of environmental, social and spiritual awareness. A cavalcade of workshops on everything from mindfulness to holistic health takes place during the day, followed by live music at night, and to wrap things up, the obligatory fire ceremony.

Cosmic Convergence CULTURAL
(www.cosmicconvergencefestival.org; festival pass Q1120; Dec-Jan) Held in San Marcos for

three days over the new year, Cosmic Convergence is an arts, spirit and eco festival. Expect everything from Maya religion to permaculture to new-tech.

Sleeping

★Circles HOSTEL $
(☎3327-8961; www.circles-cafe.com; dm/s/d Q100/175/200) Near the top of the path from the dock is this casual hostel/cafe with an attached bakery and coffee roaster to provide the essentials of a good stay. Upstairs are two private rooms and a thoughtfully designed dorm with curtains on each bunk. A chill-out terrace looks over a garden with shady cushioned nooks.

Dragon Hotel BOUTIQUE HOTEL $$
(☎3109-7707; www.eldragonhotel.com; r from Q470;) This lakefront spread created by a North American artist could be the wackiest of San Marcos lodgings. Signs of artistic exuberance pop up everywhere, from the dining area with its hanging spheres to the waterfront deck/bar with its trademark serpent, but not at the expense of luxury. Uniquely designed rooms feature plasma TVs, loft beds and private terraces.

Posada Schumann HOTEL $$
(☎5202-2216; www.laposadaschumann.com; s/d with breakfast from Q345/500, r without bathroom Q185) Set in gardens that stretch right to the shores of Lago de Atitlán, Posada Schumann has neat rooms in stone or wooden cottages, some with kitchens. An idyllic cafe deck looks over the water. Don't miss the igloo-shaped sauna (included in the room rate, along with kayaks). San Marcos' main dock is right outside the gate.

Hostal del Lago HOSTEL $$
(☎3227-9077; dm Q80, s/d Q200/250, without bathroom Q150/200) This ramshackle locale by the lakefront east of the center has a theatrical flair, with impromptu performances on a regular basis. Enthusiastically managed, it shelters legions of global drifters who settle into a series of psychedelically painted cottages. You can feed on lovely vegetarian food in the cafe (mains from Q35) or join the free daily yoga sessions on a raised platform by the water.

Eating

★Comedor Konojel GUATEMALAN $
(daily specials Q30) This cheerily painted clapboard canteen serves up big healthy portions of Guatemalan food according to a changing daily menu to help support a wider feeding program and other community projects in the area around San Marcos. Doing good rarely tastes so delicious.

Allala JAPANESE $
(☎5166-8638; mains Q35-45; 3-9pm Thu-Tue;) This groovy little shack can be found by the creek east of the village. Japanese owner Seiko makes a mean miso soup, plus vegetarian sushi and tempura platters, and the plum wine is divine. All this, and complimentary cheesecake for dessert. Service can be slow, but the funky decor gives you something to look at.

Moonfish HEALTH FOOD $
(sandwiches & burritos Q30; 7:30am-8pm Wed-Mon;) Along the main thoroughfare west of the square, Moonfish whips up hippie-friendly fare including tempeh sandwiches, tofu scrambles and fine falafel with ingredients fresh from the garden.

Restaurante Fé INTERNATIONAL $$
(mains Q55-80; 7:30am-10pm;) Fé, about midway down the main trail, offers informal candlelit dining in a pleasant, open-air hall with a tree in the middle. The pastas, pan-fried fish and particularly the curries are all well worth savoring here, and the mulligatawny stew is excellent. A good place to while away the evening.

Information

Visit San Marcos (www.visit-sanmarcos.com) A useful village information board, with directory and events listings.

Getting There & Away

Boats run throughout the day between San Marcos and Panajachel (Q20, 20 minutes). The last dependable boat to Santa Cruz La Laguna and Panajachel departs about 5pm.

A gravel road runs east from San Marcos to Tzununá and a paved one west to San Pablo, where it meets the road running from the Interamericana to San Pedro La Laguna. You can travel between San Marcos and San Pedro by pickup, with a transfer at San Pablo.

Santa Cruz La Laguna

POP 9400

Santa Cruz fits the typically dual nature of the Atitlán villages, comprising both a waterfront resort (home of the lake's scuba-diving outfit) and an indigenous

WORTH A TRIP

THE END OF THE WORLD?

On a secluded cliff facing the volcanoes is one of Guatemala's most spectacular hotels, **La Casa del Mundo Hotel & Café** (☎5218-5332; www.lacasadelmundo.com; Q355-700). It features sumptuous gardens, lake swimming from Mediterranean-style terraces, and a wood-fired hot tub overhanging the lake. The best rooms seem to float above the water, with no land visible beneath. Every room is outfitted with comfortable beds, Guatemalan fabrics and fresh flowers. Reservations are recommended.

The restaurant prepares a toothsome four-course dinner (Q85 to Q95), served family style. You can rent kayaks (Q50 per hour) for exploring the lake.

Kaqchiquel village. The village is about 600m uphill from the dock (there are *tuktuks* if you don't fancy the stiff walk). It's a lovely spot, with relaxing accommodations, activities on the water and a complete lack of hustle.

Activities

ATI Divers DIVING

(☎5706-4117; www.atidivers.com) Lago de Atitlán is one of the rare places in the world where you can dive at altitude without using a dry suit, and ATI Divers offers trips from Santa Cruz. These include a four-day PADI open-water diving certification course (Q220), as well as a PADI high-altitude course (Q750) and fun dives (Q480) for beginners.

Courses include accommodations at its base at La Iguana Perdida.

The lake fills a collapsed volcanic cone with bizarre geological formations and aquatic life such as cichlids, which spawn near an active fault line where hot water vents into the lake. Diving at altitude brings its own challenges – you need better control over your buoyancy, visibility is reduced and you cannot leave the lake the day of your final dive due to the change in atmospheric pressure. During the rainy season the water clouds up, so the best time to dive is between October and May.

Los Elementos Adventure Center KAYAKING

(☎5359-8328; www.kayakguatemala.com; kayak per hour Q60, 2hr tour Q220, 2-day tour Q1250) This outfit offers kayaks and paddleboards to explore the lake, ranging from rental by the hour to fully supported and guided multiday kayak and hiking tours around Atitlán. Its two-day paddle-and-hike tour includes a visit to Santa Catarina Palopó, followed by kayaking along the lake's northern shore and hiking along the old Maya trail through Tzununá and Jaibalito.

Sleeping & Eating

★**La Iguana Perdida** LODGE $$

(☎5706-4117; www.laiguanaperdida.com; dm Q50, s/d without bathroom Q115/150, r Q335-415; @📶) La Iguana Perdida is one of the granddaddies of Guatemala's backpacker scene, but you wouldn't know it from its ever-fresh appearance. It features a range of rooms, from a basic dorm in an A-frame cabin to the more decadent (an adobe structure with stylish furnishings and private balconies). Evening meals are served family style, making a stay here highly sociable.

The Iguana is a great hangout to enjoy the lake views and meet other travelers, go scuba diving or kayaking, or sweat it out in the sauna. There are regular evening events, from quiz nights to music and even BBQs where guests are encouraged to dive into the house dressing-up box.

Hotel Isla Verde GUESTHOUSE $$

(☎5760-2648; www.islaverdeatitlan.com; s/d cabin Q392/440, without bathroom Q296/344; 📶) This stylish, environmentally friendly lodging makes the most of its spectacular setting. A mosaic stone path winds through exuberant vegetation to the nine hillside cabins (six with private bathroom); the higher you go, the more jaw-dropping the picture-window views. Simple rooms are tastefully decorated with art and recycled elements. Bathrooms are jungle-chic affairs, and water and electricity are solar powered.

★**Café Sabor Cruceño** GUATEMALAN $

(www.amigosdesantacruz.org; breakfast Q32-45, lunch Q35-50; ⊙8am-5pm Mon-Sat) Up in the village, this brilliant community project *comedor* is run by local students who are learning to make traditional Guatemalan dishes to global tourism standards. Such Kaqchiquel fare as *subanik* (a tomato sauce of ground seeds and chilies accompanied by *tamalitos*) is prepared with locally grown herbs and veggies and served in the terrace restaurant with obligatory stunning lake views.

Getting There & Away

Santa Cruz is a 15-minute *lancha* ride from Panajachel (Q10) or 25 minutes from San Pedro (Q20). The last boat back to Pana passes at around 5:15pm.

Unless you have the sturdiest of 4WDs and it's the dry season, don't believe maps that suggest Santa Cruz has proper road access.

Chichicastenango

POP 173,300 / ELEV 2172M

Surrounded by valleys with mountains serrating the horizons, Chichicastenango can seem isolated in time and space from the rest of Guatemala. When its narrow cobbled streets and red-tiled roofs are enveloped in mist, it's downright magical. The crowds of crafts vendors and tour groups who flock in for the huge Thursday and Sunday markets lend it a much worldlier, more commercial atmosphere, but Chichi retains its mystery. *Masheños* (citizens of Chichicastenango) are famous for their adherence to pre-Christian beliefs and ceremonies, and the town's various *cofradías* (religious brotherhoods) hold processions in observance of their saints around the church of Santo Tomás.

History

Once called Chaviar, Chichi was an important Kaqchiquel trading town long before the Spanish conquest. In the 15th century the group clashed with the K'iche' (based at K'umarcaaj, 20km north) and were forced to move their headquarters to the more defensible Iximché. When the Spanish conquered K'umarcaaj in 1524, many of its residents fled to Chaviar, which was renamed Chugüilá ('Above the Nettles') and Tziguan Tinamit ('Surrounded by Canyons'). These are the names still used by the K'iche' Maya, although everyone else calls the place Chichicastenango, a name given by the Spaniards' Mexican allies.

Sights

Take a close look at the **mural** (Map p150) running alongside the wall of the town hall on the east side of the plaza. It's dedicated to the victims of the civil war and tells the story using symbology from the *Popol Vuh*.

INGUAT-authorized **guides** (Map p150; ☎5966-1162; 7a Av 7-14; ⏰8am-4pm Sun-Thu) in beige vests offer cultural walks of Chichi and up to Pascual Abaj.

★Market MARKET

(Map p150; Plaza Principal; ⏰Thu & Sun) Some villagers still walk for hours carrying their wares to reach Chichi's market, one of Guatemala's largest and a highlight of many people's trips to the country. It's a rich mix of the traditional and the tourist, where local women shopping for a new *huipile* rub shoulders with travelers looking for a textile souvenir. Sunday is the busier of the two market days, when Spanish school students and weekenders from Guatemala City descend en masse on Chichi.

At dawn on Thursday and Sunday vendors spread out their vegetables, chunks of chalk (ground to a powder and boiled with dried maize to soften it), handmade harnesses and other merchandise, and wait for customers. In the past vendors erected their stands of tree limbs and covered them with cotton sheeting each market day, but these days a sea of tin roofs remains a permanent fixture atop the plaza.

Tourist-oriented handicraft stalls selling masks, textiles, pottery and so on now occupy much of the plaza and the streets to the north. Things villagers need – food, soap, clothing, sewing notions, toys – cluster at the north end of the square and in the covered **Centro Comercial Santo Tomás** (Map p150) off the north side, whose upper deck offers irresistible photo opportunities of the fruit- and vegetable-selling business conducted below.

Iglesia de Santo Tomás CHURCH

(Map p150; 5a Av) This church on the plaza's east side dates from 1540 and is often the scene of rituals that are more distinctly Maya than Catholic. Inside, the floor of the church may be dotted with offerings of maize, flowers and bottles of liquor wrapped in corn husks; candles are arranged in specific patterns along low stone platforms. Enter through the side door rather than the front entrance and note that photography is very strictly not permitted inside.

The church's front steps serve much the same purpose as the great flights of stairs leading up to Maya pyramids (there are 20 steps, for each day of the Maya calendar). For much of the day (especially Sunday), they smolder with incense of *copal* resin, while indigenous prayer leaders called *chuchkajaues* (mother-fathers) swing censers (usually tin cans poked with holes) and chant magic words marking the days of the ancient Maya calendar and in honor of

Chichicastenango

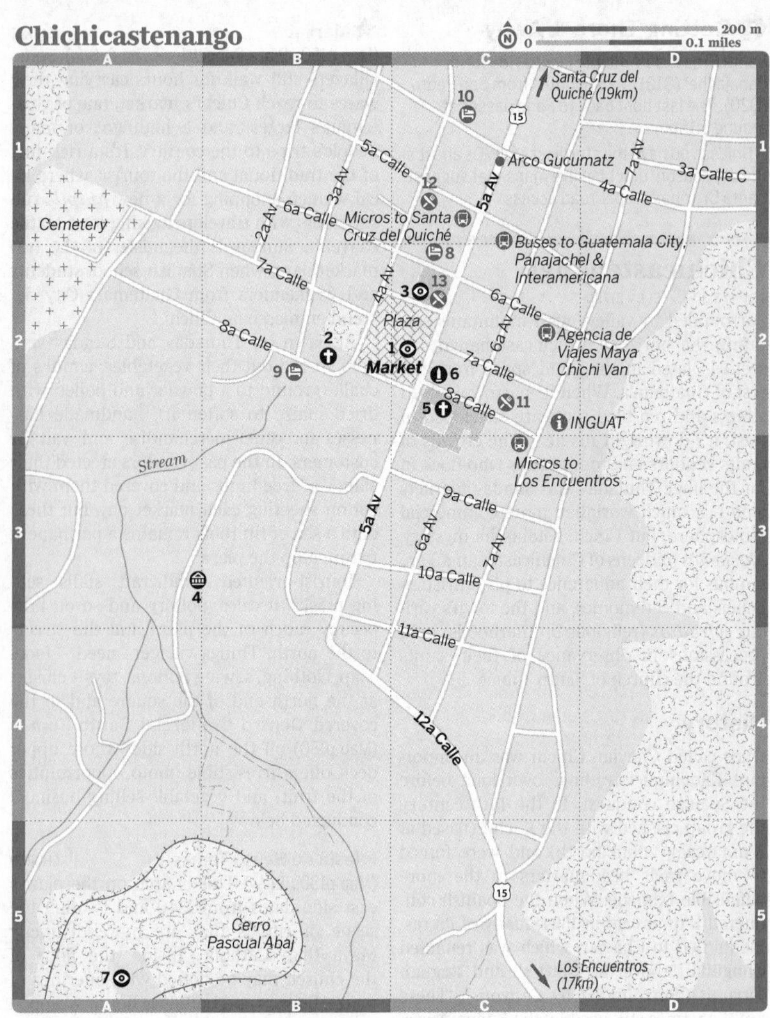

ancestors. The candles and offerings inside recall those ancestors, many of whom are buried beneath the floor just as Maya kings were buried beneath pyramids.

Capilla del Calvario CHURCH

(Map p150; 4a Av) On the west side of the plaza, this whitewashed church is similar in form and function to Santo Tomás, but smaller. Ceremonies go on continually in front of the church, as worshippers ring a bonfire of fragrant *copal,* while within, candles are placed upon blackened stone slabs.

Galería Pop-Wuj GALLERY

(Map p150; ☎4629-9327; www.galeriapopwuj.wix.com/galeriapopwuj; Casa 2-27, Calle Pascual Habaj) FREE On the way down the hill to the shrine at Pascual Abaj, you might stop into this interesting gallery. Developed as an art institute for local children with the backing of Project Guggenheim, it holds a small but important collection of oil paintings by the artist brothers Juan and Miguel Cortéz and their pupils. K'iche' classes are sometimes offered, along with the chance to experience traditional Maya ceremonies (contact the gallery in advance).

Chichicastenango

Festivals & Events

Feast of Santo Tomás CULTURAL
(Dec) This celebration of the patron saint's day goes on for most of December, starting on the 5th with an inaugural parade and culminating on the 21st when pairs of brave (some would say mad) men fly about at high speeds suspended from a tall, vertical pole. Traditional dances, concerts and fireworks also feature.

Quema del Diablo CULTURAL
(Burning of the Devil; Dec 7) In this ceremony, residents burn their garbage in the streets and usher a statue of the Virgin Mary to the steps of the Iglesia de Santo Tomás. There are lots of incense and candles, a marimba band and a fireworks display that has observers running for cover.

Sleeping & Eating

If you want to secure a room the night before the Thursday or Sunday market, it's a good idea to call or arrive early the day before.

Hotel Girón HOTEL $
(Map p150; 5527-1101; hotelgiron@gmail.com; 6a Calle 4-52; s/d/tr Q150/200/450; P) It won't win any prizes for decor, but this motel-style place a block north of the plaza is functional and reliable. It's reached through a shopping alley, so it's slightly removed from the hubbub of the town center. Get a room on the 1st floor if you can. Prices include breakfast.

Posada El Arco GUESTHOUSE $$
(Map p150; 3469-1590; 4a Calle 4-36; s/d Q244/305) Near the Arco Gucumatz, this homey, solar-powered spread is one of Chichi's more original accommodations. All nine rooms are idiosyncratically appointed, with Maya weavings, colonial bedsteads and fireplaces. Rooms 3, 4, 6 and 7 have views over the tranquil rear garden and northward to the mountains. Well-read owner Pedro likes to converse in English. Reservations are a good idea.

Mayan Inn HOTEL $$$
(Map p150; 2412-4753; www.mayaninn.com.gt; 8a Calle A 1-91; s/d/tr Q630/700/1110;) Founded in 1932, the inn today encompasses several restored colonial houses on either side of 8a Calle. The courtyards are planted with tropical flora and the walls draped in indigenous textiles. Each of the 16 rooms is individually appointed, with carved armoires and fireplaces. Those on the south side have the best views. The **restaurant** (breakfast from Q25, mains Q70-125; 7am-10pm) here does some of Chichi's finest cuisine.

★ **Villa Cofrades** CAFE $
(Map p150; Centro Comercial Santo Tomás; 7am-7pm Wed, Thu, Sat & Sun;) This charming cafe is tucked into the outside corner of Centro Comercial Santo Tomás and is a gem if you want to step back from the bustle of the market but still get a view of the action outside. It's decorated with an eccentric eye – old typewriters, prints, cutlery installations and auction house catalogs.

Los Asados GUATEMALAN $
(Map p150; cnr 4a Av & 5a Calle; breakfast from Q15, daily specials Q30) A cheery 1st-floor restaurant set back from the market hubbub, Los Asados is good for filling breakfasts, sandwiches and big grill plates. Always keep an eye on the menu of the day, which is usually good and filling.

Casa San Juan GUATEMALAN $$
(Map p150; 7756-2086; 6a Av 7-30; mains Q40-65; 10am-9:30pm Tue-Sun) One of the more stylish eateries, the San Juan occupies a beautiful colonial structure beside Santo Tomás with candlelit dining in various salons. Offerings range from burgers and sandwiches to more traditional fare, including good *chiles rellenos* laced with zesty salsa.

DON'T MISS

CHICHI'S STREET FOOD

The real food action in Chichicastenango is in the central plaza, where attentive *abuelitas* (grandmas) ladle chicken soup, beef stew, tamales and *chiles rellenos* from huge pots as their daughters and granddaughters minister to the throngs of country folk sitting at long tables covered with oilcloth. What are called tamales here are made of rice and laced with sauce. Sliced watermelon and papaya can be had at other stalls. On non-market evenings, you'll find enchiladas and *pupusas* in front of the cathedral, served with *atole de plátano*, a warm plantain beverage spiked with cinnamon.

Information

Chichi's many banks all stay open on Sunday, and there are plenty of ATMs.

ATM (cnr 5a Av & 6a Calle)

Banco Industrial (6a Calle 6-05) Visa/MasterCard ATM.

Getting There & Away

Buses (Map p150) heading to Panajachel, Quetzaltenango and all other points reached from the Interamericana arrive and depart from 5a Calle near the corner of 5a Av, one block uphill from the Arco Gucumtaz. You can also catch a micro to Santa Cruz del Quiché (Map p150) here. Buses approaching from the south go up 7a Avenida, dropping off passengers at the **gas station** two blocks east of the central plaza.

Microbuses to Los Encuentros (Map p150) leave from in front of the Telgua building on 7a Avenida.

Agencia de Viajes Maya Chichi Van (Map p150; ☎5007-2051; mayachichivan@yahoo.es; 6a Calle 6-45) offers shuttles to Guatemala City (Q125), Antigua (Q90) and Panajachel (Q55) on Thursday and Sunday at 2pm, plus a service to San Cristóbal de las Casas in Mexico at 7am daily. In most cases at least five passengers are needed. It also runs tours to K'umarcaaj near Santa Cruz del Quiché, Nebaj and elsewhere.

Santa Cruz del Quiché

POP 130,300 / ELEV 1979M

Without Chichicastenango's big market and attendant tourism, Santa Cruz – or just El Quiché – presents a less self-conscious slice of regional life and is refreshingly free of competition for tourist lucre. Just 19km north of Chichi, Santa Cruz is the capital of Quiché department, drawing a diverse populace on business and administrative affairs. The main market days are Thursday and Sunday, boosting the bustle considerably. Travelers who come here usually do so to visit K'umarcaaj, the ruins of the old K'iche' Maya capital, or to change buses en route further north.

The most exciting time to be here is mid-August during the Fiestas Elenas, a week of festivities and a proud display of indigenous traditions. It all leads up to the *Convite Femenino,* when El Quiché's women don masks and dance up a storm to marimba accompaniment.

Sights

El Quiché's main draw is the ruins of K'umarcaaj just outside the town, but there are several points of interest around the central tripartite plaza. The top square is flanked on its east side by Gobernación (the departmental government palace), the middle one by the cathedral and the *municipalidad* (town hall), and the bottom one by the big domed events hall, in front of which stands a statue of K'iche' warrior Tecún Umán in a fierce posture. The main market occupies a series of buildings east of the plaza.

K'umarcaaj ARCHAEOLOGICAL SITE

(Q'um'arkaj, Utatlán; Q30; ⏲8am-4pm) The ruins of the ancient K'iche' Maya capital of K'umarcaaj remain a sacred site for the Maya, and contemporary rituals are customarily enacted here. Archaeologists have identified more than 80 large structures in 12 groups, but only limited restoration has been done. The ruins have a fine setting, shaded by tall evergreens and surrounded by ravines. Bring a flashlight.

The kingdom of K'iche' was established in late Postclassic times (about the 14th century) by a mixture of indigenous people and invaders from the Tabasco–Campeche border area in Mexico. King Ku'ucumatz founded K'umarcaaj which, owing to its naturally fortified position, commanded an extensive valley, and conquered many neighboring settlements. During the long reign of his successor, Q'uik'ab (1425–75), the K'iche' kingdom extended its borders to Huehuetenango, Nebaj, Rabinal and the Pacific Slope. At the same time, the Kaqchiquel, a vassal people who once fought alongside the K'iche', rebelled, establishing an independent capital at Iximché.

When Pedro de Alvarado and his Spanish conquistadors hit Guatemala in 1524, it was the K'iche', under their king Tecún Umán, who led the resistance against them. In the decisive battle fought near Quetzaltenango on February 12, 1524, Alvarado and Tecún engaged in mortal combat. Alvarado prevailed. The defeated K'iche' invited him to visit K'umarcaaj. Smelling a rat, Alvarado enlisted the aid of his Mexican auxiliaries and the anti-K'iche' Kaqchiquel, and together they captured the K'iche' leaders, burnt them alive in K'umarcaaj's main plaza and then destroyed the city.

The museum at the entrance will help orient you. The tallest of the structures round the central plaza, the **Templo de Tohil** (a sky god), is blackened by smoke and has a niche where contemporary prayer-men regularly make offerings to Maya gods. The L-shaped ball court alongside it has been extensively restored.

Down the hillside to the right of the plaza is the entrance to a long tunnel known as the *cueva*. Legend has it that the K'iche' dug the tunnel as a refuge for their women and children in preparation for Alvarado's coming, and that a K'iche' princess was later buried in a deep shaft off this tunnel. Revered as the place where the K'iche' kingdom died, the *cueva* is sacred to highland Maya and is an important location for prayers, candle burning, offerings and chicken sacrifices.

If there's anyone around the entrance, ask permission before entering. Inside, the tunnel (100m long or so) is blackened with smoke and incense and littered with candles and petals. Use your flashlight and watch your footing: there are several side tunnels and at least one of them, on the right near the end, contains a deep, black shaft.

The ruins of K'umarcaaj are 3km west of El Quiché. Gray 'Ruinas' microbuses depart from in front of the cathedral in Santa Cruz every 20 minutes (Q1). The last one back is at 6:50pm.

Sleeping & Eating

The hotels are located between the Parque Central and the bus terminal.

For budget grub, there's plenty of grilling action going on around and within the market.

Hotel Rey K'iche HOTEL $

(☎7755-0827; 8a Calle 0-39, Zona 5; s/d/tr Q160/225/290; 📶) Between the bus station and plaza, the Rey K'iche is excellent value with well-maintained, brick-walled rooms around a quiet interior, and affable staff. There's free drinking water and a decent cafe upstairs serving breakfast and dinner. All things considered, it's the best place to stay.

El Sitio Hotel HOTEL $$

(☎7755-3656; elsitiohotel@gmail.com; 9a Calle 0-41, Zona 5; s/d/tr Q175/300/400; P📶) From the outside, this business-class hotel two blocks north of the bus terminal could almost be a modern evangelical church. Though rather sterile with a cavernous lobby, rooms are modern and well maintained and have a bit of local-style decor.

Restaurant El Chalet STEAK $$

(☎7755-0618; 1a Calle 2-39, Zona 5; mains Q60-70; ⏲7am-9pm) The specialty here is grilled meats, served with homemade salsa. You could make a light meal of the tortilla-sized portions. Dining is beneath an arbor flanked by a strip of garden. It's part of a posh hotel/conference center a few blocks east of the big clock tower.

Getting There & Away

El Quiché is the jumping-off point for the remote reaches of northern Quiché department, which extends all the way to the Mexican border. The main **bus station**, a dusty lot in Zona 5, is four blocks south and two blocks east of the plaza. Microbuses for Chichicastenango depart from the corner of 5a Calle and 2 Av.

BUSES FROM SANTA CRUZ DEL QUICHÉ

DESTINATION	COST (Q)	DURATION (HR)	FREQUENCY (DAILY)
Chichicastenango	10	40min	Frequent
Guatemala City	35	3	Every 10 minutes 3am-5pm
Huehuetenango	25	2	Half-hourly 5am-6pm
Nebaj	20	2	Half-hourly 6am-7pm
Quetzaltenango	25	3	Hourly 5am-6pm
Uspantán	30	2-2½	Frequent 5:30am-7pm

Nebaj

POP 106,200 / ELEV 2000M

Hidden in a remote fold of the Cuchumatanes mountains north of Sacapulas is the Triángulo Ixil (Ixil Triangle), a 2300-sq-km zone comprising the towns of Santa María Nebaj, San Juan Cotzal and San Gaspar Chajul, as well as dozens of outlying villages and hamlets. The local Ixil Maya people, though they suffered perhaps more than anybody in Guatemala's civil war, cling proudly to their traditions and speak the Ixil language. Nebaj women are celebrated for their beautiful purple, green and yellow pom-pommed hair braids, scarlet *cortes,* and their *huipiles* and *rebozos* (shawls) featuring bird and animal motifs. Nebaj is a good base for hiking – the three-day hike to Todos Santos is particularly lovely. While you're in town, visit the unexpectedly good museum dedicated to the region's history.

Sights & Tours

Centro Cultural Kumool MUSEUM

(5a Av 1-32; Q20; 9am-noon & 1-6pm Mon-Fri, 8am-1pm Sat) This small museum is something of an unexpected gem for a town of Nebaj's size. It displays a collection of mostly ceramic objects excavated in the Ixil region, all arranged by historical period. Among the more interesting pieces are a ceremonial ax with a skull handle and a giant funerary urn with a jaguar face, plus some well-preserved polychrome vases. If you're a Spanish-reader, the small library of books on local history and culture is excellent.

Iglesia de Nebaj CHURCH

(Parque Principal) This formidable church dominates the south side of Parque Principal. Inside, to the left of the entrance, is a memorial to Juan José Gerardi, who as bishop of Quiché witnessed human rights abuses here. Soon after he released a report about these atrocities, Gerardi himself was assassinated. Several hundred simple wooden crosses around the monument memorialize the Nebaj inhabitants who were murdered during the civil war and since. Outside, a bright mural celebrates Ixil culture.

Guías Ixiles HIKING

(5847-4747; www.nebaj.com; 3a Calle, El Descanso Bldg, Zona 1; 8am-12:30pm & 2-5pm) Guías Ixiles offers half-day walks to Las Cascadas (Q55 for one person plus Q25 for each extra person), a series of waterfalls north of town, or around town with visits to the sacred sites of the *costumbristas* (people who still practice non-Christian Maya rites). Guías Ixiles also leads three-day treks over the Cuchumatanes to Todos Santos Cuchumatán. Some Spanish is required.

Sleeping & Eating

Hotel Turansa HOTEL $

(4887-8584; cnr 5a Calle & 6a Av; s/d from Q85/150; P) This friendly, central establishment – just a block from the Parque Principal – has decent-sized rooms with big comfy beds and flat-screen TVs along plant-draped balconies. Top-floor triples open onto a sunny terrace; lower rooms get noise from the courtyard parking area.

Hotel Santa María HOTEL $$

(4212-7927; www.hotelsantamarianebaj.com; cnr 4a Av & 2a Calle; s/d Q150/250; P) Scarlet woven bedspreads, carved-wood headboards and other Ixil handicrafts decorate the bright, spotless rooms at this well-maintained property three blocks northwest of the main plaza. There's a restaurant (breakfast not included) and – on the off chance you get sick in Nebaj – a clinic shares the same entrance with the hotel.

Hotel Villa Nebaj HOTEL $$

(7756-0005; www.hotelvillanebaj.com; Calz 15 de Septiembre 2-37; s/d/tr Q150/250/350; P) Behind the elaborate facade is a neat, modern hotel with fountains in the courtyard and elaborate paintings of *nebajenses* in fiesta wear. Rooms on three levels have a dash of style, with colorful bedspreads, carved headboards and piping-hot showers. Rooms at the front get a lot of street noise, so ask for one in the rear annex.

Comedor El Si'm GUATEMALAN $

(3a Av; breakfast Q30; 7am-9pm) This place off the main plaza is great for a gut-stuffing *desayuno* (breakfast), served with a bonus bowl of *mosh* (warm cereal) and freshly baked cookie, and it refills your coffee cup. It's usually crammed with local characters by 8am.

El Descanso INTERNATIONAL $

(5847-4747; www.nebaj.com; 3a Calle, Zona 1; mains Q25-35; 6:30am-9:30pm;) This cozy restaurant features a bar and lounge areas in Nebaj's most alternative ambience. A range of sandwiches, salads, pastas and soups is served, as well as Western and Guatemalan breakfasts. Popular with foreign volunteers.

Information

There is a **5B ATM** in the town hall building, opposite the park.

Banrural (8am-4:30pm Mon-Fri, 7-11am Sat) In a little shopping center underneath the Parque Principal; changes dollars and euros.

Getting There & Away

The bus terminal is just below the market. Microbuses bound for Santa Cruz del Quiché, via Sacapulas, go every half-hour from 4am until 5pm (Q20, two hours), departing from behind the church at the corner of 5a Av and 7a Calle. To head west to Huehuetenango or east to Uspantán and Cobán, change at Sacapulas.

Microbuses to Chajul (Q15, 45 minutes) depart every 20 minutes or so until 6pm from in front of the Hotel Villa Nebaj, on Calz 15 de Septiembre.

The main bus terminal, behind the market, mainly serves outlying villages such as Tzalbal, Vicalama and Palop; one bus travels all the way to Guatemala City (Q50, 5½ hours) via Chichicastenango, departing around 2am.

Uspantán

POP 83,400

Uspantán, a town halfway between Huehuetenango and Cobán along the 7W road, is set amid sky-high scenery. The town itself is quiet and charming, if short of actual attractions, but the setting is stunning, in a fertile valley at the base of green forested mountains over which a bank of clouds rolls in each afternoon. Women wear lacy, loose-fitting *huipiles* in bright orange or pink.

Founded by the Uspanteko Maya around the 6th century AD, it was originally dubbed Tz'unun Kaab' – place of hummingbirds. The severe repression it experienced during the armed conflict of the 1980s forged indigenous leader Rigoberta Menchú, who grew up a five-hour walk through the mountains in the village of Laj Chimel. Cardamom is grown here, and pigs and sheep are raised on the surrounding slopes.

As ever, life centers on the central plaza; the covered market streets around its edge are worth exploring.

Sleeping & Eating

Hotel Don Gabriel HOTEL $

(7951-8540; hoteldongabriel@yahoo.es; 7a Av 6-22; s/d Q90/160; P) Rooms at this excellent-value lodging, just around the corner from the Parque Central, have plenty of thick blankets for the evening chill. If possible, choose a room on the top level opening onto a Gaudí-esque terrace with various plant-laden gazebos and fabulous views of the mountains. Downstairs is a neat and clean little restaurant serving breakfast from 7am.

Restaurante Mexicana MEXICAN $

(breakfast from Q20, mains Q25-50; 7am-9:30pm) Half a block down from the church end of the main plaza, this well-signed restaurant has just one smallish room but a large menu and generous serves of Mexican and Guatemalan dishes. Breakfasts are hearty, as are the burritos, quesadillas and plates of grilled meats. With luck, you'll end up with control of the TV remote to turn the blast down.

Getting There & Away

Microbuses for Quiché (Q30, 2½ hours), via Sacapulas, leave whenever full from Uspantán's **bus terminal** on 6a Calle, three blocks west of the Parque Central, until 7pm. For Cobán (Q35, three hours), microbuses go hourly from 4am to 3:30pm; a 35km stretch of that journey is over a frequently poor road surface. For Nebaj, there are a couple of direct microbuses (coming from Cobán), though it's easier to get a microbus to Sacapulas where you'll find frequent connections up to the Ixil Triangle.

Quetzaltenango

POP 166,700 / ELEV 2367M

Quetzaltenango is Guatemala's second city. It has a great atmosphere – not too big, not too small, enough foreigners to support a good range of hotels and restaurants, but not so many that it loses its national flavor. The Guatemalan 'layering' effect is at work in the city center – once the Spanish moved out, Germans moved in and their architecture gives the zone a somber, even Gothic, feel.

The city's name might be a mouthful, but locals kindly shorten it to Xela (*shell*-ah), an abbreviation of the original K'iche' Maya name, Xelajú.

Xela is popular with travelers with time to settle in to a place and work on their Spanish. It also functions as a base for a range of spectacular hikes through the surrounding countryside – the ascent to the summit of Volcán Tajumulco (Central America's highest point) and the three-day trek to Lago de Atitlán, to name a couple.

History

Quetzaltenango came under the sway of the K'iche' Maya of K'umarcaaj when they began their great expansion in the 14th century. Before that it had been a Mam Maya town. It was near here that the K'iche' leader Tecún Umán was defeated and killed by the Spanish conquistador Pedro de Alvarado in 1524.

The town prospered in the late-19th-century coffee boom, with brokers opening warehouses and mostly German *finca* (plantation) owners coming to town to buy supplies. Wealthy Quetzaltenango briefly declared independence in 1896, during one of the country's periodic dictatorships. Its boom busted when a combined earthquake and eruption of Santa María in 1902 wreaked mass destruction. Still, the city's position at the intersection of roads to the Pacific Slope, Mexico and Guatemala City guaranteed it some degree of prosperity. Today it's again busy with commerce, of the indigenous, foreign and *ladino* (a person of mixed indigenous and European parentage) varieties.

Sights

Parque Centro América PLAZA

(Map p162) Most of Xela's sights crowd in and around the broad central plaza. It's a great place for a stroll or to sit and people-watch. It was originally two separate parks, designed by Italian architect Alberto Porta in the 19th century; these were combined in a 1930s update into its current oblong shape. The most notable of the monuments scattered along its expanse is a rotunda of Ionic columns dedicated to the composer Rafael Álvarez Ovalle.

Cemetery CEMETERY

(Map p158; Parque El Calvario, Zona 1; ⌚6am-5:30pm) Quetzaltenango's enormous cemetery is a pleasant and fascinating green space for a walk. To the left of the main entrance, visit the grave of the gypsy Vanushka, spurned and shamed by her wealthy lover until she died of a broken heart. Flowers are still left at her grave by those seeking better fortune in affairs of the heart. We recommend only visiting Friday to Sunday during the day, when there are many people around.

Cerro el Baúl VIEWPOINT

(Map p158) This wooded hill is a popular weekend destination for city dwellers, for its wonderful views across Xela's broad plain and to the volcanos that fringe it. There's a small cafe, some surprisingly fast and scary kids' slides and a giant obelisk with great Maya warrior Tecún Umán carved in relief – legend claims he is buried on this spot.

Centro Intercultural de Quetzaltenango CULTURAL CENTER

(Map p158; 4a Calle & 19a Av, Zona 3) FREE Quetzaltenango's railroad station, 1km east of the Templo de Minerva along 4a Calle, lay dormant for many years until the city converted it into this center, which now houses schools of art and dance, plus three interesting museums.

Museo de Arte MUSEUM

(Map p158; 4a Calle & 19a Av, Zona 3; donation requested; ⌚9am-1pm & 3-7pm) An interesting if chaotic collection of some 400 paintings by Guatemala's leading modernists is exhibited here, including works by Efraín Recinos, Jorge Mazariegos and the landscape artist José Luis Álvarez. Most prominently displayed are the fantastic canvases of Rodrigo Díaz, who also happens to be the curator.

Museo Ixkik' MUSEUM

(Map p158; ☎5653-5585; 4a Calle & 19a Av, Zona 3; donation requested Q35; ⌚9am-5pm Mon-Fri) This museum is devoted to Maya weaving, with traditional outfits arranged by region. Director Raquel García is an expert on the symbols and meanings of indigenous clothing and provides interesting commentary.

Activities & Tours

There are many exciting walks and climbs to be done from Xela. **Volcán Tajumulco** (4220m), 50km northwest, is the highest point in Central America, and is a challenging one-day trek from the city or two days with a night camping on the mountain. This includes about five hours of walking up from the starting point, Tuhichan (2½ hours by bus from Xela).

With early starts, **Volcán Santa María** (3772m), towering to the south of the city, and the highly active **Santiaguito** (2488m), on Santa María's southwest flank, can both be done in long mornings from Xela, though their tough, slippery trails are recommended only for seasoned hikers. You start walking to both at the village of Llanos del Pinal, 5km south of Xela (Q5 by bus), from where it's four to five hours up to the summit of Santa María. Getting too close to Santiaguito is dangerous, so people usually just look at it from a point about 1½ hours' walk from Llanos del Pinal. Popular non-volcano hikes include the three-day walk from Xela to Lago de Atitlán, and the six-day hike from Nebaj to Todos Santos Cuchumatán.

★**Monte Verde Tours** TOURS

(Map p162; ☎5729-6279; www.monte-verdetours.com; 13a Av 8-34, Zona 1) Highly recommended local trekking and cultural tourism outfit, with knowledgeable and friendly guides. Itineraries close to Xela include tours to Zunil and Fuentes Georginas, day hikes up Santa María and overnight treks on Tajumulco. It also ranges south to Takalik Abaj and its nearby coffee and rubber plantations.

EntreMundos VOLUNTEERING

(Map p162; ☎7761-2179; www.entremundos.org; 6a Calle 7-31, Zona 1; ⊙2-4pm Mon-Thu) EntreMundos is a trusted solidarity organisation that works with NGOs and community groups, offering skill-building workshops to local NGO workers. Its website has details of 100 projects all over Guatemala looking for volunteers, and its free bilingual bimonthly magazine features articles about social development and human rights issues, as well as local volunteer opportunities. Entre Mundos asks a consultation fee of Q25 for drop-in volunteers wanting to be placed.

Guate Guides ADVENTURE

(Map p162; ☎5195-7734; www.guateguides.com; 6a Calle 15-16, Zona 1) This small, locally run outfit offers tours to area volcanoes, villages and nature reserves, with an emphasis on quality equipment and knowledgeable commentary. Among the excursions are half-day cycling trips to San Andrés Xequl via the Samalá river valley, climbs up Santa María and Tacaná volcanoes, and photography tours to the quetzal reserve near San Marcos.

Yoga House YOGA

(Map p162; www.yogahousexela.wordpress.com; 9a Av 6-68, Zona 1; per class/week Q20/50) The best place to practice yoga in Quetzaltenango. There are daily hatha yoga classes aimed at either beginner or intermediate levels, as well as Ashtanga yoga. On Saturdays there are free fitness training sessions where you 'only pay in sweat and tears.'

Adrenalina Tours TOURS

(Map p162; ☎7761-4509; www.adrenalinatours.com; 13a Av & 4a Calle, Pasaje Enríquez, Zona 1) Provides a range of trips in the Xela area, including to Laguna de Chicabal, Fuentes Georginas and El Aprisco nature reserve, plus weeklong itineraries focused on Maya cosmology and Guatemala's natural attractions.

Quetzaltrekkers ADVENTURE

(Map p158; ☎7765-5895; www.quetzaltrekkers.com; Diagonal 12 8-37, Zona 1) Most of the guides at this outfit are foreign volunteers (experienced trekkers can join their ranks). It offers one-day hikes to Fuentes Georginas and Santa María volcano, three-day trips to Lago de Atitlán and six-day treks from Nebaj to Todos Santos Cuchumatán run on a weekly basis; check the calendar to see when they go. Based at the rear of the Casa Argentina hotel.

Courses

Quetzaltenango's many language schools attract students from around the world, and the city makes for a different, possibly more studious, scene than heavily touristed Antigua.

Standard weekly prices start at Q900/1000 for four/five hours of instruction per day, Monday to Friday. Add around Q350 to Q450 for room and board with a local family. Some places charge up to 20% more for tuition in the June to August high season, and many require nonrefundable registration fees. Extras range from movies, dance and cooking classes to talks on Guatemalan politics and culture.

The women's cooperative **Trama Textiles** (Map p162; www.tramatextiles.org; 3a Calle 10-56, Zona 1) offers backstrap weaving classes. Options range from a simple demonstration of techniques (Q40) to a 20-hour course in which students produce an embroidered table runner (Q675).

★**Proyecto Lingüístico Quetzalteco de Español** LANGUAGE

(Map p158; ☎7763-1061; www.plqe.org; 5a Calle 2-40, Zona 1) This collectively managed and politically minded language institute also runs the **Escuela de la Montaña**, a limited-enrolment language-learning program in a rural zone near the town of Colomba. Intensive courses in K'iche' are also offered, along with classes on Latin American history and literature.

Centro de Estudios de Español Pop Wuj LANGUAGE

(Map p158; ☎7761-8286; www.pop-wuj.org; 1a Calle 17-72, Zona 1) As well as running Spanish

Quetzaltenango

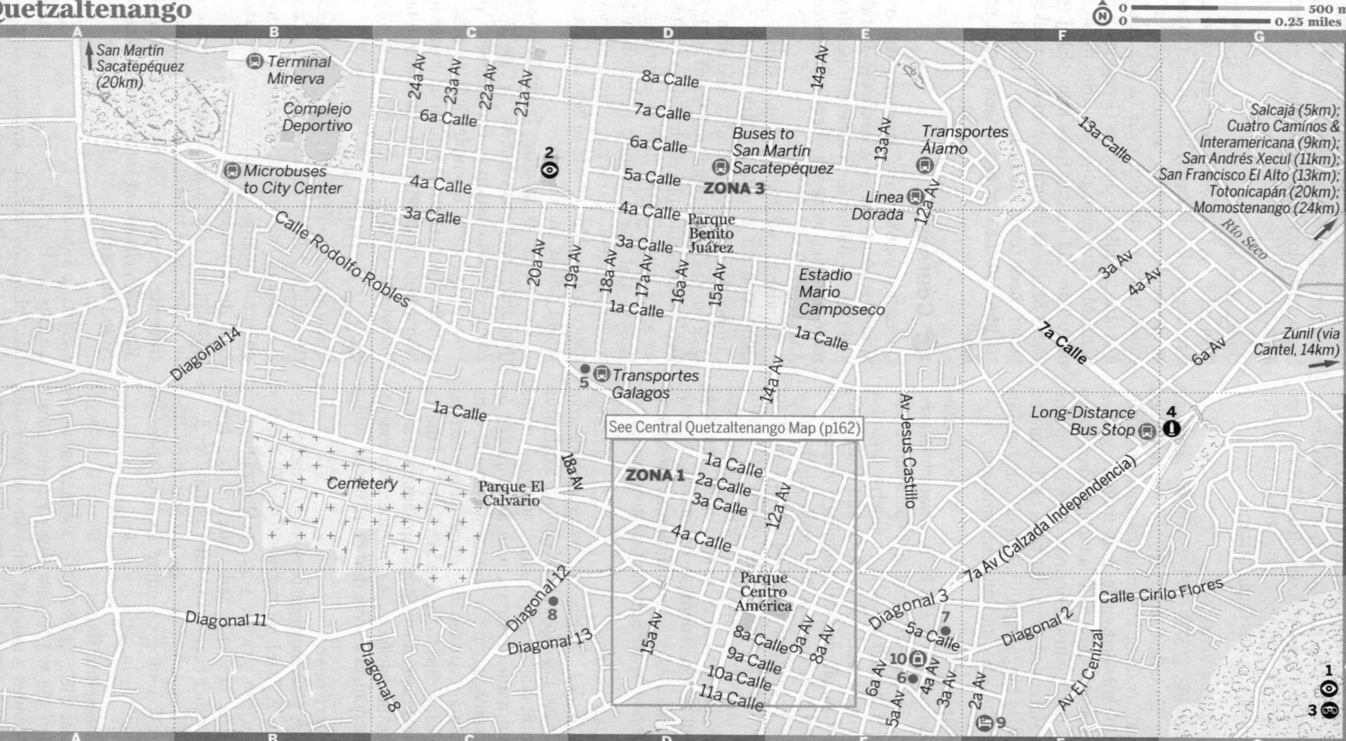

500 m
0.25 miles
San Martín Sacatepéquez (20km)
Terminal Minerva
Complejo Deportivo
Microbuses to City Center
24a Av
23a Av
22a Av
21a Av
8a Calle
7a Calle
6a Calle
6a Calle
5a Calle
4a Calle
4a Calle
3a Calle
3a Calle
1a Calle
Buses to San Martín Sacatepéquez
ZONA 3
Parque Benito Juárez
14a Av
13a Av
12a Av
Transportes Álamo
Linea Dorada
13a Calle
Salcajá (5km); Cuatro Caminos & Interamericana (9km); San Andrés Xecul (11km); San Francisco El Alto (13km); Totonicapán (20km); Momostenango (24km)
Río Seco
Calle Rodolfo Robles
20a Av
19a Av
18a Av
17a Av
16a Av
15a Av
Estadio Mario Camposeco
1a Calle
3a Av
4a Av
7a Calle
6a Av
Zunil (via Cantel, 14km)
Diagonal 14
Transportes Galagos
14a Av
Av Jesus Castillo
Long-Distance Bus Stop
1a Calle
See Central Quetzaltenango Map (p162)
Cemetery
Parque El Calvario
18a Av
ZONA 1
1a Calle
2a Calle
3a Calle
12a Av
4a Calle
7a Av (Calzada Independencia)
Parque Centro América
Calle Cirilo Flores
Diagonal 11
Diagonal 12
Diagonal 13
Diagonal 8
15a Av
8a Calle
9a Calle
10a Calle
11a Calle
9a Av
8a Av
Diagonal 3
5a Calle
Diagonal 2
6a Av
5a Av
4a Av
3a Av
2a Av
Av El Cenizal

Quetzaltenango

Sights

1 Cemetery G4
2 Centro Intercultural de Quetzaltenango C1
3 Cerro el Baúl G4
4 Monumento a la Marimba G3
Museo de Arte .... (see 2)
Museo Ixkik' .... (see 2)

Activities, Courses & Tours

5 Centro de Estudios de Español Pop Wuj D2
6 El Quetzal Spanish School E4
7 Proyecto Lingüístico Quetzalteco de Español E4
8 Quetzaltrekkers C4

Sleeping

9 Casa San Bartolomé F4

Shopping

10 Pixan E4

classes, Pop Wuj's profits go to rural development projects in nearby K'iche' villages, in which students can participate.

Inepas LANGUAGE
(Instituto de Español y Participación en Ayuda Social; Map p162; ☎7765-1308; www.inepas.org; 15a Av 4-59) Guatemalan social issues are woven into the Spanish lessons at this Unesco-recognized NGO that promotes educational development in rural communities, and students can participate in a variety of worthy projects. The institute offers a selection of inexpensive accommodations as well as homestays.

El Quetzal Spanish School LANGUAGE
(Map p158; ☎7761-2784; www.elquetzalspanish.com; 7a Calle 4-24, Zona 1) One of the few indigenous-owned and -run Spanish schools in town, offering plenty of activities.

Festivals

Feria de la Virgen del Rosario CULTURAL
(Feria Centroamericana de Independencia; Sep/Oct) Held in late September or early October, this is Xela's big annual party. Students create colorful 'flower' carpets of sawdust upon the streets of the city, taxi drivers shoot fireworks and the sirens of the fire trucks wail. Residents kick up their heels at a fairground on the city's perimeter and there's plenty of entertainment across town, including a battle of the brass bands in the Parque Centro América. An international Spanish-language literary competition, hosted by the city, runs simultaneously.

Sleeping

With a continual influx of foreign volunteers and language students, Xela counts numerous long-stay options. Some guesthouses offer furnished apartments and most language institutes can set up homestays with local families. Local rentals are listed in the classified section of the publication *XelaWho*.

★ **Kasa Kiwi** HOSTEL $
(Map p162; ☎7765-4251; www.kasakiwi.com; 9a Av 8-38, Zona 1; dm Q50, r with/without bathroom Q170/120; Wi-Fi) Kasa Kiwi has quickly established itself as a top player on Xela's hostel scene. Generously sized dorms mean that everyone gets a bed not a bunk, and there are also a handful of private rooms, a kitchen and helpful staff. The relaxed roof terrace-bar clinches the deal, with rare views across the town to the mountains.

Casa Seibel HOSTEL $
(Map p162; ☎7765-2130; www.casaseibel.com; 9a Av 8-10, Zona 1; dm/r Q50/120; Wi-Fi) Incorporated into a late-19th-century Xela house, Casa Seibel is cozy and comfortable. Set around two plant-filled courtyards, its dorms and private rooms (sharing two bathrooms, one with a tub) have attractive wood floors and painted ceilings and retain some original furniture and character; plenty of shelves and closet space.

Guests can mingle in the shared kitchen and TV lounge, or tinkle the ivories of the old piano.

Casa Nativos HOSTEL $
(Map p162; ☎7765-4723; www.casanativos.com; Pasaje Enríquez, 13a Av, Zona 1; dm Q40, d without bathroom Q125; Wi-Fi) One component of a cultural center occupying the rear of the Pasaje Enríquez, this Euro–Guate-run hostel contains basic but stylishly renovated rooms that accent the vintage beauty of the building; some feature balconies. There's a two-room apartment for long-term stays, including use of a shared kitchen.

Hotel Kiktem-Ja HOTEL $
(Map p162; ☎7761-4304; www.hotelkiktem-ja.com; 13a Av 7-18, Zona 1; s/d/tr Q135/200/270; P) Set in an atmospheric 100-year-old house downtown, the Kiktem-Ja is all squeaky floorboards at weird angles, stone arches and squiggly wood columns along foliage-draped

corridors. Rooms are spacious with sturdy bedsteads, cozy fireplaces, arched windows and pretty tiled bathrooms. Breakfast is not available.

Posada Catedral Hotel GUESTHOUSE **$$**

(Map p162; ☎7765-2472; www.hotelposadacatedral.com; 9a Av 6-47, Zona 1; s/d incl breakfast Q300/400) A cozy guesthouse centered on the obligatory courtyard, with clean white rooms and dark-wood colonial-style furniture. The rooms on the upper level are slightly brighter and lovelier with skyline views, but it's a welcoming place across the board. There's a small bar-restaurant tucked into the courtyard corner.

Hostal Casa Doña Mercedes BOUTIQUE HOTEL **$$**

(Map p162; ☎7765-4687; 6a Calle 13-42, Zona 1; s/d Q190/300, without bathroom Q100/180;) Two blocks west of Parque Centro América is this good-value, quiet establishment. Neat rooms have a bit of colonial flair with burnished wood floors and wicker bedsteads, and there's plenty of space to lounge around. Well-equipped guest kitchen.

Casa San Bartolomé B&B **$$**

(Map p158; ☎7761-9511; www.casasanbartolome.com; 2a Av 7-17, Zona 1; s/d/tr Q175/225/336; P) In the family for generations, this atmospheric old residence has been converted into a cozy B&B. All six rooms have beautiful furniture and modern art. Guests may prepare meals in a shared kitchen and take tea on the lovely and leafy upper terrace. Located in a quiet neighborhood a 15-minute walk east of the park.

★**Casa Morasan** BOUTIQUE HOTEL **$$$**

(Map p162; ☎7765-0616; www.casamorasan.com; 12a Av 8-21, Zona 1; d/tr/ste from Q500/650/700) It's difficult not to be charmed by Casa Morasan. Set in a restored town house, rooms cluster around a courtyard with trickling fountain, and lots of old wooden features and tile work offset by gleaming whitewash. Rooms are a comfortable mix of traditional and contemporary design, with crisp linens and modern bathrooms. If you fancy some self-catering, the suite has a small kitchen.

Eating

Quetzaltenango has an excellent selection of places to eat in all price ranges. Cheapest are the food stalls on the lower level of the central market, where snacks and main-course plates are sold for Q10 or less. Most restaurants are just a few minutes' walk from Parque Centro América.

★**Aj de Lunas** GUATEMALAN **$**

(Map p162; ☎7761-0097; 9a Calle 11-16, Zona 1; lunch combos Q25; 8am-9pm Mon-Sat;) This simple but cheerful dining hall is a good place to savor Xela home cooking, with daily specials like *jocón* (stew with tomatillo and cilantro) and *caldo de patas* (cow foot soup) served with a pile of tortillas and little dishes of lemons and tiny chilies. Vegetarian options are available.

★**Esquina Asiatica** ASIAN **$**

(Map p162; ☎7763-0316; 9a Av 6-79, Zona 1; starters Q15-30, mains Q25-40; 8am-9pm Mon-Sat, 8am-1pm Sun) This charming upstairs restaurant refreshes palates with generous plates from around Asia – Chinese dumplings, Indonesia satay, pad thai, Vietnamese spring rolls and more – against a backdrop of vintage travel posters. Early risers will enjoy delicious non-Asian breakfasts including Parmesan avocado on toast and ultra-filling fruity yogurt parfait with chia. There are regular buffet events and live music. Alcohol is served.

La Red Kat GUATEMALAN **$**

(Map p162; www.cafered.org; 8a Av 5-19, Zona 1; weekly specials Q50; 11am-5pm Mon, 10am-10pm Tue-Sat;) An alternative cultural center focusing on the economic reintegration of returning migrants, La Red Kat also provides grants for young chefs in training, which translates into gourmet meals at popular prices. Locally grown greens go into salads, soups and burritos, and there are nightly specials. Meals are served in a pretty patio and the various salons around it.

Café Canela GUATEMALAN **$**

(Map p162; ☎7761-6654; 6a Calle 15-16, Zona 1; lunch menus Q20; 7am-3pm Mon-Fri;) For breakfast and lunch on weekdays, *la nicaragüense* owner has a simple setup with a sunny patio and alternative vibe. You'll find creative variations on the essential *menú del día* (Q20), nicely dressed salads and tasty soups. There are three set lunch choices daily including a vegan option. Wash it down with a fresh juice (Q12).

Xelapan BAKERY **$**

(Map p162; 12 Av 5-44, Zona 1; breakfast Q24-26; 6am-8pm) This centrally located branch of the city-wide bakery chain is worth stopping into just to admire the fancy pastries on display, or to grab a bag of fresh cookies to go. The little cafe at the rear, often packed with Guatemalan families, serves fine breakfasts, notably the 'Sheca Cabezona,' with scrambled eggs stuffed into Xela's signature pastry.

Café Nativos CAFE $

(Map p162; ☎7765-4723; 13a Ave, Zona 1; breakfast Q25-30; ⏰10am-10pm) Part of a hostel/arts center in the Pasaje Enríquez, Café Nativos is an inviting place with good natural fare, espresso, French toast for breakfast, falafel and tofu in *mole*. A terrific balcony terrace, with counter along the edge, looks right at the deco wonder of the ex-Gutierrez bank building.

Panque Waffles INTERNATIONAL $

(Map p162; 6a Calle 10-25, Zona 1; waffles/burgers from Q25/38; ⏰9am-9pm; 📶) A good recipe for any restaurant is to do one or two things, and do them well. Panque Waffles nails it with, um, waffles, as well as brilliant burgers. Throw in some coffee and juices, decent wi-fi and some urban shabby chic, and you can see why it's so popular with Xela hipsters tapping away on their MacBooks.

Tacorazon MEXICAN $

(Map p162; 12a Av, Zona 1; burritos Q25; ⏰noon-10pm Mon-Sat, noon-5pm Sun) Burrito lovers need go no further than Tacorazon to fill their boots. Conveniently tucked into a corner across from the main park, this bright place does deliciously stuffed burritos made to order in increasingly monstrous sizes. A plate of fries with guacamole makes the perfect side, and if you're not going for takeout, the in-house mojitos aren't too bad either.

★**Sabor de la India** INDIAN $$

(Map p162; ☎7765-2555; 15a Av 3-64, Zona 1; mains Q50-70; ⏰noon-10pm Tue-Sun; 📶🖊) Authentic south Indian fare is whipped up here by a fellow from Kerala. Servings are huge; the *thalis* – platters of curried veggies, chicken or beef – are highly recommended, and the paneer (cheese) is almost as good as anything you'd find on the subcontinent itself. Perennially popular.

La Stampa Bistro INTERNATIONAL $$

(Map p162; 4a Calle, cnr of Parque Centro América, Zona 1; mains from Q45; ⏰8am-10pm Sun-Wed, 8am-11pm Thu-Sat) This cute bistro just off the central plaza is liberally decorated with printing paraphernalia – the owner's great-grandfather ran Xela's first printing workshop. The menu has a bit of everything – steaks, fresh pasta and salad dishes – and there's a good wine list. There's breakfast too, making it ideal for early starts as well as romantic dinners.

OFF THE BEATEN TRACK

AROUND XELA

The beautiful volcanic country around Xela offers up numerous exciting day trips. For many, the volcanoes themselves pose irresistible challenges. You can feast your eyes and soul on the yellow church at **San Andrés Xecul**, hike to the ceremonial shores of **Laguna Chicabal**, or soak in the idyllic hot springs at **Fuentes Georginas**. Or simply hop on a bus and explore the myriad small traditional villages that pepper this part of the highlands. Market days are great opportunities to observe locals in action, so Sunday and Wednesday in **Momostenango**, Monday in **Zunil**, Tuesday and Saturday in **Totonicapán** and Friday in **San Francisco El Alto** are good days to visit.

Drinking & Nightlife

Coffee and hot chocolate fuel much of Xela's day-to-day life, and there are plenty of places to grab a cup. Xela's Zona Viva revolves around the Teatro Municipal, with discos and clubs popping up along 1a and 2a Calles and up 14 Av.

★**Salón Tecún** PUB

(Map p162; Pasaje Enríquez, Zona 1; ⏰9:30am-12:30am) On the plaza end of the Pasaje Enríquez, alive day and night with a healthy mix of Guatemalans and foreigners quaffing Cabro by the liter, the Tecún claims to be the country's longest-running bar (since 1935). It also serves good pub food, and frequently has someone picking out songs on their guitar. An essential Xela experience.

★**Café La Luna** CAFE

(Map p162; ☎7761-4354; 8a Av 4-11, Zona 1; ⏰11am-9pm Mon-Fri, 4-9pm Sat; 📶) For chocolate aficionados, this is a shrine. Made from scratch on the premises, the chocolate is velvety smooth and served in a variety of beverages: the chocolate cappuccino is especially good. Groups of friends gather in the various salons, which are littered with vintage bric-a-brac.

Central Quetzaltenango

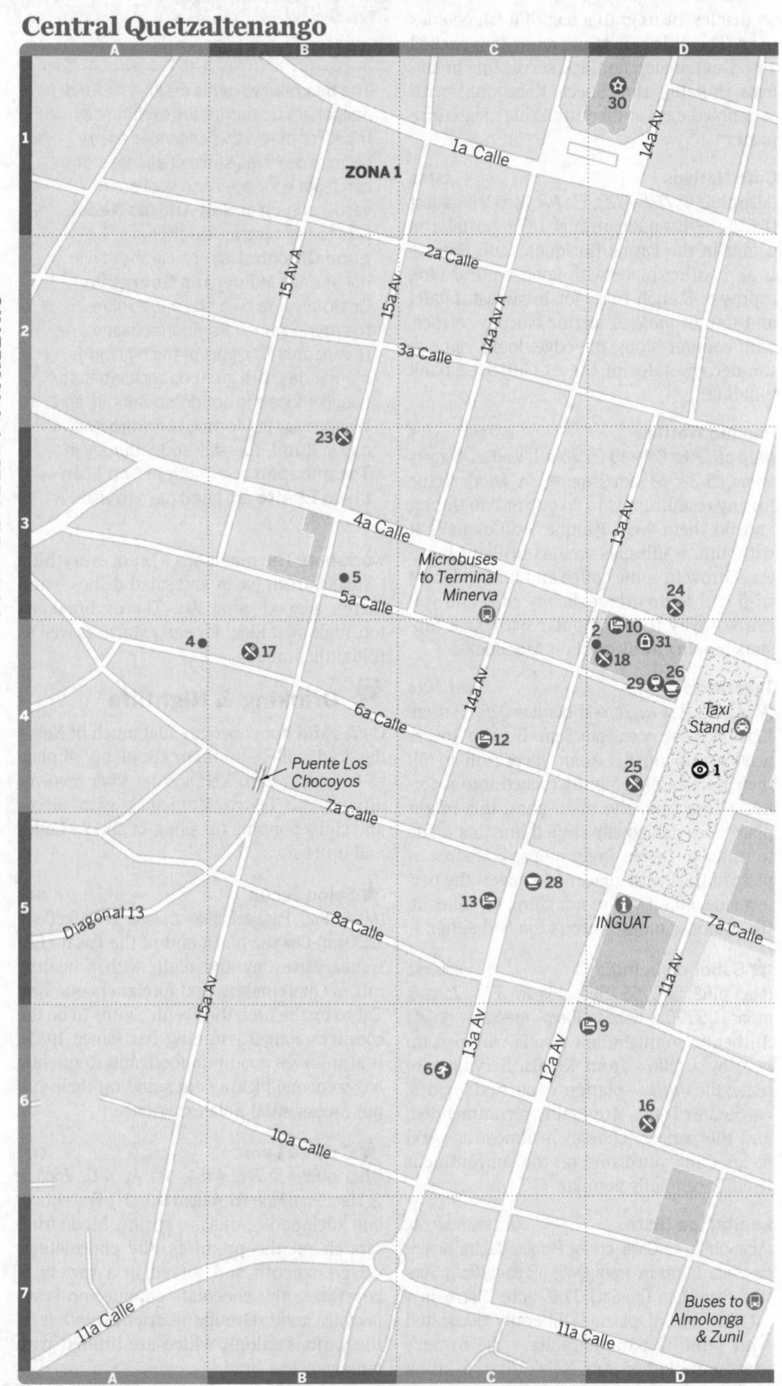

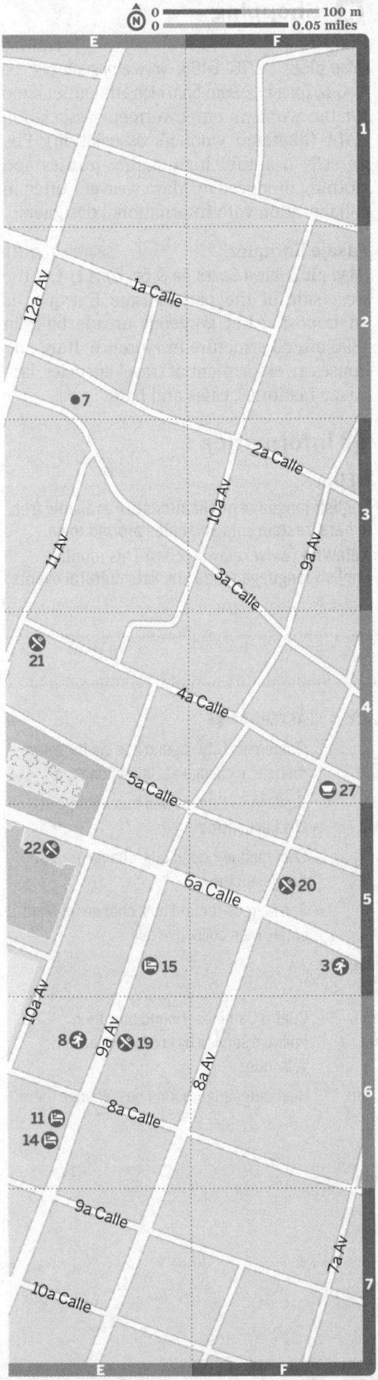

Central Quetzaltenango

Sights

1 Parque Centro América D4

Activities, Courses & Tours

2 Adrenalina Tours D4
3 EntreMundos F5
4 Guate Guides A4
5 Inepas B3
6 Monte Verde Tours C6
7 Trama Textiles E2
8 Yoga House E6

Sleeping

9 Casa Morasan D6
10 Casa Nativos D4
11 Casa Seibel E6
12 Hostal Casa Doña Mercedes C4
13 Hotel Kiktem-Ja C5
14 Kasa Kiwi E6
15 Posada Catedral Hotel E5

Eating

16 Aj de Lunas D6
17 Café Canela B4
18 Café Nativos D4
19 Esquina Asiatica E6
20 La Red Kat F5
21 La Stampa Bistro E4
22 Panque Waffles E5
23 Sabor de la India B3
24 Tacorazon D3
25 Xelapan D4

Drinking & Nightlife

26 Café El Balcón del Enríquez D4
27 Café La Luna F4
28 El Cuartito C5
29 Salón Tecún D4

Entertainment

30 Teatro Municipal D1

Shopping

31 Pasaje Enríquez D4

El Cuartito CAFE

(Map p162; 13a Av 7-09, Zona 1; 10am-11pm;) This offbeat cafe-bar is a point of reference for travelers and language students, with quirky decor and art installations. It serves a good range of breakfasts, vegetarian snacks, herbal teas and organic coffee just about any way you want it, plus some creative cocktails – how about a raspberry mojito? There's regular live music.

Café El Balcón del Enríquez CAFE

(Map p162; 12a Av 4-40, Pasaje Enríquez; 8am-10pm) With specially designed viewing counters overlooking the Parque Centro América, this lively cafe-bar on the upper level of the Pasaje Enríquez makes a nice perch for morning espresso or evening cocktails; great terrace views.

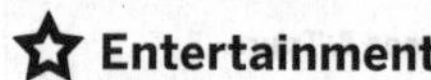

Entertainment

Parque Centro América is a popular place for an evening stroll. The music scene is particularly strong in Xela. Many of the town's restaurants, cafes and bars double as performance venues between Wednesday and Saturday – to see what's on, pick up a copy of *XelaWho*.

Teatro Municipal THEATER
(Map p162; ☎7761-2218; www.teatromunicipalquetzaltenango.org; 14a Av & 1a Calle, Zona 1) Quetzaltenango's grand neoclassical theater north of the center is the main venue for plays, concerts and dance performances. An elaborate two-tiered curved wooden balcony has private boxes for prominent families. During the day, it's sometimes possible to pop in to admire the interior, which dates from 1895.

Shopping

Pixan CLOTHING
(Map p158; ☎7761-6408; www.amaguate.org; 5a Av 6-17, Zona 1; ⏰9am-5pm Mon-Fri) Outlet shop for the women's empowerment association AMA (highland women's association), Pixan sells beautiful high-quality textiles and clothing produced by Maya weavers, often in collaboration with international designers.

Pasaje Enríquez SHOPPING CENTER
(Map p162; btwn Calles 4a & 5a, Zona 1) On the west side of the park, Pasaje Enríquez is an imposing but gorgeous arcade built in 1896 after a structure in Florence, Italy, and houses an assortment of travel agencies, language institutes, cafes and bars.

Information

MEDIA

English-language publications are available free in bars, restaurants and cafes around town.

XelaWho (www.xelawho.com) This monthly English-language magazine lists cultural events,

BUSES FROM QUETZALTENANGO

DESTINATION	COST (Q)	DURATION (HR)	FREQUENCY	ALTERNATIVE
Antigua				Guatemala City–bound bus via the Interamericana; change at Chimaltenango
Chichicastenango	25	2	Half-hourly, 8am-5pm	Guatemala City–bound bus; change at Los Encuentros
Ciudad Tecún Umán (Mexican border)	40	3	Hourly	Coatepeque-bound bus; change for Ciudad Tecún Umán
El Carmen/Talismán (Mexican border)				San Marcos–bound bus; change for Malacatán, then collective taxi
Guatemala City	40	3½	Every 15min, 2am-5pm	
Huehuetenango	25	2	Every 15min, 4am-6pm	Cuatro Caminos–bound bus; then Pullman service by Los Halcones and Velasquez
La Mesilla (Mexican border)	40	4	4 buses, 7am-2:15pm	Huehuetenango-bound bus; change there
Panajachel	30	2	Hourly, 9am-7pm	
Retalhuleu	15	1	Every 10min, 5am-7pm	
San Andrés Xequl	10	30min	Half-houly, 6am-3pm	
San Pedro La Laguna	35	3hr	Hourly, 10:30am-5pm	

has a handy map and offers an irreverent take on life in Xela and Guatemala as a whole.

EntreMundos (p157) Publishes a bimonthly magazine, which has plenty of information on political developments and volunteer projects in the region.

MEDICAL SERVICES

Rainy season brings regular floods to Xela, and with it lots of diarrheal sicknesses – it's very easy to succumb, so pay extra attention to hygiene and hand-washing.

Clínico La Fe (☎7794 3232; www.facebook.com/LaboratorioClinicoLAFE; 12a Av C-12, Zona 1) Trusted private clinic offering the full battery of laboratory tests for diagnoses. Offers free home visits.

Hospital Privado Quetzaltenango (☎7774-4700; www.hospitalprivadoquetzaltenango.com; Calle Rodolfo Robles 23-51, Zona 1; ⊙24hr) For 24-hour emergency and ambulance service. Usually has an English-speaking doctor on staff. Recommended but can be expensive, so check you have appropriate medical insurance.

Hospital San Rafael (☎7761-4381; 9a Calle 10-41, Zona 1; ⊙24hr) Foreign insurance policies accepted.

MONEY

There are numerous ATMs at the banks around Parque Centro América.

Banco Industrial (4a Calle 11-38, Zona 1; ⊙9am-6pm Mon-Fri, 9am-1pm Sat) Also changes US dollars.

TOURIST INFORMATION

There's a plethora of tourist maps circulating, of which *Xelamap* is the best. Look for it at language schools and hotels.

INGUAT (Map p162; ☎7761-4931; www.vivexela.visitguatemala.com; 7a Calle 11-35, Zona 1; ⊙9am-5pm Mon-Fri, 9am-1pm Sat) Usually staffed by an English speaker; at the southern end of Parque Centro América.

ℹ Getting There & Away

BUS

All 2nd-class buses depart from **Terminal Minerva** (Map p158; 7a Calle, Zona 3), a dusty, crowded yard in the west of town, unless otherwise noted. If you're getting here by public transport, get off at the Templo de Minerva and walk through the market to the buses.

Leaving or entering town, buses bound for Salcajá, Cuatro Caminos, San Francisco El Alto and Totonicapán make a **stop** (Map p158) east of the center at the Rotonda, a traffic circle on Calz Independencia, marked by the **Monumento a la Marimba** (Map p158). Getting off here when you're coming into Xela saves the 10 to 15 minutes it will take your bus to cross town to Terminal Minerva.

First-class companies operating between Quetzaltenango and Guatemala City have their own terminals, including **Linea Dorada** (Map p158; ☎7767-5198; www.lineadorada.com.gt; 5a Calle 12-44, Zona 3), **Transportes Álamo** (Map p158; ☎7763-6966; 6a Calle 12-13, Zona 3) and **Transportes Galagos** (Map p158; ☎7761-2248; Calle Rodolfo Robles 17-43, Zona 1).

SHUTTLE MINIBUS

Xela travel agencies all sell tickets for shuttle minibuses to all major destinations including Antigua (Q150), Chichicastenango (Q150), Panajachel (Q125), Guatemala City (Q225), Coban/Lanquín (Q360), Flores (Q500) and San Cristóbal de Las Casas, Mexico (Q225).

ℹ Getting Around

Terminal Minerva is linked to the city center by **microbuses** (Map p158), charging Q1.25 for the 10- to 15-minute ride. From the terminal, walk south through the market to the intersection by the Templo de Minerva, where you'll see the vehicles waiting on the south side of 4a Calle. Going from the center to the terminal, catch **microbuses** (Map p162) on 14a Av north of 5a Calle. **Taxis** (Map p162; Parque Centro América) await fares at the north end of Parque Centro América; a ride to the Terminal Minerva should not cost more than Q30 during the day.

The Rotonda bus stop on Calz Independencía is served by 'Parque' microbuses running to the center. INGUAT (p165) has information on other city bus routes.

Huehuetenango

POP 126,000 / ELEV 1909M

Often used as a stop off on the journey to or from Mexico, or as a staging area for forays deeper into the Cuchumatanes mountain range, Huehuetenango has a welcoming if scruffy character. 'Huehue' *(way-way)* packs in plenty of eating and sleeping options along with some striking mountain scenery, and in Zaculeu has a Maya site well worth a visit.

Huehuetenango was a Mam Maya region until the 15th century, when the K'iche', expanding from their capital K'umarcaaj (near present-day Santa Cruz del Quiché), pushed them out. But the weakness of K'iche' rule soon brought about civil war, which engulfed the highlands and provided a chance for Mam independence. The turmoil was still unresolved in 1525 when Gonzalo de Alvarado, the brother of Pedro, arrived to conquer Zaculeu, the Mam capital, for Spain.

Huehuetenango

Huehuetenango

Sights

1 Catedral de Huehuetenango C2
2 Municipalidad B1
3 Parque Central C1

Sleeping

4 Hotel Casa Blanca A2
5 Hotel El Centro D1
6 Hotel San Luis de la Sierra A2
7 Hotel Zaculeu B1

Eating

8 Cafetería Las Palmeras C2
9 La Fonda de Don Juan B1
10 La Tinaja B3

Sights

Zaculeu ARCHAEOLOGICAL SITE

(Q50; 8am-4pm) A remnant of the Mam capital, the Zaculeu archaeological zone was 'restored' by the United Fruit Company in the 1940s, leaving its pyramids, ball courts and ceremonial platforms covered by a thick coat of graying plaster. It's the sort of restoration that probably makes archaeology purists scream, but for casual visitors the site, set amid pleasant lawns, goes a long way in simulating the appearance of an active religious center.

With ravines on three sides, the Postclassic religious center Zaculeu ('White Earth' in the Mam language) occupies a strategic defensive location that served its Mam Maya inhabitants well. It finally failed, however, in 1525, when Gonzalo de Alvarado, aided by Tlaxcalan and K'iche' forces, laid siege to the site for two months. It was starvation that ultimately defeated the Mam.

An excellent museum at the site holds, among other things, skulls and grave goods found in a tomb beneath Estructura 1, the tallest structure at the site.

Zaculeu is 4km west of Huehuetenango center. Buses to the site (Q2.50, 15 minutes) leave about every 30 minutes between 7:30am and 6pm from in front of the **school** (Map p166) at the corner of 2a Calle and 7a Av. A taxi from the town center costs Q30 one way. One hour is plenty of time to look around the site and museum.

Parque Central PLAZA

(Map p166) Huehuetenango's main square is shaded by cylindrical ficus trees and surrounded by the town's imposing buildings: the **municipalidad** (Town Hall; Map p166) (with a band shell on the upper floor) and the imposing neoclassical **church** (Map p166). For a bird's-eye view of the situation, check out the little relief map of Huehuetenango department, which lists altitudes, language groups and populations of the various municipal divisions.

Sleeping

Hotel San Luis de la Sierra HOTEL $

(Map p166; ☎7764-9217; hsanluis@gmail.com; 2a Calle 7-00; s/d Q120/190; P 📶) The simple, smallish rooms here have pine furniture and homey touches, and the hotel remains pleasantly aloof from the racket outside. The real attraction, though, is the rambling coffee plantation out back, with paths for strolling.

Hotel Zaculeu HOTEL $$

(Map p166; ☎7764-1086; www.facebook.com/HotelZaculeu; 5a Av 1-14; s/d/tr Q130/250/340; P @ 📶) The long-standing Zaculeu has plenty of character, and despite its advanced age it remains quite spiffy. Rooms in the 'new section' (20-plus years old) are a bit pricier but larger and more stylish. The sprawling patio area, overflowing with plants and chirping birds, is conducive to lounging, as is the bar. There's a restaurant for dinners as well as breakfast.

Hotel Casa Blanca HOTEL $$

(Map p166; ☎7769-0777; hotelcasablancahuehue@hotmail.com; 7a Av 3-41; s/d Q190/230; P 📶) Hanging ferns and sculpted shrubs grace the attractive courtyard here, ringed by spacious, modern rooms with arched pine ceilings and good hot showers. The patio restaurant out back serves up good-value set lunches (Q25), and its Sunday breakfast buffet (Q40) is a major deal. Given how busy the road outside it is, the rooms themselves are amazingly quiet.

BUSES FROM HUEHUETENANGO

DESTINATION	COST (Q)	DURATION (HR)	FREQUENCY	ALTERNATIVE
Antigua				Guatemala City–bound bus; change at Chimaltenango
Barillas	50	6	Microbuses half-hourly 2am-4:30pm	
Cobán	45	7	Microbus at 1pm Mon-Sat from El Calvario gas station	
Gracias a Dios (Mexican border)	60	5	Hourly 3am-1pm by Chiantlequita	
Guatemala City	70	5	5 Pullman buses by Velázquez Plus 5:30am-2:30pm	
La Mesilla	20	2	Every 15min, 3am-7pm by Transportes Los Verdes	
Nebaj				Microbus to Sacapulas for connections to Nebaj
Panajachel				Guatemala City–bound bus; change at Los Encuentros
Quetzaltenango	25	2	Every 15min, 3:30am-7pm	
Sacapulas	20	2	Frequent microbuses 5:30am-5:30pm	Via Aguacatán
Santa Cruz del Quiché	25	2	Frequent microbuses 5am-5pm	
San Pedro Soloma	25	3	Hourly microbuses 4:30am-2:30pm from El Calvario gas station	
Todos Santos Cuchumatán	20	2	Every 30min, 3am-3pm from El Calvario gas station	

Hotel El Centro HOTEL $$
(Map p166; ☎7764-8966; hotelcentro@hotmail.com; 3a Calle 2-65, Zona 1; s/d Q125/250; P 📶) Good-value midrange hotel with well-appointed rooms behind its sometimes dusty blue plate-glass exterior. There's underground parking via the corner entrance.

Eating

★**La Tinaja** GUATEMALAN $
(Map p166; ☎7764-1513; 4a Calle 6-51; set menus Q25; ⏰noon-10pm) As much a cultural center as a cafe, the home of historian-gourmet Rolando Gutiérrez has an interesting library and a collection of old clocks, radios and namesake *tinajas* (urns), all displayed in a series of inviting salons. Aside from quesadillas and tamales, you'll find such local snacks as *sangüichitos* (Huehue-style sandwiches) and *rellenitos* (fried stuffed plantain balls).

Cafetería Las Palmeras GUATEMALAN $
(Map p166; 4a Calle 5-10; mains Q27-50; ⏰7am-8:30pm; 📶) Popular Las Palmeras features a breezy upper level with views over the Parque Central. The *caldo de pollo criollo* (Q30) is a must, brimming with chicken, *güisquil* (a squash-like vegetable) and corn. On Saturdays there are tasty tamales.

La Fonda de Don Juan PIZZA $$
(Map p166; 2a Calle 5-35; pizzas Q45-75; ⏰24hr) The place for Huehue's night owls and early risers, the red-and-white fronted La Fonda serves varied Guatemalan and international fare including good-value pizzas and breakfasts. And yes, it really is open all hours.

Information

There are plenty of ATMs in the banks close to the main plaza, including **Banco Industrial** (6a Av 1-26).

Getting There & Away

The **bus terminal** is in Zona 4, 2km southwest of the plaza along 6a Calle. A number of companies ply the same routes, though information is not posted in any coherent fashion. Microbuses leave from the south end of the station. Another stop, for microbuses to Cobán and Barrillas, via Soloma and San Mateo Ixtatán, is by a **gas station** at El Calvario, at the corner of 1a Av and 1a Calle, four blocks northeast of the Parque Central.

For Guatemala City, two lines run Pullman buses from their own private terminals: **Transportes Los Halcones** (☎7765-7985; 10a Av 9-12, Zona 1) leaves seven times a day 1am to 3:30pm (Q77), with deluxe service (Q90) at 7am, 10:30am and 2pm; **Linea Dorada** (☎7768-1566; www.lineadorada.com.gt; 8a Calle 8-70, Zona 1) departs at 11pm (Q100).

Buses to Zaculeu (p166) leave from near the Hotel San Luis de la Sierra, or take a private **taxi**. (Map p166)

Todos Santos Cuchumatán

POP 2980 / ELEV 2470M

Way up in the highlands, this community is nestled at the bottom of a deep valley and bordered by beautiful forested slopes. Todos Santos has excellent walking in the hills, and its horse-racing festival at the start of November draws thousands of visitors.

Unusually for the highlands, it's the men's dress here that is the more eye-catching. Men wear red-and-white-striped trousers, little straw hats with blue ribbons, jackets with multicolored stripes and thick woven collars. Women's *cortes* are navy with a royal blue pinstripe. It's a close-knit but friendly community, which suffered great violence during Guatemala's civil war, and although it's photogenic, people are very sensitive about tourists blithely snapping away. Saturday is the main market day; there's a smaller market on Wednesday.

If you're coming to Todos Santos in the wet season (mid-May to November), bring warm clothes, as it's cold up here, especially at night.

Sights & Activities

Hiking in the Cuchumatanes is a major draw for visitors to Todos Santos. January to April are the best months for hitting the trails through the rugged countryside, but you can usually walk in the morning, before the weather closes in, year-round.

Museo Balam MUSEUM
(☎5787-3598; Cantón Twitnom; Q40; ⏰8am-6pm) Todos Santos' museum is on a hilly rise on the eastern edge of town. The small but fascinating collection of outfits and masks, traditional kitchen implements, archaeological finds and musical instruments comes to life when Fortunato, its creator and a community leader, is there to provide commentary.

Iglesia Todos Santos CHURCH
(Parque Centrale) Todos Santos' Catholic church is a modest whitewashed affair, but it's worth popping in to see the beautiful painted wooden ceiling, with its brightly

TODOS SANTOS' BIG DAY

Todos Santos Cuchumatán is renowned for its wildly colorful horse races, the highlight of **El Día de Todos los Santos**, a no-holds-barred annual celebration held on November 1. It's the culmination of a week of festivities and an all-night spree of male dancing to marimbas and *aguardiente* (cane liquor) drinking on the eve of the races, which are often sponsored by *todosanteros* diaspora abroad. The races are part competition, part chance for the bravado of riding up and down as fast as possible while getting progressively drunker the whole day long (with a break for lunch). Horses are brought from across the region; ironically few people in Todos Santos still keep them.

The authentically local event attracts throngs of inhabitants from surrounding communities who gather on a grassy hillside alongside the sand track or upon the rooftops opposite to observe the riders decked out in their finest traditional garb. Todos Santos, incidentally, is the only place in Guatemala where the Day of the Dead is not observed on November 1, since that day is reserved for a celebration of autonomy within Huehuetenango province. Instead, the traditional visit to the cemetery is postponed to the following day, when graves are decorated and marimbas serenade groups of mourners as they arrive to pay their respects.

decorated carved angels emerging from the heavens to watch over the congregation.

Red de Turismo Natural y Cultural de Huehuetenango HIKING
(☎4051-5597; www.turismoruralguatemala.com/roberto-jeronimo; hikes from Q250) This network of ecologically oriented guides throughout the department is locally represented by Roberto Jerónimo Bautista. He leads hikes to the isolated mountain community of San Juan Atitán, where the women wear dazzling *huipiles*, in about six hours, returning by bus to Todos Santos. The trail climbs through old-growth forest to summits that afford views all the way to the Mexican border.

Mam Trekking HIKING
(☎5206-0916; rigoguiadeturismo@yahoo.com; hikes from Q100) Knowledgeable, English-speaking *todosantero* Rigoberto Pablo Cruz leads walks around the Parque Regional Todos Santos Cuchumatán, including a climb to the peak of La Torre, followed by a descent to La Maceta. In addition, Rigoberto leads walks to Tzunul, a community where men weave women's *cortes* on a loom and women weave men's shirt collars by hand.

Sleeping & Eating

★Hotel Casa Familiar HOTEL $
(☎5737-0112; hotelyrestaurante_casafamiliar@yahoo.com; s/d Q125/200;) This cheerfully run guesthouse uphill from the main plaza has a selection of cozy rooms with hardwood floors, traditional textile bedspreads, good hot showers and private terraces (the roof terrace has excellent hillside views). Have a breakfast bowl of *mosh* (porridge) or fresh-baked banana bread at the cafe downstairs, where lunch and dinners are also available for Q35 to Q40. The staff are well versed in helping arrange local treks, and also weave their own fabrics that are on sale in the shop next door.

Hotelito Todos Santos HOTEL $
(☎3030-6950; s/d Q75/150) South of the plaza, up a side street that branches left, this trusted hotel has small and bare but well-scrubbed rooms with tile floors and firm beds. It's on several levels, and the higher you go the better the views – room 15, one of the four private bath units in the tower, has particularly good views over the valley. Breakfast is available but not included in the rate.

Comedor Katy GUATEMALAN $
(meals Q20-40; ⏲7:30am-8pm) Women in traditional garb attend to great vats bubbling over glowing embers at this rustic cook shack just above the central plaza. There are tables on a terrace overlooking the market activity.

Getting There & Away

Buses depart from the main street between the plaza and the church, leaving for Huehuetenango (Q20, two hours) between 4:30am and 2pm. It's a spectacular drive, though the switchbacks can be a bit nervy when you're in the hands of a chicken bus driver. Buses continue on to Guatemala City. Microbuses going as far as Tres Caminos (the junction with the Huehue–Barillas highway) leave throughout the day, whenever they fill up. A Huisteca bus heads for La Mesilla around 5am.

THE PACIFIC SLOPE

Separated from the highlands by a chain of volcanoes, the flatlands that run down to the Pacific are universally known as La Costa. It's a sultry region – hot and wet or hot and dry, depending on the time of year – with rich volcanic soil good for growing coffee, palm-oil seeds and sugarcane.

The culture is overwhelmingly *ladino* (mixed indigenous and European heritage), and even the biggest towns are humble affairs, with low-rise houses and the occasional palm-thatched roof.

Archaeologically, the big draws here are Takalik Abaj and the sculptures left by pre-Olmec civilizations around Santa Lucía Cotzumalguapa.

Guatemalan beach tourism has always been rather underdeveloped, but modest El Paredón is growing in popularity as a surf and backpacker destination, while a larger scene in Monterrico is helped along by a nature reserve protecting mangroves and their inhabitants.

Retalhuleu

POP 96,200

Retalhuleu, or Reu (*ray*-oo) as it's known to most Guatemalans, is a small town packed with fine old buildings. In the early 20th century it was an important trading center, with a railway that linked cotton-producing lowlands to the steamer trade on the Pacific coast. Its best days might be behind it, but the area around the plaza is worth exploring, along with the atmospherically abandoned and overgrown train station.

Most people visit for access to the Maya ruins at Takalik Abaj, but if you're up for some serious downtime, a couple of world-class fun parks are just down the road.

Sleeping & Eating

There are decent street food options around the plaza in the evening; the dining rooms of the Hotel Posada de Don José and the **Hotel Astor** (☎7771-2559; 5a Calle 4-60, Zona 1; mains Q60-120; ⏰7:30am-11pm) both offer more refined dining options. The modern **La Trinidad Mall** (5a Av) has all the chain restaurants popular in Guatemala.

Hotel Astor HOTEL $$
(☎7957-8300; www.hotelastorguatemala.com; 5a Calle 4-60, Zona 1; s/d Q285/400; P ❄ ≋) The Astor is one of Reu's older and loveliest hotels, set in a low red building that was well located to serve the traffic from the old train line. Pretty rooms sit around a lush courtyard in old colonial style. There's a good restaurant and bar.

Hotel Posada de Don José HOTEL $$
(☎7771-0180; www.posadadedonjose.com; 5a Calle 3-67, Zona 1; r from Q375; P ❄ ≋) A beautiful mid-19th century hotel built around a huge swimming pool. Swan dives from the top balcony are tempting, but probably unwise. Rooms are spacious, comfortable and very slick after a recent refit. The hotel's large Guatemalan art collection – there are canvases everywhere – is a particular delight.

La Quinta HOTEL $$
(☎7771-0872; www.hotellaquintaguatemala.com; cnr 5a Avenida & 5a Calle, Zona 1; s/d incl breakfast Q235/300; P ❄) This modern hotel just off the main square has a bit of contemporary style, once you get past the slightly industrial-looking common areas (tempered at least by the green courtyard). Service is good.

Information

Both **Banco Agromercantil** (5a Av, Zona 1) and **Banco Industrial** (cnr 6a Calle & 5a Av, Zona 1) change US dollars and have ATMs.

Getting There & Away

Most buses traveling along the Carretera al Pacífico detour into Reu. Shared taxis (Q10) are the best way to get to El Asintal (for Takalik Abaj). Look for station wagons with 'Asintal' painted on the windshield around the bus stop and plaza.

BUSES FROM RETALHULEU

DESTINATION	COST (Q)	DURATION (HR)	FREQUENCY
Champerico	15	1	every few minutes, 6am-7pm
Guatemala City	55-95	3	every 15min, 2am-8:30pm
Quetzaltenango	25	1½	every 30min, 4am-6pm
Santa Lucía Cotzumalguapa	30	2	every 15min, 2am-8:30pm
Tecún Umán (Mexican border)	25	1½	every 20min, 5am-10pm

Most buses make two stops in town, at the **main terminal** (5a Av, Zona 5) and a smaller **bus station** (10a Calle, Zona 1).

Parque Arqueológico Takalik Abaj

About 25km northwest of Retalhuleu, the Parque Arqueológico Takalik Abaj is a fascinating archaeological site set amid coffee, rubber and cacao plantations. Takalik Abaj was an important trading center in the late Preclassic period, before AD 250, and forms a historical link between Mesoamerica's first civilization, the Olmecs, and the Maya. The Olmecs flourished from about 1200 to 600 BC on Mexico's southern Gulf coast, but their influence extended far and wide, and numerous Olmec-style sculptures have been found at Takalik Abaj.

The city, which had strong connections with the town of Kaminaljuyú (in present-day Guatemala City), was sacked in about AD 300 and its great monuments, especially those in Maya style, were decapitated. Some monuments were rebuilt after AD 600 and the site retained a ceremonial and religious importance for the Maya, which it maintains to this day. Maya from the highlands regularly come here to perform ceremonies.

Tours

★Takalik Maya Lodge TOURS
(www.takalik.com; per person Q100) Takalik Maya Lodge runs fascinating tours of its plantations, which are rich in tropical produce from coffee to macadamia nuts. Highlights include sucking the sweet seeds of a just-picked cacao pod and poking the pungent elastic exudation of a freshly tapped rubber tree. Tours are year-round, but if you want to see the coffee being processed, visit between December and April.

Sleeping & Eating

Takalik Maya Lodge is something of an accommodation treat and has a lovely restaurant offering reasonably priced meals (mains Q55 to Q100). Otherwise, Retalhuleu is the place for accommodations. The site has a small snack shop for refreshments, but El Asintal offers basic comedores.

★Takalik Maya Lodge HOTEL $$
(☎2334-7693; www.takalik.com; farmhouse/bungalows Q450/600; P ⊛) Set on the grounds of a working farm 2km past the entrance to Takalik Abaj (and on top of a large, unexcavated section of it), this is by far the most comfortable place to stay in the area. Accommodations options include the old farmhouse and a gorgeously atmospheric electricity-free house amid the trees (lanterns are provided – it's a lot cozier than it sounds).

Check the website for package deals including accommodations, meals and tours of the plantations.

Getting There & Away

To reach Takalik Abaj by public transportation, catch a shared taxi from Retalhuleu to El Asintal (Q9, 30 minutes), which is 12km northwest of Reu and 5km north of the Carretera al Pacífico. Less frequent buses leave from a bus station on 5a Av A, 800m southwest of Reu plaza, about every half hour from 6am to 6pm. Pickups at El Asintal provide transportation on to Takalik Abaj (Q5), 4km further by paved road. You'll be shown around by a volunteer guide, whom you will probably want to tip (Q20 per person is a good baseline). You can also visit Takalik Abaj on tours from Quetzaltenango.

Champerico

POP 41,900

Built as a shipping point for coffee and cotton during the boom of the late 19th century, Champerico, 38km southwest of Retalhuleu, is a sweltering sort of spot, and the beach destination of choice for anyone based in Quetzaltenango.

It's a modest and slightly scruffy place, but presents an interesting picture of regular Guatemala at play that's a long, corrective way from a trending Instagram post.

Head to the end of the town until you hit the 'boardwalk' at the beach, where there are countless restaurants and tourist shacks. Beware of strong waves and an undertow if you go in the ocean, and stay in the clearly marked central part of the beach: muggings have been known outside this area.

Sleeping & Eating

Hotel Maza HOTEL $$
(☎7773-7180; s/d Q180/270; ❄) With large clean rooms just across the road from the beach, Hotel Maza is the best bet on the beach, but don't expect too many frills.

7 Mares SEAFOOD $
(mains Q40-90; ⏲8am-7pm) One of a handful of similarly styled restaurants in the beach zone, 7 Mares offers a small shaded swimming pool, dining area and upstairs deck that catches good breezes and views. Naturally, go for the fresh seafood.

RETALHULEU'S FUN PARKS

If you have children along, or your own inner child is fighting to get out, head to one of these two gigantic theme parks next door to one another on the Quetzaltenango road, about 12km north of Retalhuleu.

Both Xocomil and Xetulul are run by Irtra (Instituto de Recreación de los Trabajadores de la Empresa Privada de Guatemala; Guatemalan Private Enterprise Workers' Recreation Institute), which administers several fun sites around the country for workers and their families. Between them, the two sites comprise the most popular tourist attraction in Guatemala, with over a million visitors a year.

With a distinct Guatemalan theme, **Parque Acuático Xocomil** (☎7772-9400; www.irtra.org.gt; Carretera CITO, Km 180.5; adult/child Q100/50; ⊙9am-5pm Thu-Sun) is world-class water park that offers aquatic diversions for all ages (under-fives must have a flotation device, but you can hire one for Q20). Among the 14 waterslides, two swimming pools and two wave pools are re-creations of Maya monuments from Tikal, Copán and Quiriguá. Visitors can bob along a river through canyons flanked with ancient temples and Maya masks. Three real volcanoes – Santiaguito, Zunil and Santa María – can be seen from the grounds.

Parque de Diversiones Xetulul (☎7722-9450; www.irtra.org.gt; Carretera CITO, Km 180.5; adult/child Q100/50; ⊙10am-5pm Fri-Sun) is a surprisingly well-organised amusement park, with first-class rides for all ages. Themed areas include representations of a Tikal pyramid, historical Guatemalan buildings and famous buildings from many European cities. An all-you-can-ride bracelet costs Q50 on top of admission.

If you're coming for a long weekend or similar, it's worth noting that you can buy a joint ticket for Q140 that gives 48-hour access to both parks.

Set on lush, tropical grounds that feature swimming pools, a spa bath, various sports fields and probably the most impressive minigolf course in the country, the **Irtra Hostales** (☎7722-9100; www.irtra.org.gt; Carretera CITO, Km 180; r with fan/air-con from Q250/300; P❄📶🏊) complex has the best accommodations for miles around (and isn't too far from the two parks). There are seven main buildings within the complex, each decorated in a different style – Colonial, Mediterranean, Polynesian, Indonesian, Thai, African, Maya – but rooms are spacious, modern and comfortable throughout. Prices listed range wildly. Its quieter from Sunday to Wednesday; Thursday to Saturday nights (when the parks are open) the place packs out and prices rise considerably. The San Martín complex is the cheapest (rooms are frequently less than Q200), while the glitzier Paljunoj complex weighs in at around Q800.

Any bus heading from Retalhuleu toward Quetzaltenango will drop you at Xocomil, Xetulul or the Irtra Hostales (Q10, 30 minutes). From Quetzaltenango, any Retalhuleu-bound bus will do the same (Q15, one hour).

Getting There & Away

Regular buses connect Champerico with other Pacific Slope towns, Quetzaltenango and Guatemala City. The **bus stop** is two blocks back from the beach on the road out of town. The last buses back to Quetzaltenango (Q30, 2½ hours) leave at about 6pm, and a bit later for Retalhuleu (Q15, one hour).

El Paredón

POP UNDER 1000

El Paredón (formerly known as Sipacate) is barely more than a single street at the end of a hard earth road that can feel like a long way from anywhere, but it's a town well on the way to becoming Guatemala's surf capital. Waves here average 1.8m, with the best breaks between December and April.

There's a thriving backpacker scene here amid the tropical greenery and palm-thatched houses, and a local development NGO, La Choza Chula, that runs tours to the local mangroves, salt farms and turtle feeding grounds, as well as arranging cooking classes.

There's a laid-back atmosphere in El Paredón and it's easy to lose more than few days doing very little. Future development plans are much discussed among locals however, with both excitement and nervousness about what a proposed paved road might bring to such a sleepy town.

Activities & Tours

All of the guesthouses offer surfing, typically charging around Q100 per day for board hire, as well as lessons for around Q120.

★La Choza Chula TOURS

(www.lachozochula.org; 9.30am-4:30pm) This local NGO is deeply involved in community tourism, alongside its education and environmental programs. Its most popular boat tour options are wildlife spotting and traditional fishing in the nearby mangroves (Q115), and to El Paredón's turtle feeding grounds and salt farms (Q185), as well as an introduction to local cuisine with cooking classes (Q90). All tours are minimum two people.

Sleeping

El Paredón's accommodations scene is small but thriving, running the line from party hostels to boutique guesthouses. La Choza Chula can also arrange homestays with local families (from Q100 per night with breakfast).

Driftwood Surfer HOSTEL $

(3036-6891; www.driftwoodsurfer.com; dm Q75, d with/without bathroom Q375/250;) El Paredón's undisputed party hostel, the Driftwood was quick to arrive in the town and set the pace with its beachfront location and swim-up pool bar. The dorms are a bit cramped, but the air-conditioning is welcome and most guests prefer to be out with the surf breaks, on the sun deck or playing drinking games in the bar.

Cocori GUESTHOUSE $

(www.cocorilodge.com; dm Q100, cabañas Q250, suites with kitchen Q450;) Cocori occupies a long strip of land down to the beach. There are a couple of cute *cabañas,* and some nice family-sized suites with their own kitchen, but the absolute draw is the thatched dorm above them with 360-degree views, where the breeze keeps you cool and you sleep and wake to the sound of the waves. Heavenly.

Soul Food Kitchen & Guesthouse GUESTHOUSE $

(3286-6473; www.facebook.com/SoulFoodKitchenElParedon; d with/without bathroom Q250/150;) This simple guesthouse has a selection of airy whitewashed rooms with mosquito nets. It's a relaxed and quiet place, but just as much of a draw is the restaurant (noon to 3pm and 6pm to 9pm) serving up big, delicious plates of Thai and Indian curries along with big bowls of noodles (all with vegetarian options). A breakfast menu was in the planning during research.

★Hotel Paredon Surf House BOUTIQUE HOTEL $$

(4994-1842; www.paredonsurf.com; dm Q205, stilt bungalow d/tr Q570/750, suites Q810-1025;) This charming beachfront guesthouse has a variety of different options, including thatched private rooms, generous dorms on stilts overlooking the ocean, and family-sized suites with open-air showers. It's well run with a relaxed, modest restraint. All prices are half-board, and beds are netted. The bar-restaurant closes early (by 9:30pm) to ensure that guests get a quiet night's sleep.

Swell BOUTIQUE HOTEL $$

(www.swellguatemala.com; d from Q450, pool suites Q750;) This 'surf and lifestyle' hotel was on the cusp of opening when we visited, and it looked a treat. Designed by the architect owner, it has a selection of options from thatched rooms on stilts catching the ocean breeze to achingly cool crisp white suites facing the pool, all fitted out with great locally made wooden furniture.

Eating

Sandra's GUATEMALAN $

(mains Q25-45; 8am-8pm) Popular open-sided restaurant that serves up a bit of everything, but leans heavily toward seafood (especially *ceviche*). Vegetarians are well covered, and all mains come with enormous side dishes. One long-term El Paredón resident argued with us that Sandra's has the best guacamole in the country, and it's certainly worth the visit to do a taste test.

Yoli's GUATEMALAN $

(breakfast Q20, pasta Q20-35; 8am-8pm) A good thatched spot near the beach for breakfasts, fruit smoothies and plates of pasta. There's usually a seafood-centered dish of the day that's worth trying.

Information

El Paredón had barely any internet access when we most recently visited, but the town was being cabled to allow it to get online properly in 2019.

There are no ATMs in El Paredón, so plan accordingly.

Getting There & Away

There are two daily tourist shuttles between El Paredón and Antigua (Q120, two hours). Tickets are sold in every travel agency in Antigua or book through your El Paredón guesthouse. Pacifico Surf Transport (p143) also runs a weekday shuttle to Santiago de Atitlán (Q150, three hours).

By public transport, take the ferry across the river (Q10) and then a *tuk-tuk* to El Paredón (Q20, 20 minutes), from where buses leave throughout the day to Guatemala City (Q45, 3½ hours) – change at La Democracía or Escuintla for onward connections.

Monterrico

POP 2400

The coastal area around Monterrico is a totally different Guatemala. Life here is steeped with a sultry, tropical flavor, with rustic wooden-slat and thatched-roof architecture and awesome volcanoes that shimmer in the hinterland. It's fast becoming popular with foreigners as a beach break from Antigua or Guatemala City. On weekdays it's relatively quiet, but on weekends and holidays it teems with Guatemalan families.

Monterrico itself is a coastal village with a few small, inexpensive hotels right on the beach, a large wildlife reserve and two centers for the hatching and release of sea turtles and caimans. The beach here is dramatic, with powerful surf crashing onto black volcanic sand at odd angles. This wave-print signals that there are riptides; deaths have occurred at this beach, so swim with care. Behind the town is a large network of mangrove swamps and canals, part of the 190km Canal de Chiquimulilla.

Sights & Activities

Biotopo Monterrico-Hawaii WILDLIFE RESERVE

(Reserva Natural Monterrico) This reserve, administered by Cecon (Centro de Estudios Conservacionistas de la Universidad de San Carlos), is Monterrico's biggest attraction. The 20km-long nature reserve of coast and coastal mangrove swamps is bursting with avian and aquatic life. The reserve's most famous denizens are the endangered leatherback and ridley turtles, which lay their eggs on the beach in many places along the coast. The mangrove swamps are a network of 25 lagoons, all connected by mangrove canals.

Boat tours of the reserve, passing through the mangrove swamps and visiting several lagoons, take 1½ to two hours and cost Q75 to Q100 per person. It's best to go just on sunrise, when you're likely to see the most wildlife. If you have binoculars, bring them along for birdwatching; January and February are the best months. Locals will approach you on the street (some with very impressive-looking ID cards) offering tours, and you can arrange tours through hotels, but if you want to support the *tortugario* arrange a tour directly through Tortugario Monterrico, which, incidentally, has the most environmentally knowledgeable guides.

Some travelers have griped about the use of motorboats because the sound of the motor scares off the wildlife. If you're under no time pressure, ask about arranging a paddled tour of the canal.

Tortugario Monterrico WILDLIFE RESERVE

(Q50; 8am-1pm & 2-5pm) The Cecon-run Tortugario Monterrico is just a short walk east down the beach from the end of Calle Principal and then a block inland. Several endangered species of animals are raised here, including leatherback, olive ridley and green sea turtles, caimans and iguanas.

There's an interesting interpretative trail and a little museum with pickled displays in bottles. The staff offer lagoon trips, and night walks (Q50) from August to December to look for turtle eggs. Around sunset nightly from September to January on the beach in front of the *tortugario,* workers help release baby turtles. You're welcome to observe, but despite what everybody else is doing, refrain from using flash cameras and flashlights.

Proyecto Lingüístico Monterrico LANGUAGE

(5475-1265; www.monterrico-guatemala.com/spanish-school.php; Calle Principal) This place, about 250m from the beach, is quite professional. Classes are generally held outdoors in a shady garden. You can study in the morning or afternoon, depending on your schedule. Twenty hours of study per week costs Q750, plus Q670 for a seven-night homestay.

Sleeping & Eating

Monterrico has a decent enough selection of hotels on two roads that run left and right parallel to the beach at the end of Calle Principal. Prices are on a shifting scale: weekends are more expensive than weekdays, but stays of three nights or more frequently attract discounts.

There are many simple seafood restaurants on Calle Principal. Even better, try the simple shacks with umbrellas and tables on the beach itself and sink a cold drink over a plate of fish or garlic shrimp while watching the waves. Most hotels have restaurants serving whatever is fresh from the sea that day.

Johnny's Place HOTEL $

(☎5812-0409; www.johnnysplacehotel.com; dm Q45, r without bathroom Q190, r with air-con from Q320, bungalow from Q600; P❄≋) Johnny's is the first place you come to turning left on the beach. It's got a decent atmosphere and attracts a mix of backpackers and family groups. The cheaper rooms are far from glamorous, but have fans and screened windows. Pay extra and things start to get very swish.

Every pair of bungalows shares a BBQ and small swimming pool. There's also a larger general swimming pool. The bar-restaurant overlooks the sea and is a popular hangout: the food is not gourmet, but there are plenty of choices and imaginative *licuados* (fresh fruit drinks) and other long cool drinks.

Brisas del Mar HOTEL $

(☎5517-1142; incl breakfast s/d with fan Q100/200, with air-con Q150/300; P❄≋) One block back from the beach, this popular option offers good-sized rooms, an open-sided thatched 2nd-floor dining hall with excellent sea views, and a large swimming pool.

Hotel Pez de Oro BUNGALOW $$

(☎5232-9534; s/d Q400/500; P≋) This funky place has comfortable little huts and bungalows scattered around a palm tree–shaded property. The color scheme is a cheery blue and yellow, and the rooms have some tasteful decorations and large overhead fans. The excellent restaurant, with big sea views, serves up great Italian cuisine and seafood dishes.

Hotel Atelie del Mar HOTEL $$$

(☎5752-5528; www.hotelateliedelmar.com; s/d incl breakfast from Q415/630; P❄⊜≋🐾) This is one of the swankiest hotels in town, with lovely landscaped grounds and spacious, simple and beautiful rooms with netted beds. It's got the best swimming pool around, along with the widest menu and an on-site art gallery.

★Taberna El Pelicano ITALIAN, SEAFOOD $$

(mains Q60-150; ⊙noon-2pm & 6-10pm Wed-Sun) This cheery thatched orange restaurant is one of the best places to eat in town, with the widest menu and most interesting food. Look for excellent salads (Q80), plenty of cleverly prepared fish (from Q90) and a range of jumbo shrimp dishes (Q175), as well as daily specials.

ℹ Information

There is a **Cajero 5B ATM** in the center of town.

ℹ Getting There & Away

The quickest and easiest way to get to Monterrico is undoubtedly with a shuttle from Antigua (Q80, two hours) or Guatemala City (Q150, three hours). The shuttles fill quickly leaving Monterrico, so book the day before if you can.

There is a daily direct bus to Guatemala City, departing at 5am (Q80, three hours). This travels via Iztapa and Escuintla, from where you can change for connections to Antigua or other destinations.

Alternatively, it can be fun to take the 30-minute boat ride to Avellana (Q5) along the Canal de Chiquimulilla, a long mangrove canal. Boats start at 4:30am and run more or less every half-hour or hour until late afternoon. There are also car ferries (Q100 per vehicle). From Avellana, there are half-hourly buses to Guatemala City via Taxisco and Escuintla. From Taxisco there are regular buses to the El Salvador border at Ciudad Pedro de Alvarado.

CENTRAL GUATEMALA

Stretching from the steamy lowland forests of El Petén to the dry tropics of the Río Motagua valley, and from the edge of the Western Highlands to the Caribbean Sea, this is Guatemala's most diverse region.

The Carretera al Atlántico (Hwy 9) shoots eastward to the sea from Guatemala City, passing the turnoffs for the wonderfully preserved ruins of Copán (Honduras), Quiriguá with its impressive stelae, and Río Dulce, a favored resting spot for Caribbean sailors and gateway to the Refugio de Vida Silvestre Bocas del Polochic (Bocas del Polochic Wildlife Reserve). While you're here, don't miss the gorgeous boat ride down the Río Dulce to Lívingston, the enclave of the Garifuna people.

The north of the region is lush and mountainous coffee-growing country. The limestone crags around Cobán attract cavers the world over, and the beautiful pools and cascades of Semuc Champey rate high on Guatemala's list of natural wonders.

Salamá & Around

A wonderful introduction to the Baja Verapaz region's not-too-hot, not-too-cold climate, the area around Salamá hosts a wealth of attractions, both post-colonial and indigenous.

Salamá itself is known for its ornate church (complete with grisly depiction of Jesus) and bustling Sunday market. A photogenic ex-sugar-mill-turned-museum and impressive stone aqueduct can be found in the neighboring town of **San Jerónimo**.

Sleeping & Eating

There are restaurants and cafes around the plaza. The meat-stuffed flour tortillas at **Antojitos Zacapanecos** (7954-5691; cnr 6a Calle & 8a Av; mains Q27-50; 10am-9pm) are not to be missed.

Hotel Real Legendario HOTEL $
(7940-0501; www.hotelreallegendario.com; 8a Av 3-57; s/d/tr Q115/160/180; P) You'll recognize this place, three blocks east of the plaza, by the pale yellow exterior and the stands of bamboo in the parking lot. The clean, secure rooms have fan, hot-water bathroom and cable TV.

Los Molinos HOTEL $$
(5762-8714; hotellosmolinos@outlook.com; Calle Los Molinos Lote 3145; s/d Q160/220; P@) A brand new, spick-and-span spot on the outskirts, best for folks with cars or those who don't mind a taxi once in a while. The almost Italian chic, the eat-off-the tile floors, minimalist decor and on-site restaurant make it a nice stop. It's a 10-minute drive from Salamá.

Getting There & Away

Buses leave Salamá's downtown **bus station** frequently for Cobán (Q20, 1½ to two hours), Guatemala City (Q40, 3½ hours) and neighboring villages.

Biotopo del Quetzal

Along Hwy 14, 34km beyond the La Cumbre turnoff for Salamá, is the Biotopo Mario Dary Rivera nature reserve, commonly called **Biotopo del Quetzal** (4499-3236; Hwy 14 Km 160.5; Q40; 7am-4pm), just east of Purulhá village.

You need a fair bit of luck to see a quetzal, as they're rare and shy, though you have the best chance of seeing them from March to June. Even so, it's well worth stopping to explore and enjoy this lush high-altitude cloud-forest ecosystem, which is the quetzal's natural habitat. Early morning or early evening are the best times to watch out for them – they're actually more prevalent around the grounds of the nearby hotels.

The reserve has a visitors center, a little shop for drinks and snacks, and a camping and BBQ area. The ruling on camping changes from time to time. Check by contacting Cecon (p117), which administers this and other biotopes.

Two excellent, well-maintained nature trails wind through the reserve: the 1800m **Sendero los Helechos** (Fern Trail) and the 3600m **Sendero los Musgos** (Moss Trail). As you wander through the dense growth, treading on the rich, spongy humus and leaf mold, you'll see many varieties of epiphytes (air plants), which thrive in the reserve's humid atmosphere.

Sleeping & Eating

★ **Ranchitos del Quetzal** HOTEL $$
(4130-9456; www.ranchitosdelquetzal.com; Hwy 14 Km 160.5; s/d/tr Q200/300/350; P) Carved out of the jungle on a hillside 200m away from the Biotopo del Quetzal entrance, this place has good-sized simple rooms with hot showers. Reasonably priced, simple meals (mains from Q30) are served, and there are vegetarian options. The best reason to be here is the wealth of info you'll get from the friendly staff, and the chance to be next door to the biotope.

Foxes visit in the evening, as does a host of interesting birds, which the staff will happily identify for you. The other options may be more luxurious, but if you're here for the nature (and who isn't?!), this is a perfect choice. A trail for quetzal viewing leads up into the hills. There's also a path along a gorgeous, lush river to a beautiful waterfall.

Hotel Restaurant Ram Tzul HOTEL $$$
(5908-4066; www.ramtzul.com; Hwy 14 Km 158; camping per person Q75, s/d Q422/645; P) This slightly faded place features a restaurant/sitting area in a tall, thatched-roofed structure with fire pits. The rustic, upscale theme extends to the rooms and bungalows, which are spacious and nicely decorated. The hotel property includes waterfalls and swimming spots.

Getting There & Away

Any Monja Blanca bus (Q65 to Q85) to or from Guatemala City will set you down at the park entrance. Heading in the other direction, it's best to flag down a bus or microbus to El Rancho (Q35) and change there for your next destination.

Those with a car will find it very convenient.

Cobán

POP 280,000 / ELEV 1320M

Once a gritty spot that tourists passed through, Cobán has become a destination in its own right and one of the best in the area (outside Guatemala City) for decent food, a range of hotels and activities. For tourists it remains a great hub for taking in the surrounding natural wonders – such as Semuc Champey (p182) – in a series of day trips.

The town was once the center of Tezulutlán (Tierra de Guerra, or 'Land of War'), a stronghold of the Rabinal Maya.

In the 19th century, when German immigrants moved in and founded vast coffee and cardamom *fincas* (plantations), Cobán took on the aspect of a German mountain town, as the *finca* owners built town residences. The era of German cultural and economic domination ended during WWII, when the USA prevailed upon the Guatemalan government to deport the powerful *finca* owners, many of whom actively supported the Nazis.

Sights & Activities

Orquigonia GARDENS

(☎4740-2224; www.orquigonia.com; Hwy 14 Km 206; Q50; ⊙7am-5pm) Orchid lovers and even the orchid-curious should not miss the wonderfully informative guided tour of this orchid sanctuary just off the highway to Cobán. The 90-minute to two-hour tour takes you through the history of orchid collecting, starting with the Maya, as you wend your way along a path in the forest. There are sweet little cabins on the grounds where you can stay for Q550 to Q750 per night, as well as campsites (Q40). The last entry is at 4pm, as people must be out by 5pm.

Parque Nacional Las Victorias PARK

(Map p178; 3a Calle, Zona 1; Q15; ⊙8am-4:30pm, walking trails 9am-3pm) This forested 82-hectare national park, right in town, has ponds, BBQ and picnic areas, children's play areas, a lookout point and kilometers of trails. The entrance is near the corner of 9a Av and 3a Calle. Most trails are very isolated – consider hiking in a group. You can **camp** (campsite per person Q50) here.

Templo El Calvario CHURCH

(Map p178; 3a Calle, Zona 1) You can get a fine view over the town from this church atop a long flight of stairs at the north end of 7a Av. Indigenous people leave offerings at outdoor shrines and crosses in front of the church, and it's an interesting stop if you have time. Don't linger here after dark, though, as muggings are not unknown in this area.

The **Ermita de Santo Domingo de Guzmán** (Map p178), a chapel dedicated to Cobán's patron saint, is 150m west of the bottom of the stairs leading to El Calvario.

Chicoj Cooperative COFFEE TOUR

(☎5524-1831; www.coffeetourchicoj.com; tours Q60) Just 15 minutes out of town by bus, this is a community tourism initiative offering 2km, 45-minute tours of its coffee farm. Halfway through there's the standard stop for a canopy zip-line tour. The tour winds up with a cup of coffee made from beans grown and roasted at the farm.

Cobán tour operators offer this tour for Q160, but you can easily catch a bus from the stop near the police station on 1a Calle, which goes straight to the village of Chicoj.

Aventuras Turísticas TOURS

(Map p178; ☎7951-4213; www.facebook.com/aventurasturisticascoban; 1a Calle 5-34, Zona 1; prices vary; ⊙8am-9pm) Leads tours to Laguna Lachuá, the Grutas de Lanquín, Rey Marcos and Parque Nacional Cuevas de Candelaria, as well as to Semuc Champey, Tikal, Ceibal and anywhere else you may want to go. It will customize itineraries, and prices depend on the location and number of people in the group. Guides speaking French, English or Spanish are available. It has a WhatsApp number: +502-3021-2169.

Festivals & Events

Rabin Ajau CULTURAL

(Estadio Verapaz) A stunning 'beauty pageant' of sorts, featuring the region's top talent dressed in their traditional finery, Rabin Ajau is not to be missed if you're in the area. Get tickets early, though, as the event sells out every year. It's held in the last week of July or the first week of August.

Cobán

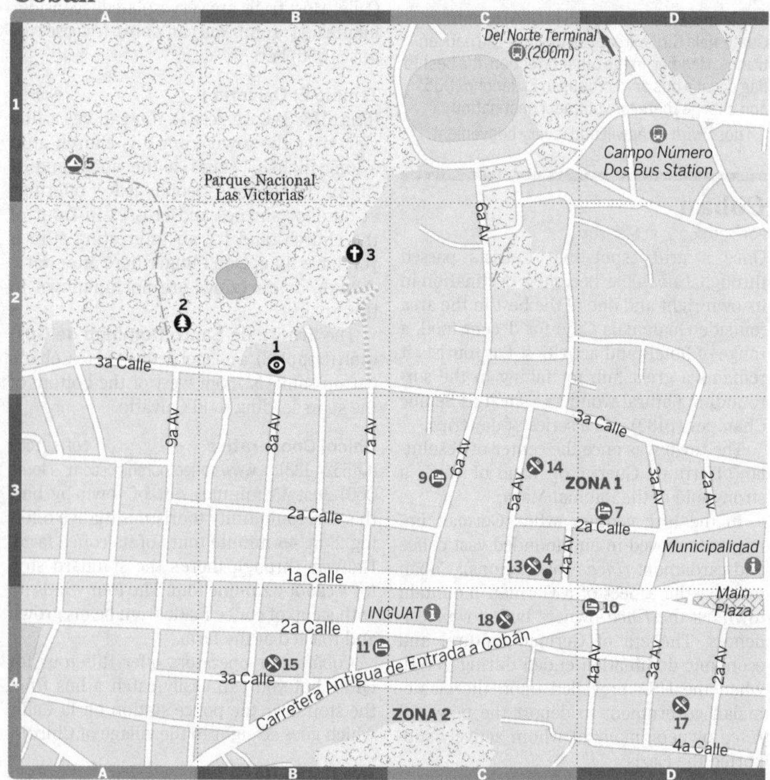

Sleeping

When choosing a room in Cobán, you may want to ensure that the showers have hot water; it can be cold in these parts.

★Casa Tenango HOSTEL $
(Map p178; ☎7952-3664; www.facebook.com/casatenango; 3a Av A 2-50, Zona 1; s/d with bathroom Q80/150, dm/s/d without bathroom Q45/60/110; P ⊜ ☎) What this place lacks in frills (no pool, no bar) it more than makes up for in warmth, with a large kitchen, several common areas that are good for meeting people, and clean rooms. The dorms have large lockers and some rooms feel more like a boutique hotel than a hostel. Best are the owners, who greet each guest like they're family.

Hotel La Paz HOTEL $
(Map p178; 6a Av 2-19, Zona 1; s/d Q98/183; P) This cheerful budget hotel, 1½ blocks north and two blocks west of the plaza, is an excellent deal. It has many flowers to brighten up the otherwise simple decor.

Casa Duranta HOTEL $$
(Map p178; ☎7951-4716; www.casaduranta.com; 3a Calle 4-46, Zona 3; s/d Q305/427; P ⊜ ☎) Some rooms at this carefully restored, eclectically decorated place are excellent value, while others are a bit cramped for the price. Tile floors grace most of the rooms, and there's a lovely courtyard. Have a look around if you can. There's also an on-site restaurant. Some rooms have street noise.

Hotel Central HOTEL $$
(Map p178; ☎7952-1442; 1a Calle 1-79, Zona 1; s/d Q137/260; P ☎) Reasonably sized rooms and lovely outdoor sitting areas make this a decent choice. Try for a room at the back for better ventilation and views out over the town.

Posada de Don Antonio HOTEL $$
(Map p178; ☎7951-1792; 5a Av 1-51, Zona 4; s/d Q265/415; P ⊜ ☎) MC Escher's famous

Cobán

Sights

1 Ermita de Santo Domingo de Guzmán ... B2
2 Parque Nacional Las Victorias ... A2
3 Templo El Calvario ... B2

Activities, Courses & Tours

4 Aventuras Turísticas ... C3

Sleeping

5 Campground ... A1
6 Casa Duranta ... F4
7 Casa Tenango ... D3
8 Hotel Central ... E3
9 Hotel La Paz ... C3
10 Hotel La Posada ... D4
11 Pensión Monja Blanca ... B4
12 Posada de Don Antonio ... F3

Eating

13 Casa Chavez ... C3
14 El Peñascal ... C3
15 Kardamomuss ... B4
16 La Abadia ... F4
17 La Casa del Monje ... D4
18 Xkape Koba'n ... C4

Relativity painting could have been inspired by the multiple staircases in the lobby here, but this atmospheric two-story place provides some of the best-value accommodations in town. Rooms are spacious and have double beds, high ceilings and attention to detail. Breakfast (Q30 to Q50) in the patio area is a great way to start the day.

Pensión Monja Blanca HOTEL $$

(Map p178; ☎7952-1712; 2a Calle 6-30, Zona 2; s/d Q200/300, without bathroom Q150/200; P ⊗ ☎) This place is peaceful despite being on busy 2a Calle. After walking through two courtyards, you come to a lush garden packed with fruit and hibiscus trees around which the spotless rooms are arranged. Each room has an old-time feel to it and is furnished with two good-quality single beds with folksy covers. Also has cable TV.

The hotel's central location and tranquil atmosphere make it a good place for solo women travelers.

Hotel La Posada HOTEL $$$

(Map p178; ☎7952-1495; www.laposadacoban.com.gt; 1a Calle 4-12, Zona 2; s/d Q480/560) Just off the plaza, this colonial-style hotel is Cobán's best, though streetside rooms suffer from traffic noise. Its colonnaded porches are dripping with tropical flowers and furnished with easy chairs and hammocks. The rooms are a bit austere, with plenty of religious relics around the place, but they have nice old furniture, fireplaces and wall hangings of local weaving.

Eating

Most of the hotels in Cobán come with their own restaurants. In the evening, food trucks (kitchens on wheels) park around the plaza and offer some of the cheapest dining in town. As always, the one to go for has the largest crowd of locals hanging around and chomping down.

★Xkape Koba'n GUATEMALAN $

(Map p178; ☎7951-4152; 2a Calle 5-13, Zona 2; snacks Q35, mains Q50-90; ⊙7am-8pm Mon-Fri, from 9am Sat) The perfect place to take a breather or while away a whole afternoon, this beautiful, artsy little cafe has a lush garden out back. Some interesting indigenous-inspired dishes are on the small menu. The cakes are homemade, the coffee is delectable and there are some handicrafts for sale.

★La Abadia FUSION $$

(Map p178; cnr 1a Calle & 4a Av, Zona 3; mains Q90-160; ⊙6-9:30pm Mon-Sat) Cobán's dining scene has improved dramatically over the years and this is part of the finer dining scene. The surrounds are refined yet relaxed, the menu offers a great selection of local, international and fusion dishes, and there's a good wine list too.

La Casa del Monje STEAK $$

(Map p178; ☎7951-3845; 3a Calle 2-24, Zona 2; mains Q59-115; ⊙6:30am-10pm; 📶) Guarded by the 'iron friar,' Cobán's best steakhouse is set in a lovely colonial-era monastery a few blocks from the park. If you're not in the mood for big chunks of meat, local dishes like *kaq'ik* (turkey stew) are recommended.

El Peñascal GUATEMALAN $$

(Map p178; 5a Av 2-61, Zona 1; mains Q75-160; ⊙11:30am-9pm) Probably Cobán's finest stand-alone restaurant, El Peñascal has plenty of regional specialties, Guatemalan classics, mixed-meat platters, seafood and snacks in a relaxed, upscale setting.

Kardamomuss FUSION $$

(Map p178; ☎7952-3792; kardamomussfusioncoban@gmail.com; 3a Calle 5-34, Zona 2; mains Q60-130; ⊙7am-10pm; P📶) The widest menu in town is at this chic place, which is in a location so new even the geckos haven't found it yet. Billing itself as 'fusion' food, it takes a pretty good stab at Indian, Chinese and Italian dishes, with locally grown cardamom as the featured ingredient. Creative cocktails and mocktails make it well worth the detour.

Casa Chavez INTERNATIONAL $$

(Map p178; ☎7951-4620; 1a Calle 4-25, Zona 1; breakfast Q25-30, lunch & dinner mains Q50-100; ⊙6am-9pm; 📶) Set in a lovely old house, Casa Chavez offers an ample, if uninspired, menu. Still, the location is great, and breakfast out back overlooking the garden and hills beyond is hard to beat.

ℹ Information

The banks listed here change US-dollar cash and traveler's checks.

Banco G&T (1a Calle; ⊙9am-7pm Mon-Fri, to 1pm Sat) Has a MasterCard ATM.

Banco Industrial (cnr 1a Calle & 7a Av, Zona 1; ⊙9am-6pm Mon-Fri, 10am-2pm Sat) Has a Visa ATM.

INGUAT (Map p178; ☎4210-9992; 2a Calle 5-12, Zona 2; ⊙9am-5pm Mon & Tue, Thu-Sat) Has an office a couple of blocks from the plaza.

Municipalidad (Town Hall; Map p178; ☎7952-1305, 7951-1148; 1a Calle, Zona 1; ⊙8am-4pm Mon-Sat) Switched-on young staff work in an office behind the police office.

ℹ Getting There & Away

The Hwy 14 leg connecting Cobán with Guatemala City (via Hwy 9) is the most traveled route

BUSES FROM COBÁN

DESTINATION	COST (Q)	DURATION (HR)	FREQUENCY/ HOURS	DEPARTURE LOCATION
Biotopo de Quetzal	15	1	1am-5pm	Monja Blanca
Cahabón	30	4	7am-4pm	Transportes Martínez
Chisec	25	2	6am-4pm	Del Norte
Fray Bartolomé de Las Casas	50	4	6am-4pm	Del Norte
Guatemala City	50-80	5	1am-5pm	Monja Blanca
Lanquín	25	2½	7am-4pm	Transportes Martínez
Nebaj	50	5	2 buses; 6am, 1pm	Del Norte
Playa Grande, for Laguna Lachuá	50	3½	6am-4pm	Del Norte
Raxruhá	35	3	6am-4pm	Del Norte
Salamá	20	2	6am-5pm	Del Norte
San Pedro Carchá	3	20min	6am-7pm	In front of Monja Blanca
Sayaxché	50	4	6am-4pm	Del Norte
Tactic	6	40min	6am-5pm	Campo Número Dos
Uspantán	30	3½	6am-5pm	Del Norte

between Cobán and the outside world, though you can arrive via other routes as well. The road north through Chisec to Sayaxché and Flores is now paved all the way, providing much easier access than before to El Petén. The off-the-beaten-track routes west to Huehuetenango and northeast to Fray Bartolomé de Las Casas and Poptún are partly unpaved and still provide a bit of adventure. Always double-check bus departure times, especially for less frequently served destinations.

Buses leave from a variety of points around town, with some early morning departures from the market. Unless otherwise specified below buses leave frequently – hourly, every 30 minutes, or more often – between the times shown in the table.

Be aware that the road to Uspantán and Nebaj is prone to landslides; get the latest before setting out.

Around Cobán

Throughout the region around Cobán, there are scores of villages where you can experience traditional Maya culture in some of its purest extant forms. One such place is **San Cristóbal Verapaz**, a Poqomchi' Maya village set beside Laguna Chicoj, 19km west of Cobán. During **Semana Santa** (Easter Week), local artists design elaborate *alfombras* (carpets) of colored sawdust and flower petals rivaled only by those in Antigua.

San Cristóbal is also home to the Centro Communitario Educativo Pokomchi (Cecep), an organization dedicated to preserving traditional and modern ways of Poqomchi' life. Cecep inaugurated the **Museo Katinamit** (☎7950-4896; cecep@itelgua.com; Calle del Calvario 0-33, Zona 3, Q10, with guide Q20; ⏲8am-1pm & 2-5pm Mon-Sat), which recreates a typical Poqomchi' house. It also offers volunteer and ethno-tourism opportunities.

Lanquín

POP 29,000

One of the best excursions to make from Cobán is to the pretty village of Lanquín, 61km to the east. People come for two reasons: to explore the wonderful cave system just out of town and as a jumping-off point for visiting the natural rock pools at Semuc Champey (p182).

Sights & Activities

Grutas de Lanquín CAVE

(adult/child 5-12yr Q30/10, tubing Q5; ⏲8am-6pm) These caves are about 1km northwest of the town, and extend for several kilometers into the earth. There is now a ticket office here. The first cave has lights, but do take a powerful flashlight (torch) anyway in case of emergencies. You'll also need shoes with good traction as inside it's slippery with moisture and bat droppings.

Though the first few hundred meters of the cavern have been equipped with a walkway and lit by diesel-powered electric lights, much of this subterranean system is untouched. If you are not an experienced spelunker, you shouldn't wander too far into the caves; the entire extent has yet to be explored, let alone mapped.

As well as featuring funky stalactites, mostly named for animals, these caves are crammed with bats. Try to time your visit to coincide with sunset (around 6pm), when hundreds of them fly out of the mouth of the cave in formations so dense they obscure the sky. For a dazzling display of navigation skills, sit at the entrance while they exit. Please be aware that bats are extremely light-sensitive, and tempting as it may be, flash photography can disorient and, in some cases, blind them.

ADETES RAFTING

(☎5069-3518; www.guaterafting.com) This excellent community tourism initiative is based in Aldea Saquijá, 12km out of Lanquín. It offers rafting trips led by well-trained community members on the Río Cahabón. Prices range from Q260 to Q360 per person for a two- to five-hour trip. To get to the headquarters, catch any bus leaving Lanquín headed toward Cahabón.

Sleeping & Eating

The food is pretty good in Lanquín – there are some good-priced *comedores* (cheap eateries) in the town, and most of the hotels offer gringo-friendly menus.

Zephyr Lodge HOSTEL $$

(☎5168-2441; www.zephyrlodgelanquin.com; dm Q105, r Q350-500; P 📶 🏊) Lanquín's self-admitted party hostel is all class – great rooms with spectacular views, decent dorms and some good hangout areas, including the big thatched-roof bar/restaurant. The river is a five-minute walk downhill. Wi-fi goes off at 8pm, however, meaning there's all the more reason to party with your new-found friends instead of hanging out with your computer or phone.

El Muro HOSTEL $$
(☎4904-0671; www.elmurolanquin.net; dm Q50, r Q150-250;) By far the best option in the town itself, El Muro is a happy little hostel/bar featuring good-sized dorms and rooms. Most have attached bathrooms and fans, and all have breezy balconies overlooking the hills or garden. Hammocks are a nice way to relax. Also has a bar, a restaurant and games.

Rabin Itzam HOTEL $$
(☎5699-1402, 4913-8927; s/d Q173/288, s/d without bathroom Q92/184) A no-frills budget hotel in the center. The beds sag a bit, but rooms upstairs at the front (without bathroom) have good valley views. Good discounts outside Semana Santa.

Restaurante Champey GUATEMALAN $
(☎3000-6130; mains Q25-60; ⏲7:30am-11pm;) This large outdoor eatery halfway between town and El Retiro serves up good-sized plates of steak, eggs and rice and gets rowdy and beer-fueled at night. Vegetarian options are also available.

Information

Banrural (⏲24hr) On Lanquín's main square. Changes US dollars and traveler's checks, and has an ATM.

Getting There & Away

Overnight tours (p177) to Grutas de Lanquín and Semuc Champey, offered in Cobán for Q400 per person, are the easiest way to visit these places, but it's really not that complicated to organize yourself. Tours take about two hours to reach Lanquín from Cobán; the price includes a packed lunch.

Buses operate several times daily between Cobán and Lanquín, stopping at the **square** before continuing to Cahabón. There are eight buses to Cobán (Q25, 2½ hours) between 6am and 5:30pm. Shuttles for Semuc Champey (Q25 one way) leave at 9:30am (book at your hotel) and pickups (Q25) leave whenever they are full, half a block from the main square.

If you're heading toward Río Dulce, a back road exists, although it's unpaved for most of the way and gets washed out in heavy rains. Transportation schedules along here are flexible at best. Ask around to see what the current situation is. A daily shuttle (Q180, six hours) runs on this road and is the most reliable, easy option. Book at any of the hotels.

If it's been raining heavily and you're driving, you'll need a 4WD vehicle, as sections of the road between Lanquín and Semuc Champey are too steep for a normal vehicle to have traction. The road from San Pedro Carchá to El Pajal, where you turn off for Lanquín, is paved. The 11km from El Pajal to Lanquín is not. You can head on from Lanquín to Flores in 14 to 15 hours via El Pajal, Sebol, Raxruhá and Sayaxché. The road from El Pajal to Sebol is now paved. Or you can head from Lanquín to Sebol and Fray Bartolomé de Las Casas and on to Poptún.

Semuc Champey & Around

Eleven kilometers south of Lanquín, along a rough, bumpy, slow road, is **Semuc Champey** (Q50; ⏲8am-5pm), famed for its great 300m-long natural limestone bridge, on top of which is a stepped series of pools with cool, flowing river water good for swimming. The water is from the Río Cahabón, and much more of it passes underground, beneath the bridge. Though this bit of paradise is difficult to reach, the beauty of its setting and the perfection of the pools, ranging from turquoise to emerald-green, make it worth it. Many people consider this the most beautiful spot in all Guatemala.

If you're visiting on a tour, some guides will take you down a rope ladder from the lowest pool to the river, which gushes out from the rocks below. Plenty of people do this and love it, though it is a bit risky.

Sleeping & Eating

★**Utopia** HOSTEL $$
(☎3135-8329; www.utopiaecohotel.com; campsites per person Q30, hammock/dm Q35/70, r with/without bathroom Q315/285;) Set on a hillside overlooking the small village of Semil, 3km from Semuc Champey, this is the most impressive setup in the area. Every type of accommodations imaginable is available, from nice riverside cabins to campsites. The restaurant/bar (serving vegetarian family-style meals) has fantastic valley views, and the stretch of river that it sits on is truly idyllic.

The turnoff to Semil is 2km before Semuc Champey. From there it's about 1km to the hotel. Call from Lanquín (or drop into the office at the crossroads where the bus arrives) for free transport out here.

El Portal HOSTEL $$
(☎4091-7878; dm Q60, r with/without bathroom Q250/150;) About 100m short of the entrance to Semuc Champey, this is the obvious choice for convenient access to Semuc. There's only electricity from 6pm to 11pm, but the well-spaced wooden huts built on the bank sloping down to the river are by far

the best accommodations deal in the area. Meals and tours are available.

Getting There & Away

If you're into walking, the 2½-hour trip from Lanquín is a fairly pleasant one, passing through lush countryside and simple rural scenes, and if you change your mind, it's easy to flag down a ride the rest of the way.

Pickups run from the plaza in Lanquín to Semuc Champey – your chances of catching one are better in the early morning and on market days: Sunday, Monday and Thursday. Expect to pay somewhere between Q25. All the Lanquín hotels and hostels run shuttle services out here too.

Fray Bartolomé de Las Casas

This town, often referred to simply as Fray, is a way station on the back route between the Cobán/Lanquín area and Poptún. This route is dotted with traditional Maya villages where only the patriarchs speak Spanish, and then only a little. This is a great opportunity for getting off the 'gringo trail' and into the heart of Guatemala.

Fray is substantial considering it's in the middle of nowhere, but don't let its size fool you. This is a place where the weekly soccer game is the biggest deal in town, chickens languish in the streets and siesta is taken seriously.

Accommodations options are very limited here. **Hotel La Cabaña** (☎7952-0097; 2a Calle 1-92, Zona 3; r per person with/without bathroom Q75/50) is about the best in town.

Eating options are few – try **Restaurante Doris** (☎3011-3396; ⏲7am-9pm) on the main street. Otherwise, grab a steak (with tortillas and beans, Q20) at the informal BBQ shacks that open up along the main street at night.

At least two daily buses depart from the plaza for Poptún (Q40, five hours). Buses for Cobán leave hourly between 4am and 4pm. Some go via Chisec (Q50, 3½ hours). Others take the slower route via San Pedro Carchá. Buses stop at the plaza before going eastward to the stop at the other side of town. Heading west, they leave from the station but will pick up travelers at the plaza before continuing onward.

EL ORIENTE

Heading east from Guatemala City brings you into the long, flat valleys of the region Guatemalans call El Oriente (the East). It's a dry and unforgiving landscape of stunted hillsides covered in scraggly brush. It's tough out here and the cowboy hats, boots, buckles and sidearms sported by a lot of the men in the region fit well against this rugged backdrop.

Most travelers pass through on their way to Copán in Honduras or to visit the pilgrimage town of Esquipulas. Further east, the landscape becomes a lot more tropical and you'll see plenty of fruit for sale at roadside stalls. If you've got some time in this area, a quick side trip to the ruins at Quiriguá is well worth your while.

Chiquimula

POP 106,000

Thirty-two kilometers south of Río Hondo on Hwy 10, Chiquimula is a major market town for all of eastern Guatemala. For travelers it's not a destination but a transit point. Your goal is probably the fabulous Maya ruins at Copán in Honduras, just across the border from El Florido. There are also some interesting journeys between Chiquimula and Jalapa, 78km to the west.

Sleeping & Eating

There's a string of *comedores* (cheap eateries) on 8a Av behind the market. At night, snack vendors and taco carts set up along 7a Av opposite the plaza, selling the cheapest eats in town.

Hotel Hernández HOTEL $
(☎7942-0708; 3a Calle 7-41, Zona 1; s/d with fan Q80/120, with air-con Q120/200; P ⊖ ❄ ≋ ☒) It's hard to beat the Hernández – it's been a favorite for years and keeps going strong, with its central position, spacious, simple rooms and good-sized swimming pool.

Hotel Posada Don Adan HOTEL $
(☎7942-3924; 8a Av 4-30, Zona 1; s/d Q120/180; P ⊖ ❄) The Don offers the best deal in this price range – neat, complete rooms with TV, fan, air-con, a couple of sticks of furniture and good, firm beds. It locks the doors at 10pm.

Hostal Casa Vieja HOTEL $$$
(☎7942-7991; hostalcasaviejachiquimula@hotmail.com; 8a Av 1-60, Zona 2; s/ste Q350/600; P ⊖ ❄ ≋) A short walk from the center, Hostal Casa Vieja is the best hotel in town. Rooms are delicately decorated and the garden areas are lovely. The whole place radiates a tranquility sorely missing in the rest of town. Laundry service and meals are also available.

Casa Lú GUATEMALAN $$

(☎5927-2562; Parque El Calvario; mains Q30-70; ⏰10:30am-10:30pm) This chic, black-and-red restaurant has the look of a sushi shop but serves a variety of local Guatemalan dishes as well as the requisite pizzas, pastas and burgers, and some decent cocktails too. The frozen margarita (grande) is colossal and a nice way to beat the Chiquimula heat.

Charli's INTERNATIONAL $$

(☎7943-8559; 7a Av 5-55, Zona 1; mains Q60-120; ⏰8am-9pm) Chiquimula option with a wide menu featuring pasta, pizza, seafood and steaks, all served up amid chilly air-con, with relaxed and friendly service.

Information

Banco G&T (7a Av 4-75, Zona 1; ⏰9am-8pm Mon-Fri, 10am-2pm Sat) Half a block south of the plaza. Changes US dollars and traveler's checks, and gives cash advances on Visa and MasterCard.

Getting There & Away

Several companies operate buses and microbuses, arriving and departing from the **bus station area** (11a Av, btwn 1a & 2a Calles). **Litegua** (☎7942-2064; www.litegua.com; 1a Calle, btwn 10a & 11a Avs), which operates buses to El Florido (the border crossing on the way to Copán) and Flores, has its own bus station a half block north. For the Honduran border crossing at Agua Caliente, take a minibus to Esquipulas and change there. If you're headed to Jalapa, you'll need to go to Ipala to make the connection. For Río Dulce, take a Flores bus or a Puerto Barrios bus to La Ruidosa junction and change there. If you're going to Esquipulas, sit on the left for the best views of the basilica housing the shrine of El Cristo Negro.

Esquipulas

POP 66,000

From Chiquimula, Hwy 10 goes south into the mountains, where it's a bit cooler. After an hour's ride through pretty country, the highway descends into a valley ringed by mountains, where Esquipulas sits. Halfway down the slope, about 1km from the center of town, there is a *mirador* (lookout) from which you get a good view. The reason for a trip to Esquipulas is evident as soon as you catch sight of the place, dominated as it is by the towering Basílica de Esquipulas, its whiteness shimmering in the sun.

History

This town may have been a place of pilgrimage before the Spanish conquest. Legend has it that the town takes its name from a noble Maya lord who ruled this region when the Spanish arrived and who received them in peace.

With the arrival of the friars, a church was built, and in 1595 an image that came to be known as El Cristo Negro (Black Christ) was installed behind the altar. In response to the steady increase in pilgrims to Esquipulas, a huge new church was inaugurated in 1758, and the pilgrimage trade has been the town's livelihood ever since.

Sights

Basílica de Esquipulas BASILICA

(11a Calle) A massive structure that has resisted the power of earthquakes for almost 250 years, the basilica is approached through a pretty park and up a wide flight of steps. The impressive facade and towers are floodlit at night. And if waiting hours to view a famed 'Black Christ' is your cup of tea, this is the right place to do it.

Inside, the devout approach the surprisingly small El Cristo Negro (Black Christ) with extreme reverence, many on their knees. Incense, murmured prayers and the scuffle of feet fill the air. When there are throngs of pilgrims, you must enter the church from the side to get a close view of the famous shrine. Shuffling along quickly, you may get a good glimpse or two before being shoved onward by the crowd behind you. On Sundays, religious holidays and (especially) during the **Cristo de Esquipulas festival** (January 14 to 15), the press of devotees is intense. On weekdays, you may have the place to yourself, which can be very powerful and rewarding.

Centro Turístico Cueva de las Minas CAVE

(☎4979-9086; Q30; ⏰7am-6pm) This has a 50m-deep cave (bring your own light), grassy picnic areas and the Río El Milagro, where people come for a dip and say it's miraculous. The cave and river are 500m from the entrance, which is behind the basilica's cemetery, 300m south of the turnoff into town on the road to Honduras. Refreshments are available. Note that (unlike some internet descriptions) this river does NOT go into the cave, so no tubing or wading is possible.

Sleeping

Esquipulas has an abundance of places to stay. On holidays and during the annual Cristo de Esquipulas festival, every hotel in town is filled, whatever the price; weekends are superbusy as well, with prices substantially higher. These rates reflect weekend prices. On weekdays (excluding the festival period), there are *descuentos* (discounts). For cheap rooms, look in the streets immediately north of the towering basilica.

Hotel Monte Cristo HOTEL $$
(7943-1453; 3a Av 9-12, Zona 1; s/d Q220/257, without bathroom Q98/122; P) Good-sized rooms with a bit of furniture and hot showers. A policy of not letting the upstairs rooms until the downstairs ones are full might see you staying at ground level.

Hotel Mahanaim HOTEL $$
(7943-1131; 10a Calle 1-85, Zona 1; s/d Q150/300; P) This establishment is on five levels around a covered courtyard. Rooms are comfortable but plain. It wouldn't be such a good deal if it weren't for the big covered swimming pool out back.

Hotel Vistana al Señor HOTEL $$
(7943-4294; hotelvistana@gmail.com; 1a Av 'A' 1-42; s/d Q350/450; P) By far the best deal in this price range are these sweet little rooms just south of the market. There's an attractive common balcony area with good views upstairs.

Hotel Portal de la Fe HOTEL $$$
(7943-4124; 11a Calle 1-70, Zona 1; s/d Q350/600; P) One of the few hotels with any real style in town and a fun spiral staircase in the main lobby. Subterranean rooms are predictably dark, but upstairs the situation improves considerably.

Eating

Restaurants are slightly more expensive here than in other parts of Guatemala. Budget restaurants are clustered at the north end of the basilica's park, where hungry pilgrims can find them readily.

Restaurante Calle Real GUATEMALAN $
(7943-0537; 3a Av; mains Q35-90; 7:30am-9pm Mon-Fri, 8am-10pm Sat & Sun) Typical of many restaurants here, this big eating-barn turns out cheap meals for the pilgrims. It has a wide menu, florescent lighting and lots of paintings of the basilica on the wall.

GETTING TO EL SALVADOR

Between Chiquimula and Esquipulas (35km from Chiquimula and 14km from Esquipulas), Padre Miguel junction is the turnoff for Anguiatú, at the border with El Salvador, which is 19km (30 minutes) away. Minibuses pass by frequently, coming from Chiquimula, Quetzaltepeque and Esquipulas.

The border at Anguiatú is open 24 hours, but you're best crossing during daylight. Plenty of trucks cross here. Across the border there are hourly buses to the capital, San Salvador, passing through Metapán and Santa Ana.

City Grill STEAK $$
(7943-1748; cnr 2a Av & 10a Calle, Zona 1; mains Q50-150; 7:30am-9pm Mon-Fri, 7am-10pm Sat & Sun) The best steakhouse in town (featuring some of the best steaks for miles around) also serves up some decent seafood and pasta dishes. The pizza is worth a look-in too.

Restaurant El Angel CHINESE $$
(7943-1372; cnr 11a Calle & 2a Av, Zona 1; mains Q50-70; 8am-9pm) This main-street Chinese eatery does all the standard dishes, plus steaks and a good range of *licuados* (milkshakes). Home delivery is available, and it has daily specials on the cheap too.

La Rotonda FAST FOOD $$
(7943-3038; 1a Av 'A' 10-30, Zona 1; mains Q40-180; 8am-10pm) Opposite Rutas Orientales bus station, this is a round building with chairs arranged around a circular open-air counter under a big awning. It's a welcoming place – clean and fresh. There are plenty of options to choose from, including pizza, pasta and burgers.

Information

Banco Internacional (3a Av 8-87, Zona 1; 8am-6pm Mon-Fri, 9am-1pm Sat) Changes cash and traveler's checks, gives cash advances on Visa and MasterCard, is the town's American Express agent and has a Visa ATM.

Getting There & Away

Buses to Guatemala City (Q65 to Q75, four to five hours) arrive and depart hourly from 1:30am to 4pm from the **Rutas Orientales bus station** (7943-1366; cnr 11a Calle & 1a Av 'A', Zona 1), near the entrance to town.

Minibuses to Agua Caliente (Honduran border; Q20, 30 minutes) arrive and depart across the street, leaving every half-hour from 5am to 5pm; taxis also wait here, charging the same as minibuses, once they have five passengers.

Minibuses to Chiquimula (Q15, 90 minutes, every six minutes) depart from the east end of 11a Calle (next to Plaza Pepsi).

Transportes Guerra (cnr 5a Av & 10a Calle, Zona 1) goes to Anguiatú (El Salvador border; Q15, 80 minutes, every 30 minutes, between 6am and 6pm).

There are three buses daily for Flores/Santa Elena (Q120, eight hours) from the **Transportes María Elena** (☎7943-0957; 11a Calle 0-54, Zona 1; ⏲4am-8pm) office, departing at 4:30am, 8:30am and 1:30pm. It passes Quiriguá (Q45, two hours), Río Dulce (Q60, four hours) and Poptún (Q90, six hours).

Quiriguá

POP 4800

Quiriguá archaeological site is only 50km from Copán as the crow flies, but the lay of the land, the international border and the condition of the roads make it a journey of 175km. Quiriguá is famed for its intricately carved stelae – the gigantic brown sandstone monoliths that rise as high as 10.5m, like ancient sentinels, in a quiet well-kept tropical park.

From Río Hondo junction it's 67km along Hwy 9 to the village of **Los Amates**, where there are a couple of hotels, a restaurant, food stalls, a bank and a small bus station. Quiriguá village is 1.5km east of Los Amates, and the turnoff to the ruins is another 1.5km to the east. The 3.4km access road leads south through banana groves.

History

Quiriguá's history parallels that of Copán, of which it was a dependency during much of the Classic period. Of the three sites in this area, only the present archaeological park is of interest.

Quiriguá's location lent itself to the carving of giant stelae. Beds of brown sandstone in the nearby Río Motagua had cleavage planes suitable for cutting large pieces. Though soft when first cut, the sandstone dried hard in the air. With Copán's expert artisans nearby for guidance, Quiriguá's stone carvers were ready for greatness. All they needed was a great leader to inspire them – and to pay for the carving of the huge stelae.

That leader was K'ak' Tiliw Chan Yo'at (Cauac Sky; r 725–84), who decided that Quiriguá should no longer be under the control of Copán. In a war with his former suzerain, Cauac Sky took Uaxaclahun Ubak K'awil (King 18 Rabbit) of Copán prisoner in 737 and later had him beheaded. Independent at last, Cauac Sky commissioned his stonecutters to go to work, and for the next 38 years they turned out giant stelae and zoomorphs dedicated to his glory.

Cauac Sky's son Sky Xul (r 784–800) lost his throne to a usurper, Jade Sky. This last great king of Quiriguá continued the building boom initiated by Cauac Sky, reconstructing Quiriguá's Acrópolis on a grander scale.

Quiriguá remained unknown to Europeans until the explorer and diplomat John L Stephens arrived in 1840. Impressed by its great monuments, Stephens lamented the world's lack of interest in them in his book *Incidents of Travel in Central America, Chiapas and Yucatan* (1841).

Stephens tried to buy the ruined city in order to have its stelae shipped to New York, but the owner, Señor Payes, assumed that Stephens (being a diplomat), was negotiating on behalf of the US government and that the government would pay. Payes quoted an extravagant price, and the deal was never made.

Between 1881 and 1894, excavations were carried out by Alfred P Maudslay. In the early 20th century all the land around Quiriguá was sold to the US-based United Fruit Company and turned into banana groves. The company is gone, but the bananas and Quiriguá remain. Restoration of the site was carried out by the University of Pennsylvania in the 1930s. In 1981 Unesco declared the ruins a World Heritage Site, one of only three in Guatemala (the others are Tikal and Antigua).

Sights

Quiriguá Archaeological Site ARCHAEOLOGICAL SITE

(Q80; ⏲8am-4:30pm) Despite the sticky heat and (sometimes) bothersome mosquitoes, Quiriguá is a wonderful place. The giant stelae on the **Gran Plaza** (Great Plaza) are all much more worn than those at Copán. To impede further deterioration, each has been covered by a thatched roof. The roofs cast shadows that make it difficult to examine the carving closely and almost impossible to get a good photograph, but somehow this does little to inhibit one's sense of awe.

Seven of the **stelae**, designated A, C, D, E, F, H and J, were built during the reign of Cauac Sky and carved with his image. Stela E is the largest Maya stela known, standing some 8m above ground, with another 3m or so buried in the earth. It weighs almost 60,000kg. Note the exuberant, elaborate headdresses; the beards on some of the figures (an oddity in Maya art and life); the staffs of office held in the kings' hands; and the glyphs on the sides of the stela.

At the far end of the plaza is the Acrópolis, far less impressive than the one at Copán. At its base are several **zoomorphs**, blocks of stone carved to resemble real and mythic creatures. Frogs, tortoises, jaguars and serpents were favorite subjects. The low zoomorphs can't compete with the towering stelae in impressiveness, but as works of art, imagination and mythic significance, the zoomorphs are superb.

Sleeping & Eating

Posada de Quiriguá BOUTIQUE HOTEL **$$**
(5349-5817; www.facebook.com/posadadequirigua; s/d Q160/300; P) The Posada de Quiriguá gets high marks, not only for lovely rooms and a gracious owner, but also for delicious Japanese food that's served there. There are only a few rooms, and when the owner is traveling the *posada* is closed, so advance reservations are essential.

Getting There & Away

Buses running Guatemala City–Puerto Barrios, Guatemala City–Flores, Esquipulas–Flores or Chiquimula–Flores will drop you off or pick you up here. If you're heading for the **hotel** (7934-2624; s/d Q80/150; P), make sure you get dropped at the *pasarela de Quiriguá* (the pedestrian overpass). Buses will also drop you at the turnoff to the archaeological site if you ask.

From the highway it's 3.4km to the archaeological site – Q5 to Q10 by *tuk-tuk* (three-wheeled motor taxi), but if one doesn't come, don't fret: it's a pleasant walk (without luggage) through banana plantations to get there.

If you're staying in Quiriguá village or Los Amates and walking to the archaeological site, you can take a shortcut along the railroad that goes from the village through the banana fields, crossing the access road very near the entrance to the archaeological site. A *tuk-tuk* from Quiriguá village to the site should cost around Q20.

Out on the main highway buses pass frequently for Río Dulce (Q35, two hours), Chiquimula (Q35, two hours) and Puerto Barrios (Q25).

Lago de Izabal

Guatemala's largest lake, to the north of Hwy 9, is starting to earn its place on travelers' itineraries. Most visitors checking out the lake stay at Río Dulce town, by the long, tall bridge where Hwy 13, heading north to Flores and Tikal, crosses the Río Dulce, which empties out of the east end of the lake. Downstream, the beautiful river broadens into a lake called El Golfete before meeting the Caribbean at Lívingston. River trips are a highlight of a visit to eastern Guatemala. If you're looking for lakeside ambience minus the Río Dulce congestion and pace, head to Chapin Abajo, west of Mariscos or El Estor near the west end of the lake, both of which give access to the rich wildlife of the Bocas del Polochic river delta. There are many undiscovered spots in this area waiting to be explored, so don't limit yourself.

Río Dulce

POP 7200

At the east end of the Lago de Izabal, this town still gets referred to as Fronteras – a hangover from the days when the only way across the river was by ferry, and this was the last piece of civilization before embarking on the long, difficult journey into El Petén.

Times have changed. A huge bridge now spans the water and the Petén region's roads are some of the best in the country. The town sees most tourist traffic from yachties – the US Coast Guard says this is the safest place on the western Caribbean for boats during hurricane season. The rest of the foreigners here are either coming or going on the spectacular river trip between here and Lívingston.

Sleeping

Many places in Río Dulce communicate by radio, but all are reachable by telephone. The bar at Bruno's (p188) will radio your choice of place to stay if necessary.

Hotel Kangaroo HOTEL **$**
(5363-6716, in English 4513-9602; www.hotelkangaroo.com; dm Q60, r Q160-180, bungalow Q220-250; @) On the Río La Colocha, just across the water from El Castillo de San

RÍO DULCE CRUISES

Tour agencies in town offer day trips up the Río Dulce to Río Dulce town (departing at 9:30am and 2:30pm), as do most local sailors at the Lívingston dock. Many travelers use these tours as one-way transportation to Río Dulce, paying Q125 one way. It's a beautiful ride through tropical jungle scenery, with several places to stop on the way.

While a boat ride on the Río Dulce is not to be missed, if you're coming from Guatemala City or Puerto Barrios it makes much more sense to catch a boat from Puerto Barrios to Lívingston and do the tour on your way out.

Shortly after you leave Lívingston, you pass the tributary Río Tatin on the right, then will probably stop at an **indigenous arts museum** set up by **Asociación Ak' Tenamit** (☎5908-3392; www.aktenamit.org), an NGO working to improve conditions for the Q'eqchi' Maya population of the area. The river enters a gorge called **La Cueva de la Vaca**, its walls hung with great tangles of jungle foliage and the humid air noisy with the cries of tropical birds. Just beyond that is **La Pintada**, a rock escarpment covered with graffiti. Further on, a **thermal spring** forces sulfurous water out of the base of the cliff, providing a chance for a warm swim. The river widens into **El Golfete**, a lakelike body of water that presages the even more vast expanse of Lago de Izabal further upstream.

On the northern shore of El Golfete is the **Biotopo Chocón Machacas**, a 72-sq-km reserve established within the Parque Nacional Río Dulce to protect the beautiful river landscape, the valuable forests and mangrove swamps and their wildlife, which includes such rare creatures as the tapir and above all the manatee. A network of 'water trails' (boat routes around several jungle lagoons) provides ways to see other bird, animal and plant life of the reserve. You can stay here, at the community-run lodge Q'ana Itz'am in Lagunita Salvador, but you will have to arrange transportation separately.

Boats will probably visit **Islas de Pájaros**, a pair of islands where thousands of waterbirds live, in the middle of El Golfete. From El Golfete you continue upriver, passing increasing numbers of expensive villas and boathouses, to the town of Río Dulce, where the soaring Hwy 13 road bridge crosses the river, and on to El Castillo de San Felipe on Lago de Izabal.

You can also do this trip starting from Río Dulce.

Felipe, this beautiful, simple Australian-Mexican-run place is built on stilts in the mangroves. Its restaurant's beguiling menu (mains Q50 to Q100) features some Aussie classics and probably the best Mexican food you're likely to find outside of Mexico.

Bruno's HOTEL **$$**
(☎7930-5721; www.brunoshotel.com; camping per person Q25, dm Q50, s Q100-220, d Q200-500; P ❄ 📶 🏊) A path leads down from the northwest end of the bridge to this riverside hangout for yachties needing to get some land under their feet. The dorms are clean and spacious and the building offers some of the most comfortable rooms in town, with air-con and balconies overlooking the river. It's well set up for families and sleeps up to six.

Casa Perico HOSTEL **$$**
(☎7930-5666; www.casa-perico.com; dm Q60, s/d without bathroom from Q110/160, cabins Q220; 📶) One of the more low-key options in the area, this place is set on a lovely little inlet about 200m from the main river. Cabins are well built and connected by boardwalks. It offers tours all up and down the river and puts on an à la carte dinner (mains Q40 to Q90).

If you want the one cabin with a bathroom, make sure you book ahead.

El Tortugal BUNGALOW **$$**
(☎7742-8847; www.tortugal.com; r/bungalow from Q420/513; 📶) The best-looking bungalows on the river are located here, a five-minute *lancha* (small motorboat) ride south from town. There are a few rooms too. There are plenty of hammocks, the showers are seriously hot and kayaks are free in the morning for guest use.

Hotel Backpackers HOSTEL **$$**
(☎7930-5168, 7930-5480; www.hotelbackpackers.com; dm Q30-50, r with/without bathroom from Q250/120; @ 📶) Across the bridge from Río Dulce town, this is an old backpacker favorite, set in a rickety, waterside building with basic rooms and dorms. The bar kicks on here at night, with karaoke at times. Visitors are

warned to avoid having food in their backpacks as it may be nibbled at night by rats.

If you're coming by *lancha* (small motorboat) or bus, ask the driver to let you off here to spare yourself the walk across the bridge.

Eating

Most of the hotels in town have restaurants. Bruno's serves good breakfasts and gringo comfort food and has a full bar. **Hacienda Tijax** (7930-5505; www.tijax.com; s/d from Q339/439, without bathroom Q123/223; P) is a popular lunch spot – give it a call and it'll arrange to have you picked up.

★**Sundog Café** INTERNATIONAL $
(4999-6972; sandwiches Q50, mains Q35-115; noon-9pm, bar to 11pm) Down a laneway opposite the Litegua bus office (200m up the main street past the end of the bridge), this open-air riverfront bar-restaurant makes sandwiches and offers a few vegetarian dishes, brick-oven pizzas and fresh juices, as well as great views. It's also the place to come for unbiased information about the area.

Cafe Paris CRÊPES $
(7930-5038; crepes Q25-55; 7am-9pm) This cafe/hotel offers very tasty coffee and espresso drinks, plus passable croissants. While its crepes might not quite pass muster at a bistro on the Champs-Élysées, they're a decent respite from the Guatemalan breakfast norm. Wi-fi is spotty.

Information

If you need to change cash or traveler's checks, visit one of the banks in town, all on the main road. **Banco Industrial** (9am-4pm Mon-Fri) has a Visa ATM. There's also a trustworthy Visa/MasterCard ATM inside the **Dispensa Familiar** (CA-13; 8am-8pm) supermarket, also on the main street.

The local online newspaper **Chisme Vindicator** (www.riodulcechisme.com) has loads of information about Río Dulce.

Getting There & Away

BUS

The **Litegua bus office** (7930-5251; 5am-8pm) is on the north side of the bridge. Seven buses depart for Guatemala City daily (Q80 to Q100).

Minibuses leave for Puerto Barrios (Q25, two hours) when full, near the Litegua bus station.

There's a daily shuttle to Lanquín (Q180, five hours), leaving from in front of the Sundog Café at 1:30pm.

Minibuses leave for El Estor (Q20, 1½ hours, 7am to 6pm hourly) from the San Felipe and El Estor turnoff in the middle of town.

BOAT

From the main dock, shared *lanchas* (small motorboats; one way/round-trip per person Q125/250) go down the Río Dulce to Lívingston, usually requiring eight to 10 people. The trip is a beautiful one, making a 'tour' of it, with several stops along the way. Boats usually leave from 9am to about 2pm. There are regular, scheduled departures at 9:30am and 2pm. Pretty much everyone in town can organize a *lancha* service to Lívingston and most other places you'd care to go, but they charge more.

San Felipe

The fortress and castle of San Felipe de Lara, **El Castillo de San Felipe** (Q25; 8am-5pm), about 3km west of Río Dulce town, was built in 1652 to keep pirates from looting the villages and commercial caravans of Izabal. Though the fortress somewhat deterred the buccaneers, a pirate force captured and burned it in 1686. By the end of the next century, pirates had disappeared from the Caribbean, and the fort's sturdy walls served as a prison.

Eventually the fortress was abandoned and became a ruin – the present fort was reconstructed in 1956.

Today the castle is protected as a park and is one of the Lago de Izabal's principal tourist attractions. In addition to the fort itself, there are grassy grounds, BBQ and picnic areas, and the opportunity to swim in the lake. The place rocks during the **Feria de San Felipe** (April 30 to May 4).

Near El Castillo, **Hotel Don Humberto** (7930-5051; s/d Q48/86; P) offers basic rooms with big beds and good mosquito netting. It's nothing fancy, but is more than adequate for a cheap sleep.

Getting There & Away

San Felipe is on the lakeshore, 3km south of Río Dulce. It's a beautiful 45-minute walk between the two towns, or take a minivan (Q15, every 30 minutes). In Río Dulce it stops on the corner of the highway and road to El Estor; in San Felipe it stops at the entrance to El Castillo.

Boats coming from Lívingston will drop you in San Felipe if you ask. The Río Dulce river tours usually come to El Castillo, allowing you to get out and visit the castle if you like, or you can come over from Río Dulce by private *lancha* (small motorboat).

El Estor

POP 21,100

The major settlement on the northern shore of Lago de Izabal is El Estor, a friendly, quiet town with a lovely setting, which provides an easy jumping-off point for Bocas del Polochic, a highly biodiverse wildlife reserve at the west end of the lake. The town is also a staging post on a possible route between Río Dulce and Lanquín.

Sleeping & Eating

Restaurante Típico Chaabil HOTEL $

(☎7949-7666, 7949-7272; 3a Calle; s/d Q75/150; P ⊖) Although they go a bit heavy on the log-cabin feel, the rooms at this place, at the west end of the street, are the best deal in town. Get one upstairs for plenty of light and good views. The restaurant here, on a lovely lakeside terrace, cooks up delicious food, such as *tapado* (Garifuna casserole).

The water here is crystal clear and you can swim right off the hotel's dock.

Hotel Vista al Lago HOTEL $$

(☎7949-7658, 7949-7205; 6a Av 1-13; s/d/tr Q150/225/300) Set in a classic historic building down on the waterfront, this place has plenty of style, although the rooms themselves are fairly ordinary. Views 'of the world's largest swimming pool,' from the upstairs balcony are superb. Rooms with fans have negotiable prices always lower than those with air-con.

Hotel Villela HOTEL $$

(☎4930-5043; 6a Av 2-06; s/d/tr Q130/255/380; P ⊖ 📶 ❄) The rooms are less attractive than the neat lawn and trees they're set around, but some are airier and brighter than others. All have fan and bathroom. Significant discounts in the off season.

Information

Banrural (cnr 3a Calle & 5a Av; ⊙8:30am-5pm Mon-Fri, 9am-1pm Sat) Changes US dollars and Amex traveler's checks and has an ATM.

Fundación Defensores de la Naturaleza (☎7949-7237, 3011-7575; https://defensores.org.gt; cnr 5a Av & 2a Calle; ⊙hours vary) Administers the Refugio de Vida Silvestre Bocas del Polochic and the Reserva de Biosfera Sierra de las Minas, among other projects.

Getting There & Away

El Estor is most easily reached from Río Dulce via a new paved road. Combis cost Q20 and run between 5am and 7pm.

You can get to Lanquín by taking the truck that leaves El Estor's Parque Central at 10:30am for Cahabón (Q40, four to five hours), and then a bus or pickup straight on from Cahabón to Lanquín the same day. Coming the other way involves changing in Cahabón, sometimes meaning an overnight there.

Refugio de Vida Silvestre Bocas del Polochic & Reserva de Biosfera Sierra de las Minas

The Refugio de Vida Silvestre Bocas del Polochic (Bocas del Polochic Wildlife Reserve) covers the delta of the Río Polochic, which provides most of Lago de Izabal's water. A visit here affords great birdwatching and howler-monkey observation. The reserve supports more than 300 species of birds – the migration seasons, September to October and April to May, are reportedly fantastic – and many varieties of butterflies and fish. You may well see alligators and, if you're lucky, glimpse a manatee. Ask in El Estor for boat guides. The reserve is managed by the Fundación Defensores de la Naturaleza, whose research station, the **Estación Científica Selempim** (☎3011-7507; https://defensores.org.gt; camping/dm per person Q20/50), just to the south in Reserva de Biosfera Sierra de las Minas, is open for ecotourism visits. Contact Defensores' El Estor office for bookings and further information.

To explore the reserves, you can use canoes free of charge, take boat trips (Q250 to Q400) or walk any of the three well-established trails.

Getting There & Away

You can get to the Estación Científica Selempim by special hire (Q600 for a boatload of up to 12 people).

Puerto Barrios

POP 117,000

Port towns have always had a reputation for being slightly dodgy, and those acting as international borders doubly so. Puerto Barrios has an edgy feel; for foreign visitors, it's mainly a jumping-off point for boats to Punta Gorda (Belize) or Lívingston, and you probably won't be hanging around.

Because of its spacious layout, you must walk or ride further in Puerto Barrios to get from place to place. For instance, it's 800m from the bus terminals by the market in the

OFF THE BEATEN TRACK

FINCA IXOBEL

Finca Ixobel is 5km south of the regional commercial center of Poptún, from where you can take a taxi (Q50) or *tuk-tuk* (Q20 to Q30). Otherwise, any bus or minibus along Hwy 13 can drop you at the turnoff, from where it's a 15-minute walk to the lodge. Departing, most buses will stop on the highway to pick you up, but not after dark.

The best way to get to Poptún from Flores/Santa Elena is to take a minibus from the main terminal (Q30, every 10 minutes, 5am to 7pm); tell the driver where you're heading and they'll drop you at the lodge. Coming from Guatemala City or Río Dulce, all Santa Elena–bound buses make a stop in Poptún.

The **Finca Ixobel lodge** (☎5410-4307; www.fincaixobel.com; campsite/dm Q40/55, private room s/d Q205/355, without bathroom Q100/155, tree house from Q150/275; P @) is an ecological resort/bohemian hideaway set amid pine forest and patches of jungle between Flores and Río Dulce in southeast Petén. With a friendly, relaxed atmosphere, a wide range of activities, accommodation options and lip-smacking homemade meals, it's a great place to meet fellow travelers.

town center to the Muelle Municipal at the end of 12a Calle, from which passenger boats depart. Very few businesses use street numbers – most just label which street it's on, and the cross streets it's in between.

Sleeping & Eating

Hotel Lee HOTEL $

(☎7948-0830; 5a Av, btwn Calles 9a & 10a; s/d with fan Q57/100, d with air-con Q180; P) This is a friendly, family-owned place, close to the bus terminals. Typical of Puerto Barrios' budget hotels, it offers straightforward, vaguely clean rooms. The little balcony out front catches the odd breeze.

Puerto Bello HOTEL $$

(☎7948-0525; 8a Av, btwn Calles 18 & 19; s/d Q255/440; P @) By far the best-looking hotel in town, marred only by its slightly out-of-the-way location. The rooms are spacious and modern and the lovely garden and pool (with waterslide!) area is a blessing year-round.

Hotel Europa HOTEL $$

(☎7948-1292; 3a Av, btwn Calles 11a & 12a; s/d with fan Q87/170, with air-con Q145/290; P) Near the public dock and thus convenient, this spot has clean rooms with TV, arranged around a parking courtyard, but check that the rate you're given isn't higher than the prices the hotel lists in the lobby.

Kaffa CAFE $

(☎7942-9175; 8a Av, btwn Calles 7a & 8a; sandwiches & breakfast Q25-40; ⌚8am-9:30pm Tue-Sun) A hip coffee shop in Puerto Barrios? Who would have guessed! The coffee and the breezy deck overlooking the park are both excellent.

★**Restaurante Safari** SEAFOOD $$

(☎7948-0563; cnr 1a Calle & 5a Av; seafood Q45-125; ⌚10am-9pm; P) The town's most enjoyable restaurant is on a thatch-roofed, open-air platform right over the water about 1km north of the town center. Locals and visitors alike love to eat and catch the sea breezes here. Excellent seafood of all kinds, including the specialty *tapado* – that great Garifuna soup (Q110).

Chicken and meat dishes are less expensive than seafood. If the Safari is full, the Cangrejo Azul next door offers pretty much the same deal, in a more relaxed environment.

Information

Immigration Office (cnr 12a Calle & 3a Av; ⌚7am-6pm) A block from the Muelle Municipal. Come here for your entry or exit stamp if you're arriving from or leaving for Belize. If you're leaving by sea, there is a Q80 departure tax to pay. If you are heading to Honduras, you can get your exit stamp at another immigration office on the road to the border at Corinto.

Getting There & Away

BUS

Minibuses (cnr 6a Av & 9a Calle) to Chiquimula (Q45, 4½ hours), via Quiriguá, leave every half-hour from 3am to 4pm. Minibuses to Río Dulce (Q25, two hours) leave from the same location.

Transportes Litegua (☎7948-1172; cnr 6a Av & 9a Calle) has frequent services to Guatemala City (Q100 to Q150, five to six hours), via Quiriguá and Río Hondo. *Directo* services avoid a half-hour detour into Morales.

GETTING TO HONDURAS

Minibuses leave for the Honduran frontier (Q30, 1½ hours) every 20 minutes from 5am to 5pm, from 6a Av outside the market in Puerto Barrios. They stop en route to the border at Guatemalan immigration, where you may be required to pay Q10 for an exit stamp. Honduran entry formalities will leave you around L60 lighter.

One semi-express minibus per day departs at 7am (Q75), from the Muelle Municipal (city dock).

BOAT

Boats depart from the **Muelle Municipal** (city dock) at the end of 12a Calle.

Regular *lanchas* (small motorboats) depart for Lívingston (Q35, 30 minutes, eight daily) between 5:30am and 5:30pm. Buy your ticket as early as you can on the day (you can't book before your day of departure) – spaces are limited and sometimes sell out.

Outside these regular times, *lanchas* depart whenever they have six people ready to go and cost Q50 per person.

Most of the movement from Lívingston to Puerto Barrios is in the morning, returning in the afternoon. From Lívingston, your last chance of the day may be the 5pm *lancha*, especially during the low season when fewer travelers are shuttling back and forth.

Lanchas also depart from the Muelle Municipal three times daily for Punta Gorda in Belize (Q200, one hour) at 10am, 1pm and 2pm. The 10am departure arrives in time for the noon bus from Punta Gorda to Belize City. Tickets are sold at the dock. Before boarding you also need to get your exit stamp at the nearby immigration office (p191) and pay Q80 in departure tax (US$10).

If you want to leave a car in Puerto Barrios while you visit Lívingston for a day or two, there are plenty of *parqueos* (parking lots) around the dock area that charge around Q50 per 24 hours. Many of the hotels offer this service too.

Lívingston

POP 7000

Lívingston is unlike anywhere else in Guatemala. Its Garifuna people, their colors, culture, rhythms, flavors, and disposition, are the best reason to visit – nowhere else in Guatemala will you find such a friendly, fun and relaxed vibe. But it's not just the people: good beaches are nearby and the slow-and-easy take on life is enchanting. Here boats lie derelict in picturesque decay; people paddleboard or kayak lazily amid refreshing ocean breezes; and pelicans soar overhead as happy hour starts in late afternoon. It's just lovely.

Though the town is most easily and cheaply visited from nearby Puerto Barrios, the approach along the Río Dulce is worth the extra time: it's so wild it was used as the location for the TV series *The New Adventures of Tarzan*. The river's mist-shrouded cliffs, thick jungle, jade-colored water (which hides numerous manatees) make arriving in this quirky Caribbean town all the more memorable.

Sights & Activities

Beaches in Lívingston itself are disappointing, as buildings or vegetation come right down to the water's edge in most places. Those beaches that do exist are often contaminated; however, there are better beaches within a few kilometers to the northwest. You can reach **Playa Quehueche** near the mouth of the Río Quehueche by taxi (Q30) in about 10 minutes. The best beach in the area is **Playa Blanca** (Q20), around 12km from Lívingston. This is privately owned and you need a boat to get there.

Rasta Mesa CULTURAL CENTER

(☎4459-6106; www.rastamesa.com; Barrio Nevago; ⏰9am-2pm, cooking class 6pm) This is a friendly, informal, enthusiastic cultural center where you can drop in for classes in Garifuna cooking (Q125 per person, fish stew Q150), drumming (Q125 per person) and dancing (Q125), or even get a massage (from Q250). It also offers volunteering opportunities.

Tours

A few outfits in Lívingston offer tours that let you get out and experience the natural wonders of the area. **Happy Fish Travel** (☎7947-0661; www.happyfishtravel.com; Calle Principal, Happy Fish restaurant; ⏰7am-10pm) is one of the standbys, but you can get excellent information and arrange tours with your hotel or hostel, and in some cases that's more reliable.

The popular ecological tour/jungle trip (Q70) takes you for a walk through town, out west up to a lookout spot and on to the Río Quehueche, where you take a half-hour canoe trip down the river to Playa Quehueche. Then you walk through the jungle to **Los**

Siete Altares (The Seven Altars; Q20), hang out there for a while, then walk back down the beach to Lívingston. This is a great way to see the area, and the friendly local guides can also give you a good introduction to the Garifuna people who live here.

The Playa Blanca tour goes by boat first to Los Siete Altares and then on to Playa Blanca, the best beach in the area, for two or three hours. This trip goes with a minimum of two people and costs Q100 per person.

Happy Fish offers a return boat trip (Q220) just along the canyon section of Río Dulce (the most interesting and picturesque part), which gives you more time to enjoy the trails, birdwatching and so on than the 'tour' given on the public *lanchas* (small motorboats). It also runs tours to **Cueva del Tigre**, a community-run tourism project 8km from Lívingston (Q175 for a tour, or they'll tell you how to get there on your own).

Also popular are day/overnight trips to the **Cayos Sapodillas** (or Zapotillas), well off the coast of southern Belize, where there is great snorkeling (Q560/1200 for one/two days). A minimum of eight people is required and exit taxes and national-park fees (US$30 in total) are separate.

Festivals & Events

Garifuna National Day CULTURAL
(Nov 26) Celebrated with a variety of cultural events.

Sleeping

Prices in Lívingston hit their peak from July to December – outside these months many midrange and top-end places halve their rates.

Casa de la Iguana HOSTEL $
(7947-0064; www.casadelaiguana.com; Calle Marcos Sánchez Díaz; hammocks/dm Q25/50, cabins with/without bathroom Q200/120;) A five-minute walk from the main dock, this happy-to-admit-it party hostel offers good-value cabins, camping and hammocks. The cabins are wooden affairs, with simple decoration. Happy hour here leads, hours later, to beer pong...which comes with a roulette wheel of fates that befall the losers: most involve drunkenness, nudity, or a combination. So don't come planning on going to sleep at nine.

★ **Casa Rosada** HOSTEL $$
(7947-0303; www.restaurantcasarosada.com; Calle Marco Sánchez Días; dm/bungalow Q80/200;) Casa Rosada is a one-stop spot that manages somehow to do it all, and do it well. The owner, Ismael, is a wealth of knowledge about the area and can arrange tours, set up performances and offer advice or suggestions, as well as handle issues that come up. Bungalows (all with clean shared bathrooms) are delightful, as is the food.

You need to order up to two hours early to have dinner, but the restaurant is open the rest of the day for walk-ins, and has great coffee, good breakfasts and tasty margaritas. The dock and hammocks make it easy to jump on boats or just lounge the day away. It's Lívingston slow luxury at its best.

★ **Casa Nostra** BOUTIQUE HOTEL $$
(7947-0842; www.livingstoncasanostra.com; Calle Marcos Sánchez Díaz; d without bathroom Q200, ste Q450;) A lovely spot right on the water with (on a good day) views of Honduras from the upper floor, the Casa Nostra is a place that feels like home. Owner Stuart makes incredible food, the staff are friendly, and the spot exudes just the right balance of casualness and style. Pick-ups and drop-offs are available from the dock.

Even if you're staying elsewhere, don't miss the chance to swing by for one of Casa Nostra's seafood pizzas, a delight even for those who are picky about their seafood.

Dos Arboles HOSTEL $$
(7947-0530; www.dosarbolesguate.com; dm/r/bungalow Q85/250/350;) A relative newcomer in what was the Vecchia Toscana, Dos Arboles is a fun, hip hostel and more, with live-music shows, a lovely pool with hummingbirds, and experienced owners who know what makes a place tick. Any closer to the water and you'll be wading. Good mosquito nets mean that you'll actually get some sleep here too.

Hotel Ríos Tropicales HOTEL $$
(7947-0158; Calle Principal; s/d/tr Q100/200/300;) The Ríos Tropicales has a variety of big, well-screened rooms facing a central patio with plenty of hammocks and chill-out space in the 2nd-floor lounge. Rooms have private bathrooms but no air-con.

Eating

Food here is relatively expensive because most of it must be brought in by boat. There's fine seafood, though, and some unusual flavors for Guatemala, including coconut and curry. *Tapado,* a rich stew made from fish, shellfish and coconut milk, spiced with cilantro, is the delicious local specialty.

Open-air eateries dot Calle Principal, and many hotels' restaurants are also delicious.

★Restaurante Buga Mama SEAFOOD $$
(☎7947-0198; Calle Marcos Sánchez Díaz; mains Q70-120; ⏲6am-9pm Tue-Sun; 📶) This place enjoys the best location of any restaurant in town, and profits go to the Asociación Ak' Tenamit (p188), an NGO with several projects in the area. There's a wide range of seafood, homemade pasta, curries and other dishes on the menu, including a very good *tapado* (Q110). Most of the waiters here are trainees in a community sustainable-tourism scheme, so be forgiving if the service is lacking.

Restaurante Gaby GUATEMALAN $$
(☎7947-0858; Calle Marcos Sánchez Díaz; mains Q35-180; ⏲7am-9pm) For a good honest feed in humble surrounds, you can't go past Gaby's. She serves up the good stuff: lobster, *tapado* (Q80), rice and beans, and good breakfasts at good prices. The *telenovelas* (soap operas) come free.

Happy Fish SEAFOOD $$
(☎7947-0661; www.happyfishtravel.com; Calle Principal; mains Q75-165; ⏲7am-10pm; 📶) One of the bustling main-street spots, Happy Fish will try to sell you tours as well as something to eat. There's a slick, marketed, inauthentic feel, but the spot remains popular. The requisite *tapado* (Q100) is here, plus a good range of other options.

Drinking

A handful of bars down on the beach to the left of the end of Calle Principal attract travelers and locals at night. It's very dark down here, so take care. Music ranges from *punta* (a Garifuna dance) to salsa, merengue, even electronica. Saturday is the party night.

Happy hour is an institution. Every restaurant has discounts on something.

Adventurous drinkers should try *guifiti,* a local concoction made from coconut rum, often infused with herbs. It's said to have medicinal properties.

ℹ Information

DANGERS & ANNOYANCES

Lívingston has a few hustlers who are famous for asking you for money 'to fund a Garifuna school or orphanage,' which they quickly pocket. Sometimes this involves a visit to a 'school, destroyed by hurricane,' which is really just a derelict house. Don't be sucked in.

Use mosquito repellent, especially if you go out into the jungle; mosquitoes here carry both malaria and dengue fever.

IMMIGRATION

Immigration Office (Calle Principal; ⏲6am-7pm) Issues entry and exit stamps for travelers arriving direct from or going direct to Belize or Honduras, charging Q80 for exit stamps. Crossing in via Corinto (Honduras) is Q30. Outside business hours, you can knock for attention at any time.

MONEY

Banrural (Calle Principal; ⏲9am-5pm Mon-Fri, to 1pm Sat) Changes US dollars and traveler's checks, and has an ATM.

ℹ Getting There & Away

Frequent boats come downriver from Río Dulce and across the bay from Puerto Barrios. There are also boats from Honduras and Belize.

People coming from Guatemala City or Antigua will likely want to take a Litegua express bus to Puerto Barrios (Q125), then take a boat to Lívingston (Q35), which is the cheapest and fastest way to arrive.

Happy Fish (p192) operates combined boat and bus shuttles to the Honduran city of La Ceiba (the cheapest gateway to Honduras' Bay Islands) for around Q550 per person, with a minimum of four people. Leaving Lívingston at 6am or earlier will get you to La Ceiba in time for the boat to the islands, making it a one-day trip, which is nearly impossible to do independently.

There's also a boat that goes direct to Punta Gorda (Belize) daily at 7am (Q250, 1½ hours), leaving from the **public dock**. In Punta Gorda, the boat connects with a bus to Placencia and Belize City. The boat waits for this bus to arrive from Placencia before it sets off back for Lívingston from Punta Gorda at about 10:30am.

If you are taking one of these early international departures, get your exit stamp from immigration in Lívingston the day before.

EL PETÉN

Vast, sparsely populated and jungle-covered, Guatemala's largest and northernmost department is a wonderland of exploration. Whether it's the mysteries of the Classic Maya, the bounty of the jungle or the chance to lounge lakeside that inspires you, it's all here in abundance. How deeply you choose to delve into the Maya legacy will depend on your willingness to get your feet muddy. The towering temples of Tikal can be reached by tour from just about anywhere, while more remote sites such as El Mirador and Piedras Negras require days of planning and further days of jungle trekking. The Reserva de Biósfera Maya (Maya Biosphere Reserve) covers virtually the entire northern third of El Petén, and together with its counterparts in Mexico and Belize forms a multinational wildlife haven that spans more than 30,000 sq km.

Sayaxché

POP 147,000 / ELEV 133M

Sayaxché, on the south bank of the Río de la Pasión, 61km southwest of Flores, is the closest town to around 10 scattered Maya archaeological sites, including Ceibal, Aguateca, Dos Pilas, Tamarindito and Altar de Sacrificios. You could stay here for weeks exploring all of them, but most travelers opt for just a few, and many skip the town proper entirely for the lovely riverside hotels an hour or so away by *lancha* (small motorboat).

Besides its strategic position between Flores and the Cobán area, Sayaxché has a riverside appeal all its own, with rickety motorboats and funky barges floating trucks across the broad waterway. If you want to explore a part of Guatemala that most tourists overlook, stop here for a night or a week and see what you can see.

Sleeping & Eating

Hospedaje Yaxkín BUNGALOW $

(4913-4879; Barrio La Esperanza; bungalow per person with/without bathroom Q50/35) East of the center are these 15 rustic cabins scattered around a wooded tract. A big open-air restaurant serves pastas, tacos and river fish (Q50). It's two blocks south and three blocks east of the church. A taxi will zip you from the ferry to the hotel for Q25 to Q80 depending on the time of day.

Hotel Del Río HOTEL $$

(7928-6138; hoteldelriosayaxche@hotmail.com; s/d Q125/200, with air-con Q175/250;) A few steps to the right of the wharf (with your back to the river) is this modern hotel. It's the cushy choice, with huge, sparkling rooms alongside and above an airy lobby.

Café Maya GUATEMALAN $$

(4641-9753; Calle del Ferry; mains Q45-95; 7am-9pm) About the best bet for grub in town is this casual, open-air hall, a popular gathering place both morning and evening. Aside from the usual eggs and beans, it does *pinchos* (brochettes) served with abundant portions of salad, beans and rice, and fries; the papaya smoothies are heavenly. Chicken, fish and pasta are the lunch/dinner options.

Information

Banrural (8:30am-5pm Mon-Fri, 9am-1pm Sat) Just downhill from the church toward the river. Changes dollars and euros; a nearby branch has a Cajero 5B ATM.

Getting There & Away

Southbound from Sayaxché, several microbuses head for Cobán (Q55, four hours) between 5am and 3pm. Every 25 minutes or so, Raxruhá-bound microbuses go to the San Antonio junction (Q35, 1½ hours), from where there are frequent departures for Cobán. Vehicles depart from a lot near the ferry dock. From the north side of the Río de la Pasión, microbuses leave for Santa Elena every 15 minutes from 5:45am to 6:30pm (Q25, 1½ hours).

For river transportation, contact **Viajes Don Pedro** (4580-9389; servlanchasdonpedro@hotmail.com; 8am-5pm).

Ceibal

With its strategic position along the west bank of the Río de la Pasión, the independent kingdom of **Ceibal** (Q60; 8am-4pm) amassed considerable power controlling commerce along this key stretch of the waterway. Though architecturally less amazing than some other sites, the river journey to Ceibal is among the most memorable, as is hiking below the jungle canopy with monkeys howling overhead.

There's a large scale model of the site by the entrance. The ceremonial core of the city covers three hills, connected over steep ravines by the original causeways. Smallish temples, many of them covered with jungle, surround two principal groups, A and D. In front of some temples, and standing seemingly alone on paths, are magnificent stelae, their intricate carvings still in excellent condition.

It takes about two hours to explore the site. Bring mosquito repellent and snacks and water.

Viajes Don Pedro in Sayaxché runs *lanchas* (small motorboats) here (Q700 for up to five passengers). The fee should include a guide, who may actually be the boatman. In

El Petén

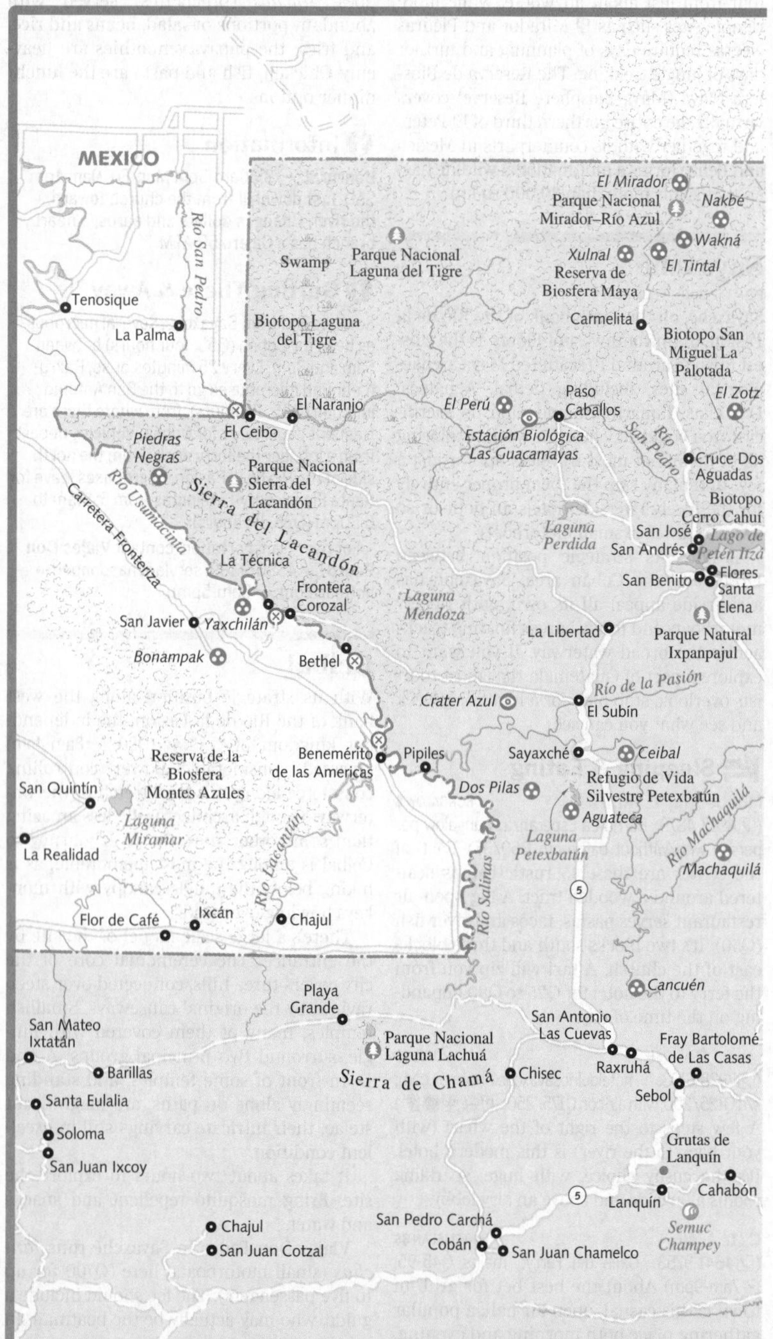
MEXICO
Río San Pedro
Tenosique
La Palma
Swamp
Parque Nacional Laguna del Tigre
Biotopo Laguna del Tigre
El Mirador
Parque Nacional Mirador–Río Azul
Nakbé
Wakná
Xulnal
El Tintal
Reserva de Biosfera Maya
Carmelita
Biotopo San Miguel La Palotada
El Zotz
El Perú
Paso Caballos
Estación Biológica Las Guacamayas
Río San Pedro
Cruce Dos Aguadas
Biotopo Cerro Cahuí
El Ceibo
El Naranjo
Piedras Negras
Parque Nacional Sierra del Lacandón
Río Usumacinta
Carretera Fronteriza
Sierra del Lacandón
Laguna Perdida
San José
San Andrés
Lago de Petén Itzá
San Benito
Flores
Santa Elena
La Técnica
Frontera Corozal
Laguna Mendoza
Parque Natural Ixpanpajul
San Javier
Yaxchilán
La Libertad
Bonampak
Bethel
Río de la Pasión
Crater Azul
El Subín
Benemérito de las Americas
Pipiles
Sayaxché
Ceibal
Reserva de la Biosfera Montes Azules
Refugio de Vida Silvestre Petexbatún
San Quintín
Dos Pilas
Aguateca
Laguna Miramar
Río Machaquilá
La Realidad
Laguna Petexbatún
Machaquilá
Río Lacantún
Río Salinas
5
Flor de Café
Ixcán
Chajul
Cancuén
Playa Grande
San Antonio Las Cuevas
San Mateo Ixtatán
Parque Nacional Laguna Lachuá
Fray Bartolomé de Las Casas
Raxruhá
Barillas
Sierra de Chamá
Chisec
Sebol
Santa Eulalia
Soloma
Grutas de Lanquín
San Juan Ixcoy
5
Cahabón
Lanquín
Semuc Champey
San Pedro Carchá
Chajul
Cobán
San Juan Chamelco
San Juan Cotzal

high season, ask the lancheros about joining a tour group.

Alternatively, Ceibal can be reached overland: get any minibus heading south from Sayaxché on Hwy 5 (toward Raxrujá and Chisec) and get off after 9km at Paraíso, from where it's an 8km walk east down a dirt track to Ceibal. About 2km in, where the road bends left by a small farmhouse, continue straight uphill to enter the park – there's no sign. In the rainy season check with locals first that this stretch is passable.

Flores & Santa Elena

POP 73,000

With its pastel houses cascading down from a central plaza to the emerald waters of Lago de Petén Itzá, the island town of Flores evokes Venice or something Mediterranean. A 500m causeway connects Flores to its humbler sister town of Santa Elena on the mainland, which then merges into the community of San Benito to the west. The three towns actually form one large settlement, often referred to simply as Flores.

Flores proper is by far the most attractive base. Small hotels and restaurants line the streets, many featuring rooftop terraces with lake views. Residents take great pride in their island-town's gorgeousness, and a promenade (partly submerged now due to lake levels rising) runs around its perimeter.

Santa Elena is where you'll find banks, buses and a major shopping mall.

History

Flores was founded on a *petén* (island) by the Itzáes, who came here after being expelled from Chichén Itzá on Mexico's Yucatán Peninsula, probably in the mid-15th century. They called it Tah Itzá (place of the Itzá), which the Spanish later corrupted to Tayasal. Hernán Cortés dropped in on King Canek of Tayasal in 1525 on his way to Honduras, and the meeting was, amazingly, peaceable. Cortés left behind a lame horse, which the Itzáes fed on flowers and turkey stew. When it died, the Itzáes made a statue of it, which, by the time a couple of Spanish friars visited in 1618, was being worshipped as a manifestation of the rain god Chac. It was not until 1697 that the Spaniards brought the Itzáes of Tayasal – by some distance the last surviving independent Maya kingdom – forcibly under their control. The Spanish soldiers destroyed its many

Flores

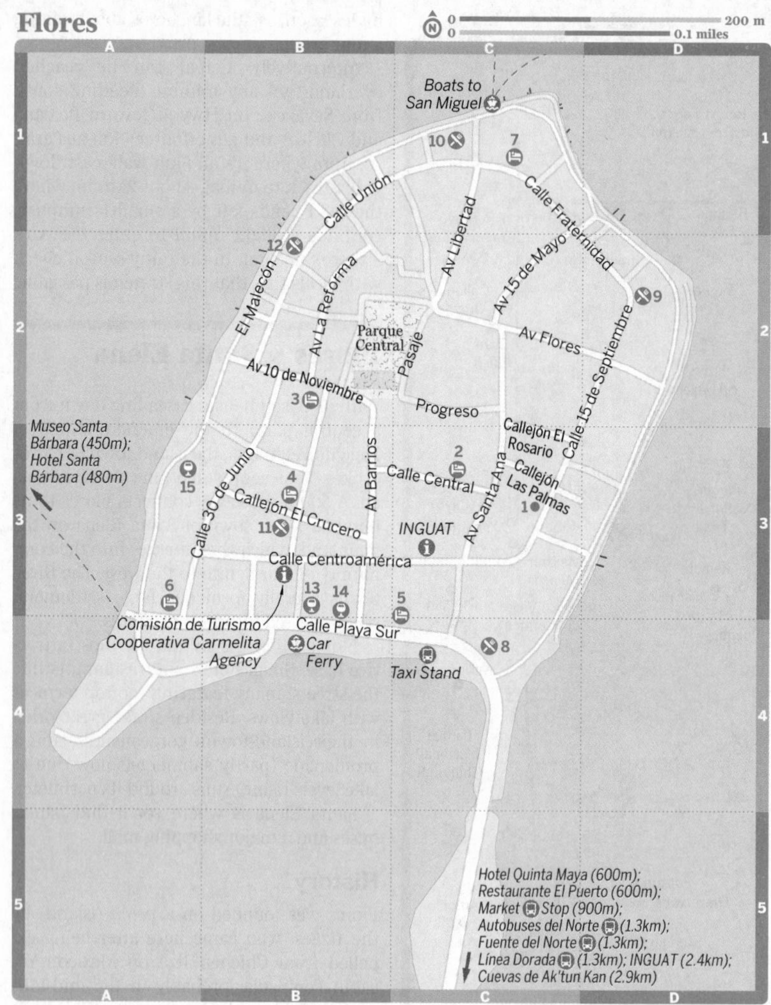

pyramids, temples and statues, and today you won't see a trace of them, although the modern town is doubtless built on the ruins and foundations of Maya Tayasal.

Sights & Activities

Museo Santa Bárbara MUSEUM

(7926-2813; www.radiopeten.com.gt; Isle of Santa Bárbara; Q25; 8am-5pm) On an islet to the west of Flores, this little museum holds a grab bag of Maya artifacts from nearby archaeological sites, plus some old broadcasting equipment from Radio Petén (88.5 FM), which still broadcasts from an adjacent building. Phone ahead to get picked up (Q10 per person) at the dock behind **Hotel Santana** (Map p198; 7867-5123; www.santanapeten.com.gt; Calle 30 de Junio, Flores; d/tr Q600/700;).

Cuevas de Ak'tun Kan CAVE

(Q35; 7am-5pm) Try spelunking at the impressive limestone caverns of Ak'tun Kan, which translates from Q'eqchi' Maya as 'Cave of the Serpent.' The cave-keeper provides the authorized interpretation of the weirdly shaped stalagmite and stalactite formations, including the Frozen Falls, the Whale's Tail and the Gate of Heaven, the last within a great hall where bats flutter in the

Flores

crevices. The provided helmets have a small light inside them. Explorations take 30 to 45 minutes. It's 2km south of Flores; take a *tuk-tuk* there (Q15).

Arcas VOLUNTEERING
(Asociación de Rescate y Conservación de Vida Silvestre; 7830-1374, volunteer coordinator 5690-6762; www.arcasguatemala.org/volunteering; initial week US$250, per subsequent week US$200) This Guatemalan NGO has a rescue and rehabilitation center for wildlife on the mainland northeast of Flores, where volunteers can assist in feeding animals, such as macaws, parrots, jaguars and coatis, that have been rescued from smugglers and the illegal pet trade. The fee covers food and accommodations.

Sleeping

Except for a few upscale properties along Santa Elena's waterfront, Flores is by far the more desirable place to stay, though the former's hotels are often good value.

Hostel Los Amigos HOSTEL $
(Map p198; 7867-5075, 4495-2399; www.amigoshostel.com; Calle Central, Flores; dm Q100-120, r Q220; @) Far and away the most popular backpackers' haven in El Petén, this hostel has grown organically in its 15 years of existence and now includes various sleeping options, from six- and 10-bed dorms to a tree house (Q200). An annex around the corner is quieter, with seven originally designed rooms.

All the global traveler's perks are here in abundance: herbal steam bath, massage, pool table, hammocks, heaping helpings of food, yoga and cut-rate jungle tours. It also offers bike tours around the area.

Despite the good-time atmosphere, it's lights out after 10pm, but the fun goes on in an ingeniously soundproofed night lounge upstairs.

La Posada de Don José HOTEL $$
(Map p198; 7867-5298; cnr Calle del Malecón & Calle Fraternidad, Flores; dm Q75, r with/without air-con Q250/175;) Near the northern tip of the island, this is an old-fashioned establishment (check the lobby for a portrait of the founder) with rocking chairs scattered around a plant-laden patio and a friendly family that knows your name. The lake level has reclaimed the *malecón* (jetty) here, making the rear terrace infinitely more peaceful than further down. Besides the neat little rooms, there's a spacious fan-cooled dorm in back.

Hotel Quinta Maya HOTEL $$
(7926-4976; www.hotelquintamaya.com; 6a Av & 4a Calle; s/d/tr Q275/390/490; P) Newly rebranded, this comfortable hotel offers large rooms arranged around a pleasant courtyard. There's a restaurant, airport transfers and a travel agent on-site.

Hotel La Mesa de los Mayas HOTEL $$
(Map p198; 7867-5268; mesamayas@hotmail.com; Av La Reforma, Flores; s/d Q125/200, with air-con Q150/250;) Standing alongside a narrow alley, the Mesa is terrific value. Its 19 rooms are neatly furnished, with pyramidal headboards, checkered bedspreads and reading lamps; some feature plant-laden balconies. There's a restaurant on the 1st floor.

Hotel Petenchel HOTEL $$
(Map p198; 7867-5450; escalofrio_puga@hotmail.com; Calle Playa Sur, Flores; s/d Q150/230, with air-con Q200/270;) Just off the causeway, this comfy hideaway has six spacious rooms, all with firm beds and high arched ceilings, set around a lush garden. Get breakfast burritos at the attached cafe, called Escalofrío ('chill').

Hotel Santa Bárbara HOTEL $$$

(7926-2813; http://radiopeten.com.gt; cabins incl breakfast Q750;) Part of a trio that includes a museum (p198) and a cafe, this is a perfect retreat from the hubbub of Flores on an islet just five minutes west by *lancha* (small motorboat; included in price). Three comfy cabins with big beds and tile floors overlook the lake past a garden brimming with coconut palms and a ceiba tree.

Hotel Isla de Flores HOTEL $$$

(Map p198; 2476-8775; www.hotelisladeflores.com; Av La Reforma, Flores; s/d Q570/663;) This island hotel sports an understated tropical style that's highly appealing. Hardwood beams frame bone-white walls with floral motifs that are echoed on cool stone floors, and large firm beds back up on painted headboards. Though it doesn't stand on the lakeshore, the plank-deck roof terrace, with a small pool, commands fantastic views over the whole island.

Enjoy mojitos and fusion cuisine in the equally stylish street-level restaurant-bar.

Eating

Flores has loads of pizza, pasta and burger options, often unimpressive. Nevertheless, a few local gems rise above the pack, and the scene seems to be changing for the better… and tastier.

★**Maple y Tocino** CAFE $

(Map p198; 7867-5294; www.facebook.com/mapleytocino; btwn Calle La Union & El Malecón; mains Q29-54; 7am-9pm Sun-Thu, to 10pm Fri & Sat) An amazing spot for breakfasts and lunches, ranging from smoothies and frappés (some topped with a fresh doughut!) to waffles, pizza, sandwiches and wraps. Tasty coffee and espresso drinks and, to top it all, a view of the lake (and the now submerged *malecón*).

Cool Beans CAFE $

(Map p198; 5571-9240, 7867-5400; Calle 15 de Septiembre, Flores; breakfast Q25-35; 7am-10pm Mon-Sat;) Also known as Café Chilero, this laid-back place is more clubhouse with snacks than proper restaurant, featuring salons for chatting, watching videos or laptop browsing. The lush garden with glimpses of the lake makes a *tranquilo* spot for breakfast or veggie burgers. Be warned – the kitchen closes at 9pm sharp.

Restaurante El Peregrino GUATEMALAN $

(Map p198; 7867-5701; Av La Reforma, Flores; mains Q35-60; 7am-10pm) Part of the hotel of the same name, this humble *comedor* serves heaping helpings of home-cooked fare such as *caldo de panza* (beef belly stew; Q40) and breaded tongue. Ask for the daily lunch specials (Q30).

★**Terrazzo** ITALIAN $$

(Map p198; 7867-5479; Calle Unión, Flores; pasta Q70-90; 11am-10pm) Inspired by a chef from Bologna, this Italian gourmet restaurant covers a romantic rooftop terrace. The fettuccine is produced in house, the pizzas (made of seasoned dough) are grilled rather than baked, and the fresh mint lemonade is incredible. All this, and the service is the most attentive in town. Happy hour, 5pm to 9pm, includes a variety of Q10 drinks.

★**Antojitos Mexicanos** STEAK $$

(Don Fredy; Map p198; 3130-5702; Calle Playa Sur, Flores; grilled meats Q60-70; 7-10:30pm; P) Every evening at the foot of the causeway these characters fire up the grill and char steak, chicken and pork ribs of exceptional quality. Their specialty is *puyazo* (sirloin) swathed with garlic sauce. Sit outside facing the twinkly lights on the lake or, if it's raining, inside under a tin roof. Staff behave with all the formality of an elegant restaurant.

Note that this can be a slow spot when they're just starting the grill.

Don Fredy himself often plays DJ, spinning tunes that range from Spanish translations of Sinatra's 'My Way' to modern Top 40.

Restaurante El Puerto SEAFOOD $$

(4211-8668, 5510-5023; 1a Calle 2-15, Santa Elena; mains Q90-130; 11am-11pm) Seafood is the star attraction at this breezy, open-air hall by the lakefront in Santa Elena, with a well-stocked bar at the front. It's an ideal setting to enjoy shellfish stews, popular *ceviches* or the famous *pescado blanco* – white fish from the lake.

Drinking & Nightlife

Flores' little Zona Viva is traditionally the strip of bars along Calle Playa Sur, but there's also action around the bend, along the lakefront promenade north of Hotel Santana.

El Trópico BAR

(Map p198; Calle Playa Sur, Flores; 5pm-1am Mon-Sat) Longest running of the bars along the southern bank, El Trópico supplies tacos and *cerveza* (beer) to a mostly older Guatemalan clientele. It's quiet at sunset, but many *gallos* (tortilla sandwiches) later, the pulse picks up and DJs work the crowd.

Qué Pachanga CLUB
(Map p198; El Malecón, Flores; ⏲2pm-1am) One of a pair of lively nightspots round the west side of the island, this room gets heavy most evenings, when young Guatemalans decked out in their tightest possible jeans gyrate to a continuous barrage of throbbing reggaetón and *cumbia* (Colombian dance tunes).

Jamming BAR
(Map p198; Calle Playa Sur, Flores; ⏲5pm-1am) One of several nightlife venues along the southern bank, Jamming sports a reggae theme, though there's more beer guzzling than ganja smoking. It attracts a younger set of middle-class Guatemalans, and by 8pm you can expect at least a few to be twerking to appreciative onlookers.

BUSES & MICROBUSES FROM SANTA ELENA

DESTINATION	COST (Q)	DURATION (HR)	FREQUENCY & NOTES
Belize City	160	4½-5	**Línea Dorada** (☎7924-8535) leaves at 7am, returning from Belize City at 1pm. This bus connects with boats to Caye Caulker & Ambergris Caye.
Bethel/La Técnica (Mexican border)	50	4-4½	**Fuente del Norte** (☎7926-2999; ⏲24hr) also departs at 6am.
Carmelita	80	4½	Microbus transport possible, but unreliable. Private transport best, usually arranged via your tour operator.
Cobán	80-125		Take a bus or minibus to Sayaxché, from where connecting microbuses leave for Cobán.
El Ceibo/La Palma (Mexican border)	50	4	El Naranjo–bound microbuses depart every 20min, 4am-6pm, stopping at the El Ceibo junction, from where there are shuttles to the border (Q15, 15min). Some go all the way to El Ceibo (Q55). At La Palma, on the Mexican side, you can find transport to Tenosique, Tabasco (one hour), & onward to Palenque or Villahermosa.
El Remate	20	45min	ATIM microbuses leave every 30min 6:30am-7pm. Buses & minibuses to/from Melchor de Mencos will drop you at Puente Ixlú junction, 2km south of El (p206)
Guatemala City	130-205	8-9	Línea Dorada runs 1st-class buses at 8am, 8pm & 9pm (Q205). **Autobuses del Norte** (☎7924-8131; ⏲24hr) has buses at 9pm & 10pm (Q180). Fuente del Norte runs at least 11 buses between 4am & 10pm (Q130), including 5 deluxe buses (Q180),
Melchor de Mencos (Belizean border)	30-50	2	Microbuses go about every hour 5am-6pm. Fuente del Norte leaves at 2:30am, 5am, 6am & 4:30pm.
Poptún	30	2	Microbuses, via Dolores, every 10min 5am-10pm.
Puerto Barrios	270	6	No direct buses. Take a Guatemala City–bound Fuente del Norte bus & change at La Ruidosa junction (Q90-150), south of Río Dulce.
Río Dulce	140	4	Take a Guatemala City–bound bus with Fuente del Norte or Línea Dorada.
San Andrés/San José	8-10	35-40min	Microbuses depart around every 15min 5am-6:40pm, from the left side of the terminal entrance.
Sayaxché	23	1½	Microbuses depart about every 15min 5:35am-6pm.
Tikal	30-80	1¼hr	8 microbuses by ATIM from 6am to 3:20pm, the last returning at 5pm. You could also take the Uaxactún-bound bus (Q40) at 2:15pm or 3:40pm, which goes a bit slower.

1

5

ANDY KRAMER/ALAMY STOCK PHOTO ©

CLAUDE LETIEN/GETTY IMAGES ©

1. **Feast of Santo Tomás (p151)**
Colour and traditional dress at the annual celebration of Chichicastenango's patron saint.

2. **San Andrés Xecul (p161)**
This town's exuberant yellow church is a sight to behold.

3. **Textile-weaving (p222)**
There are a variety of traditional weaving techniques still popular in Guatemala today.

4. **Lívingston (p192)**
The Caribbean town of Lívingston is the place to go to experience Garifuna culture.

5. **Semuc Champey (p182)**
A series of natural limestone pools ideal for swimming.

SVETLANA BYKOVA/SHUTTERSTOCK ©

Information

EMERGENCY

Regional Hospital de San Benito Petén (7932-1111; San Benito; 24hr) One of the largest hospitals in the region. Emergency service available.

Police Station (7926-1365; Calle Límite 12-28, San Benito)

MONEY

Many travel agencies and places to stay will change cash US dollars and sometimes traveler's checks, though at poorer rates than the banks. There are plenty of banks with ATMs along 4a Calle in Santa Elena.

5B Cajero ATM (7am-8:30pm) In Marlin Espadas tour agency, opposite the Ramada Tikal.

Banco G&T Continental (Maya Mall Petén, 1a Calle 6-17, Santa Elena; 10am-7pm Mon-Sat, to 6pm Sun) Has an ATM.

Banco Industrial (Metroplaza Mundo Maya, 1a Calle, Santa Elena; 9am-4pm Mon-Fri, 10am-2pm Sat) This reliable ATM is in the shopping mall opposite the airport.

Super Fotomart (Calle 30 de Junio, Flores; 6am-1am) Convenience store with an ATM, opposite Hotel Casona de la Isla.

TOURIST INFORMATION

Comisión de Turismo Cooperativa Carmelita Agency (Map p198; 4836-9423, 7867-5629; Calle Centroamérica, Flores; Tikal tour per person Q150, El Mirador 5-day/4-night per person Q1925; 8am-8pm) Flores agency for this Carmelita-based cooperative of trekking guides.

INGUAT (Map p198; 3128-6906; info-ciudadflores@inguat.gob.gt; Calle Centroamérica, Flores; 8am-4pm Mon-Fri, sometimes Sat & Sun) The official INGUAT office provides basic information. There's another branch (3128-6905, 7926-0533; info-mundomaya@inguat.gob.gt; Aeropuerto Internacional Mundo Maya; 7am-7pm Tue-Thu, 7-11am & 3-7pm Fri-Mon) at the airport.

Getting There & Away

AIR

Aeropuerto Internacional Mundo Maya is on the eastern outskirts of Santa Elena, 2km from the causeway connecting Santa Elena and Flores. **Avianca** (www.avianca.com) has two flights daily between here and Guatemala City. The Belizean airline **Tropic Air** (7926-0348; www.tropicair.com; Aeropuerto Internacional Mundo Maya) flies once a day to/from Belize City, charging around Q1432 each way for the one-hour trip. It leaves at 8:30am daily.

BUS

Long-distance buses use the **Terminal Nuevo de Autobuses** in Santa Elena, 1.5km south of the causeway along 6a Av. It is also used by a slew of aka *expresos* (microbuses), with frequent services to numerous destinations. Second-class buses and some micros make an additional stop at 5a Calle, in the **market area** (the 'old' terminal) before heading out. You can reduce your trip time by 15 minutes by going straight to the market, though the vehicle may be full by then.

As always, schedules are highly changeable and should be confirmed before heading out.

SHUTTLE MINIBUS

Most hotels and travel agencies can book shuttles, and they will pick you up from where you're staying. Returns leave Tikal at 12:30pm, 3pm and 5pm. If you know which round-trip you plan to be on, ask your driver to hold a seat for you or arrange one in another minibus. If you stay overnight in Tikal and want to return to Flores by minibus, it's a good idea to reserve a seat with a driver when they arrive in the morning.

Getting Around

A taxi from the airport to Santa Elena or Flores costs Q60 (or Q20 per person in a shared ride). There's a **taxi stand** (Map p198) on Calle Playa Sur in Flores. *Tuk-tuks* will take you anywhere between or within Flores and Santa Elena for Q20; the *tuk-tuk* service stops after 7pm. For lake travel, catch a **boat** (Map p198; one way Q5-20; 6am-midnight) from Flores, or (if you need it) the **car ferry** (Map p198; car & driver Q15, per additional passenger Q2; 5am-9:30pm).

El Remate

This peaceful spot at the eastern end of Lago de Petén Itzá makes a good alternative base for Tikal-bound travelers – it's more relaxed than Flores and closer to the site, and its lakeside living has a ramshackle vibe all of its own. People come here to bask in life-affirming slowness, so don't expect pumping discos or craft cocktails. This is all about the *cerveza* (beer) and the view.

El Remate begins 1km north of Puente Ixlú, where the road to the Belize border diverges from the Tikal road. The village strings along the Tikal road for 1km to another junction, where a branch heads west along the north shore of the lake.

El Remate is known for its wood carving, which you can buy from stalls along the main road.

Sights & Activities

Most El Remate accommodations can book two-hour boat trips for birdwatching or nocturnal crocodile spotting (each Q150 per person). Try **Hotel Mon Ami** (3010-0284; Jobompiche Rd; dm/s/d Q75/150/200, s/d without bathroom Q100/150;), which also offers sunset lake tours with detours up the Ixlú and Ixpop rivers (Q200 per person).

Biotopo Cerro Cahuí OUTDOORS
(Q40; 7am-4pm) Comprising a 7.3-sq-km swath of subtropical forest rising up from the lake over limestone terrain, this nature reserve offers mildly strenuous hiking and excellent wildlife-watching, with paths to some brilliant lookout points. As a bonus, there's an adjacent lakeside park with diving docks for a refreshing conclusion to the tour.

More than 20 mammal species roam the reserve, including spider and howler monkeys, white-tailed deer and even the elusive Mesoamerican tapir, though sightings are rare. Birdlife is rich and varied, with the opportunity to spot toucans, woodpeckers and the famous ocellated turkey, a big bird resembling a peacock. Trees include mahogany, cedar, *ramón* and cohune palm, along with many types of bromeliads, ferns and orchids.

A network of loop trails ascends the hill to three lookout points, affording views of the whole lake and of Laguna Salpetén to the east. The trail called **Los Escobos** (4km long, about 2¼ hours), through secondary growth forest, is good for spotting monkeys.

The admission fee includes the right to camp or sling your hammock under small thatch shelters inside the entrance. There are toilets and showers. The reserve is 1.75km west along Jobompiche Rd from El Remate.

Sleeping

Hotels here range from budget hostels to fancy resorts, with most falling into the category of clean and economical family-run spots. Most are set up for swimming in – and watching the sun set over – the lake.

Posada Ixchel HOTEL $
(3044-5379; hotelixchel@yahoo.com; s/d/tr Q90/140/190) This family-owned place near the village's main junction is a superior deal, with spotless, wood-fragrant rooms featuring fans and handcrafted mosquito nets. The cobbled courtyard has inviting little nooks with tree-log seats.

Hostal Hermano Pedro HOSTEL $
(5164-6485; www.hhpedro.com; Calle Camino Biblico 8055; dm/s/d incl breakfast Q80/80/160;) About 150m from the north-shore junction, this two-level wooden structure has a relaxed environment, with plenty of hammocks in the patio and along the verandas. Recycled elements are cleverly incorporated into the decor of the spacious rooms, which feature big fans and lacy curtains. Guests can use the kitchen. It's Q50 for a dorm without breakfast.

★**Alice Guesthouse** BUNGALOW $$
(3087-0654; www.facebook.com/aliceguesthouseguatemala; dm Q70, bungalow with/without bathroom Q230/200;) As in Wonderland, that is. Fruit of the budding imaginations of a Franco-Belgian pair, this slightly remote spread looks not at the lake but at a swath of jungle. Free-form, friendly and fun, it has dorms in fanciful huts with conical thatch roofs, a pair of neat colorful cabins and a tropical shower in a roundhouse, all connected by pebbly paths.

An open-air kitchen is the domain of a chef imported from Nantes. To reach Alice, go down the Jobompiche road about 1.5km; a signed track on the right angles uphill. The lake is a short walk away.

★**Posada del Cerro** BUNGALOW $$
(5376-8722; www.posadadelcerro.com; Jobompiche Rd; dm/s/d/tr/apt Q100/220/330/450/550;) This ecologically sound option blends into the jungle, close enough to Biotopo Cerro Cahuí to hear monkeys howl the evening in. Ten thoughtfully furnished rooms occupy stone-and-hardwood houses and solitary huts scattered over the hillside; one is open to the woods with its own lake-view deck. It also has an eight-bed hut and an apartment that sleeps four to five. Herbs from the forest are stirred into local recipes in the neat, thatched-roof restaurant.

Gringo Perdido Ecological Inn RESORT $$
(2334-2305; www.hotelgringoperdido.com; Jobompiche Rd; campsite Q50, s/d inclu breakfast & dinner Q360/700;) Ensconced in a paradisaical lakefront setting within the Cerro Cahuí biosphere reserve, this jungle-style lodge offers a bank of rooms with full-wall roll-up blinds to give you the sensation of sleeping in the open air. A few lakeside bungalows offer a bit more seclu-

sion. It also has a grassy campground with thatched-roof shelters for slinging hammocks, and a large bookcase lending library.

The Gringo Perdido is 3km along the north shore from the main Tikal road.

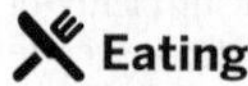

Eating

Desayunos El Árbol CAFE $
(☎5950-2367; breakfast mains Q30-40, dinner mains 40-60; ⏰6am-2pm & 5-9pm Thu-Tue) This gringo-friendly shack sports a lovely, lake-view terrace, a fine setting for healthy breakfasts, including granola, pancakes and omelets. Sandwiches come with a side of salad, and the smoothies are just grand. It's 50m south of the crossroads.

★ **Las Orquídeas** ITALIAN $$
(☎5701-9022; Jobompiche Rd; pastas Q55-120; ⏰noon-9pm Tue-Sun; P) Almost hidden in the forest, a 10-minute walk along the north shore from the Tikal junction, is this marvelous open-air dining hall. The genial Italian owner-chef blends *chaya,* a local herb, into his own tagliatelle and *panzarotti* (smaller version of calzones). There are tempting desserts too.

Information

Horizontes Mayas (☎5773-6193; www.horizontesmayas.com; Ruta a Tikal) You can change US dollars and euros (at poor rates), or check your email, at this multi-service agency by the junction. It's also a good bet for shuttle services or (by reservation) tours to Tikal, Yaxhá and numerous other destinations.

Getting There & Away

El Remate is linked to Santa Elena by frequent minibus service (Q25) from 5:30am to 6pm daily.

For Tikal, a collective shuttle departs at 5:30am, starting back at 2pm (one way/round-trip Q30/50). Any El Remate accommodations can make reservations. Or catch one of the **ATIM** (☎5905-0089) or other shuttles passing through from Santa Elena to Tikal from 5am to 3:30pm.

For taxis, ask at **Hotel Sun Breeze** (☎5898-2665; infosunbreezehotel@gmail.com; Main Rd; s/d Q150/200, with air-con Q200/250; P ⊖ ❄ ☎). A one-way ride to Flores costs about Q250; a round-trip to Tikal costs Q350.

For Melchor de Mencos on the Belizean border, get a minibus or bus from Puente Ixlú, 1km south of El Remate (Q60, 1¼ hours). Additionally, Horizontes Mayas offers private departures to Belize City (Q400) via Melchor.

Tikal

The most striking feature of **Tikal** (☎2367-2837; www.tikalnationalpark.org; Q150; ⏰6am-6pm) is its towering, steep-sided temples, rising to heights of more than 44m, but what distinguishes it is its jungle setting. Its many plazas have been cleared of trees and vines, its temples uncovered and partially restored, but as you walk from one building to another you pass beneath a dense canopy of rainforest amid the rich, loamy aromas of earth and vegetation. Much of the delight of touring the site comes from strolling the broad causeways, originally built from packed limestone to accommodate traffic between temple complexes. By stepping softly you're more likely to spot monkeys, agoutis, foxes and ocellated turkeys.

Tikal is a popular day trip from Flores or El Remate, so it is much quieter in the late afternoon and early morning, which makes an overnight stay an attractive option.

History

Tikal is set on a low hill, which becomes evident as you ascend to the Gran Plaza from the entry road. Affording relief from the surrounding swampy ground, this high terrain may explain why the Maya settled here around 700 BC. Another reason was the abundance of flint, used by the ancients to make clubs, spear points, arrowheads and knives. The wealth of this valuable stone meant good tools could be made, and flint could be traded for other goods. Within 200 years the Maya of Tikal had begun to build stone ceremonial structures, and by 200 BC there was a complex of buildings on the site of the Acrópolis del Norte.

Classic Period

The Gran Plaza was beginning to assume its present shape and extent by the time of Christ. By the dawn of the Early Classic Period, around AD 250, Tikal had become an important religious, cultural and commercial city with a large population. King Yax Ehb' Xooc, in power about 230, is looked upon as the founder of the dynasty that ruled Tikal thereafter.

Under Chak Tok Ich'aak I (King Great Jaguar Paw), who ruled in the mid-4th century, Tikal adopted a brutal method of warfare, used by the rulers of Teotihuacán in central Mexico. Rather than meeting their adversaries on the battlfield in hand-to-hand combat, the army of Tikal used auxiliary units to encircle the enemy and throw spears to kill them from a distance. This first use of 'air power' among the Maya of Petén enabled Siyah K'ak' (Smoking Frog), the Tikal general, to conquer the army of Uaxactún; thus Tikal became the dominant kingdom in El Petén.

By the middle of the Classic Period, in the mid-6th century, Tikal's military prowess and its association with Teotihuacán allowed it to grow until it sprawled over 30 sq km and had a population of perhaps 100,000. But in 553, Yajaw Te' K'inich II (Lord Water) came to the throne of Caracol (in southwestern Belize), and within a decade had conquered Tikal and sacrificed its king. Tikal and other Petén kingdoms suffered under Caracol's rule until the late 7th century when, under new leadership, it apparently cast off its oppressor and rose again.

Tikal's Renaissance

A powerful king named Ha Sawa Chaan K'awil (682–734; also called Ah Cacao or Moon Double Comb), 26th successor of Yax Ehb' Xooc, restored not only Tikal's military strength but also its primacy in the Maya world. He conquered the greatest rival Maya state, Calakmul in Mexico, in 695, and his successors were responsible for building most of the great temples around the Gran Plaza that survive today. King Ah Cacao was buried beneath the staggering height of Templo I.

Tikal's greatness waned around 900, but it was not alone in its downfall, which was part of the mysterious general collapse of lowland Maya civilization.

Rediscovery

No doubt the Itzáes, who occupied Tayazal (now Flores), knew of Tikal in the Late Postclassic Period. Perhaps they even came here to worship at the shrines of old gods. Spanish missionary friars who moved through El Petén after the conquest left brief references to these jungle-bound structures, but their writings moldered in libraries for centuries.

It wasn't until 1848 that the Guatemalan government sent out an expedition, under the leadership of Modesto Méndez and Ambrosio Tut, to visit the site. This may have been inspired by John L Stephens' bestselling accounts of fabulous Maya ruins, published in 1841 and 1843 (though Stephens never visited Tikal). Like Stephens, Méndez and Tut took an artist, Eusebio Lara, to record their archaeological discoveries. An account of their findings was published by the Berlin Academy of Science.

In 1877 the Swiss Dr Gustav Bernoulli visited Tikal. His explorations resulted in the removal of carved wooden lintels from Templos I and IV and their shipment to Basel, where they are still on view in the Museum für Völkerkunde.

Scientific exploration of Tikal began with the arrival of English archaeologist Alfred P Maudslay in 1881. Others continued his work, Teobert Maler, Alfred M Tozzer and RE Merwin among them. Tozzer worked at Tikal on and off from the beginning of the 20th century until his death in 1954. The inscriptions at Tikal were studied and deciphered by Sylvanus G Morley.

Archaeological research and restoration was carried on by the University of Pennsylvania and the Guatemalan Instituto de Antropología e Historia until 1969. Since 1991 a joint Guatemalan–Spanish project has worked on conserving and restoring Templos I and V. The Parque Nacional Tikal (Tikal National Park) was declared a Unesco World Heritage Site in 1979.

Sights

Gran Plaza

The entry path comes into the Gran Plaza around the **Templo I**, the Templo del Gran Jaguar (Temple of the Grand Jaguar). This was built to honor – and bury – Ah Cacao. The king may have worked out the plans for the building himself, but it was actually erected above his tomb by his son, who succeeded him to the throne in AD 734. The king's rich burial goods included stingray spines, which were used for ritual bloodletting, 180 jade objects, pearls and 90 pieces of bone carved with hieroglyphs. At the top of the 44m-high temple is a small enclosure of three rooms covered by a corbeled arch. The sapodilla-wood lintels over the doors were richly carved; one of them was removed and is now in the Basel Museum für Völkerkunde. The lofty roofcomb that crowned the temple was originally adorned with reliefs and bright paint. When it's illuminated by the afternoon sun, it is still possible to make out the figure of a seated dignitary.

Although climbing to the top of Templo I is prohibited, the views from **Templo II** just across the way are nearly as awe-inspiring. Templo II, also known as the Temple of the Masks, was at one time almost as high as Templo I, but it now measures only 38m without its roofcomb.

Tikal

SURVEYING THE CLASSIC MAYA KINGDOM

Constructed in successive waves over a period of at least 800 years, Tikal is a vast, complicated site with hundreds of temples, pyramids and stelae. There's no way you'll get to it all in a day, but by following this itinerary you'll see many of the highlights. Before setting out be sure to stop by the visitor center and examine the scale model of the site. The small ❶ **Museo Sylvanus G Morley** usually houses a wealth of artefacts, although the majority of its contents (other than Stela 31) are currently located in the CCIT research center while the museum is indefinitely under restoration. Present your ticket at the nearby ticket booth and when you reach the posted map, take a left. It's a 20-minute walk to the solitary ❷ **Templo VI**. From here it's a blissful stroll up the broad Calzada Méndez to the ❸ **Gran Plaza**, Tikal's ceremonial core, where you may examine the ancient precinct of the ❹ **North Acropolis**. Exit the plaza west, and take the first left, along a winding path, to ❺ **Templo V**. Round the rear to the right, a trail encircles the largely unexcavated South Acropolis to the ❻ **Plaza de los Siete Templos**. Immediately west stands the great pyramid of the ❼ **Mundo Perdido**. From here it's a quick stroll and a rather strenuous climb to the summit of ❽ **Temple IV**, Tikal's tallest structure.

TOP TIPS

➡ Bring food and water.

➡ All tickets, including sunrise/sunset, must be purchased in advance or at the entry gate. No tickets are sold inside the park.

➡ If you enter after 3pm, your ticket is good for the next day.

➡ Stay at one of the onsite hotels to catch the sunset/sunrise.

➡ To watch the sunset/sunrise from Temple IV, you'll need to purchase an additional ticket (Q100).

➡ Bring mosquito repellent.

Templo IV
Arrive in the late afternoon to get magically tinted photos of Temples I, II and III poking through the jungle canopy. Sunrise tours offer mystical mists that lift as the sun finally appears.

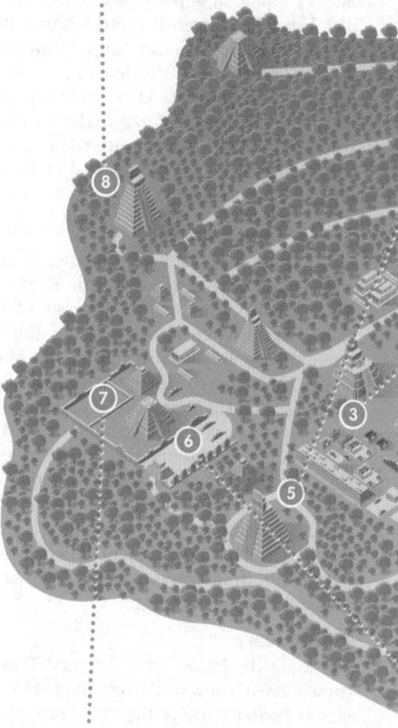

Mundo Perdido
This 'Lost World' features two impressive pyramids and some smaller structures, and the *talud-tablero* design hints at influences from distant Teotihuacán.

FRANCISCO SANDOVAL GUATE/

Templo V

As steep as it is massive, Tikal's second tallest temple (52m) has unusual rounded corners. Tempting as it may seem to climb, the broad front staircase is off-limits.

KOBBY DAGAN/SHUTTERSTOCK ©

Gran Plaza

Though the surreally tall Templo I, a mausoleum to the Late Classic ruler Ah Cacao, is off-limits to climbers, you're welcome to ascend the almost-as-tall Templo II across the plaza.

MICHAEL ZYSMAN/SHUTTERSTOCK ©

North Acropolis

Amid the stack of smaller and much older temples that rise up the hillside north of the plaza, take a peek beneath the two thatched shelters on a ledge to find a pair of fearsome masks.

4

Ticket Booth

1

Posted Map

Visitor Centre

CCIT

2

Museo Sylvanus G Morley

Volumes have been written about the remarkably preserved Stela 31, a portrait of the ruler Stormy Sky crowning himself, flanked by spear-toting warriors in the attire of (ally or overlord?) Teotihuacán.

Templo VI

The secluded temple has a lengthy set of glyphs inscribed on the back of its lofty roof comb, recording the lineage of successive kingdoms. Be patient: the contents of the weathered slab may take some effort to discern.

FRANCISCO SANDOVAL GUATE/SHUTTERSTOCK ©

Plaza de los Siete Templos

Seven miniature temples line up along the east side of this grassy courtyard. Climb the larger 'palace' at the south end to get a sightline along the septet.

MATYAS REHAK/SHUTTERSTOCK ©

Nearby, the **Acrópolis del Norte** (North Acropolis) significantly predates the two great temples. Archaeologists have uncovered about 100 different structures, the oldest of which dates from before the time of Christ, with evidence of occupation as far back as 600 BC. The Maya built and rebuilt on top of older structures, and the many layers, combined with the elaborate burials of Tikal's early rulers, added sanctity and power to their temples. The final version of the acropolis, as it stood around AD 800, had more than 12 temples atop a vast platform, many of them the work of King Ah Cacao. Look especially for the two huge, powerful wall masks, uncovered from an earlier structure and now protected by roofs. On the plaza side of the North Acropolis are two rows of stelae. These served to record the great deeds of the kings, to sanctify their memory and to add power to the temples and plazas that surrounded them.

Acrópolis Central

South and east of the Gran Plaza, this maze of courtyards, little rooms and small temples is thought by many to have been a palace where Tikal's nobles lived. Others think the tiny rooms may have been used for sacred rites and ceremonies, as graffiti found within them suggest. Over the centuries the configuration of the rooms was repeatedly changed, suggesting that perhaps this 'palace' was in fact a noble or royal family's residence and alterations were made to accommodate groups of relatives. One part of the acropolis provided lodgings for archaeologist Teobert Maler (1842–1917) when he worked at Tikal.

Templo III

West of the Gran Plaza, across the Calzada Tozzer (Tozzer Causeway) stands **Templo III**, still undergoing restoration. Only its upper reaches have been cleared. A scene carved into the lintel at its summit, 55m high, depicts a figure in an elaborate jaguar suit, believed to be the ruler Dark Sun. In front of it stands Stela 24, which marks the date of its construction, AD 810. From this point, you can continue west to Templo IV along the Calzada Tozzer, one of several sacred byways between the temple complexes of Tikal.

Templo V & Acrópolis del Sur

Due south of the Gran Plaza, **Templo V** is a remarkably steep structure (57m high) that was built sometime between the 7th and 8th centuries AD. It consists of seven stepped platforms and, unlike the other great temples, has slightly rounded corners. A recent excavation of the temple revealed a group of embedded structures, some with Maya calendars on their walls. Tempting as it may seem, you are not allowed to scale the broad central staircase.

Excavation is slow to progress on the mass of masonry just west of the temple, known collectively as the **Acrópolis del Sur** (South Acropolis). The palaces on top are from the Late Classic Period (the time of King Moon Double Comb), but earlier constructions probably go back 1000 years.

Plaza de los Siete Templos

To the west of the Acrópolis del Sur is this broad grassy plaza, reached via a path to its southern edge. Built in the Late Classic Period, the seven **temples** with their stout roofcombs line up along the east side of the plaza. On the south end stand three larger '**palaces**'; on the opposite end is an unusual **triple ball court**.

El Mundo Perdido

About 400m southwest of the Gran Plaza is **El Mundo Perdido** (Lost World), a complex of 38 structures with a huge pyramid in their midst, thought to be essentially Preclassic (with some later repairs and renovations). The pyramid, 32m high and 80m along the base, is surrounded by four much-eroded stairways, with huge masks flanking each one. The stairway facing eastward is thought to have functioned as a platform for viewing the sun's trajectory against a trio of structures on a raised platform to the east, a similar arrangement to the astronomical observatory at Uaxactún. Tunnels dug into the pyramid by archaeologists reveal four similar pyramids beneath the outer face; the earliest (Structure 5C-54 Sub 2B) dates from 700 BC, making this pyramid the oldest Maya structure at Tikal.

A smaller **temple** to the west, dating from the Early Classic Period, demonstrates Teotihuacán's influence, with its *talud-tablero* (stepped building) style of architecture.

Templo IV & Complejo N

Templo IV, at 65m, is the highest building at Tikal and the second-highest pre-Columbian building known in the western hemisphere, after La Danta at El Mirador. It was completed about AD 741, probably by order of Ah Cacao's son, Yax Kin, who was depicted on the carved lintel over the middle doorway (now in a museum in Basel, Switzerland), as the western boundary of the ceremonial precinct. A steep wooden staircase leads to the top. The view east is almost as good as from a helicopter – a panorama across the jungle canopy, with (from left to right) the temples of the Gran Plaza, Temple III, Temple V (just the top bit) and the great pyramid of the Mundo Perdido poking through.

Between Templo IV and Templo III is **Complejo N**, an example of the 'twin-temple' complexes erected during the Late Classic Period. This one was built in AD 711 by Ah Cacao to mark the 14th *katun*, or 20-year cycle, of *baktún* 9. The king himself is portrayed on the remarkably preserved Stela 16 in an enclosure just across the path. Beside the stelae is Altar 5, a circular stone depicting the same king accompanied by a priestly figure in the process of exhuming the skeleton of a female ruler.

LIDAR, A NEW ERA

This process of rediscovery is continuing, and improvements in LIDAR (Light Detection and Ranging) scanning have made it possible to map and identify ever more sections of the regions's forests and swamps. This has led to spectacular discoveries and scientists are currently estimating that the Tikal complex, once estimated at 6000 structures, may exceed 10,000. Even more fascinating, newly discovered structures indicate that people may have occupied areas considered far too swampy to live in today.

These recent and ongoing rediscoveries make it impossible to speak with absolute authority of the real size and scope of cities such as Tikal. What's unequivocal is that this is without a doubt the most important ruin in Guatemala and a must-see on many tourists' lists.

Templo de las Inscripciones (Templo VI)

Templo VI is one of the few temples at Tikal to bear written records. On the rear of its 12m-high roofcomb is a long inscription – though it will take some effort to discern it in the bright sunlight – giving us the date AD 766. The sides and cornice of the roofcomb bear glyphs as well. Its secluded position, about a 25-minute walk southeast of the Gran Plaza along the Calzada Méndez, makes it a good spot for observing wildlife. From here, it's a 20-minute hike back to the main entrance.

Northern Complexes

About 1km north of the Gran Plaza is **Complejo P**. Like Complejo N, it's a Late Classic twin-temple complex that probably commemorated the end of a *katun*. **Complejo M**, next to it, was partially torn down by the Late Classic Maya to provide building materials for a causeway, now named after Alfred P Maudslay, which runs southwest to Templo IV. **Grupo H**, northeast of Complexes P and M, with one tall, cleared temple, had some interesting graffiti within its temples.

Complejo Q and **Complejo R**, about 300m north of the Gran Plaza, are very Late Classic twin-pyramid complexes with stelae and altars standing before the temples. Complex Q is perhaps the best example of the twin-temple type, as it has been partly restored. Stela 22 and Altar 10 are excellent examples of Late Classic Tikal relief carving, dated to AD 771.

Museums

CCIT MUSEUM

(Centro de Conservación e Investigación de Tikal; ⌚8am-4pm) FREE This Japanese-funded research center is devoted to the identification and restoration of pieces unearthed at the site. The 1300-sq-meter facility has a huge cache of items to sort through, and you can watch the restorers at work. Though not strictly a museum per se, it features an excellent gallery on the different materials used by Maya craftspeople.

The center is home to the **Museo Sylvanus G Morley** (Museo Cerámico; Museum of Ceramics; Q30, also valid for Museo Lítico; ⌚8am-4pm) for an indefinite period while that museum is under restoration.

Museo Lítico MUSEUM

(Stone Museum; Q30, also valid for Museo Sylvanus G Morley; ⌚8am-4pm) The larger of Tikal's two museums is in the visitors center. It houses a number of carved stones from the ruins. The photographs taken by pioneer archaeologists Alfred P Maudslay and Teobert Maler of the jungle-covered temples in various stages of discovery are particularly striking. Outside is a model showing how Tikal would have looked around AD 800.

BIRDWATCHING AT TIKAL

As well as howler and spider monkeys romping through the trees of Tikal, the plethora of birds flitting through the canopy and across the green expanses of the plazas is impressive. The ruined temple complexes present ideal viewing platforms for this activity, often providing the ability to look down upon the treetops to observe examples of the 300 or so bird species (migratory and resident) that have been recorded here. Bring binoculars and a copy of *The Birds of Tikal: An Annotated Checklist*, by Randell A Beavers, available at the visitors center shop. Tread quietly and be patient, and you'll probably see some of the following birds in the areas specified:

Templo de las Inscripciones Tody motmots, four trogon species and royal flycatchers

El Mundo Perdido Two oriole species, keel-billed toucans and collared aracaris

Complejo P Great curassows, three species of woodpecker, crested guans, plain chachalacas and three tanager species

Aguada Tikal (Tikal Reservoir) Three kingfisher species, jacanas, blue herons, two species of sandpiper, and great kiskadees

Entrance path Tiger herons sometimes nest in the huge ceiba tree located here

Complejo Q Red-capped and white-collared manakins

Complejo R Emerald toucanets

Tours

Family-owned, local **Gem Trips** (☎4051-3805, 4214-9514, USA 530-853-4329; www.gemtrips.com; Tikal sunrise US$150) offers excellent sunrise tours as well as guided trips to Tikal and other Maya sites, while archaeologist **Roxy Ortiz** (☎5197-5173; www.tikalroxy.blogspot.com) has years of experience trekking throughout the Maya world.

Multilingual guides are available at the information kiosk. These authorized guides display their accreditation card, listing the languages they speak. Before 7am the charge for a half-day tour is Q100 per person for three to six people. After that you pay for a group tour (Q600).

Sleeping & Eating

Staying overnight enables you to relax and savor the dawn and dusk, when most of the jungle birds and animals can be seen and heard (especially the howler monkeys). Other than camping, there are only three places to stay, and tour groups often have many of the rooms reserved. Almost any travel agency in Guatemala offers Tikal tours, including lodging, a meal or two, a guided tour and transportation.

Along the right-hand side of the access road stands a series of little *comedores* (eateries). All are open from about 6:30am to 8:30pm daily. Another restaurant is in the visitors center, with pastas and hamburgers among the offerings. If you want to spend all day at the ruins without having to make the 20- to 30-minute walk back to the *comedores*, carry food and water with you.

Campground CAMPGROUND $
(campsite per person Q50, hammock with mosquito net Q85) Across the road from the visitors center, the campground covers a large, grassy area and has a clean bathroom block and thatched shelters for hanging hammocks. Pay for your campsite at the main ticket booth. You don't need a reservation as there's plenty of room.

Tikal Inn HOTEL $$$
(☎7861-2444; www.tikalinn.com; s/d/bungalow Q500/730/720; P 📶 🏊) Built in the late '60s, this resort-style lodging offers rooms in the main building and thatched bungalows alongside the pool and rear lawn, with little porches out front. All are simple, spacious and quite comfortable. The most secluded accommodations are the least expensive, in a handful of cabins at the end of a sawdust trail through the forest.

Jungle Lodge HOTEL $$$
(☎7861-0446; www.junglelodgetikal.com; s/d Q680/772, without bathroom Q359/423; P 📶 🏊) Nearest of the hotels to the site entrance, this was originally built to house archaeologists working at Tikal. Self-contained bungalows, plus a bank of cheaper units, are well spaced throughout rambling, jungle grounds. Some newer suites feature jungle-chic decor and

outdoor rain-showers. The restaurant-bar (mains Q80 to Q100) serves veggie pastas, crepes and other international dishes in a tropical ambience.

Jaguar Inn HOTEL $$$

(☎7926-2411; www.jaguartikal.com; campsite per person Q50, with tent Q115, s/d/tr Q532/639/852; P ❄ @ 🛜) The inn of choice for youthful, independent travelers has duplex and quad bungalows with thatched roofs and hammocks on the porches, plus a smart little restaurant with a popular terrace out front. For those on a tight budget there are tents for rent on a platform.

ℹ Orientation

The archaeological site is at the center of the 550-sq-km Parque Nacional Tikal. The road from Flores enters the park 19km south of the ruins. From the parking lot at the site, it's a short walk back to the junction where there's an information kiosk. Immediately south of this junction, a **visitors center** (⏲8am-4pm) sells books, maps, souvenirs, hats, insect repellent, sun block and other necessities; it also houses a restaurant and museum (p211). Near the visitors center are Tikal's hotels, a campground, a few small *comedores* and a modern research center containing a second museum (p211).

It's a five-minute walk from the ticket control booth to the entry gate. Just beyond, there's a large map posted. From here, it's a 1.5km walk (20 minutes) southwest to the Gran Plaza. From the Gran Plaza west to Templo IV, it's more than 600m.

ℹ Information

Everyone (even those staying inside the park at one of the hotels) must purchase an entry ticket *in advance* at the initial gate on the road in (or at Banrural locations such as Flores or Guatemala City). Note that *tickets are no longer available anywhere inside the entry gate* – that includes sunrise tour tickets. You purchase in advance and then use them as needed at the time/day of your choice.

Seeing the sunrise from Templo IV at the west end of the main site is possible from about October to March, but to enter the park before or after visiting hours you must purchase an additional ticket for Q100, as this is not covered in the normal park entry. You must also have a guide.

The core of the ancient city takes up about 16 sq km, with more than 6000 structures, to which an additional 4000 have recently been identified by LIDAR technology, making this one of the largest Maya cities ever discovered. To visit all the major building complexes, you must walk at least 10km, so wear comfortable shoes with good rubber treads that grip well. The ruins here can be slick from rain and organic material, especially during the wet season. Bring plenty of water, as you'll be walking around all day in the heat.

Please don't feed the coatis (pisotes) that wander about the site.

ℹ Getting There & Away

Eight ATIM (p206) microbuses depart Flores between 6:30am and 3pm (Q30 to Q80, 1¼ hours). They return from Tikal at noon, 1:30pm, 3pm and 6pm. You could also take the Uaxactún-bound bus from the market of Santa Elena at 3:30pm, which is a bit slower.

From El Remate, a collective shuttle departs at 5:30am for Tikal, starting back at 2pm (one way/round-trip Q30/50). Any El Remate accommodations can make reservations.

If traveling from Belize, get a Santa Elena–bound microbus to Puente Ixlú, sometimes called El Cruce, and switch there to a northbound microbus for the remaining 36km to Tikal. Heading from Tikal to Belize, start early and get off at Puente Ixlú to catch a bus or microbus eastward. Be wary of shuttles to Belize advertised at Tikal: these have been known to detour to Flores to pick up passengers! And do not purchase any tickets for ruins (or anything else) from so-called vendors on the bus.

Uaxactún

POP 700 / ELEV 175M

Uaxactún (wah-shahk-*toon*), 23km north of Tikal along an unpaved road through the jungle, was Tikal's political and military rival in Late Preclassic times. It was conquered by Tikal's Chak Tok Ich'aak I (King Great Jaguar Paw) in the 4th century, and was subservient to its great sister to the south for centuries thereafter, though it experienced an apparent resurgence during the Terminal Classic, after Tikal went into decline.

Villagers make an income from collecting chicle, *pimienta* (allspice) and *xate* (low-growing palm, exported to Holland for floral arrangements) in the surrounding forest. In the *xate* warehouse at the west end of town, women put together bunches of the plants for export.

Much of the attraction here is the absolute stillness and isolation. Few visitors make it up this way.

👁 Sights

Research performed by the Carnegie Institute in the 1920s and '30s laid the groundwork for much of the archaeological study that followed in the region, including the excavations at Tikal.

The fee of Q50 to enter Uaxactún is collected at the gate to Tikal National Park, though there is no ticket control at the site itself.

Grupos B & A

About a 20-minute walk to the northwest of the airstrip are Grupo B and Grupo A, the latter featuring the more formidable structures around the city's main square. **Palacio V**, on the east side of the square, is considered a model for Tikal's North Acropolis. In 1916 the American archaeologist Sylvanus G Morley uncovered a stelae dating from the 8th *baktún* at Grupo A. Thus the site was called Uaxactún, meaning 'eight stone.' Behind Palacio V, along a path back toward the village, is the imposing **Palacio A-XVIII**, affording the most panoramic view of the site from its summit.

Stela 5, at Grupo B, displays Tikal's signature glyph, from which archaeologists deduced that Uaxactún was under that city's sway by the date inscribed, 358.

Grupo E

The buildings here are grouped on five low hills. From the airstrip find the sign pointing to Grupo E between the Catholic and Evangelical churches on the right side, from where it's a 10- to 15-minute walk. The most significant temple here is **Templo E-VII-Sub**, among the earliest intact temples excavated, with foundations going back perhaps to 2000 BC. The pyramid is part of a group with astronomical significance: seen from it, the sun rises behind **Templo E-I** on the longest day of the year and behind **Templo E-III** on the shortest day. The four jaguar and serpent masks affixed to the main temple's staircase were painstakingly restored in 2014 by a group of Slovak archaeologists, but then covered up again for conservation. Viewed from Templo E-VII-Sub, the sun sets behind **Templo E-II** at the start of spring and fall. **Templo E-V** is part of a complex of unexcavated temples at Grupo E. **Templo E-X** is the tallest and possibly the oldest of a set of temples at Grupo E.

Sleeping & Eating

If you arrive here by public bus, you'll need to spend the night, since the only return trip is early in the morning. There are two places to stay: one basic, the other rustic.

A few basic cookshacks provide food, including **Comedor Uaxactún** (mains Q35-50; 8am-8pm) and **Comedor Imperial Okan Arin** (4132-5709; mains Q25-40; 7am-10pm), and the village's main lodging prepares all meals.

Posada & Restaurante Campamento El Chiclero HOTEL $
(campamentochiclero@gmail.com; campsite/r per person Q30/75) On the north side of the airstrip, this place has 10 spartan, institutional green rooms underneath a thatched roof, with decent mattresses and mosquito-netted ceilings and windows. Clean showers and toilets are in an adjacent outbuilding; lights out is 9pm. Perky owner Neria does the best food in town (Q75 for soup and a main course with rice).

Aldana's Lodge HUT $
(7783-3931; posadaaldana@gmail.com; campsite/r per person Q20/40) To the right off the street leading to Grupos B and A, the Aldana family offers seven clapboard cabins, with thin mattresses on pallets. Father and son Alfido and Héctor Aldana lead tours to jungle sites such as El Zotz (Q3000) and El Mirador (Q2000), and Amparo prepares good meals.

Getting There & Away

A Pinita bus leaves the main terminal of Santa Elena for Uaxactún (Q40) at 2pm, then migrates to the market terminal, finally leaving town at 2:30pm. This bus passes through El Remate around 3:30pm and Tikal by 5pm. The following day it starts back for Santa Elena from Uaxactún at 7am. This means you'll need to spend two nights in Uaxactún to see the ruins. Otherwise, private tours from El Remate to Uaxactún and back by **Casa de Don David** (5949-2164; www.lacasadedondavid.com; Jobompiche Rd; s/d incl breakfast or dinner from Q248/468; restaurant 6:30am-9pm;) can be arranged on a case-by-case basis.

If you're driving, the last chance to fill your fuel tank as you come from the south is at Puente Ixlú, just south of El Remate. During the rainy season (from May to October, sometimes extending into November), the road from Tikal to Uaxactún can become pretty muddy. From Uaxactún, unpaved roads lead to other ruins at El Zotz (about 30km southwest), Xultún (35km northeast) and Río Azul (100km northeast).

Yaxhá

The Classic Maya sites of Yaxhá, Nakum and El Naranjo form a triangle that is the basis for a national park covering more than 370 sq km and bordering the Parque Nacional Tikal to the west. Yaxhá, the most visited of the trio, stands on a hill between two sizable lakes, Lago Yaxhá and Lago Sacnab. The setting, the sheer size of the site, the number of excellently restored buildings and the abundant jungle flora and fauna all make it particularly worth visiting. There are also some stunning views from the tallest pyramid, which looks out over the lagoons. Not surprisingly, the foot traffic here is far less than at more popular, easy-to-reach sites.

The site is 11km north of the Puente Ixlú–Melchor de Mencos road, accessed via an unpaved road from a turnoff 32km from Puente Ixlú and 33km from Melchor de Mencos.

Sights

East Acropolis & Structure 216 ARCHAEOLOGICAL SITE

Near the site entrance is the high point of Yaxhá (literally): Structure 216 in the East Acropolis. Also called the Temple of the Red Hands, because red hand prints were discovered there, it towers over 30m high, affording views in every direction.

North Acropolis ARCHAEOLOGICAL SITE

The trio of pyramidal temples at the North Acropolis are built atop older structures dating back to 100 BC. Comprising of seven platforms, the northernmost temple rises above the jungle foliage. As you enter the complex, look for the remnants of giant stucco masks beneath the thatched roof on the right.

Getting There & Away

Agencies in Flores and El Remate offer organized trips to Yaxhá, some combined with Nakum and/or Tikal. Horizontes Mayas (p206) in El Remate runs tours (Q125 per person, minimum three people), including guide and entrance fee, at 7am and 1pm, returning at 1pm and 6:30pm. Otherwise, take a Melchor de Mencos–bound microbus and get off at Restaurante El Portal de Yaxhá, opposite the Yaxhá turnoff; it can arrange transport to the site by pickup truck or motorcycle (Q200 return). *Colectivos* from Flores charge Q200 as well.

El Mirador

Buried within the furthest reaches of the Petén jungle, just 7km south of the Mexican border, the Late Preclassic metropolis at **El Mirador** (Lookout; www.miradorbasin.com; 24hr) FREE contains possibly the largest cluster of buildings of any single Maya site, among them the biggest pyramid ever built in the Maya world. Ongoing excavations have only scratched the surface, so many are still hidden beneath the jungle.

El Mirador was so-named by local *chicheros* (chicle harvesters) for the excellent views provided by some of the pyramids. **La Danta** (the Tapir) looms 70m above the forest floor. **El Tigre** is 55m high with a base covering 18,000 sq meters. At its height, the city spread over 16 sq km and supported tens of thousands of citizens. It was certainly one of the greatest Maya cities of the Preclassic era.

Getting There & Away

A visit to El Mirador involves an arduous jungle trek of at least five days and four nights (it's about 60km each way), with no facilities or amenities aside from what you carry in and what can be rustled from the forest. During the rainy season, especially September to December, the mud can make it extremely difficult; February to June is the best period to attempt a trek. Alternatively, you can go by helicopter.

TREKKING

The trip usually departs from a cluster of houses called Carmelita, 82km up the road from Flores. The **Comisión de Turismo Cooperativa Carmelita** (7867-5629; www.turismocooperativacarmelita.com), a group of INGUAT-authorized guides, can make all arrangements for a trek to El Mirador, with optional visits to the Preclassic sites of Nakbé, El Tintal, Wakná and Xulnal. Travelers who participate in these treks should be in good physical shape, able to withstand high temperatures (average of nearly 38°C; 100.4°F) and humidity (average 85%) and be prepared to hike or ride long distances (up to 30km per day).

On the first day of a typical itinerary, you hike six hours to El Tintal, where you camp for the night. On the second day, after a look around El Tintal, you proceed through denser forests to El Mirador and set up camp there. The next day is reserved for exploring El Mirador. Five-day hikers will simply return the way they came. Those with six or more days will hike southeast to arrive at Nakbé and camp there. The next day the expedition begins the return, possibly stopping for the night at the site of La Florida. On day six, you head back to Carmelita.

For a five-/six-day trip, the cooperative charges Q1925/2240 per person in a group of at least three people. The fee includes tents, hammocks and mosquito netting; all meals and drinking water; Spanish-speaking guide; mules and muleskinners; and first-aid supplies. An English-speaking guide is available for an extra charge.

Two buses daily travel from Flores to Carmelita, at 5am and 1pm (Q80). Generally you take the morning bus and start hiking straight away if your guide hasn't arranged private transportation.

It's also possible to get El Mirador from Uaxactún, a longer but gentler approach since there are fewer *bajos* (seasonal swamps) and it's less affected by agricultural clearing, so you're underneath the jungle canopy from the outset. Going this route has become very unusual, so you'll need to plan things yourself well ahead of time rather than depending on catching a group tour. Posada Campamento del Chiclero (p214) or Aldana's Lodge (p214) will be your best chance of getting solid info on what is available and costs (currently Q2000 per person). On the first leg of the journey you're driven in a monster truck to a campground at the former *chichero* camp of Yucatán, a five-hour journey. The next morning the group is outfitted with mules and proceeds to another camp, La Leontina, a four-hour tramp through the jungle. The following day it's a three-hour walk to Nakbé. After visiting that site, the expedition continues to El Mirador. The journey back follows the same route in reverse.

HELICOPTER

If hiking, camping and mosquito-swatting isn't your cup of tea, you can go the easy way: by helicopter. During selected periods throughout the year, **TAG Airlines** (☎ 4218-5485, Guatemala City 2380-9494; www.tag.com.gt; Aeropuerto Internacional Mundo Maya; US$399; ⏲ 6am-7:30pm) offers chopper packages from Flores to El Mirador for as little as US$399 per person. Prices and availability fluctuate constantly, so contact the airline ahead of time to find out about the current schedule. Going by air means a short visit of only four to five hours, so there's far less chance to explore the ruin, but (weather permitting) you will have time to hike up to La Danta and El Tigre as well. The chopper leaves early in the morning and returns to Flores around 3:30pm. Water and snacks are provided, but bring sunscreen, repellent and plenty of camera batteries.

UNDERSTAND GUATEMALA

Guatemala Today

Guatemala is a nation with a bright tourism scene, but one that continues to struggle economically and politically. More than half its population is under the age of 25, with a similar proportion living below the poverty line. Gang violence and the still-unresolved aftermath of the civil war are countered by the boundless energy (if limited resources) of Guatemala's grassroots organizations. Successive governments may continue to make promises, but Guatemalans rely on each other to deliver solutions.

Neither Corrupt nor a Thief?

Guatemala was ahead of the American curve when Jimmy Morales, a popular TV personality, was inaugurated as president in January 2016. He swept into power after the impeachment of former president Otto Pérez Molina on corruption charges, running on the slogan 'Ni corrupto, ni ladrón' (neither corrupt nor a thief).

The country has found the reality of the Morales government rather more sobering than its early promise. The evangelical president's close ties to the military – the core of Guatemala's political elite – has led to stagnation on human rights issues, including the paring back of the country's human rights commission and an unsuccessful attempt to expel the UN's top representative. After concerns about his own presidential campaign funding, Morales pushed Congress into passing a law granting him immunity from prosecution, and has proposed further amnesties for those convicted of illegal spending.

A Political Eruption

The national conversation dramatically switched its focus on June 3, 2018, when Fuego erupted south of Antigua. In the country's deadliest eruption since 1929, around 160 people were killed and thousands were left homeless. Across Guatemala, communities pulled together to collect supplies to help the victims, but foreign aid groups were only allowed restricted access to help. Protests later broke out over alleged mismanagement of relief funds as well as the wider governmental response to the eruption, further tarnishing the Morales administration in the eyes of many Guatemalans. Continued delays over the resettling of those displaced mean that Fuego is likely to cast a long shadow into the 2019 election season.

The Global Picture

Global policy continues to affect Guatemala, not least in its relationship with the USA.

REMOTE MAYA SITES

The Petén region is full of archaeological sites in various stages of excavation. Some are harder than others to get to; tour operators in Flores and El Remate can help you reach them, but they require advance planning. Here are a few of the more intriguing ones that you might want to check out:

San Bartolo Discovered in 2003, this site features one of the best-preserved Maya murals with a depiction of the creation myth from the Popul Vuh (the Maya 'Bible'). It's approximately 40km northeast of Uaxactún, near the Río Azul.

Piedras Negras On the banks of the Río Usumacinta amid black cliffs, these remote ruins have impressive carvings and a sizable acropolis complex. It was here that part-time archaeologist Tatiana Proskouriakoff deciphered the Maya hieroglyphic system. She requested to be buried here after her death in 1985, but due to the civil war that did not happen. Finally, 10 years later, her remains were placed beneath a simple gravestone at the top of Structure J23.

La Blanca Located along the Río Mopan near the Belize border, this palatial complex may have flourished as a trading center in the Late Classic Period. The acropolis is notable for its remarkably preserved stone walls and an abundance of graffiti. Excavation was done by a Spanish team. The **Mayan Adventure** (Map p198; ☎5830-2060; www.the-mayan-adventure.com; Calle 15 de Septiembre; ⏰bookings Mon-Fri), based in Flores, leads tours here.

El Zotz This sprawling site occupies its own biotope abutting Tikal National Park. Of the three barely excavated temples, one, the Pirámide del Diablo, can be scaled for views all the way to Tikal. Stick around till dusk to see how the place gets its name – 'The Bat' in Maya. Researchers from the University of Southern California uncovered 23 masks within the tombs of the largest pyramid. INGUAT-authorized guides from the community of **Cruce Dos Aguadas** (☎5039-1188), 42km north of Flores, lead tours here, a 24km hike east through the jungle.

Río Azul Up near the corner where the Belize, Guatemala and Mexico borders meet, this medium-sized site fell under the domain of Tikal in the Early Classic Period and became a key trading post for cacao from the Caribbean. Most notable are the tombs with vibrant painted glyphs inside. Campamento El Chiclero (p214) in Uaxactún leads a recommended excursion.

El Naranjo Major excavations and restorations are happening at this immense site 12km from the Belize border. In the process archaeologists have ascertained that the city was more densely populated than Tikal and possibly larger. Ruled by Princess Six Sky, daughter of a Dos Pilas governor, Naranjo conquered neighboring kingdoms and produced some of the most refined art in the Maya world. Contact **Río Mopán Lodge** (Map p262; ☎7926-5196; avinsa@yahoo.com; r with/without air-con Q188/150; P❄☜) about visiting the site.

Jimmy Morales was the first international leader to follow Donald Trump's recognition of Jerusalem as the capital of Israel, announcing that the country would move its embassy from Tel Aviv to the city. Guatemala-Israeli ties have always been close, but the plan provoked condemnation from Arab states. The Middle East is an important market for Guatemala's cardamom exports, and threats of a boycott still hang in the air.

A particularly sensitive subject in rural Guatemala has to do with large (often foreign-administered) projects such as hydroelectric dams and mineral mines. Local indigenous organizations are currently campaigning against the International Development Bank–funded Pojom II and San Andres hydroelectric dams in northern Huehuetenango province, saying that it threatens local livelihoods as well as water supplies.

The Slow Road to Recovery

Despite the promise of the 1996 peace accords, the road to recovery from the civil war has been a slow and painful one. Official recognition of some atrocities has been an important step in the recovery process, however reluctant it appeared to some observers. Though President Morales has stated he does not believe the genocide in the Ixil Triangle ever took place, the exhumation of clandestine cemeteries used by the military to bury 'disappeared' dissidents continues, and in December 2017 172 newly identified victims were reburied in the area. More than 35,000 people remain missing, and the mandated reparation measures have never been fully put in place.

Some war criminals have been brought to justice. So far the heftiest penalty to be handed down was to ex-Military Commissioner Lucas Tecún, who was sentenced to 7710 years in prison. Former dictator Efraín Ríos Montt was tried and convicted of genocide, but a later court ruling overturned the verdict. Despite his alleged senility, he is currently being retried.

Grassroots Movement

In the face of official indifference and/or inability to deal with the country's myriad problems, many community-based organizations and NGOs are moving in to fill the void. Large segments of the Guatemalan population have become active in volunteer work, focusing on everything from neighborhood watch–type programs in areas unpatrolled by police to larger efforts focusing on food security and housing for the poor.

The mass protests against the old Pérez Molina government and now the Jimmy Morales presidency, mainly non-politically aligned and organized chiefly through social media, have sparked a continued interest in politics among young Guatemalans, with alliances being formed from previously disparate groups, and a strengthening of civil society.

History

Earliest estimates put humans in what is now Guatemala as far back as 11,000 BC. The prevailing theory is that they got here by walking across an ice bridge from Siberia. The development of agriculture and resulting improvement in the stability of the food supply led to population growth, the development of early art forms and a language that is traceable to what many Maya speak today.

Rise & Fall of the Maya

Further developments in agriculture and increases in population gave these early civilizations time and resources to develop artistic and architectural techniques.

Between 800 BC and AD 100, population centers such as El Mirador and Kaminaljuyú grew with trade and conquest and hundreds (if not thousands – many are yet to be uncovered) of temples and ceremonial centers were built. Guatemala's most famous Maya site, Tikal, came into its own around the start of the Classic period – AD 250.

The history of these – and many other – city states was troubled at best, characterized by broken military alliances, food shortages and droughts.

By the early 16th century, Maya civilization was already in trouble. Some centers, such as El Mirador, had already been abandoned and others, such as Tikal and Quiriguá, had shrunk to the size of minor towns. Theories suggest that many abandoned El Petén in favor of the highlands, setting up capitals in K'umarcaaj, Iximché, Zaculeu and Mixco Viejo.

Relocation didn't bring peace, though – soon Toltec tribes, having abandoned the Yucatán, moved in and began to take control. Infighting among tribes, overpopulation and the resulting strain on the food supply combined to make conditions very favorable to the Spanish when they arrived in 1523.

Conquest & Colonization

The Spanish didn't just walk on in, as many think. Spirited resistance was met, most notably from the K'iche' (Quiché; in a famous battle led by Tecún Umán, near present-day Quetzaltenango). Neighboring Kaqchiquel not only refused to join forces with the K'iche', they joined the Spanish and fought against them.

It didn't take long for the Spanish to turn on the Kaqchiquel, though, and pretty soon most of the Maya were under Spanish control, the exceptions being the Rabinal (who have largely maintained their culture) and the Itzáes, who, hidden out on the island of Flores in El Petén, were unconquered until 1697.

Independence & the 19th Century

By the time thoughts of independence from Spain began stirring among Guatemalans, society was already rigidly stratified. Angered at being repeatedly passed over for advancement, Guatemalan *criollos* (Guatemalan-born Spaniards) successfully rose in revolt in 1821. Independence changed little for Guatemala's indigenous communities, who remained under the control of the church and the landowning elite.

During the short existence of the United Provinces of Central America, liberal president Francisco Morazán (1830–39) instituted reforms aimed at correcting three persistent problems: the overwhelming power of the church; the division of society into a Hispanic upper class and an indigenous lower class; and the region's impotence in world markets.

But unpopular economic policies, heavy taxes and an 1837 cholera epidemic led to an indigenous uprising that brought conservative Rafael Carrera to power. Carrera ruled until 1865 and undid many of Morazán's achievements.

The liberals regained power in the 1870s under president Justo Rufino Barrios, a coffee-plantation owner who embarked on a program of modernization – constructing roads, railways, schools and a modern banking system – and did everything possible to encourage coffee production, including promoting forced relocation and labor. Succeeding governments generally pursued the same policies, maintaining control by a wealthy minority and repression of opposition.

The Early 20th Century

From 1898 to 1920, Manuel Estrada Cabrera ruled as a dictator, bringing progress in technical matters but placing a heavy burden on all but the ruling oligarchy. He fancied himself a bringer of light and culture to a backward land, styling himself the 'Teacher and Protector of Guatemalan Youth.'

When Estrada Cabrera was overthrown, Guatemala entered a period of instability that ended in 1931 with the election of General Jorge Ubico, who modernized the country's health and social welfare infrastructure but was forced into exile in 1944.

Philosopher Juan José Arévalo came to power in 1945, establishing the nation's social security system, a bureau of indigenous affairs, a modern public health system and liberal labor laws. His six years as president saw 25 coup attempts by conservative military forces.

Arévalo was succeeded in 1951 by Colonel Jacobo Arbenz Guzmán, who looked to break up estates and foster high productivity on small farms. But in 1954 (in one of the first documented covert CIA operations) the US government orchestrated an invasion from Honduras led by two exiled Guatemalan military officers. Arbenz was forced to step down and land reform never took place. Violence, oppression and disenfranchisement ensued, fueling the formation of left-wing guerrilla groups.

Civil War

During the 1960s and '70s, economic inequality and the developing union movement forced oppression to new heights. Amnesty International estimates that 50,000 to 60,000 Guatemalans were killed during the political violence of the 1970s. In 1976 an earthquake killed about 22,000 people and left around a million homeless.

In 1982 General José Efraín Ríos Montt initiated a 'scorched earth' policy. Huge numbers of people – mainly indigenous men – from more than 400 villages were murdered in the name of anti-insurgency, stabilization and anticommunism. An estimated 15,000 civilians were tortured and massacred; 100,000 refugees fled to Mexico. In response, four guerrilla organizations united to form the URNG (Guatemalan National Revolutionary Unity).

In August 1983 Ríos Montt was deposed in a coup led by General Oscar Humberto Mejía Victores, but human-rights abuses continued. The USA suspended military aid, and 1985 saw the election of civilian Christian Democrat Marco Vinicio Cerezo Arévalo – but the military had secured immunity from prosecution and armed conflict festered in remote areas.

The Signing of the Peace Accords

In 1996 Álvaro Enrique Arzú Irigoyen of the middle-right PAN (Partido de Avanzada Nacional) was elected. In December he and the URNG signed peace accords ending the 36-year civil war – a war in which an estimated 200,000 Guatemalans were killed, a million were left homeless and untold thousands 'disappeared.'

The accords called for accountability for the armed forces' human-rights violations and resettlement of one million refugees. They also addressed the identity and rights of indigenous peoples, health care, education and other basic social services, women's rights, the abolition of compulsory military service and the incorporation of the ex-guerrillas into civilian life.

It's been a rocky road since the war's end. The greatest challenge to peace stems from inequities in the power structure. It's estimated that 70% of the country's arable land is owned by less than 3% of the population. According to a UN report, the top 20% of the population has an income 30 times greater than the bottom 20%. Or, as many Guatemalans will tell you, there are seven families who 'own' Guatemala.

Guatemala in the 21st Century

Any hopes for a truly just and democratic society have looked increasingly frayed in the years since 1996. International organizations regularly criticize the state of human rights in the country and Guatemalan human-rights campaigners are threatened or simply disappear on a regular basis. The major problems – poverty, illiteracy, lack of education and poor medical facilities (all much more common in rural areas, where the Maya population is concentrated) – remain a long way from being solved.

The 1999 presidential elections brought Alfonso Portillo of the conservative Frente Republicano Guatemalteco (FRG) to power. Portillo fled the country at the end of his presidency in the face of allegations that he had diverted US$500 million from the treasury to personal and family bank accounts. Having evaded prosecution for years, Portillo was extradited to the USA to face charges of laundering money using US banks. He was sentenced to almost six years in jail, and was released in 2018.

The Central America Free Trade Agreement (CAFTA; TLC or Tratado de Libre Comercio, in Spanish) was ratified by Guatemala in 2006. Supporters claim it frees the country up for greater participation in foreign markets, while detractors state that the agreement is a bad deal for the already disenfranchised rural poor.

The 2007 presidency of Álvaro Colom was dogged by corruption claims, from straight-out vote buying to back-room deals granting contracts to companies who had contributed to his campaign fund. His eventual departure left the door open for hard-line ex-civil war general Otto Pérez Molina to take office in early 2012.

Pérez Molina's election was always going to be controversial – he was a general in Ríos Montt's army in the period where the worst atrocities occurred, in the regions where they occurred. Guatemalans had grown tired of the growing lawlessness in their country, though, and turned a blind eye to history in the hope that Molina would deliver on his two campaign promises – jobs and security.

Despite some heavy-handed reactions to protesters (the army killed seven and wounded 40 in one incident at an anti-dam and anti-mining protest), Pérez Molina did little to combat real crime, and his early presidency was plagued by vague rumors of corruption in the administration. In April 2015, the UN anti-corruption agency CICIG issued a report and things got a whole lot less vague.

The report claimed several senior members of the Pérez Molina administration were involved in taking bribes from importers in return for reduced customs fees. Within days, mass protests were organized over social media and tens of thousands turned out in downtown Guatemala City. Vice president Roxana Baldetti was the first to go – she resigned in early May, unable to explain how she paid for her US$13 million helicopter, among other things.

In the following months more than 20 officials resigned and many were arrested as the scandal snaked its way to the top. Mass protests continued as more findings were released. Baldetti was arrested in August amid calls for Pérez Molina's impeachment. The president hung on for a few weeks more, then resigned in the face of impending impeachment. He was arrested in early September.

Culture

The National Psyche

You'll be amazed when you first reach Guatemala just how helpful, polite and unhurried Guatemalans are. Everyone has time to stop and chat and explain what you want to know. Most Guatemalans like to get to know other people without haste, feeling for common ground and things to agree on.

What goes on behind this outward politeness is harder to encapsulate. Few Guatemalans exhibit the stress, worry and hurry of the 'developed' nations, but this obviously isn't because they don't have to worry about money or employment. They're a long-suffering people who don't expect wealth or good government but make the best of what comes their way – friendship, their family, a good meal, a bit of good company.

Outwardly, it appears that family ties are strong, but beneath the surface you may find that the real reason that three generations live together in one house has more to do with economics than affection.

Guatemalans are a religious bunch – agnostics and atheists are very thin on the ground. People will often ask what religion you are quite early in a conversation. Unless you really want to get into it, saying 'Christian' generally satisfies. Orthodox Catholicism is gradually giving way to evangelical Protestantism among the *ladinos* (persons of mixed indigenous and European race), with the animist-Catholic syncretism of the traditional Maya always present.

Some say that Guatemala has no middle class, just a ruling class and an exploited class. It's true that Guatemala has a small, rich, *ladino* ruling elite; it also has an indigenous Maya population, which tends to be poor, poorly educated and poorly provided for.

But as well as these two groups, there's a large group of poor and middle-class *ladinos,* with aspirations influenced by education, TV, international popular music and North America (of which many Guatemalans have direct experience as migrant workers) – and maybe by liberal ideas of equality and social tolerance. This segment of society has its bohemian/student/artist circles whose overlap with educated, forward-looking Maya may hold the greatest hope for progress toward an equitable society.

Lifestyle

The majority of Guatemalans live in one-room brick or concrete houses, or traditional *bajareque,* with roofs of tin, tiles or thatch. They have earth floors, a stove/fireplace and minimal possessions – often just a couple of bare beds and a few pots. Thus live most of Guatemala's Maya majority, in the countryside, in villages and in towns.

The few wealthier Maya and most *ladino* families have larger houses in towns and the bigger villages, but their homes may still not be much more than one or two bedrooms and a kitchen that also serves as a living area. Middle-class families in the wealthier suburbs of Guatemala City live in good-sized one- or two-story houses with gardens. The elite few possess rural as well as urban properties – eg a comfortable farmhouse on the Pacific Slope, or a seaside villa.

Despite modernizing influences, traditional family ties remain strong. Extended-family groups gather for weekend meals and vacations. Old-fashioned gender roles are strong too: many women have jobs to increase the family income but few have positions of power. Homosexuality barely raises its head above the parapet: only in Guatemala City is there anything approaching an open gay scene, and that is pretty much for men only.

The CIA's World Factbook states that more than half of all Guatemalans live in poverty. The official national minimum wage is only Q81 (about US$10) per day – and not everyone is entitled even to this. An established school teacher can earn around Q1950 (about US$250) per month. Poverty is most prevalent in rural, indigenous areas, especially the highlands. Wealth, industry and commerce are concentrated overwhelmingly in sprawling, polluted Guatemala City.

People

The great majority of Guatemala's 15 million people live in the highland strip from Guatemala City to Quetzaltenango, the country's two biggest cities. Many towns and large villages are dotted around this region. Some 49% of the population lives in towns and cities, and nearly half are aged under 19.

Some 41% of Guatemalans are indigenous, but this line is blurred as many people have indigenous blood, but some choose not to describe themselves as such. Nearly all of this indigenous population is Maya, although there is a very small population of non-Maya indigenous people called the Chinka' (Xinca) in the southeastern corner of the country. The four biggest Maya groups – the K'iche' (Quiché), Mam, Q'eqchi' (Kekchí) and Kaqchiquel – are most densely concentrated in the highlands. The rest of Guatemala's population is nearly all *ladinos* – descended from both the Maya and European (mostly Spanish) settlers. There are also a few thousand Garifuna (descended from Caribbean islanders and shipwrecked African slaves) around the Caribbean town of Lívingston.

Maya languages are still the way many Maya communicate, with over 20 separate (and often mutually unintelligible) Maya languages spoken in different regions of the country. It's language that primarily defines which Maya people someone belongs to. Though many Maya speak some Spanish, it's always a second language – and there are many who don't speak any Spanish at all.

Religion

Roman Catholicism is the predominant religion in Guatemala, but it is not the only religion. Since the 1980s evangelical Protestant sects, around 58% of them Pentecostal, have surged in popularity, and it is estimated that 30% to 40% of Guatemalans are now evangelicals. These numbers continue to grow as evangelical churches compete hard for further souls.

Catholicism's fall can also be attributed in part to the civil war. Catholic priests were (and still are) outspoken defenders of human rights, and attracted persecution from dictators at the time, especially from Ríos Montt. As a result, many Catholic churches in rural areas simply closed down during this time and evangelical ones moved in to fill the vacuum.

The number of new evangelical churches in some towns and villages, especially indigenous Maya villages, is astonishing. You will undoubtedly hear loud Guatemalan versions of gospel music pouring out of some of them as you walk around, and in some places loudspeakers broadcast the music and its accompanying preaching across entire towns.

Catholicism in the Maya areas has never been exactly orthodox. The missionaries who brought Catholicism to the Maya in the 16th century permitted aspects of the existing animistic, shamanistic Maya religion to continue alongside Christian rites and beliefs. Syncretism was aided by the identification of certain Maya deities with certain Christian saints and survives to this day. A bizarre example is the deity known, among other things, as Maximón.

The Maya still worship at a number of places sacred since ancient times, bringing offerings and sacrificing chickens to gods who predate the arrival of the Spanish. Each place has its own different set of gods – or at least different names for similar gods.

Visitors might also be able to observe traditional Maya ceremonies in places such as the Pascual Abaj shrine (Map p150) at Chichicastenango, the altars on Laguna Chicabal outside Quetzaltenango, or El Baúl near Santa Lucía Cotzumalguapa, but a lot of traditional rites are off-limits to foreigners.

Arts

Literature

Guatemalan writer Miguel Ángel Asturias (1899–1974) won the Nobel Prize for Literature in 1967. Best known for his thinly veiled vilification of Latin American dictators in *El señor presidente,* Asturias also wrote poetry (collected in *Sien de alondra,* published in English as *Temple of the Lark*). Other celebrated Guatemalan writers include poet Luis Cardoza y Aragón (1901–92) and short-story master Augusto Monterroso (1921–2003). Gaspar Pedro Gonzáles' *A Mayan Life* is claimed to be the first novel written by a Maya author.

Music

Music is a very important part of Guatemalan society, and a source of pride is that the marimba (xylophone) may have been invented here (although some claim it was brought from Africa by slaves). The Maya also play traditional instruments including the chirimía (of Arabic origin and related to the oboe) and reed flute.

Guatemalan tastes in pop music are greatly influenced by the products of other Latin American countries. Reggaetón is huge – current favorites being Pitbull, Nicky Jam and J Balvin.

The only record label seriously promoting new Guatemalan artists (mostly in the urban/hip-hop vein) is Guatemala City–based Outstanding Productions.

Guatemalan rock went through its golden age in the '80s and early '90s. Bands from this era such as Razones de Cambio, Bohemia Suburbana and Viernes Verde still have their die-hard fans. The most famous Guatemalan-born musician is Ricardo Arjona.

Weaving

Guatemalans make many traditional *artesanías* (handicrafts), both for everyday use and to sell. Crafts include basketry, ceramics and wood carving, but the most prominent are weaving, embroidery and other textile arts practiced by Maya women.

The *huipil* (a long, woven, white sleeveless tunic with intricate, colorful embroidery) is one of several types of garment that have been worn since pre-Hispanic times. Other colorful types include: the *tocoyal,* a woven head-covering often decorated with bright tassels; the *corte,* a piece of material 7m or 10m long that is used as a wraparound skirt; and the *faja,* a long, woven waist sash that can be folded to hold what otherwise might be put in pockets.

Colorful traditional dress is still predominant generally in the heavily Maya-populated highlands, but you'll see it in all parts of the country. The variety of techniques, materials, styles and designs is bewildering to the newcomer, but you'll see some of the most colorful, intricate, eye-catching and widely worn designs in Sololá and Santiago Atitlán, near Lago de Atitlán; Nebaj in the Ixil Triangle; Zunil near Quetzaltenango; and Todos Santos and San Mateo Ixtatán in the Cuchumatanes mountains.

Landscape & Wildlife

The Land

Consisting primarily of mountainous forest highlands and jungle plains, Guatemala covers an area of 109,000 sq km. The western highlands hold 30 volcanoes, reaching heights of more than 4200m southwest of Huehuetenango. In the Cuchumatanes range, land not cleared for Maya *milpas* (cornfields) is covered in pine forests, although these are dwindling rapidly.

The Pacific Slope holds rich coffee, cacao, fruit and sugar plantations. Down along the shore the volcanic slope meets the sea, yielding vast, sweltering beaches of black volcanic sand.

Guatemala City lies at an altitude of around 1500m. To the north, the Alta Verapaz highlands gradually give way to El Petén, whose climate and topography is similar to the Yucatán: hot and humid or hot and dry. Southeast of El Petén is the banana-rich valley of the Río Motagua, dry in some areas; it's moist in others.

Guatemala is at the confluence of three tectonic plates, resulting in earthquakes and volcanic eruptions. Major quakes struck in 1773, 1917 and 1976. Its dynamic geology includes a tremendous system of surface-level and subterranean caves. This karst terrain riddles the Verapaces region and has made Guatemala a popular spelunking destination. Surface-level caves have been used for Maya ceremonies since ancient times.

Animals & Wildlife

The country's abundance of animals includes 250 species of mammal, 600 bird species, 200 species of reptile and amphibian, and numerous butterflies and other insects.

The national bird, the resplendent quetzal, is often used to symbolize Central America. Though small, the quetzal is exceptionally beautiful. The males sport a bright red breast, brilliant blue-green across the rest of the body and a spot of bright white on the underside of the long tail.

Other colorful birds include toucans, macaws and parrots. Boasting the ocellated turkey (or 'Petén turkey') – a large, impressive, multicolored bird reminiscent of a peacock – Tikal is a birdwatching hot spot, with some 300 tropical and migratory species sighted to date. Several woodpecker species, nine types of hummingbirds and four trogon species are just the beginning of the list. Also in the area are large white herons, hawks, warblers, kingfishers, harpy eagles (rare) and many others.

Although Guatemala's forests host several mammal and reptile species, many remain difficult to observe. Still, visitors to Tikal can enjoy the antics of the omnipresent *pizotes* (coatis, a tropical mammal related to raccoons) and might spy howler and spider monkeys.

Other mammals deeper in the forest include jaguars, ocelots, pumas, peccaries, agoutis, opossums, tapirs, kinkajous (nocturnal arboreal mammals), *tepezcuintles* (pacas; white-spotted brownish rodents), white-tailed and red brocket deer, armadillos and very large rattlesnakes. Reptiles and amphibians in the rest of Guatemala include at least three species of sea turtle (leatherback, *tortuga negra* and olive ridley) and two species of crocodile (one found in El Petén, the other in the Río Dulce). Manatees also frequent the waters around Río Dulce.

Guatemala has over 8000 plant species in 19 different ecosystems, ranging from coastal mangrove forests to mountainous interior pine forests to high cloud forests. El Petén supports a variety of trees, including mahogany, cedar, ramón and sapodilla.

The national flower, the *monja blanca* (white nun orchid), is said to have been picked so much that it's now rare in the wild. Nevertheless, the country has around

NATIONAL PARKS & PROTECTED AREAS

Guatemala has 92 protected areas, including biosphere reserves, national parks, protected biotopes, wildlife refuges and private nature reserves. Even though some areas are contained within other, larger ones, they amount to 28% of the national territory.

Many of the protected areas are remote and hard to access by the independent traveler; the list below outlines those that are easiest to reach and/or most interesting to visitors, but excludes the volcanoes, nearly all of which are protected, and areas of mainly archaeological interest.

Parque Nacional Tikal Diverse jungle wildlife among Guatemala's most magnificent Maya ruins.

Parque Nacional Laguna del Tigre A remote, large park within the Reserva Maya, featuring freshwater wetlands. Wildlife includes scarlet macaws, monkeys and crocodiles.

Parque Nacional Mirador-Río Azul A national park within the Reserva Maya containing the archaeological site of El Mirador.

Parque Nacional Río Dulce The beautiful jungle-lined lower Río Dulce between Lago de Izabal and the Caribbean serves as a manatee refuge.

Parque Nacional Grutas de Lanquín A large, bat-infested cave system 61km east of Cobán.

Biotopo del Quetzal An easily accessible cloud-forest reserve sheltering howler monkeys and birds (and possibly a quetzal).

Biotopo Cerro Cahuí A forest reserve beside Lago de Petén Itzá offering abundant wildlife spotting and good walking trails.

Refugio de Vida Silvestre Bocas del Polochic Guatemala's second-largest freshwater wetlands, at the western end of Lago de Izabal. Abundant birdwatching (more than 300 species).

Reserva Natural Monterrico-Hawaii Covers beach and wetlands, protecting birdlife and marine turtles.

600 species of orchid, a third of which are endemic.

Guatemala also has the perfect climate for *xate* (sha-tay), a low-growing palm that thrives in El Petén and is prized in the developed world as a flower-arrangement filler.

Environmental Issues

Environmental consciousness is not largely developed in Guatemala, as vast amounts of garbage strewn across the country will quickly tell you. Despite the impressive list of parks and protected areas, genuine protection for those areas is harder to achieve, partly because of official collusion to ignore the regulations and partly because of pressure from poor Guatemalans in need of land. Deforestation is a problem in many areas, especially El Petén, where jungle is being felled at an alarming rate not just for timber but also to make way for cattle ranches, oil pipelines, clandestine airstrips, new settlements and new maize fields cleared by the slash-and-burn method.

On the more populous Pacific side of the country, the land is mostly agricultural or given over to industry. The remaining forests in the Pacific coastal and highland areas are not long for this world, as local communities cut down the remaining trees for heating and cooking fuels.

Nevertheless, a number of Guatemalan organizations are doing valiant work to protect their country's environment and biodiversity. NGOs can be good resources for finding out more about Guatemala's natural parks and protected areas.

SURVIVAL GUIDE

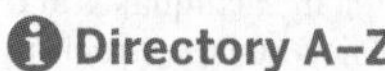

Directory A–Z

ACCESSIBLE TRAVEL

Guatemala is not the easiest country to negotiate for travelers with a mobility issues. Although many sidewalks in Antigua have ramps and cute little inlaid tiles depicting a wheelchair, the streets are cobblestone, so the ramps are anything but smooth and the streets worse.

Many hotels in Guatemala are old converted houses with rooms around a courtyard; such rooms are wheelchair accessible, but the bathrooms may not be. The most expensive hotels have facilities such as ramps, elevators and accessible toilets. Transportation is the biggest hurdle for travelers with limited mobility: travelers in a wheelchair may consider renting a car and driver as the buses will prove especially challenging due to lack of space.

Antigua-based **Transitions** (www.transitions foundation.org) is an organization aiming to increase awareness and access for people with disabilities in Guatemala.

Download Lonely Planet's free Accessible Travel guides from http://lptravel.to/Accessible Travel.

ACCOMMODATIONS

It's generally not necessary to book your accommodations in advance. If, however, you're planning on being in Antigua or down at the beach during Semana Santa, the sooner you book the better.

Hotels From desperate dives out by the bus terminal to fancy-pants boutique numbers, there is no shortage of options.

Hostels Starting to make a dent in the budget accommodations scene, especially in backpacker-favored destinations such as Antigua, Quetzaltenango and around Lago de Atitlán.

Homestays Generally organized through Spanish schools, these are a great way to connect with local culture.

CHILDREN

Young children are highly regarded in Guatemala and can often break down barriers and open doors to local hospitality.

However, Guatemala is so culturally dense, with such an emphasis on history and archaeology, it's easy to overwhelm kids. That said, the ruins at Tikal (p206) should inspire all ages – if scrambling over ruins that aren't just home to an ancient civilization but also featured in several *Star Wars* movies isn't enough, there are also plenty of howler and spider monkeys to spot.

To keep kids entertained, try to make a point of breaking up the trip with visits to places such as Guatemala City's **Museo de los Niños** (Children's Museum; Map p114; ☎2475-5076; www.museodelosninos.com.gt; 5a Calle 10-00, Zona 13; Q40; ⏰8:30am-noon & 1-4:30pm Tue-Fri, 9:30am-1:30pm & 2:30-6pm Sat & Sun) and **Museo de Historia Natural** (Natural History Museum; Map p114; ☎2334-6065; Calle Mariscal Cruz 1-56, Zona 10; Q10; ⏰8am-3pm Mon-Fri), **Autosafari Chapín** (☎2222-5858; www.autosafarichapin.com; Carretera a Taxisco, Km 87.5; adult/child Q60/50; ⏰9:30am-5pm Tue-Sun), and Retalhuleu's Xocomil (p172) water park and Xetulul (p172) theme park. Most Spanish schools are open to kids too, and many older children will enjoy activities such as zip-lining, kayaking and horseback riding.

For general information on traveling with children, have a look at Lonely Planet's *Travel with Children*.

CUSTOMS REGULATIONS

Normally customs officers won't look seriously in your luggage and may not look at all. Guatemala restricts import/export of pretty much the same things as everybody else (weapons, drugs, large amounts of cash etc).

EMBASSIES & CONSULATES

Australia, New Zealand and Ireland do not have diplomatic representation in Guatemala; their nearest embassies are in Mexico City. All of the following are in Guatemala City:

Belizean Embassy (☎2367-3883; www.embajadadebelize.org; 5a Av 5-55, Europlaza 2, Office 1502, Zona 14; ⏰9am-noon & 2-4pm Mon-Fri)

Canadian Embassy (☎2363-4348; www.guatemala.gc.ca; 13a Calle 8-44, 8th fl, Edificio Edyma Plaza, Zona 10; ⏰8am-12:30pm & 1-4:30pm Mon-Thu, 8am-1:30pm Fri)

French Embassy (☎2421-7370; www.ambafrance-gt.org; 5a Av 8-59, Zona 14; ⏰9am-noon Mon-Fri & by appt)

German Embassy (☎2364-6700; http://guatemala.diplo.de; Av La Reforma 9-55, Edificio Reforma 10, 10th fl, Zona 10; ⏰9am-noon Mon-Fri)

Honduran Consulate (☎2332-6281; embhond@intelnet.net.gt; Av La Reforma 6-64, Zona 9; ⏰9am-1pm Mon-Fri)

Mexican Embassy (☎2420-3400; https://embamex.sre.gob.mx/guatemala; 2a Av 7-57, Zona 10; ⏰8am-12:30pm Mon-Fri)

Netherlands Consulate (☎2296-1490; guatemala@nlconsulate.com; Carretera a El Salvador Km 14.5, Santa Catarina Pinula; ⏰9am-1pm Mon-Fri)

Salvadoran Embassy (☎2245-7272; http://embajadaguatemala.rree.gob.sv; 15a Av 12-01, Zona 13; ⏰8:30am-12:30pm & 1:15-3:30pm Mon-Fri)

UK Embassy (☎2380-7300; www.gov.uk/world/guatemala; 16a Calle 0-55, 11th fl, Torre Internacional, Zona 10; ⏰7:30am-12:30pm & 1:30-4:30pm Mon-Thu, to 11:30am Fri)

US Embassy (☎2326-4000; http://guatemala.usembassy.gov; Av La Reforma 7-01, Zona 10; ⏰7am-3:30 Mon-Thu, to noon Fri)

SLEEPING PRICE RANGES

The following price ranges refer to a double room with bathroom in high (but not absolute peak) season. Unless otherwise stated, taxes of 22% are included in the price.

$ less than Q200

$$ Q200–550

$$$ more than Q550

FOOD

What you eat in Guatemala will be a mixture of Guatemalan food, which is nutritious and filling without sending your taste buds into ecstasy, and international traveler-and-tourist food, which is available wherever travelers and tourists hang out. Your most satisfying meals in both cases will probably be in smaller eateries where the boss is in the kitchen themselves.

INTERNET ACCESS

Wi-fi is becoming readily available across the country, but can only really be counted on in large and/or tourist towns. Most (but not all) hostels and hotels offer wi-fi, as do many restaurants. If you have trouble finding a signal, try a Pollo Campero fast-food restaurant – they're in pretty much every town of any size and all offer free, unsecured access.

Internet cafes typically charge between Q5 and Q10 an hour – they're less common than they used to be but most towns still have one.

LEGAL MATTERS

You may find that police officers in Guatemala are, at times, somewhat unhelpful. Generally speaking, the less you have to do with the law, the better.

Whatever you do, don't get involved in any way with illegal drugs – even if the locals seem to do so freely. As a foreigner you are at a distinct disadvantage and you may be set up by others. Drug laws in Guatemala are strict, and though enforcement may be uneven, penalties are severe. If you do get caught doing something you shouldn't, your best line of defense is to apologize, stay calm and proceed from there.

While many commentators claim that corruption is rife in Guatemala, don't take this to mean you can buy your way out of any situation. If it does seem that you can 'make everything go away' by handing over some cash, proceed cautiously and tactfully.

LGBTIQ+ TRAVELERS

Few places in Latin America are outwardly gay-friendly and Guatemala is no different. Technically, homosexuality is legal for persons over 18 years, but the reality can be another story, with harassment and violence against gays too often poisoning the plot. Don't even consider testing the tolerance for homosexual public displays of affection here.

Though Antigua and Guatemala City have palatable – if subdued – scenes, affection and action are still kept largely behind closed doors. Keep your eye out for Pride events in these cities, as well as Quetzaltenango. Mostly, though, LGBTIQ+ travelers in Guatemala will find themselves keeping it low-key and pushing the twin beds together.

The best information site, **Gay Guatemala** (www.gayguatemala.com), is in Spanish.

MONEY

Guatemala's currency, the quetzal (ket-sahl, abbreviated to Q), has been fairly stable at around Q7.5 = US$1 for years. The quetzal is divided into 100 centavos.

Banks change cash but *casas de cambio* (currency-exchange offices) are usually quicker and may offer better rates.

ATMs

You'll find ATMs *(cajeros automáticos)* for Visa/Plus System cards in all but the smallest towns, and there are MasterCard/Cirrus ATMs in many places too, so one of these cards is the best basis for your supply of cash in Guatemala. The 5B network is widespread and particularly useful, as it works with both Visa and MasterCard cards.

Be aware that card skimming is a problem in Guatemala. Avoid ATMs that are left unguarded at night (ie those in the small room out the front of the bank) and look for one that is in a secure environment (such as those inside supermarkets or shopping malls). Failing that, keep your hand covered when entering your PIN and check your balance online.

Bargaining

Haggling is pretty much a national pastime in Guatemala. Treat it as a game, and if you feel you're getting ripped off, just walk away. Don't haggle in small stores and restaurants; always haggle in markets and with taxi drivers.

Cash

Cash is king in Guatemala, although carrying too much of it makes getting robbed a bigger pain than it would otherwise be. Some towns suffer from change shortages: always try to carry a stash of small bills. Keep a small supply of low-denomination US dollars (which are accepted pretty much anywhere, at various rates of exchange) as an emergency fund.

While everybody accepts dollars, you will almost always get a better deal by paying in quetzals.

Currencies other than the US dollar are virtually useless, although a small handful of places now change cash euros.

Credit Cards

Many banks give cash advances on Visa cards, and some on MasterCard. You can pay for many purchases with these cards or with American Express (Amex) cards – particularly in higher-end hotels and restaurants. Paying with credit card can attract service charges of up to 5% – be sure to ask if there is a *recargo* (transaction fee).

Tipping

A 10% tip is expected in restaurants (often automatically added to your bill in tourist towns such as Antigua). In small *comedores* (basic, cheap eateries) tipping is optional, but follow local practice and leave some spare change.

Homestays Better to buy a gift than give cash.

Hotels Q10 per bag.

Restaurants 10% maximum (if not already included).

Taxis Not customary.

Trekking and tour guides Q50 per person per day (optional).

OPENING HOURS

Hours provided are general guidelines, but there are many variations. Restaurant times, in particular, can vary by up to two hours either way.

The *Ley Seca* (dry law) stipulates that bars and *discotecas* must close by 1am, except on nights before public holidays; it is rigidly followed in large cities and universally mocked in smaller towns.

Banks 9am–5pm Monday to Friday, 9am–1pm Saturday

Bars 11am–1am

Cafes and restaurants 7am–9pm

Government offices 8am–4pm Monday to Friday

Shops 8am–noon and 2–6pm Monday to Saturday

PHOTOGRAPHY

Photography is a sensitive subject in Guatemala. Always ask permission before taking portraits, especially of Maya women and children. Don't be surprised if your request is denied. Children often request payment (usually Q1) in return for posing.

➡ In certain places, such as the church of Santo Tomás in Chichicastenango, photography is forbidden.

➡ Maya ceremonies (should you be so lucky to witness one) are off-limits for photography unless you are given explicit permission to take pictures.

➡ If local people make any sign of being offended, put your camera away and apologize immediately, both out of decency and for your own safety.

➡ Never take photos of army installations, men with guns or other sensitive military subjects.

POST

The privatised Guatemalan postal service is currently suspended, due to a years-long contract dispute with the government. For the time being, the only option for sending or receiving mail/packages is through an international courier. FedEx, UPS and DHL all operate in Guatemala.

PUBLIC HOLIDAYS

Guatemalan public holidays include the following:

New Year's Day (Año Nuevo) January 1

Easter (Semana Santa; Holy Thursday to Easter Sunday inclusive) March/April

Labor Day (Día del Trabajo) May 1

Army Day (Día del Ejército) June 30

Assumption Day (Día de la Asunción) August 15

Independence Day (Día de la Independencia) September 15

Revolution Day (Día de la Revolución) October 20

All Saints' Day (Día de Todos los Santos) November 1

Christmas Eve afternoon (Víspera Navidad) December 24

Christmas Day (Navidad) December 25

New Year's Eve afternoon (Víspera de Año Nuevo) December 31

SAFE TRAVEL

Guatemala is a mostly safe destination but crime can happen.

➡ The most frequently reported type of nasty incident involves robbery on walking trails.

➡ The days of robbers targeting tourist buses out on the open highway seem to be thankfully in the past, although some tourists in rental cars have been targeted.

➡ The crime you're most likely to become a victim of involves pickpocketing, bag-snatching, bag-slitting and the like in crowded streets, markets, bus stations and on buses, but also in empty, dark city streets.

EATING PRICE RANGES

The following price ranges refer to a standard main course, including taxes but not including tip.

$ less than Q50

$$ Q50–150

$$$ more than Q150

➡ There are dedicated tourist police in Guatemala City and Antigua. Elsewhere, **Proatur** (☎ in English 1500; http://proatur.visitguatemala.com) offers 24-hour assistance to tourists and is a good initial point of contact if you get into difficulty.

TELEPHONE

Guatemala has no area or city codes. When calling within Guatemala, just dial the eight-digit local number. When calling from other countries, dial the international access code (00 in most countries), then the Guatemala country code (502), then the eight-digit local number. The international access code from Guatemala is 00.

Cell Phones

Roaming is expensive in Guatemala. Most travelers buy a local SIM card (if you have an unlocked phone) or a local prepaid phone on arrival. ID is required to buy both. 4G is increasingly available.

There are three cell companies in the country. **Tigo** (www.tigo.com.gt) and **Claro** (www.claro.com.gt) have the best coverage; **Movistar** (www.movistar.com.gt) tends to be cheaper but has poor coverage outside major towns.

TOILETS

➡ You cannot throw *anything* into Guatemalan toilets, including toilet paper, because of poor sewage drains. Bathrooms are equipped with some sort of receptacle (usually a small wastebasket) for soiled paper.

➡ Toilet paper is not always provided, so always carry some. If you don't have any and need some, asking a restaurant worker for *un rollo de papel* (a roll of paper), accompanied by a panicked facial expression, usually produces fast results.

➡ Public toilets are rare. Use the ones at cafes, restaurants, your hotel and archaeological sites. Buses rarely have toilets on board and if they do, don't count on them working.

TOURIST INFORMATION

Guatemala's national tourism institute, **INGUAT** (El Instituto Guatemalteco de Turismo; www.visitguatemala.com), has information offices in major tourist areas. A few towns have departmental, municipal or private-enterprise tourist information offices. Proatur, a joint private-government initiative, operates a useful 24-hour toll-free advice and assistance hotline.

VISAS

Citizens of the USA, Canada, EU countries, Norway, Switzerland, Australia, New Zealand, Israel and Japan are among those who do not need a visa for tourist visits to Guatemala. On entry into Guatemala you will normally be given a 90-day stay. (The number '90' will be written in the stamp in your passport.)

Citizens of some Eastern European countries are among those who do need visas to visit Guatemala. Inquire at a Guatemalan embassy well in advance of travel.

Guatemala is part of the Centro America 4 (CA-4) trading agreement with Nicaragua, Honduras and El Salvador. Upon entry to the CA-4 region, travelers are given a 90-day stay for the entire region. You can get this extended once, for an additional 90 days, for around Q120. Do this at the **Departamento de Extranjería** (Foreigners Office; Map p110; ☎ 2411-2411; www.migracion.gob.gt; 6a Av 3-11, Zona 4; ⏲ 8am-2:30pm Mon-Fri) in Guatemala City. Along with the fee you currently need two passport photos, photocopies of of your passport and the front andback of a valid credit card. Extensions are usually issued in 24 hours.

Travelers may find it easier to leave the CA-4 region (Belize and Mexico are the most obvious, easiest options), after which you can return to the region to start all over again. Some foreigners have been repeating this cycle for years.

Visa regulations are subject to change – it's always worth checking with a Guatemalan embassy before you go.

VOLUNTEERING

Volunteer programs abound in Guatemala, but not all are created equal. If you're interested in giving something back, remember that the best schemes should be designed with their beneficiaries in mind, not just to make their participants feel good about themselves, and volunteers shouldn't join programs to do something they're not qualified for back home.

Most volunteer posts require basic or better Spanish skills and a minimum time commitment. Depending on the organization, you may have to pay for room and board for the duration of your stay. Before making a commitment, read the fine print and ask lots of questions.

Short-term placements in orphanages have been a staple of Guatemalan volunteering for years. Unicef and other child-protection organizations have pointed out the damage that can be done to children's welfare by such programs, and no reputable scheme should allow volunteers such access to children.

Lonely Planet strongly encourages those considering volunteering to do research and make informed, responsible choices. One source of information on trusted volunteer opportunities is Quetzaltenango-based EntreMundos (p157), which works with a large variety of local NGOs that welcome skilled volunteers.

WEIGHTS & MEASURES

Guatemala uses the metric system for weights and distances; some food items such as meat, sugar and coffee sold in pounds; gasoline is sold by the *galón* (US gallon).

WOMEN TRAVELERS

Women should encounter no special problems traveling in Guatemala. The primary thing you can do to make it easy for yourself while traveling here is to dress modestly. Modesty in dress is highly regarded, and if you practice it, you will usually be treated with respect.

Shorts should really be worn only at the beach, not in town, and especially not in the highlands. Skirts should be at or below the knee. Going braless is considered provocative. Many local women swim with T-shirts over their swimsuits.

Women traveling alone can expect plenty of attention from talkative men. Often they're just curious and not out for a foreign conquest. It is, of course, up to you how to respond, but there's no need to be intimidated. Consider the situation and circumstances, and stay confident. Try to sit next to women or children on the bus. Local women rarely initiate conversations, but usually have lots of interesting things to say once the ball is rolling.

While there's no need to be paranoid, the possibility of rape and assault does exist. Use your normal traveler's caution – avoid walking alone in isolated places or through city streets late at night, and skip hitchhiking.

WORK

Some travelers find work in bars, restaurants and places to stay in Antigua, Panajachel or Quetzaltenango, but wages are usually barely above survival pay. If you're looking to crew a yacht, there's always work being offered around the Río Dulce area, sometimes for short trips; sometimes to the USA and further afield. Check noticeboards and online forums for details.

Getting There & Away

AIR

There are direct flights from the USA with most major US airlines. **AeroMexico** (www.aeromexico.com) and **Interjet** (www.interjet.com) fly direct from Mexico City. **Avianca** (www.avianca.com/gt) has flights to Guatemala City from most Central American capitals. If you are coming from elsewhere, you will almost certainly be changing planes in the USA, Mexico or elsewhere in Central America.

LAND

Where possible, cross borders as early in the day as possible. Onward transportation tends to wind down in the afternoon and border areas are not always the most salubrious places to hang around late. There is no departure tax when you leave Guatemala by land, although many border officials will ask for an illicit Q10.

Guatemala has official border crossings with all of its neighboring countries. Check visa requirements before arrival. Many nationalities do not require tourist visas and will be given a 90-day stay upon entry, though citizens of some countries do need visas.

GOVERNMENT TRAVEL ADVICE

The following government websites offer travel advisories and information on current hot spots. Bear in mind that these sites are updated occasionally and are obliged to err on the side of caution – the vast majority of travelers visit Guatemala and don't experience any of the reported problems.

Australian Department of Foreign Affairs (www.smartraveller.gov.au)

Canadian Department of Foreign Affairs (https://travel.gc.ca/travelling)

New Zealand Ministry of Foreign Affairs (www.safetravel.govt.nz)

UK Foreign Office (www.gov.uk/foreign-travel-advice)

US State Department (http://travel.state.gov)

Belize

- Melchor de Mencos (GUA) – Benque Viejo del Carmen (BZE)

El Salvador

- Ciudad Pedro de Alvarado (GUA) – La Hachadura (ES)
- Valle Nuevo (GUA) – Las Chinamas (ES)
- San Cristóbal Frontera (GUA) – San Cristóbal (ES)
- Anguiatú (GUA) – Anguiatú (ES)

Honduras

- Agua Caliente (GUA) – Agua Caliente (HND)
- El Florido (GUA) – Copán Ruinas (HND)
- Corinto (GUA) – Corinto (HND)

Mexico

The busiest and most useful border crossings:

- Ciudad Tecún Umán (GUA) – Ciudad Hidalgo (MEX)
- El Carmen (GUA) – Talismán (MEX)
- La Mesilla (GUA) – Ciudad Cuauhtémoc (MEX)

RIVER

There are two possible crossings from Mexico's Chiapas State to El Petén – the most commonly used one crosses at the Mexican town of Frontera Corozal by boat to either La Técnica or Bethel in Guatemala. Frontera Corozal has good transport connections to Palenque in Mexico

DEPARTURE TAX

Guatemala levies a departure tax of US$30 on outbound air passengers, which should be included in your fare. If it's not, it has to be paid in cash US dollars or quetzals at the airline check-in desk.

and there are regular buses from La Técnica and Bethel to Flores/Santa Elena, Guatemala.

The other theoretical river route from Mexico into Guatemala's Petén department is up the Río de la Pasión from Benemérito de las Américas, south of Frontera Corozal, to Sayaxché, but there are currently no immigration facilities or reliable passenger services along this route.

SEA

Public boats connect Punta Gorda in Belize with Lívingston and Puerto Barrios in Guatemala. The Punta Gorda services connect with bus services to/from Belize City.

There is a Q80 departure tax when leaving Guatemala by sea.

Getting Around

AIR

At the time of writing the only scheduled internal flights were between Guatemala City and Flores, a route operated daily by **Avianca** (www.avianca.com) and **TAG** (www.tag.com.gt).

BICYCLE

Guatemala's mountainous terrain and occasionally terrifying road conditions make for hard going when it comes to intercity pedaling. That said, if you have your wits about you, cycling is a great way to get around smaller towns – Antigua, Quetzaltenango and San Pedro La Laguna are among the towns where you can rent reasonable mountain bikes (you don't want skinny wheels here) by the hour, day, week or longer. There are bike shops in almost every town where you can buy a new bike starting from around Q800.

BOAT

The Caribbean town of Lívingston is only reachable by boat, across the Bahía de Amatique from Puerto Barrios or down the Río Dulce from the town of Río Dulce – both great trips. In Lago de Atitlán fast fiberglass *lanchas* (motorized boats) zip across the waters between villages – by far the best way to get around.

BUS

Buses go almost everywhere in Guatemala, and the buses will leave you with some of your most vivid memories of the country. Most of them are ancient school buses from the USA and Canada. Many travelers know these vehicles as chicken buses, after the live cargo accompanying many passengers. They are frequent, crowded and cheap. Expect to pay around Q10 to Q15 for an hour of travel.

Chicken buses will stop anywhere, for anyone. Helpers will yell '*hay lugares!*' (eye loo-*gar*-ays), which literally means 'there are places.' The space they refer to may be no more than a sliver of air between dozens of locals mashed against one another. These same helpers will also yell their bus's destination in voices of varying hilarity and cadence; just listen for the song of your town. Tall travelers will be especially challenged on these buses. To catch a chicken bus, simply stand beside the road with your arm out parallel to the ground.

Some routes, especially between big cities, are served by more comfortable buses with the luxury of one seat per person. The best buses are labeled 'Pullman,' '*especial*' or '*primera clase.*' Occasionally these may have bathrooms (but don't count on them working), TVs and even food service.

Pullman routes always originate or end in Guatemala City.

In general, more buses leave in the morning (some leave as early as 2am) than the afternoon. Bus traffic drops off precipitously after about 4pm; night buses are rare and not generally recommended.

Distances in Guatemala are not huge and, apart from the Guatemala City–Flores run, you won't often ride for more than four hours at a time. On a typical four-hour bus trip you'll cover 175km to 200km for Q60 to Q100.

For a few of the better services you can buy tickets in advance, and this is generally worth doing as it ensures that you get a place.

On some shorter routes, minibuses, usually called 'microbuses,' are replacing chicken buses. These are operated with the same cram-'em-all-in principle and can be even more uncomfortable because they have less leg room. Where neither buses nor minibuses roam, *picop* (pickup) trucks serve as de facto buses; you hail them and pay for them as if they were the genuine article.

At least a couple of times a month, a chicken bus plunges over a cliff or rounds a blind bend into a head-on collision. Newspapers are full of gory details and diagrams of the latest wreck, which doesn't foster affectionate feelings toward Guatemalan public transportation.

SHUTTLE BUS

Heavily advertised shuttle minibuses run by travel agencies provide comfortable and quick transport along all the main routes plied by tourists. They're much more expensive than buses but a lot more convenient – they usually offer a door-to-door service from your hotel, with scheduled meal and bathroom breaks. The most popular shuttle routes include Guatemala City airport–Antigua, Antigua–Panajachel, Panajachel–Chichicastenango and Lanquín–Antigua.

Note that you'll sometimes be asked to swap vehicles halfway through a journey so individual shuttles can quickly return to their city of origin. It's a way of keeping costs down, but a bit of a surprise the first time the driver leaves you at a gas station waiting for your onward connection.

CAR & MOTORCYCLE

You can drive in Guatemala with your home-country driver's license or with an International Driving Permit (IDP). Guatemalan driving etiquette will probably be very different from what you're used to back home: passing on blind curves, ceding the right of way to vehicles coming uphill on narrow passes and deafening honking for no apparent reason are just the start. Expect few road signs and no indication from other drivers of what they are about to do. Do not pay any attention to turn signals – they are rarely used and even more rarely used to indicate a turn in the direction they would seem to be. Hazard lights generally mean that the driver is about to do something foolish and/or illegal.

A vehicle coming uphill always has the right of way. *Túmulos* are speed bumps that are generously (sometimes oddly) placed throughout the country, usually on the main drag through a town. Use of seat belts is obligatory, but generally not practiced.

Navigating colonial-era street plans, which often control traffic with devilish one-way systems, can be a nightmare.

In Guatemala driving at night is a bad idea for many reasons, not the least of which are armed bandits, drunk drivers and decreased visibility.

Every driver involved in an accident that results in injury or death is taken into custody until a judge determines responsibility.

If someone's car breaks down on the highway (particularly on curvy mountain roads), they'll warn other drivers by putting shrubs or small branches on the road for a few hundred meters beforehand. Annoyingly, they rarely pick them up afterwards but if you're driving and you see these, it's best to be cautious and slow down.

HITCHHIKING

Hitchhiking in the strict sense of the word is generally not practiced in Guatemala because it is not safe. However, where the bus service is sporadic or nonexistent, pickup trucks and other vehicles may serve as public transport. If you stand beside the road with your arm out, someone will stop. You are expected to pay the driver as if you were traveling on a bus and the fare will be similar. This is a reliable system used by locals and travelers, and the only inconvenience you're likely to encounter is full-to-overflowing vehicles – get used to it.

Any other form of hitching is never entirely safe, and we don't recommend it. Travelers who hitch should understand that they are taking a small but potentially serious risk.

LOCAL TRANSPORTATION

Bus

Public transportation within towns and cities outside of Guatemala City is chiefly provided by newish, crowded minibuses. They're useful to travelers mainly in the more spread-out cities such as Quetzaltenango and Huehuetenango. Guatemala City has its own forms of bus services – the old red buses (not recommended for safety reasons) and the newer fleets of TransMetro and TransUrbano buses.

Taxi

Taxis are fairly plentiful in most significant towns. A 10-minute ride can cost about Q60, which is relatively expensive – expect to hear plenty of woeful tales from taxi drivers about the price of gasoline. Except for some taxis in Guatemala City, they don't use meters: you must agree upon the fare before you set off – best before you get in, in fact. Uber is available in Guatemala City and Antigua.

If you feel reluctant to take on the Guatemalan roads, an interesting alternative to car hire can be to hire a taxi driver for an extended time. This often works out only slightly more expensive than renting and gives you all the freedom and comfort without the stress of having to drive.

Tuk-Tuk

If you've spent any time in Asia, you'll be very familiar with the *tuk-tuk,* a three-wheeled minitaxi nominally seating three passengers and a driver, but obviously capable of carrying twice that amount.

Named for the noise their little lawnmower engines make, *tuk-tuks* are best for short hops around town – expect to pay somewhere around Q5 to Q10 per person. Hail them the way you would a normal taxi.

Belize

POP 388,000

Includes ➡

Best Places to Eat

- ➡ Hidden Treasure (p250)
- ➡ Guava Limb Cafe (p267)
- ➡ Hibisca by Habaneros (p245)

Best Places to Stay

- ➡ Black Rock Lodge (p271)
- ➡ Belize Boutique Resort & Spa (p254)
- ➡ Matachica Beach Resort (p249)
- ➡ Turtle Inn (p278)

Why Go?

With one foot in the Central American jungles and the other in the Caribbean Sea, pint-sized Belize is packed with islands, adventure and culture. The Belize Barrier Reef is the second largest in the world, after Australia's, and with more than 100 types of coral and some 500 species of tropical fish, it's pure paradise for scuba divers and snorkelers. Inland, a vast (by Belizean standards) network of national parks, wildlife sanctuaries and protected areas offers a safe haven for wildlife, which ranges from the industrious parades of cutter ants to tapirs, noisy howler monkeys and the shy jaguar. The country is also home to one of the world's most mysterious civilizations – the ancient Maya – and brims with archaeological sites that date from the Maya heyday (AD 250–1000), where enormous steps lead to the tops of tall stone temples and yield 360-degree jungle views.

When to Go

Belize City

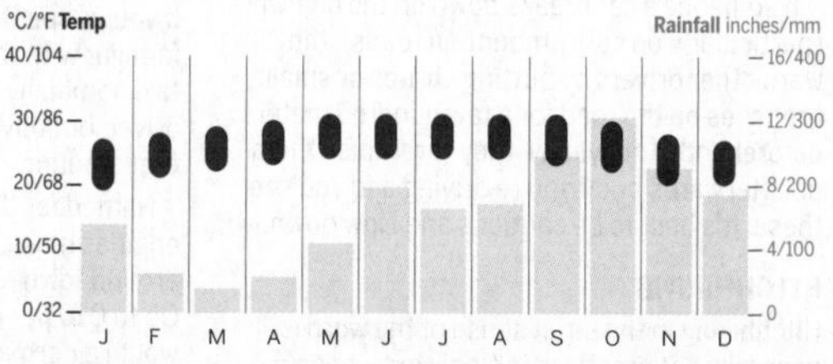

Dec–Apr Sunny skies, prices rise, reservations key during peak season.

Nov & May Fewer tourists, lower prices, attractions open across the region.

Jun–Oct Heavy rain, hurricanes possible, few tourists, prices drop, some businesses close.

Entering the Country

There are well-traveled land border crossings between Belize and Mexico to the north and Guatemala to the west. Border formalities are straightforward between both countries.

ONE-WEEK ITINERARY

Start in **Belize City** but head straight to the water taxi terminal and book a ticket to laid-back **Caye Caulker** or more upbeat **San Pedro** on Ambergris Caye. Either place makes a good base for exploring the reef.

After two or three days on the cays, return to Belize City and catch the bus straight to **San Ignacio**. This relaxed traveler town in Cayo District is the base for visiting Actun Tunichil Muknal cave, Caracol, Xunantunich, Barton Creek Cave and more. If you only have time for one, we recommended **Actun Tunichil Muknal cave**. Track back down the Hummingbird Hwy to **Hopkins** for some beach time and Garifuna drumming. Finish with a visit the chocolate factory at **Maya Center** and make the excellent detour into the 'jaguar reserve' of **Cockscomb Basin Wildlife Sanctuary**.

Essential Food & Drink

Cowfoot soup Glutinous soup flavored with an actual cow's heel.

Gibnut Small native rodent sometimes eaten barbecued.

Horchata A milky-white, thick juice made from rice.

Habanero sauce Try Marie Sharp's 'Not for Wimps'!

Chirmole Known as 'black dinner,' this Maya chicken stew has a dark chili sauce.

Top Tips

➡ Book island accommodations in advance, especially in high season. Many lodges offer free boat transfers for guests.

➡ Build some flexibility into your itinerary; you might find remote attractions such as caves closed if it's too wet, or accommodations on your island of choice booked out.

➡ Avoid driving at night. Highways are unlit, speed bumps unmarked and you risk hitting a local wandering on the road.

➡ Bring US dollars in currency along with your credit/debit cards. Some banks won't touch euros or other foreign currencies.

FAST FACTS

Currency Belize Dollar (BZ$)

Visas For most nationalities, visas are issued upon entry for up to 30 days.

Money ATMs are widely available.

Capital Belmopan

Emergency ☎911

Languages English, Kriol, Garifuna, Spanish

Exchange Rates

Australia	A$1	BZ$1.43
Canada	C$1	BZ$1.52
Euro zone	€1	BZ$2.29
Guatemala	Q1	BZ$0.26
Japan	¥100	BZ$1.82
Mexico	M$1	BZ$0.11
New Zealand	NZ$1	BZ$1.38
UK	UK£1	BZ$2.67
USA	US$1	BZ$2.02

Daily Costs

➡ Double room in a budget hotel: BZ$50–120; in a midrange hotel BZ$120–350

➡ Street-food stalls or self-catering: BZ$3–10; dinner and drinks at local restaurants: BZ$15–35

Resources

Lonely Planet (www.lonelyplanet.com/belize)

Belizean Journeys (www.belizeanjourneys.com)

Belize Tourism Board (www.travelbelize.org)

Belize Highlights

❶ **Caye Caulker** (p241) Availing yourself of the amazing array of aquatic activities – from kitesurfing and paddleboarding to snorkeling and diving.

❷ **Actun Tunichil Muknal** (p271) Doing some serious spelunking in Belize's most dramatic cave.

❸ **San Pedro** (p247) Enjoying a sunset cocktail on the deck of a sailboat cruising offshore.

❹ **Lighthouse Reef** (p252) Descending into the darkness of the Blue Hole Natural Monument.

❺ **Caracol** (p269) Exploring these remote and ancient Maya ruins.

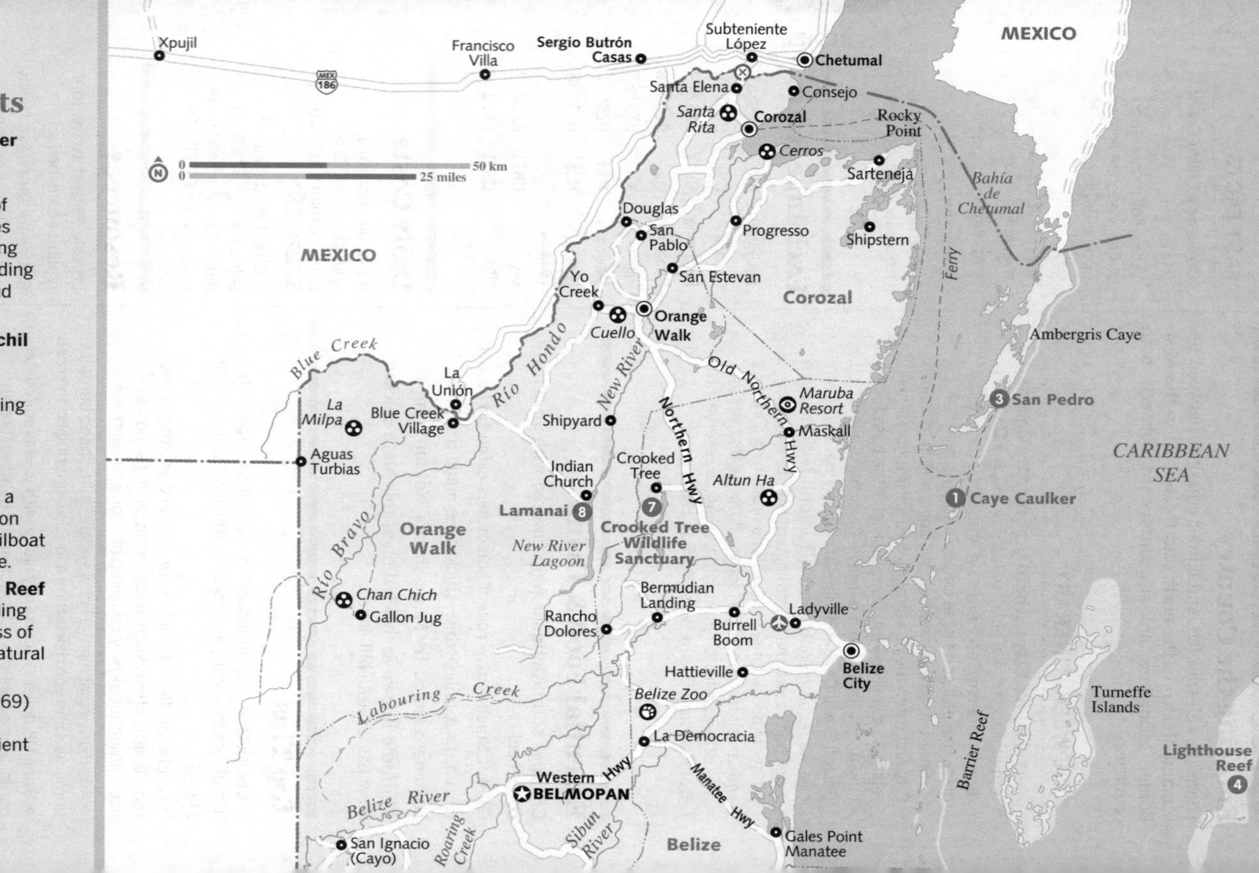

6 Placencia (p277) Eating, drinking, slacking and snorkeling at the mainland 'cay you can drive to.'

7 Crooked Tree Wildlife Sanctuary (p256) Cruising the lagoon and marveling at the birdlife.

8 Lamanai (p254) Taking the boat trip down the New River to this jungle-covered Maya site.

9 Hopkins (p275) Enjoying Garifuna drumming and Creole cooking in this laid-back beach village.

10 Deep South (p283) Discovering Maya villages, chocolate factories and archaeological sites.

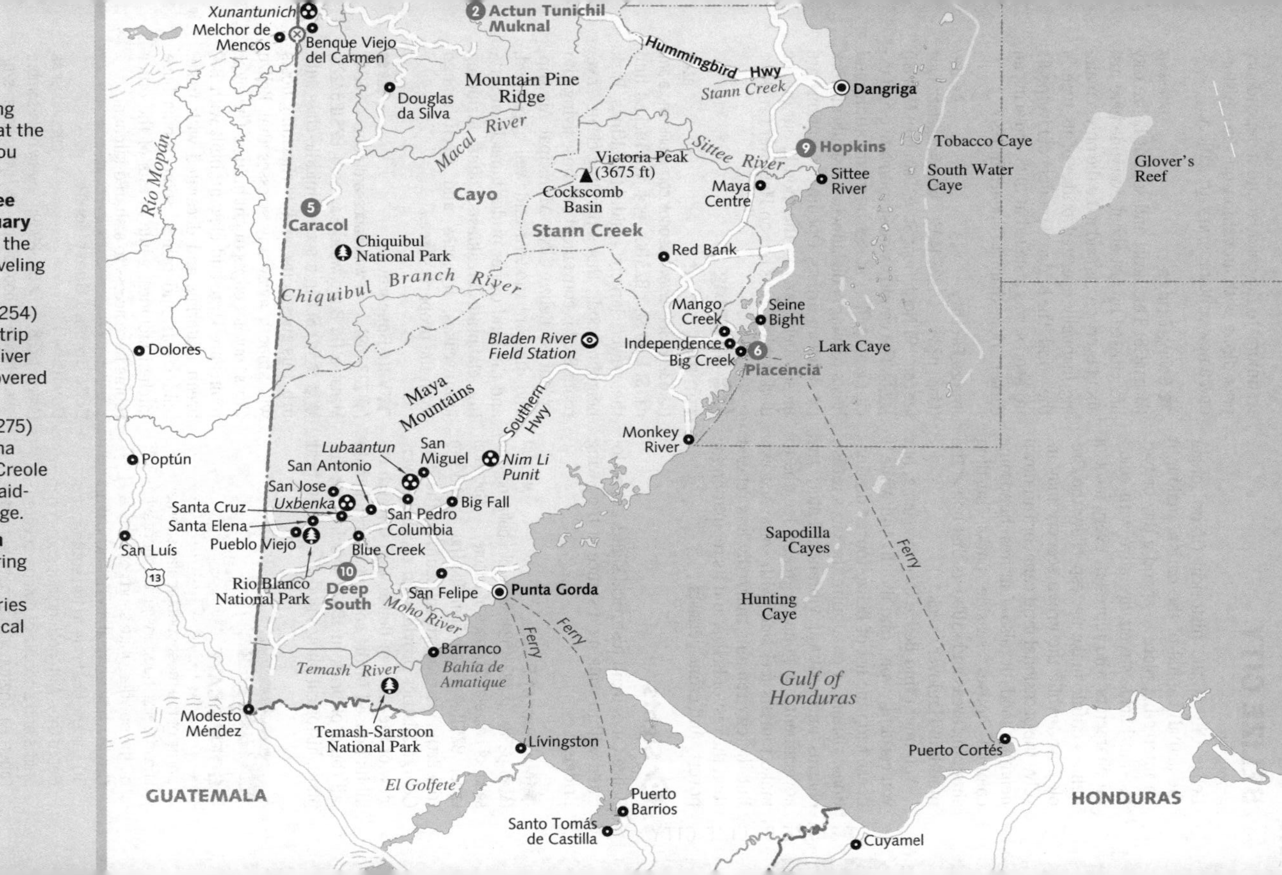

BELIZE CITY

POP 61,760

Belize City is the historical (if no longer the actual) capital of the nation, making it an interesting place to spend a day or two. Its ramshackle streets are alive with colorful characters who represent every facet of Belize's ethnic make up, especially the Creoles. And while the urban scenery may involve the occasional fetid canal or run-down neighborhood, it also features handsome colonial houses, seaside parks, bustling shopping areas and sailboats that bob at the mouth of Haulover Creek.

You might find Belize City menacing, but you certainly won't find it dull. And while it doesn't top the list of Belize tourist destinations, visitors often admire the city's raffish charms and cultural vibrancy. Lately the government has gone to greater lengths to make tourists feel safe, with some success. But the city remains markedly less relaxed than the rest of Belize, and its reputation for poverty and crime persists.

Sights

Belize City's main historical sights are all located within walking distance of the Swing Bridge.

★Museum of Belize MUSEUM

(Map p238; ☎223-4524; www.nichbelize.org/museum-of-belize-and-houses-of-culture; Gabourel Lane; BZ$10; ⏲9am-5pm Tue-Thu, to 4:30pm Fri & Sat) This modern museum in the Fort George District provides an excellent overview of the story of Belize, told through exhibits housed in the country's former main jail (built of brick in 1857). Fascinating displays, historical photos and documents bear testimony to the colonial and independence eras, along with an exhibit on slave history and a new contemporary art gallery.

DON'T MISS

GOFF'S CAYE

Some of the most spectacular snorkeling in Belize happens just a short swim off the powder-white sands of **Goff's Caye**, a tiny, uninhabited island just a 30-minute boat ride to the southeast of Belize City. With nothing but some coco palms and a couple of palapa-covered (open-air shelter with a thatched roof) picnic tables, the idyllic island sits right beside the Belize Barrier Reef and a healthy community of resident corals, lobsters, stingrays, colorful fish and more.

★Swing Bridge LANDMARK

(Map p238) This heart and soul of Belize City life, crossed by just about everyone here just about every day, is said to be the only remaining manually operated bridge of its type in the world. The bridge, a product of Liverpool's ironworks, was installed in 1923, replacing an earlier bridge that had opened in 1897.

Image Factory GALLERY

(Map p238; ☎223-1493; www.imagefactorybelize.com; 91 North Front St; ⏲9am-5pm Mon-Fri) FREE The country's most innovative and exciting art gallery stages new exhibitions and hosts regular book launches, usually of work by Belizean artists. Opening receptions are mostly held early in the month, out on the deck, which looks out on Haulover Creek.

Sleeping

TBG B&B B&B $

(☎632-2838; www.facebook.com/guillermo.alamina; St Luke St; r BZ$110; P❄🛜) Tucked into the newer, largely residential Kings Park neighborhood, this sparkling-clean, five-room B&B is convenient for those flying into or out of Belize City's Municipal Airstrip. The digs are modern and well appointed, and the kind owner prides himself on serving elaborate breakfasts, often including johnnycakes, fry-jacks and fresh mango from the property's tree.

★Villa Boscardi B&B $$

(☎223-1691; www.villaboscardi.com; 6043 Manatee Dr, Buttonwood Bay; s/d BZ$185/225; ❄@🛜≋) Set in a secure middle-class suburb, this guesthouse and its charming hosts will smooth away any stresses that Belize City's rougher edges might induce. The eight rooms are large and elegant, built with Belizean materials and decorated with fresh, bold colors and prints. Some rooms have kitchen facilities, while guests of the other rooms have access to a shared kitchen.

Bella Sombra Guest House Downtown GUESTHOUSE $$

(Map p238; ☎631-8989; www.bella-sombra-guest-house-bz.book.direct; 36 Hydes Lane; s/d/tr BZ$100/140/180; P❄🛜) A fantastic midrange guesthouse bang in the middle of downtown with large, spotless modern rooms boasting good mattresses and all the mod-cons, including huge flatscreen TVs.

Most rooms have a kitchenette with a sink, microwave and fridge, while some have large writing desks. The rooftop terrace is a great place to drink a beer and watch the sunset. Advance reservations essential.

The friendly owners also run Bella Sombra King's Park, a more homey option targeted at long-term guests and located near the Municipal Airstrip.

D'Nest Inn B&B **$$**
(☎223-5416; www.dnestinn.com; 475 Cedar St; s/d/tr incl breakfast from BZ$144/179/214; ❄📶) Your hosts Gaby and Oty have evidently put a lot of care into this retreat on the northern edge of town. The individually decorated rooms have four-poster beds, handmade quilts and plenty of Victorian-era antiques. Even more enticing, a lush garden beckons with blooming orchids and allamandas, singing birds and quiet corners.

Belize River Lodge LODGE **$$$**
(☎225-2002, USA 888-275-4843; www.belizeriverlodge.com; 2-/7-night fishing all-inclusive package (double occupancy) BZ$4121/10,631; ❄📶) Belize's oldest fishing lodge remains one of its best. Set in lush, tropical grounds close to the airport, this gleaming mahogany gem is a comfortable and convenient riverside base for anglers. An included airport pick-up involves a short boat ride, and trips to the nearby river mouth, Caribbean sea and some idyllic flats and mangrove-lined lagoons are equally speedy.

Radisson Fort George Hotel HOTEL **$$$**
(Map p238; ☎223-3333; www.radisson.com; 2 Marine Pde Blvd; r BZ$545-621; P❄@📶≋) Available at the city's top hotel are 102 conservatively decorated rooms with all the comforts. While offering international-class service, the Radisson avoids the cultural detachment that often comes with such packages, with local woods, furnishings and decorations conferring genuine Belizean character.

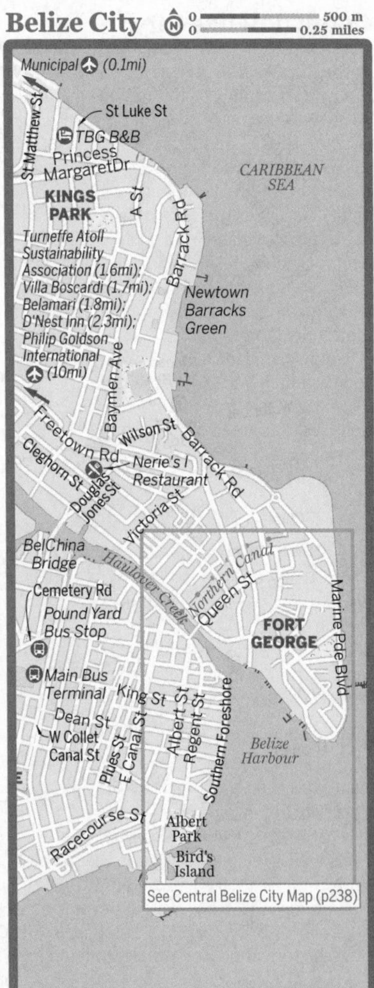

Eating

★**Nerie's II Restaurant** BELIZEAN **$**
(Map p238; ☎223-4028; cnr Queen & Daly Sts; mains BZ$10-18; ⏰8am-10pm Mon-Sat, to 3pm Sun) Nerie's offers most accompaniments imaginable to rice and beans, including curried lamb, stewed cow foot, lobster and deer. Begin with a choice of soups, including chicken, *escabeche* (with chicken, lime and onions), *chirmole* (with chicken and a chili-chocolate sauce) or cow foot, and finish with cassava pudding. Nerie's has another outlet – **Nerie's I Restaurant** (☎224-5199; 12 Douglas Jones St; mains BZ$10-18; ⏰7:30am-4:30pm Mon-Sat) – on the north side.

Dario's Meat Pies BELIZEAN **$**
(Map p238; ☎203-5197, 605-0587; 33 Hydes Lane; meat pies BZ$1.25; ⏰5am-3pm Mon-Sat) Ask any local who makes the best meat pies and they'll tell you without hesitation: Dario's. Get in the line (which will probably wrap around the block) and choose from beef or chicken. They're shipped all over the country, but it's best to buy them oven fresh at the source.

Central Belize City

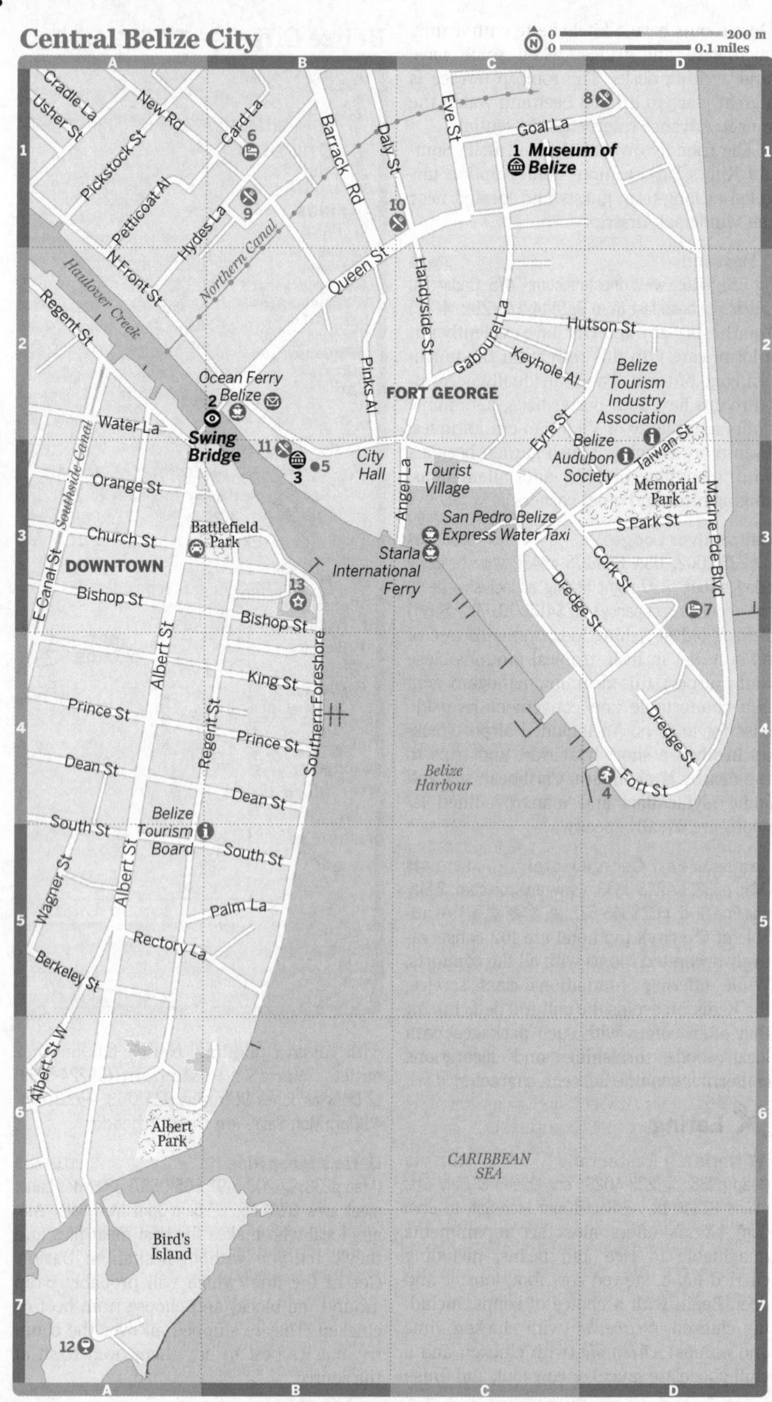

Central Belize City

★**Belamari** INTERNATIONAL **$$**
(☎615-2075; 63 Seashore Dr; pasta BZ$21-34, mains BZ$26-65; ⊙noon-10pm Tue-Thu, to 11pm Fri & Sat, to 10pm Sun) This open-air, seaside restaurant in Buttonwood Bay is a chic new spot for cocktails, and all the better if you make a meal of it. The menu spans several continents, with everything from Brazilian shrimp stew to mushroom chicken marsala to pork schnitzel. And though the kitchen's a bit poky, the breezy dining area and ocean views are lovely.

★**Spoonaz Photo Cafe** CAFE **$$**
(Map p238; ☎223-1043; www.facebook.com/spoonazorlater; 89 North Front St; johnnycakes BZ$2.25, mains BZ$10-25; ⊙7am-6pm Mon-Thu, to 7pm Fri & Sat, to 2:30pm Sun; bar until 10pm) An oasis in downtown Belize City, this cosmopolitan cafe serves quality coffee as well as paninis and sandwiches. There is a smart air-conditioned lounge area inside, but you really want to be under the green cloth umbrellas out the back watching the sailboats bobbing on Haulover Creek and working your way through the cocktail list.

Om Shanti Cafe VEGAN **$$**
(Map p238; ☎227-2247; www.omshantibelize.com/cafe-and-gift-shop; 10 Fort St; mains BZ$10-20; ⊙8:30am-6:30pm Mon-Sat; 📶) 🌿 This fantastic new vegan cafe in Fort George is just the thing after a challenging Ashtanga class in the attached **yoga studio** (Map p238; ☎610-0882; per class BZ$25, packages available; ⊙see website for class schedule), or a massage at the wellness center, all set in a gorgeously restored waterfront abode. Menu selections include papaya *ceviche*, vegan nachos and vegan cashew cheese, and the soups, juices and desserts are also phenomenal.

Celebrity Restaurant INTERNATIONAL **$$**
(Map p238; ☎223-7272; www.celebritybelize.com; cnr Marine Parade Blvd & Goal Lane; mains BZ$16-40; ⊙11am-11pm) We love Celebrity because it is a semi-swanky place that is not inside a hotel. The place has an extensive menu that includes American favorites, such as steaks and sandwiches, Mexican fare like fajitas and quesadillas, plenty of pasta dishes and a few Mediterranean surprises such as hummus, kofta and kebabs.

Drinking & Entertainment

★**Bird's Isle Restaurant** BAR
(Map p238; ☎207-6500; Bird's Island; ⊙10:30am-2:30pm Mon-Fri, 5:30pm-9pm Wed, to midnight Thu, to 10pm Fri, 10:30am-10pm Sat) Bird's Isle may be the best that Belize City has to offer. An island oasis at the southern tip of town, it manages to defy the urban grit that lies just a few blocks away. Locals and tourists alike flock to the *palapa* to partake of sea breezes, fresh-squeezed juice and cold beers.

Bliss Centre for the Performing Arts PERFORMING ARTS
(Map p238; ☎227-2110; www.nichbelize.org; Southern Foreshore) Operated by the Institute for Creative Arts, the revamped Bliss Centre has a fine 600-seat theater that stages a variety of events throughout the year. Look for concerts of traditional Belizean music and shows celebrating Belize and its culture. Annual events include the **Belize Film Festival** and the **Children's Art Festival** in May.

Information

DANGERS & ANNOYANCES

You'll likely spend most of your time in the commercial and Fort George districts, both of which are safe during daylight. However, note the following:

- Be wary of overly friendly strangers.
- Don't flash signs of wealth.
- Don't leave valuables in the hotel.

- Don't use illicit drugs.
- Avoid deserted streets.
- The Southside district (south of Haulover Creek and west of Southside Canal) sees frequent, gang-related violent crime, but non-intergang crime (petty and violent) is also an issue.
- Stay on main roads or take taxis when going to or from bus terminals and stops.
- After dark, always take taxis and don't go anywhere alone.

INTERNET ACCESS

S&L Travel (Map p238; ☎227-7593, 227-5145; www.sltravelbelize.com; 91 North Front St) Air-con internet near the water-taxi docks.

MEDICAL SERVICES

Belize City has the best medical facilities in the country.

Belize Medical Associates (☎223-0302; www.belizemedical.com; 5791 St Thomas St; ⏲emergency services 24hr) is one of several good private facilities.

Karl Heusner Memorial Hospital (☎223-1671, 223-1548; www.khmh.bz; Princess Margaret Dr; ⏲emergency services 24hr) is the city's largest public hospital.

MONEY

All banks exchange US or Canadian dollars, British pounds and, usually, euros. Most ATMs are open 24 hours, though it's highly recommended that you visit them during daylight hours.

Belize Bank (60 Market Sq; ⏲8am-3pm Mon-Thu, to 4:30pm Fri) The ATM is on the north side of the building. There is another **Belize Bank ATM** (North Front St) that is convenient for water taxis.

Scotia Bank (cnr Albert & Bishop Sts; ⏲8am-3pm Mon-Thu, to 4:30pm Fri)

POST

Main Post Office (Map p238; ☎227-2201; North Front St; ⏲8am-4pm Mon-Thu, to 3:30pm Fri)

TELEPHONE

Digi (☎223-1800; www.livedigi.com; Regent St; ⏲8am-5pm Mon-Fri) Pick up SIM cards for mobile devices at this downtown shop.

TOURIST INFORMATION

Belize Tourism Board (BTB; Map p238; ☎227-2420; www.travelbelize.org; 64 Regent St; ⏲8am-5pm Mon-Thu, to 4pm Fri) Pick up maps, magazines and all sorts of information relating to travel around Belize. This is also where you will find the cruise-ship schedule, which is published in a handy booklet.

Belize Tourism Industry Association (BTIA; Map p238; ☎227-1144; www.btia.org; 10 Taiwan St; ⏲8am-noon & 1-5pm Mon-Thu, to 4pm Fri) The BTIA is an independent association of tourism businesses, actively defending 'sustainable ecocultural tourism.' The office provides leaflets about the country's regions, copies of its *Destination Belize* annual magazine (free), and information on its members, which include many of Belize's best hotels, restaurants and other tourism businesses. The website has lots of information.

Turneffe Atoll Sustainability Association (☎670-8272; www.turneffeatollsustainabilityassociation.org; 1216 Blue Marlin Av, downstairs from OAS; ⏲8am-5pm Mon-Thu, to 4pm Fri) Manages the Turneffe Atoll Marine Reserve.

ℹ Getting There & Away

AIR

Belize City has two airports: **Philip Goldson International Airport** (BZE; Belize City; ☎225-2045; www.pgiabelize.com), which is 11 miles northwest of the city center off the Philip Goldson Hwy; and the Municipal Airstrip (TZA), around 2 miles north of the city center. All international flights use the international airport. Domestic flights on both local carriers are divided between the two airports, but those using the Municipal Airstrip are cheaper (often significantly). The following domestic airlines fly from Belize City:

Maya Island Air (☎223-1403, 223-1140; www.mayaislandair.com; Belize City Municipal Airport) Operates flights to Dangriga, Placencia, Punta Gorda, San Pedro (Ambergris Caye) and Orange Walk. From the international airport, the airline also serves Corozal, Mexico.

Tropic Air (☎224-5671; www.tropicair.com; Belize City Municipal Airport) Flights to Dangriga, Placencia, Punta Gorda, San Ignacio, Belmopan and San Pedro. From the international airport, the airline also serves Flores, Guatemala; Roatán, Honduras; and Cancún, Mexico.

BOAT

There are two water-taxi companies on North Front St offering similar services to Caye Caulker and San Pedro. On Fridays there's also a ferry to Dangriga that continues on to Honduras.

San Pedro Belize Express Water Taxi (Map p238; ☎223-2225; www.belizewatertaxi.com; Brown Sugar Mall, Front St) Professionally run water-taxi service with nine departures a day (approximately every hour from 8am to 5pm) to Caye Caulker (one way/return BZ$36/56, 45 minutes) and San Pedro (one way/return BZ$56/76, 1½ hours). Also operates one daily boat to and from Caye Caulker to Chetumal, Mexico (via San Pedro).

Ocean Ferry Belize (Map p238; ☎223-0033; www.oceanferrybelize.com; North Front St)

Runs boat services to Caye Caulker (one way/return BZ$19/30, 45 minutes) and San Pedro (one way return BZ$29/50, 1½ hours) out of the old Caye Caulker Water Taxi terminal. Leaves Belize City for both destinations at 8am, 10:30am, 1:30pm, 3pm and 5:30pm.

Starla International Ferry (Map p238; ☎628-0976; Brown Sugar Mall, Front St) Leaves from the San Pedro Belize Express terminal at 9am on Fridays, stopping in Dangriga (BZ$160) before continuing on to Puerto Cortés, Honduras (an additional BZ$110). The whole trip takes 5½ hours. On Monday the boat makes a return trip, arriving in Belize City at 4:30pm.

BUS

Belize City's **main bus terminal** (West Collet Canal St) is the old Novelo's terminal next to the canal, which now sports a faded Rastafarian red, gold and green paint job. Most buses leave from here, although local buses within Belize District to destinations such as Ladyville and Burrell Boom leave from around the corner at the **Pound Yard bus stop** (Cemetery Rd).

Getting Around

Philip Goldson International Airport The taxi fare to/from the international airport is BZ$50 for one to two passengers and BZ$60 for three and BZ$70 for four passengers. Alternatively walk the 1.6 miles from the airport to the Philip Goldson Hwy, where fairly frequent buses pass heading to Belize City. There is no public transport to/from the Municipal Airstrip.

Municipal Airstrip Taxis cost around BZ$10 to the center of town. There is no public transport to/from the international airport.

Main Bus Terminal Taxis line up outside the bus terminal. They supposedly work on a turn basis but there always seems to be plenty of debate among drivers.

TAXI

Taxis (Map p238) cost around BZ$10 for rides within the city, give or take; if it's a long trip from one side of town to the other, expect to be charged a bit more. Confirm the price in advance with your driver. Most restaurants and hotels will call a taxi for you.

NORTHERN CAYS

Daydream a little. Conjure up your ultimate tropical island fantasy. With more than 100 enticing isles and two amazing atolls, the chances are that one of Belize's northern cays can match this dream and make it a reality.

If you imagined stringing up a hammock on a deserted beach, there is an outer atoll with your name on it. Pining to be pampered? You can choose from an ever-growing glut of ritzy resorts on Ambergris Caye. San Pedro is prime for dancing the night away to a reggae beat, while Caye Caulker moves at a slower pace.

But the islands are only the beginning: only a few miles offshore, the Belize Barrier Reef flourishes for 190 awe-inspiring miles, offering unparalleled opportunities to explore canyons and coral, to come mask to snout with nurse sharks and stingrays, and to swim with schools of fish painted every color of the palette.

Caye Caulker

POP 2000

'No Shirt, No Shoes…No Problem.' You'll see this sign everywhere in Belize, but no place is it more apt than Caye Caulker. On this tiny island, where cars, too, are blissfully absent, dogs nap in the middle of the dirt road and suntanned cyclists pedal around them. The only traffic sign on the island instructs golf carts and bicycles to 'go slow,' and that directive is taken seriously.

In place of hassles, Caulker offers balmy breezes, fresh seafood, azure waters and a fantastic barrier reef at its doorstep. The easygoing attitude is due in part to the strong Creole presence on the island, which pulses to a classic reggae beat and is home to a small community of Rastafarians. This has long been a budget traveler's mecca, but in recent years tourists of all ages and incomes have begun to appreciate the island's unique atmosphere.

Activities & Tours

★RandOM Yoga YOGA

(Map p242; ☎637-4109; www.randomyoga.com; Pasero St; ⏰9am) A couple of floors above the **Namaste Cafe** (Map p242; salads & sandwiches BZ$12; ⏰7:30am-4:30pm Mon-Sat; 📶) , this excellent, long-standing yoga studio offers daily, 9am classes and occasional sunset classes on an open-air platform with a distant ocean view. The donation-based and consistently high-caliber classes are run by long-time island expat and top-notch owner/instructor Jessie Wigh. She and her husband also offer weeklong retreats.

★Contour WATER SPORTS

(Map p242; ☎615-8757; www.contourbelize.com; Front St; rentals per hour/half-day/full day BZ$25/60/80; ⏰8am-6pm) This well-run

Caye Caulker

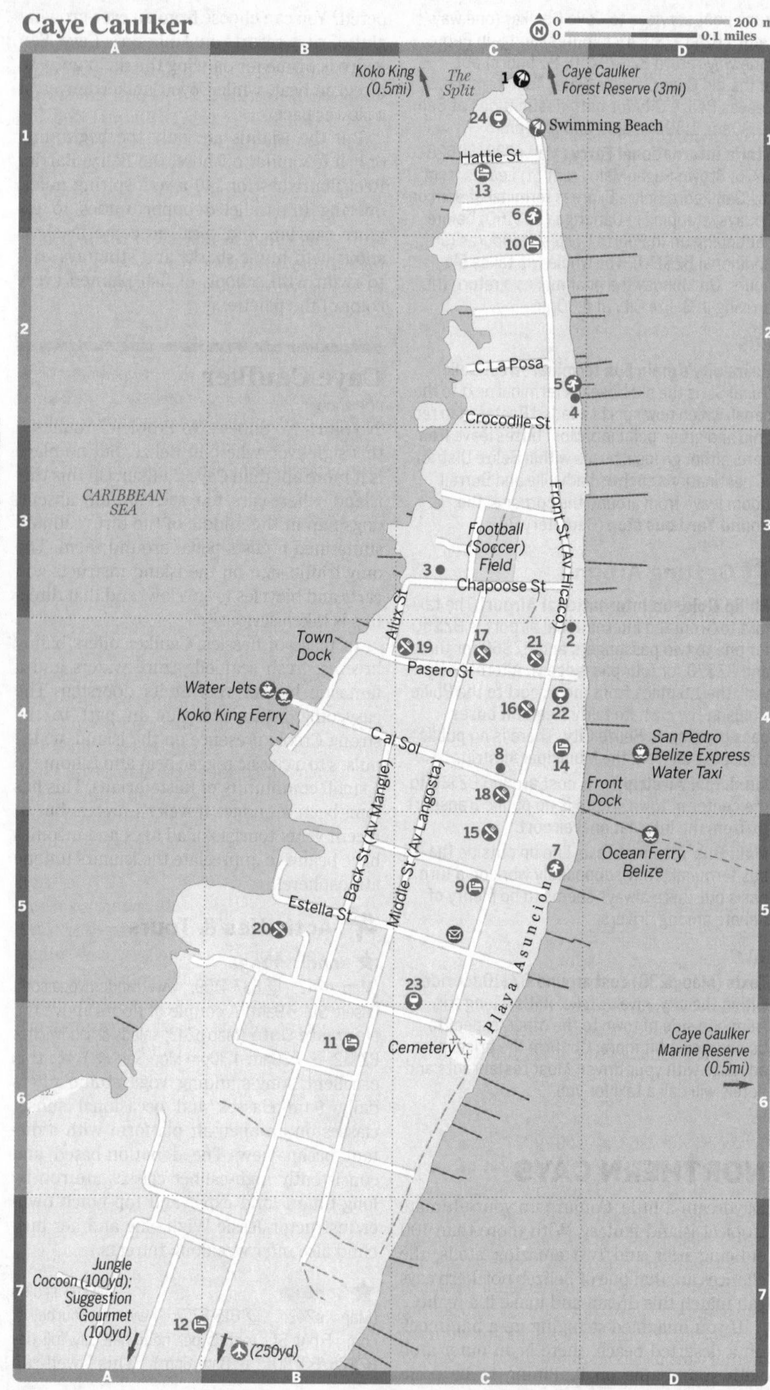

Koko King (0.5mi)
The Split
Caye Caulker Forest Reserve (3mi)
Swimming Beach
Hattie St
C La Posa
Crocodile St
CARIBBEAN SEA
Football (Soccer) Field
Chapoose St
Front St (Av Hicaco)
Alux St
Town Dock
Pasero St
Water Jets
Koko King Ferry
C al Sol
San Pedro Belize Express Water Taxi
Front Dock
Back St (Av Mangle)
Middle St (Av Langosta)
Ocean Ferry Belize
Estella St
Playa Asuncion
Caye Caulker Marine Reserve (0.5mi)
Cemetery
Jungle Cocoon (100yd); Suggestion Gourmet (100yd)
(250yd)
200 m
0.1 miles

Caye Caulker

shop brings something different to the world of Caulker aquatic recreation: taking visitors through mangroves or on sunset tours on paddleboards. It also rents out its quality equipment.

★ Anda De Wata Tours ADVENTURE

(Map p242; ☎226-0640, 607-9394; www.snorkeladw.com; Front St) Does floating on an inner tube pulled behind a slow-moving boat sound like a dream come true? Anda De Wata's 90-minute sunset boat-and-float tour (BZ$70; all-you-can drink, rum punch included) may be your own personal paradise. The company also offers great snorkeling tours around local reefs, including complimentary professional photos, and flyovers to check out the Blue Hole.

Richard's Adventures & Estuary Tours WILDLIFE

(Map p242; ☎602-0024; Playa Asuncion; snorkeling & croc tour per person BZ$70) Local guide and conservationist Richard Castillo not only excels at spotting marine life around the reefs, but he is also the only guide who can bring guests to the new crocodile reserve within **Caye Caulker Forest Reserve**. He is part of the team that installed the 1-mile boardwalk through the mangrove swamp, and is a virtual encyclopedia on the habitat.

Belize Diving Services DIVING

(Map p242; ☎226-0143; www.belizedivingservices.com; Chapoose St; ⊙8am-6pm) Professional and highly recommended dive shop that runs PADI-certification courses and offers immersions around the local reefs, as well as offshore dives at Turneffe North and the Blue Hole. It also offers advanced technical dive training and organizes trips to local cave systems.

Stressless Eco Friendly Tours SNORKELING, FISHING

(Map p242; ☎624-6064; www.stresslessecofriendlytours.com; Calle al Sol) This professional operation stands out in the crowded snorkeling market for its great customer service, focus on sustainability and passionate guides. It offers a condensed version of the classic Hol Chan/Shark Ray Alley trip, along with charter excursions and trips to Goff's Caye. Some snorkeling trips conclude with sunset *ceviche,* rum punch and a beach bonfire.

Caveman Tours SNORKELING

(Map p242; ☎226-0367; www.cavemansnorkelingtours.com; Front St; half-/full-day trips BZ$70/130; ⊙8:30am-6:30pm) Captain Caveman's guides offer extremely popular snorkeling trips throughout local waters, as well as manatee-watching expeditions and occasional private trips to Goff's Caye and Swallow Caye. The Captain is serious, safety conscious and very attentive to customer needs. His office is inside the handicraft market.

Kitexplorer KITESURFING

(Map p242; ☎652-7308; www.kitexplorer.com; Front St; equipment rental per hour/half-day/full day BZ$120/200/300; ⊙8am-6pm) Offers a two-hour introductory course (BZ$360) or a six-hour basic course (BZ$980), as well as equipment rental. Also offers windsurfing classes and has stand-up paddleboards. Located at the northern end of the island near the Split.

Sleeping

Yuma's House Belize HOSTEL $
(Map p242; ☎206-0019; www.yumashousebelize.com; Front St; dm/s/d BZ$38/75/90; 📶) This fun and freshly painted hostel is just a few steps from the water-taxi dock, giving it a prime location in the center of town and at the water's edge. It takes full advantage of the choice positioning with a dock for guests and a breezy, palm-shaded garden complete with hammocks and picnic tables from which to admire the view.

Maxhapan Cabanas CABIN $
(Map p242; ☎226-0118, 610-4993; maxhapan04@hotmail.com; 55 Pueblo Nuevo; s/d/tr BZ$100/110/120; ❄📶) In an unexpected location south of town, Maxhapan has three sweet, yellow *cabañas* clustered around a sandy yard complete with an elevated *palapa* with hammocks and a bring-your-own bar, where guests can gather. Natural light floods the spotless, modern cabins, which are equipped with fridges, air-con and TV. Your host, Louise, guarantees your comfort and happiness.

★**Jungle Cocoon** BUNGALOW $$
(☎630-8396; Av Mulche; r BZ$218; 📶) Jungle-shrouded and dripping with character, this octagonal bungalow has to be Caye Caulker's most romantic stay. The bedroom is spacious, with lovely hardwood flooring and tasteful art, but the bathroom is the real treat, offering a sitting area complete with a drum set, and lots of natural touches, including a live tree surrounded by conch shells.

Large windows on each of the bungalow's eight sides highlight the lush tropical landscaping, and the adjacent private garden is an ideal spot to take morning coffee and baked goods from **Suggestion Gourmet** (mains BZ$20; ⊙7:30am-5pm & 6-8:30pm), the property's fabulous restaurant.

★**Oasi** GUESTHOUSE $$
(Map p242; ☎623-9401; www.oasi-holidaysbelize.com; Back St; apt BZ$190-210; ❄📶🏊) 🍃 Set around blooming tropical gardens featuring an inviting pool, this excellent guesthouse has just four elegant apartments with lovely wide verandas (hung with hammocks, of course). Woven tapestries and warm hues enrich the interiors, which are equipped with full kitchens, sofas and quality bathrooms. There's also a small bar and Italian restaurant, **Il Baretto** (Map p242; Av Mangle; ⊙7:30pm Sat), that hosts lively concerts and events.

Amanda's Place GUESTHOUSE $$
(Casita Cariñosa; Map p242; ☎226-0547; www.cayecaulkercasita.com; Front St; apt BZ$190, house BZ$200-390; ❄📶🏊) Amanda offers a variety of accommodations on leafy grounds with a nice pool a block from the beach. On one side of the property there is a modern three-bedroom *casita* with a rooftop terrace. The main building looks over the road to the water and has two art-filled studios with kitchenettes downstairs and a traditional Belizean-style apartment upstairs.

★**Sea Dreams Hotel** B&B $$$
(Map p242; ☎226-0602; www.seadreamsbelize.com; Hattie St; r BZ$272, apt BZ$370-480; ❄📶) A lovely guesthouse on the north side of the island, Sea Dreams offers a rare combination of easy access and sweet tranquility. Spend the day lounging around the Split, then retreat to the cozy accommodations just a few steps away. Original paintings by local artists adorn the colorful walls of the rooms and apartments, which are elegant and comfortable.

★**Caye Reef** BOUTIQUE HOTEL $$$
(Map p242; ☎610-0240; www.cayereef.com; Front St; apt BZ$558-598; ❄📶🏊) The six apartments at Caye Reef have been designed with the utmost attention to detail – from the original artwork hanging on the walls to the swinging hammocks hanging on the private balconies. Room prices rise with the floor, with the most expensive rooms on the third floor.

Eating

Errolyns House of Fry Jacks BELIZEAN $
(Map p242; Middle St; BZ$1.50-6; ⊙6:30am-2pm & 6:30-9pm Tue-Sun) Who said Belize had to be expensive? Locals and travelers alike descend on this neat takeout hut to chow down on the island's best-value breakfast – delicious golden fry-jacks (deep-fried dough) filled with any combination of beans, cheese, egg, beef or chicken. Cheap, filling and delicious.

Amor Y Café BREAKFAST $
(Map p242; ☎610-2397; Front St; breakfast BZ$6-12.50; ⊙6am-2pm; 🖉) There's no contest when it comes to the most popular breakfast spot on the island – this place is always busy, but you won't have to wait long for a table on the shaded porch overlooking Front St. Take your pick from freshly squeezed juices, scrambled eggs or homemade yogurt topped with fruit – and don't miss out on the freshly brewed coffee (with espresso ice cubes!).

★ Caribbean Colors Art Café

HEALTH FOOD $$

(Map p242; ☎605-9242; Front St; mains BZ$10-25; ⏰7am-2:30pm Fri-Wed; 📶) What began as a **gallery** (Map p242; ⏰7am-2:30pm; 📶) for owner and artist Lee Vanderwalker has morphed into a top-notch cafe. And the art's still on the walls. While you browse you can treat yourself to a coffee or a cool smoothie, then sit down for a fresh and healthy breakfast, salad or sandwich. There are lots of veggie and vegan options too.

Little Kitchen Restaurant

BELIZEAN $$

(Map p242; ☎667-2178; off Luciano Reyes St; mains BZ$15-25; ⏰6-11am, noon-4pm & 6-10pm) Elba Flower's Little Kitchen is a 3rd-floor, open-air restaurant on Caulker's southwestern side serving traditional (yet artfully done) Belizean dishes such as curry shrimp, coconut red snapper and excellent conch fritters (to name just a few). Portions are big and it's outstanding value, although we have some concerns about immature lobsters on the menu – make sure yours is legal size.

★ Il Pellicano

ITALIAN $$$

(Map p242; ☎226-0660; Pasero St; mains BZ$25-42; ⏰5:30-9:30pm Tue-Sun) Head to the lagoon side of the island to find this great garden restaurant preparing a small, but constantly changing, selection of outstanding classic Italian dishes including flavorful homemade pastas and the best pizza on the island. Accompany your meal with Italian wine served by the glass or bottle, and be sure to sample the excellent desserts.

★ Hibisca by Habaneros

INTERNATIONAL $$$

(Map p242; ☎626-4911; cnr Front St & Calle al Sol; mains BZ$32-58; ⏰5:30-9:30pm Fri-Wed) Caulker's poshest restaurant is located in a brightly painted clapboard house in the center of town. Here chefs prepare gourmet international food, combining fresh seafood, meat and vegetables with insanely delicious sauces and flavors. Wash it down with a fine wine or a jug of sangria.

🍷 Drinking & Nightlife

Barrier Reef Sports Bar & Grill

SPORTS BAR

(Map p242; ☎226-0077; Front St; ⏰9am-midnight) Perennially popular with expats and international visitors alike, this waterfront beach bar serves fantastic international food and all kinds of drinks. There is often live music and major sporting events are shown on the many flat-screen TVs. It's pretty much the only place on the island that you are always guaranteed to find a social atmosphere.

I&I Reggae Bar

BAR

(Map p242; ☎668-8169; Luciano Reyes St; ⏰4pm-1am Mon-Wed, to 2am Thu-Sat) I&I is the island's most hip, happening spot after dark, when its healthy sound system belts out a reggae beat. Its three levels each offer a different scene, with a dance floor on one and swings hanging from the rafters on another. The top floor is the 'chill-out zone,' complete with hammocks and panoramic views. A great place for a sunset drink.

WHERE'S THE BEACH PARTY?

Koko King (☎626-8436; www.facebook.com/KokoKingCayeCaulker; ⏰10am-midnight) For those looking to kick it on the soft white sand and in the docile sea, tropical cocktail in hand, surrounded by like-minded travelers, Koko King reigns supreme. It's an all-in-one sort of beach party, with a fully stocked bar, a tasty Caribbean restaurant and a plethora of beach games and water toys – you can easily spend all day here. Arriving involves a quick ferry trip (Map p242; complimentary if you spend BZ$20 at the beach, which you prove with a wristband) or self-guided kayaking, paddleboarding or swimming adventure across the Split. If you get here early, it's worthwhile to rent a swing bed (BZ$50) or a shaded spot behind the beds (BZ$25). For true Koko King diehards, on-site We'Yu Boutique Hotel (rooms from BZ$200) opened in late 2018, which comes in handy when the place throws its famous full-moon parties.

The Split (Map p242) A narrow channel that splits Caye Caulker into two, the Split has clean, deep waters free of seaweed, making it one of the island's best swimming areas. This is particularly true following the recent construction of a seawall, a wading area with sheltered picnic tables, a spa, some restaurants and a kayak and paddleboard rental shop. The loud music and rowdy crowd at the adjacent bar, Lazy Lizard (Map p242; ⏰10am-11pm), will either enhance or dampen your experience, depending on what you're looking for.

DON'T MISS

SECRET BEACH

The island's worst-kept secret is a dreamy stretch of northwestern shoreline that has nonetheless retained the name Secret Beach. Getting here is a big part of the allure, as it requires a 45-minute golf cart ride north of San Pedro and across much of the North Island, over steamy lagoons and hauntingly beautiful mangrove swamps where crocodiles lurk.

The reward for your effort is an away-from-it-all kind of paradise that San Pedro once was, completely off thegrid and featuring soft white sands, clear turquoise waters, yummy seafood shacks and as many tropical cocktails as you can slurp. The anchoring establishment out here is **Wayne's World** (mains BZ$20-25; ⊙10am-5pm; 🛜), a restaurant and bar under the same ownership as the area's first (and only) lodgings, **Paradise on the Caye** (☎615-2042; www.paradiseonthecaye.com; r incl breakfast BZ$190; 🛜). Other highlights include the posh **Maruba Beach Klub** (☎610-3775; ⊙9am-5pm) 🍃, with its techno beats and brightly colored lounge pillows, and **Blue Bayou** (☎623-8051; www.facebook.com/pg/bluebayoubelize; ⊙10am-5pm), a small, family-owned hideaway with partly submerged picnic tables and a convivial vibe.

Paddleboards, kayaks and canoes are available for rent at Wayne's World, and there's also beach volleyball, cornhole and a wandering hair-braider. For the best bites at the beach, hit up the food shack **Aurora's** and try the BBQ grouper or fish tacos.

ℹ Information

Take care with belongings left in hotel rooms – especially in some of the more rustic accommodations south of town – as room robberies are regularly reported. If your room doesn't lock properly, ask for another and make use of the hotel safe if one is available.

There is a basic health center on the island, but if you really need medical attention you're better off heading directly to Belize City.

Atlantic Bank (Middle St; ⊙8am-3pm Mon-Fri, 9am-noon Sat) Has a pair of fairly reliable ATMs, although make sure you have some cash before you arrive in case they are out of service.

Caye Caulker BTIA (www.cayecaulkervacation.com) The official site of the Caye Caulker branch of the Belize Tourism Industry Association (BTIA).

Caye Caulker Health Center (☎226-0166, emergency 668-2547; ⊙8am-noon & 1-5pm Mon-Fri) Just off Front St, two blocks south of Calle al Sol.

Cayeboard Connection (☎206-0022; Front St; per hour BZ$12; ⊙9am-9pm) Internet access and printing; sells coffee and books.

GoCayeCaulker.com (www.gocayecaulker.com) General information for visitors.

Post Office (Map p242; Estella St, Caye Caulker Health Center Bldg; ⊙8am-noon & 1-4:30pm Mon-Thu, to 4pm Fri)

ℹ Getting There & Away

AIR

Maya Island Air (☎226-0012; www.mayaislandair.com) and **Tropic Air** (☎226-0040; www.tropicair.com) connect Caye Caulker with San Pedro and Belize City. The airline offices are at the southern end of the island.

BOAT

There are two companies running boats from Caye Caulker to Belize City and San Pedro.

Ocean Ferry Belize (Map p242; ☎226-0033; www.oceanferrybelize.com) runs boats from the main dock on Calle al Sol. Departuress to Belize City (one way/return BZ$19/30; 45 minutes) at 6:30am, 8:30am, 9am, 10:30am, noon, 1:30pm and 4:30pm. Boats to San Pedro (one way/return BZ$19/30; 30 minutes) go at 8:45am, 11:15am, 2:15pm, 3:45pm & 6:15pm.

San Pedro Belize Express Water Taxi (Map p242; ☎226-0225; www.belizewatertaxi.com) departs from the pier in front of the basketball court. Services to San Pedro (one way/return BZ$18/28) depart at 8:45am, 9:45am, 11:15am, 12:45pm, 2:15pm, 3:45pm, 4:45pm, 5:15pm and 6:15pm, and to Belize City (one way/return BZ$18/28) at 6:30am, 7am, 8am, 9am, 10:30am, noon, 1:30pm, 3:30pm and 5pm.

The docks are beside each other on the reef side of the island.

San Pedro Belize Express Water Taxi also runs a service to Chetumal, Mexico, every other day via San Pedro. **Water Jets** (Map p242; ☎20 6-0010; www.sanpedrowatertaxi.com; lagoon dock) runs the same service on alternate days.

ℹ Getting Around

Caulker is so small that most people walk everywhere. A couple of golf-cart taxis hang out around Front St and charge BZ$5 to BZ$7 per short trip around town.

You can rent a golf cart at **Buddy's Golf Cart Rentals** (☎628-8508; buddysgolfvartrentals@gmail.com; Middle St; per hour/day/24hr BZ$25/100/150), but bicycle rental is far cheaper and just as fast a way to get around. You can rent bikes at grocery stores, tour operators and hotels.

Ambergris Caye & San Pedro

POP 16,444

The undisputed superstar of Belize's tourism industry, 'La Isla Bonita' strikes an impressive and perhaps even magical balance of large-scale tourism development with a fun, laid-back atmosphere. Sure it gets busy – especially in high season when an endless procession of golf carts clogs the narrow streets of the main town, San Pedro – but it's still the kind of place where it's acceptable to hold up traffic while you greet an old acquaintance.

Complaints about over-development aside, Ambergris Caye remains an archetypal tropical paradise where sun-drenched days are filled with fruity drinks and water sports. There are plenty of simple pleasures to be had, from riding a bike along a windswept beach path to wading in crystal-clear waters. And the island's most valuable asset, the flourishing barrier reef a half-mile offshore, is the epicenter of the country's snorkeling and diving industries and the source of its most imaginative culinary scene.

Sights & Activities

★Hol Chan Marine Reserve DIVE SITE

(☎226-2247; www.holchanmarinereserve.org; national park admission BZ$20) At the southern tip of Ambergris, the 6.5-sq-mile Hol Chan Marine Reserve is probably Belize's most oft-visited diving and snorkeling site. It offers spectacular coral formations, plus a rich abundance and diversity of marine life – not to mention its proximity to the cays. Hol Chan is Maya for 'Little Channel,' which refers to a natural break in the reef known as Hol Chan Cut. The channel walls are covered with colorful corals, which support an amazing variety of fish life, including moray eels and black groupers.

Although the reef is the primary attraction of Hol Chan, the marine reserve also includes sea-grass beds and mangroves. The sea grass provides a habitat for nurse sharks and southern stingrays, which lend their name to **Shark Ray Alley**. Snorkelers have the chance to get up close to both species, due mainly to the fact that the animals are used to getting fed by tour boats.

All dive operators and nautical tours offer trips to Hol Chan. For information and displays on marine life, visit the Hol Chan Visitors Center (p251).

★ACES WILDLIFE WATCHING

(American Crocodile Education Sanctuary; Map p248; ☎623-7920; www.americancrocodilesanctuary.org; Esmeralda St; BZ$100; 6:45-9pm) A fantastic nighttime crocodile tour through the mangrove lagoon on the west side of the island. It's run by a local nonprofit that researches the reptiles and handles problematic ones. Tour lasts about three hours and departs from the Office restaurant.

★Ecologic Divers DIVING

(Map p248; ☎226-4118; www.ecologicdivers.com; 1-/2-/3-tank dive BZ$112/180/247) A high-end dive shop with great customer service and solid environmental credentials. It offers all the local dives, fishing expeditions and boat cruises. Management promises small groups, with one dive master to every six divers on all immersions. Also recommended for dive courses.

★Science & Soul Wellness YOGA

(☎615-0089; www.scienceandsoulwellness.com; Mahogany Bay; yoga class from BZ$40, massage from BZ$180; 9:30am-6pm) This gorgeous and professionally run wellness center is a reason in itself to book at stay at Mahogany Bay, the posh new 'townlet' about 2.5 miles south of San Pedro. The yoga studio is the first in Belize to offer aerial classes, which cater to all levels of experience, and the instructors are top-notch.

Searious Adventures SNORKELING, SAILING

(Map p248; ☎226-4202, 636-3001; www.seariousadventuresbelize.com) A long-running and respected outfit that offers a variety of adventures on the water and on the mainland. Combine snorkeling and sailing with the catamaran snorkel tour (BZ$146), which includes three snorkeling stops and a remote BBQ on the way from San Pedro town to Mexico Rocks.

Ak'bol Yoga YOGA

(☎626-6296, 226-2073; www.akbol.com; Mile 2.25, North Island; classes BZ$30; 9am Mon-Sat, 10am Sun) With two open, thatch-roof yoga studios (one at the end of the dock), Ak'bol offers daily walk-in classes, in addition to

San Pedro (Ambergris Caye)

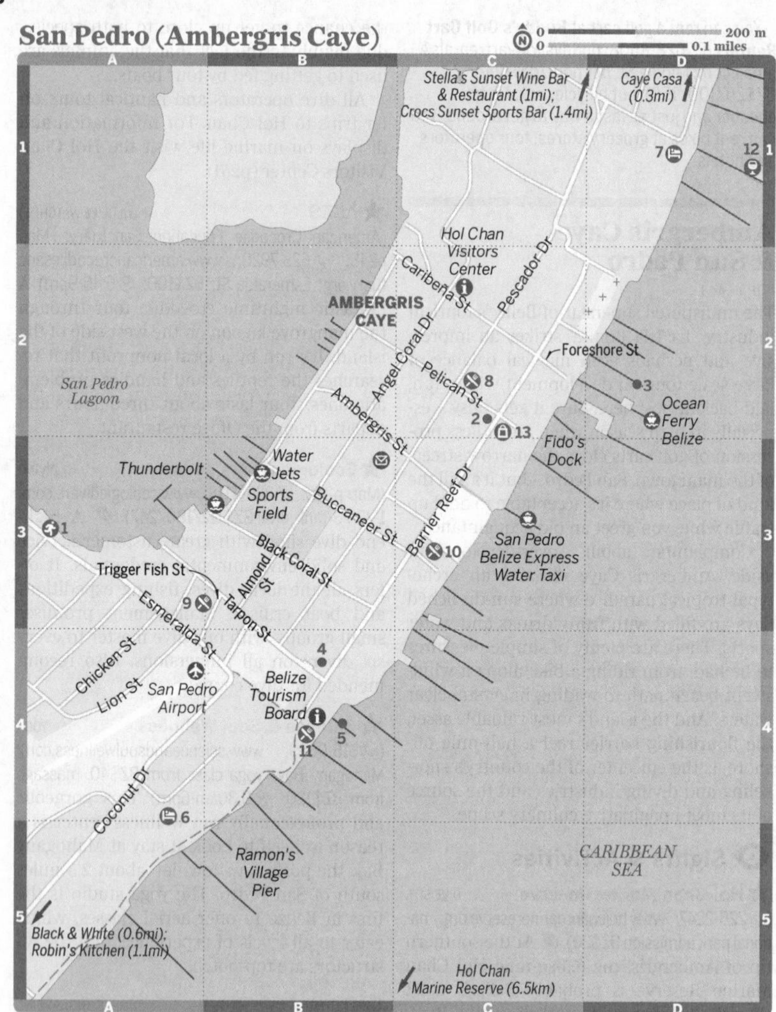

the week-long yoga retreats that are scheduled throughout the year. The retreats vary in price, but always include seven nights' accommodation, all buffet meals (minus one dinner) and all the yoga, with at least two classes offered per day.

Tours

★Belize Food Tours FOOD
(Map p248; ☎615-1321; www.belizefoodtours.com; cnr Barrier Reef Dr & Pelican St; food tours from BZ$124, cooking classes BZ$150) For a delicious introduction to all things yummy in Belize, hop on a fabulous food tour run by one of the island's pioneering families. The lunch tour, 'Belizean Bites,' and dinner tour, 'Savor Belize,' both meander through San Pedro's mom-n-pop kitchens, sampling a wide variety of authentic dishes and drinks hailing from Belize's many cultural influences.

Seaduced by Belize BOATING
(Map p248; ☎226-2254; www.seaducedbybelize.com; Tarpon St, Vilma Linda Plaza; ⏰7am-6pm; 👪) Offers a range of sailing trips, including a sunset cruise and a full-day trip to Caye Caulker. Also runs good-value outings to spot manatees at Swallow Caye (BZ$210 plus

San Pedro (Ambergris Caye)

Activities, Courses & Tours
1 ACES.......A3
2 Belize Food Tours.......C2
3 Ecologic Divers.......D2
4 Seaduced by Belize.......B4
5 Searious Adventures.......B4

Sleeping
6 Ramon's Village.......A4
7 Sandbar.......D1

Eating
8 DandE's Frozen Custard.......C2
9 El Fogón.......A3
10 Estel's Dine by the Sea.......C3
11 Wild Mango's.......B4

Drinking & Nightlife
12 Palapa Bar.......D1

Shopping
13 Belizean Arts Gallery.......C2

a BZ$30 park fee), including lunch at Goff's Caye and snorkeling. Other tours include visits to Bacalar Chico and a recommended full-day trip to Robles Beach, complete with snorkel stops and beach BBQ.

Sleeping

Accommodations on Ambergris Caye skew toward the high end, particularly outside of San Pedro, and the best spots tend to book up fast in high season, between December and May. Almost all hotels accept major credit cards, though you may pay a surcharge. For apartments, suites and condominiums, check www.ambergriscaye.com.

Sandbar HOSTEL $
(Map p248; ☎226-2008; www.sanpedrohostel.com; Boca del Rio Dr; dm/r BZ$30/120; ❄📶) A tight budget no longer means having to bed down in a stifling room on a backstreet. San Pedro's only waterfront hostel is easily its best. The bright private rooms have big sliding doors leading onto a balcony with Caribbean vistas, while the air-conditioned dorms are well designed with privacy curtains and individual power sockets for each bed.

★ **Daydreamin' Bed & Breakfast** B&B $$
(☎601-3306; www.daydreaminbelize.com; Tres Cocos; BZ$185-200; ❄📶🏊) With just four tidy cabins and a delicious **cafe** (Tres Cocos; ⏰7am-2pm) perched around a small, relaxing pool, this North Island getaway is easily one of Ambergris' most charming. The owner is an absolute class act, and her relaxed professionalism is palpable throughout the property. The elegant units are constructed from nine types of local hardwood, each featuring a unique design. Adults only.

★ **Ak'bol Yoga Resort** RESORT $$
(☎626-6296, 226-2073; www.akbol.com; North Island; s/d BZ$80/116, cabañas BZ$333-380; 📶🏊) Yogis, rejoice! Ak'bol, or 'Heart of the Village,' is a sweet retreat in a near-perfect location about 1 mile north of town on the North Island. The seven colorful *cabañas* have delightful details, such as handcrafted hardwood furniture and mosaic sinks with conch shell faucets. Enjoy plantation-style shutters that open to the sea and mosaic-tiled showers that are open to the sky.

★ **Caye Casa** BOUTIQUE HOTEL $$$
(☎226-2880; www.cayecasa.com; Boca del Rio Dr; r/ste/villa BZ$250/325/425; ❄📶🏊) At the quiet northern end of San Pedro town, Caye Casa stands out for its simplicity, sophistication and utter loveliness. The sweet colonial-style *casitas* and villas offer thatched-roof porches with wonderful sea views, fully stocked kitchens with stainless-steel appliances and limestone countertops, spacious tiled bathrooms and inviting king- and queen-sized beds.

★ **Victoria House** RESORT $$$
(☎226-2067, in USA 800-247-5159; www.victoria-house.com; Sea Grape Dr; r from BZ$420, casitas BZ$710, villas BZ$900-4200; ❄📶🏊) This elegant beach resort is one of the oldest on the island, but is meticulously maintained and shines like new. It's fronted by a beautiful, wide beach shaded by palms, while the grassy grounds center on two excellent pools. Rooms are in thatched-roof *casitas*, or colonial-style 'plantation' houses, with a sophisticated white-on-white scheme that oozes luxury.

★ **Matachica Beach Resort** RESORT $$$
(☎226-5010; www.matachica.com; Mile 5.5, North Island; r BZ$655-1725; P❄📶🏊) Vying for the title of 'swankiest resort,' Matachica is extravagant, exotic and eclectic. This place is serious about the idea of tropical luxury, so down duvets and Frette linens cover the mosquito-netted beds, and each

thatched-roof cottage boasts classic furniture and private patios...hung with hammocks, of course. The luxury villas have private terraces and outdoor hot tubs.

Ramon's Village RESORT $$$
(Map p248; 226-2071; www.ramons.com; Coconut Dr; r/ste from BZ$337/709;) Guests love the exotic, faux-jungle setting at this luxurious beach resort with a giant Maya mask known as 'Rey Ramon' overlooking the grounds. Thatched-roof *cabañas* are surrounded by lush greenery and flowering hibiscus and bougainvillea, allowing for plenty of privacy. Beachfront *cabañas* are front and center, with uninhibited Caribbean vistas; seaside *cabañas* are set back a bit.

Eating

Although there are plenty of options for cheap street food, tacos and fry-jacks (deep-fried dough), at a sit-down place it's unlikely you'll pay less than BZ$50 per person – Ambergris Caye is easily the most expensive restaurant scene in Belize. That said, the island also offers the country's freshest seafood and most innovative chefs, so diners usually get their money's worth.

★ **DandE's Frozen Custard** ICE CREAM $
(Map p248; 660-5966; www.dande.bz; Pescador Dr; ice cream from BZ$6; 2-9:30pm;) Don't be confused by 'frozen custard.' It's basically high-quality ice cream, made with eggs for extra richness, then churned as it freezes for dense creaminess. The flavors change frequently, often featuring local fruity flavors such as coconut, sour sop and mango. Alternatively you can't go wrong with 'not just' vanilla. DandE's also makes sorbet, but don't forgo the frozen custard.

★ **Truck Stop** FOOD HALL $$
(226-3663; www.truckstopbz.com; North Island; mains BZ$15-27; noon-9pm Wed-Sun;) This absurdly cool shipping-container food park doubles as Ambergris Caye's entertainment hub, offering movie nights, adult spelling bees, live music, farmers markets and backyard games such as ping pong and cornhole. And there's a pool! And a bar! And a dock over the lagoon with a funny (but true) warning about crocodiles.

★ **Robin's Kitchen** JAMAICAN $$
(651-3583; Sea Grape Dr; mains BZ$14-25; 7am-9pm Sun-Thu, to 5:30pm Fri, 6:30-9pm Sat) At this simple, small roadside restaurant south of town, Jamaican BBQ king Robin prepares the best jerk chicken and fish this side of Kingston. Dishes are spicy but with subtle flavors, and his sauces are also to die for. If you catch your own fish, Robin will prepare it for you any way you like and will only charge for sides.

Black & White GARIFUNA $$
(605-2895; gariculenter@gmail.com; Villa Dr; mains BZ$20-35; 9am-9pm) Adorned in tropics-themed tablecloths, local art and charming lattice, this little restaurant serves up Garifuna specialties including *hudut* (red snapper prepared in coconut milk with spices and pounded plantains) and cassava bread, the staple food of the group's ancestors. The restaurant doubles as a cultural center, and occasionally hosts educational performances involving Garifuna history, lifestyle and drumming traditions.

El Fogón BELIZEAN $$
(Map p248; 671-1277, 206-2121; www.elfogonbelize.com; 2 Trigger Fish St; mains BZ$17-45; 11am-9pm Mon-Sat) At first glance the ambience doesn't seem to match the price tag at this backstreet eatery, but once the food arrives you'll not be too worried about the lack of chic design. El Fogón serves up wonderfully prepared classic Belizean Creole cuisine including plenty of fresh seafood cooked to perfection. The conch is especially tasty.

Estel's Dine by the Sea BREAKFAST $$
(Map p248; 226-2019; www.ambergriscaye.com/estels; Buccaneer St; breakfast BZ$12-20, mains BZ$15-35; 6am-9pm;) This long-standing breakfast favorite is basically an extension of the beach – complete with sandy floors and ocean breezes. Stop by for a breakfast burrito, some Maya eggs or an eye-opening coffee. Breakfasts are served until 4pm, but there are also sandwiches, burgers, fish and chips, and burritos on the chalkboard menu.

★ **Hidden Treasure** CARIBBEAN $$$
(226-4111; www.hiddentreasurebelize.com; 4088 Sarstoon St; mains BZ$29-68; 5-9pm Wed-Mon;) Living up to its name, Hidden Treasure is a gorgeous open-air restaurant in an out-of-the-way residential neighborhood (follow the signs from Coconut Dr). Lit by candles, the beautiful bamboo and hardwood dining room is the perfect setting for a romantic dinner, which might feature almond-crusted grouper, blackened snapper

with bacon-wrapped shrimp, or pork ribs with a ginger-pineapple BBQ glaze.

★ **Wild Mango's** INTERNATIONAL $$$
(Map p248; ☎226-2859; 42 Barrier Reef Dr; mains BZ$20-48; ⊙11:30am-9pm Mon-Sat; ☎) Exuding a carefree, casual ambience (as a beachfront restaurant should), this open-air restaurant manages to serve up some of the island's most consistent and creative cuisine. With a hint of the Caribbean and a hint of Mexico, the dishes showcase fresh seafood, Cajun spices and local fruits and vegetables. The place is usually packed – come early or make a reservation.

Drinking & Entertainment

★ **Stella's Sunset Wine Bar & Restaurant** WINE BAR
(☎602-5284; www.stellasmile.com; Mile 1, Tres Cocos, North Island; ⊙4-9pm Mon-Wed, Fri & Sat, 8am-1pm Sun) Stella's is a classy but unpretentious wine bar set in a lovely garden on the edge of the San Pedro Lagoon that affords fine sunset views. Sit on lounge chairs under the trees or at a table in the *palapa* and work your way through two dozen different whites and reds.

Crocs Sunset Sports Bar BAR
(☎610-0026; North Island; ⊙11am-11pm) A new go-to for sunset, this open-air, triple-decker bar has large-screen TVs and picture-perfect views over the lagoon.

Palapa Bar BAR
(Map p248; ☎226-3111; www.palapabarandgrill.com; San Pedro; ⊙10am-11pm) This over-the-water *palapa*, a mile south of San Pedro bridge, serves burgers and tacos, and is a fantastic place for tropical drinks any time of day. There's no law against drinking and floating, so when it's really hot you are invited to partake of a bucket of beers while relaxing in an inner tube.

Shopping

Belizean Arts Gallery ART
(Map p248; www.belizeanarts.com; 18 Barrier Reef Dr; ⊙9am-10pm Mon-Sat) This is one of the country's best shops for local art and handicrafts, selling ceramics, wood carvings, Garifuna drums and antiques alongside affordable and tasteful knickknacks. You'll also find a decent selection of paintings by local and national artists. Rainforest-flora beauty products, including soaps, are on sale too. It's inside Fido's.

Information

Don't leave anything unattended in a golf cart that you're hoping to see later, especially in the center of San Pedro. And be sure to lock the steering wheel. The island isn't a dangerous place, but opportunistic theft is common.

San Pedro has both private and public health facilities, but for serious conditions you would want to get to Belize City.

You can exchange money easily in San Pedro, and US dollars are widely accepted. Most accommodations accept card payment, but many restaurants are cash only.

Ambergris Caye (www.ambergriscaye.com) Excellent island information and a lively message board.

Atlantic Bank (Barrier Reef Dr; ⊙8am-3pm Mon-Fri, 9am-noon Sat)

Belize Bank (Barrier Reef Dr; ⊙8am-3pm Mon-Thu, to 4:30pm Fri)

Belize Tourism Board (Map p248; ☎226-4532; Barrier Reef Dr; ⊙8am-noon & 1-5pm Mon-Fri) Goverment tourism office with limited practical information.

Hol Chan Visitors Center (Map p248; ☎226-2247; Caribeña St; ⊙8am-noon & 1-5pm Mon-Fri, 8am-noon Sat-Sun) Information and displays on marine life.

Hyperbaric Chamber (☎615-4288, 226-2851; belize@sssnetwork.com; Lion St; ⊙24hr) Center for diving accidents – it's in front of the Maya Island Air terminal.

Post Office (Map p248; Pescador Dr; ⊙8am-noon & 1-4:30pm Mon-Thu, to 4pm Fri)

San Carlos Medical Clinic, Pharmacy & Pathology Lab (☎226-2918, emergencies 627-3462; 28 Pescador Dr; ⊙7am-9pm) Private clinic treating ailments and performing blood tests.

San Pedro Policlinic (☎226-2536, emergency 660-2871; Sea Grape Dr; ⊙in-patient services 8am-8pm Mon-Fri, to noon Sat; emergencies 24hr) A public health clinic with 24-hour emergency services.

Getting There & Away

AIR

The San Pedro airstrip is just south of the town center on Coconut Dr. The Tropic Air terminal is at the north end of the strip, right on Coconut Dr, while the Maya Island Air terminal is on the west side of the strip. All flights depart between 6am and 5pm.

Tropic Air (☎226-2012; www.tropicair.com; Coconut Dr) Hourly flights operate to/from Belize City's Philip Goldson International Airport (one way/return BZ$178/315, 18 minutes), as well as around a dozen flights to the Belize City Municipal Airstrip, 12 miles closer to town (one

DON'T MISS

THE BLUE HOLE NATURAL MONUMENT

At the center of Lighthouse Reef is the world-famous **Blue Hole Natural Monument** (www.belizeaudubon.org; national park admission BZ$60; ⏲8am-4:30pm), an incomparable natural wonder and unique diving experience. It may not involve a lot of undersea life, but it remains a recreational diver's best opportunity for a heart-pounding descent into a majestic submarine sinkhole. The chance of spotting circling reef sharks and the occasional hammerhead further sweeten the deal.

In the 1970s, underwater pioneer Jacques Cousteau explored the sinkhole and declared the dive site one of the world's best. Since then the Blue Hole's image – a deep azure pupil with an aquamarine border surrounded by the lighter shades of the reef – has become a logo for tourist publicity and a symbol of Belize. The hole forms a perfect 1000ft-diameter circle on the surface and is said to be 430ft deep, but as much as 200ft of this may now be filled with silt and other natural debris.

Divers drop quickly to 130ft, from where they swim beneath an overhang, observing stalactites above and, sometimes, a few reef sharks. Although the water is clear, light levels are low, so a good dive light will enable further appreciation of the rock formations. Because of the depth, ascent begins after eight minutes; the brevity of the dive may disappoint some divers. The trip is usually combined with other dives at Lighthouse Reef, and many divers will tell you that those other dives are the real highlight. But judging from its popularity – most dive shops make twice-weekly runs to the Blue Hole – plenty want to make the deep descent.

On day trips the Blue Hole will be your first dive, which can be nerve-racking if you're unfamiliar with the dive master and the other divers, or if you haven't been underwater lately. It may be worth doing some local dives with your dive masters before setting out cold on a Blue Hole trip. An alternative is to take an overnight trip to Lighthouse Reef, where there's a dive shop offering a livelier (and more athletic) Blue Hole experience.

Long Caye Diving Services (☎601-5181, in USA 305-600-2585; www.itzalodge.com/diving; Itza Lodge; per dive BZ$140) owner Elvis Solis has been inside the Blue Hole more than 500 times, and has mapped out a unique course that he offers to small groups who are either staying at Itza Lodge, where the dive shop is based, or traveling independently. The dive begins on the northern stretch of the Blue Hole, drops to 130ft, and at around 80ft brings divers through a couple of small caves where squirrel fish and nurse sharks tend to lurk. The safety stop is a long one, around 25 minutes, and is achieved while circling the rim of the Blue Hole, where sea fans, sponges, turtles, barracudas and other reef dwellers can be spotted.

The coral around this shallow perimeter will appeal to snorkelers as well, though the trip is expensive and you'll probably have to tag along on a dive boat. Diving or snorkeling, the trip involves two hours each way by boat in possibly rough, open waters. There's a BZ$60 marine-park fee for visiting Blue Hole, and that is usually on top of the dive fees.

way/return BZ$116/206, 15 minutes). There are also four flights a day to Caye Caulker (one way/return BZ$106/156, five minutes). Additional flights depart for Corozal (one way/return BZ$151/267, 20 minutes, five daily), Orange Walk (one way/return BZ$172/304, 20 minutes, three daily), Belmopan (one way/return BZ$255/450, 40 minutes, three daily) and San Ignacio near the Guatemalan Border (one way/return BZ$310/547, 55 minutes, three daily).

Maya Island Air (☎226-2485; www.mayaisland air.com; ⏲6:30am-6pm) Runs regular flights to Philip Goldson International Airport (one way BZ$146 to BZ$233, return from BZ$293 to BZ$464, 20 minutes) and Belize Municipal Airstrip (one way BZ$83 to BZ$135, return BZ$166 to BZ$310, 20 minutes) with some services stopping on Caye Caulker. Also has four or five flights daily to Corozal and one to Orange Walk. Check website for latest schedules.

BOAT

There are two water-taxi companies running the route between San Pedro and Belize City via Caye Caulker, both departing from docks on the reef side of the island.

San Pedro Belize Express Water Taxi (Map p248; ☎226-3535; www.belizewatertaxi.com; San Pedro public dock) runs services to Caye Caulker (one way/return BZ$30/50, 30 minutes) and Belize City (one way/return BZ$40/70, 1½ hours) at 6am, 6:30am, 7:30am, 8:30am, 10am, 11:30am, 1pm, 3pm and 4:30pm.

Ocean Ferry Belize (Map p248; ☎226-2033; www.oceanferrybelize.com; Caribeña Foreshore) runs regular boat services to Caye Caulker (one way/return BZ$19/30, 30 minutes) and Belize City (one way/return BZ$29/50, 1½ hours). Boats leave San Pedro at 6am, 8am, 10am, 1pm and 4pm.

Thunderbolt (Map p248; ☎631-3400; Black Coral St) operates a daily service between San Pedro and Corozal in northern Belize (one way/return BZ$50/90, two hours) departing from behind the football field on the lagoon side of the island.

There are also departures every morning around 8am for Chetumal, Mexico (one way BZ$100 to BZ$110, two hours) from the **International Departures Dock** (Buccaneer St) on the lagoon side of town, with companies **Water Jets** (Map p248; ☎226-2194; www.sanpedrowatertaxi.com) and San Pedro Belize Express Water Taxi taking turns to make the run.

Getting Around

You can walk into the center of town from the airport terminals in five minutes and the walk from the boat docks is even shorter.

Minivan taxis ply the streets looking for customers. Official rates are BZ$7 during the day and BZ$10 at night to anywhere in the town center. For hotels outside the center negotiate the rate before hopping in.

There is a small **toll bridge** over the San Pedro river. Pay a ridiculous BZ$5 for each 20m crossing on a golf cart. Bicycles cross for free.

NORTHERN BELIZE

Northern Belize comprises two districts: Corozal and Orange Walk, both traversed by the straight, flat Philip Goldson Hwy. Off the main road, adventurous travelers will find pretty fishing villages, pristine jungles, ancient Maya cities and anachronistic Mennonite communities.

Community Baboon Sanctuary

No real baboons inhabit Belize; but Belizeans use that name for the Yucatán black howler monkey *(Alouatta pigra)*, an endangered species that exists only in Belize, northern Guatemala and southern Mexico and is one of the largest monkeys in the Americas. The **Community Baboon Sanctuary** (CBS; www.howlermonkeys.org; nature walk/river tour/villages tour BZ$14/28/50; ⏲8am-5pm) is a community-run, grassroots conservation operation that has engineered an impressive increase in the primate's local population.

CBS occupies about 20 sq miles, spread over a number of Creole villages in the Belize River valley. More than 200 landowners in seven villages have signed pledges to preserve the monkey's habitat by protecting forested areas along the river and in corridors that run along the borders of their property. The black howlers have made an amazing comeback here, and the monkeys now roam freely around the surrounding area.

CBS Museum & Visitor's Center MUSEUM
(☎245-2009, 245-2007, 622-9624; baboonsanctuary@hotmail.com; Bermudian Landing; adult/child BZ$14/7; ⏲8am-5pm; P) In a newly constructed building, CBS Museum & Visitor's Center has a number of good exhibits and displays on the black howler, other Belizean wildlife and the history of the sanctuary. Included with the admission fee is a 45-minute nature walk on which you're likely to get an up-close introduction to a resident troop of black howlers. Along the way the trained local guides also impart their knowledge of the many medicinal plants.

Sleeping

Howler Monkey Resort LODGE $$
(☎607-1571; www.howlermonkeyresort.bz; cabins BZ$250-270; P❄☎) Ed and Melissa Turton's beautiful, rustic jungle lodge consists of eight cabins of varying size and proximity to the river, set on 20 jungle-filled acres above a bend in the Belize River. This is the place to come to hear the howler monkeys roar at night and watch birds, agouti, iguana and even the occasional crocodile roam during the day.

Getting There & Away

Bermudian Landing is 27 miles northwest of Belize City and 9 miles west of Burrell Boom. Buses depart from the CBS Museum & Visitor's Center to Belize City (BZ$5 to BZ$8, one hour) very early in the morning, with additional departures at noon and 3:30pm from Monday to Saturday. Buses leave Belize City from the corner of Amara Ave and Cemetery Rd at 12:15pm, 3:25pm, 5pm, 5:20pm and 8pm.

Altun Ha

Altun Ha (www.nichbelize.org/altun-ha/; BZ$10; ⏲8am-5pm), the Maya ruins that have inspired Belikin beer labels and Belizean banknotes, stands 31 miles north of Belize City, off the Old Northern Hwy. While smaller and less imposing than some other Maya sites in the country, Altun Ha, with its immaculate central plaza, is still spectacular and well worth the short detour to get here.

The original site covered 1500 acres, but what visitors today see is the central ceremonial precinct of two plazas surrounded by temples.

Located in splendid isolation, the **Belize Boutique Resort & Spa** (☎225-5555, USA 800-861-7001, USA 815-312-1237; www.belizeresortandspa.com; Mile 40.5 Old Northern Hwy; r BZ$460, junior ste BZ$540, ste BZ$850, villas BZ$1050-1250; P ❄ 📶 🏊) resort takes the jungle-lodge-and-spa concept to extremes of expensive pampering. There are luxurious amenities and a slew of health and rejuvenation treatments. Lush tropical grounds harbor individually designed rooms in a variety of African, Creole, Maya and even Gaudíesque styles – including honeymoon and 'fertility' suites and a jungle tree house.

Lamanai

Perhaps the most fascinating Maya site in Northern Belize, **Lamanai** (www.nichbelize.org; BZ$10; ⏲8am-5pm) lies 24 miles south of Orange Walk Town up the New River (or 36 miles by unpaved road). The ruins are known both for their impressive architecture and marvelous setting, surrounded by dense jungle overlooking the New River Lagoon. Climbing to the top of the 125ft High Temple to gaze out across the vast jungle canopy is an awe-inspiring experience that is not to be missed.

Most visitors approach Lamanai by guided river trip from Orange Walk not just to avoid the long and bumpy road, but also to take advantage of the river trip itself, which goes deep into the home of the countless colorful and unusual birds that live in the area. Many guides who do the 1½-hour river trip are experts in both archaeology and the area's wildlife, making it an especially worthwhile experience. The river voyage passes through some of the most beautiful jungle and lagoon country in Northern Belize, and the Mennonite community of Shipyard, before reaching Lamanai itself. There are a number of excellent tour guides in Orange Walk who specialize in the journey.

For those who can afford it, the classy **Lamanai Outpost Lodge** (☎670-3578, USA 954-636-1107; www.lamanai.com; r from BZ$315; P @ 📶) is the perfect riverside option for fully exploring Lamanai. About 1 mile south of the ruins, the outpost is perched on a hillside just above the lagoon, and boasts panoramic views from its bar and gorgeous open-air dining room.

Getting There & Away

If you decide to go without a guide, you can get to the village of Indian Church (next to Lamanai) from Orange Walk, but the bus goes only twice a week on Monday and Friday. You'll need to find somewhere to spend a few nights while waiting for your return bus.

Orange Walk Town

POP 13,700

Orange Walk Town is many things to many people: agricultural town, economic hub, Mennonite meeting place, street-food city... but it is not generally considered a tourist town. The town itself, just 57 miles from Belize City, doesn't have much to keep travelers around for more than a day or two, but it is the premier base from which to make the superlative trip to the ruins of Lamanai and longer excursions into the wilds of Northern Belize. Orange Walk has a fine location beside the New River, which meanders lazily along the east side of town, and there are a few very nice (and reasonably priced) hotels and restaurants for visitors who choose to hang around for a bit.

Sleeping

St Christopher's Hotel HOTEL $

(☎302-1064; www.stchristophershotelbze.com; 10 Main St; r with fan/air-con BZ$80/120; P ❄ 📶) The flowering gardens and riverside setting make this otherwise nondescript hotel an attractive place to stay. The rooms themselves are spacious but plain. Riverboat trips to Lamanai pick you up right from the hotel grounds and your hosts – the Urbina family – are attentive and welcoming, in a low-key, unassuming sort of way.

Lamanai Landings HOTEL $$

(☎670-7846; Mile 51 Philip Goldson Hwy, Tower Hill; r BZ$160-200; ❄ 📶) On the New River Lagoon about 7km south of Orange Walk, this hotel is perfectly placed for trips to Lamanai and a variety of other adventure tours. All rooms face the lagoon and have balconies, air-con, modern bathrooms and cable TV. The on-site *palapa* restaurant is a great spot to enjoy the water views.

El Gran Mestizo RESORT **$$**
(☎322-2290; www.elgranmestizo.bz; 1 Naranjal St; dm BZ$30, cabañas BZ$130-160, family cabins BZ$200; P ❄ 📶) If you don't mind being a little way out of the center, El Gran Mestizo is a fantastic little resort on the banks of the New River. The compact *cabañas* are cozy and equipped with fridge, TV, air-con and comfy beds, while the premium cabins have a full kitchen and split-level living. There's even an immaculate six-bed dorm for budget travelers.

OFF THE BEATEN TRACK

DREAMY DIGS

Located in the middle of a 200-sq-mile private reserve in the far western corner of Orange Walk District, **Chan Chich Lodge** (☎223-4419, USA 800-343-8009; www.chanchich.com; Gallon Jug; cabañas incl breakfast BZ$750-950, villas with air-con BZ$1300; P @ 📶 🏊) is one of Belize's original ecolodges. The supremely comfortable thatched cabañas are built from local hardwoods, surround the partly excavated ruins of an ancient Maya plaza and feature wooden slat walls that open up to the sounds of nature.

Eating & Drinking

Come n' Dine Restaurant BREAKFAST, BELIZEAN **$**
(☎302-0311; Philip Goldson Hwy; dishes BZ$8-40; ⏱6am-5pm) Unassuming and unexpected, this roadside restaurant serves some of the best Belizean food around. Located right next to the gas station on a crook of the Philip Goldson Hwy just a couple of miles south of town, it's well placed for road-trippers (but also worth the trip if you are staying in town). Look for excellent stews, steaks and stir-fries.

★**Aegea Blue's** INTERNATIONAL **$$**
(☎628-0090; Main St, Banquitas Plaza; mains BZ$18-40; ⏱11am-11pm Wed-Sun) Aegea Blue's benefits from its lovely location on the New River and breezy garden setting. Like its sister restaurant in Corozal, the highlight here is the stone pizza oven but the menu has plenty of international dishes such as pasta, steaks and tacos, plus Belizean standards.

The cocktail bar here is among the most civilized places in Orange Walk for an evening drink.

Cocina Sabor BELIZEAN **$$**
(☎322-3482; Philip Goldson Hwy; mains BZ$15-45, light meals BZ$10-25; ⏱11am-10pm Wed-Mon) This welcoming place on the highway has a large menu of Belizean and international fare, from rice and beans to authentic pasta and flavorsome steak served in the spotless air-conditioned timber dining room. During the day it serves light meals such as burgers and wraps. Service is prompt and courteous, and there's a well-stocked bar.

Maracas Bar & Restaurant BELIZEAN **$$**
(☎322-2290; 1 Naranjal St; mains BZ$10-34; ⏱11:30am-10pm Wed-Sun, to 11pm Fri & Sat) For good eats in a fantastic natural riverside setting, take a taxi down to this restaurant at the El Gran Mestizo on the banks of the New River south of town. For the full experience pick a table in one of the waterside *palapas* and choose from Belizean, Mexican, seafood and international dishes on the ample menu.

Information

Belize Bank (34 Main St) ATM accepts all major credit cards.

Post Office (cnr Queen Victoria Ave & Arthur St; ⏱8am-5pm Mon-Thu, to 4pm Fri)

Scotia Bank (cnr Park & Main Sts) Accepts all cards.

Getting There & Away

Orange Walk is the major Northern Belize bus hub for buses plying the Corozal–Belize City route. There are half a dozen companies servicing this route and around 30 buses a day going in each direction. All long-distance buses, including services to Belize City, Corozal, Chetumal and Sarteneja, stop at the Dunn St **bus terminal** west of the cemetery. It was supposed to be a temporary facility and locals are still waiting for a permanent bus station.

Buses to rural destinations around Orange Walk District, such as **Copper Bank** (Progresso St), leave from various points around the market. Schedules are subject to change, so ask in advance around the market or at your hotel.

Buses heading north from Orange Walk begin at 6:45am and run until around 9:15pm. Heading south to Belize City, buses begin at 4:45am and run until 8:30pm. The trip to Belize City takes around two hours and costs BZ$5 to BZ$8; the trip to Corozal is slightly quicker and cheaper.

CROOKED TREE WILDLIFE SANCTUARY

Between November and April, migrating birds flock to the lagoons, rivers and swamps of the massive **Crooked Tree Wildlife Sanctuary** (CTWS; www.belizeaudubon.org; BZ$8; ⌚8am-4:30pm), which is managed by Belize Audubon. The best birdwatching is in April and May, when the low level of the lagoon draws thousands of birds into the open to seek food in the shallows. That said, at any time between December and May, birdwatchers are in for hours of ornithological bliss.

Boat-billed and bare-throated tiger herons, Muscovy and black-bellied whistling ducks, snail kites, ospreys, black-collared hawks and all of Belize's five species of kingfisher are among some 300 species recorded here. Jabiru storks, the largest flying bird in the Americas, with wingspans of up to 8ft, congregate here year-round but are particularly easy to spot in April and May.

At the entrance to the village, just off the causeway, stop by the **CTWS Visitor Center** (☎223-5004; ⌚8am-4:30pm) to browse the interesting displays, books and information materials for sale. It's here that you'll be asked to pay your admission fee. The helpful, knowledgeable staff will provide a village and trail map, as well as information on expert local bird guides. Some ccommodations options:

Beck's Bed & Breakfast (☎633-3398; www.becksbedandbreakfast.com; r BZ$196-327; P ❄ 📶 🏊) Tucked into a five-acre plot in Crooked Tree's interior, this pine forest–shrouded B&B offers the town's most sumptuous digs. The colonial-style home contains just three guest rooms, tastefully and lavishly appointed, and a fully equipped kitchen where amicable host Becky whips up authentic Belizean breakfasts. Outside, a lovely courtyard leads to a relaxing swimming pool surrounded by greenery.

Crooked Tree Lodge (☎365-6611, 626-3820; www.crookedtreelodgebelize.com; campsites per person BZ$20, cabañas BZ$175-225; P 📶) Mick is a British pilot who served for years in Belize; Angie was born and bred in Crooked Tree. This kind couple has found their little plot of paradise in Crooked Tree and installed beautifully crafted wood *cabañas*, all with private porches overlooking the lagoon and providing perfect sunrise views. The self-service waterfront bar and open-plan dining room are wonderful and welcoming.

Corozal Town

POP 12,300

Just 9 miles south of Mexico and 29 miles north of Orange Walk Town, Corozal sits charmingly on the soapy-blue waters of Corozal Bay and has a vibe different from any other town in Belize, with its obvious Mexican influence. Most of the town's wealth comes from its position as a commercial and farming center, rather than from tourism. In fact the town's fledgling tourism sector has been hit hard by the direct boat service between San Pedro and Chetumal, which has seen many travelers bypass Corozal altogether.

But Corozal remains a fine place to be a tourist as it escapes the holiday-ville atmosphere that haunts some other places in Belize. With ocean breezes, affordable hotels, fine food and easy access to the rest of the district, Corozal is worth a stop on the way to or from Mexico – if not a detour from your Belizean itinerary further south.

Sights

★Corozal House of Culture HISTORIC SITE

(Map p258; cnr 2nd St South & 1st Ave; ⌚9am-5pm Mon-Fri) FREE Built in 1886, this fine old Spanish Colonial building once housed a bustling market beside the old customs house. It was one of only 11 buildings spared by Hurricane Janet in 1955. Today the historic building houses a cultural center and museum with exhibits of local artifacts. It's also a de facto tourist office; pick up a copy of the *Corozal Town Historical Walk* leaflet for a short self-guided stroll. (See the Facebook page at www.facebook.com/CHOCNICH for monthly events.)

Santa Rita RUINS

(BZ$10; ⌚8am-6pm) Santa Rita was an ancient Maya coastal town that once occupied the same strategic trading position as present-day Corozal Town, namely the spot between two rivers – the Río Hondo (which now forms the Belize–Mexico border) and the New River (which enters Corozal Bay south of town). Much of Santa Rita remains unexcavated, but it's worth a short excursion out of town to explore the site.

Sleeping

Hotel Maya HOTEL $
(Map p258; ☎422-2082; hotelmaya@btl.net; 7th Ave, South End; d BZ$85, s/d with air-con BZ$95/120;) Run by the very friendly Rosita May, the Hotel Maya is a long-time favorite of budget-conscious travelers. Rooms are clean and homey, and enlivened by colorful bedspreads and paintings by local artists. Apartments are available for long-term rentals. In addition to being a licensed travel agent, Rosita is also a great source of local information.

Hok'ol K'in Guest House GUESTHOUSE $
(Map p258; ☎422-3329; www.corozal.net; 89 4th Ave; s/d/tr with fan BZ$77/104/109, with air-con BZ$92/120/130; @) With a Maya name meaning 'rising sun,' this modern, well-run, small hotel overlooking the bay may well be the best value in town. The large, impeccably clean rooms are designed to catch sea breezes. Each has two double beds, a bathroom and a balcony with hammock. Hok'ol K'in also has a cafe serving meals at reasonable prices (breakfasts are particularly good).

★**Serenity Sands** B&B $$
(☎669-2394; www.serenitysands.com; 50 Serenity Lane; d incl breakfast BZ$200-210, house BZ$220; P) Located about 3 miles north of Corozal Town, this B&B is off the beaten track, off the grid and out of this world. The remote beachside setting – guests have free use of the private beachfront pool – offers the perfect combination of isolation and accessibility, and the four spacious upper-story rooms are decorated with locally crafted furniture and have private balconies.

★**Almond Tree Resort** RESORT $$
(☎422-0006; www.almondtreeresort.com; 425 Bayshore Dr; r BZ$210-380; P) Tucked away on the bay south of town, Almond Tree is a gorgeous little 10-room resort and Corozal's most luxurious central offering. Most of the stylish suites have wonderful sea views, Caribbean-style furniture, Maya and Mexican artworks and modern bathrooms. Deluxe suites have full kitchenettes. The whole place is centered on lush grounds and a glorious swimming pool.

Eating & Drinking

★**Wood House Bistro** ASIAN $
(Map p258; ☎636-0209; 1st Ave; dishes BZ$9-30; noon-10pm Wed-Mon) Wood House is a real standout among the Chinese restaurants in Corozal (and Belize in general). The dining area is open-air, with solid timber furniture, a Caribbean-style bar and a world music soundtrack. The food is eclectic, offering more than the usual fried chicken. Singapore-style noodles are especially good, as are the dumplings, spicy wontons and extensive seafood offerings.

Venky's Kabab Corner INDIAN $
(Map p258; ☎402-0546; 5th St South; dishes BZ$10-15; 9am-9pm) Chef Venky is the premier – and, as far as we know, only – Hindu chef in Corozal, cooking excellent Indian meals, both meat and vegetarian. The place is not much to look at on the inside – in fact there is just one table that is usually covered in assorted clutter – but the food is excellent and filling.

Corozo Blue's PIZZA, BELIZEAN $$
(☎422-0090; Philip Goldson Hwy; mains BZ$15-35; 10am-midnight Sun-Thu, 10am-2am Fri & Sat;) The waterfront location at this semi-enclosed, stone-hewn restaurant and day resort is unbeatable, with indoor, beachfront and garden seating offering a spectacular view of the bay. It's popular for the stone-oven wood-fired pizzas, late breakfasts and formidable steaks, but also burgers and Belize standards such as rice and beans and *ceviche*.

Jam Rock BAR
(Map p258; ☎402-2205; 1st Ave; 11am-midnight Wed-Mon) In a park right by the bay, this open-air watering hole catches plenty of breeze and is popular with expats and locals alike. Tasty meals are served from noon to 10pm, the bar is well stocked and there's a convivial tropical vibe.

Information

Belize Bank (cnr 5th Ave & 1st St North; 9am-4pm Mon-Fri) Situated on the plaza; ATM accepts most international credit cards.

Corozal Hospital (☎422-2076; Santa Rita Rd; 24hr) This hospital is located northwest of the center of town on the way to Chetumal (Mexico).

Corozal House of Culture Can help with local information, including a self-guided historical walking tour.

Corozal Town

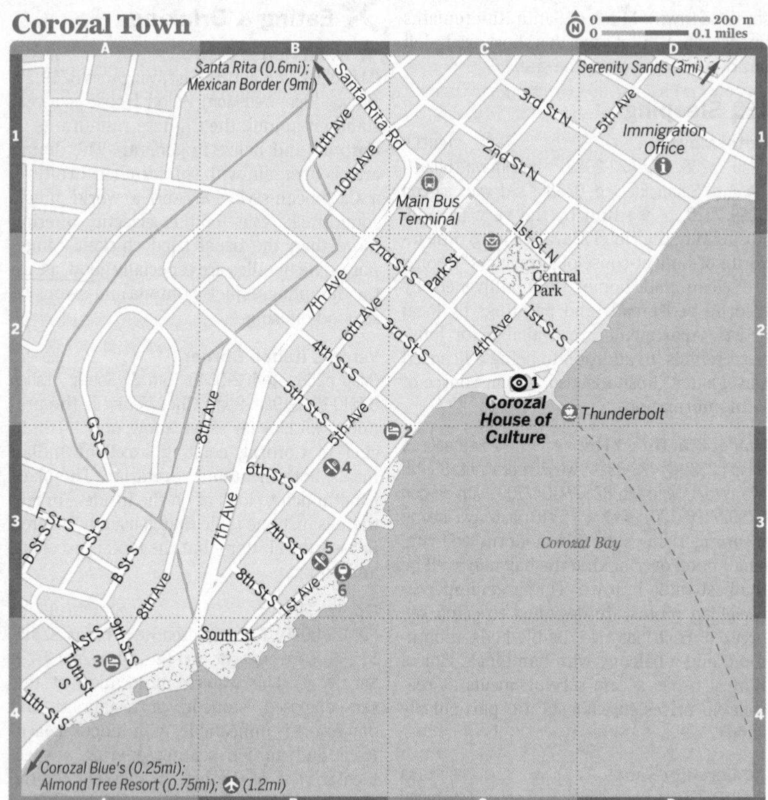

Corozal Town

Immigration Office (Map p258; ☎402-0123; 4th Ave; ⏰8am-4pm Mon-Thu, to 3:30pm Fri) Provides 30-day visa extensions for most nationalities.

Post Office (Map p258; 5th Ave; ⏰8:30am-noon & 1-4:30pm Mon-Thu, to 4pm Fri) On the site of Fort Barlee, facing the plaza.

Getting There & Away

AIR

Corozal's airstrip (CZH) is a couple of miles south of the town center in Ranchito. Taxis (BZ$10) meet incoming flights. Both **Tropic Air** (☎226-2012; www.tropicair.com) and **Maya Island Air** (☎422-2333; www.mayaislandair.com) fly in and out of Corozal with direct flights to San Pedro.

BOAT

Corozal is connected to Sarteneja and San Pedro by regular boat. **Thunderbolt** (Map p258; ☎422-0026, 610-4475; 1st Ave) is the town's main water-taxi service, and while the advent of the Chetumal to San Pedro boat has made this journey less popular, crossing the border by bus and taking this boat is significantly cheaper.

It leaves Corozal at 7am, returning from San Pedro at 3pm, stopping at Sarteneja only on request. The trip to Sarteneja takes 30 minutes and costs BZ$25/50 one way/return; San Pedro is two hours away and will cost you BZ$50/90 one way/return.

BUS

Corozal's **main bus terminal** (Map p258) is a key stop for nearly all of the myriad bus lines that ply the Philip Goldson Hwy down to Orange Walk and Belize City. At last count, 30 buses daily were doing the 2½-hour run from Corozal Town to Belize City, from 3:30am until 7pm; there are half a dozen buses in the other direction on the 15-minute run to the Mexican border, with the last coming through around 4pm. There are a couple of very early direct buses to Belmopan via Orange Walk at 3am and 3:30am.

Sarteneja

POP 3500

If you came to Belize in search of sparkling blue waters, delicious fresh seafood, fauna-rich forests and affordable prices, look no further than Sarteneja (sar-ten-*eh*-ha). This tiny fishing and shipbuilding village, located near the northeastern tip of the Belizean mainland, is a charming base from which to explore both the nautical and jungle treasures of the region.

Sights & Activities

Shipstern Conservation & Management Area NATURE RESERVE

(660-1807; www.visitshipstern.com; BZ$10; 8am-5pm) Run by a nonprofit organization, this large nature reserve, which protects 43 sq miles of semideciduous hardwood forests, wetlands, lagoons and coastal mangrove belts, has its headquarters 3.5 miles southwest of Sarteneja on the road to Orange Walk. Lying in a transition zone between Central America's tropical forests and a drier Yucatán-type ecosystem, the reserve's mosaic of habitats is rare in Belize. You can also stay overnight here.

Sarteneja Tour Guide Association ADVENTURE

(621-6465; North Front St; 9am-5pm) This cooperative of enthusiastic young guides rents out kayaks (BZ$10/50 per hour/day) and runs tours around Sarteneja and to the ruins at Cerro Maya. It also organizes boat trips to remote Bacalar Chico at the northern trip of Ambergris Caye (BZ$160 per visitor). The office is on the main waterfront.

Sleeping

Shipstern Nature Reserve Bungalows LODGE $

(660-1807; www.visitshipstern.com; Shipstern Conservation & Management Area; dm/s/d BZ$40/80/100) Located 3 miles out of town, these four bungalows are a great choice for visitors intending to take early nature tours or looking to be surrounded by wilderness. The air-con rooms have private bathroom and open out onto a screened porch for enjoying the sounds of the jungle.

Backpackers Paradise CABAÑAS, CAMPGROUND $

(607-1873, 423-2016; www.cabanasbelize.wordpress.com; Bandera Rd; camping BZ$12, s/d/tr BZ$45/55/60, cabañas BZ$50/66/70, family house BZ$60/80/90;) Peaceful, sustainable and affordable, this laid-back and very rustic spot set on lush grounds is a 15-minute walk from the beach and is a good base for budget travelers. Apart from camping, there's a range of fairly basic screened *cabañas,* some with private bathrooms, and two excellent Mennonite-built freestanding houses sleeping four to six people.

BELIZE CITY TO BELMOPAN

Formerly the Western Hwy and still referred to as such by many locals, the George Price Hwy stretches from Belize City through the village of Hattieville, and on to Belmopan and Cayo District.

Sights

★Belize Zoo ZOO

(625-3604, 822-8000; www.belizezoo.org; Mile 29 George Price Hwy; adult/child BZ$30/10; 8:30am-5pm, last entry 4:15pm) If most zoos are maximum-security wildlife prisons, then the Belize Zoo is more like a halfway house for wild animals that can't make it on the outside. A must-visit on any trip to Belize District, the zoo has many animals you're unlikely to see elsewhere – several tapirs (a Belizean relative of the rhino) including a baby, *gibnuts,* a number of coatimundi (they look like a cross between a raccoon and a monkey), scarlet macaws, white-lipped peccaries, pumas and many others.

Monkey Bay Wildlife Sanctuary WILDLIFE RESERVE

(664-2731, 822-8032; www.monkeybaybelize.com; Mile 31.5 George Price Hwy; 7am-5pm) A natural, privately protected area just off one of the country's main highways, this 1070-acre wildlife sanctuary and environmental education center offers lodging and activities for casual travelers, as well as internship activities for those with a more long-term interest in Belize. A well-stocked library provides plenty of reference and reading matter on natural history and the country.

★Nohoch Che'en Caves Branch Archaeological Reserve CAVING
(Map p262; park admission BZ$10; ⌚8am-5pm) This extensive network of limestone caves northwest of Belmopan is super-popular for cave-tubing, kayaking and spelunking. The Caves Branch River flows through nine caves, providing ideal conditions for floating through on a rubber tube or allowing for exploration of side passages that lead to other caves, such as the spectacular Crystal Cave.

WESTERN BELIZE (CAYO DISTRICT)

Cayo District is Belize's premier adventure and eco-activity region. The lush environs of the Wild West are covered with jungle, woven with rivers, waterfalls and azure pools, riddled with caves and dotted with Maya ruins ranging from small, tree-covered hills to massive, magnificent temples. Cahal Pech, Xunantunich, El Pilar and the mother of all Belizean Maya sites, Caracol, are all in Cayo.

Belmopan

POP 19,460

Like many purpose-built capital cities around the world, Belmopan can seem a bit dull at first glance. Wide ordered streets, empty urban parklands and drab government buildings conspire to give it a desolate feel. The exception is the vibrant central market area, where cheap food stalls and incoming buses provide some welcome activity.

But this is the national capital, a major transport hub, a place to extend your visa and an easygoing university city with a decent range of restaurants. More importantly, it's a useful base for exploring nearby caves, national parks, the Hummingbird Hwy and most of the attractions in eastern Cayo.

Sights & Activities

The main market days are Tuesday and Friday, when stallholders come from all over the district to sell produce.

George Price Center for Peace & Development MUSEUM
(☎822-1054; www.gpcbelize.com; Price Center Rd; ⌚8am-5pm Mon-Thu, to 4pm Fri) FREE This museum and conference center celebrates the life of Belize's beloved statesman and first prime minister after independence, George Price, who died in 2011. As well as photographs and information panels, there's an archive of documents and letters written by Price.

Guanacaste National Park NATIONAL PARK
(Map p262; George Price Hwy; BZ$5; ⌚8am-4:30pm) Belize's smallest national park was declared in 1990 and is named for the giant guanacaste tree on its southwestern edge. The tree survived the axes of canoe-makers but has now died naturally, though it still stands in its jungle habitat. The 51-acre park, off the highway at the Belmopan turnoff, is framed by Roaring Creek and the Belize River, with 2 miles of hiking trails that will introduce you to the abundant local trees and colorful birds.

Sleeping

★El Rey Hotel HOTEL $
(☎822-3438; www.elreyhotel.com; 23 Moho St; s/d/tr from BZ$90/100/110, ste BZ$180/190/200; P❄☜) Northeast of town, El Rey is Belmopan's best budget offering, an affordable and welcoming place with 12 plain, clean ground-floor rooms equipped with private bathroom, TV and wi-fi, plus one budget room available for BZ$70. All rooms have air-con, there's a small cafe and tours can be booked here.

★Hibiscus Hotel HOTEL $$
(☎633-5323, 822-0400; www.hibiscusbelize.com; Market Sq; s/d BZ$110/120; ⌚reception from 2pm Mon-Sat; P❄☜) Close to Belmopan's lively marketplace, this neat little place has just six motel-style rooms. Comforts include king and twin-sized beds, flat-screen cable TV, bath tubs, and tea and coffee facilities. There's an eco angle – some of the profits go to support local avian conservation and rescue projects – and the decent Corkers restaurant and bar is upstairs.

★Market Food Stalls MARKET $
(Market Sq; from BZ$2; ⌚6am-6pm) For a cheap meal, you can't beat the food stalls in the market square. They serve quick-fire Mexican snacks such as burritos and *salbutes* (mini-tortillas, usually stuffed with chicken), as well as Belizean standards such as beans and rice or cow-foot soup, or omelets and fry-jacks for breakfast.

★**Caladium Restaurant** BELIZEAN, SEAFOOD $
(☎822-2754; Market Sq; mains BZ$5-35; ⊙7:30am-8pm Mon-Fri, to 7pm Sat; ❄) In the market area, the Caladium is regarded by many as Belmopan's best restaurant. The intimate dining room goes well with the menu of Belizean favorites, such as fried fish and coconut rice, stew beef and BBQ chicken. Well-made burgers sit comfortably alongside Belizean treats such as lobster creole. Open early for breakfast.

Scotchies JAMAICAN $
(Map p262; ☎832-2203; 7753 Hummingbird Hwy; mains BZ$7-15; ⊙11am-9pm Mon-Thu, to 9:30pm Fri & Sat; 📶) Scotchies is a Jamaican transplant serving smoky jerk chicken and pork, sausage, wings and ribs, along with sides such as mashed sweet potato, yam, breadfruit and Red Stripe beer. Dining is in a cool garden beneath one of the octagonal thatched *palapas*.

ℹ Information

Belize Bank (Constitution Dr) and **Scotiabank** (Constitution Dr) keep regular banking hours and have 24/7 ATM access.

Darah Travel (☎822-3272; www.belizetravelservices.com; 21 Moho St) This Belmopan-based travel agency can organise flights, transfers and adventure tours throughout Cayo and Southern Belize.

Immigration Office (☎822-3860; Mountain View Blvd, ⊙8am-5pm Mon-Thu, to 3:30pm Fri) Cayo's big new immigration office offers 30-day visa extension stamps for BZ$50. It gets busy, so arrive early.

Western Regional Hospital (☎822-0666; off N Ring Rd) Just north of the city center, this is the only emergency facility between Belize City and San Ignacio.

Post Office (⊙8am-noon & 1-5pm Mon-Thu, to 4:30pm Fri)

US Embassy (p288) From visa and passport information to marriage advice and hurricane preparedness tips, the US embassy can help. The website is comprehensive and easy to navigate.

ℹ Getting There & Away

AIR

Belmopan's tiny airstrip is just a few miles east of the city.

Tropic Air (☎226-2012; www.tropicair.com) has three daily flights to San Pedro (BZ$260, 55 minutes) and Belize City Domestic (BZ$142, 25 minutes), and two to Belize City International (BZ$190, 25 minutes).

BUS

Belmopan's **bus terminal** (☎802-2799; Market Sq) is Cayo's main transit hub, and all buses (regardless of company) heading south or west from the Belize District, as well as north and west from Dangriga (and points south), stop in Belmopan. Along the George Price Hwy, buses head east to Belize City (BZ$6, one hour) and west to San Ignacio (BZ$3, one hour) and Benque Viejo del Carmen (BZ$4, 1½ hours) every half-hour from 6am to 7pm. Along the Hummingbird Hwy, buses go south to Dangriga (BZ$7, two hours) once or twice an hour from 6:45am until 7:15pm. From Dangriga, most buses continue on to Punta Gorda (BZ$20, 5½ hours).

ℹ Getting Around

The city center, within the ring road, is compact and easily negotiated on foot. Taxis gather outside the bus terminal. A short fare around town is BZ$5.

Hummingbird Highway

The lyrically named Hummingbird Hwy is one of the prettiest drives in Belize, winding its way through jungle, citrus orchards and impossibly small villages as it skirts the northern edges of the Maya Mountain range between Belmopan and Dangriga. Passing cave and jungle adventure activities, on a clear day the road affords plenty of postcard-perfect vistas. You can drive the 55-mile length of it in two hours, but along the way are some excellent ecolodges and budget accommodations, just begging for an overnight stay.

Sights & Activities

St Herman's Blue Hole National Park NATIONAL PARK
(Map p262; BZ$8; ⊙8am-4:30pm) The 575-acre St Herman's Blue Hole National Park contains St Herman's Cave, one of the few caves in Belize that you can visit without a guide. The visitors center (where flashlights can be rented for BZ$3) is 11 miles along the Hummingbird Hwy from Belmopan. From here a 500yd trail leads to St Herman's Cave. A path leads 200yd into the cave alongside an underground river – to go any further you'll need a guide.

Caves Branch Adventures ADVENTURE
(Map p262; ☎610-3451; www.cavesbranch.com; Mile 41.5 Hummingbird Hwy; tours per person BZ$150-500) At Ian Anderson's the signature adventures include jungle treks, river

Western Belize

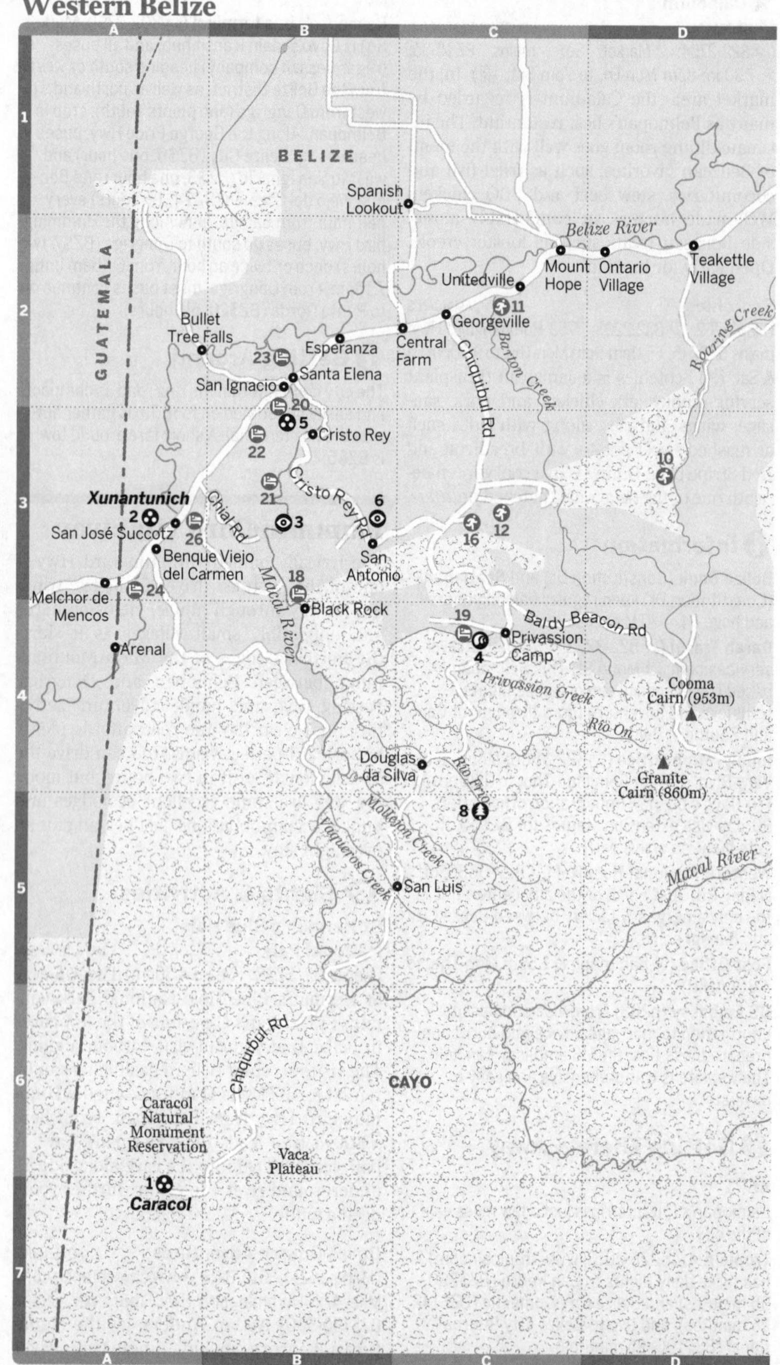

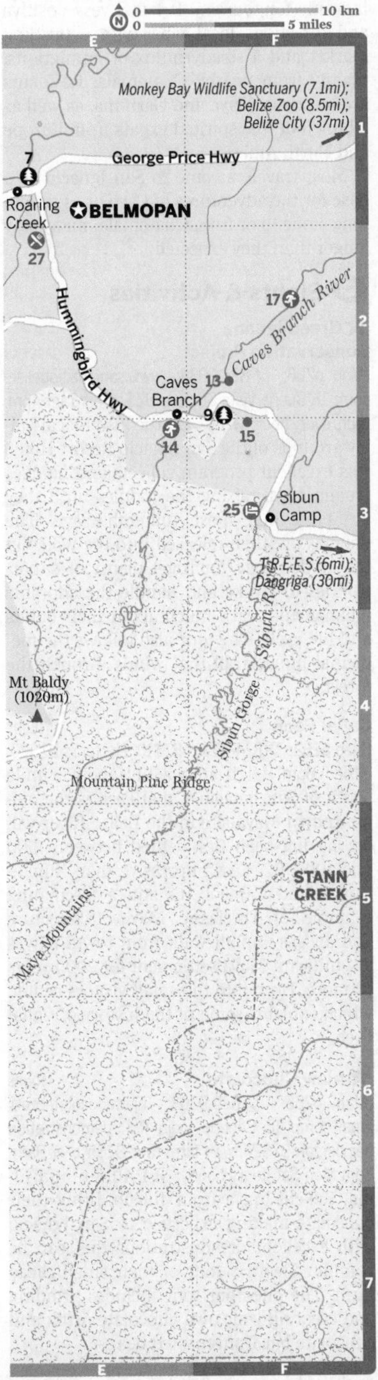

Western Belize

Top Sights

1 Caracol A7
2 Xunantunich A3

Sights

3 Belize Botanic Gardens B3
4 Big Rock Falls C4
5 Cahal Pech B3
6 García Sisters' Place B3
7 Guanacaste National Park E1
8 Mountain Pine Ridge Forest Reserve C5
9 St Herman's Blue Hole National Park F2

Activities, Courses & Tours

10 Actun Tunichil Muknal D3
11 Belize Wildlife & Referral Clinic C2
12 Calico Jack's C3
13 Caves Branch Adventures F2
14 Lamanai Chocolate E3
15 Maya Guide Adventures F3
16 MET Outfitters & Lodge C3
17 Nohoch Che'en Caves Branch Archaeological Reserve F2

Sleeping

18 Black Rock Lodge B3
19 Blancaneaux Lodge C4
20 Cahal Pech Village Resort B2
Ian Anderson's Caves Branch Jungle Lodge .... (see 13)
21 Lodge at Chaa Creek B3
22 Log Cab-Inn B3
23 Midas Resort B2
24 Río Mopán Lodge A3
25 Sleeping Giant Rainforest Lodge F3
26 Trek Stop A3

Eating

27 Scotchies E2

cave and waterfall cave expeditions, and the Black Hole Drop. Adventure activities are exclusive, exciting and depart from the excellent lodge just off the Hummingbird Hwy.

Maya Guide Adventures TOURS

(Map p262; ☎600-3116; www.mayaguide.bz; caving from BZ$170, overnight jungle tours from BZ$300) Highly experienced Kekchí Maya guide Marcos Cucul runs jungle survival tours ranging from overnight to multiple nights. Tours feature trekking, leadership and survival skills with the night spent suspended in Hennessy hammocks. With over a decade's experience as an area guide, Cucul enjoys an excellent reputation.

Sleeping

T.R.E.E.S CABIN $

(Toucan Ridge Ecology & Education Society; ☎669-6818, 665-2134; Mile 27.5 Hummingbird Hwy; bunkhouse BZ$40, s/d cabin BZ$125/140, without bathroom BZ$80/100;) T.R.E.E.S is part field station and part ecofriendly lodge, welcoming research students, interns, birders and passing backpackers alike. The operation is nonprofit, with proceeds going into community conservation projects and ecotourism. There are lectures in biodiversity, field courses and guided activities, along with yoga, hiking and village tours.

★Ian Anderson's Caves Branch Jungle Lodge LODGE $$$

(Map p262; ☎Belize 610-3452, USA & Canada 866-357-2698; www.cavesbranch.com; Mile 41.5 Hummingbird Hwy; d cabañas & bungalows BZ$340-$492, d, ste & tree houses BZ$588-$1182;) Hidden away in dense jungle off the Hummingbird Hwy, Ian Anderson's is a 90-sq-mile private estate that acts as a base for a variety of exclusive jungle activities on the property. Accommodations are superb jungle-chic, and guests can indulge themselves in the beautiful riverside pool and hot tub, and enjoy meals and cocktails at the family-style restaurant overlooking the river.

Sleeping Giant Rainforest Lodge LODGE $$$

(Map p262; ☎822-0037, toll free 888-822-2448; www.vivabelize.com/sleeping-giant; Mile 36.5 Hummingbird Hwy; r BZ$480-880, penthouse BZ$1120;) The swanky Sleeping Giant has 20 rooms either garden-facing in the main lodge or in vast individual cottages, *casitas* or suites scattered around a lush garden. They feature mod-cons such as air-con, espresso machine and local hardwood furniture, while the best have gorgeous bathrooms with skylight tubs or Jacuzzis.

San Ignacio

POP 21,150

San Ignacio is the heart and soul of the Cayo District, a vibrant traveler center from where all roads and activities fan out. Together with twin-town Santa Elena, on the east bank of the Macal River, this is the main population center of Cayo, with lots of good budget accommodations, decent restaurants and frequent transport.

But as much as it is geared to travelers, San Ignacio is no inland San Pedro, existing only for tourism. It has a very positive and infectious local vibe, with a bustling market and a steady influx of immigrants, mainly from nearby Guatemala. Residents are mestizos, Maya and Garifuna, as well as a bunch of free-spirited expats from Europe and North America.

Most travelers come to San Ignacio as a base for the adventures of Cayo or as a stepping stone to or from Guatemala; many stay longer than they expected.

Sights & Activities

★Green Iguana Conservation Project GARDENS

(Map p266; ☎824-2034; www.sanignaciobelize.com; 18 Buena Vista St; tour BZ$18; 8am-4pm, tours every hour;) On the lush Macal Valley grounds of the San Ignacio Resort Hotel, this excellent program collects and hatches iguana eggs, raising the reptiles until they are past their most vulnerable age. The iguanas are then released into the wild. On the guided tour you'll get plenty of opportunities to stroke and handle the adorable iguanas and learn much about their habits and life cycle. The tour also follows the medicinal jungle trail that winds through the forest.

Cahal Pech RUINS

(Map p262; ☎824-4236; BZ$10, 2hr tours BZ$20; 6am-6pm) High atop a hill about a mile south of San Ignacio, Cahal Pech is the oldest-known Maya site in the Belize River valley, having been first settled between 1500 and 1000 BC. Less impressive than Xunantunich and Caracol, it's still a fascinating example of Preclassic Maya architecture and an easy uphill walk from town. It was a significant Maya settlement for 2000 years or more. Drop into the small visitors center, which explains some of the history of Cahal Pech.

★Ajaw Chocolate TOURS

(Map p266; ☎635-9363; ajawchocolatebze@gmail.com; 16 Benque Viejo Rd; demonstration per person BZ$24, with farm tour BZ$50; 9am-6pm Mon-Sat, tours hourly;) Adrian and Elida, Kekchí Maya from Toledo, bring their chocolate-making expertise to San Ignacio with excellent demonstrations that can be combined with a tour of their small cacao farm. The one-hour tour includes grinding and creating your own chocolate drink and chocolate bar from roasted beans.

Tours

San Ignacio, or the lodges around it, are the natural base for visiting the cultural and natural riches of the Cayo region. There are numerous tour operators on Burns Ave and most hotels organize the same tours working with the same operators.

Trips to Actun Tunichil Muknal (p271) and Barton Creek Cave can only be done with a guide, while Caracol is usually visited by vehicle convoy.

David's Adventure Tour ADVENTURE
(Map p266; 804-3674; www.davidsadventuretours.com; Savannah St; canoe tours BZ$60-90, Barton Creek BZ$150) Based just across the street from the Saturday market, David's is an experienced operator offering ecofriendly tours to sites throughout the area, specializing in river canoe trips, cave adventures and overnight jungle treks.

Pacz Tours TOURS
(Map p266; 824-0536; www.pacztours.net; 30 Burns Ave; tours BZ$90-300) Offers reliably excellent service and knowledgeable guides to Actun Tunichil Muknal and Tikal, plus kayaking, river canoeing and horseback riding, as well as shuttle transfers all over Cayo.

Carlos the Caveman CAVE TOUR
(669-7619; www.carloscaveman.com) Cayo native Carlos Panti has a high level of cave and cultural knowledge, and specializes in small-group spiritually themed journeys into the Actun Tunichil Muknal cave.

Sleeping

San Ignacio has the best range of good-value budget accommodations (including camping) in Belize, with a few excellent midrange places as well. More luxurious options – some of the best in Belize – are the jungle and mountain lodges out of town.

Bella's Backpackers HOSTEL $
(Map p266; 824-2248; www.bellasinbelize.com; 4 Galvez St; dm BZ$25-30, d with/without bathroom BZ$90/60;) Bella's is a classic backpackers, with rustic charm, bohemian travelers of all ages floating about and a sociable rooftop chill-out area with hammocks and couches. Well-laid-out dorms with sturdy timber bunk beds and bathrooms are complemented by a few private rooms with screened-in windows and a rock-motif bathroom. Bella also has a jungle lodge at Cristo Rey.

Casa Blanca Guest House GUESTHOUSE $
(Map p266; 824-2080; www.casablancaguesthouse.com; 10 Burns Ave; s/d/tr BZ$50/70/90, with air-con BZ$75/100/120;) Intimate, immaculate and secure, Casa Blanca is everything you need from a budget guesthouse. Decent-sized rooms have clean white walls and crisp fresh linens. Guests have a comfy sitting area, a clean kitchen and a breezy balcony from which to watch the world go by.

Midas Resort HOTEL $$
(Map p262; 824-3172; www.midasbelize.com; Branch Mouth Rd; cottage/cabañas/casitas BZ$152/175/370, d/f BZ$235/370;) In a budget town, Midas stands out as one of San Ignacio's better midrange choices. The large pool, funky bar and friendly staff complement an interesting array of accommodations from hotel-style rooms in the main building to cottages, *cabañas* and a two-bedroom *casita* at the back of the property. It's in a quiet location a five-minute walk north of the market.

Rainforest Haven Inn HOTEL $$
(Map p266; 674-1984; www.rainforesthavens.com; 2 Victoria St; r BZ$130, 2-bedroom apt BZ$150;) Rainforest Haven is a good find if you're looking for midrange comfort at an almost budget price. The five rooms have air-con, flat-screen TV with cable, fridge, wi-fi and hot-water showers. The two-bedroom apartment boasts a full kitchen – a steal for families or groups. There's a cool chill-out spot on the 2nd floor.

Cahal Pech Village Resort RESORT $$
(Map p262; 824-3740; www.cahalpech.com; Cahal Pech Hill; d/cabañas/ste BZ$215/270/330;) Atop Cahal Pech hill, half a mile up from the town center, you can enjoy fine views from this upscale family resort. The resort has 21 bright, tile-floored, air-con rooms, nine family suites and 27 dreamy thatch-roof *cabañas*. The amazing two-level cascading pool (nonguests BZ$10) is a great place to cool off.

★ **San Ignacio Resort Hotel** HOTEL $$$
(Map p266; 824-2034; www.sanignaciobelize.com; 18 Buena Vista St; s/d from BZ$400/480, ste BZ$890-1320;) The most upscale hotel in San Ignacio by a considerable margin (Queen Elizabeth stayed here, as the photos in the lobby attest), this is boutique luxury but with welcoming, professional staff and a serene location just uphill from the town center. Beyond the pool area the

San Ignacio

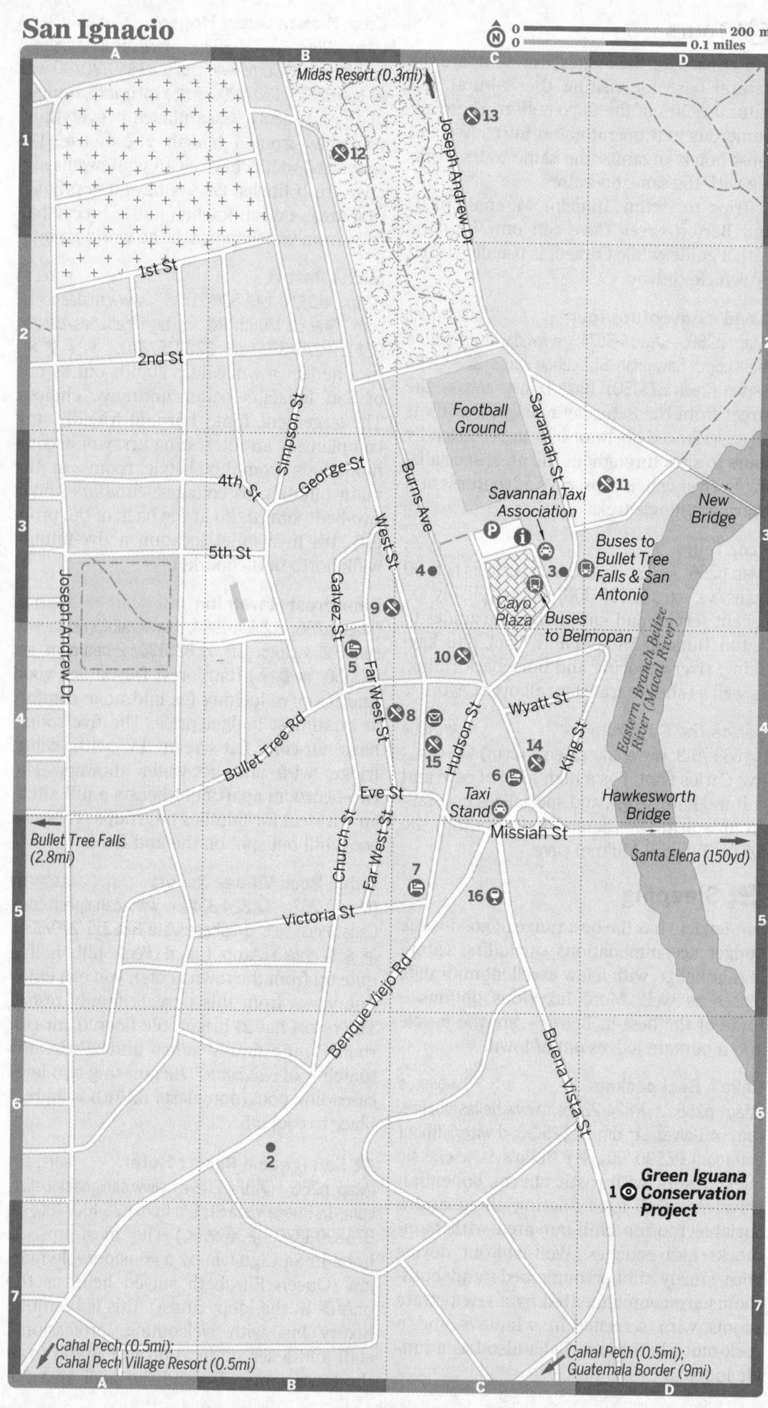
0 200 m
0 0.1 miles
Midas Resort (0.3mi)
Joseph Andrew Dr
1st St
2nd St
Simpson St
4th St
George St
5th St
West St
Burns Ave
Football Ground
Savannah St
Savannah Taxi Association
New Bridge
Buses to Bullet Tree Falls & San Antonio
Cayo Plaza
Buses to Belmopan
Galvez St
Far West St
Bullet Tree Rd
Hudson St
Wyatt St
King St
Eastern Branch Belize River (Macal River)
Eve St
Taxi Stand
Hawkesworth Bridge
Missiah St
Bullet Tree Falls (2.8mi)
Santa Elena (150yd)
Church St
Victoria St
Benque Viejo Rd
Buena Vista St
Green Iguana Conservation Project
Cahal Pech (0.5mi); Cahal Pech Village Resort (0.5mi)
Cahal Pech (0.5mi); Guatemala Border (9mi)

property is backed by jungle and home to the excellent Green Iguana Conservation Project (p264).

Eating

★Cenaida's — BELIZEAN $

(Map p266; 631-2526; Far West St; mains BZ$7-12; 11am-9pm Mon-Tue & Thu-Sat, to 5pm Wed) One of the best places in town for authentic traditional Belizean food, Cenaida's is a no-frills diner serving rice and beans, stew chicken and cow-foot soup, along with burritos and fajitas.

Farmers Market — MARKET $

(Map p266; from 5am Sat) Saturday is the big market day in San Ignacio when traders come from all over Cayo to sell fresh produce, handicrafts and clothing. The dozen or so food stalls set up in the middle of the action serve quick-fire street food – cheap and tasty. Smaller versions of the market happen most other days of the week.

Pop's Restaurant — DINER $

(Map p266; 824-3366; www.popsbelize.com; West St; breakfast BZ$4-15; 6:30am-3pm) You may feel like you're in a *Seinfeld* episode at this friendly diner with booth seating. The best omelets in town, along with waffles and good coffee, make this San Ignacio's worst-kept breakfast secret and a cozy place to while away the morning. Good subs and burgers at lunchtime.

★Guava Limb Cafe — INTERNATIONAL $$

(Map p266; 824-4837; www.guavalimb.com; 79 Burns Ave; mains BZ$16-45; 11am-10pm Tue-Sat, to 5pm Sun;) One of San Ignacio's slickest restaurants, boutique Guava Limb is set in an adorable turquoise two-story building with a serene outdoor garden area. Fresh organic ingredients are sourced from the owners' farm or local providers to create an eclectic international menu that might include Indonesian *gado gado,* a Middle Eastern platter or conch *ceviche.*

Eva's — BREAKFAST, BELIZEAN $$

(Map p266; Burns Ave; mains BZ$12-35; 6am-10pm;) Open early for breakfast, Eva's is a popular traveler hangout at the busy end of Burns Ave. The menu is pretty standard fare with Belizean and Western breakfasts, Belizean rice and beans, Creole curry, Tex-Mex, burgers, steaks and pasta. The street-side seating is a good spot for a cold beer and people-watching.

Ko-Ox Han-nah — BELIZEAN, INDIAN $$

(Map p266; 623-0019; 5 Burns Ave; breakfast BZ$7-16, Belizean mains BZ$10-12, Asian mains BZ$22-32; 6am-9pm;) The name means 'let's go eat' in Maya, but Han-nah's is far from just another Belizean restaurant. The eclectic menu features an intriguing range of Indian dishes, such as lamb curry and Burmese shrimp curry, with all food sourced from local farms. Breakfasts are good, while lunch and dinner are a mix of Mexican, burgers and Indo-Asian.

Hode's Place — BELIZEAN, AMERICAN $$

(Map p266; 804-2522; Branch Mouth Rd; mains BZ$6-30; 9am-10pm;) Locals love this rambling barn-sized place just north of the city center. A large terrace restaurant opening onto a citrus orchard and kids' playground, it's a popular spot with families or for an evening drink. Friendly service and satisfying food – from burritos and fajitas to steaks, seafood and rice and beans – complete the recipe.

★Running W Steakhouse — INTERNATIONAL, STEAKHOUSE $$$

(Map p266; San Ignacio Resort Hotel, 18 Buena Vista St; mains BZ$24-65; 7am-9:30pm Mon-Thu,

SUMPTUOUS STAY

Owned by movie director Francis Ford Coppola (who keeps a personal villa, 'the Francis Ford Coppola Villa,' complete with attendant and private pool; yours for BZ$1800 per night), the indulgent **Blancaneaux Lodge** (Map p262; ☎824-3878, USA 800-746-3743, USA 866-356-5881; www.thefamilycoppolahideaways.com/en/blancaneaux-lodge; cabañas BZ$770-1200, 2-bedroom villas BZ$1470; P) offers 20 thatched cabañas and luxury villas, spread around beautifully manicured gardens, with some looking right over the picturesque Privassion Creek.

to 10:30pm Fri-Sun, 9am-2:30pm Sun brunch;) One of San Ignacio's top dining splurges, the restaurant at the San Ignacio Resort Hotel is named for the owner's Running W ranch that supplies most of the best meat in western Belize. Steaks are a specialty, including Black Angus rib eye, but there's also a wide range of thoughtfully prepared international and Belizean dishes.

Dine in the air-conditioned restaurant or out on the romantic, candlelit balcony patio overlooking the pool and jungle. There's an attached bar with slick service.

Crave House of Flavour INTERNATIONAL $$$
(Map p266; ☎824-3707; 24 West St; mains BZ$16-45; 6-9pm) A gourmet addition to San Ignacio's dining, Crave is a tiny and intimate restaurant with just a few tables inside and out. The changing menu is broad-ranging but has a strong Italian, steakhouse and BBQ flavor. Highlights include rib eye, baby back ribs, oven roasted rabbit or spicy roasted lobster tail. Great for that romantic meal or splurge.

Drinking

Soul Project BAR
(Map p266; ☎653-1855; Buena Vista Rd; 6-11pm Wed & Fri;) Soul Project is a sweet bar and venue where local artist, filmmaker and conservationist Daniel Velazquez works hard to create a space for local and visiting artists and musicians. And he makes his own herbal fruit wine. It's only open Wednesday and Friday, so find out what's going on and definitely pencil in a night out here. It's below the Old House Hostel.

Information

Belize Bank (Burns Ave), **Scotiabank** (cnr Burns Ave & King St) and **Atlantic Bank** (Burns Ave) have ATMs that accept international Visa, MasterCard, Plus and Cirrus cards.

Cayo Welcome Center (Map p266; ☎634-8450; Savannah St, Cayo Plaza; 8am-5pm Mon-Fri, to 4pm Sat) The only tourist office in the Cayo District, this is a helpful, air-conditioned modern place in the central plaza. As well as some local exhibits, a short film about the region runs on a loop.

Post Office (Map p266; ☎824-2049; West St)

Getting There & Away

San Ignacio (surprisingly) has no bus station. Buses stop in the market plaza en route to/from Belize City (regular/express BZ$9/10, two hours), **Belmopan** (Map p266; Savannah St) (BZ$4, one hour) and Benque Viejo del Carmen (BZ$2, 30 minutes). Buses run in both directions about every half-hour from 3:30am to 7pm, with a less frequent service on Sunday.

From a **vacant lot** (Map p266) on Savannah St, buses go to San Antonio (BZ$3, 35 minutes) five or six times a day, Monday to Saturday and to Bullet Tree Falls (BZ$1, 15 minutes) roughly hourly from 10:30am to 5pm Monday to Saturday.

Several tour companies also run charter shuttle buses around Cayo and further afield. Sample fares include Guatemala border (BZ$50) and Belize City (BZ$150).

To really explore Cayo, a car is useful, preferably with good off-road capabilities and high clearance. Local car-hire companies include **Cayo Auto Rentals** (☎824-2222; www.cayoautorentals.com; 81 Benque Viejo Rd).

Several taxi stands are dotted around the town center; **Savannah Taxi Association** (Map p266; ☎824-2155; Savannah St; 24hr) is San Ignacio's main central taxi stand. Sample fares are BZ$25 to the Guatemalan border (9 miles), BZ$60 round-trip to Xunantunich, and BZ$80 to BZ$100 one-way to the Mountain Pine Ridge lodges. Taxis to Bullet Tree Falls (*colectivo*/private BZ$4/20) go from **Wyatt St** (Map p266; Benque Viejo Rd), just off Burns Ave.

Getting Around

San Ignacio is small enough that you can easily walk to most places of interest. If you're driving, note that parking can be difficult in the city center. Also pay attention to the one-way traffic system; Hawkesworth Bridge is one way leaving San Ignacio while New Bridge enters town north of the market and a new ring road allows you to bypass the town center completely.

Short taxi rides around town cost BZ$5.

Mountain Pine Ridge & Caracol

South of San Ignacio and the Western Hwy, the land begins to climb toward the heights of the Maya Mountains, whose arching ridge forms the border separating Cayo District from Stann Creek District to the east and Toledo District to the south.

In the heart of this highland area, 200 sq miles of submontane (ie on the foothills or lower slopes of mountains) pine forest is the **Mountain Pine Ridge Forest Reserve** (Map p262) FREE. The sudden switch from tropical rainforest to pine trees as you ascend to the Mountain Pine Ridge – a broad upland area of multiple ridges and valleys – is a little bizarre and somewhat startling. The reserve is full of rivers, pools, waterfalls and caves; the higher elevation means relief from both heat and mosquitoes. Beyond Mountain Pine Ridge is the spectacular Maya Ruin of Caracol.

Sights & Activities

★Caracol ARCHAEOLOGICAL SITE

(Map p262; BZ$30; 8am-4pm, convoy departs 9am) Once one of the most powerful cities in the entire Maya world, Caracol now lies enshrouded by thick jungle near the Guatemalan border, a 52-mile, roughly two- or three-hour drive from San Ignacio. Sitting high on the Vaca Plateau, this is the largest Maya site in Belize, having possibly stretched over 70 sq miles at its peak around AD 650. Nearly 40 miles of internal causeways radiate from the center to large outlying plazas and residential areas.

At its height, the city's population may have approached 150,000, more than twice as many people as Belize City has today. Though they had no natural water source, the people of Caracol dug artificial reservoirs to catch rainwater and grew food on extensive agricultural terraces. Its central area was a bustling place of temples, palaces, busy thoroughfares, craft workshops and markets. Caracol is not only the preeminent archaeological site in Belize but also exciting for its jungle setting and prolific birdlife. At the ticket office, a small visitors center outlines Caracol's history and has a helpful scale model, while a museum houses much of the sculpture found at Caracol. There are toilets, picnic tables and a small gift shop. Be sure to bring food, water and, if you're driving, a spare tire. Overnight stays are not permitted.

Big Rock Falls WATERFALL

(Map p262) The small but powerful Big Rock Falls on Privassion Creek are, for many, more impressive than the Thousand Foot Falls – not least because you can get up close and swim in the pools below. Take the road toward Gaïa River Lodge (signposted) and 1.5 miles past Blancaneaux Lodge turn along a track to the left marked 'Big Rock.' From the parking area it's a steep walk down (even steeper back up!), aided by timber steps.

García Sisters' Place CULTURAL CENTER

(Map p262; 671-1753; artistmai1981@gmail.com; Cristo Rey Rd, San Antonio; 7am-6pm) The García sisters display and sell a wide assortment of beautiful black-slate carvings. These five sisters developed this craft, which is now widely imitated around Belize. Their carvings, selling for between BZ$10 and BZ$200, depict a variety of subjects, including Maya deities and calendars. With advance notice the sisters also offer Maya ceremonies, blessings, massage and herbal tours.

Calico Jack's ADVENTURE SPORTS

(Map p262; 832-2478; www.calicojacksvillage.com; 7 Mile Rd, El Progresso; per person BZ$80-175; 8am-4pm) This 365-acre property boasts the largest state-of-the-art ziplining setup in Western Cayo, a nine-run, 15-platform zipline; various packages take you on different runs ranging from a 45-minute 'explorer' to a 90-minute 'ultimate adventure.' Adventurous visitors can try the jungle swing (BZ$60), which offers a trip across a canyon combined with a 55ft free-fall, or the cable walk.

MET Outfitters & Lodge HORSEBACK RIDING

(Map p262; 669-1124, USA 800-838-3918; www.metbelize.com; Mile 8 Chiquibul Rd; half-/full-day horseback rides BZ$136/200) For equestrians, nothing beats exploring the area from the back of a horse. Mountain Equestrian Trails (MET) has highly professional half-day and full-day local rides to Big Rock Falls, Barton Creek and more, as well as multiday riding packages, including accommodations in rustic *cabañas*. Expert guides can also arrange birdwatching, caving and vehicle tours.

West to Guatemala

Southwest from San Ignacio, the George Price Hwy runs across rolling countryside toward Benque Viejo del Carmen and the

Guatemalan border. There is a variety of places to stay along the highway and along diversions such as Chial Rd.

Sights

★Xunantunich RUINS

(Map p262; San José Succotz; BZ$10; ⏲7:30am-4pm) Set on a leveled hilltop, Xunantunich (shoo-nahn-too-neech) is one of Belize's most easily accessible and impressive Maya archaeological sites. Getting here is half the fun, with a free hand-cranked cable ferry taking you (and vehicles) across the Mopan River. Xunantunich may have been occupied as early as 1000 BC, but it was little more than a village. The large architecture that we see today began to be built in the 7th century AD.

From AD 700 to 850, Xunantunich was possibly politically aligned with Naranjo, 9 miles west in Guatemala. Together they controlled the western part of the Belize River valley, although the population probably never exceeded 10,000. Xunantunich partially survived the initial Classic Maya collapse of about 850 (when nearby Cahal Pech was abandoned), but was deserted by about 1000.

The site centers on Plazas A-2 and A-1, separated by Structure A-1. Just north of Plaza A-2, Structure A-11 and Plaza A-3 formed a **residential 'palace' area** for the ruling family. The dominant **El Castillo** (Structure A-6) rises 130ft high at the south end of Plaza A-1. El Castillo may have been the ruling family's ancestral shrine where they were buried and/or represented in sculpted friezes. Structures A-1 and A-13, at either end of Plaza A-2, were not built until the 9th century and would have had the effect of separating the ruling family from the rest of the population, possibly a response to the pressures that came with the decline of Classic Maya civilization at that time.

You can climb to the top of El Castillo to enjoy a spectacular 360-degree view. Its upper levels were constructed in two distinct phases. The first, built around 800, included an elaborate plaster frieze encircling the building; the second, built around 900, covered over most of the first and its frieze. The frieze on the east end of the building and part of the western one have been uncovered by archaeologists; these depict a series of Maya deities, with Chaac, the rain god, probably the central figure at the east end. The friezes you see today are replicas, with the originals underneath for safekeeping.

South of El Castillo is a partly overgrown area of lesser structures (Group C) that were abandoned as the city shrank after 900, leaving El Castillo (formerly at the center of the ancient city) on the southern edge of the occupied area.

There's a visitors center just past the ticket office. Inside are archaeological finds from the site, including pottery and jewelry, an interesting burial site and explanations of the El Castillo friezes.

To reach the ruins, take the ferry in San José Succotz village, then it's about 1 mile uphill to the parking lot and ticket office. Any bus from San Ignacio can drop you at the ferry point.

Belize Botanic Gardens GARDENS

(Map p262; ☎824-3101; www.belizebotanic.org; admission only BZ$16, per person self-guided/guided tour BZ$15/30; ⏲7am-5pm, last entry 3pm) The magnificent Belize Botanic Gardens, accessed from the grounds of Sweet Songs Jungle Lodge, hold samples of roughly one-quarter of the approximately 4000 species of plants in Belize. The bountiful 45-acre zone boasts 2 miles of trails, many fruit trees and four different Belizean habitats: wetlands, rainforest, Mountain Pine Ridge (with a lookout tower) and medicinal plants of the Maya.

Sleeping & Eating

★Trek Stop LODGE, CAMPGROUND $

(Map p262; ☎823-2265; www.thetrekstop.com; Mile 71 Western Hwy; camping per person BZ$14, d/tr/q with bathroom BZ$150/200/240, s/d without bathroom BZ$50/80; P@🛜≋) Trek Stop is a good option if you want to get out of San Ignacio on a budget and be close to Xunantunich. The backpackers' outpost consists of well-made timber cabins in a jungle setting just off the highway. There's an ecovibe but it has electricity and wi-fi. Plenty of hangout space, above ground pool and a cool little restaurant.

Log Cab-Inn CABAÑAS $$

(Map p262; ☎824-3367; www.logcabinn-belize.com; Mile 68 Western Hwy; d BZ$215, d cabañas BZ$260-325; P❄🛜≋) The name says it all, with 20 well-designed *cabañas* built from mahogany logs and furniture crafted at the on-site carpentry workshop. All *cabañas* have air-con, hot showers and cable TV, and the whole property is set on a citrus- and palm-dotted hillside. Meals are served in an open-air restaurant and bar overlooking a pool area.

ACTUN TUNICHIL MUKNAL

Actun Tunichil Muknal (Map p262; guided tour BZ$190) – the Cave of the Stone Sepulchre – is one of the most unforgettable and adventurous underground tours you can make in Belize. The guided trip into ATM takes you deep into the underworld that the ancient Maya knew as Xibalba. The entrance to the 3-mile-long cave lies in the northern foothills of the Maya Mountains.

Most people arrive on a guided tour from San Ignacio, Belmopan or the coastal resorts, but it's also possible to arrange a guide and self-drive.

The experience is moderately strenuous, starting with an easy 45-minute hike through the lush jungle, crossing Roaring Creek three times (your feet will be wet all day). At the wide, hourglass-shaped entrance to the cave, you'll don your helmet, complete with headlamp. To reach the cave entrance, you'll start with a bracing swim across a deep pool (about 15ft across), so you must be a reasonably good swimmer (or request a life jacket). From here, follow your guide, walking, climbing, twisting and turning your way through the blackness of the cave for about an hour.

Giant shimmering flowstone rock formations compete for your attention with thick, calcium-carbonate stalactites dripping from the ceiling. Phallic stalagmites grow up from the cave floor. Eventually you'll follow your guide up into a massive opening, where you'll see hundreds of pottery vessels and shards, along with human remains. One of the most shocking displays is the calcite-encrusted remains of the woman whom Actun Tunichil Muknal is named for. In the cave's Main Chamber, you will be required to remove your shoes; wear socks to protect the artifacts from the oils on your skin.

The trip takes about eight hours from San Ignacio, including a one-hour drive each way. A number of San Ignacio–based tour companies do the trip for around BZ$190 per person, including transportation, admission, lunch and equipment. You must be accompanied by a licensed guide (of which there are around 30). Cameras are no longer allowed inside the cave due to an incident involving a clumsy traveler, a dropped camera and the breaking of priceless artifacts.

★ **Black Rock Lodge** RESORT **$$$**
(Map p262; ☎834-4038, 834-4049; www.blackrocklodge.com; cabins BZ$280-430, ste BZ$490; P 📶) High up the Macal in beautiful Black Rock Canyon, this is a stunning setting for a jungle adventure. Slate-and-wood cabins are fan-cooled and have lovely verandas overlooking the river and up toward towering cliffs. Black Rock is all about the location and activities; you can hike pristine trails, ride a horse to Vaca Falls or canoe down the Macal River.

★ **Lodge at Chaa Creek** ECOLODGE **$$$**
(Map p262; ☎824-2037; www.chaacreek.com; Chaa Creek Rd; d/tr cottages BZ$390/270, d ste BZ$860, d villas BZ$1120; P 📶 🏊) Consistently rated among the best lodges in Belize, and with good reason, Chaa Creek's tropical gardens and beautifully kept thatched cottages are spread across a gentle slope above the Macal River. Chaa Creek blossomed from an overgrown farm more than 40 years ago. The cottages, decorated with Maya textiles and local crafts, have decks, fans and private bathrooms.

SOUTHERN BELIZE

Southern Belize is the country's most absorbing cultural melting pot, with a strong Garifuna influence around Dangriga and Hopkins, and Belize's largest Maya population down in Toledo. Nature is rich here too, where open savanna and citrus-filled farmland give way to forested hills dotted with Maya villages, ruins and national parks primed for adventurous jungle trekking.

Dangriga

POP 10,200

Dangriga is the largest town in Southern Belize, and the spiritual capital of the country's Garifuna people. Despite sharing a similar ramshackle appearance and funky coastal vibe with Belize City, Dangriga doesn't have a big-city feel and is generally a safe place to explore.

Sights

Pen Cayetano Studio Gallery GALLERY
(Map p272; ☎628-6807; www.cayetano.de; 3 Aranda Cres; adult/student BZ$5/3; ⏲9am-5pm

Dangriga

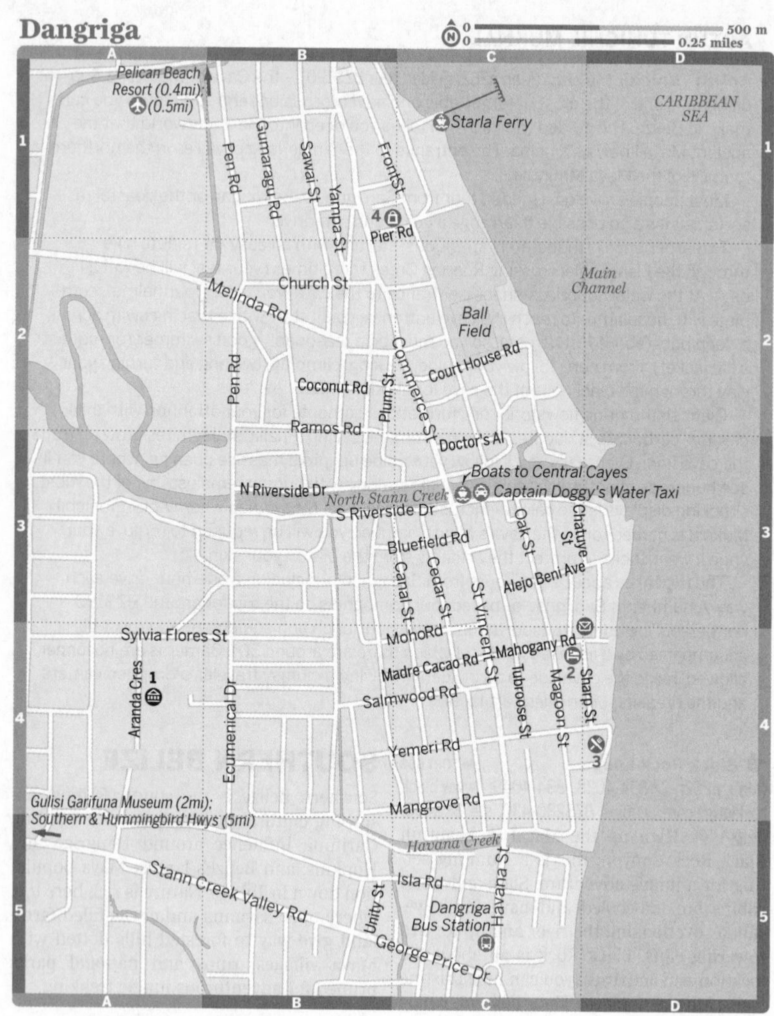

Mon-Fri, Sat & Sun by appointment) Renowned throughout Belize for his art and music, Pen Cayetano's workshop and gallery displays Garifuna artifacts and crafts. It also has works of art and music by Pen, and the textile artwork of his wife, Ingrid, available for sale. Among the unique items are drums made of turtle shells, which sell for around BZ$50.

Gulisi Garifuna Museum MUSEUM

(☎669-0639; www.ngcbelize.org; Hummingbird Hwy, Chuluhadiwa Park; BZ$10; ⏱10am-5pm Mon-Fri, 8am-noon Sat) This museum, operated by the National Garifuna Council (NGC), is a must for anyone interested in the vibrant Garifuna people. It brings together artifacts, pictures and documents on Garifuna history and culture, including an exhibit on the life and music of the late Garifuna musician Andy Palacio. A free guided tour is included with admission. The museum is 2 miles out of town; ask any bus heading out of Dangriga to drop you here.

Marie Sharp's Factory FACTORY

(☎532-2087; www.mariesharps.bz; 1 Melinda Rd; ⏱7am-4pm Mon-Fri) The super-hot bottled sauces that adorn tables all over Belize and beyond are made from habanero peppers

Dangriga

Sights

Sleeping

Eating

Shopping

here at Marie Sharp's Factory, 8 miles northwest of town on Melinda Rd. Free tours are usually offered during business hours (by advance reservation), and the factory shop sells hot sauces and jams at outlet prices. If you can't make it to the factory, Marie Sharp's also has a **store** (Map p272; ☎522-2370; 3 Pier Rd; ⏰8am-noon & 1-5pm Mon-Fri) in Dangriga.

Festivals & Events

Garifuna Settlement Day CULTURAL

On November 19 Dangriga explodes with celebrations to mark the arrival of Garifuna in Dangriga in 1832. Dangrigans living elsewhere flock home for the celebrations. Drumming, dancing and drinking continue right through the night of the 18th to the 19th, while canoes reenact the beach landing in the morning. Book ahead for accommodations.

Sleeping & Eating

★D's Hostel HOSTEL $

(Map p272; ☎502-3324; 1 Sharp St; dm/d BZ$25/100; ❄📶) Dangriga's one and only hostel is a local institution, kept in great condition by friendly owner Dana. The eight-bed dorm has individual fans and lockers, while the two spacious private rooms have either two or three double beds, air-con, kitchenette and private bathroom. The inflatable beds are unusual but comfy enough.

Pelican Beach Resort RESORT $$

(☎522-2044; www.pelicanbeachbelize.com; 1st St; s/d BZ$210/270, ste s/d BZ$260/330; P❄📶) The Pelican is the most 'upscale' choice in Dangriga but still has a faded 1950s air about it. The hotel is on the northern fringe of town, close to the small airport and fronting the Caribbean Sea. Clean but uninspiring rooms come with TV, air-con (some have fans but sea-facing verandas) and colorful local artwork.

★Tuáni Garifuna BELIZEAN $

(Map p272; ☎502-0287; 1734 Southern Foreshore; meals BZ$10-25; ⏰7am-10pm; 📶) Belizean and Garifuna dishes such as *hudut* (fish with plantain in coconut curry), pigtail, fried plantain and stew beans are the specialty at this lovely little waterfront restaurant and bar. Also good for a local breakfast of fryjacks and johnnycakes or just a cold beer on a warm evening.

Information

Belize Bank (Commerce St), **Scotia Bank** (Commerce St) and **First Caribbean International Bank** (Commerce St) all have 24-hour ATMs that accept international Visa, MasterCard, Plus and Cirrus cards. The latter charges an outrageous US$5 fee for transactions.

Immigration Office (☎522-3412; St Vincent St; ⏰8am-5pm Mon-Thu, to 4:30pm Fri) Offers 30-day visa extension stamps for BZ$50.

Post Office (Map p272; ☎522-2035; Mahogany Rd) Next to Bonefish Hotel.

Getting There & Away

AIR

From Dangriga airport (DGA), **Maya Island Air** (☎522-2659; www.mayaislandair.com) and **Tropic Air** (☎226-2012; www.tropicair.com) fly direct to Belize City, Placencia and Punta Gorda several times daily.

BOAT

Starla Ferry (Map p272; ☎628-0976) between Belize City and Puerto Cortes (Honduras) stops at the main boat dock in Dangriga at 11am every Friday, departing at noon (BZ$120).

Dangriga is the departure point for trips to Belize's central cays, as well as for chartered trips up and down the coast. The best spot to arrange **boat transport** (Map p272) is just outside the Riverside Café on South Riverside Dr. Stop by before 9am, or the afternoon before, to check when boats will be leaving. The more people you can get for one trip (within reason), the cheaper it works out per person.

Boats usually go daily to Tobacco Caye (BZ$40 per person), but can also be chartered to Thatch Caye, South Water Caye and Glover's Reef. The upmarket lodges on these islands will also organize a boat for you, but check if it's included with your accommodations; if not, it's cheaper to charter from the boatmen here.

The colorful Captain Doggy's 25ft **boat** (Map p272; ☎627-7443; captaindoggy@gmail.com) travels between Dangriga and all of the cays. He also does custom day trips with spearfishing, island stops and lunch for BZ$100.

WORTH A TRIP

COCKSCOMB BASIN WILDLIFE SANCTUARY

The **Cockscomb Basin Wildlife Sanctuary** (BZ$10) is Belize's most famous sanctuary and one of its biggest protected areas. This great swath of tropical forest became the world's first jaguar sanctuary in 1984, thanks to the efforts of American zoologist Alan Rabinowitz. Today this critical biological corridor is home to an estimated 40 to 50 jaguars and a vast array of other animal, bird and botanical life.

The unpaved, 6-mile road to the sanctuary starts at the village of Maya Center, on the Southern Hwy, 5 miles south of the Hopkins turnoff. The sanctuary office, where you pay admission, is at the end of the road. The office has trail maps (BZ$5) plus a few gifts, soft drinks and chocolate bars for sale. You can also rent binoculars (BZ$5 per day).

The visitor sighting book records instances of people spotting jaguars (often on the drive in), so it is possible. But, despite its size, the sanctuary itself isn't big enough to support a healthy breeding population of jaguars. However, its position adjacent to other reserves and swaths of jungle make it part of a biological corridor that, many believe, offers promise for the jaguar's future in Central America.

Belize's four other wild cats, the puma, ocelot, margay and jaguarundi, also reside in and pass through the sanctuary, as do tapirs, anteaters, armadillos (the jaguar's favorite prey – crunchy on the outside, but soft and chewy on the inside), brocket deer, coatimundis, kinkajous, otters, peccaries, tayras iguanas, local rodents such as gibnuts, and other animals native to the area.

The sanctuary is also home to countless birds: over 290 feathered species have been spotted. Egrets, hummingbirds, the keel-billed toucan, king vulture, great curassow and scarlet macaw are just a few that live in or pass through the park.

There's also a thriving community of black howler monkeys living close to the visitors center. If you don't see them near the center, you'll definitely hear their eerie, cacophonous howling if you stay overnight. Large boa constrictors, small (and deadly poisonous) fer-de-lances and tiny coffee snakes are some of the snakes that call the sanctuary home.

BUS

A major transit point for all bus companies servicing Southern Belize, Dangriga's main **bus station** (Map p272; Havana St) is near the roundabout at the southern end of town. There are frequent buses to Belize City (regular/express BZ$12/14, two hours), Belmopan (BZ$8, 1½ hours), Punta Gorda (BZ$14, 2½ hours) and San Ignacio (BZ$12, 2¼ hours), and a handful of direct services to Hopkins (BZ$5, 30 minutes) and Placencia (BZ$10, 1½ hours).

Central Cays

Less crowded, lesser known and often less expensive than the cays in the north, the central cays – most of them private islands – off Belize's central coast are smack in the middle of some of the country's most amazing diving, snorkeling and fishing sites.

Each of the islands has at least one resort. **Tobacco Caye** has the main budget accommodations, while Glovers Reef offers week-long budget resort stays.

In most cases the resorts will arrange boat transfers. The central cays are best reached from Dangriga, but charters also run from Hopkins and Placencia.

Sleeping

★Glover's Atoll Resort CABIN $

(☎532-2916; www.glovers.com.bz; per person per week campsite/dm BZ$298/398, cabins BZ$498-698;) Occupying the Glover's northeast cay, this little backpackers' island paradise is the perfect, affordable island getaway. The private 10-acre island has 16 cabins (overwater and on the beach), a basic dorm and eight private campgrounds. Most travelers take the weekly deal, which includes boat transfers from Sittee River, but nightly 'drop-in' rates are also available, starting from BZ$24 for camping.

Tobacco Caye Paradise CABIN $$

(☎532-2101; www.tobaccocaye.com; d cabañas incl meals BZ$160;) This is the most romantic deal on Tobacco with the only overwater bungalows on the island. Paradise has six brightly painted *cabañas* perched on stilts over the water with private baths and cold-water showers. Verandas look out toward the reef where the water is shallow enough to wade in.

★Thatch Caye Resort RESORT $$$

(☎1-800-435-3145, 603-2414; www.thatchcayebelize.com; cabañas & bungalows BZ$400-790, overwater bungalows BZ$950; [icons]) The most luxurious of the South Caye private island resorts, Thatch Caye has 13 beautiful thatched-roof, air-conditioned *cabañas* and overwater bungalows built from local hardwoods and set on stilts, connected by paths winding through native mangroves. The resort features an excellent social-hub bar-restaurant (add BZ$300 per person for an all-inclusive package), the overwater Starfish Bar and a dazzling array of activities.

Hopkins & Sittee Point

POP 1500

The friendly, slightly scruffy, coastal village of Hopkins attracts travelers looking to soak up sea breezes and Garifuna culture. It's an unpretentious place to meet other travelers or satisfied expats and makes a good base for explorations to the cays, reefs and islands to the east, and the jungles, mountains and parks to the west.

About 1.5 miles south of Hopkins, Sittee Point is a small community where high-end beachfront resorts and a few interesting independent restaurants gather.

Activities

Hopkins is a fine place from which to access some of Belize's best dive sites. The barrier reef is less than a 40-minute boat ride away, and Glover's Reef is about 90 minutes on a fast skiff. Diving and snorkeling can be arranged through several outfits in Hopkins and nearby Sittee Point.

Lebeha COURSE

(☎650-2318; Front St, North Side; lessons per person per hour BZ$20) Local Garifuna drummer Jabbar Lambey and his wife Dorothy run Lebeha both as an educational and cultural center for locals and as a general happening spot for travelers interested in Garifuna drumming. Lessons for individuals and groups are available, and there's drumming most nights from 7pm. Full-moon drumming parties are an especially great reason to visit.

Hopkins Stand-up Paddleboarding WATER SPORTS

(☎650-9040; www.suphopkins.com; Sittee River Rd, Sittee Point; paddleboarding tours BZ$140-270) This outfit offers stand-up paddleboarding (SUP) tours on the Sittee River with a mind-blowing two-hour evening bioluminescence paddle or a half-day paddle in search of wildlife. Combination paddle and snorkel tours are also available.

Belize Underwater DIVING

(☎670-7298; www.belizeunderwater.com; Sittee River Rd, Sittee Point; 2 dives BZ$270, 3 dives Glover's Reef BZ$470) Belize Underwater is a PADI-certified dive shop offering scuba instruction and trips to South Water Caye, Thatch Caye and Glover's Reef.

Hopkins Kulcha Tours TOURS

(☎661-8199; www.hopkinskulchatours.weebly.com; South Side; tours BZ$110-300) Charlton Castillo will take you birdwatching, hiking or on a tour of Maya ruins. Tours explore Stann Creek, Cayo and beyond.

Sleeping

★Funky Dodo HOSTEL $

(☎676-3636; www.funkydodo.bz; Main St, South Side; d with bathroom BZ$69-86, dm/d without bathroom BZ$25/57; [icon]) Hopkins' only hostel is indeed a funky place, with a tightly packed village of rustic timber cabin rooms and dorms inhabiting a leafy garden. Backpackers swing in hammocks reading books, while others roll out yoga mats. The best rooms are the upper-level Tree Top rooms with their own deck. There's also a communal kitchen, tour desk and bike hire.

★Coconut Row Guesthouse GUESTHOUSE $$

(☎675-3000, USA 518-658-3677; www.coconutrowbelize.com; Front St; d BZ$210-230, cabins BZ$230-250, apt BZ$280-300; [icons]) The colorfully painted Coconut Row boasts some of the finest beachfront rooms in Hopkins. The five main rooms are spacious and spotless, and come with air-conditioning, fridge, coffee-maker and king-sized beds, while two of them are full two-bedroom apartments. In the adjoining property are three excellent freestanding beachfront log cabins. The latest addition is the Coconut Husk restaurant.

Whitehorse Inn GUESTHOUSE $$

(☎651-7961; www.whitehorseguesthouse.com; Main St, South Side; r BZ$120-180, bungalows BZ$200; [icons]) This plush new beachfront guesthouse brings a level of space and comfort at a price that's probably unmatched elsewhere in Hopkins. The four rooms in the main house and two freestanding sea-facing *cabañas* are warmly furnished, air-con cooled and fitted with mini kitchens (fridge, microwave) and TV. Stay a week and get a night free. Highly recommended.

All Seasons Guest House GUESTHOUSE $$
(☎523-7209; www.allseasonsbelize.bz; Main St, South Side; r BZ$130-170, cabañas BZ$218-238; P ❄ 📶) With its brightly painted two-bedroom *cabañas* (cabins) and cozy guest-house rooms, All Seasons has some of the cutest accommodations in the village. All rooms have air-con, coffee-makers and hot showers. There's a great patio out front with a grill and picnic area. The location is good, at the south end of town and a short walk to the beach.

Tipple Tree Beya HOTEL $$
(☎615-7006; www.tippletreebelize.com; Main St, South Side; r BZ$90-110, 1-/2-bedroom apt BZ$206/350; 📶) 🍃 This sturdy wooden beachside place features three cozy, clean, fan-cooled rooms sharing a sociable veranda beneath the owner's quarters upstairs. In an adjacent building are some excellent self-contained apartments that would suit a family or group. The owner implements a number of sustainable practices including composting, recycling and keeping the place as energy efficient as possible.

★**Hamanasi Adventure & Dive Resort** RESORT $$$
(☎533-7073, USA 877-552-3483; www.hamanasi.com; Sittee River Rd; r BZ$840-970, tree house BZ$1140-1450; P ❄ 📶 🏊) The premier resort of the area, Hamanasi (Garifuna for 'almond tree') combines the amenities of a top-class dive resort with an array of inland tours and activities, all on a gorgeous 400ft private beachfront. All of Hamanasi's rooms and suites face the sea, except for the popular wood-floored tree houses, which hide among the foliage behind the beach.

★**Beaches & Dreams** BOUTIQUE HOTEL $$$
(☎523-7259; www.beachesanddreams.com; Sittee River Rd; tree house BZ$300, d cabañas BZ$350, ste BZ$400; P ❄ 📶 🏊) Beaches & Dreams is a sweet little family-run resort with direct beach access, an inviting pool area and the highly regarded **Barracuda Bar & Grill** (mains BZ$22-58; ⊙7am-9pm; 📶). Rooms include the 'Bird's Nest,' with a loft area, while the beachfront *cabañas* have sea views and hammocks on the veranda. Bikes and kayaks are available for guests.

Hopkins Bay Resort RESORT $$$
(☎523-7284; www.hopkinsbaybelize.com; Front St, North Side; 1-/2-/3-bedroom villas incl breakfast BZ$500/890/1180; P ❄ 📶 🏊) This flashy resort at the far northern end of Hopkins feels worlds away from the village life, with two pools, an absolute beachfront position and luxurious villas. Take out a free kayak or relax under the Rum Shack, an inviting sea-facing *palapa* bar and restaurant. Significant discounts are available off-season or with promo rates.

Eating & Drinking

Kat's Coffee CAFE $
(Main St, South Side; mains BZ$5-9, coffee BZ$2.50-5; ⊙7am-6pm; 📶) A top spot for breakfast, this tiny main-street shack offers bagels, fruit cups packed with granola and yogurt, smoothies, juices and, of course, filter and espresso coffee.

Gecko's BELIZEAN $$
(☎629-5411; Main St, North Side; mains BZ$15-30; ⊙noon-9pm Mon & Wed-Sat; 📶 🌿) Gecko's gets ticks for cheap tacos; vegetarian, vegan and gluten-free dishes; an interesting range of specials; and a breezy open-air dining space and bar just north of the main intersection.

Thongs Cafe CAFE $$
(Main St; mains BZ$10-23; ⊙7am-3pm; 📶) This cute Caribbean-meets-Euro-style cafe is a cool spot for breakfast or a light lunch of salad, wraps and specials such as quesadillas or meatballs. Smoothies are good – if you're detoxing try the Green Fusion with spinach, cucumber and pineapple. Service can be slow, so browse the gift shop with designer T-shirts and vintage clothing while you wait.

★**Chef Rob's** SEAFOOD $$$
(☎523-7225; www.chefrobbelize.com; Sittee River Rd; mains BZ$37-59, 4-course dinner BZ$59-79; ⊙noon-9pm Tue-Sat; 📶) Well-known locally for his sublime seafood creations and steaks cooked over hot rocks, Chef Rob's changing menu here might include sautéed red snapper, grilled jumbo shrimp kebabs or rib eye in rum sauce. Put together a four-course meal from BZ$59. The waterfront dining area at Parrot Cove is suitably romantic.

★**Driftwood Beach Bar** BAR, LIVE MUSIC
(North Side; ⊙10am-10pm Thu-Tue, to midnight Sat & Tue) Ever-popular Driftwood has moved closer to the center of the village but still has a great beachfront location, Hopkins' best drumming nights, and pizza (from BZ$16) and tacos (BZ$10). This is a popular social hub and party place: Tuesday is the big night with Garifuna drumming, but there are also weekend events and beach BBQs.

Information

There's a solitary **Belize Bank ATM** (Main St; 24hr) at the main intersection in the town center. If it's out of action the nearest banks are in Dangriga.

Getting There & Away

There are two daily buses from Hopkins to Dangriga (BZ$5, 30 minutes) and Placencia (BZ$5, one hour). Many travelers hitch or take a taxi (BZ$20) the 4 miles to the Southern Hwy junction and pick up any passing bus going north or south from there. A taxi to Hopkins from Dangriga costs BZ$80.

Placencia

POP 1500

Placencia, a true beach-holiday strip poking out from the mainland, is enduringly popular with North American expats and tourists. Perched at the southern tip of a long, narrow, sandy peninsula, the village has long enjoyed a reputation as 'the cay you can drive to' – a fully paved 27-mile road heads off the Southern Hwy via Maya Beach and Seine Bight to the tip of the peninsula.

Placencia can be a lot of fun, but how you feel about it really depends on what you're looking for. If it's laid-back ambience, varied accommodations, boat access to private islands and some of the best restaurants in Southern Belize, this beachfront hangout may be for you.

Activities & Tours

Diving, snorkeling, fishing, kayaking and trips to inland adventures are all available from Placencia and there are plenty of operators who can organize activities.

★Splash Dive Center DIVING, TOURS

(Map p278; 523-3058; www.splashbelize.com; Main St) Splash teaches PADI courses to divers of all levels, as well as offering diving and snorkeling tours to islands and reefs throughout the area. Owner Patty Ramirez is a patient and professional instructor, making her suitable for first-time divers and experts alike. As Quest Tours, Patty and partner Ralph also lead tours inland, including trips to Maya ruins and jungles.

★Taste Belize Tours FOOD & DRINK

(Map p278; Main St; day tours from BZ$250) Belize's premier culinary tours include Maya chocolate tours, Garifuna, Creole and Maya cooking tours, and spice farm trips. You can also taste cacao chocolate the Placencia shop.

King Lewey's Island Resort ISLAND

(Map p278; 543-4010; www.kingleweysisland resort.com; day tour BZ$100-240) If you're after a bit of island time on a budget, this pirate-themed resort on a tiny island about 12 miles from Placencia is a fun place for a day trip. Naturally there's a restaurant and bar, and water sports such as kayaks, paddleboards, fishing and snorkeling gear. Or just laze around in the hammock.

Seakunga Adventure ADVENTURE

(523-3644; www.seakunga.com; Mile 18 Placencia Rd; 1-/4-day kayaking tours BZ$160/2400) On the peninsula, just past Seine Bight, Seakunga runs fully supported multiday river and ocean kayaking tours and a range of adventure trips. It rents out windsurfing equipment (per day BZ$80, lessons BZ$160) and it started Placencia's first kiteboarding school.

Sleeping

★Placencia Hostel HOSTEL $

(Map p278; 627-0104; colinbelize@yahoo.com; Main St; dm/d BZ$35/60) Backpackers have more options in Placencia now, with the opening of this excellent place. Run by welcoming local Chris, it's more like a guesthouse than a hostel, with a range of private fan-cooled rooms. The doubles with private bathroom are a bargain, especially by Placencia standards. There's a small kitchen, laundry service and bikes for rent.

Anda Di Howse HOSTEL $

(Map p278; 631-1614, 523-3306; pandora_gaudino @yahoo.com; Sidewalk; dm BZ$25;) 'Under the House' was Placencia's first genuine hostel, with an absolute beachfront location, no less. Owner Pandora has designed a functional 10-bed dorm beneath her stilt home, with timber floors, spring mattresses, individual fans, lockers and spotless bathrooms. It's a cozy space with full kitchen and small veranda. Rent a tent or hammock and camp for BZ$15.

Casa Placencia APARTMENT $

(630-7811; www.casaplacencia.com; Placencia Rd; r BZ$110, apt per week BZ$1300;) On the quiet northern end of town, long-running Casa Placencia offers beautifully decorated rooms with kitchenettes, cable TV and wi-fi. There's an organic garden with bananas, mangoes and papayas, and a chill-out spot with an above-ground pool

Placencia

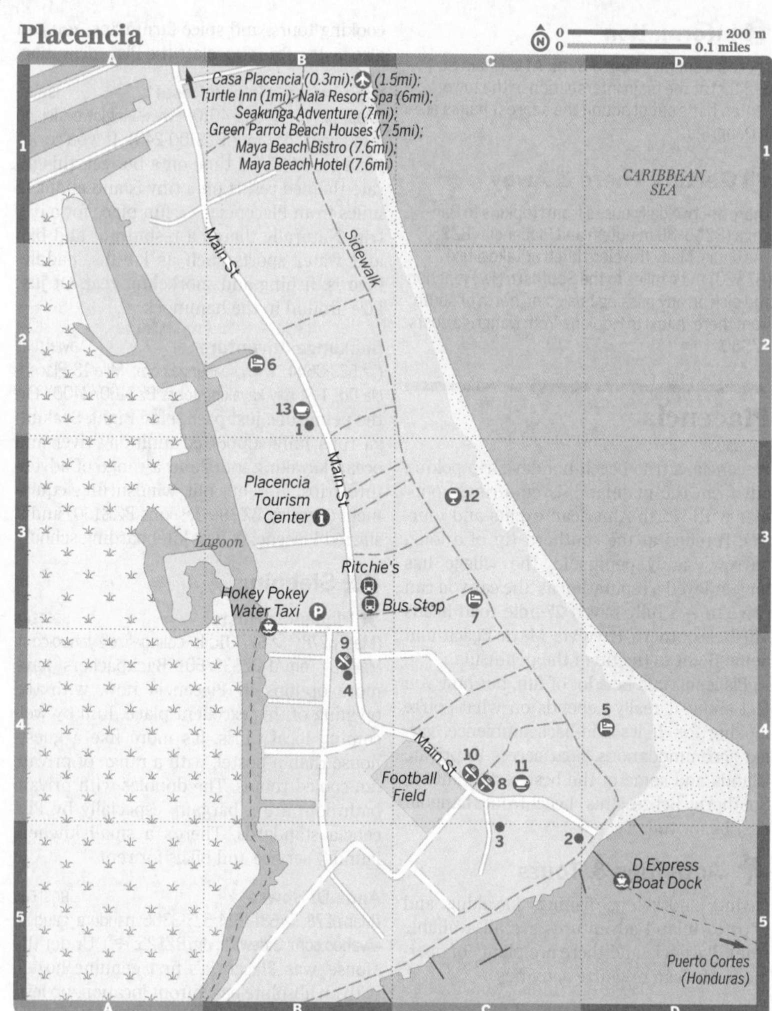

and BBQ at the back. The one- and two-bedroom apartments come with full kitchen and are perfect for families. Free bikes.

Serenade Hotel HOTEL **$$**

(Map p278; ☎523-3113; www.serenadeplacencia.com; Sidewalk; d BZ$130-170; P❄📶) This big old two-story house on the Sidewalk has nine spacious brightly painted rooms and are very reasonable by Placencia standards with air-con, microwave, minifridge, cable TV and bathrooms with hot showers. The better upper-floor rooms have sea views and the beach is just steps away.

★ **Turtle Inn** LODGE **$$$**

(☎523-3486, USA 800-746-3743; www.thefamilycoppolahideaways.com/en/turtle-inn; Placencia Rd; cottages BZ$638-2038, villas BZ$1300-3858; P📶🏊) The last word in ultra-chic luxury (with price tag to match), this Balinese-themed lodge is owned by the family of Francis Ford Coppola, where the director himself maintains his own Belizean villa. The thatch-roofed cottages and villas are a combination of opulence with a hint of the rustic, while signature Italian fine dining can be found at the Mare Restaurant.

Placencia

Activities, Courses & Tours

Sleeping

Eating

Drinking & Nightlife

★ **Maya Beach Hotel** HOTEL $$$

(533-8040; www.mayabeachhotel.com; Maya Beach; r BZ$280-400, ste BZ$500; P) The Maya Beach has 10 delightful, individually furnished and decorated rooms facing the beach. The smallest is cozy but most are spacious and thoughtfully designed, all with air-conditioning, custom-made furniture, kitchenettes and balconies or verandas. There's a cool little pool and swimming off the private jetty, and guests have free use of kayaks and stand-up paddleboards.

Naïa Resort Spa SPA HOTEL $$$

(523-4600; www.naiaresortandspa.com; off Placencia Rd, Cocoplum; studios BZ$750-850, 1-/2-/3-bedroom villas from BZ$970/1600/1990) Naïa is the newest luxury resort on the Placencia peninsula with a full-service day spa and spectacular beachfront villas. The beach houses and villas, many with private plunge pools, are spacious, private and luxuriously appointed with kitchenettes, modern artworks and full-length French windows opening onto balconies or verandas.

Green Parrot Beach Houses CABAÑAS $$$

(533-8188, USA 734-667-2537; www.greenparrot-belize.com; 1 Maya Beach; d BZ$350; P) Green Parrot offers six quirky timber beach houses and two stilted thatched *cabañas*, all on the beach. All-wood interiors, high ceilings and huge screened-in windows maximizing breezes are features. *Cabañas* have thatched roofs and open-air showers with a tropical feel. Guests have free use of bicycles, snorkeling equipment, kayaks and glass-bottom canoes, and the restaurant serves breakfast, lunch and dinner.

Eating

★ **Tutti Frutti** ICE CREAM $

(Map p278; Main St; 1/2 scoops BZ$4/5; 9am-9pm Thu-Tue) If you don't like the ice cream here, you won't like ice cream anywhere. It's that simple. The Italian gelato is even better and the 18 flavors on display are constantly changing – from salted caramel to Ferrero Rocher.

Chachi's ITALIAN $

(Map p278; 523-3305; Main Rd; pizza slice BZ$5-8; 11am-11pm) Chachi's is a fine addition to Placencia's main street scene: a sociable pizza joint and cocktail bar downstairs and breezy live music bar upstairs. Pizzas are available by the slice or you can buy a whole one and build your own toppings, including housemade sausage or blue cheese. Sip a cocktail or sangria and see what's happening upstairs.

★ **Omar's Creole Grub** SEAFOOD $$

(Map p278; 605-7631; Main St; mains BZ$10-45; 7am-9pm Sun-Thu, to 4pm Fri, to 6pm Sat) Omar's has been around a long time and still serves some of the freshest seafood in town. Step into the small and rustic streetside shack and choose from crab, lobster, shrimp or conch prepared as either traditional Creole, Caribbean curry or coconut curry. There's also burgers and burritos, and omelets for breakfast. BYO alcohol only.

★ **Maya Beach Bistro** INTERNATIONAL $$$

(533-8040; www.mayabeachhotel.com; Maya Beach; lunch BZ$18-40, dinner BZ$14-58; 7am-9pm) Maya Beach Hotel's popular bistro is a Placencia landmark, offering excellent international dishes using fresh local ingredients. This is the place where restaurant folk come n their days off to eat seafood and coconut chowder, lobster bread pudding or cacao pork. The waterfront view is fine, service is friendly and you can swim in the small pool.

★ **Rumfish** FUSION $$$

(Map p278; 523-3293; www.rumfishyvino.com; Main St; tacos BZ$9, small plates BZ$10-22, mains BZ$35-55; noon-midnight, kitchen closes 10pm) Rumfish is a gastro-style wine bar Central-American–style. Head up to the balcony of the beautiful old timber building and sample starters such as Peruvian *ceviche* or specialty mains such as Yucatán chicken or Caribbean fish stew. Gourmet tacos are BZ$18 for two. Imported wines, beers and cocktails, and a breezy veranda complete the picture.

Drinking & Nightlife

Brewed Awakenings CAFE
(Map p278; Main St; ⏲6am-9pm Mon-Sat, to 5pm Thu; 📶) The imaginative name extends to the drinks with perfectly brewed espresso coffee (BZ$3.50 to BZ$7) and a range of flavored seaweed shakes (BZ$7 to BZ$8; the seaweed acts as a thickener and is said to contain various healthy vitamins). Great for an early-morning caffeine fix.

Barefoot Bar BAR
(Map p278; ☎523-3515; Sidewalk; ⏲11am-midnight; 📶) Occupying prime beach real estate, Placencia's most happening spot for drinking and entertainment has live music five nights a week, fire dancing on Wednesdays, full-moon parties, horseshoe-tossing comps and more. Happy hour is from 5pm to 6pm, with discount beer and cheap rum. The menu has a big range of Mexican snacks, pizza and burgers.

Above Grounds COFFEE
(Map p278; ☎634-3212; www.abovegroundscoffee.com; Main St; ⏲7am-4pm Mon-Sat, 8am-noon Sun; 📶) 🍃 This coffee-shop stilt shack offers great coffee drinks, bagels, muffins and people-watching from the raised wooden veranda deck (coffee from BZ$3 to BZ$7; snacks BZ$2 to BZ$9). All coffee is Guatemalan organic, sourced directly from the farmers. It also has organic chocolate drinks, fresh juice, free wi-fi and good tunes.

ℹ Information

Belize Bank (Pompass Rd) and **Scotiabank** (⏲8:30am-2:30pm Mon-Thu, to 4pm Fri) are both on the main drag and have 24/7 ATM access. There's an Atlantic Bank branch on the far north end of town.

There's no shortage of info on Placencia, both on the web and around Belize. In town, head to the **Placencia Tourism Center** (Map p278; ☎523-4045; www.placencia.com; ⏲9am-5pm Mon-Fri), down a lane opposite Scotia Bank (look for the sign). This private BTIA (Belize Tourism Industry Association) office has friendly staff who can offer local information such as transport info. Pick up a copy of the free monthly *Placencia Breeze*.

ℹ Getting There & Around

BOAT

The **Hokey Pokey Water Taxi** (Map p278; ☎665-7242; one way BZ$10; ⏲hourly from 6:45am to 6pm, or 5pm Sunday) is a great way to arrive or depart Placencia. The scenic 10-minute boat ride along Mango Creek brings you to the administrative town of Independence/Mango Creek; from Independence bus station (BZ$5 taxi ride from the boat dock) you can connect with any of the buses that traverse the Southern Hwy.

The 45-passenger **D Express** (Map p278) sails from Placencia municipal pier to Puerto Cortés, Honduras (BZ$130, 4½ hours including immigration time) at 9am on Friday. Tickets are sold on board or ask at **Nite Wind Tours** (Map p278; ☎660-6333, 503-3487; Main St; tours BZ$45-385; ⏲8am-5:30pm). The return trip leaves Puerto Cortés at 11am on Monday.

BUS

Ritchie's (Map p278; ☎523-3806) bus line has one daily bus to Belize City at 6:15am (BZ$20, 4½ hours) and three buses to Dangriga (BZ$10, 1¾ hours) Monday to Saturday, from where you can transfer to Belmopan and points beyond. Buses to Dangriga leave at 7am, 12:45pm and 2:30pm (2:30pm only on Sunday) from the **bus stop** (Map p278) on Main St opposite the Hokey Pokey Water Taxi.

Two Bebb Line buses between Placencia and Dangriga at 10:30am and 5:30pm stop at Hopkins. Alternatively, ask to be let off at the Hopkins junction and call a taxi from there.

Travelers heading to Toledo should take the Hokey Pokey Water Taxi (p280) to Independence; from the Independence bus stand (taxi BZ$5) you can connect with any of the James Line buses that traverse the Southern Hwy.

ℹ Getting Around

Cars, motorbikes and golf buggies can be hired along the Placencia peninsula; try **Barefoot Services** (☎523-3066; www.barefootservicesbelize.com; Placencia Rd; ⏲8:30am-5:30pm Mon-Fri) or **Captain Jak's Rentals** (☎628-6447; www.captainjaks.com; Main St; ⏲7am-5pm).

Punta Gorda

POP 6030

Punta Gorda (or PG) is a slightly ramshackle coastal settlement down in the Deep South of Toledo. Once known to travelers mainly as a port to get the boat across to Guatemala or Honduras, it's increasingly attracting visitors looking to chill out in the south and as a base for exploring surrounding Maya villages and culture, and the remote southern cays.

Activities

★Cotton Tree Chocolate Factory FOOD & DRINK
(Map p282; ☎621-8776; www.cottontreechocolate.com; 2 Front St; ⏲8am-noon Mon-Sat & 1:30-5pm Mon-Fri) FREE Cotton Tree offers a good opportunity to buy some local chocolate and learn a bit about the process. Beans are sourced from Toledo Cacao Growers Association, promoting both fair trade and local production. The owner happily offers tours of the small factory, and there's a gift shop selling only locally made handicrafts, including soaps, cacao-bean jewelry and, obviously, chocolate bars.

Warasa Garifuna Drum School COURSE
(☎632-7701; www.warasadrumschool.com; New Rd; drum lessons BZ$25, half-day package BZ$125; ⏲by appointment) Local drummer Ronald Raymond (Ray) McDonald teaches Garifuna beats at his Warasa Garifuna Drum School on New Rd (about 15 minutes' walk out of town). There are one-on-one classes and group lessons. McDonald also performs and lectures about Garifuna culture at Hickatee Cottages.

Maroon Creole Drum School COURSE
(☎632-7841, 668-7733; methosdrums@hotmail.com; Joe Taylor Creek Rd; ⏲by appointment) Those looking to study with a master will find the trip to Emmeth Young's drum school well worth it. When he's not touring the country performing, one of Belize's most respected Creole drummers hosts drum-making workshops and group presentations. It costs BZ$25 an hour for drum lessons, or BZ$250 for a few days learning both drumming and drum making.

TIDE Tours TOURS
(☎722-2129; www.tidetours.org; Hopeville) Ecofriendly TIDE Tours is a subsidiary of the Toledo Institute for Development and Environment (TIDE), running conservation and ecotours throughout the Toledo area, including inland adventures to caves and waterfalls, birding trips to Payne's Creek National Park and cultural tourism to local Maya villages. TIDE also does boating adventures out to the southern cays, including snorkeling, fishing and diving tours.

Sleeping

A Piece of Ground HOTEL $
(☎665-2695; www.apieceofground.com; 1050 Pelican St; dm/d BZ$38/78;) Also known locally as Backa Jama's, this funky, sociable four-story place has a ground-floor hostel with two dorms (one with air-con) and four spotless guesthouse rooms with attached bathroom on the second floor. Keep going up the stairs to the popular restaurant, serving chicken dishes and American-style burgers and fries, and the rooftop bar.

Tate's Guest House GUESTHOUSE $
(Map p282; ☎722-0147; tatesguesthouse@yahoo.com; 34 Jose Maria Nunez St; r BZ$75-90, units BZ$125-150;) Former postmaster Mr Tate keeps his guesthouse in immaculate condition and it's the best budget deal in the town center. The six rooms inside the mauve two-story facade, set in a little garden with a gazebo, are all air-conditioned and good value at these rates. Two are self-contained, with kitchenettes, and all come with cable TV and hot showers.

★Coral House Inn BOUTIQUE HOTEL $$
(Map p282; ☎722-2878; www.coralhouseinn.com; 151 Main St; d incl breakfast BZ$220-240, ste BZ$290;) This sublime seaside inn at the southern end of town boasts a lovely garden and in-ground swimming pool. Enormous rooms are stylishly designed, giving the place a classic (but not at all pretentious) colonial feel. A spacious veranda overlooks the sea on one side and a quaintly picturesque old cemetery on the other.

Hickatee Cottages RESORT $$
(☎662-4475; www.hickatee.com; cottages BZ$170-230, d BZ$160, ste BZ$270-290;) Serene Hickatee Cottages is a beautiful and unique solar-powered resort that leaves as light an ecological footprint as possible. There are three fully furnished cottages, two spacious suites and the Hickatee Den, a small detached unit that sleeps two and overlooks the tiny plunge pool. The property features both garden and wild jungle space, and a 3-mile trail network.

★Blue Belize Guest House B&B $$$
(Map p282; ☎722-2678; www.bluebelize.com; 139 Front St; ste BZ$170-340; @) It's impossible not to feel a calming sense of space and relaxation at Blue Belize, with its waterfront location, lush garden and enormous rooms in a pair of connected two-story houses. The six breezy and beautifully decorated suites are more like serviced apartments than hotel rooms, offering well-furnished living rooms and kitchenettes, in addition to a comfortable master bedroom.

Punta Gorda

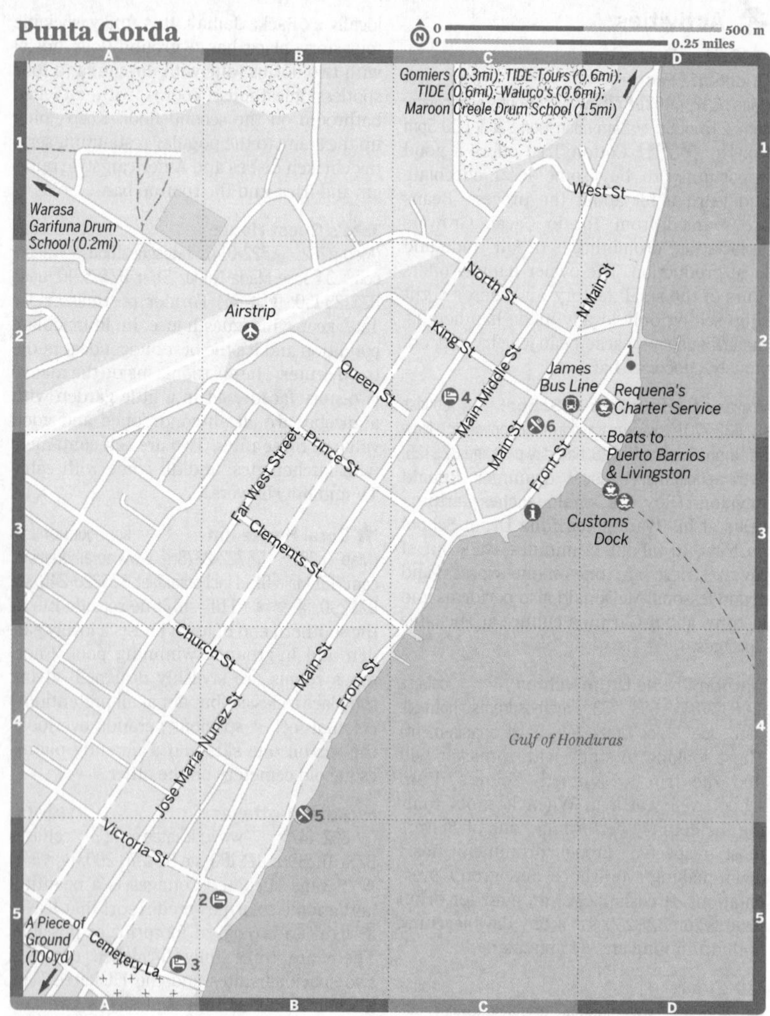

Eating & Drinking

★Gomiers VEGETARIAN $

(Southern Hwy, Hopeville; meals BZ$5-17; 8am-10pm;) Gormiers has moved from his little green shack to a new location across from the waterfront north of town. It's still the best place in PG for organic vegetarian and vegan cuisine, a variety of tofu-based creations, veggie lasagna and a few fish dishes. Look out for live reggae nights on Fridays.

★Snack Shack CAFE $

(Map p282; Main St; mains BZ$7.50-12; 7am-3pm Mon-Fri, to noon Sat) With a breezy upper deck overlooking Main St, this is the best spot in town for all-day Western or Belizean breakfasts, served alongside brain-freezing slushies, juices and shakes.

★Asha's Culture Kitchen SEAFOOD $$

(Map p282; 722-2742; 74 Front St; mains BZ$15-30; noon-10pm, closed Tue dinner) Twisted lobster, baked barracuda, cracked conch, whole snapper and lionfish fingers – and the best waterfront deck in PG. There's a lot to like about Asha's, where seafood is the specialty and the sea breezes are fine. A standard meal includes a choice of main from the blackboard menu and two sides (garlic

Punta Gorda

Activities, Courses & Tours
1 Cotton Tree Chocolate Factory..........D2

Sleeping
2 Blue Belize Guest House......................B5
3 Coral House Inn....................................A5
4 Tate's Guest House..............................C2

Eating
5 Asha's Culture Kitchen.........................B4
6 Snack Shack..C2

mashed potato is a winner). Service can be slow but it's worth the wait.

Waluco's BAR
(☎702-2129; Front St, Hopeville; ⏰11:30am-midnight Tue-Sun; 📶) This big, breezy *palapa,* a mile northeast of town, is a popular weekend spot, especially for Sunday sessions when the BBQ fires up and everyone goes swimming off the pier opposite. There's cheap bar food, and Garifuna drummers sometimes play here.

Information

Belize Bank (30 Main St) and **Scotia Bank** (1 Main St) both have 24-hour ATMs accepting most international cards.

Customs & Immigration (☎722-2022; Front St; ⏰9am-5pm Mon-Fri) This is your first port of call when coming to Punta Gorda by boat from Guatemala or Honduras; it should also be your last stopping place when leaving by sea (there's a departure tax of BZ$40). Head here for visa extensions too.

Punta Gorda Tourism Information Center (Map p282; ☎722-2531; Front St; ⏰8am-5pm Mon-Fri) PG's little BTIA tourist office can answer general questions and has village bus timetables. If they have it, pick up a free copy of the local tourist paper *Toledo Howler.*

TIDE (☎722-2274; www.tidebelize.org; One Mile San Antonio Rd) The Toledo Institute for Development and Environment is responsible for a range of community conservation projects in the Deep South, both in the inland forests and the marine parks.

Getting There & Away

AIR

Tropic Air (☎722-2008; www.tropicair.com) has five daily flights to Belize City and Belize City International (BZ$370, one hour), and one to Placencia (BZ$150, 20 minutes) and Dangriga (BZ$226, 40 minutes). **Maya Island Air** (☎722-2856; www.mayaislandair.com) also flies four times daily to Belize City, Placencia and Dangriga for similar prices. Specials are often available, and ticket offices are at the **airstrip** (PND; Map p282).

BOAT

At the time of writing there were two daily **boat services** (Map p282) to Puerto Barrios in Guatemala at 9am and 2pm. There was also one daily boat to Livingstone at 2pm (BZ$60). Boats depart from the municipal pier in front of the customs and immigration office, where you'll need to clear customs.

Requena's Charter Service (Map p282; ☎722-2070; 12 Front St) operates the *Mariestela,* departing Punta Gorda at 9am daily for Puerto Barrios, Guatemala (BZ$60, one hour), and returning at 2pm. Tickets are sold at the office and the **customs dock** (Map p282) down the street.

At the time of writing, a shuttle boat between Punta Gorda, Barranco and Monkey River was under consideration.

BUS

James Bus Line (Map p282; ☎702-2049, 722-2625; King St) has hourly buses from Punta Gorda to Belize City (regular/air-con BZ$26/28, seven hours) from 4am to 4pm. Buses stop at Dangriga (BZ$14/15, 3½ hours) and Belmopan (BZ$20/22, 5½ hours). Another regular service runs to Independence (for Placencia). All buses leave from the **main bus station** on King St and cruise around PG a bit before heading north.

Toledo Villages

Visitors to Belize's Deep South have a unique opportunity to simultaneously experience both ancient and contemporary Maya culture. Over 60% of the population of Toledo District is Maya and these people, across more than 30 villages, have done a great deal to keep their culture alive and intact.

Big Falls & Indian Creek

On the Southern Hwy, about 20 miles from Punta Gorda, Big Falls is a small village with a number of cultural and adventure attractions. This is a good starting point for the Toledo cultural circuit taking in San Miguel and San Pedro Columbia.

★**Living Maya Experience** CULTURAL CENTER
(☎Chiacs 632-4585, Cals 627-7408; livingmayaexperience@gmail.com; Big Falls; tours per person BZ$20-30; ⏰by appointment) Two Kekchí families in Big Falls village have opened up

their homes as a cultural experience for visitors and both are excellent. The Cal family demonstrates ancient Maya lifestyle from tortilla- and chocolate-making to traditional instruments and an exploration of their self-sufficient garden. With the Chiac family, you can learn to make woven Maya crafts – baskets, hammocks or bags.

Nim Li Punit RUINS
(☎822-2106; BZ$10; ⏰8am-5pm) The Maya ruins of Nim Li Punit stand atop a natural hill half a mile north of the Southern Hwy, near the village of Indian Creek. The site is notable for the 26 stelae found in the southern Plaza of the Stelae. Four of the finest are housed in the stela house beside the visitors center.

San Pedro Columbia

Around 20 miles northwest of Punta Gorda is the village of San Pedro Columbia, the largest Kekchi Maya community outside Guatemala.

Sights & Activities

Lubaantun RUINS
(BZ$10; ⏰8am-5pm) The Maya ruins at Lubaantun, 1.3 miles northwest of San Pedro Columbia, are built on a natural hilltop and display a construction method unusual in the ancient Maya world of mortar-less, neatly cut, black-slate blocks. Archaeologists postulate that Lubaantun, which flourished between AD 730 and 860, may have been an administrative center regulating trade, while nearby Nim Li Punit was the local religious and ceremonial center. The Maya site comprises a collection of seven plazas, three ballcourts and surrounding structures.

Eladio's Chocolate Adventure FOOD & DRINK
(☎624-0166; eladiopop@gmail.com; per person BZ$60) In San Pedro Columbia village, passionate local Eladio Pop will take you on a tour of his cacao farm, followed by a traditional chocolate-making demonstration and Maya lunch.

San Antonio

The largest Mopan Maya community in Belize, San Antonio was founded in the mid-19th century by farmers from San Luis Rey in the Petén, Guatemala. A wooden idol (of San Luis) was taken from the church in San Luis Rey by settlers who returned to Guatemala to retrieve their saint. The idol remains in the beautiful stone church in San Antonio, which has wonderful stained-glass windows with Italian and Irish names on them (because the glass was donated by parishioners from St Louis, Missouri).

San Antonio has a large concentration of cacao farmers growing cacao for export and use in Belizean-made chocolate products.

Río Blanco National Park NATIONAL PARK
(BZ$10; ⏰7am-5pm) The 105-acre Río Blanco National Park, just west of Santa Elena village, is a compact protected wildlife area that's home to a variety of flora and fauna. The highlight for visitors is definitely Río

FOOD OF THE GODS

The cacao plant, and the chocolate that derives from it, have always been important in Maya society, and is known to the Maya as the 'food of the gods.' Traditional methods of fermenting, drying and roasting the cacao beans, then grinding them by hand, are still practiced in the Toledo District, and chocolate-making cottage industries can be found in a number of places in Belize. The **Chocolate Festival of Belize** celebrates all things chocolate in Punta Gorda in May.

Cotton Tree Chocolate Factory (p281) in Punta Gorda is a good place to sample and buy local chocolate products, while Taste Belize Tours (p277) in Placencia offers culinary tours to chocolate factories.

Other chocolate-making enterprises open to tourists in Belize include **Ixcacao Maya Belizean Chocolate** (☎742-4050; www.ixcacaomayabelizeanchocolate.com; San Felipe village; tours per person BZ$60-100; ⏰9am-5pm) and Eladio's Chocolate Adventure in Toledo, **Che'il Chocolate Factory** (☎660-3903; juliosaqui@gmail.com; Southern Hwy; tours per person BZ$35; ⏰shop 7am-5:30pm, tours 9am, 11am, 1pm & 3pm or by appointment) in Maya Center, **Lamanai Chocolate** (Map p262; ☎621-9127; www.lamanaichocolate.com; Hummingbird Hwy; chocolate tour BZ$25; ⏰8am-5pm) near Belmopan and Ajaw Chocolate (p264) in San Ignacio.

Blanco Falls, a beautiful 20ft-high waterfall leading into a clear swimming hole just a five-minute walk in from the ranger station. Steps lead down to a platform for swimming and a concrete path has been constructed leading to a swing bridge across the river.

Blue Creek

Part Kekchí and part Mopan Maya, Blue Creek is split by the pretty, blue-green-tinted namesake river. Howler monkeys inhabit the surrounding hilly jungles, otters live along the creek and green iguanas are plentiful. For travelers Blue Creek is an appealing destination for its cave and jungle walks.

Near Blue Creek is the **Tumul'kin School of Learning**, a Maya boarding school that hosts students from throughout Toledo and other parts of Belize, providing a learning venue that inculcates pride in being Maya and gives students an education that values traditional knowledge.

UNDERSTAND BELIZE

Belize Today

Belize is finally booming. After years in the shadow of its neighbors, Central America's youngest and least populated nation is suddenly seen as the next big thing in Caribbean tourism, the country's major source of employment and investment. Visitor numbers doubled in the past decade, and the challenge moving forward is one of balancing the needs of the tourism industry with Belizeans' desire to protect the environment and maintain the low-key lifestyle that makes their country so appealing.

In 2018 Dean Barrow's UDP government made its most important environmental move to date – indefinitely banning offshore oil drilling and exploration in all its waters to protect the delicate barrier reef. The legislation was widely applauded by conservationists and the tourism industry, and was key to Unesco removing the World Heritage-listed reef from its endangered list. Add to this a stable decade-old government offering compulsory education and you have the makings of a tiny, extraordinarily beautiful country that's spreading its wings.

That said, economic prosperity remains elusive for most Belizeans. A few entrepreneurs have made big money, and a small middle class survives from business, tourism and other professions. But many more Belizeans live on subsistence incomes in rudimentary circumstances.

History

Don't be fooled into believing that Central America's youngest independent nation is short on history. Though independence came only in 1981 (peacefully, we might add), many Belizean families trace their connection to the land back for many generations. Most Belizeans have a story to tell about the role played by their relatives in the creation of the nation they now proudly call home.

Belize Before Columbus

Belize certainly earns its place on the Ruta Maya – ruins are everywhere and the Maya population is still thriving, particularly in the southwest. The Maya have been in Belize since the first human habitation. One of the earliest settlements in the Maya world, Cuello, was near present-day Orange Walk. Maya trade routes ran all through the country, and the New River, Río Hondo and Belize River all played an important role in early trade and commerce. Important archaeological sites such as Cahal Pech, near San Ignacio, and Lamanai date from this period.

Pirate's Paradise

Lack of effective government and the onshore safety afforded by the barrier reef attracted English and Scottish pirates to Belizean waters during the 17th century. They operated freely, capturing booty-laden Spanish galleons. In 1670, however, Spain convinced the British government to clamp down on the pirates' activities. Most of the unemployed pirates went into the logwood business.

During the 1780s the British actively protected the loggers' interests, at the same time assuring Spain that Belize was indeed a Spanish possession. But this was a fiction. By this time, Belize was already British by tradition and sympathy, and it was with relief and jubilation that Belizeans received the news, on September 10, 1798, that a British force had defeated the Spanish armada off St George's Caye.

Into the 19th Century

With the diminishing importance of logging, Belize's next trade boom was in arms, ammunition and other supplies sold to the Maya rebels in the Yucatán who fought the War of the Castes during the mid-19th century. The war also brought a flood of refugees from both sides to Belize.

In 1859 Britain and Guatemala signed a treaty that gave Britain rights to the land, provided that the British built a road from Guatemala to the Caribbean coast. The treaty still stands, and the road, long ignored, is only now being constructed. Many Guatemalan-made maps show most of Belize south of the Hummingbird Hwy as being part of Guatemala.

Independence & Beyond

The country's first general election was held in 1954, and the People's United Party (PUP) won handsomely on leader George Price's pro-independence platform. On September 21, 1981, the colony of British Honduras officially became the independent nation of Belize.

In modern politics, Belize is a parliamentary democracy within the Commonwealth, where the monarch of Britain is the head of state but executive power rests with the government. Since 2008 the government and ruling party has been the center-right United Democratic Party (UDP), led by Dean Barrow, with the opposition People's United Party (PUP) holding the remaining seats in parliament.

Culture

The National Pysche

Rule number one in Belize: give respect and you'll get respect. Belizeans are friendly and curious by nature, but often wait to see what you're like before deciding how they're going to be.

Belize's long association with the UK has left some odd legacies. Perhaps because of this (and the language thing), the country is more closely aligned with the USA than with other Central American countries. Many Belizeans also identify more closely with the Caribbean than they do with Central American culture.

People

Belize is a tiny country, but it enjoys a diversity of ethnicities that is undeniably stimulating and improbably serene. Four main ethnic groups – mestizo, Creole, Maya and Garifuna – comprise 76% of the population. The remaining 24% includes East Indians (people of Indian subcontinent origins), Chinese, Spanish, Arabs (generally Lebanese), the small but influential group of Mennonites, and North Americans and Europeans who have settled here in the last couple of decades.

The Maya of Belize make up almost 11% of the population and are divided into three linguistic groups. The Yucatec Maya live mainly in the north; the Mopan Maya in the southern Toledo District; and the Kekchí Maya in Western Belize and also in the Toledo District. Use of both Spanish and English is becoming more widespread among the Maya. Traditional Maya culture is strongest among the Maya of the south.

Southern Belize is the home of the Garifuna (or Garinagus, also called Black Caribs). The Garifuna are of South American indigenous and African descent.

Music

Music is by far the most popular art form in Belize, from the reggae-soaked cays to the ribcage-rattling tunes pumped out on every bus in the country. Styles are much more Caribbean than Latin – after a few weeks you'll be an expert on calypso, soca, steel drums and, quite possibly, reggae.

Punta rock is the official musical style of Belize. Its origins are from the music of the Garifuna – drum heavy with plenty of call and response. This music is designed to get your hips moving. Probably the most famous punta rocker is Pen Cayetano, who has a studio and gallery in Dangriga.

The parranda style, which owes its roots to more traditional Garifuna arrangements with acoustic guitar, drums and shakers, is most widely associated with artists such as Paul Nabor and the late Andy Palacio.

Brukdown, another Belizean style, was developed by Creoles working in logging camps during the 18th and 19th centuries. It involves an accordion, banjo, harmonica and a percussion instrument – traditionally a pig's jawbone is used, the teeth rattled with a stick.

The Maya of Belize are off on their own tangent when it comes to music. Most notable here is the flute music of Pablo Collado and the traditional marimba (played with large wooden xylophones, double bass and drum kit) of Alma Beliceña.

Landscape & Wildlife

The Land

Belize is mostly tropical lowland, typically hot and humid for most of the year. Rainfall is lightest in the north and heaviest in the south. The southern rainforests receive almost 4m of precipitation annually, making the south the country's most humid region.

An exception to Belize's low-lying topography and hot, sticky climate can be found in the Maya Mountains, which traverse western and southern Belize at elevations approaching 1000m. The mountains enjoy a more pleasant climate than the lowlands – comfortably warm during the day and cooling off a bit at night.

The country's coastline and northern coastal plain are largely covered in mangrove swamp, which indistinctly defines the line between land and sea. Offshore, the limestone bedrock extends eastward into the Caribbean for several kilometers at a depth of about 16.5ft (5m). At the eastern extent of this shelf is the second-longest barrier reef in the world (after Australia's Great Barrier Reef).

Wildlife

The lush tropical forests contain huge ceiba trees as well as mahogany, guanacaste and cohune palms, all festooned with orchids, bromeliads and other epiphytes and liana vines. Much of the shorelines of both the mainland and the islands are cloaked in dense mangrove.

Baird's tapir is Belize's national animal. The *gibnut* or *tepezcuintle (paca)*, a rabbit-size burrowing rodent, is abundant. Other tropical animals include the jaguar, ocelot, howler monkey, spider monkey, peccary, vulture, stork and anteater.

There are 60 species of snake in the forests and waters of Belize, but only a handful are poisonous: the fer-de-lance, the coral snake and the tropical rattlesnake are especially dangerous.

Belize's birdlife is varied and abundant, with hummingbirds, keel-billed toucans, woodpeckers and many kinds of parrots and macaws.

National Parks & Protected Areas

About 44% of Belizean territory, a little over 4062 sq miles, is under official protection of one kind or another, either by national organizations or private trusts. Much of the Maya Mountain forest south of San Ignacio is protected as the Mountain Pine Ridge Forest Reserve and Chiquibul National Park. There are smaller parks and reserves, including marine reserves, throughout the country.

Environmental Issues

Belize takes environmental issues quite seriously, and much has been done to protect the endangered species that live within its borders. Species under threat include the hawksbill, green and leatherback sea turtles, the Morelet's and American crocodiles, the scarlet macaw, the jabiru stork and the manatee.

Despite the impressive amount of protected territory, and having the highest relative forest cover in Central America, deforestation in Belize has been slow and steady since independence. Agriculture and aquaculture, development and illegal harvesting all contribute to the felling of the forests, which is taking place at a rate of 0.6% per year.

Development along the coast has catered to the growing demands of tourists, with entire islands bought and sold for the construction of resorts. Construction of buildings and paving of the roads on Ambergris Caye has dramatically changed the aesthetics and the atmosphere of that island, once a sleepy outpost and now a destination for package-tourists and partiers. Of course, there is no hard and fast rule about how many tourists are too many or how much development is too much. Many Belizeans compare their country to Cozumel or Cancún, and they are proud of the way that ecotourism is preserving their paradise.

SURVIVAL GUIDE

Directory A–Z

ACCESSIBLE TRAVEL

Belize lacks accessibility regulations and many buildings are on stilts or have uneven wooden steps. You won't see many ramps for wheelchair access and there are very few bathrooms designed for visitors in wheelchairs.

More difficulties for wheelchair users come from the lack of footpaths, as well as plentiful rough and sandy ground. With assistance, bus travel is feasible, but small planes and water taxis might be a problem.

ACCOMMODATIONS

Budget Within this range the best value is usually provided by small, often family-run guesthouses. Only the cheapest budget options have shared bathrooms or cold showers. This also includes the few backpacker hostels providing dorm accommodations, and camping.

Midrange Midrange embraces many hotels, more-comfortable guesthouses, and most of the small-scale lodges and resorts. Many places in this range have their own restaurants and bars, and offer arrangements for activities, tours and other services. The range of accommodations and service is wide within this category.

Top End Top-end accommodations can be seriously sumptuous. These are resorts, lodges and classy hotels with large, well-appointed rooms and plenty of other facilities, from restaurants and bars to private beaches, spas, pools, horse stables, dive shops and walking trails. Many have their own unique style and atmosphere created with the help of architecture, decor, location and layout.

CUSTOMS REGULATIONS

Duty-free allowances on entering Belize:

- 1L of wine or spirits
- 200 cigarettes, 250g of tobacco or 50 cigars

It is illegal to leave the country with ancient Maya artifacts, turtle shells, unprocessed coral and fish (unless you have obtained a free export permit from the Fisheries Department). It is also illegal to take firearms or ammunition into or out of Belize.

EMBASSIES & CONSULATES

A few countries have embassies in Belize. Many others handle relations with Belize from their embassies in countries such as Mexico or Guatemala, but may have an honorary consul in Belize to whom travelers can turn as a first point of contact. Unless noted, all embassies are located in Belize City.

Australian High Commission (www.trinidadandtobago.embassy.gov.au) The Australian High Commission in Trinidad & Tobago handles relations with Belize.

Canadian Honorary Consulate (223-1060; belize-city@international.gc.ca; Newtown Barracks 8, Rennaisance Tower; 8:30am-3pm Mon-Thu, to noon Fri)

German Honorary Consulate (223-0896; kay@karlmenzies.com; 104 Barrack Rd)

Guatemalan Embassy (223-3150; embbelice1@gmail.com; 8 A St, Kings Park; 8:30am-5pm Mon-Fri)

Honduran Embassy (224-5889; embahn.embajadabelize@gmail.com; 6 A St, Kings Park; appointments 9am-noon Mon-Fri)

Mexican Consulate (223-0193; consular@embamex.bz; cnr Wilson St & Newtown Barracks Rd; 8am-noon & 3-4pm)

Mexican Embassy (822-0406; https://embamex.sre.gob.mx/belice; Embassy Sq, Belmopan; 8am-5pm Mon-Fri)

Netherlands Honorary Consulate (223-2953; mchulseca@gmail.com; cnr Baymen Av & Calle Al Mar)

UK High Commission (822-2146; http://ukinbelize.fco.gov.uk; Embassy Sq, Belmopan; 8am-noon & 1-4pm Mon-Thu, 8am-2pm Fri)

US Embassy (822-4011; https://bz.usembassy.gov; Floral Park Rd, Belmopan; 8am-noon & 1-5pm Mon-Fri)

INTERNET ACCESS

With plenty of wi-fi and affordable 4G in Belize, internet cafes are virtually nonexistent these days. Even remote hotels and lodges will usually have limited wi-fi where guests can access the internet, but occasionally you'll be completely off-grid.

For those traveling with laptops and smartphones, most accommodations have wireless access in the rooms or in common areas, as indicated by the icon. This access is fairly reliable, but is easily overburdened if there are several people working simultaneously.

Public wi-fi hotspots have not really taken off in Belize, but getting hooked up to the 4G network with a local SIM card is a reliable way of getting online when there's no wi-fi around.

LGBTIQ+ TRAVELERS

Male homosexuality only became legal in Belize in 2016, when the Supreme Court found the anti-sodomy laws to be unconstitutional. The country's first official Pride march was held in 2017. Generally speaking, Belize is a tolerant society with a 'live and let live' attitude. But underlying Central American machismo and traditional religious belief mean that same-sex couples should be discreet. Some useful resources:

International Gay & Lesbian Travel Association (www.iglta.org) General information on gay and lesbian travel in Latin America.

Purple Roofs (www.purpleroofs.com) Includes some listings in San Pedro and Cayo District.

Undersea Expeditions (www.underseax.com) Scuba-diving company that sometimes offers live-aboard trips to the Blue Hole.

MONEY

The Belizean dollar (BZ$) is pegged to the US dollar at two to one (BZ$1 = US$0.50). Nearly every business in Belize accepts US dollars and prices are often quoted in US dollars at resorts and hotels – always check in advance whether you're paying in Belize dollars or US dollars.

Bargaining

Bargaining is not common in Belize with the notable exception of outdoor souvenir markets, where everything is negotiable. When business is slow, it's possible to obtain a discount on hotel rooms, golf-cart rentals and other tourism services, although this is usually limited to a quick back-and-forth rather than hard-edge bargaining.

Credit Cards

Credit cards are accepted at most hotels, restaurants and shops.

Tipping

Tipping is not obligatory but is always appreciated if guides, drivers or servers have provided you with genuinely good service. Some hotels and restaurants add an obligatory service charge to your check (usually 10%).

Hotels Not needed but baggage porters appreciate a small gratuity.

Restaurants Round up the check between 5% and 10%.

Taxis Tips are not expected.

Tour guides In high-volume areas, tour guides are used to receiving tips.

OPENING HOURS

Outside of banks, phone companies and government offices, you'll generally find most opening hours to be flexible. Restaurants and bars tend to keep longer hours during high season, but will also close early if they wish (if business is slow etc).

Banks 8am–3pm Monday to Thursday and 8am–4pm or 4:30pm Friday

Pubs and bars Noon to midnight (or later)

Restaurants and cafes 7am–9:30am (breakfast), 11:30am–2pm (lunch) and 6pm–8pm (dinner)

Shops 9am to 5pm Monday to Saturday, some open Sunday

PUBLIC HOLIDAYS

Many of Belize's public holidays are moved to the Monday nearest the given date in order to make a long weekend. You'll find banks and most shops and businesses shut on these days. Belizeans travel most around Christmas, New Year and Easter, and it's worth booking ahead for transportation and accommodations at these times.

New Year's Day January 1

Baron Bliss Day March 9

Good Friday March or April

Holy Saturday March or April

Easter Monday March or April

Labor Day May 1

Sovereign's Day May 24

National Day September 10

Independence Day September 21

Day of the Americas October 12

Garifuna Settlement Day November 19

Christmas Day December 25

Boxing Day December 26

SLEEPING PRICE RANGES

The following price ranges refer to a double room with bathroom during high season. Unless otherwise stated, a tax of 9% is added to the price.

$ less than BZ$120

$$ BZ$120–350

$$$ more than BZ$350

SAFE TRAVEL

Belize has fairly high levels of violent crime, but most areas frequented by travelers are safe and by taking basic precautions visitors are unlikely to experience any serious problems. The most likely issues for travelers involve opportunistic theft, both while out and about, and from hotel rooms.

In order to minimize the risks:

- Keep your bag in the overhead rack or under your seat on long-distance buses rather than at the back of the bus.
- Make sure windows and doors lock correctly in your room, especially in remote beachside huts, and use hotel safes where provided.
- Ask hotels and restaurants in major urban areas to phone a trusted taxi.

TELEPHONE

Belize has no regional, area or city codes. Every number has seven digits, all of which you dial from anywhere in the country. When calling Belize from other countries, follow the country code with the full seven-digit local number.

Cell Phones

Local SIM cards can be used in most unlocked international cell phones with the notable exception of phones from some operators in the USA.

EATING PRICE RANGES

The following price ranges refer to a standard meal – rice, beans, meat or fish and a side. Only the fanciest places tend to have service charges, but tipping is always appreciated.

$ less than BZ$15

$$ BZ$15–35

$$$ more than BZ$35

TOURIST INFORMATION

Belize Tourism Board (www.travelbelize.org) The official tourist agency has information offices in Belize City and San Pedro.

Belize Tourism Industry Association (p240) An independent association of tourism businesses, actively defending 'sustainable ecocultural tourism.' The Belize City office provides information about the whole country and it also runs small information offices in some key destinations. The website has a plethora of information.

VISAS

Information on visa requirements is available from Belizean embassies and consulates, and the Belize Tourism Board (www.travelbelize.org). At the time of writing, visas were not required for citizens of EU, Caricom (Caribbean Community) and Central American countries, nor Australia, Canada, Hong Kong, Israel, Mexico, New Zealand, Norway, Singapore, Switzerland and the USA. A visitors permit, valid for 30 days, will be stamped in your passport when you enter the country. In most cases this can be extended by further periods of one month (up to a maximum of six months) by applying at an immigration office (there's at least one in each of Belize's six districts). For further information you can contact the Immigration & Nationality Department (p261) in Belmopan.

VOLUNTEERING

There are a lot of opportunities for volunteer work in Belize, especially on environmental projects. In some cases, you may have to pay to participate (costs vary).

Belize Audubon Society (Map p238; ☎223-4987, 223-5004; www.belizeaudubon.org; 16 Taiwan St) Invites volunteers who are available to work for at least three months to assist in the main office or in education and field programs. Divers can volunteer for marine research projects. For rural sites, volunteers should be physically fit and able to deal with rustic accommodations.

Belize Wildlife & Referral Clinic (Map p262; ☎615-5159; www.belizewildlifeclinic.org; ⊙8:30am-5pm) Offers short-term internships in wildlife medicine for veterinary and non-veterinary students. Various scholarships and work exchanges are available for students with sincere interests and skills, and the clinic is flexible and always interested in speaking with potential interns and long-term volunteers.

Cornerstone Foundation (www.cornerstonefoundationbelize.org) This NGO, based in San Ignacio, hosts volunteers to help with AIDS education, community development and other programs. Most programs require a two-week commitment, plus a reasonable fee to cover food and housing.

Earthwatch (www.earthwatch.org) Paying volunteers are teamed with professional scientific researchers to work on shark conservation projects.

Monkey Bay Wildlife Sanctuary (p259) Monkey Bay's programs provide opportunities in education, conservation and community service. It also has many links to other conservation organizations in Belize.

Maya Mountain Research Farm (☎630-4386; www.mmrfbz.org) The 70-acre organic farm and registered NGO in Toledo offers internships for those interested in learning about organic farming, biodiversity and alternative energy.

Oceanic Society (☎USA 800-326-7491; www.oceanicsociety.org; St. George's Caye; family education program per person BZ$5000, voluntourism/snorkeling program per person BZ$6400) Paying participants in the society's expeditions assist scientists in marine research projects on St George's Caye and around the Turneffe Atoll.

Plenty International (www.plenty.org) Has opportunities for working with grassroots organizations (such as handicraft cooperatives) and schools, mostly in Toledo District.

ProWorld Service Corps (www.proworldvolunteers.org) Like a privately run Peace Corps, ProWorld organizes small-scale, sustainable projects in fields such as healthcare, education, conservation, technology and construction, mostly around San Ignacio in Cayo.

T.R.E.E.S (p264) Internships and volunteer placements are available at this nonprofit conservation organisation on the Hummingbird Hwy.

Volunteer Abroad (www.volunteerabroad.com) A sort of clearing house for volunteer opportunities around the world. The database includes a few dozen organizations that work in Belize.

WEIGHTS & MEASURES

The imperial system is used. Note that gasoline is sold by the (US) gallon.

Getting There & Away

AIR

Philip Goldson International Airport (p240), at Ladyville, 11 miles northwest of Belize City center, handles all international flights. With Belize's short internal flying distances it's often possible to make a same-day connection at Belize City to or from other airports in the country.

Non-Belizeans pay fees that total US$55.50 when flying out of Belize City on international flights. This includes the US$3.75 Protected Areas Conservation Trust (PACT) fee, which helps to fund Belize's network of protected natural areas. Most major carriers include this tax in the price of the ticket.

BORDER CROSSINGS

When departing Belize by land, non-Belizeans are required to pay fees that total BZ$40 (US$20) in cash (Belizean or US dollars). Of this, BZ$7.50 is the Protected Areas Conservation Trust (PACT) fee, which helps to fund Belize's network of protected natural areas.

Mexico

There are two official crossing points on the Mexico–Belize border. The more frequently used is at Subteniente López–Santa Elena, 9 miles from Corozal Town in Belize and 7 miles from Chetumal in Mexico. The all-paved Philip Goldson Hwy runs from the border to Belize City.

The other crossing is at La Unión–Blue Creek, 34 miles southwest of Orange Walk Town near the Río Bravo Conservation and Management Area. A new highway runs between Blue Creek and Orange Walk.

If you are crossing from Mexico to Belize, you will have to hand in your Mexican tourist card to Mexican immigration as you leave and pay a US$30 tourist tax (payable in US dollars or Mexican pesos).

Mexican bus company ADO (www.ado.com.mx) runs excellent air-conditioned express bus services twice daily from Cancún (M$840, 10 hours) to Belize City via Corozal and Orange Walk. The Cancún bus stops in Playa del Carmen and Tulum and can drop passengers directly at Cancún airport on the return leg. The buses do not enter Chetumal town in either direction. Note that the overnight bus arrives at the border in the early hours of the morning, when you'll need to leave the bus, hand in your Mexican tourist card and pay a US$30 exit fee before entering Belize.

Many regular Belizean buses ply the Philip Goldson Hwy between Belize City and Chetumal. In Chetumal, buses bound for Corozal Town (BZ$4, one hour), Orange Walk Town (BZ$8, two hours) and Belize City (BZ$14 to BZ$16, four hours) leave from the north side of Nuevo Mercado, about 0.75 miles north of the city center. Leaving from Belize, buses mostly depart in the morning; from Chetumal, afternoon departures are more common.

Additionally, an air-conditioned tourist bus (BZ$50, three hours) runs daily between the San Pedro Belize Express Water Taxi Terminal and Chetumal.

Guatemala

The only land crossing between Belize and Guatemala is a mile west of the Belizean town of Benque Viejo del Carmen at the end of the all-paved George Price Hwy from Belize City. The town of Melchor de Mencos is on the Guatemalan side of the crossing. The border is 44 miles from the Puente Ixlú junction (also called El Cruce) in Guatemala, where roads head north for Tikal (22 miles) and southwest to Flores (18 miles). The road is fully paved.

The Southern Hwy now extends to the Guatemalan border in the south, but there is no official border crossing here.

Two companies run express buses to/from Guatemala. From the San Pedro Belize Express Water Taxi terminal in Belize City, you can go to Flores (BZ$50 to BZ$55, five hours) at 10am and 1pm. From Flores there are frequent connections to Guatemala City.

You can also take any of the frequent westbound Belizean buses to Benque Viejo del Carmen and then use the local service to the border.

SEA

It's possible to arrive in Belize by boat from three neighboring countries.

The only fee you have to pay when leaving Belize by sea from Placencia is the BZ$7.50 (US$3.75) Protected Areas Conservation Trust (PACT) fee. It's payable in cash (Belizean or US dollars).

Those leaving from Punta Gorda or using the water-taxi service from Caye Caulker/San Pedro to Chetumal are required to pay the regular departure tax of BZ$40.

Getting Around

Air Maya Island (www.mayaislandair.com) and Tropic Air (www.tropicair.com) fly between all major towns in Belize. Planes are small, flights are short and fairly affordable.

Car & Motorcycle Driving is on the right. All major highways are paved, but few have decent shoulders and painted dividing lines. Speed bumps are common but not all are marked.

Boat Caye Caulker and Ambergris are serviced by ferries from Belize City, and there is also a boat from Corozal to Ambergris with a possible Sarteneja stop.

Bus Most public travel in Belize is done by bus. All towns are serviced by one or more of a bewildering variety of private bus services, and you can usually flag down a bus on the highway.

El Salvador

☎503 / POP 6.2 MILLION

Includes ➡

Why Go?

Wanted: public relations expert to rebrand Central America's most underrated country. Criteria: passion for adventure and dispelling travel myths. Reward: the honor of righting a travel wrong.

El Salvador suffers horribly from bad press. While gang violence still dominates international headlines – and keeps so many adventurous travelers at bay – the vast majority of this beautiful country remains untouched by 'the troubles.'

Those visitors who do make the effort are invariably impressed by the warm welcome they receive and by just how much this tiny country has to offer: world-class surfing on empty, dark-sand beaches; coffee plantations clinging to the sides of volcanoes; pretty villages; and sublime national parks. There are few crowds outside the capital, San Salvador, which itself has more swagger than its Central American counterparts. There is only so much encouragement we can give; it's now up to you. Please inquire within.

Best Places to Eat

- Beto's (p304)
- Rustico Bistro (p303)
- R&R (p327)
- Tunco Veloz (p314)
- La Cocina de Ma'Anita (p340)

Best Places to Stay

- La Tortuga Verde (p337)
- Casa Verde (p316)
- Hotel Anáhuac (p327)
- Los Almendros de San Lorenzo (p343)

When to Go

San Salvador

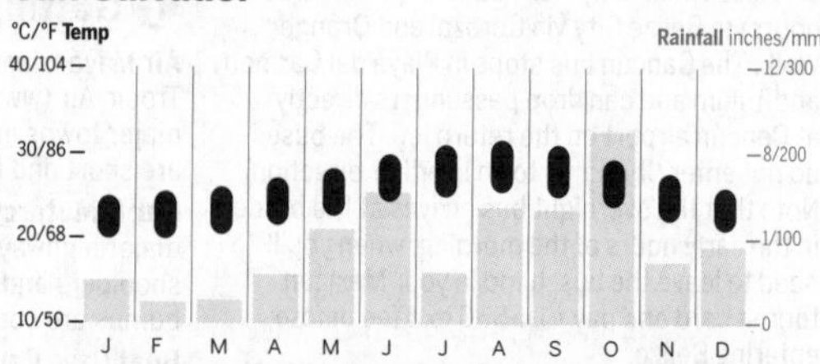

Dec–Jan The landscape is verdant after the rainy season and the weather is perfect.

May–Aug The surf gets heavy. Early August brings the celebration of El Salvador's patron saint.

Jul–Nov It's turtle-nesting season along the 300km Pacific Ocean coastline.

Entering the Country

There are four border crossings from Guatemala: through San Cristóbal, from where buses run to Santa Ana, through Las Chinamas close to Ahuachapán, through La Hachadura, near the Pacific coast, and through Anguiatú near Metapán in the north.

From Honduras, El Poy in the north El Salvador and El Amatillo in the east are the options.

EL SALVADOR IN ONE WEEK

Most of El Salvador's star attractions are squeezed into the compact western region, making it possible to explore them all in just a week. The friendly city of **Santa Ana** is a good place to start. From here you can take day trips to **Parque Nacional Los Volcanes** to climb Volcán Santa Ana, visit the Maya ruins at **Tazumal**, and take a boat trip on the shimmering waters of **Lago de Coatepeque**.

Next, head southwest to Juayúa and spend a few days working your way up the **Ruta de las Flores**, sampling coffee, exploring local villages and bathing in natural pools. From **Ahuachapán**, at the western end of the Flowers Route, make the short bus journey to **Tacuba**, the jumping-off point for forays into the lush virgin wilderness of **Parque Nacional El Imposible**. Potential adventures include rappelling down (and jumping off) waterfalls and mountain-biking to a pristine, mangrove-fringed beach at Barra de Santiago. Return to Ahuachapán and take the highway east to **San Salvador**; continue your journey from there.

Essential Food & Drink

Pupusas Cornmeal tortillas with savory fillings; *the* Salvadoran staple.

Nuégados Fried yucca dumplings with sugarcane syrup.

Panes Chucos Vegan-friendly soy hot dogs.

Riguas Sweet cornmeal cakes wrapped in a leaf and grilled.

Top Tips

- El Salvador is small and its attractions are easily accessible. To avoid lugging luggage on and off crowded buses, consider basing yourself in one place and making day trips.
- Plan in advance to avoid traveling after dark. Always check bus times to make sure you don't get stranded.
- Salvadorans tend to eat well at breakfast and lunchtime, and come evening there may be nothing available but *pupusas*. Take your main meal at midday for a better range of options.

FAST FACTS

Currency US dollar (US$)

Visas A visa is generally not required for stays of under 90 days, although a $10US tourist card is obligatory for the citizens of certain countries.

Money ATMs are plentiful, and credit cards, particularly Visa, are widely accepted.

Capital San Salvador

Emergency ☎911

Languages Spanish, Nahuat

Exchange Rates

Australia	A$1	US$0.70
Canada	C$1	US$0.76
Euro zone	€1	US$1.14
Japan	¥100	US$0.90.
New Zealand	NZ$1	US$0.68
UK	UK£1	US$1.33

Daily Costs

- Dorm bed: US$7–10; double room in a midrange hotel: US$20–60
- Bean-and-cheese *pupusa:* US$0.25; lunch for two in a restaurant: US$12–20

Resources

Lonely Planet (www.lonelyplanet.com/el-salvador)

Ministry of Tourism (www.elsalvador.travel)

SalvaNATURA (www.salvanatura.org)

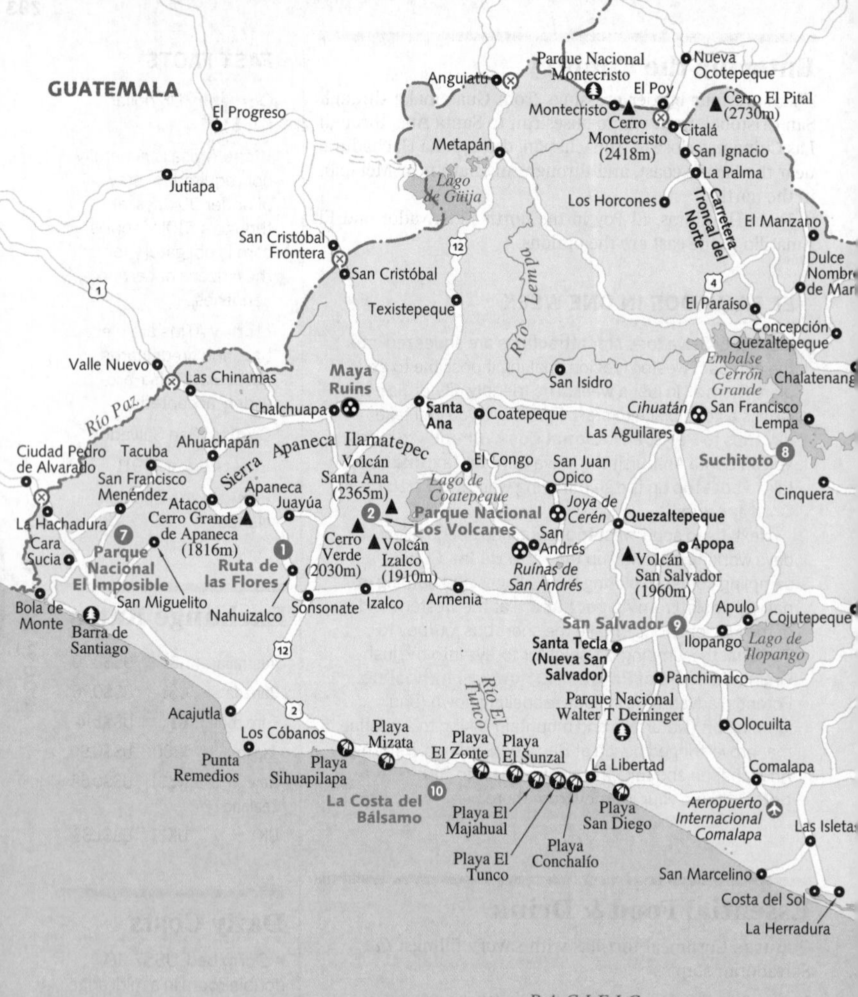

El Salvador Highlights

1 Ruta de las Flores (p323) Tracking your gourmet coffee from plantation to cup.

2 Parque Nacional Los Volcanes (p318) Hiking the park's active peaks.

3 Bahía de Jiquilisco (p333) Kayaking through mangroves and boat trips.

4 Perquín (p339) Learning about El Salvador's troubled past at sobering civil war sites.

5 Eastern Beaches (p337) Tackling the wild east, starting in Playa Esteron.

6 Maya Ruins (p320) Exploring the sites of Tazumal and Joya de Cerén.

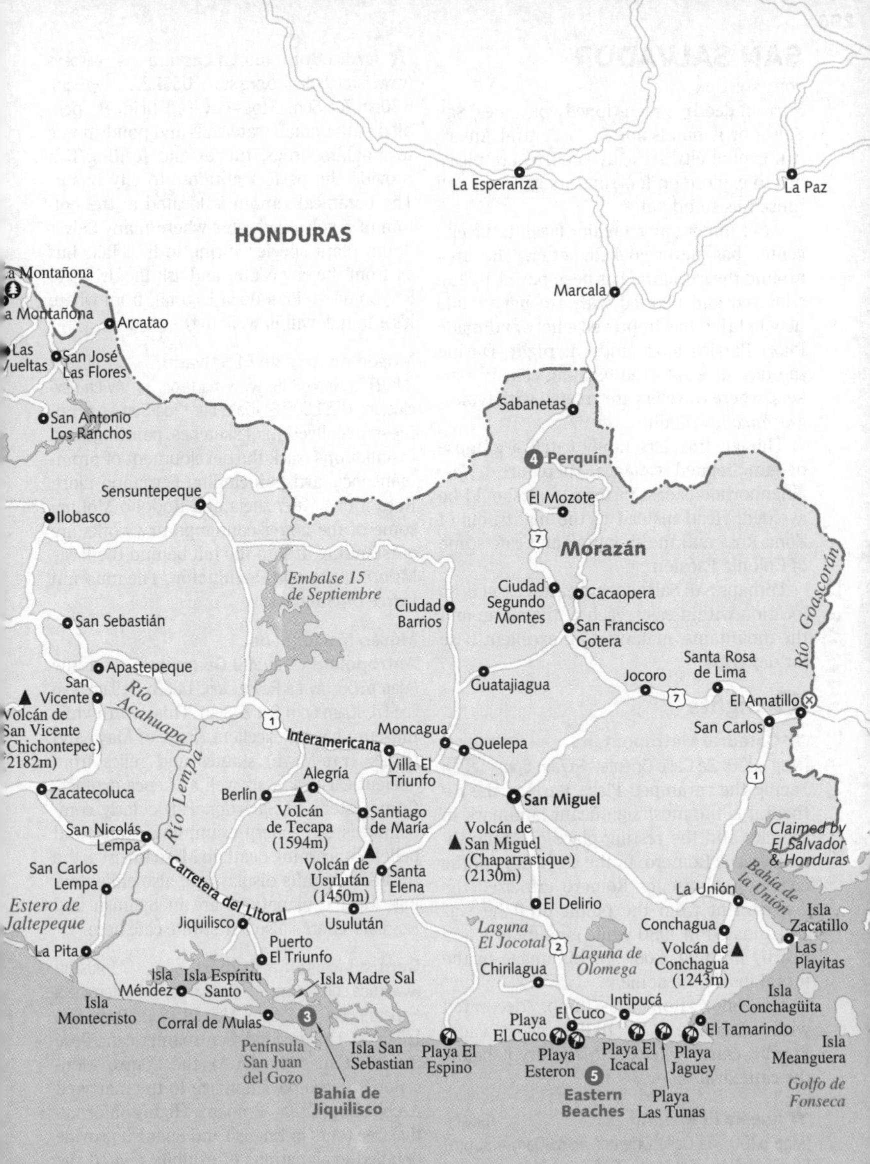

7 **Parque Nacional El Imposible** (p327) Hiking through virgin forest and rappelling down shimmering waterfalls.

8 **Suchitoto** (p341) Strolling cobbled streets in this relaxing artists' retreat.

9 **San Salvador** (p296) Getting a cultural fix at the capital's galleries, churches and museums.

10 **La Costa del Bálsamo** (p312) Kicking back at Playa El Tunco: surf, party, repeat.

SAN SALVADOR

POP 1.1 MILLION

Surrounded by green-tipped volcanoes, San Salvador is handsome for a Central American capital city. Its leafy suburbs are pleasant to explore on foot, and its galleries and museums stand out.

After undergoing a major facelift, the city center has never looked better. The area around the cathedral has been paved, pedestrianized and planted with greenery, while new lighting has improved safety and made Plaza Barrios look pretty at night. During the day, dive into the teeming *centro* markets, where travelers are greeted with typical *guanaco* hospitality.

Though travelers rarely catch a glimpse of gang-related violence, there are a few neighborhoods east of town that should be avoided. Head instead to the nightspots of Zona Rosa and the shopping and cafe scene of Colonia Escalón.

Perhaps San Salvador's greatest asset is its location within easy reach of the ocean and the mountains, making it an excellent base for day trips.

Sights

★Catedral Metropolitana CATHEDRAL

(Map p300; 2a Calle Oriente; 7am-5pm) FREE Facing the revamped Plaza Barrios, the cathedral is the most significant landmark in the city and the resting place of Archbishop Óscar A Romero. In the early days of the civil war, Monseñor Romero criticized the government from the pulpit until he was assassinated in 1980 while giving Mass at a nearby hospital. Look for his image in the mural inside the dome.

Monseñor Romero's tomb, decorated with a sculpture by Italian artist Paolo Borghi, can be viewed in the crypt below the cathedral.

★Iglesia El Rosario CHURCH

(Map p300; 4a Calle Oriente; 8:30am-4:30pm) Designed by sculptor Ruben Martinez and completed in 1971, Iglesia El Rosario is radically beautiful. Arguably the finest church in Central America, its nondescript concrete exterior conceals an arched roof and a rainbow of natural light rushing across the altar and bouncing off the metal and rock. The father of Central American independence, Padre Delgado, is buried here – quite happily, we imagine.

★Jardín Botánico La Laguna GARDENS

(www.jardinbotanico.org.sv; US$1.25; 9am-5:30pm Tue-Sun) Moss-covered bridges, pebbled paths, small waterfalls and ponds home to croaking frogs, turtles and feeding fish provide the perfect antidote to city bustle. The botanical garden is located at the bottom of a volcanic crater where many Salvadoran plant species spring to life. Take bus 44 from the city center and ask the driver to let you off at 'Plan de la Laguna,' from where it's a 1km downhill walk to the garden.

Museo de Arte de El Salvador MUSEUM

(MARTE; Map p306; www.marte.org.sv; Av La Revolución; US$1.50; 10am-6pm Tue-Sun) An impressive collection of sketches, paintings and installations track the development of prominent local artists including Fernando Llort, Rosa Mena Valenzuela and Rodolfo Molina; some of the larger contemporary works are outstanding. It's up the hill behind the large **Monumento a la Revolución**. The museum is free on Sundays.

Museo Nacional de Antropología David J Guzmán MUSEUM

(Map p306; Av La Revolución; US$3; 9am-5pm Tue-Fri, 10am-6pm Sat & Sun) This worthwhile museum has an excellent range of Maya and Olmec (pre-Maya) statues and relics from ancient Cuscatlan, as well as Lenca artifacts from eastern El Salvador. Particularly compelling is the gallery examining rituals and beliefs concerning death in Mesoamerica; the traditional crafts displays are also enlightening. Most explanations are in Spanish and English. There's also a first-rate cafe here.

Centro Monseñor Romero MUSEUM

(www.uca.edu.sv/cmr; Calle de Mediterraneo; 8am-noon & 2-6pm Mon-Fri, 8-11:30am Sat) FREE At Universidad Centroamericana José Simeón Cañas (La UCA), the Centro Monseñor Romero pays homage to the martyred Archbishop Oscar Romero. Highly informative free tours in English and Spanish provide detailed explanations of exhibits related the life and work of Monseñor Romero, and pay tribute to other victims of the civil war, including the six Jesuit priests murdered on the UCA campus in 1989.

The scene of their assassination – now a rose garden – can be visited, and the room where mother and daughter Elba and Celina Ramos were killed on same day has been preserved. Don't miss the chapel, which displays evocative works by artist Fernando Llort.

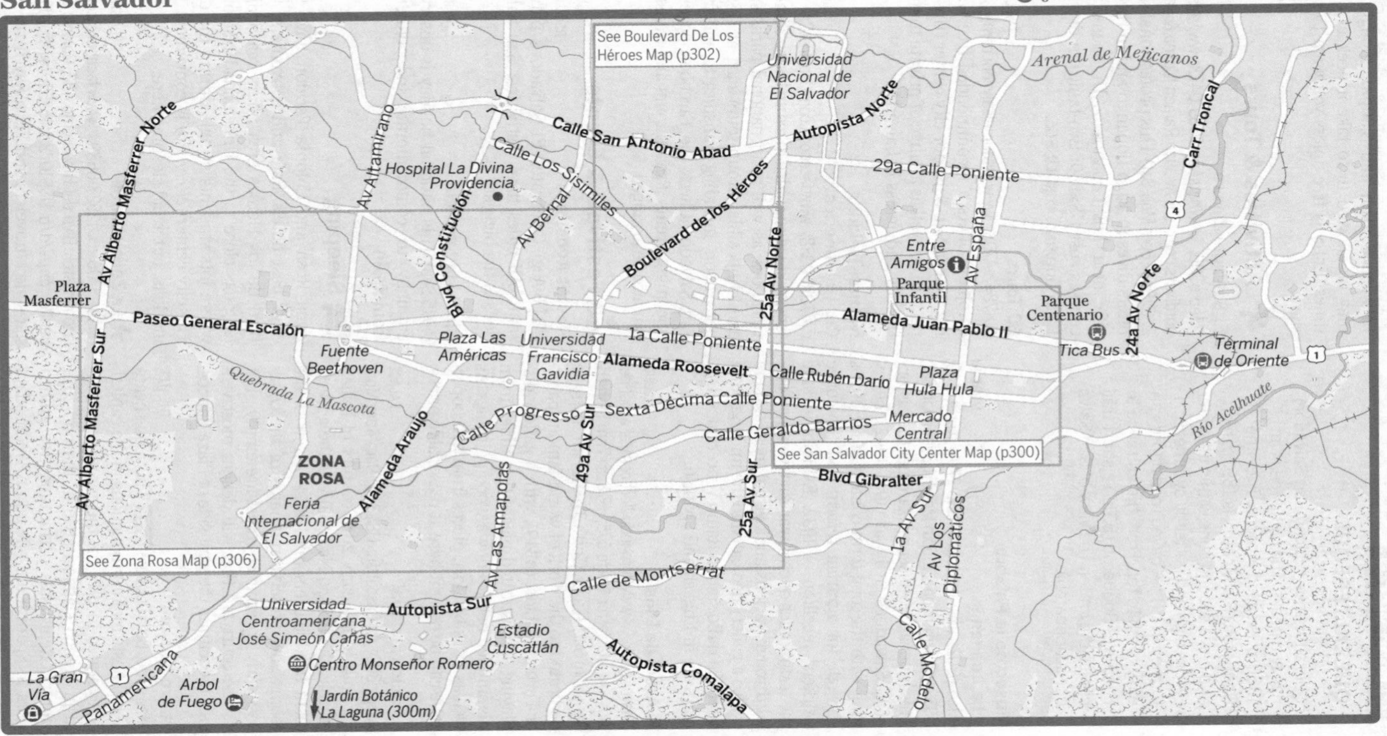
San Salvador
0 2 km
0 1 mile
See Boulevard De Los Héroes Map (p302)
Universidad Nacional de El Salvador
Arenal de Mejicanos
Carr Troncal
Av Alberto Masferrer Norte
Av Altamirano
Calle San Antonio Abad
Autopista Norte
Calle Los Sisimiles
Hospital La Divina Providencia
29a Calle Poniente
Boulevard de los Héroes
Av Bernal
Blvd Constitución
25a Av Norte
Entre Amigos
Av España
24a Av Norte
Parque Infantil
Parque Centenario
Plaza Masferrer
Paseo General Escalón
Alameda Juan Pablo II
Plaza Las Américas
Universidad Francisco Gavidia
1a Calle Poniente
Tica Bus
Terminal de Oriente
Fuente Beethoven
Alameda Roosevelt
Calle Rubén Darío
Plaza Hula Hula
Av Alberto Masferrer Sur
Quebrada La Mascota
Sexta Décima Calle Poniente
Calle Progresso
49a Av Sur
Mercado Central
Río Acelhuate
Calle Geraldo Barrios
See San Salvador City Center Map (p300)
ZONA ROSA
Alameda Araujo
Av Las Amapolas
Blvd Gibralter
25a Av Sur
1a Av Sur
Feria Internacional de El Salvador
Av Los Diplomáticos
See Zona Rosa Map (p306)
Calle de Montserrat
Universidad Centroamericana José Simeón Cañas
Autopista Sur
Estadio Cuscatlán
Autopista Comalapa
Calle Modelo
Centro Monseñor Romero
La Gran Vía
Panamericana
Arbol de Fuego
Jardín Botánico La Laguna (300m)

DON'T MISS

QUEZALTEPEQUE

Quezaltepeque (Volcán San Salvador) has two peaks. The higher peak, at 1960m, is called Picacho. The other, Boquerón (Big Mouth), is 1893m high and has a second cone within its crater – 45m high and perfectly symmetrical – formed in 1917. A paved road affords an easy climb to top. From the entrance to Parque El Boquerón (p310) a short trail circles the crater. The view of San Salvador is unbeatable.

Museo de la Palabra y La Imagen MUSEUM
(Map p302; www.museo.com.sv; 27 Av Norte 1140; US$2; ⌚8am-noon & 2-5pm Mon-Fri, 8am-noon Sat) This innovative museum examines the history of El Salvador's civil war (1981–1992), beginning with the long-term context of the 1920s struggle for agrarian reform and the coffee workers' rebellion of 1932. Exhibits include the testimonies of civil war survivors presented through various audiovisual means; there is also a gallery dedicated to the underground guerrilla radio station Radio Venceremos. Displays are in English and Spanish.

El Arbol de Dios GALLERY
(Map p306; www.fernando-llort.com/el-arbol-de-dios; Av Masferrer Norte 575; ⌚8am-7pm Mon-Fri, 9am-6pm Sat) FREE 'God's Tree' is an institute dedicated to the work of world-famous painter Fernando Llort (p349), with a gallery displaying sophisticated pieces that differ from his simpler, better-known wood paintings. As well as work by Llort, pieces from his cooperative can be bought here at reasonable prices.

Palacio Nacional PALACE
(Map p300; Av Cuscatlán; US$3; ⌚9am-4pm Mon-Fri) Built in the early 20th century of Italian marble, the Palacio Nacional was the government headquarters until 1974. A few of the rooms now preserve remnants of the country's early governance (most are empty), but it's the courtyard that will delight most visitors. It occupies the west side of Plaza Barrios.

Teatro Nacional THEATER
(Map p300; Calle Delgado) FREE This aging beauty still hosts major productions in the capital. Inaugurated in 1917, the theater was renovated in French classical style in the mid-20th century. Rehearsals permitting, free guided tours in Spanish are offered on Wednesdays between 8:30am and 3:30pm, though you may be allowed in to take a peek at other times. Entry is free unless you want to see a show.

Activities & Tours

El Salvador Divers DIVING
(Map p306; ☎WhatsApp 7069-0473; www.elsalvadordivers.com; cnr Av Juan Ramon Molina & Pasaje 2; ⌚9am-6pm Mon-Sat) This professional shop offers dives in Lago Ilopango and in the Pacific near Los Cóbanos. PADI open-water courses cost US$350; two-tank fun dives in Lago Ilopango cost US$65.

EC Tours WALKING
(☎7842-4708; www.ectourselsalvador.com) This company offers a recommended free walking tour of San Salvador city center (tips expected), as well as a range of private tours in the city and across El Salvador.

Natural Trekking Central America HIKING
(☎7016-0938; www.facebook.com/NatTrekCA) Offers good-value guided hikes up lesser-climbed volcanoes, as well as in national parks such as El Imposible. Group tours start at US$25 per person, including transport to and from San Salvador. Check the Facebook page for upcoming events. Private tours and transfers can also be arranged.

Festivals & Events

Fiestas Agostinas RELIGIOUS
(⌚1-6 Aug) Celebrates El Salvador's patron saint. All cities have festivities; San Salvador's is the biggest.

Dia de Indepencia PARADE
(⌚15 Sep) This national holiday is observed annually to commemorate independence from Spain.

Sleeping

Zona Rosa and Colonia Escalón have the city's best hotels. Safe and convenient, the Blvd de los Héroes area offers reasonable lodgings close to the Universidad Nacional where lots students mingle during the day. The city center *(el centro)* is convenient for markets, but avoid sleeping here.

★La Zona Hostel HOSTEL $
(Map p306; ☎2528-6689; www.facebook.com/lazonahostel; Blvd del Hipódromo 436, Colonia San Benito; dm/s/d/tr US$10/35/45/55; ❄📶) This self-styled 'travelers spot' is a key fixture in

the capital's budget accommodation stocks. Perfectly located for the Zona Rosa action and opposite the Tica Bus stop in a safe, prosperous neighborhood, La Zona has colorful dorms, well-appointed private rooms and comfortable communal areas. A great place to trade travel tips over a cold beer.

★Cumbres del Volcán Colonia Escalón HOSTEL **$**

(Map p306; ☎2207-3705; www.cumbresdelvolcan.com; 85a Av Norte 637; dm US$10-12, d US$20, tr US$30-45; ❄📶) In the leafy Colonia Escalón neighborhood, 'Volcano Summit' offers popular dorm rooms downstairs and four color-themed private rooms on the 2nd floor. The communal lounge is large and quiet, and the shared kitchen and terrace are ideal for meeting other independent travelers. It's within walking distance of some of San Salvador's best restaurants.

La Almohada HOSTEL **$**

(Map p302; ☎2260-7380; www.facebook.com/almohadahostal; Calle Berlín 220; dm/s US$12/15; 📶) The socially conscious Almohada hostel supports a local kids' charity by selling a cheap place to rest in a welcoming, communal atmosphere. The quiet, suburban location is safe for walking and there are a few restaurants within easy reach, though many guests will happily settle for the large shared kitchen and common areas.

★Cumbres del Volcán Flor Blanca HOSTEL **$$**

(Map p306; ☎2556-9803; www.cumbresdelvolcan.com; cnr Sexta-Decima Calle Pte & 37 Av Sur; dm US$7, r US$30-35; 🚭📶) This well-run hostel occupies an airy 1950s mansion close to Parque Cuscatlán in the Flor Blanca neighborhood. The spacious, modern kitchen, bright courtyard and homey common areas are big pluses, and upstairs the private rooms are huge. It's a convenient base for exploring the city center, 2km to the east, but nightlife options in the area are limited.

Arbol de Fuego HOTEL **$$**

(☎2557-3601; www.arboldefuego.com; Av Antiguo Cuscatlan, Colonia La Sultana; incl breakfast s US$60-70, d US$70-80; ❄@📶) 🍃 Named for the red-flowered 'Fire Tree' outside, Arbol de Fuego is the pick of the hotels in the quieter Antiguo Cuscatlan area south of the city. The rooms are impeccably presented, featuring colorful local fabrics and natural soaps; those upstairs are a little brighter. The breakfast garden is an oasis.

The owners have invested heavily in making the property as environmentally conscious as possible and even run seminars on sustainability for nonguests.

Hotel Villa del Angel HOTEL **$$**

(Map p306; ☎2223-7171; www.villadelangelhotel.com; 71 Av Norte 219; s/d/tr incl breakfast from US$70/75/87; ❄📶) The Angel offers a peaceful retreat in the city, with a range of bright, oversized rooms arranged around a pretty garden and terraces. The location is convenient for accessing Galerías Escalón. English is widely spoken.

SAINT ÓSCAR ROMERO

Óscar Arnulfo Romero has long been revered as a hero and martyr in his homeland, and now it's official. In 2018, three years after some 250,000 people attended a beatification ceremony in San Salvador, Pope Francis gave his approval for Romero's sainthood. Romero was canonized on October 14, 2018.

A passionate advocate for social justice, Archbishop Romero was shot dead on March 24, 1980, while celebrating Mass at the **Hospital La Divina Providencia** (El Hospitalito; www.hospitaldivinaprovidencia.org; cnr Calle Toluca & Av Rocio; ⌚8am-noon & 2-5pm Mon-Fri, 8am-noon Sat) FREE in San Salvador. His path to sainthood was previously blocked by conservatives in the church and is viewed by many as long overdue. In El Salvador, confirmation of Romero's sainthood has been received with joy and pride.

In San Salvador, the excellent Centro Monseñor Romero (p296) examines the life and work of Romero. His tomb can be visited in San Salvador Cathedral (p296).

No one was brought to justice for Romero's murder, but in 2017 a judge reopened the case. New trials in a number of cases related to the civil war have been made possible by a Supreme Court ruling that overturned the 1993 General Amnesty Law. Another high-profile case recently reopened involves 18 former military officials and their alleged involvement in the massacre at El Mozote (p341).

San Salvador City Center

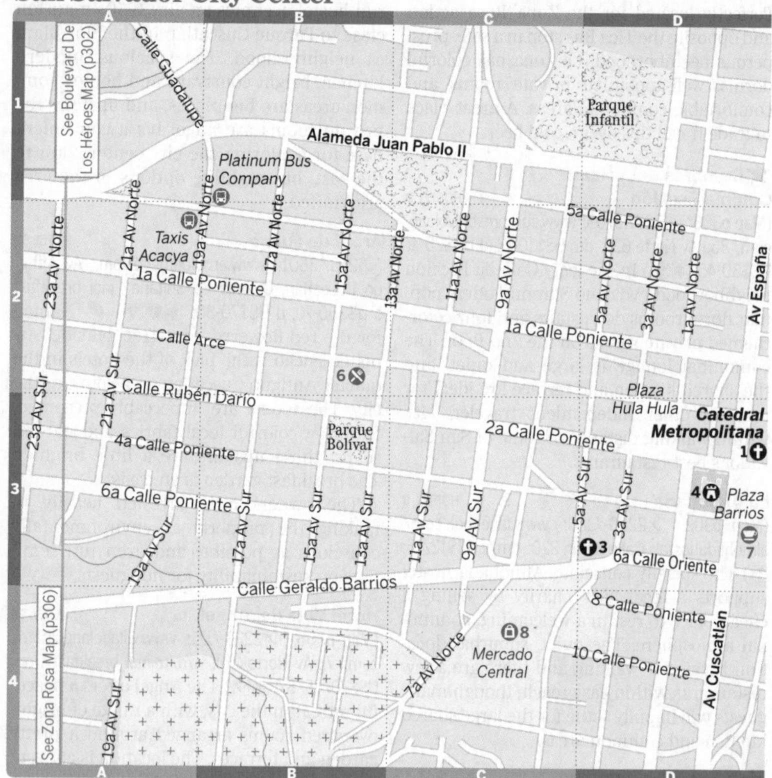

La Posada del Rey I

HOTEL $$

(Map p306; ☎2264-5245; laposadadelrey@gmail.com; Pasaje Dordely 4425, Colonia Escalón; s/d/tr US$53/65/74; ❄@☎☒) This stalwart of Colonia Escalón still turns out well-sized rooms with plush beds to tour groups, business folk and solo travelers. The numerous staff are always smiling, there's a relaxing patio area with a dipping pool and the paint job will cheer the jet lag. The surrounding area is pleasant for walking.

Hostal Armonía

HOTEL $$

(Map p302; ☎2225-6124; www.armoniahostal.com; 35a Av Norte; s/d/tr US$34/42/50; ❄☎) This neat guesthouse offers excellent value and prompt, courteous service, though it is short on communal areas. The 14 rooms are spacious and well appointed. It's a smart option for those wanting a little peace and convenience; look for the white arches.

Hotel Villa Florencia Zona Rosa

HOTEL $$

(Map p306; ☎2243-7164; www.hotelvillaflorencia.com; Av La Revolución; s/d/tr incl breakfast US$65/75/88; ❄@☎) A number of excellent cultural and dining options within close walking distance make this small hotel a favorite among return travelers to San Salvador. It isn't particularly cheap, but the small rooms are modestly lavish and the stone courtyard is a refuge from the heat. It's also close to the stop for buses to Guatemala and Honduras.

International Guest House

HOTEL $$

(Map p302; ☎2226-7343; i_guesthouse@hotmail.com; 35a Av Norte 9 bis; s/d/tr incl breakfast US$25/35/45; @☎) Competition for customers brings out the best in the International, overseen by the charmingly effusive Alma. Wi-fi is fast, beer is chilled and the beds are just right. There's a cozy feel to the plant-filled common areas, and there's a garden with hammocks out back.

San Salvador City Center

Top Sights

1 Catedral Metropolitana D3
2 Iglesia El Rosario E3

Sights

3 Iglesia El Calvario D3
4 Palacio Nacional D3
5 Teatro Nacional E3

Eating

6 Pollo Bonanza B2

Drinking & Nightlife

7 Café de El Salvador D3

Shopping

8 Mercado Central C4
9 Mercado Ex-Cuartel F3

Hotel El Torogoz HOTEL **$$**

(Map p302; ☎2225-8483; www.hoteleltorogoz.com; 35a Av Norte 7B; s/d incl breakfast with bathroom US$35/45, without bathroom US$27/42; @≋) There are better rooms in town than those on offer at this relaxed family-run hotel, but El Torogoz' big appeal lies in its leafy gardens and inviting swimming pool.

Hotel Tazumal HOTEL **$$**

(Map p302; ☎2235-0156; www.hoteltazumalhouse.com; 35a Av Norte 3; s/d/tr incl breakfast US$35/45/55; @ 📶) In an area with numerous small hotels offering similar rooms, Tazumal stands out for its homey communal spaces, natural light and pretty courtyard. Not much English is spoken, so dust off the phrasebook.

★**Nico Urban Hotel** BOUTIQUE HOTEL **$$$**

(Map p306; ☎2528-4200; www.nicourbanhotel.com; Blvd del Hipódromo 605, Colonia San Benito; s/d incl breakfast US$153/172; ❄📶) Zona Rosa is rosier for Nico Urban Hotel, El Salvador's most upscale boutique hotel. The six rooms are minimalist in design, yet spacious enough to swing a yoga mat. The stone floors, sheltered lawn garden and pure cotton sheets cancel out the need for a swimming pool, while the furniture and art selections create a sanctuary of good taste. The hotel also has a gin bar and restaurant that rivals anything in town.

Clarion Suites Las Palmas APARTMENT **$$$**

(Map p306; ☎2250-0800; www.choicehotels.com/clarion; Blvd del Hipódromo, Colonia San Benito; ste from US$150; ❄@≋) These suites have kitchenettes with large fridges and microwaves plus there's discreet staff, space to dance and a fabulous rooftop pool, making Las Palmas a smart choice for families or groups looking for a base close to the Zona Rosa nightlife. The decor gives off a business hotel vibe, but there are great views from the upper floors. Rates drop on weekends.

Eating

★**Pollo Bonanza** SALVADORAN **$**

(Map p300; Calle Arce 525, City Center; mains $2.75; ⏰9:30am-6pm Mon-Sat, to 3pm Sun) Locals claim the broiled chicken at this simple downtown diner is the best in the country. For more than 30 years, Bonanza has been pulling in lunchtime crowds with generous portions of *pollo* cooked in a wood-fired oven, served with *escabeche* (picked cabbage) and fries. Arrive early or be ready to wait in line.

Boulevard De Los Héroes

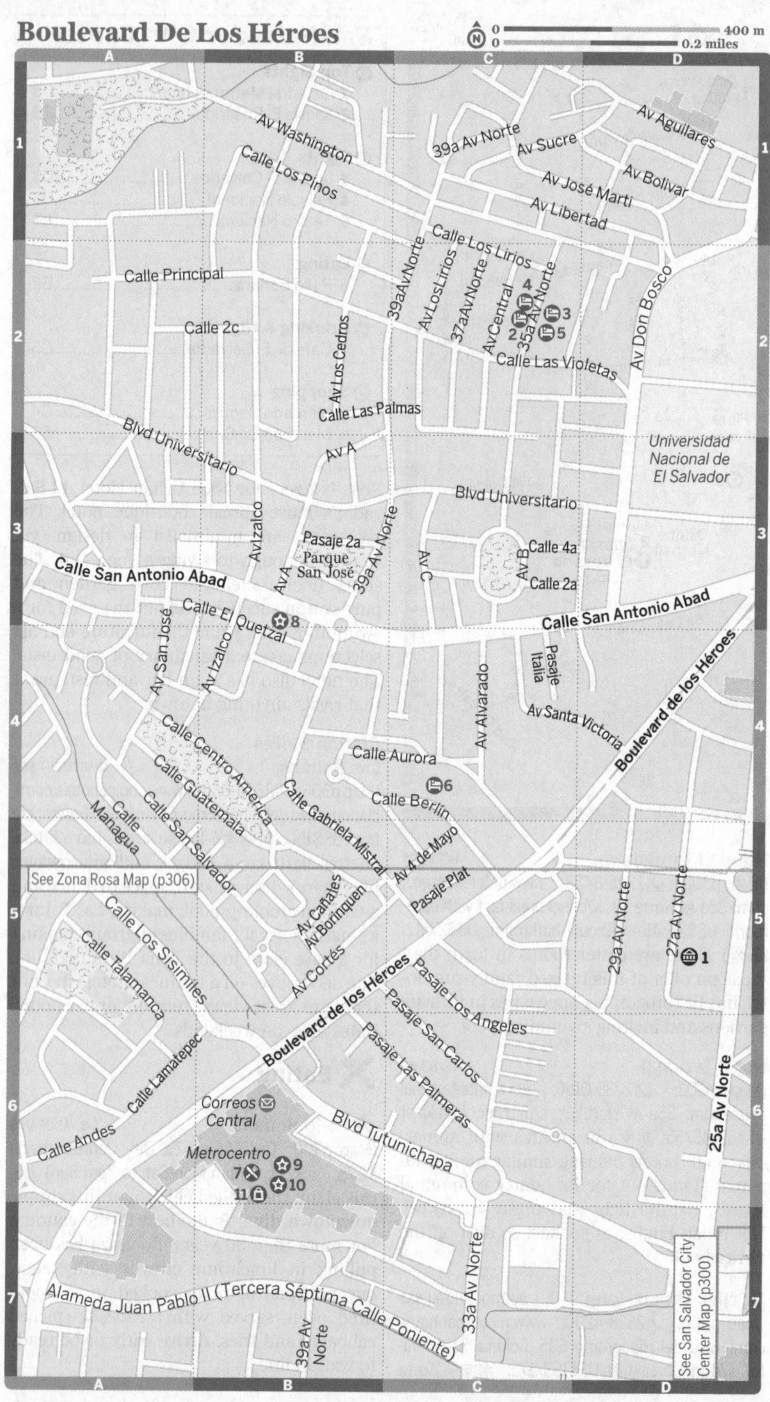

EL SALVADOR SAN SALVADOR

Boulevard De Los Héroes

Sights

1 Museo de la Palabra y La Imagen D5

Sleeping

2 Hostal Armonía C2
3 Hotel El Torogoz C2
4 Hotel Tazumal C2
5 International Guest House C2
6 La Almohada C4

Eating

7 Café Maquilishuat B6

Entertainment

8 Café La 'T' B3
9 CineMark B6
10 Teatro Luis Poma B6

Shopping

11 La Ceiba Libros B6

Food Trucks STREET FOOD $
(Map p306; Av La Revolución, Colonia San Benito; mains US$3-7; 11:30am-2:30pm & 6-9:30pm Mon-Sat, noon-4pm Sun) Near the Monumento a la Revolución in San Benito you'll find food trucks selling burgers, *arepas* (stuffed corn tortillas), grilled meats, *chocobananos* (frozen bananas dipped in chocolate) and more. Wash it down with a mojito from the Kombi 2Go cocktail van.

Café Maquilishuat SALVADORAN $
(Map p302; Av Los Andes, Metrocentro; mains US$2.25-4.50; 7:30am-7pm Mon-Sat, 9am-5:30pm Sun;) Named after the pinkish national tree of El Salvador, this *típico* is a reliable option for a cheap bite. The menu of local staples changes daily, with plenty of vegetarian options.

★ **Rustico Bistro** BURGERS $$
(Map p306; 2224-5656; 3a Calle Poniente 3877, Colonia Escalón; mains US$6-11; noon-3pm Mon & Tue, noon-3pm & 6-9:30pm Wed-Sat) Rustico rivals any burger place in the world as far as we're concerned. The buns are thick and fresh and the patties must weigh half a cow. Try the pulled-pork sandwiches with tamarind sauce and wash it all down with a jar of fruit juice or a cold Cadejo beer.

★ **El Sopón Típico** SALVADORAN $$
(Map p306; Paseo General Escalón, Colonia Escalón; mains US$5-15; 11am-9pm) Simple, fresh and delicious local food is the order of the day at this famous *típico* restaurant on a busy corner beside Galerías Escalón. Winning dishes include *marisco en crema* (seafood with cream) and *sopa de chorizo* (soup with sausage), but it's hard to fault much.

Olas Permanentes SEAFOOD $$
(Map p306; 2264-5954; www.olaspermanentes.restaurant; Calle El Mirador 127, Colonia Escalón; mains US$7-20; noon-10:30am Sun-Wed, to midnight Thu, to 1am Fri & Sat) If you don't go to the beach, the beach comes to you, or so goes the tagline of this buzzy, marine-themed restaurant and bar. The breezy terrace overlooks Plaza Palestina, while the arty interior decor features wave-like mosaics, sculptures by local artists and shell-covered light fittings. Seafood dishes here are good value; try the *coctel de camaron* (prawn cocktail).

Mile Time VEGETARIAN $$
(Map p306; 2264-9980; www.facebook.com/MileTimeEscalon; 11a Calle Poniente 4134, Colonia Escalón; mains US$4-8.50; 11:30am-9pm Mon-Sat;) Faux-meat never tasted so good. The full gamut of Asian and Western vegan and vegetarian dishes is served at this impressive restaurant in Escalón. The *sopa agripicante* (sweet and sour soup) is divine, and the dessert menu is extensive.

Le Croissant FRENCH $$
(Map p306; 2223-2575; www.lecroissant.com.sv; Blvd del Hipódromo, Colonia San Benito; breakfast US$4-8.50, mains US$4.25-10; 7:30am-6:30pm) A range of freshly baked French pastries, brunches, quiches, salads and sandwiches are served at this chic patisserie located in an upscale furniture store. The coffee is decent and it makes a handy breakfast stop if you're staying in Zona Rosa.

El Cafe de Don Pedro SALVADORAN $$
(Map p306; 2260-2011; www.elcafededonpedro.com; cnr 39a Av Norte & Alameda Roosevelt, Colonia Flor Blanca; mains US$4-12; 24hr) The grilled meats and breakfast specials are the highlights of this 24-hour restaurant, located in a partially open-air 1950s diner. The food can be hit-or-miss, but staff are bubbly and there's ample parking and dirt-cheap beer.

Típicos Margoth SALVADORAN $$
(Map p306; 2263-3340; 77a Av Norte, Colonia Escalón; mains US$4-7.50; 7am-9:30pm) While service is not always as *margoth* (bubbly and extroverted) as advertised, this self-serve family-run restaurant is a tasty initiation into Salvadoran cuisine. The *antojitos* (small dishes) are a good place to start; finish with *plátanos* (plantain) and cinnamon cream.

WORTH A TRIP

LOS PLANES DE RENDEROS

This hillside district, 12km to the south of San Salvador, is famous for **Puerta del Diablo** (Devil's Door). Two towering boulders, reputedly one single stone split in two, form a lookout with fantastic views. During the war this place was an execution point, the cliffs offering easy disposal of the bodies.

The boulders are 2km past the family-friendly **Parque Balboa** (US$3; 8am-4pm), where you will reputedly find some of the best *pupusas* in the land. Take bus 12, 'Mil Cumbres' (US$0.30, 20 minutes), from the east side of the Mercado Central, at 6a Calle Poniente. If you're driving, head down Av Cuscatlán until you see the signs.

★**Beto's** SEAFOOD $$$

(Map p306; 2263-7304; cnr 85a Av Norte & Pasaje Dordely, Colonia Escalón; mains US$7-21; 11am-11pm Mon-Thu, to midnight Fri & Sat, to 10pm Sun;) Colonia Escalón is the place to be seen lingering over crustaceans, and Beto's has the perfect mix of lunchtime work crowd and Salvadoran elite dining on anything that moves under the sea. Service is disarmingly good. The lengthy menu also features meat dishes, pasta and pizza.

Drinking & Nightlife

San Salvador has a healthy and diverse nightlife. Zona Rosa is the most popular locale, with plenty of smoky dance floors and live bands jamming until well after midnight, while a more refined crowd can be found around Colonia Escalón. Outside town, Paseo El Carmen in Santa Tecla is the nightspot à la mode, with alfresco cafes and thumping bars on weekends.

★**Cadejo Brewing Company** CRAFT BEER

(Map p306; 2223-3180; www.cervezacadejo.com; Calle La Reforma 222, Colonia San Benito; 11:30am-11pm Mon-Thu, to midnight Fri & Sat, 10am-8pm Sun) Craft beer has landed in El Salvador! This popular brewpub offers seven Cadejo beers on tap; a sampler of six costs US$5. Try the Suegra (mother-in-law) – an IPA that's strong, sweet and bitter with plenty of personality (just like the brewer's own *suegra*). Free brewery tours are usually held at 5pm; call ahead to confirm.

Nómada COCKTAIL BAR

(Map p306; 7803-3788; Blvd del Hipodrómo; noon-3pm & 6pm-1am Mon-Sat) Take a seat and watch the mixologists at work at this chic, low-lit cocktail bar that could hold its own in New York or London. In-house creations include the Nómada, a blend of passion fruit, chiltepe chilies, lemon and Tíc Táck (a local sugarcane liquor).

Café de El Salvador COFFEE

(Map p300; Av Cuscatlán, Edificio Centro, 2nd fl; 8:30am-5pm Mon-Fri, 8am-noon Sat) Inside the Museo Banco Hipotecario (admission free) at Plaza Barrios is this excellent coffee shop, offering an air-conditioned escape from the heat and an expertly brewed latte or espresso made with your choice of bean. There are six different local varieties available; a map shows which part of the country the coffee was grown.

Mercado Cuscatlán ROOFTOP BAR

(Map p306; cnr 25 Av Sur & Calle Gerardo Barrios; market 6am-3am, bars 11:30am-10pm Sun-Thu, to midnight Fri & Sat) The magnificent murals adorning the outer walls of this gleaming new market are reason enough to take a look. Inside there are two floors of market stalls and a rooftop *mirador* (viewpoint) with several bars and cafes that get lively on weekends. The most popular is **La Taberna**, with DJs and dancing on Friday and Saturday nights.

La Ventana BAR

(Map p306; 2557-0198; 83a Av Norte 510; noon-11pm Mon-Wed, to 2am Thu-Sat) The Ventana has been in business for more than two decades, which is quite an achievement in a city like San Salvador. The beer comes first though, with a huge list of ales to choose from to accompany a solid pub-style menu (mains US$7 to US$15). Crepes are also available for a bit of variety.

Barbass BAR

(Map p306; 79a Av Norte 725, Colonia Escalón; 7:30am-late Tue-Sat) Rock and roll ain't noise pollution at this reverberating den, which hosts local guitar heroes and an all-ages crowd. The walls are covered in engrossing street art. Tattoos are not a prerequisite for entry, though they will be appreciated.

Republik BAR

(Map p306; 2240-0041; www.facebook.com/barrepublik; Calle La Reforma 243-247; 3pm-1am Wed-Sun) Irish bar Republik is the most consistently lively venue in Zona Rosa. Live cover bands and CD-spinning DJs entertain a well-dressed crowd who dance in groups and drink mojitos and buckets of bottled beer on reserved tables. Check the Facebook page for upcoming events.

Scape GAY
(Map p306; www.facebook.com/scapedisco; Prolongación Juan Pablo II; ⏲9pm-2:30am Thu-Sat) Gay disco heaven on weekends.

☆ Entertainment

★Café La 'T' LIVE MUSIC
(Map p302; Calle San Antonio Abad 2233; ⏲10am-9:30pm Mon-Wed, to 11pm Thu-Sat) The country's finest musicians appear intermittently at this down-tempo cafe set aside from the hullabaloo. Ska, jazz, blues, salsa: just turn up and try your luck. There's light food, booze and good coffee.

Teatro Luis Poma THEATER
(Map p302; ☎2210-3828; www.teatroluispoma.com; Blvd de los Héroes, Metrocentro; US$7) Contemporary performances across all genres at San Salvador's most respected theater. Naturally, it's at the mall.

CineMark CINEMA
(Map p302; ☎2261-2001; Blvd de los Héroes, Metrocentro, 3rd fl) Our favorite of the big cinema groups.

Shopping

Xocolatísimo CHOCOLATE
(Map p306; www.xocolatisimo.com.sv; Blvd del Hipódromo 548; ⏲9am-7pm Mon-Fri, to 6pm Sun) Since most of the country's cacao is exported, quality Salvadoran chocolate can be hard to find, but this chocolatier is the exception. The award-winning truffles and bars sold here are made with cacao from Hacienda San José Real de la Carrera in Usulután; the beautiful packaging makes it perfect for gifts.

Galerías Escalón MALL
(Map p306; www.galerias.com.sv; Paseo General Escalón; ⏲10am-8pm) Galerías has three air-conditioned levels of upscale clothing and jewelry stores, electronics stores, cellphone offices, banks and a cinema. The mall is constructed around a beautifully restored 1950s mansion, which sits within the main atrium and houses stores and a gallery.

Mercado Central MARKET
(Map p300; 6a Calle Ote; ⏲7:30am-6pm Mon-Sat, to 2pm Sun) Salvadoran city life at full throttle, the Mercado Central is the local favorite for clothes and electronics.

DON'T MISS

PARQUE CUSCATLÁN

West of the center in Colonia Flor Blanca is **Parque Cuscatlán**, a public park that was undergoing a US$4.6 million dollar makeover at research time. As well as state-of-the-art landscaping and lighting, improvements include expanding the art gallery and building a new cultural center and sports center.

One block south of the park on 25 Av Sur is Mercado Cuscatlán, a swanky new market in a four-story building, with two floors of vendors' stalls, a public library and a rooftop *mirador* with wonderful views across San Salvador and beyond. So far the market hasn't been the success that planners hoped, but the rooftop bars are popular on weekends.

La Gran Vía MALL
(cnr Carretera Panamericana & Calle Chiltiupán; ⏲10am-8pm) Large mall with a number of international chains, cafes, restaurants and a cinema.

Mercado Ex-Cuartel MARKET
(Map p300; Calle Delgado; ⏲7:30am-6pm Mon-Sat, to 2pm Sun) The Mercado Ex-Cuartel is a difficult place to navigate, but be patient and you'll find handmade hammocks and embroidered fabrics from across the country.

La Ceiba Libros BOOKS
(Map p302; Blvd de los Héroes, Metrocentro, 1st fl; ⏲9am-7pm Mon-Sat, 10am-5pm Sun) Stock up on Salvadoran history and literature in Spanish. There are four branches in the capital.

ℹ Orientation

San Salvador follows the same grid pattern as most Central American cities. Unfortunately, signage is sparse in the central area (check for names on the street curbs). From the zero point at the cathedral, Av España goes north and Av Cuscatlán south; Calle Arce runs to the west and Calle Delgado to the east.

Avenidas (avenues) run north–south, and change from Sur (South) to Norte (North) when they cross the major east–west artery (Calles Arce and Delgado). Likewise, avenues are odd- or even-numbered depending on whether they are west or east of the north–south artery (Avs

Zona Rosa

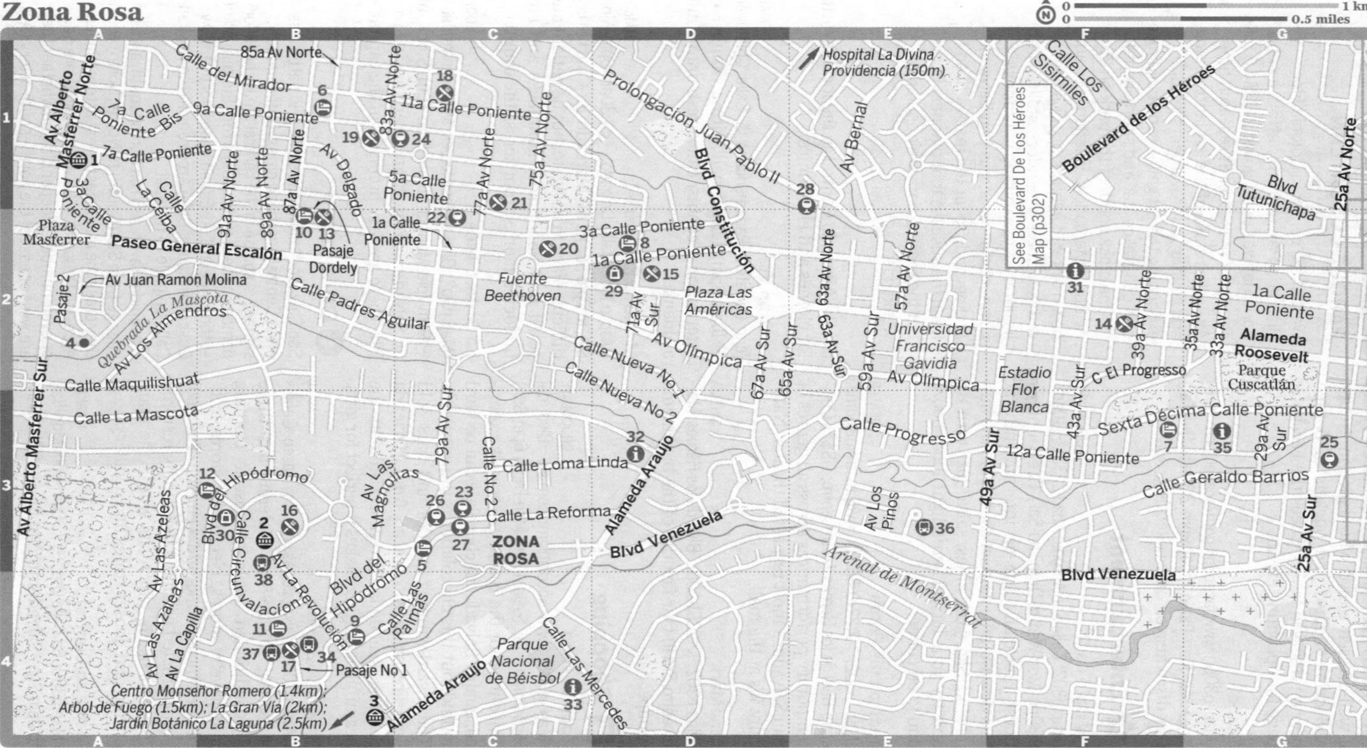

0
1 km
0
0.5 miles
Calle del Mirador
85a Av Norte
Av Alberto Masferrer Norte
7a Calle Poniente Bis
9a Calle Poniente
7a Calle Poniente
3a Calle Poniente
Calle La Ceiba
Plaza Masferrer
Paseo General Escalón
91a Av Norte
89a Av Norte
87a Av Norte
Av Delgado
83a Av Norte
11a Calle Poniente
5a Calle Poniente
77a Av Norte
75a Av Norte
1a Calle Poniente
Pasaje Dordely
Pasaje 2
Av Juan Ramon Molina
Quebrada La Mascota
Av Los Almendros
Calle Padres Aguilar
Fuente Beethoven
3a Calle Poniente
1a Calle Poniente
71a Av Sur
Plaza Las Américas
Prolongación Juan Pablo II
Blvd Constitución
Av Bernal
Hospital La Divina Providencia (150m)
63a Av Norte
57a Av Norte
See Boulevard De Los Héroes Map (p302)
Calle Los Sisimiles
Boulevard de los Héroes
Blvd Tutunichapa
25a Av Norte
1a Calle Poniente
39a Av Norte
35a Av Norte
33a Av Norte
Alameda Roosevelt
Parque Cuscatlán
Av Olímpica
Calle Nueva No 1
Calle Nueva No 2
67a Av Sur
65a Av Sur
63a Av Sur
59a Av Sur
Universidad Francisco Gavidia
Av Olímpica
Estadio Flor Blanca
43a Av Sur
C El Progresso
Sexta Décima Calle Poniente
29a Av Sur
Calle Maquilishuat
Calle La Mascota
Av Alberto Masferrer Sur
79a Av Sur
Calle No 2
Calle Loma Linda
Alameda Araujo
Calle Progresso
49a Av Sur
12a Calle Poniente
Calle Geraldo Barrios
Blvd del Hipódromo
Av Las Magnolias
Calle La Reforma
ZONA ROSA
Blvd Venezuela
Av Los Pinos
25a Av Sur
Av Las Azeleas
Calle Circunvalación
Av La Revolución
Blvd del Hipódromo
Calle Las Palmas
Arenal de Montserrat
Blvd Venezuela
Av Las Azaleas
Av La Capilla
Pasaje No 1
Parque Nacional de Béisbol
Calle Las Mercedes
Alameda Araujo
Centro Monseñor Romero (1.4km); Arbol de Fuego (1.5km); La Gran Vía (2km); Jardín Botánico La Laguna (2.5km)

Zona Rosa

Sights
1 El Arbol de Dios A1
2 Museo de Arte de El Salvador B3
3 Museo Nacional de Antropología David J Guzmán B4

Activities, Courses & Tours
4 El Salvador Divers A2

Sleeping
5 Clarion Suites Las Palmas C3
6 Cumbres del Volcán Colonia Escalón B1
7 Cumbres del Volcán Flor Blanca F3
8 Hotel Villa del Angel D2
9 Hotel Villa Florencia Zona Rosa B4
10 La Posada del Rey I B2
11 La Zona Hostel B4
12 Nico Urban Hotel B3

Eating
13 Beto's B2
14 El Cafe de Don Pedro F2
15 El Sopón Típico D2
16 Food Trucks B3
17 Le Croissant B4
18 Mile Time C1
19 Olas Permanentes B1
20 Rustico Bistro C2
21 Típicos Margoth C1

Drinking & Nightlife
22 Barbass C2
23 Cadejo Brewing Company C3
24 La Ventana C1
25 Mercado Cuscatlán G3
26 Nómada C3
27 Republik C3
28 Scape E1

Shopping
29 Galerías Escalón D2
30 Xocolatísimo B3

Transport
31 Centro Nacional de Registros F2
32 Corporación Salvadoreña de Turismo D3
33 Ministerio de Medio Ambiente C4
34 Platinum Bus Company B4
35 SalvaNatura G3
36 Terminal de Occidente E3
37 Tica Bus B4
38 Transportes del Sol B3

Cuscatlán and España). So, 5a Av Sur is south of Calle Arce and west of Av Cuscatlán (because it's odd-numbered). Calles (streets) are similarly ordered, only using Oriente (East) and Poniente (West). It's confusing to the visitor at first, but you'll quickly learn the orderliness of it. The odd/even thing can be tricky, ie 25a Av is one block from 27a Av, but it is more than 25 blocks from 26a Av!

From the city center, 1a Calle Poniente and Calle Rubén Darío, to the north and south of Arce respectively, are the main roads to the wealthier west.

Information

DANGERS & ANNOYANCES

Crime is still a serious problem in San Salvador. Travel light, avoid wearing flashy jewelry and watches, and stay aware of your belongings, especially on buses, in market areas and among street crowds. If you are held up, just hand over the goods. In most areas of the city you should take taxis after 8pm; Zona Rosa and Colonia Escalón are the exception, but use your judgment and don't take risks. The city center has improved in recent years but is still best avoided after dark; if you do venture in, take a taxi to and from Plaza Barrios and stick to well-lit areas.

Accidents between cars and pedestrians are not uncommon; be extra careful crossing the street. Pedestrians don't have the right of way and no car will chivalrously cede it to you.

HEALTH

Pollution is a consistent pest, seemingly locked in place by the surrounding mountains. Thick vehicle exhaust, especially from buses, can leave you with runny eyes and a sore throat.

Hospital Bloom (☎2225-4114; www.hospitalbloom.gob.sv; cnr Blvd de los Héroes & Av Gustavo Guerrero)

Hospital Diagnóstico Escalón (☎2506-2000; www.hospitaldiagnostico.com; Paseo General Escalón 99)

MAPS

Centro Nacional de Registros (IGN; Map p306; ☎2593-5000; www.cnr.gob.sv; 1a Calle Poniente; ⊙7:30am-4pm Mon-Fri)

MONEY

Banks and 24-hour ATMs are found throughout the capital, issuing US dollars. Malls and service stations usually have reliable, safe ATMs.

Banks

Banco Credomatic Branches are located in the *centro* and next to the Super Selectos supermarket, in the Centro Comercial San Luis, off Calle San Antonio Abad. Changes traveler's checks or gives cash advances on MasterCard.

Citibank ATMs that accept all cards are located in Metrocentro Mall and Galerías Mall.

Branches change traveler's checks and can give cash advances on Visa cards.

POST

Correos Central (Map p302; ☎2260-3210; Blvd de los Héroes, Metrocentro; ⊙7:30am-5pm Mon-Fri, 8am-noon Sat)

TOURIST INFORMATION

Corporación Salvadoreña de Turismo (Corsatur; Map p306; ☎914, 2201-4000; www.elsalvador.travel; Alameda Araujo; ⊙9am-4pm) Has an excellent website.

SalvaNatura (Map p306; ☎2202-1515; www.salvanatura.org; 33 Av Sur 640; ⊙8am-12:30pm & 2-5:30pm Mon-Fri) Manages Parque Nacional El Imposible and Parque Nacional Los Volcanes.

Tourist Police (POLITUR; ☎Central Office 2511-8300, Zona Rosa 2263-3904; www.politurelsalvador.com)

Getting There & Away

AIR

Monseñor Óscar Arnulfo Romero International Airport (☎2349-9455; www.elsalvadorinternational.com) Located 44km southeast of San Salvador.

INTERNATIONAL BUSES

Bus companies **Tica Bus** (Map p306; ☎2243-1188; www.ticabus.com; Blvd El Hipodrómo 301, Hotel Meson de Maria; ⊙8am-7pm) and **Platinum** (Map p306; ☎2241-8705; www.platinumcentroamerica.com; Bvd El Hipódromo, Pasaje 1, Local 415, Colonia San Benito) have offices convenient locally right next to each other and close to several hostels and hotels in Zona Rosa, as well as offices in the city center.

Transportes del Sol (Map p306; ☎2133-7800; www.transportedelsol.com; Calle Circunvalación 149; ⊙office 8am-6pm Mon-Fri, to 4pm Sat & Sun) also has an office in Zona Rosa.

Tica Bus has services to Guatemala City at 6am and 3pm (US$20, five hours) from the Hotel Meson de Maria in Zona Rosa and **Hotel San Carlos** (☎2243-1188; www.ticabus.com; Calle Concepción 121) in the city center. Reserve one to two days in advance and arrive at the departure point a half-hour early. From Guatemala City it leaves for the Mexican border at Tapachula, Chiapas, at 7am (US$42, seven hours).

Going east, Tica Bus leaves the San Salvador at 5am and arrives in Managua, Nicaragua, between 6pm and 7pm (US$35). The bus leaves Managua at 6am the following morning and arrives in San José, Costa Rica, between 3pm and 4pm (US$62). It then leaves at noon for Panama (US$102), where you arrive between 4am and 5pm on the third day.

Platinum (Map p300; ☎2281-1996; www.platinumcentroamerica.com; 19a Av Norte) offers deluxe services to Guatemala City (US$35), San Pedro Sula (US$49), Tegucigalpa (US$40) and Nicaragua (US$56).

Transportes del Sol has buses to Guatemala City leaving at 7am and 4pm (US$25) and Antigua at 7am (US$45) and 4pm (US$75). To Nicaragua, buses leave for Managua at 1am and 6:30am (US$50). Buses to San José in Costa Rica (via Nicaragua) leave at 1am (US$65).

Getting Around

BUS

San Salvador's bus network is extensive, from large smoke-spewing monsters to zippy microbuses. Fares are US$0.30 to US$0.35.

Buses run frequently from 5am to 7:30pm daily; fewer buses run on Sunday. Services stop between 7:30pm and 8:30pm; microbuses run later, until around 9pm. After 9pm you'll have to take a taxi.

In the center, it is fastest to walk a few blocks away from Plaza Barrios to catch your bus. Key routes:

Bus 9 Goes down 29a Av Norte alongside the Universidad de El Salvador. Then it turns east toward the city center, heading past the cathedral and up Independencia past Terminal de Oriente.

Bus 26 Passes Plaza Barrios and Parque Zoológico on its way to Terminal de Sur.

Bus 29 Goes to Terminal de Oriente via the center. Buses stop between Metrocentro and MetroSur.

Bus 30 Heads downtown and is the best way to get to and from bus 138 to the airport. Pick it up behind Metrocentro or at Parque Libertad in the center.

Bus 30B A very useful route, especially from Blvd de los Héroes. The bus goes east on Blvd Universitario, then southwest down Blvd de los Héroes to Metrocentro. From there it goes west along Alameda Roosevelt. It then turns south at 79a Av and continues along Blvd del Hipódromo to Av Revolución, then returns on Alameda Araujo, Roosevelt and 49a Av Sur back to Metrocentro.

Bus 34 Runs from Terminal de Oriente to Metrocentro then down to the Zona Rosa, turning around right in front of MARTE art museum. Passes Terminal de Occidente on its return.

Bus 42 Goes west along Calle Arce from the cathedral and continues along Alameda Roosevelt. At El Salvador del Mundo, it heads southwest along Alameda Araujo, passing the Mercado de Artesanías and Museo Nacional de Antropología David J Guzmán, and continues down the Carretera Interamericana, passing La Ceiba de Guadalupe.

BUSES FROM SAN SALVADOR

San Salvador has three main terminals for national long-distance buses.

Buses serving all points east and a few northern destinations arrive and depart from the **Terminal de Oriente** (Alameda Juan Pablo II), on the eastern side of the city. To get to the terminal, take bus 9, 29 or 34 from the city center; bus 29 or 52 from Blvd de los Héroes; bus 7C or 34 from Terminal de Occidente; or bus 21 from Terminal de Sur. Frequent departures are as follows; note that faster *especial* services are available for La Unión and San Miguel.

DESTINATION	BUS	COST (US$)	DURATION (HR)
Chalatenango	125	1.50	2
El Poy (Honduran border)	119	1.80	3
Ilobasco	111	1.10	1½
La Palma	119	1.80	2¾
La Unión	304	3.25	4
San Miguel	301	3-5	3
San Vicente	177	1	1½
Suchitoto	129	0.90	1½

Buses serving all points west, including the Guatemalan border, arrive and depart from the **Terminal de Occidente** (Map p306; Blvd Venezuela, near 49a Av Sur). To get here, take bus 34 from the city center; bus 44 from Blvd de los Héroes (get off at Blvd Venezuela and walk a few blocks west to the terminal); or bus 7C or 34 from Terminal de Oriente. Frequent departures are as follows:

DESTINATION	BUS	COST (US$)	DURATION (HR)
Ahuachapán	203/203e	1.25/2.30	3/1¼
Cerro Verde	Santa Ana bus then 248	0.90	40min
Joya de Cerén	201 to Opico turnoff then 108	0.85	1¾
La Hachadura	205 to Sonsonate then 259	1.55	3½
La Libertad	102	0.70	1
Lago de Coatepeque	Santa Ana bus then 242	0.90	40min
Las Chinamas	205 to Ahuachapán then 263 or minibus	1.60	2½
Los Cóbanos	205 to Sonsonate then 257	1.30	2½
Metapán	201A	2.50	1¾
Ruínas de San Andrés	Santa Ana bus 201	0.85	40min
San Cristóbal	498	1.30	3
Santa Ana	201	0.90	1¼
Sonsonate	205/205e	1/1.50	1½

In the south of the city, **Terminal de Sur** (Autopista a Comalapa), also called Terminal San Marcos, serves destinations to the south and southeast. To get here take bus 26 or microbus 11B from the city center or bus 21 from Terminal de Oriente. Departures include the following; note that a faster *especial* service is available for Usulután.

DESTINATION	BUS	COST (US$)	DURATION (HR)
Costa del Sol	495	1.25	2½
Puerto El Triunfo	185	1.60	2
Usulután	302	1.70	2½

Bus 101 Goes from Plaza Barrios in the center, past Metro Sur, the anthropology museum, La Ceiba de Guadalupe and on to Santa Tecla.

CAR & MOTORCYCLE

Avoid driving through the city center. The traffic gets snarled in daytime and the area is unsafe at night. It's quickest to take major thoroughfares. One-way streets have signage or an arrow painted on the pavement.

TAXI

Taxis are plentiful but unmetered, so negotiate a price in advance. A ride in town should cost between US$5 and US$10 during daytime. Rates go up a few dollars late at night. License plates beginning with 'A' indicate a registered taxi; in theory they can be held accountable for problems. If you don't spot a passing taxi, call **Taxis Acacya** (Map p300; 2271-4937, airport 2339-9282; www.taxisacacya.com; cnr 19a Av Norte & 3a Calle Poniente) or **Acontaxis** (2523-2424; www.acontaxis.com).

CENTRAL EL SALVADOR

San Salvador lies in the 'valley of the hammocks,' skirted by makeshift communities clinging precariously to sloping land and with Maya ruins dotting its fringe. It is also surrounded by steep volcanic peaks that offer hiking opportunities and visits to small artists' towns and coffee *fincas* (plantations) elevated from the heat. The coast is a short drive to the south; La Libertad, the main port, marks the start of a world-class surf voyage.

Santa Tecla

POP 133,601

As San Salvador has started to creak under social and infrastructure difficulties, the city of Santa Tecla (or Nueva San Salvador), 15km southwest, has slowly gentrified, particularly in the area around Paseo El Carmen, which has a young, artsy vibe. This pedestrian-only strip turns into a market each weekend, then into a happening nightspot, with food stalls, cafes, bars, restaurants and even furniture stores serving a noticeably relaxed crowd.

Sights

Parque El Boquerón PARK

(US$3; 8am-5pm) El Salvador's most accessible volcano is El Boquerón (the mouth), one of Volcán San Salvador's two peaks. An easy trail leads around the crater, offering views of San Salvador to one side and a smaller cone within the crater, a mini-me volcano formed by an eruption in 1917. To get here, take the 103 bus from Santa Tecla (30 minutes).

Sleeping & Eating

A number of guesthouses and hostels are popping up around Paseo El Carmen. Santa Tecla's excellent transport links make it a good base for exploring San Salvador and western El Salvador.

★**La Casa de Izel** HOSTEL $$

(2566-6695, 7925-3037; www.lacasadeizel.com; Av Manuel Gallardo 3; dm/s/d US$12/25/35, with air-con s/d US$45/55) Behind stained glass windows is an elegant house that's been decorated with real flair to create a homey, relaxing hostel. With artwork on the walls and retro furniture, the four-bed dorms and private rooms are charming. There's a well-equipped kitchen and book exchange. The roof terrace is the perfect place to chill before hitting Paseo Carmen.

Hotel Jardin del Carmen HOTEL $$

(2519-6487; www.hoteljardindelcarmen.com; 7a Calle Oriente 7-8; s/d US$35/40;) Located near the eponymous pedestrian-only area, Carmen offers spacious tiled room and a large grassy garden that's ideal for kids. Staff are cheerful and there are generous discounts for longer stays.

El Cafecito CAFE $

(cnr Paseo El Carmen & 1 Av Norte; sandwiches US$4; 2-8:30pm Sun & Tue-Thu, to 10:30pm Fri & Sat) Get your caffeine fix at this airy corner cafe. The food ranges from paninis to waffles and crepes.

★**El Sopón Don Guayo** SALVADORAN $$

(2228-9394; 5a Av Norte 2-6; meal combos US$5-7.50; 9:30am-4pm) *Sopa de Gallina* is a Salvadoran specialty and this family-run restaurant is the perfect place to try it. Whole chickens are first roasted in a wood-fired oven before being made into tasty soup, served with tortillas.

Teklebab MIDDLE EASTERN $$

(7910-1482; 5a Av Norte 2-13; mains US$6-14; 6pm-11:30pm Mon-Wed, to 1:30am Thu-Sat) Expect excellent Turkish-influenced cuisine in this hip restaurant and bar with the requisite hookah lounge.

Shopping

Fundación Emprendedores Por El Mundo ARTS & CRAFTS
(www.facebook.com/emprendedoresPM; Paseo El Carmen, near 1 Av Norte; 2-8:30pm Tue-Sun) Run by a group of young Salvadoran creatives, this shop sells the products of more than 50 entrepreneurs from around the country. Items include hand-painted tins, indigo-dyed shirts, bags, jewelry and soaps.

Getting There & Away

Bus 102 from La Libertad costs US$1 and takes 45 minute.

A taxi to/from San Salvador costs about US$12.

La Libertad

POP 16,885

La Libertad is the first port of call for many travelers fleeing the capital in search of Pacific Coast surf beaches and all the misadventure that entails. Its no picture postcard, but the notorious **Punta Roca** wave breaking before a bustling fish market and *malecón* creates a striking urban image hard to manufacture elsewhere in the world. Its reputation as dangerous is not unfounded, but it's hardly the wild west many pundits suggest.

Beyond the beach, La Libertad is an important commercial center – thanks mostly to the port – with more energy, souped-up buses and loud-mouthed touting than you'd expect for a town of such modest proportions. Most travelers bypass it for the more chilled-out beaches to the west, or the Deininger national park to the east, but it's an ideal stop to stock up on supplies, or to experience a midsize, working-class Salvadoran city within minutes of your hammock.

Sights & Activities

La Libertad fills up with city dwellers on weekends. The beach is rocky and covered with large black boulders, and the riptide, along with sewage, makes the water uninviting in the rainy season (May to October). If you just want to frolic in waves, hit the Costa del Bálsamo or go 4km east to sandy Playa San Diego.

Parque Nacional Walter T eininger NATIONAL PARK
(US$3; 8am-4pm) About 4km north of La Libertad, along the Comalapa road, Parque Nacional Walter T Deininger is named for the German settler who donated the land. It includes two types of forest: *caducifolio,* which sheds its leaves in summer, and *galería,* which retains its foliage year-round. It's a 15-minute ride from La Libertad – catch bus 187.

Hospital de Tablas de Surf SURFING
(7944-3632; www.facebook.com/hospitaldetablas; 3a Av Norte 27-8, Playa La Paz) Surf doctor Saul has expanded Hospital de Tablas de Surf into the neighboring premises, so there's even more space for repairing, renting and selling boards. Just knock if it appears closed.

Sleeping & Eating

La Libertad has a few rough motels that are best avoided unless you really can't make it slightly further west to Playa El Tunco and beyond. A number of excellent seafood restaurants line the *malecón.*

Punta Roca Surf Resort HOTEL $$
(2352-4628; Playa El Cocal; d US$60;) Run by the same couple who own the famous restaurant on the point in La Libertad city, this popular local resort is a day-tripper's delight for the spacious pool area; by night it's a quiet, low-key resort. Nothing fancy, but the sincere hospitality and the comfortable beds make it work.

AST Surf Hotel HOTEL $$
(2306-2110; www.astelsalvador.travel; Calle Principal Malecón Turístico; s US$50-80, d US$75-95, tr US$100-125;) The best accommodations in Puerto de la Libertad is this passable option with direct access to the waves. Breakfast is included in the rates and pricier rooms have terraces and ocean views. There are only six rooms, so book ahead.

★ **Punta Rocamar** SEAFOOD $$
(2315-4100; cnr 5a Av Sur & 4a Calle Poniente; mains US$7-16; 9am-7pm Mon-Thu, to midnight Fri & Sat, to 10pm Sun) Overlooking the point is the pride of expatriate surfer Robert Rotherham, who has been feeding the notoriously fussy surf community for decades. The *gringo frijolero* (grilled fish or meat with beans, vegetables, avocado and tortillas, $10) will satisfy a whole gang of grommets. The generous shakes, smoothies and cocktails are best taken at sunset. Live music most weekends.

Information

DANGERS & ANNOYANCES

La Libertad is known as a bastion for organized and not-so-organized crime, so be mindful of wandering aimlessly, especially at night. It is best

WORTH A TRIP

RUINS NEAR SAN SALVADOR

Joya de Cerén (US$3; ⏲9am-4pm Tue-Sun) Known as the Pompeii of America, Unesco World Heritage Site Joya de Cerén was a small Maya settlement that was buried under volcanic ash when the Laguna Caldera Volcano erupted in AD 595. Residents fleeing the eruption left behind a wealth of everyday items that provide clues about ancient planting, home building and food storage. Preserved structures include the village shaman's house and the *tamascal* sweat lodge. There is excellent signage in English and Spanish. A small museum (closed for renovations during our last visit) displays artifacts and models of the villages. One compelling piece is a small dish showing fingerprints smeared in the remains of an interrupted meal. To get here, take bus 201 (US$0.85) from San Salvador (36km) or Santa Ana (42km) to the turn off for Opico, and then bus 108 (10 minutes, US$0.50) from outside the gas station at Sitio del Niño. Get off after crossing the bridge over the Río Sucio; the ruins are signposted.

Ruinas de San Andrés (adult/child US$3/free; ⏲9am-4pm Tue-Sun) In 1977 a step pyramid and a large courtyard with a subterranean section were unearthed at this site, inhabited by Maya between AD 600 and 900. Experts believe that up to 12,000 people lived here. These peaceful ruins are 33km west of San Salvador and 300m north of the highway in the Valle de Zapotitán. Take the Santa Ana bus 201 from San Salvador's Terminal de Occidente and get off at Km 33 at the sign for the ruins. The city once dominated the Valle de Zapotitán and possibly the neighboring Valle de las Hamacas, where San Salvador is now situated. If combining this with a visit to Joya de Cerén, visit Joya de Cerén first, then catch any bus on the highway for the short distance to San Andrés.

Parque Arqueológico Cihuatán (US$3; ⏲9am-4pm Tue-Sun) The modest ruins of Cihuatán were once an immense urban area alongside the Río Guazapa, possibly the largest pre-Columbian city between Guatemala and Peru. Today Cihuatán makes a convenient excursion for those staying in the capital and helps to contextualize San Salvador's modern-day settlement. From San Salvador's Terminal de Oriente, take bus 119 toward Chalatenango (1½ hours) and get off 2km beyond Aguilares; ask the driver to let you off at the ruins. It's a 900m walk to the site.

to avoid the area southeast of the plaza at night (there's better nightlife on the *malecón* anyway).

Strong rip currents proliferate throughout the coast. Lifeguards work only on weekends in La Libertad and Playa San Diego. Avoid eating the black clams if you want to keep catching waves.

MONEY

Banco Agrícola Opposite the tourist office.

POST

Post Office (☎2335-3002; Complejo Turístico, Puerto de la Libertad; ⏲8am-4pm Mon-Fri, to noon Sat) Near 2a Av Norte.

TOURIST OFFICE

Tourist Office (Plaza del Muelle; ⏲9am-12:30pm & 1:10-5pm)

ℹ Getting There & Away

There is no bus terminal. Bus 102 goes to and from San Salvador (US$1.50, one hour). In San Salvador, catch it at its terminal behind Parque Bolivar or at Terminal de Occidente. In La Libertad, buses leave from the corner of 4a Av Norte and Calle Gerardo Barros.

To Sonsonate, take bus 287 (US$1.25, 2½ hours, 6:15am and 1:45pm only) from the bus stop at 2a Calle Poniente, or take bus 192 to Playa Mizata and change.

You can also go directly from the airport – it's about the same distance as San Salvador. Take the microbus to the *puente a Comalapa* (Comalapa overpass) a few minutes away. A path leads up onto the intersecting road; from there it's 100m to the town of Comalapa, where bus 187 leaves every 20 minutes to La Libertad (US$0.60).

ℹ Getting Around

Bus 80 goes west from La Libertad to Playa El Tunco and Playa El Sunzal (US$0.25, every 15 minutes 4:30am to 6pm) or east to Playa San Diego (US$0.30, every 15 minutes 5:40am to 6pm). Buses leave from 4a Av Norte at 2a Calle Oriente.

For Playa El Zonte or Playa Mizata take bus 192 (US$0.50, every 30 minutes 7am to 5:30pm).

La Costa del Bálsamo

Welcome to surfing paradise, El Sal style. Starting at the tough port city of La Libertad, the coastal highway glides west past two-break, black-sand beaches in the one part of El Salvador that young travelers and ocean lovers gravitate toward without exception.

Playa El Tunco parties hard on weekends, but press on a few clicks away from the city, circle down like an eagle and you'll soon have the glistening ocean, awash with turtles, dolphins and huge leaping fish, all to yourself. **Playa El Zonte** is the best place to learn surfing or rent a fisher's boat for the morning.

The region takes its name from the valuable aromatic oil extracted here by burning the bark of live balsam trees. Today only a handful of trees remain and cotton has become the main cash crop.

Sleeping

Playa El Tunco

Playa El Tunco has the most sleeping and eating options, and the largest travel 'scene' in El Salvador for both locals and tourists. There is a lot fun to be had, waves to be surfed and hangovers to be nursed. The 'Pig' *(el tunco)* refers to the rocky formation just offshore.

Papaya Lodge HOSTEL $
(2389-6027; www.papayalodge.com; Playa El Tunco; dm with/without air-con US$10/8, r with/without air-con US$50/25) Papaya's is a big-hearted hostel with a youthful vibe, plenty of hammocks for lounging when the surf's flat and a guest kitchen. The property is set back from the beach but near several bars, and the enthusiastic surf community can raise the decibels when trading stories.

Meals and snacks are available at the on-site bar, and board rental (US$15 per day) and classes (US$15 per hour, plus board hire) can also be arranged.

La Sombra HOSTEL $
(www.surflibre.com; Playa El Tunco; dm/d/tr without bathroom US$7/18/21, d/tr with bathroom US$30/45;) La Sombra is an upbeat little hostel that punches above its weight. The tidy dorm rooms are the best value in El Tunco and the small pool does the trick, plus there's a guest kitchen, working wi-fi and BYO booze!

★**Hotel Mopelia** HOTEL $$
(www.hotelmopelia-salvador.com; Playa El Tunco; s/d from US$15/20, with air-con US$35/40;) This large property is a magnet for travelers who appreciate the thoughtfulness and space afforded by the owner's business model. Mopelia offers 12 rooms at a variety of price points, dotted around a relaxing garden, with plenty of hammocks and a small pool. The bar stocks one of the most extensive beer selections in El Salvador.

★**La Guitarra** HOTEL $$
(2389-6398; www.surfingeltunco.com; Playa El Tunco; s/d/tr with fan US$20/40/60, s/d/tr with air-con from US$30/65/110;) You won't find accommodations closer to the waves than the beachside rooms at this rock-music-themed El Tunco sleep-easy; the garden rooms are quieter and closer to reception. The grassy area by the pool and table tennis encourage interactivity between guests. Reduced rates for longer stays. Live music fills the bar on weekends, so be prepared.

Eco del Mar HOTEL $$
(www.ecosurfelsalvador.com; Playa El Tunco; r incl breakfast US$48-78;) One of Tunco's more discreet places is the Eco del Mar. This two-story building uses plenty of wood, including for its pleasant veranda, sitting area and external staircases. The rooms are larger than average and feature breakfast tables, fridges, cooking facilities and TVs. Excellent value for a small family. Cash only.

El Sunzalito HOTEL $$
(2406-3647; www.facebook.com/Elsunzalito; Playa El Tunco; d US$30-50;) A neat pool, grassy lawns, a well-equipped guest kitchen and a ban on music makes this quiet hotel a good option for families. Rooms are small and sparsely furnished but spotless, and the place is generally wellmaintained.

Boca Olas BOUTIQUE HOTEL $$$
(2389-6333; www.bocaolas.com; Playa El Tunco; d incl breakfast US$146-170;) Boca Olas has upped the sophistication of little Tunco with this manicured, high-end offering, which has two fine pools (complete with swim-up bar), plush rooms and professional service. The two-bedroom suites (US$280) are ideal for small groups. The seafood restaurant here is also recommended.

Tekuani Kal BOUTIQUE HOTEL $$$
(2355-6500; www.tekuanikal.com; Playa El Tunco; r incl breakfast US$61-117;) The 21 rooms at this quirky boutique hotel have real personality, such as the tree-house suite, which is constructed around a large trunk with a balcony in the canopy. Suites with ocean views offer uninterrupted views of the waves plus racks for storing surfboards.

Playa El Sunzal

There are wooden shacks aplenty and gringo surfers hanging out between sets. A few new places have opened up here, but it's still very much on the quiet side.

B Boutique Hotel BOUTIQUE HOTEL $$$
(7574-9664; www.bboutiquehotel.com; Carretera Litoral Km 45.9; d incl breakfast US$350; P) Just outside Playa El Sunzal is the finest upscale accommodations in El Salvador. This small hotel is remarkably discreet, with only four rooms overlooking an infinity pool and the Pacific Ocean beyond. The fabulous seafood restaurant, Beto's, is on the premises.

Playa El Zonte

A one-way path off the highway leads to Playa El Zonte, where time passes even more slowly than the locals walk. This is the best option for learning to surf, and for getting some respite from the Tunco party scene. A couple of excellent high-end accommodations have opened here.

Esencia Nativa HOSTEL $
(7737-8879; www.esencianativa.com; Playa El Zonte; dm/s/d US$10/27/34, s/d with air-con US$38/48;) El Zonte's one road leads to Escencia Nativa, and rightly so. This low-key hostel is where most travelers linger, irrespective of where they choose to sleep. The pool is a winner and it will take some serious swell to get you away from your pizza at the restaurant replete with ocean views. Long-time local Alex is your font of knowledge.

Canegue Hostal HOSTEL $
(7207-8669; www.facebook.com/caneguehostal; Playa El Zonte; dm/r US$10/20, hammocks & camping US$5) Canegue is a no-frills hostel run by local surfer Zancudo, who loves to chat with guests. The private rooms and dorms are nothing special, but it's right by the beach and the hammocks are a good deal.

El Dorado BOUTIQUE HOTEL $$
(7859-4212; www.surfeldorado.com; Playa El Zonte; s/d from US$31/66;) Across the river from the main 'drag' is El Dorado, a stylish resort run by an enterprising French-Canadian couple and staffed by a team of locals. Direct access to the waves will get you out of bed, while the presentation of the rooms with bamboo artwork, quality linens and stone showers will keep you primed for the next session. From November to May there is a minimum stay of one week.

★ **Puro Surf Hotel** BOUTIQUE HOTEL $$$
(6148-7782; www.purosurf.com; Playa El Zonte; dm US$78, d incl breakfast US$236;) Every detail of this slick hotel and surf academy has been designed with surfers in mind. Each room has been impeccably decorated using Salvadoran materials and has a balcony with views, while the infinity pool might just tempt you away from the waves. The luxurious dorm is the perfect place to chew the fat with fellow surfers.

Eating

★ **Covana Seaside Kitchen** INTERNATIONAL $$
(6148-7782; Playa El Zonte; mains US$8-18; 8am-8:30pm Mon-Thu, to 9pm Fri & Sun, to 10pm Sat;) Such impressive architecture is a surprising find in the beach hamlet of El Zonte, but the lofty dining room at Puro Surf is a stunning spot. A soaring, palm-thatch roof frames ocean views, while polished concrete floors and contemporary furnishings complete the look. The menu of fresh local seafood, healthy salads and snacks lives up to the setting. There's a well-stocked bar and decent coffee too.

★ **Tunco Veloz** ITALIAN $$
(2406-5689; Playa El Tunco; mains US$8-10; 7am-11pm) The thin-crust pizzas at the Speedy Pig are good anytime of day – topped with spinach and egg for breakfast, or laden with whatever you might fancy for lunch or dinner. Homemade pastas and gnocchi are also on the menu, and a decent wine list tops things off.

Loroco Bistro SALVADORAN $$
(7725-5744; Playa El Tunco; mains US$6-8; 7am-1pm Mon & Tue, 7am-1pm & 5-10pm Wed-Sun) This laid-back bistro with open-air seating serves great local breakfasts (US$3 to US$3.50). Come evening, candles add a romantic touch, while the menu of pizzas, burgers, schnitzels, salads and *ceviche* is excellent value and some of the best food in town.

Esquina La Comadre SALVADORAN $$
(Playa El Tunco; mains US$4-12; 8am-10pm) Popular with hungry surfers, this unassuming corner spot punches out generous portions of tacos, seafood and rice dishes to all who stop by.

WORTH A TRIP

PANCHIMALCO

Set on the green slopes of Cerro Chulo, Panchimalco is a small town renowned for its religious festivals, particularly Palm Sunday, when residents march through the streets bearing decorated palm fronds. Early May's **Fería de Cultura de las Flores y las Palmas** features palm artistry, folk dancing and fireworks.

Inhabited by descendants of the Pipils, Panchimalco has reinvented itself as an artists' enclave. You can visit a number of working galleries here and purchase work from leading national artists at reasonable prices.

Bus 17 departs for Panchimalco from Av 29 de Agosto on the south side of the Mercado Central in San Salvador.

Coyote CAFE **$$**
(Playa El Tunco; mains US$5.50-9.50; ⏲9am-9pm Wed-Mon) Get your fill of tempting breakfasts, smoothies, coffee and in-between-surf food at this American-style cafe near the beach.

La Bocana SEAFOOD **$$**
(Playa El Tunco; mains US$5-20; ⏲7am-10pm) It's on the beach, seats a hundred-plus people, has an oversupply of waiters and a long menu of pretty much anything you feel like. It gets raucous once the sun sets, but then again, so do you after a six-hour lunch.

Dale Dale Cafe CAFE **$$**
(☎7080-0263; Playa El Tunco; sandwiches US$4-8; ⏲6am-5pm) If you crave a less Latin American start to the day, then try a smoothie, herbal tea, mug of Americano or stack of fluffy pancakes at this moderately upscale place on the main drag. Go on! *(Dale dale!)*

Drinking & Nightlife

★Monkey Lala BAR
(☎2228-3992; Playa El Tunco; ⏲2-8pm Mon & Tue, 10am-8pm Wed & Thu, 9am-10pm Fri & Sat, 9am-8pm Sun) Everyone's favorite Tunco sunset spot is this gorgeous cocktail bar, east of the main beach. Crisp electronic beats are the default sound, as well-heeled locals and savvy travelers mingle above the sand.

★Cadejo La Libertad CRAFT BEER
(☎2346-2828; Carretera Litoral Km 45, Playa El Sunzal; ⏲11:30am-8:30pm Mon-Thu, to midnight Fri, 7:30am-midnight Sat, 7:30am-7pm Sun) Perched on a clifftop west of Playa El Sunzal is this branch of the San Salvador brewery (p304), serving the country's best beer with ocean views. There's plenty of tasty bar snacks and seafood available, making it a place where you'll want to linger. At research time a pool area was in the works.

Beach Life Café BAR
(Calle Principal, Playa El Tunco; ⏲5pm-12:30am Mon-Thu, to 1:30am Fri & Sat, 3pm-12:30am Sun) After sunset at the beach, Tunco's party crowd heads to this thatch-roofed shack to dance into the small hours. Drink offers, live music and friendly vibes keep things cool.

Information

There are several ATMs in El Tunco, but none in El Zonte. Bring sufficient cash.

Getting There & Away

Bus 102A from San Salvador and bus 80 from La Libertad go as far as Playa El Sunzal. Beyond that, take the less frequent bus 192.

Bus 287 connects La Libertad and Sonsonate, passing the beaches along the way. It leaves La Libertad twice daily at 6:15am and 1:45pm.

WESTERN EL SALVADOR

Western El Salvador may be a small region, but it contains the majority of the country's attractions. The cloud forest and conical splendor of Parque Nacional Los Volcanes, the mysterious and at times unvisited Maya ruins at Tazumal, the Ruta de las Flores, and a volcanic lake are all within a 90-minute drive of Santa Ana, the charming provincial capital with the finest plaza in El Salvador.

From the wilds of Parque Nacional El Imposible near the Guatemalan border – where you can find pumas, boars and tigrillos – traverse waterfalls until you pick up the famed Flower Route, a pin-up region of hot springs, food fairs and artisan villages.

Indeed, if you fly into San Salvador, you can reach it all in a day and end at the far western tip at Barrio de Santiago, a windswept beach with massive surf where turtles lay eggs by moonlight.

Santa Ana

POP 176,660

Only 65km from the capital, Santa Ana is a mid-sized El Salvadoran city, the long-standing coffee wealth of which is reflected in its architecture, some of the most magnificent in Central America. There's a relaxed confidence in the wide, tree-lined streets and colorful houses, and Santanecos are genuinely proud of their growing cultural scene. Smart travelers are choosing Santa Ana as an alternative base to the capital for exploring Volcán Santa Ana, Lago de Coatepeque, the Maya ruins at Tazumal and Joya de Cerén, or the Ruta de las Flores.

Sights

Catedral de Santa Ana CATHEDRAL
(Map p317; 1a Av Norte; 7am-noon & 2-6pm) FREE The most notable sight in Santa Ana is its large neo-Gothic cathedral, which was completed in 1913. Exquisite ornate moldings cover the church's front, while interior pillars and high archways are painted in slate and pink stripes, enhancing a sense of stillness and spaciousness. A spooky figure of the city's patron saint, Nuestra Señora de Santa Ana, greets you as you enter.

Teatro de Santa Ana THEATER
(Map p317; 2447-6268; cnr Av Independencia Sur & 2a Calle Poniente; US$1.50; 9am-noon & 1-5pm Tue-Sat) The Teatro de Santa Ana is an opulent Renaissance-style building constructed using funds from an export tax on coffee beans. The epitome of wealth, excess and culture, it features stained-glass windows, marble staircases and immaculate detail. In 1933 it was converted into a movie house, and, after a hefty facelift, is now a theater again (tickets around US$5).

Sleeping

★ **Casa Verde** HOSTEL $
(Map p317; 7840-4896; www.facebook.com/hostalcasaverde; 7a Calle Poniente; dm/s/d/tr US$10/25/30/35;) Carlos and his team at Casa Verde display the kind of resourceful, conscientious hospitality that makes this country such a joy. From the roof terrace, all post-travel calm will be restored, particularly at sunset. Dorm rooms are generously sized, with single-level beds, small tables and ample storage, plus there are two spotless kitchens and a lounge area to meet other travelers.

Hostal Vital Yek HOSTEL $
(Map p317; 2421-2276; www.facebook.com/vitalyek.sv; Av Independencia Sur, btwn Calles 15 & 17 Oriente; dm US$10, d with/without bathroom US$36/30) Vital Yek is a fun addition to the Santa Ana travel scene. Popular with local musicians and artists, the narrow hangout area is covered in graffiti and plant life. Rooms are comfortable, there's a small kitchen, and the garden and terrace are a plus. Plans for expansion are in the works.

Casa Frolaz B&B $
(2440-1564; casafrolaz@yahoo.com; 29a Calle Poniente; dm/d US$9/23) Francisco is a cultured gentleman who politely scrutinizes travelers' itineraries from the comfort of his splendid open home. Each double room has a small balcony and guests can use the kitchen and garden. It's located in a quiet street.

A small cafe on the ground floor serves salads, sandwiches and pancakes (US$6 to US$7.50) during the day and hosts occasional low-key events (such as coffee tastings) on weekend evenings.

Villa Napoli B&B $$
(7985-6021; www.villanapoli.hostel.com; Quinta del Moral Km 62-63; d/tr US$30/37;) Rosa is a natural host and the Napoli is a restful, stylish guesthouse on the road out of Santa Ana, where the gardens grow wilder and the houses were built for an extended family. The pool area will lure you in for the long term.

Eating

Santa Ana has numerous high-quality eating options, some more refined than others. Look out for *panes chucos*, soy-meat hot dogs sold by street vendors that are a local specialty, and *nuégados*, deep fried balls made with corn or yucca dough.

El Sin Rival ICE CREAM $
(Map p317; Calle Libertad Oriente; cones US$0.50-1; 9am-6pm Wed-Mon) This outfit has been making ice cream and sorbet (and amazing fruit cones) for decades; also look out for the carts around the main square. Try the tart *arrayán* (a bittersweet local fruit) or *mora* (blackberry).

Restaurante Rincón Típico SALVADORAN $
(2440-5697; www.facebook.com/Rincontipicosantaana; 3a Av Sur; mains US$3-5; 7:30am-5pm;) This is a terrific place to try hearty Salvadoran stews, barbecued meats, fresh

Santa Ana

Santa Ana

Sights
1 Catedral de Santa Ana C1
2 Teatro de Santa Ana C1

Sleeping
3 Casa Verde B2
4 Hostal Vital Yek C4

Eating
5 Artisant C1
6 Café Expresión Cultural B3
7 El Sin Rival D2
8 Pastelería Ban Ban C2

Drinking & Nightlife
9 Café Téjas B4
10 Simmer Down C1

salads and house specialty *sopa de gallina* (chicken soup). The homemade soft drinks are a hit. There is often live music on weekends.

Artisant INTERNATIONAL $
(Map p317; 2441-3139; Callejón Sur de Catedral 6; mains US$4-6; 7am-8pm Sun-Thu, to 10pm Fri & Sat;) Generous breakfasts plus paninis, burgers, salads and huge sandwiches made with homemade bread are served at this chic downtown cafe behind the cathedral. Vegan options available on request.

Pastelería Ban Ban BAKERY $
(Map p317; Av Independencia Sur; pastries US$0.50-2.50; 6:30am-7pm Mon-Thu, to 8pm Fri-Sun) Ban Ban is all over the country, but it started in Santa Ana and the locals like to celebrate their hometown each mid-afternoon over sublime cakes and pastries.

★ **Café Expresión Cultural** CAFE $$
(Map p317; 2440-1410; 11a Calle Poniente, btwn 6a & 8a Av Sur; mains US$4-6.50; 7am-8pm Mon-Sat;) This versatile establishment is a favorite among intellectuals and artists who come for the live music and small bookstore.

Tourists and young lovers enjoy the big breakfasts, fine coffee and accessible art. Ignore the nefarious street life and take refuge in the outside garden.

Inna Jammin INTERNATIONAL $$
(☎2400-5757; Av Indepencia Sur; pizzas small/large US$5/10; ⊙11am-11pm Tue-Sun;) The Rasta vibe flows over two levels at this restaurant with a broad international menu. The pizzas are rated highly, the Salvadoran grills are great and the cocktails are generously poured. The atmosphere is reason enough to come; reggae tunes blast (occasionally live) and young Santanecos celebrate life for the sake of it.

Drinking & Nightlife

There's a growing bar scene in Santa Ana, but places go in and out of fashion with the seasons. Ask locals for tips on current Santa Ana hot spots.

★**Café Téjas** CAFE
(Map p317; ☎2447-2110; www.facebook.com/cafetejas.santaana; Av Independencia Sur; ⊙1-11pm Wed-Sat, to 9pm Sun & Mon;) Retro furniture, chunky wooden decking and jungly gardens help create a chill vibe at this sprawling cafe, where vinyl records provide the tunes. Come for a lunchtime sandwich and *licuado* (smoothie), or for tapas-style snacks and beer later on. Live music most Saturdays pulls in the crowds.

Simmer Down BAR
(Map p317; ☎2484-7511; 1a Av Norte; ⊙10am-2am) Overlooking the cathedral, this busy bar serves ice-cold beer, pizza and pasta (mains US$8 to US$15) and has a festive atmosphere week-round. The natural wooden furniture belies the urban setting.

Information

MEDICAL SERVICES

Hospital Cáder (☎2447-1010; www.hospitalcader.com; 5A Calle Oriente 10)

Hospital San Juan de Dios (☎2435-9500; 17 Av Sur)

MONEY

Banco Agrícola (3a Calle Oriente; ⊙8am-4pm Mon-Fri, to noon Sat)

Banco Cuscatlan (cnr Independencia Sur & 3a Calle Oriente; ⊙8am-4pm Mon-Fri)

POST

Post Office (Map p317; Av Independencia Sur; ⊙8am-5pm Mon-Fri)

Getting There & Away

Several destinations are served by Santa Ana's main **bus terminal** (Map p317; cnr 10a Avenida Sur & 15a Calle Poniente), including Ahuachapán, Juayúa, Sonsonate and San Cristóbal (Guatemalan border). For Las Chinamas (Guatemalan border) take any Ahuachapán bus and transfer.

For San Salvador, take bus 210 from the main bus terminal to the **TUDO terminal** west of town, where you can catch the 201 (US$0.90, 1¼ hours).

Bus 235 to Metapán (US$0.90, 1½ hours) departs from the corner of Av F Moraga Sur and 13a Calle Poniente. For Anguiatú (Guatemalan border) take bus 235 to Metapán and transfer.

Bus 248 to Parque Nacional los Volcanes (Cerro Verde; US$0.90, 1¾ hours) departs from **La Vencedora Terminal** (Map p317; cnr Av F Moraga Sur & 11a Calle Poniente), one block west of Parque Colón, at 7:30am and makes the return journey from Cerro Verde at 4pm.

Parque Nacional Los Volcanes

With three major volcanoes in hiking distance, the bird-filled forests and barren peaks of **Parque Nacional Los Volcanes**

BUSES FROM SANTA ANA

DESTINATION	BUS	COST (US$)	DURATION (HR)
Ahuachapán	210	0.75	1
Chalchuapa (Tazumal)	218	0.25	½
Juayúa	238	0.50	1
Lago de Coatepeque	220	0.40	1¼
San Cristóbal (Guatemalan border)	236	0.50	1
San Salvador *directo*	201	1	1½
San Salvador *especial*	201e	1.30	1¼
Sonsonate	216	0.75	1¼

(park entry US$3, guided volcano climb US$7; ⏲8am-5pm) are a trip highlight for many visitors to El Salvador.

Active **Volcán Izalco** is the youngest in the group. Its cone began forming in 1770 from a belching hole of sulfuric smoke and today stands 1910m high. Izalco erupted throughout the 20th century, spewing smoke, boulders and flames. Today this bare, perfect cone stands devoid of life in an otherwise fertile land.

Without Izalco's stark drama but 400m higher, **Volcán Santa Ana** (also known as Ilamatepec) is El Salvador's third-highest point. Its eruption in October 2005 triggered landslides that killed two coffee pickers and forced the evacuation of thousands. The summit affords spectacular views of a steep drop into the crater on one side and Lago de Coatepeque on the other.

Activities

Four-hour guided hikes up Volcán Santa Ana (Ilamatepec) and Volcán Izalco leave at 11am sharp (meaning you can't do both in one day), with a minimum of 10 people. Since the Santa Ana climb is more popular, guided hikes are pretty much guaranteed. If you plan to climb Izalco (a steeper, more challenging climb) it's best to come on a weekend when there is more chance that there will be a group going up; there is nearly always a guided hike on Sundays. Wear sturdy shoes and bring a jacket. In addition to the US$3 park entry fee, there is a US$1 guide tip and a further US$6 park fee to climb either volcano.

A short alternative is a 40-minute nature trail around Cerro Verde that offers views of the lake and Volcán Santa Ana. Volunteer guides can take you around the trail for a tip.

All hikes start from the parking lot at Cerro Verde, near the park entrance.

Sleeping & Eating

In the parking lot near the starting point for guided volcano hikes are several food stalls selling local breakfasts, *pupusas*, fresh fruit and *nuégados* (fried yucca-dough balls). If you're staying overnight bring supplies from Santa Ana or Sonsonate.

Cerro Verde Cabins CABIN $
(☎2260-9249, 7294-7255; 4-/6-bed cabins US$35/55) These simple cabins at Cerro Verde in Parque Nacional Los Volcanes have bunk beds and bathrooms with hot water, and are located steps away from the starting point for hikes up Volcán Santa Ana and Volcán Izalco. Bed linen isn't provided. Bring your own food and water. No kitchen.

Cabañas Campo Bello CABIN $$
(☎2271-0853; www.campobello.com.sv; San Blas; camping per person US$5, 1-/2-bed cabins US$50/55) Wake up in a concrete igloo surrounded by volcanoes, in a landscape resembling Teletubbyland. Bizarrely beautiful. On the road up to Cerro Verde, follow signs to the right 2km before the entrance to the park.

Casa de Cristal CABIN $$
(☎2483-4713; www.facebook.com/CasaCristalOficial; Finca San Blas; cabins per person US$12-18) Casa de Cristal has rustic *cabañas* and a campground; it's located in San Blas on the road up to Casa Verde. It also organizes guided hikes.

Information

For safety reasons, solo hiking is still not advised, despite huge improvements in recent years.

Getting There & Away

Arrive by 11am as the guided hikes leave just once a day. The easiest, surest route is to come from Santa Ana, where bus 248 (US$0.90) goes all the way to the park entrance at Cerro Verde. However, the bus departs from the La Vencedora Terminal in Santa Ana at 7:30am and arrives in Cerro Verde about 1½ hours later, meaning a wait of around two hours for the hike to begin. The bus back to Santa Ana leaves Cerro Verde at 4pm, about an hour after returning from the hike.

If you're driving, Parque Nacional Los Volcanes is 67km from San Salvador via Sonsonate or 77km via the more scenic route toward Santa Ana.

Lago de Coatepeque

Approaching Lago de Coatepeque via road, visitors are struck by the dramatic beauty of the 6km-wide sparkling blue caldera. You'll notice many cars slowing down at the *mirador* when the lake first comes into view. It's also remarkably free of crowds – mostly as the majority of properties dotting the lake's edge are privately owned by San Salvador's elite – and you can swim, dive or splash about in a boat without fear of the dreaded blue-green algae, an algal bloom that can cause skin irritations and sickness if ingested.

For around US$5, day-trippers can enjoy lake access at one of the hotels on the northeast shore. For US$20 you can rent a boat for a couple of hours.

Sleeping & Eating

Amacuilco Hostal HOSTEL $
(7009-8620; hostalamacuilco@hotmail.com; El Congo; dm/d US$8/25;) This popular hostel is in the small village of El Congo at the top of the road into Coatapeque. The sleeping options include tidy dorms and five double rooms. There's a kitchen, a compact pool in a tropical garden, a book exchange and recommended Spanish lessons.

El Gran Mirador SEAFOOD $$
(7860-2044; mains US$7-15; 9am-9pm) Eat fresh *mojarro* fish from the lake at this seafood restaurant with 'the view.' It's at Km 53 on the road down from El Congo to the lake.

Getting There & Away

Buses 220 and 242 depart Santa Ana for the lake every half-hour (US$0.50, 45 minutes).

Chalchuapa

POP 84,510

The plains town of Chalchuapa is known as the home of Tazumal, a pre-Columbian settlement featuring the finest ruins in El Salvador. These Maya ruins are an unexpected highlight for many travelers, though don't go comparing them to those found elsewhere in Central America.

Chalchuapa's friendly central neighborhood of low-rise multicolored houses with crumbling colonial exteriors is pleasant to walk around, and the town has some excellent places to eat.

Sights & Activities

In the nearby suburbs, **Laguna Cuzcachapa** is a natural sulfur pond and a mystical place of great significance in Maya culture. Locals suggest coming here when faced with difficult decisions, but beware the siguanaba (a mythical creature that poses as a beautiful woman to lure solo male travelers)! You can swim in natural spring-water pools at **El Trapiche** (location of the first Maya settlement in 2000 BC) or jump into a waterfall in **Salto El Espino**.

★**Tazumal** RUINS
(7a Calle Oriente; US$3; 9am-4pm Tue-Sun) In the K'iche' language Tazumal means 'pyramid where the victims were burned.' Archaeologists estimate that the verdant 10-sq-km Tazumal area – much of which is still buried under Chalchuapa's housing – was first settled around 5000 BC. The latest works, inaugurated in December 2006, restored the original stone-and-mortar construction of much of the ruins. A chain-link enclosure prevents visitors walking on the pyramids, but their close proximity to everyday Salvadoran life connects the site to the present in a powerful way.

A **museum** displays artifacts that show active trade as far away as Panama and Mexico, with explanations in Spanish. Other finds, including the Estela de Tazumal, a 2.65m-high basalt monolith inscribed with hieroglyphics, are at the Museo Nacional de Antropología David J Guzmán (p296) in San Salvador.

Casa Blanca RUINS
(Carretera Km 78; US$3; 9am-4pm Tue-Sun) Across the highway from Chalchuapa town center and the Tazumal site sits Casa Blanca, home to some Preclassic Maya ruins set in attractive woodland. An excellent museum with detailed explanations in English and the pleasant, peaceful surroundings make this site well worth your while. There's also an indigo workshop where you can dye your own fabrics.

RastaMaya Tours TOURS
(7878-0155; www.rastamaya.com; 5 Av Sur Casa 6, Barrio Apaneca, btwn Calles 1a & 3a Oriente) Based near the ruins of Tazumal, former English teacher Jorge and his vibrant young team put real heart into curating offbeat adventures. Tours like Aguas Termales (Hot Springs) and Ruta Ancestral are a lot of fun.

Sleeping & Eating

When it comes to culinary offerings, little Chalchuapa punches above its weight. The town is known for the prevalence of *chilate,* a nourishing drink made of corn, served with *camote* (sweet potato) and sugary *buñuelos* (cassava), as well as its *yuca* (yam) with roast pork – a national delicacy. The stalls lining the road into Tazumal serve excellent *comida típica* (regional specialities).

Hostal Las Flores GUESTHOUSE $$$
(2408-5117, 2444-0194; 5a Calle Oriente 13; dm/d US$20/110;) The former colonial residence of a wealthy Santaneco, this beautifully restored guesthouse consists of a dozen bright rooms with original features and antique furniture, a tiled internal courtyard and flourishing garden. There are plans to add a Jacuzzi.

★Pan La Esperanza BAKERY $

(cnr 1a Calle Oriente & Av 2 de Abril Sur; ⌚7am-6pm Mon-Sat) Delectable pastries, bread and buns are baked fresh every day using owner Beatriz' closely guarded recipes. Sweet treats such as passion-fruit muffins as well as savory sandwiches and snacks can be devoured at the cafe or packed up to take on the road. Good coffee too.

Jade SALVADORAN $

(7a Calle Oriente; mains US$1-2; ⌚9:30am-7pm) *Yuca con chicharrón* (yam with roast pork) is the only thing on the menu here, so your only decision is what size portion to order. Go for large!

Getting There & Away

Take bus 218 from Santa Ana (US$0.30, 30 minutes, half-hourly). A sign on the main road through Chalchuapa points toward the Tazumal ruins, about a five-minute walk from the highway.

Metapán

POP 19,145

There's a strong sense of pride among the citizens of this hot agricultural capital, which makes a charming detour from the wilds of the bigger cities. The restored colonial town square, dominated by the impressive Iglesia de San Pedro, is a pleasant place to stroll around.

Metapán is a comfortable and convenient base for forays into Parque Nacional Montecristo (p322), the country's most inaccessible and exotic national park, which can only be reached by 4WD.

Sights & Activities

Iglesia de San Pedro CHURCH

(Av Benjamin E Valiente) FREE Metapán's town square features the glorious Iglesia de San Pedro, the jewel in a restored old quarter where the sense of civic pride is palpable. In the park opposite, languid Salvadoran family life carries on into the evening.

Reserva Ecologica El Limo NATURE RESERVE

(Carrertera Km 122.5, northbound) Fourteen kilometers north of Metapán is the lush Reserva Ecologica El Limo, home to incredible *cascadas* (waterfalls). Drivers near the turnoff to Frontera Anguiatú will offer to drive you there for about US$30; otherwise try Hostal Villa Limón.

Apuzunga Water Park RAFTING

(☎7205-1288; www.apuzunga.com; US$3; ⌚7am-5pm) Apuzunga is one of the better known and most developed of the thermal-springs resorts in El Salvador. The real plus here are the rapids, running below the bar-restaurant. They are surprisingly fast after the wet season. Rafting trips cost US$50 per person for a group of six; book ahead.

Lago de Güija OUTDOORS

On the El Salvador–Guatemala border, Lago de Güija is a beautiful fishing and birdwatching wetland. In the dry season you can hike to archaeological sites and find rock carvings along the shore. Swimming is dependent on the extent of the blue-green algae, but boat trips can be arranged with local operators.

The lake is several kilometers south of Metapán and 30km north of Santa Ana along CA12. To get there, take a Santa Ana–bound bus and get dropped off at the junction to the lake. It is a 2km walk from there.

Sleeping & Eating

Hostal de Metapan HOSTEL $

(☎2402-2382; 2a Calle Oriente; r US$22; ❄📶) The owners make every effort to make guests feel welcome in this functional, small hotel close to the bus station. The interior design feels like the set of a 1990s TV romance.

Hostal Villa Blanca HOTEL $$

(☎2402-3383; www.hostalvillablancametapan.com; Av Isidro Menéndez 4; s/d US$30/45; ❄📶) The smartest choice in town is this well-run hotel in the quaint old quarter. The pristine tile floors keep the place cool, while the spacious rooms are brightened up by colorful furniture. It's popular with honeymooners and hikers. Staff can help arrange day trips to Parque Nacional Montecristo (p322).

Hostal Villa Limón HOSTEL $$$

(☎2442-0149; www.facebook.com/hostalvilla.limon; cottages US$80-115; 🏊) Hostal Villa Limón is a collection of three forest cottages that can each sleep four people comfortably, possibly more. It is located 14km north of Metapán near a spectacular waterfall at Reserva Ecologica El Limo. Call ahead to arrange pick-up from Metapán; if driving, take the dusty road towards Frontera Anguiatú then continue straight until you see the signs.

Balompie Sports Bar & Cafe CAFE $$

(☎2402-3567; 3 Av Norte 17; mains US$3-10; ⌚11am-11pm Tue-Sun) Fronting the town square and backing onto Metapán's football stadium, this incongruously good sports bar is more than a place to sink beers and cheer on *Los Caleros*. Here you can sit on a sunny terrace and savor Salvadoran food. Entrance is via a concrete arch leading to a staircase.

Information

Scotiabank (Av Ignacio Gómez; 8am-4:30pm Mon-Fri, to noon Sat)

Getting There & Away

The **bus terminal** sits on the highway facing the entrance to town. For Santa Ana, take bus 235 (US$0.90, 1½ hours). San Salvador bus 201A (US$2.50, 1¾ hours) departs seven times daily. Bus 235 and microbuses go to the Guatemalan border at Anguiatú (US$0.50, 30 minutes); the last leaves at 6:30pm.

Parque Nacional Montecristo

In the northwestern reaches of El Salvador, the forest touches the sky. At the highest point of **Parque Nacional Montecristo** (MARN office in San Salvador 2455-5192; www.marn.gob.sv/parque-nacional-montecristo-2; US$10; 7:30am-3pm, last admission 1pm), the borders of El Salvador, Honduras and Guatemala converge at a point known as El Trifinio (2418m). Here cloud-forest oaks and laurel trees, some growing to 30m, form a dense canopy impenetrable to sunlight. The forest floor provides a habitat for abundant exotic plant life including mushrooms, lichens, mosses and tree ferns up to 8m tall. The temperature averages between 10°C (50°F) and 15°C (59°F) and relative humidity hovers at 100%.

Animals seen (albeit rarely) include pumas, anteaters, skunks, spider monkeys, agoutis and coyotes, while nearly 100 bird species – including quetzals, green toucans and white-faced quails – make the forest their home.

Sights

Hacienda San Jose MUSEUM
(8am-noon & 1-3pm) Near the park entrance, a charming hacienda with pretty gardens holds a small interpretative center with displays on the park's flora and fauna, including taxidermy.

Jardín de los Cien Años GARDENS
At Los Planes, this enchanting garden has more than 70 species of orchid as well as towering oaks and other plants, many of which are labeled. Don't miss the *arbol de amor* (the love tree), two cyprus trees that are joined together in an embrace.

Activities

Several hiking trails begin from Los Planes (about 1900m), a grassy clearing in a bowl at the foot of Cerro Montecristo. A 1.2km trail leads through fragrant pine forest with views of the park and surrounding area; a second trail leads to waterfalls where it's possible to swim.

The walk you are probably looking for, though, is the one to **El Trifinio** (2418m). The park highlight, the trail is a tough 7km climb through dense, misty cloud forest; allow five hours for the hike. At the summit a plaque marks the borders of the three countries, and the views are some of the most incredible in Central America. From December to April, certified local guides wait by the park entrance to offer their services and usually charge about US$25.

To climb up to El Trifinio in one day you'll need to be at the park gates at 7:30am to begin the hike from Los Planes by 8:30am and be back down in time to leave the park before it closes at 3pm.

Although advance permission from the **Ministerio de Medio Ambiente** (MARN; Map p306; 2267-6276; www.marn.gob.sv; Alameda Araujo/Carretera Santa Tecla Km 5.5; 8:30am-12:30pm & 1:10-4:30pm Mon-Fri) is officially required to enter the park, during the week it's usually possible for day-trippers to simply turn up and pay admission at the gates. On weekends or public holidays you may be turned away if you haven't reserved ahead, as there is a limit on the number of people admitted to the park. Note that the area above Los Planes is closed from May to November, the breeding season of the local fauna.

Sleeping & Eating

Los Planes Campsite CAMPGROUND $
(MARN in San Salvador 2455-5192; www.marn.gob.sv/parque-nacional-montecristo-2; camping per person US$6, 8-bed cabin US$35; check-in 7:30am-12:30pm) To fully explore Parque Nacional Montecristo it's best to spend the night in a tent (if you have your own gear) or in one of two cute wooden eco-cabins, which have small gas-powered kitchens, solar-powered lights and BBQs. It gets cool here at night so bring a good sleeping bag. Book ahead.

Tienda Roxana SALVADORAN

(Los Planes; mains US$2; ⌚7am-8pm) A family serves typical local fare at their idyllically located home, near the campgroud at Los Planes. With advanced warning they can prepare *sopa de gallina* (chicken soup; US$20, feeds six), using one of their own free-range chickens. They also have a small store selling a few basic supplies and snacks.

Getting There & Away

Getting to Los Planes is a challenge. If you have a 4WD, you can drive there (22km from Metapán). Drivers in Metapán charge US$80 to US$100 for the round-trip.

If you wait at the park turnoff on the main road in the early morning, you may be able to catch a ride with the rangers or residents of a small village in the park, but there are no guarantees, and the trip back remains unresolved. You can walk from the turnoff to the gate (5km), but you can't walk beyond that without a private vehicle – that's the rule.

Ruta de las Flores

Traveling the Ruta de las Flores, slowly and purposefully, is like a meander through the story of El Salvador. It's a beautiful series of villages, each with a mix of colonial architecture in indigenous tones. Those who like the good life can feast on local food, particularly at the weekend markets, browse the craft *tiendas* (stores) or undertake firsthand research into why El Salvadoran coffee is renowned across the world. If the pace is too slow, you can hit the Cordillera Apaneca, a volcanic mountain range filled with waterfalls, mountain-bike trails, and pine forest hikes where white flowers bloom in May.

In 1932 this region witnessed the horrible Peasant Massacre, when mostly Nahuatl coffee farmers were slaughtered by government troops following an attempted insurrection and mass protest. The actual number of deaths is still unknown, but 30,000 people is a close estimate.

Getting There & Away

Bus 249 runs frequently between Sonsonate and Ahuachapán, stopping in all the towns along the way, including Juayúa, Apaneca and Ataco.

Ahuachapán

POP 38,110

Ahuachapán is either the beginning or end of the Ruta de las Flores, depending on which direction you roll. Either way, it's a prosperous, provincial capital that supplies 15% of the country's electrical power thanks to the wonders of geothermal energy. There are some attractive colonial buildings, but for travelers it's mostly a jumping-off point for trips to Parque Nacional El Imposible or Ataco.

Ahuachapán bubbles with geothermal activity, evidenced in the steaming mud pits found in the area. **Los Ausoles**, aka *los infernillos* (the little hells), is a series of hot springs 20km north of town. Ask at your hotel for guides; if you have a car, it's easy enough to explore them on your own.

Sleeping & Eating

La Casa de Mamapán HOTEL **$$**

(☎2413-4747; www.lacasademamapan.com; cnr 2a Ave Sur & Pasaje La Concordia; r incl breakfast US$50-80; P❄📶) Mamapan is a 19th-century house opposite Plaza Concordia that celebrates authentic Salvadoran life in the food, artwork and quiet respectfulness of the owners. The rooms are modest and functional, with comfortable, dark wooden beds and very clean bathrooms, and there's a terrace overlooking the church.

Termales de Santa Teresa RESORT **$$**

(☎2423-8041; www.termalesdesantateresa.com; r per person incl breakfast & dinner from US$60; ⌚day visits 8am-10pm) In a region famed for its hot springs, the sprawling set of pools at Santa Teresa surpasses expectations. You can opt for the bathing only (US$10), or sleep it off in kitsch splendor. Beauty treatments, massages and mud packs are also available. From Ahuachapán, take the road toward Ataco for 2km, turn left at the sign and continue for 2km.

Hotel Casa Blanca HOTEL **$$**

(☎2443-1505; cnr 2a Av Norte & Calle Barrios; s/d US$33/60; ❄📶) Set inside an old mansion filled with colonial-style furniture, this slightly ostentatious hotel is a fine choice to start or end your journey down the Ruta de las Flores. The eight rooms are a little cluttered and the color schemes startling, but the beds are comfy. Take your coffee in the internal courtyard, which speaks to an earlier time.

Las Mixtas SALVADORAN **$**

(2a Av Sur, btwn Calles 3a & 1a Oriente; mains US$3-5; ⌚7am-8pm Mon-Fri, to 9pm Sat, 11am-9pm Sun) Colorful, convivial and teeming with young couples, Las Mixtas serves, you guessed it, *mixtas*, which is basically a sloppy sandwich filled with too much of everything, including pickled vegetables. Locals rave about the ice-cold *licuados* (fresh fruit drinks).

Típicos Kolo Kolo SALVADORAN **$**
(cnr Av Tranceico Menéndez Sur & 1a Calle Oriente; mains US$2.50; ⏲6am-4pm) You can't miss this cheery corner place that's painted inside and out with bright murals celebrating local life. Salvadoran breakfasts, buffet lunches and *pupusas* hit the spot.

Information

Banco de America Central (3a Calle Oriente; ⏲8am-5pm Mon-Fri, to noon Sat) Changes Amex and Visa traveler's checks.

Getting There & Away

Buses for Tacuba, Santa Ana and Sonsonate line Av Menéndez at 10a Calle Oriente, one block north of Parque Central. Buses for the Guatemalan border at Las Chinamas leave from 8a Calle Poniente, at the northwest corner of Parque Menéndez. Buses for San Salvador leave from the new terminal just past the gas station on Carretera 13, the road toward Santa Ana.

Ataco

POP 12,882

Many people leave Ataco with a new favorite village in El Salvador with brightly colored murals and artisan markets, cobblestone streets and colonial-era buildings, a congenial mountain setting and excellent, cheap dining and sleeping options, this sleepy Flower Route destination even gets a little festive on Saturday nights with live music spilling into the streets.

The next town along, **Salcoatitán**, was founded by the pre-Columbian Pipils and has lots of tiny art galleries down cobblestone streets.

Tours

Ask at the tourist office for guide services to explore the countryside. Options include **Salto de Chacala**, a 50m waterfall on the Río Matala, and **Chorros del Limo**, a spring that forms a broad pool ideal for a dip.

El Carmen Estate FOOD & DRINK
(☎2243-0304; www.elcarmenestate.com; tour per person US$6; ⏲9am-4pm) Hour-long tours explain the coffee-growing process and end with a tasting of Finca el Carmen's gourmet beans. In English and Spanish.

Sleeping & Eating

Segen Hostel HOSTEL **$$**
(☎2450-5832; www.facebook.com/segenhostel.ataco; Calle Poniente 3; s/d US$25/40; ❄📶) Not much has changed in recent years at one of Ataco's best little hostels. Rooms are adequate for the price, the rooftop balcony is still a great place to watch the village go about its business, and the hosts still fuss over their guests. Entrance is via a locked gate; don't worry, someone's always home, usually Eduardo, the English-speaking owner.

Los Portones de Ataco HOTEL **$$**
(☎2432-8853, 6114-8030; www.losportonesdeataco.webstudio503.com; 2a Av Sur 2; s/d US$35/50; 📶) Go through the *portones* (gates) and past a charming cafe and interior garden to reach six neat rooms, tucked away at the back of this youthful, nicely designed property. Rooms have private bathrooms and cable TV, and are decorated with local artwork.

Out front, Cafe La Estancia is the perfect place to people watch while sampling Ataco's famous coffee.

Villa Santo Domingo HOSTEL **$$**
(☎2450-5442; hotel.villasantodomingo@gmail.com; cnr 1a Av Norte & Calle Central; d US$30; @📶) Pretty gardens and a spread of local antiques and artwork round out a very

BUSES FROM AHUACHAPÁN

DESTINATION	BUS	COST (US$)	DURATION (HR)
Las Chinamas	263 or minibus	0.50	40min
San Salvador	202	1.25	3
San Salvador *especial*	202e	2.30	1¼
Santa Ana	210	0.50	1
Sonsonate *directo*	23	1.25	1½
Sonsonate via Ataco & Juayúa	249	0.95	2
Tacuba	264 or Ruta 15	0.70	¾

pleasant hotel experience. Rooms face an internal courtyard and have original stone floors and thick walls.

El Carmen Estate BOUTIQUE HOTEL $$$
(☎2243-0304; www.elcarmenestate.com; La Casona d/tr/q incl breakfast US$88.50/100/112, Quinta El Carmen d incl breakfast from US$65; ❄📶) The ubiquitous Cafe Ataco brand hails from this charming *finca*, which has been operating since the 1930s. The original house, **La Casona**, has been converted into a luxurious boutique hotel, set in lush gardens and with several elegant common areas including a library and bar. A second building, **Quinta el Carmen**, is a fabulous option for families with plenty of room to run around.

★ **Tayua** INTERNATIONAL $$
(cnr 5a Calle Oriente & 2a Av Norte; mains US$6.50-13; ⏲5:30-8pm Wed & Thu, noon-10pm Fri & Sat, noon-6:30pm Sun; 📶✎) On weekends, Tayua is one of the most lively spots in little Ataco. Homemade pizza, salads and gourmet sandwiches use fresh herbs from the garden out back, while the decadent sweet pastries are perfect for dunking in coffee. Live music bobs up on occasion, and purchasable artwork adorns the walls.

Vocho Pizza PIZZA $$
(1a Av Sur; pizzas US$5-6; ⏲noon-9pm Tue-Sun) It's a little gimmicky, sure, but a Volkswagen Beetle that's been converted into a food truck with a functioning wood-fired pizza oven is hard to pass by. Take a seat in the wood-cabin dining room while you wait for your thin crust pizza to be baked outside.

Shopping

Diconte-Axul ARTS & CRAFTS
(cnr 2a Av Sur & Calle Central; ⏲8:30am-6pm) This store is popular for its homemade textiles, tie-dyes and hand-painted objects.

Market MARKET
(2a Av Sur; ⏲7am-7pm) Ataco's sprawling market makes for a fascinating stroll.

Information

Scotiabank (cnr 2a Av Sur & Calle Central)

Tourist Information Kiosk (⏲7am-7pm Sat & Sun) Sits at the entrance to town. You can pick up a handy street map here.

Getting There & Away

Bus 249 stops on the corner of 2a Calle Oriente and 4a Av Sur. It heads north to Ahuachapán (US$0.35, 15 minutes); and south to Apaneca (US$0.25, 10 minutes), Juayúa (US$0.70, 30 minutes) and Sonsonate (US$0.80, one hour). Frequency is every 15 minutes.

Apaneca

POP 8597

Apaneca means 'river of the wind' in Nahuatl, and there is a definite cooling in the air in El Salvador's second-highest town (1450m). One of the country's prettiest places to visit, its cobbled streets and colorful adobe houses are blissfully peaceful during the week, but come alive with increasing numbers of visitors on weekends. Apaneca's cottage craft industry is highly revered and the surrounding Sierra Apaneca Ilamatepec is a hiker's paradise.

The beautiful **Iglesia San Andres** was one of the oldest churches in the country until the 2001 earthquake reduced it to rubble, but it has been rebuilt with a similar appearance.

Sights & Activities

The crater lakes **Laguna de las Ninfas** and **Laguna Verde**, north and northeast of town, are within hiking distance. The former is swampy, reedy and rife with lily pads; the latter is deep and cold. For directions or a guide stop by the tourist kiosk at the plaza (open weekends only).

Finca Santa Leticia FARM
(☎2433-0357; www.hotelsantaleticia.com; Carretera de Sonsonate Km 86.5; ⏲archaeological park 9am-5pm) Finca Santa Leticia is a coffee farm, hotel and restaurant just south of Apaneca. The highlight here is the small on-site **archaeological park** (admission US$8; call ahead) displaying two pot-bellied figures carved from huge basalt boulders, weighing between 6350kg and 11,000kg. Experts speculate that these 2000-year-old chubbies were created by early Maya in deference to their rulers.

Apaneca Canopy Tours ADVENTURE
(☎2433-0554; Av 15 de Abril; 1½hr tour US$35) An excellent zip-line experience covering 13 cables and 2.5km of mountain forest. Tours leave daily at 9:30am, 11:30am and 3pm.

Buggy Buggy Apaneca Aventura ADVENTURE
(☎2612-7034; www.503apanecabuggies.wix.com/apanecaadventure; 4a Av Norte; 2hr tour for 2 people US$70) A convoy of dirt buggies in the

quiet village of Apaneca jolts the senses, but it is good, honest, dirty fun to roar down to Laguna Verde with this popular outfit. Tours run at 9am, 11am, 1pm and 3pm.

Sleeping

Hostal Il Piemonte HOSTEL **$**
(☎7739-5830, 2406-5987; 2a Av Sur 4; dm US$8, s/d with bathroom US$20/35, s/d without bathroom US$15/25;) Italian Massimo has opened his home (and his action-figurine collection) to budget travelers, and the town is better for it. Natural light fills the well-kept rooms and hikers will appreciate the homemade pasta.

Jardín Hostal HOTEL **$$**
(☎2407-3784; www.jardinhostal.com; cnr 2a Calle Poniente & 1a Av Sur; s/d without bathroom US$20/25, d with bathroom US$35-45;) In a pleasant corner building covered in greenery, the Jardín has simple rooms with exposed brick walls; most access a wraparound balcony with mountain views. It's a well-run place with helpful staff and a relaxed atmosphere. Breakfast is available in the 1st-floor cafe (US$3.25 to US$4.50).

Eating & Drinking

The upscale restaurants on the highway offer the inevitable *buena vista* and a relaxed atmosphere to dally in. Otherwise you'll find plenty of local food in the village, but not much after dark.

Plaza Apaneca MARKET **$**
(1a Av Sur; mains US$2.50-6; 7am-8pm) In a fancy new building comprised of lofty brick arches and plenty of wood, this food court facing the park offers ham, eggs and beans, and *atole* (a corn-based drink), as well as chicken dishes and *pupusas*. Look out for *piñas locas*, a cocktail of rum, pineapple and cream served in a hollowed-out pineapple.

★**El Jardin de Celeste** INTERNATIONAL **$$**
(☎2433-0277; www.eljardindeceleste.com; Km 94; mains US$8-17; 7am-6pm;) This heavenly garden venue is one of the culinary highlights of the region and warrants stopping for a meal or, at the very least, coffee and cake. Located between Apaneca and Ataco, Celeste is best enjoyed with friends, laughing, eating and celebrating the subtropical splendor.

Cafe Albania CAFE
(☎7349-5124; 8am-5pm Mon-Fri, to 6pm Sat & Sun;) The hedge labyrinth (admission US$3) here is the talk of the town, but it's the sublime views across mist-covered mountains that won us over. Call in for a cup of delicious coffee from the Albania finca, accompanied by pancakes or a slice or cake.

It's just off the main road, on the other side from Apaneca village center; look for the sign.

Shopping

Axul Artesanías ARTS & CRAFTS
(www.facebook.com/axulartesania; Av Central Norte; 9am-6pm) This store sells a range of handicrafts made by local artists and artisans, including beautiful handwoven tablecloths, painted boxes and jewelry. Bike rental available (US$2 per hour).

There's an artsy cafe here too, serving good local coffee; on weekends it also serves sandwiches and other meals (mains US$4.50 to US$10.50).

Information

There are no banks in town; the closest ATM is in Ataco or Juayúa.

A tourist information booth operates on the plaza on weekends.

Getting There & Away

Buses drop off and pick up on the main street, right in front of the market. Bus 249 plies the route between Ahuachapán and Sonsonate, stopping in Apaneca every half-hour. The last bus leaves between 6pm and 7pm. Ask a local to be sure.

Juayúa

POP 9936

Juayúa (why-ooh-ah) is the most-visited town on Ruta de las Flores due to its attractive cobbled streets, weekend food fair, and nearby waterfalls and hot springs. The fresh mountain air led to a rich indigenous settlement here and Nahuatl roots can still be seen in the craft aesthetic.

Cristo Negro (Black Christ), an important religious statue carved by Quirio Cataño in the late 16th century and housed in the church, is significant both as a symbol of change and for its obvious beauty.

Juayúa has a tumultuous past. Indigenous uprisings in the region ignited the revolutionary movement of 1932. Backed by the coffee elite, government forces brutally quelled the ill-organized insurrection.

Festivals & Events

Fería Gastronómica FOOD & DRINK
(Sat & Sun) A popular food fair held every weekend in the main square. Guinea pig and frog skewers headline an ambitious menu; less risky fare includes *riguas de coco* (fried coconut and cornmeal) and the ubiquitous *elote loco* (crazy corn) slathered with parmesan cheese and mustard.

Activities

A recommended place to hike and swim is **Los Chorros de Calera**, a series of falls spewing from fractured cliffs. The **Ruta de las Seite Cascadas** follows the Río Bebedero over seven scenic drops. Ask Hotel Anáhuac or Casa Mazeta for a guide, which is recommended due to reported robberies en route. Other guided excursions include lake visits, coffee tours and waterfall rappels.

Sleeping

★**Casa Mazeta Hostal** HOSTEL $
(English 7252-8498, Spanish 2406-3403; www.casamazeta.com; 1 Calle Poniente 22; dm US$12, d with/without bathroom US$32/26, tr US$36; @) Mazeta is a wonderful small hostel overseen by English owners who have decorated the converted home with panache. The double rooms are decorated with local fabrics and antique furniture, and the dorms are the stuff of guidebook legend, filled with character and free from dust. There's a good-sized shared kitchen and a wealth of information on the area to hand. Their seven waterfalls tour (US$20 per person) is recommended.

★**Hotel Anáhuac** HOSTEL $$
(2469-2401; www.hotelanahuac.com; cnr 1a Calle Poniente & 5a Av Norte; dm/s/d US$11/20/30;) To many travelers, Hotel Anáhuac is synonymous with Juayúa. Space is used effectively throughout, from the internal garden to the upstairs double room above the trees to the spare bathroom near the entrance. Owner César is incredibly knowledgeable about the region and knows even more about coffee; do not miss the tour of his plantation and roastery (US$20).

Hotel Juayúa HOTEL $$
(2469-2109; www.hotel-juayua.com; Final Av 6; dm US$12, r incl breakfast US$35-60;) This charming property is perfect for families looking for a little run-around room. Lounging on the manicured lawn by the sparkling swimming pool with flowering coffee plantations in the background is pretty easy to get used to. Some rooms are brighter than others, but all are spacious and stylish in a rustic kind of way.

The eight-bed dorm is perfect for those on the budget seeking a quiet place to stay.

Eating & Drinking

Taquería la Guadalupana MEXICAN $
(Calle Merceditas Caceres Poniente; mains US$3-9; 10:30am-9pm Tue-Sun) Gaudy and loud (the owner is a karaoke fan), Guadalupana serves upstanding Mexican food without much fanfare.

★**R&R** SALVADORAN $$
(2452-2083; Calle Mercedes Caceres Poniente; mains US$7-12; 11:30am-9pm Wed-Mon) R&R is still the finest restaurant in Juayúa, and possibly in the whole Ruta de las Flores. Chef Carlos puts a twist on steaks, salads and Mexican food. Even when Juayúa is quiet, the tables at this small, brightly painted corner building are filled with happy diners.

Restaurante San José SALVADORAN $$
(2469-2349; 2a Calle Poniente; mains US$5-7.50; 9am-7pm) On the main square in one of Juayúa's oldest buildings, the San Jose serves grilled beef, chicken and seafood dishes along with a few more exotic items such as grilled rabbit. There's a well-stocked bar and a cheery sunflower-themed decor.

★**Occalli Cafe** COFFEE
(2452-2783; 3a Av Sur; 7:30am-6:30pm Thu-Tue) Offers a fine selection of gourmet local beans brewed using a variety of methods, plus breakfasts, sandwiches and cakes.

Information

Juayutur (Plaza de Juayúa; 9am-5pm Sat & Sun) Juayúa's tourist agency dispenses information about the town and area excursions from its kiosk on the east side of the plaza.

Scotiabank (Calle Monseñor Óscar Romero)

Getting There & Away

Bus 249 has services northwest to Apaneca (US$0.60, 20 minutes), Ataco (US$0.70, 30 minutes) and Ahuachapán (US$0.90, one hour) and also south to Sonsonate (US$0.80, 45 minutes) during daylight hours. Buses leave every 15 minutes from the park, or from four blocks west on weekends. For Santa Ana, bus 238 (US$0.75, 40 minutes) goes direct, leaving a few blocks west of Parque Central six times daily.

Sonsonate

POP 72,591

Sonsonate is a dusty city at the foot of Ruta de las Flores, which many travelers will pass through en route to beaches and volcanoes. There's a slightly rural feel in the jeans and boots of the cattlemen, and a few attractive colonial-era buildings. There's not much need to hang about though, particularly at night, unless you're in town during **Semana Santa**, when half the province descends.

Sleeping & Eating

Hotel Plaza HOTEL $$

(☎2451-6626; cnr 9a Calle Oriente & 8a Av Norte; s/d/tr US$36/42/47; ❄≋) This yellow, flat-roofed property has a good swimming pool and a restaurant, and is located in a pleasant neighborhood. Its rooms are an ode to 1980s creature comforts, which appeal when darkness encroaches and you can simply travel no further.

★Café La Casona INTERNATIONAL $

(3 Calle Poniente, btwn 1 & 3 Avs Norte; sandwiches US$2-4, pizzas US$8; ⏰8am-6pm; ❄📶) An oasis amid the hot dusty streets of downtown Sonsonate, Café La Casona serves some of the country's best coffee as well as smoothies, sandwiches with yucca chips, freshly baked pizzas and homemade desserts like basil cheesecake, coconut flan and lemon pie. It's located in a beautifully restored and stylishly decorated old building – there's even a room with swings.

Information

Banco Agrícola (cnr Calle San Antonio del Monte & Av Rafael Campos; ⏰8am-4pm Mon-Fri, 8:30am-noon Sat)

Getting There & Away

Take a taxi or bus 53C from the central park to the bus station, 2km east of the city center. Buses to San Salvador leave from outside the terminal.

The terminal also serves Izalco (bus 53A), Nahuizalco (bus 53D) and Acajutla (bus 252). For Parque Nacional El Imposible take any La Hachadura bus to Puente Ahuachapío or Cara Sucia (US$0.50, 30 minutes). An alternative for Barra de Santiago is to take bus 259 to the turnoff and catch a pickup.

Tacuba

POP 5055

Tacuba is a small, pretty mountain outpost known to travelers as the access point for the wilds of Parque Nacional El Imposible. At 680m and atop a one-way road, the lush, green setting mesmerizes first-time visitors with its sense of isolation.

★Imposible Tours ADVENTURE

(☎2417-4202; www.imposibletours.com; Hostal de Mamá y Papá; tours from US$25, 2-day Barra de Santiago tour US$70) It's worth going out of the way for an Imposible Tour. Effervescent Manolo knows this land backward and forward and his passion for his backyard is infectious. Tours run from two hours to three days, depending on how deep into Imposible you are willing to venture. Cascading down waterfalls, hiking through virgin forest or mountain-biking to Barra de Santiago are all on offer.

Hostal de Mamá y Papá HOSTEL $

(☎2417-4202; www.imposibletours.com; 10a Calle Poniente, btwn Av Cuscatlan & 1a Ave Sur No 1; dm/d US$9/20; 📶) Mamá runs Tacuba's best hostel, and luckily it exceeds expectations for

BUSES FROM SONSONATE

DESTINATION	BUS	COST (US$)	DURATION (HR)
Ahuachapán via Juayúa, Apaneca & Ataco	249	0.95	2
Barra de Santiago	285	1	1¼; departs 10am & 5pm
La Hachadura	259	0.85	1¾
La Libertad	287	1.30	2½
La Perla	261	0.80	1½
Los Cóbanos	257	0.45	40min
San Salvador *directo*	205	1	1½
San Salvador *especial*	205	1.50	1½
Santa Ana	216	0.75	1¼

such a remote town. All the action takes place in the trellised garden where guitar music accompanies delicious home-cooked breakfasts. Rooms are large and well priced, and include hot showers. There's an upstairs chill-out area with sublime views, while Manolo from Imposible Tours will attend to your every need.

Getting There & Away

Bus 264 (US$0.70, 45 minutes, every 30 minutes 5:30am to 6pm) goes to Ahuachapán from the main plaza.

Parque Nacional El Imposible

This **park** (Salvanatura 2279-1515; US$6; 8am-4pm) is the largest park in El Salvador and is named for the perilous gorge – now spanned by a bridge – that regularly claimed the lives of farmers and pack mules transporting coffee to the Pacific port. Decreed a national park in 1989, it sits in the Apaneca Ilamatepec mountain range between 300m and 1450m above sea level, and encompasses eight rivers that feed the watershed for Barra de Santiago and the mangrove forests along the coast.

Edging Guatemala, the mostly primary forest of Parque Nacional El Imposible shimmers with rivers and beautiful waterfalls. Hiking can get muddy and steep, but it rewards with panoramas of misty peaks and the gleaming Pacific Ocean. The best time to visit is October to February, as the rainy season hinders travel. Entry is via one of two points – either from the north or the southeast.

The main San Benito entrance is on the southeast side, beyond the hamlet of San Miguelito. If entering from the north via Tacuba, you don't need to pay, but you should be with a guide as it gets dense pretty quickly. Try Imposible Tours for a range of excellent options.

Patient wildlife spotters may see pumas, tigrillos, wild boars, antelopes and anteaters, while birders will thrill to black-crested eagles, king hawks, motmots and hundreds of other bird species. Butterflies are also in abundance.

Three large camping areas with toilets and grills are within walking distance of the visitors center; the furthest one (a 20-minute walk) is the least crowded. Bring your own gear.

Activities

Los Enganches HIKING

An ideal picnic spot, this big swimming hole is reached by a trail (3.5km one way), which passes **Mirador El Mulo** and descends steeply. Along the way you'll pass **Mirador Madre Cacao**, with views of the southeastern part of the park. Look for agoutis and coatis.

Cerro El Leon HIKING

A tough 8km circuit tops out on one of the park's highest peaks (1113m), starting in a lush, humid gorge and climbing through dense forest. This trail offers terrific panoramic views. Allow several hours and bring plenty of water.

Piedra Sellada HIKING

A 4km trail leads to a swimming spot and a stone etched with Maya writings. Take the Los Enganches trail; just before the end another trail cuts upriver 1km to Piedra Sellada.

Getting There & Away

From Sonsonate catch bus 259 toward La Hachadura and get off at Cara Sucia (US$0.90). From there, a bus leaves at 11am and a pickup at 2pm (both US$2, one hour) for the main entrance. The trucks return to Cara Sucia every morning at 5:30am and 1:30pm (confirm times at the visitors center). If you think you might miss the pickups in Cara Sucia, you may be able to cut them off at Puente Ahuachapío (bridge), a few kilometers short of Cara Sucia. If the pickups have already passed, you may be able to hitch a ride (13.5km). You can also visit the park from the northern side via Tacuba.

EASTERN EL SALVADOR

Most travelers race down the Carretera Interamericana in search of El Salvador's western attractions or, if heading east, the Nicaraguan border. However, the wild east of the country is a diverse geographical region that warrants greater consideration.

The quaint village of Alegría, the visceral war history around Morazán and the long, sandy surf beaches near El Cuco and Las Flores will give even the most worldly traveler something to savor. They see only fleeting traffic from nearby cities such as San Miguel, a city with a distinctly cavalier attitude. Real off-the-beaten-track coastal adventure is found at Bahía de Jiquilisco, where birdlife soars, and in tiny fishing villages with little contact with the outside world.

WORTH A TRIP

BEACHES NEAR SONSONATE

From Sonsonate there's easy access to the coastal points of **Los Cóbanos**, a fishing village on a secluded reef that features the country's best snorkeling and diving, and **Barra de Santiago**, a protected mangrove forest reserve where you can swim with cayman crocodiles, canoe with local fishers and search for ancient ruins in the muddy shores. To stay on a huge, unspoiled ocean beach, contact Hostal de Mamá y Papá (p328) in Tacuba, who can arrange a hike through Parque Imposible to the beach, where accommodations in a large house await.

Water Quest (☎7160-8361; www.waterquestelsalvador.com; Los Cóbanos Hotel) Professional outfit offering open-water courses (US$275) and reef dives (US$65). Based at Los Cóbanos Hotel.

La Cocotera (☎2245-3691; www.lacocoteraresort.com; Barra de Santiago; r per person incl meals US$195;) Located on the rugged oceanfront of Barra de Santiago, near the Guatemalan border, these six luxury apartment–style rooms with king-sized beds open onto a long, empty beach surrounded by coconut and mango trees. Only 4WDs can make it here across the sandbank, but you can approach by boat if you request it.

Silence descends once the sun sets; there's neither TV nor internet and, sometimes, there aren't even any other guests. The attention to locally sourced, environmentally sustainable materials throughout the property is exemplary.

History

Prior to the war, subsistence farming was long the primary means of survival here. The inevitable demand for nationwide land reform resonated throughout the poorer communities, and the northeast in particular became a fierce guerrilla stronghold. Far from the capital, these mountainous areas witnessed horrific atrocities – none worse than at El Mozote – but barely a village was spared from the fighting, and the resilience of the locals will stir visitors for generations to come.

Cojutepeque, Ilobasco & San Sebastian

A few towns of interest lie between San Salvador and San Vicente on the Carretera Interamericana. **Cojutepeque**, 32km east of San Salvador, is a small town best known for the Cerro las Pavas (Hill of the Turkeys), featuring an outdoor shrine to the Virgen de Fátima, brought here from Portugal in 1949. Religious pilgrims come on Sundays and on May 13, **El Día de la Virgen**.

Further along the highway (54km east of San Salvador or 22km east of Cojutepeque) is the turnoff to **Ilobasco**, a town famous for ceramics known as *sorpresas*. Most depict religious imagery and rural scenes in minute detail; others are deliciously racy. Upon entering the town a string of *artesanía* shops lines Av Carlo Bonilla. The annual **crafts fair** runs September 24 to 29.

Another 8.5km east along the Interamericana is the road to **San Sebastián**, known for woven hammocks and textiles.

Getting There & Away

Cojutepeque In San Salvador, catch bus 113 from the Reloj de Flores, just west of the Terminal de Oriente (45 minutes, US$0.45).

Ilobasco Take bus 111 or 142 from the Terminal de Oriente in San Salvador (one hour, US$0.60) or from Cojutepeque.

San Sebastián Take bus 111 from Cojutepeque (80 minutes, US$1.10).

San Vicente

POP 44,369

San Vicente is dwarfed by pointy Volcán Chichontepec in the Jiboa Valley. Look out for the equally dramatic behemoth of **Torre Kiosko**, an otherworldly clock tower that juts from the farmland like some Disneyland ride gone haywire. The town is also known as the home of many *cumbia* musicians.

El Pilar, a beautiful colonial church built in the 1760s, was badly damaged by an earthquake; despite renovations, it remains closed.

Activities

Volcán Chichontepec HIKING

The double-peaked Volcán Chichontepec (also known as Volcán de San Vicente) offers a moderate climb through coffee plantations. Book a guide through the tourist office at least one day in advance. Transport to the trailhead, a guide and a police escort costs US$20 for one person and US$30 for two.

There are two potential starting points for the climb to the peak: one is a three-hour hike to the top, the other is a 90-minute hike to the top. The first part of the longer hike is unshaded.

Note that the road to the trailhead passes through private property, so you must be accompanied by a tourist office–appointed guide with the relevant permissions.

Wear sturdy boots and bring a sweater, plus plenty of food and water.

Sleeping & Eating

Hotel Pablo Tesák HOTEL $$

(☎2393-0012; rosaelena_valencia@yahoo.com; Calle Dr Jacinto Castellanos 25; s/d/tr US$25/31/43; ❄📶) San Vicente's smartest sleeping option is Hotel Pablito Tesak, which has 33 rooms arranged around a courtyard parking lot. After climbing Chinchontepec you can relax on a terrace with views of the volcano's pointy summit.

★**Dulcería Villalta** SWEETS $

(7 Calle Poniente 4; sweets $0.25; ⏲7:30am-5pm Mon-Sat, to 3pm Sun) Since 1860 the Villalta family has been making *camote* (sweet potato) sweets using traditional methods. Now in her nineties, Señora Villalta can still be found at the store keeping an eye on quality control.

Casa Vieja SALVADORAN $$

(1a Calle Poniente, near 3a Av Sur; mains US$5-8.25; ⏲6:30am-9pm) A reliable restaurant for satisfying plates of grilled meats, tacos or *pan relleno* (filled bread; US$3), San Vicente's specialty bread rolls stuffed with avocado, chicken, egg, salad and tomato sauce.

Information

Banco Agrícola (2a Av Sur)

Tourist Office (☎2314-2424; Av José Maria Cornejo; ⏲8am-4pm Sun-Fri)

Getting There & Away

All buses pass by the Parque Central after leaving the **bus terminal** up the hill on 6a Calle and 15 Av. Beat the crowds at the park without hoofing it to the terminal by catching buses at 6a Calle and 2a Av. For Alegría, catch an eastward bus from the Carretera Interamericana and transfer at Villa El Triunfo.

Alegría

POP 15,000

Happiness is an elusive state, but at least towns like Alegría exist to remind us to stop and smell the rose bushes in the town square. Arriving via a slow mountain pass, visitors are struck by the tranquility of the place – that a *mirador* so grand could be seen from a family's kitchen table. There's not much to do per se – you can walk the town in half an hour – but a day at the lagoon, or an afternoon cafe-hopping and buying flowers and local crafts, could make for a wonderful rest day between hikes in the surrounding area.

Activities

Hiking options include a scenic 2km walk up to the beautiful **Laguna de Alegría** (US$0.25; ⏲8am-6pm); its icy waters are said to be medicinal.

Don't miss the view from the **Mirador de las Cien Grados** – an overlook at the top of 100 steps. You can also take a walk along the road toward **Berlín**, another pretty mountain village.

Ask at the Tourist Agency (p332) about hiring a guide and other local hikes.

BUSES FROM SAN VICENTE

DESTINATION	BUS	COST (US$)	DURATION (HR)	DEPARTURES
Ilobasco	530	0.60	1	6:50am, 11am, 4pm
San Miguel	301 from the turnoff at the highway	1.50	1½	last bus 6pm
San Salvador	116	1	1½	last bus 6pm
Zacatecoluca	177	0.60	50min	every 20 min; last bus 5pm

Sleeping

Cabañas La Estancia de Daniel CABIN $
(2628-1030, 7876-5344; 2a Av Sur; s/d US$15/25;) The best value in Alegría is found at this house two blocks west of the plaza, which has four *cabañas* in a flowery garden. Owner Betty will prepare breakfast on request (US$2.50).

★Hostal & Cafe Entre Piedras HOTEL $$
(2313-2812; entrepiedras.alegria@hotmail.com; Av Camilo Campus; s/d US$16/32;) Easily the best digs in Alegría, Entre Piedras uses cooling slate tile to perfection, offset by wood paneling and slick bathrooms. There's a charming courtyard cafe where you can try one of the specialty chocolate dishes, or dine on pizzas or paninis (mains US$5 to US$6). Book ahead on weekends.

Casa del Huéspedes la Palma B&B $$
(2628-1012; per person US$15;) This eccentric family home cluttered with religious carvings, photos and bric-a-brac serenades as an informal hostel with four spare, tiled rooms. Two rooms, with a double and bunk beds, are suitable for families. Coffee is served on the plaza.

Eating & Drinking

Cartagena SALVADORAN $$
(mains US$5-13; 8am-8pm;) Ignore the overpriced rooms and come instead for the views and lovely gardens. The beer is cold and the lunch servings of grilled meat and sides can be easily shared. It's a couple of blocks downhill from the plaza.

Restaurante Mi Pueblito SALVADORAN $$
(Av Camilo Campus; mains US$6-10; 8am-7pm) Huge plates of chicken, rice, beans and salad are served at this old staple run by an industrious family. There are stirring views over mist-covered hills. The restaurant is half a block east of the main square.

La Fonda BAR
(2628-1198; https://lafondadealegriasv.jimdo.com; Final Calle Gólgota; 10am-8pm Mon-Fri, 9am-8pm Sat & Sun) If you find yourself in need of a cocktail or a stiff whisky, this is the place to come: this restaurant has the best-stocked bar in town. Soak it up with *pupusas* or a typical Salvadoran grilled chicken or meat dish (mains US$6.50 to US$12.50). It's two blocks down from the square.

Information

There is an ATM at the mayor's office but it's unreliable. The next nearest ATM is in Santiago de María or Berlín.

Tourist Agency (2605-5119; cnr 1a Av Norte & 1a Calle Poniente; 7am-4pm)

Getting There & Away

Alegría sits between the Interamericana and Litoral highways and is accessible from either side. From Carretera Interamericana, catch a minibus from Villa El Triunfo to Santiago de María (US$0.25, 15 minutes), where buses leave hourly for Alegría (US$0.35, 45 minutes).

Usulután

POP 71,636

The eponymous capital of Usulután Department is a noisy market town at the foot of Volcán de Usulután (1450m). For most travelers, Usulután will probably serve as a way station to Bahía de Jiquilisco and the lovely Playa El Espino. You can also easily reach the mountain hamlet of Alegría from here.

Lito's Comida Mexicana MEXICAN $$
(2624-4926; cnr Calle Dr Federíco Penado & 1a Av Norte; mains US$4.50-8.50; 6am-9:30pm) A

BUSES FROM USULUTÁN

DESTINATION	BUS	COST (US$)	DURATION (HR)
Playa El Cuco	373	1.50	2
Puerto Parada	350	0.30	½
San Salvador *directo*	302	2	2½
San Salvador *especial*	302	2.30	1½
Santiago de María (change for Alegría)	348	1	1
Zacatecoluca	302	0.80	1½

large Mexican place with open windows and a sizzling BBQ. The *tortas* (meat sandwiches) cooked out front are delicious, as are the sizable tacos.

Information

Scotiabank (Carratera El Litoral, btwn Avs 6a & 8a Sur)

Getting There & Away

Usulután's main **bus terminal** is 1.5km east of the Parque Central (taxi US$3); buses to San Salvador leave from here. The **San Miguel terminal** is west of town, but passengers can board along 1a Calle Oriente, a block south of the Parque Central. The San Miguel bus is No 373 (US$0.80, 1½ hours); take it to connect to La Unión.

Buses to Santiago de María (where you can change for Alegría), Puerto El Triunfo and San Salvador all take 4a Calle west through the center of town. Since most buses travel this route you don't necessarily have to go to the terminal (unless you want a seat).

For Playa El Espino, buses 351 and 358 (US$1.25, 1½ hours) leave from a **small lot** 100m west of main terminal, across from a supermarket. For Puerto El Triunfo take bus 363 (US$0.55, one hour) from a **lot** along the highway. Buses to Santiago de María leave from a **small terminal** to the west of the main San Salvador terminal.

Bahía de Jiquilisco

With kilometer after kilometer of white sand pounded by surf and inland mangroves facing volcanoes, Bahía de Jiquilisco beckons. El Salvador's largest estuary is a Unesco biosphere reserve and an important breeding zone for the endangered hawksbill turtle. The inland sector is a habitat for gray egrets, pelicans and other waterbirds.

This protected area is refreshingly pristine and undeveloped, and there is plenty to do here, from kayaking through the mangroves to fishing and birdwatching.

Fishing communities in the bay include **Corral de Mulas** and **La Pirraya**, and there are sheltered sandy beaches at **Punta San Juan** and **Isla Madre Sal**. Also called Isla Jobal, **Isla Espíritu Santo** has endless coconut groves and a coconut-oil processing plant.

Sleeping & Eating

Hotel Solisal RESORT **$$**
(2243-2290, 7890-2638; info@hotelsolisal.com; Corral de Mulas; r for 3/5 people incl boat trip US$40/60;) Highly recommended for groups (though solo travelers could make it work), the Solisal is famed for its floating restaurant in Corral de Mulas, on the calm peninsula of San Juan del Gozo. Lodge in a variety of wooden rooms on stilts, where the birdlife will flash by your window and the fish will dance by your back door.

★**Puerto Barillas** RESORT **$$$**
(2632-1802, 2675-1131; www.puertobarillas.com; Canal Barillas; tree house incl breakfast for 1-3 people US$95, apt incl breakfast for 1-6 people US$200;) It's worth blowing the budget to stay at this well-run resort in a truly memorable setting. Puerto Barillas is located at the heart of a unique biosphere, where flashy international yachts moor in search of solitude. The accommodations are in simple tree houses and more luxurious apartments surrounded by woodland, a short walk from the resort's waterfront pool and restaurant.

It's a fun place to stay with a playground for kids and plenty of other family-friendly activities on offer, including cycling tours to a local cacao farm (US$20 for two people), kayaking in the mangroves (from US$12 per person) and boat trips around the bay (from US$100 for up to five people). Juanita the resident alligator lives under a bridge and a troop of spider monkeys can be spotted in the neighboring forest. The hotel works closely with environmental groups to protect hawksbill turtle nesting sites and monitor migratory birds. If you don't have a car, take the bus as far as Usulután and arrange to be collected from there.

Getting There & Away

The gateway to Bahía de Jiquilisco, Puerto El Triunfo, is best sped through, preferably by boat. The last bus to Puerto El Triunfo from Usulután is at 4:40pm; the last one back to Usulután is at 5:30pm. From the highway turnoff, take bus 377 to San Miguel (US$1.40, 2½ hours, last bus 2:50pm) or bus 185 to San Salvador (US$1.65, two hours, every 30 minutes, last bus 2:50pm).

San Miguel

POP 218,410

Founded in 1530 and dwarfed by Volcán Chaparrastique, San Miguel is El Salvador's second-largest city and a provincial capital with plenty of swagger. For the traveler, there are some colonial-era buildings in the center, though it remains mostly an important

San Miguel

San Miguel

Sights

1 Museo Regional del Oriente D4

Sleeping

2 Europa Guest House A1
3 Hotel Plaza Floresta A4

Eating

4 El Barrilito B3
5 Los Chipotles D4
6 Pastelería Lorena A2

transport hub, halfway point between the mountains of Morazán and the Pacific Ocean beaches, and a base for excursions up the volcanic hinterland.

San Miguel is best known for the biggest party in El Salvador, the Carnaval de San Miguel. For the rest of the year, nightlife returns to normal, but as San Miguel has more strip clubs per capita than any other city in Central America, most visitors stick to the flash new malls along Av Roosevelt for their entertainment fix.

Sights & Activities

Museo Regional del Oriente MUSEUM

(Map p334; 15a Calle Oriente; US$3; 9am-4pm Mon-Sat) The small collection of pottery includes pieces found at Quelepa, with explanations in English and Spanish. There's not much to see here but the exhibitions are well thought out, and the museum is probably the best attraction in the city itself.

Ruinas de Quelepa ARCHAEOLOGICAL SITE

FREE Archaeology buffs will appreciate the Ruinas de Quelepa, grassy mounds covering 40 terraced ceremonial platforms, largely unexcavated. Lenca inhabited the site between the 2nd and 7th centuries AD, trading with Copán in Honduras as well as with Mexico. To visit the site, you must first go to the mayor's office in Quelepa and request a police escort. The ruins are 2.5km outside town.

Many of the impressive finds here are currently in storage, but there are plans to open a museum.

Quelepa is 8km west of San Miguel; from the cathedral take the No 90 Moncagua bus (US$0.60, 30 minutes).

Volcán Chaparrastique HIKING

Strong hikers can tackle 2130m Volcán Chaparrastique, aka Volcán de San Miguel, a towering cone southwest of the city. The top affords gaping views of the coast and a patchwork of rolling farmland. The crater is hundreds of meters deep, with a jumble of boulders at the bottom. Europa Guest House offers guided climbs for US$25 per person.

Moncagua Piscinas Naturales SWIMMING

(Turicentro El Capulin; US$1; 7am-5pm) These pretty natural pools are best visited during the week, when there are fewer people and the water is clearer. The pools flow into caves and are surrounded by greenery. Moncagua is 12km west of San Miguel. Take bus 90 from the cathedral. Don't bring valuables.

Festivals & Events

Fiestas Patronales RELIGIOUS

(Nov) Every November San Miguel honors the Virgen de la Paz with Fiestas Patronales, marking the occasion with holy processions and enormous, colorful sawdust carpets. Save yourself for its blowout finale, **Carnaval**, a citywide party held the last Saturday of November.

Sleeping & Eating

★**Europa Guest House** GUESTHOUSE $

(Map p334; 2639-2042, 7528-6952; Polígono 20, Calle Suiza 1, Colonia Hirleman; dm US$12, d with/without bathroom US$27/25;) This family home turned guesthouse in a leafy neighborhood is a pleasant place to stay. There's a large kitchen, a garden with hammocks and five spacious rooms. Owner and proud Migueleño Mauricio is a font of knowledge and runs an informal free tour to San Miguel's market. Guided climbs up Volcán Chaparrastique and horseback riding are also available.

There are bicycles on hand for exploring the city. Laundry costs US$2. Spanish classes also offered.

Hotel Plaza Floresta HOTEL $$

(Map p334; 2640-1549; florestahotel@yahoo.com; Av Roosevelt 704; s/d/tr incl breakfast US$36/50/54;) A welcoming local family does a fine job of managing this hotel on Av Roosevelt. The internal courtyard with swimming pool is a relaxing place to hang out, while the standard, tiled rooms across two levels are airy, clean and surprisingly quiet.

Pastelería Lorena BAKERY $

(Map p334; Av Roosevelte Norte; cakes US$0.20-3; 7am-7pm) El Salvador's most famous bakery started here. A glass of *horchata* and a slice of *Maria Luisa* (jam cake) are the business.

Los Chipotles MEXICAN $$

(Map p334; 7167-7355; 4a Av Sur 704; mains US$4.25-6; 4-10pm Wed-Sun) Mexican Florinda serves the city's best tacos at this fun Mexican joint with bright yellow walls and a leafy courtyard.

El Barrilito SEAFOOD $$

(Map p334; 2660-2344; 5a Calle Poniente 403; US$5-12; 10am-11pm) Feast on seafood cocktails, fresh juices and *pupusas* at this cavernous San Miguel institution.

Drinking & Nightlife

Zona Zero BAR

(www.zonazero.com.sv; Av Roosevelt; 11am-2am) For a pumping night out savvy Migueleños head to Zona Zero, where there are low-lit bars, karaoke mics and thumping dance floors, all in one complex. There's regular live music too; check the website for upcoming acts.

Information

DANGERS & ANNOYANCES

Although gang violence has quieted down with new security measures, the area around the bus terminal in the city center is still the wrong place to be once the sun sets.

IMMIGRATION

Immigration Office (Migración; 2660-0957; cnr 15a Calle Oriente & 8a Av Sur; 8am-4pm Mon-Fri)

MONEY

Banco Cuscatlán (cnr 4a Calle Oriente & Av Barrios)

Scotiabank (8a Calle Poniente)

POST

Post Office (Map p334; 3a Calle Oriente near 4a Av Sur; ⌚8am-5pm Mon-Fri, to 1pm noon)

Getting There & Away

BUS

San Miguel's **bus terminal** (Map p334; 6a Calle Oriente) has clearly marked bus lanes, but ask around for schedules. Take a taxi to your hotel if you arrive at night.

For the Honduran border, the El Amatillo bus 330 (announced as Santa Rosa; US$2, 1½ hours) leaves at 10-minute intervals from 4am to 6pm. For Perquín, bus 332 (US$1.75, three hours) leaves at 6:20am, 9:50am, 10:20am, 12:40pm and 3:20pm. Alternatively, take 328 to San Francisco Gotera and transfer to a pickup.

CAR

Alamo Rent A Car (☎2367-8040; www.alamoelsalvador.com; Av Roosevelt Sur)

La Unión

POP 26,739

While some pockets of the town retain a salt-crusted colonial charm, La Unión is the kind of place even the saltiest sea dogs are keen to avoid, and there's little to keep you here but an overdue boat headed for Nicaragua. The heat can be brutal too; even dogs whimper at noon.

Playa Las Tunas and Playa Jaguey are good beaches on the coast west of La Unión. For some respite from the heat, plus views of the gulf, head to **Conchagua**, at the base of the imposing volcano of the same name. The panoramas are knee-trembling.

Sleeping & Eating

The budget choices in town are sketchy; **Comfort Inn** (☎2665-6565; Calle a Playitas Carretera Panamericana Km 2.8; s/d incl breakfast US$70/82;) on the highway is by the far the best place to stay.

Amanecer Marino SEAFOOD $$$
(☎2604-4645; www.amanecermarino.com.sv; cnr 3a Calle Oriente & 9a Av Norte; mains US$10-20; ⌚10am-10pm) Fresh seafood is the star of the show at this cheery family restaurant at the port. Try the *Mariscada 'Devuelvame La Vida'* ('bring me back to life' seafood platter with lobster and prawns); we're told it's the ultimate hangover cure. The views across the Golfo de Fonseca will also clear the head.

Information

Immigration Office (☎2526-3409, 2604-4375; cnr Av General Cabañas & 7a Calle Poniente; ⌚6am-10pm Mon-Sat) Next door to the post office; the sign says Control Migración. You must stop by here if you're arriving or departing by boat from Nicaragua or Honduras. Some agencies offering the boat trip will arrange the paperwork for you, meaning you don't need to go to the office, but be sure to check.

Plaza Médica Vida (☎2604-2065; Calle General Menéndez, btwn 7a & 9a Avs Sur; ⌚24hr)

Scotiabank (3a Calle Oriente, near 1a Av Norte; ⌚8am-5pm Mon-Fri, to noon Sat) Has a 24-hour ATM.

Getting There & Away

The **bus terminal** is on 3a Calle Poniente between 4a and 6a Avs Norte. For El Amatillo at the Honduran border take Santa Rosa de Lima bus 342 (US$1, one hour) to San Carlos and transfer to bus 330 at the turnoff.

Boat service from La Unión to Coyolitos, Honduras, and the port of Potosí, Nicaragua, is very infrequent. **Mario Calleja** (☎7540-6048) sometimes makes the trip. You could also ask at Amanecer Marino; the staff may be able to help. Tortuga Verde in El Cuco arranges the trip to Nicaragua via La Unión for their guests; they

BUSES FROM SAN MIGUEL

DESTINATION	BUS	COST (US$)	DURATION (HR)	FREQUENCY (DAILY)
El Cuco	320	1	1½	every 30min
La Unión	324	0.90	1¼	hourly
Marcala, Honduras	426	4	5½	4 daily
Puerto El Triunfo	377	1.60	2	3 daily
San Salvador	301	2.20	3	every 30min
San Salvador *especial*	301	5	2	hourly
Usulután	373	0.80	1½	hourly

may know of a boat that's going. If you book with Tortuga Verde, the price is US$250 for a private boat for up to four people, or US$75 per person to join an existing group.

As a last resort, the land route may not be too exciting, but neither is hanging out in La Unión.

Beaches near La Unión

Southwest of the unspoiled coastal forest of Bosque Conchagua sits a long, sweeping sandy beach that was once the sole preserve of surfers, San Miguelites and sea turtles. But the word is out, and these days more and more travelers are finding their way down to this beautiful stretch of coast, which remains for the large part supremely peaceful and untouched.

Beaches

For many travelers **Playa Esteron** is the pick of the beaches, partly due to its accessible, clean surf and coconut trees, and also because it's home to La Tortuga Verde eco-resort.

About 3km west is **Playa El Cuco**, which is popular with weekenders from San Miguel. There are plenty of good, cheap seafood restaurants in the sandy town square and a sizable surf break out front.

Further west, **Playa Las Flores** is a beauty and a prime surfing point suitable for beginners from December to February. From June to September it's best left to the pros.

The once blissfully deserted **Punta Mango** is also attracting more visitors, with several new hotels opening up recently. You can access the famed Punta Mango break by boat from either Las Flores or El Cuco.

Broad and sandy **Playa Jaguey** is another good beach between El Tamarindo and El Cuco, with moderate surf. Private homes front the beach but you can still use it. There are no facilities.

Playa Las Tunas is also pleasant enough, with a wide, flat beach reaching 100m to an estuary. The seafood restaurants get rowdy on weekends.

Sleeping & Eating

There are many good sleeping options along this stretch of coast – both to the east and west of El Cuco town – with new places opening all the time, especially at Playa Las Flores.

Casa de Canela HOSTEL $
(2612-6820; www.azulsurfclub.com; Playa El Cuco; dm/d US$10/25;) The only hostel in El Cuco proper is Casa de Canela, a well laid-out property on the town's main street. Wi-fi is only available during the day, but there's a kitchen and lounge, and the location is convenient. Best of all you can use the pool and facilities at sister property Azul Surf Club (p338), 1km to the east.

Mama Cata HOSTEL $
(2619-9173; casacata1@hotmail.com; Playa Las Flores; r with/without air-con US$35/20;) Mama Cata will sort you out for a cheap, clean room right by the breaks. She will also cook, and treat you like the reckless young person you have become.

★**La Tortuga Verde** RESORT $$
(7338-9646; www.latortugaverde.com; Playa Esteron; dm/s/d US$10/12/18, d with air-con US$25-70, house US$200;) Hidden across three beachfront properties linked by sandy, low-lit paths and shaded by coconut trees is La Tortuga Verde. Here, with the help of local employees, New York native Tom Pollack has created a ridiculously enjoyable eco-resort to suit all budgets.

BUSES FROM LA UNION

DESTINATION	BUS	COST (US$)	DURATION (HR)
Conchagua	382A	0.50	20min
El Tamarindo	383	1	1¼
Las Playitas	418	1	1
San Miguel	324	1	1¼
San Miguel *especial*	324	1	1
San Salvador	304	3.25	4
San Salvador *especial*	304	6	3
Santa Rosa de Lima	342	1	1

LOCAL KNOWLEDGE

EL SALVADOR'S TOP SURF SPOTS

With 16 right-hand point breaks and 28°C (82°F) water swarming with sea turtles, what's not to love? Our favorites:

Punta Roca Iconic for a reason. Central America's best wave is often compared to South Africa's J Bay. A rocky bottom makes it fast and strong. Bring just your board – theft is common on the walk to the point.

Las Flores A fast sandy point break best at low tide. Picture a hollow take-off ending on a black-sand beach. A 300m ride is possible – welcome to the Wild East. From here you can also reach the infamous Punta Mango by boat. Don't drop in!

Playa El Sunzal The most popular wave in El Salvador; a fun, consistently big right-hander with a seasoned surf crowd.

Playa El Zonte Oodles of foam and plenty of instructors on hand make this pretty, largely protected beach an ideal place to learn.

Playa El Palmarcito A bit of a secret, this little beauty can serve up tasty waves for all levels when conditions are right.

There's a sparkling swimming pool, sunset bar, yoga studio, turtle hatchery, and day spa (best massage for miles!). The reputable on-site restaurant serves meals to locals and astounded travelers who can't quite believe what they've stumbled into, while a volunteer program enables some to trade their services for free board.

Various boat trips, excursions, parties and spontaneous activities take place at your desire; just enter into the spirit of the place, smile and wave to the ever-present camera. If traveling to/from Nicaragua, you can catch a fast boat for US$75, which is a glorious way to cross a border.

La Tortuga Verde is 3km east of El Cuco. Once you reach El Cuco, turn left and follow the gravel road for roughly 3km. La Tortuga Verde is on the right.

Papaya Lodge Las Flores HOSTEL $$

(☎2619-9091; papayalasflores2017@gmail.com; Playa Las Flores; dm/s/d US$15/35/50, s/d with air-con US$45/60;) Neat thatched bungalows arranged around a pool help create a mellow vibe at this hostel, which opened in 2017. There are boards to rent (US$15 per day) and it's a five-minute walk down a sandy path from the palm-filled grounds to gorgeous Las Flores beach. With a bar and restaurant on-site, post-surf relaxation beckons.

Azul Surf Club RESORT $$

(☎2612-6820; www.azulsurfclub.com; Playa El Cuco; d/tr incl breakfast US$80/90;) Azul Surf Club is an attractive family-run surf resort with a range of accommodations options right on a beautiful, quiet stretch of beach. Surf lessons and board rental are available, including at Playa Mango, accessed by boat. Owner Lisette is passionate about her community and runs service projects in the area.

Hotel Miraflores HOTEL $$

(☎7890-4751; www.elhotelmiraflores.com; Playa Las Flores; s/d/tr incl breakfast US$70/82/95;) Hotel Miraflores has elevated views of the famed Las Flores wave and respectable rooms. The pool area overlooking the beach invites all day-long lounging.

Information

Be aware of jellyfish and manta rays, especially around El Cuco. Shuffle while walking out.

There is no ATM in El Cuco. Bring sufficient cash from San Miguel.

Getting There & Away

La Unión Bus 383 takes a circular route to El Tamarindo (US$1, 70 minutes); it passes Las Tunas and Jaguey on the way.

San Miguel Catch bus 320 to Playa El Cuco (US$1, 1½ hours, every 30 minutes, 5:30am to 4pm). Buses are less frequent on Sundays.

Golfo de Fonseca Islands

This archipelago near the coast of Nicaragua was once the playground of 17th-century pirates. Today it is home to small fishing villages, pretty pepper-colored coves and warm waters. The raw ocean setting is memorable, whether you are whizzing to the border or just cruising about in a speedboat chartered from El Cuco in search of a seafood lunch at Isla Meanguera.

La Tortuga Verde (p337) in El Cuco offers recommended day trips to Isla Meanguera (US$35 to US$75 per person depending on group size).

Getting There & Away

La Unión has services to Zacatillo (US$2, 20 minutes) and Meanguera (US$2.50, 1½ hours) from the pier. Departure times vary, but are generally from 10:30am, returning at 5am the next day. Day-trippers have to arrange a private pick-up.

A private 'express' *lancha* costs from US$60 round-trip to Meanguera. Agree on a price before the journey starts, and pay only half up front to ensure your return trip. You could also contact **Golfo de Fonseca Boat Tours** (☎7930-4878, 2604-4645; www.amanecermarino.com.sv; boat for up to 12 people US$60-200) for a quote.

Ferries for the islands also depart from Las Playitas, further down the coast.

Morazán

The northeastern Morazán Department is a small agricultural region interspersed with rugged mountain forest. The cooler climate attracts visitors from San Miguel, as does the country's cleanest river, the Río Sapo, and the opportunity for countless hikes to waterfalls and old hideaways from the civil war. The museum in Perquín and a memorial in El Mozote are powerful displays of reconciliation and remembrance, while indigenous traditions survive in villages around San Francisco Gotera, the department capital.

Activities

This quiet corner of the country has some truly beautiful and still undeveloped natural wonders to discover.

At the *aguas termales* (hot springs) near El Rosario, you can bathe in a beautiful *pila* (bath) perfectly made for two. It's a 40-minute drive south of Perquín, then a one-hour hike to the Río Araute. Nearby, **El Salto waterfall** is only for the truly adventurous. To get here you must walk along the slippery banks of the Río Araute.

Near San Fernando, 6km east of Perquín, is **La Cascada del Chorrerón**, the most impressive and most accessible waterfall in the region. The water comes from a permanent, natural spring and the area was the site of one of the bloodiest battles of the civil war, La Batalla del Moscardon. From San Fernando, you can hike for 2km through a *reserva natural* along smooth terrain. The 40m-high waterfall streams into a beautiful crater that is perfect for swimming.

Perquín

POP 3862

A visit to the former FMLN headquarters in the mountain town of Perquín is paramount to understanding El Salvador's brutal civil war. It was in these hills that the opposition garnered its most loyal support, and despite vigorous bombing campaigns, the military was unable to dislodge the guerrilla forces. The town itself is small but the stunning pine forest surroundings can be seen at every turn, the mountain climate is agreeable and the war museum makes a trip here the highlight of El Salvador for many visitors.

Sights

Museo de la Revolución Salvadoreña MUSEUM

(Calle Los Héroes; US$2; 8:30am-5pm) A few blocks north of the park is this excellent little museum that charts the causes and course of the Salvadoran civil war. Highlights include the collection of antiwar posters from throughout the world, the stark color photos of life inside guerrilla camps, the incredible assortment of Soviet and US weapons, and the stories of those who died in action; there is also a crater left by a 500lb bomb. It makes for a somber, stirring visit.

The museum is also the contact point for ex-guerrilla guides who can help put the exhibits in context and provide detailed explanations. Their stories are compelling, though not many guides speak English. They can also take visitors on fascinating guided trips throughout the war zone. The most popular destination is El Mozote (p341).

Campamento Guerrillero MUSEUM

(☎7536-8747; Calle Los Héroes; US$1, guided trips per group US$20; 7am-4:30pm) This reconstructed guerrilla camp features *tatús* (cave hideouts) and underground shelters connected by rickety rope bridges and dirt tracks in a patch of partially cleared woodland. It's next to the museum, uphill and to the north of the main square.

Sites within the camp include the remains of the downed helicopter that carried Lieutenant Colonel Domingo Monterrosa, head of the notorious Atlacatl Battalion, to his death. You'll see the equipment of the FMLN's clandestine station Radio Venceremos (We Will Win Radio), part of an elaborate hoax that used a radio transmitter rigged with explosives to bring Monterrosa's helicopter down.

Activities & Tours

Mountainous Perquín offers excellent hiking and river swimming. An abundance of orchids and butterflies make it a prime birdwatching zone – 12 varieties of oriole have been spotted, along with the rare chestnut-headed oropendola. For guides, consult Serafin Tours or ask at the museum.

Serafin Tours TOURS
(7901-9328, 2613-8032; www.facebook.com/SerafinTousrRutadePaz) Offers recommended tours of Perquín and the surrounding area, including to El Mozote and El Chorrerón waterfall.

Swimming

The **Río Sapo** is one of three rivers cutting through the forest – you can swim or camp here after visiting El Mozote. It's about a 45-minute walk and well worth the effort. The beautiful upper watershed has lots of welcoming communities, such as **Cumaro** where you can swim in a water hole or wander past coffee and sugar plantations. **Quebrada de Perquín** is a smaller, craggier creek, also good for swimming.

Hiking

Cerro de Perquín is a 10-minute hike from town, while **Cerro el Pericón** is a longer haul. Both offer gorgeous views.

Sleeping & Eating

Hostal Perquín Real HOSTEL $
(2680-4020; per person US$10) In a prime location, this plant-filled hostel charges a fair price for clean rooms and relaxing common areas. The showers are icy cold though, so be prepared. It's located at the south entrance of town.

★**Hotel Perkin Lenca** HOTEL $$
(2680-4046, 7287-6510; www.perkinlenca.com; Carretera a Perquín Km 205; s/d incl breakfast from US$20/30, cabins US$40-65;) On the road into Perquín is a reputable and attractive mountain retreat hand-built by an American expatriate who excels in community projects. Finished with wood, the rooms and cabins are wholesome and spacious, all with hot water. Hiking and cultural tours are readily available. The views from the restaurant are superb.

Concina Lenca SALVADORAN $
(mains US$1-2.50; 6:30am-8pm) This convivial *típico* on the square serves the usual Salvadoran breakfasts, *comida a la vista* (canteen-style local food) for lunch, and a huge selection of *pupusas* in the evening.

La Cocina de Ma'Anita SALVADORAN $$
(Hotel Perkin Lenca; mains US$5-9; 7am-8pm;) Mostly organic and always tasty, Anita's is an all-day affair that, aside from the usual breakfast and lunch spread, serves heartier meals such as the Perkin *parillada* (BBQ; US$8.60) and *churrasco tipico* (steak; US$8). Diners also enjoy wall-length windows and homemade preserves. It's at the Hotel Perkin Lenca.

Getting There & Away

The CA7 north of San Miguel to the Honduran border is in good shape. Bus 332 runs from San Miguel to Perquín (US$1.50, three hours) at 6am, 7am, 9:50am and 12:40pm. Alternatively, there's the more frequent bus 328 to San Francisco Gotera (US$0.75, two hours), from where pickups go on to Perquín (US$0.75, one hour). The last bus back to San Miguel is at 4pm; the last pickup to Gotera leaves at 5:40pm, but you have to catch the 5pm to make the last Gotera–San Miguel bus.

NORTHERN EL SALVADOR

The small province of Chalatenango constitutes the northern region of El Salvador, where mountains run to the Honduran border. It's a very pretty, peaceful area, easily accessible from both San Salvador and the Honduran border.

Suchitoto – everyone's favorite Salvadoran colonial town – is deservedly the area's most well-known attraction. On some weekends it can feel like the cultural center of Central America, and it makes a fabulous base for a visit to the country.

La Palma is an atypical artists' hangout, famous for naïve art that continues to capture the imagination, while hiking trips from San Ignacio and Miramundo are among the

WORTH A TRIP

EL MOZOTE

On December 11, 1981, government soldiers terrorized and executed the residents of this northern hill village. It's estimated that 978 people died: of the 143 victims uncovered, 131 were children. El Mozote is now a destination for those paying homage to the massacre. A tribute includes bright murals painted on the church, depicting the town as it once was and as its children hope it will be again one day. There is also a plaque bearing the names of those who died and a rose garden planted over the collective grave of the massacred children.

Next to the church there is a small artisan shop; buying something here helps the local community. It's best to visit with a guide – Serafin Tours and Museo de la Revolución Salvadoreña (p339) run trips here. Once in the village, local Spanish-speaking guides may approach you to talk about the site. Please remain respectful.

Official recognition of the El Mozote massacre was a long time coming, but after three decades of political resistance an international ceremony was held in the small mountain village in 2011. New roads welcomed visiting dignitaries and relatives of victims spoke of the impact the event has had on their lives.

A striking **monument** was also constructed to honor those killed in the conflict. It features silhouettes of children and is surrounded by figures in peaceful resistance from around the world.

Meanwhile, human rights groups continue to campaign for justice for the victims. In 2016, 35 years after the massacre, the Supreme Court ruled the 1993 General Amnesty Law to be unconstitutional, allowing the case against 18 high-ranking former military officials to be reopened. Since 2017 more than 30 survivors and witnesses of the El Mozote massacre have appeared in a court in San Francisco Gotera to give testimonies. At press time the trial was ongoing.

El Mozote is 10km southeast of Perquín. From Perquín, walk or take a pickup 3km south to a fork in the highway. El Mozote is 10km from the paved road; the 332 Jateca-bound bus passes here at 8am. On the way you'll pass Arambala, once decimated by air raids. The same bus returns from El Mozote at 12:30pm and can drop you at the turnoff. Combine this trip with a visit to Río Sapo, a 30-minute walk from El Mozote.

best in the country. The commercial hub of Chalatenango (p345) is a proud farming town with a strong community spirit.

Suchitoto

Located 50km northeast of San Salvador, wondrous little 'Suchi' is the cultural capital of the country. Every weekend the cobbled streets come alive as Suchi fills with weekenders. For the entire month of February, the entire town celebrates its resident artists and the small galleries swell with domestic tourists. None of this is new, however; when indigo ruled the marketplace and the beautiful Spanish church was packed daily, Suchitoto was the pride of the province.

Architecture buffs will love the colonial buildings, while outdoor types can choose between numerous hikes to waterfalls, caves and beautiful Lago Suchitlán, with trails beginning just meters from town. Suchitoto is also a bird migration zone with over 200 species. Thousands of hawks and falcons fill the skies as the seasons change, and birds of all sorts nest in the relative safety of the lake islands.

History

It is believed that Yaqui and Pipil peoples settled in the area some 1000 years ago. El Salvador's capital was established near here in the early 16th century. More recently, some of the earliest fighting of the civil war began in Suchitoto, accompanied by much destruction and emigration. Today the town has rebounded to become the highland seat of national tourism.

Sights & Activities

Southwest of town, the former FMLN hideout of Volcán Guazapa is a popular horseback riding (six-hour trip US$30) destination operated by an independent cooperative. Visitors can check out *tatús,* clever dugout hideouts, as well as craters and bomb shells. Book trips through the tourism office (p344).

WORTH A TRIP

CINQUERA

The former FMLN stronghold of Cinquera has transformed itself into a successful example of grassroots tourism. The friendly community has initiated a series of projects that have helped it to rebound from the horrors for the civil war. Ex-guerrillas share firsthand accounts of the conflict at a **war museum**. A terrific little **forest park** is great for a short hike and waterfall swim, and there's a sustainable **iguana farm** for the herpetophiles.

The road into Cinquera is terrible. Bus 482 (US$0.80, one hour) leaves Suchitoto at 9:15am and 2pm and makes the return journey from Cinquera at 6:30am and noon, making it difficult to visit as a day trip without your own vehicle. Gringo Tours runs a recommended tour to Cinquera, including private transport to and from Suchitoto (US$50 per person).

★Centro Arte para la Paz CULTURAL CENTER
(☎2335-1080; www.capsuchitoto.org; 2a Calle Poniente 5; US$2; ⏲8am-noon & 1-4pm Tue-Sun) Opened in 2000 as a charitable initiative to support victims of domestic violence, the Centro Arte para la Paz now organizes a range of cultural activities from its premises in a beautiful, old Dominican convent. There's a small museum (admission US$2) and gallery, a cafe and even a self-catering dorm with respectable facilities (usually for groups; reserve ahead). The community spirit alone makes it a lovely place to visit.

Cascadas Los Tercios WATERFALL
Geologic oddity Cascadas Los Tercios tumbles over a cliff of tightly packed hexagonal stone spires. The waterfall underwhelms when water is low (often), but the rock formation and the trip there are captivating enough. It's 1.5km east of town toward Cinquera, but don't hike solo as some robberies have been reported; book a trip through Gringo Tours.

Indigo Workshop ARTS CENTER
(cnr 4a Av Sur & 2a Calle Poniente, Casa Municipal de la Mujer; ⏲8am-4:30pm) This center, founded to support women in rural communities, offers traditional indigo dyeing demonstrations and can show you how to dye your own T-shirt (US$25), scarf (US$20) or sarong (US$25). Workshops last about one hour. There are also ready-dyed pieces for sale.

Casa de los Recuerdos Alejandro Cotto MUSEUM
(Av 15 de Septiembre 103; US$3; ⏲9am-noon & 2-5pm Tue-Fri, 9am-5pm Sat & Sun) The former home of El Salvador's most successful film director, the late Alejandro Cotto, is now a museum. Many of Cotto's personal belongings, artwork, awards and furniture have been preserved here, and the building is a fine example of a wealthy Salvadoran home. Don't miss the lake views from the end of the garden.

Turicentro San Juan SWIMMING
(US$1; ⏲pool 8am-5pm) Down at Lago Suchitlán is a tourist complex with several restaurants selling local fare plus a 25m swimming pool (US$3). It's busy with local families on weekends, but quiet during the week. To get here from Suchitoto take bus 3 from outside the tourist office on the main square (10 minutes, US$0.30).

Courses & Tours

Pájaro Flor Spanish School LANGUAGE
(☎2327-2366, 7230-7812; www.pajaroflor.com; 4a Calle Poniente 22) Pájaro Flor Spanish School offers 20 hours of accomplished private instruction for US$160. Homestays can also be arranged.

★Gringo Tours TOURS
(☎7860-9435; www.elgringosuchitoto.com; 8a Av Norte 9) Californian Roberto ('El Gringo') has been offering tours of El Salvador from his home in Suchitoto for more than 10 years, and his wealth of knowledge and experience shows in the quality of the itineraries on offer, ranging from *pupusa* classes to week-long trips. Birding and local history are particular strengths. Roberto is extremely helpful and a good point of contact for tips and advice.

★Suchitoto Adventure Outfitters TOURS
(☎2335-1859, 7921-4216; www.suchitotoadventureoutfitters.net; Final Pasaje Cielito Lindo 7) There really aren't many places left in

El Salvador where René Barbon has not roamed firsthand. Kayaking, fishing and physical pursuits are his strength, but he is equally knowledgeable about history and culture. Day trips include a visit to Lago de Ilopango to the east of San Salvador, and to the war history and rainforest park at Cinquera.

Boat Trips BOATING
(Puerto San Juan; per hour US$30; ⏲6am-6pm) Boat trips on the lake for up to 10 people leave from the lake shore at Turicentro San Juan. There is a better chance of linking up with others to share the cost on weekends.

Festivals & Events

Festival de Maíz CULTURAL
(⏲Aug) Suchitoto's corn-harvest festival involves religious processions and street parties centering on the Parque Central.

Sleeping

Posada Blanca Luna HOSTEL $
(☎2398-1056; hotelblancaluna@gmail.com; 1a Calle Oriente; s with/without bathroom US$10/6, d US$13-25; 📶) A small, peaceful hostel tucked a block behind the church. Rooms on the 2nd floor have private bathrooms (no hot water), while the simple singles downstairs are separated by thin partition walls. The terrace is the place to congregate while enjoying lovely views of the sunset over Suchi.

El Tejado HOTEL $$
(☎2335-1769; 3a Av Norte 58; d incl breakfast US$60-75; ⏲pool 10am-5pm Mon-Fri, 9am-5pm Sat & Sun; ❄📶🏊) It's worth paying extra for a room with a view here – the lake is spectacular – and the private terraces are another plus. Overall the hotel has a feeling of space and is well maintained. Nonguests can use the huge pool for US$3.50. It's also a good spot for a beer.

Hostal Vista al Lago HOSTEL $$
(☎7310-1854; 2a Av Norte 18; s/d US$20/30; 📶) The views at this leafy premises are simply incredible. Enter through an unremarkable reception area, where the rooms are also a little gloomy. But press on into the garden and check out the newer double rooms, which is where you'll find the famous vistas. The owners are cheerful and happy to leave you to your own electronic devices.

★**Los Almendros de San Lorenzo** BOUTIQUE HOTEL $$$
(☎2335-1200; www.hotelsalvador.com; 4a Calle Poniente; d/ste incl breakfast from US$120/150; ❄📶🏊) Without a doubt this boutique hotel, set in a restored 200-year-old home, is one of the best places to stay in El Salvador. High-end Salvadoran art, antique and modern furnishings, custom-made doors and several gurgling fountains set the scene for immaculate rooms with high ceilings, large tile bathrooms and classy, simple decor.

In addition to enjoying rooms that are hard to leave, guests can lounge in the luxurious library, at the well-tended pool or in the lush garden. A fine restaurant and hip lounge-bar complete the experience.

Eating

Suchimex MEXICAN $
(☎6106-0908; Pasaje el Cerrito; mains US$4-5; ⏲11am-11pm Tue-Sun) A fun Mexican joint turning out decent burritos and tacos that go down well with a margarita or two.

★**La Lupita del Portal** INTERNATIONAL $$
(☎2335-1429; Calle San Marcos; mains US$4-12; ⏲7:30am-9pm Sun-Thu, to 11pm Fri & Sat) Now flanked by *pupusa* joints, Lupey's is still a reliable restaurant and drinking spot overlooking the central park. The menu features salads, sandwiches, pizza and grills, plus large fruit shakes. Breakfast (US$5 to US$6) is served until 11am.

Casa 1800 INTERNATIONAL $$
(www.facebook.com/casa1800suchitoto; Av 15 de Sepiembre 61; mains US$6-21; ⏲9am-5pm Mon-Fri, 8am-8pm Sat & Sun; 📶) Blissful lake views from a wooden deck beneath the trees make Casa 1800 a sound choice. The menu of grilled meats, fish, sandwiches and pizzas is on the pricey side, but you're paying a premium for the setting. Three guest rooms in the old house here are tastefully decorated but share bathrooms (double including breakfast US$60).

Drinking & Nightlife

★**Café Literario Eluney** COFFEE
(www.facebook.com/eluneycafe; 1a Av Sur; ⏲8am-6pm Mon-Fri, to 8pm Sat & Sun) Juan José and Marisol have fitted their small, artsy coffee shop with books to browse, and use the space to host live poetry readings, literary discussions and occasional jazz nights. There's also a gallery displaying an excellent

range of products made by independent Salvadoran artisans, such as handmade soap, pineapple jam, loroco pesto, flavored honey and jewelry.

El Necio BAR

(6a Calle Oriente; ⌚6pm-midnight Tue-Sat) A straight-up drinking den with a revolutionary flavor in the stiff drinks. Jerry and friends rotate the political paraphernalia with great zeal. You can learn as much about the country's history in a night as you could by reading a book devoted to the subject.

Shopping

Arte Añil FASHION & ACCESSORIES

(☎2335-1080; Calle San Marcos; ⌚8am-6pm) Local indigo artist Irma Guadrón runs a cozy shop that specializes in high-quality indigo-dyed pieces; each one is meticulously handcrafted, and she caters to a variety of clients all over the world.

Orientation & Information

La Iglesia Santa Lucía stands on the east side of the Parque Central, the town center. Signs to the lake lead you a block east of the park, left onto 3a Av Sur, then down steeply to the water (about 1km). You can also follow the street that forms the park's western edge (Av 15 de Septiembre); it merges with 3a Av Sur several blocks down. Parque San Martín is two blocks west and two blocks north of the town center.

A 24-hour **HSBC ATM** is found on the town square.

Tourism Office (☎2335-1739; Calle San Marcus; ⌚8am-4pm)

Getting There & Away

From San Salvador's Terminal de Oriente take bus 129. To return, the same bus departs from the corner of 1a Calle Poniente and 4a Av Sur, a block west of Parque Centenario. By car, go toward Cojutepeque on the Interamericana. When you get to San Martín, turn left at the Texaco sign.

If you're headed north, catch bus 163 to Las Aguilares (US$0.75, one hour), where buses pass for Chalatenango, La Palma and the El Salvador–Honduras border. A slower but more scenic option is to take a boat (US$5, 20 minutes) or car ferry (US$1/10 per person/car) across Lago de Suchitlán to San Francisco Lempa and from there catch bus 643 to Chalatenango (US$0.80, 45 minutes). The last one leaves at 3pm.

La Palma

Starring murals upon murals in the rainbow-colored, naïve art–style made famous by local boy Fernando Llort (p349), La Palma is a tiny village that makes a big splash. A two-hour drive north of San Salvador, the clean mountain air and access to exceptional hiking trails is reason enough to visit, but given that every bus stop, spare wall and park bench screams at you in thick pastel daubs, the playful irreverence keeps you happily grounded.

These bright, primitive images of mountain villages, *campesinos* (farmers) or Christ are synonymous with the modern Salvadoran art movement. Llort taught local residents how to create the same images and started a successful cooperative.

When it is time to move on, there are challenging peaks to ascend. Serious hikers often prefer lodging in the neighboring village of **San Ignacio** as it's closer to the main trails.

Sights

★**La Semilla de Dios** ARTS CENTER

(cnr 3a Calle Poniente & 5a Av Norte; ⌚8am-4pm Mon-Sat, 9am-4pm Sun) Local cooperative La Semilla de Dios, founded in 1977 by Fernando Llort, crafts quality products in workshops behind the store. If you ask permission you can wander through the workshops and watch the painters and woodworkers at work.

Activities

Cerro El Pital (2730m) is the highest peak in El Salvador, but thanks to an access road it is also one of the easiest to hike. From nearby San Ignacio, bus 509 to Las Pilas leaves you at Río Chiquito near the trail. It's about 1½ hours to the top, where spectacular views await. You will know you've reached the summit when you find the concrete block marking it. It's private property, so bring US$5 to cover admission.

Once there, ask for directions to **Piedra Rajada**, a huge rock a half-hour walk from the summit, accessed by a nerve-racking log bridge spanning a 25m drop. Don't try this one in wet weather. With a day's notice the Tourist Office can arrange transport to Río Chiquito and a guide for the walk, or contact local guides José Samuel Hernández (7554-2608) or Patricia Morales (7214-0921).

OFF THE BEATEN TRACK

CHALATENANGO & THE HIGHLANDS

'Chalate' is the capital of the mountainous Chalatenango province in the country's north. There's a lovely daily rhythm here, as the narrow streets fill with farm trucks laden with fruit, sugarcane, indigo and coffee en route to the morning market, where you might just meet a cowboy.

It's a pleasant place to walk around as you catch glimpses of the spectacular La Peña mountains and the Cerro Verde further west, both likely destinations if you've made it this far. Another popular day trip is to Lago Suchitlán to the east.

The stains of history are hard to erase here. There's a real contrast between the ambitious, city-bound youth and a generation of leather-skinned subsistence farmers recounting tales of FMLN might. The large military garrison on the plaza was built during wartime to rein in revolutionary activity in this FMLN stronghold.

The countryside around Chalatenango climbs into dry forest studded with toothy peaks and rugged tawny hills. The small villages in this remote area have stunning landscapes and compelling histories. **La Montañona** is a pine-forest reserve at 1600m with prime views and pre-Columbian rock carvings. The civil war left several *tatús* (cave hideouts), including one used by clandestine guerrilla radio station Radio Farabundo, as well as an underground guerrilla hospital. Northwest of Chalate, **Concepción Quezaltepeque** is a hammock-making center. You'll see women threading them along the side of the road. Beyond the Río Sumpul, **Arcatao** is a beautiful village in the mountains bordering Honduras. Ask in the municipal office about tours of the *tatús*, which attest to Arcatao's former role as an FMLN stronghold.

The pinnacle of awesome forest views is in **Miramundo**, a small, aptly named community perched on a steep hillside. Back at Río Chiquito, follow the right-hand fork for about an hour to Miramundo. Right on the trail is the ridgetop Hostal Miramundo . From Miramundo it's a three-hour (12km) downhill hike to La Palma.

Sleeping & Eating

Hostal Posada Real HOTEL **$**
(☎2335-9009; www.facebook.com/restauranteposadareal; r per person US$10) Freshly painted rooms with colorful murals and a pleasant courtyard garden brighten up this simple family-run place. The price is good, but there's no hot water.

It's on the main road, just before the main square on the way into town.

Hotel La Palma HOTEL **$$**
(☎2335-9012, 2305-8483; www.hotellapalma.com.sv; Barrio El Tránsito; s/d US$21/35; @ ≋) A long-standing retreat catering to large groups, this mountain getaway bordered by the Río La Palma is nonetheless a decent choice for individuals due to a yummy restaurant and well-kept grounds. The brightly painted rooms are elevated and look into the trees, while staff are attentive. It's just before town to the right of the main road.

Hostal Miramundo HOTEL **$$**
(☎2219-6252; www.hostalmiramundo.com; San Ignacio; 2-person cabin US$60, q US$65) These rooms and cabins in the woods near San Ignacio are a good choice if you plan to hike. You can walk to Río Sumpul and El Pital from the doorstep, then take a hot shower and sleep in a lovely, firm bed.

La Cafeta CAFE **$**
(www.facebook.com/cafetalapalma; Calle Gerardo Barrios; sandwiches US$1.75-2.50, pastries US$1-2; ⏲9am-7pm Mon-Sat; ☎) Gourmet coffee from the hills surrounding La Palma plus the best homemade cakes, pastries and cookies in town are the order of the day at this cheery cafe. Also sells breakfasts and sandwiches.

Cartagena MEXICAN **$**
(☎2305-8741; Calle Gerardo Barrios; mains US$1.50-2.85; ⏲9am-8pm Sat-Thu) Satisfying, freshly prepared tacos, burritos, quesadillas and enchiladas as well as tasty *licuados* (smoothies) are available here.

Information

Banco Azteca (Calle la Ronda)
Tourist Office (☎2335-9076; Parque Municipal; ⏲9am-12:30pm & 1:10-5pm) Very helpful; Spanish only.

Getting There & Away

Bus 119 runs every half-hour from San Salvador's Terminal de Oriente to the El Salvador–Honduras border at El Poy, stopping at La Palma (US$1.80, 2¾ hours). Some enter San Ignacio, 3km to the north; others drop you off at the entrance. From San Ignacio you can catch the bus to El Pital and its environs.

Bus 509A to Las Pilas, passing through Río Chiquito, leaves San Ignacio at 7am, 9:30am, noon, 2pm and 4pm and returns at the same times.

From La Palma the 509 bus to Los Planes via Miramundo (25 minutes) and Río Chiquito (45 minutes) leaves at 10:45am and 2:45pm. It makes the return journey from Río Chiquito at 11.45am and 3pm, passing Miramundo 20 minutes later.

UNDERSTAND EL SALVADOR

El Salvador Today

Over the past few years, El Salvador has been in and out of the international spotlight due to ongoing problems with gang-related violence. This disturbing trend undermined the early years of President Salvador Sanchez Cerén, a former guerrilla soldier who was elected in 2014 and oversaw a number of well-received social-welfare initiatives and educational reforms.

But a worse blow was yet to come. In 2016 ex-president Mauricio Funes fled to Nicaragua after prosecutors began investigating him on suspicion of personal enrichment while in office. The corruption scandal has cast a shadow over the FMLN (Farabundo Martí National Liberation Front) and Cerén's presidency.

The victory of ARENA (Nationalist Republican Alliance) in the 2018 legislative elections in which only 42% of the electorate voted (in El Salvador voting is obligatory) spoke more about general disillusionment with what many now view as corruption on both the left and the right. If anyone came out of the elections a winner it was rising star Nayib Bukele, whose name was scrawled across some spoiled ballots in support of a presidential bid ('Nayib 19'). A former FMLN politician who was kicked out of the party by political rivals in 2017, Bukele gained broad support for his populist policies as mayor of San Salvador and is expected to form a new party – the New Ideas Movement – and run for office in the 2019 presidential elections.

History

Mesoamerica

Paleo-Indian peoples populated El Salvador as early as 10,000 years ago, leaving their mark with cave paintings in modern Morazán. Around 2000 BC the Olmecs followed, leaving as their legacy the Olmec Boulder, a giant head sculpture similar to those from Mexico, found near Casa Blanca.

El Salvador was once a key regional trading center. Archaeological remains reveal diverse influences, from Pipil, Teotihuacan and Maya in the west to Lenca, Chorti and Pok'omama in the east. The step pyramid ruins at Tazumal, San Andrés and Casa Blanca show 3000 years of nearly constant pre-Hispanic habitation.

BOOKS TO READ BEFORE YOU VISIT

Major Salvadoran authors are available in translation. Joan Didion's *Salvador* is a moving account of the early days of the war. Nonfiction about the civil war includes *Massacre at El Mozote* by Mark Danner and *Rebel Radio*, a fascinating, firsthand account of clandestine radio stations operated by FMLN guerrillas.

Óscar Romero: Memories in Mosaic, by María López Vigil, is a recommended account of the clergyman's life and political conversion told by those who knew him. *When the Dogs Ate Candles*, by Bill Hutchinson, is an anecdotal history of the conflict based on interviews with refugees. Archaeology buffs can read about Central America's Pompeii in *Before the Volcano Erupted: The Ancient Ceréen Village in Central America* by Payton Sheets.

La Diaspora is an important novel by Horacio Casellanos Moya that communicates the experience of living in exile.

When Spanish conquistador Pedro de Alvarado arrived in 1524, he saw a country dominated by Pipils, descendants of Toltecs and Aztecs. These northern peoples (from modern-day Mexico) dubbed their home Cuscatlán, 'Land of Jewels.' Their maize-based farming economy flourished enough to support several cities and a sophisticated culture with pursuits that included hieroglyphics, astronomy and mathematics. Their dialect is related to modern Nahuat.

From Indigo to Independence

Spanish rule started with a year-long struggle against the Pipil. The Spaniards prevailed and laid claim to the land, transforming it into plantations of cotton, balsam and indigo. Agriculture boomed throughout the 1700s, with indigo the number-one export. A small group of Europeans, known as the '14 families,' controlled virtually all of the colony's wealth and agriculture, enslaving indigenous peoples and Africans to work the land.

Conflict simmered under this gross imbalance of power. A revolt against Spain in 1811 was led by Padre (Father) José Delgado. While it failed, it planted a seed of discontent. Independence was gained 10 years later, on September 15, 1821, when El Salvador became part of the Central American Federation.

Pushing for land reform, Anastasio Aquino led an indigenous rebellion in 1883. Though it was subdued and Aquino was executed, he became a national hero. El Salvador withdrew from the Central American Federation in 1841, but Independence Day continues to be celebrated on September 15.

In Comes Coffee

In the late 19th century, synthetic dyes undermined the indigo market, and coffee took the main stage. A handful of wealthy landowners expanded their properties, displacing indigenous people. Coffee became the most important cash crop and *cafetaleros* (coffee plantation owners) earned purses full of money that was neither taxed nor redistributed as reasonable wages to the workers. By the 20th century, 95% of El Salvador's income derived from coffee exports, but only 2% of Salvadorans controlled that wealth.

The 20th Century

The government vigorously eradicated union activity in the coffee industry during the 1920s. In January 1932 Augustín Farabundo Martí, a founder of the Central American Socialist Party, led an uprising of peasants and indigenous people. Under Maximiliano Hernández Martínez' orders, the military responded brutally by systematically killing anyone who looked indigenous or supported the uprising. La Matanza (the Massacre) resulted in the death of 30,000 individuals, including Martí, who was killed by firing squad. The FMLN (Frente Farabundo Martí para la Liberación Nacional) revolutionary army would later take up his name in his honor.

Over the course of the 1970s, landlessness, poverty, unemployment and overpopulation became serious problems. In government, the polarized left and right tangled for power through coups and electoral fraud. In 1972 José Napoleon Duarte, cofounder of the Christian Democrat Party (Partido Demócratico Cristiano; PDC), ran for president supported by a broad coalition of reform groups. When his victory was denied amid allegations of fraud, protests followed. The military averted an attempted coup, and the right responded to increasing guerrilla activity by creating 'death squads.' Thousands of Salvadorans were kidnapped, tortured and murdered.

In 1979 a junta of military personnel and civilians overthrew President Carlos Humberto Romero and promised reforms. When promises were not met, opposition parties banded together as the Frente Democrático Revolucionario (FDR) and allied with the FMLN, a revolutionary army composed of five guerrilla groups for whom armed struggle appeared to be the only means of change. The successful revolution in Nicaragua in 1979 had encouraged many Salvadorans to demand reforms. One of them was Monsignor Oscar Romero, a formerly conservative priest who took up the cause of the people.

On March 24, 1980, outspoken Archbishop Romero was assassinated while saying Mass in the chapel of the San Salvador Divine Providence Cancer Hospital. His murder ignited an armed insurrection that same year that was to turn into a civil war.

Civil War

The rape and murder in late 1980 of four US nuns performing relief work in El Salvador prompted the Carter administration to suspend military aid. But in 1981 the newly elected Reagan administration, bristling from the threat of Nicaragua's socialist revolution, pumped huge sums into the moribund Salvadoran military. Uncle Sam's support would effectively prolong the conflict. When guerrillas gained control of areas in the north and east, the Salvadoran military retaliated by decimating villages. In 1981 the US-trained elite Atlacatl Battalion killed more than 700 men, women and children in El Mozote, Morazán. As many as 300,000 citizens fled the country.

In 1982 Major Roberto D'Aubisson, founder of the extreme-right ARENA party, became president of the legislative assembly and enacted a law granting the legislative body power over the president. D'Aubisson created death squads targeting, among others, trade unionists and agrarian reformers. In response, the FMLN offensive blew up bridges, cut power lines and destroyed coffee plantations and livestock – anything to stifle the economy. When the government ignored an FMLN peace proposal, the rebels refused to participate in the 1984 presidential elections, which Duarte won over D'Aubisson. For the next few years the PDC and FMLN engaged in peace talks unsuccessfully. Death squads continued pillaging, and the guerrillas continued to undermine military powers and jeopardize municipal elections.

The Price of Peace

Hopes for peace rose in 1989, when the FMLN offered to participate in elections if the government agreed to a postponement to ensure democratic polls. Its calls were ignored and Alfredo Cristiani, a wealthy ARENA businessman, was elected president. The FMLN's response was a major attack on the capital. In retaliation the military killed an estimated 4000 'leftist sympathizers.'

UN-mediated negotiations began between the government and FMLN in April 1990. Among the first agreements was a human-rights accord signed by both parties. Yet violent deaths actually increased in 1991 when a UN mission arrived to monitor human rights.

On January 16, 1992, a compromise was finally signed. The FMLN became an opposition party, and the government agreed to various reforms, including dismantling paramilitary groups and death squads, and replacing them with a national civil police force. Land was to be distributed to citizens and human-rights violations investigated. But instead the government gave amnesty to human-rights abusers, a decision that in 2016 was finally ruled unconstitutional by the Supreme Court, allowing trials against suspected perpetrators to begin.

During the course of the 12-year civil war, an estimated 75,000 people were killed.

Modern Currents

The FMLN has mostly proven to be a model example of a former guerrilla organization transitioning to mainstream politics. Skeptics argued that Salvadorans would always prefer conservatives. However, this all changed in 2009 when Mauricio Funes led the FMLN to power in a popular victory. The FMLN narrowly achieved re-election in 2014 under the leadership of Salvador Sánchez Cerén, but the party received only 25% of votes in the 2018 legislative elections, losing out to ARENA.

An ongoing issue for the ruling administration has been how to deal with the two major criminal gangs in the country. Also known as M-13, or Mara Salvatrucha, and Barrio 18, these gangs of roughly 100,000 across Central and North America were formed in the USA in response to orchestrated attacks by Mexican gangs. Deported en masse from the USA between 2000 and 2004, the *maras* became heavily involved in drug cartels, guns, the sex trade and illegal immigration.

Both the carrot and the stick have failed to have a lasting impact on the gang problem, as successive governments have struggled to curtail the violence. A heavy-handed approach by the right-wing ARENA party in the 2000s led to numerous high-profile arrests but arguably exacerbated the retaliation, while a carefully brokered 'truce' between the rival gangs in 2012 proved only a temporary reprieve.

Record body counts in 2015 earned El Salvador the dubious distinction of having the world's 'highest murder rate.' International media continues to frame the progress of the country in relation to this damning statistic. In January 2017, newspapers picked up the story that for the first time in two years, El Salvador had passed a whole day without any reported homicides.

BEHIND THE SCENES OF NAÏVE ART

Holy scenes, strange birds, unabashed rainbow colors: the childlike images of Fernando Llort have come to symbolize hope in a war-torn Central America. Compared to Miró and Picasso, Llort differs with earnest iconography and flat tropical hues in a style dubbed primitive modern.

Ironically, this strong Latin American identity was forged when Llort went to France to study architecture and then theology. Religious symbols are recurring motifs in his artwork. He prefers the rough and everyday to the exalted.

When Llort returned to El Salvador in the early 1970s, he arrived to the tensions and violence leading up to the civil war. Llort moved to La Palma, a distant mountain town in the north, to take refuge. The apparent simplicity of a life in harmony with nature further informed his style. He started La Semilla de Dios (God's Seed; p344), a workshop to teach others his craft and professionalize local artisans.

Llort has since lived in San Salvador and abroad, but the workshop is still going strong in his former studio. You can find his work in the White House, MoMA and the Vatican.

Culture

The National Psyche

Salvadorans are strong-willed people who are very welcoming to travelers. With an estimated third of the population residing in the USA, they are nostalgic for their country of birth and often fiercely idealistic about the future. There is at times a palpable frustration with the progress of the nation.

The civil war still looms large in people's minds, as it must – the memories are too searing to forget. At the same time, Salvadorans are genuinely dismayed to learn that many foreigners know little about El Salvador beyond the war. They will eagerly volunteer information and assistance.

Lifestyle

Remittances sent home from the roughly two million Salvadorans living abroad, which account for 20% of the national GDP, provide a measure of stability to the economy and greatly influence how people live. Poverty and unemployment persist, with about 35% of the population living below the poverty line, mostly in rural areas. That said, El Salvador enjoys the highest minimum wage in Central America (US$225 per week) and is notably more prosperous than neighboring Honduras and Nicaragua.

Religion

El Salvador is a very religious country. Once staunchly Catholic, like the rest of Latin America, El Salvador is experiencing an explosive growth of evangelical churches. Their fiery services seem to have brought fresh energy to faith. Town-square services with booming speakers are becoming an all-too-typical way of spreading 'the word.' Protestant churches now account for almost 50% of believers.

Before and during the war, priests and missionaries were often outspoken critics of government repression – many, such as Archbishop Oscar Romero, were killed for their stands.

Arts

El Salvador's artisanal products can be innovative and high quality. Fernando Llort's naïve art inspired an industry of brightly painted crafts in childlike motifs in the community of La Palma. Guatajiagua in Morazán produces black pottery with a Lenca influence and Ilobasco is known for its *sorpresas,* intricate miniatures hidden in ceramic shells.

Poetry is beloved in El Salvador. Iconoclastic poet Roque Dalton was exiled for radical politics. He eventually returned home to aid the guerrilla cause but was executed by his own side due to suspicion that he was a CIA operative. Notable works include *Taberna y otros lugares* (1969), a political vision in verse, and *Miguel Marmol* (1972). Progressive poet Claudia Lars wrote spare, bold erotic poetry and is considered one of the country's foremost writers.

Writing under the pen name Salarrué, lauded writer Salvador Efraín Salazar Arrué published *Cuentos de barro* (Tales of Mud) in 1933, marking the beginning of Central America's modern short-story

NATIONAL PARKS & PROTECTED AREAS

El Salvador has only four official national parks, but there is a number of locally or privately administered reserves.

Barra de Santiago (p330) A remote bar of mangrove-fringed estuaries and beaches on the Pacific coast.

Cerro El Pital (p344) El Salvador's highest peak. *Torogoz* (blue-crowned motmots) and quetzals can be observed on its piney slopes.

La Laguna de Alegría (p331) An emerald-green lake fed by hot springs, in the crater of dormant Volcán de Tecapa. Ocelots and coatis are among the wildlife inhabiting primary-growth forest surrounding the lake. In 2015 the lake receded to record-low water levels.

Laguna El Jocotal This freshwater lagoon east of Usulután is an important sanctuary for migratory birds from October to March.

Parque Nacional El Imposible (p327) Near El Salvador's western limit; one of the country's last remnants of original tropical forest with waterfalls, views and numerous endangered plant and animal species.

Parque Nacional Los Volcanes (p318) A volcano-crater forest with amazing views of nearby Izalco and Santa Ana volcanoes. Highlights include emerald toucanets, motmots and hummingbirds.

Parque Nacional Montecristo (p322) A mountainous cloud-forest reserve at the borders of El Salvador, Honduras and Guatemala. Wildlife includes pumas, spider monkeys and agoutis. Giant ferns, orchids and bromeliads are abundant.

Parque Nacional Walter T Deininger (p311) This dry tropical forest on the Pacific coast is the habitat for 87 bird species, deer and pacas.

genre. Likewise, Manlio Argueta's *One Day of Life* (1980), a tale of a rural family with the backdrop of the civil war, is considered a modern classic. Matilde Elena Lopez is a playwright who wrote a gripping 1978 play based on the life of indigenous leader Anastasio Aquino.

One of the more compelling contemporary Salvadoran novelists is Horacio Castellanos Moya. His translated *Senselessness* (2004) is a burning black comedy about government-sponsored violence.

Films *Romero* (1988), produced by Ellwood Kieser, and *Salvador* (1986), directed by Oliver Stone, offer Hollywood versions of the civil war. *Innocent Voices* (2004) looks at the civil war from a child's perspective and was nominated for an Oscar.

Landscape & Wildlife

The Land

The Land of Volcanoes, El Salvador has two volcanic ranges spanning east to west, spicing the views (as well as daily life) with a little drama. Much of the land is deforested, but mountains in the far north are blanketed in pine and oak, jagged rock formations and cloud forests. The Río Lempa bisects the country with a fertile swath of land. While El Salvador is the only Central American country not to have a Caribbean coast, there is over 300km of Pacific coastline bordering mangroves, estuaries and tropical dry forest. Lakes and freshwater lagoons provide drinking water and recreation.

Wildlife

El Salvador was drastically deforested over the 20th century. As a result, many species of plants and animals ceased to exist in the country. However, national parks and protected lands still maintain good biodiversity.

The country has over 800 animal species. Almost half are butterflies; bird species are second in number, with about 330 resident species (and 170 migratory), including quetzals, toucans, herons, kingfishers, brown pelicans, egrets, parakeets and sandpipers. Illegal bird trafficking continues to pose a problem, in particular macaws from Nicaragua.

The remaining mammal species number around 200 and can be seen mostly in reserves. They include opossums, anteaters, porcupines, agoutis, ocelots, spider monkeys and white-tailed deer.

In all about 90 animal species are in danger of extinction, including marine turtles, armadillos and over 15 types of hummingbird.

With so much of the land cultivated, few original plants still exist. Small stands of balsam trees survive along the western Pacific coast (dubbed the Costa del Bálsamo) and mangroves line many estuaries. Parque Nacionales Montecristo and El Imposible offer the widest variety of indigenous plants, and Parque Nacional Los Volcanes offers good vegetation. Plants in these areas include mountain pines, oaks, figs, magueys, ferns and orchids.

Environmental Issues

Deforestation is a major cause for concern, coupled with relatively high population density, which disrupts the regeneration of ecosystems. Today a mere 14% of the country is forested, with only a minuscule 2% to 5% of that primary forest. As a result, many native species have become endangered or extinct.

El Salvador has also copped the brunt of many natural disasters in recent years. Earthquakes in 2001 brought on landslides and destroyed buildings, killing 1159 people; the eruption of Santa Ana volcano in October 2005, coupled with Hurricane Stan's torrential rains, unleashed scores of landslides, with the largest loss of life occurring in poor areas built on steep slopes or riverbanks. In 2009 massive floods killed 200 people and devastated large tracts of land and housing within 50km of the capital.

Another particularly volatile year for seismic activity was 2012, while 2015 saw the San Miguel volcano spew gas above the second-largest city in the land.

Río Lempa, a crucial watershed for the country, suffers from pollution due to decades of pesticide use and the destabilizing effects of global warming. Community leaders have labeled damage to the protected biosphere around Bahía de Jiquilisco an environmental emergency and a government response is being closely monitored by climate-change watchdogs.

One recent high-profile environmental case in the country concerned an Australian- and Canadian-owned gold-mining operator, Pacific Rim, which attempted to sue El Salvador for US$250 million for refusing to allow it to dig for gold in the country. In 2016 an international tribunal ruled against the mining company and ordered it to pay the Salvadoran government US$8 million in legal costs. The ruling bolstered the cause of community activism across the globe.

SURVIVAL GUIDE

Directory A–Z

ACCESSIBLE TRAVEL

There are many people with disabilities in El Salvador – most victims of war-related violence – but there are still limited services or amenities to make their lives easier. There are few well-maintained ramps and handrails, and few services for the visually and hearing impaired. However, all travelers, including those with disabilities, will find Salvadorans extremely friendly and eager to help.

ACCOMMODATIONS

El Salvador has an excellent range of small hotels and backpacker hostels, particularly in San Salvador and western El Salvador.

Camping and *eco-albergues* (ecohostels; basic shared cabins, some with modest kitchen facilities) are found around popular outdoor destinations. Bring your own camping equipment.

Prices go up during the first week of August (summer holidays) and Semana Santa (Easter week), when it's also best to book ahead.

CHILDREN

El Salvador is a very Christian, family-centered society, so children are always welcomed. Some tips:

- Suchitoto, Ruta de las Flores and Alegría are generally relaxed, family-friendly places to visit.
- La Costa del Bálsamo has fabulous beaches, but the ocean is dangerous for weak swimmers.
- Camping is potentially excellent, but some experience is needed as facilities are not great.
- Buses are often packed full and traveling on public transport with children is challenging in El Salvador.

CLIMATE

The *invierno* (wet season) is from May to October, and the *verano* (dry season) is from November to April. During the rainy season, it usually only rains at night.

In San Salvador the maximum temperature varies from 27°C (80°F) in November to 30°C (86°F) in March and April; the minimum temperatures range from 16°C (61°F) in January and

SLEEPING PRICE RANGES

The following price ranges refer to a double room with bathroom. Unless otherwise stated, breakfast is not included in the price.

$ less than US$25

$$ US$25–80

$$$ more than US$80

February to 20°C (68°F) in March. The coastal lowlands are the hottest region.

CUSTOMS REGULATIONS

People entering El Salvador are permitted to bring in the following:

- 200 cigarettes or 25 cigars and cigarillos or 250g of tobacco
- Up to 12L of alcoholic beverages
- Up to six units of perfume
- Other articles up to a value of US$500

All visitors leaving and entering El Salvador go through customs. Be prepared for bag checks at both airports and land borders.

EMBASSIES & CONSULATES

Australian Consulate (☎2298-9447; consuladohonorarioelsalvador@gmail.com; 12a Calle Poniente 2028, Colonia Flor Blanca)

Canadian Embassy (☎2279-4655; www.canadainternational.gc.ca/el_salvador-salvador; 63a Av Sur, Centro Financiero Gigante, Local 6; ⏱8:30am-noon Mon-Fri)

Dutch Consulate (☎2296-1490; sjo@minbuza.nl; Alameda Araujo, Edificio Unicomer, 5a fl)

French Embassy (☎2521-9000; www.sv.ambafrance.org; 1a Calle Poniente 3718; ⏱9am-noon Mon-Fri)

German Embassy (☎2247-0000; www.san-salvador.diplo.de; 7a Calle Poniente 3972, Colonia Escalón; ⏱8am-11:30am Mon-Thu, to 11am Fri)

Guatemalan Embassy (☎2271-2225; embelsalvador@minex.gob.gt; 15a Av Norte 135, btwn Calle Arce & 1a Calle Poniente, Colonia Escalón; ⏱8am-4pm Mon-Fri)

Honduran Embassy (☎2264-7841; www.embajadahonduraselsalvador.com; 89a Av Norte 561, btwn 7a & 9a Calles Poniente, Colonia Escalón; ⏱9am-noon & 2-5pm Mon-Fri)

Irish Consulate (☎2263-8236; rmurray@agrisal.com; Pasaje Francisco Campos 160, Colonia Escalón)

Mexican Embassy (☎2248-9900; https://embamex.sre.gob.mx/elsalvador; cnr Calle Circunvalación & Pasaje 12, Colonia San Benito; ⏱8am-5pm Mon-Fri)

Nicaraguan Embassy (☎2263-8770; 7a Calle Poniente, Colonia Escalón; ⏱9am-4:30pm Mon-Fri)

UK Consulate (☎2511-5757; britishembassy.elsalvador@fco.gov.uk; Torre Futura, 14th fl, Colonia Escalón; ⏱7:30am-4:30pm Mon-Thu, to 11:30am Fri)

US Embassy (☎2501-2999; https://sv.usembassy.gov; Blvd Santa Elena, Antiguo Cuscatlán; ⏱7:30-11:30am Mon-Fri)

FOOD

A typical Salvadoran breakfast includes eggs, beans or *casamiento* (rice and beans mixed together), fried plantains, cheese, tortillas and coffee or juice. *Panaderías* (bakeries) usually offer morning cakes and coffee. *Almuerzo* (lunch) is the largest meal of the day.

More often than not, an evening meal is El Salvador means *pupusas*. Also popular are *panes*, a baguette sliced open and stuffed with chicken, salsa and pickled vegetables.

HEALTH

El Salvador has a burdened public health system, and an excellent private system with well-trained professionals. Vigilance is required in mosquito-prone areas near the coast and during the rainy season when dengue fever outbreaks can occur.

You can easily get access to a top doctor in San Salvador, but you will have to pay significant fees up-front.

Health insurance is highly recommended and necessary for the better hospitals.

Recommended Vaccinations

- Hepatitis A
- Hepatitis B
- Malaria
- Rabies
- Typhoid
- Yellow Fever

Tap Water

Tap water is generally very good in El Salvador; however, in poorer areas it is best to always boil before drinking.

INTERNET ACCESS

Wi-fi is available at many restaurants and cafes and nearly all hostels and hotels in urban areas. Many rural areas also have wi-fi, though a few remote places are off the grid. Some towns now have free wi-fi in public spaces, although the connection is not very reliable.

Internet cafes are becoming less common, but can still be found in most urban centers. Expect to pay between US$0.50 and $1 per hour.

LANGUAGE

Spanish is the national language. In a few indigenous villages just a handful of people still speak the Nahuat language of the Pipil, but there is increasing interest in preserving it. Many Salvadorans pick up some English working in the USA, Australia and elsewhere, which means you are more likely to meet English speakers here than in neighboring countries.

Courses

Suchitoto has an excellent Spanish schools, and locals there are used to conversing with traveling language students. Playa El Tunco is also a pretty good place to find a qualified language tutor.

LEGAL MATTERS

Law enforcement is strict and effective, from beat cops to border officials. Police are entitled to stop buses and search people and bags. If arrested, cooperate and call your embassy, although if you have committed a crime there's little your embassy can do. Even minor offenses require jail time.

LGBTIQ+ TRAVELERS

Gay people receive little tolerance. Numerous recent attacks on members of the LGBTIQ+ community have gone unpunished. Some hotels refuse to rent a room with one bed to two men; women will encounter less scrutiny. In San Salvador, the area around Blvd de los Héroes has cultural centers and clubs that are gay friendly. Gay organization **Entre Amigos** (☎2206-8400; https://entreamigoslgbti-sv.org; 17a Calle Poniente 142, Barrio San Miguelito; ⏲10am-5pm Mon-Fri) is the most established in the country.

MAPS

➡ Corsatur and the Ministry of Tourism offer glossy maps of El Salvador and the capital, available at some hotels and tour offices.

➡ Simple maps of hiking trails are sometimes available at visitors centers.

MONEY

In January 2001, El Salvador adopted the US dollar as its official currency, replacing the colón. Bring some US dollars with you, preferably in US$20 bills and smaller. The border crossings have money changers.

Credit cards are widely accepted, though many establishments add a surcharge. Visa and MasterCard are more common than American Express.

A VAT of 13% applies to all goods and services; it is usually factored into prices.

ATMs

ATMs are found in most cities and towns. Banco Agrícola, Scotiabank and Banco Cuscatlán have the largest networks of ATMs. Visa and MasterCard cards generally work well, but try more than one machine should your initial attempt fail. Look for safer locking cabins when withdrawing money, and avoid taking out cash at night.

Bargaining

Bargaining is less common here than it is in other Central American countries. A little back-and-forth is common with taxi drivers and market shopkeepers, but hard bargaining can seem a bit rude.

Tipping

Restaurants Tip 10%

Taxis It is not customary to tip taxi drivers, though rounding up the amount is appreciated

OPENING HOURS

Some offices and stores close at lunchtime, between noon and 2pm, but this practice is fading.

Businesses & stores 9am–6pm weekdays

Government offices 8am–4pm weekdays

Banks 8am–4pm or 5pm weekdays; most open Saturday morning as well

Restaurants Dinner is early; 4pm is *pupusa* hour

PUBLIC HOLIDAYS

New Year's Day January 1

Semana Santa Easter

Labor Day May 1

Mother's Day May 10

Father's Day June 17

Feast of San Salvador August 6

Independence Day September 15

All Souls' Day November 2

Christmas Day December 25

SAFE TRAVEL

Attacks on tourists in El Salvador are rare and crime shouldn't deter travelers from visiting.

➡ Gang violence is concentrated in neighborhoods with little appeal to travelers. Police control most tourist areas, so don't be overly nervous.

EATING PRICE RANGES

The following price ranges refer to a standard meal.

$ less than US$5

$$ US$5–15

$$$ more than US$15

- Avoid traveling at night. After dark it's best to take a taxi, particularly in San Salvador, San Miguel, Sonsonate, La Unión and La Libertad.
- Take commonsense precautions: carry as little as possible on day trips and avoid toting expensive items.
- Weapons are widespread, so never resist a robbery.
- Make copies of important documents; carry a copy with you and email a copy to yourself.

TELEPHONE

- The country code when calling El Salvador from abroad is 503.
- Phone numbers usually have eight digits; there are no internal area codes.
- Some internet cafes offer web-based calling.

Cell Phones

Claro, Tivo, Digicel and Movistar all provide decent service and affordable, ubiquitous prepaid SIM cards that work in Australian and European cell phones. You will need a passport to sign up initially.

US travelers should be aware that CDMA-only phones cannot use GSM SIM cards.

TOURIST INFORMATION

- El Salvador has decent tourist offices in the more popular areas, including Suchitoto, Ruta de las Flores, La Libertad and Perquín; however, hotel owners are often the best resources.
- In the capital you'll find the office of Corporación Salvadoreña de Turismo (p308), which offers brochures and flyers.

VISAS

- A visa is not required for stays of up to 90 days for citizens of the USA, Canada, Australia, New Zealand, Switzerland or the European Union, among other countries.
- Citizens of the USA, Canada, Australia, Bulgaria, Croatia and Romania among other countries must buy a US$10 tourist card on arrival, valid for 90 days.
- Citizens of the European Union (except Bulgaria, Croatia and Romania), New Zealand and most South and Central American countries do not require a tourist card.

Central America-4 Agreement

The Central America-4 agreement allows for travel between the borders of Guatemala, Honduras, El Salvador and Nicaragua for up to 90 days, with one passport stamp and one US$10 tourist card (unless you are a from a country that is exempt from needing a tourist card).

A full visa – if you a from a country which requires one – costs US$30.

VOLUNTEERING

In San Salvador's Blvd de los Héroes area, Centro de Intercambio y Solidaridad (CIS; www.cis-elsalvador.org) is a center for peace and social justice that provides opportunities for volunteers to teach English to low-income Salvadoran adults and learn Spanish. There's a 10-week minimum commitment and teachers get half-price Spanish classes in return. It can also provide information about NGOs working on various issues, including community development, gang intervention, the environment and more. CIS cannot arrange an actual volunteer position, but can point you in the right direction.

In Bahía de Jiquilisco, the Eastern Pacific Hawksbill Initiative (ICAPO; www.hawksbill.org) is a non-profit organization dedicated to hawksbill turtle conservation. Volunteers help monitor, measure and tag turtles. Placements cost US$280 per week, including meals and accommodations.

WEIGHTS & MEASURES

The metric system is used.

WORK

There are no publicized working opportunities in El Salvador for travelers, though teaching English or surfing is sometimes done on an ad hoc basis. Those looking to stay longer term are invariably involved in volunteer community projects.

ℹ Getting There & Away

AIR

Flights to and from the USA sell out quickly around Christmas and Easter, so book well in advance to avoid excessive costs.

La Costa del Bálsamo is as close to the airport as San Salvador, so it is easy to avoid the capital if you so desire.

Airports & Airlines

The Monseñor Óscar Arnulfo Romero International Airport (p308) is 44km southeast of San Salvador. A major Latin American hub, it is also a gateway to North American cities.

The following airlines are among those providing services to El Salvador.

American (☎24hr 2298-0777; www.aa.com; cnr 89a Av Norte & Calle del Mirador, World Trade Center I; ⏲9am-7pm Mon-Fri, to 1pm Sat)

Avianca (☎2267-8222; www.avianca.com; Paseo General Escalón, Galerías Escalón; ⏲9am-7pm Mon-Fri, to 5pm Sat)

Copa (☎2209-2672; www.copaair.com; cnr 89a Av Norte & Calle del Mirador, World Trade Center I; ⏲8am-6pm Mon-Fri, to noon Sat)

Delta (☎2275-9292; www.delta.com; cnr 89a Av Norte & Calle del Mirador, World Trade Center I; ⏰8am-6pm Mon-Fri)

United (☎2207-2040; www.united.com; Av de la Revolución, Sheraton Presidente Hotel; ⏰8am-6pm Mon-Fri, to noon Sat)

BORDER CROSSINGS

Unless you arrive by plane, you will already have the CA-4 visa when you arrive at an El Salvadoran border.

Guatemala

➡ The San Cristóbal–El Progreso border is open 24 hours, but you should cross during daylight hours. From Santa Ana, take bus 236 to San Cristóbal (US$0.50, one hour, every 20 minutes). Buses on the other side of the border go to El Progreso. The last bus back from San Cristóbal is at 6pm.

➡ The Las Chinamas–Valle Nuevo border is open 24 hours, but it's best to cross in daylight. Buses leave Ahuachapán from Parque Menéndez every 15 minutes (US$0.50, 5am to 7:30pm) for the Guatemalan border. After crossing the border it's 300m to the bus stop for service to Guatemala City via Cuilapa. The Tica Bus passes every half-hour and is safer than 2nd-class service. The last bus from the border to Ahuachapán is at 5:45pm.

➡ The La Hachadura–Ciudad Pedro de Alvarado border is open 24 hours, but it's best to cross in daylight. Bus 259 from Sonsonate (US$0.85, 1¾ hours) drops you right at the border; Salvadoran and Guatemalan immigration posts are at the far side of the complex. In Guatemala, the bus stop is 1km away; bicycle taxis cost US$0.50. Buses for Guatemala City leave every half-hour via Chiquimulilla and Escuintla. The last bus from La Hachadura to Sonsonate is at 6pm.

➡ From Metapán, microbuses run every half-hour (40 minutes) to the Anguiatú–Chiquimula border (open 24 hours, but more reliably from 6am to 7pm). On the Guatemalan side, buses run frequently to Chiquimula (one hour, last bus at 5:30pm) and onward to Guatemala City (three hours, last bus from Chiquimula at 3:30pm). This is the quickest route to Nueva Ocotopeque or Copán Ruínas, Honduras. In El Salvador, the last bus from the border to Metapán is at 6:30pm.

Honduras

➡ The bus from La Palma drops you about 100m from the El Salvador–Honduras border (open 24 hours) at El Poy, where you pay a US$3 administrative fee to enter Honduras. From El Poy, you can take a bus or *colectivo* (shared taxi) to Nueva Ocotepeque, Honduras. From there buses leave hourly for San Pedro Sula. For Copán Ruinas, transfer at La Entrada.

➡ The last bus to El Poy from La Palma (bus 119, US$0.50, 30 minutes) leaves at 7pm. The last bus south from El Poy to San Salvador leaves around 4pm.

➡ From San Miguel's main bus terminal, bus 330 (US$2, one hour) via Santa Rosa de Lima drops you 50m from El Amatillo on the Salvadoran border. From here a bridge crosses into Honduras; you pay US$3 to enter. Honduran buses then go to Choluteca (1½ hours) and on to Tegucigalpa (3½ hours). The last bus from El Amatillo to San Miguel goes at 6:30pm. From La Unión bus terminal, take bus 342 (US$1, one hour) to Santa Rosa de Lima and take the 330 bus from there.

Nicaragua

➡ From El Amatillo in Honduras, microbuses run from 5:30am to 5pm across the southern tip of Honduras to the Nicaraguan border town of Guasaule (US$6 depending on number of passengers, two hours). Walk 200m for the connections that reach León and Managua.

CAR & MOTORCYCLE

If you drive into El Salvador, you must show a driver's license (an international driving permit is accepted) and proof that you own the vehicle. You must also fill out extensive forms. Car insurance is available and advisable but not required. Vehicles may remain in El Salvador for 30 days. If you wish to stay longer, it's best to leave the country and drive back in rather than attempt to deal with the Transport Ministry.

SEA

El Salvador shares the Golfo de Fonseca with Honduras and Nicaragua. Boats occasionally ferry passengers between La Unión (El Salvador), Coyolito, Amapala or San Lorenzo (Honduras), and Potosí (Nicaragua). Going by sea does not save time since there are no scheduled passenger boats and land crossings are relatively close.

La Tortuga Verde (p337) offers boat crossings from La Unión to Potosí (Nicaragua).

ℹ Getting Around

El Salvador has excellent bus networks and most travelers happily bounce between long-distance coaches and souped-up old American school buses. There are no trains, and few travelers bother renting a car.

AIR

Flying within El Salvador is neither cost effective nor easily accessible. Some well-heeled execs fly private planes between San Miguel and San Salvador, and Puerta Barillas in Bahía de Jiquilisco has a helicopter pad, but most folk here stay grounded.

BICYCLE

Cycling is popular in El Salvador, both as a recreational activity and means of transport.

In San Salvador, a good point of contact is cycling enthusiasts **Ciclistas Urbanos** (☎7432-0241; www.facebook.com/asociacionciclistasurbanos). They can provide information about the **Cicleada Urbana Nocturna**, a weekly Thursday-night group-cycling event in the capital.

Mountain-biking is possible near Perquín in Morazán – ask at Perkin Lenca (p340) or Serafin Tours (p340).

BOAT

You'll need to use a boat to get around Bahía de Jiquilisco in eastern El Salvador and for any trips in the Golfo de Fonseca, near La Unión. Otherwise water transportation is rare.

BUS

- Hypercolored American school buses run frequently to points throughout the country and are very cheap (US$0.25 to US$5). Some weekend fares increase by up to 25%.
- Routes to some eastern destinations have different categories: *ordinario, especial* and *super especial*. The last two options cost more, but they are faster and more comfortable.
- Most intercity bus services begin between 4am and 5am and end between 6pm and 7pm.

CAR & MOTORCYCLE

Most roads in El Salvador are paved, but traffic is not easy to negotiate and roads are not particularly well signed.

Police set up checkpoints, especially on roads to border crossings. Carjacking is a problem, as is getting parts stolen off your parked car. Don't drive alone in areas of ill repute and always park in safe places. Car insurance is a good idea, but not required.

Rental cars are available in San Salvador and San Miguel and can be delivered elsewhere. The following are in San Salvador:

Alamo Uno Rent a Car (☎2367-8000; www.alamoelsalvador.com; Blvd del Hipódromo 426; ⏲5:30am-7:30pm)

Avis (☎2500-2800, airport 2339-9268; www.avis.com.sv; 43a Av Sur 127, Colonia Flor Blanca; ⏲8am-6pm Mon-Fri, to noon Sat)

Budget (☎2259-5400, airport 2259-5402; www.budget.com; 85a Av Norte 648, Colonia Escalón; ⏲8am-5pm Mon-Fri, to noon Sat)

Quick Rent a Car (☎2229-6959; www.quickrentacar.com.sv)

HITCHHIKING

Buses or collective pickups go just about anywhere you could want to go, so hitching isn't usually necessary. Both men and women usually hop in the back of pickup trucks. Hitchhiking is never entirely safe, and we don't recommend it. Travelers who hitch should understand that they are taking a small but potentially serious risk.

Honduras

POP 9.1 MILLION

Includes ➡

Best Places to Eat

- Roatán Oasis (p408)
- Cafe at La Casa de Cafe (p381)
- Mango Café (p413)
- Galeano Cafe (p363)

Best Places to Stay

- D&D Brewery (p373)
- La Villa de Soledad (p400)
- La Madrugada (p376)
- La Casa de Café (p381)

Why Go?

White beaches fringed by the world's second-largest barrier reef, jungle-covered mountains cut by raftable white-water rivers and home to an astounding number of bird species, exquisite Maya ruins, colonial, cobblestone villages, fresh seafood grilled on the beach...Yes, all this is found in Honduras, a country often hurried through or avoided entirely due to its dangerous image.

After a decade in which the country spiraled into a whirlwind of terrible violence, Honduras has very definitely begun – with a few hiccups – the journey back from the abyss. While the challenges ahead are still significant and travel here still means bumpy roads with no seatbelts, things haven't looked this positive for years. It's important to take care in the cities and the country is certainly not for the fainthearted, but other than that, Honduras is back open for business and just waiting to be discovered.

When to Go

Tegucigalpa

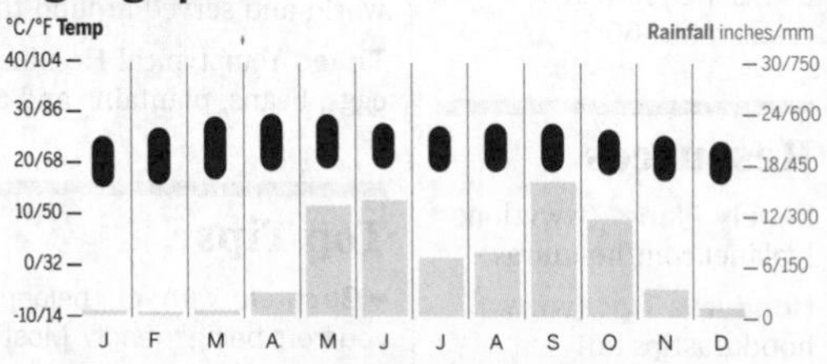

Oct–Feb Rainy season on the north coast and islands, but dry in the interior.

Mar–Apr Hot and dry everywhere, with temperatures soaring inland.

Jun–Sep Peak season for viewing whale sharks in Utila.

FAST FACTS

Currency Lempira (L)

Visas Most travelers do not require visas to enter Honduras, and simply receive 90-day tourist cards on arrival.

Money Big towns and cities have plentiful ATMs.

Capital Tegucigalpa

Emergency ☎911

Language Spanish (and English in the Bay Islands)

Exchange Rates

Australia	A$1	L17.33
Canada	C$1	L18.55
Euro zone	€1	L27.77
Japan	¥100	L21.92
New Zealand	NZ$1	L16.64
UK	UK£1	L32.39
USA	US$	L24.42

Daily Costs

➡ Double room in a budget hotel: L400; in a midrange hotel: L800

➡ Simple meal: L80–120; dinner in a top-end restaurant: L600

Resources

Lonely Planet (www.lonelyplanet.com/honduras)

Honduras Tips (www.hondurastips.hn)

Honduras Travel (www.hondurastravel.com)

Bay Islands Voice (www.bayislandsvoice.com)

Entering the Country

It's possible to enter Honduras from all three of its neighbors. Border crossings include Corinto and El Florido (Guatemala), El Amatillo and El Poy (El Salvador), and Guasaule, Leimus and Las Manos (Nicaragua). It's also possible to reach Honduras by boat from Belize. You can often choose between luxury international bus or much less expensive but time-consuming local buses.

HONDURAS IN TWO WEEKS

Entering Honduras at the El Florido border, you'll hit a key attraction immediately: the stunning ruins of **Copán**. Budget at least a couple of days in the area, taking in the temples and surrounding sights before making a short hop west to the atmospheric highland town of **Gracias** with its hot spring and Lencan villages. Then it's a long day on the road to the coastal city of **La Ceiba**.

Set sail from here for either **Roatán** or **Utila** and indulge in some serious beach and reef time, snorkeling, diving and living the dream. Back on the mainland, sign up for a rafting trip down the exquisite **Río Cangrejal**, then it's south to **Lago de Yojoa** for an artisanal brew or two, hiking and boat trips. Finish off with a night in either colonial, tranquil **Comayagua** or the bustling capital of **Tegucigalpa**.

Essential Food & Drink

Baleadas Fresh flour tortilla filled with beans, cheese and more.

Salva Vida The country's official beer is light, crisp and often feels like a lifesaver.

Sopa de caracol Conch soup cooked Garifuna-style with coconut milk and spices.

Pinchos Grilled kebabs of beef or chicken.

Honduran coffee Hailed as some of the best in the world and served around the country.

Tipico Your typical Honduran meal features meat or eggs, beans, plantains and a slice of soft sour cheese.

Top Tips

➡ Be careful with your belongings, but don't let that care stop you from being friendly. Most Hondurans are kind, helpful and love talking to foreigners.

➡ Spanish makes life easier, but a huge percentage of the country speaks English so it's not entirely necessary either.

➡ Eat *baleadas* at places that make fresh tortillas on the spot – it makes all the difference.

TEGUCIGALPA

POP 1.19 MILLION

Ringed by forested hills in a highland valley, sprawling Tegucigalpa enjoys a relatively fresh, mild climate and a spectacular setting. It's a bustling and dynamic place, but one that many travelers minimize their time in or skip over entirely. This is a shame, as while Tegus (as all locals call it) is no beauty – streets are choked with traffic and its resultant pollution, and crime stats are high – it's a fascinating place, with some good museums, restaurants and the air of a place on the up. Keep your ear to the ground and you'll discover a dynamic young urban scene led by emerging artists, musicians, DJs and designers.

Sights

Downtown Tegus is the neglected heart of the nation, a cluster of once elegant but now faded streets where *ropa americana* (used clothing) outlets have replaced department stores. For a feel of the city, stroll the pedestrianized Calle Peatonal, visit a couple of the city's decent museums and grab a snack at the market.

★Museo para la Identidad Nacional MUSEUM
(MIN; Map p368; www.min.hn; Av Miguel Paz Barahona; L100; ⏲9am-5pm Tue-Sat, 11am-5pm Sun) If you hit only one sight in Tegus, head here. The museum is housed in the gorgeously renovated 19th-century former Palace of Ministries. It's a superb overview of the nation's history and identity through modern exhibits. Displays are in Spanish, but there are free tours in English by excellent guides four times a day (also ask for French or German tours).

Parque Naciones Unidas El Picacho NATIONAL PARK
(L25; ⏲8:30am-5pm) This small hilltop park 6km from downtown has busy walking trails, but the main reason to visit is to stand at the feet of the approximately 20m high **El Cristo del Picacho** (entry L10) that you may have seen lit up, hovering high above the city at night. There are sweeping views over the city from up here.

Centro de la Cultura Garinagu de Honduras CULTURAL CENTER
(Map p368; ☎2222-0511; Plaza Morazán; ⏲8am-5pm Mon-Sat) FREE It's well worth dropping by this cultural center, and situated right on the Parque Morazán, which is handicrafts, clothing and tools on display, as well as a library and information about the Garifuna people. Employees will also be able to tell you where you can see Garifuna dance troupes performing their incredibly athletic and sensual dance moves.

Plaza Morazán PLAZA
(Map p368; Av Miguel de Cervantes) At the center of the city is the Plaza Morazán, often called Parque Central by locals – this is Tegucigalpa's hub. A statue of former president Francisco Morazán on horseback sits at its center. An elaborate baroque **cathedral** dating from the 18th century overlooks the square: step inside and you'll find an intricate altar of gold and silver.

Basílica de Suyapa CHURCH
(Anillo Periferico 2) The most important church in Tegucigalpa – and therefore in Honduras – is this neo-Gothic basílica. La Virgen de Suyapa is the patron saint of Honduras; in 1982 a papal decree made her the patron saint of all Central America. Construction of the basilica, which is famous for its large stained-glass windows, began in 1954.

Iglesia Los Dolores CHURCH
(Map p368; Av Máximo Jeréz) This striking church, which dominates an otherwise unremarkable plaza, has some attractive religious art. Its facade contains figures representing the Passion of Christ – his unseamed cloak, the rooster that crowed three times – all crowned by the more indigenous symbol of the sun.

Sleeping

Downtown Tegucigalpa is generally quite safe during the day, although you should be on your guard at all times and always take taxis at night. Comayagüela is a much dodgier part of town: wandering around here, day or night, is not recommended. Colonia Palmira is the safest but pricier neighborhood, but still be on guard – again, taxis are the best option at any time.

★Palmira Hostel HOSTEL $
(Map p364; ☎9972-9666; www.palmirahostel.com; Av Republica del Peru; hammock/dm/r L120/216/695; 📶) This excellent, clean and highly secure hostel is run by Hernán, an English-speaking local who goes beyond the call of duty to help visitors get as much out of Tegus as possible. There's a kitchen, communal area and free afternoon tours of

Honduras Highlights

1. **Utila** (p410) Blissing out in dive-bum heaven, with beautiful marine life and wild nightlife.
2. **Copán** (p384) Gazing at extraordinary Maya stone carvings and epic ancient structures near a charming, cobblestone village.
3. **Cayos Cochinos** (p401) Being dazzled by the bluest waters and finest beaches.
4. **Río Cangrejal** (p399) Getting in touch with nature as white water powers through a majestic jungle.
5. **Lago de Yojoa** (p373) Drinking craft beer, paddling on

lakes, hiking to mountains and exploring coffee plantations.

6 **Roatán** (p404) Living it up in this upscale destination, including dining and enjoying world-class diving.

7 **The Moskitia** (p414) Exploring Central America's last untamed wilderness on an adventurous route to Nicaragua.

8 **Trujillo** (p403) Soaking up everyday life in this small town with a quirky history, lovely beaches and charming locals.

downtown Tegus on offer. It's a great place to meet other travelers; staff can give excellent local advice. Note that there's no sign so book in advance so they know you're coming!

★ La Ronda HOSTEL $
(Map p368; ☎9949-9108; www.larondahostel.com; cnr Calle La Ronda & Av Máximo Jeréz; dm/r L240/L600; ❄📶) Downtown's coolest accommodations are run by Juan Pablo, a one-time Honduran reggaetón star, and the place has easygoing, artsy vibe. Simple but spotless dorms and a couple of private rooms (sleeping up to four) are arranged around a sociable terrace, while downstairs there's a hip and popular bar (that shuts at 10pm) and a good restaurant.

Hotel Boston HOTEL $
(Map p368; ☎9719-0538; nuevohotelboston@yahoo.es; Av Máximo Jérez 321; s/d/tw/q from L375/500/675/800; @📶) This downtown hotel is in a once-grand, now-faded building with ancient tiled floors, high ceilings and two guest lounges that will make you feel you've been transported to 1937. Choose between street-facing rooms that are incredibly spacious but get traffic noise, or cheaper but smaller and darker options to the rear. Some mattresses are *very* soft. Free coffee and motherly service.

★ Hotel MacArthur HOTEL $$
(Map p368; ☎2237-9839; www.hotelmacarthur.com; Av Lempira 454; incl breakfast s/d with fan L966/1269, with air-con L1222/1551; ❄📶🏊) This hotel has a strong Honduran flavor, with an inviting butter-yellow lobby full of old photographs of the city. Rooms are spotless, large, decorated in comforting warm hues and full of natural light. New beds and exposed brick wall details add a modern edge. Try to nab a terrace room overlooking the street. The pool is one of the capital's best.

Apart Hotel Plaza Colonial HOTEL $$
(Map p368; ☎2222-7727; 504 Calle Hipolito Matute; r L716-818, apt L1073) The colonial-style, mustard-yellow building here with a tiled interior courtyard laden with ferns is one of the prettiest in downtown Tegus. The rooms, however, are small, dark and perfectly functional but not that special. The apartments with kitchenettes and living rooms are good for longer stays (negotiate the price) – apartments 8 and 9 have terraces and are a bit brighter.

FERIA DE SUYAPA

The Virgin of Suyapa, the patron saint of Honduras, is **celebrated** (⏲early Feb) in her eponymous Tegucigalpa suburb of Suyapa from around February 2 to 11. February 3 is the saint's day. Expect huge crowds and multiple religious ceremonies in and around the Basílica de Suyapa.

Hotel Otoch Balam B&B B&B $$
(Map p364; ☎2238-2747; Calle Republica de Brasil, Palmira; s/d/tr L1350/1550/1800; P❄📶) Perhaps the homiest choice in Tegucigalpa, the big, modern, plush rooms are in a spacious house behind a very secure gate in a quiet but central part of Palmira. The breakfast area with self-serve cereal and snacks feels a little industrial, but the warm service and cool Copan-inspired murals on the walls will bring you back to feeling at home again.

Casa Bella HOTEL $$
(Map p364; ☎2262-6000; www.casabellahn.com; Calle Principal s/n, Colonia Palmira; r incl breakfast from L1400; P⊖❄📶) This very comfortable, excellent-value hotel has a fantastic location in the heart of Colonia Palmira, within easy walking distance of many restaurants and bars. Its mustard-colored, sponge-painted public areas give way to surprisingly tasteful modern rooms, featuring attractive, darkwood furniture and local handicrafts. Suites are enormous, and all rooms have fridges, safes and cable TV. Staff speak excellent English.

Eating

There's a dearth of choice downtown, where fast-food joints rule. Colonia Palmira has an impressive selection of upscale, international offerings for a well-worth-it splurge.

★ Mercado Los Dolores HONDURAN $
(Map p368; Av Paulino Valladares; snacks L20-70; ⏲11am-3pm) At the side of Iglesia Los Dolores, these stands inside a covered market offer a variety of tempting cheapie lunchtime street-food dishes, including *pupusas* (cornmeal stuffed with cheese or refried beans), lots of soups and *tapado* (Caribbean seafood stew). For *baleadas* (flour tortillas filled with various ingredients) head straight to **Beleadas Dolores**, which has been a Tegus favorite since 1980.

Mini Cafeteria HONDURAN $
(Map p368; mains L34-75; ⏲5-11:30am) A Tegucigalpa breakfast institution since 1973, everyone will tell you they love this place but

no one can remember the name. The specialty is *burritas*, tortillas stuffed with a variety of fillings (scrambled egg, cheese, deep fried pork skin, beans and more) and piled on top of each other. Size 'small' is huge and the medium can easily feed two people.

Baleadas Express FAST FOOD $

(Map p364; cnr Avs La Paz & Juan Lindo, Texaco; baleadas L20-55; ⏲7am-11pm) As hard as it is to imagine a gas station fast-food outlet being one of the best eating options in the city, within 24 hours in Tegus you will almost certainly meet a local who will wax lyrical about the fantastic *baleadas* (thick flour tortillas containing fried beans, cheese, meat, eggs and other fillings) served up here. It's a chain so you'll find other outlets around the country.

Pupusería El Patio HONDURAN $

(Map p364; Blvr Morazán, Colonia Palmira; pupusas L30-55; ⏲11am-1:30am) On weekends this beer hall of a place can be a riot, with tables overflowing with bottles and families belting out the karaoke. *Pupusas,* tacos and other typical Honduran fare are the main items on the menu – groups should go for the Plato de Variedad, which introduces all of the Honduran staples and serves three to four people.

★Galeano Cafe CAFE $$

(Map p364; ☎2263-8096; Plaza San Martín, Colonia Palmira; mains L155-175; ⏲7am-9pm Mon-Sat, 9am-7pm Sun; 📶) This very hip cafe rocks both an industrial and upcycling look, with brushed concrete fittings and salvaged wood furniture. It's an absolute lifeline though, as it does great coffee, enormous smoothies served up in glass jars, crepes and panini – try the delicious *pero aguacatero* – as well as breakfasts and pastries. Upstairs is a terrace and Tegus' hippest clothing store as well.

Café Paradiso CAFE $$

(Map p368; ☎2222-3066; www.paradisoblog.wordpress.com; Av Miguel Paz Barahona 1351; mains L100-250; ⏲10am-10pm Mon-Sat; 📶🖉) An intimate, bohemian hangout, this is the place to find Tegus' creative types. The decor (with an excess of curios and lots of paintings) and layout (multiple rooms set off a central covered patio) are unusual. Food-wise, you can snack on a pastry for just L35 or feast on a filet mignon for L250. Art-house movies are shown at 6:30pm Tuesday; poetry readings at 6:30pm Thursday.

★Pisco PERUVIAN $$$

(Map p364; 5 Calle; mains L165-330) You can't beat this classy and delicious Peruvian restaurant in Palmira for a special night out – or for a welcome change from Honduran basics. The menu here is divided by ingredients such as lemon, octopus or shallot. Each dish has a photo on the menu that will whet your appetite and the real plates do not disappoint. Paeo Republica de Argentina changes to 5 Calle, so the address of Pisco is 5 Calle.

Claudio's Italian Bistro ITALIAN $$$

(Map p364; ☎2235-7738; Av Ramón Ernesto Cruz; mains L230-425; ⏲11am-10pm; 📶) Claudio's attracts a well-heeled crowd and makes for a good break from local cuisine. There's superb pizza and a variety of pasta dishes, seafood and grilled meats. The downstairs wine shop and dining room give way to an attractive alfresco terrace upstairs, and even though the decor can be tacky (those candlesticks!), it's otherwise a sophisticated and friendly option.

Café Honoré INTERNATIONAL, DELI $$$

(Map p364; ☎2239-7566; 5a Calle/Paseo República de Argentina 1941, Colonia Palmira; sandwiches L140-398, mains L270-635; ⏲8:30am-11pm Mon-Sat; 📶) This is a mecca for the Honduran elite, and if you're yearning for gourmet treats this is the place. The deli section has Parma ham and French cheese, while the large street terrace, complete with mod-Asian decor, makes a great place to blow the budget on a pricey gourmet sandwich, burger, salad or pasta dish. Honoré also delivers to wherever you're staying.

Drinking & Nightlife

Colonia Palmira is your best bet for a night out, with several bars along Bulevar Morazán and Paseo de Republica de Argentina. However, as security issues have dogged the city in recent years, Tegus' nightlife generally starts directly after work and tends to wind down by midnight.

★Honduras Brewing Company BREWERY

(Map p364; ⏲5-10pm Tue-Fri, 2-10pm Sat) The Honduras brewery crafts five beers that would thrive in any beer-loving city. Each is named after a passage of the Honduran national anthem. The India Virgin Pale Ale is light yet buttery and flavorful, and the Ondas Bravias Irish Red Ale is nice and malty without being too heavy.

Tegucigalpa

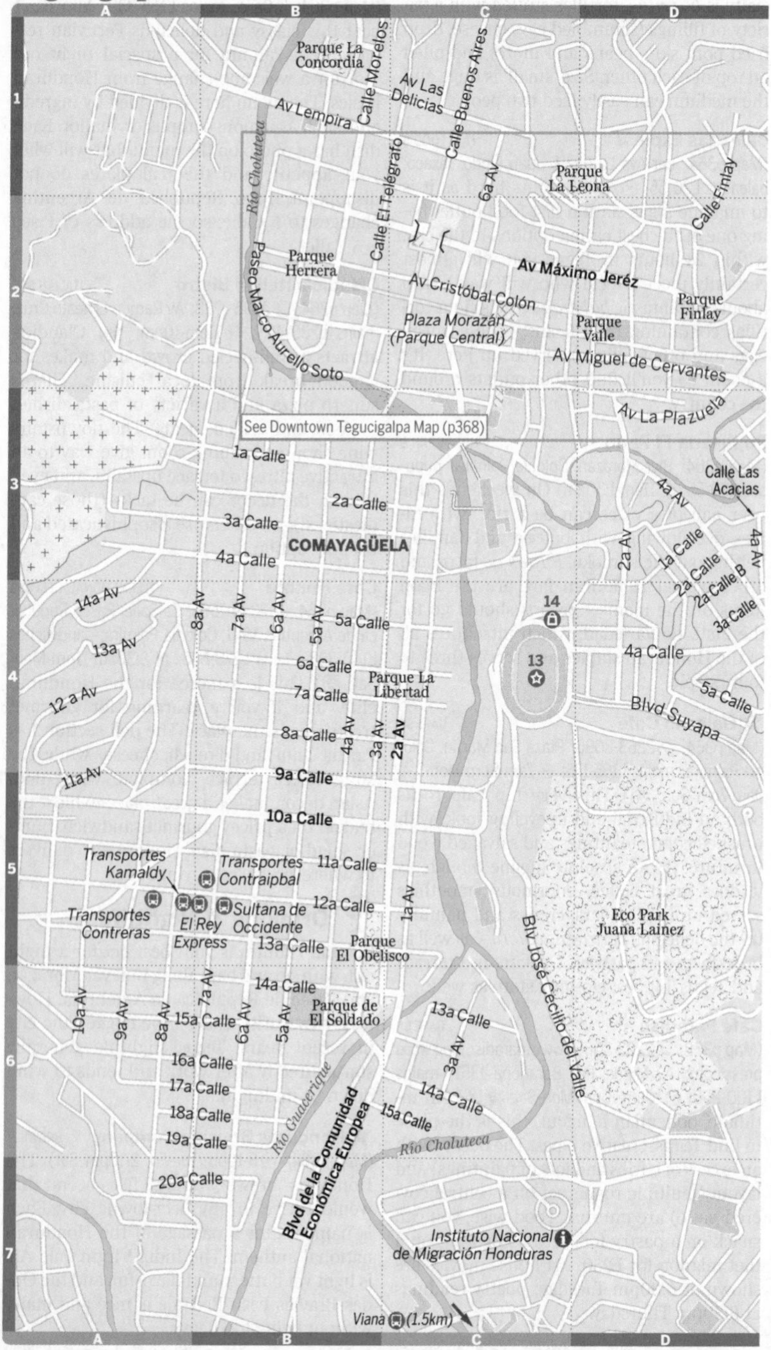

A B C D

Parque La Concordia
Calle Morelos
Calle Buenos Aires
Av Las Delicias
Av Lempira
Río Choluteca
Calle El Telégrafo
6a Av
Parque La Leona
Calle Finlay
Paseo Marco Aurelio Soto
Parque Herrera
Av Máximo Jeréz
Av Cristóbal Colón
Parque Finlay
Plaza Morazán (Parque Central)
Parque Valle
Av Miguel de Cervantes
Av La Plazuela
See Downtown Tegucigalpa Map (p368)
1a Calle
Calle Las Acacias
2a Calle
4a Av
3a Calle
COMAYAGÜELA
2a Av
1a Calle
4a Av
4a Calle
2a Calle
2a Calle B
14a Av
8a Av
7a Av
6a Av
5a Av
5a Calle
14
3a Calle
13a Av
13
4a Calle
6a Calle
12 a Av
7a Calle
Parque La Libertad
5a Calle
Blvd Suyapa
8a Calle
4a Av
3a Av
2a Av
11a Av
9a Calle
10a Calle
Transportes Kamaldy
Transportes Contraipbal
11a Calle
Transportes Contreras
El Rey Express
Sultana de Occidente
12a Calle
1a Av
13a Calle
Parque El Obelisco
Eco Park Juana Lainez
Blv José Cecilio del Valle
10a Av
9a Av
8a Av
7a Av
15a Calle
6a Av
5a Av
14a Calle
Parque de El Soldado
13a Calle
3a Av
16a Calle
17a Calle
14a Calle
18a Calle
15a Calle
19a Calle
Río Guacerique
Río Choluteca
20a Calle
Blvd de la Comunidad Económica Europea
Instituto Nacional de Migración Honduras
Viana (1.5km)

A B C D

HONDURAS

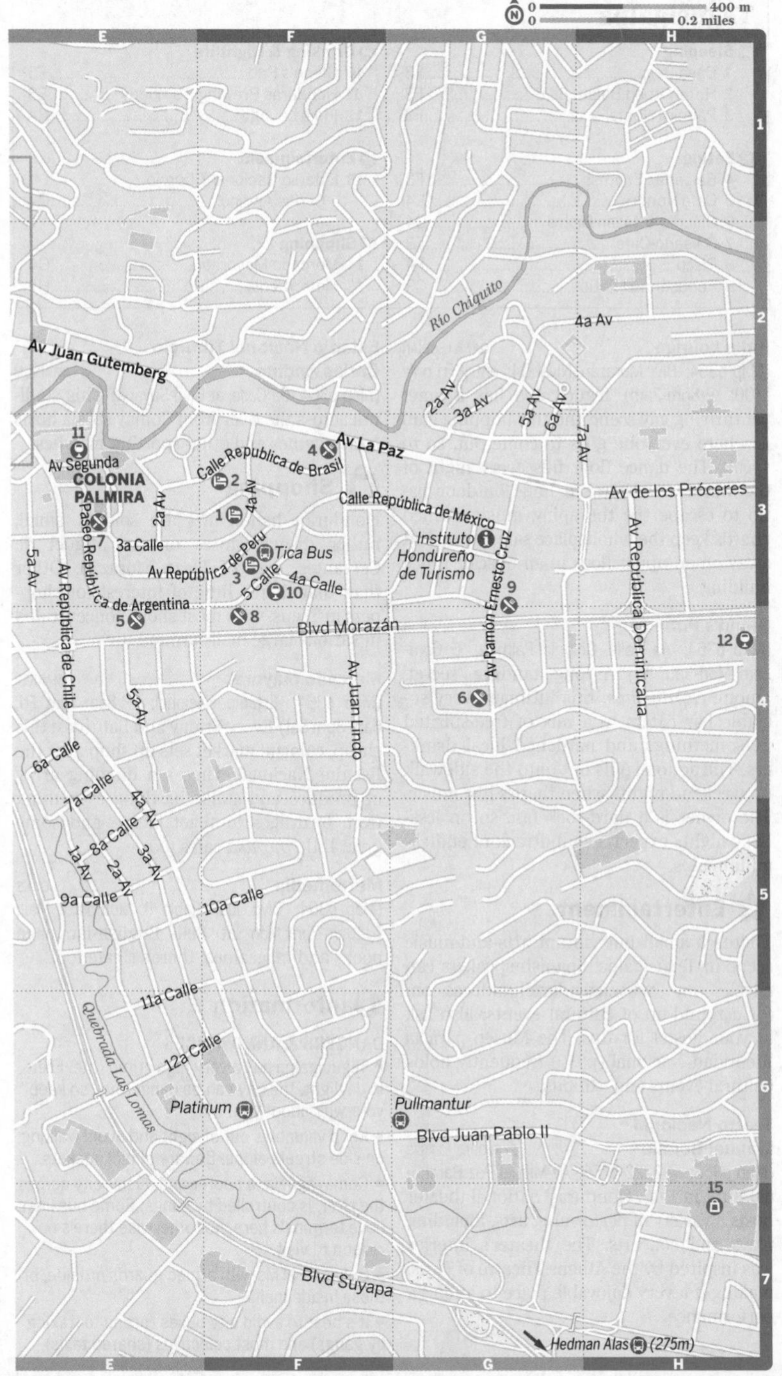

0 400 m
0 0.2 miles
E
F
G
H
1
2
3
4
5
6
7
Río Chiquito
4a Av
Av Juan Gutemberg
2a Av
3a Av
5a Av
6a Av
7a Av
Av La Paz
11
Av Segunda
COLONIA
PALMIRA
Calle Republica de Brasil
4
2
1
4a Av
2a Av
Paseo República de Argentina
7
3a Calle
Av de los Próceres
Calle República de México
Instituto
Hondureño
de Turismo
Tica Bus
Av República de Peru
3
5 Calle
4a Calle
10
9
Av Ramón Ernesto Cruz
Av República Dominicana
5a Av
Av República de Chile
5
8
Blvd Morazán
12
6
Av Juan Lindo
5a Av
6a Calle
7a Calle
4a Av
8a Calle
1a Av
2a Av
3a Av
9a Calle
10a Calle
11a Calle
12a Calle
Quebrada Las Lomas
Platinum
Pullmantur
Blvd Juan Pablo II
15
Blvd Suyapa
Hedman Alas (275m)

Indie Lounge GAY & LESBIAN
(Map p364; Blvr Morazán, Nivel C4; entry Fri only L100; 8pm-2am) Tegucigalpa has a quiet yet thriving gay scene and this hopping club is where everyone goes to come out, so to speak. The dance floor fills every night of the week, and there's a huge outdoor patio to escape the thumping music. Armed guards keep the whole place safe. It's tucked away on an upper floor in an upscale office building.

Glenn's Pub PUB
(Map p364; 4a Calle, Colonia Palmira; 6pm-2am Mon-Sat;) A long-standing 'secret' among *capitalinos,* this intimate, very sociable bar caters to a mix of free-spirited 20-somethings and hardened local drinkers. The action spills out onto the sidewalk on weekend nights when there's live music. The owner is a hard-rock fan, so on less-busy nights expect a soundtrack of endless guitar solos.

Entertainment

There's a small but vibrant arts-and-music scene in Tegucigalpa. Spanish speakers can check out www.agendartehonduras.com for a round-up of cultural events; also ask at your hostel for tips. The Museo para la Identidad Nacional (p359) frequently holds cultural events and exhibits.

Teatro Nacional Manuel Bonilla PERFORMING ARTS
(Map p368; 2222-4366; Av Miguel Paz Barahona) Built in 1912, Honduras' national theater hosts a variety of performing arts, including plays and concerts. The theater's interior was inspired by the Athens Theatre of Paris, making it a very enjoyable place to attend a performance.

Estadio Nacional Tiburcio Carías Andino STADIUM
(Map p364; 9a Calle, at Blvd Suyapa) This stadium across the river from Comayagüela hosts soccer games and other sporting matches.

Shopping

Honduran handicrafts are sold at small, rather dismal stores on Av Miguel de Cervantes, east of Plaza Morazán. Other than that there's little of interest for shoppers in Tegus, with most shops concentrated in various large malls around town.

Mercado Mayoreo MARKET
(Map p364; Estadio Nacional; 8am-5pm Fri, 6am-3pm Sat) Every Friday and Saturday, this cheap, colorful market sets up shop near the Estadio Nacional. There's a dazzling array of produce and stalls, hawking everything from birdcages to vegetables – and some great little *pupusa* cafes too.

Metromedia BOOKS
(Map p364; Blvd Juan Pablo II, Multiplaza Mall; 10am-7pm Mon-Sat) Sells English-language books and magazines; there's a cafe too.

Information

DANGERS & ANNOYANCES

- Tegucigalpa has a very high crime rate. Even in daylight, the city can be dangerous, so keep your wits about you.
- Keep valuables out of sight and avoid walking on side streets alone. Beware of pickpockets.
- Comayagüela, a poorer and dirtier city across the river, is controlled by gangs. Some bus lines have terminals here, but otherwise there's no reason to visit.
- Only use ATMs with armed guards outside, or those inside malls.
- It's best to avoid city buses (prone to 'taxing' by gangs) and most *colectivos* (shared taxis),

apart from busy ones that go short distances in the city center or are specific to the airport.

➡ At night, unless you're walking a short distance on busy streets, take a taxi.

EMERGENCY & MEDICAL SERVICES

Ambulance	☎195
Police	☎199

Honduras Medical Center (☎2280-1500; www.hmc.com.hn; Av Juan Lindo; ⏰24hr) One of the best private hospitals in the country, with English-speaking doctors and state-of-the-art equipment.

MONEY

ATMs are dotted about the city: at the airport, on the northeast corner of Parque Central, in the Hedman Alas bus terminal and in the shopping malls.

Banco Atlántida (Parque Central; ⏰9am-4pm Mon-Fri, 9am-2pm Sat) Has a 24-hour ATM.

Citibank (Blvr Morazán, Centro Comercial Plaza Criolla; ⏰8am-4pm Mon-Fri, 9am-1pm Sat) One of several banks here.

HSBC (Blvr Morazán; ⏰8am-5pm Mon-Fri, 9am-1:30pm Sat) Has an ATM.

Exchanging money can be difficult in Tegucigalpa as most money changers will only accept crisp, unmarked 50 and 100 US dollar bills.

POST

Downtown Post Office (Map p368; cnr Av Miguel Paz Barahona & Calle El Telégrafo; ⏰8am-5pm Mon-Fri, 8am-1pm Sat)

TOURIST INFORMATION

Instituto Nacional de Migración Honduras (Map p364; ☎2235-7381; www.inm.gob.hn; Colonia El Prado, Blvd Kuwait; ⏰7am-5pm Mon-Fri) Handles immigration matters.

Instituto Hondureño de Turismo (IHT; Map p364; ☎2222-2124; www.letsgohonduras.com; cnr Av Ramón Ernesto Cruz & Calle República de México, 1st fl; ⏰9am-5pm Mon-Fri) A helpful tourist office, with good general information and lots of glossy leaflets. But don't expect too much practical information.

ℹ Getting There & Away

AIR

The **airport** (TGU; ☎2234-0106; www.interairports.hn; CA-5) is 6.5km south of central Tegucigalpa. A taxi from the center of town costs around L120, though going into the city from the airport costs around L220 to L250.

BUS

Frustratingly, there's no central bus station in Tegus, meaning that bus lines are scattered all over the city. Unfortunately many bus depots are in Comayagüela, the least safe area of town – though a spate of recent gang attacks has led to several companies relocating to safer areas in eastern Tegus, and now few 1st-class bus companies run their services from there.

In general you'll need to know which bus you want to take rather than simply turning up at a bus terminal and waiting, so calling ahead is always a smart move.

International & Long-Distance Buses

There are four recommended international bus companies:

Hedman Alas Connects Tegus with San Salvador and Guatemala City. Two departures offices: one in Comayagüela and a far nicer terminal located behind Multiplaza Mall in the southeast of the city.

Platinum (Map p364; ☎2225-5415; www.platinumcentroamerica.com; Juan Manuel Gálvez 1521) Goes to El Salvador, Guatemala and Nicaragua.

Pullmantur (Map p364; ☎2232-0216; www.pullmantur.com; Blvr Juan Pablo II, Hotel Marriott) Connects Tegus with San Salvador and Guatemala City.

Tica Bus (Map p364; ☎2291-0022; www.ticabus.com; Palmira Hostel) Goes to El Salvador, Guatemala, Nicaragua and the Mexican border, and has connections to Costa Rica and Panama.

Long-distance buses for domestic services include the following:

Colinas de Oro (☎9523-1637; Centro Comercial la Alhambra, Colonia Kennedy)

El Rey Express (Map p364; ☎2237-8561)

Hedman Alas (☎2516-2273; www.hedmanalas.com; Blvd Centro America, Colonia Tres Caminos)

Sultana de Occidente (Map p364; ☎2238-8507; www.sultanaexpress.webs.com)

Transportes Contreras (Map p364; ☎2238-8984; 12a Calle)

Transportes Cotraipbal (Map p364; ☎2237-1666; 7a Avenida)

Transportes Kamaldy (Map p364; ☎2220-0117; 12a Calle)

Viana (☎2225-6583; www.vianatransportes.com; Blvr Fuerzas Armadas)

ℹ Getting Around

TO/FROM THE AIRPORT

Aeropuerto Internacional Toncontín Located 6.5km south of the center of Tegucigalpa. Local buses run from the airport to Comayagüela, but it's far safer to catch a taxi due to security concerns on city buses; or grab a **colectivo van** (Map p368; L12), which connects the airport

Downtown Tegucigalpa

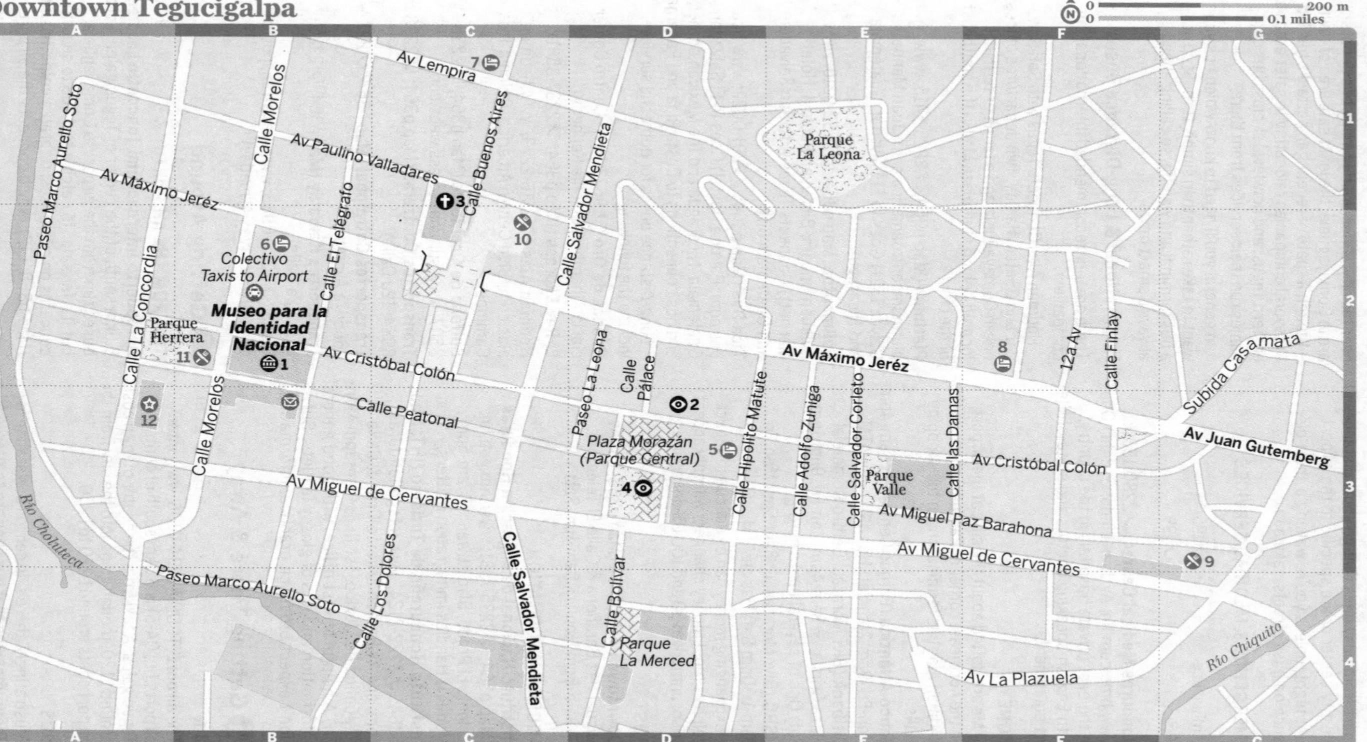

Downtown Tegucigalpa

Top Sights
1 Museo para la Identidad Nacional......B2

Sights
2 Centro de la Cultura Garinagu de Honduras D3
3 Iglesia Los Dolores......C1
4 Plaza Morazán......D3

Sleeping
5 Apart Hotel Plaza Colonial......D3
6 Hotel Boston......B2
7 Hotel MacArthur......C1
8 La Ronda......F2

Eating
9 Café Paradiso......G3
10 Mercado Los Dolores......C2
11 Mini Cafeteria......B2

Entertainment
12 Teatro Nacional Manuel Bonilla......A3

with a stop on Calle Morelos, five blocks west of Parque Central.

BUS

City buses vary from cheap, former US school buses (L10) to faster minibuses known as *rapiditos* (L15), both of which can be dirty and dangerous. Theft is common and gangs sometimes target buses. Stick to taxis.

CAR & MOTORCYCLE

Care hire rates start at L720 per day. **National/Alamo** (2239-1537, airport 2233-4962; www.alamo.com; Blvr San Juan Bosco; 8am-6pm Mon-Sat) and the other major international companies can be found at the airport – as well as local agency **Econo Rent-a-Car** (2235-2105, airport 2291-0108; www.econorentacarhn.com; Calle El Trapiche; 7am-7pm Mon-Fri, 7am-5pm Sat & Sun).

TAXI

Taxis cruise all over town; a ride costs L80 to L150 depending on the distance. It's always best to call a trusted taxi company rather than stopping one on the street. **Teguber** (www.ferby.stolz-engineering.com:8888/teguber) is Tegus's answer to Uber and works via an app that's worth downloading if you're going to spend any amount of time in the city. For a reliable traditional taxi company, try **Radio Taxi Mall** (2232-4067 2232-2352; www.facebook.com/rtmall1998), which responds to phone and Facebook Messenger inquiries. If you find a driver you like, take their number so you can hire them throughout your stay.

WESTERN HONDURAS

Honduras' heartland of high, cool mountains, wildlife-rich forests and undulating coffee fields isn't on most foreign travelers' itineraries and that's their loss. Those that do come here can expect a genuine welcome and to brush elbows with the colorful Lenca culture, have plenty of chances to warm up in natural hot springs and drink some excellent coffee. The top attraction is easily the impressive Maya ruins of Copán, closely followed by the colonial charm of towns such as Copán Ruinas and Gracias.

Hikers will love the spectacular trails inside the Montaña de Celaque cloud forest, while there's dazzling birdlife and wonderful scenery around idyllic Lago de Yojoa, which has established itself as the only major stop in this region on the Central American backpacker trail.

San Pedro Sula is the economic powerhouse of the nation and a travel hub; though it has little to offer visitors, so few hang around.

Comayagua

POP 152,050

Comayagua was the first capital of Honduras and an important religious and political center for over three centuries, until power shifted to Tegucigalpa in 1880. The town's rich past is evident in its fine old churches, an impressive cathedral and its colonial plazas. A very Catholic city, it's *the* place in Honduras to witness Easter celebrations. Once the new, nearby Palmerola International Airport opens to become Honduras's main point of entry, the town will become a great alternative place to overnight instead of grittier San Pedro Sula or Tegucigalpa.

Right next to Palmerola Airport is a huge air base used by the US military. It formed a base for US forces in the 1980s when the Contra war was raging in Nicaragua. Today about a thousand soldiers are stationed here, and you'll often see off-duty soldiers relaxing in town.

Sights

Sights are clustered around the beautiful Parque Central.

Cathedral CHURCH

(Parque Central; 7am-8pm) Comayagua's impressive cathedral is the largest colonial-era place of worship in Honduras. Built between

AROUND TEGUCIGALPA

The gorgeous area around Tegucigalpa features one of Honduras' most impressive national parks, Parque Nacional La Tigra, as well as several attractive mountain towns perfect for day trips. Among them is **Santa Lucía**, a charming old colonial mining town with a spectacular vista over the capital, 14km to the east. There's a striking 18th-century *iglesia* (church) and historic streets to explore.

Parque Nacional La Tigra (☎ Jutiapa 2265-1891, Rosario 2265-3167; L240; ⊙ 8am-4pm, last entrance 2pm) encompasses a cloud forest and eight hiking trails. There's an abundance of (elusive) wildlife – from pumas to peccaries – as well as towering trees, lichens and large ferns, bromeliads and orchids. It can be chilly up here: bring adequate clothing.

The camping fee for the national park is L120 per person; there are simple shelters at both park entrances where walkers can overnight (L200 per person).

For somewhere really special to stay, the two-room **Cabaña Mirador El Rosario** (☎ 2767-2141; r L650) is perfect, with stunning views and delicious home-cooked food. The German owners Jorge and Monika will pick you up if you call ahead.

1685 and 1715, it's adorned with intricate wooden carvings and gold-plated altars. The cathedral's most interesting feature is its ancient Moorish clock, dating from around AD 1100, which was originally located in the Alhambra in Granada, Spain.

Museo Regional de Arqueología MUSEUM
(6a Calle NO; L92; ⊙ 8am-4pm) This lovely museum is housed in a former presidential palace, a one-story, tiled-roof house with a beautiful, manicured garden at the center. Inside you'll find Comayagua's history from the prehistoric to today, the highlights being some ancient Lenca artifacts, including a stela, polychrome ceramics, jade jewelry and petroglyphs. Most descriptions are in Spanish only.

Parque Nacional Montaña de Comayagua NATIONAL PARK
(Panacoma; L70) Spanning more than 300 sq km of primary and secondary forest, Panacoma (which is managed by Ecosimco) has two main hiking trails leading through the cloud forest, from near the small village of Río Negro, 42km north of Comayagua, to waterfalls.

Sleeping & Eating

Hotel America Inc HOTEL $
(☎ 2772-0630; www.hotelamericainc.com; cnr 1a Av NO & 1a Calle NO; s/d from L600/1075; ❄ 📶 🏊) A very orange place (inside and out) in the busy, not-as-secure-feeling-as-a-few-blocks-north market area, this modern hotel is only a few minutes' walk to Parque Central. The cheaper singles are plain but great value; the more expensive rooms are big but a bit pricey for what you get. Ask for a room with a window as not all have them.

Hotel Antigua Comayagua HISTORIC HOTEL $$
(☎ 2772-0816; www.hotelantiguacomayagua.com; cnr 6a Calle NO & 2a Av NO; s/d incl breakfast L1400/1550; ❄ 📶 🏊) This is the best option in town: a super-secure, well-cared-for property with a wonderful pool and spacious, smart rooms, many of which have balconies. The hotel has its own nightclub as well, which can mean some noise on the weekend. It's just around the corner from Parque Central and has great hot-water showers but terrible wi-fi.

★ **Cafe Tío Juan** CAFE $
(Parque Central; drinks L35-65; ⊙ 7am-9pm; 📶) This hip and friendly second-story coffee joint overlooking the main plaza offers you great, hot or cold organic coffee from nearby Marcala, inspirational wall quotes and delicious slices of cake or banana bread. There are also a few tables downstairs on the street outside – perfect for people-watching over an espresso.

Ricardo's HONDURAN $$$
(Parque Central; mains L140-450; ⊙ 7:30am-10pm; 📶) Right on the Parque Central, this classy restaurant offers the best view in town from its tables on the plaza and its myriad atmospheric dining rooms bursting with curios and character. It's quite pricey, but the set lunch (L81) is excellent value, and the seafood, grilled meats and selection of yummy sauces are of a surprisingly high standard.

Drinking & Nightlife

La Gota de Limón BAR

(5a Calle NO; ⏲10:30am-7pm Sun-Wed, to 2am Thu-Sat) An upscale bar-lounge that operates as an (underused) cafe in the day. On weekend nights it morphs into one of the town's best bars, drawing a fashionable crowd, with DJs playing a mix of salsa, merengue and Latin hits. There's usually no cover charge.

Orientation

Heading north into town from the main San Pedro Sula–Tegucigalpa highway, you'll pass through the market area after 750m, then hit the Parque Central in another 250m.

Streets are defined according to the compass: NO for *noroeste* (northwest), NE for *noreste* (northeast), SO for *suroeste* (southwest) and SE for *sureste* (southeast).

Information

There are several banks with ATMs around Parque Central. **Banco Credomatic** (Parque Central & 1a Av NO; ⏲8am-noon & 1-4pm Mon-Fri) is the most reliable, and if that doesn't work try **Banco Atlántida** (1a Av NO; ⏲8am-5pm Mon-Fri, 9am-1:30pm Sat).

Ecosimco (Ecosistema Montaña de Comayagua; ☎2772-4681; ecosimco@yahoo.com.mx; Edifico Pasaje Andara Flores, Calle del Comercio; ⏲9am-noon & 1-5pm Mon-Fri) Offers information about the Parque Nacional Montaña de Comayagua; you can pay the entry fee here too. It's 500m north of town – look for the big green gates.

Getting There & Away

Comayagua is connected to Tegucigalpa (L50, two hours, every 20 minutes) by very regular buses, including those run by **Transportes Catrachos** (☎2772-0260; cnr 1a Calle SO & 1a Av NO), **Transportes Contreras** (☎2772-4618; Av 3a SO) and El Rey Express; pick up El Rey buses on the highway on the south side of town. All buses running between San Pedro Sula and Tegucigalpa pass by the entrance to Comayagua on the main highway.

Transportes Catrachos and El Rey Express also operate buses to San Pedro Sula (L92, three hours, every 30 minutes). Buses to Marcala (L60, 1½ hours) leave just outside the **Transportes Rivera bus terminal** (cnr 2a Calle SO & 1a Ave NO), departing hourly from 6am until 1pm, and again at 3pm.

La Esperanza

POP 12,960

Up in the highlands, pretty, bustling La Esperanza is the highest city in Honduras (1770m) as well as one of the friendliest. Indigenous influence is strong here – you will see many women wearing the distinctive, colorful Lenca headdress. The city is known for its markets that seem to be almost everywhere, and are at their biggest and boldest on Saturday and Sunday. It's a great place to shop for vibrant Lenca woven goods from scarves to ponchos, any day of the week. Note that it can get decidedly chilly here!

Sights

La Esperanza is more a town to wander through aimlessly than chase down specific sights.

La Gruta CHAPEL

(⏲9am-4pm) This curious sight is perhaps La Esperanza's most notable building: a small cave now converted into a chapel, complete with a cute facade built into the cliffside. It's easy to spot from all over the town – just follow the pedestrianized street from Parque Central and walk up the very cool hand-carved stairs. There are nice views over town from the top.

Casa de la Cultura MUSEUM

(Av Morazán; ⏲noon-4pm Mon-Fri) FREE This small cultural center has a couple of rooms devoted to Lenca culture, including some excellent ceramics and weavings.

Sleeping

Hotel Las Margaritas HOTEL $

(s/d/tr L550/885/1100; 📶) This spotless, well-cared for business-style hotel has massive rooms with hot water and strong wi-fi. Free coffee and filtered water add a nice touch. Lovely Grethel, who runs the place, speaks excellent English and can answer most questions about La Esperanza.

★**Posada Papa Chepe** HOTEL $$

(☎2783-0443; posadapapachepe@gmail.com; Parque Central; s/d/tr/q L850/1000/1200/1450; 📶) An unexpected charmer on La Esperanza's Parque Central, Papa Chepe's features a wild and wonderful courtyard heaving with plants and flowers surrounded by a series of well-appointed rooms with high ceilings and good hot-water showers (a necessity in this climate). There's a small restaurant at the back, a coffee shop with decent espresso, and arts and crafts for sale.

Eating & Drinking

Restaurants tend to be fairly samey here, though do look out for local dishes containing *choros* (wild mushrooms).

La Hacienda Lenca HONDURAN **$$**

(Av España; mains L120-180; ⏲9am-10pm) A block east of Parque Central, this cavernous, upscale-feeling place is full of heavy wood furniture and has a few dining areas including a patio. The waitstaff are super friendly and the food is good, with typical Honduran fare, burgers, fajitas, big breakfasts and *choros* dishes when they're in season.

La Casa Vieja BURGERS **$$**

(Parque Central; burgers L165-275; ⏲11am-10pm Tue-Thu, to 11pm Fri & Sat, to 9pm Sun; 📶) Famous for its burgers – the king of which is La Big Daddy (made with 450g of beef) – La Casa Vieja also does chicken wings and breaded shrimp, veggie burgers, cocktails and cheesecake. It's a cool space, with a wood-beamed roof and friendly service.

MarDu Arte Cafe Y Vino CAFE

(coffee L25-45, wine L60-75) Settle into this cozy cafe, with bright colored walls, comfy couches and local art on the walls, to sip a hot cup of joe, or try one of the locally produced (quite sweet) fruit wines. There are also cold drinks and cocktails plus basic sandwiches, pizza and baked goods on offer.

Shopping

★**Artesanias Togopala** TEXTILES

(⏲8am-4pm Mon-Fri, to noon Sat) This little shop just east of Parque Central has a huge selection of gorgeous, handwoven Lenca ponchos, shawls, scarves and more. You'll likely find one of the artists weaving on a loom when you go in. Colors range from very bright local favorites to neutrals that are hard to find elsewhere.

Information

For cash, there's a **Banco Atlántida** (Av Los Proceres) one block north of Parque Central.

Getting There & Away

Busy Terminal Carolina is the main bus station and is 800m east of the center, past the bridge. Hop on any Tegucigalpa-bound bus for Comayagua (L90, 2½ hours).

Marcala

POP 29,860

Marcala is a tiny, dusty (or muddy depending on the season) highland town with a strong indigenous heritage. It lies at the southern end of Honduras' 'Ruta Lenca' – a collection of Lenca villages and a stronghold of Lencan culture. The town itself is tranquil but it's definitely not a looker. It sits in prime coffee country, however; the smell of coffee roasting permeates the streets. Several hikes in the surrounding area take in picturesque waterfalls and caves, but few foreigners make it here aside from those buying coffee for export.

Cooperativa RAOS ECOTOUR

(☎9987-8920, 2764-3779; www.cooperativaraos.org; ⏲8am-4pm Mon-Fri, to noon Sat) FREE Cooperativa RAOS, on the road toward La Esperanza, is Honduras' first organic farming cooperative. It now represents over 200 small producers, providing work in the region. Tours are usually for coffee buyers, but if you call in advance the *cooperativa* will happily pick you up at its office in Marcala and give you a makeshift tour of the coffee factory. No English is spoken.

Sleeping & Eating

La Casona HOTEL **$**

(☎2764-5311 9696-7269; s/d L400/500; 📶) The best option in this small town, La Casona

BUSES FROM LA ESPERANZA

DESTINATION	COST (L)	DURATION (HR)	FREQUENCY
Gracias	90	1½	5 daily
Marcala	45	¾	every 30min
San Pedro Sula	120	4	hourly
Santa Rosa de Copán	140	2½	daily
Tegucigalpa	120	4	hourly

is a basic, concrete hotel that's friendly and clean but a bit dark. It's a block or so from the church, but there's a second location out near the Cooperativa RAOS coffee factory. Ask for a room at the front of the building, as these have terraces. There's also hot water.

Casa Gloria HONDURAN $$
(Parque Central; mains L60-210; ⏲8am-9pm; 📶) An attractive colonial-style place that offers buffet dining – *pollo asada* (grilled chicken), *bistek* (steak) and some veggie options – during the day and service with a smile. It was undergoing a massive renovation when we passed so should be the nicest-looking place in town once it's finished.

Information

For cash head to **Banco Atlántida** (⏲8am-4:30pm Mon-Fri, to noon Sat), at the entrance to town, which has an ATM.

Getting There & Away

Buses leave from various points, but all pass the **Texaco gas station** at the east end of the main road in and out of town. If you arrive here, ask for directions to walk into town (about five minutes) or grab a taxi (L20).

Foreign travelers are not permitted entry to El Salvador at the nearby border crossing of Sabanetas (locals are allowed to pass through, though). Save yourself a frustrating journey and use alternative crossings.

Lago de Yojoa

Largely undeveloped and ringed by mountains and dense tropical forest, Lago de Yojoa is an exceptionally scenic oasis. Thanks to the indefatigable efforts of a local microbrewery owner to promote the region, the lake is now *the* most popular spot for travelers breaking the journey between the Bay Islands and Nicaragua.

Lago de Yojoa's birdlife is world-class: the latest species count is up to 485 – over half the total in Honduras – including the elusive quetzal. You can also hike to remote waterfalls and the summit of Santa Bárbara, visit coffee plantations, go zip-lining or kayak on the lake itself (swimming is possible but the lake is shallow and chock-full of vegetation).

Peña Blanca is the main transportation hub near the lake; it's a bustling but uninteresting commercial town. Los Naranjos, an otherwise unremarkable village some way down the road, is where most travelers base themselves at D&D Brewery.

Activities

Boat trips on the lake are an essential experience, involving an early start and paddling along the totally undeveloped western side of the lake. Here the magnificent birdlife includes toucans and fish eagles; you may well also see large iguanas and monkeys. Expect to pay L450 per person for a morning tour in a rowing boat or paddling yourself with a kayak with a guide.

A **three-waterfall hike** runs through the foothills of Parque Montaña Nacional de Santa Bárbara (p374) – a delightful day hike through coffee country and traditional settlements. The main attraction here is a stunning series of falls, dubbed La Escalada de los Gigantes (Giants' Stairs) by locals, from where there are sweeping views. D&D Adventures charges L675 for this hike, including transportation.

★**D&D Adventures** ADVENTURE
(☎9994-9719; www.ddadventures.com; D&D Brewery, Los Naranjos; day trips from L250) This excellent outfit has enthusiastic, English-speaking guides and is the best way to explore the more remote areas around Lago de Yojoa. Trips include the fantastic three-waterfall hike; birdwatching, kayaking, caving and coffee tours are also offered.

Sleeping & Eating

★**D&D Brewery** LODGE $
(☎2544-0052, 9994-9719; www.ddbrewery.com; Los Naranjos; campsites/dm per person L85/150, r with/without bathroom from L420/300; 🅿❄📶) 🍃 Having created Honduras' most pioneering

BUSES FROM MARCALA

DESTINATION	COST (L)	DURATION (HR)	FREQUENCY
Comayagua	70	2	8 daily
La Esperanza	45	¾	every 30min
San Pedro Sula	200	5	1 daily
Tegucigalpa	110	3½	hourly

PARQUE NACIONAL MONTAÑA DE SANTA BÁRBARA

Overlooking Lago de Yojoa, the **Parque Nacional Montaña de Santa Bárbara** FREE is home to the majestic Montaña de Santa Bárbara (aka El Maroncho, as many locals call it). At 2744m it's the second-highest peak in Honduras – and looks absolutely mammoth from afar. A protected area since 1987, the park is a 321-sq-km combination of tropical, pine and cloud forest. It is also composed entirely of limestone, which means there are lots of caves and tunnels, and no visible water at higher elevations, as it is absorbed by the porous rock.

Parque Nacional Montaña de Santa Bárbara does not have any tourist infrastructure – trails are unmarked although a few have been recently cut by D&D Brewery (p373), and there are no campgrounds or park services.

and ethically run hotel, brewery and coffee roastery, American Bobby Durrette is now busy attracting backpackers to Lago de Yojoa (with considerable success). The simple but spotless and comfortable rooms set amid the thick jungle are amazing value and there are tons of options from camping to a huge, more luxurious room with terrace for L1050.

El Cortijo del Lago HOTEL $
(9906-5333, 2608-5527; www.elcortijodellago.com; dm/d L250/625;) This hotel is one of the only places in the area on the lakeshore itself. The spacious dorm has aircon and the rooms share an atmospheric, screened-in communal area with lake views. The freestanding *cabaña* is the best room and well worth requesting when you book. Outside of Honduran holidays, you'll likely have the place to yourself.

Finca Paradise CABAÑAS $$$
(9502-8189, 9995-1875; r/cabin L840/2375) This beautiful coffee plantation is a magical place to stay. The simple rooms have hot water and are very clean, but the real attraction here is the two tree-house-style cabins that sleep six people each. The structures are fairly simple (and definitely not for the vertiginous), have wraparound balconies and are perfect for enjoying the sounds of the forest.

El Dorao Cafe CAFE $
(Peña Blanca; panini L40-60; 7am-7pm;) An unbelievable find in sleepy Peña Blanca, this smart and cool place has fused local coffee-growing expertise with the needs of the cosmopolitan city dweller. The result is a wonderful cafe serving up excellent coffee, cakes (try the passion-fruit cheesecake), waffles and a daily changing range of panini. It's on the left immediately after the turnoff toward Los Naranjos.

D&D Brewery INTERNATIONAL $$
(9994-9719, 2544-0052; www.ddbrewery.com; Los Naranjos; mains L100-280; 8am-8pm) Besides offering craft beers brewed right on the premises, this restaurant also offers excellent food – try the blueberry pancakes, burgers or sumptuous chicken enchiladas. The local coffee is also fabulously smooth and service doesn't get much friendlier anywhere in Honduras.

Getting There & Away

The small town of Peña Blanca acts as a transportation hub for the lake.

Hedman Alas (2516-2273; www.hedmanalas.com; 3a Calle NO & 8a Av NO; 5am-6pm) now provides direct Lago Yojoa services (stopping at the La Guama police station) to/from several destinations including La Ceiba (L500, six hours), San Pedro Sula (L200, two hours), Tegucigalpa (L200, three hours), Copan Ruinas (L790, five hours) and Antiqua, Guatemala (L1343, 12 hours). Meanwhile Tica Bus has exclusive services for guests to D&D Brewery (p373) bookable only on the D&D Brewery website, from the police station in La Guama to Leon (L960, eight hours) and Managua (L960, 10 hours), Nicaragua.

For cheaper local buses from San Pedro Sula, get an El Mochito–bound chicken bus from the main terminal to the village of Los Naranjos (L50, two hours, every 30 minutes). The bus stops within 300m of the D&D Brewery.

From Tegucigalpa, there's a direct daily bus to Los Naranjos and Peña Blanca from the Mercado Mama Chepa in Comayagüela, which leaves at 1pm daily (L135, four hours). Ask for the bus going to Las Vegas, Santa Barbara and tell the driver where you wish to get off. Alternatively get a San Pedro Sula–bound bus to La Guama (L97, three hours, more than 20 daily). From there, take another bus to Peña Blanca (L15, 15 minutes, every 15 minutes) from where you can either get a bus or *mototaxi* to Los Naranjos, 6km away.

Around Lago de Yojoa

If you like the great outdoors, the gorgeous region around Lago de Yojoa will keep you busy for days. Here the rolling, verdant landscape conceals rushing rivers, extraordinary waterfalls, spectacular caves, coffee plantations, important archaeological sites and extremely rich flora and fauna, all of which can be explored on your own or with the passionate, English-speaking guides of D&D Adventures (p373).

Sights

Pulhapanzak WATERFALL

(www.pulhahn.com; L80; ⏲6am-6pm) This magnificent 43m waterfall on the Río Lindo is 17km north of Lago de Yojoa (and also an easy day trip from San Pedro Sula). Surrounded by lush forest, it's a privately run beauty spot where guides will lead you along a fun, challenging path behind the waterfall (L300). There's good swimming and ziplining (L550) right over the falls.

Parque Nacional Cerro Azul Meambar NATIONAL PARK

(☎8881-2553; L168) East of Lago de Yojoa, this well-maintained national park boasts kilometers of trails leading to waterfalls, caves and untouched cloud forest. There's also a visitors center, lodge and restaurant here. The entrance is via a turnoff from La Guama on the main CA-5 highway. Frequent pickups head to Santa Elena; from there, walking to the park's Panacam Lodge takes about one hour.

Parque Eco-Arqueológico Los Naranjos NATIONAL PARK

(☎9654-0040; L140; ⏲8am-4pm) On the northwest side of the lake, this park was first occupied around 1300 BC, and is thought to be the largest Preclassic-era Lenca archaeological site. The main reason to visit, however, is the wildlife. The park has 6km of trails that wind through the forest over hanging bridges and on a lakeside boardwalk, providing fantastic opportunities for birdwatching.

The ruins themselves are not terribly interesting: they're made of clay, so have been only semi-excavated, to protect them from environmental damage. The little museum near the entrance has a few nice pieces of pottery and information panels.

Cuevas de Taulabé CAVE

(☎9545-0095; L96; ⏲8am-4pm) Around 20km south of the Lago de Yojoa is the entrance to the Cuevas de Taulabé, a network of underground caves with unusual stalactite and stalagmite formations. Admission includes a guide – a tip may get you to some of the less-visited areas. So far the caves have been explored to a depth of 12km, with no end in sight.

Sleeping

Panacam Lodge LODGE $$

(☎8881-2553, Tegucigalpa 9865-9082; www.panacam.com; Parque Nacional Cerro Azul Meámbar; campsites L200, d incl breakfast L1680; ❄📶) This high-quality lodge makes an excellent base for the Parque Nacional Cerro Azul Meámbar. Comfy rooms are in the lodge, but sturdy double-occupancy cabins with terraces and calming views over the forrest are expected to be completed in 2019. The terrace of the on-site international-style restaurant is lined with hummingbird feeders and you'll see several species – plus possibly a scavenging coati.

Getting There & Away

To reach the Pulhapanzak waterfall from San Pedro Sula, take an El Mochito chicken bus (L45, one hour) and get off at San Buenaventura, from where it's a well-marked 15-minute walk. The last bus back passes through San Buenaventura around 4pm. The El Mochito bus also passes through Los Naranjos, meaning it's easy to reach the falls from D&D Brewery.

To get to Parque Nacional Cerro Azul Meambar, there are buses from Peña Blanca to La Guama (L25, 20 minutes, every half-hour). In La Guama you then need to take a minibus bound for Santa Helena and pay the driver L250 for the trip up into the park.

San Pedro Sula

POP 639,000

The business and industrial capital of Honduras, San Pedro generates almost two-thirds of the country's GDP, with thousands employed in giant *maquila* (clothes-weaving) factories. It's wealthier and more sophisticated yet less interesting than Tegucigalpa. Despite its reputation for gang violence, tourists are rarely targeted and the town feels safer – whether it is or not – than the capital.

Indeed, the city is on an upswing, falling from the world's most violent city (outside of a war zone) in 2015 to number 26 in 2018. The city is doable for travelers for a day or two, but you should still be cautious, especially after dark.

Few linger, however: there are few sights, little cultural life, and the sultry climate can be oppressive. Since San Pedro's international airport is a main entry point and its bus station a crucial travel hub, you're very likely to pass through.

Sights & Activities

The heart of the city around the Parque Central is run-down but full of life.

Museo de Antropología e Historia de San Pedro Sula MUSEUM
(☎2557-1874; cnr 3a Av NO & 4a Calle NO; L75; ⊙9am-4pm Mon & Wed-Sat, to 3pm Sun) This airy two-story museum walks visitors through the history of the Valle de Sula from its pre-Columbian days to the modern era. The pottery collection is especially lovely and there are English information sheets.

Parque Nacional Cusuco NATIONAL PARK
(L220; ⊙8am-4:30pm) Just 45km from San Pedro Sula, but remarkably difficult to access, Parque Nacional Cusuco is a cloud forest nestled in the impressive Merendón mountain range. The park has abundant wildlife, including parrots, toucans and a large population of quetzals, best spotted from April to June.

Its highest peak is Cerro Jilinco (2242m). The visitors center (where guides can be hired) is the starting point for five different hiking trails. Two trails – **Quetzal** and **Las Minas** – pass waterfalls and swimming holes.

JungleXpedition HIKING
(☎9762-6620; www.junglexpedition.com; 19 Avenida, San Pedro Sula) The experts on Parque Nacional Cusuco, JungleXpedition's English-speaking owner Juan Paz builds and maintains trails inside the park, has contacts in all the communities and has generously supported efforts to improve the lives of locals living inside the park. Daily rates for hiking trips start at L2040 per person (minimum three participants) and include 4WD transport and all meals.

Coca-Cola HIKING
FREE Hike to the giant Coca-Cola sign on the mountain over San Pedro Sula for views over the city. It's safe even for solo walkers in the company of lots of locals trying to get fit. Round-trip, the walk takes around 1½ hours (it's about 6km all up). A taxi to the entry gate from town costs L50 to L80.

Sleeping

Aging budget hotels are mostly in the downtown area south of Parque Central, an area that's very dodgy after dark. Hostels and guesthouses tend to be in the more suburban areas of the city, and some way from downtown.

Dos Molinos B&B B&B $
(☎2550-5926; www.dosmolinos.hostel.com; cnr 13a Calle SO & 8a Av SO, Barrio Paz Barahona; dm L530, s/d/tr incl breakfast L530/750/880;) Here's a spotless, brightly painted yet aging, family-run B&B. Blanca and her family are exceptionally kind hosts and, though they speak little English, guests quickly feel right at home. All rooms, including the 'dorms' (actually just a twin and triple whose beds are sold individually), have fans and their own cold-water bathrooms.

La Hamaca HOSTEL $
(☎9868-3270, 2510-5174; www.lahamacahostel.com; 10 Calle SO, btwn 26 & 27 Av; dm with/without air-con L600/500, r with/without bathroom L1500/750; @) This excellent party hostel is a five-minute taxi ride from the bus station. It's run by a dynamic team of young Hondurans (all English speakers), who give superb up-to-date travel advice. Rooms and dorms are spacious, if a little aged, and there's a terrific lounge, games room, kitchen and garden. It's definitely a social place, but parties move elsewhere after 11pm.

★**La Madrugada** HOSTEL $$
(☎2569-6085; www.lamadrugadahostel.com; 8 Calle NO, btwn 8 & 9 Av NO; dm/r L240/600;) This hostel downtown takes up an entire block – it's the impressive conversion of a mansion that retains some original features, including beautifully tiled floors. Dorms are spacious, bright and enjoy generous bathrooms with hot water, while private rooms each sleep up to four. There's a pleasant bar and social area, a pool table and an expansive outside area.

La Posada B&B $$
(☎2566-3312; www.laposadahn.com; 21 Calle A, btwn 9 and 11 Avs, Colonia Universidad casa 172; s/d/q L1176/1320/1750;) This is a great bargain given the quality of the elegant house, the cleanliness, the beautiful rooms

and the very welcoming and helpful family owners. There's a guests' kitchen and garden and it's four blocks from a mall and restaurants in a leafy, wealthy area – the nicest area of the city.

Eating

San Pedro Sula is no culinary capital and you'll find mostly fast food and basic Honduran fare. Upscale places, where you'll find a few decent international options, are mainly located on Circunvalación. There's also a whole bunch of cheap and cheerful *comedores* at Mercado Guimilito.

Pastelitos Miriam BAKERY $
(11 Calle NE; pastelitos L18; 6:30am-noon) San Pedro Sula's breakfast favorite is this diner-style restaurant that pumps out deep-fried *pastelitos* – half-moon shaped pies filled with all sorts of yumminess. Choose from the Italiano with ham, cheese and pepperoni, to the more unusual Cubana, a salty-sweet mix of gooey hot cheese and guava jelly. Eat in or take a box to go.

★ **Angeli Gardens** HONDURAN $$
(2556-5891; Jardines del Recuerdo; mains L210-355; 8am-10pm Tue-Sun) So the food is just OK (the Honduran plates for two or more people are your best bet), but the setting here in a lush garden at the edge of a mountain makes it a romantic getaway. Beautiful jungle trails meander from the restaurant so you can hike in the mountains for up to two hours before or after your meal.

Enjoy your meal with beer brewed at the on-site Cerveceria Del Bosque. There's even a zip-line canopy tour in the works. A taxi here should cost L80 to L100, or you can call to arrange a pick-up at your hotel.

Sobre Mesa CAFE $$
(3276-3619; Hotel Holiday Inn Express; mains L90-250; 8am-9:30pm) The antidote to fried food, here you'll find soups, salads, sandwiches, hearty breakfasts and light meals all made with health-conscious, organic ingredients. Then, of course, you'll deserve one of their house-made decadent cakes, pastries or gelato.

Drinking & Nightlife

The *zona viva,* which hugs the inside of the Circunvalación between 7a Calle SO and 11a Calle SO, is home to the main concentration of bars and clubs.

Cerveceria Del Bosque BREWERY
(9861-8037; Jardines del Recuerdo; 325mL beer L65; 4-10pm Tue-Fri, noon-10pm Sat, 11am-5pm Sun) A cozy spot with gravel floors, picnic benches and plenty of plants, San Pedro Sula's hip brewery makes four decent beers from a very light pilsner to a dark porter. You can eat at Angeli Restaurant and hike forest trails from the garden setting.

Information

The city's malls also have banks with ATMs.

BAC/Bamer (5a Av NO, btwn 1a & 2a Calles NO; 9am-5pm Mon-Fri, to noon Sat)

Banco Atlántida (Parque Central; 8:30am-5pm Mon-Fri, 9am-1pm Sat)

Mesoamérica Travel (2558-6447; www.mesoamerica-travel.com; 32 Avenida) Professional agency that does interesting upscale tours, including national park trips throughout Honduras.

Post Office (cnr 9a Calle & 3a Av SO; 7:30am-5pm Mon-Fri, 8am-noon Sat)

Tourist Police (2550-0001; cnr 12a Av NO & Blvr Morazan; 24hr) No English is spoken here.

DANGERS & ANNOYANCES

- San Pedro Sula's notorious crime mostly involves gangs, and travelers rarely get caught up in big trouble. However, do be very cautious.
- Avoid being flashy with your belongings and dress with restraint (save the shorts for the beach).
- Downtown is dodgy after nightfall. Use taxis to get around – don't risk the local buses at any time of day.

Getting There & Away

AIR

San Pedro Sula's modern **Aeropuerto Internacional Ramón Villeda Morales** (SAP; 6689-3261) is served by daily direct flights to many major cities in Central America and several US cities. Domestically there are connections to Tegucigalpa, La Ceiba, Puerto Lempira and the Bay Islands (usually via La Ceiba). The airport is on SPS-Tela Hwy CA-13, about 14km southeast of the city center.

BUS

All buses depart from designated bays in the modern, well-organised **Terminal Gran Central Metropolitana** (2516-1616; Av Circunvalación), 6km south of the Parque Central. There's also a large mall and food court here. The terminal entrance has a handy directory; Hedman Alas (p374) buses have their own terminal at the rear. To head into town from here, use taxis from the official rank, not freelance drivers.

Getting Around

BUS

It's best not to use local buses as they are subject to frequent robberies and 'taxing' by gangs.

CAR & MOTORCYCLE

Car rental agencies in San Pedro Sula with airport offices include the folllowing:

Econo Rent-A-Car (☎2668-1884; www.econorentacarhn.com; Airport)

Hertz (☎2580-9191; www.hertz.com; Airport)

Thrifty (☎2668-2427; www.thrifty.com; Airport)

TAXI

Average fares around town are L50 to L120. From the bus station to the center is around L100; to the airport is about L350. Fares rise substantially after 9pm.

Copán Ruinas

POP 39,490

The town of Copán Ruinas, often simply called Copán, is a beautiful place, paved with cobblestones and lined with white adobe buildings with red-tiled roofs. It's also one of the most charming and traveler-oriented places in Honduras, with a friendly local population, widely spoken English and some great hotels and restaurants. Many people come here just to see the famous nearby Maya ruins, but with plenty of other attractions in the town and nearby, there's reason enough to linger.

INTERNATIONAL BUSES FROM SAN PEDRO SULA

DESTINATION	COST (L)	DURATION (HR)	BUS LINE	PHONE	FREQUENCY
Antigua, Guatemala	1205	9	Hedman Alas	☎2516-2273	daily
Guatemala City, Guatemala	1067	8	Hedman Alas	☎2516-2273	daily
Managua, Nicaragua	980	12	Tica Bus	☎2220-0579	daily
San Jose, Costa Rica	1632	33	Tica Bus	☎2220-0579	daily
San Salvador, El Salvador	720	8	King Quality/ Platinum	☎2516-2167	daily

DOMESTIC BUSES FROM SAN PEDRO SULA

DESTINATION	COST (L)	DURATION (HR)	BUS LINE	PHONE	FREQUENCY
Agua Caliente	230	5	Congolón	☎2553-1174	every 2hr
Comayagua	92	3	Catrachos, El Rey Express		every 30min
Copán Ruinas	140	3	Casasola	☎2516-2031	4 daily
La Ceiba	150-420	3-4	7 bus lines incl Hedman Alas, Viana, Diana Express		every 15-30min
Lago de Yojoa	296	2	Hedman Alas	☎2516-2011	3 daily
Puerto Cortés	76	1-1½	Impala	☎2665-0606	every 15min
Santa Rosa de Copán	100	3	Toritos y Copanaecos	☎2516-2045	every 30min
Tegucigalpa	150-710	4-4½	6 bus lines incl El Rey Express, Hedman Alas, Sultana, Viana		every 15-30min
Tela	90	2	7 bus lines incl COTUC, Mirna, Tela Express		every 15-30min
Trujillo	230	7	Cotuc	☎2520-7497	8 daily

Sights

Though the archaeological site is the main attraction of the Copán region, there are other fine places to visit in the area, including several museums in and around town.

Tea & Chocolate Place AGRICULTURAL CENTER
(2651-4087; 4-6pm Mon-Sat) This charming place is a research center that doubles as a tea and gift shop every afternoon to support the important reforestation work carried out by its environmental charity. Enjoying a cup of tea (try the cacao and spice) on the wonderful veranda is something of a rite of passage in Copán Ruinas. Take a *mototaxi* to get here or walk the kilometer uphill from town.

Museo Digital de Copán MUSEUM
(Map p380; Parque Central; L69; 1-9pm) This museum opened in late 2015 as a gift to the people of Copán from Japan and contains some interesting old photographs. The main reason to visit, though, is to watch the excellent 12-minute video on demand that's a great primer before you visit the Copan Archaeological Site.

Memorias Frágiles GALLERY
(Map p380; 2651-3900; Palacio Municipal, Parque Central; 8am-5pm Mon-Fri) FREE This fascinating photo exhibition was a gift from Boston's Peabody Museum; it features a collection of rare photos detailing the first archaeological expeditions to Copán at the turn of the 20th century. Many of these proved essential in later restoration work, as the photos showed the site decades beforehand and offered clues to how the various stone hieroglyphs had lain.

Museo de Arqueología Maya MUSEUM
(Map p380; 2651-4437; Parque Central; L69; 2-9pm) The Museo de Arqueología Maya is worth a visit. The exhibits include some of the best excavated ceramics, fragments from the altars and the supports of the Maya ruins, an insight into the Maya's sophisticated use of calendars and a re-creation of a female shaman's tomb. Some descriptions have English translations.

Macaw Mountain Bird Park ZOO
(2651-4245; www.macawmountain.org; L230; 9am-5pm) Around 2.5km outside Copán Ruinas is an extensive private reserve aimed at saving Central American macaws. There are plenty of them here, along with toucans, motmots, parrots, kingfishers and orioles, all flying around in spacious, humanely constructed cages. In the 'Encounter Center' uncaged birds fly onto your shoulders or hands and you can pose for photos with them.

Casa K'inich MUSEUM
(Map p380; 2651-4105; off Av Centroaméricano; L30; 8am-noon & 1-5pm Tue-Sun) Casa K'inich includes an interactive re-creation of the ancient football game practiced by the Copán residents more than a millennia ago. Displays are in three languages: English, Spanish and Ch'orti'. Kids might get a kick out of the stela with a cutout hole to poke their heads through.

Courses & Tours

Guacamaya Spanish Academy LANGUAGE
(Map p380; 2651-4360; www.guacamaya.com; Calle de las Gradas, off Av Copán) Offers a package of 20 hours of one-on-one tuition for L3840. For L2400 more you can have full board and lodging with a local family.

Ixbalanque Spanish School LANGUAGE
(Map p380; 2651-4432; www.ixbalanquespanish.com; Av los Jaguares) Offers 20 hours of one-on-one instruction in Spanish for L6240 per week, including a homestay with a local family that provides three meals a day.

Welchez Copan Coffee Tours ECOTOUR
(Map p380; www.cafehonduras.com; half-day tours L960) These morning or afternoon tours take guests to Finca Santa Isabel where some of the finest coffee beans in the region are grown. The hillsides are also teeming with birds, so bring binoculars! The price includes a delicious meal at a charming ranch.

Alexander Alvarado BIRDWATCHING
(9751-1680; alexander.alvarado469@gmail.com) English-speaking Alexander Alvarado runs birdwatching tours in Copán and all over Honduras.

Basecamp Tours ADVENTURE
(Map p380; 2651-4695; www.basecamphonduras.com; Calle de la Plaza) Located inside Café ViaVia, this outfit offers a range of original and adventurous tours around the local area on foot (L230 to L460) and horseback (L345, three hours). The highly recommended two-hour 'Alternative Copán' walking tour (L230) delves beneath the glossy surface of the town and investigates the reality of life for many Hondurans.

Copán Ruinas

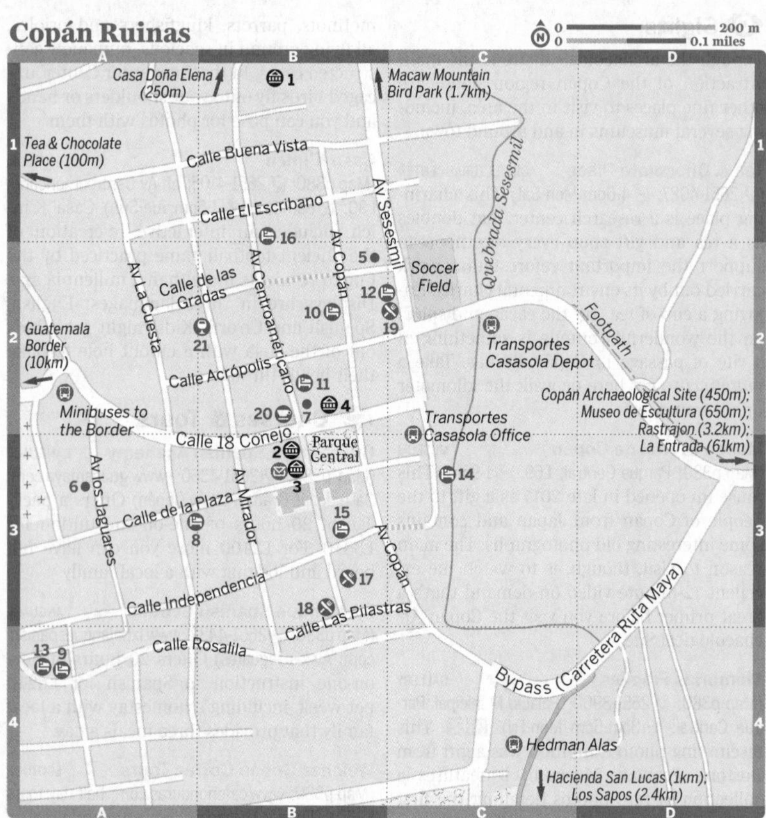

Sleeping

Madrugada Copan HOSTEL $

(Map p380; www.madrugadacopan.com; dm/s/d from L240/360/480;) Situated in a colonial-style hacienda next to a bougainvillea-lined creek and near the town center, this place opened in late 2017 and is oriented specifically to backpackers. Rooms are simple but tastefully furnished and are cooled by overhead fans. There's a hammock-strewn terrace to chill on and a kitchen for guests use, and there's a friendly vibe.

Café ViaVia HOTEL $

(Map p380; 2651-4652; www.viaviacafe.com/en/copan/hotel; Calle de la Plaza; r L230;) This small, Belgian-run, European-style hotel has five very simple, spotless rooms with hot-water bathrooms, tiled floors and good beds. There are hammocks, a small garden and enough space to chill out. It's a great place to come for tourist information, and also has a lively bar attached, which – be aware – can get noisy. Overall it's an amazing deal.

Hotel La Posada HOTEL $

(Map p380; 2651-4059; www.laposadacopan.com; Av Centroaméricano; s/d L495/760;) Good value, tranquil and comfortable, La Posada is only half a block from the plaza. Its 19 cheery rooms are set around leafy patios, are comfortable and clean, and have hot-water bathroom, fan and TV. It has a local feel and is great value.

Hostel Iguana Azul HOSTEL $

(Map p380; 2651-4620; www.iguanaazulcopan.com; Calle Rosalila; dm/s/d L200/400/450;) This colonial-style home has eight comfy bunk beds in two rooms and a shared bathroom with hot water; four private rooms sleep two. There's also a pretty back garden. The communal area has books and lots of travel information, and there's a fridge but

Copán Ruinas

Sights

1 Casa K'inich ... B1
2 Memorias Frágiles ... B3
3 Museo de Arqueología Maya ... B3
4 Museo Digital de Copán ... B2

Activities, Courses & Tours

Basecamp Tours ... (see 8)
5 Guacamaya Spanish Academy ... B2
6 Ixbalanque Spanish School ... A3
7 Welchez Copan Coffee Tours ... B2

Sleeping

8 Café ViaVia ... A3
9 Hostel Iguana Azul ... A4
10 Hotel & Hostal Berakah ... B2
11 Hotel La Posada ... B2
12 Hotel Mary ... B2
13 La Casa de Café ... A4
14 Madrugada Copan ... C3
15 Plaza Yat B'alam ... B3
16 Terramaya ... B1

Eating

Cafe at La Casa de Cafe ... (see 13)
17 Café San Rafael ... B3
Café ViaVia ... (see 8)
18 Carnitas Nia Lola ... B3
19 Casa Ixchel ... C2
Comedor Mary ... (see 12)

Drinking & Nightlife

20 Café Welchez ... B2
21 Sol de Copán ... B2

no kitchen. This is backpacking elegance at its finest: even a room-cleaning service is included.

★La Casa de Café B&B $$

(Map p380; ☎2651-4620; www.casadecafecopan.com; Calle Rosalila; s/d incl breakfast L1275/1512; ❄📶) This impeccably decorated B&B has rooms adorned with carved wooden doors and Guatemalan masks. The setting is stunning – the view from the lawn over the copious and delicious breakfast service is of morning mists rising around the Guatemalan mountains in the distance. North American owner Howard is a mine of local information and staying here feels like being his personal guest.

Casa Doña Elena GUESTHOUSE $$

(☎2651-4029; www.casadonaelena.com; Av Centroaméricano; s/d/tr incl breakfast L700/1200/1440; ❄📶) This lovely, family-run hilltop place enjoys some great views of the town and surrounding valley and has a beautifully tended garden shared by its seven individually named rooms. The rooms themselves are simple but spacious and clean, and a good breakfast is included in the price. It's a 10-minute stiff uphill walk from the center of town.

Hotel Mary HOTEL $$

(Map p380; ☎2651-4673; www.comedormary.com; Av Sesesmiles; s/d L1050/1180; ❄📶) This nicely presented place has very sweet rooms that are brightly painted and well maintained. There's hot water, ceiling fans, attractive traditional bed covers and a pretty garden to boot. Air-conditioning costs an extra L230 per night.

★Terramaya BOUTIQUE HOTEL $$$

(Map p380; ☎2651-4623; www.terramayacopan.com; Av Centroaméricano; s/d incl breakfast from L2090/2280; ❄📶) This ultra-comfortable, flawlessly run, stylish gem hovers somewhere between a B&B and boutique hotel, offering six terra-cotta-tiled, cream linen-draped rooms, a flowery backyard garden and a candlelit terrace with misty-eyed mountain views. Upstairs rooms offer spectacular balconies with vistas out to the mountains beyond – room 6 is to die for. It's fantastic value and a worthy splurge.

Plaza Yat B'alam BOUTIQUE HOTEL $$$

(Map p380; ☎2651-4338; www.yatbalam.com; Calle Independencia; s/d/tr from L1600/1850/2100; P❄📶) Each of the four beautiful rooms here is spacious and comes with all the usual comforts, as well as minibar and DVD player (the hotel has a selection of movies you can borrow). The whole place is pleasantly decorated with a mix of colonial and indigenous furnishings.

Eating

★Cafe at La Casa de Cafe INTERNATIONAL $$

(Map p380; ☎2651-4620; www.casadecafecopan.com; mains L50-175; ⏱7am-8pm) Inspired by trips the owners have taken around the world, you'll find homemade, healthy and fresh delights here from tamales to perfectly spiced curries. The pancakes, egg dishes and smoothies at breakfast are superb, as are the lunchtime sandwiches on bread sometimes still warm from the oven. Chefs use plenty of vegetables, herbs, spreads and delicious fillings like pan-fried tilapia (cichlid fish).

Casa Ixchel CAFE $$

(Map p380; Av Sesesmiles; mains L90-250; 7am-6pm;) There's a friendly welcome at this serious coffee-lover's place, where locally grown Casa Ixchel Arabica coffee is the fuel of choice and the espresso machine is rarely out of use. There's a great little back patio for eating and drinking in the sunshine, and a brunchy menu for tasty breakfasts and light lunches.

Comedor Mary HONDURAN $$

(Map p380; Av Sesesmiles, Hotel Mary; mains L88-250; 7am-9pm;) This charming space comprises a garden for alfresco dining and a dining room full of dark wood furniture where excellent *pupusas* (L12 to L25 each) are served up. *Comida típica* is also redefined here (try the *lomito de res a la plancha,* a grilled beef tenderloin); service is uncharacteristically friendly and the atmosphere is upscale. Don't miss it.

Café ViaVia INTERNATIONAL $$

(Map p380; www.viaviacafe.com/en/copan; Calle de la Plaza; breakfast L60-95, mains L95-150; 7am-10pm;) This terrific restaurant serves breakfast, lunch and dinner in a hip, convivial atmosphere, with tables next to a garden courtyard or overlooking the street. The organically grown coffee it prepares is excellent, the bread is homemade and there's always a good selection of vegetarian and meat-based dishes on offer.

★**Café San Rafael** CAFE, DELI $$$

(Map p380; Av Centroaméricano; sandwiches L160-200; 11am-11pm Tue-Sat, 8am-6pm Sun & Mon;) This smart cafe serves organic coffee grown at its *finca* (ranch), though it's mostly known for its delicious cheeses (platters L150 to L700). Breakfasts (L100 to L200) are a filling splurge, while the toasted sandwiches (try the excellent steak and provolone) are a great lunch option. Half the place is in a beautiful garden patio and the other is indoors and very modern.

Carnitas Nia Lola HONDURAN $$$

(Map p380; Av Centroaméricano; mains L180-455; 7am-10pm;) Two blocks south of the plaza, this open-air restaurant has a beautiful view toward the mountains over corn and tobacco fields. It's a relaxing place with simple and economical food; the specialties are charcoal-grilled chicken and beef. Happy hour starts at 6:30pm.

Drinking & Nightlife

★**Sol de Copán** BREWERY

(Map p380; Av Mirador; mains L130-180; 2-10pm Tue-Sat;) A terrific, German-owned microbrewery in a basement pub. The owner, Thomas, is friendly and makes sure everyone's regularly topped up with pilsner or lager. Delicious German sausages are served, and there's live music some nights too. If you're lucky, Thomas might show you his fermenting vats out the back. Sit at a big table to meet locals and other travelers.

Café Welchez CAFE

(Map p380; 2651-4202; near Parque Central; mains L150-200; 7am-5pm;) This very pleasant two-floor place does excellent coffee and cake and has a charming terrace with Parque Central views. Good breakfasts are available, including French toast, eggs Benedict and a 'full American.' Sandwiches, soups and salads complete the offerings.

Information

Police (2651-4060; Calle de la Plaza; 24hr) Located 300m west of the park.

Post Office (Map p380; Calle de la Plaza; 8am-noon & 1-5pm Mon-Sat) A few doors from the plaza.

Proyecto Clinico Materno Infantil (Hwy CA-11; 24hr) The only hospital in the area specializes in pediatrics and obstetrics, but no one is turned away. It's in El Jaral, 20km northeast of Copán Ruinas on Hwy CA-11.

MONEY

US dollars can be changed at most banks, though Guatemalan quetzals at present can only be changed on the black market. The following banks have ATMs that accept foreign cards.

BAC (Parque Central; 9am-5pm Mon-Fri, to noon Sat) Exchanges US dollars and has a 24-hour ATM.

Banco Atlántida (cnr Calle Independencia & Av Copán) Changes US dollars and has an ATM.

Banco de Occidente (cnr Calle 18 Conejo & Av Copán) On the plaza; changes US dollars and gives cash advances on Visa and MasterCard.

Getting There & Away

An airport opened here in 2015, but it has never received commercial flights and no one expects it to in the near future.

BUS

Casasola (Map p380; 2651-4078; Av Sesesmiles) buses arrive and depart from an open-air **bus depot** (Map p380; 2651-4078) at the entrance to town, where destinations include

San Pedro Sula (L140, three hours, five daily) and Santa Rosa de Copán (L100, three hours, hourly), from where you can connect easily to Tegucigalpa.

Minibuses to/from the **Guatemalan border** (Map p380) (L25, 20 minutes, every 20 minutes) run between 6am and 5pm from near the town's cemetery at the end of Calle 18 Conejo. On the Guatemala side, buses to Esquipulas and Chiquimula leave the border regularly until about 5pm.

You can book popular shuttle buses at either Basecamp Tours (p379) or **Hotel & Hostal Berakah** (Map p380; ☎9951-4288, 2651-4771; www.hotelberakahcopan.hostel.com; Av Copán; dm/d/tw L174/400/450) to Antigua (L600, six hours), Guatemala City (L600, five hours), San Salvador (L880, five hours), stopping at Santa Ana or Tunco (both L960, 4½ hours); there's one shuttle to Leon and Managua in Nicaragua (L2040, 12 hours) and also one to La Ceiba (L960, seven hours), Lago de Yojoa (L480, six hours) and to the San Pedro Sula airport (L480, four hours). Note that many shuttles only run when there are enough people.

Hedman Alas (Map p380; ☎2651-4037; Carretera a San Lucas Km 62) has a modern terminal just south of town, where you can get daily 1st-class buses to San Pedro Sula and the airport (L395, three hours), Tegucigalpa (L790, eight hours), Lago Yajoa (L790, six hours), La Ceiba (L731, seven hours) and Tela (L731, six hours).

Around Copán Ruinas

The forested hills around Copán Ruinas include a few interesting sights that are well worth visiting while you're staying in the town.

Sights & Activities

Rastrajon ARCHAEOLOGICAL SITE
(L70) Situated for defense on a mountainside, the earth shifting due to subterranean water flow here has left the remains twisted into unusual formations. This site was occupied both before and after the long Copan dynasty making it unique in the valley; it contains exceptional sculpture. It's about 2km trip beyond the main site behind the Clarion Hotel (L30 by *mototaxi*).

Los Sapos ARCHAEOLOGICAL SITE
(Hacienda San Lucas; L30) The *sapos* (toads) are old Maya stone carvings, set along a hiking trail in the hills next to Hacienda San Lucas (they'll give you a map). The site is connected with Maya fertility rites and is one of a few with similar stone carvings. There are dozens here and it's fun to try to pick them out in the pile of stones.

Luna Jaguar Spa Resort SPA
(www.lunajaguarsparesort.com; from L250; ⏲9am-9pm) This gorgeous hot springs is 24km north of Copán Ruinas – an hour's drive through mountains and coffee plantations. The Popol Nah area features pools in the river, where the boiling-hot spring mixes with cool river water. More posh is the Spa Acropolis section offering herbal steam baths, massage stations and more, scattered around the hillside and connected by stone pathways.

Finca El Cisne HORSEBACK RIDING
(☎2651-4695; www.fincaelcisne.com; tours from L2000) Visiting this working farm 24km from Copán Ruinas is more like an agri-eco experience than a tour. Founded in the 1920s and still operating, the *finca* mainly raises cattle and grows coffee and cardamom. Full-day and overnight packages include guided horseback riding through the forests, and tours of the coffee and cardamom fields and processing plants. Day tours are L2000.

Sleeping & Eating

★**Hacienda San Lucas** HISTORIC HOTEL $$$
(☎2651-4495; www.haciendasanlucas.com; s/d/tr incl breakfast L2860/3300/3960; 📶) This magical place some 3km south of town enjoys sweeping views from its wonderfully maintained gardens. It's a rustic yet charming experience with adobe-constructed, candlelit rooms and a tail-wagging dog to welcome you. The rooms have stone floors, terra-cotta roofs and are decorated with locally made handicrafts, while the on-site restaurant is superb. The Los Sapos archaeological site is on the property.

★**Hacienda San Lucas** HONDURAN $$$
(☎2651-4495; www.haciendasanlucas.com; 3-/4-courses L600/750) Set on farmland overlooking Copán Ruinas, this wonderful place – worth the effort to get here and the price – has some of the best food in the region. The romance of dining on a several-course meal by candlelight in the restored farmhouse can't really be exaggerated. Cuisine draws heavily on traditional ingredients and techniques. Reserve at least a day ahead.

Getting There & Away

Access from Copán Ruinas is easy and cheap using the town's *mototaxis*.

Copán Archaeological Site

One of the most important of all Maya civilizations lived, prospered, then mysteriously crumbled around the Copán archaeological ruins, a Unesco World Heritage Site. During the Classic period (AD 250–900), the city at Copán Ruinas culturally dominated the region. The architecture is not as grand as that across the border in Tikal, but the city produced remarkable sculptures and hieroglyphics, and these days you'll often be virtually alone at the site, which makes it all the more haunting.

The ruins are a pleasant 1km stroll outside of Copán. A visitors center, an excellent sculpture museum and a cafe and gift shop are close to the main entrance. The guides at the Asociación de Guías Copán really know their stuff and hiring one is a worthwhile investment.

History

Pre-Columbian History

People have been living in the Copán Valley since at least 1200 BC; ceramic evidence has been found from around that date. Copán must have had significant commercial activity since early times, as graves showing marked Olmec influence have been dated to around 900 to 600 BC.

In the 5th century AD one royal family came to rule Copán, led by a mysterious king named Mah K'ina Yax K'uk' Mo' (Great Sun Lord Quetzal Macaw), who ruled from 426 to 435. Archaeological evidence indicates that he was a great shaman, and later kings revered him as the semidivine founder of the city. The dynasty ruled throughout Copán's florescence during the Classic period.

We know little about the subsequent kings who ruled before 628. Only some of their names have been deciphered: Mat Head, the second king; Cu Ix, the fourth king; Waterlily Jaguar, the seventh; Moon Jaguar, the 10th; and Butz' Chan, the 11th.

Among the greatest of Copán's kings was Smoke Imix (Smoke Jaguar; r 628–95), the 12th king. Smoke Imix built Copán into a major military and commercial power in the region. He may have taken over the nearby princedom of Quiriguá, as one of the famous stelae at that site bears his name and image. By the time he died in 695, Copán's population had grown substantially.

Smoke Imix was succeeded by Uaxaclahun Ubak K'awil (18 Rabbit; r 695–738), the 13th king, who willingly took the reins of power and pursued further military conquest. In a war with King Cauac Sky, his neighbor from Quiriguá, 18 Rabbit was captured and beheaded. He was succeeded by K'ak' Joplaj Chan K'awiil (Smoke Monkey; r 738–49), the 14th king, whose short reign left little mark on Copán. Smoke Monkey's son, K'ak' Yipyaj Chan K'awiil (Smoke Shell; r 749–63), was, however, one of Copán's greatest builders. He commissioned the city's most famous and important monument, the great Escalinata de los Jeroglíficos (Hieroglyphic Stairway), which immortalizes the achievements of the dynasty from its establishment until 755, when the stairway was dedicated. It is the longest inscription ever discovered in the Maya lands.

Yax Pasaj Chan Yopaat (Sunrise or First Dawn; r 763–820; also known as Yax Pac, Yax Pasaj Chan Yoaat and Yax Pasah), Smoke Shell's successor and the 16th king, continued the beautification of Copán. The final occupant of the throne, U Cit Tok', became ruler in 822, but it's not known when he died.

Until recently, the collapse of the civilization at Copán had been a mystery. Now archaeologists have begun to surmise that near the end of Copán's heyday the population grew at an unprecedented rate, straining agricultural resources. In the end, Copán was no longer agriculturally self-sufficient and had to import food from other areas. The urban core expanded into the fertile lowlands in the center of the valley, forcing both agricultural and residential areas to spread onto the steep slopes surrounding the valley. Wide areas were deforested, resulting in massive erosion that further decimated food production and brought flooding during rainy seasons. Interestingly, this environmental damage of old is not too different from what is happening today – a disturbing trend, but one that meshes with the Maya belief that life is cyclical and history repeats itself. Skeletal remains of people who died during Copán's final years show marked evidence of malnutrition and infectious diseases, as well as decreased life spans.

The Copán Valley was not abandoned overnight – agriculturists probably continued to live in the ecologically devastated valley for maybe another one or two hundred years. But by the year 1200 or thereabouts even the farmers had departed, and the royal city of Copán was reclaimed by the jungle.

Copán Archaeological Site

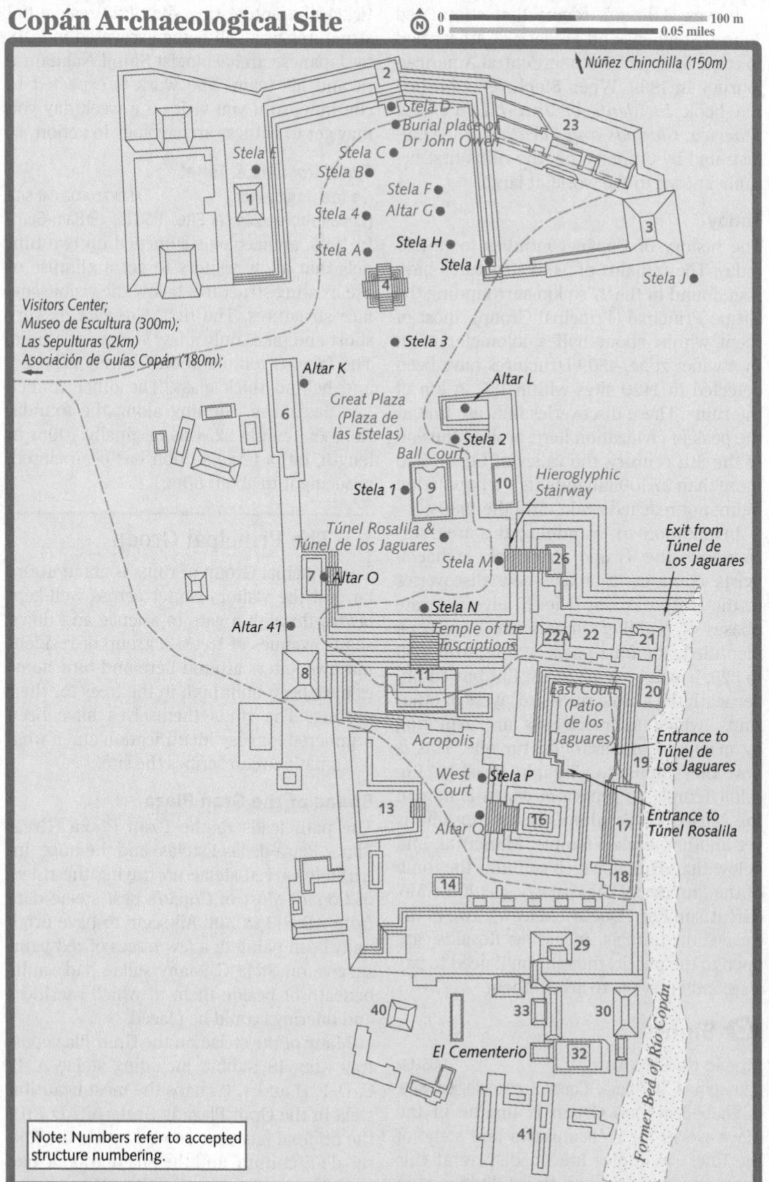

European Discovery

The first known European to see the ruins was a representative of Spanish King Felipe II, Diego García de Palacios, who lived in Guatemala and traveled through the region. On March 8, 1576, he wrote to the king about the ruins he found here. Only about five families were living here at the time, and they knew nothing of the history of the ruins. The discovery was not pursued, and almost three centuries went by before another Spaniard, Colonel Juan Galindo, visited the ruins and made the first map of them.

It was Galindo's report that stimulated John L Stephens and Frederick Catherwood to come to Copán on their Central American journey in 1839. When Stephens published the book *Incidents of Travel in Central America, Chiapas and Yucatan* in 1841, illustrated by Catherwood, the ruins first became known to the world at large.

Today

The history of Copán continues to unfold today. The remains of 3450 structures have been found in the 27 sq km surrounding the Grupo Principal (Principal Group), most of them within about half a kilometer of it. In a wider zone, 4509 structures have been detected in 1420 sites within 135 sq km of the ruins. These discoveries indicate that at the peak of civilization here, around the end of the 8th century, the valley of Copán had more than 27,500 inhabitants – a population figure not reached again until the 1980s.

In addition to examining the area surrounding the Grupo Principal, archaeologists continue to make new discoveries in the Grupo Principal itself. Five separate phases of building on this site have been identified; the final phase, dating from 650 to 820, is what we see today. But buried underneath the visible ruins are layers of other ruins, which archaeologists are exploring by means of underground tunnels. This is how they found the Templo Rosalila (Rosalila Temple), a replica of which is now in the Museo de Escultura. Below Rosalila is yet another, earlier temple, Margarita, and below that, Hunal, which contains the tomb of the founder of the dynasty, Yax K'uk' Mo' (Great Sun Lord Quetzal Macaw). Two of the excavation tunnels, including Rosalila, are open to the public, though you'll need to pay a second entry fee to access them.

Sights

Museo de Escultura MUSEUM
(Museum of Sculpture; Copan Archaeological Site; US$7; ⏲8am-6pm) Copán is unique in the Maya world for its sculptures and some of the finest examples are on display at this impressive museum, which is fully signed in English. Entering the museum is an experience in itself: you go through the mouth of a serpent and through its entrails before suddenly emerging into the bright main hall.

Núñez Chinchilla ARCHAEOLOGICAL SITE
One hundred and fifty meters north of the Grand Plaza and included on the Copan site ticket, this interesting site of 23 residential structures was still being excavated in 2018 by Japanese archaeologist Shinji Nakuamura and his team. The work is expected to continue, so if you visit on a week day you may get to witness archaeology in action.

Túnel Rosalila & Túnel de los Jaguares ARCHAEOLOGICAL SITE
(Copan Archaeological Site; US$15; ⏲8am-6pm) In 1999, archaeologists opened up two tunnels that allow visitors to get a glimpse of pre-existing structures below the visible surface structures. The first, **Rosalila**, is very short and takes only a few visitors at a time. The famous temple is only barely exposed, and behind thick glass. The other tunnel, **Los Jaguares**, running along the foundations of Temple 22, was originally 700m in length, but a large section has been closed, reducing it to about 80m.

The Principal Group

The Principal Group of ruins is about 400m beyond the visitors center across well-kept lawns, through a gate in a fence and down shady avenues of trees. A group of resident macaws loiters around here and bird houses have been built high in the trees for their nesting. The ruins themselves have been numbered for easy identification and a well-worn path circumscribes the site.

Stelae of the Gran Plaza

The path leads to the **Gran Plaza** (Great Plaza; Plaza de las Estelas) and the huge, intricately carved stelae portraying the rulers of Copán. Most of Copán's best stelae date from AD 613 to 738. All seem to have originally been painted; a few traces of red paint survive on Stela C. Many stelae had vaults beneath or beside them in which sacrifices and offerings could be placed.

Many of the stelae on the Gran Plaza portray King 18 Rabbit, including stelae A, B, C, D, F, H and 4. Perhaps the most beautiful stela in the Gran Plaza is **Stela A** (AD 731); the original has been moved inside the Museo de Escultura, and the one outdoors, like many here, is a reproduction. Nearby and almost equal in beauty are **Stela 4** (AD 731); **Stela B** (AD 731), depicting 18 Rabbit upon his accession to the throne; and **Stela C** (AD 782), with a turtle-shaped altar in front. This last stela has figures on both sides. **Stela E** (AD 614), erected on top of Estructura 1

(Structure 1) on the west side of the Gran Plaza, is among the oldest.

At the northern end of the Gran Plaza at the base of Estructura 2, **Stela D** (AD 736) also portrays King 18 Rabbit. On its back are two columns of hieroglyphs; at its base is an altar with fearsome representations of Chac, the rain god. In front of the altar is the **burial place of Dr John Owen**, an archaeologist with an expedition from Harvard's Peabody Museum who died during excavation work in 1893.

On the east side of the plaza is **Stela F** (AD 721), which has a more lyrical design than other stelae here, with the robes of the main figure flowing around to the other side of the stone, where there are glyphs. **Altar G** (AD 800), showing twin serpent heads, is among the last monuments carved at Copán. **Stela H** (AD 730) may depict a queen or princess rather than a king. **Stela I** (AD 692), on the structure that runs along the east side of the plaza, is of a person wearing a mask. **Stela J** (AD 702), further off to the east, resembles the stelae of Quiriguá in that it is covered in glyphs, not human figures.

Ball Court & Hieroglyphic Stairway

South of the Gran Plaza, across what is known as the Plaza Central, is the Juego de Pelota (Ball Court; AD 731), the second largest in Central America. The one you see is the third one on this site; the two smaller courts were buried by this construction. Note the macaw heads carved atop the sloping walls. The central marker in the court is the work of King 18 Rabbit.

South of the Juego de Pelota is Copán's most famous monument, the Escalinata de los Jeroglíficos (Hieroglyphic Stairway; AD 743), the work of King Smoke Shell. Today it's protected from the elements by a canvas roof. The flight of 63 steps bears a history (in several thousand glyphs) of the royal house of Copán; the steps are bordered by ramps inscribed with more reliefs and glyphs. The story told on the inscribed steps is still not completely understood because the stairway was partially ruined and the stones jumbled, but archaeologists are using 3D-scanning technology to make a digital version of the original, with the hope of one day reading it in its entirety.

At the base of the Hieroglyphic Stairway is **Stela M** (AD 756), bearing a figure (probably King Smoke Shell) dressed in a feathered cloak; glyphs tell of the solar eclipse in that year. The altar in front shows a plumed serpent with a human head emerging from its jaws.

Beside the stairway, a tunnel leads to the **tomb of a nobleman**, a royal scribe who may have been the son of King Smoke Imix. The tomb, discovered in June 1989, held a treasure trove of painted pottery and beautiful carved-jade objects that are now in Honduran museums.

Acrópolis

The lofty flight of steps to the south of the Hieroglyphic Stairway mounts the **Templo de las Inscripciones** (Temple of the Inscriptions). On top of the stairway, the walls are carved with groups of hieroglyphs. On the south side of the Temple of the Inscriptions is the **Patio Occidental** (West Court), with the **Patio Oriental** (East Court), also called the **Patio de los Jaguares** (Court of the Jaguars) to its east. In the West Court, check out **Altar Q** (AD 776), among the most famous sculptures here; the original is inside the Museo de Escultura. Around its sides, carved in superb relief, are the 16 great kings of Copán, ending with its creator, Yax Pasaj Chan Yopaat. Behind the altar is a sacrificial vault in which archaeologists discovered the bones of 15 jaguars and several macaws that were probably sacrificed to the glory of Yax Pasaj Chan Yopaat and his ancestors.

This group of temples, known as the Acrópolis, was the spiritual and political core of the site – reserved for royalty and nobles, a place where ceremonies were enacted and kings buried.

The East Court also contains evidence of Yax Pasaj Chan Yopaat – his **tomb**, beneath Estructura 18. Unfortunately the tomb was discovered and looted long before archaeologists arrived. Both the East and West Courts hold a variety of fascinating stelae and sculptured heads of humans and animals. To see the most elaborate relief carving, climb Estructura 22 on the northern side of the East Court. This was the **Templo de Meditación** (Temple of Meditation) and has been heavily restored over recent years.

Tours

Asociación de Guías Copán TOURS
(☎2651-4018; guiascopan@yahoo.com; Archaeological Park US$30, tunnels US$15, Sepulturas US$18) It's a good idea to visit the site with a guide, who can help to explain the ruins and bring them to life. Guides work for the

DON'T MISS

EL BOSQUE & LAS SEPULTURAS

Excavations at El Bosque and Las Sepulturas have shed light on the daily life of the Maya in Copán during its golden age. Las Sepulturas, once connected to the Gran Plaza by a causeway, may have been the residential area where rich and powerful nobles lived. One huge, luxurious residential compound seems to have housed some 250 people in 40 or 50 buildings arranged around 11 courtyards. The principal structure, called the **Palacio de los Bacabs** (Palace of the Officials), had outer walls carved with the full-sized figures of 10 men in fancy feathered headdresses; inside was a huge hieroglyphic bench. To get to Las Sepulturas you have to go back to the main road, turn right, then right again at the sign (2km from the Gran Plaza).

The walk to get to **El Bosque** is the real reason for visiting it, as it's removed from the main ruins. It's a 5km (one hour) walk on a well-maintained path through foliage dense with birds, though there isn't much of note at the site itself save for a small ball court. Still, it's a powerful experience to have an hour-long walk on the thoroughfares of an ancient Maya city all to yourself. To get to El Bosque, go right at the hut where your ticket is stamped. Be sure to slather on the insect repellent before you set off and it's advised not to go alone.

cooperative Asociación de Guías Copán and prices are for groups of up to five people. You can find them at the entrance to the parking lot.

Getting There & Away

The Copán archaeological site is a kilometer from Copán Ruinas proper and can be walked easily enough. An alternative is to take a *mototaxi* from the town (L20 per person). To get between the Archaeological Park and Sepulturas you can walk the 2km or hire a *mototaxi* (L20 per person each way).

Gracias

POP 12,800

Gracias is a small, tranquil cobblestoned town that's one of the prettiest and most historic settlements in Honduras. For a brief time in the 16th century, it was the capital of all Spanish-conquered Central America and traces of its former grandeur remain in its centuries-old buildings, colonial churches and impressive fort. It's been in a state of slow but charming decline ever since, and today the pace of life here rarely moves beyond walking.

Founded in 1526 by Spanish Captain Juan de Chávez, its original name was Gracias a Dios (Thanks to God). Eventually the town's importance was eclipsed by Antigua (Guatemala) and Comayagua.

The main reason many people to come to Gracias is to explore the mountainous, forested countryside around the town itself and perhaps climb El Cerro de las Minas (2849m) in Parque Nacional Montaña de Celaque, the country's highest peak.

Sights

Gracias is a charming place to wander around. As well as the famous fortress, the town has several colonial *iglesias* (churches), including **San Marcos** on the Parque Central (whose facade, oddly, does not face the plaza).

Most of the area's other attractions, including some fine hot springs, are a few kilometers out of town.

Fuerte de San Cristóbal FORTRESS
(8am-4pm) FREE Built in response to the tumultuous times of the 18th century, the striking Fuerte de San Cristóbal has fantastic views of Gracias and the San Marcos church below. Beyond that, there's not much else to see up here, save for the **tomb of Juan Lindo**, a Honduran who was the former president of both El Salvador (1841–42) *and* Honduras (1847–52).

Museo Casa Galeano MUSEUM
(2625-5407; L30; 8am-6pm) This museum is located in a beautiful, ancient colonial house with high ceilings, carved timber posts and delightful paint-chipped walls with floral designs. Its contents (faded photos, old coins) are pretty mediocre and labeling is only in Spanish. There are plans to improve the collection, however, so check out what's there!

Jardín Botánico GARDENS
(8am-5pm Mon-Sat, to noon Sun) The city's botanical garden is at the southern end of

town, five blocks south of the old Mercado Municipal, and takes up half a city block. Local flora can be admired all year long from a paved path that meanders through the park.

Activities & Eating

Ángel at Jardín Cafe Hostel, does excellent various tours, while Carlos at **Finca Bavaria** (2656-1372; Calle Lopez Garcia; 6pm-midnight;) specializes in birdwatching. Good tours can also be organised at the Hotel Guancascos. Guides are abundant and most hotels work with ones they know and trust.

Expect to pay L1000 for two-day hikes in Parque National Montaña de Celaque, L850 for waterfall rappelling and L850 for a day of birdwatching.

Sleeping

Jardín Cafe Hostel HOSTEL $
(2656-1244; jardincafegracias@gmail.com; Av Circunavalacion; dm L470, r L700-950;) The big private rooms and spacious four-bed dorms here are good value, with modern style and hot water bathrooms. All look over the garden cafe area of the restaurant, which clears out around 10pm. Ángel, the owner, offers birdwatching, hiking and rappelling and local opal mine tours. The only drawback is the location on a busy road at the edge of town.

★**Hotel Guancascos** HOTEL $$
(9920-0711; www.guancascos.com; Av Eleuterio Galeano Trejo; dm/s/d incl breakfast from L360/800/1150;) This memorable, Dutch-run place boasts immaculately clean and good-value rooms set off shady paths that meander through the hotel's leafy plot, perched on the hillside under the town's fortress. All plants are labeled, and woodpeckers and hummingbirds are frequently seen. Rooms 13 and 14 share a gorgeous patio area with stellar town views, while the five-bed dorm is great value.

Hotel Real Camino Lenca HOTEL $$
(2656-1932; www.realcaminolencahotel.com; Calle Jeremias Cisneros; r incl breakfast from L1550;) The place to go if you want to be served by staff in black tie, the Camino Lenca has aging rooms leading off a plant-filled atrium inside a colonial-era building. The rooms themselves are comfortable and have large flatscreen TVs, though many lack natural daylight. There's a popular bar on the rooftop and a restaurant downstairs. Reserve ahead.

Posada de Don Juan HOTEL $$$
(2656-1020; www.posadadedonjuanhotel.com; Av Dr Juan Lindo; r from L1900;) This is definitely the fanciest choice in town, with a stylish lobby (draping bougainvillea, artsy B&W photographs of town); modern-ish, clean and spacious rooms; and an excellent pool and a good restaurant.

Eating & Drinking

Cafetería Artesenías El Jarrón HONDURAN $
(Av Medina; mains L75-120; 7am-8pm;) A bustling, atmospheric place that does a lot of lunchtime trade: the buffet (L120) is a great deal, with lots of veggie dishes. You sit at polished log tables, and there's a garden patio at the rear. Lencan handicrafts and ceramics are also sold here and tours can be arranged.

★**Kandil Pizza Y Cafe** PIZZA $$
(Av Medina; pizzas L115-440; 11:30am-10pm Tue-Sun;) Flying the flag for contemporary aesthetics in the rustic Lencan hills, Kandil is a beautifully designed place where modish decor juxtaposes with colonial-style tradition. You can sit either inside its sleek main dining room or outside in the shady courtyard. It's famous for its cocktails and pizza so stay awhile and hang out with the arty crowd.

Jardín Café INTERNATIONAL $$
(2656-1244; Av Circumvalecion; mains L150-220; 7.30am-10pm Mon-Sat, to 4pm Sun;) This hip and cozy place has some of the best food in town. As the name suggests it's cafe-style with tables in a main room, out in a garden patio or up on a 2nd story rooftop to enjoy the sunset. Pizza, burgers and more are all good, but the Honduran-style meals with plenty of sides are where this place shines.

Restaurante Guancascos INTERNATIONAL, HONDURAN $$
(Hotel Guancascos; mains L95-180; 7am-9pm;) A wonderful terrace restaurant at the Hotel Guancascos, from where you can gaze over Gracias' terra-cotta-tiled rooftops and the Lencan highlands. Great for breakfast (L70 to L90), a filling sandwich, a veggie plate or pan-fried fish. There's efficient service, excellent fresh juices and wine by the glass.

Plaza Cafe COFFEE
(Parque Central; drinks L20-60; ⏲7am-8:40pm; 📶) Occupying the two-story hexagonal structure in the middle of the town's central square, this is the best place in town to enjoy an espresso, cappuccino, flavored coffee or *granita* (iced fruit drink) and a doughnut – the coffee comes from the nearby Finca Santa Elena. The upstairs seating area is a great place for people-watching.

Shopping

Envasados Dulces Lorendiana FOOD
(Av Dr Juan Lindo; ⏲7:30am-7pm Mon-Sat, to noon Sun) An incredible find, this little store has shelves stacked floor-to-ceiling with hundreds (thousands?) of jars filled with pickled vegetables, chutneys and fruit wines, all prepared by the owner. A takeout portion costs L25. It's 250m southwest of the Parque Central.

Information

There are at least four ATMs around town, including **Banco Atlantida** (Calle Jeremias Cisneros; ⏲9am-5pm Mon-Fri).

Hospital Dr Juan Manuel Galvez (☎2656-1100; Carretera a Santa Rosa de Copán; ⏲24hr) Very basic hospital near the entrance to town.

Post Office (Calle San Christobal; ⏲8am-noon & 2-5pm Mon-Fri, 8-11am Sat) One block southeast of Parque Central.

Getting There & Away

Most buses leave from the **terminal**, which is on the ring road just northwest of the fortress. It's a busy and confusing place, and you'll have to ask which of the myriad big buses or minivans to get on (tickets are sold on board). Destinations include Santa Rosa de Copán, San Pedro Sula and La Esperanza; the Tegucigalpa buses are luxury models and quite comfortable. Change at Santa Rosa de Copán for Copán Ruinas and at La Esperanza for Comayagua.

Around Gracias

The rolling green countryside around Gracias includes two very popular thermal springs, several traditional Lenca villages and some superb canyon scenery, where zip lining is available in the village of La Campa. La Campa is also the best place in the region to buy red earth-toned Lenca pottery, found in artist studios all around town.

Activities

★**Canopy Extremo** ADVENTURE SPORTS
(☎9756-9801; www.facebook.com/canopyextrem/; La Campa; L720) This is the craziest zip line in all of Honduras, if not Central America. Some six lines soar over the steep, rocky river valley, with enormous drops below. Safety is respected, some instructors speak English and the course takes around two hours. Definitely call ahead so that you're expected, and request the free pick-up from Gracias.

Centro Turístico Terma del Río HOT SPRINGS
(www.termasdelrio.com; L150; ⏲7am-9pm) Located 7km from town on the road to Santa Rosa de Copán, Centro Turístico Terma del Río is a relaxed and family-oriented hot spring. There's also a cool-water swimming pool, camping, simple lodging and a zip line. Catch any bus heading to Santa Rosa to get here.

Aguas Termales Presidente HOT SPRINGS
(L60; ⏲7am-11pm) The hot springs at Aguas Termales Presidente are one of Gracias' main attractions. About 6km southeast of town, the hot springs have several pools at various temperatures. To get here take a *mototaxi* from Gracias (L80) and either negotiate a waiting fee or try to flag one heading back once you're done.

Sleeping

★**Hostal JB** GUESTHOUSE $
(☎9547-7356; La Campa; r L500) One of the prettiest places to stay on the Ruta Lenca, this is more like a huge house with clay-tiled patios, a big garden and window-lit rooms. Each room has a single and queen-sized bed equipped with thick comforters; guests

BUSES FROM GRACIAS

DESTINATION	COST (L)	DURATION (HR)	FREQUENCY
La Esperanza	90	1½	frequent
San Pedro Sula	150	4	4 daily
Santa Rosa de Copán	50	1½	every 30min
Tegucigalpa	200	6	hourly

NUEVA OCOTEPEQUE

Dust-blown Nueva Ocotepeque is a crossroads town, with a lot of traffic to the nearby borders at Agua Caliente (Guatemala) and El Poy (El Salvador). It's not a pleasant place, and you're strongly advised to avoid spending the night here. If you do, take care after dark.

Few travelers stay here, but if you get stuck there are some adequate hotels, including the good-value **Hotel Turista** (☎2653-3639; 3era Av General Francisco Morazán; s/d L400/550, d without bathroom L300;).

Two long-distance bus companies serve Nueva Ocotepeque: **Congolón** (☎2653-3064) is half a block south of the Parque Central, while **Sultana** (☎2653-2405) is two blocks north of the *parque*. Buses to Agua Caliente and El Poy depart from the **Transportes San José terminal** two blocks north of the *parque*.

For Tegucigalpa, take a San Pedro Sula bus and transfer. For Santa Rosa de Copán, take any San Pedro Sula bus.

share a kitchen and a spacious living room with sofas, folk art and high wood-beamed ceilings. It's just before the church.

Hotel Real Camino Lenca La Campa BUNGALOW **$$**
(☎2617-6470; www.realcaminolencahotel.com; La Campa; d incl breakfast L1450;) Opened in late 2017, this is the fanciest place for miles, with picturesque white bungalows with ceramic tile roofs, spreading over a flowery hillside. The interiors are comfortable and new, but rather bland, and all have views of the nearby zip lines over the canyon. There's a small pool and a restaurant on-site, and the staff are helpful and professional.

Getting There & Away

Both thermal springs are best reached by *mototaxi* (L80) from Gracias. Buses head from Gracias to La Campa (L25, one hour, four daily) and normally continue on to San Manuel Colohete (L35, two hours), a further hour away.

NORTHERN HONDURAS

The lush, tropical northern region of Honduras has seduced visitors for centuries with its natural wonders and easy Caribbean vibe. Between the beaches are mangrove swamps and jungle reserves that scream out to be explored. Rafting the white waters of the Río Cangrejal is *the* big-ticket experience, but there's also fine hiking in Parque Nacional Pico Bonito and the unique flavor and rhythms of the coast's Garifuna villages. Finally, isolated Trujillo, the last stop before the Moskitia, is a charming slice of the old Caribbean, with some wonderful beaches nearby and superb mountain scenery behind it.

Despite all the region has to offer, many visitors simply travel through here en route to the Bay Islands or Belize, and see nothing more than the drab charms of Puerto Cortés, Tela or La Ceiba. Avoid the towns and make a beeline for the countryside!

Omoa

POP 47,290

Omoa feels like the end of the road, and indeed this unremarkable town 18km west of Puerto Cortés sees few visitors. Despite this fact, it's an attractive little resort on a broad curving bay that makes for great sunsets, even if, due to coastal erosion, the brown-sugar beach is minimal. There's a historic fort and a clutch of seafood restaurants along the seafront.

Sights

Fortaleza de San Fernando de Omoa FORT
(☎2658-9167; L88; 8am-4pm Mon-Fri, 9am-5pm Sat) Omoa's claim to fame is this colossal Spanish fortress. Built in brick and coral between 1759 and 1777 under orders from King Fernando VII of Spain, the fortress was intended to protect the coast from Caribbean piracy, though in 1779 it was captured by the British. It's in excellent condition and the fine visitors center and museum provide a satisfying historical background.

Sleeping & Eating

Roli's Place HOSTEL **$**
(☎2658-9082; www.omoa.net/roli.html; campsites/hammocks/dm per person L90/100/120, s/d L300/350, s/d without bathroom L180/250;

WORTH A TRIP

EXPLORING LA CAMPA & AROUND

This beautiful little whitewashed town is set to birdsong, strewn with coffee beans drying on the pavement and surrounded by mountain views. Stroll the friendly pottery shops, visit the striking, baroque **Iglesia De Santa Maria** or just sit on a shady bench in the town square and watch the very mellow world go by. Many people visit to go zip-lining across the exceedingly high river gorge, but if you want a break from the modern world, consider staying here overnight or more.

An 18km drive west of La Campa, **Parque Nacional Montaña de Celaque** (L120) is one of Honduras' most impressive national parks and boasts El Cerro de las Minas, the country's highest peak (2849m), which is covered in lush forest. The park contains the headwaters of several rivers, a majestic waterfall visible from the entire valley, and very steep slopes, including some vertical cliffs.

The park is rich in plant and animal life: pumas, ocelots and quetzals live here, but they are rarely seen. More commonly sighted are butterflies, monkeys and reptiles.

) This tired, Swiss-owned hostel on a big grassy plot is a lovely place to hang out, and is just 70m from the beach. The well-furnished double rooms, complete with cable TV, are a steal; there's also a decent dorm and a shady campground. Freebies include ocean-going kayaks and bikes. It's not a party hostel and there are rules, but it's very relaxing.

Family Restaurante SEAFOOD $$$
(mains L190-600; 11am-9pm) The best of Omoa's seafront seafood restaurants is always teeming with lip-smacking diners, and has a view through blooming birds of paradise over the sea. All the local favorites here are done to perfection, from grilled fish or coconut-y conch soup to garlic grilled lobster.

Getting There & Away

There are hourly connections (L25, 30 minutes) to/from Puerto Cortés; some buses will branch off the highway and drop passengers at the beach, which is about 1.5km away.

Roli's Place (p391) runs shuttles on demand to La Ceiba or Puerto Barrios in Guatemala.

Puerto Cortés

POP 126,010

Puerto Cortes is where you may arrive from or depart to Belize or Guatemala. If you've just arrived, don't worry: Honduras only gets better from here. Unfortunately the country's main port is a thoroughly depressing and ugly town. If you need to overnight for the ferry, Omoa is a far more attractive base, though most people head straight for San Pedro Sula or beyond.

Festivals & Events

Garifuna Day CULTURAL
(Apr 12) This annual holiday for Garifuna communities commemorates the day in 1797 when the Garifuna arrived in Honduras.

Sleeping

Hotel El Centro HOTEL $
(2665-1160; 3a Av, btwn 2a & 3a Calles E; r with fan/air-con from L450/650;) This hotel is a secure and clean option in the center of town: a good choice for backpackers.

Prince Wilson Hotel HOTEL $$
(9864-7760; s/d with air-con L700/950;) This decent place is your best bet for the ferry, as it's right by the dock. Rooms are clean and comfortable, and staff are helpful. It's easily the best located and most secure option.

Getting There & Away

BOAT

D-Express (9991-0778, 2665-0726) runs to Big Creek, Belize City and Placencia (all L1320) at 11:30am on Mondays. The **dock** is next door to Restaurant El Delfin in Barra la Laguna, 3km southeast of the center. If arriving in Puerto Cortés by bus, ask the driver to let you off at the Laguna intersection, then cross the street and walk toward the bridge, where you'll find the ticket office and immigration authorities. You'll need to be at the dock by 10am to complete paperwork and then board. The return trip from Belize departs Fridays at 9:30am from Placencia and 10:30am from Big Creek.

Note that it may be cheaper and easier for you to get to Belize via the Guatemalan port of Puerto Barrios.

BUS

Buses for San Pedro Sula (L76, one hour, every 15 minutes until 5:30pm) leave from a **terminal** on 4a Av between 3a and 4a Calles. Buses for the Guatemalan border at Corinto leave roughly hourly (L65 to L90, two hours) via Omoa (L25, 30 minutes).

Tela

POP 99,290

Many people pass through Tela or even stay a night or two to visit the fantastic Lancetilla Botanical Garden, the largest botanical garden in the Americas. The two nearby nature reserves – Jeannette Kawas and Punta Izopo – are both wonderful excursions as well, and within easy striking distance of town.

Tela itself is a run-down urban resort whose beaches are, sadly, full of trash and in many places simply unsafe even during daytime. Its town center is loud, busy, paint-chipped and definitely not safe after dark, while its hotels and restaurants are overpriced.

Tela is crammed with Honduran vacationers during Semana Santa (Holy Week before Easter), and often on weekends, but the rest of the time things are pretty *tranquilo*.

Sights & Activites

The main attraction of Tela itself is its **beaches**, which stretch for miles around the bay. Most are littered, but west of town in front of Hotel Villas Telamar there's a pale, powdery stretch that is kept impeccably clean. Beach beds can be rented by nonguests, but only when occupancy is low at the resort. Beaches further afield, while much cleaner, can be risky to visit.

Garífuna Tours BOATING
(☎2448-1069; www.garifunatours.com; 9a Calle NE, at 5a Ave NE) A professional, established agency that offers tours, including full-day boat excursions to Parque Nacional Jeannette Kawas (L925), full-day kayaking in Punta Izopo (L850) and trips to Cayos Cochinos (L1375). There's also an excellent tour to the various Garifuna villages, including a visit to Lancetilla Botanical Gardens (L1375). Tours require a minimum of six people and fill easily on weekends.

Sleeping & Eating

Hotel Bertha PENSION $
(☎2448-3020; 2a Av NE & 7a Calle NE; r with fan/air-con from L450/700; ❄) A classic old-school *pensión* in a quiet location. What's great about this place is that the friendly family owners aren't doing anything fancy, but provide very decent, small, clean rooms, all with en suite bathrooms (cold water), at affordable prices. Don't expect a particularly warm welcome, though. It's a five-minute walk inland from the beach.

★Maya Vista Hotel y Restaurante HOTEL $$
(☎2448-1497; www.mayavista.com; 8a Calle NE, btwn 9a & 10a Av NE; s/d/tr from L1450/1650/2180; ❄📶≋) Easily the best place to stay in Tela, this architecturally interesting place on a hilltop in the middle of town has a fine selection of rooms with tasteful decor, many of which enjoy sweeping views over Tela and the sea, with spectacular sunsets. There is also a fantastic, though pricey, restaurant on-site (mains L160 to L595), which specializes in seafood.

Auto Pollo Al Carbón FAST FOOD $
(11a Calle NE, at 2a Av NE; chicken L43-185; ⏲7am-11pm) Roast chicken served under a corrugated-iron roof in a down-home, red-and-white-painted open-air shack, a wishbone's throw away from the Caribbean. You can grab a quarter-chicken and a salad here for just L58.

Luces del Norte SEAFOOD $$
(cnr 11a Calle NE & 5a Av NE; mains L190-395; ⏲7am-9pm; 📶) Settle in to the homey and colorful wooden Caribbean-style premises to enjoy locally renowned seafood (the paella is particularly noteworthy). It also serves up a variety of pasta dishes, omelets and filling breakfasts.

★César Mariscos Restaurante SEAFOOD $$$
(Calle Peotonal frente al mar; mains L290-404) This is the Honduran favorite, and a reason many city folk come to Tela. Combine grilled lobster sold by weight and dripping with garlic butter with a perfect people-watching spot right on the beach. Other specialties include conch soup and coconut breaded shrimp; dishes come with homemade, hot and crispy coconut bread and an outrageous chunky hot sauce. Very splurge-worthy.

Information

There are plenty of ATMs in the center of Tela. One reliable one is **Banco de Occidente** (Parque Central; ⏲8am-5:30pm Mon-Fri, 8:30am-1pm Sat).

Fundación Prolansate (☎2448-2042; www.prolansate.org; cnr 7a Av & 8a Calle NE; ⊙8am-5:30pm Mon-Thu, to 4:30pm Fri) Promotes sustainable tourism in Tela and has information on Lancetilla Botanical Gardens and Punta Sal (in the Parque Nacional Jeannette Kawas).

Post Office (4a Av NE; ⊙8am-4pm Mon-Fri, 8am-noon Sat)

Tourist Police (☎9713-6731; cnr 11a Calle NE & 4a Av NE; ⊙24hr)

DANGERS & ANNOYANCES

Tela is a poor city and not a safe place after dark. Avoid walking any distance at night, particularly anywhere poorly lit or along the beach.

Don't take anything of value to the beach. During the day, also avoid walking alone beyond the Hotel Villas Telamar Resort on the western end of the beach and the La Ensenada Beach Resort pier on the eastern end.

Getting There & Around

Slow **'chicken' buses** (cnr 9a Calle NE & 9a Av NE) leave Tela every 20 minutes for La Ceiba (L50, 2½ hours, 4am to 6pm) from the long-distance terminal at the corner of 9a Calle NE and 9a Av NE. For quicker direct buses, take a taxi to the gas station on the highway, from where **buses** to La Ceiba (L80) and San Pedro Sula (L92) depart regularly.

Transportes Tela Express (2a Av NE) operates nine daily direct buses (seven on Sunday) to San Pedro Sula (L90, two hours) from its terminal. **Hedman Alas** (☎2448-3075; Aleros Gas Station; ⊙8am-5pm) has a daily connection to San Pedro Sula (L165, two hours) and also to La Ceiba (L195, two hours).

Local **buses** (cnr 11a Calle & 8a Av) to the Garifuna villages near Tela depart from a dirt lot on the corner of 11a Calle and 8a Av.

Tela has many taxis; a ride in town costs L25. A taxi to Triunfo de la Cruz, La Ensenada or Tornabé is around L120 to L150.

Around Tela

The region surrounding the town of Tela is a fascinatingly diverse place. Within a relatively small area you'll find some great beaches, several nature reserves, thriving Garifuna villages and one of the world's largest botanical gardens.

Sights

Parque Nacional Jeannette Kawas NATIONAL PARK

(L160) This national park a half-hour boat ride from Tela has several white-sand beaches, including the pretty **Playa Cocalito**. Offshore coral reefs make for reasonable **snorkeling**, and howler monkeys, boa constrictors, toucans and very shy jaguars live in the forest. You can arrange day trips, which include **hiking**, snorkeling and hanging out on the beach. Tela's travel agencies run tours here.

Refugio de Vida Punta Izopo WILDLIFE RESERVE

(L90) Rivers entering the Punta Izopo Wildlife Refuge spread out into a network of canals that channel through the tangle of mangrove forest. Monkeys, turtles and even crocodiles live here, as well as many species of birds. Gliding silently through the mangrove canals, you can often get close to many forms of wildlife.

Garifuna Villages

Several idyllic villages populated by the Garifuna are within easy reach of Tela. Each has rustic (sometimes stilted) houses right on the beach, with fishing canoes resting on the sand and the azure waters of the Caribbean lapping against the shore.

The closest village is attractive little **La Ensenada**, 3km east along the arc of the beach from Tela, just before you reach the point. There are a few basic places to stay, but seafood restaurants in La Ensenada tend to only open on the weekend. The next town northeast is larger **El Triunfo de la Cruz**, the most developed of the Garifuna villages; it lacks the peaceful ambience of the other settlements. West of Tela, it's 8km to **Tornabé**, a large Garifuna settlement where you can set up boat tours. Past Tornabé, the beach road continues for several more kilometers to **Miami**, a beautiful village of *palapa*-roofed (thatched) huts on a narrow sandbar; it's the most traditional and least changed of the villages on this strip. Boats can be hired here (L2200 for up to seven people) for trips into Parque Nacional Jeannette Kawas.

Sleeping

Coco Cabañas CABAÑAS $

(☎3335-4599; www.hotelcaraibe.com; Triunfo de la Cruz; cabañas L500; 📶) These very rustic, double-occupancy cabins on the beach are built out of recycled bottles, bamboo and other eco-friendly materials. The owner is lovely, there are mosquito nets on the beds, hot-water bathrooms, kitchenettes and you have waves lapping right out the door. Breakfast is available and you can organize local tours here.

Getting There & Away

Buses to the Garifuna villages depart from the local bus terminal in Tela. There are two routes: one heading west to Tornabé; the other heading east to El Triunfo de la Cruz. Buses on both routes depart hourly from around 7am to 5pm Monday to Saturday; the fare ranges from L15 to L22, and journeys take about 30 to 45 minutes to reach the villages. You can also take a *colectivo* taxi for around L50.

Lancetilla Jardín Botánico

One of the largest tropical gardens in the world, the **Lancetilla Botanical Garden & Research Center** (2408-7806; www.esnacifor.hn; L190; 7am-5pm) was founded by the United Fruit Company in 1926 and is still an active center for scientific study. The gardens are a delight to visit – a tropical wonderland of plant species from all corners of the globe. There are 636 species of Asiatic fruit trees, including many varieties of lycee, mango, durian, mangosteen and jackfruit. Trails are well marked.

Birdlife also thrives at Lancetilla – hundreds of species have been spotted. Each year on December 14 and 15 the Audubon Society conducts a 24-hour bird count; you can participate if you're here then. Migratory species are present from November to February.

There's a **visitors center** (2408-6715; 7am-4pm) where you can hire a guide (L150 per hour), though tours are only available in Spanish.

Accommodations are available on the site, with **cabins** (2408-6715; tw/cabin L545/760;) with three individual beds and private bathrooms. Book through the visitors center.

Getting There & Away

Lancetilla is 6km southwest of the center of Tela. A round-trip taxi ride will cost around L230.

La Ceiba

POP 204,140

La Ceiba is known as Honduras' good-time town: 'Tegucigalpa thinks, San Pedro Sula works and La Ceiba parties,' so the saying goes. Certainly this port city's buzzing nightlife makes it a mecca for fiesta-hungry Hondurans, though nearly all the action is over the estuary in Barrio La Isla, the city's *zona viva* (nightlife district). Elsewhere expect searing heat and punishing humidity (and take care after dark).

There's otherwise little of interest in Ceiba itself: local beaches are polluted and unsafe and the downtown has a crumbling, neglected air, although it's all lively and friendly. Despite this, most travelers will find themselves here at some point as Ceiba is the transportation hub for the Bay Islands, as well as a great base for exploring the Pico Bonito National Park, the idyllic Cayos Cochinos and the world-class white water on the Río Cangrejal.

Sights & Activities

Parque Swinford PLAZA

(Map p396; Av La República, btwn 7a & 8a Calles; 6am-6pm) FREE Parque Swinford is a lush, tropical botanical oasis in the heart of La Ceiba, complete with a restored train carriage from the area's railway heyday.

Tourist Options HIKING, DIVING

(Map p396; 9978-8868, 9982-7534; www.hondurastouristoptions.com; Av La República) This travel agency runs trips to Garifuna villages and day trips to Cayos Cochinos (from L1000 per person). It also runs diving trips, day trips to Trujillo and birdwatching tours.

Festivals & Events

Carnaval CULTURAL

(late May) The city reaches its good-time peak at Carnaval, when it's crammed with revelers. Saturday is the biggest day, with parades, costumes, music and celebrations in the streets.

Sleeping & Eating

Accommodations are fairly uninspiring in La Ceiba. Staying in the center is convenient, although it is eerily quiet at night (when you shouldn't walk the streets). There are far better options outside the city amid the tropical jungle by the Río Cangrejal.

There are some good eating options in La Ceiba, and you'll have the choice of great seafood pretty much everywhere you go. **La Línea**, a strip where La Ceiba's old railway runs on Av La República, is where you can find street food – including delicious *baleadas* (tortillas stuffed with refried beans and other fillings) – 24 hours a day.

La Ceiba

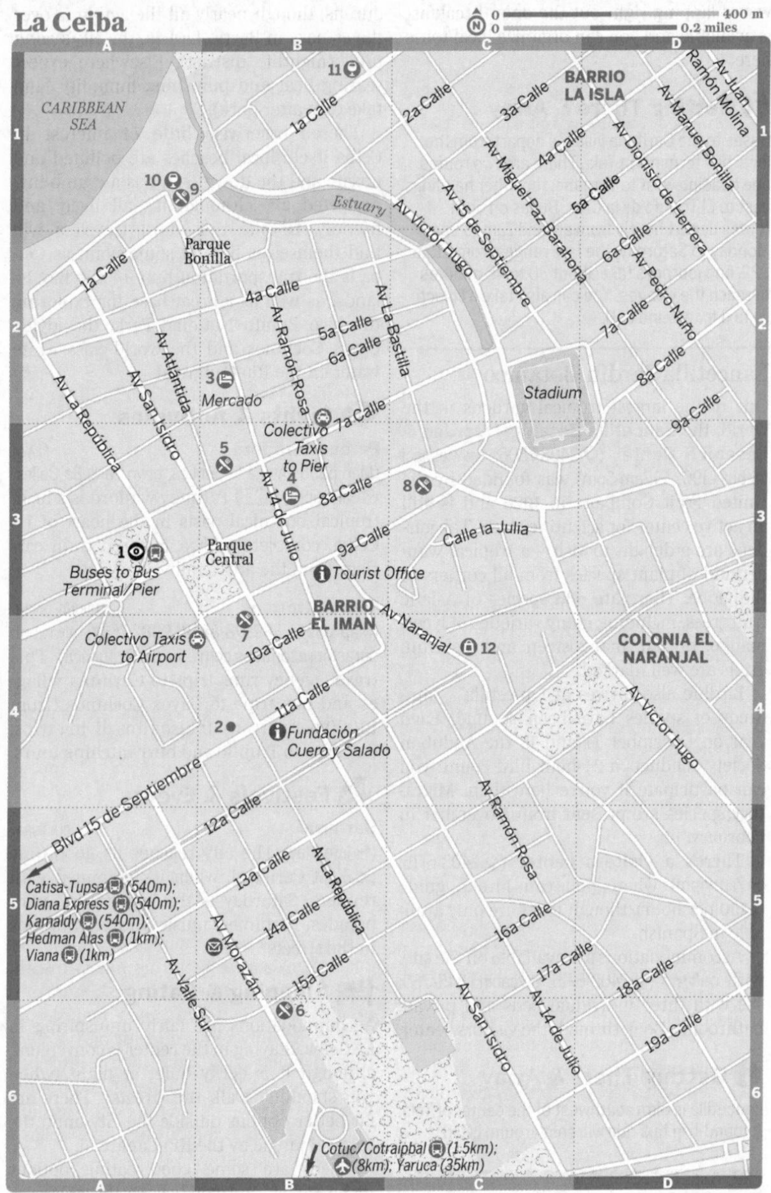

Guacamayos Backpackers HOSTEL $
(Map p396; ☎8763-1410; Av 14 de Julio; dm/r L195/350; ❄📶) This hostel is dingy, unsecure and basic, but functional, central and cheap. The common space is a few chairs around a small TV and a table with open bottles of whiskey and Coke. Dorms have three to four beds and rooms have private hot-water bathrooms.

Casa de Espana BOUTIQUE HOTEL $$
(Map p396; www.casadeespana.com; Av 14 de Julio; s/d/tw/q from L700/1300/1700/1900; ❄📶) This safe, clean and very well-located hotel

La Ceiba

is lovingly run by Carlos and Jennifer. Decorative and cozy touches from throw pillows to framed mirrors are everywhere and there's a fantastic rooftop restaurant/lounge area with a sea view, where hearty, large breakfasts are served and other meals can be ordered. Rooms are small but have good beds and linens.

Cobel HONDURAN $
(Map p396; 2 baleadas L35) A great stop for cheap, filling and delicious *baleadas* in clean surroundings and in the heart of town.

Jugos Chapala JUICE BAR $
(Map p396; Av San Isidro; drinks around L35; 7:30am-7pm) This terrific juice bar has an incredible choice of juices and shakes, including a bunch of fruits you'll have never even heard of. Each drink can come with myriad extras (including oats, cornflakes and fiber). It's a godsend if you're feeling fruit and vegetable deprived. Price depends on ingredients.

Pupusaría Universitaria HONDURAN $
(Map p396; 1a Calle, near Av 14 de Julio; pupusas L29, mains L130-175; 10am-10pm Sun-Fri) This excellent budget haunt inside a clapboard-and-bamboo building serves up big flavors at moderate rates, including *pupusas* (cornmeal mass stuffed with cheese, crispy pork and/or refried beans), tacos and succulent *pinchos* (kebabs). It's popular with a young crowd of students, and the staff are friendly.

★Ki'boc Café HONDURAN, INTERNATIONAL $$
(Map p396; 4a Av, btwn 8a & 9a Calles; mains L50-138; 7am-7pm Mon-Fri, 8am-7pm Sat, 8am-noon Sun;) This friendly place is about as bohemian as Ceiba gets, with a civilized and artsy feel, welcoming staff and organic coffee. The filling breakfasts are the best in town and include delicious Honduras-style *chilaquiles,* fruit salad, French toast, omelets and several types of flan. There's a book exchange, a little terrace and an air-conditioned interior with paintings and mismatched decor.

★El Jardín de Susana HONDURAN $$$
(Map p396; 2440-0061; 15a Calle & Av Morazán; mains L250-340; 10am-2:30pm & 5-10pm Wed-Mon) Totally unsigned (look for the green house with tables in the courtyard), Susana's Garden cooks up a storm. Famous for its salad bar (yes, those are fresh vegetables – you are not hallucinating), this might be the only place to serve zucchini in Honduras. The salad bar costs from just L140. Mains are meaty or full of fresh seafood, and delicious.

Drinking & Nightlife

★La Casa del Jaguar BAR
(Map p396; off 1a Calle; 5-11pm Mon-Sat) This is one of Ceiba's more interesting drinking establishments, a curious, enclosed beach bar with a tree-house feel and lots of nooks, crannies and corners to get cozy in. It's famous locally for the owner's homemade liquors – he dubs it (with a wink) 'the only organic bar in Honduras.' The crowd is bohemian and parties on the weekend go late.

La Palapa BAR, CLUB
(Map p396; Av 15 de Septiembre; 11am-11pm Sun-Wed, to 2am Thu-Sat) This huge, upscale, two-story, thatched-roof bar-restaurant just off the beach is a *zona viva* mainstay. It draws a wealthy and hedonistic party crowd, though many come here for the excellent seafood as much as to dance it all off afterward. Of the two dance floors, the upstairs one is free, while the downstairs one has a varying cover charge.

Shopping

Souvenirs El Buen Amigo ARTS & CRAFTS
(Map p396; Av Naranjal s/n, Barrio El Iman; 8am-6:30pm Mon-Sat) This small family-run place sells Honduran *artesanías* (handicrafts), including Lencan pottery, wood carvings and hammocks. It's a good spot to pick up souvenirs.

Information

There are several ATMs in the city center and around, including **Banco Atlántida** (Av San Isidro; ⏲9am-noon & 1-5pm Mon-Fri).

Tour companies are your best bet for booking travel services, though La Ceiba's **Tourist Office** (Map p396; ☎2440-3044; 9a Calle; ⏲8am-4:30pm Mon-Fri) tries to be helpful (no English is spoken). There's also an excellent tourism website at www.visitalaceiba.com.

Hospital Eurohonduras (☎2440-0927; Av Atlántida; ⏲24hr) Between 1a Calle and the beach.

Immigration Office (☎2442-0638; 1a Calle, cnr Av 14 de Julio; ⏲7:30am-3:30pm Mon-Fri) Can extend entry stamps and visas.

Post Office (Map p396; cnr Av Morazán & 14a Calle; ⏲8am-4pm Mon-Fri, 8am-noon Sat)

Tourist Police (☎2441-0860; Residencial El Toronjal; ⏲24hr) Three blocks south of Carretera a Tela.

Getting There & Away

AIR

La Ceiba's **Aeropuerto Golosón** (LCE) is 10km west of La Ceiba, on the highway to Tela. Flights leave frequently for San Pedro Sula, Tegucigalpa, the Bay Islands and the Moskitia.

AeroCaribe (☎3364-7688, 2442-1088; www.aerocaribehn.com; 13a Calle) Flies to Guanaja and several destinations in the Moskitia, including Puerto Lempira and Brus Laguna.

Aerolíneas Sosa (☎2443-1399, airport 2440-0692; www.aerolineassosa.com; Av San Isidro, btwn 8a & 9a Calles) Regular connections to Roatán, Utila and Puerto Lempira.

Lanhsa (☎2442-1283; www.lanhsa.com; Airport) Connects Ceiba with Roatán, Guanaja, Puerto Lempira and Tegucigalpa.

BOAT

Ferries to the Bay Islands operate from the **Muelle de Cabotaje** pier, about 8km east of town. From the bus terminal or from town, taxis charge about L100. A **colectivo** (Map p396) will cost L25 and goes from the town center from 7a Calle; there's no *colectivo* on the way back. To get to the ferry pier from the center of La Ceiba, take a bus from Av La República.

The modern, comfortable **Galaxy Wave** (☎2445-1775; www.roatanferry.com) sails twice daily to Roatán (L900, 1¼ hours). To Utila, the modern **Utila Dream** (☎9450-8133; www.utilaferry.com; Muelle de Cabotaje; one way L200; ⏲9:30am & 4pm daily) leaves twice daily for Utila (L600) and takes 45 minutes.

Sea sickness can affect passengers on all the above services, especially if the sea is rough – plan accordingly as bags are not provided.

BUS

The main bus terminal is at **Mercado San José**, about 1.5km west of central La Ceiba. Local

BUSES FROM LA CEIBA

DESTINATION	COST (L)	DURATION (HR)	BUS LINE	FREQUENCY
Antigua (Guatemala)	1285	11	Hedman Alas	2 daily
Copán Ruinas	731	7	Hedman Alas	2 daily
La Unión-Cuero y Salado	33	1½	Main Terminal	every 45min Mon-Sat, hourly Sun
Lago de Yojoa	500	5	Hedman Alas	4 daily
Sambo Creek/Corazal	20	1	Main Terminal	every 35min
San Pedro Sula	150	3½	Diana Express	6 daily
	138	3½	Catisa-Tupsa	hourly 5am-6pm
	300	3	Hedman Alas	3 daily (via San Pedro Sula airport)
	420	3	Viana	4 daily
Tegucigalpa	265	7	Kamaldy	4 daily
	710	6½	Viana	4 daily
	537	6½	Hedman Alas	2 daily
Tela	72	2	Kamaldy	4 daily
	54	2	Main Terminal	every 25min
Trujillo	160	3	Cotuc/Cotraipbal	hourly
Yaruca/Río Cangrejal	25	½	Main Terminal	5 daily, or any Las Mangas bus

buses run between this terminal and the central plaza (L9), or you can take a *colectivo* taxi (L20). Buses marked 'Terminal' head to the station from the **bus stop** (Map p396) at Av La República between 7a Calle and 8a Calle.

La Ceiba is a big transportation hub, and there are even services connecting Ceiba to Antigua in Guatemala, as well as shuttles to/from Copán Ruinas. Most non-luxury buses use the main terminal – **Diana Express** (☎2509-4886; www.transportedianaexpress.jimdo.com), **Catisa-Tupsa** (☎2441-2539) and **Kamaldy** (☎2441-2028; www.transporteskamaldy.com) all have offices there – but there are some exceptions. The **Viana** (☎2441-2230; www.vianatransportes.com; Blvr 15 de Septiembre) bus terminal is another 500m further west along the same road; you'll find **Hedman Alas** (☎2441-5347; www.hedmanalas.com) across the street. **Cotuc/Cotraipbal** (☎2441-2199) buses for Trujillo leave from terminals on Carretera a Tela.

Getting Around

There are numerous car rental agencies in La Ceiba. The airport is the best place to compare prices. Agencies include **Avis** (☎2441-2802; www.avis.com.hn; Airport) and **Econo Rent-A-Car** (☎2441-5079, 2441-5080; www.econorentacarhn.com; Airport; ⏲8am-5pm).

Colectivo taxis in La Ceiba charge a standard L25 per person, going up a bit after 8pm.

TO/FROM THE AIRPORT

Any non-express bus heading west from the main bus terminal in La Ceiba can drop you at the airport. **Colectivo taxis** (Map p396) from the Parque Central pass the airport (L25); you must wait for the taxi to fill up. A normal taxi costs around L200.

Taxis in the official rank outside the airport charge about L200 to La Ceiba; if you go to the main road and flag down a *colectivo* it's L25 per person.

Around La Ceiba

The area around La Ceiba is a knockout, and by far the best reason to visit the city. Indeed, many travelers prefer to stay in the surrounding areas rather than in La Ceiba proper, all the better to enjoy the Parque Nacional Pico Bonito, the stunning Río Cangrejal, the beautiful beaches of Cayos Cochinos or the wildlife of Refugio de Vida Silvestre Cuero y Salado.

Río Cangrejal

Surging through the jungle, the turquoise Río Cangrejal is rightly renowned as Central America's premier rafting experience. Even if you've zero intention of dipping an oar in its foaming waters, the region makes a stunning base for all manner of adventure sports, birdwatching or just chilling by the river. The scenery is spectacular, the air is mountain-fresh and there are some excellent places to stay strung out along the riverside.

Activities

Most visitors are here to raft or kayak the Cangrejal, but there's also mountain biking, horseback riding, swimming and great rainforest hiking. You can book with the lodge you're staying at, or with a travel agency in La Ceiba.

Hiking

Just uphill from the Jungle River Lodge, right by the visitors center (p400), a rope bridge extends over the Cangrejal to the other side of the river, allowing hiking access into the heart of Parque Nacional Pico Bonito. Omega Lodge (p400) also has several well-marked trails on its grounds.

★Omega Tours ADVENTURE
(☎9745-6810, 9631-0295; www.omegatours.info; Omega Lodge) Set up by a former international kayaker, Omega offers professionally run white-water rafting (from L1400 including lunch), kayak and canoe trips, horseback riding, mountain biking, and jungle- and river-hiking tours. All trips include a free night at its jungle lodge.

Guaruma Servicios HIKING
(☎2442-2673; www.guaruma.org; hiking guides per day incl park entrance fee L360-525) A worthwhile operation dedicated to boosting opportunities for the local community through sustainable tourism. It's based at the small village of Las Mangas in Río Cangrejal.

Horseback Riding

Horseback riding is offered at Omega Lodge (p400) for L1500 per half day. All the horses live at the lodge and are very well cared for.

White-Water Rafting

The Río Cangrejal offers superb white-water rafting. The scenery is immense, with the river coursing through rainforest that's part of the Parque Nacional Pico Bonito. You've a good chance of seeing herons, kingfishers and toucans.

There are two main sections of the Cangrejal: the upper part is hard-core, offering real Class IV and V thrills, rapids and speed. After very heavy rain it may not be possible to raft here. The lower section offers year-round Class III rafting, with the river surging around giant boulders.

Whichever section you choose, you'll need an experienced, competent guide – accidents have occurred in the upper section of the Cangrejal after heavy rainfall, when conditions can be particularly treacherous. Always check out the situation first with your tour operator (you can book through your lodge).

La Moskitia Ecoaventuras RAFTING
(www.lamoskitia.hn; half-day rafting tours L1075) Eco-minded Jorge Salaverri was a pioneer of rafting the Rio Cangrejal and he's still going strong, with his sons often leading tours. He's also one of the few and probably most knowlegable guides to the Moskitia region (he's originally from just across the border of Puerto Lempira in Nicaragua) and can lead tours or help you visit independently.

Jungle River Tours ADVENTURE
(2416-5009, 9681-6466; www.jungleriverlodge.com) This agency organizes white-water rafting, mountain biking, canopy tours on a questionably maintained zip line, hiking tours and other trips.

Sleeping & Eating

La Moskitia Adventuras Lodge LODGE $
(2441-3279; www.lamoskitia.hn; road to Yaruca Km 9; tents L250;) A very basic riverside lodge with a stunning position overlooking the roaring Cangrejal – you'll be mesmerized by the view. Accommodations are in sturdy army tents with real beds. Meals can sometimes be made on request, or you can use the kitchen or walk to nearby Omega Lodge to eat. Dorms are planned for the future. It's very rafting oriented.

Jungle River Lodge LODGE $
(9681-6466, 2416-5009; www.jungleriverlodge.com; road to Yaruca Km 7; dm/d/tr from L250/750/850, meals from L120;) It's haphazardly run, but Jungle River Lodge is perched on a ledge with a magnificent perspective of the Río Cangrejal valley – the outdoor bar-restaurant here has one of Honduras' greatest vistas. New dorms are tiled and clean (skip the dark older dorms at the same price), while woodsy rooms are screened in with mosquito nets and have private hot-water bathrooms.

★ **Omega Lodge** LODGE $$
(9631-0295; www.omegatours.info; incl breakfast s/d from L1550/1900, s/d cabins from L840/1200, camping per person L240;) A beautifully conceived and constructed ecolodge, Omega is surrounded by thick jungle, which means it doesn't have views. But it *is* very thoughtfully conceived: solar power, a chemical-free pool and ecofriendly waste-management are all at the heart of the lodge's philosophy. The owners are experts of rafting on the Río Cangrejal and offer many excellent trips. Food is outstanding, with plentiful vegetarian choices.

★ **La Villa de Soledad** B&B $$$
(9967-4548; www.lavilladesoledad.com; d incl breakfast L1550-2630;) Imagine a modern Italian villa with cathedral ceilings, add some Mexican touches including a few hammocks and put it all in the middle of a peaceful, verdant jungle chirping with birdsong. Yes it's a splurge, but your lempira goes a long way at this sumptuous, impeccably run place that quickly feels like home.

Getting There & Away

Most lodges here will arrange for transport from La Ceiba, including pick-ups at the airport, bus station or the Muelle de Cabotaje (the ferry pier). As all the lodges are on the main road, you can also get on a bus to Yaruca or Las Mangas (L25, 30 minutes) at the main terminal in La Ceiba.

Parque Nacional Pico Bonito

Looming over La Ceiba, the densely forested mountain of Pico Bonito forms one of Honduras' best-known national parks (entrance fee L190). It harbors some abundant wildlife, including jaguars, armadillos and monkeys.

There are two entrances. Most people go through the Río Cangrejal entrance, where there's a **visitors center** (10km down road to Yaruca; 7am-4pm) next to a suspension bridge over the roaring river (L40 to access for photos). Conveniently, it's on the same road as the Río Cangrejal river lodges. From the visitors center there's a lovely trail (24 km or four hours round-trip) through lush mountainside forest to **El Bejuco waterfall**.

The second park entrance is in the village of El Pino about 15km west of La Ceiba on the highway to Tela. You'll need to prearrange guides in La Ceiba for the moderately difficult three-hour hike to **Cascada Zacate** (L190 per person incl park entrance fee) waterfall (17km one way). If you want to stay here you'll find rustic cabins at the **Centro Ecoturístico Natural View** (☎3302-2456; r L600; ❄☒).

Getting There & Away

Any bus headed toward Tela or San Pedro Sula can drop you at El Pino (L23, 30 minutes). To get to the Río Cangrejal side, jump on a bus to Yaruca or Las Mangas (L25, 30 minutes) at the main terminal in La Ceiba.

Cayos Cochinos

White sands that look like a hallucination are lapped by equally astounding blue water. The phenomenally beautiful Cayos Cochinos (Hog Islands), just 17km from the mainland, can easily be visited as a day trip from the La Ceiba region and are one of the most beautiful places in all of Honduras. Access is by motorized canoe from Nueva Armenia or Sambo Creek, east of La Ceiba.

The two Hog Islands, the 13 tiny coral cays and the seas around them comprise a marine reserve – it's illegal to anchor on the reef, and commercial fishing is prohibited. Consequently, the reefs are pristine and the fish abundant. Diving and snorkeling are excellent around the islands, with black coral reefs, wall diving, cave diving, seamounts and a plane wreck. The islands are also known for their unique pink boa constrictors and the strength of the local Garifuna culture.

Sleeping & Eating

Most people visit Cayos Cochinos for the day, but if you want to play Robinson Crusoe there are *extremely* rustic *cabañas* (L150 to L500) with sand floors and damp, saggy beds, available on Chachauate Cay; ask around on the beach. There are also two comfortable, modern cabins with private bathrooms at **Laru Beya** (☎9489-6058; www.facebook.com/CayosCochinosHonduras; dm L280) at the east end of the main island. Other options around these islands are upscale dive resorts.

Day-trip packages will include either a picnic lunch or a BBQ on the beach, and if you stay over on Chachauate Caye, your host will cook meals for you for (L80 to L200 per meal). There aren't many other eating options save a few shacks selling fish and seafood, or the restaurant at Laru Beya.

Getting There & Away

Access to Cayos Cochinos is by motorized canoe from Nueva Armenia or Sambo Creek, east of La Ceiba. It's possible to go independently to the cays, although you won't save much money, and local boat operators are unlikely to have a radio or life jackets.

Lots of La Ceiba tour operators offer tours to the cays: this is the best way to visit. Agencies charge around L1000 per person (minimum six people) for a full-day trip. You can also visit on a day trip from Roatán, but expect to pay at least triple the price.

Sambo Creek

Some 21km east of La Ceiba, Sambo Creek is a thriving Garifuna fishing village. It's a slightly scruffy but fascinating place where you'll see women in striking attire and traditional headdresses. A *punta* (traditional Garifuna dance) party is never far away. The beach is a lovely stretch of sand, which most of the year is pretty clean, though trash washes up after storms.

Activities

Sambo Creek Canopy Tour & Spa ADVENTURE

(☎3355-5481; spa incl transportation to/from La Ceiba L1000) Sambo Creek Canopy Tour has an absolutely gorgeous spring-fed hot waterfall river complete with several bathing pools that get cooler the further you walk downstream. Included is a body and face smear of local mud to draw out toxins and an outdoor full-body massage. It's especially nice after tackling the adrenaline-charged 18-zip-line canopy cruise (add L500).

Sleeping & Eating

Centro Turístico Sambo Creek PENSION $

(☎9587-0874; mauricioelvir@yahoo.com; per person with/without air-con L360/215; ❄📶) Run by the La Ceiba–based travel agency Tourist Options, this cheap place right on the beach is a great place to lay your head in Sambo Creek if your budget is tight.

Villa Helen's GUESTHOUSE $$

(☎2408-1137; www.villahelens.com; r L957-1075, cabins from L1200; ❄📶☒) The best deal in town, this hotel boasts a tropical bar and restaurant as well as gorgeous gardens and a decent pool. The rooms are fairly basic, but come with hot-water bathrooms and small refrigerators. There are also seven cabins, most of which come with living rooms and kitchens.

Kay's Place HONDURAN **$$**
(meals L145-600; ⌚9:30am-10pm) This breezy top-floor, beachside restaurant has fantastic views over the beach and does good fish, seafood and meat grills, as well as beach-bum-worthy cocktails. There's often live Garifuna music here and the owner has a warm smile for everyone.

ℹ Getting There & Away

Colectivo taxis (L30, 40 minutes) leave when there are four people from Ave San Isidro and 4a Calle in La Ceiba. Buses from La Ceiba's main bus terminal to Sambo Creek (L20, one hour) leave every 30 minutes throughout the day.

Refugio de Vida Silvestre Cuero y Salado

On the coast about 30km west of La Ceiba, this wetland reserve protects varied and abundant wildlife: manatees are the most famous (and the hardest to see), but there are also howler and white-faced monkeys, sloths, agoutis (rabbit-sized rodents), iguanas, caimans and around 200 bird species.

The small town of **La Unión** is the gateway to Cuero y Salado. From there, you catch a train to a visitors center, where a L250 entrance fee is collected and tours can be organized. Two-hour guided **canoe tours** (L200 for two people, plus L250 per guide) are by far the best way to explore the reserve.

For further information, contact **Fundación Cuero y Salado** (FUCSA; Map p396; ☎2443-0117; 11a Calle, btwn Avs San Isidro & Av La República; ⌚8am-5pm Mon-Fri, 8-11am Sat) in La Ceiba.

ℹ Getting There & Away

To get to the reserve, take a bus to La Unión from La Ceiba's main terminal (L33, 1½ hours, every 45 minutes). From La Unión, jump on the *trencito* (railcar) for the 9.5km ride (L260, hourly 7am to 2pm) on an old banana railroad to the visitors center. The last railcar returns from the visitors center at 2:30pm; the final bus from La Unión to La Ceiba is at 4pm.

Alternatively, book a tour with a travel agency in La Ceiba, which will cost nearly the same and save you a lot of trouble.

Trujillo

POP 62,560

Isolated, plucky Trujillo is the end of the line for the Honduran mainland: beyond it lies the virtually roadless jungle of the Moskitia, so there's a frontier-town vibe about the place. The town's setting is magnificent, with soaring mountains in the distance and the wide arc of the Bahía de Trujillo – a brilliant blue expanse of water that has seen the sails of Columbus and many a famous buccaneer – spread out before it. Trujillo boasts some interesting history, excellent nearby beaches and a slow-moving Caribbean air you won't find anywhere else on Honduras' northern coastline.

For years the town has been talked up as Honduras' next big tourism thing. Every so often the town is swamped by cruise travelers, and the weekends see tons of Honduran visitors, but thankfully the rest of the time things carry on as they always have done in this delightful, semi-forgotten place.

◉ Sights

You can sense the town's tumultuous history during a quick stroll around Trujillo's historical core. Many fine Caribbean-style wooden houses remain around the Parque Central, and of course there's the fascinating old fort, which offers sweeping views over the bay.

Trujillo also has a lovely shoreline, though trash sometimes washes up on its beaches. The best beaches are a few kilometers west of town. Just off the coast, 2km east of Casa Kiwi on the road to Puerto Castillo, is the wreck of a sunken ship that's good for **snorkeling**; close to the shore, it's easily accessible from the beach.

Around 5km east of Trujillo, **Laguna de Guaimoreto** functions as a wildlife refuge and has a complex system of canals and mangrove forests that provide shelter to abundant bird, plant and animal life (including the elusive manatee). Thousands of migratory birds refuel here between November and February. You can hire rowing boats or canoes (and even someone to paddle for you) by the old bridge between Trujillo and Puerto Castillo. Expect to pay around L3000 for a two-hour excursion.

The nearby, friendly and traditional Garifuna villages of Santa Fe, San Antonio and Guadeloupe are a short bus ride away.

Trujillo

Top Sights

Sleeping

Eating

★Fortaleza Santa Bárbara de Trujillo FORT

(Map p403; L69; ⏲9am-5pm) High above the waves, gazing over the Caribbean toward the European motherland, this 17th-century Spanish fortress could not have a more evocative position. Though its ruined remains are not that impressive visually, it's still an inspirational spot to reflect on the forces and characters that shaped the history of the North American continent.

Grave of William Walker CEMETERY

Just west of town, where the Río Cristales flows into the sea, is the ancient and fascinating town cemetery. Here lies the grave of William Walker, who died in Trujillo shortly after his ill-fated bid to conquer Central America.

Sleeping & Eating

Hotel Emperador PENSION $

(Map p403; ☎2434-4446; r with/without air-con L600/300; ❄📶) This central hotel has 10 basic but cute, clean and homey rooms to the side of a remarkable Caribbean building, which dates back to 1787. It's run by a busy, large and friendly family. Check out the time-warp atmosphere in the adjoining cafe while you're here.

★Tranquility Bay CABAÑAS $$$

(☎9928-2095; www.tranquilitybayhonduras.com; apartments/cabañas from L1890/2130; ❄📶) This fantastic place is definitely a splurge, but it's well worth it: spacious, attractive and clean wooden cabins sleeping up to four people each face the best beach in Trujillo and are surrounded by luscious gardens. Apartments and town houses are closer to town. There's a restaurant here, and a menagerie, including a rescued capuchin and a white-faced monkey.

Du Monde Cafe y Te CAFE $

(Map p403; light meals L70-80) A wonderful little find, this classy, cozy cafe has indoor or outdoor seating overlooking the street and the best coffee in town. Small meals like nachos with chili or grilled cheese sandwiches are also available alongside tempting baked goods.

Café & Sabores HONDURAN $

(Map p403; Calle Principal; baleadas L12-30, mains L80-120; ⏲6am-9pm Mon-Sat, to 1pm Sun; ❄📶) This agreeable diner-like cafe is a good spot for breakfast and always has five or six set-lunch choices. Excellent *licuados* (fresh-fruit drinks) are refreshing, and its *baleadas* (thick flour tortillas stuffed with various fillings) are famous for good reason. There's an air-conditioned room at the rear.

Cafe Vino Tinto HONDURAN $$

(Map p403; mains L90-250, pizzas L160-300; ⏲noon-10pm; 📶) Just below the plaza, this atmospheric little restaurant serves up wonderful sea views, along with great wood-fired pizzas, quesadillas and fresh fish and seafood. Red wine is available by the glass (L60) and you may be lucky enough to meet English owner Jon, a passionate local historian and a mine of information about the town's history and the neighboring Moskitia.

Information

There are two ATMs in Trujillo, but it's a good idea to bring extra cash in case they aren't working.

Banco Atlántida (Parque Central; ⏰8am-4:30pm Mon-Fri, 8:30am-noon Sat) Has a 24-hour ATM.

Banco Occidente (2a Calle & Calle Principal; ⏰8am-noon & 1:30pm-5pm Mon-Fri)

Police (☎2434-4054; Parque Central)

Post Office (Map p403; 4a Calle; ⏰8am-4pm Mon-Fri, 8-11am Sat)

Tourist Office (Map p403; ☎2434-3140; Parque Central; ⏰8am-4pm Mon-Fri) English-speaking staff can help you here.

Getting There & Away

Note that the highway between Trujillo and La Ceiba passes a notorious drug-smuggling route into the Moskitia. It's lined with many police checkpoints.

BOAT

A ferry from the **pier** connects Trujillo to Guanaja (L800, 1½ hours), one of the Bay Islands, but its timetable is rather vague. On days when it runs, it leaves Trujillo at around 1pm, though its frequency changes according to demand. At the time of research it was generally leaving at least every other day. In the other direction, the boat leaves Guanaja at around 8am, arriving in Trujillo by around 10am.

There are no scheduled departures to the Moskitia region from Trujillo, but fishing and cargo boats do sail there occasionally from the town's pier from July to February, so ask around.

BUS

Two bus companies, **Cotuc** (☎2444-2181) and **Cotraipbal** (☎2434-4932), operate from two small bus terminals 1km and 2km west of the Parque Central respectively, with direct (speedy) and ordinary services. There's another small terminal closer to town, where local chicken buses and the services through Olancho depart.

From the two terminals, buses leave for San Pedro Sula (L230, seven hours, eight daily) via La Ceiba (L160, three hours) and Tela (L200, five hours); most leave during the morning, with the last bus at 3pm. There are also three daily buses to Tegucigalpa (L360, 10 to 11 hours) from here.

Local buses (Map p403) go from a stop by the old cemetery to the Garifuna villages of Santa Fe, San Antonio and Guadalupe.

BAY ISLANDS

Spectacular diving and snorkeling draws visitors from around the world to the three Bay Islands (Islas de la Bahía) – Roatán, Utila and Guanaja – located between 25km and 50km off the north coast of Honduras. Their reefs are part of the second-largest barrier reef in the world, and teem with fish, coral, sponges, rays, sea turtles and even whale sharks.

Diving here is very affordable, but lodging and food on the islands can be more expensive than on the mainland. Low-key Utila is the fun, budget island (and very popular with backpackers), while Roatán is much, much bigger, has better beaches and is decidedly more sophisticated. Diving is also good on Guanaja, though costs are far higher here than the other two islands.

The rainy season here runs roughly from October or November to February. March and August are the hottest months; at other times sea breezes temper the heat.

Roatán

POP 69,500

Roatán is the largest and most developed of the Bay Islands. Long and thin (50km long, but only 2km to 4km wide), the island is (like neighboring Utila) a diving and snorkeling paradise – virtually its entire coastline is fringed by an astonishingly diverse coral reef teeming with tropical fish. On land, exquisite white-sand beaches like West Bay, a mountainous interior of pine-forested hills and the remote wild east of the island (once a pirate hangout) beg to be explored.

Roatán attracts a far more midrange crowd than Utila, and has fewer budget options. Nearly all backpackers base themselves in West End, where most of the shoestring places are located along with a lively and fun traveler's scene.

Gigantic cruise ships visit Roatán regularly, but dock at Coxen Hole or Mahogany Bay. You'll probably see minivans full of cruise-shippers around the island's hot spots during the day.

West End

Curled around two small turquoise bays and laced with coconut palms, West End is a chilled-out world apart where independent

Bay Islands

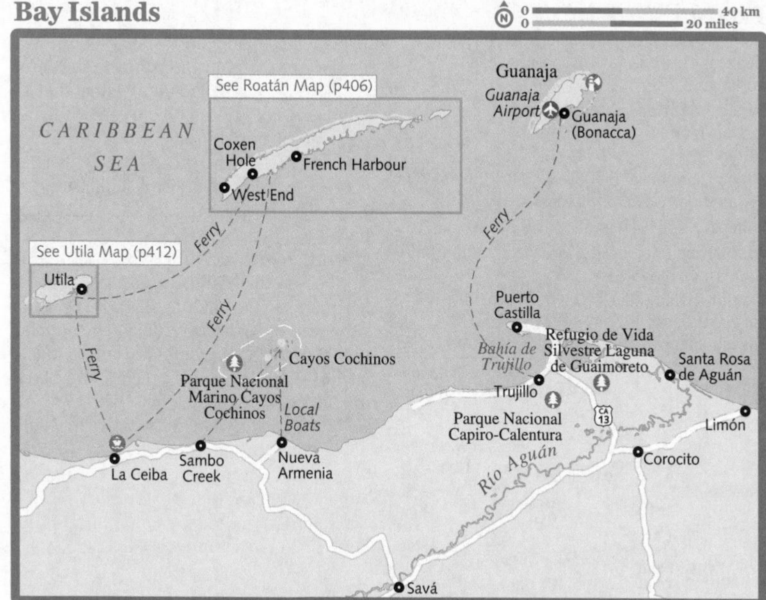

travelers – rather than package tourists – mingle, lounge, swim, party and, of course, go diving. Its quirky main street is lined with sea-facing restaurants, boutiques selling sarongs and jewelry, reggae bars and tons of dive schools. Everything you need is within walking distance.

Even though many accommodations and eating options are geared toward the midrange market, you'll find some great budget places here, plus there's a fun community of travelers to socialize with.

Sights & Activities

Roatán Marine Park MARINE RESERVE
(2445-4206; www.roatanmarinepark.com) Originally set up in 2005 with the aim of protecting the reef system around the West End and Sandy Bay, the Roatán Marine Park now covers the whole island. This nonprofit organization campaigns strongly to conserve the marine environment – Roatán's reefs are under enormous pressure, both from construction and the sheer amount of visitors. Four boats patrol the shoreline; people fishing illegally (using nets, harpoons or traps) have been jailed.

The park office rents out snorkeling equipment (L120 per day).

Beaches & Snorkeling

Half Moon Bay, which forms the northern part of the West End, is a lovely sandy bay with shallow, sheltered water. Swim out to the anchored **iSoar Fun Boat** FREE to swing on the super-fun rope swing. Snorkeling is OK along the south shore here, but nearby West Bay is far better.

Snorkeling equipment can be rented (L120 per day) from numerous places in West End: we suggest you go to the Marine Park office, as then your money will go toward helping to protect the reef.

Diving

Roatán is a diver's paradise with many wrecks, walls and cracks just minutes offshore. Prices are some of the lowest you'll find anywhere in the world and rival those on Utila. There is a slew of dive shops throughout the region, but a few of the top spots are **West End Divers** (9565-4465; www.westenddivers.com; dives from L830, open water course L7150), **Grand Bleu** (www.grandbleudiving.com; dives from L850, open water courses L8350), **Native Sons** (2445-4003; www.roatandivingnativesons.com; dives from L1300, open water course L6675) and **Roatán Divers** (9949-3781; www.roatandiver.com; dives from L1000, open water course L8950). Training and courses in **free diving** are also now available in West End.

Roatán

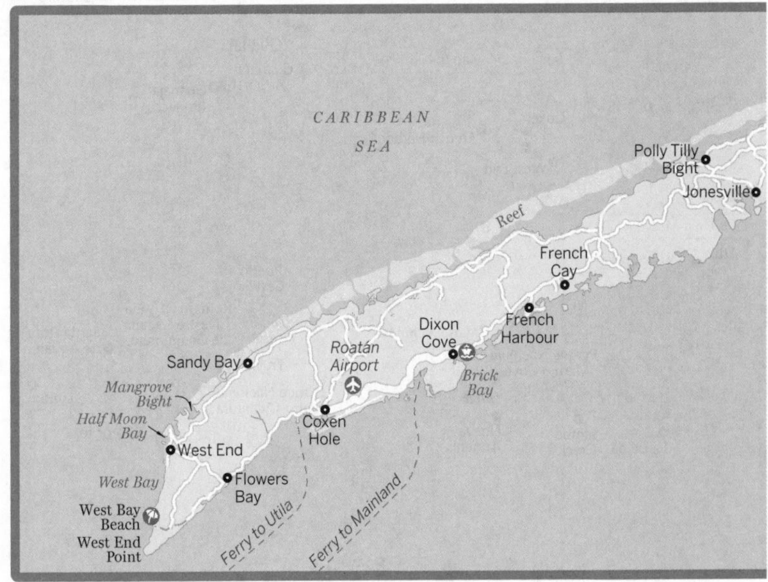

Deep-Sea Submarine

Roatán Institute of Deep Sea Exploration ADVENTURE
(☎3359-2887; www.stanleysubmarines.com; dives from L12,000) Karl Stanley takes passengers to depths of up to 300m, 450m or 600m in his small, yellow submarine. Since light doesn't penetrate to those depths, those who dare to take the ride can witness some extraordinary marine life, including elusive six-gilled sharks.

Horseback Riding

El Rancho Barrio Dorcas HORSEBACK RIDING
(☎9687-1067; www.barriodorcasranch.com; 2hr rides per person from L950) This well-organised outfit runs horseback rides along the beach and mangroves, or special night rides on full-moon nights.

Sleeping

There is a handful of budget choices for backpackers in West End. Some inexpensive places are linked to dive schools, so if you book a course you'll get a discounted room. Otherwise there are some fabulous boutique-style midrange options that can spill over into the top-end price range.

★Chillies HOSTEL $
(☎2445-4003; www.hotelchilliesroatan.com; Half Moon Bay; dm/d L300/600, cabin rooms from L700, private cabins from L950; 📶) The best backpacker choice for those tired of dorms, the rustic but pleasant cabins here spread back into a jungle-like garden – Half Moon Bay's beach is just across the street. Budget rooms and dorms are on the small side and have access to a communal kitchen. Two-bedroom cabins share a kitchen, while private cabins have their own kitchens.

★Buena Onda HOSTEL $
(☎9770-0158; www.hbuenaonda.com; dm L300, s with/without bathroom L650/500, d with/without bathroom L900/700; 📶) Run by a welcoming, worldly Spanish traveler, this excellent place is perfectly set up, with stylish dorms that have lovely bamboo beds, good mattresses, lockers and giant art canvases. The heart of the operation is a very social, open-plan kitchen and living room. Otherwise swing in a hammock on the rooftop terrace and expect to meet plenty of other travelers.

Georphi's Tropical Hideaway CABAÑAS $
(☎2445-4104; www.georphis.com; dm from L240, r with/without bathroom L800/600, cabins from L840; ❄📶) This sprawling collection of wooden cabins in dark, tree-shaded grounds

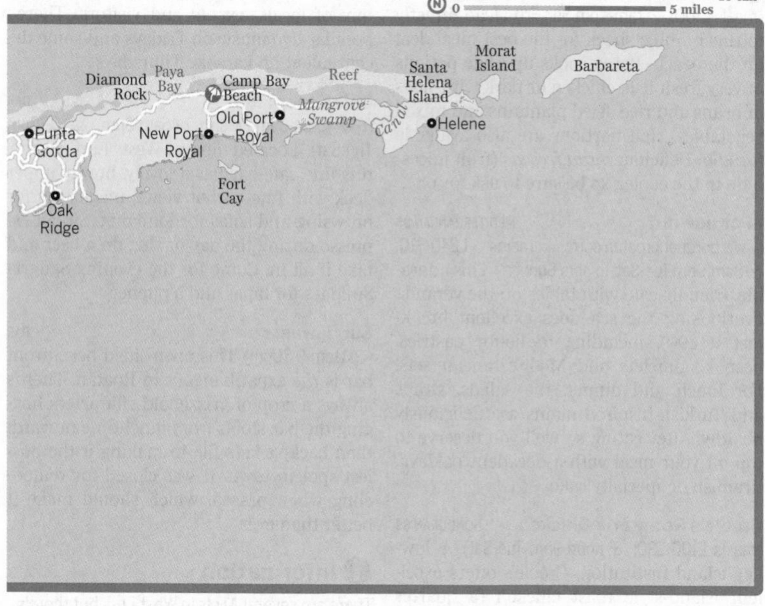

is in the middle of West End and moments from the sea. The screened cabins are sturdy (though basic) structures – some with kitchen – that all have a private patio with hammocks. Shared kitchens are minuscule but functional. It's great value, management is friendly and it's very popular.

Posada Arco Iris HOTEL **$$**

(☎2445-4264; www.hotelarcoirisroatan.com; s/d/tr with fan L1000/1150/1300, apt from L1580; ❄@📶) A fine choice in a shady setting behind Half Moon Bay, this Argentine-owned place has very well-presented rooms and apartments with kitchens, all brightened up with weavings and tribal art. You'll pay more for air-con and an ocean view, but for groups it can work out to be reasonably affordable. There is free kayak use for guests and there's an excellent on-site restaurant.

Posada Las Orquideas HOTEL **$$**

(☎2445-4387; www.posadalasorquideas.com; s/d with fan L860/1000, with kitchen L1150/1300; ❄@📶) This stylish, white-linen-draped and well-run place is at the very end of West End on the quiet and secluded peninsula overlooking the bay of Mangrove Bight. Rooms are smart and spacious, with those on the 3rd floor priced higher for their sea views. There's a jetty that's exclusively for guests, though the water here is brackish.

Land's End Resort HOTEL **$$**

(☎9979-9324; www.landsendroatan.com; r from L1400; ❄📶🏊) This aging hotel facing a spectacular ocean panorama has a few comfy, cheaper rooms that lack ocean views but are decent value. There's a concrete saltwater infinity pool, a bar-restaurant, reef access via a ladder into the sea and a giant, open-mouthed Great White shark statue; and it's all a 10-minute walk from the West End action.

Eating

Food in West End is surprisingly affordable if you skip the tourist-oriented restaurants. For the cheapest eats, look out for **baleada vendors** at various spots along the main strip: they serve up the wheat-flour tortillas at L20 to L45 per hit.

★**Tacos Raul** TACOS **$**

(tacos L45; ⏲7am-midnight Sun-Thu, to 2am Fri & Sat) This rustic outdoor stall fries up some of the best *el pastor* (pork) tacos in the country. Topped with *chimole* (chopped salsa), two make a large meal. The *gringas* (tortillas filled with melted cheese) are filled with delicious, fresh cheese imported from the mainland. Top everything with Raul's fiery homemade hot sauce and you have a meal to remember.

Keith's BBQ BARBECUE $
(meals L100; ⊙7am-4pm Sun-Fri) Head directly to this humble shack for the best meal deal on the beach. Reina cooks up huge potions of very fresh fish, chicken or pork with sides of beans and rice, fried plantains and mixed vegetables. Half portions are also available for L60. Delicious *agua frescas* (fruit juices) hide in the cooler, so be sure to ask for one.

¿Por qué no? MEDITERRANEAN $$
(www.porquenoroatan.com; mains L240-310; ⊙8am-9pm Tue-Sat, to 3pm Sun;) This adorable, friendly cafe with tables on the veranda overlooking the sea does excellent breakfasts (L190), including to-die-for pastries, bespoke omelets and Mediterranean sets. For lunch and dinner, the salads, wraps and Turkish-inspired mains are deliciously healthy. After eating so well you deserve to top off your meal with a decadent baklava, tiramisu or specialty cake.

Creole's Rotisserie Chicken HONDURAN $$
(mains L100-230; ⊙noon-9pm Tue-Sat) A low-key island institution, Creole's offers excellent island-style roast chicken (a quarter chicken is L80), plus shrimp and fish mains. Choose from eight different *fixins* (side dishes) – including coconut rice, carrot salad, coleslaw and red beans – to accompany your main. Round it out with a slab of rum cake and you're set. Dining is on an open-sided deck facing the beach.

★**Roatán Oasis** INTERNATIONAL $$$
(9484-6659; www.roatanoasis.com; mains L295-450; ⊙5-8:30pm Mon-Fri;) If you're going to splurge on a meal on Roatán, go here. The gorgeous Oasis uses seasonal and locally sourced produce to create delectable creations such as duck confit risotto or scallop and shrimp ravioli. Come Monday through Wednesday nights for the three-course set meal (available from 5pm to 7pm) that's amazing value from L580. Cocktails are out of this world.

Drinking & Nightlife

The West End drag is lined with bars where live music or DJs play come dusk. Partying is limited, with most visitors getting up to dive the next day, but it's the liveliest place on the island.

Blue Marlin BAR
(www.bluemarlinroatan.com; ⊙noon-midnight Mon-Thu, to 2am Fri & Sat, to 10pm Sun) A highly welcoming bar-restaurant with superb sunset views from the rear deck. Draws a good mix of locals, expats and visitors. There's popular live music on Fridays and some decent talent on karaoke Thursdays.

Cafe Escondido BAR
(⊙7:45am-3pm Mon, 7:45am-3pm & 6-10pm Thu-Sat) Located above West End Divers, this fine cafe-bar has a lovely, breezy upper deck with fine harbor views, magazines for browsing and sofas for lounging. Sip an espresso during the day or slug on a beer and take it all in. Come for the evening Sangria Sundays for tapas and a pitcher.

Sundowners BAR
(⊙11am-9:30pm) This open-sided beachfront bar is *the* expat hangout in Roatán. There's always a crop of grizzly old characters hogging the bar stools from lunchtime onward; then backpackers file in making it the busiest spot in town. It was closed for remodeling when passed, which should make it better than ever.

Information

There are several ATMs in West End, but there's been a problem with some being loaded with card readers that steal your bank information. A safer option is to take a taxi to Coxen Hole where there are safe ATMs inside banks with guards.

Getting There & Away

From the airport, private taxis charge L350 to West End. If you walk to the highway outside the airport, transportation is cheaper: *colectivos* charge L50.

From the ferry terminal, official taxis ask for L500 to West End. A cheaper alternative is to walk 150m to the main road and catch a *colectivo* (L60).

Far East

Oak Ridge is old time-y Roatán, home to pirate-like locals and expats who have washed up on sailboats. It's accessed mostly via waterways that run through mangroves, the town itself and out to the cays. The best way to experience it is to hook up with a **Mangrove Tour** (per person around L1000).

East of Oak Ridge, a dirt road snakes along the wildly beautiful forested spine of the island rising above isolated bays, beaches and mangroves. There are turnoffs for the Garifuna settlement of **Punta Gorda** and the old pirate stronghold of **Port Royal**, but the main attraction is stunning **Camp Bay Beach** – a wonderful, undeveloped strip of pale sand.

Continue further east for the dense pines of the **Port Royal National Park**. Unfortunately there was a car-jacking incident on the road to Camp Bay in 2018, so check the safety status before driving out here.

Sleeping & Eating

Reef House HOTEL $$

(☎9487-0521; www.reefhouselodge.com; d incl breakfast L1900; ❄☜) Out on Oak Ridge Cay, this colorful diver's haunt offers a whole different experience from the hotels in Western Roatán. You'll get taken around by boat, meet locals, play garden games and dive pristine reefs few other dive operators visit. There's a natural swimming hole in the reef and snorkeling right off the beach.

★**Temporary Cal's Cantina** FUSION $$

(☎9985-8539; mains L140-325; ⊙10am-8pm Tue-Fri) This place is packed nightly by those willing to drive to this out-of-the-way location between Oak Ridge and French Harbor. Wooden tables on a beautiful garden patio overlook a panorama from jungle to sea. Everything from the jerk chicken to the fried conch or smoked pork chop is delectable. For something lighter, try the yummy fish tacos (L140).

La Sirena SEAFOOD $$$

(☎8867-5227, 3320-6004; Camp Bay; meals L200-450; ⊙11am-8pm) This remote restaurant is housed in a fairly run-down building on stilts over the water. Inside, however, you'll be served some of Roatán's best seafood, so it's worth the long, rough drive from the east of the island. The road here had experienced problems with armed bandits when we passed, but it is usually safe. Check on the status before going.

Drinking & Nightlife

★**Hole in the Wall** BAR

(mains L400; ⊙10am-7pm) There's a party going on, way out in the mangroves at this over-the-water bar only accessible by boat (including on mangrove tours). Slip onto a stool next to fellas straight out of *Pirates of the Caribbean*, grab a beer or something stronger and try your gaming luck by tossing a ring onto a hook on the wall. There are also meals and snacks on offer.

French Harbour

An important port, French Harbour has a large fishing, shrimp and lobster fleet, but other than the quirky appeal of **Arch's Iguana Farm** (☎2455-7743; www.archsiguanaandmarinepark.com; L220; ⊙8am-4pm) in French Cay, just outside town, there's little of interest here.

Sandy Bay

About 4km northeast of West End, Sandy Bay is a quiet little community popular with expats. Here the **Carambola Botanical Gardens** (☎2445-3117; www.carambolagardens.com; L240; ⊙8am-5pm) covers a protected hillside, with several nature trails filled with orchids, spice plants, an 'iguana wall' and lots of wandering agoutis (rodent-like animals). As the name suggests, there's a decent beach here. It's a more chilled-out alternative to West End.

Sleeping & Eating

Roatán Backpackers Hostel HOSTEL $

(☎9714-0413; www.roatanbackpackers.com; dm/s/d from L240/360/620, apt L860; ☜❄) This well-organized hostel in and around a homey colonial house has multiple room categories, a communal kitchen and a pool and sunbathing patio – it even has its own waterfall. Sleepy Sandy Bay Beach is a short walk away and busy West End is a five-minute, L30 *colectivo* taxi ride away. It's not the most convenient location, but the prices can't be beat.

Sunken Fish INTERNATIONAL $$$

(☎2407-2070; www.tranquilseas.com; Tranquil Seas Eco-Lodge & Dive Center, Sandy Bay; meals L220-550; ⊙7:30am-10pm; ✎) The in-house restaurant of a lodge and dive center, the Sunken Fish is open to the public all day and enjoys a fantastic setting overlooking the sea – one particularly apt for impressive sunsets. The eclectic and delicious menu offers seafood and Garifuna cuisine, along with Spanish, Honduran and even Thai influences. Great food deals at happy hour (4pm to 6pm).

Information

There is a hospital on Roatán, but it's rudimentary and rarely used even by locals, who prefer to travel to La Ceiba for treatment. For basic medical assistance, **Clinica Esperanza** (☎2445-3234; www.clinicaesperanza.org; ⊙7:30am-6pm Mon-Fri) in Sandy Bay is your best bet.

West Bay

Here is a paradisical Caribbean white-sand beach, one of the prettiest in Honduras, fringed with coconut palms and with an azure sea filling the horizon. Two decades ago backpackers reveled in its natural majesty, but today a line of uninspiring resort hotels dominates palms and coastal pines.

It's a great place for a day trip, however. Head to the far southern end of the kilometer-long beach, close to the volcanic rocks, to claim a slice of dreamy beach and enjoy spectacular snorkeling. You can also pay a fee (usually around L300 per person) to use the facilities – many resorts will credit the fee toward drinks or food at their bar/restaurants. There are good sandwiches, coffee and cake to be had at **Java Vine** (www.javavine.com; sandwiches from L130; ⏲7:30am-5pm Mon-Fri, 8am-2pm & 3-5pm Sat & Sun; 📶), a friendly cafe and wine bar; it's also one of the few independent and budget-oriented places to eat in West Bay.

Time your visit carefully, however: when a cruise ship moors, up to 5000 people can be disgorged on poor old West Bay, and sunbeds that normally go for L100 will get jacked up to L500.

Utila

POP 4160

Honduras' most popular backpacker haunt, little Utila is also one of the cheapest places in the world to learn how to dive. You'll meet people here daily who came to get certified, went home, sold all their stuff and came back on a one-way ticket. Utila's sublime tropical beauty and chilled-out vibe makes it hard to not to entertain that idea yourself at least once.

The island is only about 13km long and 5km wide, and is focused around Utila Town, the island's only settlement, which is set on a curving bay with two small beaches and dozens of hotels, restaurants, bars and dive shops. There are few roads and much of the island is impenetrable wilderness accessible only by sea.

Another draw: juvenile whale sharks – gentle giants measuring up to 6m long – are spotted around the island. Spotting one is like winning the ocean jackpot.

Sights

Whale Shark & Oceanic Research Center AQUARIUM

(☎3373-1307; https://wsorc.org; Main St E; snorkeling trips L1400; ⏲9am-4pm Mon-Sat) This center studies whale sharks and monitors the coral reef. It offers regular snorkeling trips to track down whale sharks and spear invasive lion fish. If the whale sharks are found, everyone dons snorkeling gear and jumps into the ocean with them – an unforgettable experience. The idea is not to disturb the animals and to promote sustainable whale shark encounters.

Bando Beach BEACH

(L72) Utila Town's privately run beach is a small strip of white sand, a few lounge chairs, some shady palms and a lively bar. You can take a dip here, but the water is shallow and too full of sea grass for swimming or snorkeling, Turn right from the harbor and head to the very end of Main St.

Iguana Research & Breeding Station WILDLIFE RESERVE

(☎2425-3946; www.utila-iguana.de; L60; ⏲9:30am-noon & 1:30-5pm Mon-Fri) Up the hill from the town center, this great place studies and protects the highly endangered Utila iguana *(Ctenosaura bakeri)*, which is known locally as 'the swamper.' Visitors get to see plenty of these fascinating, spiny-tailed critters. Four excellent naturalist-themed tours (L240 to L400) to bat caves and beyond are offered; there are volunteer opportunities available as well.

Activities

Diving

Utila has some superb dive sites. The north side of the island offers spectacular wall diving, with bountiful pelagic life including rays and sharks, and usually excellent visibility. It's great for drift- and deep-diving.

The southern sites are more suited to beginners, with shallower water, though the coral is in a less pristine condition. The seamount **Black Hills** often offers the most prolific marine life, including schools of horse-eyed jacks, while the wreck *Halliburton 211* is a deep-dive thrill.

Utila is rightly famous for the magnificent **whale sharks** that gather here all year. An encounter with one of these creatures will be the highlight of any visit – but diving with them is not permitted. Snorkeling with them is an option, but be sure to do so with an ethically minded, research-centered organization such as the Whale Shark & Oceanic Research Center.

Most dive shops start a course every day or two, and many offer instruction in various languages. Prices hardly vary at all, so take a good look around and talk to the instructors before you decide to sign up. Safety and conservation are key concerns; stick with dive shops that are members of Udsec (Utila Dive Safety & Environment Council). Most schools offer free or discounted accommodations if you take a course. PADI open-water dive courses take three or four days and prices hover around L7000.

Free-diving courses are now available at **Free Dive Utila** (☎9730-3424; www.freediveutila.com; Main St E).

Alton's Dive Center DIVING
(☎2425-3704; www.diveinutila.com; 2-tank dive L1600, open water course L8400) Friendly and welcoming, this dive school has up-to-date gear and free dorm accommodations (with diving) or more upscale rooms (doubles L1000 per night) right on the dock. It attracts a younger backpacker crowd of serious divers. It's 300m east of the main intersection.

Underwater Vision DIVING
(☎2425-3103; www.utilascubadiving.com; 2-tank dive L1400, open water course L7190) One of the busiest dive schools on the island and with a strong party vibe, Underwater Vision offers professional tuition in English, Spanish, German, French, Swedish and Italian. Discounted accommodations are in great dorms in the connected and classy Trudy's (p412) hotel, where there's a good place to swim at the small beach.

Captain Morgan's Dive Centre DIVING
(☎2425-3349; www.divingutila.com; Main St; 2-tank dive L1300, open water course L6900) Right opposite the dock, Captain Morgan's selling point is that it offers more trips to the north coast and its immense drop-offs than any other dive center. There's an outdoor teaching area, small beach and new wetsuits. Accommodations are in a good hotel, the Pirate's Bay Inn, next door.

Utila Dive Centre DIVING
(UDC; ☎2425-3326; www.utiladivecentre.com; 2-tank dive L1850, open water course L8400) The largest diving operation in Utila, UDC is very serious about safety. The school offers five dive boats, lots of tech diving and rebreather courses and instruction. Students are separated from certified divers; accommodations at the Mango Inn (p413) are excellent.

Ecomarine DIVING
(Gunter's Dive Shop; ☎2425-3350; www.ecomarineutila.com; 2-tank dives L1440, open water courses L6900) The longest-established dive shop on the island, it's a 10-minute walk west of the dock and is low-key and unpretentious, with small classes and solid PADI instruction. The backpacker lodge across the street is free for students.

Kayaking, Canoeing & Paddleboarding

Paddling from Utila Town to **Rock Harbour** is a wonderful day trip. The route goes via Oyster Bed Lagoon and Lower Lagoon and along a mangrove canal. There's a good beach at Rock Harbour that's very private. Many dive schools offer free kayaks or paddleboards for customers.

Snorkeling

Utila offers exceptional snorkeling, though you'll have to make a bit of an effort to access a good reef. Many dive shops rent out snorkel gear (around L150 per day), and most dive schools allow snorkelers to tag along on dive boats for a small fee (around L100).

The best place to snorkel off Utila itself is from Neptune's Restaurant (p413), accessed by free boat shuttle from town. Otherwise there's some snorkeling at **Chepes Beach**, at the western end of Main St, but the water is very shallow close to shore.

Nature Tours

Few visitors make it much beyond Utila Town and the reefs offshore, but the swampy interior of the island is fascinating to explore.

The Iguana Research & Breeding Station offers excellent tours (L240 to L400) to bat caves and a dead lagoon and a kayaking trip through the mangroves.

Boat Trips

Many local fishers have signs in their windows for boat tours; prices start at L1000 per boat. They can take you to Water Cay, to Rock Harbour via the mangrove canal, through the lagoon, and to other places.

Sleeping

Expect to be greeted at the pier by a bunch of brochure-carrying touts giving you the hard sell. Many dive shops have good, cheap (or free) accommodations if you sign up for

Utila

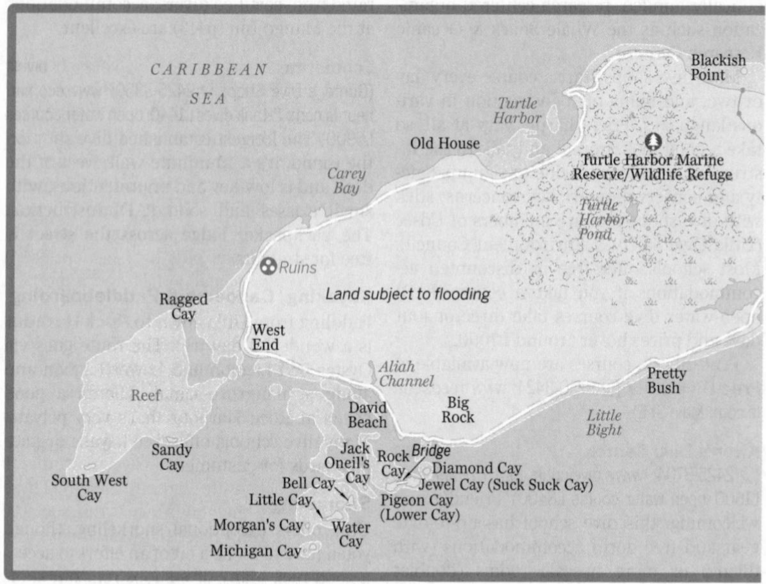

a course, though such offers only apply on days when you're diving or on the course.

★ The Venue HOSTEL $

(☎9505-5760; www.thevenueutila.com; r L330; 📶) This hip place is situated right on a beautiful mangrove river with Chepes Beach steps away at the opposite end. The small rooms are sliced like a pie into in an octagonal building, have two bunk beds apiece and share a bathroom. A few bigger double rooms were in the works when we passed. Kayaks and stand-up paddleboards are available to rent (L100 per hour).

★ Rubi's Inn HOTEL $

(☎2425-3240; rubisinn@yahoo.com; Main St E; s/d L480/600, ste with air-con L1320; ❄📶) Owned by a charming local couple, this small hotel has 12 spotless, spacious rooms with polished floors and fresh linen in a wooden waterfront building. Rooms on the upper deck glimpse the sea, and the corner 'honeymoon suite' has uninterrupted views. There's a private dock for swimming and sunbathing, hammocks for chilling in, and a guests' kitchen.

Sea Side Utila Hostel HOTEL $

(☎2425-3150; Main St W; r with/without air-con L840/480; ❄📶) A 10-minute walk west of the dock, this bright, well-maintained place with simple colonial charm has a tranquil location close to Chepes Beach. Rooms have two double beds and are available either with air-con or a fan (a far cheaper option). There's also a guests' kitchen. You'll enjoy the sweeping Caribbean views from the shared balcony.

★ Jade Seahorse BOUTIQUE HOTEL $$

(☎2425-3270; www.jadeseahorseutila.com; cabins L1800-2525; ❄📶) Welcome to this hillside, arty oasis where about half the surfaces are covered in colorful, whimsical mosaics of glass, tile and more. Each of the six comfy cabins is unique. We particularly loved the blue and bright Mono Lisa in the shade of a tamarind tree. The Asian-inspired on-site restaurant is one of the island's best, as is the Treetanic Bar (p414).

Hotel Trudy HOTEL $$

(☎2425-3103; www.utilascubadiving.com; Main St E; dm/r/ste L300/1080/2140; ❄📶) A delightful base, this locally owned place has a fantastic oceanfront plot to enjoy, with a small beach-volleyball court and a cafe that makes for a relaxing and sociable stay. Dorms are small but have polished wooden floors and sea views from the communal balcony. The shared bathrooms have hot water. Divers with Underwater Vision get discounted rates.

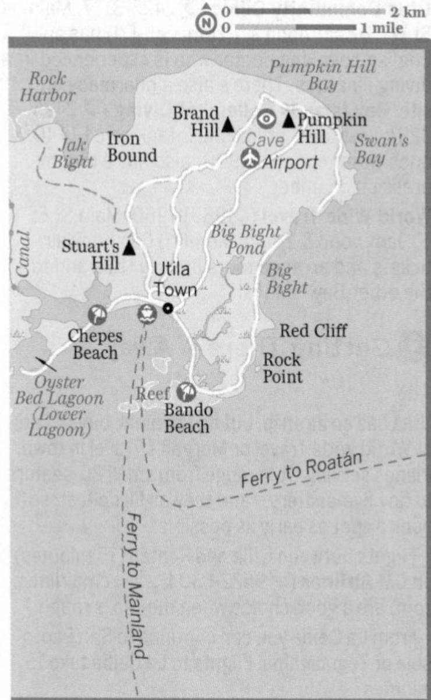

Mango Inn HOTEL $$$
(☎2425-3326; www.mango-inn.com; Cola de Mico; s/d incl breakfast from L2000/2200, cabins incl breakfast from L3270; ❄📶🏊) Linked to Utila Dive Center, this excellent place is straight up the hill from the pier. Well-constructed timber room blocks and cabins are scattered around a garden shaded by mango trees; the pool area and cafe are just great and the whole place is exceptionally well run. All accommodations include a hearty breakfast. This is a good choice for families.

Eating

Utila Town has a good selection of eating options for such a small settlement, from cheapo *baleadas* to fine dining. Several places to stay also have kitchens where you can cook. Poorly stocked supermarkets dot Main St.

Camilla's Bakery BAKERY $
(☎9969-6360; mains L71-140; ⏰6:30am-2pm & 5-9pm Sun-Tue; 📶) Our favorite breakfast stop on Utila serves fresh bread and homemade bagels with all kinds of toppings, as well as delicious egg dishes, quiche, smoothies and croissants. There's a lot of French *savoir faire* going on and even the self-service coffee is top notch. At night it turns into Pizza Nut and churns out fantastic, cheesy pies (around L200).

★Neptune's Restaurant & Bar INTERNATIONAL $$
(mains L155-210; ⏰9am-5:30pm) Hop on the free shuttle (every half-hour) near the Coral View Dive Center to get to this day trip-worthy bar-restaurant on a gorgeous white sand beach. The best snorkeling on mainland Utila is right off the dock. Fill your belly with good burgers, tacos, salads and vegetarian options plus an excellent fresh raw tuna and avocado poke tower appetizer.

Hotspot Cafe CAFE $$
(Main St W; mains L90-150; ⏰6am-5pm Mon-Sat; 📶) With real coffee and an enormous whiteboard menu that includes breakfasts, smoothies, burgers, wraps and a popular steak sub, this cute, brightly painted shack lives up to its name – it heaves with divers and backpackers throughout the day. There are relatively few tables, but the sociable counter is a great place to meet new people.

RJ's CARIBBEAN $$
(Main St E; mains L150-200; ⏰5:30-9pm Wed, Fri & Sun) Ask anyone on the island where you can find Utila's best food and they'll tell you RJ's without hesitation. While that may be due more to the local taste for traditional Caribbean cooking than anything else, this friendly place does excellent pork and seafood dishes, all accompanied by a sea of trimmings. Note the odd opening hours, and come early.

★Mango Tango INTERNATIONAL $$$
(☎3211-9469; mains L275-390; ⏰8am-10pm; 📶) Housed in an over-the-water building that takes in views from three sides, Mango Tango has some of the best food in town. Try the Galician-style octopus, homemade shrimp and ricotta ravioli or filet mignon with chimichurri from the interesting international menu while enjoying the sea breezes. Start with a world-class cocktail and finish with a Better Than Sex Big Tiramisu.

Mango Café PIZZA, INTERNATIONAL $$$
(☎2425-3410; Mango Inn, Cola de Mico; mains L180-240, pizzas from L170; ⏰6am-2pm & 5-10pm; 📶) Owned by Andrea, an Italian who's lived in Utila since the 1990s, this place specializes in authentic thin-crust pizza from a purpose-built brick oven. The menu runs from egg sandwiches and burritos to seared

tuna, coconut shrimp and wine-poached snapper fillet; there's always a daily special too. If you eat here you're welcome to use the hotel pool and sunbeds.

Drinking & Nightlife

The party scene is strong in Utila, which at times feels like a cool college town revolving around a small diving university. There's usually a special night of the week when each bar fills up, so ask around.

★ Treetanic BAR

(Cola de Mico; 8pm-midnight Sat-Tue & Thu, to 1am Wed & Fri) Owned by Neil, an eccentric American artist, this psychedelic mango-treetop bar is somewhere you just have to see while visiting Utila. It always draws a cast of local characters and is definitely one of the more fun places on the island. The 'Dark Moon' night during the new moon is one of the best parties on the island.

Islanders BAR

(beer 12oz/tasting flight L90/160) Serving El Bosque craft beers brewed in San Pedro Sula, Islanders is a new, low-key spot for quality brews and even better views from the over-the-sea terrace. Wine, cocktails and light meals like burgers and nachos are also served.

Relapse BAR

(11am-midnight) Overlooking Chepes Beach from an over-the-water covered deck, this colorful hammock- and pillow-strewn drinking hole is an oasis of chill during the day and gets progressively livelier through to nighttime.

Skid Row BAR

(Main St W; 10am-11pm) This is everything a hard-drinking bar should be, with a leaky tin roof, concrete floor, pool table, dart board, an excess of wizened characters and a long-suffering bartender. All visitors are cordially invited to take up the 'Giufity Challenge' – downing shots of a Garifuna herb-enhanced moonshine. Decent pub grub, including Tex-Mex dishes and burgers, is also available, as is delivery.

Information

Morgan's Travel (2425-3161; www.utilamorganstravel.com; 8am-5:30pm Mon-Fri, 8am-noon Sat) Arranges plane tickets off the island and taxis to and from the airport. Next to the pier.

Utila Community Clinic (2425-3137; Main St W; 8am-noon & 1-2pm Mon-Fri) has an English-speaking doctor who is experienced in diving illnesses. There's also a pharmacy on-site. **Bay Islands College of Diving** (2425-3291; www.dive-utila.com; 2-tank dive L1440, open water course L7900) also has a recompression chamber.

World Wide Travel (9891-1960; Main St E; 9am-noon & 2-5pm Mon-Fri) Can book air tickets and arrange tours around Utila and to the other Bay Islands.

Getting There & Away

AIR

Utila has an airstrip, but no terminal; buy tickets at World Wide Travel or Morgan's Travel in town. Planes serving Utila range from small 20-seaters to tiny five-seaters – and they all fill up fast, so book a spot as early as possible.

Flights between Utila and Roatán (15 minutes) on **CM Airlines** (9522-5304; www.cmairlines.com) are a good choice when the sea is rough.

From La Ceiba you can continue to San Pedro Sula or Tegucigalpa. Flights to La Ceiba take 15 minutes.

BOAT

The **Utila Dream** (2425-3191; www.utilaferry.com) sails twice a day to/from La Ceiba (L600, 45 minutes) and once per day to/from Roatán (L700, one hour). Arrive 30 minutes before your boat's departure.

Getting Around

You can walk the entirety of Utila's Main St in about 20 minutes.

Bikes are available from many places by the hour/day/week for L25/100/600, though they're generally poorly maintained rust buckets.

THE MOSKITIA

The Moskitia (named for the Moskito people who live here, not the bloodthirsty insects) is one of the region's last frontiers of untamed wilderness. Huge expanses are virtually untouched jungle, and when combined with magnificent wetland and savanna habitats it's no wonder the region is often dubbed Central America's Amazon. You'll primarily hear the Moskito language spoken near the coasts, although most people also easily communicate in Spanish.

Manatees, tapirs and jaguars all thrive here, but aren't easy to spot. Crocodiles can be seen in the waters, while the birdlife, including macaws and fish eagles, is outstanding.

A visit to this region is not for the faint-hearted – access is tricky and conditions are rustic at best. Transport and safety are improving, however, and a trip through the Moskitia is a very adventurous way to cross into Nicaragua. *Lancha* voyages through rivers, past savannas and across great lagoons are a highlight.

Getting There & Away

AeroCaribe (2442-1088; www.aerocaribehn.com; La Ceiba) and **Lanhsa** (9450-1025; www.lanhsahn.com) fly between Puerto Lempira and La Ceiba (L3100) daily. AeroCaribe also has regular flights between Puerto Lempira and Brus Laguna (L1400), Ahuas (L1150) and Wampusirpe (L1530).

Take an early bus from Trujillo (L45, 1½ hours) or La Ceiba (L100, 2½ hours) to Tocoa, from where overloaded *pailas* (pickup trucks) leave from the market area at between 9am and 10am for Batalla (L400 to L500, four to six hours). From Batalla, *colectivo* boats head to Palacios (L60, five minutes), Raista (L250, two hours) and several other destinations as far as Brus Laguna (L550, four hours). From Brus Laguna, there is transport onward to Puerto Lempira (L1100, seven hours) via Ahuas (L500, 3½ hours). Note that you may get stuck in Ahaus for a day or more if there aren't enough people for the *lancha* to Puerto Lempira.

To return, take an early-morning *lancha* to Batalla for a 7am truck to Tocoa. Tocoa has bus connections to both La Ceiba and Trujillo (roughly hourly until 4pm).

Laguna de Ibans

The small traditional coastal communities around Laguna de Ibans are a cluster of small settlements – **Cocobila**, **Raista** and **Belén** are a short walk apart, but nearly everyone stays is Raista because of the friendly, well-run accommodations there.

You can swim in the murky sea here but jellyfish can spoil the experience, so a dip in the freshwater lagoon is a better choice. If you get the chance, take in **Plaplaya**, a lovely, traditional Garifuna village a short boat ride from Raista, where giant leatherback sea turtles nest and are released by volunteers between April and July.

Sleeping & Eating

Your only eating options are at hotels.

★**Raista Eco Lodge** LODGE $
(8926-5635, 2433-8220; Raista; r per person L180) A pioneer of Moskitia ecotourism, Raista Eco Lodge has rustic but comfortable rooms, mosquito nets and excellent home cooking (meals L100). The Bodden family, who run the place, are extremely friendly and knowledgeable. Guests get a free village and beach walk and you can organize turtle- or caiman-spotting tours. It can also arrange travel to Las Marías and other destinations.

Getting There & Away

Heading inland, you can arrange private *lanchas* to Las Marías (return L5000, five to six hours) or hope for a *colectivo lancha* (L500 per person). Heading east to Batalla and west as far as Brus Laguna daily *colectivo lanchas* are quite reliable.

Reserva de la Biósfera del Río Plátano

The Río Plátano Biosphere Reserve is a magnificent nature reserve, declared a World Heritage Site in 1980. A vast, unspoiled and untamed wilderness, it's home to extraordinary animal life, including a number of endangered species. The best time to visit is from November to July, though birdwatchers should come in February and March, when many migratory birds are here.

One of the best places to experience all this nature is in **Las Marías**, a village in the heart of the reserve with around 100 Miskito and Pech families. There is no running water or electricity here, though there are a few generators.

Short trails around the village are good for birding, but for longer trips it's essential to hire a guide and arrange camping equipment and food. Guides do not speak English. Bookings are difficult to organize in advance and not really necessary.

Tours

Popular short tours in the reserve include a twilight crocodile-spotting walk and a day trip by boat to see some petroglyphs. Arduous longer trips into primary rainforest include a two-day hike up wildlife-rich **Cerro Baltimore** and a three-day expedition to the summit of **Pico Dama** (840m), both of which require several guides.

LA CUIDAD BLANCA: LEGEND TO DISCOVERY

A national legend and subject of countless TV programs and articles, the search for La Ciudad Blanca (Spanish for 'The White City') has gone on in Honduras since 1516, when Spanish conquistador Hernán Cortés wrote about rumors of a region of extreme wealth. Most of the subsequent and numerous searches and finds have been hoaxes, some of them having much international fanfare before being debunked.

Then in 2012, a team led by documentary filmmaker Steve Elkins and the Honduran government used lidar mapping that revealed two large settlements. Excitement grew that they may have found Ciudad Blanca. A ground expedition to one of the areas in 2015 determined that the site was a Pre-Columbian city. The story was widely covered in *National Geographic* and in the best-selling book *The Lost City of the Monkey God* by Douglas Preston, who was on both expeditions. Some archaeologists specializing in the region, however, have called the story hype and that many conclusions are being jumped to. The ancient inhabitants of Mosquitia are not Maya and are one of the least-known cultures in Central America, so there is little previous knowledge to work from.

In 2018 Honduras's president Juan Orlando Hernandez inaugurated an Archaeological Research Center dedicated to the finds, in the El Aguacata sector of Olancho Province. The center is unfortunately in a very-out-of-the way location for most travelers to Honduras to visit. The archaeological site itself is so deep in the jungle that it takes days or a helicopter to visit. Scientists on the expedition believe it had no human presence for around 500 years.

Sleeping & Eating

Several basic lodgings, including Hospedaje Doña Justa, will cook you simple meals on request. There are no other eating options.

Hospedaje Doña Justa HOTEL $
(☎9966-9234; Las Marías; r without bathroom per person L150) Super friendly, the Doña Justa is a thatch-roofed building with several airy rooms overlooking a huge flower garden. Each room is well kept and has decent beds with mosquito nets. There's a big patio with lots of hammocks, perfect for whiling away an afternoon with a book. Meals (L60 to L100) are prepared upon request.

Getting There & Away

There are a few weekly *colectivo lanchas* (small motorboats) between Las Marías and Raista, but you may have to hang around a few days to catch one; these cost L500 per person one way. A round-trip chartered boat ride from Raista costs around L5000 for up to three people (five to six hours); the boat operator will wait in Las Marías for two or three nights for the return leg. Boats are also available to/from Brus Laguna for higher prices.

Palacios

Palacios will be the first place you stop in Moskitia if you're taking the overland route from within Honduras. The river setting is lovely, but it's a rather lawless place that won't be a regional highlight. If you arrive to Batalla too late, however, you may end up having to sleep here. Don't venture out at night and take care of your belongings.

There is a *comedor* in town, which serves up very cheap meals.

Hotel Moskitia (☎9996-5648; r L180) is Palacios' best sleeping option, though it's still very basic. The best part is the lake view from the balconies.

Getting There & Away

Colectivo canoes will run you across the lake from Batalla (L60, five minutes).

There are also regular flights on **AeroCaribe** (☎3312-8978; www.aerocaribehn.com) to/from Puerto Lempira (L1960).

Brus Laguna

Beside the lagoon of the same name, Brus Laguna is a lively, dusty town and an accessible entry point to the Moskitia, as it has an airport and direct boat service to Batalla. You can also head to Raista or even straight to Las Marías from here. It does feel much dodgier here, however, than Raista or Puerto Lempira, especially after dark, and there's a heavy Honduran military presence due to narco activities. That said, the stunning *lancha* trip between Brus Laguna and Raista makes a visit worthwhile; you'll almost definitely have to spend a night here if your overlanding to or from Nicaragua.

There are a few basic eateries serving typical Honduran fare and cheap but good *baleadas*.

Worth the extra lempira if you want a good night's sleep, the pastel purple, two-story, concrete **Ciudad Blanca** (☎3165-0250; s/d L400/600) hotel has good-sized clean rooms that are hugely better than anything else in town. To find it, walk two blocks down the main drag from the boat dock then turn left. It's a block or two from here on the left.

Getting There & Away

AeroCaribe (p415) connects La Ceiba (one way L3100) and Puerto Lempira (one way L1400) with Brus Laguna daily. From Batalla, *lanchas* (small motorboats) head to Brus Laguna between 3pm and 5pm (L550, four hours). Change boats in Ahaus to get to Puerto Lempira (L1100, seven hours).

Puerto Lempira

Situated on the inland side of the Laguna de Caratasca, Puerto Lempira is the largest town in the Moskitia. If you've come through the region overland from the Honduran side, you'll feel like you've reached a metropolis, although in reality it's just a large village with mostly dirt roads, a large pier, three supermarkets, a hospital, an ATM and good air connections. It's a friendly enough place if you say *'buenos dias'* to people. The drug cartels are still going strong here, but they've learned to keep their activities fairly low-profile and are not a threat if you use common sense and keep out of their business.

The favorite day trip from Puerto Lempira is to the serene Miskito village of **Mistruk**, 18km south of town on the banks of the lovely Laguna de Tansing. You can hire a truck to take you for around L1000.

Tours

La Moskitia Ecoaventuras (p400) has decades of experience in the Moskitia, and owner Jorge Salaverri is a native of the region. He has several tours from overland and backpacker-style to deluxe and more comfortable. The biggest advantage of a tour is that activities are arranged (boating, fishing, birdwatching etc) in places where it can be difficult to arrange activities independently.

Another good person to speak to is Jon Tompson, owner of Vino Tinto (p403) in Trujillo, who has traveled widely in the region.

Sleeping & Eating

For cheap eats, your best options are the cafeterias near the pier that sell delicious *baleadas,* tacos and *tipico* meals. Head to Hotel Pinares or Hotel Yu Baiwan if you're looking for something a little bit more sophisticated.

★Hotel Yu Baiwan HOTEL $

(☎9568-2142, 2433-6348; off Calle Principal; r L550) The best deal in town, the Yu Baiwan feels like a beach resort with a white-sand beach and palm trees lining the lagoon directly in front. Rooms are old but big, spotless and comfortable and service is friendly. To get here, look for a narrow concrete passageway off Calle Principal, a half-block from the pier.

Hotel El Sol HOTEL $

(r L350) The only decent very low budget choice in town, the El Sol really is sunny, with bright colored walls, potted plants everywhere and vibrant faux brick wall paintings in the rooms. The terrace has wooden benches and overlooks the street. It's one block up and two blocks to the left from the pier.

Hotel Pinares HOTEL $$

(☎2433-6681; Av 10; r with/without air-con L950/750; ❄≋) Right on the lagoon, this is a comfortable, friendly choice in Puerto Lempira, with aging yet very large rooms surrounding a plant-filled courtyard. The highlight is the pool that sits enclosed by fencing next to the lagoon – but you can still see the lagoon and catch its breezes. The air-conditioning doesn't function during Puerto Lempira's frequent power outages.

Getting There & Away

AeroCaribe and Lanhsa (p415) fly to/from La Ceiba (L3100) daily. AeroCaribe also has regular flights to Palacios (L1960), Brus Laguna (L1400), Ahuas (L1150) and Wampusirpe (L1530). Alternatively, boats head to Ahuas where you can connect with boats to Brus Laguna.

There are daily morning pickup trucks to the Nicaragua border (L200, four hours). Stamp out then take a *lancha* to cross the river to get stamped in to Nicaragua in Leimus. Pickup trucks leave from here to Waspan, where you'll probably have to stay overnight before catching transportation further afield.

Southern Honduras & Isla del Tigre

POP 9690

Honduras touches the Pacific with a 124km coastline on the Golfo de Fonseca. This perpetually and often infernally hot coastal plain is dominated by agribusinesses: sugarcane, African palm plantations and shrimp farms.

While it's a much-traveled region (the Interamericana crosses through Honduras here), there's little of interest to travelers – except perhaps Isla del Tigre, which has some charm.

Isla del Tigre is an inactive volcanic island off the southern coast of Honduras, with a highest point of 783m. It's a dramatic place covered in thick forest and with some decent beaches that attract droves of locals but very few foreigners.

Its main town is **Amapala**, a scruffy fishing village with picturesque, crumbling clapboard architecture. Black-sand **Playa Negra**, in the north of the island, is arguably the island's best beach, though there are several other totally undeveloped stretches elsewhere here.

Sleeping & Eating

Accommodations in Isla del Tigre are more expensive than on the mainland. There are few budget options, but the good-value favorite is Paz Camping Playa Negra on beautiful Playa Negra.

Isla del Tigre's Playa Grande offers a plethora of eateries.

Paz Camping Playa Negra HOTEL **$$**
(☎9978-2761; r from L1440; ❄☎) This family-run block hotel set against a jungle hillside has terraces overlooking chilled-out Playa Negra. There are seven clean rooms, a little pool, an on-site restaurant and a fun atmosphere. Hiking and fishing tours can also be arranged.

Information

There are no ATMs on Isla del Tigre and the closest one is in San Lorenzo on the mainland. Smaller hotels don't accept credit cards, so bring plenty of cash!

Getting There & Away

If you're only passing through southern Honduras, it's less than three hours by bus between the borders of El Salvador and Nicaragua. Heading east to Nicaragua you're sure to pass through the large city and transportation hub of Choluteca, which has little to detain you, though there are plentiful banks and facilities.

If you are headed to Isla del Tigre, small *colectivo* boats (L25, 20 minutes) depart from the town of Coyolito, 30km from the Interamericana, but you'll have to wait until the boat fills up with 10 passengers. Otherwise you can pay L120 for a private boat trip (the preferred, hassle-free choice).

Buses go to Coyolito from the town of San Lorenzo (L30, one hour, every 40 minutes until 5:30pm) from the terminal behind San Lorenzo's prefabricated market, or from a dusty turnoff 2km north of town. San Lorenzo can be reached by buses that run by Blanquita or San Benito from Tegucigalpa (L90, two hours, every 40 minutes).

Getting Around

Minibuses (L15) from Amapala circuit halfway around the island past beaches. You can also grab a *mototaxi*.

UNDERSTAND HONDURAS

Honduras Today

Welcome to Central America's bad boy: Honduras has for years been the regional cautionary tale about what goes wrong when corruption, drugs and poverty intersect. But this ever-plucky nation refuses to be pigeonholed and has been fighting back steadily against its dangerous international reputation. Murder rates – while still sky-high – are dropping, security is better than it has been for years and, despite some hiccups here and there, things are finally looking up for one of the region's least-appreciated destinations.

The original banana republic, Honduras has been ignored or kicked about for most of its existence. But in 2012 the nation finally became newsworthy – the United Nations announced the country had become the murder-rate capital of the world. But by 2015 Honduras had lost the title to neighboring El Salvador, and by 2017 San Pedro Sula (the roughest city) had fallen to a staggering 26 on Business Insider's 'Most Dangerous City's' list, though by any standards, the security situation in the country remains dire. It's not only the day-to-day threat of attack or robbery that Hondurans have to consider as they go shopping, drive a car or board a bus. Extortion or 'war taxing' practiced by gangs in poor barrios hikes up costs for the whole nation: street vendors have to pay to pitch a stall and transportation companies have to pay so their buses can pass through gang-controlled territory. Sky-high crime rates curb inward investment, so prospective employers avoid Honduras because of huge security costs. Armed guards stand in front of just about everything. Tourism suffers, and even the Peace Corps pulled out in 2012, citing safety concerns.

The political situation is similarly disappointing. National Party of Honduras candidate Juan Orlando Hernández assumed the Honduran presidency in 2014 and then, in defiance of a law against re-election, won a second term in late 2017. Protests broke out decrying the election a fraud and at least 17 people were killed. A conservative, Hernández (known to locals by his initials JOH) has been credited with seeing murder rates drop, but he has also been powerless to make any serious inroads on that age-old Honduran issue of corruption, even being indirectly implicated in it himself.

Given the status quo, many have voted with their feet and sought a new life in the USA or elsewhere. An estimated million Hondurans live north of the border; according to *La Prensa* newspaper their remittances home for 2014 were some US$3.4 billion, or about 17% of the Honduran economy. There's barely a family in the whole nation that does not have a member in 'El Norte.'

History

Honduras has had a rough deal over the centuries. Things got off to a sparkling start when the Maya civilization emerged in Copán, but then the Spaniards came and trampled all over the territory. Marauding pirates added to the mix in the 17th century.

Independence brought a brief respite, but for virtually the entire 20th century Honduras was dominated by distant, powerful forces as giant US fruit companies and, later, the US military set up shop in the nation.

Early History

The earliest humans are thought to have arrived in Honduras around 9000 BC, though almost nothing is known about their lives other than that they were hunter-gatherers. By around 2000 BC settlements started cropping up across the land.

It was over a millennia more before the Maya site of Copán Ruinas began to flourish, as sculptors carved stone stelae unequaled in the Maya world and mathematicians and astronomers calculated uncannily accurate calendars and planetary movements. For hundreds of years, a good slice of the Maya Classic Period (AD 250 to 900), the city dominated the region culturally, until its decline in the 9th century AD.

THE FOOTBALL WAR

Legendary football (soccer) manager Bill Shankly once said, 'Some people believe football is a matter of life and death. It is much more important than that.' Even Mr Shankly might have balked at the sporting rivalry between Honduras and El Salvador, which spilled off the pitch and onto the battlefield in the 1969 Guerra de Fútbol – the notorious Football War.

Tensions did not suddenly break out on the stadium terraces. In the 1950s and 1960s, a flagging economy forced 300,000 Salvadorans to seek better conditions in Honduras. However, the Honduran economy was itself ailing, and Salvadorans began to be targeted as scapegoats. In June 1969 Honduran authorities started throwing Salvadoran immigrants out of the country. A stream of Salvadoran refugees followed, alleging Honduran brutality.

In the same month, the two countries were playing World Cup qualifying matches against each other. At the game in San Salvador, Salvadorans attacked Honduran fans, defiling the Honduran flag and mocking the anthem. Across the border, angry Hondurans then turned on Salvadoran immigrants. Tempers frayed further and the El Salvador army invaded Honduran territory on July 14, capturing Nueva Ocotepeque. Honduras retaliated with air strikes. A ceasefire was called after only six days, but around 2000 Hondurans lost their lives, while thousands of Salvadorans fled home.

Spanish Colonization

Columbus, on his fourth and final voyage, landed near present-day Trujillo in 1502, naming the place Honduras ('depths' in Spanish) for the deep waters off the north coast.

He established a town (Trujillo), Honduras' first capital in 1525, but the gleam of silver from the interior soon caught the eye of the conquistadors: in 1537 Comayagua, midway between the Pacific and Caribbean coasts, became the new capital.

Indigenous people put up fierce resistance to the invasion, although this was weakened by their vulnerability to European-introduced diseases. The sternest resistance was from Lempira (chief of the Lenca tribe, who's considered a national hero), who led a force of 30,000 against the Spanish before he was assassinated. By 1539 resistance was largely crushed.

British Influence

By the beginning of the 17th century, Spanish colonists were coming under regular attack from rival imperial forces – especially the British. Merchants from Britain, attracted by the mahogany and hardwoods of the Honduran Caribbean coast, established settlements there and on the Bay Islands.

Britain eventually ceded control of the Caribbean coast to the Spanish, but continued to influence the region. In 1797 slaves rebelled on the Caribbean island of St Vincent. The British shipped thousands to the island of Roatán, where they mixed with indigenous people. Eventually these people, the Garifuna, crossed to the mainland and founded settlements along the coast.

Independence

After gaining its independence from Spain in 1821, Honduras was briefly part of independent Mexico and then a member of the Central American Federation. The Honduran liberal hero General Francisco Morazán was elected president in 1830. The union was short-lived, however, and Honduras declared itself a separate independent nation in 1838.

Liberal and conservative factions wrestled and power alternated between civilian governments and military regimes – such that the country's constitution would be rewritten 17 times between 1821 and 1982. Honduras has also experienced literally hundreds of coups, rebellions and power seizures since achieving independence.

The 'Banana Republic'

Around the end of the 19th century, US traders marveled at the rapid growth of bananas on the fertile north coast (just a short sail from southern USA). US entrepreneurs bought land for growing bananas, and three

READING UP

Want more background? Leaf your way through the following books:

➡ *Enrique's Journey* (Sonia Nazario; 2006) A runaway from Tegucigalpa searches for his mother in the USA.

➡ *Bananas: How the United Fruit Company Shaped the World* (Peter Chapman; 2007) Great insight on the banana giant's impact on Central America.

➡ *The Mosquito Coast* (Paul Theroux; 1981) A vivid fictional account of life in the jungle.

➡ *The United States, Honduras, and the Crisis in Central America* (Donald E Schulz and Deborah Sundloff Schulz; 1994) Discusses the role of the US in Central America during the region's tumultuous civil wars.

➡ *Prisión Verde* (Ramón Amaya-Amador; 1950) Life on a banana plantation by a political writer.

➡ *El Humano y la Diosa* (The Human and the Goddess; 1996), *Los Barcos* (The Boats; 1992) and *The Big Banana* (Roberto Quesada; 1999) One of Honduras' leading novelists.

➡ *The works of Juan Ramón Molina* (1875–1908) Perhaps the country's best-loved poet.

➡ *The Lost City of the Monkey God* (Douglas Preston; 2017) A riveting read about the search and possible discovery of the legendary Cuidad Blanca ruins in Moskitia.

companies – including the Standard (later United Fruit) company – bought up huge chunks of land.

Bananas provided 11% of Honduras' exports in 1892, 42% in 1903 and 66% in 1913. The success of the industry made the banana companies extremely powerful within Honduras, with policy and politicians controlled by their interests.

20th-Century Politics

The USA increasingly came to influence Honduran affairs. In 1911 and 1912, US marines were dispatched to the nation to 'protect US investments.'

A two-month strike in 1954 – in which as many as 25,000 banana workers and sympathizers participated – remains a seminal moment in Honduran labor history. Unions were recognized, and workers gained rights that were unheard of in neighboring Central American countries.

From the late 1950s, the military steadily began to take a much more important role in the country's governance, via coups and political pressure. Long periods of military rule alternated with civilian presidents throughout the 1960s and 1970s. This cycle was finally ended with the 1981 democratic presidential elections.

The 1980s

During the 1980s Honduras was surrounded by revolutions and conflict. In July 1979 the revolutionary Sandinista movement in Nicaragua overthrew the Somoza dictatorship, and Somoza's national guardsmen fled into Honduras. Civil war broke out in El Salvador in 1980 and internal conflict worsened in Guatemala.

Honduras became the focus of US policy and strategic operations in the region, backed up by General Gustavo Álvarez, who supported an increasing US military presence. Under Ronald Reagan huge sums of money and thousands of US troops were funneled into Honduras; refugee camps of Nicaraguans in Honduras were used as bases for a US-sponsored covert war against the Nicaraguan Sandinista government, known as the Contra War.

Public alarm grew as hundreds of leftists in Honduras 'disappeared' and the US militarization of Honduras ramped up. By 1984 General Álvarez was exiled by fellow officers, and the Honduran government suspended US training of the Salvadoran military within its borders.

In Washington the Reagan administration was rocked by revelations it had illegally used money from arms sales to Iran to support anti-Sandinista Contras. Large demonstrations followed in Tegucigalpa, and in November 1988 the government refused to sign a new military agreement with the USA. With the election of Violeta Chamorro as president of Nicaragua in 1990, the Contra War ended.

Modern Currents & Coups

Through the presidential administrations of Rafael Leonardo Callejas Romero (1990–94) and Carlos Roberto Reina Idiaquez (1994–98), Honduras struggled economically. Then in 1998 Honduras was dealt a devastating blow as Hurricane Mitch killed thousands and caused widespread devastation (estimated at US$3 billion), setting the economy back years. In 2001 Ricardo Maduro from the National Party was elected president, via promises to reduce crime. But despite pouring huge resources into the problem, crime levels rose. In 2006 José Manuel Zelaya Rosales, a cowboy hat–wearing rancher, was elected president. He aligned himself with other Latin American left-wing leaders (such as Hugo Chávez) but in 2009 his plan to rewrite the constitution – thereby making himself eligible for a second term – provoked a political crisis. The Supreme Court ordered Zelaya be removed from office – many countries viewed his expulsion as a coup – and he was exiled in the Dominican Republic.

Democratic elections followed, and Nationalist party candidate Porfirio 'Pepe' Lobo, a center-right conservative with backing from the nation's oligarchy, was voted in. Lobo's presidency racked up foreign debts of over US$5 billion, while ongoing financial turmoil left state workers, including teachers and the military, unpaid. Conservative Juan Orlando Hernández was elected in 2014 and though he has been hit with non-stop corruption allegations, managed to lower the country's violence statistics. He made himself eligible for a second term and, unlike Zelaya, got away with it in 2017. His second win was met by violent protests claiming he had manipulated votes and stolen the election.

Culture

Honduras is a complex ethnic, religious and cultural melting pot that you need to understand in order to make the most of any journey here. The legacy of its rich and turbulent history can be seen everywhere, from the Garifuna settlements of former slaves (who remain quite apart from the rest of the population) to the Bay Islands' distinctly British feel and the indigenous populations such as the Lenca and Moskito peoples, many who still speak their native languages.

The National Psyche

Generalizations don't – and shouldn't – come easily for a country with such wide-ranging cultures. The *ladino* (someone of mixed indigenous and European parentage) business employee will have a different outlook from the Garifuna fisher, who may not have much in common with a Lencan subsistence farmer. However, Hondurans are less likely to reach a collective flashpoint than their neighbors, at least historically.

It's this easygoing nature that probably defines the national psyche more than anything else. Other Central Americans, particularly those from El Salvador, tend to view it as laziness, which is a tad harsh. For Western visitors this lack of a sense of urgency can be occasionally frustrating, but it is important to remember that attitudes toward service are very different from, say, the USA. For Hondurans, a steady, laid-back demeanor is the way things are done. A sense of reserve is often maintained – few Hondurans are in-your-face loud and assertive.

Lifestyle

Lifestyles in Honduras vary as widely as the country's shockingly unequal social spectrum. The fortunate economic elite often lead an Americanized lifestyle, driving SUVs and shopping in air-conditioned malls. Far more commonly, Hondurans are forced to scratch out a living. Poverty is perhaps at its most shocking in poor urban barrios, where there's a constant threat of violence.

Lack of opportunities have forced many to seek jobs in the USA, which has an estimated one million Hondurans, over 60% of them undocumented.

Hondurans are hugely family-oriented. They often have a wider family network than many Europeans or North Americans are used to – aunts, uncles, grandparents, cousins and even more distant relatives often play a significant role in family life.

Another attitude in Honduran society is machismo. Women's wages are much lower than men's and reported levels of domestic abuse are quite high.

People

Around 90% of Hondurans are mestizo, with a mixture of Spanish, indigenous and African heritage. One of the most ethnically diverse regions of Honduras is the Moskitia, home to Miskito and Pech people, as well as tiny numbers of Tawahka (fewer than 3000) around the Río Patuca.

Over 50,000 Garinagu (Afro-Carib Garifuna people) live on Honduras' north coast, spread between the Moskitia and the Guatemalan border. Thousands of other people with African ancestry also live on the north coast and Bay Islands.

The indigenous Tolupanes (also called Jicaque or Xicaque) live in small villages dotting the departments of Yoro and Francisco Morazán. Some 38,000 Ch'orti' Maya are found around Copán Ruinas, while the large Lenca group (as many as 300,000) live in southwestern Honduras.

Many of Honduras' elite are of white (Spanish and European) stock, but there are also small numbers in the Bay Islands who trace their (distant) roots back to Britain.

Honduras also has perhaps 100,000 people of Arab descent, mainly Catholic and Orthodox Christians originally from Palestine and the Levant.

Religion

Honduras has traditionally been an overwhelmingly Roman Catholic country, but this has changed considerably in the last few decades with the rise of the evangelical movement. Unlike Guatemala, few indigenous customs or beliefs have been integrated into Christian worship. There are also small numbers of Orthodox Christians, Jews and Muslims. Tegucigalpa and San Pedro Sula both have synagogues and mosques.

Arts

The Garifuna are known for their incredible dances. If you get a chance to see Ballet Folklórico Garífuna, don't miss it.

Musician-politician Aurelio Martínez (who was a deputy in Honduras' Congress for four years) is the star of the *punta* (traditional Garifuna music and dance) scene; his *Garífuna Soul* and *Laru Beya* albums receive rave reviews all over the world.

There's a thriving visual arts scene. Julio Visquerra (b 1943) paints in a style that's been called 'magical realist'; José Antonio Velásquez (1906–83) was a renowned primitivist painter. Urban Maeztro is the pseudonym of a Honduran street artist who makes provocative, Banksy-style work. Lovers of graphic novels should check out Honduran Independent Comics (www.hiccomics.com). Tegucigalpa's Museo para la Identidad Nacional (p359) is the best place to see exhibits by up-and-coming artists.

Landscape & Wildlife

Honduras is a country of breathtaking natural beauty, with a huge range of bird, mammal, reptile and plant species. However, illegal logging, ranching encroachment on protected lands and under-resourced authorities are putting this under threat. While the environment has plenty of defenders, it faces a tough struggle against developers, corruption and plain ignorance.

The Land

Countries don't come that big in Central America, but Honduras weighs in as the second-largest (after Nicaragua), with an area of 112,090 sq km. Its coastline includes a 644km Caribbean stretch and 124km on the Pacific side, as well as the Bay Islands and other islets. The fertile north is by far the most developed area – its banana plantations have long been a mainstay of the economy.

Much of the Honduran interior is mountainous, with peaks reaching 2849m. There are many fertile highland valleys, but no active volcanoes. Extensive wetland areas, swamps and mangrove forests are dotted along the north coast.

NATIONAL PARKS & PROTECTED AREAS

Almost a fifth of Honduran territory is officially protected as a national park or reserve, but all too often the government lacks the resources – or the political will – to stop development and deforestation. Important protected areas, including marine reserves, include the following:

Lancetilla Botanical Garden (p395) This botanical gardens has more than 1200 plant species and hundreds of bird species. Near Tela.

Parque Nacional Cusuco (p376) A cloud forest with a large population of quetzals. Near San Pedro Sula.

Parque Nacional Jeannette Kawas (p394) Habitats include mangrove swamps, a small tropical forest, beaches and offshore reefs. Near Tela.

Parque Nacional Montaña de Celaque (p392) An elevated plateau that includes Honduras' highest peak. Near Gracias.

Parque Nacional Pico Bonito (p400) High biodiversity, dense forests and many waterfalls. Near La Ceiba.

Refugio de Vida Punta Izopo (p394) Includes tropical wet forest, mangroves and wetlands. Near Tela.

Refugio de Vida Silvestre Cuero y Salado (p402) The largest manatee reserve in Central America. Monkeys and birdlife also abound. Near La Ceiba.

Reserva de la Biosfera del Río Plátano (p415) A World Heritage Site, the Río Plátano covers 5251 sq km of lowland tropical rainforest. In the Moskitia.

Roatán Marine Park (p405) Protects the entire coastline of the island and includes some outstanding coral formations. On Roatán.

Tawahka Asangni Biosphere Reserve Tropical rainforest on the ancestral lands of the Tawahka people. In the Moskitia.

Turtle Harbor Marine Reserve Turtle Harbor is a marine park popular with divers. On Utila.

BIRDS IN HONDURAS

Over 700 bird species have been recorded in Honduras. The Lago de Yojoa is an avian mecca, and national parks and reserves provide excellent opportunities for spotting toucans, parrots and raptors. Quetzals are found in cloud-forest national parks, including Cusuco, Celaque and La Tigra.

Migratory birds flock to wetlands and lagoons along the north coast from November to February. A successful breeding and reintroduction program has resulted in the scarlet macaw, the Honduran national bird, recolonizing the Copán valley, where there's also an excellent bird park.

Wildlife

There is a dazzling array of plant and animal species in Honduras. Jaguars, tapirs, crocodiles and the mighty Ceiba tree are found in tropical zones; in the cloud forests rare butterflies flit among the orchids and magnificent pines; while whale sharks and sea turtles swim in the country's turquoise Caribbean waters.

It is the sheer variety of habitats here that allows so many different species to thrive. Honduras has mangroves, freshwater lakes, oceans, lagoons, cloud forests, pine forests and tropical rainforests (considerably more than Costa Rica).

Much of the habitat is under threat from deforestation. Endangered species include the scarlet macaw (the national bird), Utilan iguana, manatee, quetzal, jaguar and tapir. Their future depends on just how much protection Honduras' protected areas can really offer.

Environmental Issues

Deforestation is the most pressing environmental issue facing Honduras today. Though Honduras' forests are the densest in Central America, they're disappearing fast – around 2% is lost each year. A Voluntary Partnership Agreement between Honduras and the EU was agreed to in 2018 so that only legally obtained timber could be exported to Europe. However, illegal timber exports to the USA and Caribbean islands continue.

Activists who oppose loggers, developers or ranchers are regularly threatened, and even killed. In 2015 Honduras was named the 'deadliest country in the world to be a land and environmental defender' by environmental NGO Global Witness (the title more recently went to Nicaragua). The Punta Sal reserve near Tela is now the Parque Nacional Jeannette Kawas, named after the campaigner who opposed construction plans and was murdered. The 2016 murder of Berta Cáceres, who protested the construction of Agua Zarca Dam across a river sacred to her Lenca people, received worldwide news coverage.

There are myriad other environmental concerns. Honduras lost two-thirds of its mangrove forests between 1980 and 2003. Vast plantations of African palms are spreading along the north coast, a monocultural environment that provides little in the way of habitat for wildlife; parts of the Reserva de la Biósfera del Río Plátano are being encroached upon by ranchers, slashing and burning jungle for cattle fields.

SURVIVAL GUIDE

ℹ Directory A–Z

ACCESSIBLE TRAVEL

Honduras lacks facilities for disabled travelers, other than in upscale hotels and resorts. Wheelchair-bound visitors will find it difficult to negotiate towns because of poor-quality sidewalks and cobblestones. Public transportation is not geared to less-able travelers, though the ferries to Roatán do offer wheelchair access.

ACCOMMODATIONS

In most towns you can get a functional room with a bathroom and a fan for around L350 to L550. In the big cities and the Bay Islands, costs are higher (L500 to L1000).

You'll find hostels with dorm beds in Tegucigalpa, Copán Ruinas, Utila, Roatán, La Ceiba and San Pedro Sula. Costs vary from L175 to L300 a bed.

CHILDREN

Like most of Latin America, Honduras is very open and welcoming of children. There's no taboo about bringing children to restaurants or performances, and pregnant women are ushered to the front of the line in banks, government offices and many private businesses.

Travelers will be hard-pressed to find child-specific amenities like car seats, high chairs and bassinets, except perhaps in top-end hotels and resorts. Disposable diapers (nappies), wipes, formula and other basics, however, are available in most large supermarkets.

CLIMATE

Confusingly, there are two rainy seasons in Honduras. On the north coast, it rains year-round, but the wettest months are from September to February. During this time floods can occur, impeding travel and occasionally causing severe damage. The south and west of the country has a different, distinct rainy season between May and October.

The mountainous interior is much cooler than the humid coastal lowlands. Altitude affects temperatures greatly: in places like Tegucigalpa (975m) and Gracias (803m) the heat rarely gets too oppressive.

Hurricane season is June to November.

CUSTOMS REGULATIONS

Customs checks are pretty lax; while police and customs officers are entitled to search you at any time, especially in border areas, they rarely do. Even searches at the airport tend to be perfunctory, though you have to submit your luggage to an x-ray upon entering and exiting Honduras. The exception is if something about your appearance or demeanor suggests to the officer you may be carrying drugs.

EMBASSIES & CONSULATES

Most embassies are in Tegucigalpa. British citizens are represented by their embassy in Guatemala; the nearest Dutch and Canadian embassies are in Costa Rica, and the nearest Australian, Irish and New Zealand embassies are in Mexico City.

Belizean Embassy (☎2238-4614; consulado belice@yahoo.com; Av República de Chile, Centro Comercial Hotel Honduras Maya)

El Salvadoran Embassy (☎2232-4947; http://embajadahonduras.rree.gob.sv; Diagonal Aguán 2952, Colonia Altos de Miramontes; ⏲7:30am-noon & 2-4pm Mon-Fri)

French Embassy (☎2232-5444; www.ambafrance-hn.org; Calle 4, Blvd Juan Pablo II; ⏲7:30am-1pm & 2-4:30pm Mon-Fri)

German Embassy (☎2275-9292; www.tegucigalpa.diplo.de; Av República Dominicana 925; ⏲8am-4pm Mon-Fri)

Guatemalan Embassy (☎2231-1543; www.honduras.minex.gob.gt; Calle Bonn)

Nicaraguan Embassy (☎2232-4290; www.cancilleria.gob.ni; Av Choluteca, Bloque M-1, No 1130, Colonia Lomas de Tepeyac; ⏲9am-5pm Mon-Fri)

US Embassy (☎2236-9320; http://honduras.usembassy.gov; Av La Paz; ⏲7:30-11:30am Mon-Fri)

INTERNET ACCESS

Wi-fi is fairly ubiquitous in Honduras, with nearly every hotel and hostel offering it for free (even if, in many cases, the signal doesn't always reach every room). Many public squares and other government institutions offer free access (though these services are rarely very reliable), as do many restaurants, bars and cafes. Many hotels offer internet terminals.

LEGAL MATTERS

There are tourist police in towns including San Pedro Sula and Tela, but as very few officers speak English, don't expect too much help. Police officers in Honduras aren't immune to corruption – if you have any problem with the police, contact your embassy immediately.

LGBTIQ+ TRAVELERS

Honduras is rather a contradictory place for gay people. While on the one hand same-sex marriage and adoption are both banned in the constitution, it is also illegal to discriminate against people on the grounds of their sexuality. Gay people are visible in society here, though open displays of affection between gay or lesbian couples are unusual, and even risky in some situations. Despite that, there are small yet active gay and lesbian communities in all major cities, though most socializing takes place online.

MONEY

ATMs

➡ There are cash machines in cities and towns throughout the country, though don't rely on them working in small towns.

➡ ATM robberies are common: never use them at night, unless you're in a secure environment such as a mall.

➡ In daytime use ATMs inside banks that have armed guards on patrol outside.

Bargaining

Crafts are fairly rare in Honduras, so you won't have to haggle while shopping. Prices for many services are fixed, so there shouldn't be any need to bargain: in large cities, for example, both *colectivos* and private taxis have a single fixed price for rides around town. Ask at your hotel what taxis should cost – if you get in knowing what the price should be, most drivers won't argue.

Cash

➡ The unit of currency in Honduras is the lempira (L), which is divided into 100 centavos.

➡ Many establishments give prices in US dollars, and are happy to accept payment in them too.

SLEEPING PRICE RANGES

The following price ranges refer to a double room with bathroom. Taxes are included in the price.

$ less than L1000

$$ L1000–1500

$$$ more than L1500

EATING PRICE RANGES

The following price ranges refer to the typical cost of a main course.

$ less than L100

$$ L100–200

$$$ more than L200

➡ Banks will exchange US dollars and occasionally euros, although some will insist on clean, crisp bills only and no $20 bills. Bring your passport.

Credit Cards

➡ Visa and MasterCard are accepted at most midrange and top-end hotels, as well as at some hostels, but expect a 5% to 10% credit card surcharge (which makes using them quite expensive in the long run).

➡ Cash advances on cards are available at most banks in case of emergency.

Exchange Rates

The US dollar and (to a lesser extent) the euro are the only foreign currencies that are easily exchanged in Honduras; away from the borders you will even find it difficult to change the currencies of neighboring countries.

Taxes

Restaurants and hotels are supposed to always include VAT in their prices, but it is not always included in hotel-room prices, so be sure to ask when booking. Many hotels will give you a room without VAT charged as long as you do not require a receipt.

Tipping

Tipping is not common in *comedores,* cafes or simple restaurants, but is appreciated. Upscale restaurants will automatically add a 10% service charge to your bill.

OPENING HOURS

Businesses are generally open during the following hours.

Banks 8:30am–4:30pm Monday to Friday and 8:30am–noon Saturday

Bars noon–midnight daily

Restaurants 7am or 8am–9pm daily

Shops 9am–6pm daily

PUBLIC HOLIDAYS

New Year's Day January 1

Day of the Americas April 14

Semana Santa (Holy Week) Thursday, Friday and Saturday before Easter Sunday

Labor Day May 1

Independence Day September 15

Francisco Morazán Day October 3

Día de la Raza (Columbus Day) October 12

Army Day October 21

Christmas Day December 25

SAFE TRAVEL

➡ Be cautious in cities, especially San Pedro Sula and Tegucigalpa, which both have gang problems (though travelers are rarely targeted). Walking in the center in daytime is usually fine.

➡ Don't show off your belongings, never walk alone or down side streets, and keep an eye out for people approaching you: daylight robbery is common.

➡ Always take a cab at night.

➡ Watch yourself on the north coast, especially on the beach.

➡ It's best not to walk alone on city beaches in Tela or La Ceiba.

➡ Use ATMs inside banks to avoid potential skimmers that steal your bank information.

TELEPHONE

The country code for Honduras is 504. There are no area codes, and all telephone numbers in the country (both cell and landlines) have eight digits.

Cell Phones

Honduras has widespread cell coverage; Claro and Tigo are the two main providers. SIM cards (usable with unlocked phones) are easily available from any operator (bring your passport) for around L100. Most deals will get you 3G data as well as calling credit. Phone credit *(saldo)* can be topped up in many places, including small stores.

VISAS

Citizens of the EU, Australia, Canada, Japan, New Zealand and the USA normally receive free, 90-day tourist cards when entering the country. This also applies to nationals of the countries signed up to the CA-4 border agreement – Guatemala, Nicaragua, Honduras and El Salvador.

Other nationalities, including most Asian and African countries, have to apply for a visa in advance from a Honduran embassy, and pay a fee of US$30.

Once inside Honduras you can apply for a one-time 30-day extension (US$20) at the main immigration office (p367) in Tegucigalpa (travelers have reported problems gaining extensions in other offices). Or just take a trip outside the CA-4 border agreement area (Belize and Costa Rica are nearest) for at least three days, then get a new 90-day visa upon re-entering Honduras.

VOLUNTEERING

A number of organizations offer volunteer opportunities in Honduras, on projects ranging from building homes to teaching English.

The website www.transitionsabroad.com has a long list of groups that run volunteer programs here, from large operations like **Casa Alianza** (www.casa-alianza.org) to the tiny Utila Iguana Research & Breeding Station (p410).

WEIGHTS & MEASURES

The metric system is used in Honduras.

WOMEN TRAVELERS

Honduras is still a male-dominated society. Personal safety is the biggest concern for female travelers. Most women do not feel threatened while traveling alone in Honduras, but it certainly pays to adopt an assertive demeanor.

WORK

Most independent travelers who stay in Honduras to work do so on the Bay Islands; dive instructors are almost exclusively foreigners, and many people completing dive-master training raise a little extra cash working as waiters or bartenders in West End, West Bay or Utila. Most do not have work permits and leave every three to six months to get a new tourist visa.

Getting There & Away

AIR

Frequent direct flights connect Honduras with other Central American capitals and destinations in the USA. There are no direct flights to Europe.

Airports & Airlines

Palmerola Airport, estimated to be completed in 2019, is expected to become Honduras's largest international airport. Otherwise, San Pedro Sula's airport, Tegucigalpa and Roatán also have international departures and arrivals including to Atlanta, Houston and Miami in the US.

Honduras has no national airline. Airlines flying to Honduras include **Aeroméxico** (www.aeromexico.com), **American Airlines** (www.aa.com), **Avianca** (www.avianca.com), **Copa** (www.copa.com), **Delta** (www.delta.com), **Spirit Airlines** (www.spirit.com), **Sunwing** (www.sunwing.ca), **TAG** (www.tag.com.gt), **Tropic Air** (www.tropicair.com) and **United** (www.united.com).

LAND

Border crossings include Corinto and El Florido (Guatemala), El Amatillo and El Poy (El Salvador), and Guasaule, Leimus and Las Manos (Nicaragua).

There are four main luxury-class international bus companies serving Honduras from neighboring countries: Platinum, Pullmantur, Tica Bus and Hedman Alas.

The two hubs for international departures are San Pedro Sula and Tegucigalpa. From these two cities you can get to San Salvador (El Salvador); Guatemala City, Antigua and Santa Elena/Flores (Guatemala); Managua (Nicaragua); San José (Costa Rica); and Panama City (Panama).

It's also possible to take local buses, crossing the border on foot and picking up another bus on the other side. This is cheaper but far slower.

Guatemala

To Guatemala, the main crossings are at El Florido, Agua Caliente and Corinto. There's no official fee to leave Honduras or enter Guatemala, but immigration officials often ask for a dollar or two.

The 24-hour border at Agua Caliente is a half-hour bus ride from Nueva Ocotepeque. Buses connect the Honduran and Guatemalan immigration posts, which are 2km apart. From the Guatemalan side buses go to Esquipulas, where you can connect to Guatemala City or Flores.

The 24-hour border at El Florido is 9km west of Copán Ruinas and connected by very regular minibus services (L25, 20 minutes, every 20 minutes). If you're on a trans-border bus or shuttle bus you'll have to get off and clear customs and immigration on both sides of the frontier. Moneychangers will approach you, usually offering decent rates. There's also a bank on the Guatemalan side.

The Guatemalan border at Corinto (open 6am to 9pm) is a 51km bus ride southwest of Omoa (L48, 1½ hours, every hour). Buses to the border leave from the main highway and will drop you at a set of *comedores*. From there, walk through immigration procedures. Microbuses waiting on the Guatemalan side connect to Puerto Barrios.

El Salvador

To El Salvador, the main crossings are El Poy and El Amatillo; the crossing at Sabanetas near Marcala is *not* open for foreigners.

The El Salvador border at El Poy (open 24 hours) is a short bus ride from Nueva Ocotepeque (L18, 15 minutes, every 20 minutes to 7pm). On both sides, the bus drops you about 100m from the border, from where you walk across and catch a bus onward. On the Salvadoran side, buses leave frequently for San Salvador and La Palma.

> **ETIQUETTE**
>
> Hondurans are fairly easygoing, and it's unusual for them to be easily upset or annoyed by foreigners not knowing cultural norms.
>
> It's polite to greet people in Spanish when you first see them each day: *buenas días* (in the morning), *buenas tardes* (after midday) or *buenas noches* (after dark).
>
> Men tend to shake hands when they meet. Women often embrace one another, but tend to remain on nodding terms with men, unless they know them well.

DEPARTURE TAX

If you fly out of Honduras, you must pay L880 (US$40) in departure tax at the airport. The domestic departure tax is L44 (US$2). These prices are often included in your tickets: you'll be told at check-in whether or not you need to pay.

There are buses from Choluteca in Honduras' south to the Salvadoran border at El Amatillo (L55, two hours, every 20 minutes until 6:30pm).

Nicaragua

Crossings to Nicaragua are at Guasaule, El Espino, Las Manos and Leimus. In southern Honduras, buses run from Choluteca to the Nicaraguan border at Guasaule (L30, 45 minutes, every 20 minutes 6am to 6pm).

For the El Espino border you'll have to travel via San Marcos de Colón, from where there's very regular transportation (L20, 15 minutes).

For Las Manos, buses run from Tegucigalpa (L97, 2½ hours, three daily).

From Leimus pickup trucks head to Puerto Lempira (L200, four hours) mornings only.

SEA

The only scheduled international passenger boat services to/from Honduras are the small boats that run weekly from Puerto Cortés to Belize.

If you arrive or depart from Honduras by sea, be sure to clear your paperwork (entry and exit stamps, if necessary) immediately with the immigration office in Puerto Cortés.

Getting Around

AIR

Domestic air travel in Honduras is fairly pricey, though the safety record is generally good. There are connections from La Ceiba, Tegucigalpa and San Pedro Sula to Utila and Roatán, and also between the three major cities themselves. Routes also open up the Moskitia and the Bay Island of Guanaja from La Ceiba.

BICYCLE

On the mainland there are few opportunities to rent bikes, as heavy traffic, bad roads and the danger of being robbed are big deterrents.

Bikes really come into their own on the Bay Islands, particularly little Utila, where there is very little traffic – riding around here is both safe and fun.

BOAT

Passenger ferries operate between La Ceiba and the Bay Islands and Utila and Roatan.There's a regular ferry between Trujillo and Guanaja, the third of the Bay Islands.

In the Moskitia, almost all transportation is by water. There are also water taxis on Roatán from West End to West Bay, and from Coyolito on the Golfo de Fonseca over to the Isla del Tigre.

BUS

Buses are a cheap and easy way to get around Honduras, though there are also some very fancy (and consequently far more costly) services. The first buses of the day often start very early in the morning; the last bus usually departs in the late afternoon. Buses on major highways run later.

On major bus routes, you'll often have a choice between taking a *directo* (direct) or a *parando* (an ordinary bus that makes many stops). Microbuses or *rapiditos* are minivan-like buses.

City buses are not recommended due to safety issues – gangs 'tax' transportation companies and occasionally assault drivers.

CAR & MOTORCYCLE

Driving on the highway in Honduras is like playing in the advanced level of a video game. Many locals drive at insane speeds (to avoid the perceived threat of carjacking), but it can be safe to drive in Honduras as long as you're mindful of your speed and drive defensively.

The main highways are paved and mostly in reasonable condition; most are also toll roads, which means regular but meager payments (around L20) for drivers. Away from the highways, roads tend to be quite rough and sometimes they're unsurfaced: conditions can vary wildly according to rainfall and the time of year, ranging from acceptable to impassable. Always check with locals on your route before you head off, and bear in mind that many navigation systems will send you along the most direct route, rather than the best road – getting local knowledge is always key.

Rental cars are available in Tegucigalpa, San Pedro Sula and La Ceiba, and on Roatán. Prices start at L650 a day for an economy car. Motorcycles and scooters can be rented on Utila and Roatán.

TAXI

Taxis are everywhere in Honduran towns. It's very common to share a ride in many places, so each passenger pays around L20. If you want a private ride, rates start at about L60. Fares increase at night.

In the major cities, *colectivos* (shared taxis) ply a number of prescribed routes, costing around L20 to L35 per passenger.

Three-wheeled *mototaxis* (tuk-tuks) are very common in small towns and villages, but they're not allowed to operate in big city centers. Expect to pay about half what you would in a taxi: typically a ride around town costs L10 to L25 per person.

Nicaragua

POP 6.3 MILLION

Includes ➡

Best Places to Eat

- Miss Dell's Kitchen (p447)
- Asados Doña Tania (p437)
- Darinia's Kitchen (p496)

Best Places to Stay

- La Bastilla Ecolodge (p487)
- La Posada Azul (p462)
- Casa Lucia (p437)

Why Go?

Nicaragua offers travelers volcanic landscapes, colonial architecture, sensational beaches, remote, idyllic islands, wave-battered Pacific beaches and pristine forests. Colonial architecture comes in two distinct flavors. The elegant streetscapes of Granada, Nicaragua's best-preserved colonial town, have been entrancing travelers for centuries. Working-class León offers a different experience where crumbling 300-year-old houses and churches are interspersed with revolutionary murals, and architectural masterpieces. The great outdoors are relatively untamed – at many key attractions, there are no signs and few crowds – making this so-called 'land of lakes and volcanoes' a fantastic place for an independent adventure. Whether it's dipping your toes into the crystalline Caribbean or paddling out to the crashing waves of the pounding Pacific, Nicaragua's beaches always deliver the goods. Few destinations have such beauty as Nicaragua, yet remain undeveloped.

When to Go

Managua

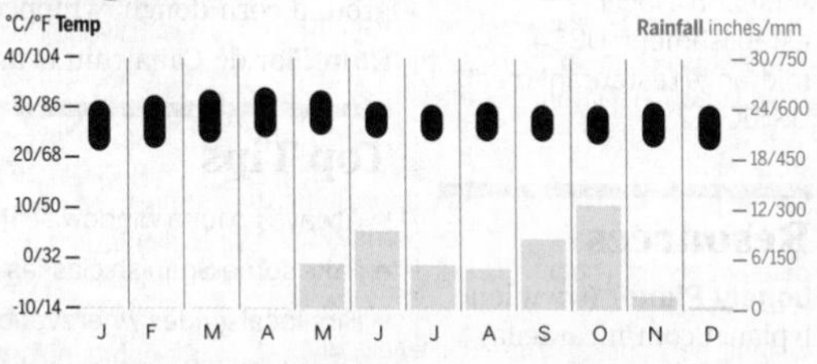

Dec–Apr
Hot, sunny and dry conditions throughout the country.

May–Oct
The biggest swell on the Pacific side pulls a crowd to the best breaks.

Nov
Cool weather and green countryside make for the best trekking.

FACT FACTS

Currency Córdoba (C$), US dollar (US$)

Visas Generally not required for stays up to 90 days.

Money ATMs are widespread in most midsize towns.

Capital Managua

Emergency Fire ☎115 (from cell phones ☎911), police ☎118, ambulance ☎128

Language Spanish

Exchange Rates

Australia	A$1	C$23.42
Canada	C$1	C$25.08
Costa Rica	₡100	C$5.43
Euro zone	€1	C$37.55
Japan	¥100	C$29.58
New Zealand	NZ$1	C$22.50
UK	UK£1	C$43.79
USA	US$1	C$32.97

Daily Costs

- Dorm bed: US$9–15; double room in a midrange hotel: US$20–45
- Meal in a local establishment: US$4; midrange restaurant meal: US$10–12

Resources

Lonely Planet (www.lonelyplanet.com/nicaragua)

Vianica.com (www.vianica.com/traveling)

Intur (www.intur.gob.ni)

Entering the Country

Nicaragua shares borders with Costa Rica and Honduras. Generally, Nicaraguan border crossings are chaotic (there are no signs anywhere), but the procedure is fairly straightforward provided you have your documents in order. Two of the busiest border crossings – with Honduras and Costa Rica – are open around the clock, while the rest have limited opening hours.

TWO-WEEK ITINERARY

If you've limited time in Nicaragua, a trip through the southwest is big on awesome and small on hours in the bus. Kick off your trip in charismatic **Granada**. Spend three nights taking in the wonderful streetscapes, and visiting the museums and churches. From here, you can head out for day trips or overnighters to the lush crater at **Laguna de Apoyo**, the lyrical artisan villages known as **Pueblos Blancos**, or to the **Mombacho** and **Masaya** volcanoes and protected wild preserves.

Next head down the highway to San Jorge, from where you'll take the ferry across to the out-of-this world **Isla de Ometepe** with its twin volcanoes and endless outdoor activities. From there, it's across the isthmus to the Southern Pacific Beaches. Most people begin and end their beach time in the funked-out international beach village of **San Juan del Sur**, but definitely plan on spending a night or two on the surf beaches north and south of here. If you are headed north from here, you won't want to miss a stop off in **León**.

Essential Food & Drink

Gallo pinto Daily staple: red beans boiled with garlic, mixed with rice fried with onion and red pepper.

Quesillo Tortilla stuffed with cheese, topped with pickled onions and sour cream.

Nacatamal Spiced chicken and vegetables cooked inside ground corn dough, wrapped in a banana leaf.

Rum Flor de Caña rum is among the best in the world.

Top Tips

- Always go for a window seat in public transport.
- Take some Spanish classes.
- Hire local guides wherever possible.
- Forget about keeping a tight schedule. Allow extra days in your trip, especially if you're traveling by public transport.
- Take advantage of the hearty Nicaraguan-style breakfast served at most hotels – it will get you through most of the day.
- Have your hostel or hotel to call you taxi (discuss the price before getting in).

MANAGUA

POP 1.03 MILLION / ELEV 83M

Managua is not the easiest place to get your head around. It has no discernible center; its attractions are scattered around its many neighborhoods and the trick is to know when to go where.

Stay a day or two and you will see that big, bad Managua ain't so bad after all, and that this truly is the heartstring that holds the nation's culture and commerce together. Skip it altogether, and you miss out on the revolutionary landmarks, vibrant dining and nightlife scenes and a slice of down-to-earth urban life that you're unlikely to see anywhere else.

Aside from diving into the spirited whirl of sprawling markets, improbable electric trees, remarkable street art and impressive monuments, Managua also gives you easy access to nearby lagoons, the nature reserve of Chocoyero-El Brujo, plus a smattering of fun beaches like Pochomil.

History

A fishing encampment as early as 6000 years ago, Managua has been an important trading center for at least two millennia. When Spanish chronicler Fernández de Oviedo arrived in 1528, he estimated Managua's population at around 40,000; most of these original inhabitants fled to the Sierritas, the small mountains just south, shortly after the Spanish arrived. The small town, without even a hospital or school until the 1750s, didn't really achieve any prominence until 1852, when the seemingly endless civil war between Granada and León was resolved by placing the capital here.

The clever compromise might have worked out better had a geologist been at hand: Managua sits atop a network of fault lines that have shaped its history ever since. The late 1800s were rocked by quakes that destroyed the new capital's infrastructure, with churches and banks crumbling as the ground flowed beneath their feet. In 1931 the epicenter was the stadium – dozens were killed during a big game. In 1968 a single powerful jolt right beneath what's now Metrocentro mall destroyed an entire neighborhood.

And on the evening of December 23, 1972, a series of powerful tremors rocked the city, culminating in a 6.2 magnitude quake that killed 11,000 people and destroyed 53,000 homes. The blatant siphoning of international relief funds by President Somoza touched off the Sandinista-led revolution, which was followed by the Contra War, and the city center, including the beautiful old cathedral, was never rebuilt. Rather, it was replaced by a crazy maze of unnamed streets, with shacks that turned into shanties that turned into homes and later buildings. There have been some efforts to resurrect the old city center – the restoration of the Malecón (waterfront) was certainly a promising development – but new construction had come to a standstill at research time due to the outbreak of violence in April 2018.

Sights & Activities

★Antigua Catedral CATHEDRAL

(Catedral de Santiago; Map p436; 14 Av Sureste, Área Monumental) The hollow shell of Managua's Old Cathedral remains Managua's most poignant metaphor, shattered by the 1972 earthquake – and slowly undergoing

WARNING: POLITICAL UNREST IN NICARAGUA

At the time of writing, the situation on the ground in Nicaragua remains volatile. The use of deadly force by riot police and government-funded Sandinista mobs against largely unarmed protesters led to locals barricading themselves in their neighborhoods and erecting roadblocks. There has been looting of small businesses and the torching of some government buildings. The fighting has been fiercest at night and concentrated in the areas of Masaya and the capital city of Managua. Granada and León have also been impacted. Many locals are under a self-imposed curfew. The violence has seemingly subsided from the summer of 2018 during which, at last count, 300 people were killed – mostly unarmed protesters by the police and government-funded supporters. Members of the clergy have also been targets of violence. President Daniel Ortega steadfastly refuses to call new elections before 2021, in spite of calls to do so by a large proportion of the population.

Foreigners are not deliberately targeted by the violence, but if you're unlucky, you can get caught up in it, so make sure you get the latest information before traveling to or around Nicaragua.

Nicaragua Highlights

1. **Isla de Ometepe** (p455) Scrambling to the summits for views to everywhere and beyond on this lush and lovely island.
2. **Corn Islands** (p493) Swimming through crystal-clear Caribbean waters.
3. **Granada** (p443) Savoring the architectural delights and spirited streets of this colorful city.
4. **León** (p467) Hitting the bohemian bars of this buzzing city to find out why the revolution wasn't televised.
5. **Southern Pacific Coast** (p460) Charging the big waves and relaxing in chill surf towns.
6. **Reserva Natural Laguna de Apoyo** (p449) Swimming in clear waters, or lazing about in a hammock.
7. **Matagalpa** (p484) Discovering the heart of the hardworking highlands in this earthy town.

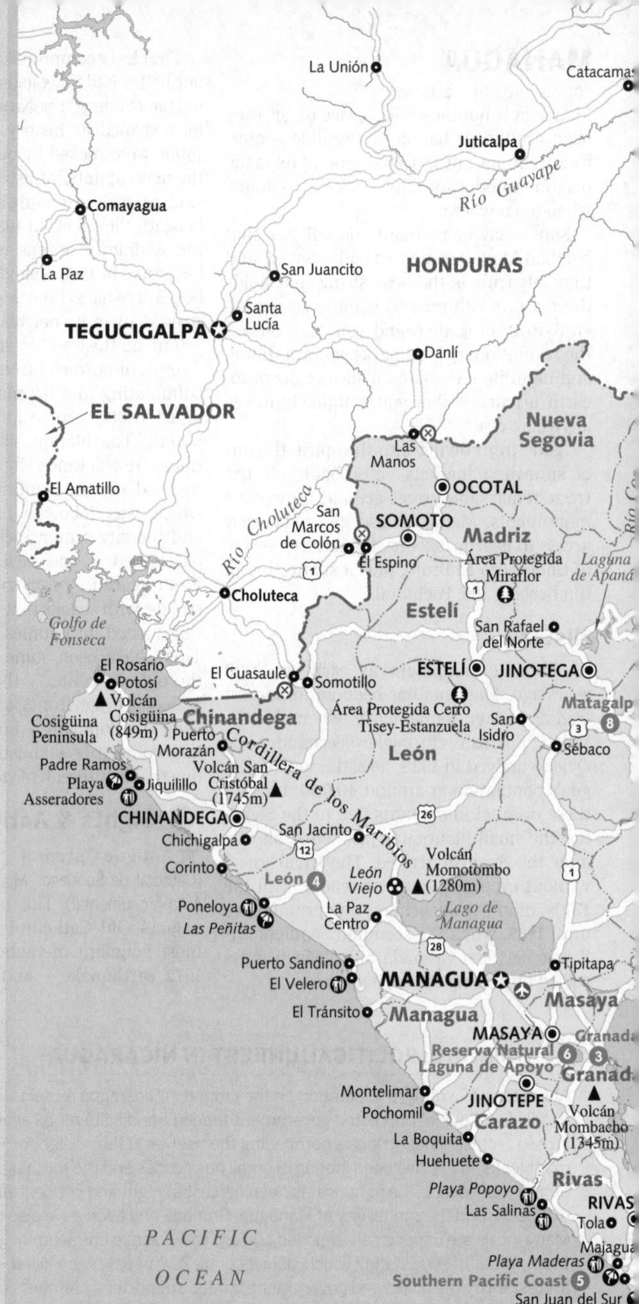

Cabo Gracias a Dios
Laguna Bismuna
Río Coco (Segovia)
Leimus
Waspám
Bismuna Tara
Río Patuca
La Troquera
Cordillera Entre Ríos
San Andres
Río Wawa
Luciana
Dákura
Río Waspuk
Atlántico Norte
Sisin
Laguna Pahara
Reserva de Biosfera Bosawás
BILWI (PUERTO CABEZAS)
Yulú
Kukalaya
Lamlaya
Río Bocay
Rosita
Costa de Miskitos
Laguna Karatá
Jinotega
Siuna
El Empalme
El Ocote
Laguna Wounta
Wiwili
El Cuá
Cordillera Isabelia
Valle Kuikuinita
Río Prinzapolka
Yaoska
Kangrina
Río Tuma
Matagalpa
Río Grande de Matagalpa
Barrera
Karawala
San José
Barra de Río Grande
San Ramón
Río Kurinwas
Matiguás
Chamarro
Tortuguero
Tasbapauni
Atlántico Sur
Boaco
Orinoco
BOACO
El Ayote
Laguna de Perlas
Pearl Keys
Río Kama
Camoapa
Laguna de Perlas
Chontales
El Alto
San Lorenzo
Río Escondido
El Rama
Corn Islands 2
JUIGALPA
Isla El Muerto
BLUEFIELDS
7
Río Rama
Río Ojecuapa
San Ubaldo
Bahía de Bluefields
CARIBBEAN SEA
Isla Zapatera
Lago de Nicaragua
Río Tepenaguasapa
Morrito
Monkey Point
Altagracia
Volcán Concepción (1610m) 1
Río Punta Gorda
Punta Gorda
San Jorge
San Miguelito
Río San Juan
La Virgen
Isla de Ometepe
Archipiélago de Solentiname
Río Maíz
Bahía Punta Gorda
Sapoá
Peñas Blancas
SAN CARLOS
El Ostional
Boca de Sábalos
La Cruz
Los Chiles
El Castillo
1
San Juan del Norte (Greytown)
Río Frío
COSTA RICA
7 Río San Juan
Barra del Colorado

Managua

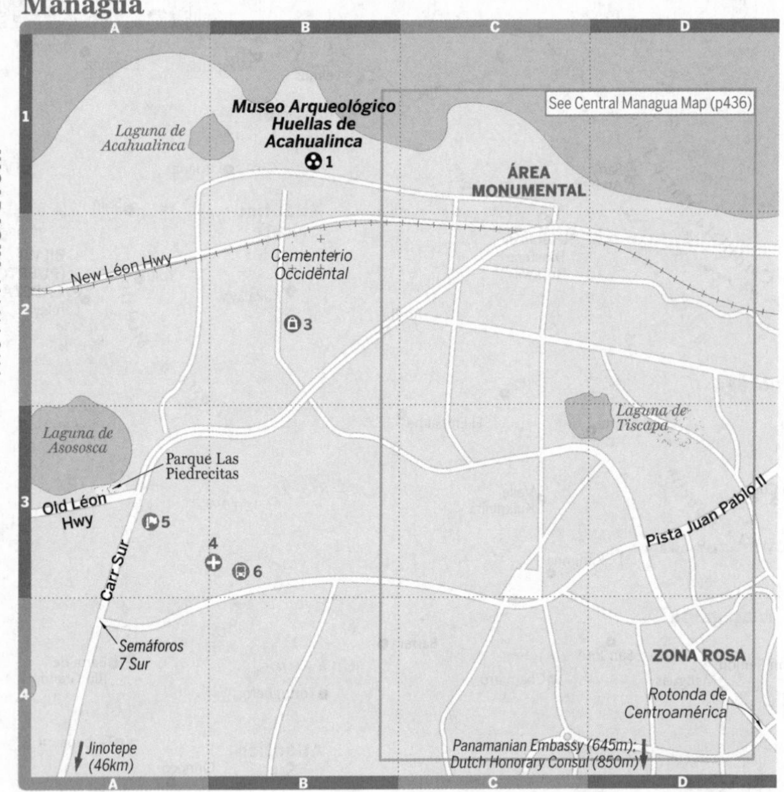

Managua

Top Sights

1 Museo Arqueológico Huellas de Acahualinca B1

Drinking & Nightlife

2 DeLaFinca Cafe E3

Shopping

3 Esperanza En Acción B2

Information

4 Hospital Alemán-Nicaragüense B3
5 US Embassy A3

Transport

6 Mercado Israel Lewites B3
7 Mercado Mayoreo H3
8 Mercado Roberto Huembes E4

restoration. Though its neoclassical facade is beautiful and serene, attended by stone angels and dappled in golden light, its interior is empty and off-limits: a cathedral without a heart in a city without a center.

★Museo Arqueológico Huellas de Acahualinca ARCHAEOLOGICAL SITE

(Map p434; 2266-5774; Calle Museo de Acahualinca, Barrio Acahualinca; US$3; 8am-4pm Mon-Fri) Discovered by miners in 1874, these fossilized tracks record the passage of perhaps 10 people – men, women and children – as well as birds, raccoons, deer and possum across the muddy shores of Lago de Managua some 6000 to 8000 years ago. Despite early speculation that they were running from a volcanic eruption, forensics specialists have determined that these folks were in no hurry – and, interestingly, were fairly tall at between 145cm and 160cm. Come here by taxi (US$2 to US$4).

National Assembly Pedestrian Walk PUBLIC ART

(Map p436; Av Central) East of the National Assembly along Av Central is a pedestrian

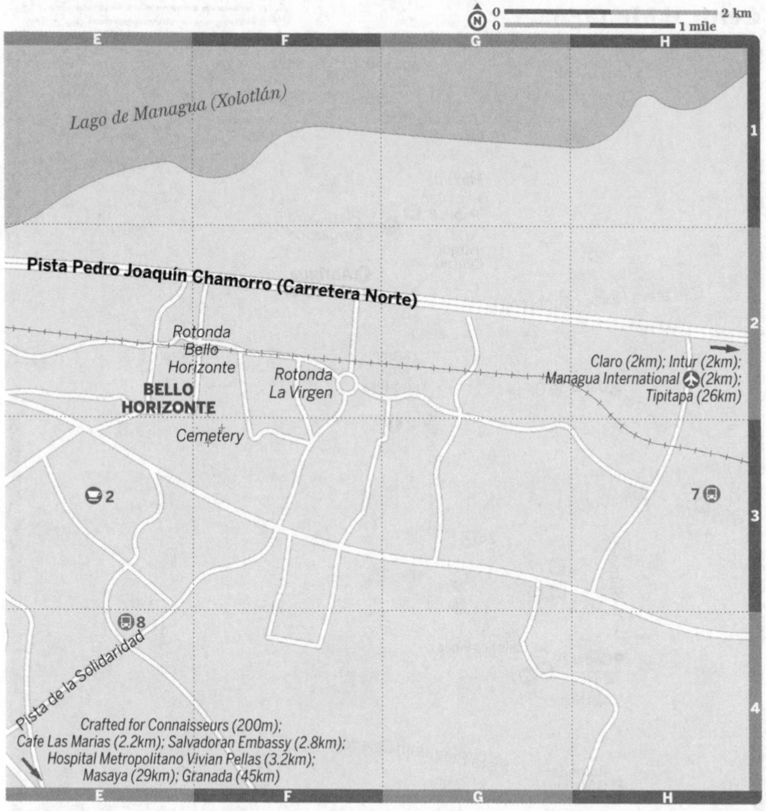

walk with open-air exhibits on Nicaragua's history, featuring everything from historic photos of Sandino to evocative pictures of pre-earthquake Managua. It's a great path to take if you're walking from Barrio Bolonia to the lakefront, especially if you're interested in Nicaragua's political and literary histories.

★Claudio Perez Cruz OUTDOORS
(5889-89105; https://casaluciamanagua.com) Based at Casa Lucia (p437), young, knowledgeable, bilingual Claudio is extremely passionate about Nicaragua and all it has to offer. He has contacts all over the country and can either travel with you or make arrangements for you, depending on your interests and the amount of time you have. Exploring Managua with him is a blast.

Nica on Pedals MOUNTAIN BIKING
(Map p436; 8281-1512; www.nicaonpedals.com; Monte de los Olivos, 1c N, 1c O, ½c N, Casa 55, Colonial Los Robles) Based at **Managua Backpackers Inn** (Map p436; 2267-0006; www.managuahostel.com; 15 Av Sureste, Monte de los Olivos, 1c N, 1c O, ½c N, Casa 56, Los Robles; dm/s/d from US$10/22/30;), these guys offer an active, adrenaline-packed way of exploring Nicaragua's great outdoors. They take you downhill biking on Ventarron Hill, just outside Managua, with great views of Volcán Masaya (US$63 per person), where there are several trails of varying difficulty.

Sleeping

★La Bicicleta Hostal HOSTEL $
(Map p436; 2225-2557; www.labicicletahostal.com; Calle San Juan, Restaurante La Marsellaise, 2½ c E, Villa Santa Fe; dm US$13, r with/without bathroom US$32/40;) At this sustainably built hostel in a stellar location, dorms and guest rooms are named after bicycles – try the Tandem for two people, or the Penny Farthing if there's four of you;

Central Managua

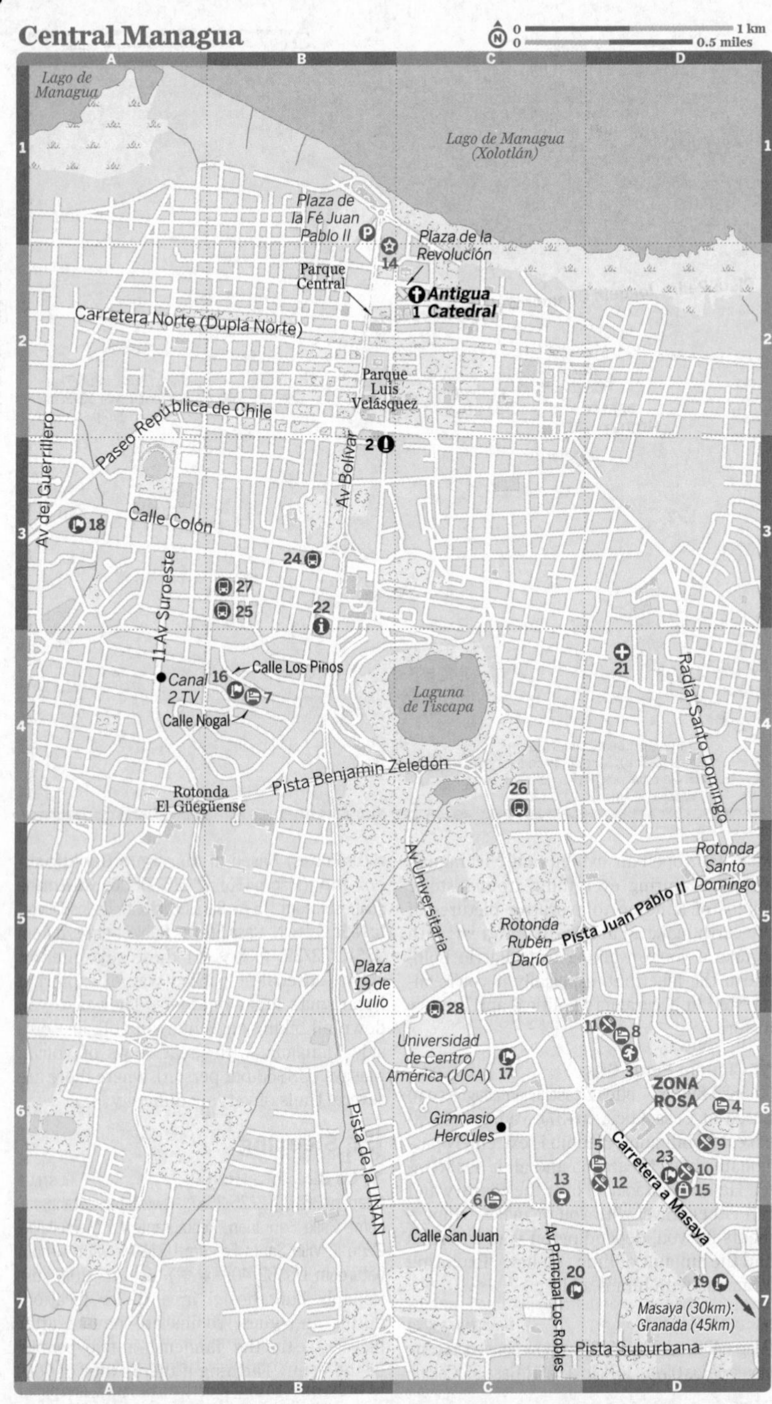

0 1 km
0 0.5 miles
Lago de Managua
Lago de Managua (Xolotlán)
Plaza de la Fé Juan Pablo II
14
Plaza de la Revolución
Parque Central
1 Antigua Catedral
Carretera Norte (Dupla Norte)
Parque Luis Velásquez
Paseo República de Chile
2
Av del Guerrillero
Av Bolívar
18
Calle Colón
24
11 Av Suroeste
27
25
22
21
Radial Santo Domingo
Canal 2 TV
16
Calle Los Pinos
7
Calle Nogal
Laguna de Tiscapa
Pista Benjamin Zeledón
Rotonda El Güegüense
26
Av Universitaria
Rotonda Santo Domingo
Rotonda Rubén Darío
Pista Juan Pablo II
Plaza 19 de Julio
28
11
8
3
Universidad de Centro América (UCA)
17
ZONA ROSA
4
Pista de la UNAN
Gimnasio Hercules
9
5
23
10
Carretera a Masaya
12
15
13
6
Calle San Juan
Av Principal Los Robles
20
19
Masaya (30km); Granada (45km)
Pista Suburbana

Central Managua

Top Sights
1 Antigua Catedral C2

Sights
2 National Assembly Pedestrian Walk B3

Activities, Courses & Tours
3 Nica on Pedals D6

Sleeping
4 Casa Lucia D6
5 Hotel Casa Colonial D6
6 La Bicicleta Hostal C6
7 La Posada del Arcangel B4
8 Managua Backpackers Inn D6

Eating
9 Asados Doña Tania D6
10 De Muerte Lenta D6
11 Don Cándido D6
12 Terraza Peruana D6

Drinking & Nightlife
13 Estación Central C6

Entertainment
14 Teatro Nacional Rubén Darío B2

Shopping
15 Nostalgia de Nicaragua Cigar D6

Information
16 Canadian Embassy B4
17 Costa Rican Consulate C6
18 French Embassy A3
19 German Embassy D7
20 Honduran Embassy C7
21 Hospital Bautista D4
22 Intur Central B3
23 Mexican Embassy D6

Transport
24 Central Line B3
25 Tica Bus B3
26 Transnica C4
27 Transporte del Sol B3
28 UCA Minivans C5

all are individually styled with inspirational quotes on walls and good beds. There's a lovely hammock-strung garden and a guest kitchen, but the biggest shout-out goes to the super-helpful staff.

★Casa Lucia B&B $$

(Map p436; ☎8898 9105; https://casaluciamanagua.com; 33 Calle Sureste, frente Parque Los Robles, Planes de Altamira No 1; s/d US$35/45; ❄📶) In a quiet, walkable neighborhood, this cheery, peach-colored, family-run B&B stands out not just for its warm hospitality, but also for the its wonderful host, Claudio. A young, bilingual Managuan, he's very passionate about his city and can show you places you're unlikely to discover by yourself. Your morning coffee is likely to be among the best in the country too.

★La Posada del Arcangel GUESTHOUSE $$$

(Map p436; ☎2254-5212; www.hotellaposadadelarcangel.com; Calle Los Pinos, Canal 2 TV, 100m O, 150m S, Barrio Bolonia; r from US$60; ❄📶) There's much to love about colonial-style Posada de Arcangel, from the quirky art collection and leafy garden to the guest rooms with crimson accents, bold splashes of contemporary art, and hand-carved wooden furnishings, including four-poster beds. The included breakfast is excellent too, and owners go above and beyond the call of duty to be helpful.

Hotel Casa Colonial BOUTIQUE HOTEL $$$

(Map p436; ☎7967-4883; http://casa-colonial-boutique.hotelsinmanagua.com; Carretera a Masaya Km 4.5, del Restaurante Tip Top 75m O, No 10, Planes de Altamira; s/d from US$55/65; P❄📶🏊) This intimate, hacienda-style hotel has an attractive arched breakfast patio centered on a babbling fountain. Dark-wood furniture, high ceilings, and heavy wooden beams are the rooms' defining features, along with subtle illumination. Head into the surrounding streets for dining and nightlife.

Eating

★De Muerte Lenta ICE CREAM $

(Map p436; ☎8272-9877; www.facebook.com/demuertelenta.ni; frente Parque Altamira, Planes de Altamira; ⏰11:30am-7:30pm) This diminutive ice-cream stall kills you softly with its 12 flavors of ice cream on a stick. It's some of the best ice cream you'll ever have; we're particularly partial to mint with brownie chunks.

★Asados Doña Tania NICARAGUAN $

(Map p436; ☎2270-0747; www.facebook.com/asadosdonatania; Hotel Colón, 1c S, ½c O, Los Robles; mains US$3-5; ⏰4:30-10:30pm Sun-Fri) Come evening, Managuans make their way to this *fritanga* temple where Doña Tania has perfected her craft over 20 years. There is only one thing worth ordering: strips of marinated meat, smoky and seared and bursting with flavor, plus sides of *gallo pinto, ensalada criolla* (salad of onions, peppers and tomatoes), fried plantain and fried cheese. Portions are large enough to get your through a siege.

★Terraza Peruana PERUVIAN $$
(Map p436; ☎2278-0013; de la Pasteleria Sampson, 100m N; mains US$5-12; ⊙noon-11pm Tue-Sun) Set on a cool front balcony overlooking a leafy side street, refined Terraza's authentic Peruvian menu takes you from coastal *ceviches* (marinated seafood) and *tiraditos* (Japanese-Peruvian raw fish), to high Andean cuisine. Classics such as *anticuchos de corazón* (ox-heart skewers) and *suspiro limeño* (dulce de leche and meringue-based dessert) are present and correct. Don't miss a cocktail from the pisco list.

Cafe Las Marias CAFE $$
(☎2231-2524; www.facebook.com/lasmariascafe; Uniplaza Las Colinas, primera entrada, 3c E; sandwiches US$6-8; ⊙7am-8pm Mon-Fri, 8am-8pm Sat, 8am-6pm Sun; ❄📶✎) At this bang-on-trend cafe you can peruse the map of Nicaragua's coffee-growing regions while deciding which way you want your superlative brew: chemex, V60, aeropress, cold press… There's a decent supporting cast of zucchini muffins, imaginative sandwiches and salads too.

★Don Cándido STEAK $$$
(Map p436; ☎2277-2485; https://restaurantedoncandido.com; de donde fue el Chaman 75 vrs al Sur, 15 Av Sureste, Los Robles; steaks US$18-35; ⊙noon-10pm Mon-Fri, 2pm-midnight Sat & Sun; ❄📶) All heavy wooden beams, exposed brick walls and contemporary art, this smart steakhouse means business. Choose from a sizable list of cuts of meat – from the beautifully grilled sirloin with crisped ribbons of fat, the T-bone and New York steak to short ribs and baby back ribs. The wine list spans the world, but is particularly strong on Spanish tipples.

Drinking & Entertainment

★DeLaFinca Cafe COFFEE
(Map p434; ☎2252-8974; www.delafincanicaragua.com; Parque El Dorado, costado Sureste; ⊙7am-8pm Mon-Fri, 8am-7pm Sat & Sun; 📶) No self-respecting coffee connoisseur should miss out on visiting this altar to the coffee bean, whose owner comes from generations of coffee farmers and who has perfected *viñedo* – a novel coffee bean fermentation method. Come here to buy beans and to sample the best of Nicaragua's single origin coffees, each prepared using the method that best suits each one.

★Estación Central CRAFT BEER
(Map p436; ☎2225-3274; Av Gabriel Cardinal, del Hospital Monte España, 2½c N, Planes de Altamira; ⊙4-10pm Mon & Tue, 4pm-midnight Wed-Fri, noon-1am Sat, noon-10pm Sun) The pick of the neighborhood bars, hip and relaxed Estación Central is your first port of call for the best range of Nicaraguan craft beers, from the original Moropotente brews to Erdmann's, Pinolera, Campo and La Porteña. There are quite a few Belgian beers also, plus decent bar food, served to the tune of some ambient beats.

Teatro Nacional Rubén Darío THEATER
(Map p436; ☎2266-3630; www.tnrubendario.gob.ni; Av Bolívar, Área Monumental; ⊙hours vary) One of the few Managua buildings to survive the 1972 earthquake, this 'temple to Nicaraguan art and culture' often has big-name international offerings on the main stage. It's worth trying to catch some experimental jazz or performance art in the smaller Sala Experimental Pilar Aguirre. Prices vary.

Shopping

★Nostalgia de Nicaragua Cigar CIGARS
(Map p436; ☎2270-1450; Carretera a Masaya, frente Casino Pharaoh; ⊙10am-10pm Mon-Sat, 10am-4pm Sun) Step inside the humedor to choose from Nicaragua's finest cigars, hand-rolled in Mombacho and Estelí. Look out for Joya de Nicaragua, Padrón, AJ Fernández, Don Pepín García and other top brands. You can sample the wares in the attached lounge.

Crafted for Connaisseurs GIFTS & SOUVENIRS
(☎2278-1478; www.facebook.com/craftednica; Carretera a Masaya Km 6.5, contiguo a Café las Flores; ⊙11am-9pm Mon-Sat) Mostly a gourmet food store, Crafted for Connaisseurs sells boxes of handmade Nicaraguan Momotombo chocolates, superb Cielo Isla coffee, plus other single origin coffees, and has an excellent wine selection. There are also some premium cigars for sale, and some evenings (Thursday to Saturday) there's a short and sweet tapas menu to go with wine tastings.

Esperanza En Acción ARTS & CRAFTS
(Map p434; ☎8388-2844; www.esperanzaenaccion.org; Casa de Ben Linder, de la Estatua Monseñor Lezcano, 3c S, ½c E, Barrio Monseñor Lezcano;

9am-5pm Mon-Fri)  An excellent selection of fair-trade crafts from all over Nicaragua, made by 31 groups of local artisans. There is exquisite pottery, woven bags, jewelry, single origin coffee, toys and weavings. Proceeds go to the artisans themselves and help some of the most economically disadvantaged corners of the country.

Information

DANGERS & ANNOYANCES

Managua has a reputation for being a dangerous city, and with fairly good reason. But by using common sense and general caution, you can avoid problems.

- Don't flash expensive items.
- Look at the map before venturing out on a walk.
- Make ATM transactions during daylight hours.
- Ask your hotel or hostel to call you a taxi instead of hailing one in the street.
- Carry only as much money as you'll need for the day.

EMERGENCY & IMPORTANT NUMBERS

Ambulance (Cruz Roja)	128
Fire	115 (emergency), 2222-6406
Police	118 (emergency), 2249-5714

INTERNET ACCESS

Free wi-fi can be found in the vast majority of accommodations and, increasingly, at cafes and restaurants.

MEDICAL SERVICES

Managua has scores of pharmacies – some open 24 hours (just knock) – and the nation's best hospitals.

Hospital Alemán-Nicaragüense (Map p434; 2249-3368; Carretera Norte Km 6) Modern equipment and German-speaking staff.

Hospital Bautista (Map p436; 2264-9020; www.hospital-bautista.com; Casa Ricardo Morales Avíles, 2c S, 1½c E, Barrio Largaespada) Some English-speaking staff and modern facilities.

Hospital Metropolitano Vivian Pellas (2255-6900; www.hospitalvivianpellas.com; Carretera a Masaya Km 9.75) Best hospital in the country, with English-speaking staff.

MONEY

Managua has scores of banks and ATMs, most on the Visa/Plus system. BAC, with machines at Metrocentro mall, Managua International Airport and Plaza España, accepts MasterCard/Cirrus debit cards and gives US dollars and córdobas. Any bank can change US dollars and many businesses accept them.

TELEPHONE

You can purchase a SIM card to make your cell-phone function on local networks, or make phone calls from your hotel. There's a handy **Claro** (8am-7pm) outlet inside the Managua Airport building.

TOURIST INFORMATION

Intur Central (Nicaraguan Institute of Tourism; Map p436; 2254-5191; www.visitanicaragua.com; Hotel Crowne Plaza, 1c S, 1c O; 8am-5pm Mon-Fri) Flagship tourism office with heaps of flyers. There's another office (p510) at the airport in the international terminal, next to the luggage belt in the arrivals area, where English-speaking staff can recommend hotels, confirm flights and share flyers.

Marena Central (Ministry of the Environment & Natural Resources; 2263-2830; Carretera Norte Km 12.5) Bring ID to the inconveniently located headquarters if you want to get info on most of Nicaragua's 82 protected areas.

INTERNATIONAL BUS SERVICES FROM MANAGUA

Tica Bus (p512) is located in a terminal in the heart of Barrio Martha Quezada and has the following services.

DESTINATION	COST (US$)	DURATION (HR)	FREQUENCY
Antigua, Guatemala	77-89	33	5am, 11am
Guatemala City	63-74	30	5am, 11am
Panama City	75-107	34	6am, 7am, noon, 1pm
San José, Costa Rica	29-44	10	6am, 7am, noon, 1pm
San Pedro Sula, Honduras	46	12	5am
San Salvador, El Salvador	40-52	11	5am, 11am
Tegucigalpa, Honduras	30	7	5am

Getting There & Away

AIR

Managua International Airport (MGA; www.eaai.com.ni; Carretera Norte Km 11) is a small, manageable airport about 30 to 45 minutes from most hotels.

The smaller, more chaotic domestic terminal is adjacent to the main building.

Departures to the USA include flights to Houston with United Airlines (www.united.com), Miami and Dallas with American Airlines (www.americanairlines.com) and Fort Lauderdale with

NATIONAL BUS SERVICES FROM MANAGUA

DESTINATION	COST (US$)	DURATION (HR)	DEPARTURES	FREQUENCY	LEAVES FROM
Boaco	2.20	3	4am-6:30pm	every 15min	Mayoreo
Carazo (serving Diriamba & Jinotepe)	1.40	1	4:30am-6:20pm	every 20min	Lewites
Chinandega/El Viejo	2.70	3	5am-6pm	every 30min	Lewites
Chinandega minibus	3	2	4am-6pm	when full	Lewites
El Astillero	3	3	3pm	daily	Huembes
El Tránsito	1.20	1½	11:15am, 12:40pm, 2pm	3 daily	Lewites
Estelí	3	2	5:45am-5:45pm	hourly	Mayoreo
Granada	0.75	1	4am-6pm	every 15min	Huembes
Granada minibus	1.25	1	6am-8pm	when full	UCA
Jinotega	3.50	4	4am-5:30pm	hourly	Mayoreo
Jinotepe minibus	1.15	1	5am-8pm	when full	UCA
Juigalpa	2	4	3:15am-10pm	every 20min	Mayoreo
La Paz Centro	1.60	1½	6:15am-8pm	every 30min	Lewites
León *expreso* (via New Hwy & La Paz Centro)	1.85	1½	10am-6:30pm	every 2hr	Lewites
León *ordinario* (via Old Hwy)	1.50	2	5am-7pm	every 20min	Lewites
León minibus	2.75	1½	4am-6pm	when full	Lewites
León minibus	2.75	1½	5am-9:15pm	when full	UCA
Masatepe minibus	1.10	1	6:30am-6:30pm	every 20min	Huembes
Masaya	0.50	1	5:30am-9pm	every 30min	Huembes
Masaya minibus	0.90	½	6am-9pm	when full	UCA
Matagalpa	2.25	2¾	3am-6pm	hourly	Mayoreo
Mateare	0.30	40min	5:50am-6:30pm	every 2hr	Lewites
Naindame	1	1½	11am-3:30pm	every 20min	Huembes
Ocotal	4.25	3½	5am-5pm	hourly	Mayoreo
Pochomil/Masachapa	1.30-1.60	2	6am-7pm	every 20min	Lewites
Río Blanco	5	4	9:15am-12:15pm	hourly	Mayoreo
Rivas *expreso*	3.25	1½	8:30am-1pm	6 daily	Huembes
Rivas *ordinario*	2	2	4am-6pm	every 30min	Huembes
San Carlos	7.50	9	5am-6pm	6 daily	Mayoreo
San Juan del Sur *expreso*	3.25	2½	9:30am-5:30pm	6 daily	Huembes
San Marcos minibus	1	1	4am-6pm	when full	Huembes
Somoto	4	4	5am-6pm	8 daily	Mayoreo
Ticuantepe minibus	0.40	40min	4am-6pm	when full	Huembes

Spirit Airlines (www.spirit.com). Copa Airlines (www.copaair.com) serves San José, Costa Rica, Panama City and Guatemala City, while Avianca (www.avianca.com) flies to San Salvador.

Domestic carrier La Costeña (www.lacostena.com.ni) has regular service to Bluefields, the Corn Islands, Siuna, Isla Ometepe, San Carlos, Río San Juan, Bonanza, Puerto Cabezas and Waspán.

BUS

Managua is the main transportation hub for the country, with several major national bus and van terminals, plus a handful of international bus lines (most grouped in Barrio Martha Quezada).

National Buses & Minivans

Buses leave from three main places: **Mercado Roberto Huembes** (Map p434; Pista de la Solidaridad) for Granada, Masaya and southwest Nicaragua; **Mercado Israel Lewites** (Map p434; semáforos de Mercado Israel Lewites, 1c N) for León and the northern Pacific; and **Mercado Mayoreo** (Map p434; frente Aduana Managua) for the Caribbean coast and the northern highlands. Some also leave from the Mercado Oriental, mainly to rural destinations not covered here.

It's faster, more comfortable and a bit more expensive to take **minivans from UCA** (Map p436; frente UCA), pronounced 'ooka', or *expreso* (express) versus *ordinario* (regular) services.

Shuttle Buses

There are established shuttle pick-ups from Managua Airport with the likes of **Adelante Express** (☎2568-2083; www.adelanteexpress.com), **Casa Oro** (Map p461; ☎2568-2415; www.casaeloro.com; cnr Av Ral & Calle Vandervilt) and **Bigfoot Hostel** (Map p468; ☎8852-3279; www.bigfoothostelleon.com/shuttle; BanPro, ½c S) that whisk travelers straight off to Granada (US$25), León (US$15), San Juan del Sur (US$25) and other popular destinations along the west coast. Hostels in Managua also offer direct shuttle services to all of these destinations. All remote hotels and surfing lodges offer pick-up from Managua Airport.

CAR

Driving in Managua presents the usual challenges of driving in a big city, but it's perfectly manageable as long as you have a good GPS (the Maps.me app is very useful) and you know where you're going. International car rental companies have offices at Managua airport and around the city.

ℹ Getting Around

BUS

Local buses are frequent and crowded and unless you actually live in Managua or are a serious penny-pincher, these convoluted local bus routes with unmarked bus shelters are not useful to travelers. Backpackers prefer to spend a bit more on a taxi to travel around the city.

International Buses

Transnica (p512) serves Costa Rica and Honduras, and has offices over on the other side of the laguna.

Costa Rica (US$29, nine hours, four daily at 5am, 7am, 10am & noon) To San José. There's also a luxury bus (US$38) that leaves daily at 1pm.

Honduras (US$30, 10 hours, one daily at 11:30am) For Tegucigalpa.

Transporte del Sol (p512) daily buses leave for San Salvador (US$50, 13 hours, two daily at 3am & 10am), Guatemala City (US$70, six hours, one daily at 3am) and San José (US$35, 9½ hours, daily at noon).

Central Line (Map p436; ☎2254-5431; www.transportescentralline.com; Rotonda Hugo Chávez Frías, 1c S, 1½c O) offers one daily bus to San José, Costa Rica (US$29, eight hours), with stops in Granada and Rivas.

CAR & MOTORCYCLE

Take care and stay vigilant if driving in Managua at night – even if you have a rental car, consider getting a taxi, and make sure your car is in a guarded lot. At research time, navigating Managua after dark by car was highly inadvisable due to road blocks.

TAXI

- Most taxis in Managua are *colectivos*, which pick up passengers as they go. There are also more expensive private taxis based at the airport, shopping malls, Mercado Roberto Huembes and other places. These are safer, but regular taxis also always congregate close by.
- Licensed taxis have red plates and the driver's ID above the dash; if yours doesn't, you're in a pirate taxi. This is probably OK, but don't go to the ATM, and beware of scams no matter what kind of taxi you're in.
- At night, take only licensed taxis – there has been an increase in reports of taxi drivers robbing passengers after dark.

Around Managua

Masachapa & Pochomil

POP UNDER 1500

An easy day trip from Managua, the twin villages of Masachapa and Pochomil are so close together that they might as well be one. They tend to attract weekenders from the capital and a contingent of surfer visitors. A handful of bars, hotels and restaurants are

Around Managua

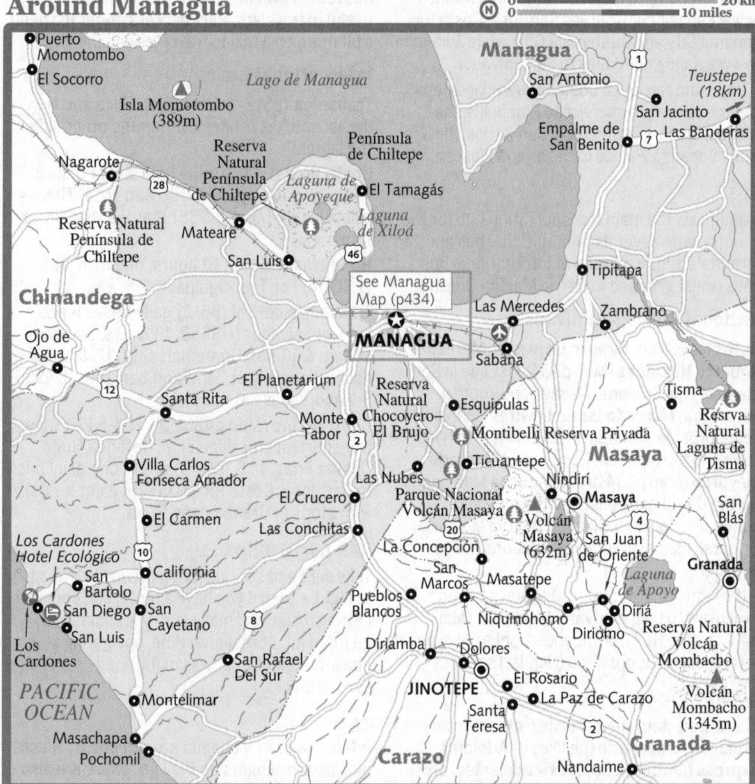

dotted along the sleepy, unpaved streets. Some will rent out surfboards.

The better hotels are on the beach in Pochomil, south and across the river from Masachapa. There's a cluster of thatch-roofed restaurants in Pochomil, all comparable and predominantly serving seafood. Most hotels have their own restaurants.

Casa del Titito HOTEL **$$$**
(☎8484-7724; www.casadeltitito.com; San Rafael del Sur, Pochomil; r US$70;) Right on the beach and featuring an outdoor pool, this easygoing hotel with a breezy hammock area overlooking the waves is a good budget pick with a complimentary Nicaraguan breakfast. French, English and Spanish are spoken.

ℹ Getting There & Away

For Masachapa, get off at the *empalme* (T intersection).

Buses run from Pochomil and Masachapa to Managua's Mercado Israel Lewites (p441) (US$1.30 to US$1.60, two hours) roughly every 30 minutes from 8am to 5pm.

The two villages are a straightforward drive along the paved NIC-2 and NIC-8. NIC-10 is a shortcut toward León.

San Diego

POP UNDER 500

As you drive through cane fields when you turn off Hwy 10, the tarmac gives way to packed dirt, and you can smell the salty tang of the sea. Then you're in San Diego, a one-street village with an uncrowded beach and some world-class waves for surfers of all abilities.

San Diego is an excellent surfing destination. Los Cardones is a beach break suitable for beginners and intermediates. Asuchillo (1½ hours' walk from San Diego or a 10-minute jetski ride) is an excellent beach break with consistent barrels, while Hemmies, a 15-minute walk away, is a fast, hollow reef break for experts only.

Prices at Los Cardones Hotel Ecológico include all meals, while Mind The Gap Nica has a restaurant and a kitchen for self-caterers.

Mind The Gap Nica HOSTEL **$**
(☎5859-7050; http://mindthegapnica.com; Playa San Diego; dm/s/d US$15/25/30, camping per person US$5; 📶) This beachfront hostel attracts steady local traffic; they come for the fish tacos and beer and the live music on weekends; surfing guests get all of the above, plus breezy, basic rooms a stone's throw from the surf. There are boards for rent and even an on-site spa with massages for sore muscles and a Mexican-style temescal sweat lodge.

Los Cardones Hotel Ecológico LODGE **$$$**
(☎8364-5925; www.loscardones.com; Carretera Montelimar Km 49, 15km O, Finca Del Mar Beach Community; 2-person bungalows/cabañas without bathroom incl all meals US$214/146; 📶) Just south of San Diego village, this rustic ecolodge has great food and some of the best surfing in Nicaragua, just steps from your hammock. Owners offer fishing, snorkeling and horseback riding, and sea turtles lay their eggs on the beach. The whole operation is low-impact (solar energy, composting toilets) and also family friendly, with surf breaks for kids under 12 years.

Getting There & Away

Buses run from Managua's Mercado Israel Lewites (p441) to San Cayetano (US$2, 1½ to two hours, every 45 minutes from 5am to 5pm); get off at the California crossroads, 1.5km from San Cayetano, and then either hitch a ride for the remaining 13km to San Diego, or pay a tuk-tuk to drive you. If driving, take NIC-12 north from Managua, then NIC-10, and turn off at California; the last 8km to the beach is unpaved and bumpy. You can also arrange to be picked up directly from Managua airport.

GRANADA & THE MASAYA REGION

This geographically rich area boasts a number of Nicaragua's most vaunted attractions, including the spellbinding town of Granada. The area is also rich in biodiversity. Wildlife abounds on the flanks of Volcán Mombacho, and Parque Nacional Volcán Masaya is one of the country's most visibly active craters. Lush tropical forest surrounds the banks of the crystalline Laguna de Apoyo, and Las Isletas on Lago de Nicaragua make for another fine swim setting.

Just west of Granada, the Pueblos Blancos (White Villages) stand amid a highland coffee-growing region rich in pre-Columbian traditions. These charming towns are an excellent place to observe some of Nicaragua's most beautiful craftwork in the making.

Granada

POP 100,496 / ELEV 62M

Nicaragua's oldest town is also its most beguiling and photogenic. It's no wonder many travelers use the city as a base, spending at least a day bopping along cobblestone roads from church to church in the city center, then venturing out into the countryside for trips to nearby attractions.

Just out of town, adventures take you to an evocative archipelago waterworld at Las Isletas and fun beaches at the Peninsula de Asese. Volcán Mombacho has walking trails, not to mention a few hot springs dotted around its foothills. The Laguna de Apoyo is another must-see: its clear turquoise waters and laid-back waterfront lodges offer a splendid natural respite.

Culturally curious travelers might consider a trip to community-tourism operations in nearby villages such as Nicaragua Libre, or out to Parque Nacional Archipiélago Zapatera, home to one of the most impressive collections of petroglyphs and statues in the country.

History

Nicknamed 'the Great Sultan,' in honor of its Moorish namesake across the Atlantic, Granada was founded in 1524 by Francisco Fernández de Córdoba, and is one of the oldest cities in the New World. It was constructed as a showcase city, the first chance that the Spanish had to prove they had more to offer than a bizarre religion and advanced military technology. The city still retains an almost regal beauty, each thick-walled architectural masterpiece faithfully resurrected to original specifications after every trial and tribulation.

A trade center almost from its inception, Granada's position on the Lago de Nicaragua became even more important when the Spanish realized that the Río San Juan

Granada

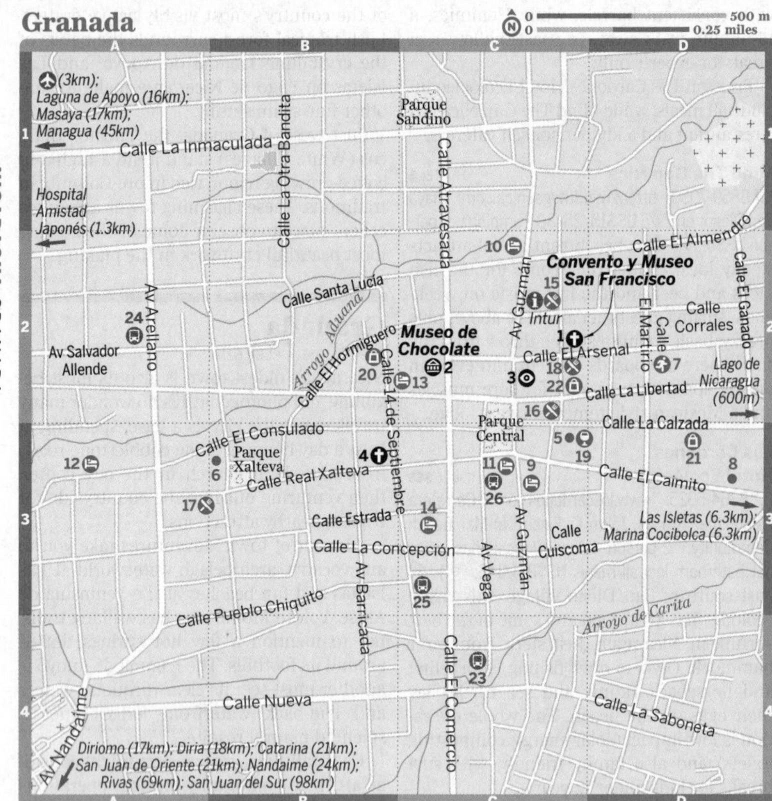

was navigable from the lake to the sea. This made Granada rich – and vulnerable. Between 1665 and 1670, pirates sacked the city three times.

Undaunted, Granada rebuilt and grew richer and more powerful, a conservative cornerstone of the Central American economy. After independence from Spain, the city challenged the colonial capital and longtime Liberal bastion León for leadership of the new nation.

Tensions erupted into full-blown civil war in the 1850s, when desperate León contracted the services of American mercenary William Walker and his band of 'filibusterers.' Walker defeated Granada, declared himself president and launched a conquest of Central America – and failed. Walker was forced into a retreat after a series of embarrassing defeats, and as he fell back to his old capital city, he set it afire and left in its ashes the infamous placard: 'Here was Granada.'

The city rebuilt – again. And while its power has waned, its importance as a tourist center and quick escape from bustling Managua keeps the city of Granada vibrant.

Sights & Activities

★Convento y Museo San Francisco

CHURCH

(Map p444; 2552-5535; Plaza de los Leones 1c N, 1c E; US$5; 8am-4pm Mon-Fri, 9am-4pm Sat & Sun) One of the oldest churches in Central America, Convento San Francisco boasts a robin's egg–blue birthday-cake facade and houses both an important convent and one of the best museums in the region. The highlight is the museum that focuses on Nicaragua's pre-Columbian people. Don't miss the Zapatera statuary, two solemn regiments of black-basalt statues, carved between AD 800 and 1200, then left behind on the ritual island of Zapatera.

Granada

Top Sights
1 Convento y Museo San Francisco........C2
2 Museo de Chocolate..........C2

Sights
3 Casa de los Leones & Fundación Casa de los Tres Mundos..........C2
4 Iglesia La Merced..........B3

Activities, Courses & Tours
5 Adventour Nicaragua..........C3
6 Casa Xalteva..........B3
Corazón Trips..........(see 10)
7 Las Tortilla Cooking School..........D2
8 Nicaragua Mia Spanish School..........D3

Sleeping
9 Casa del Agua..........C3
10 Hotel Con Corazón..........C2
11 Hotel Gran Francia..........C3
12 Hotel La Polvora..........A3
13 Lemon Tree Hostel..........C2
Mansión de Chocolate..........(see 2)
14 Oasis Hostel..........C3

Eating
15 Bocadillos Tapas Kitchen & Bar..........C2
16 Cafe del Arte..........C2
17 Espressonista..........A3
18 Miss Dell's Kitchen..........C2

Drinking & Nightlife
19 Nectar..........C3

Shopping
20 Cooperativa El Parche..........B2
21 Soy Nica..........D3
22 The Garden Shop..........C2

Transport
23 Buses to Destinations South..........C4
24 Buses to Managua..........A2
25 Buses to Masaya..........C3
26 Microbuses to Managua..........C3

★ Museo de Chocolate MUSEUM

(Map p444; ☎2552-4678; www.chocomuseo.com; Calle Atravesada, frente Bancentro; chocolate workshop adult/child US$21/12; ⏰7am-6:30pm;) FREE Granada's new chocolate museum is excellent if you're traveling with children: the 'beans to bar' chocolate workshop, where participants learn to roast and grind cocao beans, and mold their very own Nicaraguan chocolate bar, is hands-on fun for all ages. Cigar-making workshops are also held here. The museum is at the **Mansión de Chocolate hotel** (Map p444; ☎2552-4678; www.mansiondechocolate.com; Calle Atravesada, frente Bancocentro; r/tr from US$77/101;), which also has a chocolate-oriented spa and a popular buffet breakfast (US$7), plus a great swimming pool you can use for an extra US$6.

Iglesia La Merced CHURCH

(Map p444; cnr Calle Real Xalteva & Av 14 de Septiembre; bell tower US$1; ⏰11am-6pm) Perhaps the most beautiful church in the city, this landmark was built in 1534. Most come here for the spectacular views from the **bell tower** – especially picturesque at sunset. Originally completed in 1539, it was razed by pirates in 1655 and rebuilt with its current baroque facade between 1781 and 1783. Damaged by William Walker's forces in 1854, it was restored with the current elaborate interior in 1862. Today Catholics come here to see the Virgen de Fatima.

Casa de los Leones & Fundación Casa de los Tres Mundos NOTABLE BUILDING

(Map p444; ☎2552-4176; http://c3mundos.org/es/inicio; Parque Central, 50m N; ⏰8am-6pm) Founded in 1986 by Ernesto Cardenal, the Fundación Casa de los Tres Mundos moved to elegant Casa de los Leones in 1992. Casa Los Leones was built in 1720, but what you see now is a reconstruction, since William Walker burned down the original. At the entrance, a board lists special events: poetry readings, classical ballet, folkloric dance and free movies. During regular business hours, you can enjoy the beautiful mansion, historical archive, cafe and art displays.

Corazón Trips TOURS

(Map p444; ☎2552-8852; www.hotelconcorazon.com; Calle Santa Lucia 141) Located inside the **Hotel Con Corazón** (Map p444; ☎2552-8852; Calle Cervantes, Parque Central, 3c N; s/d/tr/f US$75/91/117/139;), this nonprofit tour operator offers well-organized trips including bike tours, cooking classes and trips to Mombacho.

Courses & Tours

Las Tortilla Cooking School COOKING

(Map p444; ☎5503-2805; Calle El Martirio 305, entre Calle La Libertad y El Arsenal; basic class US$45 per person; ⏰cooking classes 10:30am & 4:30pm) A really fun, hands-on experience that teaches you all about the origins and methods of Nicaraguan cuisine. Spend two or three hours learning to make five typical dishes and throw in a market tour (US$15) to learn about the ingredients.

Casa Xalteva LANGUAGE

(Map p444; 2552-2993; www.casaxalteva.org; Calle Real Xalteva, Iglesia Xalteva, 25m N; 1-week language course from US$160; 8am-5pm Mon-Fri) Next to the church of the same name, Casa Xalteva also runs a program providing breakfast and education for street kids, as well as language classes and homestays.

Nicaragua Mia Spanish School LANGUAGE

(Map p444; 7779-0209; www.facebook.com/nicaraguamiaschool; Calle El Caimito, alcaldía, 3½ c E; 1 week all-inclusive per person US$280) Run by a women's co-op, with a range of teaching methods and years of experience.

Adventour Nicaragua OUTDOORS

(Map p444; 5760-6733; www.adventournicaragua.com; Calle Calzada, el catedral, ½c E; 8am-9pm) Ramiro and his passionate, professional team run highly recommended tours of Las Isletas, Isla Zapatero, Volcán Mombacho (from US$25) and Granada itself, with small groups accompanied by bilingual guides. Shuttles available to destinations across the country too.

Livit Water WATER SPORTS

(8580-7014; www.livitwater.com; Marina Cocibolca; SUP tours per person from US$40) Scott and Gea run professional SUP tours on the water, both here and in Laguna Apoyo, with pick-up from Granada. Combine your SUP (stand-up paddleboarding) experience with yoga or half-day tours up Volcán Mombacho.

Festivals & Events

International Poetry Festival PERFORMING ARTS

(www.festivalpoesianicaragua.com; 2nd week in Feb) This festival brings together scores of wordsmiths, artists and musicians – not just Nicaragua's finest, but also poets from all over Latin America and around the world as well. Events are held in open spaces in front of major landmarks.

Fiestas de Agosto RELIGIOUS

(3rd week Aug) Granada celebrates the Assumption of Mary with fireworks, concerts in the park, horse parades and major revelry by the lakefront.

Sleeping

Oasis Hostel HOSTEL $

(Map p444; 2552-8005; www.nicaraguahostel.com; Calle Estrada 109, Mercado Municipal, 1c N, ½c O; dm/s/d US$8/15/20;) A five-minute walk from the main square, this hostel is a Granada institution. It's extremely well run, with numerous daily shuttles and activities, and the owners are really clued-up about backpacker needs: there is generous locker space, free international phone calls, kitchen, ample breakfast and more. Rooms are basic, but then they're not the main attraction here.

Lemon Tree Hostel HOSTEL $

(Map p444; 8912-8764; www.lemontreehostels.com; Calle La Libertad, Parque Central, 2c O; dm/r US$10/35;) A boutique hotel in its previous incarnation, this is the grandest hostel in Granada – all vast ceilings, graceful courtyard, spa and hammocks strung around the pool. The huge doubles share facilities, though, as do the dorms. Staff are happy to arrange excursions and shuttles.

Casa del Agua HOTEL $$

(Map p444; 8872-4627; www.casadelaguagranada.com; Av Guzmán, Parque Central, ½c S; d/tr from US$40/50;) Spacious rooms surround a small pool (with a suspended swing) in a prize location just off Parque Central. Furnishings inside this beautiful colonial building are all new and tastefully selected, and owner Gerry is a treasure trove of local knowledge. There's a fully stocked kitchen for guest use, on-site bike rentals and a pancake breakfast.

★ **Hotel Gran Francia** HISTORIC HOTEL $$$

(Map p444; 2552-6000; www.lagranfrancia.com; Av Guzmán, Parque Central, ½c S; r from US$110;) Just off the main plaza, this elegant hotel is set in an opulent historic building, with hardwood floors, hand-painted sinks, wrought-iron detail and heavy wooden beams in its characterful rooms. Across the street, the Gran Francia's restaurant, bar and lounge (set in William Walker's former home) are equally impressive.

Hotel La Polvora BOUTIQUE HOTEL $$$

(Map p444; 2552-1227; www.hotellapolvora.com; Calle El Consulado, Fortaleza La Polvora, ½c E, 1c N, 1c E; r from US$75;) Barring the sound of church bells, nothing is likely to disturb your rest at this intimate boutique hotel on a quiet residential street, near the namesake fort. Beyond the beautifully tiled lobby there are just 10 comfortable rooms, most with rocking chairs on the terrace or balcony. Liam and his staff go above and beyond the call of duty.

Eating & Drinking

★Bocadillos Tapas Kitchen & Bar INTERNATIONAL $$
(Map p444; ☎2552-5089; www.bocadillosgranada.com; frente Convento San Francisco; dishes US$4-8; ⊙noon-9pm;) The interior leafy courtyard of this stylish yet casual restaurant is an ideal setting for a cocktail (including some original ones!), a local craft beer or two or three, and imaginative tapas that span the globe, from spicy samosas and pulled pork sliders to Thai noodle salad and roasted garlic hummus. There's a handful of substantial dishes too.

Cafe del Arte NICARAGUAN $$
(Map p444; ☎2552-6461; Calle Cervantes, el catedral, 1c E, ½c N; mains US$4-7; ⊙7:30am-9pm) Sit in the courtyard, filled with greenery and paintings by local artists, and savour an excellent coffee and an ample nica breakfast.

★Miss Dell's Kitchen FUSION $$$
(Map p444; ☎2552-2815; cnr Calle Cervantes & Calle El Arsenal; mains US$10-14; ⊙5:30pm-midnight) Mellow jazz plays in the background at this candlelit spot, with a mural of a rooster, Mr Beautiful, gracing the back wall. The rooster belonged to Miss Dell, a Haitian cook, whose recipes have been adapted by the chef for the short and sweet menu. The *piri piri pescado* (fish in a chilli sauce) is one of the best things we've ever tried, anywhere.

Espressonista FUSION $$$
(Map p444; ☎2552-4325; www.facebook.com/espressonistacoffee; Calle Real Xalteva, frente Iglesia de Xalteva; mains US$10-18; ⊙noon-8pm Wed-Sun;) Tall ceilings, hand-carved furniture and gilded mirrors give this place a certain old-world grandeur, but the succinct menu is as contemporary as it gets, with French influences. Feast on the likes of mackerel and passion-fruit *ceviche* (marinated seafood), rabbit confit and ox cheek à la bourguignonne, along with some of Granada's best gourmet coffee.

Nectar BAR
(Map p444; www.facebook.com/NectarNicaragua; Calle La Calzada, Parque Central, 1½c E; dishes US$5-8; ⊙11am-11pm) This place wears many hats and we like all of them. It's a small lounge-bar with a good list of cocktails and local craft beers (come for happy hour). In high season it often gets visiting DJs and live rock bands to liven the place up. Internationally inspired light dishes and snacks make up the creative menu.

Shopping

★The Garden Shop ARTS & CRAFTS
(Map p444; www.gardencafegranada.com; Calle La Libertad, Parque Central, 1c E; ⊙9am-6pm;) A fantastic addition to the popular Garden Café, this sustainably minded boutique offers crafts, jewelry, clothing and artwork produced through NGOs and fair-trade organizations throughout Nicaragua. Artisans from Chinandega, Diriamba, Granada, Masatepe, Managua and Masaya are all represented here; you can also buy coffee beans and postcards, and there's a good-sized book exchange at the entrance.

Soy Nica FASHION & ACCESSORIES
(Map p444; ☎2552-0234; www.facebook.com/soynica.dk; Calle La Calzada, Iglesia de Guadelupe, 100m O; ⊙9am-6pm Mon-Thu, to 8pm Fri & Sat, to 2pm Sun) Come here for stylish purses, shoulder bags, belts and other accessories made of Nicaraguan leather. You can see them being made at the workshop next to the store.

Cooperativa El Parche ARTS & CRAFTS
(Map p444; ☎8473-7700; Calle 14 de Septiembre, Hostal Entre Amigos) Inside the Hostal Entre Amigos, this excellent gift shop sells crafts made by local artisans. What makes it special are the items made of recycled products and local materials, and your purchase helps to support recyclable art in rural communities.

Information

DANGERS & ANNOYANCES

- Always take a cab after dark between the lake and the Centro Turístico.
- Avoid cycling to Peninsula de Asese due to occasional robberies.

EMERGENCY & IMPORTANT NUMBERS

Ambulance (Cruz Roja)	☎2552-2711
Police	☎2552-2929

MEDICAL SERVICES

For serious medical emergencies, it's best to go to Managua.

Hospital Amistad Japonés (☎2552-2022; Carretera a Masaya–Granada Km 45; ⊙24hr)

The most frequently recommended private hospital is out of town, on the road to Managua. Basic emergency care.

TOURIST INFORMATION

Check at hostels and tour operators for the latest tourist info.

Intur (Map p444; ☎2552-6858; www.visitanicaragua.com; Calle Corrales; ⊙8am-5pm Mon-Fri) The Granada branch of the national tourist office has up-to-date transportation schedules, a reasonable city map, and lots of information and flyers.

Getting There & Away

BOAT

Marina Cocibolca (☎2552-2269; desvio a Posintepe), about 2km southeast of town, has boats for Las Isletas and Parque Nacional Archipiélago Zapatera.

BUS

Granada doesn't have one central bus terminal.

Buses to Managua (Map p444; Calle El Tamarindo) (US$0.75, 1½ hours, every 20 to 30 minutes, from 5am to 7pm), arriving at Managua's Mercado Roberto Huembes, depart from the lot just north of the old hospital on the western edge of town. **Microbuses to Managua** (Map p444; Calle Vega) (US$1, one hour, every 20 minutes, from 5am to 7pm), arriving at UCA in Managua, leave from the convenient lot just south of the Parque Central on Calle Vega; change at UCA for microbuses and chicken buses to León.

Buses to Masaya (Map p444; Calle 14 de Septiembre) (US$0.50, 30 minutes, every 20 to 30 minutes, from 4:30am to 4:30pm) leave from two blocks west of the Mercado Municipal, around the corner from Palí. Change in Masaya for buses to Tipitapa (US$0.25, one hour, every 45 minutes from 3:30am and 5:50pm), and in Tipitapa for buses to Estelí (US$1, three hours, every 45 minutes) or Matagalpa (US$1, three hours, every 30 minutes from 4am to 7pm).

Buses to destinations south (Map p444; Mercado Municipal, 1c S) leave from a block south of the market, across from the Shell petrol station.

Carazo (US$0.75, 45 minutes, every 20 minutes, from 6am to 5:05pm) For San Marcos, Diriamba (with connections to the Carazo beaches) and Jinotepe.

Catarina & San Juan de Oriente (US$0.60, 30 minutes, 6am to 6pm, every 30 to 60 minutes)

Rivas (US$1.10, 2½ hours, seven daily, from 6:30am to 3pm) Early afternoon buses will allow you to make the last boat to Isla de Ometepe. Change in Rivas for chicken buses to San Juan del Sur and San Jorge.

Around Granada

Reserva Natural Volcán Mombacho

This looming 1345m **volcano** (☎2552-5858; www.mombacho.org; Empalme de Guanacaste, Carretera Granada–Nandaime Km 50; park entrance per car/pedestrian US$20/5, mariposario US$2; ⊙8am-5pm) is the defining feature of the Granada skyline. It's been a few decades since it has acted up, but it is still most certainly active and sends up the periodic puff of smoke. It's easy to get to the crown of cloud forest, steaming with fumaroles and other bubbling volcanic activity beneath the misty vines and orchids. Take a tour from Granada or drive yourself.

The area has thriving rural communities, coffee farms and cooperatives along its foothills, and the volcano's slopes, covered in ferns and cloud forest, are home to howler monkeys, dozens of bird species, and many of Nicaragua's shy mammals, including the jaguarundi.

Managed by the Fundación Cocibolca, Reserva Natural Volcán Mombacho does the crucial work of maintaining this important ecosystem, and visitors are welcome to explore the volcano's three hiking trails (of varying difficulty), or else go horseback riding through its picturesque rural communities. It's particularly rewarding to overnight on the volcano's misty slopes and be welcomed in the morning by the incomparable chorus of howler moneys and birds.

While many visitors come to the park on a day trip and sleep in nearby Granada, there are several excellent lodgings on the volcano slopes, from a party hostel and rustic cabins to an upscale ecolodge.

The park's visitor center has a basic cafeteria, and there's a popular cafe halfway up the volcano.

Treehouse Nicaragua HOSTEL $
(☎8569-0191; www.treehousenicaragua.com; Carretera Granada–Nandaime Km 57.5; hammock/dm/d/tr US$8/10/25/40; 📶) After the effort of the uphill hike, you find yourself in the canopy on the slopes of Volcán Mombacho, amid troops of howler monkeys. At night, beers are cracked open, guests and staff jam on musical instruments and revelry continues into the wee hours at this 'treehouse for adults' before you fall asleep in your hammock. Day visits are available.

Albergue Rural Nicaragua Libre GUESTHOUSE $$
(☎8965-7017; www.ucatierrayagua.org; Entrada de Monte Verde, 500m SE, El Coyolar; r US$25) The rustic guesthouse at **Nicaragua Libre** (☎2552-0238; per person guided tour US$5; ⏲tours by reservation) is a good place to base yourself for excursions in the area. Hosts Donald and Rene are happy to show guests around the rural cooperative and take you horseback riding to a nearby swimming hole. Simple guest rooms have beds with mosquito nets.

El Respiro Ecolodge LODGE $$$
(☎8951-9573; www.elrespiroecolodge.com; Carretera Granada–Nandaime Km 55, Camino El Momón; r US$100-150;) Living up to its name ('breath' or 'break'), El Respiro offers the opportunity to connect with nature, and go hiking and horseback riding along the volcano slopes, but without roughing it or having your room invaded by tiny jungle denizens. The three rooms and the *casita* (cottage) come with four-poster beds and open-air showers; join hosts Romain and Emi for dinner.

Getting There & Away

You can take any Nandaime bus from Granada and ask to be let off at the entrance. From here, you'll walk two steep kilometers (stay left where the road splits) to the spot where the eco-mobiles pick up passengers for the uphill drive.

Some visitors come by organized tour from Granada. If you drive yourself, bear in mind that you need a 4WD to drive to the viewpoint near the summit; a city car will only get you halfway up the volcano, up to **Cafe Las Flores** (☎8768-9678; Empalme de Guanacaste, 4km E; mains US$5-7; ⏲9am-5pm).

Reserva Natural Laguna de Apoyo

A vision in sapphire set into a lush forest crater, this 200m-deep, 200-centuries-old crater lake is said to be the country's cleanest and deepest. You can easily visit the area as a day trip from Granada. The warm undersea fumaroles feed the healing and slightly salty waters, howler monkeys bark overhead every morning and there's a cool air that make this a favorite respite for travelers.

While technically a natural reserve, this wild area has plenty of hotels dotting the lake's shore and limited environmental protection by the various agencies that claim jurisdiction. Tread lightly.

Some visitors are content with just taking in the view from the crater's edge in Catarina or Diriá. But it's well worth making your way to the bottom for one of the finest swims you'll ever enjoy. A tiny village lies at the bottom of the paved road into the crater, accessible via an often unsigned turnoff about 15km north of Granada, along the Carretera a Masaya.

Monkey Hut HOSTEL $
(☎2520-3030; www.themonkeyhut.net; El Triangulo, 200m N; dm/s/d/cabins US$16/48/52/90;) This popular waterfront hostel (US$7 day use for nonguests) features a small beach on the edge of the lake, terraced lounge and picnic areas, plus a floating dock with plenty of kayaks, inner tubes and other flotation devices. Overnight guests have kitchen and grill access; choose between dorms, private rooms or a freestanding cabin. The restaurant food is hit-and-miss.

★**Casa Marimba** B&B $$$
(☎2520-2837; www.casamarimba.com; El Triangulo, 1.6km NE; r US$55-75, f US$120;) Run by three friends, this sweet five-room B&B offers the best lakeside accommodations – individually styled rooms, meals involving lovingly grown organic veggies and herbs from their own garden, and lake access. Ideal for romancing your sweetie or just getting away from it all for a few tranquil days.

Getting There & Away

Many hotels and hostels on the lake offer daily shuttle transportation to and from Laguna de Apoyo from Granada (from US$3.50 one way), including options for day visitors and overnight guests.

Outside the posted shuttle times, you could also arrange a taxi from Granada (US$12 to US$15), Masaya (US$10 to US$12) or Managua (US$30 to US$40) to the door of your hotel or destination in Laguna de Apoyo.

Public 'La Laguna' buses run all the way down to Laguna Apoyo from the market in Masaya at 10:30am and 3:30pm (US$0.90, 45 minutes); the last bus departs Laguna Apoyo at 4:30pm. Hourly buses from Masaya (US$0.70) run roughly between 6am and 6pm, dropping passengers off near the crater rim, from where it's a half-hour, 2km descent.

If driving, you have to take the unsigned minor road toward the Laguna; the turnoff is 15km north of Granada, along the Carretera a Masaya (Hwy 4).

Isla Zapatera

Isla Zapatera, a dormant volcano rising to 629m from the shallow waters of Lago de Nicaragua, is an ancient ceremonial island of the Chorotega and male counterpart to more buxom Isla de Ometepe, whose smoking cone can be seen after you take the three-hour hike to the top. The island and surrounding archipelago of 13 islets comprise the 45-km-sq **Parque Nacional Archipiélago Zapatera**, designated to protect not only the wildlife-rich remaining swaths of virgin tropical dry and wet forest, but also the unparalleled collection of **petroglyphs** and **statues** left here between 500 and 1500 years ago by the Nahuatl, to whom the islands were an important sacrifice spot and burial ground.

About 500 people live here quasi-legally, fishing and subsistence farming and hoping that no one puts pressure on Marena (Ministry of the Environment and Natural Resources) to do anything about it. Visitors get a glimpse of their unique life.

There is no potable water on the island, nor any place to buy supplies. Bring your own food from Granada. There are basic meals (US$3 to US$6) available at the Sonzapote community's rural lodge. Hotel Bahía Zapatera prices include delicious home-cooked meals, while homestays arrange simple meals on request.

★Hotel Bahía Zapatera HOTEL **$$$**
(☎8884-0606, 8864-0521; www.hotelzapatera.com; Bahia Zapatera; d incl all meals & tours US$297;) Overlooking Isla el Muerto across the water, Isla Zapatera's wonderful hotel is run by knowledgeable Rafael. It consists of four comfortable bungalows with hammocks, and meals include fresh grilled fish and fruit juices. Also included are extensive tours of Isla Zapatera and the archipelago, nature walks for the whole family, birdwatching and more.

ℹ Getting There & Away

The island is about 20 to 90 minutes by boat (depending on weather and the boat) from the Asese port of Granada. Catch a ride with locals in a shared boat (US$8) or organize transportation with the Isla Zapatera Community (www.zapatera.blogspot.com). The most reliable option involves going with Zapatera Tours, whose tours include travel to and from the island by speedboat.

Isletas de Granada

With an islet for every day of the year (there are 365 in total), this spectacular archipelago, within easy reach of Granada, was created during a spectacular eruption by Volcán Mombacho some 20,000 years ago. Several hundred fishing folk make the islets their home; if you're out on the water after daybreak, you can see them casting their nets among the herons and other birdlife, as their kids paddle their dugout canoes to school. Many visitors come by day trip from Granada, but it's much more rewarding to spend the night on one of the islands. Ecolodge stays include full board. There are several basic island eateries as well, frequented by boat tours.

★Isleta El Espino BOUTIQUE HOTEL **$$$**
(☎7636-0060; www.isletaelespino.com; r US$135-210;) Kayaking at dawn among the reeds and the herons, delicious meals, yoga, massages and a chance to disconnect from it all are on offer at this island ecolodge. Isleta El Espino is a study in luxurious tranquility, and whether you stay in a lakefront *casita* or the jungly Treetop Rancho, you're guaranteed seclusion and stellar views of Volcán Mombacho.

Jicaro Island Lodge BOUTIQUE HOTEL **$$$**
(☎2558-7702; https://jicarolodge.com; r from US$450;) Close to the northern end of the peninsula, this Londoner-owned boutique hotel takes its eco-credentials very seriously, with its use of solar power, water filtration, hiring of locals and investment in local community education. Expect spacious, breezy two-story *casitas* with hammocks, local ingredients turned into gourmet meals, and plenty of activities, from kayaking and SUP (stand-up paddleboarding) to yoga and local tours.

ℹ Getting There & Away

From the Cocibolca marina (p448) in Granada, set-price tours include a 30-minute boat jaunt (US$2 per person or US$40 per yacht), a nature tour (US$16 per person), a thorough tour of the islets (US$40 to US$80) and a full day on Isla Zapatera (US$180). Don't expect to haggle over the prices.

Masaya

POP 125,800 / ELEV 248M

Coming from Granada, Masaya may seem a bit down at heel. This is a very workaday little town, unexceptional but for a few things: a proliferation of excellent artisans and a picturesque, crumbling *malecón* (waterfront walkway). Nicaraguan tourists, by the way, always make sure their visit coincides with one of Masaya's many spectacular festivals, and there are cultural exhibitions and dances every Thursday evening.

Dangers & Annoyances

Since April 2018, Masaya has become both an epicenter of violence and a symbol of resistance against the Ortega government. At the time of writing, Masaya was a ghost town, and the situation on the ground remained very volatile.

Getting There & Away

Minivans (Parque San Miguel) to Managua's Universidad Centro America (US$0.90, 30 minutes) leave the park in front of Iglesia de San Miguel (when full); services peter out late afternoon. Other buses (US$0.50) and minivans arrive and depart from the **bus station** (Blvd Doctor Manuel Maldonado) at the eastern side of the Mercado Municipal.

Parque Nacional Volcán Masaya

Described by the Spaniards as the gates of hell, the craters that comprise **Volcán Masaya National Park** (☎2528-1444; Carretera a Masaya Km 23; day/evening US$4/10; ⏲9am-4:30pm & 5:30-7:30pm) are the most easily accessible active volcanoes in the country. The two volcanoes at the park, **Masaya** and **Nindirí**, together comprise five craters. Of these, **Cráter Santiago** is still very active and bubbling with red-hot lava. The park entrance is just 7km from Masaya on the Managua highway and most tour operators in Granada run evening trips to the crater. The lava is more impressive at night.

The park has 20km of hiking trails, though at the time of research they were closed to visitors, but you could hike the 5km to the Plaza de Oviedo to see the bubbling lava of the Santiago crater.

The Plaza de Oviedo is a clearing located by the Santiago crater's rim and named after the 16th-century Spanish monk who, suspecting that the bubbling lava was gold, descended to the crater with a bag and small shovel – and came back alive.

Most outfitters in Granada offer a night tour (around US$10 per person, 3½ hours) that involves a convoy of cars driving up to the summit at an assigned time from the visitor centre, just as darkness falls.

Whether you hike or take tour, you will be allowed exactly 15 minutes at the crater lookout point (the time limit is due to the fumes drifting up, and also the smell of sulfur is strong).

If you speak Spanish, have a wander around the attractive **museum** (free admission) at the visitor information center (p452), with impressive natural history displays and beautiful murals, and a **butterfly garden**.

There's no camping at the park. Most travelers stay in nearby Granada or Masaya, but the La Mariposa Spanish School & Eco Hotel is located at the base of the volcano. You can pick up water and basic snacks at the visitors' center (p452).

La Mariposa Spanish School & Eco Hotel LODGE **$$$**
(☎8669-9455; www.mariposaspanishschool.com; El Cruce, 50m E, Carretera a La Concepción, San Juan de la Concepción; per week per person incl

BUS SERVICES FROM MASAYA

DESTINATION	COST (US$)	DURATION (HR)	DEPARTURES (DAILY)
Carazo (Diriamba & Jinotepe)	0.30-0.50	1¼	every 30min, 5am-6pm
Catarina, Diriomo & Diriá	0.30-0.50	40min	every 20min, 6am-5pm
Catarina, San Juan de Oriente, Niquinohomo & Masatepe	0.50	1¼	every 30min, 5am-6pm
Granada	0.50	40min	every 30min, 5am-6pm
Laguna de Apoyo entrance	0.40	20min	at least hourly, 5am-5pm
Managua	0.50	1	every 20min, 5am-5pm
Matagalpa	3	3	5:30am & 6am

classes, accommodations & activities US$520; 📶) 🌿 Just out of San Marcos, on the road to Ticuantepe, is one of Nicaragua's prettiest Spanish schools. Set on the rolling hillside at the base of Volcán Masaya, this wonderful school-hotel minimizes impact through the use of solar electricity, water recycling and reforestation. The setting is lush; afternoon activities include hikes and horseback rides.

ℹ Information

Pay your park entry fee (US$4 by day, US$10 at night) and any guides' fees at the entrance to the park.

The **visitor information center** (⏲ 9am-4.30pm & 5.30-7.30pm) has a good natural history museum (Spanish only) that introduces you to the mysteries of volcanoes.

ℹ Getting There & Away

The park entrance is signposted off NIC-4 7km north of Masaya. Travelers who come here on organized tours have transportation included in the price.

Any Managua-bound bus from Masaya or Granada can drop you at the entrance, but it's a steep, hot climb to the crater; hitchhiking is definitely possible, if you're up for it. Alternatively, consider taking a round-trip taxi from Masaya (around US$10) or Granada (around US$15 to US$20), including an hour's wait at the top.

Los Pueblos Blancos

Originally built from the chalky, pale volcanic tuff upon which this pastoral scene is spread, this series of rural communities, often called the White Villages or Pueblos Blancos, once shimmered a blinding white amid the pale-green patchwork of pasture and jungle.

Today the centuries-old buildings have been painted and the shady roads are paved. Most days the roads between the villages are lined with stands selling vividly painted *artesanías* (handicrafts). Each town has its specialty: handcrafted ceramics, homemade sweets, wooden furniture or freshly cut flowers. The region is also famous for its *curanderos* (folk healers). The villages are most often visited as a day trip from Granada, but take the time to explore and the inner workings of life in rural Nicaragua may reveal themselves.

Catarina

POP 8500

At the crossroads of Los Pueblos Blancos, Catarina is known for its spectacular **mirador** (Viewpoint; 300m Oeste del centro) over Lago de Nicaragua and Laguna de Apoyo, and for its *viveros* (nurseries) that supply ornamental plants for households across Nicaragua.

ℹ Getting Around

Catarina is a popular stop on Granada–Masaya tours. There are also microbuses for destinations throughout the *meseta*, and tuk-tuks that you can hire, while buses run regularly between the *mirador* (viewpoint) and destinations including the following:

Granada (US$0.50, 30 minutes, at least hourly, 6am to 6pm)

Managua (US$0.60, 50 minutes, half-hourly, 6am to 6pm) Arrives/departs Mercado Roberto Huembes.

Masaya (US$0.40, 30 minutes, half-hourly, 6am to 6pm)

If driving, avoid the insanely busy parking lot by the *mirador*.

Diriá & Diriomo

POP 12,300

Diriomo, home to a number of so-called 'witch doctors,' has long been known as the Witch Capital of the Meseta and it is here that people come if they're looking to curse an enemy, cure an ailment or bewitch a paramour. Most healers work out of their homes, which are unsigned. Ask at the *alcadía* (mayor's office). It's also famous for its *cajetas* (rich, fruit-flavored sweets), *chicha bruja* (an alcoholic corn beverage) and even stiffer *calavera del gato* ('skull of the cat' – drink at your own risk).

Diriá, a twin town across the road, boasts **Mirador el Boquete** (Calle Laguna de Apoyo), the less-touristed overlook of Laguna de Apoyo, where the viewpoint features a few eating places that get packed with families on weekends. From the lookout, there's a steep, half-hour trail to the bottom, where a muddy little beach offers access to the bright-blue water for swimming.

ℹ Getting There & Away

Buses leave almost hourly from Diriomo for Mercado Huembes in Managua (US$0.80) and every 40 minutes for Masaya (US$0.50). If you're in a rush (or heading south), make your way out onto the highway and flag down any passing bus.

To get to the *mirador*, take any Niquinohomo-bound bus (US$0.50, every 30 minutes) from Diriá, which will stop in the city center. It's a 2km walk or a quick taxi ride to the lookout.

Masatepe

POP 20,600

This photogenic colonial town has well-kept plazas and churches, and is renowned for two things: the exuberant horse parade in June that's part of its *fiestas patronales,* and its carpenters, who make Nicaragua's finest furniture, showcased at Masatepe's old train station which has been reincarnated as one of the better **artisan markets** (Carretera Masatepe-Masaya; ⏲9am-6pm) in the country.

Towering over Masatepe's attractive central plaza, **Iglesia San Juan Bautista** is home to El Cristo Negro de La Santísima Trinidad, whose feast days mean a month of parties between mid-May and mid-June, and features nationally famous folkloric dances like La Nueva Milpa, Racimo de Sacuanjoche and Masatepetl. The sweeping adobe makes a fine colonial centerpiece, but it's the views from its gates, of fuming Volcán Masaya, that add depth to your prayers.

Around Masatepe, you'll find competing restaurants serving the hearty *mondongo* tripe stew, and hole-in-the-wall eateries specializing in local specialites like *tamagus,* which are like a *nacatamale* (banana-leaf-wrapped bundle of cornmeal, meat, vegetables and herbs), but made with sticky rice instead of cornmeal.

Centro Ecoturístico Flor de Pochote ECOLODGE **$$**
(☎8885-7576; www.flordepochote.com; Iglesia Católica de Masatepe, 4km N, El Pochote; cabins US$35; P 📶 ≋) This beautiful ecolodge lies within the Reserva Natural Laguna de Apoyo, perched right on the crater rim. The cabins (which sleep two) scattered around the 10-hectare *finca* (farm) are made from natural materials. There are lots of activities on-site, from birdwatching to biking; the owners also make wine. It's a 4km downhill walk or taxi ride from Masatepe. Reservations required.

ℹ Getting There & Away

Buses leave the Parque Central **bus stop** (Parque Central) half-hourly for Masaya (US$0.40) and Mercado Roberto Huembes in Managua (US$1.30, one hour), while minivans make the run to Jinotepe (US$0.50, 15 minutes) when full. Alternatively, take a tuk-tuk between the villages.

San Juan de Oriente

POP 2800

This attractive colonial village – known to some as the sister 'bewitched village' of Catarina – is renowned for its artisanal traditions. San Juan de Oriente, indeed, has been in the pottery business since before the Spanish conquest, and 95% of the residents are artisans. While production of inexpensive and functional pottery for local consumption is still important, the recent generations of craftspeople have upped their game. A number of the local masters are international award winners who exhibit abroad, and their vases, plates, pots and other creations are exquisitely decorated and very fairly priced.

At the time of writing, this town had experienced a big drop off in tourism as a result of the political unrest which began in 2018, further information see p431.

There's no infrastructure here for overnight guests; luckily, you're close to Granada.

BUYING CERAMICS IN SAN JUAN DE ORIENTE

There is no better place in Nicaragua to buy fine ceramics, with many pieces true works of art. You can find San Juan de Oriente ceramics in Granada, but for the best pieces, you have to visit the mother lode directly. Quality varies, and several shops along the main street sell crude, cheap, mass-produced vases, wind chimes and other tat; ignore those and head straight for the workshops of the village's renowned artists.

Transporting ceramics can be tricky and most ceramics masters don't offer shipping. It's best to come with your own packing material and FedEx your treasure home; alternatively, the following websites sell pieces from San Juan de Oriente and offer international shipping: www.nicaraguanartpottery.com and www.nicaceramicart.com. These are also good introductions to the most prominent artists and the styles of work you're likely to come across.

There are a couple of very basic food options in village, but for more of a dining experience, head to nearby Masatepe or Granada.

★**Galería de Helio Gutiérrez** ART
(☎8230-9892; ⏰8am-5pm) The recipient of more international awards than any other master in the village, Helio combines geometric, traditional and contemporary design elements in his unique ceramics and is known as the father of the contemporary potter movement in San Juan de Oriente. Pieces start from US$130.

Red Clay ART
(☎8687-0484; ⏰9am-5pm) This stellar shop mostly stocks high-end pieces by Miguel Maldonado, winner of national and international awards, which blend traditional and contemporary design. There are also a number of excellent pieces by Gregorio Bracamonte, a master of pre-Columbian design who excels at making intricate jaguar vessels, decorated with natural dyes.

ℹ Getting There & Away

Buses leave more or less hourly for Granada (US$0.50, one hour) from the **bus stop** (Parque Central) on San Juan de Oriente's Parque Central. Alternatively, flag down any passing bus making the Granada–Rivas run on the highway. A more convenient option is a tuk-tuk (US$0.50 to Catarina, US$2 to Granada).

Carazo Towns

Southwest of the Pueblos Blancos, several coffee-growing highland towns offer a refreshingly cool climate and a couple of wide, sandy beaches along the coast. Carazo is central in Nicaraguan history and myth. It's not only where the first Nicaraguan coffee was sown but also where the nation's most famous burlesque, *El Güegüense,* was anonymously penned in the late 17th century.

The main attractions here are the twin cities of **Diriamba** and **Jinotepe**. Diriamba is considered the birthplace of coffee production in Nicaragua; it was already a bustling settlement when the Spanish arrived. Today it has a pleasant central plaza and interesting European-style architecture that dates back to the coffee boom. Jinotepe is famous in Nicaragua for its neoclassical architecture and locally produced ice cream, and has a lively, youthful vibe due to a large student population.

ℹ Getting There & Away

Jinotepe is a transportation hub, and the big, confusing **bus station** (Carretera Panamericana) is six blocks east of the Parque Central, across the Panamericana (Pan-American Hwy). Microbuses to Managua line up directly on the highway.

SOUTHWESTERN NICARAGUA

Packed with attractions, the southwest offers up some of Nicaragua's hallmark vistas and adventures. Surfers have been hitting this coastline for years, drawn by perfect, uncrowded waves and laid-back surfing encampments around San Juan del Sur. No trip to the southwest would be complete without a few days of kayaking, swimming, hiking and biking on Isla de Ometepe.

Rivas

POP 34,357

Rivas' strategic position on the only sliver of land between the Pacific and Atlantic oceans made it an essential stop along the

CATCHING THE BOAT FROM SAN JORGE

Just 15 minutes from the bustle of Rivas is the port town of San Jorge, lined with inexpensive seafood restaurants and casual bars. From the ferry terminal, where there's guarded parking (US$3) for your car and a regular boat service to Isla de Ometepe, up to 18 boats make the trip from San Jorge to Isla de Ometepe (US$1.50 to US$3, one hour) each day between 7am and 5:45pm, though not all sail reliably. There's no need to reserve ahead. Passengers simply board and pay on the boat. However, if you're trying to put your car onto a ferry you might have to kill some time: there's often a short waiting list.

Buses leave San Jorge for Rivas (US$0.25) almost hourly from the ferry terminal. Alternatively, *colectivo* taxis between the Rivas bus terminal and the San Jorge ferry terminal should cost around US$1. Several shuttle operators in Granada (US$20) and San Juan del Sur (US$18) offer direct, convenient drop-offs at the ferry terminal.

arduous overland crossing to San Juan del Sur during the Gold Rush. Now, with all the development on the southwestern beaches and Ometepe, it is once again an important trading and transport hub.

If you have some time to kill in town, a **museum** (☎2563-3708; Mercado, 1c S, 1c E; US$2; ⏰9am-noon Mon-Sat) in a 200-year-old house is the place to go. Inside you'll find some moth-eaten taxidermy, a wall of myths and legends and, best of all, a well-signed (in both English and Spanish) collection of pre-Columbian artifacts, many of them discovered by the Santa Isabela Archaeological Project.

Rivas has plenty of cheap eats, with the very cheapest clinging to the outside of the chaotic *mercado* (market). Nothing to wow your palate, though.

Getting There & Away

BUS

The main **Terminal de Buses** (☎8669-0330; Frente mercado) is adjacent to the *mercado*. You can catch more luxurious long-distance buses (most headed to and from Managua, not Granada) at the **long-distance bus stop** (Carretera Panamericana) just north of the exit to San Jorge. If you're headed south to Costa Rica, catch a **Transnica** (☎2563-5397; www.transnica.com; Carretera Panamericana) bus or **Tica Bus** (☎8877-1407; www.ticabus.com; Frente Estadio Yamil Rios) on its way to San José (US$35 to US$45) from Managua.

Several express buses to Managua's Mercado Roberto Huembes start in San Jorge and pass through Rivas, stopping at the Puma gas station by the traffic circle, a 10-minute walk from the Terminal de Buses. Four express buses from Managua to Peñas Blancas also stop at the Puma gas station; check times locally.

MINIBUS & TAXI

Colectivos (shared taxis or minibuses) run regularly to San Jorge (US$0.70) and San Juan del Sur (US$2). Private taxi drivers also hang around the bus terminal, waiting to scoop up travelers who need a ride to the Tola beaches or San Juan del Sur. They'll quote a wide range of prices, depending on exactly where you're going (and whether you're toting a surfboard,) but it shouldn't cost more than US$20 to San Juan del Sur, or more than US$35 per carload to the Tola beaches.

Isla de Ometepe

POP 29,800

Ometepe never fails to impress. Its twin volcanic peaks ('fire' and 'water'), rising up out of Lago de Nicaragua, have captured the imagination of everyone from precolonial Aztecs (who thought they'd found the promised land) to Mark Twain (who waxed lyrical about it in his book *Travels with Mr Brown*) – not to mention the relatively few travelers who make it out here. The island's fertile volcanic soil, clean waters, wide beaches, wildlife population, off-the-beaten track farmstays, archaeological sites and dramatic profile are quickly propelling it up traveler must-see lists.

More than 1700 petroglyphs have been found on Ometepe, making this a DIY archeologists' fantasy island.

Activities

Some of the island's tourist attractions are hard to find or even a bit dangerous – take that active volcano, for example. Sometimes it's just worth hiring a guide.

The island's two volcanoes can be ascended from Moyogalpa or Altagracia for **Volcán Concepción** (Map p456), and Fincas Magdelena, El Porvenir and Hacienda Mérida for **Volcán Maderas** (Map p456). Guided ascents of Concepción cost around US$40 per person; Maderas is less expensive. The uphill slog to Cascada San Ramoń (p460), more a walk than a hike, makes for an excellent half-day trip.

Relatively less challenging hikes abound, including to the halfway point up Maderas on the Finca Magdalena trail, and **El Floral** (Map p456), a five- to seven-hour round-trip to a viewpoint about 1000m up Concepción (around US$30 per person).

Tours

Many tour operators are based in Moyogalpa. However, just about any lodging on the island can organize horseback riding and tours. Guides are not really necessary for San Ramón waterfall or Reserva Charco Verde, although it's always easier to have someone else arrange transportation.

After various tourists got lost and died climbing volcanoes solo, it's now illegal to climb the volcanoes without a guide. Guides are available at or near the major trailheads in Altagracia, Moyogalpa, Balgüe and Mérida. Another place where it's worth having a guide along is a kayak cruise of the Río Istiam – they know where all the animals are.

Isla de Ometepe

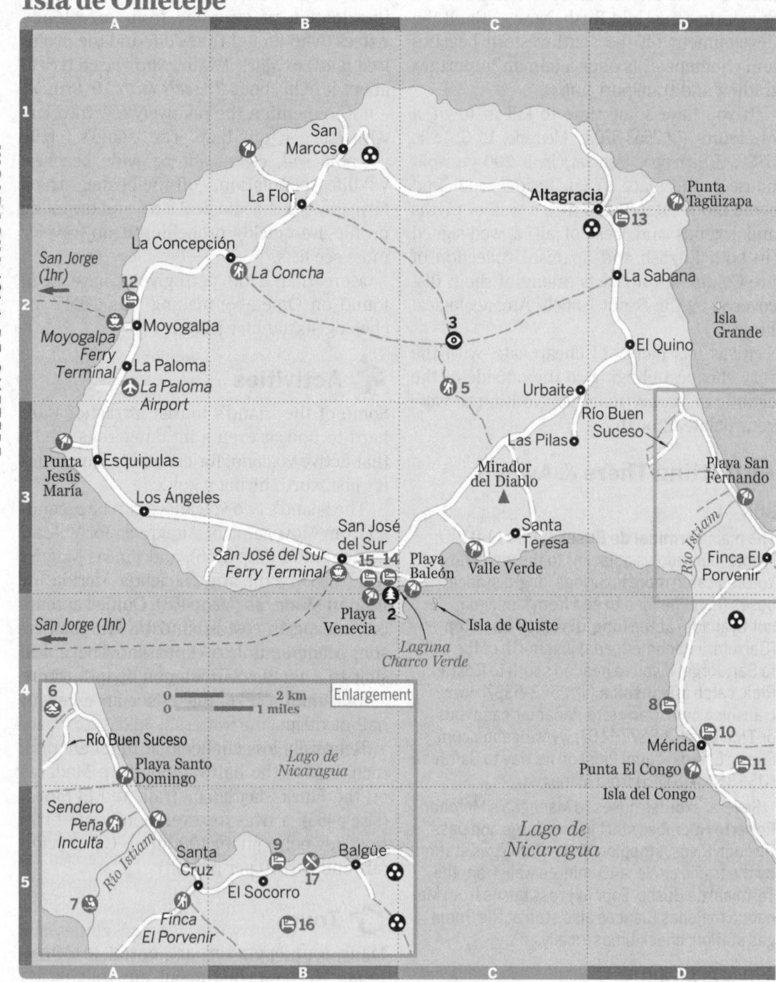

Getting There & Away

AIR

On Thursdays and Sundays at noon, La Costeña Airlines flies 12-seater aircraft from Managua to La Paloma Airport (around US$80, 20 minutes) – an airstrip some 2km south of Moyogalpa. From Ometepe, the flights continue to San Carlos and San Juan del Norte.

BOAT

Up to 15 boats and ferries ply the 17km route daily between San Jorge on the mainland and the **Moyogalpa ferry terminal** (El muelle; Map p456; Calle Santa Ana), Ometepe's main port. Departures are between 7am and 5:45pm (US$1.50 to US$3, one hour); some are more reliable than others. There are departures from San Jorge to the **San José del Sur ferry terminal** (Map p456; El muelle) at 9:30am, 2pm and 5pm. Between November and February, winds can make the sea rough, particularly in the afternoon; consider taking a car ferry instead of a smaller boat. The Ferry Schedules page on www.ometepenicaragua.com has up-to-date departure information.

Most boats can transport bikes and other equipment without a problem. If you're loading your car onto the ferry, you might have to wait, depending on availability; otherwise, no reservations are required. Passengers pay on the boat.

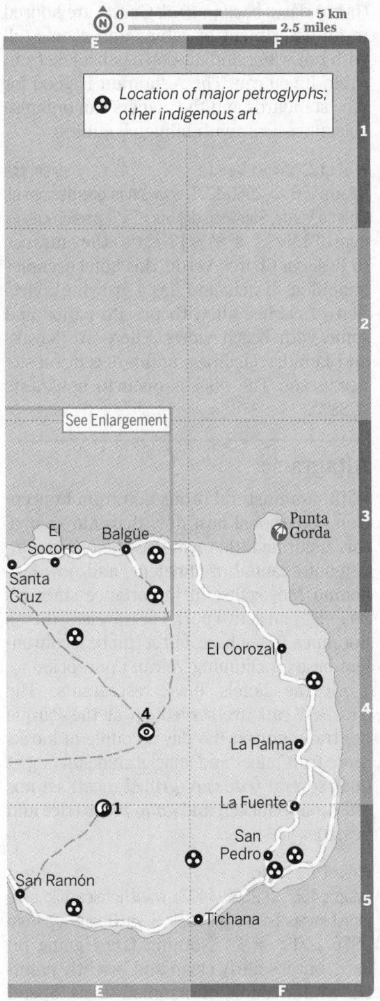

Isla de Ometepe

Sights

1 Cascada San Ramón ... E5
2 Reserva Charco Verde ... B4
3 Volcán Concepción ... C2
4 Volcán Maderas ... E4

Activities, Courses & Tours

5 El Floral ... C2
Hari's Horses ... (see 10)
6 Ojo de Agua ... A4
7 Río Istiam ... A5

Sleeping

8 Caballito's Mar ... D4
9 El Pital Chocolate Paradise ... B5
10 Finca Montania Sagrada ... D4
11 Finca Mystica ... D4
12 Hospedaje Soma ... A2
13 Hotel Castillo ... D2
14 Hotel Charco Verde ... B3
15 Hotel Finca Venecia ... B3
16 Totoco Ecolodge ... B5

Eating

17 Café Campestre ... B5

Moyogalpa

Moyogalpa is home to the ferry terminal for hourly boats from the mainland, and, as such is the nerve center for Ometepe's nascent tourist industry. There are numerous guesthouses, budget hotels and restaurants here, and many of the island's tour companies; it's also base camp for the climb up Volcán Concepción. However, it's not exactly an island paradise you'll want to linger in.

Cultu Natural OUTDOORS
(☎8364-7211; NIC-64, al lado de supermercado; Volcán Concepción ascents US$30, waterfall hike US$15; ⏰9am-5pm) Friendly Danilo and his team get great feedback from travelers for their combination of local knowledge and bilingual tours to Ometepe's biggest attractions. Ascents of Volcán Concepción, kayaking at dawn, the waterfall hike, horseback riding and more can be organized here.

Green Expeditions Ometepe OUTDOORS
(☎8421-1439; www.facebook.com/greenometepe; Frente a Hospedaje Central; Volcán Concepción trek per person US$25; ⏰9am-5pm) This highly regarded operator runs trekking tours up Volcán Concepción with bilingual guides and transport included. The motorbikes for rent are in excellent condition.

Hospedaje Soma GUESTHOUSE $$
(Map p456; ☎2569-4310; www.hospedajesoma.com; Frente del Instituto J.R. Smith; dm US$12, r with/without bathroom US$40/30, 2-person cabins with air-con/fan US$70/60; ❄📶) Book ahead at this relaxed but professionally run guesthouse, a 10-minute walk from the ferry dock. Choose between a dorm, private room or cabin, all scattered around a large and beautiful tropical garden. The German owners are helpful with planning excursions around the island and have folders full of useful info about the island.

★ Cornerhouse CAFE $$
(☎2569-4177; www.thecornerhouseometepe.com; Muelle 1c E; mains US$4-7; ⊙7am-5pm Mon-Fri, to 3pm Sat;) Easily the most stylish eating venue on this corner of the island. All-day breakfast is served at this rustic-chic cafe just uphill from the port; the menu features eggs Benedict with roasted tomatoes and fresh basil. There are also gourmet sandwiches and salads (including a great one with papaya and toasted almonds) and wi-fi. It's part of the **Cornerhouse B&B** (El muelle, 1c O; s/d/tr US$25/35/45;).

Information

Banco Lafise (El muelle, 200m E)

BanPro Credit (El muelle, 3c E) Accepts Visa. Not always operational.

Police Station (☎2569-4231; El muelle, 3c E, 1c S)

Getting Around

Moyogalpa has the greatest choice of motorbike, ATV and scooter hire places on the island. It typically costs US$15/day for a scooter, US$25/day for a motorbike and US$60/day for an ATV. Vehicle condition varies, so shop around before you commit to renting.

Charco Verde & Isla de Quiste

On the southern side of Concepción lies a lush, less windblown clutch of beaches, centered on **Reserva Charco Verde** (Map p456; US$2; ⊙7am-5pm). The fine green Laguna Charco Verde is accessible from a short hiking trail that begins at Hotel Charco Verde.

Not only is this a lovely spot for swimming, hiking and wildlife-watching, it's also the home of Chico Largo, a tall, thin and ancient witch who often appears swimming or fishing in the lagoon. His primary duty is to protect the tomb and solid-gold throne of Cacique Nicarao, buried nearby.

Just offshore, **Isla de Quiste** is within swimming distance of the beach. Any of the area's hotels can arrange boat service and perhaps rental tents, as it's a prime camping, fishing and birding spot.

All hotels offer meals. If you're hiking in Reserva Charco Verde, it's a good idea to bring plenty of drinking water and snacks.

Hotel Finca Venecia HOTEL $$
(Map p456; ☎8887-0191; d US$30, cabins with fan/air-con from US$40/60;) With terra-cotta walls and ancient funereal urns dotted around the lush property, this *finca* (farm) dates back to 1915. Guests are housed in an assortment of cabins and rooms (all with hot water and air-con); nab a lakefront cabin if you can. The restaurant is good for nica standards and the owners can organise volcano ascents with bilingual guides.

Hotel Charco Verde CABIN $$$
(Map p456; ☎2560-1271; www.charcoverde.com.ni; Charco Verde, San José del Sur; 2-/3-person cabins from US$55/93;) Next to the entrance to Reserva Charco Verde, this hotel occupies a fabulous beach, and has a growing collection of cabins, all with private patios and some with beach views. There are kayaks and laundry facilities, and a decent on-site restaurant. The pool is open to nonguests (US$5).

Altagracia

With more natural protection from Concepción's occasional lava flow than Moyogalpa, this soporific little town was the original indigenous capital of Ometepe, and now lags behind Moyogalpa in importance since it's no longer an active port. For travelers, there's not much to see here, but it can be a convenient base for climbing Volcán Concepción.

All the hotels have restaurants. The cheapest eats are served up at the Parque Central – during the day a couple of kiosks serve fruit juices and snacks, and starting at dusk several *fritanga* (grilled meat) set-ups offer roast chicken and *gallo pinto* (rice and beans).

Hotel Castillo HOTEL $
(Map p456; ☎2569-4403; www.hotelcastillo-ometepe.blogspot.com; iglesia, 1c S, ½c O; dm/s/d from US$6/12/19;) Nothing fancy going on here, but it's fairly clean and brightly painted, with a couple of common areas. Spend a few more dollars for air-con (provided it's working) and to have your own bathroom. The restaurant (dishes US$3 to US$5) is good, and serves real coffee. You can arrange tours here, and rent bikes.

Playa Santo Domingo & Santa Cruz

Windswept sandy beaches and several good hotels lie southeast of Altagracia, on the long and lovely lava isthmus that cradles Playas Santo Domingo, San Fernando and Santa Cruz, which flow seamlessly from north to south.

GETTING AROUND ISLA DE OMETEPE

Half of the southern loop between Moyogalpa and Altagracia (the island's two major towns), that passes through San José del Sur, is a beautifully paved road. The paved road continues along Playa Santo Domingo all the way to Balgüe. The other half of the loop between Moyogalpa and Altagracia is unpaved, rough and bumpy, and best tackled on an ATV or motorcycle; the same goes for much of the loop around Volcán Maderas. The unpaved roads actually get better during the rainy season, when the jutting rocks sink into the softer ground.

The island is bigger than it looks and very few destinations are really walkable. The lack of traffic makes hitchhiking a problem (although any passing pickup will almost certainly give you a ride) – but you'll also be happy if you have your own wheels.

Heading south to Santa Cruz along the island's main road, the beach gets progressively less crowded and the waves are popular with kiteboarders.

★Río Istiam KAYAKING
(Map p456) On the south side of the isthmus, this river shimmers as it snakes through the island's lava valley. The best way to explore the river (which is really a swamp) is by kayak – you're pretty much guaranteed to see turtles, caimans and howler monkeys. Inquire at nearby hotels, like **Caballito's Mar** (Map p456; 8842-6120; www.caballitosmar.com; dm/r/cabins US$8/25/35), which offers the trip for US$25 per person.

Ojo de Agua SWIMMING
(Map p456; btwn El Quino & Santo Domingo; US$5; 7am-6pm) Take a pleasant stroll through banana plantations to the well-signed, shady swimming hole about 1.5km north of Playa Santo Domingo. The mineral-infused water in the pool here bubbles up from 35 small underground springs; with an average temperature of 22°C to 28°C (71°F to 82°F), it makes for a refreshing dip.

Santa Cruz to Balgüe

The northern side of Volcán Maderas has become one of the island's hot spots: apart from being an excellent base for volcano ascents, spread-out little Balgüe has an organic chocolate farm for you to explore, an increasing number of excellent budget accommodations and a burgeoning dining scene.

El Pital Chocolate Paradise HOSTEL $
(Map p456; 2560-3249; www.elpitalometepe.com; Santa Cruz, 1.4km del Este; camping per person US$5, dm US$10-12;) Reached via an atrociously bumpy road leading to the water, this hippie-esque place wears many hats. It's an organic cacao farm, a place to learn to make artisanal chocolate (US$15 per person), a hostel consisting of wonderfully breezy bamboo dorms, a venue hosting fire shows, guided meditation and aerial silks, and a chilled-out cafe.

Totoco Ecolodge LODGE $$$
(Map p456; 8358-7718; www.totoco.com.ni; Callejon de la Palmera, 800m arriba, Balgüe; budget casita US$45, lodge US$102; P) This gorgeous ecolodge features *cabañas* perched high above the beach on a large organic farm that runs on solar power and recycles gray water. It's not on the beach, but there's a beautiful pool with views from here to eternity. The romantic rooms are the best on the island, and the restaurant, open to the public, is excellent.

★Café Campestre INTERNATIONAL $$
(Map p456; 8571-5930; www.campestreometepe.com; Hospedaje Así es Mi Tierra, 50m O; mains US$5-10; 11:30am-9pm;) This popular cafe using local ingredients from the adjacent organic farm has something for everyone: excellent coffee, freshly baked breads, huge salads and international dishes from hummus platters to Thai curries. They do wonderful things with eggplant and you can buy local coffee and honey here.

Santa Cruz to Mérida & San Ramón

This lush part of the island feels progressively wilder and more untamed the further south you travel. Here, lush *fincas* (farms) dot the foothills of Volcán Maderas and, if you travel past San Ramón, beyond the reach of public transportation, you'll find yourself in one of the remotest parts of Nicaragua, amid indigenous villages where visitors are seldom encountered.

Your best bet for eating around here are the restaurants at the guesthouses and *fincas*. Head to Balgüe for more options.

Cascada San Ramón WATERFALL
(Map p456; US$5; ⌚8am-5:30pm) This stunning 40m waterfall is one of the jewels of the island. The 3.7km trail begins at the Estación Biológica de Ometepe. You can drive 2.2km up to the parking area, from where it's a 30- to 40-minute hike up to the waterfall, with a steep scramble near the end. At the top, the cascade tumbles down a sheer, mossy rock face into a cold pool that's fabulous for a dip on a hot day.

Hari's Horses HORSEBACK RIDING
(Map p456; ☎8383-8499; www.harishorsesnicaragua.com; Finca Montania Sagrada, Mérida) Located at the Finca Montania Sagrada, this reliable operator offers several different horseback riding outings in the vicinity of Volcán Maderas. These include rides to the San Ramón waterfall (US$50), trail rides with swimming in the lake (US$25) and, for expert riders only, a five to six-hour endurance gallop all the way around the volcano (US$100).

★**Finca Mystica** FARMSTAY $$
(Map p456; ☎8751-9653; www.fincamystica.com; Punta El Congo, 500m S, 300m E; dm/d/f US$15/42/46; ❄📶) Travelers looking for ecofriendly accommodations in the midst of lush jungle hit the mother lode with Finca Mystica. A labor of love by US expats Ryan and Angela, this eco-farm receives its guests in round cob (soil, rice straw, sand and horse manure) cabins, with a chorus of howler monkeys at dawn and nights filled with fireflies. Exceptional restaurant too.

Finca Montania Sagrada FARMSTAY $$
(Map p456; ☎8383-8499; www.fincamontaniasagrada.com; r/f US$45/75; ❄📶) At the southern end of Mérida, a bumpy road leads uphill to this Edenic property where cabins peek out from between the fruit trees. Swing in a hammock at sunset, play with the resident dogs and cats, or join owners Hari and Mirca for a cup of coffee. The restaurant serves authentic Italian food. English, Italian and German are spoken.

SOUTHERN PACIFIC COAST

Southwestern Nicaragua's Pacific beaches offer amazing surf, sand and sun. The beaches around San Juan del Sur attract more beginners and intermediate surfers, while the waves further north are where the serious surfers head. To get to the Tola beaches – El Astillero down to Playa Gigante – most travelers pass through Rivas and Tola and follow the unpaved roads to the remote strips of sand. The party town of San Juan del Sur serves as the access point for the beaches between Playa Majagual in the north downward to El Ostional.

San Juan del Sur

POP 15,762

Easygoing San Juan del Sur is the hub for exploration of Nicaragua's toned-and-tanned southern Pacific beaches. The town itself, with its clapboard Victorian houses, a towering statue of Christ on a neighboring hillside and a steady influx of young and beautiful international travelers and surfers, is Nicaragua's beach party central – Matthew McConaughey used to hang out here before the place got too popular.

And while the once-sleepy fishing village doesn't sit on an amazing stretch of coastline – you need to head just north or south for that – its half-moon, brown-sugar beach is pretty for a sunset stroll. Top it all off with a string of world-class surfing enclaves located within easy distance of town, and you have all the workings to kick off an amazing adventure on the waves.

Activities

★**Rancho Chilamate** HORSEBACK RIDING
(☎8849-3470; www.ranchochilamate.com; Escamequita; daytime/sunset ride US$79/85) Excellent horseback-riding tours at a beautiful ranch a 20-minute drive south of San Juan del Sur (round-trip transportation provided). Daily rides last around three hours and take place at low tide. Riders must be at least 18 years old. It's well worth staying out at the ranch too (rooms US$99 to US$129); guests rave about the lodgings and food.

One Love Surf School & Shop SURFING
(Map p461; ☎8251-5525; www.facebook.com/onelovenicaragua; Av Vanderbuilt; surfing lessons from US$20; ⌚8am-7pm) Gianni from One Love gets much love from rookie surfers for his patient surfing instruction. He also rents out quality boards and sells surfing gear.

San Juan del Sur

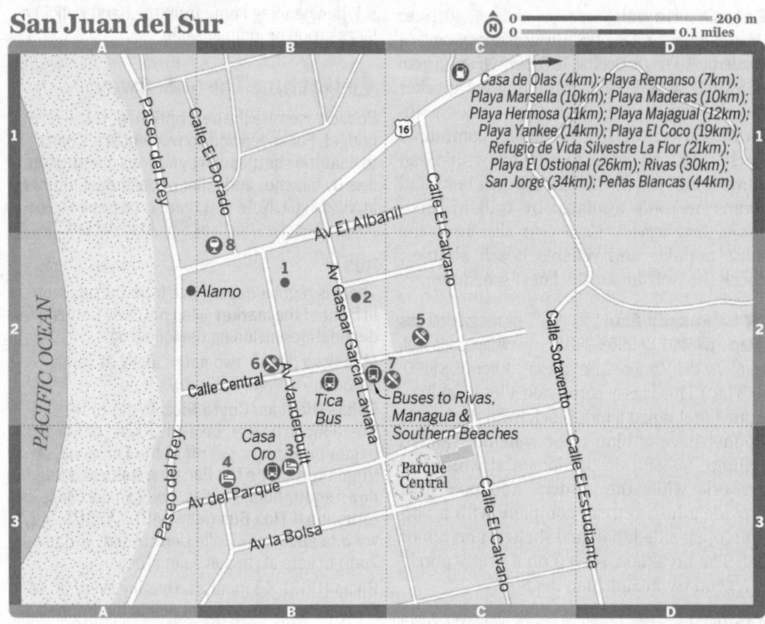

San Juan del Sur

San Juan Surf & Sport BOATING
(Map p461; ☎8984-2464; www.sanjuandelsursurf.com; Av Gaspar García Laviana, above Arena Caliente; booze cruises US$24) Though these guys also organize surfing lessons and deep-sea fishing excursions, they're particularly well known for their boozy sunset cruises, where drinks flow freely during the two-hour spin around the bay.

Festivals & Events

★**Sunday Funday** POOL CRAWL
(☎2568-2043; www.facebook.com/SundayFundayPoolCrawl; US$35; ⏲from 2:30pm) Infamous on the nica party scene, Sunday Funday is known to have involved more than 800 participants on one occasion. It's a highly organised pool/bar crawl with DJ sets, involving Hostel Pachamama, Naked Tiger and other hostels and bars (though the line-up can change). Minibuses shuttle revelers between venues as part of San Juan's most epic party.

Semana Santa RELIGIOUS
(Holy Week; ⏲Mar or Apr) Holy Week (the week before Easter) is one of the busiest times of the year in San Juan del Sur and the surrounding area. In addition to a full range of religious pageants and processions, the beaches explode with parties and celebrations.

Sleeping & Eating

Casa de Olas HOSTEL $
(☎8326-7818; www.casa-de-olas.com; Lot 6, Las Escaleras; dm/d US$16/45;) Run by a friendly Aussie couple, this is a party hostel – unashamedly so, but very wellrun and with epic hilltop views. There's a large pool, a bar, two rescued spider monkeys out back (don't give them beer!), simple dorms with thatched roofs, and communal meals. It's 3km east of San Juan del Sur, with several daily shuttles into town.

Casa Oro Hostel HOSTEL $$

(Map p461; ☎2568-2415; www.casaeloro.com; Av Vanderbuilt, Parque Central, 1c O, 50m N; dm/d from US$10/48; ❄@🛜) This rambling backpacker favorite has all the amenities – a great information center, free breakfast, communal kitchen, lounge space, rooftop bar with ocean views – and good vibes 24/7. Dorm beds and rooms are only available by walk-in: first-come, first-served. Casa Oro also runs the most popular and reliable beach shuttles; check the website for the latest schedules.

★**La Posada Azul** HISTORIC HOTEL $$$

(Map p461; ☎2568-2524; www.laposadaazul.com; Av del Parque/Calle Iglesia; d from US$100; ❄🛜🏊) This classy converted Victorian boutique hotel is just a half-block from the beach. Rooms have a blue color scheme, vaulted ceilings, tasteful decorations and whimsical artwork, while the gardens and pool area provide a lush retreat, complete with a *palapa* (open-sided thatched shelter) and honor bar. The breakfast, served on a pretty porch, is legendary in San Juan del Sur.

Asados Juanita NICARAGUAN $

(Map p461; Av Central; mains US$3-5; ⊙6-10pm Mon-Sat) Follow the plumes of smoke to this hugely popular outdoor *fritanga* (grill) where you'll choose between pork or chicken, sweet or savory plantains, and *gallo pinto* (blended rice and beans). Eat in, or take away – it's delicious and inexpensive.

★**Barrio Café** INTERNATIONAL $$

(Map p461; ☎2568-2294; www.barriocafesanjuan.com; cnr Av Vanderbuilt & Calle Central; dishes US$5-9; ⊙6:30am-10pm) Excellent coffee, gourmet breakfasts, killer *ceviche,* imaginative fusion dishes, an all-nica staff, and potent, fruity rum cocktails – what's not to like? This breezy cafe is on a centrally located corner just a block from the beach. There's a nice little boutique hotel attached (rooms US$40).

King Curry FUSION $$$

(Map p461; ☎8375-7618; www.facebook.com/pages/King-Curry/176871972510703; cnr C Central & Av Mercado; mains US$8-10; ⊙5-11:30pm) Perch at one of several communal tables and go for an Indian or Thai-style curry at this thimble-sized, candlelit place. We love both the ambience and the authentic flavors.

Information

DANGERS & ANNOYANCES

- Don't walk alone on the beach at night.
- When heading home from the bars, walk in a large group or jump in a cab.

Getting There & Away

Public buses are the best option for those on a budget. For speed and convenience, it's hard to beat the shuttles run by various operators to nearby beaches and other popular destinations in Nicaragua. Note that there is no public transport to beaches north of San Juan del Sur.

BUS

There is regular bus service from the bus stop in front of the **market** (Map p461; Av Central) to destinations including the following:

Managua (US$2, two hours, daily at 5am, 5:40am, 7am and 3:30pm)

Peñas Blancas/Costa Rica To get to the Costa Rican border, take any Rivas- or Managua-bound bus, get off at the Empalme La Vírgen turnoff on the Panamericana and flag down south-bound buses. You can purchase international **Tica Bus** (Map p461; ☎2568-2427; www.ticabus.com; Calle Central s/n; ⊙8am-7pm) tickets at its San Juan office.

Rivas (US$1, 45 minutes, roughly every 30 to 60 minutes, 6am to 6pm) Ask to be dropped at the bus stop in front of the Puma gas station to catch a Managua-bound bus (look for expreso to catch a faster bus).

Southern beaches (US$1.50, 20 minutes to one hour, three daily) Service to Playa El Coco, Refugio de Vida Silvestre La Flor and Playa El Ostional. Departure times change occasionally; call into a hostel in San Juan del Sur to see or ask about the latest posted times.

CAR

Alamo (Map p461; ☎2277-1117; www.alamonicaragua.com; Av del Mar) rents out sedans and 4WD vehicles. You'll probably want the latter, especially if you're heading to the beaches south of town. **UNO station** (Map p461; NIC-16) is the only place to get gas.

TAXI

Taxis congregate close to the market. In theory, each driver has a list of set rates for destinations outside of town, but you'll hear a small range of prices. Get together with other travelers for the best deal. Casa Oro (p441) organizes four-person taxis to Playa Gigante (US$50), Laguna Apoyo (US$70), Playa Popoyo (US$60), the Costa Rican border (US$25) and more.

Getting Around

Numerous outlets around town rent out dirt bikes (US$25 per day), quad bikes (US$65 per day) and other rugged wheeled transport that's ideal for the bumpy roads to the beaches. **Big Wave Dave's** (Map p461; ☎2568-2151;

www.facebook.com/BigWaveDavesSJDS; UNO Station, 2½c O; ⏲8am-late Tue-Sun) has the best motorbikes.

Beaches North of San Juan del Sur

The gorgeous beaches north of San Juan del Sur each have their own unique character. Playa Maderas is a surfers' beach, Playa Marsella is a place to chill out and watch the sunset, Playa Magajual is good for swimming and Playa Ocotal is a private sheltered cove. All can be easily visited on a day trip from San Juan del Sur.

Playa Maderas

A good-time-vibe backpacker and surfer hangout, this stunning beach – with a shark's fin rock at the northern end and wonderful, wide sandy stretches for sunbathing – is famed for having one of the best beach breaks in the country.

★Buena Vista Surf Club LODGE $$$
(☎8863-4180; www.buenavistasurfclub.com; Playa Maderas; s/d US$115/140; 📶) Take a right where the road dips after Parque Maderas to get to this lovely getaway with spectacular views over the bay. Six tree house–style *cabañas,* all tucked into the forest, are outfitted with beautiful natural wood, huge mirrors and comfortable beds. Traditional Nicaraguan food is served family-style; yoga and surf lessons are also on the menu.

Arte-Sano Hotel Cafe BOUTIQUE HOTEL $$$
(☎8872-9672; www.artesano-hotelcafe.com; Playa Maderas; r US$90; ❄📶🏊) Arte-Sano's infinity pool overlooks Playa Marsella from its lofty hilltop location. Bold contemporary artworks, painted cattle skulls and exquisite pottery from San Juan de Oriente decorate the vast lounge and cafe-bar area where a succinct mix of international dishes is served. Take the left turnoff steeply uphill just before reaching Playa Maderas.

Tacos Locos INTERNATIONAL $$
(Playa Maderas; dishes US$7-14) A breezy, shady taco restaurant overlooking the beach, serving passable tacos and a smattering of decent fish dishes.

ℹ Getting There & Away

Many surf shops and hostels in San Juan del Sur – including Casa Oro, which goes four times daily – offer shuttles here (US$5). Coming by car, Playa Maderas is 11km north of San Juan del Sur via a decent (though sometimes narrow) dirt road.

Playa Majagual

With its white-sand beach framed by two jutting cliffs, this beautiful bay is good for swimming – watch the riptide, though. There's no surfing off this beach, though Playa Los Playones, a two-minute walk to the south, has a strong shore break.

Hostal Matilda's HOSTEL $
(☎8456-3461; www.hostalmatilda.com; Playa Los Playones; dm/s/d from US$7/15/30) A psychedelic maze of sultry mermaids, shoals of tropical fish, Poseidons brandishing their tridents and giant frogs carrying mushroom umbrellas, this basic, family-run guesthouse consists of somewhat musty but serviceable rooms with high beds and bug netting – all just metres away from the surf.

Bar El Ranchito INTERNATIONAL $$
(Playa Majagual; mains from US$7; ⏲noon-9pm) Enjoy your grilled fish with garlic sauce, *ceviche, sopa de mariscos* (seafood soup) and grilled chicken at this basic beachfront joint that overlooks the southern end of Playa Majagual.

ℹ Getting There & Away

Majagual is 12km north of San Juan del Sur via an unpaved road that's good enough for regular cars (though getting here on an ATV or dirt bike is more fun). Several shuttle companies in San Juan offer drop-off services to Majagual (US$5); it's also possible to take one of the more frequent shuttles to nearby Playa Maderas and walk to Majagual (10 minutes).

Beaches South of San Juan del Sur

Heading south from San Juan del Sur toward the border of Costa Rica, a string of low-key beach villages offer surf breaks and sea-turtle-watching opportunities. There's an interesting wildlife refuge, but you'll also see plenty of monkeys in the trees if you just keep your eyes open while traveling along the hilly forested road. Playa Hermosa is one of the better beaches for surfing, along with Playa Yankee and Playa Remanso.

SURFING AT PLAYA YANKEE

Some 15km south of San Juan del Sur, Playa Yankee is renowned in surfer circles for its powerful point break, best at mid to high tide. Buses from San Juan del Sur to El Ostional can drop you at the turnoff for the beach, from where it's another 2km to the beach along a decent unpaved road. Bring all food and drink with you.

Playa Hermosa

This long, wide, strikingly beautiful beach was the setting for two seasons of the US TV series *Survivor*. Playa Hermosa is famous for great surfing – there are five breaks on this beach alone – and a cool, lost-in-paradise vibe. The left and right beach breaks are fun for intermediate and advanced surfers alike; sometimes the conditions are right for beginners too. It's a privately owned beach; pay an entrance fee of US$3 at Playa Hermosa Ecolodge.

Playa Hermosa Surf Camp SURFING
(7667-5436; www.playahermosabeachhotel.com; Playa Hermosa; board rental per day US$10, surfing lessons US$30) The surf camp and shop at Playa Hermosa Ecolodge offers lessons and board rentals; they have boards of all shapes and sizes. Also available here are horseback riding, snorkeling, fishing and sailing trips (to name just a few).

Playa Hermosa Ecolodge LODGE $$$
(8671-3327; www.playahermosabeachhotel.com; Playa Hermosa; dm US$25, d US$90-100;) Considered by many to be one of the best beach hostels on Nicaragua's south Pacific coast. The open-air, six-bed dorm rooms in this rustic paradise catch the breeze to stay cool at night. Private rooms upstairs have giant mosquito nets. There's a great vibe and surf scene here, with a chilled-out, open-air restaurant. Transfers from San Juan del Sur are included.

Getting There & Away

Playa Hermosa Ecolodge (p464) includes transfers to and from San Juan del Sur in its room prices and day-use passes (US$10).

Otherwise, buses stop in Playa Hermosa on their way from San Juan del Sur to Playa El Ostional (US$1.25, 35 minutes, four daily); the beach is a 3km walk from the turnoff. Casa Oro (p462) offers daily shuttles (US$10, leaving at 9:30am and 11am, returning at 4pm and 6pm).

There are several shallow stream crossings along the access road – fine for city cars during dry season and for quad bikes and high clearance vehicles the rest of the time.

Playa El Coco

POP UNDER 500

This is a world-class beach – a spectacular stretch of sparkling sand punctuated by cliffs so pretty that they grace about half of the country's tourist literature. Playa El Coco makes a great day trip from San Juan, or a handy base for visiting the nearby Refugio de Vida Silvestre La Flor.

★ **Tortugas Hostel** HOSTEL $$
(7894-7139; Playa El Coco; dm/d US$20/100;) Who needs a fancy seaside villa when you can get exceptional views of the Pacific from the infinity pool at this hilltop hostel? The location is second to none, the thatched-roofed dorms catch the breeze and the onsite restaurant serves great pasta (the owner's Italian), plus nica breakfasts. The double is very spacious but overpriced – though that's our only complaint.

Getting There & Away

Buses stop in Playa El Coco on their way between San Juan del Sur and Playa El Ostional (US$1.30, 40 minutes), departing San Juan at 7am, 11am, 1pm and 5pm. Some outfitters in San Juan del Sur also offer shuttle service (US$10), usually with a minimum of five passengers required.

Refugio de Vida Silvestre La Flor

One of the principal laying grounds for endangered olive ridley and leatherback turtles, this **wildlife refuge** (ranger station 8419-1014; US$8, campsites per tent US$15) (locally called by its shorter name, 'La Flor') is 20km south of San Juan del Sur. It's easy to visit on a guided tour from San Juan del Sur or from Playa Hermosa Ecolodge in Playa Hermosa.

Turtles lay their eggs here, usually between 9pm and 2am, between July and January, peaking in September and October, and there can be more than 3000 of them on the beaches at a time. Rangers can do guided walks on request along the short nature trails, pointing out the local flora and fauna (US$10).

When there aren't any turtles around, the park still has an attractive, undeveloped beach, a couple of monkeys on-site and a few short trails; there's a decent beach break (right and left) at the northern end. (But during turtle season there's no surfing as the beach is off-limits.)

You can camp at the reserve (US$15 per tent). The closest hotels are in Playa El Coco.

There aren't many services here; bring your food and water from town.

Getting There & Away

Buses pass near the entrance of the park on their daily trips from San Juan del Sur to Playa El Ostional (US$1.50, 50 minutes, three daily). Advise the driver of your destination, then follow the signs for around 300m.

Tola & the Tola Beaches

Tola ('land of the Toltecs') is an unassuming agricultural town. Pass through it and you hit the rugged and gorgeous nearby coastline. Once almost inaccessible and totally wild, the 30km of Tola beaches are slowly coming into their own. They still retain some of that lost-paradise feel, with top-notch surf, uncrowded sand and good vibes.

There are no banks or real grocery stores, and internet and cell-phone coverage is patchy at best, so enjoy getting away from it all.

Getting There & Away

There are eight buses daily from Rivas to Las Salinas, but while they'll get you to Playa Guasacate (Playa Popoyo), they can't be called convenient – they can drop you at the turnoffs to the other beach villages and you have to walk (or hope to hitch a ride) several kilometers to your destination. Let your driver know where you're going. There's a single direct plantation pickup truck (with benches for passengers) between Tola and Playa Gigante (Monday to Saturday).

Surf camps and hotels offer transportation to and from Managua Airport. Several taxi drivers in Playa Popoyo offer airport pick-up from Managua airport (US$70). A tourist shuttle runs at least once daily between San Juan del Sur and Playa Popoyo (US$15) with a roof rack for surfboards (US$3); ask at Casa Oro (p441) about departure times.

A taxi to Playa Gigante from Rivas costs around US$30, and around US$60 from San Juan del Sur, depending on your bargaining prowess.

Driving from Rivas, the road is unpaved once you pass through Tola, but perfectly passable in a city car in the dry season. Coming from Managua or Granada in dry season, it's possible to take the minor road from the NIC-2 highway directly to Las Salinas, though there's a minor river crossing involved.

El Astillero

POP 5815

This picture-perfect fishing village fronts a gently scalloped white-sand beach. Apart from an excellent beach break with consistent barrels, there's surf north of here (accessible when turtles aren't arriving) and, if you're serious about hitting the more elusive waves, it's possible to talk a local fisherman into helping you explore the coastline.

Hostal Las Hamacas HOSTEL **$$**
(8810-4144; www.hostalhamacas.com; Escuela, 50m S; s/d with fan US$25/30, with air-con US$40/45;) Set on a grassy lot with wide beachfront access, this laid-back guesthouse has peaceful, marine-blue rooms with comfy beds, TV and spacious bathrooms, plus a small swimming pool and – as the name suggests – plenty of hammocks to relax in.

Las Plumerias Lodge LODGE **$$$**
(8979-7782; www.lasplumerias.com; Playa Gavilan, El Astillero; surfer/non-surfer package per week incl all meals from US$750/500;) Run by French surfing instructors Etienne and Emeline, this wonderful surfers lodge is uphill from the road to El Astillero. Breezy traditional, thatch-roofed bungalows come with composting toilets and you can watch the sunset from your hammock or the pool after a day of surfing. Packages include expert surfing instruction and access to waves either by 4WD or boat.

Playa Gigante

POP UNDER 2000

This glorious crescent sweep of white sand, tucked into forested hills, was once a traditional fishing village. Today, though fishing still takes place, the popular sandy beach break right in front of the one-street Playa Gigante gets hollow and fun when conditions are perfect, attracting a steady stream of surfers and sun-seekers.

There are a handful of simple restaurants on the beach and on the road leading to it, and a small *pulpería* (general store) on the main drag.

Buena Vista HOSTEL $

(Punta del Arco; r from US$16;) High up on Punta del Arco headland at the north end of Playa Gigante, this basic but comfortable hostel with a low-key restaurant is run by a friendly local family. From your lofty hammock perch you can watch surfers playing in the waves of Playa Amarilla, north of the point.

Camino del Gigante HOSTEL $$

(8743-5899; www.gigantebay.com; Playa Gigante; dm US$10, d with/without bathroom US$39/30;) The location's the draw at this beachfront hostel: the dorms, rooms and five-person bungalow are bare-bones, but who cares? You're here for the ocean views, the mellow communal areas decked out in psychedelia, and access to great surf spots. There's a bar and restaurant, and, more importantly, the hostel runs a sunset booze cruise (US$10).

Aqua Wellness Resort RESORT $$$

(8739-2426; www.aquanicaragua.com; Redonda Bay; r/ste from US$216/378;) Overlooking a private beach cove, the elegant jungle tree houses at this excellent spa and resort have tremendous ocean views and all the high-end amenities you could wish for. The suites come with plunge pools and there's a private beach, plus lush forest on all sides. Meditation and yoga are a focus, though you can also arrange surfing, fishing and more.

Playa Jiquelite

POP UNDER 1000

With Las Cinco Playas (five beaches area) to the south and separated from Playa Popoyo to the north by the Río de Nagualapa estuary, the Jiquelite area comprises two long beaches buffeted by Pacific waves: Playa Sardina and Playa Jiquelite, separated by a tall cliff. The former attracts novice and intermediate surfers, while Playa Jiquelite, accessed via the village of Limón Dos, is the playground for expert wave riders.

Hotel Magnific Rock HOTEL $$

(8916-6916; www.magnificrockpopoyo.com; Punta Sardinas; 2-person cabins US$40, 2-person studios from US$70, 4-person apt from US$100;) Built on a magnificent rock outcropping, this friendly surfer's hotel has amazing views overlooking Playa Sardina and Playa Jiquelite. The cabins are simple, but good enough, and the studio doubles have incredible beach views. The excellent restaurant serves fish tacos, garlic shrimp, French toast and jumbo smoothies. It's 2km off the road to Las Salinas; look for the signs.

★ **Sirena Surf Lodge** GUESTHOUSE $$$

(8556-5392; www.facebook.com/sirenasurfhouse; r US$70;) The moment you step out of your room, you can bury your toes in the sand. These two beautiful rooms with king-sized beds are all individually designed by owner and surfing instructor Bella, who feeds her guests a phenomenal breakfast and is happy to organize surfing lessons, boat trips and other local excursions.

Getting There & Away

Buses from Rivas to Las Salinas (US$2.50 to US$4, two to three hours, eight daily) can drop you either by the access road to Hotel Magnific Rock, or the one to Playa Jiquelite; it's a 2km walk to the beach from either.

Playa Popoyo (Guasacate) & Around

POP UNDER 1000

Home to one of the most storied waves in Nicaragua, **Playa Popoyo** (Playa Guasacate) is a long stretch of remote coastline several kilometres northwest of the little town of **Las Salinas de Nagualapa**, named for the salt evaporation ponds you'll pass on the way in. Apart from a few surfers and fishers, this stretch of sand is almost empty, ideal for a long walk at sunset. The large, dramatic rock formations on the beach are fun to explore at low tide.

Playa Guasacate is often called Playa Popoyo (www.popoyo.com) in honor of its famed beach break near the southern end, where a shallow lagoon and slow river shift through the long, sandy beach. Don't confuse it with the community of Popoyo that was moved south of Playa Sardinas following the 1992 tsunami.

Wild Waves Surf House GUESTHOUSE $

(8578-6102; www.wildwavesnicaragua.com; De la Bocana, 250m N, Playa Guasacaste; dm/r US$14/40;) Run by friendly Italian surfer Gianni, this three-room guesthouse is the perfect retreat for serious wave-riders. The doubles have king-sized beds, there's a guest kitchen and Gianni arranges boat trips to catch waves further up and down the coast.

WORTH A TRIP

REFUGIO DE VIDA SILVESTRE RÍO ESCALANTE-CHACOCENTE

The main event at this remote wildlife refuge is the mass arrival of female turtles (at intervals between July and December), who crawl up onto the sandy shores to lay their eggs. It's an occasion worth planning a trip around, though Chacocente, as it's often called, is a year-round destination, with deserted beaches and good birdwatching.

The refuge protects five species of turtle, as well as 48 sq km of dry tropical forests and mangrove swamps. **Cosetuchaco** (☎8481-1202, 8603-3742; turtle observation US$10, beekeeper tour US$20) arranges wildlife watching.

Marena (Nicaragua's Ministry of the Environment and Natural Resources) runs a biological station here where you can camp (US$5 per person), stay overnight in hostel-style accommodations (from US$10 per person) or stop for a simple meal (US$3 to US$5).

There's currently no public transportation or regularly offered organized tours to the refuge, but if you have a 4WD you can take a signed, rough track 7km north of Salinas. Or you could walk along the shore 7km from El Astillero.

Weeklong surf packages are US$699 for beginners and from US$399 for experienced surfers.

Club Surf Popoyo HOTEL **$$**
(☎8237-7417; www.clubdelsurf.com; De la Bocana, 200m del Oeste, Playa Popoyo; s/d from US$40/50; ❄📶) Owned by a friendly Italian family, this popular hotel has six spotless and spacious rooms, as well as an excellent, authentic pizzeria that's open to the public. You're not quite on the beach – that's about 100m away – but there's good access to the Popoyo break itself, and guests rave about the helpful staff and hearty breakfast.

Casitas Pacific Hotel BOUTIQUE HOTEL **$$$**
(☎7841-4533; www.casitaspacific.com; De la Bocana, 300m N; d/q from US$72/81; ❄📶) With eight individually decorated rooms, gorgeous native-wood furniture, hammocks and swings on private terraces and thatched roofs, this two-story boutique hotel is Playa Popoyo's most stylish accommodation. The quads, with their two sets of bunk beds, are excellent value for groups of surfer friends, and Popoyo's famous beach break is a 300m-walk down the beach.

★La Vaca Loca CAFE **$$**
(☎8584-9110; www.lavacalocaguasacate.com; De la Bocana, 180m N, Playa Guasacate; mains US$5-7; ⌚Wed-Sun 8am-1pm; ❄📶) La Vaca Loca wears several hats and we love them all: it's an art house with beautifully carved furnishings; a tranquil cafe in a flowering garden, serving American breakfasts and artisanal coffee; and a B&B with just two beautiful, breezy rooms (singles/doubles US$40/50).

LEÓN & NORTHWESTERN NICARAGUA

This is Nicaragua at its fieriest and most passionate. The regional capital of León is – and will always be – a hotbed of intellectualism and independence. The city has nourished some of Nicaragua's most important political and artistic moments. Less polished but somehow more authentic than its age-old rival Granada, the city is beloved for its grand cathedral, art museum, hopping nightlife and spirited revolutionary air.

Just out of León, more than a dozen volcanic peaks wait to be climbed (some can be surfed). Along the still-crowdless beaches there's the best beach accommodations – and gnarliest surfing – in the country. And the virgin wetlands of the Reserva Natural Isla Juan Venado are not to be missed.

Further afield, you'll find the biggest mangrove forest in Central America, awe-inspiring beauty at Reserva Natural Volcán Cosigüina and unique windows into everyday Nicaraguan life in the little towns along the way.

León

POP 169,362

Intensely political, buzzing with energy and, at times, drop-dead gorgeous (in a crumbling, colonial kind of way), León is what Managua should be – a city of awe-inspiring churches, fabulous art collections, stunning streetscapes, cosmopolitan eateries, vibrant student life, fiery intellectualism, and all-week, walk-everywhere, happening nightlife. Many people fall in love with Granada, but most of them leave their heart in León.

León

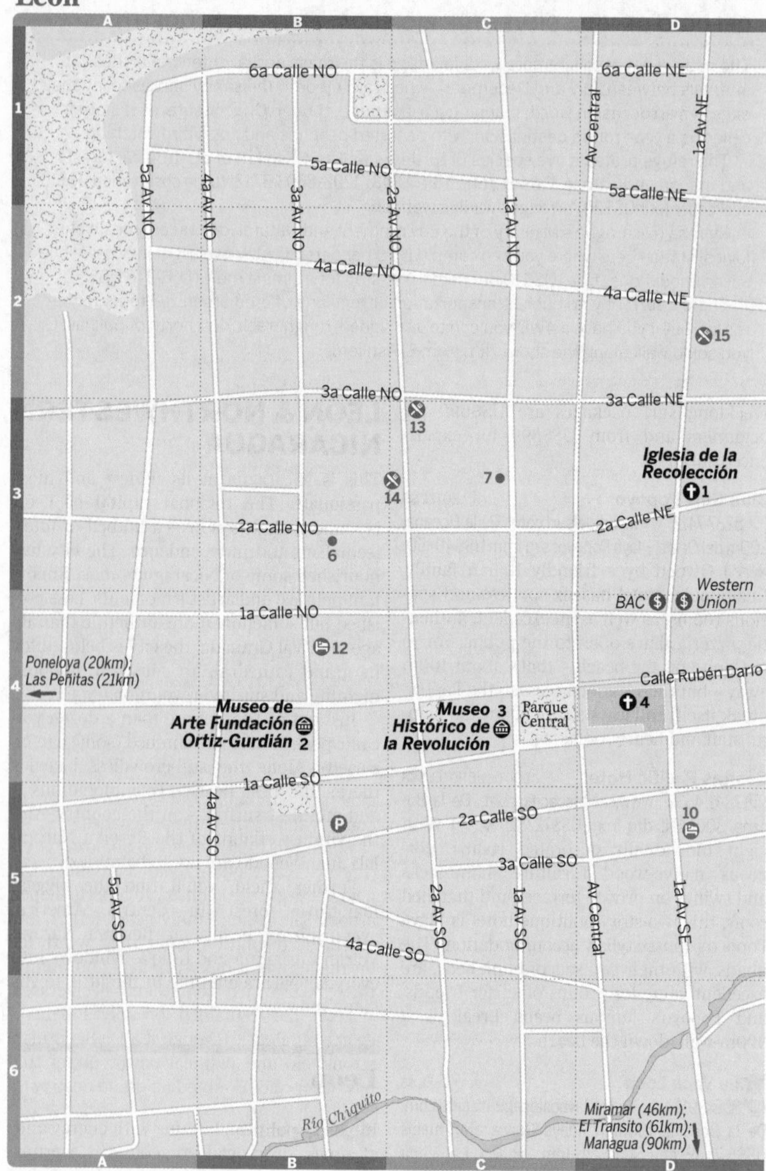

History

Originally located on the slopes of Volcán Momotombo, León was the site of some of the Spanish conquest's cruelest excesses; even other conquistadors suggested that León's punishment was divine retribution. When the mighty volcano reduced León to rubble in 1610, the city was moved to its current location, saint by saint, to sit next to the existing indigenous capital of Subtiaba.

The reprisals did not end there. Eager to win the civil war with Granada – which had, since independence, been contesting

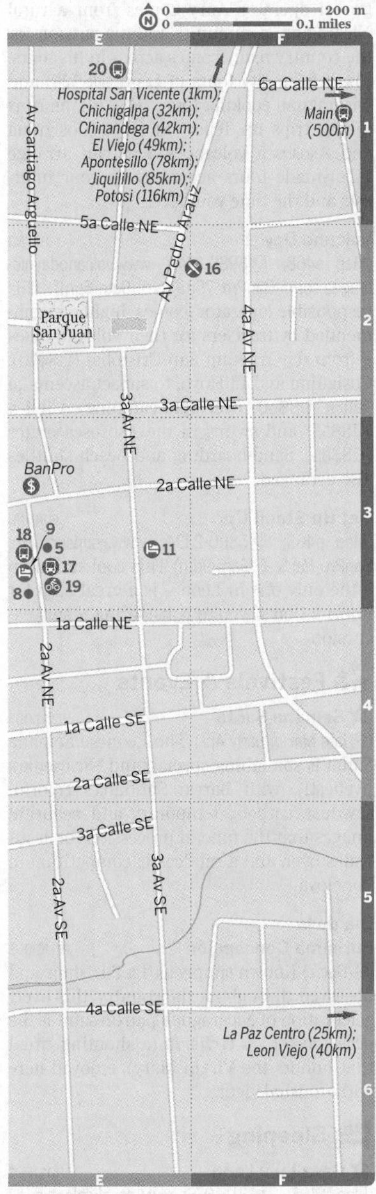

León

Top Sights
1 Iglesia de la Recolección......D3
2 Museo de Arte Fundación Ortiz-Gurdián......B4
3 Museo Histórico de la Revolución......C4

Sights
4 Catedral de León......D4

Activities, Courses & Tours
5 Get Up Stand Up......E3
6 Mas Adventures......B3
7 Tierra Tour......C3
8 Volcano Day......E3

Sleeping
9 Bigfoot Hostel......E3
10 Casa Lula León......D5
11 Guesthouse El Nancite......E3
12 Hotel El Convento......B4

Eating
13 El Desayunazo......C3
14 El Mediterraneo......C3
15 Imbir......D2
16 Mercado La Estacíon......F2

Transport
17 Bigfoot Hostel Shuttles......E3
18 Gekko Explorer......E3
19 Ruedas León......E3
20 Tica Bus......E1
Tierra Tour......(see 7)

the colonial capital's continuing leadership role – in 1853 León invited US mercenary William Walker to the fight. After the Tennessean declared himself president (and Nicaragua a US slave state), he was executed; the nation's capital was moved to Managua, and Granada's Conservatives ran the country for the next three decades.

Finally, in 1956, Anastasio Somoza García (the original dictator) was assassinated at a social event in León by Rigoberto López, a poet. The ruling family never forgot, and when the revolution came, their wrath fell on this city in a hail of bullets and bombs, the scars of which have still not been erased.

León has remained proudly Liberal – even a bit aloof – through it all, a Sandinista stronghold and political power player that has never once doubted its grand destiny.

Sights

★Museo Histórico de la Revolución — MUSEUM

(Map p468; Parque Central; US$2; 8am-5pm) León is the heart and soul of liberal Nicaragua. Stop into this museum for an overview of the Nicaraguan revolutionaries who stood up against the Somoza dictatorship, tracing national history from the devastating earthquake of 1972 to the Sandinista overthrow. The true highlight here is being shown around by the former revolutionaries who can tell you all about their role in the conflict.

★Museo de Arte Fundación Ortiz-Gurdián MUSEUM

(Map p468; www.fundacionortizgurdian.org; Parque Central, 2c O; US$3; ⏲9am-5:30pm Tue-Fri, 9:30am-5:30pm Sat, 9am-4pm Sun) Probably the finest museum of contemporary art in all of Central America, the Ortiz-Gurdián Collection has spilled over from its original home in Casa Don Norberto Ramírez,which was refurbished in 2000 to its original Creole Civil style, with Arabic tiles and impressive flagstones. The collection, spread across two buildings and surrounding greenery-filled courtyards, includes works by Picasso, Chagall, Miró and a number of noted Nicaraguan artists.

★Iglesia de la Recolección CHURCH

(Map p468; Catedral de León, 3c N; ⏲hours vary) Three blocks north of the cathedral, the 1786 Iglesia de la Recolección is considered the city's most beautiful church, a Mexican-style baroque confection of swirling columns and bas-relief medallions that portray the life of Christ. Dyed a deep yellow, accented with cream and age, the lavishly decorated facade may be what makes the cover of all the tourist brochures, but be sure to stop inside and admire the slender mahogany columns and ceiling decorated with harvest motifs.

Catedral de León CATHEDRAL

(Basílica de la Asunción; Map p468; Parque Central; ⏲8am-noon & 2-4pm Mon-Sat) FREE Officially known as the Basílica de la Asunción, León's cathedral is the largest in Central America, its expansive design famously (and perhaps apocryphally) approved for construction in much more important Lima, Peru. Leonese leaders originally submitted a more modest but bogus set of plans, but architect Diego José de Porres Esquivel, the Capitán General of Guatemala (also responsible for San Juan Bautista de Subtiaba, La Recolección and La Merced churches, among others), pulled the switcheroo and built this beauty instead.

Tours

★Mas Adventures OUTDOORS

(Map p468; ☎5765-2838; https://masadventures.com; Iglesia Zaragoza, 3c E; ⏲8am-7pm) Home-grown operator Anry comes from a rural Nicaraguan community and his passion for the country really comes across in his tours. Apart from city tours of León (US$25) and Nicaraguan cooking tours (US$20), he runs hiking trips up Telica, El Hoyo, Cosigüina and Asososca volcanoes, and can arrange tailor-made tours according to your interests and the time you have.

Volcano Day HIKING

(Map p468; ☎8980-8747; www.volcanodaynicaragua.com; BanPro, 75m S; ⏲9am-6pm) This responsible operator comes highly recommended by travelers for their volcano hikes – from day trips up San Cristóbal (US$70), Cosigüina and El Hoyo, to sunset ascents of Telica (US$40), overnight camping on Telica (US$55) and swims in the Asososca crater (US$35). Sand-boarding and beach shuttles also arranged.

Get Up Stand Up SURFING

(Map p468; ☎5800-2394; www.gsupsurf.com; BanPro, ½c S; ⏲9am-9pm) This cool surf shop – the only one in León – is a great stop for information if you're considering a surf excursion.

Festivals & Events

★Semana Santa RELIGIOUS

(⏲late Mar or early Apr) The Leonese Semana Santa is something special (and Nicaragua's liveliest!), with Barrio Subtiaba's colorful sawdust 'carpets,' temporary and beautiful images that the funeral procession for Jesus walks over, and a sandcastle competition in Poneloya.

Día de la Purísima Concepción RELIGIOUS

(⏲Dec 7) Known simply as 'La Purísima' and observed throughout the country, this lively celebration of Nicaragua's patron saint is the occasion for *La Gritería* (a shouting ritual that honors the Virgin Mary), enjoyed here with unusual vigor.

Sleeping

★Casa Lula León HOSTEL $

(Map p468; ☎2311-1076; www.casalulaleon.com; esquina SE de la Catedral, 2c S; dm US$10, r with/without bathroom US$30/25; ❄📶) Sociable without being a party hostel, Casa Lula is a budget traveler favorite, largely through the efforts of hosts Eric and Selina and the knowledgeable, helpful staff. There's a strong emphasis on outdoor activities, a large garden to chill out in, a well-equipped kitchen and spotless rooms (with big lockers in the dorm).

Bigfoot Hostel HOSTEL $

(Map p468; ☎2315-3863; www.bigfoothostelleon.com; BanPro, ½c S; dm/d from US$8/26;) With kitchen access, a miniature swimming pool, freshly made mojitos on offer, and spacious dorms and rooms with ample, secure luggage storage, this place is appealing. It's also well organised: staff run numerous tours and shuttles daily. There's a good travelers' vibe at this party hostel – staff swear the party shuts down at 10pm – and a sweet little cafe-bar out front.

Guesthouse El Nancite B&B $$

(Map p468; ☎2315-4323; 3a Av NE, btwn 2a Calle NE & 1a Calle NE; r US$35-45;) Run by helpful North American John and his lovely wife, this jaunty yellow guesthouse, decorated with Carnival masks and figures, has a handful of fan-cooled economy rooms, a couple of split-level mini-suites facing the leafy courtyard out back, characterful rooms with balconies out front, and an upstairs suite with own balcony. John's coconut pancakes are ace.

★**Hotel El Convento** HISTORIC HOTEL $$$

(Map p468; ☎2311-7053; www.elconventonicaragua.com; Iglesia de San Francisco, 20m N; s/d US$95/140;) There's atmosphere galore at this historic hotel on the grounds of one of the city's most notable convents and churches. The centerpiece garden is impressive and you're surrounded by precious artwork. Guest rooms, with exposed brick walls, are comparatively simple (as befitting a former place of worship) but comfortable, and there's a good but rather pricey restaurant.

Eating

★**Mercado La Estacíon** NICARAGUAN $

(Map p468; Parque San Juan, 1c E, 1c N; mains US$1.50; 6pm-late) Head here in the evenings for your fill of the BX, León's famous dish. BX *(bajón extremo)* was coined by local students in the 1990s; it's the local take on the *fritanga,* consisting of *gallo pinto* (rice and beans), slaw and marinated grilled beef, topped with a tortilla and a piece of omelet, and served on *bijagua* leaves. The Mama Tere's stall is the best.

★**Imbir** FUSION $$

(Map p468; ☎5728-5887; www.imbirestaurant.com; Iglesia de la Recolección, 150m N; mains US$4-9; noon-10pm Mon-Sat;) A happy marriage of Polish and Sri Lankan dishes, this eclectic restaurant does an equally good job with moreish pierogi (dumplings with multiple fillings) and curries ranging from gentle to fruity yet fiery. The shady interior courtyard is also ideal for sipping one of half-dozen local Cerro Negro craft beers, with guest beers chosen from breweries countrywide.

El Desayunazo NICARAGUAN $$

(Map p468; ☎8235-4837; www.facebook.com/leonleonnicaragua; Iglesia de la Merced, 1c O, 2c N; mains US$4-7; 6am-2pm Mon, to 9pm Tue-Sun;) Whether you're being whisked off on an early-morning tour or shuttle, or are just a fan of all-day breakfasts, this is the place for generous portions of *gallo pinto* (rice and beans) and fried plantain, pancakes with maple syrup, full English breakfasts and waffles. Good coffee too.

El Mediterraneo MEDITERRANEAN $$$

(Map p468; ☎2311-0756; 2a Av NO, Parque Rubén Darío, 2½c N; dishes US$6-13; 6pm-late) Date night? Check out one of the longer-running dining institutions in town. The decor is gorgeous, and carefully prepared seafood, pasta, meats and pizza are generally reliable, but when the place is busy, the serving staff tend to get overwhelmed. The wine list is heavy on Argentinean and Chilean wines.

Information

MEDICAL SERVICES

Hospital San Vicente (☎2311-6990; Av Pedro Aráuz) Out past the main bus terminal, the region's largest hospital is a 1918 neoclassical beauty that attracts architecture buffs as well as sick tourists.

MONEY

Several banks have ATMs that accept Visa/Plus debit cards.

BAC (Map p468; 1a Calle NE, La Unión, 10m O)

BanPro (Map p468; 2a Calle NE, Bigfoot Hostel, 20m N) ATM is open 24 hours and accepts Visa and MasterCard.

Western Union (Map p468; 1 Calle NE; 8am-6pm Mon-Sat) International cash transfers.

Getting There & Away

BUS

National Buses

Most buses leave from León's chaotic **main bus terminal** (☎2311-3909; 6a Calle NE, Palí, 1.5km E), which has a fun market area nearby (watch your wallet). If you're heading south, you'll invariably pass through Managua.

International Buses

While international bus routes heading north start in Managua, many tend to include a stop in León. Buy your bus tickets at **Tica Bus** (Map p468; ☎2311-6153; www.ticabus.com; 6a Calle NE, Palí, 1c O; ⏲8am-6pm). Buses headed south stop first in Managua, with an often lengthy wait between connections – it's better to make your own way there and take the bus from Managua.

Shuttle Buses

The quickest and most comfortable way to get between popular destinations in Nicaragua and elsewhere in Central America is by shuttle. Several operators run daily shuttles (book ahead), with private shuttles also an option. If you're headed to less popular destinations, be aware that most shuttles require a minimum of four passengers. Shuttles to San Juan del Sur that stop in Managua and Granada can take longer than direct buses. Popular operators include the following:

Bigfoot Hostel Shuttles (p441) Daily shuttles at 9:30am to San Juan del Sur (US$20) via Managua Airport, Granada (US$12) and Rivas. Daily international shuttles to Antigua, Guatemala (US$37, 2am) via El Tunco, El Salvador (US$25), and to La Ceiba, Honduras (US$65, 1am) via Tegucigalpa (US$45).

Gekko Explorer (Map p468; ☎2389-6199; www.gekkotrailsexplorer.com; BanPro, 25m S) Shuttles to Granada (US$12), San Juan del Sur (US$20) and Rivas/San Jorge (US$18). International services to Antigua, Guatemala (US$50), Copán, Honduras (US$70) and El Tunco, El Salvador (US$30).

Tierra Tour (Map p468; ☎2315-4278; www.tierratour.com; 1a Av NO, Iglesia de la Merced, 1½c N) Daily shuttles to Granada via Managua Airport (US$15) at 9:30am, and onward from Granada to San Juan del Sur (US$15) at 12:30pm.

Buses to Beaches

Buses to Poneloya and Las Peñitas (US$0.50, 40 minutes) depart hourly, 6am to 6pm, from El Mercadito in Subtiaba. Day-trippers take note: the last bus returns around 6pm too.

Another option: Bigfoot Hostel (p471) runs a daily shuttle to Las Peñitas.

Getting Around

The city is strollable, but big enough that you may want to take taxis, particularly at night. Cycling around León is not particularly pleasant, given the heat, the narrow streets and the traffic, but you can rent bikes for around US$5 to US$7 per day from hostels. **Ruedas León** (Map p468; ☎2311-6727; www.ruedasleon.com; BanPro, 80m S; ⏲8am-6pm Mon-Sat) rents out scooters, motorbikes and mountain bikes.

Pacific Beaches near León

The most accessible beaches from León are Poneloya and Las Peñitas, both an easy 20-minute bus ride from Mercadito Subtiaba in León. Las Peñitas is a popular backpacker haunt, while Poneloya is much more of a local scene.

NATIONAL BUSES FROM LEÓN

DESTINATION	COST (US$)	DURATION (HR)	FREQUENCY
Chinandega (bus)	0.80-1	1½	every 20min, 4:30am-8pm
Chinandega (microbus)	1.20	50min	4:30am-8pm, departs when full
Estelí	2.70	2½-3	6:20am & 3pm
Granada (microbus)	3	2-3	hourly
La Paz Centro	0.75	40min	every 45min
Managua (microbus)	2.75	1¼	4:30am-7pm, departs when full
Managua (Carr Nueva, via La Paz Centro) *expreso*	1.80	1¼	hourly, 5am-4pm
Managua (Carr Vieja, via Puerto Sandino) *ordinario*	1.50	1¾	every 30min, 5am-6:30pm
Masaya	2.90	2½	hourly
Matagalpa	3	2½	4:20am, 7:30am, 2:45pm
Nagarote	1	1	hourly
Rota (Cerro Negro)	0.75	2¼	5:50am, 11am, 3:30pm
Salinas Grandes	0.80	2	5:15am, 8:30am, 11:40am, 1:40pm

Next to Las Peñitas, **Reserva Natural Isla Juan Venado** (US$4.50) beckons nature lovers with its vast wetlands. This 20km-long, sandy barrier island (in some places only 300m wide) has swimming holes and lots of wildlife, including hundreds of migrating bird species, crocodiles, nesting turtles and mosquitoes galore. On one side of the uninhabited island you'll find long, wild, sandy beaches facing the Pacific; on the other, red and black mangroves reflected in emerald lagoons. Las Peñitas ranger station and various accommodations offer guided boat tours (US$55 for up to four people) and kayaking excursions (US$12 per person).

Some 32km south of León, partially paved NIC-52 branches off toward a trio of beaches: Miramar, **Playa Hermosa** and El Tránsito, 'discovered' by surfers but off the beaten track for most other travelers.

Poneloya

POP UNDER 1000

This beach has the famous name – it's highly praised in the *Viva León, Jodido* theme song – and this is where affluent Leonese come for the weekend, unlike its sister beach, Las Peñitas, which is popular with foreign surfers and sun seekers. For many travelers, Poneloya is simply the point of departure to the beautiful island of **Isla Los Brasiles**, the location of a popular surfing lodge.

★ Surfing Turtle Lodge LODGE **$$**
(☎8640-0644; www.surfingturtlelodge.com; Isla Los Brasiles, Poneloya; dm US$10, r US$35-40, cabin US$60; 📶) 🍃 The breezy 2nd-story dorm is one of the coolest spots in all of Central America, with a giant view to the ocean. Camping in pre-set-up tents or staying in a bamboo hut will save money, or you can upgrade to a cabin. From El Chepe bar in Poneloya, catch a boat (US$1) to Isla Los Brasiles, then walk 15 minutes.

Bar Margarita SEAFOOD **$$**
(☎7508-5573; www.facebook.com/bocana505; La Bocanita; mains US$7-10; ⏲10am-9pm) At the very end of the street leading to the estuary, this thatched-roof restaurant and bar serves large platters of grilled catch of the day with rice, beans and plantains, with a side helping of estuary views.

ℹ Getting There & Away

Buses (US$0.50) run between Poneloya, Las Peñitas and León (not to the center, but to El Mercadito, a small market on the western edge of town in the neighborhood called Sutiaba) roughly every 45 minutes between 4:30am and 6pm. Coming from León, the bus stops in Poneloya first, then goes up the coast to Las Peñitas.

If you're headed to Surfing Turtle Lodge, check the website for information about catching the daily shuttle (US$3 one way) from León.

Las Peñitas

POP UNDER 2000

A wide, sandy stretch of beachfront paradise fronted by a cluster of surfer hostels and boutique hotels, Las Peñitas offers the easiest access to the turtles and mangroves of Reserva Natural Isla Juan Venado. There's also good, if not spectacular, surfing here, with smallish regular waves that are perfect for beginners. Several hotels and hostels offer tours into the reserve, plus surf lessons and board rentals.

★ Mano a Mano Ecohostel HOSTEL **$**
(☎7527-5505; https://somosmanoamano.wixsite.com/hostalmanoamano; La curvita, 50m N; dm/ste US$12/60; ❄📶) 🍃 Everything a stellar hostel should be, Mano a Mano is all breezy bamboo dorms and mezzanine loft suites inside a beautiful, sustainably built structure, with seafront chill-out areas and a bar that overlooks the waves. The multi-ethnic, multi-lingual staff make everyone feel at home, point surfers toward the best waves and organize trips. You'll never want to leave.

Nayal Lodge BOUTIQUE HOTEL **$$**
(☎5715-0076; www.nayallodge.com; de la Policía, 300m E; ste US$49; P❄📶🏊) Consisting of two thatched-roofed adobe towers, this four-room hotel is run by Spanish owner Catalina and her husband, who are happy to share their extensive local knowledge. Each suite is circular, spacious and with a hammock-strung terrace; a pool and massage room are in the works, and breakfast is an excellent nica spread.

Aáki Hotel BOUTIQUE HOTEL **$$$**
(☎8988-1867; www.facebook.com/aakihotel; Entrada a las Penitas, 600m SE; d/q US$90/120; P❄📶🏊) Las Peñitas' most stylish little hotel overlooks a kidney-shaped pool and its own stretch of beach. There are only nine rooms here – spacious, bright, with bamboo accents, and with either terraces or balconies. Excellent breakfast and imaginative,

beautifully presented dishes, and a cool, minimalist interior are part of the draw.

Dulce Mareas PIZZA $$
(☎8827-1161; www.facebook.com/dulcemareas; Barca de Oro, 50m S; mains US$4.50-9; ⏰8am-9pm Wed-Sun; ✎) It's known for pizzas baked in a clay-brick oven, but this Italian-owned beachfront eatery also does breakfast and lunch – plus coffee, desserts and cold cocktails, all with a view of the water. You can also rent out rooms (double US$45).

★**La Bombora** FUSION $$$
(☎8662-9554; www.thebomboragroup.com/relax; Frente Cocteles Las Peñitas; mains US$10-17; ⏰12:30-8pm; ❄📶) Chef Marc has earned La Bombora its share of local followers with his culinary masterpieces, from slow-cooked ribs and brisket to pulled pork sliders and grilled seafood. Don't leave without trying his jalapeño margarita! There are also four snug rooms (US$60) here, brightened up with splashes of tropical art, just steps from the sea.

Getting There & Away

Buses (US$0.50) run between Poneloya, Las Peñitas and León (El Mercadito de Subtiaba) roughly every 40 minutes between 5:20am and 6.40pm. Coming from León, the bus swings through Poneloya first, then heads north to Las Peñitas. The last stop is at the parking lot outside **Barca de Oro** (☎2317-0275; www.barcadeoro.com; bayfront, frente parada de buses; ⏰7am-10pm), but you can also pick it up at a bus stop outside the hotel Playa Roca.

Another option is the daily shuttle that runs from Bigfoot Hostel (p471) in León to Las Peñitas.

In a pinch, you can also hire a taxi from León for about US$15 one way.

El Tránsito

POP UNDER 2000

This little fishing village on the coast between León and Managua sits on a hill slope around a near-perfect crescent bay. There's a strong undertow, but to the south, near the lava flows, there are protected swimming holes. El Tránsito has gained popularity with surfers, since there's something for all abilities here: four consistent year-round beach breaks. Pistols, Pangas and Main are rights and lefts, while the Corner is a left; there's also a hollow left for advanced surfers 40 minutes up the coast, and the swells are particularly powerful April to June.

Sleeping & Eating

There are several basic beachfront eateries in the village, and surf camp restaurants welcome nonguests.

There are several surfer-oriented digs here, from an all-inclusive surf camp to a basic **hostel** (☎5817-8425; http://thefreespirithostel.com; Escuela, 2c N, 1c O, ½c N; dm/d US$25/70, hippie van US$60; ❄).

Getting There & Away

Buses from Managua's Mercado Israel Lewites (p441) leave for El Tránsito at 11:15am, 12:40pm and 2pm daily (US$1.20, 1½ hours), returning at 5am, 6am and 7am. Many travelers drive themselves here. If driving, the partially paved NIC-40 to El Tránsito is bumpy but passable by regular car in dry season.

Miramar

POP UNDER 5000

Along the coast from this hard-working port town there are some 'Hawaii-sized waves,' the biggest being Puerto Sandino at the river mouth – a world-class monster! About 5km south of Puerto Sandino, at the fishing village of Miramar, there's a left point break called Punta Miramar, a beach break called Pipes, left and right barrels at Shacks (when conditions are right) and La Derechita, a right-hander. These are some of the most uncrowded waves on the Pacific Coast, frequented by serious surfers.

All surf camps have their own restaurants and there are several low-key local joints along the Miramar beach that serve seafood.

★**Vivir Surf & Fish** LODGE $$$
(☎7648-0354; http://vivirsurf.com; Miramar; s/d/tr US$101/148/195, 3-night package US$495; 📶) This Aussie-run surf camp gets rave reviews from surfers for owner Lewis' hospitality, the perfect location for hitting the waves (there are five breaks within a few minutes' walk of the camp, plus three advanced breaks accessible by boat), first-rate accommodations and plenty of camaraderie out of the water, fueled by soccer, baseball and cricket games.

Miramar Surfcamp LODGE $$$
(☎8945-1785; www.miramarsurfcamp.com; Miramar; s/d US$58/81, surfer package s/d incl meals from US$138/184; 📶🏊) For surfers of all abilities (including beginners), the location of this surf camp – and the friendly staff – are huge draws. Choose between basic air-con rooms or splurge on the digs in the Ocean

View Tower. If you're not playing volleyball on the beach in between catching breaks, you can try your hand at skateboarding the half-pipe next to the surf camp.

Getting There & Away

Surf camps offer pick-up and drop-off at Managua Airport. There are several buses daily between Puerto Sandino and León (US$0.85, 30 to 40 minutes), but Miramar is 5km south of the Puerto Sandino turnoff along a partially paved, bumpy road. Commandeer a tuk-tuk or drive yourself.

Cosigüina Peninsula Beaches

The Cosigüina peninsula is well on its way to becoming an island, worn away on two sides by brilliant estuaries and fringed with sandy beaches, ranging from the pearl-grays of Jiquilillo to coal-black at Playa Carbón.

Playa Aserradores and Playa Jiquilillo are both quiet fishing villages that are firmly on the surfing circuit, while the Reserva Natural Estero Padre Ramos is a vast mangrove wetland, ideal for kayaking and birdwatching, that's also an important breeding ground for sea turtles.

Playa Aserradores

This long, smooth stretch of sand has excellent surfing: the main attraction here is a world-class wave, El Boom – a fast, hollow beach break for experienced wave shredders only. At nearby Aposentillo there are some nice longboard swells, and waves suitable for beginners as well. Aposentillo is a quiet, spread-out village with killer sunsets and a laid-back vibe that's now missing from surfing destinations further south. Surf is best from March to October.

Las Dunas Surf Resort GUESTHOUSE **$$**
(☎8476-5211; www.lasdunassurfresort.com; Santa Maria del Mar 11; dm/casita US$15/60; ❄📶) With a clutch of pastel-colored, thatched-roofed *casitas* clustered around the pool, plus a breezy restaurant with attendant playful felines, this is one of the better budget options in Aserradores. You're a 10-minute walk from the waves too.

★ThunderBomb Surf Camp LODGE **$$$**
(☎8478-0070; https://thunderbombsurf.com; Santa María del Mar; 7-day surf package from US$1099; ❄📶) Run by Bostonian Jonathan, this excellent surf camp is all about hitting the A-frames, pipes and barrels up and down the coast. There are several excellent waves right on your doorstep, and the surf guides whisk guests off in 4WDs and boats in pursuit of the best breaks. Spacious tiled rooms, international food, yoga classes and massages seal the deal.

★Coco Loco Eco Resort RESORT **$$$**
(☎5797-4244; www.cocolocoecoresort.com; El Manzano 1, Aposentillo; 7-day surf packages from US$1245; ⊙Mar-Oct; ❄📶) 🍃 There are only two things to do in this wonderfully tranquil spot: hit the waves and do yoga. Guests are lodged in airy cabins made from sustainable local materials; delicious and nutritious meals are served communal-style to encourage mingling; and surfers are taken daily to the best spots, with post-surfing massages to relax those tired muscles.

★Al Cielo Hotel & Restaurante FUSION **$$$**
(☎8993-4840; http://alcielonicaragua.com; El Manzano 2; mains US$8-17; ⊙7am-10pm; 📶) It's well worth making the trek to this excellent French-Italian fusion restaurant on top of a hill, with fantastic sea views to complement your rum-infusion aperitif. There are *cabañas* too, in case you decide to linger (singles/doubles from US$15/25) and the French owners arrange all manner of excursions.

Getting There & Away

During dry season, the NIC-264 access road is passable in a regular car, but otherwise you'll want a 4WD vehicle for the bumpy ride from the well-signed exit off the Chinandega–Potosí Hwy.

There is only one daily bus from Chinandega to Aserradores, departing from Chinandega's Mercadito (p477) at 12:30pm (US$1, 1½ hours) and returning at 5am. Hotels and surf camps offer private transport for around US$90 for one or two people.

Playa Jiquilillo

POP UNDER 500

This endless pale-gray beach frames what you thought existed only in tales that begin: 'You should have seen it back when I was first here...' The spread-out fishing village fronts a dramatic rocky point, where tide pools reflect the reds and golds of a huge setting sun, with Cosigüina's ragged bulk rising hazy and post-apocalyptic to the north.

The region remains largely undeveloped, despite its beauty and accessibility, and it's a place to surf, enjoy the tranquility and hang out with locals, to whom non-locals are still a relative novelty.

The guesthouses here all have restaurants, and there are several village eateries both in Jiquilillo and nearby Padre Ramos.

Rancho Tranquilo HOSTEL $

(☎8968-2290; www.ranchotranquilo.wordpress.com; Los Zorros, Playa Jiquilillo; dm/s/d US$7/20/22; 📶) Run by a friendly family, this collection of bungalows and a small dorm on its private stretch of beach is a great budget choice. There's a cool bar and common area, and vegetarian dinners (US$2 to US$4.50) are served family-style. Kayaking in the mangroves and surfing lessons can be arranged. Check online for information on the area's turtle rescue program.

Rancho Esperanza GUESTHOUSE $$

(☎8680-0270; www.rancho-esperanza.com; Playa Jiquilillo; dm US$8, 2-person cabañas with/without bathroom US$35/25) 🍃 This quiet and ecofriendly collection of simple, breezy bamboo huts – which are scattered across a grassy field just slightly removed from the beach – offers volunteer opportunities in community projects related to education and environmental issues. There's also a small library of English-language books and a good breakfast (served all day).

Monty's Surf Camp LODGE $$$

(☎8473-3255; www.montysbeachlodge.com; Playa Jiquilillo; dm/d US$35/66; 📶🏊) This midrange surf camp is set right on the waterfront. Rooms are fan-cooled and the beds draped with mosquito nets. Most travelers come here on weeklong packages (singles/doubles/triples per person US$700/600/500) that include all meals, but it's entirely possible to just come for a few days, hang by the pool and watch the sunset from a hammock.

ℹ Getting There & Away

Buses to Chinandega (US$1, 1½ hours, five daily) come and go roughly between 7am and 4:30pm. Some lodgings can arrange transport if contacted in advance. NIC-58 that runs to Jiquilillo from the main NIC-12 highway is unpaved but in good condition.

Reserva Natural Estero Padre Ramos

POP UNDER 500

Less than 2km north of Playa Jiquilillo is the community of Padre Ramos, a tiny, sleepy fishing village inside the federally protected wetlands of Reserva Natural Estero Padre Ramos. The river delta is part of the largest remaining mangrove forests in Central America, and is key in the proposed **Reserva Biologica Golfo de Fonseca** (Gulf of Fonseca Biological Corridor), a wetlands conservation agreement between Nicaragua, Honduras and El Salvador.

Locals can arrange boat, kayak and birding tours of the mangroves for around US$10 to US$40 per person. Sea turtles lay their eggs here between July and December, peaking in October and November; contact Rancho Tranquilo about the turtle protection program.

Based in Padre Ramos, **Ibis Exchange** (☎8961-8548; http://ibiskayaking.com; Padre Ramos; day tours per person US$40) 🍃 offers day tours and multi-day camping and kayaking tours (two days, one night US$150 per person) of the wetland reserve, as well as multiday tours of the Pacific Coast and Volcán Consigüina climbs. These guys have an organic orchard, composting toilets and solar panels. Contact them in advance.

It's entirely possible to stay in Playa Jiquilillo, 2km away, where there are more sleeping options.

ℹ Getting There & Away

Buses from Chinandega's Mercadito run to Padre Ramos via Playa Jiquilillo (US$1, 1½ to two hours, 6:45am, 9:45am, 11:15am, 2:45pm and 4:15pm). Some lodgings in nearby Playa Jiquilillo can arrange transport if contacted in advance. NIC-58 to Jiquilillo from the main NIC-12 highway is unpaved; the last 2km to Padre Ramos is sandy. In Padre Ramos, take the estuary road rather than the beach road, or risk getting stuck in sand.

Chinandega

POP 111,300

Sultry Chinandega is the regional transport hub with a few decent hotels, a clutch of good restaurants, an excellent archaeological museum and several appealing churches. It's not a bad place to bed down for a night or two (splurge on the air-con, since it's hot as the Sahara); you're likely to acquaint yourself with this busy agricultural town if you happen to be heading toward Nicaragua's northwestern beaches or looking to explore the little-visited Volcán Cosigüina.

Sights

★Museo Enrique B Mántica MUSEUM

(☎2341-4291; Farallones Hotel, 2c E, Reparto los Angeles; US$5; ⏰8am-5pm Mon-Fri) Anyone with even a passing interest in archaeology should stop in here, one of the finest museums in the country. The beautifully displayed collection focuses on pre-Columbian ceramics and is presented in a logical timeline, from the early inhabitants up until the arrival of the Spanish. It's a little tricky to find, signposted off the NIC-24, near Farallones Hotel, amid workshops where local youth study various trades.

Iglesia Guadalupe CHURCH

(Santuario de Nuestra Señora de Guadalupe; correo, 3½c S; ⏰hours vary) Chinandega has some seriously striking churches, including the 1878 Iglesia Guadalupe, which despite the radiant – and rather grandiose – colonial-style facade has a simple, precious wood interior with an exceptionally lovely Virgin.

Sleeping & Eating

Hotel Casa Real HOTEL $$

(☎2341-7047; http://hotelcasareal.net; Parque Central, 2c S, ½c E; s/d US$30/40; ❄📶) A couple of blocks south of Parque Central, this is the nicest hotel in this part of town. Think spotless rooms, friendly management, and a belly-filling nica breakfast thrown in to boot.

Hotel Los Balcones de Chinandega HOTEL $$$

(☎2341-8994; www.hotelbalconeschinandega.com; esquina de los bancos, 1c N; s/d US$41/53; P❄📶) This colonial-style hotel is one of the nicer places to stay in Chinandega, with colorful splashes of tropical art in the simple, tiled rooms. There are, in fact, balconies, but you may choose to spend your time on the tiny roof terrace instead.

★Fritanga Las Tejitas NICARAGUAN $

(Mercado, 2c E; mains US$2-5; ⏰8am-9pm) A local institution, this *fritanga* gets packed breakfast, lunch and dinner – and mariachis could show up at any time to play some music. It's a solid buffet with a nationwide reputation and an excellent place to try traditional nica food.

La Parrillada NICARAGUAN $$

(Palí, 1c S; set lunch US$3, mains US$4-8; ⏰noon-9pm) This locals' favorite is part steakhouse, part pizzeria, part *fritanga*. Order a slab of meat or help yourself to inexpensive buffet offerings; if you can't find something you want to eat here, the chances are you're not hungry.

Getting There & Away

Most travelers make their connections through **Mercado Bisne** (Calle Central), on the south side of the city (it's best to take a cab to and from here, as it's not within easy walking distance of downtown), though some buses leave from the smaller station known as **Mercadito** (Parque Central, 1½c N).

Taxis also make the runs to El Viejo (US$3 to US$5) and Corinto (US$6 to US$8).

Bus Services from Mercadito

El Viejo (bus US$0.80, 20 minutes, every 15 minutes, 5am to 6pm; microbus US$0.60, 10 minutes, departs when full, 5am to 6pm)

Playa Aserradores (US$1, 1½ hours, daily at 12:30pm)

BUS SERVICES FROM CHINANDEGA'S MERCADO BISNE

DESTINATION	COST (US$)	DURATION (HR)	FREQUENCY
Chichigalpa (microbus)	0.30	15min	departs when full, 5am-6pm
Corinto (bus)	0.50-0.60	40min	every 15min, 4:30am-6pm
Corinto (microbus)	0.75	25min	4:30am-7pm, departs when full
El Guasaule (Honduran border; bus)	1.70	1¾	every 25min, 4am-5pm
El Guasaule (Honduran border; microbus)	2	1	departs when full, 4:30am-7pm
León (bus)	0.80	1½	every 15 min, 4am-7pm
León (microbus)	1.20	1	departs when full, 4:30am-7pm
Managua (bus)	2.70	3	hourly, 4am-5:20pm
Managua (microbus)	3	2	departs when full, 4:30am-7pm

Playa Jiquilillo and Reserva Natural Estero Padre Ramos (US$1 to $1.20, 1½ to two hours, at 6:45am, 9:45am, 11:15am, 2:45pm and 4:15pm)

Potosí (Reserva Natural Volcán Cosigüina) (US$1.50 to $1.75, 3½ hours, three daily)

Around Chinandega

We'll be frank with you: there are only two things in Chinandega's immediate environs that warrant attention from travelers. There's a beautiful colonial church in the ancient indigenous capital of El Viejo (which is of particular interest to pilgrims). Chichigalpa attracts pilgrimages of a different kind: dedicated imbibers of rum come to the famous Flor de Caña rum factory to learn the tipple's secrets.

North of El Viejo, and totally off the beaten track, you'll find the **Reserva Natural Delta del Estero Real** (Asociación Selva 8884-9156), a remote birdwatcher's paradise, while the main highway, NIC-24, snakes northeast from Chinandega, traversing wide open spaces en route to Somotillo, the last town before the border between Nicaragua and Honduras.

Chichigalpa

POP 42,000

Chichigalpa, Nicaragua cutest-named town, is best known as the source of **Flor de Caña rum**, made in seven beloved shades from crystal clear to deepest amber. The rum has been produced in the **distillery tours** (8966-8200; www.tourflordecana.com; Carretera a Chinadenga Km 120; US$10; 9am, 11am & 3pm Tue-Sun) since 1890. It's also home to **Ingenio San Antonio**, the country's largest sugar refinery, fed by the cane fields that carpet the skirts of **Volcán San Cristóbal**, which rises from the lowlands just 15km from the city center. Both the sugar refinery and the Flor de Caña distillery belong to the affluent Pellas family that has been producing rum since 1890, with a short break during the revolution. The rum factory, hosting several popular tours daily, is Chichigalpa's sole attraction.

There are no recommendable lodgings in town; most visitors come here on a day tour. Chinandega or León have numerous lodgings.

Look for street food around the Parque Central.

Getting There & Away

Microbuses to Chinandega (US$0.30, 15 minutes) depart from the market when full, from 5am to 6pm.

El Viejo

POP 49,452

Just 5km from Chinandega is the ancient indigenous capital of Tezoatega, today called El Viejo. Its **church** (costado este del Parque Central; hours vary) is the home of Nicaragua's patron saint and the venue for the country's biggest national religious event, **La Gritería**, attended by thousands of pilgrims. If you're not a pilgrim, the church is worth a quick peek if you happen to be passing through (most travelers stop by on day trips from larger towns or cities such as León and Chinandega).

In terms of food, as with most of small-town Nicaragua, the best, most fun eating to be had is at the *fritanga* (grill) stands in the Parque Central.

Getting There & Away

All buses headed north from Chinandega to Potosí or the Cosigüina beaches stop at the El Viejo *empalme* (junction) about 20 minutes after leaving Chinandega.

To Chinandega, you can get buses and minivans (US$0.60 to US$0.80, 10 to 20 minutes, every 15 minutes) from in front of the basilica. A taxi to Chinandega costs US$3 to US$5.

Drivers: note that this is the last chance for gas on the peninsula if you're heading north.

Potosí

POP UNDER 1000

This small fishing village is the main base for hiking up Volcán Consigüina and a gateway to El Salvador; regular boat services mean that you can hit El Salvador's beaches while avoiding the lengthy detour overland.

It's only worth overnighting here if you're catching the morning boat to El Salvador.

Getting There & Away

Potosí is 74km northwest of Chinandega. There are up to six buses daily between Chinandega and Potosí (US$1.50 to US$1.75, three hours). If you're driving, it's 59km along the beautifully paved Ruta 12, then 15km from the turnoff to the village, the first 12km unpaved and seriously bumpy, though passable by regular car outside wet season.

From Potosí, **Ruta del Golfo** (☎El Salvador 503-2525-6464, Nicaragua 2315-4099; www.rutadelgolfo.com) runs at least one boat per week to La Union, El Salvador (US$65, 2½ hours) across the picturesque Golfo de Fonseca, typically departing at 12:30pm, with optional 4WD pickup from León at 8:30am (US$99 total). Call ahead about departures and tickets.

Reserva Natural Volcán Cosigüina

It was once the tallest volcano in Central America, perhaps more than 3000m high, but all that changed on January 20, 1835. In what's considered the Americas' most violent eruption since colonization, this hot-blooded peninsular volcano blew off half its height in a single blast that paved the oceans with pumice, left three countries in stifling darkness for days and scattered ash from Mexico to Colombia. What remains today of Volcán Cosigüina reclines, as if spent, on the broad and jagged 872m heart of the peninsula.

Beyond all that lies the **Golfo de Fonseca**, bordered by the largest mangrove stand left in the Americas. In the other direction, around the volcano's back, **Punta Ñata** overlooks cliffs that plunge 250m into the sea; beyond lie the **Farallones del Consigüina** (also known as the Islotes Consigüina), a series of volcanic islets. There are many black-sand beaches around here for DIY exploration.

Getting There & Away

There are up to six buses daily between Chinandega and Potosí via La Piscina (US$1.50 to US$1.75, 3½ hours) that pick up and drop off close to the reserve's entrance. If you're driving, it's 59km along the paved NIC-12 from Chinandega, then 15km from the turnoff to Potosí, the first 12km unpaved and seriously bumpy; a 4WD is necessary outside the dry season.

Volcanoes near León

The Maribios chain is the epicenter of one of the most active volcanic regions on earth. Trekking up these volatile giants rewards you with tremendous views from the top, whether you go up there for sunset or camp overnight to greet the dawn. The easiest and safest way to visit the volcanoes is on a guided hike or excursion, arranged by many outfitters in León and elsewhere.

If you do decide to go to the volcanoes alone, it's a good idea to consult park management first. Marena León manages Reserva Natural Volcán Momotombo, Reserva Natural Telica-Rota and Reserva Natural Pilas-El Hoyo, which includes Cerro Negro; **Marena Chinandega** (Ministry of the Environment & Natural Resources; ☎2344-2443; www.marena.gob.ni; Iglesia Guadalupe, 1½c O; ⏲9am-4:30pm Mon-Fri) keeps tabs on Reserva Natural San Cristóbal-La Casita and Reserva Natural Volcán Cosigüina.

This area is ground zero for **volcano boarding** – also called volcano surfing. With professional outfitters and custom-made boards, you can hurtle downhill at exhilarating speeds. A half-day excursion generally includes transportation, equipment and instruction for around US$35 a person – try **Tierra Tour** (Map p468; ☎2315-4278; www.tierratour.com; Iglesia de la Merced, 1½c N; volcano boarding US$30) in León.

Reserva Natural Volcán Momotombo VOLCANO

(☎León 2311-3776) The perfect cone of **Volcán Momotombo**, destroyer of **León Viejo** (Puerto Momotombo; US$5; ⏲8am-5pm) and inspiration for its own Rubén Darío poem, rises red and black 1280m above Lago de Managua. It is a symbol of Nicaragua, the country's most beautiful threat, and has furnished at its base itself in miniature – the island of **Isla Momotombito** (389m), sometimes called 'The Child.' Most people come to climb Momotombo, a serious eight to 10-hour round-trip. Guided treks make access easier from the power plant at the trailhead.

Reserva Natural Pilas-El Hoyo VOLCANO

(☎León 2311-3776) Most people come to this reserve to see the volcano **Cerro Negro** (726m and growing), one of the youngest volcanoes in the world. Almost every guide in León offers a guided hike to the top of El Hoyo, a shadeless, two- to three-hour climb into the eye-watering fumes of the yellow-streaked crater, from where you'll shimmy downhill on a volcano board. Afterward, relax in the deliciously cool **Laguna de Asososca**, a jungle-wrapped crater lake (a popular add-on).

Reserva Natural San Cristóbal-La Casita VOLCANO

(☎Chinandega 2344-2443) Eye-catching **Volcán San Cristóbal** (1745m), the tallest volcano in Nicaragua, streams gray smoke from its smooth cone. Achieving the summit of this beauty is a serious hike: six to eight hours up, and three hours down. A guide is highly recommended, as access is difficult and dangerous and requires crossing private property. The volcano is very active, with two large eruptions at the end of 2012.

Getting There & Away

Drive yourself or arrange transportation with one of the many outfitters in León that offer organized excursions into the park.

NORTHERN HIGHLANDS

Nicaragua's Northern Highlands are off the typical backpacker route through the country, but nobody with an interest in coffee, cigars and wonderful scenery should miss them. Here colorful quetzals nest in misty cloud forests, and Nicaragua's best coffee and tobacco are cultivated with both capitalist zeal and collective spirit. With a little time and commitment you'll get pounded by waterfalls; explore Somoto's canyon; and pay tribute to the pirates, colonists, revolutionaries, artists and poets who were inspired by these fertile mountains and mingled with the open-hearted people who've lived here for generations.

On either end of the region are its two largest cities: hardworking Estelí buzzes with students, farmers and cigar moguls, while Matagalpa is slightly hipper – and better funded, thanks to nearly a century of successful coffee cultivation. All around and in between are granite peaks and lush valleys dotted with dozens of small towns and their friendly inhabitants.

Estelí

POP 125,000 / ELEV 844M

Estelí has a multifaceted soul: it's both a university town with a large number of progressive students and the main center of commerce for the rural farming communities that surround it. On weekdays you can wake up with sunrise yoga before Spanish class; on Saturday you can mingle with farmers at the massive produce market, then see them again at midnight, dancing like mad in a *ranchero* bar.

Set on the Panamericana close to the Honduran border, Estelí was a strategic gateway that saw heavy fighting and helped turn the revolution and, later, the Contra War. It's no surprise, then, that Estelí has remained one of the Sandinistas' strongest support bases. While it's not a particularly attractive place, its character and easy access to the surrounding mountains make it a popular place for backpackers to base themselves.

Sights & Tours

★Galería de Héroes y Mártires MUSEUM
(Map p481; ☎8419-3519, 2714-0942; http://galleryofheroesandmartyrs.blogspot.com; Av 1a NE & Calle Transversal; by donation; ⏲9:30am-4pm Tue-Fri) Be sure to stop by this moving gallery devoted to fallen revolutionaries, with displays of faded photos, clothes and weaponry. Check out the exhibit (with English signage) on Leonel Rugama, the warrior-poet whose last line was his best. When he and Carlos Fonseca were surrounded by 300 Guardia Nacional troops supported by tanks and planes, they were told to surrender. 'Surrender, your mother!' he famously replied, proving that a 'your mother' retort is always solid. Opening hours are irregular.

Catedral CHURCH
(Map p481; Parque Central) The 1823 cathedral has a wonderful facade and is worth a wander. A number of interesting **murals** can be seen in the surrounding blocks, although most of the original revolutionary works have long disappeared.

★Tree Huggers CULTURAL
(Map p481; ☎8405-8919, 8496-7449; www.treehuggers.cafeluzyluna.org; cnr Av 2a NE & Calle 3a NE; ⏲8am-9pm) This friendly and vibrant tour office is the local specialist for trips to Miraflor and Tisey, but also offers other interesting community tourism trips throughout the region, including Cañon de Somoto and a great-value cigar tour (US$10, including a US$2 donation per person). Friendly staff dispense a wealth of impartial information for independent travelers, and profits support excellent local social projects.

★La Gran Fabrica Drew Estate TOURS
(www.cigarsafari.com; Barrio Oscar Gamez 2) Estelí's most innovative cigar company offers all-inclusive, multiday 'Cigar Safari' tours aimed at serious cigar enthusiasts. These are upscale tours that include superb dining options and a totally immersive cultural experience aimed at the North American cigar aficionado market.

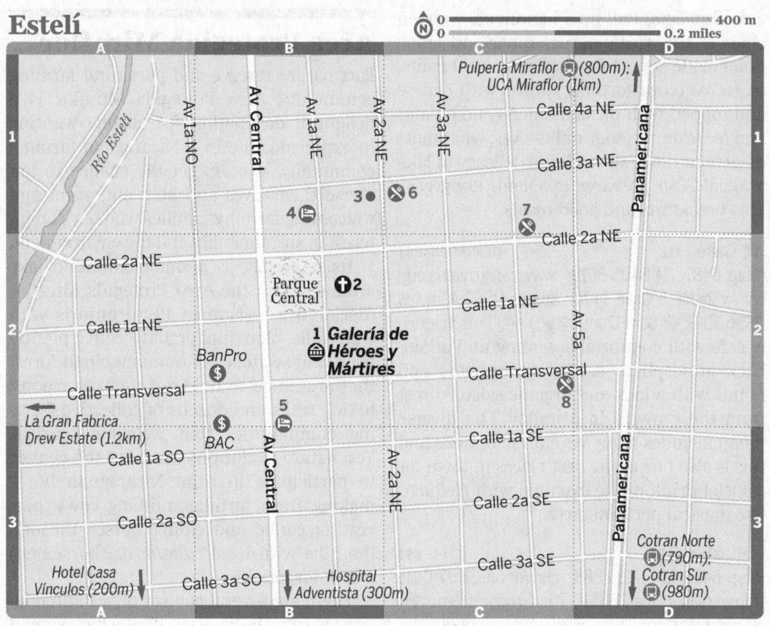

Estelí

Top Sights
1 Galería de Héroes y Mártires B2

Sights
2 Catedral B2

Activities, Courses & Tours
3 Tree Huggers B1

Sleeping
4 Hotel Los Arcos B1
5 Iguana Hostel B2

Eating
6 Café Luz C1
7 El Quesito C1
8 Pullaso's Ole C2

Sleeping & Eating

Iguana Hostel HOSTEL $

(Map p481; ☎5704-5748; www.facebook.com/jairoaiguanas; Av Central, Calle Transversal, 75m S; s/d US$10/11;) Cheap and cheerful, the Iguana has a central location and everything budget travelers need: spacious rooms, a guest kitchen and hammocks in the courtyard, though sadly there are no dorms. The whole place is charmingly painted and staff are super-friendly.

★**Hotel Casa Vínculos** HOTEL $$

(☎2713-2044; www.casavinculos.com; Almacén Sony, 1c 1/2 al Oeste; s/d incl breakfast US$31/50;) This excellent hotel is a real find. It offers eight rooms over two floors surrounding a small tree-filled courtyard, including two rooms for mobility-impaired travelers. The fan-cooled rooms positively gleam, and have comfortable mattresses and good bathrooms. Best of all, the profits from your stay go toward supporting educational programs for local children.

Hotel Los Arcos HOTEL $$$

(Map p481; ☎2713-3830; www.hotelosarcosesteli.com; cnr Av 1a NE & Calle 3a NE; s/d/tw incl breakfast with fan US$47/49/53, with air-con US$58/61/65;) Run by a nonprofit organization, Los Arcos remains the best value hotel in town, with a dream location, a roof deck with kick-ass mountain and city views, and spotless rooms with soft sheets, Spanish tiles and high ceilings. The colorfully painted rooms make up for a general lack of light – rooms at the back get the most.

El Quesito NICARAGUAN $

(Map p481; cnr Calle 2a NE & Av 4a NE, Del Asoganor, 1c N; breakfast US$1-2.50, mains US$4.50;

⏲6:30am-8pm) Pull up a handmade wooden chair at this rustic corner diner and enjoy homemade yogurt flavored with local fruits, *quesillos* (corn tortillas stuffed with cheese and topped with pickled onions and cream) and *leche agria* (sour milk) – yes, what most of us pour down the sink is a delicacy in Nicaragua! Also prepares excellent, nongreasy nica breakfasts and good meals.

★**Café Luz** INTERNATIONAL **$$**
(Map p481; ☎8405-8919; www.cafeluzyluna.org; cnr Av 2a NE & Calle 3a NE; snacks US$2-4, mains US$6.50-9; ⏲8am-11pm; 📶🌿) 🌱 This friendly cafe with comfortable seating and a laid-back atmosphere serves up burritos and fajitas with a kick and organic salads direct from the growers in Miraflor. The diverse menu includes many vegetarian options and this is also one of the best places in town for a social drink in the evening, with frequent live musical performances.

Pullaso's Ole STEAK **$$$**
(Map p481; ☎2713-4583; cnr Av 5a SE & Calle Transversal; dishes US$10-25; ⏲noon-11pm; 📶) Named for an Argentine cut of beef (the *pullaso*), this sweet, family-owned grill is the best place in town for a good steak. It serves up certified Angus beef as well as pork, chicken and chorizo dishes on its front porch and in a quaint dining room crowded with racks of South American red.

ℹ Information

MEDICAL SERVICES

Hospital Adventista (☎2713-3827, 8851-5298; Av Central, Calle 6a SO, ½c S; ⏲24hr) Private clinic with a variety of specialists.

MONEY

BAC (Map p481; Av 1a NO, Calle Transversal, 50m S) MasterCard/Cirrus/Visa/Plus ATM.

BanPro (Map p481; cnr Calle Transversal & Av 1a NO) Reliable ATM. Also changes euros and dollars.

ℹ Getting There & Away

Estelí has two bus terminals a short distance from one another: the blue-collar **Cotran Norte** (☎2713-2529; Panamericana, Calle 11a SE) is a bit of a bun fight where you'll have to cram onto provincial buses, while **Cotran Sur** (☎2713-6162; Panamericana, Calle 14a SO) is more refined, with a ticket counter and timetables. Both are located at the southern end of the city.

Área Protegida Miraflor

Part nature reserve and part rural farming community, Área Protegida Miraflor is a delightful destination for anyone wanting to experience life in a Nicaraguan farming community. Visitors get the chance to immerse themselves and help out warm and welcoming farming families who have an interest in sustainability and the environment.

Its namesake is a small mountain lake around which the Área Protegida Miraflor (declared a reserve in 1999) unfurls with waterfalls, blooming orchids, coffee plantations and swatches of remnant cloud forest that are home to hold-out monkey troops, hiking trails and dozens of collective-farming communities that welcome tourists. Yes, nature is glorious here, but the chance to participate in rural Nicaraguan life – making fresh tortillas, milking cows, harvesting coffee and riding horses through the hills with local *caballeros* (horsemen) – is unforgettable.

There are several choices of accommodations within the reserve, all of which should be booked through **UCA Miraflor** (Unión de Cooperativas Agropecuarias de Miraflor; ☎2713-2971; www.ucamiraflor.org; Gasolinera Uno Norte, 2c E, ½c N; ⏲8am-noon & 1-5:30pm Mon-Fri, 8am-3pm Sat) 🌱 or Tree Huggers (p480) in Estelí. Farmhouse rooms allow the most interaction with local families; *cabañas* have more privacy. Both options are rustic and some accommodations have pit latrines. Expect to pay around US$28 per person, including three meals.

ℹ Getting There & Away

From Estelí there are a number of daily buses heading into Área Protegida Miraflor. For much greater comfort and ease, you can also arrange 4WD transfers and/or a driver for the day via either UCA Miraflor or Tree Huggers (p480).

For Coyolito (US$0.65, 45 minutes) and La Pita (US$0.70, one hour), buses leave Estelí from **Pulpería Miraflor** (Calle 14 NE) (near the Uno gas station on the Panamericana north of town) at 5:45am and 1pm daily, returning from La Pita at 8am and 3pm.

There are three daily direct buses (except Wednesday) from Estelí's Cotran Norte bus station to Cebollal (US$0.65, 45 minutes) departing at 6am, 11am and 3:45pm.

To La Perla or El Sontule (US$0.65, one hour), take the Camino Real bus signed Oro Verde/Sontule/Puertas Azules from Cotran Norte at

2pm Monday to Saturday. The bus returns at 7am Monday to Saturday from La Perla and El Sontule.

Área Protegida Cerro Tisey-Estanzuela

Smaller, drier and less populated but every bit as gorgeous as Área Protegida Miraflor, this *other* protected area, just 10km south of Estelí, has also jumped on the tourism bandwagon. You won't see the same species diversity in Tisey (which is what locals call the region), but those rugged, pine-draped mountains, red-clay bat caves, waterfalls and marvelous vistas that stretch to Lago de Managua – and even El Salvador on clear days – are worth the trip.

It's possible to visit Tisey on a day trip from Estelí; however, the reserve's attractions are spread out all over its 93 sq km and public transportation is limited so you'll see more (and contribute more) if you spend the night at one of the lodges or homestays.

Getting There & Away

Tisey is served by two buses a day (US$1, one hour), which are marked 'La Tejera' and leave from Estelí Cotran Sur at 6:30am and 1:30pm daily except Wednesday. The buses pass Salto Estanzuela and Eco-Posada Tisey before arriving at the La Garnacha turnoff, a 1.5km walk from the community. Buses return to Estelí from the La Garnacha turnoff at 8am and 3pm daily except Wednesday.

In general, taxis won't do the trip as the road is in fairly poor condition and drivers don't want to rough up their sedans. Tree Huggers (p480) in Estelí offers round-trip transportation in pickups for US$60, which is a good option for day-trippers.

Somoto

POP 35,000 / ELEV 705M

One of Nicaragua's most enjoyable natural sites, the magnificent Cañon de Somoto should not be missed by anyone in this part of the country. It makes for a super enjoyable and exciting day excursion that combines hiking, swimming, scrambling and boating through a narrow, towering canyon from where the Río Coco, Central America's longest river, begins its epic journey to the Caribbean.

Until 2003, the nearby town of Somoto was just another sleepy place in the Honduran shadow, known locally for its donkeys and *rosquillas* (crusty cornbread rings). This was when two Czech scientists 'discovered' what the locals had known about since time immemorial: the dramatic nearby canyon that could have been designed for tourism. Overnight Somoto became a popular backpacker stopover between Honduras and Granada and is today the second most visited attraction in Nicaragua – don't miss it.

★Monumento Nacional Cañon de Somoto NATIONAL PARK

(Carretera Somoto–El Espino Km 229.5; US$2) The Coco (or Wangki), Central America's longest river, runs all the way to the Caribbean, but its first impression may be its most spectacular. Gushing from underground, it has carved solid rock into this 3km-long gorge that drops 160m, and at times is just a hair under 10m wide. Protected as Monumento Nacional Cañon de Somoto, the canyon is an unmissable experience.

Somoto Canyon Tours ADVENTURE

(8610-7642; www.somotocanyontours.org; Carretera Somoto–El Espino Km 229.5) A well-run community tourism organization based in the village of Sonis, right by the entrance to the Cañon de Somoto, Somoto Canyon Tours offers a fantastic package, including transportation from Somoto, life vest and water shoes, dry bag, entrance fee, guide, lunch and a boat trip for US$25 per visitor for the standard loop and US$30 for the longer version.

Quinta San Rafael LODGE $$$

(8449-1766; info.canondesomoto@gmail.com; entrada Cañon de Somoto; campsite per person US$10, house for up to 12 visitors US$250, cabaña for 6-8 visitors US$120) With a privileged location at the entrance to the canyon, this spacious property offers the most comfortable accommodations for miles around. The main house has two floors, with an open fireplace in the lounge and kitchen area and a wonderful deck with panoramic views of the mountains. There are also several smaller *cabañas* and camping is possible in the garden.

Getting There & Away

The bus station in Somoto itself is on the Panamericana, six blocks from the town center. Buses from Somoto to El Espino pass by the entrance to the canyon – tell the driver where you're headed and they'll drop you off.

BUSES FROM SOMOTO

DESTINATION	COST (US$)	DURATION (HR)	FREQUENCY
El Espino (Honduran border)	0.40	40min	hourly, 5:15am-5:15pm
Estelí	1.10	1¾hr	every 40min, 5:20am-5pm
Managua (*expreso*)	3.40	4hr	5am, 6:15am, 7:30am, 2pm, 3:15pm
Managua (*ordinario*)	2.50	4½hr	almost hourly, 4am-5pm
Ocotal	0.50	1hr	every 45min, 5:15am-4:30pm

Jinotega

POP 51,800 / ELEV 985M

Hidden at the bottom of a verdant valley, Jinotega, the 'City of Mists,' is enclosed on all sides by mountains dappled in cloud forests, crowned with granite ridges and pocked with deep gorges. Its setting is gorgeous, and even though the city is no colonial beauty, the wide streets and neat public squares are inviting and the climate is cool and breezy.

Few travelers make it here, but those who do enjoy visiting nearby Lago de Apanás and hiking into the misty mountains, where you can discover the local coffee industry and stroll through primary forest. Just make sure to get to **Cerro La Cruz** on a clear morning to glimpse Jinotega in all her jade glory.

And that City of Mists moniker is no joke – the average temperature is just 20°C (68°F) and the town can get 2600mm of rain annually – so bring a fleece for the cool evenings.

★**Hotel Café** HOTEL **$$$**

(☎2782-2710; Gasolinera Uno, 1c O, ½c N; s/d incl breakfast US$55/65; P❄📶) The most comfy sleep in Jinotega at this three-star property. Rooms are a little aged now, with pastel paint jobs and, in some cases, little natural light, but they're decent and have desks and fast wi-fi. Service is professional and courteous, and breakfast is good. Hyper-speed laundry service and free parking in the garage opposite are bonuses.

★**Jikao Cafe** CAFE **$$**

(www.facebook.com/jikaocafe; Hotel Café, ½c N; mains US$3-6; ⏰8am-9pm Mon-Sat, noon-9pm Sun; 📶) This lovely new place gets it all just about right: friendly staff, hip decor, excellent coffee (yes, competition is stiff here) and a scrumptious menu that couldn't be further away from *gallo pinto* if it tried – enjoy savory or sweet crepes, chimichangas, a grilled cheese sandwich or just the heavenly passion-fruit mousse.

★**Bar Jinocuba** BAR

(Alcaldía, 5c N; ⏰3-11pm Mon-Thu, to midnight Fri-Sun; 📶) A groovy bohemian bar (and guaranteed *ranchero*-free zone) with occasional, hip live-music performances and cultural events. The young owners are very knowledgeable about tourism in the region and can hook you up with independent English- and German-speaking guides to explore the surrounding mountains. Also serves Cuban and international meals.

ℹ Getting There & Away

There are two bus terminals in Jinotega; **Cotran Norte**, on the edge of the market, is little more than a chaotic parking lot, while orderly and clean **Cotran Sur** (📶) sits near the town's southern entrance and is the best terminal in the region: it has shops, departure announcements and even a waiting lounge with wi-fi.

Buses departing from Cotran Norte:

Estelí (US$1.60, two hours, 5:15am, 7am, 9am, 1pm, 2:45pm & 3:30pm)

Pantasma (Asturias) (US$1.60, 1½ hours, hourly, 4am to 4:30pm)

Pantasma (San Gabriel) (US$1.60, 1½ hours, hourly, 5:30am to 4:30pm)

San Rafael del Norte (*ordinario* US$0.70, 40 minutes; *expreso* US$1, 30 minutes, half-hourly, both 6am to 6pm)

Yalí (US$1.60, two hours, 6am, 8:30am, 10am, noon, 2:30pm and 4pm)

Buses departing from Cotran Sur:

Managua (US$2.80, 3½ hours, 4am to 4pm, 10 daily) Buy tickets at the office in Cotran Sur.

Matagalpa (US$0.85, 1¼ hours, half-hourly, 5am to 6:15pm)

Matagalpa

POP 150,600 / ELEV 902M

Matagalpa may be one of Nicaragua's biggest cities, but it remains a fairly provincial and laid-back place, an almost reluctant urban center for this most bucolic of regions. Here the nearby mountains, which soar in every direction around the city's central neighborhoods, are never far from locals' minds, not to mention the coffee produced on their hillsides, which accounts for Matagalpa's historic wealth.

The city itself is pleasant enough, with a young and friendly population who seem delighted to see visitors. It is best used, however, as a comfortable urban base for exploring the surrounding countryside, where you can hike through primary forest to gushing waterfalls, explore coffee plantations and disused mine shafts, and listen to *ranchero* troubadours jam under a harvest moon.

★Nativos Tours TOURS

(2772-7281, 8493-0932; nativotour@hotmail.com; Cancha Brigadista, 4c E) Contact English-speaking Nativo Tours for some of the most imaginative and interesting excursions available in the region. Owner-operator Guillermo is young and hugely passionate about hiking and nature, and his tours include cultural city tours, black pottery workshops, hikes up to the cross above town, horseback riding, herding cattle, visits to waterfalls and even nocturnal hiking.

★Matagalpa Tours ADVENTURE

(2772-0108, 2772-5379; www.matagalpatours.com; Parque Rubén Darío, 1c E, 20m N; tours from US$15; 8am-12:30pm & 2-6pm Mon-Fri, 8am-4pm Sat) Matagalpa Tours offers nearly a dozen interesting and enriching ways to get into this city and the surrounding countryside. In Matagalpa proper it offers urban walking tours and rents out bicycles, but its best work is done around the local mountains, where it offers both day trips and multiday excursions, including a fascinating tour of local coffee farms.

★Buongiorno Principessa GUESTHOUSE $$

(2772-2721; buongiornoprincipessa35@gmail.com; Cancha Brigadista, 2c E ½c N; dm/r incl breakfast US$12/30; wifi) This laid-back guesthouse in a narrow lane is an excellent-value base for exploring town. Dorms feature good mattresses and are not overcrowded, while private rooms are bright and welcoming. All boast fans and hot water, and are spotless. The included breakfast is top quality, but the highlight is the hammock-slung and plant-strewn rooftop terrace offering 360-degree views of Matagalpa.

★La Buena Onda HOSTEL $$

(2772-2135; www.labuenaonda.com.ni; Cancha Brigadista, 2½c E; dm/s/d US$9/25/30; wifi) Clean, centrally located and with a chilled vibe, this popular hostel in a cozy, converted house with well-furnished rooms offers spacious dorms (with private bathrooms and big lockers) and an upstairs balcony overlooking the street. There is a communal kitchen, a small garden and laundry service available. The helpful management provides plenty of information on attractions in town and beyond.

★Lunaflor INTERNATIONAL $$

(8617-8600; contiguo a tienda la Piñata; mains US$4-8; 4-10pm Mon-Sat; wifi) This fantastic arrival on Matagalpa's dining scene will be a godsend to travelers bored with typical nica cuisine, with curry and teriyaki-based dishes, bruschetta, bagels and artisanal beer topping the list of things you won't find elsewhere in the northern highlands. The whole place is gorgeous, with tables scattered under a fairy light-strewn tree on a breezy terrace.

Information

MEDICAL SERVICES

Clinica Santa Fe (2772-2690, emergency 8419-6283; Catedral, 3c N, ½c E; 24hr)

MONEY

Most banks are located on Av Martínez, a block south of Parque Morazán.

Getting There & Away

There are two main bus terminals in Matagalpa. Fairly well-organized **Cotran Sur** (2772-4659), about 800m west of Parque Rubén Darío, generally serves Managua, Jinotega and most points south.

Disorienting by comparison, **Cotran Norte** (Cotramusun) is next to the northern market and goes to mostly rural destinations in the north.

Dipilto

POP 200 / ELEV 880M

It would be hard to dream up a sweeter setting than what you'll find in this tiny mountain *pueblo* 20km north of Ocotal, and just a 30-minute drive from Honduras. Think narrow, cobbled streets, surrounded by the pine-studded, coffee-shaded Segovias, carved by a rushing, cascading river.

The majestic mountains around Dipilto are known for producing some of the best coffee in Nicaragua. Staff in the **alcaldía** (☎8429-3489) can help organize hikes through some of the town's stunning shade-grown plantations with especially trained local guides. It's also possible to arrange guided treks to quetzal nesting grounds in the cloud forest on the 1867m El Volcán.

10km north of Dipilto, **Finca San Isidro** (☎2732-2392; La Laguna; r incl breakfast per person US$20) is charming coffee hacienda with great views of the surrounding mountains, and can feed and sleep up to 10 people in rustic rooms with shared bathrooms. Spend the night and enjoy a cup of farm-fresh coffee when you get up. It's best to reserve a couple of days ahead.

Getting There & Away

Dipilto is divided into two communities, Dipilto Nuevo and Dipilto Viejo, the latter is a further 3km along the highway toward the Honduran border. The alcaldía and access to the **Santuario** is from Dipilto Nuevo. Take any bus bound for the Las Manos border crossing and ask the driver to let you out in Dipilto Nuevo (US$0.20). Buses run south to Ocotal (US$0.60, 30 minutes) and beyond every 30 minutes or so until around 5pm.

Jalapa

POP 25,000 / ELEV 687M

In a region freckled with remote mountain towns, Jalapa is one where the emerald hills are so close you can see their dips and grooves, their texture and shadows. While the town itself is not likely to win any beauty contests, the surrounding countryside boasts such dramatic natural beauty and so many adventure opportunities that the utter lack of tourism here is difficult to fathom. That said, you will almost certainly not run into other travelers here, and excursions are very much yours to arrange.

Hotel El Pantano HOTEL **$$**
(☎2737-2031; www.hotelelpantano.com; Banco Procredit, 8c O; s/d/tr incl breakfast US$20/27.50/35; 📶) Easily your best bet in Jalapa, this welcoming hotel is set on lovely, lush grounds by a creek a short walk from town. The comfy though rather aged brick rooms have cable TV and (sometimes) hot water, and you'll be serenaded by birdsong and cockerels in the mornings. Campers are welcome to pitch their tent (US$4 per night).

Pizza Giomar PIZZA **$**
(☎2737-2607; Mercado, 2½c O; pizza slice US$1, pizzas US$3-8; ⏲10am-10pm) Pretty much the only alternative to regional dishes in town, this friendly restaurant serves up surprisingly decent pizza with a smile, albeit with a blaring TV accompaniment. Order it whole or by the slice; delivery is available.

Luz de Luna NICARAGUAN **$$**
(Parque Central, 1c S; mains US$5-7.50; ⏲11am-10pm) A popular spot that serves plates of *comida típica* (regional specialties) on plastic tables that can be easily jettisoned – which is what happens when this *comedor* morphs into the closest thing to a happening nightclub in Jalapa. There's a public pool in the same building, in case you want to swim off lunch.

Getting There & Away

The **bus terminal** is just south of town, near the cemetery. The taxi drivers who hang out here are sharks, so if your bags aren't too heavy, walk a couple of blocks and hail a cab on the road.

Bus services include the following:

El Jícaro (Ciudad Sandino) (US$1.60, 1½ hours, 10:15am and 3pm) Meets buses to Murra.

El Porvenir (US$1.30, 30 minutes, hourly until 6pm)

Estelí (US$3.50, four hours, 4am and 10:50am)

Managua (US$6, 5½ hours, 3am, 4am, 9am, 9:40am,1:45pm and 5:30pm)

Ocotal (US$1.70, 2½ hours, hourly, 5am to 4pm)

La Dalia & Peñas Blancas

Easily accessible from both Matagalpa and Jinotega, the area around the hardworking rural town of La Dalia is dotted with thundering waterfalls, working coffee farms and the north's most impressive tracts of virgin forest. The undoubted star of the show is the **Reserva Natural Macizos de Peñas Blancas**, a series of spectacular stone bluffs topped by cloud forest that is inhabited by scores of monkeys as well as jaguars and other rarely seen creatures.

Getting There & Away

If traveling in a private vehicle note that the road north from La Dalia is paved until the turnoff to El Cuá, after which it is dirt and often features muddy puddles. A 4WD vehicle is highly recommended if visiting Peñas Blancas.

Buses leave Matagalpa for La Dalia (US$1.30, 1½ hours) almost hourly from 6am to 6pm. To get to Peñas Blancas, take any bus leaving Matagalpa for El Cuá and get off at 'Empalme la Manzana' – the Peñas Blancas turnoff (US$2.20, three hours). There are also two buses a day from Jinotega to Peñas Blancas. The village is 600m off the main road.

Reserva Natural Cerro Datanlí-El Diablo

The mountains towering over and buffering the eastern end of Jinotega are part of this stunning 100-sq-km reserve, which climbs well into the quetzal zone at 1650m. It's a magical place, with butterflies dancing around coffee bushes that cling to impossibly steep mountainsides in the shade of lush cloud forest. A network of trails connects communities within the reserve and makes for great hiking.

Set on a dramatic, forested mountainside at 1200m with views all the way down to Lago de Apanás, **La Bastilla Ecolodge** (☎8654-6235, 2782-4335; www.bastillaecolodge.com; dm/s/d/tr incl breakfast US$20/45/70/100; P 📶) has easily the most comfortable accommodations in the reserve. The spacious, solar-powered brick *cabañas* have red floor tiles, sparkling bathrooms with solar hot water, and sensational views over coffee plantations full of birds from the wide wooden balconies.

Getting There & Away

One daily bus leaves Cotran Norte (p485) in Matagalpa at 1:45pm for Las Nubes, passing through La Fundadora and La Esmeralda, returning at 6am. It gets full, so arrive early or you may be riding on the roof. During the coffee harvest buses also run to the area from Jinotega, but the schedule is irregular and they are usually packed.

If you miss the direct bus, it's also possible to hike into La Fundadora from Las Latas on the old Matagalpa–Jinotega highway; it's a much shorter trek than walking along the main Fundadora road but there's also less traffic, so your chances of hitching a ride are minimal.

For La Bastilla, take any Pantasma bus (via Asturias) from Jinotega and jump out at the 'empalme La Bastilla,' from where it's a tough 5km hike uphill. If you call in advance, staff from La Bastilla Ecolodge will pick you up at the turnoff (US$5). The same Pantasma bus can drop you at the village of Venencia, a short distance further down the road from La Bastilla, from where it's a 3km, one-hour walk down a rough spur road to El Gobiado. If you phone ahead to La Bastilla Ecolodge, it's possible to organize horses to save you the walk.

Reserva Natural Cerro El Arenal

A short drive from Matagalpa along the old highway north to Jinotega, this 14-sq-km nature reserve is home to cloud forest interspersed with shade-grown coffee plantations. Despite being one of the smallest nature reserves in the country, it boasts varied landscapes and a wide variety of flora and fauna. It has a pleasant, cool climate – making it an attractive destination for great hikes through ethereal forest landscapes sprinkled with orchids.

In the heart of the reserve, the secluded and intimate family-run **Aguas del Arenal lodge** (☎8886-3234, 8160-8431; aguasdelarenal@gmail.com; Carretera Matagalpa–Jinotega Km 142.5; s/d incl breakfast US$30/40, cabañas s/d/tr/q incl breakfast US$50/60/70/80; 📶) is perfect for those looking for a more laid-back coffee country experience. The 7-hectare coffee farm has five spacious and comfortable *cabañas* as well as four rooms in the main house, where you'll also find the cozy common area, complete with a fireplace.

Getting There & Away

The reserve can be accessed via a number of dirt spur roads leading off the old Matagalpa–Jinotega highway. The most used entrance is the road to Aranjuez.

One bus a day leaves from Cotran Sur (p485) in Matagalpa (US$0.70, one hour, noon) to Aranjuez, traveling into the reserve. You can also take any Matagalpa–Jinotega bus to the Aranjuez junction and hike in.

It's also possible to access the reserve from the Matagalpa–La Dalia highway, near San Antonio de Upas.

San Juan de Limay

San Juan de Limay's cobblestone and brick streets seemingly appear from the dust 44km west of Estelí to form a precious country town, known for its stone carvers and surrounded by soaring peaks.

Look for the enlightened *gorda* (pudgy lady); she's the town's signature symbol. Most often she's carved from *marmolina* (soapstone), a heavy rock that is mined in nearby Cerro Tipiscayán and carved and sanded in home workshops until it shines.

The best gallery, **Taller Casco Dablia** (☎2719-5228, 8842-5162; detras del colegio; ⌚8am-6pm), is behind the school and opposite the town square.

ℹ Getting There & Away

The road to Limay branches off the Panamericana north of Estelí, near the community of La Sirena. Buses leave the Cotran Norte (p482) in Estelí for Limay (US$1.30, 2½ hours) six times daily.

San Ramón

POP 2400 / ELEV 641M

Only 12km from Matagalpa, the small highland town of San Ramón feels a world away, with a rural sensibility and a relaxed vibe. While the town itself isn't of particular interest to travelers, the real reason to come here is to get an authentic taste of rural life among the hardworking farmers in the surrounding hills, and there are half a dozen working coffee farms nearby that offer tours and sometimes accommodations. Like many coffee *fincas* in northern Nicaragua, San Ramón's were hit hard by the outbreak of coffee rust disease in 2013 and some local farmers lost up to 80% of their crops. But growing new, hardier varieties has seen a return to almost full production at most farms in the area and the future looks bright.

Many of the villages around town offer homestays (US$35 to US$45 per visitor), which include three meals and activities. There is also a hotel in San Ramón itself – **Finca Esperanza Verde** (www.fincaesperanzaverde.com; Yucul; dm from US$17.50, budget/luxury cabaña US$30/111; P 📶) 🌿 – with lush gardens full of hummingbirds, spectacular mountain views and enchanting nature trails. This large organic farm is a fantastic place to stay whether you want to get active or just relax with a good book. The various types of accommodations are simple in design but well constructed and very comfortable, offering top vistas right from your bed.

ℹ Getting There & Away

Buses between Matagalpa and San Ramón (US$0.50, 30 minutes) run every half-hour between 5am and 7pm, leaving from Cotran Norte (p485) in Matagalpa and the park in San Ramón.

Colectivo taxis (US$0.80, 20 minutes) run on the same route from 5am to 7pm, leaving from the Parada San Ramón in Matagalpa.

CARIBBEAN COAST

Nicaragua's remote Caribbean coast often feels like an entirely separate country from 'mainland' Nicaragua; barely connected to the rest of the nation and looking out toward the Caribbean rather than inwards to Managua. Here you'll find English-speaking Creole people living side-by-side with indigenous Miskito, Mayangna, Rama and Garifuna populations; some of the country's best beaches on the Corn Islands and Pearl Keys; and various slices of wilderness bisected by wide muddy rivers, lined with thick jungle, and connected by mangrove-shrouded black-water creeks and lagoons.

Travel in the Nicaraguan Caribbean is challenging and exciting, and the rewards – including superb scuba diving, epic treks through dense rainforest, wildlife watching and fishing in the mangroves – are huge. The area is formally made up of two vast and sparsely populated autonomous regions known by their official names, Región Autónoma Atlántico Norte (North Atlantic Autonomous Region; RAAN) and Región Autónoma Atlántico Sur (South Atlantic Autonomous Region; RAAS).

ℹ Information

DANGERS & ANNOYANCES

Nicaragua's Caribbean coast is as poor as the country gets. Outside Bluefields and the Corn Islands you can expect dodgy infrastructure, frequent power cuts, nonexistent internet or cell coverage, and terrible roads.

- Bring a flashlight (torch) and enjoy those occasional bucket showers.
- Local agents for Colombian coke impresarios keep a fairly low profile, but the cocaine traffic in the region isn't bloodless.
- Tourists won't have any problems with drug-related violence as long as they refrain from purchasing and consuming cocaine.
- Given the poverty, even in seemingly innocuous small towns, stick to big-city rules: stay alert, don't wander far alone, take taxis at night and watch your valuables.

ℹ Getting There & Away

You can travel overland from Managua to the Caribbean coast, but most visitors take the frequent and inexpensive La Costeña flights. There are active airstrips in Bilwi, Waspám, Bluefields, Great Corn Island and two of the three Las Minas towns. Still, if you have more time than cash and enjoy the (really) slow lane, there are two main overland routes into the region. A new road from Nueva Guinea to Bluefields should be complete by the time you read this, the first sealed road connecting the region to the rest of Nicaragua, which will result in far shorter journey times and much more comfortable overland travel.

SIUNA–BILWI (PUERTO CABEZAS)–WASPÁM & RÍO COCO

We won't sugarcoat this: you're in for a grueling ride on a beat-up old school bus packed to the gills. It begins with a 10- to 12-hour bus ride from Managua to Siuna in Las Minas, where you can access the Reserva de Biosfera Bosawás (Bosawás Biosphere Reserve). From Siuna, it's another 10 to 12 hours on a horrendous road to Bilwi. Waspám and the Río Coco are a smoothish six hours north from there.

JUIGALPA–EL RAMA–BLUEFIELDS–CORN ISLANDS

The (much!) preferred trip to the crystalline Caribbean Sea unfurls on the smooth, paved road to El Rama, with rejuvenating side trips to the mountain towns of Boaco and Juigalpa. From El Rama, you can hop on a testing five-hour bus journey along the rutted dirt road to Pearl Lagoon, or take a convenient two-hour fast boat ride down the Río Escondido to Bluefields, from where there are twice-weekly boat services to the Corn Islands and daily speedboats to Pearl Lagoon.

Getting Around

Most local travel within the region is by *panga* – an open speedboat with an outboard motor. Tickets are much more expensive than a comparable distance by bus, and some of the craft are downright dangerous, but a lack of alternatives means you'll find yourself taking these if you travel much here.

Bluefields

POP 45,500

Named after the Dutch pirate Abraham Blauvelt, who made his base here in the 1700s, Bluefields is the beating heart of Creole culture, famed for its distinctive music, colorful dances and delicious cuisine – considered by many as the best in the country. And while it is not your typical Caribbean dream destination, if you give it a chance and get to know some of the town's ebullient locals, Bluefields' decaying tropical charm will definitely grow on you. Still, you probably won't linger too long. After all, you are just a boat ride away from the intriguing Pearl Lagoon basin, the spectacular Pearl Keys and those luscious Corn Islands.

Bluefields is the capital of the RAAS, also known as the Región Autónoma de la Costa Caribe Sur.

> **DRINKING WATER ADVISORY**
>
> Tap water on the Caribbean coast generally comes from wells or rainwater collection tanks and is usually untreated. Often it is potable, but it may also contain bacteria; bring water purification tablets if you don't want to take the risk. Bottled water is widely available and some hotels offer filtered water refills.

Sights & Activities

★Museo Histórico Cultural de la Costa Caribe MUSEUM
(CIDCA; Iglesia Morava, 2c S; US$2; 8am-noon & 2-4:30pm Mon-Fri) Learn about the Caribbean region's diverse cultures with a visit to this fascinating museum, which contains an interesting mix of historical items from the pre-Columbian era and British rule, including a sword belonging to the last Miskito king and artifacts left by the Kukra indigenous group.

★Waiku Centro de Arte CULTURAL CENTER
(www.waikuart.wordpress.com; Movistar, 15m S; 9am-7pm Mon-Sat) This excellent social project is run by two English-speaking activists, Greta and Yesi, whose small arts center displays painting, handicrafts, clothing and jewellery for sale, made by members of all six ethnic groups present in the RAAS. Above all, the center encourages reading, and it provides chairs, coffee (US$0.05 per cup!) and a book exchange.

Catholic Church & Clock Tower CHURCH
A modern white-and-green Catholic church that is more or less open to the elements. It also has an impressive matching clock tower.

Sleeping

Hospedaje Yellow House HOSTEL $
(8212-5575; www.facebook.com/HospedajeYellowHouse; El Malecón, Santa Rosa; dm/s/d/tr US$5/7/13/18;) The closest thing

Bluefields has to a hostel, the Yellow House is a brightly painted collection of buildings set in some fairly wild gardens by the waterfront in the *barrio* of Santa Rosa, a short cab ride from downtown. Rooms are ultra-basic and share bathrooms, but come with mosquito nets and use of a big kitchen.

Hotel Jackani GUESTHOUSE **$$**
(2572-0440; hoteljackani@gmail.com; frente Policia, Barrio Punta Fria; s/d/tw/tr incl breakfast US$30/40/50/60;) This super-friendly family-run hotel in front of the police station is popular with travelers thanks to its spotless rooms and warm welcome. Guests also appreciate the hot water, fast internet and the large balcony out front with views over to the bay, even if the furnishing choices in the rooms themselves are a little on the garish side.

★ **Hotel Casa Royale** HOTEL **$$$**
(2572-0675, 2572-0668; www.hotelcasaroyale.com; Calle Neysi Rios, Barrio Pointeen; r from US$70;) This fantastic hotel is easily the best choice in town, with modern, sleek and spotless rooms, an excellent location with a great view over the bay, helpful staff and an impressively good top-floor restaurant. Add to the mix a good pool and a delicious *desayuno típico* each morning, and you're onto a winner.

Eating & Drinking

★ **Cevicheria El Chino** SEAFOOD **$**
(frente Colegio Bautista; ceviche US$2; 7am-9pm) Don't leave Bluefields without trying El Chino's marvelous *ceviche*, prepared fresh every day and served in small polystyrene cups, alongside an array of auto parts at this unremarkable grocery shop. Choose from shrimp, fish, oyster or mixed and watch out for the outrageously spicy homemade 'Ass in Space' chili sauce – made with pounds of habanero chilies.

★ **Galeria Aberdeen** CAFE **$$**
(2572-2605; Mercado, 1½c O; light meals US$4-7; 8am-9pm;) Feeling just a tad too chic for grimy Bluefields, this light-filled, split-level cafe serves real coffee in addition to panini, pasta dishes, salads and other meals you won't find anywhere else. There's also a great selection of desserts and a fridge full of imported beers. The walls are covered with works by local artists and it hosts regular cultural events.

★ **Four Brothers** CLUB
(Parque Reyes, 6c S, 3c E; 8pm-4am Thu-Sun) Dance up a storm to dancehall, country and reggae on the wooden dance floor at this legendary disco ranch, comfortable in the knowledge that your dignity is protected by the extremely low-wattage lighting. It doesn't get going until after midnight. Go in a group: it sometimes gets a little rough later on.

Information

MEDICAL SERVICES

Clinica Bacon (2572-2384; Iglesia Morava, 1c S, ½c O) Private clinic with a range of specialists and a laboratory.

MONEY

BanCentro (Iglesia Morava, ½c S) Visa/Plus ATM.

BanPro (frente Iglesia) Reliable Visa/MasterCard ATM.

Getting There & Away

AIR

Take a taxi (US$0.50) to **Bluefields Airport**, where **La Costeña** (2572-2500, 2572-2750; Aeropuerto; 6am-5pm) has three daily flights to Managua (one way/round trip US$83/127, 45 minutes) and Great Corn Island (one way/round trip US$65/99, 25 minutes) and flies to Bilwi (one way/round trip US$96/148, 50 minutes) three days a week when there's enough demand. If there aren't enough passengers for the direct Bilwi flight, you'll be rerouted through Managua at no extra cost.

BOAT

Bluefields is the heart of the *panga* and shipping network connecting the various towns and settlements along the Caribbean coast. Just bear in mind that you'll often need to make journeys that don't feel particularly safe and are nearly always far from comfortable. There are three main piers from where *pangas* leave: the **Muelle Municipal** (Municipal Dock), the **Terminal Costa Atlántica** and the **Muelle Mercado**.

Following an accident in 2017, which saw the *Captain D* ferry overturn and sink, the only connection between Bluefields and Corn Island is now the government-run *Río Escondido* (US$8, five hours), which departs from the Muelle Municipal at 9am on Wednesday and Saturday, with return runs on Thursday and Sunday. There are also a number of cargo boats making the trip on irregular schedules; inquire at the docks.

For Pearl Lagoon (US$5.25, one hour), *pangas* leave when full from the Muelle Municipal throughout the day, with the last ones leaving by

4pm. There's also a weekly *panga* to San Juan de Nicaragua (US$32, three hours) that leaves the Muelle Municipal at 8:30am on Friday, returning on Wednesday. Bring bin bags for your luggage and prepare yourself for a tough journey if the water is anything other than dead calm.

Those heading to El Rama (US$8, two hours) can take a *panga* from the far more orderly and cleaner Terminal Costa Atlántica, where *pangas* are run by **Transporte Vargas** (☎2572-0724, 2572-1510; contiguo Muelle Municipal; ⏰5am-4pm) and **Transporte Jipe** (☎2572-1879; Calle Municipal; ⏰5am-4pm). These leave when full throughout the day, with the first departures between 6am and 7am and a final one at around 3pm. Transporte Vargas also runs boats to Tasbapauni and Orinoco in the greater Pearl Lagoon area.

Pangas crossing the bay to El Bluff (US$1.30, 30 minutes) leave throughout the day from Muelle Mercado when full.

BUS

There are now bus services that link Bluefields to Managua via the town of Nueva Guinea. At the time of writing, the road to Nueva Guinea was still rough in places, but passable unless there's been heavy rain, and was due to be completely sealed soon. Buses run by Transporte Vargas (and Transporte Jipe leave from the area outside the Muelle Municipal every day at 6:30am (US$12.75, seven hours).

Pearl Lagoon

POP 4900

In charming Pearl Lagoon you'll find dirt roads, palm trees, reggae music and mangrove forests, all brought to life by a friendly English-speaking Creole community that lives off the sea and still refers to Nicaraguans elsewhere in the country as 'Spaniards.' You can feel the stress roll off your shoulders as soon as you get off the boat, after a gorgeous journey down wide rivers and across glass-still lagoons. Best of all, Pearl Lagoon still sees very few tourists – which means you may well be the only foreigner buzzing through the mangroves and jungle.

Pearl Lagoon is a perfect base from which to visit the nearby Pearl Keys, where you'll find sugar-white beaches that double as turtle hatcheries, and swaying coconut palms that lull you into inner peace. You'll be glad to return here afterward, though, to enjoy cold beers and stellar local seafood on the waterfront.

There's little to see in the town itself, which is laid out along two main north–south roads: Front Rd, on the water, and another road a block inland. At the southern end of the inland road you'll find the **Moravian Church**, with its characteristic red tin roof.

★Captain Sodlan McCoy BOATING

(☎8368-6766, 8410-5197; Sunrise Hotel, Up Point) Anyone can take you to the Pearl Keys, but few know the area even half as well as Captain Sodlan McCoy, a colorful, no-nonsense fisherman who has been visiting the islands since he was a boy. A trip with Sodlan is much more than sightseeing – it's a cultural experience. He also offers birdwatching, fishing and community trips.

★Queen Lobster BUNGALOW **$$**

(☎8662-3393; Front Rd, Muelle, 200m N; s/d/tr/q US$30/40/50/60; ❄📶) Easily the best and most charming choice in Pearl Lagoon, Queen Lobster offers seven rooms on stilts over the water, with private bathrooms and hammocks on the porch. The two original rooms are made of bamboo and thatch, and are a rustic, somewhat darker affair, while the newer rooms have more modern design, air-con and enjoy more light.

Best View Hotel HOTEL **$$**

(☎8824-3962, 2572-5099; Up Point, Barrio Ivan Dixon; s/d/tr US$30/40/50; ❄📶) Jutting out into the water at the end of the sidewalk, this modern hotel catches plenty of breeze and is a good place to observe Miskito sailing canoes and local fishing boats out on the lagoon. Rooms are small but modern and come with cable TV, air-con and reliable wifi. There's also a good restaurant here.

★Casa Ulrich INTERNATIONAL **$$**

(☎8603-5173; Up Point, Muelle, 350m N; mains US$4.50-12.75; ⏰7am-10pm; 📶) Local boy and Swiss-trained chef Fred Ulrich returned to Pearl Lagoon after a long absence working in resorts all over the Americas, and has invested in his own impressive two-floor restaurant right by the water. Everything on the menu is top-notch, but the delicate shrimp pasta and the grilled fish in garlic are outstanding.

ℹ Information

There are no banks in Pearl Lagoon, so come with ample cash and plan on staying longer than anticipated. You can receive emergency cash transfers at **Western Union** (frente Muelle, Tienda Miss Isabel; ⏰9am-5pm Mon-Fri). The nearest ATM is in the village of Kukra Hill, 22km away.

Getting There & Away

Timetabled boats run to Bluefields (US$5.25, one hour) at 6am and 1pm from Pearl Lagoon's busy **wharf** (Muelle). Sign up the day before for the early boat. Throughout the day, other *pangas* coming from other communities around the lagoon stop here too.

Every Monday, Thursday and Saturday, a *panga* makes the run to Orinoco and nearby Marshall Point from Bluefields via Pearl Lagoon (US$10.50, two hours, 9am); it returns to Pearl Lagoon and Bluefields the following day. This boat can also drop travelers at the communities of Kakabila, Brown Bank and La Fe. There are *pangas* from Bluefields to Tasbapauni (US$10.50, 2½ hours) that pass Pearl Lagoon every day at 11am. Times are liable to shift depending upon the season, so you'll need to ask about departure times at the dock.

One bus (US$6.30, five hours) a day leaves Pearl Lagoon at 5:30am for El Rama, where you can connect to services to Managua and elsewhere in the country. There is also a weekly bus service to Managua (US$10.50, nine hours). The same bus returns overnight Friday to Pearl Lagoon. All bus services leave from outside the **basketball court**.

Around Pearl Lagoon

With a dozen villages belonging to three distinct ethnic groups clinging to its shores and a similar number of jungle-lined rivers feeding it, a boat trip on Pearl Lagoon can make you feel like an 18th-century explorer venturing into an intriguing new world. This is authentic, off-the-beaten-track cultural tourism at its best, and there is nothing like it anywhere else in the country.

Kakabila

Crossing the lagoon to the northwest from Pearl Lagoon town, you'll come to Kakabila, a welcoming Miskito village carpeted with soft grass and studded with mango, pear and breadfruit trees and coconut palms. There's definitely some tropical country romance happening here. To the south of town is **Tuba Creek**, a narrow, jungle-lined river that is great for wildlife spotting.

You an stay here at the community-run **Lakiya Tara** (dm US$10) guesthouse, set on a grassy point north of town with a small sandy beach. There are no restaurants in Kakabila, although simple meals can be ordered in advance at Lakiya Tara.

Getting There & Away

A private transfer from Pearl Lagoon to Kakabila will cost around US$50 for a large boat or US$20 to US$30 in a motorized canoe. Alternatively, the 9am daily public *panga* from Bluefields to Orinoco (US$11) will drop you here on request.

Orinoco

When you hear the evocative call of the *djimbe* (wood and animal-skin drum) spilling out across the rippling water from the red-earth streets of Orinoco, you know you're approaching Garifuna country.

Orinoco is home to 2000 of Nicaragua's approximately 5000 Garifuna people. Here you can learn to paddle a dugout canoe, try your hand at fishing or take the 30-minute stroll northeast along the water to **Marshall Point**, a neighboring Creole village.

There are a couple of cheap guesthouses in town, the best of which by some way is the excellent and switched-on **Hostal Garífuna** (☎8648-4985; www.hostalgarifuna.net; per person US$15).

Getting There & Away

Daily public boats run from Bluefields to Orinoco (US$11, two hours) via Pearl Lagoon, leaving from next to the municipal dock in Bluefields between 9am and 10am and passing Pearl Lagoon one hour later. A private round-trip boat transfer from Pearl Lagoon to Orinoco costs around US$120.

Pearl Keys

The snow-white, palm-shaded, turquoise-fringed Pearl Keys are home to Nicaragua's best Caribbean beaches. Located 30km out to sea from the village of Pearl Lagoon, there were once 18 pearls, but rising tides and beach erosion have trimmed the number to just 10, with more threatened by disappearance in the future.

Once communally owned by Miskito and Creole villagers on the mainland, some of the keys have been bought by foreign investors – much to the anger of locals, frustrated at lack of promised jobs and the apparent indifference of developers to the existential crisis the keys face.

Unless you're lucky enough to be visiting the exclusive **Calala Island** (www.calala-island.com; Lime Key; r incl full board from US$1450; ❄📶🏊) hotel here, you'll either be coming on a day trip from Pearl Lagoon, or spending a night on the beach as part of a tour. Either way, do not miss this dazzling string of tiny Caribbean islands, the closest thing to paradise Nicaragua has.

Getting There & Away

The only way to visit the keys is on a private boat tour. Arrange trips in Pearl Lagoon town. A day trip will typically set you back US$200 to US$300, depending on the size of your group and how many islands you want to visit.

In calm weather, it's just another hour (and another US$200) by *panga* from the keys to the Corn Islands. Considering the adventure quotient, the price and the time involved, it actually makes good sense to travel to the Corn Islands from Pearl Lagoon via the Pearl Keys, rather than doubling back to Bluefields and flying to Great Corn from there.

Las Minas

During their heyday early last century, the gold-mining towns of Las Minas bustled with immigrants from China, Europe, North America and the Caribbean looking to strike the mother lode. These days very few outsiders visit this wild and remote part of the country, and its main towns, **Siuna**, **Rosita** and **Bonanza**, are most notable for their shocking lack of infrastructure and their abundance of armed, inebriated men.

While gold panning is still popular among villagers, the gold rush is well and truly over and the only real money being made here is in Bonanza, where a large foreign-owned mine continues to operate despite criticism from environmentalists.

Siuna has a number of worthwhile attractions. Locals love the nearby, crystalline **aguas calientes** (hot springs). Take a taxi to La Bomba, then follow the trail for about an hour across private Finca Dorado to the springs. Also popular are the rocky beaches of the lazy **Río Wani**, a slow-motion, sinuous beast carving rocky sandbars and encroaching jungle with lazy grace about 11km from town.

Bonanza is the jumping-off point for **Reserva Natural Cerro Cola Blanca** and the Mayangna indigenous communities downriver on the **Río Waspuk** and **Río Pispis**. There are also a couple of great swimming holes and waterfalls around town.

If you plan to visit the mines, local tour operator **Wiwi Tours** (☎2794-2097, 8495-9820; laposadadonachella@gmail.com; Barrio Gilberto Romero) in Siuna is a good first port of call. It offers a number of overnight packages to local attractions, as well as a rugged six-day adventure into **Parque Nacional Saslaya**.

Getting There & Away

All three towns have airstrips, but only Bonanza and Siuna have daily flights to and from Managua. Make reservations in advance, as the 12-seat prop planes fill up. Flights leave Managua daily at 8am for Bonanza (US$96/148, 1½ hours) and at 9am for Siuna (one way/round trip US$82/127, one hour). Return flights to Managua leave daily from both destinations at 10am.

The road here from Managua is scenic but terrible. It's a long, hard slog in a bus from Managua to Siuna (US$18, 12 hours) and an even more challenging journey to Bonanza (US$21, 14 to 17 hours). The Río Blanco–Siuna stretch of the 12-hour hump from Managua is considered one of the country's worst. Rosita is a slightly more manageable eight-hour ride from Bilwi (US$6.50). It involves a river crossing by cable barge and lots of ceiba trees.

Getting Around

The Las Minas towns are linked by frequent – though horrendously overcrowded and slow – bus services. You can also charter taxis locally, which cuts your road time in half and quadruples your comfort level.

Corn Islands

The Caribbean coast's biggest tourist draw is actually 70km offshore, on a pair of enchanting islands with crystalline coves, horseshoe bays and underwater caves. Great Corn is larger and peopled by a Creole population that lives in colorful wooden houses, many of which are sprinkled along the main road around the island. And though tourism is the second-largest industry, behind lobster fishing, you won't see mega-developments here.

Little Corn, a tiny, jungled jewel, actually attracts more tourists, with visitors suitably seduced by myriad dining options, creatively realized beachside *cabañas,* plenty of cheap hostels and even a luxury resort. The dive sites are also more diverse on Little Corn, which explains why so many transit the larger island and head directly to this car-free utopia. During high season there can be more foreigners than locals, but the charms of *Likkle Corn,* as locals call it, cannot be overstated.

Information

Bare-bones law enforcement and the growing tourist industry have seen theft become a problem on the Corn Islands, especially from hotel rooms.

Great Corn Island

POP 7100

The larger of Nicaragua's two most lovely islands, Great Corn (called Big Corn by locals) is a wonderfully manageable and authentic slice of the Caribbean that combines some cracking stretches of golden sand beach with a rich and independently minded English-speaking culture. Here you'll find barefoot bars, commercial fishing wharfs, baseball games on the beach and smiling young lobster divers, catch in hand, wherever you go. An ever-present armada of elders sitting in rocking chairs on creaky front porches, and several jungle-swathed headlands to explore, complete the picture. It's a place where reggae and country music can coexist without irony, where fresh lobster is a staple ingredient rather than a luxury, and where the longer you stay, the less you'll want to leave.

Sights

★Long Bay — BEACH

This stunner of a beach arcs from a pile-up of local fishing *pangas* and lobster traps to a wild, jungle-covered headland at its far end. If you're looking for a place to snooze and swim in absolute tranquility, this is your destination, although be careful in the water, as the riptide can be strong and the waves very rough.

Southwest Bay — BEACH

The most popular beach on Great Corn, Southwest Bay has calmer, more sheltered water than at most other beaches on the island, though the area is more developed, with several hotels, guesthouses and restaurants lining the roadside behind it. It's a good spot to watch the sunset too.

Sleeping & Eating

★Island Roots Hostel — HOSTEL $

(☎8366-6795, 8694-7355; www.islandrootsnicaragua.com; South End; dm US$10-14, r with/without bathroom US$30/28; ❄) This superbly friendly and laid-back place opened in 2018 and feels more like staying in a private home than a hostel. There's an eight-bed dorm and three private rooms, one of which shares a bathroom with the dorm. Breakfast is an extra US$4, but all guests are free to use the communal kitchen at any time.

Hotel G&G — HOTEL $$

(☎2575-5017; martinez-downs69@hotmail.com; contiguo Pasenic, Brig Bay; r with fan US$15-25, with air-con US$25-45; ❄📶) If you don't need to be right by the water's edge, save your cash for lobster and beer and check into this friendly and laid-back hotel in town. Offering outstanding value on clean, brightly painted and spacious rooms, it's within walking distance of a fairly inviting stretch of beach and the main dock.

★Arenas Beach Resort — HOTEL $$$

(☎8851-8046, 2575-5145; www.arenasbeachhotel.com; Southwest Bay; incl breakfast s/d/tr bungalow US$117/146/175, s/d/tr US$146/187/229; ❄📶) Following a full renovation in 2017, Great Corn Island's most professionally managed resort has added a modicum of style to its already lovely beachside location. You can choose to stay in a colorful wooden bungalow room with sea views from the hammocks on the porch, or modern rooms in the main building with fantastic bathrooms boasting rain showers.

Island Bakery & Sweets — BAKERY $

(Sally Peachie; ⏲8am-7pm Mon-Sat) Head to this good old-style Caribbean bakery to indulge in all kinds of delicious sweet snacks, including fantastic cinnamon rolls, coconut pies and cakes. There's also a good variety of natural drinks – try the ginger and pineapple. Also hires out bikes (US$10 per day).

★Big Fish — SEAFOOD $$

(☎8383-8442; North End; mains US$10-14; ⏲7am-9pm; 📶) This fantastic place is run by a friendly team of locals, who give a consistently warm welcome. The menu is one of the most interesting on the island, and specialties include Jamaican jerk lobster, shrimp in jalapeño sauce and a giant seafood soup. There's a good stretch of beach outside and they also offer three comfortable rooms (US$30 to 40).

★Pizzeria Italia — PIZZA $$$

(☎8232-9103; South End; pizzas US$10-15; ⏲6-10pm Tue-Sat) While the restaurant doesn't look like much, these are certainly some of the best pizzas available along Nicaragua's Caribbean coast. We love the fact that there's a whole section for 'Pizzas with Garlic,' which may be the biggest understatement of all time, not to mention the lobster pizza, in case you can't stand an evening without a crustacean on your plate.

Information

EMERGENCY & IMPORTANT NUMBERS

Police (☎2570-1440; contiguo Aeropuerto)

INTERNET ACCESS

Wi-fi, while theoretically present in almost all hotels, is extremely unreliable and patchy on Great Corn Island. Your best bet is to come armed with a local SIM card – Movistar reception is the best here.

MEDICAL SERVICES

Hospital (☎2575-5236; Alcaldía, 500m E)

Sweet Valley Clinic (Doctor Somarriba; ☎8355-3140, 2575-5852; Costado Derecho Estadio; ⏲8am-noon & 3-6pm Mon-Fri)

MONEY

There is only one **ATM** (Brig Bay) on Great Corn Island and it does run out of money occasionally, so you should still plan ahead and carry ample cash. Only a few businesses on the island accept credit cards.

Getting There & Away

Great Corn's small **airport** is served by La Costeña, which runs flights to Bluefields (one way/round trip US$65/99, 20 minutes), with continuing service to Managua (one way/round trip US$107/164, 1¼ hours) three times a day.

The island's **port** is where boats leave for Bluefields and Little Corn. The government-run *Río Escondido* (US$8, five hours) leaves Great Corn on Thursday and Sunday at 9:30am, and travels back from Bluefields on Wednesday and Saturday at the same time. The service is extremely uncomfortable and the sea can be rough, so we don't recommend it.

There are a number of other even less comfortable fishing and cargo boats that make the Bluefields run and there is usually at least one departure on Sunday nights. Bring a hammock or you will be trying to get comfortable on the cold steel deck.

Getting Around

Taxis cost US$0.70 per person (US$1 at night) to anywhere on the island. During the day, there is one bus (US$0.35) that continuously runs a clockwise circuit, but you might have to wait a while until it passes.

Rentals are a great way to explore the island. **Corn Island Car Rental** (☎8543-9881, 2575-5222; cornislandcarentals@hotmail.com; Southwest Bay; golf cart per 2hr US$25-40, per day US$50-100, scooter or motorcycle per day US$25-46) offers scooter and golf-cart rentals, while **Lulu Scooter Rental** (☎5773-8424, 8844-9611; scooter per day US$30) offers scooters. Both will deliver your vehicle to you by arrangement.

PERILOUS WATERS

The *panga* crossing between Great and Little Corn can get extremely rough, especially during the windy season (November to January). Squalls are common (on land and sea) and swells can grow as high as 3m, throwing walls of water over the boat and its passengers. It makes for a white-knuckle, and sometimes bruising, roller-coaster ride. The back seats bounce less, but you are more likely to get wet. All passengers should make sure they have a well-fitting life vest securely fitted before departure, even when the conditions are apparently calm.

Little Corn Island

POP 800

Little Corn is the stuff of fantasy: a dreamy Caribbean escape where arty characters from all over the world have created private refuges on virgin beaches, and where ambitious chefs compete quietly to be the most sought after on the island. With no cars allowed, there's a certain old-world magic to any walk beneath the mango, coconut and breadfruit trees and on into the thick forest that buffers the northern and eastern coasts.

Backpackers love this tiny place, and make up the bulk of its visitors, though there's also plenty for midrange travelers and even a couple of top-end resorts. Whether you want to spend the day snorkeling, swimming and sunbathing at one of a dozen golden coves, or prefer to spend your time getting to know the charismatic locals in the Village, it's hard to imagine anywhere better in Nicaragua to relax and recharge.

Sights & Activities

The two best beaches on the island are **Cocal Beach** and **Otto Beach**, which are both great for swimming and have just a few non-intrusive beachside guesthouses hidden away on them.

Adventurers can also walk to the windward shore, which involves a scramble over the rocks to get to **Big Fowl House Beach**, then **Jimmy Lever Beach**, both totally wild coves where it's possible to swim. Alternatively, ramble the rugged northern shore from the Village until you find the spectacular **Goat Beach**, framed by two headlands.

Don't forget to head up to the **lighthouse**, a steel tower jutting 6m above the mango trees, where you can glimpse the island's curves and coves, and catch an outrageous sunset. Finally, if you're on Little Corn on Saturday morning, do not miss the supply boat from Bluefields arriving at the main pier around 9 or 10am. This weekly event sees hundreds of people heading to the Village with their carts to collect their groceries, and it's an incredible sight.

Kite Little Corn KITESURFING
(☎8498-5381; www.kitelittlecorn.com; Steadman's Place; ⏲8am-6pm) Soar over the turquoise waters of Little Corn with this kitesurfing school run by Nacho, an affable Spaniard who is passionate about the sport. Located on the windy side of the island, it offers two-day intensive courses (US$300) and group tuition (US$50 per hour).

Sleeping & Eating

★Green House Hostel HOSTEL **$**
(☎5877-5642; Village; dm US$10-17; 📶) The best budget option on the island, Green House is located very conveniently for the arrival jetty in the heart of the Village. It has three fan-cooled dorms, each of which has several handcrafted pine bunks with their own lockers. Each dorm has its own bathroom and access to a good kitchen and a large garden.

Ensueños BUNGALOW **$$**
(www.ensuenos-littlecornisland.com; Otto Beach; cabañas/casas from US$25/100) 🍃 Surrounded by forest and fruit orchards, and perched on a golden crescent of sand in a gorgeous sheltered turquoise cove lined by coconut palms, this enchanting place features a variety of (very!) rustic *cabañas* on stilts. There are also three idiosyncratically designed solar-powered *casas* (houses) with small kitchens a bit further back.

The entire place is rather like a set from *The Mosquito Coast*, and it's run by Ramón, a Spanish artist/naturalist/bohemian, and his family. Excellent gourmet meals are prepared on demand.

★Yemaya Island Hideaway & Spa HOTEL **$$$**
(☎8741-0122, 8239-5330; www.yemayalittlecorn.com; Otto Beach; r incl breakfast from US$279; ❄📶) Yemaya offers the most luxurious accommodations on the island and boasts professional service to match. The 17 fan-cooled rooms are stylish, bright and comfortable and offer fantastic sea views through their large glass sliding doors, which open onto porches with comfy bamboo chairs. Five of the rooms even have their own infinity plunge pools, and the beach below is sumptuous.

Baker Shop Gloria BAKERY **$**
(Village; pastries from US$0.30; ⏲5am-9pm) Delicious and moist banana, ginger and coconut breads are just some of the highlights of this super-simple local bakery. It's a great option for a cheap and filling backpacker breakfast.

★Comedor Bridget NICARAGUAN **$$**
(☎8437-7295; Village; meals US$7-10; ⏲7am-10pm) Pull up a chair on the porch of this converted family home and order the superb salt-dusted, lightly fried fish and a cold beer. Alternatively, try its mind-bogglingly good shrimp coconut curry or the great-value lobster. Bridget pioneered tourism on the island and her homey place is still your number-one choice for no-nonsense authentic local dining.

★Darinia's Kitchen INTERNATIONAL **$$$**
(☎8744-3419; dariniabonilla@gmail.com; Village; per person US$25; ⏲by reservation only; 🖉) For a truly local experience in the Village, reserve an evening meal at this ambitious and eclectic supper club. Self-taught Managua transplant Darinia cooks up a four-course feast that can easily accommodate vegetarians and vegans at her simple alfresco dining table. Food is superb, featuring fresh vegetable, fish and seafood dishes with a Thai bent and excellent desserts.

Information

ELECTRICITY

Little Corn only has power between 1pm and 6am, with its generator resting for several hours each morning. Some hotels have solar- or wind-power backups, meaning they're never without electricity, but in most cases expect to wake up sweaty when the fans stop running at dawn.

INTERNET ACCESS

Some hotels around the island have wi-fi, but it's generally unpredictable and slow. The most reliable way to be online is to get a local SIM card at Managua airport before you come – Claro gets the best 3G on the island – but you cannot buy SIM cards here or on Great Corn.

MONEY

There are no banks and certainly no ATMs on Little Corn, so bring all the cash you'll need with you. Some hotels do accept credit cards, but be sure to check before you travel.

Getting There & Away

Collective *pangas* to Little Corn (US$5, 40 minutes) leave from the pier on Great Corn at 10am and 4:30pm daily. In the other direction, boats leave Little Corn at 7am and 1:30pm from the **main pier**. Be sure to come in good time to get a ticket, as you are unable to book ahead and boats sometimes sell out during high season.

If you're taking the morning flight to Managua from Great Corn, it's best to travel back the day before. Bear in mind that the journey can get very rough and you may get soaked. Bringing garbage bags to cover your luggage is a good idea. For a smoother ride, it's possible to ride on the large cargo ships (US$2 to US$3, 1¼ hours) that supply the *islita*, but there are only a handful of departures each week – ask at the main pier in the Village.

Getting Around

Little Corn is only about 1.5km across. You can walk end to end in under an hour – which is just as well, because the only wheels on the island's jungle trails belong to wheelbarrows.

Bilwi (Puerto Cabezas)

POP 48,500

This impoverished Caribbean port town and ethnic melting pot sprawls along the coast and back into the scrubby pines on wide brick streets and red-earth roads, full of people and music, smiles and sideways glances. Old wooden churches, antique craftsman homes and ramshackle slums are knitted together with rusted sheet-metal fencing, coconut palms and mango trees. In a single stroll you'll eavesdrop on loud jagged Miskito banter, rapid-fire Spanish and lovely, lilting Caribbean English. Sure, this city has systemic problems (poverty, decay, crime), and its dilapidated infrastructure lags years behind the rest of the country. But with tasty seafood, great-value historic lodging options, and seaside indigenous communities a boat ride away, it can be as alluring as a sweet, yet slightly sketchy, new friend.

Take a stroll along the wooden boards of the historic **Muelle Viejo** (Old Pier), where both Sandino and the Contras received arms smuggled in from abroad, the former with the assistance of the town's sex workers. But the 420m-long pier's biggest moment in the spotlight was in 1961, when Somoza lent the facility to US-funded Cuban exiles to launch the disastrous Bay of Pigs invasion.

★Casa Museo Judith Kain HOTEL $
(☎2792-2225; Parque Central, 4c N, 1c O; r/tw with fan US$14/16, r/tw/tr with air-con US$25/30/35; ❄📶) In a town with an abundance of atmospheric lodging, this may be the best of the bunch. The 19 rooms occupy various buildings set back from the house-museum of a local artist. Sadly, the rooms themselves aren't all in good condition, but they do have high ceilings, the odd antique and shared access to the lovely gardens.

Comedor Alka NICARAGUAN $
(frente Parque Central; meals US$3; ⏰11am-9pm) Stop at this simple *comedor* (basic eatery) for savory and cheap eats such as fantastic barbecued beef and chicken, served with a bit of attitude. It's all in good fun and the food is as good, if not better, than many more upscale restaurants.

★Restaurante Faramhi SEAFOOD $$
(☎2792-1611; frente Aeropuerto; mains US$5-10; ⏰11am-10pm; 📶) Close to the airport, this popular restaurant serves easily the best food in town. It's a very Bilwi kind of place: the open-air dining area features seashell light shades, a random disco light and a country music soundtrack. The menu reflects the town's multi-ethnic roots, with typical seafood plates starring alongside an ensemble of good Chinese dishes.

Information

DANGERS & ANNOYANCES

- Be cautious when wandering alone even during daylight, and avoid carrying nonessential items with you.
- Take taxis after dark, as the streets are not safe to walk after sunset.
- Avoid empty side streets and the seafront if you're alone at any time of day.

MONEY

BanPro Changes dollars and has a Visa/MasterCard ATM.

Getting There & Away

Most visitors arrive in Bilwi by plane. **La Costeña** (☎2792-2282; Aeropuerto) offers three daily flights from **Puerto Cabezas Airport** (☎2792-2282) to Managua (one way/round trip US$97/149, 1½ hours) and thrice-weekly services to Bluefields (US$96/148, 50 minutes).

Getting Around

Bilwi is not the safest place to be strolling off the main streets at any time. *Colectivo* taxis around town cost US$0.30; use them for all journeys after dark, and even during the day if you're unsure of where you're going – neighborhoods can change from fine to sketchy very quickly.

Boaco

POP 57,000 / ELEV 1020M

'The City with Two Floors' was once two ranching communities separated by a steep 400m slope. They've grown together over the years, and now this *ranchero* market town, a couple of hours' drive from Managua, is a bustling agricultural hub. Being off the main highway, Boaco receives few visitors, but its charming central square and good hotels and restaurants make it a decent overnight stop for those looking to explore the region's petroglyph-studded mountain hinterland.

You can duck into two interesting churches. **Parroquia de Nuestra Señora del Perpetuo Socorro** (salida, 1c N, 2c E), down on the lower level of town, and the peach-colored **Parroquia de Santiago Apóstol** on the upper. The best views in town can be glimpsed from **Parque El Cerrito del Faro** (Parque Central, 2c N, 1½c O; ⏰10am-9pm).

BACK ROAD TO MATAGALPA

If you're heading north from Boaco and are not in any hurry, consider taking the scenic backcountry route to Matagalpa through peaceful, pastoral lands at the foot of rugged and rarely visited mountains. This is a route you're guaranteed to be virtually the only traveler on, and its rustic villages and rolling scenery make for a thoroughly relaxing drive.

Public transport on this route is very limited and it's best explored in a private 4WD vehicle. There are buses from Teustepe (US$1, one hour) to San José de los Remates at 7am and 5pm, the latter of which continues to Esquipulas.

★Tijerino's Hotel HOTEL $$

(☎2542-2798; hoteltijerinos@gmail.com; frente al Parque Central; r with/without air-con US$30/40; ❄📶) Way ahead of everything else in town, this fancy hotel on the park seems a little too smart for rural Boaco. Yes, the decor is on the garish side, but the bright, modern rooms boast ultra-comfortable bedding and are the finest for miles around. The biggest draw, however, are the two ample terraces with majestic mountain panoramas. Outstanding value.

Kónoha Café INTERNATIONAL $

(Alcaldía Municipal, ½c O; mains US$3-6; ⏰8am-10pm Mon-Sat, from 2pm Sun; 📶) There's a jazz soundtrack, good coffee and a friendly owner at this great little spot just off the Parque Central. The menu is simple rather than anything particularly exciting, but features atypical treats such as burgers, fajitas, quesadillas and crepes, as well as nachos for two people to share.

Getting There & Away

Boaco is 12km from the Empalme de Boaco junction, on the main Managua–El Rama Hwy. Local buses leave from the market. Managua-bound buses leave from the station, another 200m uphill. Matagalpa-bound folks need to take the bus to San Benito, from where there are frequent departures for Matagalpa. Bus services include:

Managua (US$1.50, two hours, half-hourly, 3:45am to 5:25pm) Express minivans (US$1.90, 1½ hours) depart when full from the market area until around noon.

San José de los Remates (US$1.25, 1½ hours, noon)

Santa Lucia (US$0.75, 30 minutes, noon and 3pm)

Juigalpa

POP 71,300 / ELEV 117M

Blessed with a wonderful setting, Juigalpa is nestled on a high plateau peering into a golden valley quilted with rangeland carved by a crystalline river. It's enclosed on all sides by the looming Serranía Amerrisque, the sheer granite faces and layered peaks of which are ripe for contemplation and adventure. To the west is a series of smaller hills and dry valleys that crumble into marsh, which then melts into Lago de Nicaragua.

The town itself, sprinkled with well-preserved colonial buildings and peopled by ranchers, rambles along both sides of the Managua Hwy. Apart from a fascinating archaeological museum, there are not a lot of attractions here and the pulse of tourism is quite faint, but it's a good place to break a journey for lunch or overnight if you're passing through.

★**Museo Arqueológico Gregorio Aguilar Barea** MUSEUM
(☎2512-0784; Parque Central, 2½c E; US$0.40; ⊙8am-noon & 1-5pm Tue-Fri, 8am-noon & 1-4pm Sat, 9am-noon & 1-3pm Sun) Mystical stone statues rise like ancient totems in the courtyard entrance here. It houses the most important collection of stelae in the country, with more than 120 basalt statues carved between AD 800 and 1500, including *La Chinita,* known as 'The Mona Lisa of Chontales.' She too has appeared at the Louvre.

Parque Palo Solo PARK
(Parque Central, 5c E) This rather lovely, beautifully tended and shady park is where couples come to whisper, cuddle and kiss beneath palm and ficus trees, and absorb a truly magnificent view of the distant Serranía Amerrisque.

★**Hotel Los Arcangeles** HOTEL **$$**
(☎2512-0847; detras Iglesia; r US$40; ❄📶) This highly atmospheric ranch-style hotel, decorated with dozens of folk-art archangels, has a variety of spotless rooms set around plant-filled corridors in a top location directly behind the cathedral. Some are too enclosed while others are spacious with high ceilings, so ask to see a few – they're all the same price. Breakfast is an extra US$5.

Palo Solo NICARAGUAN **$$**
(☎2512-2735; Parque Palo Solo; dishes US$6-12.50; ⊙11am-11pm Thu-Tue; 📶) Set on a shady patio at the western edge of Palo Solo park, this restaurant serves up tasty Nicaraguan mixed grill plates. It's not exactly fine dining, but it's lively, the food is good and the view is fantastic.

ℹ Getting There & Away

Buses to Managua, El Rama and San Carlos all leave from the **Cotran** bus terminal, across Hwy 7 from downtown (taxis there cost around US$0.60). Minivans for Managua (US$3.50) leave the Cotran when full. Passing *expreso* buses between Managua and San Carlos or El Rama do not enter the Cotran – hail them on the highway. Buses to Cuapa, La Libertad and Puerto Díaz leave from the **Mercado** (Parque Central, 1c E, ½c N; meals US$2; ⊙6am-6pm).

El Rama (US$3.50, five hours, almost hourly from 4:30am to 2:45pm)

Managua (*expreso* US$2.70, two hours, 5:45am & 1:15pm; *ordinario* US$2.20, three hours, half-hourly, 4am to 6pm)

Puerto Díaz (US$1, one hour, 5:30am, 9:30am, 11:30am and 1pm) The later buses do not always run – check at the market.

San Carlos (US$3.50, four hours, every two hours, 3am to 1:30pm)

San José de los Remates

POP 1800

Impossibly scenic and peacefully pastoral, San José de los Remates has relatively easy access to the **Reserva Natural Cerro Cumaica-Cerro Alegre**, and boasts an impressive municipal tourism program launched to help preserve its own clean water supply. Several years ago, a Boaco-based cattle-ranching operation had polluted the watershed to the point that municipal groundwater was threatened. The townspeople mobilized, convinced the rancher to grow sustainable organic coffee instead, and reforested much of the property themselves. The land is now protected as a municipal park, **Reserva Hídrica Municipal La Chorrera**, adjacent to the national reserve. Local tourism helps foot the bill, making San José an exemplary case of successful ecotourism. Visiting will please anyone with an interest in the subject.

ℹ Getting There & Away

There are buses from Teustepe (US$1, one hour) to San José de los Remates at 7am and 5pm, the latter of which continues onto Esquipulas.

Miskito Keys

Sitting 50km offshore, the Miskito Keys is a group of rocky Caribbean isles rimmed with stilted Miskito fishing villages. Their thatched over-water bungalows loom above crystalline turquoise coves that double as an ideal lobster habitat. The historic first meeting between the British pirate, Captain Sussex Camock, and his future Miskito allies took place here in 1633. Today the keys are still a haven for seafaring bad guys, so if you see any boats with Colombian plates, look the other way.

Unlike the Pearl Keys further south, this is a cultural rather than beach destination – very few of the islands have any sand at all. Most are pure rock with the odd bit of scrubby vegetation. Nevertheless, a visit to this isolated community sticking out of the

OFF THE BEATEN TRACK

RESERVA DE BIOSFERA BOSAWÁS

Buffered to the north by three neighboring reserves in Honduras, **Reserva de Biosfera Bosawás** makes up part of the largest protected expanse of rainforest north of the Amazon, itself clocking in at some 20,000 sq km. A vast wilderness crisscrossed by rivers and shrouded in dense jungle, it's a vital part of the Mesoamerican biological corridor, the land route between North and South America that is used by many migratory species of animal, and is home to some of the region's last giant anteaters, spider monkeys, jaguars, harpy eagles, tapirs and crocodiles.

Named for three geographical features that delineate the reserve – the Río Bocay, Cerro Saslaya and Río Waspuk – Bosawás is a destination for seriously intrepid adventurers and wildlife enthusiasts. Come here to explore a true wilderness, canoe down giant rivers, birdwatch and see an extraordinary array of creatures in their natural habitat.

Getting There & Away

You can begin inquiries at the Bosawás office at Marena Central (p439) in Managua, or any of the satellite offices located in most large towns bordering the reserve, where they can arrange guides and transportation, or at least point you in the right direction. It's often easiest to access the reserve through lodges on the periphery or private organizations, however, so ask around.

ocean is a fascinating experience, although it doesn't come cheap. Bring plenty of insect repellent too!

Getting There & Away

All access to the Miskito Keys is from Bilwi. From there you can arrange overnight visits for US$600 for up to six visitors, a large chunk of which goes toward transportation costs. Transport in a larger, faster *panga* for up to 12 will cost you around US$800 round-trip; **Intur** (☎2792-1564; puertocabezas@intur.gob.ni; Parque Central, 2c N; ⊙8am-4pm Mon-Fri) in Bilwi is able to recommend responsible captains. To make the journey on the cheap, you'll need to make arrangements with a lobster fisher who is already going: doable, but your return could take days. It's two hours to the keys on a fast boat, up to five on a lobster vessel, and the ride is often rough.

Waspám & the Río Coco

POP 7000

Waspám, the end of the line in Nicaragua and as about as remote as you can get here, is a poor and developmentally challenged place that nevertheless still enjoys a simple beauty: children at play, twittering flocks of parakeets in the trees, and dugout canoes plying the edges of Waspám's biggest attraction, the lazy brown waters of the Río Coco.

Known as Wangki in Miskito, the Río Coco is the longest river in Central America and links some 116 Miskito communities that run from the rainforested interior to the Caribbean coastal marshlands. This makes Waspám, its epicenter, the cultural, geographic and economic heart of the Mosquitia. The river also forms a natural border with Honduras, a fact most Miskitos prefer to ignore. You shouldn't. If you plan on crossing into Honduras, get your passport stamped at **Bilwi Migración** (Immigration Office; ☎2792-2258; contiguo la Policía; ⊙8am-4pm Mon-Fri).

The town is worth a wander. You'll see the oddly constructed **Iglesia San Rafael**, you can dangle your legs over the cinder-block outfield walls of the **baseball stadium** with the locals on weekends, and you can stroll **parque central**. Its **war monument** was erected for fallen Contras overrun by the Sandinistas, who then torched and occupied Waspám until the war was over.

Hotel Casa de la Rose HOTEL $

(☎5729-9380; frente la pista; s/d with fan US$11/15, with air-con US$18/22; ❄📶) One of Waspám's two really good hotels. Rooms are clean with fresh tiles, cable TV and a lovely wooden porch nestled in the banana palms of the gorgeous garden. It also has a terrific restaurant set in a sweet wooden *cabaña* patrolled by parrots.

★**Hotelito El Piloto** HOTEL $$

(☎8331-1312, 8642-4405; hotelitoelpiloto@live.com; Muelle, 20m S; r/tw US$25/35; ❄📶) Waspám's best all-round choice. Rooms have fresh paint and bathroom tiles, and a terrific location steps from the river. The friendly owners are a wealth of information and will happily arrange all manner of local excursions, as well as serve up quality meals.

Getting There & Away

AIR

La Costeña (☎8415-8210; Aeropuerto) planes only seat 12, so it's best to book in advance. Flights depart on Tuesday, Thursday and Saturday from Managua to Waspám (one way/round trip US$104/160, 1½ hours) at noon, and return to Managua at 1:40pm.

BUS

Buses leave for Bilwi (US$6.50, six hours) at 6am and 7am daily. Come early if you want a seat. There are also several direct buses a week to Managua (US$25, 25 hours), usually departing on Monday, Wednesday, Thursday and Saturday at around 8am.

Río Coco

Waspám's prime attractions are out of town and accessible by the Río Coco, which upriver from town forms the northern boundary of the Bosawás reserve and downriver flows to Cabo Gracias a Dios and into the Caribbean. Access is pricey but easily organized with local captains who hang around at Waspám's dock.

Getting There & Away

Expect to pay US$60 per day for boat hire plus fuel, which will make up most of the cost. You can also arrange trips through Hotelito El Piloto in Waspám, where owner Barry Watson speaks English.

RÍO SAN JUAN DEPARTMENT

The steamy Río San Juan runs from Lago de Nicaragua into the Caribbean, forming the border with Costa Rica for much of its journey through the wilderness. The thick jungle here is a haven for migratory birds and dozens of animal species including jaguars, howler monkeys, alligators, sloths and fluorescent fingernail-sized tree frogs.

It's also a place thousands of travelers simply pass through on their way to Costa Rica, ignoring the distant Archipiélago de Solentiname, and the towns and villages along Río San Juan.

Getting There & Away

The Río San Juan is an international entry point to Nicaragua with buses linking San Carlos with Los Chiles in Costa Rica across a new bridge that spans the Río San Juan.

La Costeña operates twice-weekly flights between San Carlos and Managua via Ometepe. The flight continues to San Juan de Nicaragua. You can also arrive in San Carlos and San Miguelito by bus from Managua, Juigalpa and El Rama.

All other destinations in this region are only accessible by boat from San Carlos.

San Carlos

POP 12,200

Located where Central America's biggest lake meets one of its largest rivers, the capital of the isolated Río San Juan department is the gateway to some of Nicaragua's most compelling countryside. San Carlos itself enjoys a lovely natural position surrounded by water, the silhouettes of the Islas Solentiname in one direction and distant volcanic peaks framed by rainforest in the other.

During the day the town sees plenty of travelers, which explains the bustling waterfront lined with restaurants. But when night falls, the magnificent views disappear with the setting sun and San Carlos quickly falls quiet.

San Carlos is less a tourist destination and more a place to wait for your ship, or *panga* (small motorboat), to come in, but there is beauty here – particularly on the grounds of Centro Cultural Jose Coronel Urtecho, which is set within the crumbling walls of **Fortaleza de San Carlos** (⌚9am-5pm) FREE. It's no El Castillo, but it was built in 1724 and has amazing lake and Río San Juan views. There's another old Spanish observation post, with cannons, at the end of the *malecón*.

Hotel Gran Lago HOTEL **$$**

(☎2583-0075, 8823-3488; www.grandhotelsnicaragua.com; Parque Central, 1c O, 1c S; s/d/tr incl breakfast from US$37/41/60; ❄📶) Right on the edge of the lake with views over to the Archipiélago de Solentiname, this small hotel is the best San Carlos has to offer, with a variety of rooms split over two levels. Those downstairs are a bit closed in and dark, but the bigger upstairs rooms are spacious, get plenty of light and enjoy lake views.

★ **Restaurante Kaoma** NICARAGUAN $$
(☎2583-0293; Parque Central, 1½c S; mains US$6.50-11.50; ⏰11:30am-10pm; 📶) Just about the only full-service restaurant in town, this attractively set place has old wooden floors, beamed ceilings and pleasant lake views. The extensive menu includes some excellent tender beef dishes and fish, which comes sautéed in a buttery garlic sauce or stuffed with shrimp. The fish and crab soup is also delicious.

ℹ Information

MEDICAL SERVICES

Hospital Felipe Moncada (☎2583-0244)

MONEY

There are two ATMs in town **BanPro** (frente alcaldía) on the main road through town and **Bancentro LAFISE** (Parque Central, 1c S) just off the *malecón*.

ℹ Getting There & Away

San Carlos is no longer the isolated corner of Nicaragua it once was thanks to the construction of a good road to Juigalpa and the opening of a modern bridge over the Río San Juan at Santa Fe, which links the region by road with Las Tablillas in Costa Rica.

AIR

The trip by air to San Carlos from Managua (usually via Ometepe) is spectacular, with close up fly-bys of two volcanoes, the Islas Solentiname and the Laguna de Apoyo. La Costeña (www.lacostena.com.ni) operates compact, 12-seat planes on Thursday and Sunday flying from Managua to Ometepe, San Carlos and then San Juan de Nicaragua on the Caribbean coast before returning via the same route (depending on demand). The San Carlos **airport** is a 3km, US$1 cab ride from downtown San Carlos.

BOAT

Collective riverboat services to Boca de Sábalos (US$2.85, two hours) and El Castillo (US$2.60, three hours) leave from the **Portuaria San Carlos** (Muelle Municipal), half a block west of the *mercado* (market), at noon (Monday to Saturday) and at 2:30pm (Monday, Tuesday, Friday and Saturday). Express boats to Sábalos (US$3.90, 1½ hours) and El Castillo (US$4.50, two hours) leave at 6am, 8am, 10:30am, 3:30pm and 4:30pm daily.

Boats to Islas Solentiname (US$10, 90 minutes) leave from the public dock next to Migración at 3pm daily.

Colectivo boats to Papaturro (US$3.30, five hours), for access to the **Centro Ecológico de Los Guatuzos** (☎2270-3561, 8772-9630; www.losguatuzos.com; Río Papaturro; r per person US$15), leave the Muelle Municipal at 9am on Monday, Tuesday, Wednesday and Friday. There are fast boats (US$4.75, three hours) that leave San Carlos on Saturdays at 10am.

Slow boats to San Juan de Nicaragua (US$10.50, nine to 12 hours) leave the Portuaria San Carlos at 6am on Tuesday, Thursday and Friday. Fast boats on the same route (US$20, seven hours) leave San Carlos at 6am on Tuesday and Friday.

BUS

Buses leave from the **bus terminal** in San Carlos for the following destinations:

Boca de Sábalos (US$2.20, two hours, 7am, 9am, 11am, 2pm, 4:30pm and 7pm) Buses also stop in La Esperanza.

El Rama (US$4.75, seven hours, 9am)

Juigalpa (US$3.50, four hours, 10am, 11:10am, 12:40pm and 1:30pm) Managua-bound buses (except overnight services) will also drop passengers in Juigalpa.

Managua (US$4.75, six hours, 2am, 6:30am, 8am, noon, 2:30pm, 6pm, 9pm and 10:30pm)

San Miguelito (US$1.60, two hours) Direct buses leave at 12:20pm and 1pm, but you can hop on any Managua- or Juigalpa-bound bus and get off at the San Miguelito turnoff. There are also more comfortable minibus services (US$2, two hours) that leave from the *malecón* at 10:30am and 5pm daily.

Minivans for the border crossing at Santa Fe (US$2, 30 minutes) depart when full from the terminal from 3am to 5:30pm.

Alternatively, Agua Trails (www.aguatrails.com) runs a daily shuttle service to La Fortuna in Costa Rica (US$55 per person).

BORDER CROSSING: TO LOS CHILES, COSTA RICA

The completion of the bridge over the Río San Juan at Santa Fe downstream from San Carlos sadly saw the traditional (and very scenic) river route into Costa Rica being superseded by the faster land option. This means that unless you have a private launch, you'll need to cross at Santa Fe.

The cheapest way to do this is to take a local minivan from the bus station in San Carlos across the bridge and to the border at San Pancho (US$2, 30 minutes). Vans run from 3am to around 5:30pm but the border is only open from 8am to 4pm, so there's no need to head out at dawn. Once stamped out of Nicaragua (for which you'll pay US$2), walk over to the Costa Rican immigration office and get your entry stamp before taking another bus to Los Chiles (US$1, 15 minutes) or Quesada (US$6, three hours) from where there are continuing services to San

José. There is also one direct bus a day from Las Tablillas to San José at 3pm.

If you have a private launch, begin your trip at friendly San Carlos **Migración** (☎2583-0263; Malecón; ⏰8am-5pm), where you'll have your passport stamped. When you arrive in Los Chiles, go to customs, opposite the dock, to have your bags searched, then another building about two blocks away to have your passport stamped.

At both border crossings you'll be required to pay US$12 to enter Nicaragua and US$2 upon departure. If you are leaving Costa Rica by road you will be required to pay US$7 exit fee by debit or credit card only – no cash.

UNDERSTAND NICARAGUA

Nicaragua Today

Traditionally, Nicaraguan presidents have only been permitted to serve two five-year terms, but 2014 saw the decision to abolish term limits. In November 2016, President Daniel Ortega again won the presidential election, securing a highly controversial third term. Since then Ortega has been busy dismantling Nicaragua's institutional democracy by assuming full control of the military, the police, and all branches of government. In April 2018, a series of clashes between protesters and pro-government supporters led to hundreds of deaths, with violent clashes taking place in Masaya, Managua, Granada, León and elsewhere. At the time of writing, 325 people have been killed and over 2000 injured as a result of these clashes.

Although the violent situation has simmered down somewhat, and some political prisoners have recently been released, the country is still in crisis. The economy is crumbling under the pressure of the precarious political climate, and Ortega steadfastly refuses to call new elections before 2021, in spite of calls to do so by a large proportion of the population.

History

Early History

Pre-Hispanic Nicaragua was home to several indigenous groups, including the ancestors of today's Rama, who live on the Caribbean coast, and the Chorotegas and Nicaraos on the Pacific side. The latter spoke a form of Náhuatl, the language of the Aztecs. Many Nicaraguan places retain their Náhuatl names.

By 1500 BC Nicaragua was broadly settled, and though much of this history has been lost, at least one ancient treaty between the Nicarao capital of Jinotepe and its rival Chorotegan neighbor, Diriamba, is still celebrated as the Toro Guaco.

European Arrival

Although Columbus stopped briefly on the Caribbean coast in 1502, it was Gil González de Ávila, sailing north from Panama in 1522, who would really make his mark here. He found a chieftain, Cacique Nicarao, governing the southern shores of Lago de Nicaragua and the tribe of the same name. The Spaniards thus named the region Nicaragua.

Colonial Settlement

The main Spanish colonizing force arrived in 1524, founding the cities of León and Granada. Both were established near indigenous settlements, whose inhabitants were put to work.

The gold that had attracted the Spaniards soon gave out, but Granada and León remained. Granada became a comparatively rich colonial city, with wealth due to surrounding agriculture and its importance as a trading center. Originally founded on Lago de Managua, León in time became the center for radical clerics and intellectuals, who formed the Liberal Party and supported the unification of Central America and reforms based on the French and American Revolutions.

The difference in wealth between the two cities, and the political supremacy of León, led to conflicts that raged into the 1850s, at times erupting into civil war. The animosity stopped only when the capital was moved to the neutral location of Managua.

Zelaya's Coup & US Intervention

In 1893 a Liberal general named José Santos Zelaya deposed the Conservative president and became dictator. Zelaya soon antagonized the USA by seeking a canal deal with Germany and Japan. Encouraged by Washington, which sought to monopolize a transisthmian canal in Panama, the Conservatives rebelled in 1909.

After Zelaya ordered the execution of two US mercenaries accused of aiding the Conservatives, the US government forced his resignation, sending marines as a coercive measure. Thus began a period of two decades of US political intervention in Nicaragua. In 1925 a new cycle of violence began with a Conservative coup.

The Conservative regime was opposed by a group of Liberal rebels including Augusto C Sandino, who recruited local peasants in the north of the country and eventually became leader of a long-term rebel campaign resisting US involvement.

Sandino & the Somoza Era

When the US marines headed home in 1933, the enemy became the new US-trained Guardia Nacional, whose aim was to put down resistance by Sandino's guerrillas, as documented in Richard Millett's comprehensive study *Guardians of the Dynasty: A History of the US-Created Guardia Nacional de Nicaragua and the Somoza Family.* This military force was led by Anastasio Somoza García.

Somoza engineered the assassination of Sandino after the rebel leader was invited to Managua for a peace conference. National guardsmen gunned Sandino down on his way home. Somoza, with his main enemy out of the way, set his sights on supreme power.

Overthrowing Liberal president Sacasa a couple of years later, he established himself as president, founding a family dynasty that would rule for four decades.

Rising Opposition

In 1961 Carlos Fonseca Amador, a prominent figure in the student movement that had opposed the Somoza regime in the 1950s, joined forces with Colonel Santos López (an old fighting partner of Sandino) and other activists to form the Frente Sandinista de Liberación Nacional (Sandinista National Liberation Front; FSLN).

On December 23, 1972, at around midnight, an earthquake devastated Managua, leveling more than 250 city blocks. The *Guardian* newspaper reported that, as international aid poured in, the money was diverted to Anastasio Somoza and his associates, while the people who needed it suffered and died.

By 1974 opposition was widespread. Two groups were widely recognized – the FSLN (Sandinistas) and the Unión Democrática de Liberación, led by Pedro Joaquín Chamorro, popular owner and editor of the Managua newspaper *La Prensa,* which had long printed articles critical of the Somozas.

Revolution & the FSLN

For a Nicaraguan public tired of constant violence, the last straw was the assassination of Chamorro. By mid-1978 many major towns were rising up against government forces. The Guardia Nacional's violent reprisals garnered further support for the Sandinistas.

The FAO threw in its lot with the Sandinistas, whom they now perceived as the only viable means by which to oust the dictatorship. The FSLN was well prepared to launch its final offensive in June 1979. The revolutionary forces took city after city, supported by thousands of civilians. On July 17, as the Sandinistas were preparing to enter Managua, Somoza fled the country. He was assassinated by Sandinista agents a year later in Asunción, Paraguay. The Sandinistas marched victorious into Managua on July 19, 1979.

They inherited a shambles. Poverty, homelessness, illiteracy and inadequate health care were just some of the problems. An estimated 50,000 people had been killed in the revolutionary struggle, and perhaps 150,000 more were left homeless.

The Contra War

After Ronald Reagan became US president in January 1981, relations between Nicaragua and the USA began to sour. Reagan suspended all aid to Nicaragua and, according to the Report of the Congressional Committees Investigating the Iran-Contra Affair, by the end of the year had begun funding the counterrevolutionary military groups known as Contras.

A CIA scheme to mine Nicaragua's harbors in 1984 resulted in a judgment against the USA by the International Court of Justice. The court found that the USA was in breach of its obligation under customary international law not to use force against another state and ordered it to pay repatriations to the Nicaraguan government; the

Reagan administration rejected the findings and no payments were ever made.

Nicaraguan elections in November 1984 were boycotted by leading non-Sandinistas, who complained of sweeping FSLN control of the nation's media. The Sandinistas rejected the claims, announcing that the media was being manipulated by Contra supporters. Daniel Ortega was elected president with 63% of the vote, and the FSLN controlled the National Assembly by a similar margin.

In May 1985 the USA initiated a trade embargo of Nicaragua and pressured other countries to do the same. The embargo lasted for five years, helping to strangle Nicaragua's economy.

With public opinion in the USA growing weary of the war, the US Congress rejected further military aid for the Contras in 1985. According to the congressional report into the affair, the Reagan administration responded by continuing to fund the war through a scheme in which the CIA illegally sold weapons to Iran and diverted the proceeds to the Contras. When the details were leaked, the infamous Iran-Contra affair blew up.

Polls & Peace

By the late 1980s the Nicaraguan economy was again desperate. Civil war, the US trade embargo and the inefficiencies of a centralized economy had produced hyperinflation, falling production and rising unemployment. As it became clear that the US Congress was preparing to grant the Contras further aid, Daniel Ortega called elections that he expected would give the Sandinistas a popular mandate to govern.

The FSLN, however, underestimated the disillusionment and fatigue of the Nicaraguan people. Economic problems had eclipsed the dramatic accomplishments of the Sandinistas' early years: redistributing Somoza lands to small farming cooperatives, reducing illiteracy from 50% to 13%, eliminating polio through a massive immunization program and reducing the rate of infant mortality by a third.

Politics in the 1990s

Chamorro took office in April 1990. The Contras called a heavily publicized ceasefire at the end of June. The US trade embargo was lifted, and foreign aid began to pour in.

Economic recovery was slow; growth was sluggish and unemployment remained stubbornly high. Nevertheless, in 1996, when Nicaragua went to the polls again, the people rejected the FSLN's Ortega and opted for former Managua mayor Arnoldo Alemán of the PLC, a center-right liberal alliance.

Alemán invested heavily in infrastructure and reduced the size of the army by a factor of 10, but his administration was plagued by scandal, as corruption soared and Alemán amassed a personal fortune from the state's coffers, earning himself a place on Transparency International's list of the top 10 corrupt public officials of all time.

Sandinista 2.0

After losing three successive elections, FSLN leader Ortega returned to power in the November 2006 elections, capitalizing on disillusionment with neoliberal policies that had failed to jump-start the country's economy and an *el pacto*–sponsored law that lowered the threshold for a first-round victory to 35% of the votes (Ortega received 38%).

Taking office in January 2007, Ortega proclaimed a new era of leftist Latin American unity, leaving the USA and some international investors a little jumpy. As the Ortega government found its feet, there was no sign of radical land reforms or wave of nationalizations that the business sector had dreaded and some die-hard FSLN supporters had hoped for.

The first test for Nicaraguan democracy under the new Ortega government surfaced in 2008, with countrywide municipal elections. The FSLN claimed victory in over 70% of municipalities. Opposition forces claimed widespread voter fraud and *La Prensa* labeled the election 'the most fraudulent elections in Nicaraguan history.'

Culture

The National Psyche

Nicaragua has a fierce cultural streak and prides itself on homegrown literature, dance, art, music and cuisine. This spiritual independence is a holdover not only from the revolution and Contra War, but also back to Spanish colonization, when indigenous nations won limited autonomy at enormous personal cost.

Though ideological divisions between former Contras and Sandinistas recently seemed to have been addressed and worked through, it seems that the ongoing political unrest of 2018 will lead to yet another generation of Nicaraguans to suffer the trauma of violence.

Attitudes differ from place to place. Residents of the English- and Miskito-speaking Atlantic coast rarely consider themselves part of Nicaragua proper, and many would prefer to be returned to the British Empire than suffer further oppression by the 'Spaniards' on the other side of the country. The cattle ranchers of the central highlands resist interference from the federal government, while coffee pickers in Matagalpa or students in León are willing to walk to Managua to complain to the government if they perceive that an injustice has been done.

Lifestyle

Nicaragua is a country in motion. One in five Nicas live outside the country, mostly in the USA, Costa Rica and Honduras. Waves of migration to the cities, which began in the 1950s, have left more than 59% of the population urban. Most internal immigrants are young women, and most go to Managua; men tend to follow the harvest into rural areas and the surrounding countries. Regular jobs are difficult to find, and more than half of employed Nicaraguans are in the 'informal sector' – street vendors, cleaners, artisans – without benefits or job security.

The young and the educated in big cities such as Managua, León and Granada have more disposable income, much greater exposure to social media and global trends, and a keen interest in what's happening in the world. Life in smaller towns is more laid-back and steeped in tradition, with a strong culture of hospitality. The *campesino* lifestyle is simpler still, and means long hours and hard physical labor.

Despite the country's Catholic background, couples often live together and have children without being married, especially in larger cities. Nicaraguans are generally fairly accepting of the LGBTIQ+ community, although the community is still fighting for full legal recognition.

Wealth is distributed unequally, with the moneyed elite living much as they would in Miami or elsewhere. For the vast majority of Nicaraguans, however, just putting food on the table is a daily struggle, with over 50% living below the poverty line in rural areas and perhaps a third of the country subsisting on two meals or fewer per day.

People

With 6.3 million people spread across 130,375 sq km, Nicaragua is the second-least densely populated country in Central America after Belize. The CIA World Factbook estimates that 69% of the population is *mestizo* (of mixed ancestry, usually Spanish and indigenous people), 17% white, 9% black and 5% indigenous. The most recent census reports that just over 440,000 people describe themselves as indigenous: the Miskito (121,000), Mayangna/Sumo (9800) and Garifuna (3300), all with some African heritage, occupy the Caribbean coast alongside the Rama (4200). In the central and northern highlands, the Cacaopoeras and Matagalpas (15,200) may be Maya in origin, while the Chorotegas (46,000), the Subtiavas (20,000) and the Nahoas (11,100) have similarities to the Aztecs.

Religion

Although Nicaragua's majority religion is Catholic, Nicaraguan Catholicism retains many indigenous elements, as the decor and ceremonies of churches such as San Juan Bautista de Subtiava and Masaya's María Magdelena make clear. Liberation theology also made its mark on Nicaraguan Catholicism, influencing priest and poet Ernesto Cardenal to advocate armed resistance to the Somoza dictatorship. Publicly chastised and later defrocked by Pope John Paul II, Cardenal remains a beloved religious leader. Nicaragua's incredible selection of Catholic churches and fascinating *fiestas patronales* (saints days) remain highlights of the country. Around 13% of Nicaraguans say they are atheist or agnostic, unusual in Latin America.

Arts

Nicaragua is a bright star in the firmament of Latin American literature, and poetry is the country's most important and beloved art. Rubén Darío (1867–1916), a poet who lived in León, is one of the most renowned authors in the Spanish language, and his writings have inspired literary movements and trends throughout the Latin world. Three outstanding writers emerged soon after Darío, and their works are still popular: Azarías Pallais (1884–1954), Salomón de la Selva (1893–1959) and Alfonso Cortés (1893–1969). In the 1930s the experimental 'Vanguardia' movement came on the scene, led by José Coronel Urtecho, Pablo Antonio Cuadra, Joaquín Cuadra Pasos and Manolo Cuadra. A number of leading personalities in the Sandinista leadership, including Sergio Ramírez, Rosario Murillo and Ernesto Cardenal, made literary contributions as well as political ones.

Landscape & Wildlife

With more than a 10,000 sq km of virgin forest, 19 active volcanoes, vibrant coral reefs, thriving populations of birds and butterflies, tropical fish, and various species of turtles, Nicaragua has been endowed with more than its share of natural beauty. Combine that with a low population density and very little industrialization and you'll discover that in Nicaragua, wilderness is never far away – and you'll have it mostly to yourself when you get there.

The Land

The formation of the Central American Isthmus began about 60 million years ago, connecting the two massive American continents for the first time three million years ago. Marking the volcanic crush of the Cocos and Caribbean tectonic plates, the Maribios Volcanic Chain is one of the most volcanic places in the world.

There are 40 major volcanic formations, including 28 volcanoes and eight crater lakes, among them Reserva Natural Laguna de Apoyo, with hotels and private homes, Laguna Tiscapa in downtown Managua, and Laguna Asososca, with no development at all.

The region's appeal to early colonists increased as they realized that the soil was further enriched by this striking geological feature. Earthquakes and volcanoes are a part of life along the borders of the Caribbean and Cocos plates, and you'll find very few authentic colonial buildings that haven't been touched up since the 1500s.

Nicaragua's highest mountains, however, are metamorphic, not volcanic. Running down the center of Nicaragua like an opening zipper, they rise to their greatest heights as a granite chain contiguous with the Rocky Mountains and the Andes. They go by several names, including Cordillera Dariense (after Rubén Darío). Topped with cool cloud forests above 1200m, these refreshing regions are home to some of the best national parks and protected areas. Two of the most accessible reserves up north are Área Protegida Miraflor, close to Estelí, and Reserva Natural Cerro Apante, a hike from Matagalpa. Or go deeper, to Reserva Natural Macizos de Peñas Blancas, actually part of Bosawás, the largest protected swath of rainforest north of the Amazon. It's 7300 sq km of humid tropical and subtropical forest, also accessible by the largest river in Central America, the Río Coco (560km).

Nicaragua also has the two largest lakes in Central America, Lago de Managua (1064 sq km) and Lago de Nicaragua (8264 sq km), with more than 500 islands, some protected, as well as wonderful wetlands, such as Refugio de Vida Silvestre los Guatuzos.

The Atlantic coast is worlds apart, geologically as well as culturally, from the drier, more developed Pacific side. A vast eroding plain of rolling hills and ancient volcanic plugs, here's where around 90% of the country's rainfall ends up. This is the region with the wildest protected reserves and worst access – with very few exceptions, it's difficult and relatively expensive to travel here, as most transportation is by boat. The lowlands are remarkable for their dry pine savannas and countless wetlands and have four major river systems. The easiest way in is along the Río San Juan, a Unesco biosphere reserve.

CARIBBEAN COAST

The Caribbean ('Atlantic') region occupies about half of Nicaragua's area. The 541km coastline is broken by many large lagoons and deltas. Twenty-three rivers flow from the central mountains into the Caribbean, including the Río Coco (685km), Nicaragua's longest river, and the Río San Juan (199km), which flows from Lago de Nicaragua. These define much of the borders with Honduras and Costa Rica respectively.

The Caribbean region gets an immense amount of rainfall. It is sparsely populated and covered by tropical rainforest. The largest towns are Bluefields and Bilwi (Puerto Cabezas), both coastal ports. Several small islands, including the much-visited Corn Islands (Islas del Maíz), lie off the Caribbean coast, surrounded by coral reefs.

Wildlife

Nicaragua is home to about 1800 vertebrate species, including around 250 mammals, and 30,000 species in total, including 764 bird species (551 resident and 213 migratory).

Animals are slowly working their way northward, a migration of densities that will one day be facilitated by the Mesoamerican Corridor, a proposed aisle of shady protected rainforest stretching from Panama to Mexico. Other countries in on the agreement are just getting started on the project, but Nicaragua's two enormous Unesco biosphere reserves, Bosawás and Southeast Nicaragua (Río San Juan), make up a significant chunk.

Environmental Issues

With a developing economy, poor infrastructure and limited resources, Nicaragua faces a tough task in protecting the environment at the same time as lifting its citizens out of poverty.

While there has certainly been progress in recent times, the country still faces a variety of pressing environmental issues.

SURVIVAL GUIDE

Directory A–Z

ACCESSIBLE TRAVEL

While Nicaraguans are generally accommodating toward people with mobility issues, and will gladly give you a hand getting around, the combination of cobbled streets, cracked sidewalks and stairs in pretty much every building can make life tough.

There are few regular services for disabled travelers and because of difficulties in finding suitable transport, it's easiest to go through a tour company. Vapues Tours (www.vapues.com) is an experienced local operator, specializing in accessible travel.

There are very few wheelchair-accessible toilets and bathrooms in Nicaragua, so bringing toilet-seat extensions, and wall-mountable mobility aids are highly recommended.

Download Lonely Planet's free Accessible Travel guides from http://lptravel.to/AccessibleTravel.

ACCOMMODATIONS

Outside absolute peak periods in major tourist destinations, it's rarely necessary to reserve accommodations in advance in Nicaragua.

Hospedajes These cheap guesthouses are often family-run and are sometimes the only option in smaller towns.

Hotels Larger and more polished; boutique hotels can be intimate and characterful. They offer facilities including reception and often a restaurant.

Hostels Traveler's hostels with dormitories and common areas are only found in the main tourist areas.

Ecolodges Usually at the higher end of the market, these offer comfortable rooms surrounded by nature.

Surfing lodges Offer all-inclusive surfing packages, and often shared accommodations and great food.

EMBASSIES & CONSULATES

Most embassies and consulates are located in Managua.

Canadian Embassy (Map p436; ☎2268-0433; http://travel.gc.ca/assistance/embassies-consulates/nicaragua; Calle Nogal 25, Los Pipitos, 2c E, Barrio Bolonia; ⊙8am-noon & 12:30-4pm Mon-Thu, 7:30am-1pm Fri)

Costa Rican Consulate (Map p436; ☎2276-1352; www.rree.go.cr; 28 Calle Sureste, del Seminole Plaza, 2c N, ½c O; ⊙8am-4pm Mon-Fri)

Dutch Honorary Consul (☎8787-9067; Carretera a Los Nubes, del Club Terraza, ½c N; ⊙7:30am-4:15pm Mon-Thu, 9am-1pm Fri)

French Embassy (Map p436; ☎2228-1056; www.ambafrance-ni.org; 7 Calle Suroeste, Iglesia del Carmen, 1½c O; ⊙7:30am-12:30pm & 1:30-4:30pm Mon-Thu, 7:30am-12:30pm Fri)

German Embassy (Map p436; ☎2255-6920; www.managua.diplo.de; Carretera a Masaya Km 5, Calle Erasmus de Rotterdam, del Colegio Teresiano, 1c S, 1c O; ⊙8am-5pm Mon-Fri)

Guatemalan Embassy (☎2279-9606; Carretera a Masaya Km 11.5; ⊙8am-noon & 1-4pm Mon-Fri)

Honduran Embassy (Map p436; ☎2270-2347; Edificio OPUS II, Modulo 103, semáforos Enitel Villa Fontana, 1c E, 50m N, Planes de Altamira No 3; ⊙9am-5pm Mon-Fri)

Mexican Embassy (Map p436; ☎2278-4919; http://embamex.sre.gob.mx/nicaragua; Carretera a Masaya Km 4.5, Optica Matamoros, 25m E; ⊙9am-5pm Mon-Fri)

Panamanian Embassy (☎2277-0501; https://panama.visahq.com/embassy/nicaragua; Reparto Villa Fontana, del Club Terraza, 1c E, ½c N; ⊙9am-5pm Mon-Fri)

Salvadoran Embassy (☎2276-0712; https://el-salvador.visahq.com/embassy/nicaragua; Carretera a Masaya Km 9.5, Pasaje Los Cerros 142, Las Colinas)

US Embassy (Map p434; ☎2252-7100; https://ni.usembassy.gov; Carretera Panamericana; ⊙9am-5pm)

FOOD

Many Nicaraguans eat lunch on the go, but the majority eat dinner at home, so outside tourist areas you may find eating options are reduced in the evening. Budget eateries including *comedores* (basic eateries), where you choose from a variety of ready-prepared dishes, and market stalls serve a limited range of filling dishes and set meals from US$2 to US$5. Also in this price range are *fritangas* (grills), which serve grilled meats and fried sides. Midrange eateries will have a decent-sized menu charging US$5 to US$10 per plate. Top-end establishments (mostly found in Granada, León, Managua and San Juan del Sur) will have an even better range, including dishes from around the world, costing more than US$10.

INTERNET ACCESS

Internet cafes have pretty much disappeared with the proliferation of free wi-fi in most accommodations and a growing number of restaurants, bars and cafes. Some hostels have free computers for guest use. Top-end hotels mostly have 'business centers' and often connections for laptops and wi-fi in rooms. The internet icon used in our hotel listings signifies that the hotel has a computer with internet access available to guests free of charge.

Public wi-fi is still rare outside big cities and tourist hot spots. If you're staying for a while, consider purchasing a USB modem, which works well in larger cities but is often very slow in rural areas.

Nicaragua's mobile data network is continually improving and works well in big cities but can be painfully slow in rural towns where everyone is trying to get online through one tower. SIM cards are cheap, and prepaid internet plans are also very affordable.

LEGAL MATTERS

Nicaragua's police force is notoriously corrupt and underpaid, and renowned for stopping foreign motorists, in particular, on minor or made-up charges.

For minor traffic violations or made-up offences your driver's license will normally be confiscated and you will need to go to the bank to pay your fine and then to the nearest police station to retrieve your document. This can be a pain if you are only driving through. Trying to bribe a traffic cop is a really bad idea and they're unlikely to let you off with just a warning. However, sometimes they'll 'do you a favor': instead of an official fine of US$100, they may refrain from holding onto your license if you pay them US$50. Another alternative for foreign visitors is this: if you are certain that it's a shakedown (and it will be quite obvious if it is), you have the option of surrendering your license, not paying the fine, and simply replacing your license when you get home.

If you get caught with drugs or committing a more serious crime, it won't be that easy to get away from the law.

At the time of writing, the police were involved in a violent crackdown on Nicaragua's unarmed student protestors, using live bullets and a disproportionate amount of force.

SLEEPING PRICE RANGES

Price indicators for sleeping options in our listings denote the cost of a standard double room with private bathroom.

$ less than US$20

$$ US$20–50

$$$ more than US$50

LGBTIQ+ TRAVELERS

While consensual gay sex was decriminalized in Nicaragua in 2008, attitudes have taken a bit longer to change. As in most of Latin America, gay and lesbian travelers will run into fewer problems if they avoid public displays of affection, and ask for twin beds. That said, lots of Nicaraguan gays and lesbians flaunt their sexuality, so you probably won't have much difficulty figuring out the scene.

There is a small selection of gay and lesbian bars and clubs in Managua, an underground gay scene in Masaya and a vaguely tolerant scene in Granada, but apart from that, it's a pretty straight (acting) country.

MONEY

Nicaragua's currency is the córdoba (C$), sometimes called a 'peso' or 'real' by locals. Córdobas come in coins of C$0.50, C$1 and C$5, and plastic bills of C$10, C$20, C$50, C$100, C$200 and C$500. Older plastic bills are flimsy and tear easily and some paper bills remain in circulation. Bills of C$200 and larger can be difficult to change; try the gas station.

US dollars are accepted almost everywhere, but they will be rejected if they are even slightly marked, ripped or damaged. Córdobas are usually easier to use, particularly at smaller businesses and anywhere off the beaten track – always keep at least 200 córdobas on you, preferably in smaller bills.

The córdoba is valued according to a fixed plan against the US dollar. Our listings give prices in US dollars (US$), as the costs in córdoba are more likely to fluctuate with the exchange rate.

EATING PRICE RANGES

Price indicators for eating options in our listings denote the cost of a typical main course.

$ less than US$5

$$ US$5–10

$$$ more than US$10

Bargaining

All-out haggling is not really part of Nicaraguan culture. However, a bit of bargaining over a hotel room is considered acceptable, and negotiating the price in markets or with roadside vendors is the norm.

Tipping

Tipping is not widespread in Nicaragua except with guides and at restaurants.

- **Guides** Tipping guides is recommended as this often makes up the lion's share of their salary.
- **Restaurants** A tip of around 10% is expected for table service. Some high-end restaurants automatically add this to the bill. Small and/or rural eateries may not include the tip, so leave behind a few coins.

OPENING HOURS

Opening hours vary wildly in Nicaragua as there are many informal and family-run establishments. General office hours are from 9am to 5pm.

Comedores (cheap eateries) usually open for breakfast and lunch while more formal restaurants serve lunch and dinner.

Banks 8:30am–4:30pm Monday to Friday, to noon Saturday

Comedores 6am–4pm

Government Offices 8am–noon and 1–4pm Monday to Friday, 8am to noon Saturday

Museums 9am–noon and 2–5pm

Restaurants noon–10pm

Bars noon–midnight

Clubs 9pm–3am

Shops 9am–6pm Monday to Saturday

PUBLIC HOLIDAYS

New Year's Day (January 1) Shops and offices start closing at noon on December 31.

Semana Santa (Holy Week; Thursday, Friday and Saturday before Easter Sunday) Beaches are packed, hotel rates skyrocket and everything is closed – make sure you have a place to be.

Labor Day (May 1)

Mother's Day (May 30) No one gets away with just a card – more places close than at Christmas.

Anniversary of the Revolution (July 19) No longer an official holiday, but many shops and government offices close anyway.

Battle of San Jacinto (September 14)

Independence Day (September 15)

Indigenous Resistance Day (October 12)

Día de los Difuntos (November 2) All Souls' Day.

La Purísima (December 8) Immaculate Conception.

Navidad (December 25) Christmas.

SAFE TRAVEL

Despite the fact that Nicaragua has one of the lowest crime rates in Central America, as a 'wealthy' foreigner you will at least be considered a potential target by scam artists and thieves.

- Pay extra attention to personal safety in Managua, the Caribbean region, around remote southern beaches and in undeveloped nature reserves.
- In larger cities, ask your hotel to call a trusted taxi.
- Backcountry hikers should note there may be unexploded ordnance in very remote areas, especially around the Honduran border. If in doubt, take a local guide.

TELEPHONE

- Nicaragua's calling code is 505.
- There are no area codes within Nicaragua.
- All numbers are made up of eight digits; fixed line numbers begin with 2, while cell phone numbers begin with 8, 7 or 5.
- To call abroad from Nicaragua, dial 00 + country code + area code + phone number.

Cell Phones

Local phone costs start at around US$15. You can also buy a SIM card (around US$3.50) for any unlocked GSM phone. Numerous cell-phone networks offer free roaming in Nicaragua. The two phone companies are Claro and Movistar.

TOURIST INFORMATION

Intur (☎2263-3174; www.intur.gob.ni; Managua Airport; ⏲8am-10pm), the government tourism office has branches in most major cities. It can always recommend hotels and activities (but not make reservations) and point you toward guides, though branches of Intur are usually sparsely stocked and their staff are not hugely knowledgeable.

In destinations popular with travelers, hostels are a good source of local info, as well as traveler message boards.

The *alcaldía* (mayor's office) is your best bet in small towns without a real tourist office. Although tourism is not the mayor's primary function, most will help you find food, lodging, guides and whatever else you might need. In indigenous communities, there may not be a mayor, as many still have councils of elders. Instead, ask for the president (or *wihta* in Miskito communities), who probably speaks Spanish and can help you out.

VISAS

All visitors entering Nicaragua are required to purchase a Tourist Card for US$10.

Those entering by land also pay a US$2 migration processing fee. Upon departure by land or boat there is another US$2 migration fee, while a small municipal charge – usually around US$1 – may also be levied by the local government depending on the border crossing.

VOLUNTEERING

Nicaragua has a very developed volunteer culture, traceable to the influx of 'Sandalistas' (young foreign volunteers) during the revolution. Many hostels and Spanish schools maintain lists of organizations. Also check out Volunteer South America (www.volunteersouthamerica.net) and Go Abroad (www.goabroad.com).

WOMEN TRAVELERS

The biggest problems that many solo female travelers encounter in Nicaragua are the *pirópos* (catcalls) and general unwanted attention. Nicaragua is not particularly dangerous for women, but, like always, stay alert. Dress conservatively when not on beaches (knees should be covered, though shoulders are OK), especially when in transit; avoid drinking alone at night; and – this is the hard one – reconsider telling off the catcalling guy so the situation does not escalate. Sigh.

Getting There & Away

Nicaragua is accessible by air via the international airport in Managua, by road using four major border crossings with Honduras and Costa Rica (plus another crossing to Costa Rica at San Pancho – Las Tabillas, which sees few visitors), and by boat between El Salvador and Potosí, and Costa Rica and San Carlos.

Flights, cars and tours can be booked online at lonelyplanet.com/bookings.

AIR

Upon arrival in Nicaragua by air, visitors are required to purchase a tourist card for US$10; make sure you have US currency handy.

It's worth checking fares to neighboring Costa Rica, which is an air-conditioned bus ride away and may be significantly cheaper.

Airports & Airlines

Nicaragua's main international hub is Managua International Airport (p440), a small, manageable airport that receives flights from Miami, Fort Lauderdale, Atlanta and Houston in the USA, and several major cities within Central America and Mexico City.

Nicaragua has no national airline, but is served by several major American carriers, as well as Copa and Avianca.

LAND

Visitors entering Nicaragua by land must purchase a tourist card for US$10 and pay a US$2 immigration fee. Land departures are also subject to the immigration fee.

Border Crossings

Nicaragua shares borders with Costa Rica and Honduras. Generally, Nicaraguan border crossings are chaotic (there are no signs anywhere), but the procedure is fairly straightforward provided you have your documents in order. The Honduras and Costa Rica border crossings are the busiest, and are open around the clock while the rest have limited opening hours.

Ocotal to Tegucigalpa, Honduras See the sunny Segovias and the Honduran capital at this major, business-like border. The Las Manos crossing point is efficient, although sometimes crowded.

Somoto to Choluteca, Honduras A high-altitude crossing that comes with an amazing granite canyon. Crossing point El Espino is laid-back and easy.

El Guasaule to Choluteca, Honduras The fastest route from Nicaragua, an easy cruise north from León. The El Guasaule 24-hour crossing is hectic and somewhat disorganized.

Sapoá to Peñas Blancas, Costa Rica The main, 24-hour border crossing is generally easy unless your arrival coincides with an international bus or two, in which case it could take hours. The local municipality charges an additional US$1 fee at this crossing.

San Pancho to Las Tablillas, Costa Rica Uncrowded border crossing (open 8am to 4pm daily) that uses a bridge and beautifully paved road.

Bus

International buses have reclining seats, air-conditioning, TVs, bathrooms and sometimes even food service, and are definitely safer for travelers with luggage. Crossing borders on international buses is generally hassle-free. At many borders the helper will take your passport, collect your border fees, get your stamp and return your passport to you as you get back on the bus. At the Costa Rican border post at Peñas Blancas you must complete the formalities in person.

There are direct bus services (without changing buses) to Costa Rica, Honduras, El Salvador and Guatemala, and connecting services to Panama and Mexico.

Nica Expreso (https://nicaexpreso.online.com.ni) Runs from Chinandega (via Managua) to San José, Costa Rica.

Tica Bus (Map p436; ☎8739-5505; www.ticabus.com; 9 Calle Suroeste, Barrio Bolonia) Travels to Costa Rica, Honduras and El Salvador with connecting services to Guatemala, Panama and Mexico.

Transnica (Map p436; ☎2270-3133; www.transnica.com; Metrocentro, 300m N, 50m E) Serves Costa Rica, Honduras and El Salvador.

Transporte del Sol (Map p436; ☎2422-5000; frente Tica Bus, Barrio Bolonia) Same-day service to Guatemala and El Salvador.

Car & Motorcycle

To bring a vehicle into Nicaragua, you'll need the originals and several copies of the ownership papers (in your name), your passport and a driver's license.

You'll get a free 30-day permit (lose it and you'll be fined) and you will need to purchase obligatory accident insurance for US$12. You may also be required to pay US$3 to US$4 for the fumigation of your vehicle. Your passport will be stamped saying you brought a vehicle into the country; if you try to leave without it, you'll have to pay import duty. It's possible to extend the vehicle permit twice at the DGA office in Managua before you have to leave the country.

You can drive across two border crossings to Costa Rica. The most popular is at Sapoá–Peñas Blancas near Rivas; the crossing at San Pancho-Las Tablillas in the Río San Juan sees few vehicles.

It's possible to drive across the Nicaragua–Honduras border at El Guasaule, Somoto–El Espino and Ocotal–Las Manos.

Getting Around

AIR

The hub for domestic flights is Managua International Airport (p440). Other airports are little more than dirt strips outside town (or in Siuna and Waspám, in the middle of town). The airport in San Juan de Nicaragua is located across the bay in Greytown and is one of the few airports in the Americas where you need to take a boat to get on your flight.

La Costeña (www.lacostena.com.ni) is the domestic carrier with a good safety record. It services Bluefields, Bonanza, the Corn Islands, Las Minas, Ometepe, Rosita, San Carlos (via Ometepe), San Juan de Nicaragua, Puerto Cabezas, Siuna and Waspám. Many domestic flights use tiny single-prop planes where weight is important and bags necessarily get left behind, so keep all necessities in your carry-on luggage.

Flights on all routes are grounded in bad weather, but this is actually fairly rare. Normally the worst that happens is delays. The Bluefields–Bilwi flight is typically cancelled unless there is enough demand.

BOAT

Many destinations are accessible only, or most easily, by boat. Public *pangas* (small open motorboats) with outboard motors are much more expensive than road transport – in general it costs around US$6 to US$8 per hour of travel. In places without regular service, you will need to hire your own private *panga*. Prices vary widely, but you'll spend about US$50 to US$100 per hour for four to six people; tour operators can usually find a better deal. It's easy, if not cheap, to hire boat transport up and down the Pacific coast. On the Atlantic side, it's much more difficult. While it's not common, boats do sink here and tourists have drowned – wear your life jacket.

River boats on the Río San Juan tend to be slow and fairly cheap. There are often express and regular services – it's worth paying a bit extra for the quicker version.

Following are the major departure points with regular boat service.

Bluefields To Pearl Lagoon, El Rama and Corn Island.

Corn Islands Regular boats run between Great Corn and Little Corn Islands.

El Rama To Bluefields.

San Carlos To the Islas Solentiname, the Río San Juan, the scenic border crossing to Costa Rica and several natural reserves.

Waspám The gateway to the Río Coco.

BUS

Bus coverage in Nicaragua is extensive although services are often uncomfortable and overcrowded. Public transport is usually on old Bluebird school buses, which means no luggage compartments. Try to avoid putting your backpack on top of the bus, and instead sit toward the back and put it with the sacks of rice and beans.

Pay your fare after the bus starts moving. You may be issued a paper 'ticket' on long-distance buses – don't lose it, or you may be charged again. Some bus terminals allow you to purchase tickets ahead of time, which should in theory guarantee you a seat. While buses sometimes cruise around town before hitting the highway, you're more likely to get a seat by boarding the bus at the station or terminal.

Bus terminals, which are often huge, chaotic lots next to markets, may seem difficult to navigate, particularly if you don't speak much Spanish. Fear not! If you can pronounce your destination, the guys yelling will help you find your bus – just make sure they put you on an *expreso* (express) and not an *ordinario* (ordinary bus) or you'll be spending more time on the road than you planned.

CAR & MOTORCYCLE

Driving is a wonderful way to see Pacific and central Nicaragua, but it's best to use public transportation on the Caribbean side as roads are, for the most part, terrible.

HITCHHIKING

Hitchhiking is never entirely safe, and we don't recommend it. Travelers who hitchhike should understand that they are taking a small but potentially serious risk.

Nevertheless hitchhiking is very common in rural Nicaragua, even by solo women – to find a ride, just stick out your thumb. Foreign women, particularly those carrying all their bags, should think twice before hitchhiking solo. Never hitchhike into or out of Managua.

In rural areas where bus service is rare, anyone driving a pickup truck will almost certainly stop for you. Climb into the back tray (unless specifically invited up front) and when you want to get off, tap on the cabin roof a couple of times.

You should always offer to pay the driver, which will almost always be refused.

LOCAL TRANSPORTATION

In smaller towns there are fewer taxis and more tuk-tuks (motorized three wheelers) and *triciclos* (bicycle rickshaws). They're inexpensive – around US$0.50 per person to go anywhere in town – and kind of fun. Tuk-tuks are also the easiest and quickest way to get between the Pueblos Blancos near Masaya.

TAXI

Almost all taxis in Nicaragua are *colectivos* (shared taxi or minibus), which stop and pick up other clients en route to your destination; however, it is always possible to pay a bit extra for an express service.

Managua taxis are unmetered and notorious for ripping off tourists. Always negotiate the fare before getting in. Taxis at major border crossings may also overcharge, given the chance.

Most other city taxis have set in-town fares, usually around US$0.50 to US$0.70, rising slightly at night. Ask a local how much a fare should cost before getting into the cab.

Hiring taxis between cities is a comfortable and reasonable option for midrange travelers. Prices vary widely, but expect to pay around US$10 for every 20km.

Costa Rica

☎506 / POP 4.97 MILLION

Includes ➡

Best Places to Eat

➡ La Bodega (p579)

➡ Jalapeños Central (p536)

➡ Bread & Chocolate (p552)

➡ La Ventanita (p557)

Best Places to Sleep

➡ Hostel Casa del Parque (p521)

➡ Room 2 Board Hostel & Surf School (p589)

➡ Camp Supertramp (p581)

➡ Casa de Lis Hostel (p540)

Why Go?

The bellowing of howler monkeys echoes across the treetops. Magnificent frigate birds circle high overhead, while less-than-sonorous squawking reveals a pair of scarlet macaws. Morning is breaking in the coastal rainforest. Similar scenes unfold across Costa Rica, from the dry tropical forest along the Pacific coast to the misty cloud forest at higher altitudes. Close to one-third of this country's area is protected, making it a wildlife wonderland. The flora and fauna are only part of the appeal. Annually Costa Rica attracts more than two million visitors eager to catch a wave, climb a volcano or otherwise partake of paradise.

It's never easy to maintain the delicate balance between preserving natural resources and cashing in on economic opportunity, but Ticos are tireless in their efforts. These peace-loving people are eager to share the staggering scenery, bountiful biodiversity and complete contentment of *pura vida,* the 'pure life' of Costa Rica.

When to Go

San José

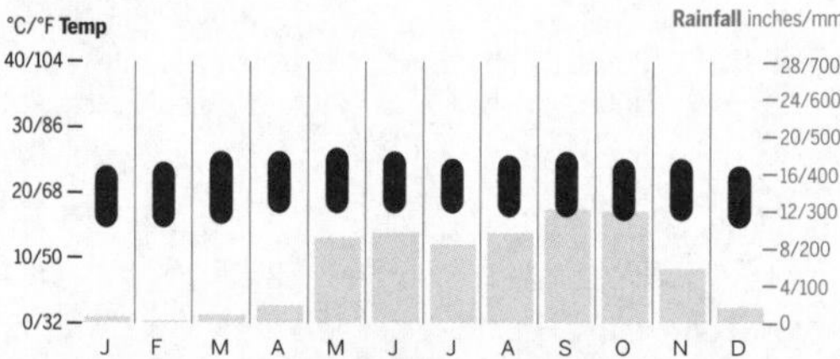

Jan–Apr
The 'dry' season sees consistently hot temperatures and sunny skies.

May–Jul
Crowds thin out and prices drop during the 'green' rainy season.

Dec
The holidays are festive, though accommodation prices skyrocket.

Entering the Country

Costa Rica shares land borders with Nicaragua and Panama. There is no fee for travelers to enter Costa Rica, but visas may be required for certain nationalities. There have also been reports of towns adding their own entry and exit fees, usually US$1.

TWO-WEEK ITINERARY

From **San José**, beeline north to **La Fortuna**. After a refreshing forest hike on the flanks of Volcán Arenal, soak in the country's best hot springs. Then do the classic jeep-boat-jeep run across **Lake Arenal**, and a bus to Monteverde, where you might encounter the elusive quetzal on a stroll through the Bosque Nuboso Monteverde. Next: beach time. Head west to the biggest party town in Guanacaste, **Playa Tamarindo,** and enjoy the ideal surf, top-notch restaurants and rowdy nightlife.

In week two, visit waterfalls and linger a bit in chilled-out **Montezuma**, where you can connect via speedboat to **Jacó**, a town with equal affection for surfing and partying. Spend half a day busing to Quepos, the gateway to **Parque Nacional Manuel Antonio**. A full day in the park starts with some jungle hikes and wildlife-watching and ends with a picnic and a dip in the park's perfect waters.

Essential Food & Drink

Guanabana Sweet and sticky fruit, also known as soursop.

Patí Caribbean version of *empanada*.

Street mango Sold in plastic bags with salt, lime juice and sometimes chili powder.

Gallo pinto Stir-fry of rice and beans.

Casado Inexpensive set meal; also means married.

Top Tips

- In Costa Rica, things have a way of taking longer than expected (Tico time). Don't overschedule, learn to relax into delays and take these opportunities to get to know the locals.
- Avoid driving at night – pedestrians, animals and huge potholes are difficult to see on Costa Rica's largely unlit roads. Also keep an eye out for impatient drivers passing on two-lane roads – tailgating is a national custom.
- Take public transport. There's no better way to get to know the country or its people.
- If you need directions, ask a few different people.
- It's often cash-only in remote areas. Keep a stash of colones or dollars, because ATMs do run out.
- Ticos use quite a lot of local slang, so even experienced Spanish speakers might need to adjust.

FAST FACTS

Currency Costa Rican colón (₡), US dollar ($)

Visas Generally not required for stays less than 90 days.

Money ATMs are ubiquitous; credit and debit cards widely accepted.

Capital San José

Emergency ☎911

Languages Spanish, English

Exchange Rates

Australia	A$1	₡431
Canada	C$1	₡462
Euro zone	€1	₡692
Japan	¥100	₡545
New Zealand	NZ$1	₡415
UK	£1	₡607
USA	US$1	₡608

Daily Costs

- Dorm bed: US$8–15; basic double room with private bathroom: US$20–50
- Meal at a *soda* (inexpensive eatery): US$3–7; at a restaurant geared toward travelers: US$5–12

Resources

Lonely Planet (www.lonelyplanet.com/costa-rica)

Costa Rica Tourism Board (www.visitcostarica.com)

Yo Viajo (www.yoviajocr.com)

Tico Times (www.ticotimes.net)

Costa Rica Highlights

1 Tortuguero (p541) Sliding silently through jungle canals in search of wildlife or volunteering to protect endangered sea turtles.

2 Puerto Viejo de Talamanca (p549) Surfing, sampling the culinary scene, lazing on the beach and partying.

3 La Fortuna (p554) Hiking the slopes of Volcán Arenal, then soothing your weary muscles with a soak in volcano-heated pools.

4 Monteverde (p561) Spotting the resplendent quetzal through the mist at one of the nearby reserves.

5 Mal País & Santa Teresa (p583) Surfing luscious breaks and feasting on farm-fresh cooking.

6 Parque Nacional Manuel Antonio (p593) Watching troops of monkeys, slow-moving sloths and gliding brown pelicans.

7 Cerro Chirripó (p605) Climbing atop Costa Rica's tallest peak to watch the sunrise.

8 Parque Nacional Corcovado (p607) Hiking the remote coast and rich rainforest in the country's premier wilderness experience.

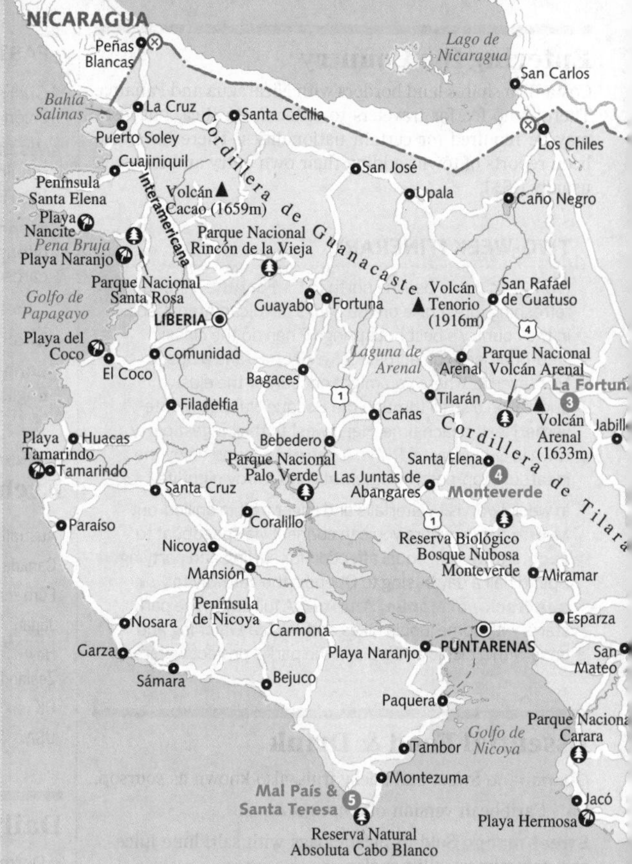

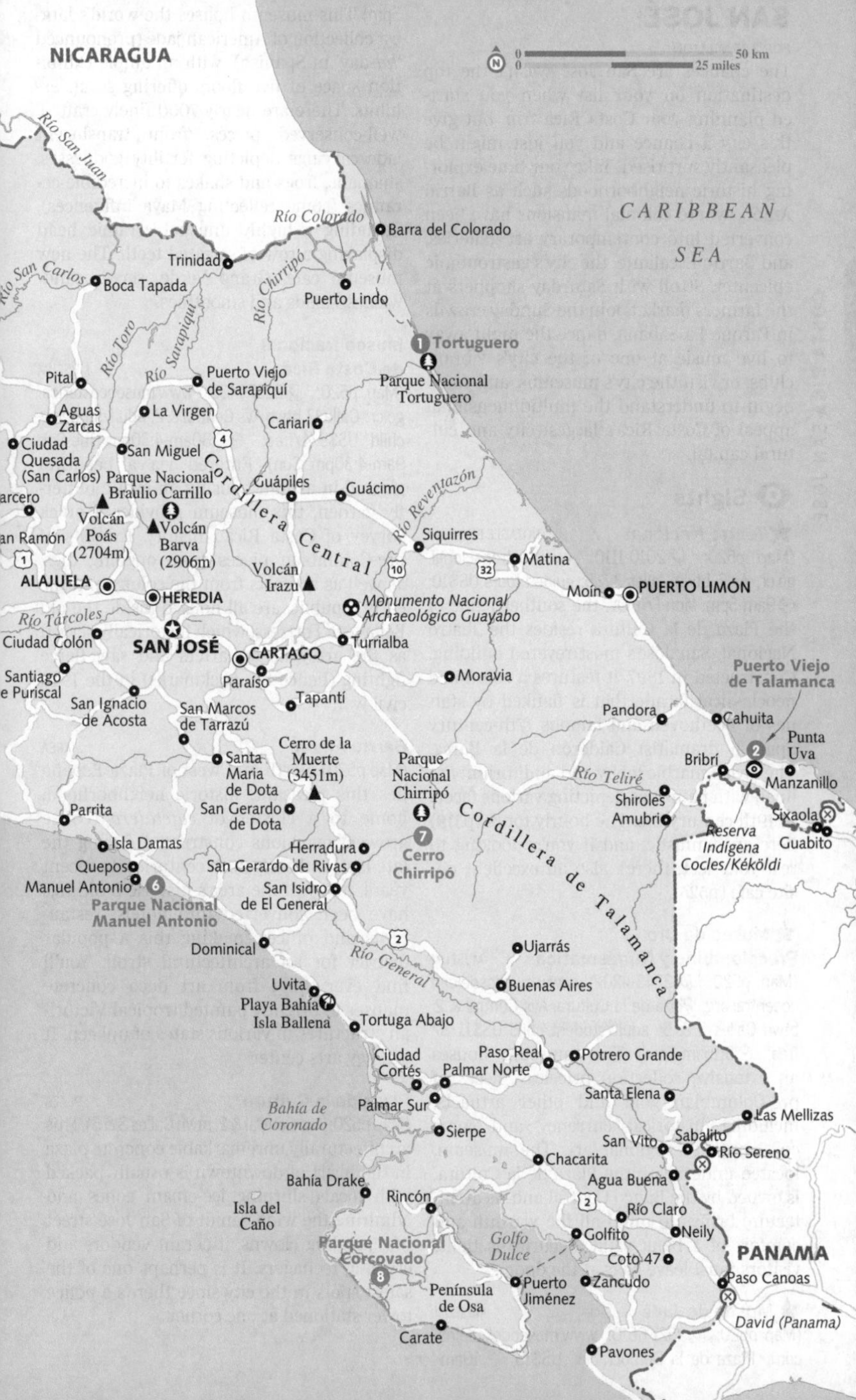

NICARAGUA
0 50 km
0 25 miles
CARIBBEAN SEA
Río San Juan
Río Colorado
Barra del Colorado
Trinidad
Río San Carlos
Boca Tapada
Río Chirripó
Puerto Lindo
Río Sarapiquí
Río Toro
1 Tortuguero
Parque Nacional Tortuguero
Pital
Puerto Viejo de Sarapiquí
Aguas Zarcas
La Virgen
Cariari
Ciudad Quesada (San Carlos)
San Miguel
Parque Nacional Braulio Carrillo
Cordillera Central
Guápiles
Guácimo
Río Reventazón
Volcán Poás (2704m)
Volcán Barva (2906m)
San Ramón
Siquirres
Matina
Volcán Irazu
ALAJUELA
HEREDIA
Moín
PUERTO LIMÓN
Monumento Nacional Archaeológico Guayabo
Río Tárcoles
Ciudad Colón
SAN JOSÉ
CARTAGO
Turrialba
Paraíso
Moravia
Santiago de Puriscal
San Ignacio de Acosta
Tapantí
Puerto Viejo de Talamanca
San Marcos de Tarrazú
Pandora
Cahuita
Cerro de la Muerte (3451m)
Santa Maria de Dota
Parque Nacional Chirripó
2
Punta Uva
Bribrí
Manzanillo
Río Teliré
Parrita
San Gerardo de Dota
Shiroles
Amubri
Sixaola
Guabito
7 Cerro Chirripó
Cordillera de Talamanca
Reserva Indígena Cocles/Kéköldi
Isla Damas
Herradura
Quepos
San Gerardo de Rivas
Manuel Antonio
6 Parque Nacional Manuel Antonio
San Isidro de El General
Dominical
Ujarrás
Río General
Uvita
Buenas Aires
Playa Bahía Isla Ballena
Tortuga Abajo
Paso Real
Potrero Grande
Ciudad Cortés
Palmar Norte
Santa Elena
Bahía de Coronado
Palmar Sur
Las Mellizas
Sierpe
Sabalito
San Vito
Río Sereno
Chacarita
Agua Buena
Bahía Drake
Rincón
Isla del Caño
Río Claro
Golfito
Neily
Golfo Dulce
Parque Nacional Corcovado
8
PANAMA
Coto 47
Puerto Jiménez
Zancudo
Paso Canoas
Península de Osa
David (Panama)
Carate
Pavones

SAN JOSÉ

POP 2.15 MILLION

The chances are San José wasn't the top destination on your list when you started planning your Costa Rica trip, but give this city a chance and you just might be pleasantly surprised. Take your time exploring historic neighborhoods such as Barrio Amón, where colonial mansions have been converted into contemporary art galleries, and Barrio Escalante, the city's gastronomic epicenter. Stroll with Saturday shoppers at the farmers market, join the Sunday crowds in Parque La Sabana, dance the night away to live music at one of the city's vibrant clubs, or visit the city's museums, and you'll begin to understand the multidimensional appeal of Costa Rica's largest city and cultural capital.

Sights

★Teatro Nacional — NOTABLE BUILDING

(Map p520; 2010-1110; www.teatronacional.go.cr; Av 2, btwn Calles 3 & 5; guided tours US$10; 9am-5pm, Mon-Fri) On the southern side of the Plaza de la Cultura resides the Teatro Nacional, San José's most revered building. Constructed in 1897, it features a columned neoclassical facade that is flanked by statues of Beethoven and famous 17th-century Spanish dramatist Calderón de la Barca. The lavish marble lobby and auditorium are lined with paintings depicting various facets of 19th-century life. The hourly tours (p519) here are fantastic, and if you're looking to rest your feet, there's also an excellent onsite cafe (p525).

★Museo de Oro Precolombino y Numismática — MUSEUM

(Map p520; 2243-4202; www.museosdelbancocentral.org; Plaza de la Cultura, Avs Central & 2, btwn Calles 3 & 5; adult/student/child US$11/8/free; 9:15am-5pm) This museum houses an extensive collection priceless pieces of pre-Columbian gold and other artifacts, including historical currency and some contemporary regional art. The museum, located underneath the Plaza de la Cultura, is owned by the Banco Central and its architecture brings to mind all the warmth and comfort of a bank vault. Security is tight; visitors must leave bags at the door.

★Museo de Jade — MUSEUM

(Map p520; 2521-6610; www.museodeljadeins.com; Plaza de la Democracia; US$15; 10am-5pm) This museum houses the world's largest collection of American jade (pronounced '*ha*-day' in Spanish), with an ample exhibition space of five floors offering seven exhibits. There are nearly 7000 finely crafted, well-conserved pieces, from translucent jade carvings depicting fertility goddesses, shamans, frogs and snakes to incredible ceramics (some reflecting Maya influences), including a highly unusual ceramic head displaying a row of serrated teeth. The new museum cafe, Grano Verde, serves sandwiches, salads and smoothies.

Museo Nacional de Costa Rica — MUSEUM

(Map p520; 2257-1433; www.museocostarica.go.cr; Calle 17, btwn Avs Central & 2; adult/student/child US$9/4/free; 8:30am-4:30pm Tue-Sat, 9am-4:30pm Sun) Entered via a beautiful glassed-in atrium housing an exotic butterfly garden, this museum provides a quick survey of Costa Rican history. Exhibits of pre-Columbian pieces from ongoing digs, as well as artifacts from the colony and the early republic, are all housed inside the old Bellavista Fortress, which historically served as the army headquarters and saw fierce fighting (hence the pockmarks) in the 1948 civil war.

Barrio Amón — AREA

(Map p520) North and west of Plaza España lies this pleasant, historic neighborhood, home to a cluster of *cafetalero* (coffee grower) mansions constructed during the late 19th and early 20th centuries. In recent years, many of the area's historic buildings have been converted into hotels, restaurants and offices, making this a popular district for an architectural stroll. You'll find everything from art deco concrete manses to brightly painted tropical Victorian structures in various states of upkeep. It is a key arts center.

Plaza de la Cultura — PLAZA

(Map p520; Avs Central & 2, btwn Calles 3 & 5) This architecturally unremarkable concrete plaza in the heart of downtown is usually packed with locals slurping ice-cream cones and admiring the wide gamut of San José street life: juggling clowns, itinerant vendors and cruising teenagers. It is perhaps one of the safest spots in the city since there's a police tower stationed at one corner.

Parque Nacional PARK

(Map p520; Avs 1 & 3, btwn Calles 15 & 19) One of San José's nicest green spaces, this shady spot lures retirees to read newspapers and young couples to smooch coyly on concrete benches. At its center is the Monumento Nacional, a dramatic 1953 statue that depicts the Central American nations driving out North American filibuster William Walker. The park is dotted with myriad monuments devoted to Latin American historical figures, including Cuban poet, essayist and revolutionary José Martí, Mexican independence figure Miguel Hidalgo and 18th-century Venezuelan humanist Andrés Bello.

Museo de Arte y Diseño Contemporáneo MUSEUM

(MADC; Map p520; ☎2257-7202; www.madc.cr; cnr Av 3 & Calle 15; US$3, 1st Tue free; ⊙9:30am-5pm Tue-Sat) Commonly referred to as MADC, the Contemporary Art & Design Museum is housed in the historic National Liquor Factory building, which dates from 1856. The largest and most important contemporary-art museum in the region, MADC is focused on the works of contemporary Costa Rican, Central American and South American artists, and occasionally features temporary exhibits devoted to interior design, fashion and graphic art.

Parque Metropolitano La Sabana PARK

(Map p526) Once the site of San José's main airport, this 72-hectare green space at the west end of Paseo Colón is home to a regional art **museum** (Map p526; ☎2256-1281; www.musarco.go.cr; east entrance of Parque La Sabana; ⊙9am-4pm Tue-Sun; 👪) FREE, a lagoon and various sporting facilities – most notably Costa Rica's **National Stadium**. During the day, the park's paths make a relaxing place for a stroll, a jog or a picnic.

Tours

★Really Experience Community TOURS

(Triángulo de la Solidaridad Slum Tour; ☎2297-7058; www.boywithaball.com; per person US$12-25, minimum group rate $100) Nonprofit Boy with a Ball wants to be clear: this is not your average slum tour. It may seem exploitative, but visiting El Triángulo, a squatter development of 2000 people north of San José, is anything but. Promising young residents lead tours, introducing guests to neighbors and community entrepreneurs. No cameras are allowed, but the conversations make a lasting impression.

Teatro Nacional CULTURAL

(Map p520; ☎ext 1114 2010-1100; www.teatronacional.go.cr/Visitenos/turismo; Av 2, btwn Calles 3 & 5; tours US$10; ⊙9am-4pm) On this fascinating tour, guests are regaled with stories of the art, architecture and people behind Costa Rica's crown jewel, the National Theater. The best part is a peek into otherwise off-limits areas, such as the Smoking Room, which features famous paintings, lavish antique furnishings and ornate gold trim.

ChepeCletas TOURS

(Map p520; ☎8849-8316; www.chepecletas.com; Sat morning walking tours per person US$10) This dynamic Tico-run company offers excellent private tours focusing on history, culture, food markets, coffee and nightlife. Its ever-changing menu of offerings also includes informative walks around San José

TALK LIKE A TICO

San José is loaded with schools that offer Spanish lessons (either privately or in groups) and provide long-term visitors to the country with everything from dance lessons to volunteer opportunities. Well-established options include the following:

Costa Rican Language Academy (Map p525; ☎2280-1685, USA 866-230-6361; www.spanishandmore.com; Calle Ronda, Barrio Dent)

Institute for Central American Development Studies (ICADS; ☎2225-0508; www.icads.org; Calle 87A, Curridabat; month-long courses with/without homestay US$1990/915)

Personalized Spanish (☎2278-3254, USA 786-245-4124; www.personalizedspanish.com; Tres Ríos)

Already speak Spanish? To truly talk like a Tico, check out the **Costa Rica Idioms** app, available for iOS. It's quite basic but defines local lingo and uses each term in a sentence. *Tuanis, mae!* (Cool, dude!)

San José

on Saturday mornings and free bike tours on Wednesdays at 7pm (and occasionally on Sunday mornings as well).

Carpe Chepe TOURS

(8347-6198; www.carpechepe.com; guided pub crawls US$20; 8pm Fri & Sat) For an insider's look at Chepe's nightlife, join one of these Friday- and Saturday-evening guided pub crawls, led by an enthusiastic group of young locals. A shot is included at each of the four bars visited. There are other offerings as well, including a hop-on, hop-off nightlife bus, food tours, a craft-beer tour and free walking tours of San José.

Festivals & Events

Las Fiestas de Zapote CULTURAL

(www.fiestas.cr/zapote; Zapote; late Dec-early Jan) Between Christmas and New Year, this week-long celebration of all things Costa Rican draws tens of thousands of Ticos to the bullring in the suburb of Zapote, just southeast of San José.

Sleeping

You'll find the cheapest sleeps in the city center, with nicer midrange and top-end spots clustered in more well-to-do districts such as Barrio Amón and La Sabana. Also

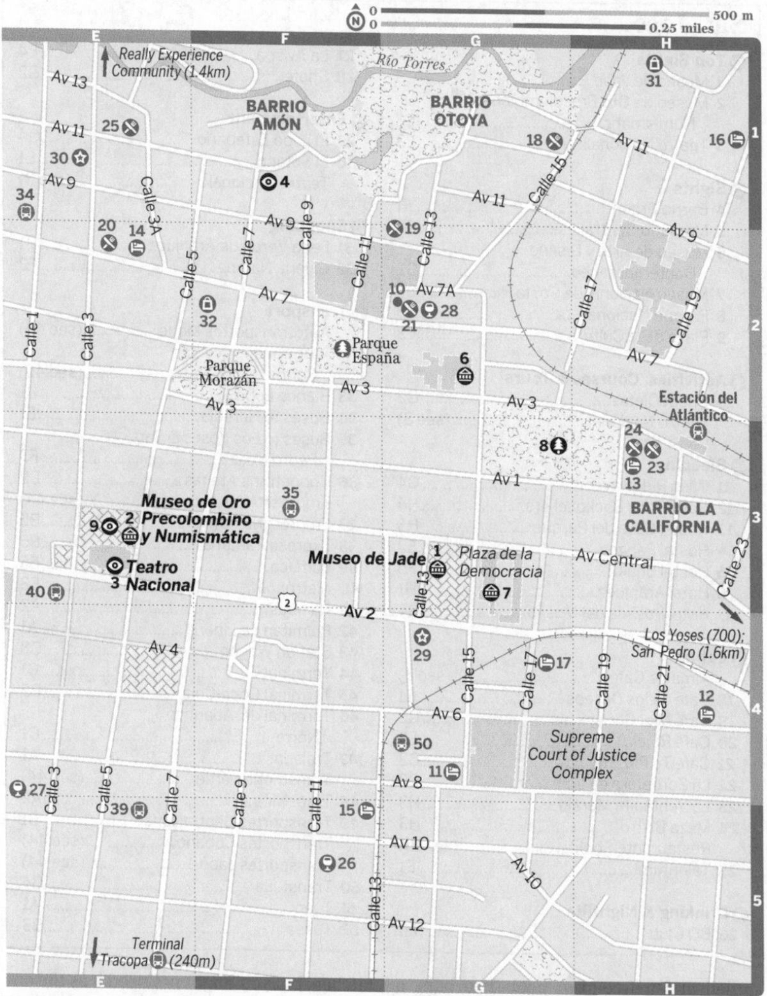

worthwhile for their charm, safety and serenity are the adjacent neighborhoods of Los Yoses and San Pedro, which lie within walking distance of downtown. For stylish options, the upscale suburbs of Escazú and Santa Ana are good choices.

Central San José

★Hostel Casa del Parque HOSTEL $

(Map p520; ☎2233-3437; www.hostelcasadelparque.com; Calle 19, btwn Avs 1 & 3; dm US$14, d with/without bathroom US$49/39;) A vintage art deco manse from 1936 houses this cozy and welcoming spot on the northeastern edge of Parque Nacional. Five large, basic private rooms (two with private bathroom), a newer seven-bed dormitory and an older 10-bed dormitory upstairs have parquet floors and simple furnishings. Enjoy some sun on the plant-festooned outdoor patio and take advantage of the shared kitchen.

Costa Rica Backpackers HOSTEL $

(Map p520; ☎2221-6191; www.costaricabackpackers.com; Av 6, near Calle 21; dm US$9-14, d without bathroom US$35;) This popular hostel has 19 basic but clean dormitories and 14 private rooms with shared bathrooms surrounding a spacious hammock-filled

San José

Top Sights
1 Museo de Jade G3
2 Museo de Oro Precolombino y Numismática E3
3 Teatro Nacional E3

Sights
4 Barrio Amón F1
5 Mercado Central C3
6 Museo de Arte y Diseño Contemporáneo G2
7 Museo Nacional de Costa Rica G3
8 Parque Nacional G3
9 Plaza de la Cultura E3

Activities, Courses & Tours
10 ChepeCletas G2
Teatro Nacional .... (see 3)

Sleeping
11 Casa Ridgway G4
12 Costa Rica Backpackers H4
13 Hostel Casa del Parque H3
14 Hostel Pangea E2
15 Hostel Shakti F5
16 Hotel Aranjuez H1
17 Hotel Posada del Museo G4

Eating
Alma de Café .... (see 3)
18 Café de los Deseos G1
19 Café Miel Garage G2
20 Café Rojo E2
21 Café Té Ría G2
22 La Sorbetera de Lolo Mora C3
23 La Ventanita Meraki H3
24 Maza Bistro H3
Restaurante Shakti .... (see 15)
25 Talentum E1

Drinking & Nightlife
26 BO Club F5
27 La Avispa E4
28 Stiefel G2

Entertainment
29 El Lobo Estepario G4
30 El Sótano E1
Teatro Nacional .... (see 3)

Shopping
31 Feria Verde de Aranjuez H1
32 Galería Namu F2

Transport
Autotransportes Mepe .... (see 46)
Autotransportes San Carlos .... (see 46)
33 Blanco Lobo B1
34 Buses to Heredia E1
35 Buses to Los Yoses & San Pedro F3
36 Coopetrans Atenas B2
Empresa Alfaro .... (see 44)
37 Empresarios Unidos B5
38 Expreso Panamá B5
39 Lumaca E5
40 Metrópoli E3
41 Nicabus A2
42 Pulmitan de Liberia A1
43 Station Wagon C3
44 Terminal 7-10 .... C1
45 Terminal Coca-Cola B2
46 Terminal del Atlántico Norte C1
47 Tralapa A1
Transmonteverde .... (see 44)
48 TransNica A2
49 Transportes Central Line B1
Transportes Cobano .... (see 44)
Transportes Jacó .... (see 44)
50 Transtusa G4
51 Tuan A1
52 Tuasa B3

garden and a free-form pool. Two bars, a restaurant and chill-out music enhance the inviting, laid-back atmosphere. Other benefits include a communal kitchen and TV lounge, free luggage storage, internet access, an on-site travel agency and low-cost airport transfers ($26).

Hostel Shakti HOSTEL $
(Map p520; 2221-4631; cnr Av 8 & Calle 13; dm/s/d incl breakfast US$18/30/40; P ❄ @) A lovely little guesthouse using bold colors and natural materials to create an oasis of calm and comfort amid the chaos of San José. Three dorms and four private rooms are dressed up with eclectic furnishings and colorful bedding. There is a fully equipped kitchen, but you might not need it as the on-site restaurant (p526) is healthy, fresh and amazing.

Casa Ridgway GUESTHOUSE $
(Map p520; 2222-1400, 2233-6168; www.casaridgwayhostel.com; cnr Calle 15 & Av 6A; incl breakfast dm US$17, s/d without bathroom US$24/38; P) A small, peaceful guesthouse on a quiet side street run by the adjacent Friends' Peace Center, a Quaker organization promoting social justice and human rights. There is a small lounge, a communal kitchen and a lending library filled with books about Central American politics and society. No smoking or alcohol is allowed, with quiet hours from 10pm to 6am.

Hostel Pangea HOSTEL $$

(Map p520; ☎2221-1992; www.hostelpangea.com; Av 7, btwn Calles 3 & 3A, Barrio Amón; dm US$14, d with/without bathroom US$45/34, ste from US$55; P@☎≋) An industrial-strength hostel – 25 dorm beds and 25 private rooms – which has been a popular 20-something backpacker hangout for years. It's not difficult to see why: it's smack in the middle of the city and comes stocked with a pool and a rooftop restaurant-lounge with stellar views. Needless to say, it's a party spot.

Hotel Aranjuez HOTEL $$

(Map p520; ☎2256-1825; www.hotelaranjuez.com; Calle 19, btwn Avs 11 & 13; d incl breakfast US$45-95; P@☎) This hotel in Barrio Aranjuez consists of five nicely maintained vintage homes that have been strung together with a labyrinth of gardens and connecting walkways. The 35 spotless rooms come in various configurations, all with a lockbox and a cable TV. The hotel's best attribute, however, is the lush garden patio, where a legendary breakfast buffet is served every morning.

Luz de Luna BOUTIQUE HOTEL $$

(Map p525; ☎2225-4919; www.luzdelunahotelboutique.com; Calle 33, btwn Avs 3 & 5; r US$46-75; ☎) A converted old mansion, this boutique hotel, restaurant and cafe is in a prime location: the heart of Barrio Escalante's Paseo Gastronómico La Luz district and its up-and-coming restaurants. Foodies who like to relax will appreciate this sanctuary and self-described 'lunar complex' for its lush gardens, hardwood floors and occasional pre-Columbian statues.

Hotel Posada del Museo GUESTHOUSE $$

(Map p520; ☎2258-1027; www.hotelposadadelmuseo.com; cnr Calle 17 & Av 2; s/d/tr/q incl breakfast US$40/51/65/79; @☎) Managed by an amiable, multilingual couple, this architecturally intriguing, 1928 vintage inn is diagonally across from the Museo Nacional. French doors line the entrances to each of the rooms, no two of which are alike. Some rooms accommodate up to four people, making this a family-friendly option. Light sleepers, take note: the hotel is adjacent to the train tracks.

La Sabana & Around

Gaudy's HOSTEL $

(Map p526; ☎2248-0086; www.backpacker.co.cr; Av 5, btwn Calles 36 & 38; dm US$13-14, r with/without bathroom US$39/35; P@☎) Popular among shoestring travelers for years, this homey hostel inside a sprawling modernist house northeast of Parque La Sabana has 13 private rooms and two dormitories. The owners keep the design scheme minimalist and the vibe mellow, with professional service and well-maintained rooms. There's a communal kitchen, a TV lounge, a pool table and a courtyard strung with hammocks.

Mi Casa Hostel HOSTEL $

(Map p526; ☎2231-4700; www.micasahostel.com; Las Américas; incl breakfast dm US$15, r with/without bathroom from US$43/40; P@☎) This converted modernist home in La Sabana has polished-wood floors, vintage furnishings and over a dozen eclectic guest rooms to choose from, including one large dorm and another room that's wheelchair-accessible. Mellow communal areas are comfortably furnished, and the shared kitchen is clean and roomy. There is a pleasant garden, a pool table, free internet and a laundry service. They also have locations in Playa Grande and Playa Cocles in Puerto Viejo, if you're headed that way.

La Rosa del Paseo BOUTIQUE HOTEL $$

(Map p526; ☎2257-3225; http://larosadelpaseo.com; Paseo Colón, btwn Calles 28 & 30; s/d/ste from US$72/80/90; P@☎) Don't let the Paseo Colón location and the small facade fool you: this sprawling Victorian-Caribbean mansion (built in 1910 by the coffee-exporting Montealegre family) has 18 spacious rooms reaching way back into an interior courtyard far from the city noise. The revamped hotel maintains the original tile floors and other historic details, including antique oil paintings and sculptures.

Colours Oasis Resort BOUTIQUE HOTEL $$

(☎2296-1880, USA & Canada 866-517-4390; www.coloursoasis.com; cnr Triángulo de Pavas & Blvr Rohrmoser; r US$55-200; ☎≋) This longtime LGBTIQ-friendly hotel occupies a sprawling Key West–style complex in the elegant Rohrmoser district (northwest of La Sabana). Rooms and mini-apartments have modern furnishings and impeccable bathrooms. Facilities include a TV lounge, pool, sundeck and Jacuzzi, as well as an international restaurant, ideal for evening cocktails.

Los Yoses & San Pedro

Locals use several prominent landmarks when giving directions, including Spoon restaurant, the Fuente de la Hispanidad fountain and Más x Menos supermarket.

★Hostel Bekuo HOSTEL $
(Map p525; ☎2234-1091, USA 1-813-750-8572; www.hostelbekuo.com; Av 8; dm US$13, d from US$32; 📶) For pure positive energy, you won't find a nicer hostel in San José. This restful spot, in a hip area of Los Yoses just a block south of Av Central, feels extremely homey, thanks to frequent backyard BBQs, a living room with piano and guitar, and a kitchen equipped with good knives, appliances and an inviting work space.

Hostel Urbano HOSTEL $
(Map p525; ☎2281-0707; www.hostelurbano.com; Calle 39; dm/d US$12/35) Within easy walking distance of the university and its nightlife, yet right on the bus line into downtown San José, this immaculate hostel is in a 1950s home opposite Parque Kennedy in San Pedro. Guests feel instantly welcome, with its open floor plan, spacious backyard, pool table, modern internet facilities and a kitchen-dining area nice enough for a dinner party.

Hostel Casa Yoses HOSTEL $
(Map p525; ☎2234-5486; www.casayoses.hostel.com; Av 8, Los Yoses; incl breakfast dm US$10-15, d with/without bathroom US$38/33; P@📶) A mellow place, this Spanish Revival–style house from 1949 is perched on a hill and offers lovely views of the valley from the front garden. Here you'll find 10 rooms (three of them dorms) of varying decor and style, all of which are spotless, with wooden floors and tiled hallways.

Hotel Ave del Paraíso HOTEL $$
(Map p525; ☎2283-6017, 2225-8515; www.hotelavedelparaiso.com; Paseo de la Segunda Republica; s/d incl breakfast US$68/79; @📶) 🌿 Decorated with beautiful mosaic tiles, this hotel run by an artsy family is set back from the busy street just far enough to permit a good night's sleep. There's a wonderful restaurant and bar, Café Kracovia (p527), owned by the same family. The university is just a two-minute walk east.

Hotel Milvia B&B $$
(☎2225-4543; www.hotelmilvia.com; cnr Calle 75 & Av 1; s/d incl breakfast US$59/69; @📶) Owned by a well-known Costa Rican artist and former museum director, this lovely Caribbean-style building offers a homey retreat from the city. Nine eclectic rooms, all dotted with bright artwork, surround a pleasant courtyard with a trickling fountain. An upstairs terrace provides views of the mountains.

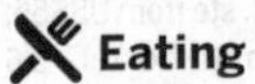

Eating

From humble corner stands dishing out gut-filling *casados* (set meals) to contemporary bistros serving fusion everything, in cosmopolitan San José you'll find the country's best restaurant scene.

Central San José

The city's hectic commercial heart has some of the cheapest eats in town. One of the best places for a budget-priced lunch is the **Mercado Central** (Map p520; www.facebook.com/Mercado-Central-de-San-José-Costa-Rica-132271433523797; Avs Central & 1, btwn Calles 6 & 8; ⏲6:30am-6pm Mon-Sat), where you'll find a variety of *sodas* serving *casados*, tamales, seafood and everything in between.

★Café de los Deseos CAFE $
(Map p520; ☎2222-0496; www.facebook.com/Cafedelosdeseos; Calle 15, btwn Avs 9 & 11; mains US$5-12; ⏲11:30am-10pm Tue-Thu, to 11pm Fri & Sat; 📶) Abuzz with artsy young bohemians, this colorful Barrio Otoya cafe makes a romantic spot for drinks (from wine to cocktails to smoothies), *bocas* (handmade tortillas with Turrialba cheese, salads, teriyaki chicken, individual pizzas) and tempting desserts. Walls are hung with the work of local artists and rooms are adorned with hand-painted tables, beaded curtains and branches entwined with fairy lights.

★Café Rojo CAFE $
(Map p520; ☎2221-2425; www.facebook.com/elcaferojo; cnr Av 7 & Calle 3; coffee US$1.50-4, mains US$7-10; ⏲noon-7pm Mon-Thu, to 8pm Fri & Sat, noon-7pm Sun; 🖉) This quaint cafe with a towering cactus out front uses the fresh produce of Costa Rica to create innovative lunch specials, such as Vietnamese noodle bowls and sandwiches with pork meatballs or caramel chicken, and mind-blowingly delicious salads. Vegans will find plenty to like here, as will coffee enthusiasts.

La Sorbetera de Lolo Mora DESSERTS $
(Map p520; ☎2256-5000; www.facebook.com/Lolomora1901; Mercado Central, Avs Central & 1, btwn Calles 6 & 8; desserts US$2-5; ⏲9:30am-5:30pm Mon-Sat) Head to the main market for dessert at this century-old local favorite that serves up fresh sorbet and cinnamon-laced

Los Yoses, Barrio Escalante & San Pedro

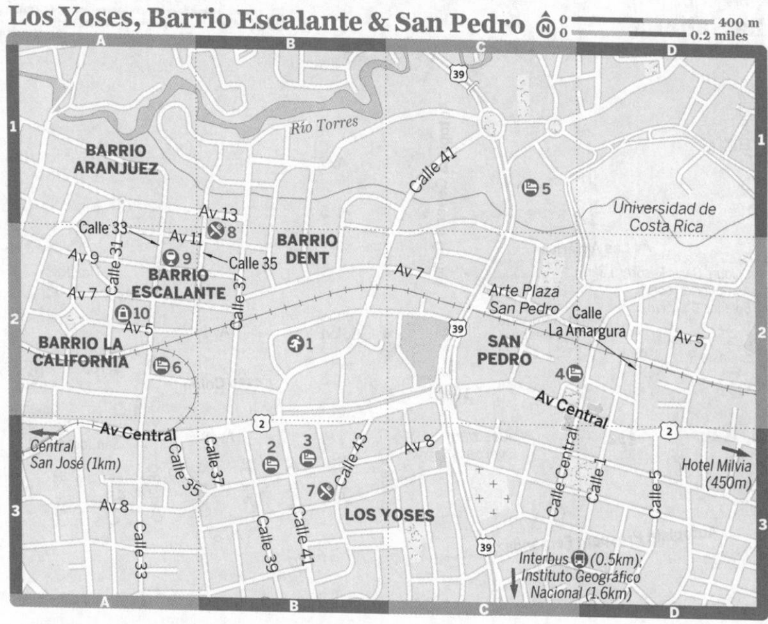

Los Yoses, Barrio Escalante & San Pedro

Activities, Courses & Tours
1 Costa Rican Language Academy B2

Sleeping
2 Hostel Bekuo B3
3 Hostel Casa Yoses B3
4 Hostel Urbano C2
5 Hotel Ave del Paraíso C1
6 Luz de Luna A2

Eating
7 El Portón Rojo B3
8 Mantras Veggie Cafe and Tea House B2

Drinking & Nightlife
9 Wilk A2

Shopping
10 Kiosco SJO A2

frozen custard. Do as the locals do and order *barquillos* (cylindrical sugar cookies that are perfect for dipping).

Alma de Café CAFE $
(Map p520; ☎2010-1119; www.teatronacional.go.cr/Cafeteria; Teatro Nacional, Av 2, btwn Calles 3 & 5; mains US$6-11; ⏲9am-7pm Mon-Sat, to 6pm Sun) One of the most beautiful cafes in the city, this atmospheric spot evokes early-20th-century Vienna. In other words, it's a perfect place to sip a cappuccino, enjoy a crepe or quiche and take in the lovely ceiling frescoes and rotating art exhibitions. The spiked coffee concoctions are an excellent midday indulgence.

Talentum CAFE $
(Restaurante Tournant; Map p520; ☎2256-6346, restaurant 2248-9523; www.galeriatalentum.com; Av 11, btwn Calles 3 & 3A; lunch specials US$8-12; ⏲restaurant noon-4pm Mon & Tue, noon-10pm Wed-Fri, 1pm-10pm Sat, gallery 11am-6pm Mon-Sat) This vibrant, quirky cultural space in a renovated mansion runs the gamut from cafe to art gallery. Sporting local artwork inside and out, with cozy seating on vintage couches and an outdoor deck, it's a fun place for a midday break. The ever-changing cultural agenda includes book signings, films, anatomical drawing classes and occasional live music. The gallery may stay open later than 6pm on Saturdays depending on the event.

Café Miel Garage CAFE $
(Map p520; www.cafemielgarage.com; Av 9, btwn Calle 11 & 13; coffee US$1-5, pastries US$2; ⏲9am-6pm Mon-Fri, 1:30-6pm Sat & Sun) This tiny cafe opened to such wild success in 2014 that the

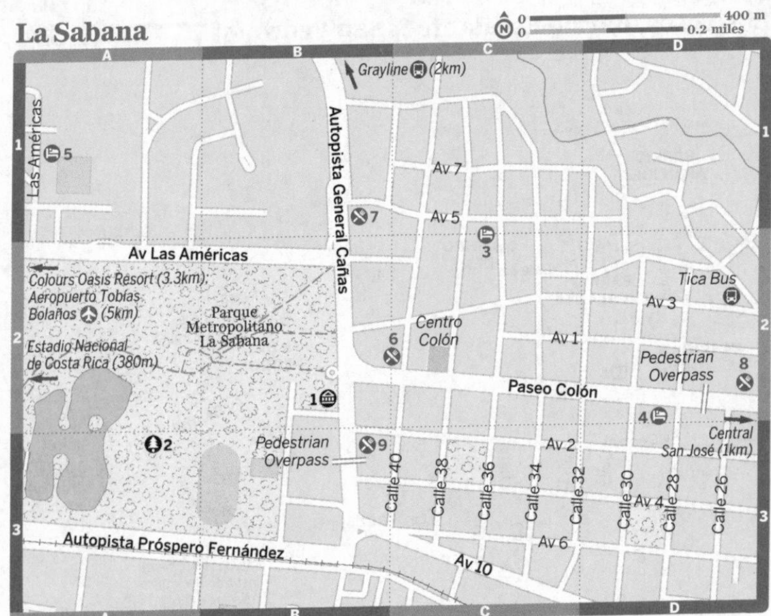

La Sabana

Sights
1 Museo de Arte Costarricense.............B2
2 Parque Metropolitano La Sabana.......A3

Sleeping
3 Gaudy's.............C2
4 La Rosa del Paseo.............D2
5 Mi Casa Hostel.............A1

Eating
6 Las Mañanitas.............C2
7 Más X Menos.............B1
8 Palí.............D2
9 Soda Tapia.............B3

owners quickly opened two more nearby. What's its secret? In addition to adorable and homey interiors, it's the artisanal products from the chefs and bakers. The mushroom *empanadas* are divine, as is the locally sourced coffee.

La Ventanita Meraki FAST FOOD $
(Map p520; 2221-8016; www.facebook.com/laventanitameraki; cnr Av 3 & Calle 21, in front of the train station; mains US$5-8; noon-midnight Tue-Thu, to 2am Fri-Sun) Ventanita means 'little window' in Spanish and Meraki means 'artistry' in Greek. Put them together and it's an accurate moniker for this fusion hole-in-the-wall: a to-go window in front of downtown's train station that serves innovative street food. Expect elaborate spins on typical fare, along with sandwiches like pumpkin butter cheese madness, and Twinkie *frito* (fried Twinkie) for dessert.

Café Té Ría CAFE $
(Map p520; 2222-8272; www.facebook.com/CafeTeRiaenAmon; cnr Av 7 & Calle 13; mains US$6, cakes US$1.50-3; 10:30am-7:30pm Mon-Fri, noon-7:30 Sat;) This petite, pet-friendly cafe in Barrio Amón is adorned with local art and replete with homey goodness. It's a perfect place to work over a few cups of morning coffee, then stay for a fresh salad, delicious sandwich or mouthwatering pastry. Vegetarians are well served.

Restaurante Shakti VEGETARIAN $
(Map p520; cnr Av 8 & Calle 13; mains US$5-10; 7:30am-6pm Mon-Fri, to 5pm Sat;) This informal neighborhood health-food outpost has simple, organic-focused cooking and freshly baked goods. Favorites include veggie burgers, along with various fish and chicken dishes, but most people come for the vegetarian *plato del día* (meal of the day) – only US$6 for soup, salad, main course and fruit drink (or US$8 with coffee and dessert thrown in)!

Maza Bistro BISTRO $$

(Map p520; 2248-4824; www.facebook.com/MazaBistro/; Calle 19, on Parque Nacional; mains US$10-12, brunch US$10-12; 9am-5pm Tue-Sun;) At this charming, alfresco restaurant attached to Hostel Casa del Parque (p521), brunch is served all day, with dishes like *huevos pochados* (a Latino version of eggs Benedict) and braised beef shank *au jus* with pickled vegetables and a fried egg. The burgers combine three kinds of meat and are also a big hit, along with daily veggie options.

La Sabana & Around

Supermarkets include **Más X Menos** (Map p526; 2248-1396; www.masxmenos.co.cr; cnr Autopista General Cañas & Av 5; 7am-midnight Mon-Sat, to 10pm Sun; P) and **Palí** (Map p526; 2256-5887; www.pali.co.cr; Paseo Colón, btwn Calles 24 & 26; 8am-8pm Mon-Sat, 8:30am-6pm Sun; P).

Soda Tapia SODA $

(Map p526; 2222-6734; www.facebook.com/sodatapia; cnr Av 2 & Calle 42; mains US$4-10, desserts US$2-7; 6am-2am Sun-Thu, 24hr Fri & Sat; P) An unpretentious '50s-style diner with garish red-and-white decor, this place is perpetually filled with couples and families noshing on grilled sandwiches and generous *casados*. If you have the nerve, try the monstrous 'El Gordo,' a pile of steak or chicken, onions, cheese, lettuce and tomato served on Spanish bread. Save room for dessert: ice cream and fruit sundaes are the specialty.

Las Mañanitas MEXICAN $$

(Map p526; 2248-1593; Calle 40, btwn Paseo Colón & Av 3; mains US$6-17; 11:30am-10pm Mon-Sat) At this authentic Mexican place near the park, well-rendered specialties include tacos in sets of four – corn tortillas accompanied by chicken, steak, sea bass or *carne al pastor* (spiced pork). Fans of *mole poblano* (central Mexico's famous chili and chocolate sauce) will also want to try it here, as the restaurant's owner hails from Puebla.

Los Yoses & San Pedro

Café Kracovia CAFE $

(2253-9093; www.cafekracovia.com; Paseo del la Segunda Republica; snacks US$4-10, mains US$8-14; 10:30am-9pm Mon, to 11pm Tue-Sat;) With several distinct spaces, from the low-lit, intimate downstairs to the outdoor garden courtyard, this hip cafe has something for everyone. Contemporary artwork and a university vibe create an appealing ambience for lunching on crepes, wraps, salads, Polish food and craft beer. It's 500m north of the Fuente de la Hispanidad traffic circle, where San Pedro and Los Yoses converge.

Mantras Veggie Cafe & Tea House VEGETARIAN $

(Map p525; 2253-6715; www.facebook.com/mantrasveggiecafe; Calle 35, btwn Avs 11 & 13; mains US$8-10; 9am-5pm;) Widely recognized as the best vegetarian restaurant in San José (if not all of Costa Rica), Mantras draws rave reviews from across the foodie spectrum for meatless main dishes, salads and desserts so delicious it's easy to forget you're eating meat-free. It's in Barrio Escalante, and there's a great brunch on Saturdays and Sundays.

El Portón Rojo PIZZA $$

(Map p525; 2224-4872; www.elportonrojo.com; cnr Av 10 & Calle 43; pizzas small US$8-10, large US$16-18; noon-3pm & 5:30-11pm Tue-Sat, 5:30pm-11pm Mon, noon-5pm Sun) Serving up some of the best pizza and sangria in the Los Yoses area, this hip restaurant doubles as a gallery. Funky local art sells right off the brick walls, and a steady influx of customers from Hostel Bekuo (p524) keeps things lively.

Drinking & Nightlife

Chepe's artsiest, most sophisticated drinking venues are concentrated north and east of the center in places like Barrio Amón and Barrio Escalante. For a rowdier, younger scene, head to Barrio la California or Calle la Amargura.

★**Stiefel** PUB

(Map p520; 8850-2119; www.facebook.com/StiefelPub; Av 5; 11:30am-2pm & 6pm-2am Mon-Sat) Two dozen-plus Costa Rican microbrews on tap and an appealing setting in a historic building create a convivial buzz at this pub half a block from Plaza España. Grab a pint of Pelona or Maldita Vida, Malinche or Chichemel; better yet, order a flight of four miniature sampler glasses and try 'em all!

★**Castro's** CLUB

(2256-8789; cnr Av 13 & Calle 22; 1pm-4am) Chepe's oldest dance club, this classic Latin American disco in Barrio México draws crowds of locals and tourists to its large dance floor with a dependable mix of salsa, *cumbia* and merengue.

Wilk BREWERY
(Map p525; www.facebook.com/wilkcraftbeer; cnr Calle 33 & Av 9; ⊙4pm-1am Tue-Sat) This Escalante pub attracts a mixed crowd of Ticos and Gringos who share an appreciation for craft brews and seriously delicious burgers (veggie included). The wide selection includes 27 craft beers on tap, including inventive concoctions of **Costa Rica Craft Brewing** (☎2249-4277; www.facebook.com/craftbeercostarica; Calle Cajeta, Brasil de Mora Ciudad Colón; ⊙10am-10pm Mon-Wed, to midnight Thu-Sat, noon-8pm Sun) and Treintaycinco. On each month's first Thursday, a crowd gathers to watch a local brewmaster invent a new beer.

☆ Entertainment

Pick up *La Nación* on Thursday for listings (in Spanish) of the coming week's attractions. The free publication *GAM Cultural* (www.gamcultural.com) and the website San José Volando (www.sanjosevolando.com) are also helpful guides to nightlife and cultural events.

★Teatro Nacional THEATER
(Map p520; ☎2010-1100; www.teatronacional.go.cr; Calles 3 & 5, btwn Avs Central & 2) Costa Rica's most important theater stages plays, dance, opera, classical concerts, Latin American music and other major events. The main season runs from March to November, but there are performances throughout the year.

El Lobo Estepario LIVE MUSIC
(Map p520; ☎2256-3934; www.facebook.com/loboesteparioc r; Av 2; ⊙11am-12:45am Sun-Thu, to 2am Fri & Sat) This artsy, two-story dive serves up good vegetarian fare and attracts some of the top local talent for live music gigs. The ceiling is also a blackboard, filled nightly with messages and drawings of the patrons' choosing.

El Sótano LIVE MUSIC
(Map p520; ☎2221-2302; www.facebook.com/sotanocr; cnr Calle 3 & Av 11; ⊙5pm-2am Mon-Tue & Thu-Sat) One of Chepe's most atmospheric nightspots, Sótano is named for its cellar jazz club, where people crowd in for frequent performances including intimate jam sessions. Upstairs in the same mansion, a cluster of elegant rooms with high ceilings have been converted into a gallery space, a stage and a dance floor where an eclectic mix of groups play live gigs.

Shopping

★Feria Verde de Aranjuez MARKET
(Map p520; www.feriaverde.org; Barrio Aranjuez; ⊙7am-12:30pm Sat) For a foodie-friendly cultural experience, don't miss this fabulous Saturday farmers market, a weekly meeting place for San José's artists and organic growers since 2010. You'll find organic coffee, artisanal chocolate, tropical-fruit ice blocks, fresh produce, leather, jewelry and more at the long rows of booths set up in the park at the north end of Barrio Aranjuez.

Galería Namu ARTS & CRAFTS
(Map p520; ☎2256-3412, USA 800-616-4322; www.galerianamu.com; Av 7, btwn Calles 5 & 7; ⊙9am-6:30pm Mon-Sat year-round, 1-5pm Sun Dec-Apr) This fair-trade gallery brings together artwork and cultural objects from a diverse population of regional ethnicities,

LGBTIQ+ SAN JOSÉ

The city is home to Central America's most thriving gay and lesbian scene. As with other spots, admission charges vary depending on the night and location (from US$5 to US$10). Some clubs close on various nights of the week (usually Sunday to Tuesday) and others host women- or men-only nights; inquire ahead or check individual club websites for listings. Many clubs are on the south side of town, which can get rough after dark. Take a taxi.

La Avispa (Map p520; ☎2223-5343; www.laavispa.com; Calle 1, btwn Avs 8 & 10; ⊙8pm-6am Thu-Sat, 5pm-6am Sun) A lesbian disco bar that has been in operation for more than four decades, La Avispa (the Wasp) has a bar, pool tables and a boisterous dance floor that's highly recommended by travelers.

BO Club (Map p520; ☎2221-0500; www.facebook.com/pages/Taller-Bo-Club/906788412753646; cnr Calle 11 & Av 10; ⊙8pm-6am Fri & Sat) A club that features everything from classic disco to electronica, as well as special themed nights. It's on the south side of town.

including Boruca masks, finely woven Wounaan baskets, Guaymí dolls, Bribrí canoes, Chorotega ceramics, traditional Huetar reed mats, and contemporary urban and Afro-Caribbean crafts. It can also help arrange visits to remote indigenous territories in different parts of Costa Rica.

Kiosco SJO ARTS & CRAFTS

(Map p525; ☎2253-8426; http://kalu.co.cr/boutique-kiosco-sj; cnr Calle 31 & Av 5; ⏰noon-8pm Tue-Fri, from 10am Sat, 10am-4pm Sun) With a focus on sustainable design by Costa Rican artisans, this sleek shop in Barrio Escalante stocks handmade jewelry, hand-tooled leather bags, original photography, stuffed animals, fashion and contemporary home decor by established designers. It's pricey, but rest assured everything you find here will be of exceptional quality. It's part of Kalu Cafe.

Orientation

San José's center is arranged in a grid with *avenidas* (avenues) running east to west and *calles* (streets) running north to south. Av Central is the nucleus of the downtown area and is a pedestrian mall between Calles 6 and 9.

Slightly further west of downtown is La Sabana, named for its huge and popular park where many *josefinos* spend their weekends jogging, swimming, picnicking or attending soccer matches.

East (and within walking distance) of the center are the contiguous neighborhoods of Los Yoses and San Pedro, the former a low-key residential area with some nice accommodations, the latter home to the tree-lined campus of the UCR, the country's most prestigious university.

Information

DANGERS & ANNOYANCES

Though Costa Rica has the lowest crime rate of any Central American country, crime in urban centers such as San José is a problem. The most common offense is opportunistic theft (eg pickpocketing and mugging). Keep a streetwise attitude, leave your car empty of valuables in a guarded lot and never put your bag in the overhead racks on a bus. Be aware that prostitutes are known for sleight-of-hand, and that they often work in pairs.

EMERGENCY

Fire	☎118
Red Cross	☎128
Traffic Police	☎2523-3300, ☎2222-9245, ☎2222-9330

MEDICAL SERVICES

Clínica Bíblica (☎2522-1000; www.clinicabiblica.com; Av 14, btwn Calles Central & 1; ⏰24hr) The top private clinic downtown has a 24-hour emergency room; doctors speak English, French and German.

Hospital CIMA (☎2208-1000; www.hospitalcima.com; Autopista Próspero Fernández; ⏰24hr) For serious medical emergencies, head to this hospital in San Rafael de Escazú. Its facilities are the most modern in the greater San José area.

POST

Correo Central (Central Post Office; Map p520; ☎2202-2900; www.correos.go.cr; Calle 2, btwn Avs 1 & 3; ⏰6:30am-6pm Mon-Fri, to noon Sat) In a gorgeous historic building near the center of town. Express and overnight services.

Getting There & Away

AIR

Aeropuerto Internacional Juan Santamaría (☎2437-2400; www.fly2sanjose.com) Outside Alajuela. Handles international flights in its main terminal. Domestic flights on **Sansa** (☎2290-4100; www.flysansa.com) depart from the Sansa terminal.

Aeropuerto Tobías Bolaños (☎2232-2820; Pavas) In the San José suburb of Pavas; services private charter and a few national flights.

BUS

Bus transportation from San José can be bewildering. There is no public bus system and no central terminal. Instead, dozens of private companies operate out of stops scattered throughout the city. Many bus companies have no more than a stop (in this case pay the driver directly); some have a tiny office with a window on the street; others operate from bigger terminals servicing entire regions.

Collectively, the following five San José terminals serve Costa Rica's most popular destinations. The chances are you'll be passing through one or more of them during your trip.

Gran Terminal del Caribe (Calle Central) This roomy station north of Av 13 is the central departure point for all buses to the Caribbean.

Terminal 7-10 (Map p520; ☎2519-9740; www.terminal7-10.com; cnr Av 7 & Calle 10) This newer bus terminal is a base for routes to Nicoya, Nosara, Sámara, Santa Cruz, Tamarindo, Jacó, Monteverde, La Fortuna and a few other places. The four-story facility has a food court, shopping center and parking lot. Although it's located in the *zona roja*, historically a dangerous area of the city, police have stepped up their patrols to reduce crime.

Terminal Coca-Cola (Map p520; Av 1, btwn Calles 16 & 18) A well-known landmark. Numerous buses leave from the terminal and the four-block radius around it to points all over Costa Rica, in particular the Central Valley and the Pacific coast. This is a labyrinthine station with ticket offices scattered all over.

Terminal del Atlántico Norte (Map p520; cnr Av 9 & Calle 12) A small, rather decrepit terminal serving the Southern Caribbean and Puerto Jiménez.

Terminal Tracopa (2221-4214; www.tracopacr.com; Calle 5, btwn Avs 18 & 20) Buses to southwestern destinations, including Neily, Dominical, Golfito, Manuel Antonio, Palmar Norte, Paso Canoas, Quepos, San Isidro de El General, San Vito and Uvita.

Domestic Bus Companies

Alfaro (http://empresaalfaro.com) Nicoya, Playa Sámara and Playa Tamarindo.

Autotransportes Caribeños (2222-0610; www.grupocaribenos.com; Gran Terminal del Caribe, Calle Central) Northeastern destinations including Puerto Limón, Guápiles, Cariari, Siquirres and Puerto Viejo de Sarapiquí; the Caribeños group encompasses several smaller companies (including Empresarios Guapileños and Líneas del Atlántico), all of which share the same terminal and customer-service phone number.

Autotransportes Mepe (Map p520; 2257-8129; www.mepecr.com; Terminal del Atlántico Norte, cnr Av 9 & Calle 12) Southern Caribbean destinations including Cahuita, Puerto Viejo de Talamanca, Manzanillo, Bribrí and Sixaola.

Autotransportes San Carlos (Map p520; 2255-4300; Terminal 7-10, cnr Av 7 & Calle 10) La Fortuna, Ciudad Quesada and Los Chiles.

Blanco Lobo (Map p520; 2257-4121; Terminal del Atlántico Norte, cnr Av 9 & Calle 12) Puerto Jiménez.

Coopetrans Atenas (Map p520; 2446-5767; www.coopetransatenas.com; Terminal Coca-Cola, Av 1, btwn Calles 16 & 18) Atenas.

Deldu (www.facebook.com/transportedeldu) Peñas Blancas.

Empresa Alfaro (Map p520; 2222-2666; www.empresaalfaro.com; Terminal 7-10, cnr Av 7 & Calle 10) Nicoya, Nosara, Sámara, Santa Cruz and Tamarindo.

Empresarios Unidos (Map p520; 2221-6600; cnr Av 12 & Calle 16) San Ramón and Puntarenas.

Lumaca (Map p520; 2552-5280; Av 10, btwn Calles 5 & 7) Cartago.

Mepe (www.mepecr.com) Cahuita, Puerto Viejo de Talamanca and Sixaola.

Metrópoli (Map p520; 2530-1064; Av 2, btwn Calles 1 & 3) Volcán Irazú.

Musoc (2222-2422; Calle Central, btwn Avs 22 & 24) San Isidro de El General and Santa María de Dota.

Pulmitan de Liberia (Map p520; 2222-0610; Calle 24, btwn Avs 5 & 7) Northwestern destinations including Cañas, Liberia, Playa del Coco and Tilarán.

Station Wagon (Map p520; 2441-1181; Av 2, btwn Calles 10 & 12) Alajuela and the airport.

Terminal Tracopa (p530) Southwestern destinations including Ciudad Neily, Dominical, Golfito, Manuel Antonio, Palmar Norte, Paso Canoas, Quepos, San Isidro de El General, San Vito and Uvita.

Tracopa (tracopacr.com) Dominical, Uvita, Golfito, Palmar, Paso Canoas, Quepos, Manuel Antonio and San Isidro de El General.

Tralapa (Map p520; 2223-5876; Av 5, btwn Calles 20 & 22) Several Península de Nicoya destinations, including Playa Flamingo, Playa Hermosa, Playa Tamarindo and Santa Cruz.

Transmonteverde (Map p520; 2645-7447; www.facebook.com/Transmonteverde; Terminal 7-10, cnr Av 7 & Calle 10) Monteverde.

Transportes Cobano (Map p520; 2221-7479; transportescobano@gmail.com; Terminal 7-10, cnr Av 7 & Calle 10) Montezuma and Mal País.

Transportes Deldú (Calle Central, Gran Terminal de Caribe) Peñas Blancas (Nicaraguan border).

Transportes Jacó (Map p520; 2290-2922; www.transportesjacoruta655.com; Terminal 7-10, cnr Av 7 & Calle 10) Jacó.

Transtusa (Map p520; 4036-1800; www.transtusacr.com; Calle 13A, btwn Avs 6 & 8) Cartago and Turrialba.

Tuan (Terminal de Buses Grecia; Map p520; 2258-2004, 2494-2139; cnr Av 5 & Calle 18A) Grecia.

Tuasa (Map p520; 2442-6900; Av 2, btwn Calles 12 & 14) Alajuela and the airport.

International Bus Companies

International buses get booked up fast. Buy your tickets in advance – and take your passport.

Expreso Panamá (Map p520; 2221-7694; www.expresopanama.com; Terminal Empresarios Unidos, cnr Av 12 & Calle 16) Panama City (Panama).

Nicabus (Map p520; 2221-2581; cnr Av 1 & Calle 20) Managua (Nicaragua).

Tica Bus (Map p526; 2296-9788; www.ticabus.com; cnr Transversal 26 & Av 3) Nicaragua, Panama, El Salvador and Guatemala.

TransNica (Map p520; 2223-4242; www.transnica.com; Calle 22, btwn Avs 3 & 5) Nicaragua and Honduras.

Transportes Central Line (Map p520; ☎2221-9115; http://transportescentralline.com; Av 9) Managua (Nicaragua).

Shuttle Bus Companies

Grayline (☎2220-2126; www.graylinecostarica.com; Av 31) and **Interbus** (☎4100-0888; www.interbusonline.com; Av 20) shuttle passengers in air-conditioned minivans from San José to a long list of popular destinations around Costa Rica. They are more expensive than the standard bus services, but they offer door-to-door service and can get you there faster.

DOMESTIC BUSES FROM SAN JOSÉ

DESTINATION	BUS COMPANY	COST (US$)	DURATION (HR)	FREQUENCY
Cahuita	Mepe	8.70	4	6am, 8am, 10am, noon, 2pm, 4pm, 6pm
Cartago	Lumaca	1.10	1	every 15min
Dominical & Uvita	Tracopa	9.40	4½-5½	6am, 3pm
Golfito	Tracopa	13.20	6½	6:30am, 7am, 3:30pm
Jacó	Transportes Jacó	4.30	2½	every 2hr 7am-5pm
La Fortuna	San Carlos	4.40	4	12:45pm, 2:45pm
Liberia	Pulmitan	8	4½	hourly 6am-8pm
Los Chiles	San Carlos	5.20	5	5:15am, 3pm
Monteverde/Santa Elena	Transmonteverde	5	4½	6:30am, 2:30pm
Montezuma/Mal País	Cobano	12.40	5½-6	6am, 6:30am, 2pm
Nicoya	Alfaro	7.20	5	5:30, 7:30am, 10am, 1pm, 3pm, 5pm
Palmar	Tracopa	10.30	6	13 daily
Paso Canoas	Tracopa	13.80	7-8	13 daily
Peñas Blancas	Deldú	8.20	6	9 daily
Playa Flamingo	Tralapa	10.30	6	8am, 10:30am, 3pm
Playa Sámara	Alfaro	7.60	5	noon
Playa Tamarindo	Alfaro	9.50	5	11:30am, 3:30pm
	Tralapa	8.90	5	7am, 4pm
Puerto Jiménez	Blanco Lobo	15	8	8am, noon
Puerto Limón	Caribeños	5.70	3	hourly
Puerto Viejo de Sarapiquí	Caribeños	4.50	2½	10 daily
Puerto Viejo de Talamanca	Mepe	10	4½	6am, 8am, 10am, noon, 2pm, 4pm, 6pm
Puntarenas	Empresarios Unidos	4.60	2½	hourly
Quepos/Manuel Antonio	Tracopa	8.10	3½	every 1-2hr
San Isidro de El General	Musoc	6.40	3	hourly 4:30am-6:30pm
	Tracopa	6.40	3	hourly
Sixaola	Mepe	12.30	5½	6am, 8am, 10am, 2pm, 4pm
Tilarán	Pulmitan	8	4	7:30am, 9:30am, 12:45pm, 3:45pm, 6:30pm
Turrialba	Transtusa	2.40	2	hourly

Getting Around

TO/FROM THE AIRPORT

International flights arrive at Aeropuerto Internacional Juan Santamaría (p529) in nearby Alajuela.

An official, metered taxi from the airport to downtown San José costs around US$30. Plan on spending extra for wait time during periods of heavy traffic.

Interbus (p531) runs shuttles between the airport and San José hotels (adult/child under 12 US$15/7).

Even cheaper are the public buses (US$1.10) operated by Tuasa (p530) and Station Wagon (p530), which pick up passengers at a stop on the main road in front of the airport. On the return trip, board at the Tuasa or Station Wagon terminal in downtown San José. Hotels can also arrange for private airport pick-up.

From downtown, the drive to the airport can take anywhere from 20 minutes to an hour (more if you take the bus).

BUS

Local buses are useful to get you into the suburbs and surrounding villages, or to the airport. Most buses run between 5am and 10pm and cost between US$0.40 and US$1.10.

Heredia Regular busesleave from Calle 1, between Avs 7 and 9.

La Sabana To catch a bus heading west from San José toward La Sabana (US$0.40), head for the convenient downtown stop at the southeast corner of Av 3 and Calle 3.

Los Yoses and San Pedro Catch eastbound buses to Los Yoses and San Pedro (US$0.50) from the northeast corner of Av Central and Calle 9.

TAXI

Red taxis can be hailed on the street day or night, or you can have your hotel call one for you.

Marías (meters) are generally used, though a few drivers will tell you they're broken and try to charge you more – especially if you don't speak Spanish. Not using a meter is illegal. The rate for the first kilometer should automatically appear when the meter starts up (at the time of research, the correct starting amount was 610 colones). Make sure the *maría* is operating when you get in, or negotiate the fare up front. Short rides downtown cost US$2 to US$4. There's a 20% surcharge after 10pm that may not appear on the *maría*.

Uber has also become a popular form of transport in the city.

CENTRAL VALLEY & HIGHLANDS

It is on the nontouristy, coffee-cultivated hillsides of the Central Valley that you'll find Costa Rica's heart and soul. This is not only the geographical center of the country but also its cultural and spiritual core. It is here that the Spanish first settled, here that coffee built a prosperous nation, and here that picturesque highland villages still gather for centuries-old fiestas. It is also here that you'll get to fully appreciate Costa Rica's country cooking: artisanal cheeses, steamy corn cakes and freshly caught river trout.

INTERNATIONAL BUSES FROM SAN JOSÉ

DESTINATION	BUS COMPANY	COST (US$)	DURATION (HR)	FREQUENCY
David (Panama)	Tracopa	21	8½	7:30am, noon
Guatemala City (Guatemala)	Tica Bus	86	48	3am, 6am, 7am, 12:30pm
Managua (Nicaragua)	Tica Bus	29-42	9	3am, 6am, 7:30am, 12:30pm
	TransNica	28	8½	2am, 4am, 5am, 9am, noon
	Central Line	29	8½	4:30am, 10am
	Nicabus	29	8	4:30am, 6:30am
Panama City (Panama)	Expreso Panamá	40	14	noon
	Tica Bus	42-58	16	noon, 11:55pm
San Salvador (El Salvador)	Tica Bus	65	20	3am, 6am, 7:30am, 12:30pm
Tegucigalpa (Honduras)	TransNica	57	16	2am

Curvy mountain roads force travelers to slow their pace. Quaint and quirky agricultural towns invite leisurely detours to farmers markets and church processions, a refreshing break from the tourist-industrial complex on the coasts. But it's not all cows and coffee – world-class rapids, resplendent quetzals and close encounters with active volcanoes all show off the rich landscape in which Costa Rica's character is rooted.

Alajuela

POP 42,975

Costa Rica's second city is home to one of the country's most famous figures: Juan Santamaría, the humble drummer boy who died putting an end to William Walker's campaign to turn Central America into slaving territory in the Battle of Rivas in 1856.

Alajuela is by no means a tourist 'destination,' but it's an inherently Costa Rican city and, in its more relaxed moments, it reveals itself as such, where families have leisurely Sunday lunches and teenagers steal kisses in the park. It's also a good base for exploring the countryside to the north.

Sights

Museo Histórico Cultural Juan Santamaría MUSEUM

(2441-4775; www.museojuansantamaria.go.cr; Av 1, btwn Calles Central & 2; 10am-5:30pm Tue-Sun) FREE Situated in a century-old structure that has served as both jail and armory, this museum chronicles Costa Rican history from early European settlement through the 19th century, with special emphasis on the life and history of Juan Santamaría and the pivotal mid-1850s battles of Santa Rosa, Sardinal and Rivas. Exhibits include videos, vintage maps, paintings and historical artifacts related to the conflict that ultimately safeguarded Costa Rica's independence.

Sleeping

Alajuela Backpackers Boutique Hostel HOTEL $

(2441-7149; www.alajuelabackpackers.com; cnr Av 4 & Calle 4; dm US$14-19, r/ste US$55/70;) This four-story place with cookie-cutter rooms may feel a tad institutional at first glance, but dig deeper and you'll discover some big pluses: free shuttles to and from the airport, air-conditioned dorms and doubles with en suite bathrooms, and a super-cool 4th-floor bar terrace where you can sip beers while watching planes take off in the distance.

Hotel Los Volcanes GUESTHOUSE $$

(2441-0525; www.hotellosvolcanes.com; Av 3, btwn Calles Central & 2; incl breakfast s/d US$55/69, with air-con US$70/81, without bathroom US$39/54;) Tranquil and centrally located, this welcoming place in a refurbished 1920s mansion has 15 rooms, from vintage units with period-style furniture and clean shared bathrooms to contemporary rooms with flat-screen TV, air-con and safe. There's an enjoyable courtyard in the back, complete with gurgling fountain. The helpful owners arrange a free airport drop-off at the end of your stay.

Hotel Pacandé B&B $$

(2443-8481; www.hotelpacande.com; Av 5, btwn Calles 2 & 4; incl breakfast r US$48-65, without bathroom US$35;) This popular, locally run option is spotlessly clean throughout, offering 10 large rooms with wood furnishings, folk-art touches and cable TV. The bright, sunny breakfast nook is a great spot for a morning brew.

Vida Tropical B&B B&B $$

(2443-9576; www.vidatropical.com; Calle 3; incl breakfast s/d US$45/55, without bathroom US$25/35;) In a quiet residential neighborhood a five-minute walk north of downtown Alajuela, this friendly house has snug, simple guest rooms awash with bright murals; two share a bathroom. The well-tended backyard is perfect for catching some sun in a hammock, and laundry service is available ($5 per load; free with three-day stay). In the backyard, kids will enjoy two playful pet rabbits.

Tacacori Ecolodge BUNGALOW $$$

(2430-5846; www.tacacori.com; d incl breakfast US$130, extra person US$20) Expat owner Nadine and her sheepdog run this peaceful retreat high above Alajuela. Four spacious bungalows with ultra-modern fixtures and abundant ecofriendly touches (solar hot water, LED lighting, dual-flush toilets) sit on a verdant hillside. Attractively priced 'Hello-Goodbye' packages and 15-minute airport transfers (from US$25) provide an incentive to begin and end your travels here.

Central Valley & Highlands

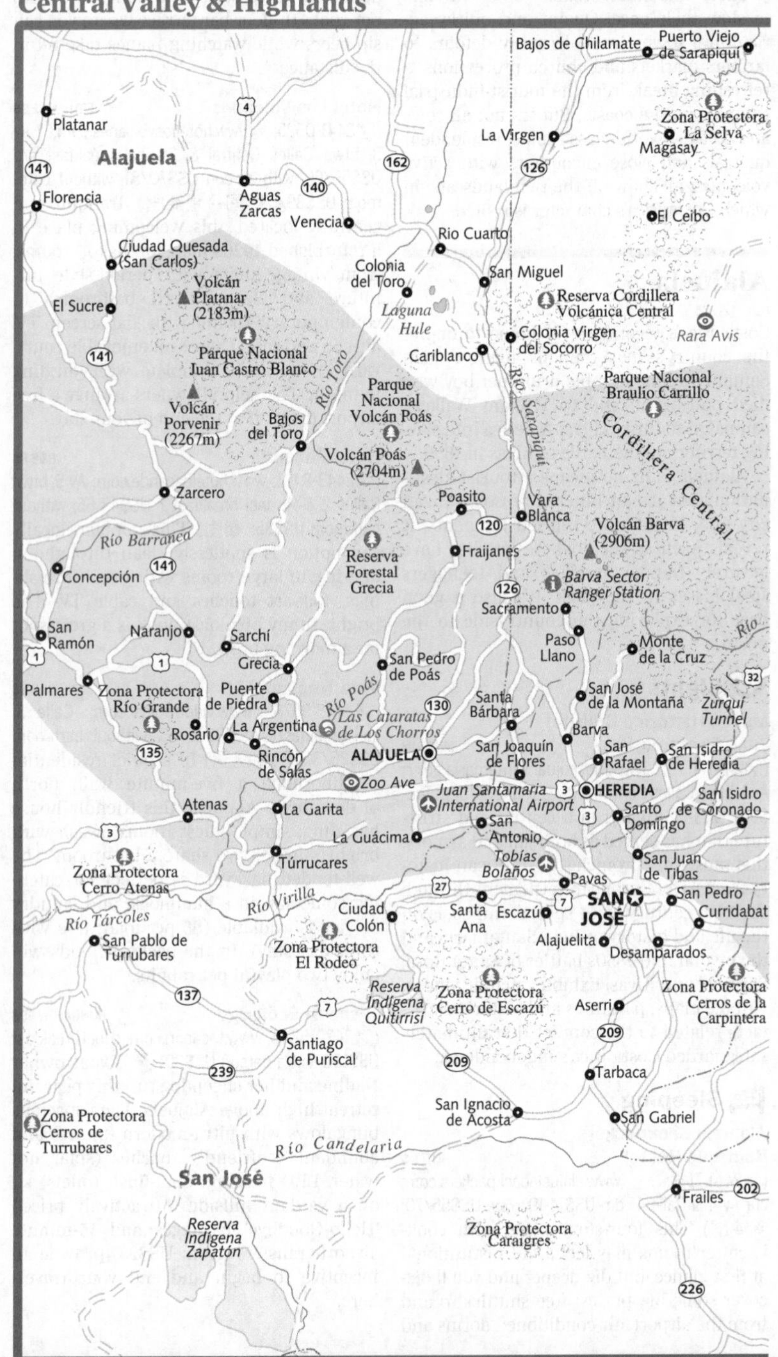

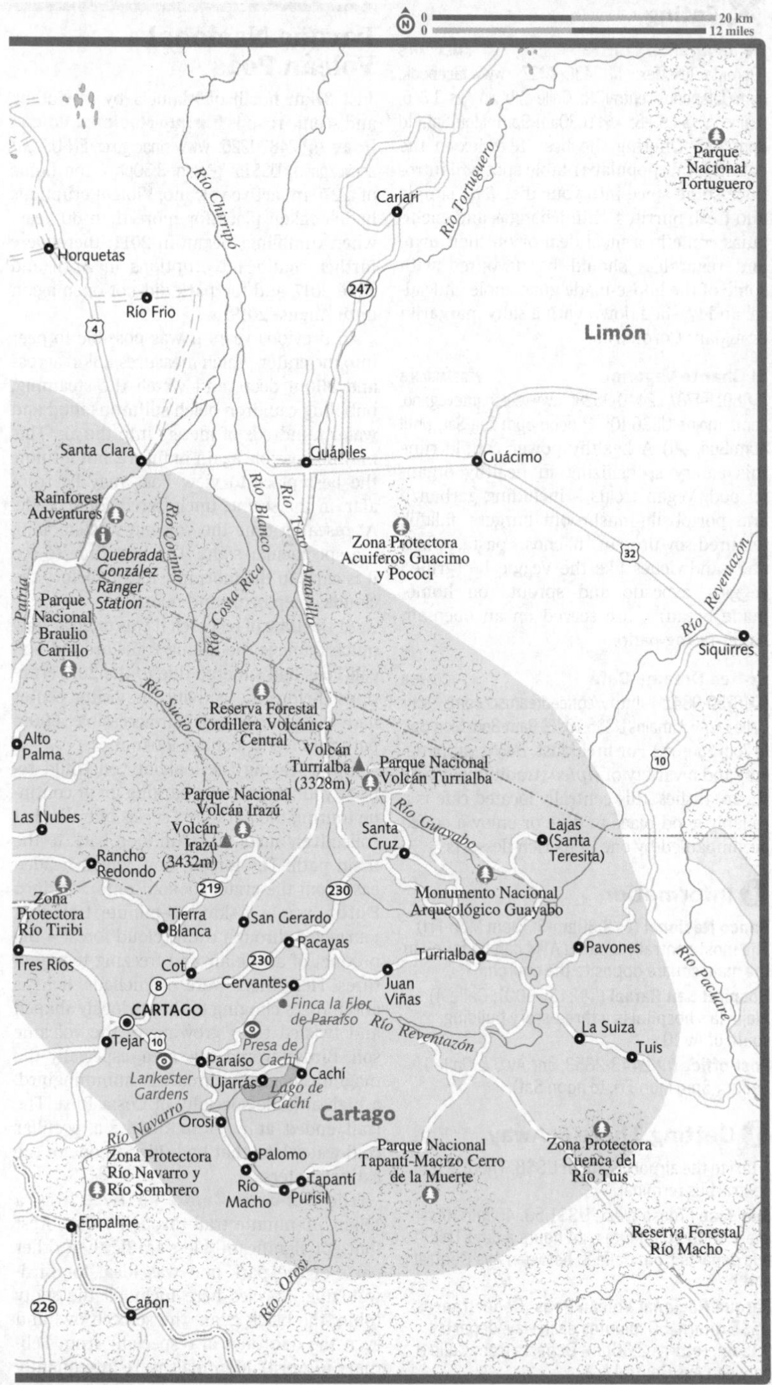

0 20 km
0 12 miles
Parque Nacional Tortuguero
Cariari
Río Chirripó
Río Tortuguero
Horquetas
Río Frio
247
4
Limón
Santa Clara
Guápiles
Guácimo
Rainforest Adventures
Río Corinto
Río Blanco
Río Toro Amarillo
Zona Protectora Acuiferos Guacimo y Pococi
32
Quebrada González Ranger Station
Río Costa Rica
Río Reventazón
Patria
Parque Nacional Braulio Carrillo
Siquirres
Río Sucio
Reserva Forestal Cordillera Volcánica Central
Alto Palma
Volcán Turrialba (3328m)
Parque Nacional Volcán Turrialba
10
Parque Nacional Volcán Irazú
Río Guayabo
Las Nubes
Volcán Irazú (3432m)
Santa Cruz
Lajas (Santa Teresita)
Rancho Redondo
219
230
Monumento Nacional Arqueológico Guayabo
Zona Protectora Río Tiribi
Tierra Blanca
San Gerardo
Pacayas
Pavones
Tres Ríos
Cot
230
Turrialba
Río Pacuare
8
Cervantes
Juan Viñas
CARTAGO
Finca la Flor de Paraíso
Río Reventazón
Tejar
10
Presa de Cachí
La Suiza
Tuis
Paraíso
Lankester Gardens
Ujarrás
Cachí
Lago de Cachí
Cartago
Río Navarro
Orosi
Zona Protectora Río Navarro y Río Sombrero
Palomo
Parque Nacional Tapantí-Macizo Cerro de la Muerte
Zona Protectora Cuenca del Río Tuis
Río Macho
Tapantí
Purisil
Empalme
Reserva Forestal Río Macho
Río Orosi
226
Cañon

Eating

★ Jalapeños Central MEXICAN $
(Comida Tex-Mex; ☎2430-4027; www.facebook.com/JalapenosCentralCR; Calle 1, btwn Avs 3 & 5; mains US$4.50-8; ⏲11:30am-9pm Mon-Sat, to 8pm Sun) Offering the best Tex-Mex in the country, this popular 11-table spot will introduce some spice into your diet. The simple and fresh burritos, chimichangas and enchiladas come in a meal deal or on their own, and regardless should be devoured with some of the house-made guacamole and salsa, and washed down with a salty margarita or a giant Coronarita.

El Chante Vegano VEGETARIAN $
(☎8911-4787, 2440-3528; www.elchantevegano.com; mains US$6-10; ⏲noon-8pm Tue-Sat, until 4pm Sun; 🌶) A healthy power couple runs this eatery specializing in healthy organic food. Vegan treats – including garbanzo and portobello-mushroom burgers, falafel, textured-soy-protein nachos, pasta, pizza and sandwiches like the Veggie Lú (grilled veggies, avocado and sprouts on home-made bread) – are served on an open-air, street-facing patio.

Coffee Dreams Café CAFE $
(☎8750-0841; http://coffeedreamscr.com; cnr Calle 1 & Av 3; mains US$5-10; ⏲9am-8pm Mon-Sat, to 7pm Sun; 🌶) For breakfast, *bocas* (appetizers) and a variety of *típico* (traditional Costa Rican) dishes, this centrally located cafe is a reliably good place to dine or enjoy a coffee accompanied by one of its rich desserts.

Information

Banco Nacional (⏲8:30am-3:30pm Mon-Fri) The most centrally located ATM can be found in the main square opposite the church.

Hospital San Rafael (☎2436-1001; Calle 4) Alajuela's hospital is a three-story building south of Av 10.

Post office (☎2443-2653; cnr Av 5 & Calle 1; ⏲8am-5pm Mon-Fri, to noon Sat)

Getting There & Away

A taxi to the airport is about US$8. There is no central bus terminal.

San José (Tuasa West; US$1.50, 45 minutes, every 10 to 30 minutes, 24 hours a day) This bus departs from Calle 8, between Avs Central and 1.

Parque Nacional Volcán Poás (Coopetransasi; US$5 return, 50 minutes each way, departs 9:15am, returns 2:30pm) Departs from Calle 8, between Avs Central & 2.

Parque Nacional Volcán Poás

Just 37km north of Alajuela by a winding and scenic road is **Parque Nacional Volcán Poás** (☎2482-1226; www.sinac.go.cr/EN-US/ac/accvc/pnvp; US$15; ⏲8am-3:30pm), the home of a 2704m active volcano. Violent eruptions hadn't taken place for more than 60 years when rumblings began in 2014; there were further significant eruptions in April and June 2017, and the park did not open again until August 2018.

In previous years it was possible to peer into the crater, which measures 1.3km across and 300m deep, and watch the steaming, bubbling cauldron belch sulfurous mud and water hundreds of meters into the air. This may be possible again in future, but for now the best place to view Poás may be from afar, in the scenic, uncluttered countryside. At research time the volcano was smoking – a spectacular sight. The best time to see it is early in the morning, ideally before the clouds creep in around noon.

At the time of research it was unclear how much damage the hiking trails around Volcán Poás had suffered due to the 2017 eruptions. Before the activity the visitor center had a paved, wheelchair-accessible 600m path that led to a crater lookout.

Upon leaving the lookout you could retrace your steps to the parking lot or continue touring the park on a series of trails that collectively made a 3.6km loop back to the main path. The longer loop, which headed east from the crater lookout onto **Sendero Botos**, was a 1.4km, 30-minute trail that journeyed through dwarf cloud forest – the product of acidic air and freezing temperatures. Here there were bromeliads, lichens and mosses clinging to the curiously shaped and twisted trees growing in the volcanic soil. Birds favored this area, especially the magnificent fiery-throated hummingbird, a high-altitude specialty of Costa Rica. The trail ended at **Laguna Botos**, a peculiar cold-water lake that had filled in one of the extinct craters.

The **Sendero Canto de Aves** was a 1.8km, 45-minute trail through taller forest that got significantly less traffic than other parts of the park and was ideal for bird-watching. Species here included the sooty robin, the black guan, the screech owl and even the odd quetzal (especially from February to April). Mammals were infrequently sighted in the park, but there were resident coyotes and the endemic montane squirrel – these have almost certainly gone in search of new pastures after the eruptions.

To return to the main path, visitors could walk via the 400m, 10-minute **Sendero Escalonia**, which finished at the restrooms just north of the visitor center.

Sleeping

There are no accommodations inside the park, but the area surrounding the volcano offers a range of options for all tastes and budgets. Some are closed due to recent eruptions, but the Peace Lodge is still open; book before you visit.

Guests feel they've stepped into a fairy tale at the **Peace Lodge** (2482-2720; www.waterfallgardens.com; d standard/deluxe/villa/deluxe villa US$430/510/710/940, additional adult/child US$40/20; P), an over-the-top lodge with exquisite villas boasting majestic valley views, private decks with Jacuzzis, fireplaces and huge bathrooms with waterfall showers. There's an animal-rescue center, hiking trails, five giant waterfalls and a trout pond where you can fish for your own lunch. This highly imaginative setting, with its multiple pools and interactive animal experiences (toucan and hummingbird feeding), will have kids over the moon.

Getting There & Away

Numerous local companies offer daily tours to the volcano (US$40 to US$100). It's much cheaper, and nearly as easy, to visit the volcano on the daily **Coopetransasi** (2449-5141) bus from Alajuela (US$5 return, 50 minutes each way, 9:15am returning 2:30pm). Due to the latest volcanic activity the bus may only reach a certain point; check with the driver before you board.

Parque Nacional Braulio Carrillo

Enter this under-explored **national park** (2206-5500, 2266-1883; adult/child US$12/5; 8am-3:30pm) and you'll have an idea of what Costa Rica looked like prior to the 1950s, when 75% of the country's surface area was still covered by forest. Here, steep hills cloaked in impossibly tall trees are interrupted only by canyons and cascading rivers. It has extraordinary biodiversity due to the range of altitudes, from steamy 2906m cloud forest alongside Volcán Barva to lush, humid lowlands on the Caribbean slope. Its most incredible feature, however, is that the southernmost point of this massive park is only 30 minutes north of San José.

Activities

Hiking

Three easy-to-moderate trails (between 1km and 2.5km) fan out from the **Quebrada González ranger station** (8am-4pm) between Guápiles and San José. On the north side of Hwy 32, the mostly flat, gravel-paved 1km **Sendero El Ceibo** is the easiest of the three, passing a giant ceibo tree, a scenic overlook and seven other marked points of interest before looping back to the ranger station. Proximity to the highway creates some distracting traffic noise here.

Sendero Botarrama is a more difficult, slightly more rugged spur trail (expect mud and exposed roots) that branches off Sendero El Ceibo and continues another 1.5km to the junction of the crystal-clear Río Honduras with the Río Sucio (Dirty River), the yellow waters of which carry volcanic minerals.

Back on the south side of Hwy 32, the 1.6km, gravel-paved **Sendero Las Palmas** is another loop trail that climbs moderately into dense rainforest – prime territory for birdwatching.

To hike 2906m Barva, the third-largest volcano in Costa Rica, head to the **Barva Sector Ranger Station** (2266-1883; 8am-3:30pm), where you'll find four trails. The **Cacho de Venado** (Deer Cuckoo trail) is around 2km through birdwatching landscape. The shorter 1km **Mirador Vara Blanca** offers a scenic lookout point. Then there's the 3km **crater walk**, which climaxes with a view of the water-filled crevice surrounded by lush vegetation, and a longer 5km hike to a scenic watering hole named **Copey Lagoon**.

Getting There & Away

Frequent buses between San José and Guápiles can drop you off at the Quebrada González station, but the return trip is more challenging. While it's possible to flag a bus down on busy Hwy 32, your luck will depend on the driver's discretion and how full the bus is.

Public buses from Heredia (US$1.40, one hour, 5:25am and 6:25am) will only get you as far as Paso Llano, 7km from the park entrance at Barva.

Cartago

POP 157,800

Cartago exists mainly as a commercial and residential center, though the beauty of the surrounding mountains helps take the edge off modern life. As in other commercial towns, expect plenty of functional concrete structures. Two worthy exceptions, however, are the striking ruins of the Santiago Apóstol Parish, an ancient site home to a number of churches since 1575, and the bright white **Basílica de Nuestra Señora de Los Ángeles** (www.santuarionacional.org; Calle 15, btwn Avs Central & 1; ⏲Mass 6am, 9am, 11am, 6pm daily, 4pm Sat & Sun). The latter is visible from many parts of the city – it stands out like a snowcapped mountain above a plain of one-story edifices. The city is thrown briefly into the spotlight every August, when pilgrims from every corner of the country descend on the basilica to say their most serious prayers.

Sleeping & Eating

Los Ángeles Lodge B&B $$

(☎2591-4169, 2551-0957; hotel.los.angeles@hotmail.com; Av 1, btwn Calles 13 & 15; s/d incl breakfast US$35/50;) With its balconies overlooking the Plaza de la Basílica, this decent B&B stands out with spacious and comfortable rooms, hot showers and breakfast made to order.

Getting There & Away

BUS

Bus stops are scattered around town. Destinations include:

Orosi (Autotransportes Mata Irola) About US$1, 45 minutes, every 15 to 30 minutes between 5:15am and 10:25pm; departs from Calle 3 between Avs 2 and 4.

San José (Lumaca) About US$1.50, 50 minutes, every 15 minutes between 4:35am and 11pm; departs from the terminal on Calle 6 between Avs 3 and 7.

Turrialba (Transtusa) US$1.60, 80 minutes, every 20 minutes to an hour between 6:15am and 11pm weekdays (less frequently on weekends); departs from Av 4 between Calles 5 and 7.

TRAIN

Train service runs between San José's Estación del Pacífico and Cartago's downtown **station** (Av 3, btwn Calles 4 & 6). The one-hour trip costs US$1. From Monday to Friday the schedule is weighted toward morning and afternoon commute hours. On Saturday trains run to San José every hour until 1:30pm. See www.incofer.go.cr for up-to-date timetable info.

Valle de Orosi

This straight-out-of-a-storybook river valley is famous for mountain vistas, a lake formed by a hydroelectric facility, a truly wild national park and coffee – lots and lots of coffee. A well-paved 32km loop winds through a landscape of rolling hills terraced with coffee plantations and valleys dotted with pastoral villages, all set against the backdrop of volcanoes Irazú and Turrialba. If you have a rental car (or good legs for cycling) you're in for a treat, though it's still possible to navigate most of the loop via public buses.

The loop road starts 8km southeast of Cartago in **Paraíso**, heads south to **Orosi**, then doubles back northeast and west around the artificial **Lago de Cachí**, passing the historic church at **Ujarrás** en route back to Paraíso. Alternatively, from Orosi you can branch south into Parque Nacional Tapantí-Macizo Cerro de la Muerte, an end-of-the-road national park with superb river and mountain scenery.

Sights & Activities

Parque Nacional Tapantí-Macizo Cerro de la Muerte NATIONAL PARK

(☎2206-5615; adult/child 6-12yr US$10/5; ⏲8am-4pm;) This 580-sq-km national park preserves the verdant northern slopes of the Cordillera de Talamanca and is the wettest reserve in the country, getting 8000mm of precipitation a year. The park's largest peak, the Cerro de la Muerte (Mountain of Death; 3451m), is also the highest point on the Costa Rican section of the Interamericana. **El Salto** is an easy 100m walk to a lookout point with waterfall and mountain views, and there are three other trails of varying difficulty.

The other trails range from 1km to 3km and run up steep slopes or along the flat riverbed. The **ranger's office** (☎2206-5615; ⏲8am-4pm) at the park entrance has maps and info on each path. Toilets, picnic tables and water are available in the park, and there are birdwatching and orchid-spotting opportunities aplenty.

Iglesia de San José Orosi CHURCH

Orosi is one of the few colonial-era towns to survive Costa Rica's frequent earthquakes,

SPANISH COURSES IN THE CENTRAL VALLEY

Spanish schools usually do packages including homestays, meals and daily language lessons.

Adventure Education Center (☎USA 800-237-2730; http://adventurespanishschool.com; 1 week with homestay US$325)

Centro Panamericano de Idiomas (CPI; ☎2265-6306, USA 1-877-373-3116; www.cpi-edu.com; private lessons from US$30, 20hr group tuition from US$460, 1-week homestay from US$200)

Intensa (☎2442-3843, USA & Canada 866-277-1352, WhatsApp 8866-1059; www.intensa.com; 1 week with 3hr tuition per day US$340, with homestay US$520; ⊙8am-8pm Mon-Fri)

Intercultura (☎2260-8480; www.interculturacostarica.com; cnr Calle 10 & Av 4; private lessons from US$26, 20hr group tuition from US$275, with 1-week homestay US$570)

Spanish by the River (Spanish at Locations; ☎2556-7380, USA 1-877-268-3730; www.spanishatlocations.com; 20/30hr per week group US$225/300, 10/20hr per week private $225/360, homestay/hostel bed per night US$24/14)

which have thankfully also spared the photogenic village church. Built in the mid-1700s, it is the oldest religious site still in use in Costa Rica. The roof of the church is a combination of thatched cane and ceramic tiling, while the carved-wood altar is adorned with religious paintings of Mexican origin.

Finca Cristina TOURS

(☎2574-6426, USA 203-549-1945; www.cafecristina.com; Hwy 224; guided tours per person US$15; ⊙by appointment 9am & 2pm) Finca Cristina, 2km east of Paraíso on the road to Turrialba at the end of a short dirt track, is an organic coffee farm. Linda and Ernie have been farming in Costa Rica since 1977, and a two-hour tour of their microprocessing plant is a fantastic introduction to the processes of organic coffee growing, harvesting and roasting.

Sleeping & Eating

Montaña Linda HOSTEL $

(☎2533-3640; www.montanalinda.com; dm US$9, guesthouse s/d/tr/q US$30/30/35/40, s/d/tr/q without bathroom US$15/22/33/40; P@🛜) A short walk southwest of Orosi's bus stop, this welcoming, chilled-out budget option has three tidy dorms and eight private rooms surrounding a homey terrace with flowers, hammocks and a wood-heated hot tub. All share a guest kitchen and six bathrooms with hot showers. Owners provide an exceptional information packet highlighting local attractions, including hot springs, waterfalls and more.

Kiri Mountain Lodge LODGE $

(☎8394-6286, 2533-2272; s/d incl breakfast from US$35/45; P🛜) About 2km before the Parque Nacional Tapantí-Macizo Cerro de la Muerte entrance, surrounded by 50 mossy hectares of land, Kiri has six rustic *cabinas* with intermittent wi-fi and hot water (but no fans), and a restaurant specializing in trout. Trails wind into the nearby Reserva Forestal Río Macho.

Getting There & Around

Autotransportes Mata Irola (☎2533-1916) runs buses (roughly US$1) every 30 minutes to Paraíso (20 minutes) and Cartago (45 minutes) from multiple stops along Orosi's main street. Transfer in Paraíso for buses to Ujarrás and Cachí (US$1.15).

Turrialba

POP 31,100

When the railway shut down in 1991, commerce slowed, but Turrialba nonetheless remained a regional agricultural center where local coffee planters could bring their crops to market. And with tourism on the rise in Costa Rica in the 1990s, this modest mountain town soon became known as the gateway to some of the best white-water rafting on the planet. By the early 2000s, Turrialba was a hotbed of international rafters looking for Class V thrills. For now, the Río Pacuare runs on, but its future is uncertain.

Activities

Most organized expeditions from Turrialba head for the Río Pacuare, which offers

WORTH A TRIP

MONUMENTO NACIONAL ARQUEOLÓGICO GUAYABO

Nestled into a patch of stunning hillside forest 19km northeast of Turrialba is the largest and most important archaeological site in the country. **Guayabo** (☎2559-1220; US$5; ⊙8am-3:30pm) is composed of the remains of a pre-Columbian city that was thought to have peaked at some point in AD 800, when it was inhabited by as many as 20,000 people. Today visitors can examine the remains of petroglyphs, residential mounds, a roadway and an impressive aqueduct system – built with rocks that were hauled in from the Río Reventazón along a cobbled 8km road. Amazingly the cisterns still work, and (theoretically) potable water remains available at the site. In 1973, as the site's importance became evident, Guayabo was declared a national monument, with further protections established in 1980. The site occupies 232 hectares, most of which remains unexcavated. It's a small place, so don't go expecting Mayan pyramids, but it's a fascinating visit nonetheless.

Guided tours (in Spanish; from US$20) are available from the monument's front desk. In high season English-speaking guides may be available.

Getting There & Away

Buses to the site were suspended at the time of writing, but would normally leave from Turrialba (about US$1, one hour); check in Turrialba to see if service has resumed. You can also take a taxi from Turrialba (round-trip fares start at US$30, with an hour to explore the park).

arguably the most scenic rafting in Central America. The river plunges down the Caribbean slope through a series of spectacular canyons clothed in virgin rainforest, through runs named for their fury and separated by calm stretches that enable you to stare at near-vertical green walls towering hundreds of meters above. The Pacuare can be run year-round, though June to October are considered the best months.

Ecoaventuras OUTDOORS
(☎8868-3938, 2556-7171; www.ecoaventuras.co.cr; white-water rafting packages per person from US$70) Ecoaventuras offers white-water rafting on the Ríos Pacuare and Pejibaye, along with horseback riding (from US$50) and mountain biking (prices depend on tour length and rider experience). Three-day rafting experiences include all meals, accommodations, equipment and a zipline tour (inquire for prices). It's 100m north and 100m west of the Rawlings Factory.

Explornatura RAFTING
(☎2556-0111, USA & Canada 866-571-2443; www.explornatura.com/en/; Av 4, btwn Calles 2 & 4) Offers rafting, mountain-biking and horseback-riding tours. A rafting day trip on the Pacuare is US$85 per person; a canyoneering and canopy tour is US$75 per person.

Loco's RAFTING
(☎2556-6035, 8704-3535, USA 707-703-5935; www.whiteh2o.com) Loco's takes guests on wild rides of varying difficulty down the Ríos Pacuare, Pejibaye and Reventazón. The outfit also runs camping trips on the Pacuare, plus canyoning and rappelling adventures. A day of rafting starts at around US$70 per person, depending on group size; prices include lunch and transport.

Sleeping & Eating

★**Casa de Lis Hostel** HOSTEL $
(☎2556-4933; www.hostelcasadelis.com; Av Central; dm/d/tr/q US$14/55/65/75, under 3yr free;) Hands down Turrialba's best value, this sweet, centrally located place is a traveler's dream. Spotless dorms and doubles with comfy mattresses and reading lamps are complemented by a fully equipped kitchen, a volcano-view roof terrace, a pretty back garden, fantastic information displays and a friendly atmosphere. There's free tea and coffee in the mornings, a book exchange and board games.

Hotel Interamericano HOTEL $
(☎2556-0142; www.hotelinteramericano.com; Av 1; s/d/tr/q US$25/35/50/65, without bathroom US$15/22/33/44; P) On the south side of the old train tracks is this basic 20-room hotel, traditionally regarded by rafters as *the*

meeting place in Turrialba. The collection of basic rooms includes some with private bathroom, some with shared bathroom and many that combine bunks with regular beds. There's also a shared kitchen, plus TVs in some of the rooms.

Hotel Wagelia HOTEL **$$**
(☎2556-1566; www.hotelwageliaturrialba.com; Av 4, btwn Calles 2 & 4; s/d incl breakfast US$55/80; P 📶) Simple, modern and clean rooms come with cable TV and face a quiet interior courtyard. A restaurant serves Tico specialties, while the pleasant terrace bar is a good place for a drink and has wi-fi.

Maracuyá CAFE **$**
(☎2556-2021; www.facebook.com/maracuya2012; Calle 2; frozen coffee around US$4, mains US$5-7; ⏰2-9:30pm Wed-Mon; 🌿) This bright-walled cafe north of Av 10 serves up one of the best coffee treats in the country – a frozen caffeine concoction with gooey *maracuyá* (passion fruit) syrup and crunchy seeds. Dishes include veggie wraps, creative salads, fried chicken and chips, and Latin American favorites such as *patacones* (fried plantains).

La Feria COSTA RICAN **$**
(☎2556-5550, 2556-0386, 8378-7979; www.facebook.com/RestauranteLaFeria; Calle 6; mains US$5-14; ⏰11am-9:30pm Wed-Mon, to 3pm Tue; 🌿) This unremarkable-looking eatery has friendly service and excellent, reasonably priced home cooking. Sometimes the kitchen gets a bit backed up, but the hearty *casados* (typical dishes with beans, rice, a small salad and a choice of protein) are well worth the wait. Caribbean chicken, salads, pasta and red snapper are also available. Find the place north of Av 4.

★Wok & Roll ASIAN **$$**
(☎2556-6756; www.facebook.com/Wok-Roll-489594887746705; Calle 1; mains US$9-16; ⏰11am-10pm Wed-Sun, 11am-3pm & 6-10pm Mon) Pan-Asian cuisine fills the menu at this eatery near the main square. Enjoy sushi rolls and sashimi, teriyaki or sweet-and-sour chicken, Thai curry, wontons and other Asian favorites, plus tempura ice cream for dessert. Wash it all down with homemade mint lemonade and honey-sweetened jasmine tea.

ℹ Getting There & Away

A modern bus terminal is located on the western edge of town off Hwy 10.

San José via Paraíso and Cartago About US$3, two hours to two hours 20 minutes, every 15 to 30 minutes from 4:30am to 9pm.

Siquirres, for transfer to Puerto Limón About US$2.50, two hours, every 30 minutes to two hours from 5:30am to 6:15pm. Schedules vary slightly on weekends.

CARIBBEAN COAST

The wildness of the Caribbean Coast thwarted 16th-century Spaniards in their quest to settle here and isolated the region for centuries afterward, making it distinctly different from the rest of Costa Rica. Influenced by indigenous peoples and West Indian immigrants, the Caribbean's culture has blended slowly and organically.

It does take a little more effort to travel here to see the nesting turtles of Tortuguero, raft the Río Pacuare or dive the reefs off Manzanillo, but you'll be glad you made the trip. Nature has thrived on this rugged and rustic coast – many visitors will meet resident sloths, hear the call of howler monkeys and spot alligators on the vast network of canals. Others tuck into the area's unique flavors, such as jerk chicken, grilled snapper and *rondón* (spicy seafood gumbo); listen to the lilt of patois; and laze around on the uncrowded palm-lined beaches.

Tortuguero Village

POP 1500

Located within the confines of Parque Nacional Tortuguero, accessible only by air or water, this bustling little village with strong Afro-Caribbean roots is best known for attracting hordes of sea turtles (the name Tortuguero means 'turtle catcher') – and the hordes of tourists who want to see them. While peak turtle season is in July and August, the park and village have begun to attract travelers year-round. Even in October, when the turtles have pretty much returned to the sea, families and adventure travelers arrive to go on jungle hikes, take in the wild national park, and canoe the area's lush canals.

Sights & Activities

Parque Nacional Tortuguero NATIONAL PARK
(☎2709-8086; www.acto.go.cr; US$15; ⏰6am-6pm, last entry 4pm) This misty, green coastal

park sits on a broad floodplain parted by a jigsaw of canals. Referred to as the 'mini-Amazon,' Parque Nacional Tortuguero is a place of intense biodiversity that includes more than 400 bird species, 60 known species of frog, 30 species of freshwater fish and three monkey species, as well as the threatened West Indian manatee. Caimans and crocodiles can be seen lounging on riverbanks, while freshwater turtles bask on logs.

More than 150,000 visitors a year come to boat the canals and see the wildlife, particularly to watch turtles lay eggs. This is the most important Caribbean breeding site of the green sea turtle, 40,000 of which arrive every season to nest. Of the eight species of marine turtle in the world, six nest in Costa Rica, and four nest in Tortuguero. Various volunteer organizations address the problem of poaching with vigilant turtle patrols.

Park headquarters is at Cuatro Esquinas, just south of Tortuguero village. Strong currents make the beaches unsuitable for swimming.

Boating

Four aquatic trails wind their way through Parque Nacional Tortuguero, inviting waterborne exploration. **Río Tortuguero** acts as the entranceway to the network of trails. This wide, beautiful river is often covered with water lilies and is frequented by aquatic birds such as herons, kingfishers and anhingas – the latter of which is known as the snakebird for the way its slim, winding neck pokes out of the water when it swims.

Caño Chiquero and **Canõ Mora** are two narrower waterways with good wildlife-spotting opportunities. According to park regulations, only kayaks, canoes and silent electric boats are allowed in these areas. Caño Chiquero is thick with vegetation, especially red guácimo trees and epiphytes. Black turtles and green iguanas like to hang out here. Caño Mora is about 3km long but only 10m wide, so it feels as if it's straight out of *The Jungle Book*. **Caño Haroldas** is actually an artificially constructed canal, but that doesn't stop the creatures – such as Jesus Christ lizards and caimans – from inhabiting its tranquil waters. Canoe rental and boat tours are available in Tortuguero village.

Hiking

Behind **Cuatro Esquinas ranger station** (☎2709-8086; www.acto.go.cr; ⏲6am-4pm), the well-trodden **main trail** is a muddy, 2km out-and-back hike that traverses the tropical humid forest and parallels a stretch of beach. Green parrots and several species of monkey are commonly sighted here. The short trail is well marked. Rubber boots are required and can be rented at hotels and near the park entrance.

A second hiking option, **Cerro Tortuguero Trail**, is also available. To reach the trailhead, guests have to take a boat to the town of San Francisco, north of Tortuguero village, where they will disembark at another ranger station and buy a ticket (US$7, plus US$4 for the 15- to 20-minute round-trip boat ride). The trail then takes visitors 1.8km up a hill for a view of the surrounding lagoon, forest and ocean. **Casa Marbella** (☎8833-0827, 2709-8011; http://casamarbella.tripod.com; r incl breakfast US$35-65, extra person US$10; @📶) in Tortuguero village can help guests organize the details and even arrange a local guide (from US$35) to take you on the trip.

Tours

Leonardo Tours OUTDOORS
(☎8577-1685; www.leonardotours.wordpress.com; nature walks from US$20, canoe/kayak tours $30/40; ⏲9am-7pm) With over a decade of experience guiding tours in the area, Leonardo Estrada brings extensive knowledge and infectious enthusiasm to his turtle, canoeing, kayaking and hiking tours.

Tinamon Tours TOURS
(☎8842-6561; www.tinamontours.de; 2½hr hikes from US$25, 2-night tour packages per person from US$100) Zoologist and 20-plus-year Tortuguero resident Barbara Hartung offers hiking, canoeing, cultural and turtle tours in German, English, French or Spanish. Tour packages, including two nights' accommodations, breakfast, a canoe tour and a hike, start at US$100 per person. Note that you'll need to pay the US$15 entrance fee for park (p541) hikes.

Castor Hunter Thomas TOURS
(☎8870-8634; www.castorhunter.blogspot.com; nature tours per person from US$35) Excellent local guide and lifelong Tortuguero resident Castor has led hikes, turtle tours and canoe tours for more than 20 years.

Sleeping

Aracari Garden Hostel HOSTEL $
(☎2767-2246; www.aracarigarden.com; dm US$13, r US$30-45; 📶) This newly renovated, tangerine-colored hostel on the south side of the soccer field has eight sparkling rooms

and relaxing shared spaces surrounded by fruit trees. A stay comes with free coffee, a shared open-air kitchen, book exchange and hammocks. The ocean is 50m away and toucans can sometimes be spotted in the trees.

La Casona CABINA $
(☎2709-8092; www.lacasonatortuguero.com; s/d/tr incl breakfast US$20/35/40;) Cute rooms with rustic touches, fans and hot showers surround a lovely garden at this family-run spot. Sit back and relax in one of the hammocks and watch hummingbirds, butterflies, iguanas and frogs visit the garden. It's on the north side of the soccer field.

Cabinas Tortuguero CABINA $
(☎8839-1200, 2709-8114; www.cabinas-tortuguero.com; dm $10, r US$25-35;) Down a side street between the boat landing and the park entrance, you'll find eight quaint bungalows surrounding a tidy garden at this popular budget spot. Rooms have hardwood floors and fans, and the property also features hammocks for lounging, a shared kitchen and a laundry service. Inquire about reduced rates in low season.

El Icaco HOTEL $
(☎2709-8044; www.hotelelicaco.com; s/d/tr/q US$25/35/40/50;) This simple lodging offers clean, brightly painted rooms and friendly service. The beachfront location is ideal, and there are plenty of hammocks from which to enjoy it. The hotel also offers access to an off-site swimming pool, along with rental housing for groups and families. Cash only. Breakfast (US$7) is available by prior arrangement.

★**Hotel Miss Junie** CABINA $$
(☎2709-8029; www.iguanaverdetours.com; incl breakfast s/d standard US$50/55, superior US$65/75;) Tortuguero's longest-established lodging, Miss Junie's is set on spacious, palm-shaded grounds strewn with hammocks and wooden armchairs. Spotless, wood-paneled rooms in a tropical plantation–style building are tastefully decorated with wood accents and bright bedspreads. Upstairs rooms share a breezy balcony overlooking the canal; the **restaurant** (mains US$9-16; ⏲7-9am, noon-2:30pm & 6-9pm) downstairs serves delicious food. It's at the northern end of the town's main street.

★**Rana Roja** LODGE $$
(☎8730-2280, 2709-8260; www.ranarojalodge.com; r/cabins per person incl breakfast US$55/75, r per person incl 3 meals US$75;) On the opposite side of the canal from Tortuguero village, this jungle hideaway is good value. The immaculate rooms are connected by elevated walkways; some rooms have private terraces and rockers, and all have tiled floors, hot showers and awesome nature views – iguanas, deer and herons are frequently spotted.

Eating

★**Taylor's Place** CARIBBEAN $
(☎8319-5627; mains US$7-14; ⏲6-9pm) Low-key atmosphere and high-quality cooking come together beautifully at this backstreet eatery southwest of the soccer field. The inviting garden setting, with chirping insects and picnic benches spread under colorful paper lanterns, is rivaled only by friendly chef Ray Taylor's culinary artistry. House specialties include beef in tamarind sauce, grilled fish in garlic sauce, and avocado and chicken salad.

Mi Niño CARIBBEAN $
(☎8460-5262; mains US$3.50-9, smoothies US$3-4; ⏲7am-10pm) The former Fresh Foods locale and new owner Juan are getting high marks for their vegetarian and vegan offerings, as well as coastal specialties like pasta in lemon sauce and garlic shrimp.

Information

There's one **ATM** in town (Banco de Costa Rica), but bring back-up cash as it may run out of money in high season.

The community's website, Tortuguero Village (www.tortuguerovillage.com), is a solid source of information, listing local businesses and providing comprehensive directions on how to get to the Tortuguero area.

Immediately to the left of the boat landing, **the local tour guides' association** (☎2767-0836; www.asoprotur.com; ⏲6am-7pm) is also a good source of tourist information, as is **Tortuguero Keysi Tours** (☎8579-9414; ⏲5:30am-6pm).

Getting There & Away

BUS & BOAT

The classic public-transit route to Tortuguero is by bus from San José to Cariari to La Pavona, then by boat from La Pavona to Tortuguero. Alternatively, Tortuguero is accessible by private boat from Moín, near Puerto Limón on the Caribbean coast (p544).

From San José's Gran Terminal del Caribe, buy a ticket at the window for one of the early buses (6:10am or 9am) to Cariari (around US$4, two to three hours). In Cariari, buy another ticket from the bus-station window to catch a local **Coopetraca** (☎2767-7590) bus (US$2.20, 11:30am and 3pm) to La Pavona (one to two hours), where you'll transfer onto the boat (US$3.50, 1pm and 4:30pm) to Tortuguero (around one hour).

On the return trip, boats leave Tortuguero for La Pavona daily at 5am, 9am, 11am and 2pm or 3pm, connecting with Cariari-bound buses at the La Pavona dock.

SHUTTLE

If you prefer to leave the planning to someone else, convenient shuttle services can whisk you to Tortuguero from San José, Arenal-La Fortuna or the southern Caribbean coast in just a few hours.

Caribe Shuttle (☎2750-0626; www.caribeshuttle.com) Shuttles from Puerto Viejo (US$75, five hours) and Arenal-La Fortuna (US$60, six hours).

Jungle Tom Safaris (☎2221-7878; www.jungletomsafaris.com) Offers one-way shuttles between Tortuguero and San José (US$45). All-inclusive one- and two-night packages (US$99 to US$152) can also include shuttles from Cahuita (US$60), Puerto Viejo (US$60) and Arenal-La Fortuna (US$60), as well as optional tours.

Ride CR (☎2469-2525; www.ridecr.com) Shuttles from Arenal-La Fortuna (US$55). Minimum two passengers.

Puerto Limón

Puerto Limón is the biggest city on Costa Rica's Caribbean coast, the capital of Limón province, and a hardworking port that sits removed from the rest of the country. Cruise ships deposit dazed-looking passengers here between October and May, but around these parts, business is measured by truckloads of fruit, not busloads of tourists, so don't expect any pampering.

A general lack of political and financial support from the federal government means Limón has not aged gracefully: it's an unlovely grid of dilapidated buildings, overgrown parks, and sidewalks choked with street vendors. Crime is more common here than in other Caribbean towns. However, despite its shortcomings, Limón can be a good base for adventurous urban explorers.

Sleeping & Eating

Find cheap eats at the *sodas* in the **central market** (Av 2, btwn Calles 3 & 4; ⏲6am-8pm Mon-Fri) and smoothies at **Fruit and Veggies Land** (☎4702-8653; Calle 7, btwn Avs 2 & 3; smoothies from US$2, meals US$2-5; ⏲11am-8pm). You can get groceries at the large **Más X Menos** (cnr Av 3 & Calle 3; ⏲7am-9pm, to 8pm Sun), or at the **Palí** (cnr Calle 7 & Av 1; ⏲8am-9pm Fri-Mon, to 8:30pm Tue-Thu) next to the Terminal Caribeño.

Hotel Miami HOTEL $
(☎2758-0490; hmiamilimon@yahoo.com; Av 2, btwn Calles 4 & 5; s/d US$32/40, with air-con US$44/60; P❄@) For its location on the main drag, this clean, mint-green place feels surprisingly serene, especially in the rooms out back. All 34 tidy rooms are equipped with cable TV and fan. Rooms with air-conditioning have hot water. Welcoming staff, common balconies overlooking the street and a secure setup mean it's the best value in town.

★**Soda El Patty** CARIBBEAN $
(☎2798-3407; cnr Av 5 & Calle 7; patí US$1.50, mains US$2-5; ⏲7am-7pm Mon-Sat) This beloved nine-table Caribbean eatery, with soccer memorabilia on the walls, serves up delicious *patí* (flaky beef turnovers stuffed with onion, spices and Panamanian peppers), along with sweet plantain tarts and heaping plates of rice-and-beans (the spicier, more flavorful version of the country's traditional *casado*).

Macrobiótica Bionatura VEGETARIAN $
(☎2798-2020; Calle 6, btwn Avs 3 & 4; ⏲8am-6:15pm Mon-Fri, to 5:15pm Sat; ✎) This macrobiotic grocery store sells healthy vegetarian foods, vitamins and some things made of soy.

Information

Though police presence has ramped up noticeably, pickpockets can be a problem, particularly in the market and along the sea wall. In addition, people do get mugged here, so stick to well-lit main streets at night, avoiding the sea wall and Parque Vargas. If driving, park in a guarded lot and remove everything from the car.

If you're traveling onward to Parismina or Tortuguero, Limón is a good opportunity to get cash and phonecards (Parismina has no ATMs, and Tortuguero's one ATM may run out of cash in high season).

Banco de Costa Rica (cnr Av 2 & Calle 1) Exchanges US dollars and has an ATM.

Scotiabank (cnr Av 3 & Calle 2; ⏲9am-5pm Mon-Fri, to 1pm Sat) Exchanges cash and has a 24-hour ATM that dispenses US dollars.

Getting There & Away

BOAT

Cruise ships dock in Limón, but smaller passenger boats bound for Parismina and Tortuguero use the port at Moín, about 7km west of town.

Tracasa buses to Moín from Puerto Limón (roughly US$1, 20 minutes) depart from Terminal Caribeño hourly from 5:30am to 6:30pm (less frequently on Saturday and Sunday). Get off the bus before it goes over the bridge.

ABACAT (Asociación de Boteros de los Canales de Tortuguero; ☎8360-7325; boat trips one way/return US$35/70) Operates regular service to Tortuguero.

Tropical Wind (☎8327-0317, 8313-7164; one way/return US$35/70) Operates shuttles between Tortuguero and Moín in high season. Discounts available for big groups.

BUS

Buses from all points west arrive at **Terminal Caribeño** (Av 2, btwn Calles 7 & 8), just west of the baseball stadium. Buses to all points south depart from **Autotransportes Mepe Terminal** (☎2758-1572; Calle 6, btwn Avs 1 & 2), on the east side of the stadium.

Manzanillo (US$5, two hours) via **Cahuita** (US$3, one hour) and **Puerto Viejo de Talamanca** (US$4, 1½ hours) Autotransportes Mepe Terminal, every one to two hours from 5am to 5:15pm.

San José (Autotransportes Caribeños; US$7, three hours) Terminal Caribeño, every 30 minutes to one hour from 4:30am to 7pm.

Sixaola (US$5.50, three hours) Autotransportes Mepe Terminal, hourly from 5am to 7pm.

Cahuita

POP 8300

Even as tourism has mushroomed on Costa Rica's southern coast, Cahuita has managed to hold onto its laid-back Caribbean vibe. Dirt roads remain off the main highways, many of the older houses rest on stilts, and chatty neighbors still converse in Mekatelyu.

Cahuita proudly claims the area's first permanent Afro-Caribbean settler: a turtle fisherman named William Smith, who moved his family to Punta Cahuita in 1828. Now his descendants, along with those of many other West Indian immigrants, run the charming eateries and brightly painted bungalows that hug this idyllic stretch of coast.

Situated on a pleasant point, the town itself has a waterfront but no beach. For that, most folks make the five-minute jaunt up the coast to Playa Negra or southeast into neighboring Parque Nacional Cahuita.

Sights

★Playa Negra — BEACH

(Map p546) At the northwestern end of Cahuita, Playa Negra is a long, black-sand beach flying the *bandera azul ecológica,* a flag that indicates that the beach is kept to the highest ecological standard. This is undoubtedly Cahuita's top spot for swimming and is never crowded. When the swells are big, this place also has a good beach break for beginners.

Parque Nacional Cahuita — NATIONAL PARK

(Map p546; ☎2755-0461, 2755-0302; US$5; ⏲Kelly Creek entrance 6am-5pm, Puerto Vargas entrance 8am-4pm) This small but beautiful park – just 10 sq km – is one of the more frequently visited national parks in Costa Rica. The reasons are simple: the nearby town of Cahuita provides attractive accommodations and easy access, and the park has white-sand beaches, a coral reef, coastal rainforest and a small lagoon, all bursting with wildlife.

There are north and south entrances to the park. Visitors who enter the park at Kelly Creek (p549) to the north are not required to pay the US$5 entrance fee, but donations are welcomed. The park service is habitually underfunded, and tourist dollars provide important support for education, conservation and maintenance programs.

Tree of Life — GARDENS

(Map p546; ☎2755-0014, 8317-0325; www.treeoflifecostarica.com; adult/child US$16/7.50; ⏲tour 11am Tue-Sun Nov-Mar) This lovingly maintained wildlife center and botanical garden 3km northwest of town on the Playa Negra road rescues and rehabilitates animals while promoting conservation through educational programs. The rotating cast of residents typically includes kinkajous, peccaries, sloths, monkeys and toucans. There's excellent English-language signage throughout. It's also possible to volunteer here; see the website for information.

Activities

Hiking

An easily navigable 8km **coastal trail** leads through the jungle from Kelly Creek to Puerto Vargas. At times the trail follows the beach; at other times hikers are 100m or so away from the sand. At the end of the first beach, Playa Blanca, hikers must ford the dark Río Perezoso (Sloth River), which bisects Punta Cahuita. Inquire about conditions before you set out: this river is generally easy enough to wade across, but during periods of heavy rain it can become impassable since it serves as the discharge for the swamp that covers the point.

Cahuita

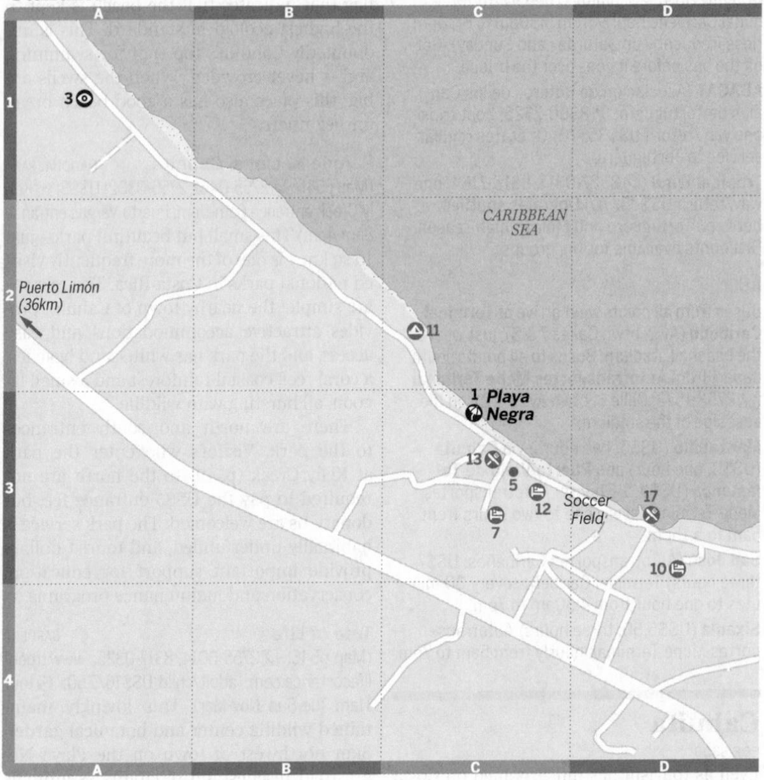

The trail continues around Punta Cahuita to the long stretch of Playa Vargas. It ends at the southern tip of the reef, where it meets up with a road leading to the Puerto Vargas ranger station. Once you reach the ranger station, it's another 1.5km along a gravel road to the park entrance. From here you can hike the 3.5km back to Cahuita along the coastal highway or catch a ride going in either direction. Buses will stop if you flag them down. They pass around every 30 minutes in each direction; fares are about US$1 – bring change in local currency.

Swimming

Almost immediately upon entering the park, you'll see the beautiful 2km-long **Playa Blanca** stretching along a gently curving bay to the east. The first 500m of beach may be unsafe for swimming, but beyond that the waves are usually gentle (look for green flags marking safe swimming spots). The rocky Punta Cahuita headland separates this beach from the next one, **Playa Vargas**. It is unwise to leave clothing or other belongings unattended when you swim.

Tours

Centro Turístico Brigitte HORSEBACK RIDING

(Map p546; ☎2755-0053; www.brigittecahuita.com; Playa Negra) Behind Reggae Bar in the heart of Playa Negra, this well-signposted backstreet spot does it all, but specializes in horseback tours (hour to full day; US$35 to US$110) and surf lessons (US$40 including board use). Brigitte also rents bicycles (US$9) and offers a laundry (US$12 a load) service. Check the website or stop by for full details. Also offers a couple of basic wood *cabinas* and two private single rooms, and serves a good brekkie.

Cahuita Tours TOURS

(Map p546; ☎2755-0000, 2755-0101; www.cahuitatours.com; ⏲7:30am-noon & 2-5pm) One of

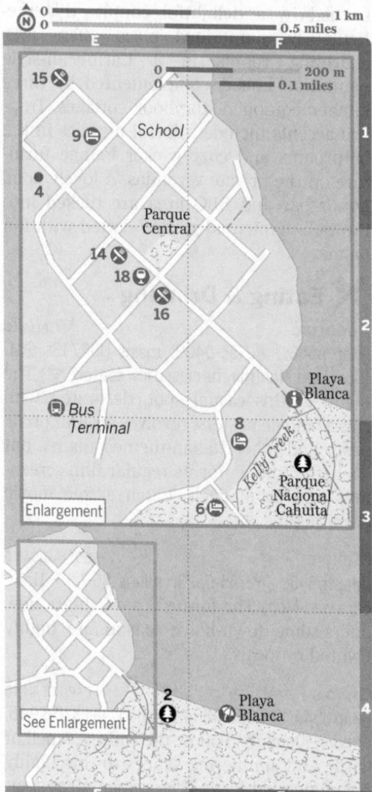

Cahuita

Top Sights

Sights

Activities, Courses & Tours

Sleeping

Eating

Drinking & Nightlife

the most established agencies in town. Offers snorkeling trips (from US$55 per person), horseback riding (US$85) and hiking tours (from US$50).

Snorkeling House TOURS

(Map p546; ☎8361-1924; www.snorkelinghouse.com; snorkeling tours adult/child from US$30/15) Local tour guide and conservationist Fernando Brown launches his excellent snorkeling tours in Cahuita national park (p545) from **Miss Edith's** (Map p546; ☎2755-0248; mains US$6-16; ⏰7am-10pm;) , his family's restaurant. The tour includes a couple of stops where reef sharks, rays and numerous fish are often spotted, and concludes with a fresh fruit snack.

Sleeping

There are two general areas to stay in Cahuita: the town center (near the national park) and the quieter north of town along Playa Negra. If you're journeying between Playa Negra and the center at night, be streetwise; better yet, cycle (with lights) or take a taxi, especially if traveling alone.

Central Cahuita

Cabinas Riverside CABINA $

(Map p546; ☎6064-0825, 8893-2252; www.facebook.com/pg/RiversideCabinsHouses; d with/without kitchen US$30/25; P) This tidy budget place just around the corner from Kelly Creek ranger station offers nine simple rooms with mosquito nets and hot showers; five units that are a bit more expensive also come with kitchens. The grassy yard abuts a swampy area perfect for spotting caimans, monkeys and sloths.

Cabinas Smith 1 & 2 CABINA $

(Map p546; ☎2755-0068, 2755-0157; s/d/tr with fan US$18/23/30, d/tr/q with air-con US$30/40/45; P❄📶) These clean rooms spanning two properties between the main drag and the waterfront are run by a friendly older couple with deep local roots. Eight units adjacent to the owners' home have TV, air-con, wi-fi and fridge; five older fan-cooled units around the corner with an outside bathroom are primarily of interest to the budget minded. All share a guest kitchen.

★ Alby Lodge BUNGALOW $$
(Map p546; 2755-0031; www.albylodge.com; d/tr/q US$60/65/70; P 📶) This fine lodge on the edge of the park has spacious landscaped grounds that attract howler monkeys and birds. Four palm-thatched, raised bungalows (two sleeping three people, two sleeping four) are spread out, allowing for plenty of privacy. High ceilings, mosquito nets and driftwood details make for pleasant jungle decor. Rooms also have safes and fans. Cash only.

Cabinas Iguana CABINA $$
(Map p546; 2755-0005; http://cabinas-iguana.com; d/tr/q US$65/80/95, 5/6 people US$110/120, d with shared bathroom US$25; P 📶 🏊) Set back from the beach on the road marked by the Reggae Bar, this family-run spot features rather worn but nicely shaded simple wood cabins with kitchens. Cabins are of various sizes and are nestled into forested grounds with abundant wildlife. The pool's a pretty place to spot nature.

Playa Negra

Cabinas Tito BUNGALOW $
(Map p546; 8880-1904, 2755-0286; www.cahuita-cabinas-tito.com; d/tr US$46/55, q US$67-72, 5-person house with kitchen US$90; P 📶) Only 200m northwest of Cahuita, yet surrounded by extensive tropical gardens, this quiet oasis offers six brightly painted, clean and simple *casitas,* plus a family-friendly Caribbean-style house with a kitchen. There's also a resident sloth named Lola, who's been living in one of the trees on the property for five years.

Camping María CAMPGROUND $
(Map p546; 2755-0091; campsites per person US$8, incl tent rental US$10; P 📶) Well-spaced campsites share a gorgeous section of waterfront near the northern end of Playa Negra, shaded by coconut palms and a variety of fruit trees. Campers have access to rudimentary cooking facilities, bathrooms with cold-water showers, hammocks, a tree swing and a BBQ area. There are power outlets throughout for phone charging. Maria also rents out her own tents.

★ Playa Negra Guesthouse BUNGALOW $$
(Map p546; 2755-0127; www.playanegra.cr; d/q US$76/90, d with air-con US$104; P ❄ 📶 🏊) Owned by a delightful couple, this meticulously maintained place offers four charming rooms in a Caribbean-style plantation house, complemented by three kitchen-equipped storybook cottages. Tropical accents include colorful mosaics in the bathrooms and cozy wicker lounge furniture on the private verandas. A lovely pool, honor bar and BBQ area are tucked into the well-manicured garden dotted with fan palms.

Eating & Drinking

Cocoricó ITALIAN $
(Map p546; 2755-0409; mains US$7-13; 4-10pm Wed-Mon, may be closed low season; 📶) The menu at this casual spot, decorated with classic movie posters, revolves around pizza, pasta and other Italian-themed mains, but it's better known for its regular film screenings and drink deals. Catch a free movie every night.

Ricky's COSTA RICAN $
(Map p546; 2755-0323; mains $5-7; 11am-6pm Wed-Mon) The former Cafe Cahuita now offers some down-home coastal fare, highly favored by locals.

Chao's Paradise CARIBBEAN $$
(Map p546; 6098-4864; seafood mains US$9-15; noon-10pm; 📶) Follow the wafting smell of garlic and simmering sauces to this highly recommended Playa Negra open-air restaurant-bar, where chef Norman has been serving up fresh catches cooked in spicy 'Chao' sauce for more than 20 years. Other dishes include shrimp and octopus in Caribbean sauce, and beef in red-wine sauce. Also has a pool table.

Sobre Las Olas SEAFOOD $$$
(Map p546; 2755-0109; pastas US$15-18, mains US$15-30; noon-10pm Wed-Mon; ✎) Garlic shrimp, seafood pasta and grilled fish of the day come accompanied by crashing waves and sparkling-blue Caribbean vistas at this sweet spot. Cahuita's top option for romantic waterfront dining, it's only a 400m walk northwest of Cahuita, on the road to Playa Negra.

Coco's Bar BAR
(Map p546; www.facebook.com/cocosbar.cahuita; noon-late) Low-key Cahuita is home to one insanely loud drinking hole. At the main intersection, you can't miss it: painted Rasta red, gold and green and cranking the

reggaetón up to 11. On some nights (usually on weekends) there's also live music.

Information

Banco de Costa Rica (9am-4pm Mon-Fri) At the bus terminal; has an ATM.

Kelly Creek Ranger Station (Map p546; 2755-0461; admission by donation; 6am-5pm) Restrooms are available at the park's northern entrance.

Puerto Vargas Ranger Station (2755-0302; US$5; 8am-4pm) At the park's southern entrance.

Getting There & Away

Autotransportes Mepe buses arrive and depart at the **bus terminal** (Map p546) 200m southwest of Parque Central. Ticket office open 7am to 6pm.

Puerto Viejo de Talamanca

This burgeoning party town is no longer a destination for intrepid surfers only; it's bustling with tourist activity. Street vendors tout Rasta trinkets and Bob Marley T-shirts, stylish eateries serve global fusion, and intentionally rustic bamboo bars pump dancehall and reggaetón. It can get downright hedonistic, attracting revelers wanting to marinate in ganja and *guaro* (a local firewater made from sugarcane).

Despite that reputation, Puerto Viejo manages to hold onto an easy charm. Stray a couple of blocks off the main commercial strip and you might find yourself on a sleepy dirt road, savoring a spicy Caribbean stew in the company of local families. Nearby you'll find rainforest fruit and cacao farms set to a soundtrack of cackling birds and croaking frogs, and wide-open beaches where the daily itinerary revolves around surfing and snoozing. If you're looking to chill a little, party a little and eat a little, you've come to the right place.

Sights

★Playa Cocles BEACH

Playa Cocles has waves for surfers who aren't keen to break skin and bones at nearby Salsa Brava (Costa Rica's biggest break). Instead, it has steep lefts and rights, which break (and often dump) on the steep sandy beach. During the right tide and swell, the best wave breaks near the island offshore; this spot produces a mellow left-hand longboarder's ride over a deep reef. Conditions are best from December to March, and early in the day before winds pick up. The organized lifeguard system helps offset the dangers of the frequent riptides.

Jaguar Centro de Rescate WILDLIFE RESERVE

(2750-0710; www.jaguarrescue.foundation; Playa Chiquita; 1½hr tours adult/child under 10yr US$20/free; tours 9:30am & 11:30am Mon-Sat;)

Named in honor of its original resident, a jaguar, this well-run wildlife-rescue center in Playa Chiquita now focuses mostly on other animals, including sloths, alligators, anteaters, snakes and monkeys. Founded by zoologist Encar and her partner Sandro, a herpetologist, the center rehabilitates orphaned, injured and rescued animals for reintroduction into the wild whenever possible.

Activities & Tours

Find one of the country's most infamous waves at Salsa Brava – a shallow reef break that's most definitely for experts only. It's a tricky but thrilling ride over sharp coral. Salsa Brava offers both rights and lefts, although the right is usually faster. Conditions are best with a southeasterly swell.

For a softer landing, try the beach break at Playa Cocles, where the waves are consistent, the white water is abundant for beginners, and the wipeouts are more forgiving. Cocles is about 2km east of town. Conditions are usually best early in the day,

BUSES FROM CAHUITA

DESTINATION	COST (US$)	DURATION (HR)	FREQUENCY (DAILY)
Manzanillo	2.40	1	6am, 9:30am, 11:30am, 1:45pm, 4pm, 6:15pm
Puerto Limón	2.40	1½	hourly 6:30am-8:30pm
Puerto Viejo de Talamanca	1.50	½	half-hourly 6am-8:30pm
San José	9	4, with 1 change in Puerto Limón	every 1-2hr 6am-4pm
Sixaola	4	2	hourly 6:30am-8:30pm

Puerto Viejo de Talamanca

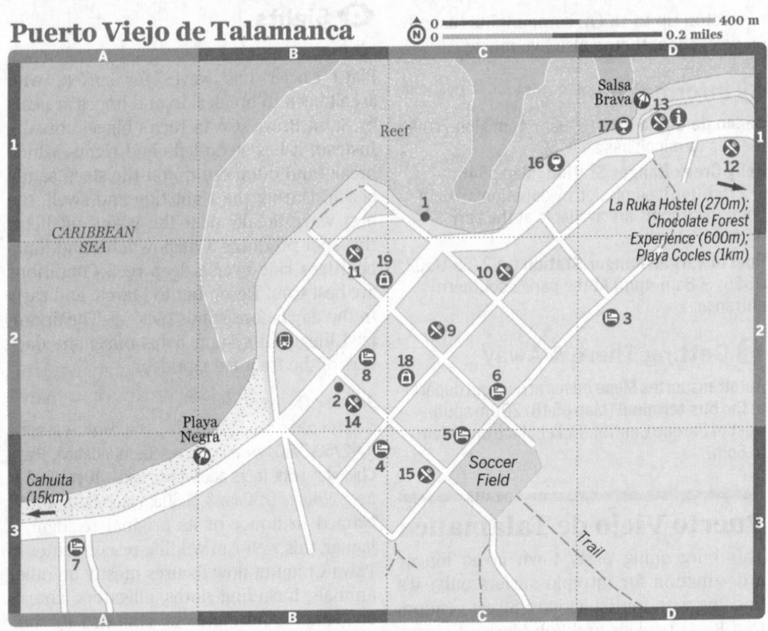

Puerto Viejo de Talamanca

Activities, Courses & Tours

1 Caribbean Surf School & Shop C1
2 Terraventuras B2

Sleeping

3 Cabinas Tropical D2
4 Hostel Pagalú B3
5 Hotel Pura Vida C3
6 Jacaranda Hotel & Jungle Garden C2
7 Kaya's Place A3
8 Lionfish Hostel B2

Eating

9 Bread & Chocolate C2
10 Café Rico C2
11 Como en mi Casa Art Café B2
12 De Gustibus D1
13 Laszlo's D1
14 Sel & Sucre B2
15 Soda Shekiná C3

Drinking & Nightlife

16 Lazy Mon C1
17 Salsa Brava D1

Shopping

18 Lulu Berlu Gallery C2
19 Organic Market B2

before the wind picks up. Meanwhile, Punta Uva (p552) has a fun, semi-fickle right-hand point for intermediates, and you can't beat the setting.

Waves in the area generally peak from December to February, but you might get lucky during the surfing mini-season between June and July. From late March to May, and in September and October, the sea is at its calmest.

Several surf schools around town charge US$40 to US$50 for two-hour lessons. Locals on Playa Cocles rent out boards from about US$20 per day.

Caribbean Surf School & Shop SURFING

(Map p550; ☎8357-7703; www.crcaribbeansurf.com; 2hr lesson US$55) Lessons by super-smiley surf instructor Hershel Lewis are widely considered the best in town. He also teaches paddleboarding.

One Love Surf School SURFING

(☎8719-4654; https://onelovecostarica.wordpress.com/about; 2hr surf lesson US$50, 1hr reiki US$50) Julie Hickey and her surfing sons, Cedric and Solomon, specialize in beginners' surf lessons, reiki and Thai massage. She also offers massage and reiki courses from US$300.

Chocolate Forest Experience TOURS
(☎2750-0504, 8341-2034; www.caribeanscr.com; Playa Cocles; tours US$28; ⏰8:30am-6pm Mon-Sat, tours 10am Mon, 10am & 2pm Tue & Thu, 2pm Fri & Sat) Playa Cocles–based chocolate producer Caribeans leads tours of its sustainable cacao forest and chocolate-creation lab, accompanied by gourmet chocolate tastings. There's also a shop with a refrigerated chocolate room where visitors can try several varieties of chocolate flavor.

Terraventuras TOURS
(Map p550; ☎2750-0750; www.terraventuras.com; ⏰7am-7pm) Offers overnight stays in Tortuguero (US$99), a cultural tour to an indigenous reserve (US$80) and a Caribbean cooking class (US$50), along with the usual local tours. It also has its very own 23-platform, 2.1km-long canopy tour (US$58), complete with Tarzan swing.

Sleeping

Cabinas Tropical CABINA $
(Map p550; ☎2750-2064; s/d/tr US$45/50/60; P ⊖ ❄ 📶) Ten spacious rooms – decorated with varnished wood and shiny tiles – surround a primly landscaped garden at the eastern end of town. The comfortable quarters are just part of the appeal: biologist owner Rolf Blancke leads excellent hikes, birdwatching excursions and rainforest tours. Ask about the collection of rare plants from around the world.

Kaya's Place GUESTHOUSE $
(Map p550; ☎2750-0690; www.kayasplace.com; d with/without air-con from US$50/27, r without bathroom from US$20; P ❄ 📶) Across from the beach at Puerto Viejo's western edge, this funky guesthouse has colorful basic rooms, ranging from dim units with shared cool-water showers to more spacious garden rooms with air-con and hot-water bathrooms. The property also includes a bungalow, a private cabin and three apartments (inquire for prices). A 2nd-floor deck is filled with hammocks with ocean views.

Jacaranda Hotel & Jungle Garden CABINA $
(Map p550; ☎2750-0069; www.cabinasjacaranda.net; s/d/tr from US$35/45/60, air-con extra US$15; P ❄ 📶) In a blooming garden intersected by mosaic walkways, this place near the soccer field has 12 simple wood *cabinas* (sleeping one to four people) with spotless ceramic-tile floors and murals of flowers. There's a small shared kitchen and patio, and yoga classes (US$10) are available. The spa offers massage and bodywork (hotel guests get 15% off treatments).

Hotel Pura Vida HOTEL $
(Map p550; ☎2750-0002; www.hotel-puravida.com; s/d/tr US$40/45/60, without bathroom US$30/35/45; P 📶) This inn opposite the soccer field doubles as a Spanish school and offers midrange amenities. Breezy, immaculate rooms feature polished wood, bright linens and ceramic-tile floors; many have charming views of the surrounding village. Showers are heated with solar power, and there's a lounge with easy chairs and hammocks. Breakfast (US$7), snacks and chilled beer are available.

La Ruka Hostel HOSTEL $
(☎2750-0617; http://larukahostel.com; dm US$10-12, r with/without bathroom US$60/46; P 📶) If the sign 'welcome all sexes, races, colors, religions, languages, shapes and sizes' doesn't lure you in, the friendly greeting from owners Dannie and Dave will. East of town, this hostel has common areas, a shared kitchen, dorms and a couple of private rooms with shared bathroom upstairs, plus a BBQ area, book exchange, and surfboard and snorkel rental.

Hostel Pagalú HOSTEL $
(Map p550; ☎2750-1930; www.pagalu.com; dm US$8, d with/without bathroom US$26/22; P 📶) A contemporary hostel with clean, airy doubles and dorms, the latter with lockers and bunk-side reading lamps. There's also a shared, open-air kitchen and a quiet lounge with tables and hammocks, plus a supply of coffee, tea and spring water for refilling your bottle.

Lionfish Hostel HOSTEL $
(Map p550; ☎2750-2143; www.facebook.com/thelionfishhostel; dm/r US$10/25; P 📶) Right off the main street in the center of the action, this hostel is tops for party people. It was started by local surfers and appeals to like-minded adventurers. The dorms are

BIKE TO THE BEACH

A bicycle is a fine way to get around town, and pedaling out to beaches east of Puerto Viejo is one of the highlights of this corner of Costa Rica. You'll find rentals all over town for about US$10 per day.

WORTH A TRIP

PUNTA UVA

Off a dirt road marked by **Punta Uva Dive Center** (2759-9191; www.puntauvadivecenter.com; Punta Uva; shore/boat dives from US$85/95) is an idyllic quiet cove that could double for a scene in the Leonardo DiCaprio film *The Beach*. There are usually a couple of locals renting out surfboards on the sand, and the reef to the right of the cove is excellent for snorkeling and surfing (but not at the same time!). When the waves are up, this spot creates a forgiving peeling right-hand wave that's suitable for intermediates.

basic and can be stuffy. Facilities include shared kitchen, fans, lockers and hot water. A fried-chicken joint on the first level keeps patrons well fed.

★Cabinas Punta Uva CABINA $$
(2759-9180; www.cabinaspuntauva.com; Punta Uva; cabinas with/without private kitchen US$90/65;) Steps from idyllic Punta Uva, this cluster of *cabinas* with tiled bathrooms, polished-wood verandas, hammocks and a shared open-air kitchen is hidden down a dead-end street in a verdant garden setting. Fall asleep to the sound of crashing waves and chirping insects and wake up to the roar of the resident howler monkeys. Wi-fi is available in common areas.

Eating

★Bread & Chocolate BREAKFAST $
(Map p550; 2750-0723; www.breadandchocolatecr.com; cakes US$3.50-4, meals US$6-9; 6:30am-6:30pm Wed-Sat, to 2:30pm Sun;) Ever had a completely homemade PB&J, with bread, peanut butter and jelly all made from scratch? That and more can be yours at this dream of a cafe, serving sandwiches, soups and salads, and (of course) the treat that gives it its name: chocolate. Served as truffles, bars, cakes, tarts and covered nuts, and in cookies (gluten-free available).

★Café Rico CAFE $
(Map p550; 2750-0510; caferico.puertoviejo@yahoo.com; breakfast US$6-8; 7am-noon Sat-Wed;) Home to some of Puerto Viejo's best house-roasted coffee, and natural smoothies such as probiotic ginger ale, this cozy garden cafe serves breakfast (yogurt and strawberries, omelets). A plethora of other services includes wi-fi, a large book exchange, laundry, plus snorkel and bike rentals.

Como en mi Casa Art Café CAFE $
(Map p550; 6069-6337; www.comoenmicasacostarica.wordpress.com; mains US$3.50-6; 8am-4pm Wed-Mon, kitchen to 2:30pm;) Owned by a friendly bohemian expat couple, this charming vegetarian cafe champions the slow food movement and makes everything from scratch, from the jams and the hot sauces to the gluten-free pancakes. Popular items include raw cakes, homemade lentil-bean burgers, and gluten-free avocado wraps, smoothies and chocolate brownies. The walls are covered in local art.

Soda Shekiná CARIBBEAN $
(Map p550; 2750-0549; mains US$6-10; breakfast 7:30-11:30am, lunch & dinner 11:30am-9pm Thu-Sun) Delicious pancake and fruit breakfasts and Caribbean home cooking can be found at this backstreet eatery with wooden slab tables on an open-air terrace. Lunch and dinner mains are served with coconut rice and beans, salad and caramelized fried bananas. It's just northwest of the soccer field. They may closer earlier on Sunday (5pm) if there's not a crowd.

Sel & Sucre FRENCH $
(Map p550; 2750-0636; meals US$4-10; noon-9:30pm Tue-Sun;) Dark coffee and fresh-fruit smoothies offer a nice complement to the menu of crepes, both savory and sweet. These delights are all prepared by the one and only chef Sebastien Flageul, who also owns the hostel next door (dorm $12, double $30 to $35). Service can be slow, but it's worth the wait.

De Gustibus BAKERY $
(Map p550; 2756-8397; www.facebook.com/degustibusbakery; baked goods from US$1; 6:45am-6pm) This bakery on Puerto Viejo's main drag draws a devoted following with its fabulous focaccia, along with slices of pizza, apple strudels, profiteroles and all sorts of other sweet and savory goodies. Eat in or grab a snack for the beach.

★Laszlo's SEAFOOD $$$
(Catch of the Day; Map p550; 8730-6185; mains US$16; 6-9pm) Whaddya get when you take a champion sport fisherman, born and raised in Transylvania, and transplant him to Puerto Viejo by way of New Jersey? Answer: an amazing, eclectic eatery with no sign and no menu that only opens when

owner Laszlo catches enough fish. The day's catch comes with garlic and parsley, homemade French fries and grilled veggies. Yum.

Drinking & Nightlife

Salsa Brava BAR

(Map p550; www.facebook.com/SalsaBravaBeachBar; cocktails from US$5; ⏲9am-2am Fri-Sun) Specializing in tacos, Caribbean bowls and sweet plantain fries, this popular spot is the perfect end-of-day cocktail stop – hit happy hour from 4pm to 6pm and you'll also catch two-for-one mojitos to enjoy while taking in the sunset over Salsa Brava surf break. On Friday and Sunday the bar brings in DJs for popular reggae nights.

Lazy Mon CLUB

(Map p550; ☎2750-2116; www.thelazymon.com; signature cocktails from US$5; ⏲noon-2:30am) Run by brothers Khalil and Abasi and their friend Rocky, Puerto Viejo's most dependable spot for live music opened in 2010. Lazy Mon draws big crowds, plays reggae, and serves two-for-one cocktails (4pm to 7pm); sometimes there's even a 'crappy hour' (10pm to midnight). Try Jamakin' Me Crzy, a potent mix of vanilla vodka, orange liquor, mango and coconut cream.

Shopping

Lulu Berlu Gallery ARTS & CRAFTS

(Map p550; ☎2750-0394; ⏲9am-9pm) On a backstreet parallel to the main road, this gallery carries folk art, clothing, jewelry, ceramics, embroidered purses and mosaic mirrors, among many other one-of-a-kind, locally made items.

Organic Market MARKET

(Map p550; ⏲6am-noon Sat) Don't miss the weekly organic market, when local vendors and growers sell snacks typical of the region, particularly tropical produce and chocolate. Arrive before 9am or the best stuff will be long gone.

Information

Be aware that though the use of marijuana (and harder stuff) is common in Puerto Viejo, it is nonetheless illegal.

As in other popular tourist centers, theft can be an issue. Stay aware, use your hotel safe, and if staying outside town avoid walking alone late at night.

Banco de Costa Rica (⏲9am-4pm Mon-Fri) Two ATMs here work on Plus and Visa systems, dispensing both colones and dollars. Sometimes they run out of cash on weekends, and they can be finicky; if one machine won't let you withdraw cash, try the other.

Banco Nacional (⏲9am-4pm Mon-Fri, ATM 6am-10pm daily) Just off the main street near the bridge into town. Dispenses colones only.

Costa Rica Way (Map p550; ☎2750-3031; www.costaricaway.info; ⏲8am-6pm) Operates a tourist-information center near the waterfront east of town, and lists hotel and restaurant info on its website and accompanying magazine, *Caribbean Way*. It is also a for-profit tour operator.

Puerto Viejo Satellite (www.puertoviejosatellite.com) A good place to look for info on local lodgings, eating and activities.

Sixaola

POP 3400

This is the end of the road – literally. Bumpy tarmac leads to an old railroad bridge over the Río Sixaola that serves as the border crossing into Panama. Like most border towns, Sixaola is hardly scenic: it's an extravaganza of dingy houses and roadside stalls selling rubber boots.

There's no good reason to stay in Sixaola, but if you get stuck, head for safe, clean **Cabinas Sanchez** (☎2754-2126; d/tr US$20/30; ❄📶).

BUSES FROM PUERTO VIEJO

All public buses arrive at and depart from the **bus stop** (Map p550) along the beach road in central Puerto Viejo. The **ticket office** is diagonally across the street.

DESTINATION	COST (US$)	DURATION	FREQUENCY
Bribrí/Sixaola	1.50/3.35	30/90min	hourly 7am-9pm
Cahuita/Puerto Limón	1.50/3.60	45min/2hr	hourly 6am-8pm
Manzanillo	1.30	30min	every 2hr 6:30am-6:45pm; less frequent on weekends
San José	10.90	5hr	7am, 7:30am, 9am, 11am & 4pm

The bus station is just north of the border crossing, one block east of the main drag.

Buses to San José (about US$14, six hours) run hourly from 6am to 1pm, and at 3pm, 4pm and 7pm, with a change in Puerto Limón (about US$7, three hours from Sixaola). All buses pass Bribrí and Cahuita.

There are also regular buses to Puerto Viejo (about US$3, one hour), running hourly between 6am and 7pm Monday to Saturday, and every two hours on Sunday.

ARENAL & NORTHERN LOWLANDS

You know about the region's main attraction: that now-dormant volcano, surrounded by old lava fields, bubbling hot springs and a stunning lake. Venture further onto the wild rivers and into the tropical jungle of the northern lowlands and you will discover real-life Costa Rica, where agricultural commerce and ecological conservation converge as a work in green progress. Stretching from the borderlands of Nicaragua south to the Cordillera de Tilarán, *fincas* (farms) of banana, sugarcane and pineapple roll across humid plains. Community tourism lives and breathes here, creating added revenue for a historically farm-based economy. You can spot a macaw in the wild, paddle into roaring rapids and cruise inky lagoons, all with lifelong resident guides, then nest in lodges that double as private rainforest reserves. When the tourist hordes get you down, make your way here for a refreshing blast of rural realism and an invigorating dose of wild beauty.

La Fortuna & Volcán Arenal

Whether you approach from the west or from the east, the drive into the Arenal area is spectacular. Coming from Tilarán in the west, the road hugs the northern bank of Laguna de Arenal. The lake and forest vistas are riveting. On either side lovely inns, hip coffeehouses and eccentric galleries appear like pictures in a pop-up book. Approaching from Ciudad Quesada (San Carlos), you'll have Volcán Platanar as the backdrop, and if the weather cooperates, the resolute peak of Arenal looms in front of you.

The volcano may be dormant, but plenty of adventure still awaits you here. There are trails to hike, waterfalls to rappel down, and sloths to spot. No matter what your preferred method of exploring – hiking, biking, horseback riding, ziplining – you can do it here. And when your body says it's had enough, you can ease into a volcano-heated pool to soak your aches away.

Sights

★Parque Nacional Volcán Arenal PARK

(☎2461-8499; adult/child US$15/5; ⏲8am-4pm, last entrance 2:30pm) From 1968 until 2010, Volcán Arenal was an ever-active and awe-striking natural wonder, producing menacing ash columns, massive explosions and streams of glowing molten rock almost daily. While the fiery night views are gone for now, this mighty mountain is still a worthy destination. Part of the Area de Conservación Arenal, the park is rugged and varied, with about 15km of well-marked trails that follow old lava flows. Hikers routinely spot sloths, coatis, howler monkeys, white-faced capuchins and even anteaters.

Parque Nacional Volcán Arenal is approximately 17km west of La Fortuna. The main park entrance is on the road to El Castillo (turn off the main road 13km west of town). It's easiest to reach the park by car or on a tour. Otherwise take any bus to Tilarán and ask the driver to let you off at the turnoff.

In 2017 a new 'sector peninsula' set of trails opened, comprising 1.2km of trails, an observation tower and scenic lake overlook. Although the last entrance to the national park is at 2:30pm, you may be allowed to enter and stay at the new sector later.

Catarata Río Fortuna WATERFALL

(www.cataratariofortuna.com; Diagonal 301; US$15; ⏲8am-5pm; P) You can glimpse the sparkling 70m ribbon of clear water that pours through a sheer canyon of dark volcanic rock arrayed in bromeliads and ferns with minimal sweat equity. But it's worth the climb down and out to see it from the jungle floor. Though it's dangerous to dive beneath the thundering falls, a series of perfect swimming holes with spectacular views tile the canyon in aquamarine. Early arrival means you might beat the crowds: the parking lot fills quickly.

Activities

Hiking

Although it's not currently active, Volcán Arenal is the big draw here. There is a well-marked trail system within the park, and several private reserves on its outskirts. Waterfalls, lava flows and crater lakes are all worthy destinations that you can reach without a guide.

In November 2017, four Dutch tourists were injured, a couple severely, when they were caught in a landslide in the off-limits area (within 4km of the crater) of Volcán Arenal. It took more than a day to rescue them and their Costa Rican guide from the mountain. So, quite literally – don't go there.

Arenal 1968 HIKING
(☎2462-1212; www.arenal1968.com; El Castillo–La Fortuna; trails US$12, mountain-bike park US$12; ⏲7am-10pm) This private network of trails along the original 1968 lava flow is right next to the park entrance. There's a *mirador* (lookout) that on a clear day offers a picture-perfect volcano view. It's 1.2km from the highway turnoff to the park, just before the ranger station.

Hot Springs

Beneath La Fortuna the lava is still curdling and heating countless bubbling springs. There are free, natural hot springs in the area that any local can point you toward (ask about 'El Chollín'). If you're after a more comfortable experience, consider one of the area's resorts.

★Eco Termales Hot Springs HOT SPRINGS
(☎2479-8787; www.ecotermalesfortuna.cr; Via 142; with/without meal US$62/40; ⏲10am, 1pm & 5pm; 👪) Everything from the natural circulation systems in the pools to the soft lighting is understated, luxurious and romantic at this gated, reservations-only complex about 4.5km northwest of town. Lush greenery surrounds the walking paths that cut through these gorgeous grounds. Only 150 visitors are admitted at a time, to maintain the ambience of serenity and seclusion.

Paradise Hot Springs HOT SPRINGS
(www.paradisehotspringscr.com; Via 142; adult/child US$28/16, with meal $45/27; ⏲11am-9pm) This low-key place has one lovely, large pool with a waterfall and several smaller, secluded pools, surrounded by lush vegetation and tropical blooms. The pools vary in temperature (up to 40°C/104°F), some with hydromassage. Paradise is much simpler than the other larger spring settings, but there are fewer people, and your experience is bound to be more relaxing and romantic.

☞ Tours

★Don Olivo Chocolate Tour TOURS
(☎6110-3556, 2469-1371; http://chocolatedonolivo.wixsite.com/chocolatedonolivo; Via 142; tour US$25; ⏲8am, 10am, 1pm & 3pm; 👪) Let Don Olivo or his son show you around their family *finca*, showing off their sugarcane, oranges and – of course – cacao plants. The process of turning this funny fruit into the decadent treat that we all know and love is truly fascinating. Bonus: lots of taste-testing along the way.

Arenal Oasis BIRDWATCHING
(☎2479-9526; www.arenaloasis.com; night/bird walks US$40/65, child under 12 half price; ⏲bird walk 6am, night tour 5:45pm) The Rojas Bonilla family has created this wild frog sanctuary, home to some 35 species of croaking critters. The frogs are just the beginning of this night walk, which continues into the rainforest to see what other nocturnal animals await. If you're more of a morning person, it also does a birdwatching tour. Reservations recommended. Located 3km from La Fortuna's center; hotel pick-up costs US$10.

Bike Arenal CYCLING
(☎2479-7150, 2479-9020; www.bikearenal.com; cnr Ruta 702 & Av 319A; rental per day/week US$25/150, half-/full-day tour US$75/110; ⏲7am-6pm) This outfit offers a variety of bike tours for all levels of rider, including a popular ride around the lake and a half-day ride to El Castillo. You can also do versions of these rides on your own. Make advance arrangements for rental and an English-speaking bike mechanic will bring the bicycle to you.

Canoa Aventura CANOEING
(☎2479-8200; www.canoa-aventura.com; Via 142; canoe or kayak trip US$57; ⏲6:30am-9:30pm) This long-standing family-run company specializes in canoe and float trips (leisurely trips aimed at observation and relaxation) led by bilingual naturalist guides. Most are geared toward wildlife- and birdwatching. Canoa is the sister company of the **Maquenque Lodge** (☎2479-7785; www.maquenqueecolodge.com; s/d/tr incl breakfast from US$105/130/155; P 📶 ≋) in Boca Tapada and can arrange an overnight stay there.

Canopy Tours & Canyoning

Arenal Paraíso Canopy Tours CANOPY TOUR
(☎2479-1100; www.arenalparaiso.com; Via 142; tours US$50; ⏲8am-5pm; 👪) A dozen cables zip across the canyon of the Río Arenal,

giving a unique perspective on two waterfalls, as well as the rainforest canopy. Also includes admission to the resort's swimming pool and 13 thermal pools, which are hidden among the rocks and greenery on the hillside.

Sky Adventures CANOPY TOUR
(☎2479-4100; www.skyadventures.travel; adult/child Sky Walk US$39/27, Sky Tram US$46/32, Sky River Drift US$72/57, Sky Limit US$81/56, Sky Trek US$81/56; ⏱7:30am-4pm) El Castillo's entry in the canopy-tour category has ziplines (Sky Trek), a floating gondola (Sky Tram) and a series of hanging bridges (Sky Walk). It's safe and well run, and visitors tend to leave smiling. A unique combo, Sky River Drift combines a zipline with tree-climbing and river tubing, while Sky Limit combines ziplining with rappel and other high-altitude challenges.

PureTrek Canyoning CANYONING
(☎2479-1313, USA toll free 1-866-569-5723; www.puretrekcanyoning.com; 4hr incl transportation & lunch US$101; ⏱7am-10pm;) The reputable PureTrek leads guided rappels down three waterfalls, one of which is 50m high. Also included: rock climbing and a 'monkey drop,' which is actually a zipline with a rappel at the end of it. High marks for attention to safety and high-quality gear. It gets some big groups, but it does a good job keeping things moving.

Check in at PureTrek headquarters, in a tree house 6km west of town. Combo trips including ATV, pedalboard and farm-to-table food options are available.

Horseback Riding

Arenal Wilberth Stables HORSEBACK RIDING
(☎2479-7522; www.arenalwilberthstable.com; 1/2hr US$40/65; ⏱7:30am, 11am & 2:30pm) Two-hour horseback-riding tours depart from these stables at the foot of Arenal. The ride takes in forest and farmland, as well as lake and volcano views. The stables are opposite the entrance to the national park, but there's an office in La Fortuna, next to Arenal Hostel Resort.

Alberto's Horse Tours HORSEBACK RIDING
(☎2479-9043, 2479-7711; www.facebook.com/albertoshorses; Ruta 702; US$85; ⏱8:30am-1:30pm) Alberto and his son lead popular horseback-riding trips to the Catarata de la Fortuna. It's a three- or four-hour trip, but you'll spend about an hour off your horse, when you hike down to the falls for a swim or a photo op. Beautiful setting, beautiful horses. Cash only. You'll find Alberto on Ruta 702, about 2km south of town.

Sleeping

Sleeping Indian Guesthouse GUESTHOUSE $
(☎2479-8431, 8446-9149; sleepingindianguesthouse@gmail.com; Av 331, near Calle 442; d incl breakfast US$45;) Named for the nearby mountain formation *(indio dormido)*, this delightful 2nd-story guesthouse's five sweet fan-cooled rooms have lofty ceilings, tile floors, colorful paint jobs and big windows. The spacious common area includes a fully equipped kitchen, balconies with volcano views, and a homey living room well stocked with books and games. Manager Heidy's artwork graces many of its walls.

Arenal Backpackers Resort HOSTEL $
(☎2479-7000; www.arenalbackpackersresort.com; Via 142; dm US$14-18, tent s/d US$35/44, r s/d US$55/86; P) The original hostel-resort in La Fortuna, this self-proclaimed 'five-star hostel' with volcano views is pretty cushy. Sleep on orthopedic mattresses and take hot showers in your en suite bathroom (even in the dorms). A step up from the dorms are the raised tents, which have double beds and electricity (but no proper walls, so you'll hear your neighbors loud and clear).

Hostel Backpackers La Fortuna HOSTEL $
(☎2479-9129; www.hostelbackpackerslafortuna.com; Calle 474; dm/s/d/tr/q US$22/46/51/71/81; P) The rooms at this rather grown up hostel are done in whites and beiges, and the courtyard is lush, lovely and strung with hammocks. Guests are invited to go down the street to the sister property, Arenal Hostel Resort, to join the party (swimming pool, bar) and then to return here for quiet, comfort and good night's sleep.

Hotel Monte Real HOTEL $$
(☎2479-9357; www.monterealhotel.com; Av 325, btwn Calles 464 & 466; incl breakfast r/ste US$95/107; P) A smart, modern property on the edge of the Río Burio. This location combines the convenience of town with the nature and rusticity of the forest – meaning lovely gardens and wildlife on your doorstep. Spacious rooms have Spanish-tile floors, stained-wood ceilings and sliding glass doors; some have a private balcony. Ask Angel, the gardener, where all the cool animals are.

La Fortuna Suites GUESTHOUSE $$
(☎8328-7447; www.lafortunasuites.com; Av 331A; d/ste incl breakfast from US$55/85; P❄📶) Here's a chance to luxuriate in some high-end amenities (Apple TV and Netflix, for example) at budget prices. We're talking high-thread-count sheets and memory-foam mattresses, custom-made furniture and flat-screen TVs, gourmet breakfast on the balcony and killer views. Despite all these perks, guests agree that the thing that makes this place special is the hospitality shown by the hosts.

La Choza Inn INN $$
(☎2479-9361, 2479-9091; www.lachozainnhostel.com; Av 331; incl breakfast dm US$10-15, s/d US$36/42; P❄@📶) With all the budget 'resorts' in town, it's refreshing to find a charming, old-fashioned, family-run inn, where facilities are basic but staff are always accommodating. Take your pick from the dark, palm-wood dorms or the attractive doubles boasting volcanic views from the balcony. A clean common kitchen and one-time free transport to Tabacón hot springs are other perks.

Arenal Hostel Resort HOSTEL $$
(☎2479-9222; www.arenalhostelresort.com; Via 142; dm/s/d/tr/q US$17/50/60/80/90; P❄@📶🏊) 🍃 A combination of hostel and resort, this sprawling place is arranged around a landscaped garden complete with hammocks, small pool, party-place bar and volcano view. All rooms are clean, spacious and air-conditioned, with en suite bathrooms. A word of warning: a recurring complaint is that reservations were 'lost' or clients were 'bumped' to Hostel Backpackers La Fortuna.

Eating & Drinking

★La Ventanita CAFE $
(☎2479-1735; El Castillo–La Fortuna road; mains US$3-5; ⏰11am-9pm; 🌱) *La Ventanita* is the 'little window' where you place your order. Soon enough, you'll be devouring the best *chifrijo* (rice and pinto beans with fried pork, capped with fresh tomato salsa and corn chips) that you've ever had, along with a nutritious and delicious *batido*. It's typical food with a twist – pulled pork and bacon burritos, for example.

Rainforest Café CAFE $
(☎2479-7239; Calle 468; mains US$7-10; ⏰7am-10pm; 📶🌱) We know it's bad form to start with dessert, but the irresistible sweets at this popular spot are beautiful to behold and delicious to devour. The savory menu features tasty burritos, *casados*, sandwiches etc. There's also a full menu of coffees, including some tempting specialty drinks (such as Mono Loco: coffee, banana, milk, chocolate and cinnamon).

Soda Víquez SODA $
(☎2479-8772; cnr Calle 468 & Av 325; mains US$5-10; ⏰8am-10pm; 🌱) Travelers adore the 'local flavor' that's served up at Soda Víquez (in all senses of the expression). It's a super-friendly spot, offering tasty *típico* (traditional dishes), especially *casados*, rice dishes and fresh fruit *batidos*. Prices are reasonable and portions ample.

Anch'io Ristorante & Pizzeria ITALIAN $$
(☎2479-7024; Via 142; mains US$10-18; ⏰noon-10pm; P📶👪) If you have a hankering for pizza, you can't do better than Anch'io, where the crust is crispy thin, the toppings are plentiful and the pie is cooked in a wood-fired oven. Start yourself off with a traditional antipasto. Accompany it with cold beer or a bottle of red. Add super service and pleasant patio seating, and you've got yourself a winner.

Chifa La Familia Feliz FUSION $$
(☎8469-6327; Calle 472; mains US$8-12; ⏰11am-10pm; 📶🌱👪) If you're looking for a change of taste – a *real* change from *casados* and pizza – check this out. *Chifa* means 'Chinese food' in Peruvian-Spanish. So what we have here is Peruvian Chinese food, which is something special indeed. The chef goes out of his way to welcome and satisfy all comers.

El Establo BAR
(☎2479-7675; Ruta 702; ⏰5pm-2am Wed-Sat) La Fortuna's raucous *sendero* bar with an attached disco fronts the bull ring and attracts an ever-enthusiastic local following. The age demographic here ranges from 18 to 88. That's almost always a good thing. And the beer's cheap, too!

Information

Centro Medico Sanar (☎2479-9420; cnr Calle 464 & Av 331; ⏰8am-8:30pm) Medical consultation, ambulance services and pharmacy.

Correos de Costa Rica (Av 331; ⏰8am-5:30pm Mon-Fri, 7:30am-noon Sat) Northeast of the Parque Central.

Getting There & Away

BUS

The **bus terminal** (Av 325) is on the river road. Keep an eye on your bags, as this is a busy transit center.

San José (Auto-Transportes San José–San Carlos; US$5, four hours, departs 12:45pm and 2:45pm) Alternatively, take the bus to Ciudad Quesada, from where there are frequent departures to San José.

Tilarán, with connection to Monteverde (Auto-Transportes Tilarán, departs from the Parque Central; US$3, 3½ hours, departs 7:30am, 12:30pm and 5pm)

Monteverde/Santa Elena (US$4, six to eight hours) Take the early bus to Tilarán, where you'll have to wait a few hours for the onward bus to Santa Elena.

TAXI-BOAT-TAXI SHUTTLE

The fastest route between Monteverde-Santa Elena and La Fortuna is the taxi-boat-taxi combo (formerly known as jeep-boat-jeep, which sounds sexy but it was the same thing). It is actually a minivan with the requisite yellow '*turismo*' tattoo, which takes you to Laguna de Arenal, meeting a boat that crosses the lake, where a 4WD van on the other side continues to Monteverde. It's a terrific transportation option that can be arranged through almost any hotel or tour operator in La Fortuna or Monteverde (US$25, four hours).

This is now the first transportation choice for many between La Fortuna and Monteverde as it's incredibly scenic and reasonably priced.

Tilarán

POP 8700

Near the southwestern end of Laguna de Arenal, the small town of Tilarán has a laid-back, middle-class charm thanks to its long-running status as a regional ranching center. Nowadays it's also the main commercial center for the growing community of expats that resides along the shores of Laguna de Arenal.

Most visitors, however, are just passing through, traveling between La Fortuna and Monteverde. Because it's situated on the slopes of the Cordillera de Tilarán, this little hub is a much cooler alternative (in climate and atmosphere) than the towns along the Interamericana.

Driving between Monteverde and Arenal, there is no good excuse for skipping **Viento Fresco** (2695-3434; www.vientofresco.net; Ruta 145, Campos del Oro; adult/child US$15/10, horseback tour US$55/45; 7:30am-5pm;), a series of five cascades, including the spectacular Arco Iris (Rainbow Falls), which drops 75m into a refreshing shallow pool that's perfect for swimming. The 1.3km of trails are well maintained, but there are no crowds or commercialism to mar the natural beauty of this place. You'll probably have the falls to yourself, especially if you go early in the day. Add on a horseback riding tour or grab lunch at the restaurant to support this family-run operation. It's 11km south of Tilarán on the road to Santa Elena.

Sleeping & Eating

Hotel Guadalupe HOTEL **$$**
(2695-5943; www.hotelguadalupe.co.cr; Av 4, near Calle 1; s/d incl breakfast US$42/60;) This modern hotel attracts traveling business types, who make themselves at home in simple rooms dressed up with jewel tones and tiled floors. Service is friendly and efficient. There is a decent restaurant on-site, as well as a swimming pool, kids' pool and hot tub. Bigger family rooms are available, but only some rooms have air-con.

Los Chiles

POP 9900

Seventy kilometers north of Muelle on a smooth, paved road through the sugarcane, and just 6km south of the Nicaraguan border, lies the sweltering farming and fishing town of Los Chiles. Arranged with dilapidated grace around a ragged soccer field and along the unmanicured banks of the leisurely Río Frío, the humid lowland village was originally settled by merchants and fisherfolk who worked on the nearby Río San Juan, much of which forms the border. Amazingly, for Costa Rica, there are street signs on every corner of this *pueblito*.

In the 1980s, American-trained Contras were a presence in town as part of the USA's subversive military actions against Nicaragua's Sandinista government.

With the opening of the new border crossing at Las Tablillas, travelers to and from Nicaragua are no longer obliged to pass through Los Chiles, but it remains an enjoyable water route to Caño Negro.

Sleeping & Eating

With the new border crossing at Las Tablillas, it's usually possible to cruise right by Los Chiles without spending the night (there's nothing to hold you here, trust us). If that doesn't work for you, you'll find a limited selection of hotels in town.

There are a few pleasant places to eat on the road down to the dock, as well as several supermarkets in town.

Hotel y Cabinas Carolina CABINA $
(☎2471-1151; Av 2A, near Calle 5; r from US$30; P❄☎) Not your typical border-town accommodations. This friendly, family-run option gets good reviews for attentive staff, spotless rooms and above-average local food. It's near the main highway, just a few blocks south of the bus station. However, there is no attendant on Sundays, so you'll have to phone to see a room.

ℹ Getting There & Away

BOAT

The boat docks are about 1km west of the bus terminal. With the opening of the land border at Las Tablillas, this river border is pretty sleepy. If you do arrange a boat across the border, before hopping on you need to stop at the **immigration office** (Migración; ☎2471-1233; Av Central (Av 0), btwn Calle 4 & Calle 6; ⏲8am-6pm), across the street from Hotel Wilson Tulipán.

BUS

All buses arrive and leave from the **terminal** (Av 1, near Calle 5) behind Soda Pamela, near the intersection of Hwy 35. **Chilsaca** (☎2460-1886; www.chilsaca.com; Plaza San Carlos) has 16 daily buses to Ciudad Quesada (US$2.25, two hours) from 4:30am to 6pm; you can transfer here for La Fortuna. Autotransportes San Carlos (p530) has two daily buses to San José (US$6, five hours), departing at 5am and 3pm. There are also three departures to Caño Negro (US$4, 40 minutes) at 5am, noon and 4:30pm. Timetables are subject to change, so always check ahead.

Sarapiquí Valley

This flat, steaming stretch of *finca*-dotted lowlands was once part of the United Fruit Company's vast banana holdings. Harvests were carried from the plantations down to Puerto Viejo de Sarapiquí, where they were shipped downriver on boats destined for North America. In 1880 a railway connected rural Costa Rica with the port of Puerto Limón, and Puerto Viejo de Sarapiquí became a backwater. Although it's never managed to recover its former glory as a transport route, the river has again shot to prominence as one of the premier destinations in the country for kayakers and rafters. With the Parque Nacional Braulio Carrillo as its backyard, this is also one of the best regions for wildlife-watching, especially considering how easy it is to get here.

Activities & Tours

White-Water Rafting

Aguas Bravas RAFTING
(☎2761-1645, 2292-2072; www.aguasbravascr.com; rafting trips US$65-85, safari float US$80; ⏲9am-5:30pm) This well-established rafting outfit has set up shop along the Río Sarapiquí (complete with on-site hostel). Aguas Bravas has two tours on offer: take a gentle safari float to spot birds, iguanas, caimans and other wildlife, or sign up to splash through 14km of 'extreme rapids' on the San Miguel section of the river. Both include a spot of lunch.

Aventuras del Sarapiquí RAFTING
(☎2766-6768; www.sarapiqui.com; river trips US$60-95) This highly recommended outfitter offers land, air and water adventures. In addition to white-water rafting (both Class II and III/IV trips), you can also fly through

BUSES FROM TILARÁN

Buses arrive and depart from the terminal half a block west of Parque Central. Be aware that Sunday afternoon buses to San José can sell out as much as a day in advance. There is no longer a direct bus service to La Fortuna or Puntarenas.

DESTINATION	COMPANY	COST (US$)	DURATION (HR)	FREQUENCY
Cañas	Transporte Villana	1	½	15 daily, 5am-7:45pm (8 Sunday)
San José	Pulmitan	7	4	5am, 7am, 9:30am, 2pm daily; 5pm Saturday and Sunday only
Santa Elena/ Monteverde	TransMonteverde	3	2½	7am, 4pm

WORTH A TRIP

CAÑO NEGRO

The remote, 102-sq-km **Refugio Nacional de Vida Silvestre Caño Negro** (☎2471-1309; www.ligambiente.com; adult/child US$5/1; ⊙8am-4pm) has long lured anglers seeking that elusive 18kg snook, and birders hoping to glimpse rare waterfowl. During the dry season water levels drop, concentrating the birds (and fish) in photogenically (or tasty) close quarters. From January to March, when migratory birds land in large numbers, avian density is most definitely world class. Stop at the ranger station first to pay the admission fee.

Thanks to improved roads, tour operators are now able to offer relatively inexpensive trips to Caño Negro from all over the country. However, you don't need them to explore the river. It's much more intriguing and rewarding to rent some wheels (or hop on a bus), navigate the rutted road into the rural flat lands and hire a local guide right in the center of Caño Negro village. It's also a lot cheaper, and it puts money directly into the hands of locals, thus encouraging communities in the area to protect wildlife.

the air on a 12-cable canopy tour. Or stay down to earth with horseback riding, mountain biking or good old-fashioned hiking. Situated just off the highway.

Sarapiquí Outdoor Center RAFTING, KAYAKING
(SOC; ☎2761-1123; www.costaricaraft.com; 2/4hr rafting trip US$65/90, guided kayak trips from US$90) David Duarte is the local paddling authority. In addition to its own rafting excursions, SOC offers kayak rental, lessons and clinics. Indie paddlers should check in for up-to-date river information. If you need somewhere to sleep before you hit the water, you can crash in the simple rooms or camp in one of the all-inclusive tents – no equipment necessary. Located about 18km southwest of Sarapiquí, off Hwy 126.

Tropical Duckies KAYAKING
(☎2761-0095, 8760-3787; www.tropicalduckies.com; off Hwy 126; adult/child US$56/50; ⊙departs 9am & 1pm) Highly recommended for beginners and families, this outfit does tours and instruction in inflatable kayaks, which allow for a fun paddle even when the river is low. Paddle on flat moving water or Class III rapids (or somewhere in between). Reserve ahead.

Boat Tours

The boat traffic at the dock in Puerto Viejo is no longer transporting commuters who have somewhere to go. Nowadays it's used primarily for tourist boats cruising the Ríos Sarapiquí and Puerto Viejo looking for birds and monkeys. On a good day, passengers might spot an incredible variety of water birds, not to mention crocodiles, sloths, two kinds of monkeys and countless iguanas sunning themselves on the muddy riverbanks or gathering in the trees.

Farm Tours

Costa Rica Best Chocolate FOOD & DRINK
(☎8501-7951, 8816-3729; adult/child US$30/20; ⊙tours 8am, 10am, 1pm & 3pm) Where does chocolate come from? This local Chilamate family can answer that question for you, starting with the cacao plants growing on their farm. The two-hour demonstration covers the whole chocolate-making process, with plenty of tasting along the way. Choose from four (chocolate) bars at the end of the tour. About 5km west of downtown Sarapiquí, on the main highway.

Organic Paradise Tour FOOD & DRINK
(☎2761-0706; www.organicparadisetour.com; adult/child US$35/14; ⊙8am, 10am, 1pm & 3pm) Take a bumpy ride on a tractor-drawn carriage and learn everything you ever wanted to know about pineapples (and peppers). The two-hour tour focuses on the production process and what it means to be organic, but it also offers real insight into Costa Rican farm culture, as well as practical tips like how to choose your pineapple at the supermarket.

Sleeping

Isla del Río HOSTEL $
(☎2766-6525; www.aguasbravascr.com; dm US$12, r with/without bathroom US$40/35, breakfast US$6; P 📶) After riding the rapids, you can hunker down at this riverside hostel, operated by Aguas Bravas (p559). It's a clean, basic setup with solid wooden beds, clean bathrooms and hearty breakfasts. There are trails for exploring, as well as an outdoor

hangout area where you can lounge in a hammock, listen to the rushing river and recall your rafting adventure.

Cabinas Laura CABINA $
(2766-6316; s/d US$25/30;) On the road to the pier, behind Banco Nacional, this place is quiet and cheap. The 22 rooms are simple but spotless, with shiny tiles, wooden furnishings and cable TV.

Posada Andrea Cristina B&B B&B $$
(2766-6265; www.posadaandreacristina.wixsite.com/andreacristina; d incl breakfast US$64;) On the edge of town and at the edge of the forest, this charming B&B is a rough-around-the-edges gem. The grounds are swarming with birds, not to mention the frogs that populate the pond. Quaint cabins all have high, beamed ceilings, colorful paint jobs and private terraces. There's also a funky tree house, built around a thriving Inga tree.

★Chilamate Rainforest Eco Retreat LODGE $$$
(2766-6949; www.chilamaterainforest.com; incl breakfast dm US$30-35, s/d/tr/q US$90/110/130/155;) Family-run and family-friendly, this is an inviting and innovative retreat, where owners Davis and Meghan are dedicated to protecting the environment and investing in community. Built on 20 hectares of secondary forest, the solar-powered cabins are basic but full of character, with hand-crafted furniture and natural air cooling. Located just off the main highway, about 5km west of Sarapiquí.

Eating & Drinking

Restaurante Mar y Tierra COSTA RICAN $
(8434-2832; mains US$8-10; 8am-10pm) You can't miss this roadside restaurant, set in an A-frame in the middle of town. The seafood and steak restaurant is popular with both locals and travelers. Try the *arroz Mar y Tierra,* a Tico take on surf and turf.

Bar & Cabinas El Río BAR
(2761-0138; noon-10pm) At the southern end of town, turn off the main road and make your way down to this atmospheric riverside hangout, set on rough-hewn stilts high above the river. Locals congregate on the upper deck to sip cold beers and nosh on filling Tico fare. From here, you can stumble right into your bed if you stay in one of the A-frame bungalows (with fan/air-con US$15/20) near the road.

Getting There & Away

The **bus terminal** (Calle Central; 5am-7pm) is right across from the park, near the Hotel El Bambú. Local buses run hourly between La Virgen and Puerto Viejo de Sarapiquí (US$1, 30 minutes) from 5am to 8pm.

Ciudad Quesada (Transportes Linaco) US$3, two hours, departs eight times daily from 4:40am to 6:30pm.

San José (Autotransportes Sarapiquí and Empresarios Guapileños) US$2.50, two hours, departs 5am, 5:15am, 5:30am, 7am, 8am, 9:30am, 11am, 1:30pm, 3pm, 4:30pm and 5:30pm.

NORTHWESTERN COSTA RICA

What did you come to Costa Rica for? To lounge on pristine beaches and ride glorious waves? To hike up volcanoes and soak in geothermal springs? To spy on birds and monkeys and get lost among ancient trees? The northwestern corner of Costa Rica packs in all this and more. Unlike any other part of the country, Guanacaste – in the far northwest – is a wide, flat expanse of grasslands and dry tropical forest, where savanna vistas are broken only by windblown trees. Further east, the Cordillera de Guanacaste rises majestically out of the plains in a line of sputtering, steaming volcanic peaks that beg exploration. Further south, higher altitudes create misty, mystical cloud forests, teeming with life. What did you come to Costa Rica for? Here it is...

Monteverde & Santa Elena

Spread out on the slopes of the Cordillera de Tílaran, this area is a sprawling chain of villages, farms and nature reserves. The biggest population center – the village of Santa Elena – runs almost seamlessly into its next-door neighbor Cerro Plano and its next next-door neighbor, tiny Monteverde (which borders the namesake reserve).

The Reserva Bosque Nuboso de Monteverde is the most famous one, but there are public and private properties of all shapes and sizes – from tiny family *fincas* to the vast Children's Eternal Rainforest – that blanket this whole area in luscious green. As a result, there are trails to hike, birds to spot, waterfalls to swim and adventures to be had everywhere you turn.

Sights

Reserva Biológica Bosque Nuboso Monteverde WILDLIFE RESERVE

(Monteverde Cloud Forest Wildlife Biological Reserve; 2645-5122; www.reservamonteverde.com; adult/student/child under 6yr US$20/10/free; 7am-4pm) This beautiful cloud forest reserve came into being in 1972, when the Quaker community (which had already set aside a third of its property for preservation), spurred on by the threat of encroaching squatters, joined forces with environmental and wildlife organizations to purchase and protect an extra 328 hectares of land. Today the reserve totals 105 sq km.

Butterfly Garden ZOO

(Jardín de Mariposas; Map p564; 2645-5512; www.monteverdebutterflygarden.com; Cerro Plano; adult/student/child US$15/12/5; 8:30am-4pm) Head here for everything you ever wanted to know about butterflies. There are four gardens representing different habitats; they're home to more than 40 species. Up-close observation cases allow you to witness the butterflies as they emerge from the chrysalis (if your timing is right). Other exhibits feature the industrious leafcutter ant and the ruthless tarantula hawk (actually a wasp that eats tarantulas) and lots of scorpions. Kids love this place, and knowledgeable naturalist guides truly enhance the experience.

Ranario ZOO

(Monteverde Frog Pond; Map p564; 2645-6320; Santa Elena; per attraction US$14, package ticket US$23, night tour US$40; mariposario 9am-3pm, frog pond to 8:30pm) Returning to its former glory as the Ranario, or Frog Pond (it's changed names a few times), this place has added an insect house and a butterfly garden. The frogs are still the highlight – about 25 species reside in transparent enclosures lining the winding indoor jungle paths. Sharp-eyed guides point out frogs, eggs and tadpoles with flashlights. Your ticket entitles you to two visits, so come back in the evening to see the nocturnal species.

Bat Jungle ZOO

(Map p564; 2645-7701; www.batjungle.com; Monteverde; adult/child US$13/11; 9am-7pm) The Bat Jungle in Monteverde is a small but informative exhibit, with good bilingual educational displays and a habitat housing almost 100 free-flying bats. Make a reservation for your 45-minute tour to learn about echolocation, bat wing aerodynamics and other amazing flying mammal facts. The bats are on a reversed day/night schedule so they are most active from 9am to 5pm.

Activities & Courses

Cerro Amigos HIKING

(Map p564) Take a hike up to the highest peak in the area (1842m) for good views of the surrounding rainforest and, on a clear day, Volcán Arenal, 20km away to the northeast. Behind **Hotel Belmar** (Map p564; 2645-5201; www.hotelbelmar.net; r US$225-255, deluxe chalets US$288-405, ste US$450-554; P@) in Cerro Plano, take the dirt road going downhill, then the next left. The trail ascends roughly 300m in 3km. Note that this trail does not connect to the trails in the Monteverde reserve (p562).

Curi-Cancha Reserve HIKING, BIRDWATCHING

(Map p564; 2645-6915, 8356-1431; www.curi-cancha.com; US$15, night tour US$20, natural history tour US$35, bird tour US$85; 7am-3pm, guided hike 7:30am & 1:30pm) Bordering Monteverde but without the crowds, this lovely private reserve on the banks of the Río Cuecha is popular among birders. There is about 10km of well-marked trails, a hummingbird garden and a view of the continental divide. Make reservations for the guided hikes, including the early-morning bird walks and specialized three-hour natural history walks.

Monteverde Institute LANGUAGE

(Map p564; 2645-5053; www.monteverde-institute.org; Monteverde; week-long courses US$390, homestay per day incl meals US$25.50) This nonprofit educational institute in Monteverde offers interdisciplinary courses in Spanish, as well as more specialized programs in tropical ecology, conservation and ecotourism, among other topics. Courses are occasionally open to the public, as are volunteer opportunities in education and reforestation.

Centro Panamericano de Idiomas LANGUAGE

(CPI; Map p564; 2265-6306; www.cpi-edu.com; Cerro Plano; weeklong classes from US$460; 8am-5pm) Specializes in Spanish-language education, with courses geared toward families, teenagers, medical professionals and retirees. For fun: optional dance and cooking classes are included in tuition fees.

WORTH A TRIP

RESERVA SANTA ELENA

The exquisitely misty 310-hectare **Reserva Santa Elena** (Reserva Bosque Nuboso Santa Elena; 2645-7107, 2645-5390; www.reservasantaelena.org; entrance adult/student US$16/9, guided hike US$17; 7am-4pm) offers a completely different cloud forest experience to Monteverde. Cutting through the veiled forest, the reserve's 12km of dewy trails see much less traffic, retaining a magic that is sometimes missing at Monteverde. Open since 1992, Santa Elena was one of the first community-managed conservation projects in the country.

The reserve itself is about 6km northeast of the village of Santa Elena; the **reserve office** (Map p564; 2645-5390; 7am-5pm Mon-Fri) is at the Colegio Técnico Profesional in town. The reserve has a simple restaurant, coffee shop and gift store. Note that all proceeds go toward managing the reserve, as well as to environmental education programs in local schools.

Tours

Finca Modelo Ecologica ADVENTURE
(2645-5581; www.familiabrenestours.com; La Cruz; treetop/canyoning/combo US$45/79/113; treetop 8am-4pm, canyoning 8am, 11am & 2pm) The Brenes family *finca* offers a number of unique and thrilling diversions. Their masterpiece is the two-hour canyoning tour, which descends six glorious waterfalls, the highest of which is 40m. No experience necessary, just an adventurous spirit. The treetop tour involves climbing a 40m ficus tree, using ropes and rappels to go up and down.

Original Canopy Tour ADVENTURE
(Map p564; 2645-5243; www.theoriginalcanopy.com; adult/student/child US$45/35/25; tours 7:30am, 10:30am & 2:30pm) The storied zipline tour that started the trend. With 15 cables, a Tarzan swing and a rappel through the center of an old fig tree, it's a lot of fun. Your adrenaline rush may not be as big as at some of the other canopy tours, but you'll enjoy smaller groups and more emphasis on the natural surroundings.

Selvatura ADVENTURE
(2645-5929; www.selvatura.com; canopy tour US$50, walkways US$30, each exhibit US$5-15; 7:30am-4pm) One of the bigger games in town, Selvatura has 3km of cables, 18 platforms and a Tarzan swing over a stretch of incredibly beautiful primary cloud forest. In addition to the cables, it has 3km of 'Treetops Walkways' and extras including a hummingbird garden, a butterfly garden and an amphibian and reptile exhibition.

Café de Monteverde FOOD & DRINK
(Map p564; 2645-7550; www.cafedemonteverde.com; Monteverde; tour adult/child US$32/15; coffee tasting 7:30am-4:30pm, tours 8am & 1:30pm) Stop by the shop in Monteverde to take a crash course in coffee and sample the delicious blends. You can also sign on for the 2½-hour tour on sustainable agriculture, which visits organic *fincas* implementing techniques such as composting and solar energy. Learn how coffee growing has helped shape this community and how it can improve the local environment.

Sabine's Smiling Horses HORSEBACK RIDING
(2645-6894, 8385-2424; www.horseback-riding-tour.com; 2hr/3hr/all-day ride per person US$45/65/105; tours 9am, 1pm & 3pm) Conversant in four languages (in addition to equine), Sabine will make sure you're comfortable on your horse, whether you're a novice or experienced. Her long-standing operation offers a variety of treks including a popular waterfall tour (three hours) and a magical full-moon tour (monthly). And yes, the horses really do smile.

Caballeriza El Rodeo HORSEBACK RIDING
(Map p564; 2645-5764, 2645-6306; elrodeo02@gmail.com; Santa Elena; US$40-55) Based at a local *finca* (farm), this outfit offers tours on private trails through rainforest, coffee plantations and grasslands, with plenty of pauses to spot wildlife and admire the fantastic landscapes. The specialty is a sunset tour to a spot overlooking the Golfo de Nicoya. *¡Que hermoso!*

Sleeping

★**Casa Tranquilo** HOSTEL $
(Map p564; 2645-6782; Santa Elena; incl breakfast dm US$12, d with/without bathroom US$35/28; P@) The wonderful Tico hospitality starts first thing in the morning with homemade banana bread or pancakes. In

Monteverde & Santa Elena

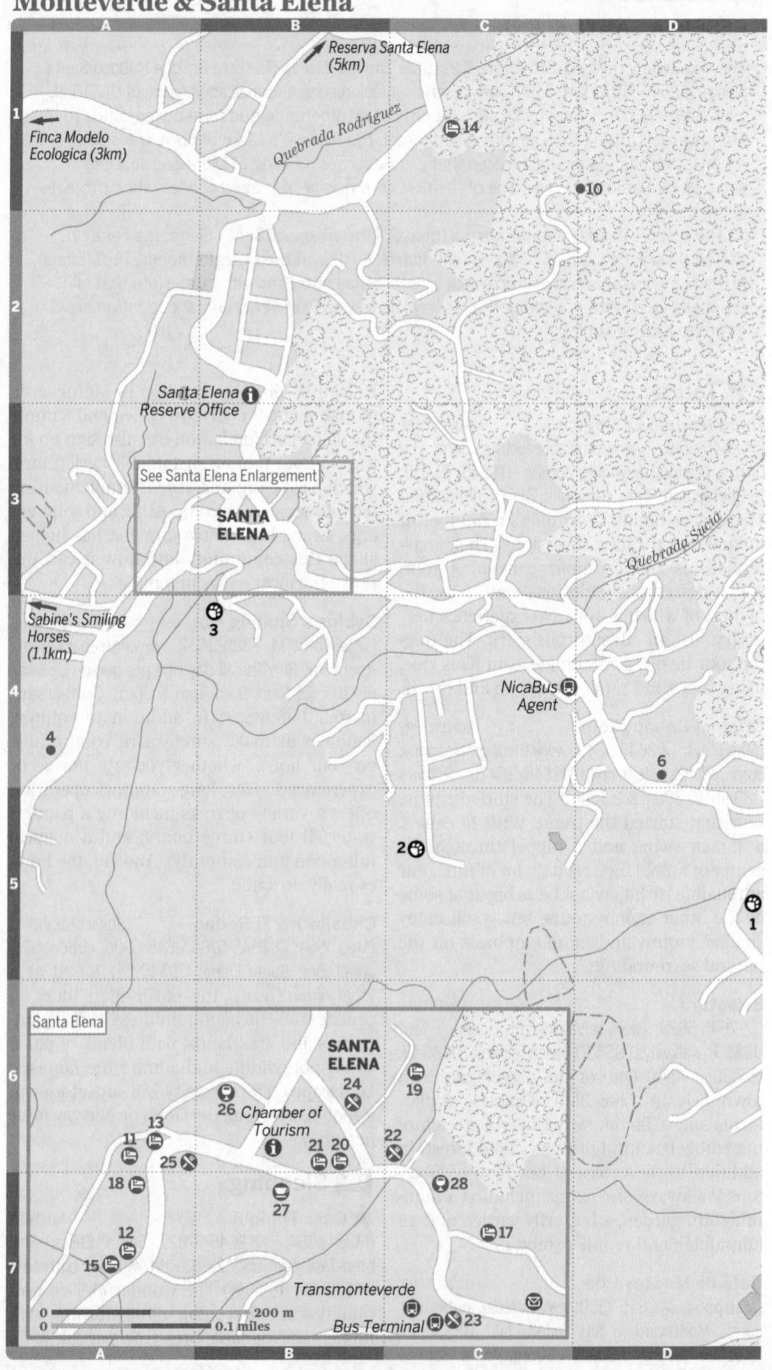

Reserva Santa Elena (5km)
Finca Modelo Ecologica (3km)
Quebrada Rodríguez
Santa Elena Reserve Office
See Santa Elena Enlargement
SANTA ELENA
Quebrada Sucia
Sabine's Smiling Horses (1.1km)
NicaBus Agent
Santa Elena
Chamber of Tourism
Transmonteverde Bus Terminal
200 m
0.1 miles

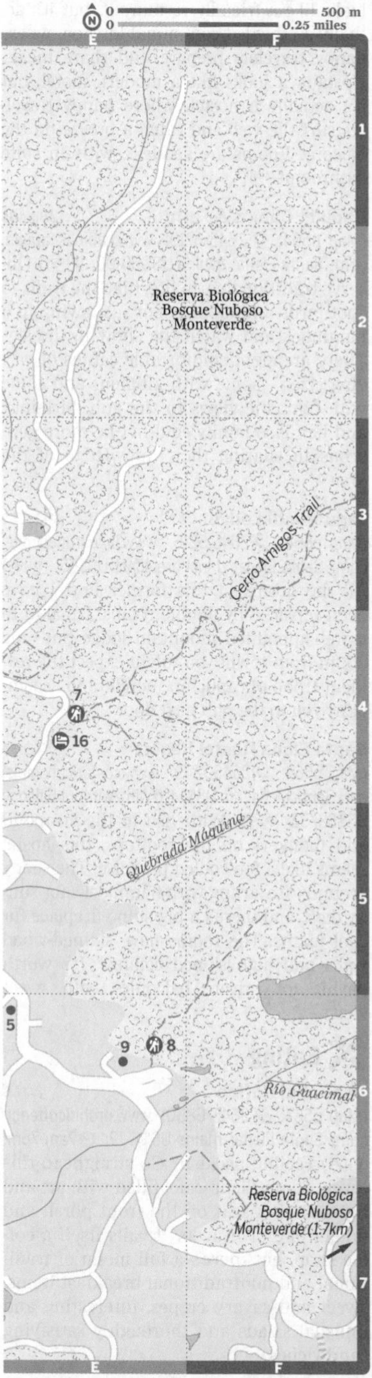

Monteverde & Santa Elena

Sights
1 Bat Jungle........D5
2 Butterfly Garden........C5
3 Ranario........B4

Activities, Courses & Tours
4 Caballeriza El Rodeo........A4
5 Café de Monteverde........E6
6 Centro Panamericano de Idiomas..... D4
7 Cerro Amigos........E4
8 Curi-Cancha Reserve........E6
9 Monteverde Institute........E6
10 Original Canopy Tour........D1

Sleeping
11 Cabinas & Hotel Vista al Golfo........A6
12 Cabinas Eddy........A7
13 Cabinas El Pueblo........A6
14 Capulín Cabins & Farm........C1
15 Casa Tranquilo........A7
16 Hotel Belmar........E4
17 Jaguarundi Lodge........C7
18 Monteverde Backpackers........A7
Pensión Santa Elena........(see 24)
19 Santa Elena Hostel Resort........C6
20 Sleepers........B6
21 Sloth Backpackers........B6

Eating
22 Orchid Coffee........C6
Passi Flora........(see 15)
23 Sabor Tico........C7
24 Taco Taco........B6
25 Toro Tinto........A6

Drinking & Nightlife
26 Bar Amigos........B6
27 Beso Cafe........B7
28 Monteverde Beer House........C7

addition to the excellent breakfast, staff lead free guided hikes, sharing their in-depth local expertise. Rooms are simple and spotless, with some featuring skylights and gulf views. Colorful murals adorn the outside, so you'll know you are in the right place.

Pensión Santa Elena HOSTEL $

(Map p564; ☎2645-5051; www.pensionsantaelena.com; Santa Elena; incl breakfast d US$32-38, d without bathroom US$28, ste US$45-60; P@🛜) This full-service hostel right in central Santa Elena is a perennial favorite, offering budget travelers top-notch service and *pura vida* hospitality. Each room is different, with something to suit every budget. The 'grand' rooms in the annex feature perks including superior beds, stone showers and iPod docks. There are also four family lofts with bunk beds.

Cabinas Eddy CABINA $
(Map p564; ☎2645-6635; www.cabinas-eddy.com; Santa Elena; d US$40-60, without bathroom US$35; P@📶) This budget spot continues to get rave reviews for its amazing breakfasts, attentive service and delightful manager Freddy (son of Eddy, by the way). The rooms are spotless, as is the fully equipped communal kitchen. The balcony is a great place to relax with a cup of free coffee and take in the view.

Monteverde Backpackers HOSTEL $
(Map p564; ☎2645-5844; www.monteverdebackpackers.com; Santa Elena; dm incl breakfast US$12-15; P@📶) Small and friendly, Monteverde Backpackers is part of the Costa Rica Hostel Network. The dorms are clean and comfy enough, the showers are hot, the location in Santa Elena is quiet and management is helpful. Freebies include coffee, hammocks and a sunset hike. Breakfast is DIY, so you can make 'em how you like 'em (eggs, that is). Dorms only.

Cabinas El Pueblo CABINA $
(Map p564; ☎2645-6192; www.cabinaselpueblo.com; Santa Elena; d incl breakfast with/without bathroom US$48/40; P@📶) On a quiet road just steps from Santa Elena town, this pleasant hostel is run by an attentive Tico couple, Marlenny and Freddy. Well-furnished rooms are bright and clean, if cramped, with new TVs. You'll also find a communal kitchen, hammocks and – most importantly – an exceedingly warm welcome. All guests are gifted a treat from the family coffee plantation.

Cabinas & Hotel Vista al Golfo CABINA $
(Map p564; ☎2645-6321; www.cabinasvistaalgolfo.com; Santa Elena; incl breakfast dm US$14, r with/without bathroom from US$37/30, ste US$50; P📶) This bright, kitschy lodge is well kept, the showers are hot and the owners will make you feel right at home. On a clear day the upstairs balconies have great views of the Golfo de Nicoya. The fully wired/wi-fi common space is furnished with beanbags. The 'suite' in the blue house next door is worth the step up in price.

Sleepers HOSTEL $
(Map p564; ☎8305-0113; www.sleeperssleepcheaperhostels.com; Santa Elena; dm/s/d incl breakfast US$12/25/30) Next to **Sloth Backpackers** (Map p564; ☎8896-3200, 2645-5793; www.hostelslothbackpackers.com; Santa Elena; incl breakfast dm/tr/q US$12/60/80, d US$40-50; P📶) in central Santa Elena. Downstairs it looks like a friendly restaurant, but it's actually a crowded communal kitchen, where happy travelers prepare and share meals. Upstairs it looks like a modern motel, but it's actually a hostel, where happy travelers surf the web and catch a breeze on the balcony. Rooms are spotless, with en suite bathrooms.

Capulín Cabins & Farm CABINA $$
(Map p564; ☎2645-6719; www.cabinascapulin.com; Santa Elena; cabina US$60-90; P📶) Observe traditional farm life, hike the trails to spot birds and monkeys or just swing in a hammock and watch the show in the sky. There are eight comfortable cabins of varying sizes – some with kitchens and some with fantastic views to the gulf. Sirlainey and her Tico family couldn't be more generous in sharing their knowledge of the area.

Jaguarundi Lodge HOSTEL $$
(Map p564; ☎2645-5216; www.jaguarundilodge.com; Santa Elena; d incl breakfast US$65; P📶) All the dorms in this former hostel have been replaced by double rooms. It's akin to a well-appointed mountain lodge but only 200m from town; you might expect the resident troop of capuchin monkeys to accompany you to the pub next door.

Santa Elena Hostel Resort HOSTEL $$
(Map p564; ☎2645-7879; www.costaricahostels.net; Santa Elena; dm US$14, d with/without balcony US$58/52; P📶) With fish in the koi pond and monkeys on the rooftops, this hostel seems like a fan-cooled paradise. The shady grounds are strung with hammocks for sunny days, and there's a big stone fireplace for cool nights. The rooms have stained-wood walls and high sloped ceilings. It's worth paying for private balconies with sweet views.

Eating

★Orchid Coffee CAFE $
(Map p564; ☎2645-6850; www.orchidcoffeecr.com; Santa Elena; mains US$8-12; ⏰7am-7pm; 📶🌿) Feeling peckish? Go straight to this lovely Santa Elena cafe, filled with art and light. Grab a seat on the front porch and take a bite of heaven. It calls itself a coffee shop, but there's a full menu of traditional and nontraditional breakfast items, sweet and savory crepes, interesting and unusual salads and thoroughly satisfying sandwiches.

★ Taco Taco MEXICAN $
(Map p564; ☎2645-7900; www.tacotaco.net; Santa Elena; mains US$5-8; ⏰11am-10pm; 📶) Quick and convenient, this *taquería* (taco stall) offers tasty Tex-Mex tacos, and burritos and quesadillas filled with shredded chicken. There's also slow-roasted short rib, roasted veggies and battered mahi-mahi. The only difficulty is deciding what to eat (though you really can't go wrong).

Choose from two locations: this, the original deck location in front of Pensión Santa Elena (p565), is perfect for people-watching, but the newer two-toned terrace restaurant next to SuperCompro is a step up in comfort.

Passi Flora VEGETARIAN $
(Map p564; ☎2645-6782; Santa Elena; mains US$7-10; ⏰noon-9pm; 🌱) Good for the body, good for the soul and good for the earth. That's what this joint strives for in its menu of vegetarian and vegan delights. It's a pretty comprehensive offering, with sandwiches, salads, pasta, rice and *rollitos (empanadas)*. It's all fresh and deliciously satisfying. Look for the Buddha mosaic and you'll know you're in the right place.

Sabor Tico SODA $
(Map p564; ☎2645-5827; www.restaurantesabortico.com; Centro Comercial, Santa Elena; mains US$5-8; ⏰11am-10pm) Ticos and travelers alike rave about this local joint. Look for tasty twists on the standard fare, such as *olla de carne* (beef soup), *chorreadas Ticas* (fried corn cakes with sour cream) and tamales (holiday fare, typically). The *gallos* (soft tortillas with delicious fillings of your choice) are a perfect alternative to the more filling *casados* (set meals) for lunch.

Toro Tinto STEAK $$
(Map p564; ☎2645-6252; www.facebook.com/torotinto.cr; Santa Elena; mains $9-14; ⏰noon-10pm) This Argentinean steakhouse lures in customers with soft lighting and a cozy brick-and-wood interior. It keeps them sated with steaks that are perfectly cut and grilled to order, plus unexpected specials and delicious desserts. The wine selection is good – mostly Chilean and Argentine – but pricey. This place will warm your cloud-soaked soul.

🍷 Drinking & Nightlife

Bar Amigos BAR
(Map p564; ☎2645-5071; www.baramigos.com; Santa Elena; ⏰noon-3am) With picture windows overlooking the mountainside, this Santa Elena mainstay evokes the atmosphere of a ski lodge. But, no, there are DJs, karaoke and pool tables plus sports on the screens. This is the one consistent place in the area to let loose, so there's usually a good, rowdy mix of Ticos and tourists.

Monteverde Beer House BEER GARDEN
(Map p564; ☎8659-2054; www.facebook.com/monteverdebeerhouse; Santa Elena; ⏰10am-10pm; 📶) It's not a brewery – contrary to the sign – but it does offer a selection of local craft beers. There's a shady deck out back and smiling servers on hand; it's a perfect atmosphere for kicking back after a day of adventures.

Beso Cafe CAFE
(Map p564; ☎2645-6874; Santa Elena; ⏰9am-7pm) We overheard someone saying, 'This is the best cup of coffee I've had in Costa Rica.' Hard to quantify in the Monteverde

BUSES FROM SANTA ELENA

DESTINATION	COMPANY	COST (US$)	DURATION (HR)	FREQUENCY (DAILY)
Las Juntas*	Transmonteverde	2.50	1½	4:20am, 3pm
Puntarenas via Las Juntas via Sardinal via Lagartos	Transmonteverde	3.5	3	4:20am, 5:30am, 6am, 3pm
Reserva Monteverde (Monteverde Cloud Forest Reserve)	local bus	1.20	½	Departs 6:15am, 7:30am, 1:20pm, 3pm; returns 6:45am, 11:30am, 2pm, 4pm
San José	Tilarán Transportes	5	3-4	5:30am, 2:30pm
Tilarán, with connection to La Fortuna	local bus	3	2½ (7 total)	5am, 7am, 11:30am, 4pm

* Buses to Puntarenas can also drop you off in Las Juntas.

region, but espressos, lattes and cappuccinos are about all they do here (plus a couple of sandwiches on offer), and they do it very well indeed.

Information

Most hotels, hostels and guesthouses are eager to assist their guests, whether by booking tours or making transportation arrangements.

Chamber of Tourism (Map p564; ☎2645-6565; Santa Elena; ⊙9am-noon & 1-7pm) Operated by the local chamber of commerce, this office promotes its member hotels and tour companies; it's not necessarily an unbiased source.

Consultorio Médico (☎2645-7778; ⊙24hr) In Cerro Plano; across the intersection from Hotel Heliconia.

Correos de Costa Rica (Map p564; Santa Elena; ⊙8am-4:30pm Mon-Fri, to noon Sat) Across from the shopping mall.

Police (☎2645-6248; Santa Elena)

Getting There & Away

BUS

Most buses stop at the **bus terminal** (Map p564; Santa Elena) across from the Centro Comercial mini-mall on the hill above downtown Santa Elena, and do not continue to Monteverde; you'll have to walk or take a taxi if that's where you plan to stay. On the trip in, keep all bags at your feet and not in the overhead bin.

Note that the bus to Tilarán does not leave from the terminal but from downtown Santa Elena, just meters down the street from the Vitosi pharmacy.

If you're traveling to Managua or Grenada in Nicaragua, you can make arrangements to meet the international bus en route on the Interamericana in Lagartos with either of the following:

Monteverde Experts (☎2645-7263; www.monteverdeexperts.com; Rte 606; ⊙8am-5pm) Agent for TicaBus.

NicaBus Agent (Map p564; ☎2645-7063; www.nicabus.com.ni/en/agencies; Cerro Plano)

TAXI-BOAT-TAXI SHUTTLE

The fastest route between Monteverde–Santa Elena and La Fortuna is via a taxi-boat-taxi combo (US$25 to US$30, four hours, departs 8am and 2pm), which can be arranged through almost any hotel or tour operator – including **Monteverde Tours** (Desafío Adventure Company; ☎2645-5874; www.monteverdetours.com; Santa Elena; ⊙7am-7pm Mon-Fri, 10am-6pm Sat & Sun) – in either town. A 4WD minivan can pick you up at your hotel and take you to Río Chiquito, meeting a boat that crosses Laguna de Arenal, where a van on the other side continues to La Fortuna. This is increasingly becoming the primary transportation between La Fortuna and Monteverde as it's incredibly scenic, reasonably priced and saves half a day of rough travel.

Liberia

POP 56,900

The sunny rural capital of Guanacaste has long served as a transportation hub connecting Costa Rica with Nicaragua, as well as being the standard-bearer of Costa Rica's *sabanero* (cowboy) culture. Even today, a large part of the greater Liberia area is involved in ranching operations, but tourism is fast becoming a significant contributor to the economy. With an expanding international airport, Liberia is a safer and more chilled-out alternative Costa Rican gateway to San José, which means more travelers are spending a night or two in this sweet town, knitted together by corrugated-tin fencing, mango trees and magnolias.

The area may be transformed by Discovery Costa Rica, a billion-dollar, 890-hectare theme park due to be built between 2018 and 2020.

Sights

Ponderosa Adventure Park WILDLIFE RESERVE

(☎2288-1000, WhatsApp 8460-1750; www.ponderosaadventurepark.com; tour incl lunch adult/child US$45/37, 3-tour package incl lunch adult/child US$75/68; ⊙8:30am-3:30pm (last tour)) Elephants, zebras, giraffes and other African animals are right at home in the dry Guanacaste heat, as you can see at this private wildlife reserve. The safari tour allows you to get up close and personal with the (sort of) wild animals. Kayaking, ziplining, horseback riding and ATVs are also on offer. The park is in El Salto, about 11km south of town on the Interamericana, halfway to Bagaces.

Sleeping & Eating

Liberia has a good selection of restaurants, both in town and on the road going out to the airport. If you're taking the bus, pick up some snacks for the road at the traditional covered **market** (Map p569; Av 7, btwn Calles 10 & 12; ⊙6am-7pm Mon-Sat, to noon Sun), conveniently located next to Terminal Liberia.

Liberia

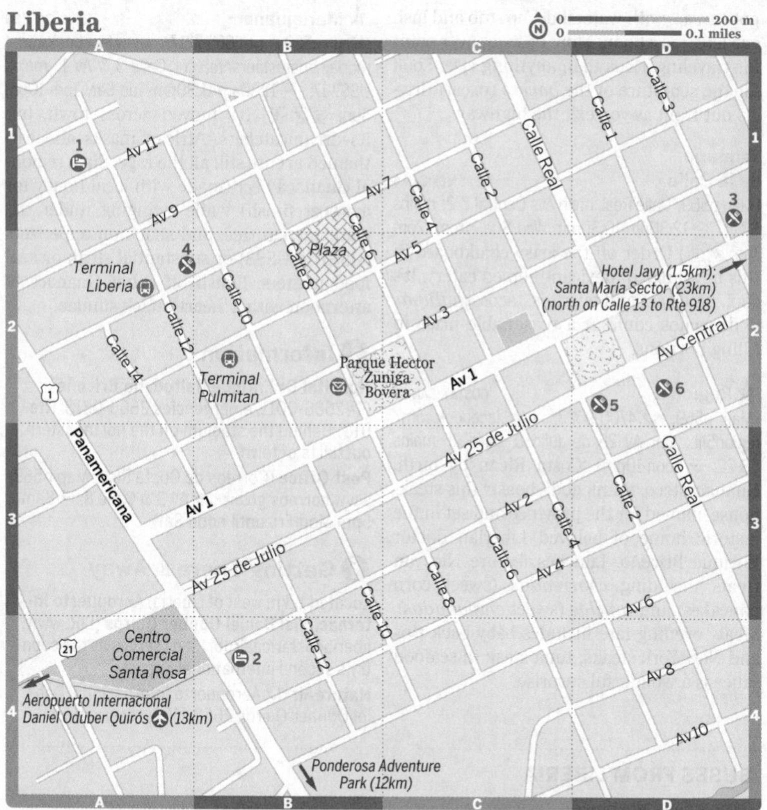

Liberia

Sleeping

Eating

Hospedaje Dodero HOSTEL $
(Map p569; ☎8729-7524, 2665-4326; www.hospedajedodero.yolasite.com; Av 11, btwn Calles 12 & 14; dm US$11, s US$17-20, d US$25-30; ❄📶) This place is super-clean, has super service and is close to the bus station. All rooms have shared bathrooms; some have air-con. There's a communal outdoor kitchen overlooking a small yard filled with flowers and hung with hammocks. It's nothing fancy, but it's very friendly. Shawn, the owner, has an incredibly comprehensive bus schedule in a three-ring binder.

Hotel Javy HOTEL $$
(☎2666-9253; www.hoteljavy.com; cnr Av 19 & Calle 19; d incl breakfast US$50; P❄📶) Isabel is your hostess with the mostest. This charming lady goes out of her way to make sure her guests are happy, not least by preparing an enormous, delicious breakfast to send you off feeling satisfied. The rooms are light-filled and comfortable, with firm beds, incongruously formal furnishings and spotless new bathrooms.

Hotel Boyeros HOTEL $$
(Map p569; ☎2666-0722; www.hotelboyeros.com; cnr Interamericana & Av 2; s/d/tr/q incl breakfast US$66/76/86/96; P❄@📶🏊) The largest hotel in Liberia feels like a cross between a dude ranch and a North American chain hotel. Rooms have comfortable furnishings and tile floors, but they are aging. The 24-hour **restaurant** gets mixed reviews. The

pool area – with waterslide, hot tub and lush gardens – is a boon. More of a stopover point for traveling Ticos than anything else. Look for the sculpture of the *boyero* (oxcart driver) out front as you exit the highway.

Taquería de la Calle MEXICAN $
(Map p569; Calle Real, btwn Avs Central & 2; mains $3-7; 12:30pm-10:30pm Wed-Sun, from 2pm Tue;) Order off the artsy chalkboard in this newfangled Mexican-themed eatery. It's cool, it's clean, and burritos, tacos, *chalupas* and nachos come at a reasonable price in filling portions.

★**Region 5** COSTA RICAN $$
(Map p569; 4700-9523; www.facebook.com/region5lib; cnr Av 25 de Julio & Calle 2; mains $8-22; noon-10pm) 'Costa Rican by birth, Guanacasteco, thank god!' boasts this steakhouse, named for the province and set in the historic home of beloved Liberian doctor Enrique Briceño. Lunches feature Nicoyan treats including *chorreadas* (sweet corn pancakes) and *tanelas* (sweet *empanadas*). Meaty evening fare includes baby back ribs and New York steaks; tuna steak in seafood sauce is a wonderful surprise.

★**Mariajuana** CAFE $$
(Map p569; 2665-7217; www.facebook.com/mariajuanarestaurante; cnr Calle 3 & Av 1; mains US$7-17; 11:30am-11:30pm Tue-Sat, 1pm-10pm Sun;) It's moved across town, but its dreamcatchers, African masks and cat-themed art are still all the rage. Sip a regional Guanaca beer (made with local honey for a sweet finish) while swinging under the giant mango tree, and snack on appetizers (US$7 to US$8) or substantial steak or seafood platters. Finish off a hot Guanacaste afternoon with a 'heart-attack sundae.'

Information

Hospital Dr Enrique Baltodano Briceño (2666-0011, emergencies 2666-0318; Rte 918) Behind the stadium on the northeastern outskirts of town.

Post Office (Correos de Costa Rica; Map p569; www.correos.go.cr; cnr Av 3 & Calle 8; 8am-5pm Mon-Fri, until noon Sat)

Getting There & Away

Located 12km west of Liberia, **Aeropuerto Internacional Daniel Oduber Quirós** (LIR; www.liberiacostaricaairport.net) serves as the country's second international airport.

NatureAir (Aeropuerto Internacional Daniel Oduber Quirós 2668-1106, reservations

BUSES FROM LIBERIA

DESTINATION (COMPANY)	COST (US$)	DURATION (HR)	TERMINAL	FREQUENCY
Cañas (Reina del Campo)*	2	1½	Liberia	Half-hourly, 5:30am-5:30pm
Curubandé	2	40min	Liberia	6:40am, noon, 5pm
La Cruz/Peñas Blancas (Arrieta)	2.50	1½-2	Liberia	5:30am, 8:30am, 9am, 11am
Nicoya, via Filadelfia and Santa Cruz (La Pampa)	2.50	1½	Liberia	Half-hourly, 4:30am-8:20pm
Playa Flamingo and Brasilito (La Pampa)	2	1½	Liberia	6am, 8am, 10am, 11am, 12:30pm, 5pm, 6pm
Playa Hermosa (La Pampa)	2	1½	Liberia	5 daily, 7:30am-5:30pm
Playa Tamarindo (La Pampa)	2	2	Liberia	7 daily, 3:50am-12:30pm; hourly, 2pm-6pm
Playas del Coco (Pulmitan)	1.50	1	Pulmitan	Half-hourly, 5am-11am, plus 12:30pm, 2:30pm, 6:30pm
Puntarenas* (Reina del Campo)	3	3	Liberia	9 daily, 5am-3:30pm
San José (Pulmitan)	8	4	Pulmitan	14 daily, 3am-10pm

* It's quicker to take the San José–bound bus and jump off when it reaches your destination.

2299-6000; www.natureair.com; ⏲6am-5pm) To/from San José.

Sansa (☎Aeropuerto Internacional Daniel Oduber Quirós 2668-1017, reservations 2290-4100; www.flysansa.com) To/from San José.

BUS

Buses arrive and depart from **Terminal Liberia** (Map p569; Av 7, btwn Calles 12 & 14) and **Terminal Pulmitan** (Map p569; Av 5, btwn Calles 10 & 12). At the time of research, Pulmitan was in the process of buying up some of the smaller rural lines.

Parque Nacional Rincón de la Vieja

Given its proximity to Liberia – really just a hop, a skip and a few bumps away – this 141-sq-km **national park** (☎2661-8139; ⏲8am-3pm Tue-Sun) feels refreshingly uncrowded and remote. The name (which translates as 'old lady's nook') comes from its steamy main attraction, the active Volcán Rincón de la Vieja (1895m). The park also covers several other peaks in the same volcanic range, including the highest, Volcán Santa María (1916m). Exhaling geothermal energy, the park bubbles with multihued fumaroles, tepid springs and steaming, flatulent mud pots, as well as a young and feisty *volcancito* (small volcano). All of these can be visited on foot via well-maintained (but often steep) trails. Note the Las Pailas sector is closed on Monday.

Activities

Hiking

From the Santa María ranger station (p572), there's 12km of hiking trails, which take in the hot springs. Since the 2012 eruptions, the trek to the summit of Rincón de la Vieja is not currently open to the public.

Sendero Las Pailas HIKING

A circular trail known as Sendero Las Pailas – about 3km in total – takes you east of Las Pailas ranger station (p572), past boiling mud pools *(las pailas)*, sulfurous fumaroles and a *volcancito*. This is the most popular (and most crowded) section of the park, as it's an easy but worthwhile trail with a lot to see.

Catarata La Cangreja HIKING

A four-hour, 5.1km (each direction) hike leads to Catarata La Cangreja, where falls drop 50m from a cliff into a small swimmable lagoon. The trail winds through forest past massive strangler figs, then to open savanna spiked with yucca on the volcano's flanks, where views stretch to the Palo Verde wetlands and the Pacific beyond.

Hot Springs

There's no better way to recover from a grueling hike than by soaking in thermal springs. Many of the springs are reported to have therapeutic properties – always a good thing if you've been hitting the *guaro cacique* (sugarcane liquor) a little too hard.

In the Sector Santa María, a trail leads 2.8km west through the 'enchanted forest,' past the lovely **Catarata Bosque Encantado** (Enchanted Forest Falls) to sulfurous hot springs. Don't soak in them for more than about half an hour (some people suggest much less) without taking a dip in the nearby cold springs, 2km away, to cool off. If you want real-deal, volcano-created thermal pools, here they are – it doesn't get more 'natural' than this.

On the fringes of the park, there are several private facilities that have thermal pools with varying temperatures: no hiking required. Many companies and hotels offer tours to these sites from Liberia.

Hot Springs Río Negro HOT SPRINGS

(☎2690-2900; www.guachipelin.com; adult/child US$30/20; ⏲9am-5pm) Set in the dry forest along the Río Negro, this magical place is managed by the **Hacienda Guachipelín** (☎2666-8075; s/d/tr/q incl breakfast US$84/102/132/152; P ❄ @ 🛜 ≋). Ten natural, stone-crafted hot pools are accessed by a lovely wooded trail, with hanging bridges leading to pools on either side of the raging river. Pools range in temperature from 28°C (82°F) to 53°C (127°F).

Sleeping

El Sol Verde CAMPGROUND $

(☎2665-5357; www.elsolverde.com; campsite US$10, tent houses US$29, d/q US$52/71; P 🛜) 🍃 The feisty German couple here offers three Spanish-tiled, wood-walled rooms. Alternatively, bed down in the camping area, where there are a few furnished tent houses, a shared outdoor kitchen, solar-heated showers and plenty of space to pitch your own tent. The mural-painted terrace is a lovely place to relax. In Curubandé village.

WORTH A TRIP

SANTA ROSA

Santa Rosa (☎2666-5051; www.acguanacaste.ac.cr; adult/child US$15/5, surfing or snorkeling surcharge US$12; ⏲8am-4pm) is the southern sector of the Area de Conservación Guanacaste. Some 30km of hiking trails weave through this tropical dry forest, offering fantastic vistas of the Cordillera de Guanacaste and the Valle Naranjo. It's also the site of two historic battles, with the small **La Casona museum** (www.acguanacaste.ac.cr/1997/ecodesarrollo/ecoturismo/museosantarosaing.html; incl in park admission; ⏲8-11:30am & 1-4pm) and **Monument de los Heroes** (incl in park admission) to prove it. Along the coast, **Playa Naranjo** (surfing surcharge US$12) is a legendary surfing beach, while **Playa Nancite** is a critical nesting site for the olive ridley turtle.

To reach the Santa Rosa sector, turn off the Interamericana at the signed entrance 35km north of Liberia. It's 7km on a paved road to the park headquarters, where you'll also find the museum, campgrounds and a **nature trail**. From here, a very rough track leads 12km to Playa Naranjo. It's a notoriously bad road, impassable during the rainy season and requiring 4WD at any time of year.

Casa Rural Aroma de Campo HOTEL $$
(☎2665-0008, reservations 7010-5776; www.aromadecampo.com; incl breakfast s/d/tr/q US$59/81/110/128, bungalow US$116; P📶✖) Near the village of Curubandé, this serene, epiphyte-hung, hammock-strung oasis has six rooms with polished hardwood floors, open bathrooms, colorful wall art, mosquito nets and a classy rural sensibility. Scattered around the property, an additional six prefab bungalows have bold colors and glass walls for better immersion in the forested setting. Delicious meals are served family-style in the courtyard.

Rinconcito Lodge LODGE $$
(☎2206-4832, 2206-4833; www.rinconcitolodge.com; San Jorge; lodge s/d US$34/47, standard s/d US$52/70, superior d US$78; P📶) Just 3km from the Santa María sector of the park, this affordable option has attractive, rustic cabins that are surrounded by some of the prettiest pastoral scenery imaginable. The cheaper rooms are tiny, but they are clean and fresh. The lodge also offers horseback riding and ziplining tours.

ℹ Information

The two main entrances to the park each have their own ranger station, where you sign in, pay admission and get free maps. Most visitors enter through **Las Pailas ranger station** (☎2666-5051; www.acguanacaste.ac.cr; adult/6-12yr/under 5yr US$15/5/free; ⏲8am-4pm Tue-Sun, no entry after 3pm) on the western flank, where most of the trails begin. The **Santa María ranger station** (☎2666-5051; www.acguanacaste.ac.cr; adult/6-12yr/under 5yr US$15/5/free; ⏲7am-4pm, no entry after 3pm), to the east, is in the Hacienda Santa María, a 19th-century *rancho* that was reputedly once owned by US President Lyndon Johnson. This is your access point to the sulfurous springs.

ℹ Getting There & Away

There's no public transportation to the park entrances, but a bus travels from Liberia to Curubandé three times daily in each direction (40 minutes). Any hotel in Liberia can arrange transport to the park for around US$20 per person. Alternatively, you can hire a 4WD taxi from Liberia for about US$40 to Las Pailas, or US$65 to Santa María, each way.

La Cruz

POP 11,100

La Cruz is the closest town to the Peñas Blancas border crossing with Nicaragua, and is the principal gateway to Bahía Salinas, Costa Rica's premier kitesurfing destination. La Cruz itself is a fairly sleepy town set on a mountaintop plateau, with lots of Tico charm and magical views of an epic, windswept bay. El Mirador or the neighboring bar are required stops to stretch your legs and widen your worldview.

🛏 Sleeping

Hotel Amalia Inn INN $
(☎2679-9618; https://hotelamalialacruz.weebly.com; Calle Central, near Av 2; s/d with fan US$25/35, with air-con US$40/50; P❄📶✖) This yellow stucco house on a cliff isn't a bad place to spend the night. Its eight homey rooms are furnished rather randomly and have attractive brick floors and wooden ceilings. Walls in the meandering house are hung with

modernist paintings by Amalia's late husband, Lester Bounds. The shared terracotta terraces have stupendous bay views.

Hotel La Mirada HOTEL $
(2679-9702; www.hotellamirada.com; Av 1; d US$44-61; P ❄ 📶) This is the town's spiffiest spot. Family owned and lovingly cared for, rooms are spacious and clean, with high, beamed ceilings and loft sleeping spaces. The biggest rooms have kitchenettes and air-con. Despite the name, there's no view to speak of. It's just off the Interamericana, 100m north and east of the Banco Nacional de Costa Rica.

Getting There & Away

The bus station is on the western edge of town, just north of the road to Bahía Salinas. A **Transportes Deldú counter** (2223-7011; www.facebook.com/transportedeldu; Rte 935; 7:30am-12:30pm & 1:30-6pm) sells tickets and stores luggage. To catch a TransNica bus to Peñas Blancas at the border and on to Managua in Nicaragua, you'll need to flag down a bus on the Interamericana.

Peñas Blancas US$1, 45 minutes, 10 almost hourly from 5am to 5:30pm.

San José via Liberia US$7, five hours, departs hourly from 5am to 7pm.

For information on the border crossing, see Border Crossings (p619).

PENÍNSULA DE NICOYA

Maybe you've come to the Península de Nicoya to sample the sapphire waters that peel left and right, curling into perfect barrels up and down the coast. Or perhaps you just want to hunker down on a pristine patch of sand and soak up some sun. By day, you might ramble down rugged roads, fording rivers and navigating ridges with massive coastal views. By night, you can spy on nesting sea turtles or take a midnight dip in the luxuriant Pacific. In between adventures, you'll find no shortage of boutique bunks, tasty kitchens and indulgent spas to shelter and nourish body and soul. Whether you come for the thrills or just to chill, the Nicoya peninsula delivers. You'll find that the days (or weeks, or months) drift away on ocean breezes, disappearing all too quickly.

Playas del Coco

Sportfishing is the engine that built Playas del Coco, while deep-sea diving has become an additional attraction. You'll mingle with foreign-born anglers and divers at happy hour (it starts rather early). That said, there is an actual Tico community here and plenty of Tico tourists. The town broadened its international sporting reputation by hosting the country's first-ever Ironman competition in June 2017.

Stroll along the grassy beachfront plaza at sunset and gaze upon the wide bay sheltered by long, rugged peninsular arms, the natural marina bobbing with motorboats and fishing *pangas* (small motorboats). All will be right in your world.

Activities

Sportfishing, sailing, scuba diving and sea kayaking are popular activities that keep the troops entertained. Sea kayaks are perfect for exploring the rocky headlands to the north and south of the beach.

Pacific Coast Stand-Up Paddle WATER SPORTS
(Pacific Coast Discovery; 8359-5118; www.pacificcoastsuptours.com; lessons US$35, tours US$65-85) Let Jorge and his crew take you out for an amazing day of paddling, exploring hidden coves, spotting dolphins and other sea creatures, and picnicking on a near-private beach. The three-hour tour even allows time for snorkeling. These guys also offer surf and snorkel tours, all of which are recommended.

Summer Salt DIVING
(2670-0308; www.costaricadivecenter.com; Las Chorreras; 2-tank dive incl equipment from US$105) This friendly Swiss-run dive shop has professional, bilingual staff. Snorkelers are also welcome on the dive boats. Follow the sign to Summer Salt.

Sleeping & Eating

Garden House at M&M HOSTEL $
(2670-0273; www.hotelmym.com; La Chorrera; dm/d incl breakfast US$20/65; ❄ 📶 🏊) There are plenty of budget *cabinas* (cabins) in Coco but this is the only proper hostel. After many changes in name and management, the property is now known as the Garden House – operated by the good folks behind Hotel M&M (p576). There are two dorm rooms, a handful of private rooms and a sweet swimming pool, all within striking distance of the beach.

Península de Nicoya

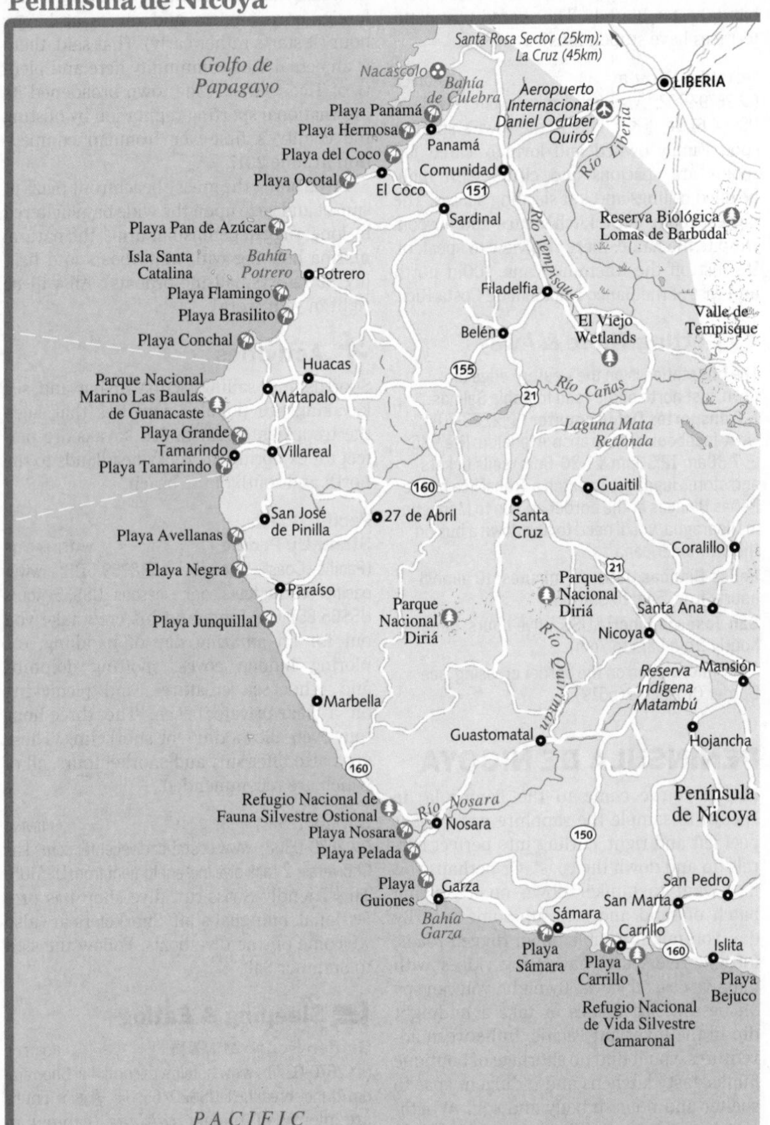
Santa Rosa Sector (25km); La Cruz (45km)
Golfo de Papagayo
Nacascolo
Bahía de Culebra
LIBERIA
Aeropuerto Internacional Daniel Oduber Quirós
Playa Panamá
Playa Hermosa
Panamá
Playa del Coco
Comunidad
Río Liberia
Playa Ocotal
El Coco
151
Sardinal
Reserva Biológica Lomas de Barbudal
Playa Pan de Azúcar
Isla Santa Catalina
Bahía Potrero
Potrero
Río Tempisque
Playa Flamingo
Filadelfia
Playa Brasilito
Valle de Tempisque
Playa Conchal
Belén
El Viejo Wetlands
Huacas
155
Parque Nacional Marino Las Baulas de Guanacaste
Matapalo
21
Río Cañas
Laguna Mata Redonda
Playa Grande
Tamarindo
Villareal
Playa Tamarindo
160
Guaitil
San José de Pinilla
27 de Abril
Santa Cruz
Playa Avellanas
Coralillo
Playa Negra
Paraíso
Parque Nacional Diriá
Parque Nacional Diriá
Santa Ana
Playa Junquillal
Nicoya
Río Quirimán
Reserva Indígena Matambú
Mansión
Marbella
Hojancha
Guastomatal
160
Península de Nicoya
Refugio Nacional de Fauna Silvestre Ostional
Río Nosara
Nosara
Playa Nosara
150
Playa Pelada
Playa Guiones
Garza
San Pedro
San Marta
Bahía Garza
Sámara
Carrillo
Playa Sámara
Playa Carrillo
160
Islita
Playa Bejuco
Refugio Nacional de Vida Silvestre Camaronal
PACIFIC OCEAN
COSTA RICA

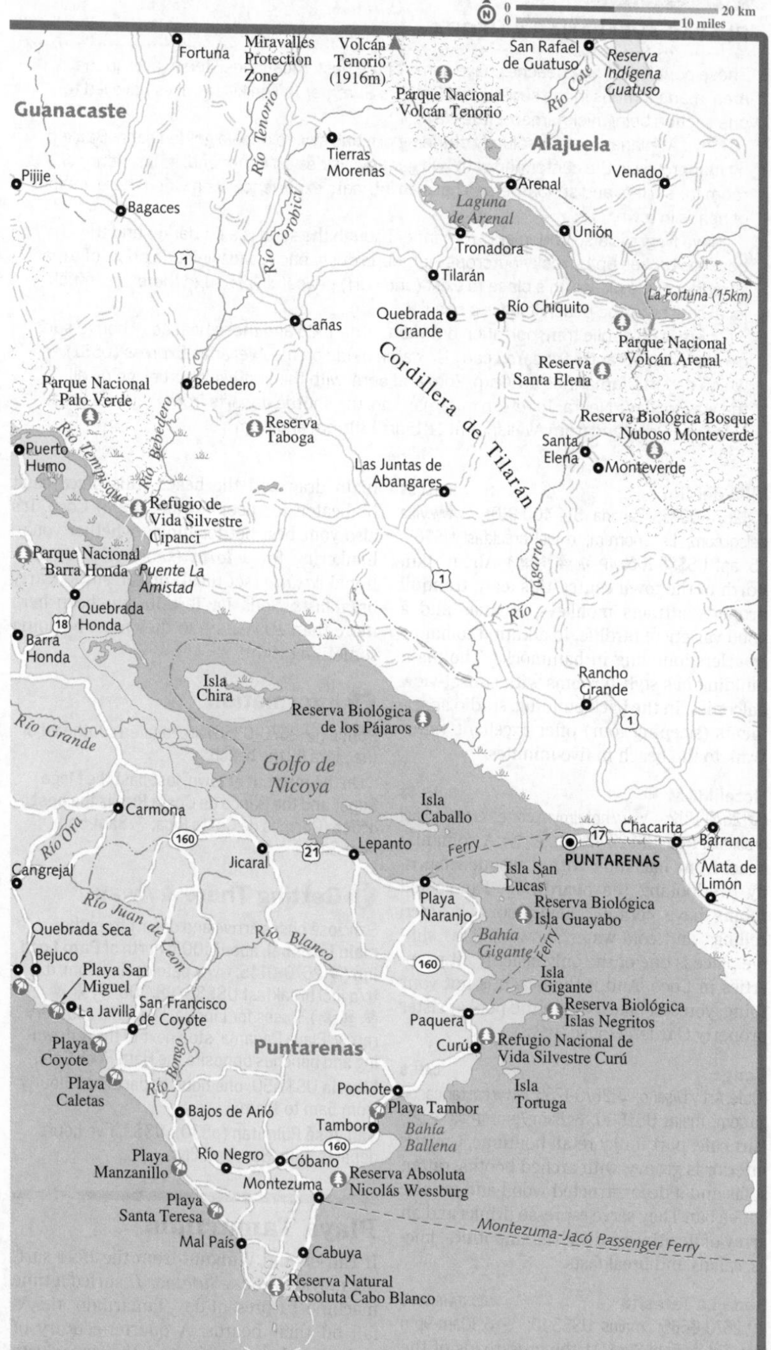

0
20 km
0
10 miles
Fortuna
Miravalles Protection Zone
Volcán Tenorio (1916m)
San Rafael de Guatuso
Reserva Indígena Guatuso
Río Cote
Parque Nacional Volcán Tenorio
Guanacaste
Río Tenorio
Alajuela
Tierras Morenas
Pijije
Arenal
Venado
Laguna de Arenal
Bagaces
Río Corobicí
Unión
Tronadora
1
Tilarán
La Fortuna (15km)
Quebrada Grande
Río Chiquito
Cañas
Parque Nacional Volcán Arenal
Cordillera de Tilarán
Reserva Santa Elena
Parque Nacional Palo Verde
Bebedero
Reserva Biológica Bosque Nuboso Monteverde
Río Bebedero
Reserva Taboga
Río Tempisque
Santa Elena
Puerto Humo
Monteverde
Las Juntas de Abangares
Refugio de Vida Silvestre Cipanci
Parque Nacional Barra Honda
Puente La Amistad
Río Lagarto
Quebrada Honda
18
Barra Honda
Isla Chira
Rancho Grande
Reserva Biológica de los Pájaros
Río Grande
Golfo de Nicoya
Isla Caballo
Carmona
Chacarita
Barranca
17
160
Río Ora
Lepanto
Ferry
Jicaral
21
PUNTARENAS
Cangrejal
Isla San Lucas
Mata de Limón
Playa Naranjo
Reserva Biológica Isla Guayabo
Río Juan de Leon
Quebrada Seca
Río Blanco
Bahía Gigante
Bejuco
Playa San Miguel
Isla Gigante
La Javilla
San Francisco de Coyote
Paquera
Reserva Biológica Islas Negritos
Playa Coyote
Puntarenas
Curú
Refugio Nacional de Vida Silvestre Curú
Playa Caletas
Río Bongo
Pochote
Isla Tortuga
Bajos de Arió
Playa Tambor
Tambor
Bahía Ballena
Playa Manzanillo
Río Negro
Cóbano
Reserva Absoluta Nicolás Wessburg
Montezuma
Playa Santa Teresa
Montezuma-Jacó Passenger Ferry
Mal País
Cabuya
Reserva Natural Absoluta Cabo Blanco

DON'T MISS

PLAYAS AVELLANAS & NEGRA

These popular surfing beaches have some of the best, most consistent waves in the area, made famous in the surf classic *Endless Summer II*. The killer waves have led to one section being nicknamed 'Little Hawaii.'

Playa Avellanas is an absolutely stunning pristine sweep of pale golden sand. Backed by mangroves in the center and with two gentle hillsides on either end, it has plenty of room for surfers and sunbathers to have an intimate experience even when there are lots of heads in town.

Playa Negra is also undeniably romantic. Though the sand is a bit darker and the beach is broken up by rocky outcrops, gorgeous dusty back roads link tide pools of expat shredders who picked this place to exist (and surf) peacefully. Though there isn't much local soul here, the beach itself is a beaut.

There is no public transportation between Tamarindo and these beaches, though surf camps often organize trips. You can also catch a ride on the Avellanas Express (p581), which departs Tamarindo at 10am, 2pm and 5pm, with the first two shuttles going all the way to Playa Negra. To return to Tamarindo, the shuttle departs from Playa Negra at 11am and 3pm, and from Avellanas at 11:15am, 3:15pm and 6pm.

Villa del Sol HOTEL **$$**
(☎2670-0085, Canada 514-400-9101; www.villadelsol.com; La Chorrera; d incl breakfast US$65-85, apt US$85-105; P ❄ @ 🛜 🏊) About 1km north of the town center, this leafy, tranquil property attracts monkeys, iguanas and a good variety of birdlife, in addition to happy travelers lounging in hammocks. The main building has stylish rooms with sunset-view balconies. In the back building, studio apartments (sleeping four) offer excellent value. Walk to the beach in five minutes.

Hotel M&M HOTEL **$$**
(☎2670-1212; www.hotelmym.com; s/d/tr incl breakfast from US$27/42/53; P 🛜) A romantic beachfront hacienda with a wooden balcony overlooking the boardwalk. Fan-cooled rooms have ceramic tiled floors, beamed ceilings and cold-water showers. This simple place is one of the only beachfront properties in Coco. And if the beach is not your thing, you can take a dip in the pool at sister property Garden House (p573).

Congo CAFE **$**
(Café, Art y Diseño; ☎2670-1265; www.costaricacongo.com; mains US$6-10; ⏰8am-7pm; P ❄ 🛜 🖉) Part cafe, part funky retail boutique, Congo's interior is groovy, with arched booths, rattan sofas and a deconstructed wood-and-granite coffee bar. They serve espresso drinks and an array of healthy sandwiches, smoothies, juices, salads and breakfasts.

Soda La Teresita COSTA RICAN **$**
(☎2670-0665; mains US$5-10; ⏰6:30am-9pm Mon-Sat, to 5pm Sun) At the crossroads of the main drag and the beach, this place can't be beaten for people-watching in Coco. It's also your best bet for lunch, whether you're hankering for a *torta* (sandwich), a traditional *casado* (set meal) or Teresita's hearty breakfasts. Soda La Teresita has been here more than 40 years – so they must be doing something right!

Information

Police (☎2670-0258) are located southeast of the plaza by the beach.

On the road out of town, just past the Mega Super and the Banco de Costa Rica is the **post office** (Correos de Costa Rica; ⏰8am-5pm Mon-Sat).

Getting There & Away

San José buses arrive and depart from the **main terminal**, about 100m north of **Pato Loco Inn** (☎2670-0145; www.patolocoinn.com; d/tr/q incl breakfast US$88/98/108; P ❄ @ 🛜 🏊 🐾). Buses for Liberia, Filadelfia and, very rarely, Playa Panama, stop next to the red awning and benches opposite the Hard Rock Cafe.

Liberia US$1.50, one hour, departs half-hourly from 5am to 11pm.

San José Pulmitan (p530); US$9, five hours, departs 4am, 8am and 2pm.

Playa Tamarindo

If Patrick and Wingnut from the 1994 surfing movie *Endless Summer II* surfed a time machine to present-day Tamarindo, they'd fall off their boards. A quarter-century of hedonism has transformed the once-dusty burg into 'Tamagringo,' whose perennial status as Costa Rica's top surf and party destination has made it the first and last stop for legions of tourists.

Despite its party-town reputation, Tamarindo offers more than just drinking and surfing. It forms part of Parque Nacional Marino Las Baulas de Guanacaste, and the beach retains an allure for kids and adults alike. Foodies will find some of the best restaurants in the country. There's a thriving market on Saturday mornings and fierce competition has kept lodging prices reasonably low. Its central location makes it a great base for exploring the northern peninsula.

Sights

Parque Nacional Marino Las Baulas de Guanacaste — PARK

(2653-0470; adult/child US$12/2, turtle tours incl park admission US$35; 8am-noon & 1-5pm, tours 6pm-2am) Las Baulas national marine park encompasses the entire beach at Playa Grande, as well as the adjacent land and 220 sq km of ocean. This is one of the world's most important nesting areas for the critically endangered *baula* (leatherback turtle). In the evenings from October to March, rangers lead tours to witness the turtles' amazing cycle of life. Canoe tours explore the mangroves, home to caimans and crocodiles, as well as numerous bird species such as the roseate spoonbill.

Activities

Surfing

Like a gift from the surf gods, Tamarindo is often at its best when neighboring Playa Grande is flat. The most popular wave is a medium-sized right that breaks directly in front of the Tamarindo Diria hotel. The waters here are full of virgin surfers learning to pop up. There is also a good left that's fed by the river mouth, though be advised that crocodiles are occasionally sighted here, particularly when the tide is rising (which is, coincidentally, the best time to surf). There can be head-high waves in front of the rocks near El Be.

More advanced surfers will appreciate the bigger, faster and less crowded waves at neighboring beaches: Playa Langosta, on the other side of the point; Playas Avellanas, Negra and Junquillal to the south; and Playa Grande to the north.

There are countless surf schools offering lessons and board rental in Tamarindo. Surf lessons hover at around US$45 for 1½ to two hours, and most operators will let you keep the board for a few hours beyond that to practice.

★ Iguana Surf — SURFING

(Map p578; 2653-0613; www.iguanasurf.net; board rental per day US$20, group/semiprivate/private lessons US$45/65/80; 8am-6pm) Iguana Surf has been giving lessons since 1989, so they probably know what they're doing. Excellent for couples, families or anyone really. The two-hour lesson includes a rash guard and locker, in addition to the surfboard. After your lesson, all gear is half-price.

Learn Improve Surf Company — SURFING

(Map p578; 8316-0509; www.learnimprovesurfcompany.com; lessons s/d US$70/90) Edgar Sanchez wants to teach you how to surf. This upstart company excels at offering instruction for all ages and abilities. It also takes more advanced wave riders on surf tours to Playa Avellanas and Playa Grande.

Kelly's Surf Shop — SURFING

(Map p578; 2653-1355; www.kellyssurfshop.com/en; board rental per day/week US$20/120, group/semiprivate/private lessons US$50/65/90; 9am-6pm) One of the best surf shops in the area, Kelly's has a terrific selection of newish boards that it rents out by the day or week. Premium boards cost a bit more. Staff are super-informative, with lessons, advice and other recommendations to get you out on the waves. You can also rent bikes here.

Diving

Tamarindo is a surf town. But that doesn't mean there's nothing to see below the waves. Enticing dive sites in the vicinity include the nearby Cabo Velas and the Islas Catalinas.

Freedive Costa Rica — DIVING

(Map p578; 8353-1290; www.freedivecostarica.com; Plaza Conchal; free diving US$35-55, snorkeling US$60, spearfishing US$155; 9:30am-5:30pm) Owner Gauthier Ghilain claims free diving is 'the most natural, intimate and pure form of communion with the underwater world.' It requires no bulky gear and minimal training. He promises a safe and super-fun environment in which to learn how to explore the deep blue sea in new ways.

Tamarindo Diving — DIVING

(Map p578; 8583-5873; www.tamarindodiving.net; 2-tank dive US$110) It's called Tamarindo Diving, although trips actually depart from

Playa Tamarindo

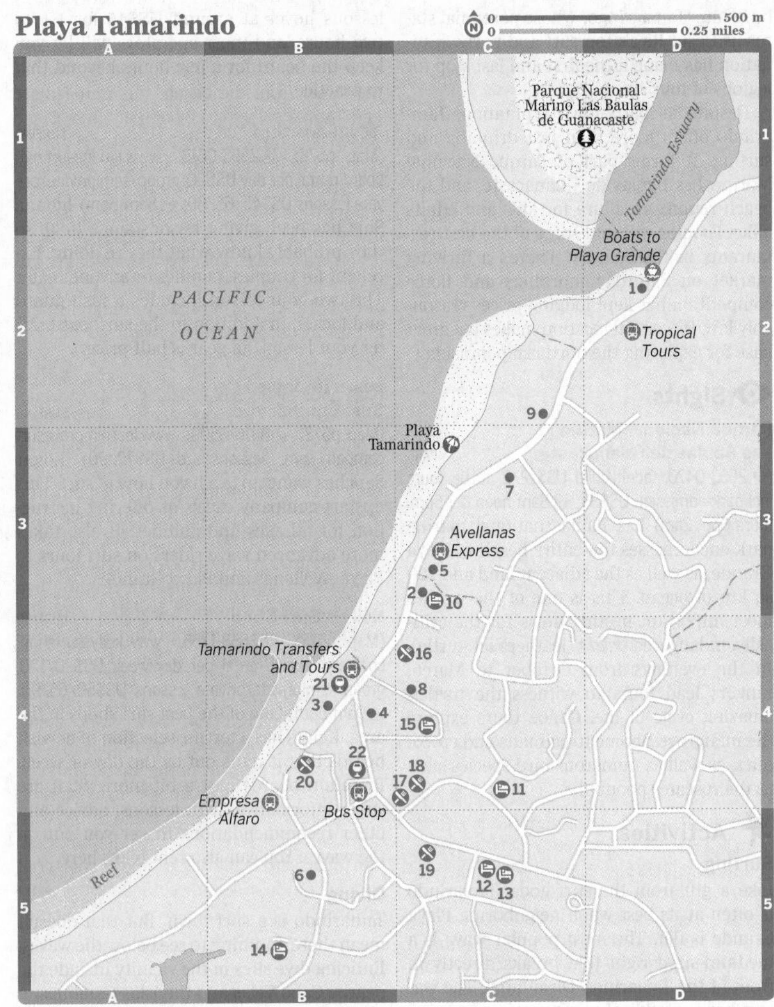

Playa Flamingo and head out to the Islas Catalinas. (It's a trade-off: you'll spend more time on the road but less time on the boat motoring to your destination.) Turtles, dolphins and whales are often spotted from the boat, while eagle rays, sharks and manta rays are lurking below the surface.

Courses

Coastal Spanish Institute LANGUAGE
(Map p578; ☎2653-2673; www.coastalspanish.com; per week from US$365) This Spanish school is right on the beach in downtown Tamarindo (which may make it more difficult to concentrate on your grammar and vocabulary). It specializes in weekly surf and Spanish packages, which include 20 hours of Spanish classes and six hours of surf instruction, as well as board rental.

Instituto de Wayra LANGUAGE
(Map p578; ☎2653-0359; www.spanish-wayra.co.cr; per week from US$335; ⏲7am-5:30pm Mon-Fri, 10am-4pm Sun) A Spanish program that offers small class sizes and an immersive experience. The school recommends (and arranges) homestays so students have more opportunities to polish up their language skills.

Playa Tamarindo

Activities, Courses & Tours

1 Asociación de Guías Locales de Tamarindo D2
2 Blue Trailz C3
3 Coastal Spanish Institute B4
4 Freedive Costa Rica B4
5 Iguana Surf C3
6 Instituto de Wayra B5
7 Kelly's Surf Shop C3
8 Learn Improve Surf Company C4
9 Tamarindo Diving C2

Sleeping

10 Blue Trailz Hostel C3
11 Hotel Mahayana C4
12 La Botella de Leche C5
13 Pura Vida Hostel C5
14 Tamarindo Backpackers B5
15 Villas Macondo C4

Eating

16 El Casado del Carro C4
17 Falafel Bar C4
18 Green Papaya C4
19 La Bodega C5
20 Surf Shack B4

Drinking & Nightlife

21 El Be! B4
22 Sharky's B4

Sleeping

Tamarindo Backpackers HOSTEL $

(Map p578; 4033-4583; www.tamarindobackpackershostel.com; dm US$15, d with/without bathroom US$50/40; P ❄ @ ☎ ≈) This attractive yellow hacienda has a great vibe that welcomes all comers. Private rooms (mostly with shared bathroom) are excellent value, with Spanish-tiled floors, mural-painted walls, beamed ceilings and flat-screen TVs. The dorms are quite clean but otherwise unspectacular. Outside, hammocks are strung in the tropical gardens and around a small pool. It's a five-minute walk to the beach.

La Botella de Leche HOSTEL $

(Map p578; 2653-0189; www.labotelladeleche.com; dm US$13-15, d US$50; P ❄ @ ☎ ≈) With a relaxed vibe, this congenial spot – aka 'the Bottle of Milk' – is recommended for its warm and attentive management, plus fully air-conditioned rooms and dormitories. Stenciled walls pretty up the otherwise plain rooms. Facilities include a shared kitchen, surfboard racks, hammocks and a TV lounge. A yoga and fitness studio was added in 2018.

Blue Trailz Hostel HOSTEL $

(Map p578; 2653-1705; www.bluetrailz.com/tamarindo-hostel; dm/r US$15/69; ❄ @ ☎) Across the street from the beach, this immaculate and intimate hostel is popular among the surfer set. Budget travelers appreciate the clean, cool dorms (with air-con) as well as the attentive service from the staff. Guests get reduced rates on boards, bikes, lessons and tours at the **Blue Trailz** (Map p578; board rental per day US$15, group/semiprivate/private surf lessons US$45/60/80; 7am-7pm) surf shop out front. Sweet. There is a minimum three-night stay during high season.

Pura Vida Hostel HOSTEL $

(Map p578; 8368-3508, 2653-2464; www.puravidahostel.com; dm US$18-20, d with/without bathroom US$60/50; ❄ @ ☎) Inside this leafy compound are dorms and private rooms accented by trippy murals and mirrored mosaics. The vibe is friendly and super-chill, especially in the common *rancho*, furnished with hammocks and rocking chairs. They sometimes organize open-mic nights, live music and fire shows in keeping with the *rockero*-themed murals in the rooms. Free bikes and boards are available too.

Hotel Mahayana HOTEL $$

(Map p578; 2653-1154; www.hotelmahayana.com; d US$65; P ❄ ☎ ≈) The Mahayana is a sweet retreat, away from the hustle and bustle of the main drag. Spotless, citrus-painted rooms are fitted with high ceilings, big windows and private terraces (with hammocks). The courtyard contains a small, cool pool and an outdoor kitchen, which is at your disposal.

Villas Macondo HOTEL $$

(Map p578; 2653-0812; www.villasmacondo.com; s/d/tr US$50/60/70, with air-con US$75/87/97, apt US$125-170; P ❄ @ ☎ ≈) Although it's only 200m from the beach, this establishment is an oasis of serenity in an otherwise frenzied town – it's also one of the best deals around. Beautiful modern villas with private hammocks and patios surround a solar-heated pool and tropical garden. Larger apartments are equipped with kitchens: ideal for families. Extra credit for naming it after Garcia-Marquez' fictional town.

Eating

★ **La Bodega** BREAKFAST, SANDWICHES $

(Map p578; 8395-6184; www.labodegatamarindo.com; Nahua Hotel; mains US$6-8; 7am-3pm

Mon-Sat, until noon Sun; 📶✏️👪) This delightful shop and cafe specializes in unique combinations of ingredients, focusing on whatever is fresh, local and organic. For breakfast, it does amazing things with eggs, while lunch is a daily changing menu of sandwiches and salads. Any time of day, you can't go wrong with its banana bread or lemon scones and a cup of freshly brewed java.

★**Green Papaya** MEXICAN $

(Map p578; ☎2652-0863; www.facebook.com/Gr33nPapaya; mains US$5-10; ⏲11am-9pm Tue-Sun; ❄📶✏️👪) Swing on up to the bar for a breakfast burrito or pull up a tree-stump stool to sample the fantastic fare. The mahi-mahi tacos are perfection in a tortilla, while non-meat-eaters will appreciate the multiple veggie options including enchiladas in creamy chipotle sauce. You'll go loco for the Chocolate Lovers dessert. Everything is funky, fresh and friendly – don't miss it.

Surf Shack BURGERS $

(Map p578; ☎2653-2346; www.facebook.com/surfshacktamarindo; mains US$5-10; ⏲11am-9pm Fri-Wed; 📶) If you are craving a big bad burger, Surf Shack has you covered with a good selection of patties, thick-cut onion rings and irresistible milkshakes. Tin-can walls and surfboard decor create a laid-back vibe, enhanced by the drinks coming from the bar. It's steps from the beach; the sea breeze is the perfect accompaniment to anything you order.

Falafel Bar LEBANESE $

(Map p578; ☎2653-1268; www.facebook.com/tamarindofalafelbar; mains US$5-10; ⏲7am-10pm Wed-Mon; ✏️) When you get tired of *casados*, head to this Middle Eastern cafe for all the faves: shawarma, falafel, tabbouleh, hummus and kebabs. The pita bread is made fresh daily. Fresh juice and coffee in the morning; a real 'bar' at night.

El Casado del Carro COSTA RICAN $

(Map p578; casados US$4; ⏲noon-3pm) Doña Rosa has been delivering top-notch *casados* from her late-model red Toyota hatchback for more than a decade. Her devoted Tico following lines up daily at noon, and she generally sells out by 2pm. You'll get your meal from hubby Salvador in a Styrofoam platter (nobody's *perfecto*), usually with yucca or plantains, rice, chicken or beef, and tasty black beans.

Drinking & Nightlife

El Be! BAR

(Map p578; ☎2653-2637; ⏲10am-10pm) Formerly Le Beach Club, this place has changed languages (and added an exclamation point!) but the cool vibe remains the same. Lounge on beach beds or hammocks and listen to the DJ's sounds. Happy hour (4pm to 7pm) features drink specials, live jazz music and fabulous sunsets. It's not a bad option for food if you're feeling peckish.

Sharky's SPORTS BAR

(Map p578; ☎8729-8274; www.sharkysbars.com; ⏲6pm-2am) If you want to catch the big game, look no further than Sharky's. Besides nine screens showing sports, there are burgers, wings and lots of beer. There's a nightly lineup of fun and games, including karaoke night on Tuesday and ladies' night on Saturday. The motto is *'un zarpe mas?'* (one last drink?). Get ready to get your drink on.

Information

Should you need medical attention, contact the **Coastal Emergency Medical Service** (☎2653-1974, emergency 8835-8074; ⏲24hr).

Backwash Laundry (⏲8am-8pm Mon-Sat) Get your filthy unmentionables washed, dried and folded.

Getting There & Away

Surfers and other beach party people flock to Tamarindo by air, bus and car. If you choose your lodgings wisely, there's no need for a car, as you can walk to the beach and book tours of other outings in the area.

The **Empresa Alfaro** (Map p578; ☎2653-0268, 2222-2666; ⏲7:30am-5:30pm Mon-Sat,

BUSES FROM TAMARINDO

DESTINATION	COMPANY	PRICE (US$)	DURATION (HR)	FREQUENCY
Liberia	La Pampa	3	2½	12 daily, 3:30am-6pm
San José	Alfaro	11	5½	3am & 5:30am
San José	Tralapa	11	5½	7am
Santa Cruz	Tralapa	2	1½	6am, 8:30am & noon

9am-3:30pm Sun) office is near the beach, while other buses depart from the **bus stop** (Map p578) in front of Pacific Park.

Private shuttle buses offer a faster (albeit more expensive) option. **Tamarindo Transfers and Tours** (Map p578; ☎2653-0505; www.tamarindotransfersandtours.com; Centro Comercial Galerías del Mar) provides comfortable and convenient transfers from Tamarindo to destinations around the country, including both airports. **Tropical Tours** (Map p578; ☎2640-0811, 2640-1900; www.tropicaltourshuttles.com) has daily shuttles that connect Tamarindo to San José, as well as to several destinations in the southern part of the Nicoya Peninsula.

Getting Around

Stop by the **Asociación de Guías Locales** (ACUATAM; Map p578; ☎2653-1687; boats to Playa Grande round-trip US$3, turtle tours US$35; ⏲7am-4pm) at the northern end of the beach to hire a boat to cross the estuary to Playa Grande. **Avellanas Express** (Map p578; one way/return US$6/12; ⏲8am-5pm) runs a surf shuttle to area beaches. There are two different 'lines' from Tamarindo: the Blue Line goes back and forth to Playa Conchal; the Green Line goes south to Avellanas and Negra. Based at Neptuno Surf Shop.

Playa Sámara

POP 4150

Is Sámara the black hole of happiness? That's what more than one expat has said after stopping here on vacation and never leaving. On the surface it's just an easy-to-navigate beach town with barefoot, three-star appeal. The crescent-shaped strip of pale-gray sand spans two rocky headlands, where the sea is calm and beautiful. But be careful, the longer you stay, the less you'll want to leave.

Activities & Courses

No matter what you like to do at the beach, you can probably do it at Playa Sámara. Expert surfers might get bored by Sámara's inconsistent waves, but beginners will have a blast. Otherwise there's hiking, horseback riding and sea kayaking, as well as snorkeling out around Isla la Chora. Take a break from the beach to explore the forested hillsides on foot or on zipline.

Pato Surf School & Camp SURFING
(☎8761-4638; www.patossurfingsamara.com; board rental per day US$15, lessons US$35-45; ⏲8am-5pm) Pato offers inexpensive and quality board rental, as well as beginner surf instruction, on the beach at the southwest end of town. The instructors are top-notch. Pay for a lesson and get free board rental for five days. Also on offer: stand-up paddle rental and lessons; kayak rental and tours; snorkel gear; and beach massages. What else do you want?

The newly christened Pato's Surf Camp encompasses three-, seven- or 10-day camps that include transport, lodging and food, as well as surf and Spanish lessons.

Intercultura Costa Rica Spanish Schools LANGUAGE
(☎2656-3000; www.interculturacostarica.com; courses per week with/without homestay US$470/315) Centro de Idiomas Intercultura is right on the beach, which makes for a pleasant – if not always productive – place to study. Language courses can be arranged with or without a family homestay. Courses for kids are also available.

Sleeping

★**Camp Supertramp** HOSTEL $
(☎2656 0190; napharddreambig@camsupertramp.com; Hojancha; campsites per person US$8, dm US$10, cabina s/d $15/25) Major move! Supertramp is now 8km southeast of Hojancha, beside the Salto de Calvo waterfall, with mountain/ocean views. The list of things to love is long: Thomas (the owner), Subwoofer (the dog), the jungle shower, the fire pit, the 1971 VW bus, the table-tennis table and the volleyball court. The vibe here is fun-filled and super chill.

El Cactus Hostel HOSTEL $
(☎2656-3224; www.samarabackpacker.com; dm US$18, d US$45-75; 📶🏊) Brightly painted in citrus colors, El Cactus is a great option for Sámara's backpacker set, especially those who prefer serenity over revelry. Fresh rooms have wooden furniture, clean linens and hot-water showers. Hammocks hang around a small pool, and a fully fitted kitchen is also available. On a side street in the center of town, 100m from the beach.

Hostel Matilori HOSTEL $
(Matilori Hostel; ☎2656-0291; www.hostelmatilori.com; dm/s/d/tw US$15/35/40/50; 🅿📶) A terrific-value hostel a block from the beach,

with private rooms (shared bathrooms) in the main house and cozy dorm rooms (sleeping four or six) in the annex. All the rooms have fresh coats of jewel-toned paints, and guests have use of a kitchen and a shady patio. Endearing owners Fran and Jen welcome you with a *cerveza* on arrival.

Hotel Casa Paraíso GUESTHOUSE **$**
(2656-0741; http://casaparaisoahorasi.com/; dm/d US$15/60;) A lovely little guesthouse tucked in behind Ahora Sí. Four simple rooms and a shared dorm are brushed in deep blues and inviting pastels, with thematic murals, high ceilings and comfy beds. Ceiling fans will keep you cool while hot-water showers will warm you up. Hostess Sylvia will overwhelm you with her charm, and there's Italian cooking at the restaurant.

Las Mariposas HOSTEL **$**
(8703-3625, 2656-0314; www.hostelmariposas.com; hammock US$8, dm US$12-15, d with/without bathroom US$38/30;) On a rough dirt road near the language school, this fun, friendly hostel guarantees a good time, with a fresh, youthful vibe. It's got wooden rooms and dorms, plenty of swaying hammocks, paper lantern lighting and a communal kitchen. Best of all, it's just 60m from the sand.

La Mansion B&B B&B **$$**
(Bed and Best Breakfast; 2265-0165; http://isamara.co/mansion/index.htm; s US$40, d US$50-80, ste US$150;) This whitewashed concrete hacienda, twirling with fans and bursting with colorful knickknacks, is on a quiet street. There's loads of charm: rooms are spacious and bright, and ex-Arizonian hostess Marlene McCauley is proud of her huge and delicious breakfast repasts. Her artwork adorns the walls and you can even buy one of her cute bird-themed postcards. Air-con is extra.

Eating & Drinking

It's not exactly a party town, but Sámara sees some action at night. All of the beach bars get busy after sunset. Lo Que Hay and Flying Taco are both technically taco bars, but after hours the emphasis is on the 'bar.' New kid on the block **Media Luna** (Tapas y Vino; 8416-1852; www.facebook.com/Media-Luna; 6pm-2am) has a more cocktail-ish, Gatsby feel.

★**Lo Que Hay** MEXICAN **$**
(2656-0811; tacos US$2, mains US$8-12; 7am-11pm) This rocking beachside *taquería* and pub offers six delectable taco fillings: fish, chorizo, chicken, beef, pork or veggie. The grilled avocados stuffed with *pico de gallo* are great. Even without tacos, a good time will be had as the bar crowd drinks into the wee small hours.

Roots Bakery BAKERY **$**
(8924-2770; www.facebook.com/rootsbakerycafeEnSamara; items US$3-5; 7am-4pm Mon-Sat, to noon Sun;) The carrot cake is really good, and the spinach quiche is better. But the cinnamon buns are otherworldly – so rich, gooey, sweet and chewy that you might have to do penance after you eat one. Required eating. Roots is on the main drag, opposite the turnoff to Carrillo. Like many places to eat in Sámara, it's cash only.

Ahora Sí VEGETARIAN **$**
(2656-0741; http://casaparaisoahorasi.com; mains US$5-11; 8am-10pm;) Sylvia of Bergamo runs this vegetarian restaurant and all-natural cocktail bar, and the fish joint next door. Expect smoothies with coconut milk, gnocchi with chive or smoked cheese, soy burgers, and imported Italian pasta. All are served on a lovingly decorated tiled patio where the chairbacks are shaped into musical notes and the menus contain inspirational quotes. Good vibes, good food.

Sámara Organics – Mercado Organico MARKET **$$**
(2656-3046; www.samaraorganics.com; smoothies & juices US$4-5; 7am-8pm) It's not cheap, but self-caterers (and anybody with a dietary restriction) will appreciate this cafe and market, well-stocked with organic produce and delicious prepared foods. Come get your healthy food fix, and enjoy the small seating area for a chat or read. On the main beach road, parallel to the water.

Flying Taco BAR
(El Taco Volador; 8409-5376; 11am-2am;) A laid-back, Tex-Mex beach bar near the soccer field. It's open for lunch – and the grub is recommended – but it's more fun to come at night, when you can also sing karaoke, play poker and drink margaritas. The Wednesday open-mic 'Taco Jam' fills the bar with musical talent of varying levels having a blast. But don't forget the tacos.

Information

La Vida Verde (Green Life; 2656-1051; greenlife@samarabeach.com; per kg US$3; 8am-6pm Mon-Sat) Drop your dirty duds off at this laundry, 75m west of Banco Nacional. Or call ahead for pick-up and delivery.

Post office (⏲8am-noon & 1:15-5:30pm Mon-Fri) In the same building as the police station, on the main road where it meets the beach.

Samara Beach (www.samarabeach.com) Surf this excellent website to get the skinny on Sámara, including a decent tourist map of the village and beach.

Samara Info Center (☎2656-2424; www.samarainfocenter.com; ⏲8am-6pm) Located in front of Lo Que Hay, the Info Center is run by the amiable Brenda and Christopher. It's basically a tour consolidator, but they can help with accommodations, restaurant recommendations, transportation and simply answering questions about Sámara and Carrillo. And they book tours.

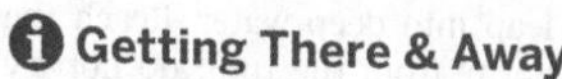

Getting There & Away

Traroc buses go to Nicoya (US$3.60, one hour) 10 times a day from 5:30am to 7pm. Heading in the opposite direction, the same buses go to Playa Carrillo.

Mal País & Santa Teresa

Santa Teresa didn't even have electricity until the mid-1990s. Then one major landowner died and his property was subdivided, and the landscape north of the Playa El Carmen intersection changed forever. These days you'll need to balance the annoyance of the omnipresent ATVs kicking up dust with the restaurants serving gob-smackingly delicious food and the yoga dens with transformational ocean views.

It's still a wonderful surfing town, though no longer a secret one, and there are plenty of great places to eat and a modicum of nightlife. The entire area unfurls along one bumpy coastal road that rambles south from Santa Teresa through Playa El Carmen and terminates in the relaxed, sleepy fishing hamlet of Mal País.

Activities

Surfing is the raison d'être for most visits to Santa Teresa and Mal País, and perhaps for the town itself. Most travelers want to do little else, except maybe stretch their muscles with a little yoga. That said, it's a gorgeous, pristine coastline: horseback riding or fishing trips can be easily arranged, as well as a fun-filled ziplining jaunt.

Sleeping

Don Jon's BUNGALOW $

(☎2640-0700; www.donjonsonline.com; Santa Teresa; dm/bungalow & tree house/apt US$20/60/110; P❄📶) Just 100m from the surf, this is the perfect base for anybody looking to 'relax to the max.' Rustic teak bungalows are creatively decorated, while attractive Spanish-tiled dorms have high-beamed ceilings and plenty of hammocks in the garden. An amazing tree-house structure not only has an appealing room but also hosts yoga classes. It's 150m past the soccer field. Not all rooms have air-con.

Casa Zen GUESTHOUSE $

(☎2640-0523; www.zencostarica.com; Santa Teresa; dm/d/tr/q incl breakfast US$15/35/42/50; P📶) This lovely Asian-inspired guesthouse is decked out in celestial murals and Buddha sculptures. The colorful but basic rooms share bathrooms and two fully equipped kitchens. Some guests have complained that the thin walls and passing traffic detract from the Zen atmosphere; we would argue that the noise is just an opportunity to practice more Zen. On the beach access road.

Cuesta Arriba HOSTEL $

(☎2640-0607; www.cuestaarriba.com; Santa Teresa; dm US$18, d US$50-60; P❄📶🏊) This is a thinking person's hostel, attracting a cultivated crowd of travelers who appreciate the orderly atmosphere. En suite bathrooms, polished concrete floors, colorful tapestries and mosaic tile embellishments look lovely in both shared and private rooms. Communal areas include a well-stocked kitchen area, a breezy terrace upstairs and a garden with hammocks. Situated 3km north of the T intersection.

Malpaís Surf Camp & Resort LODGE $$

(☎2640-0031; www.malpaissurfcamp.com; Mal País; campsite per person US$16, dm US$22, d with/without bathroom US$90/50, villa from US$108; P❄@📶🏊) There are comfortable, private *cabañas* and more luxurious digs, but the best deal at this surfers' lodge is the open-air *rancho,* with a tin roof and pebble floors, which you can share with three other surfers. Explore the landscaped tropical grounds, swim in the luscious pool, grab a cold beer in the open-air lounge and soak up the good vibes.

Eating & Drinking

Zwart Cafe CAFE $

(Zwart Art Cafe; 2640-0011; Santa Teresa; mains US$4-8; 7am-5pm;) *Zwart* means 'black' in Dutch, but this shabby-chic, artist-owned gallery and cafe is all white (or mostly – damn dust!). You'll love the surf-inspired Technicolor canvases, the lively outdoor patio and the breakfasts, including chocolate-chip pancakes. At lunch it's all about the burritos. About 2km north of the T intersection, on the right if you're heading north.

Roca Mar BAR

(2640-0250; www.facebook.com/rocamarbeachsantateresa; Santa Teresa; noon-9pm;) Tucked away at the Blue Surf Sanctuary hotel at the northern end of town, this pretty perfect beach lounge attracts a local expat crowd. Beanbags are stuck in the sand, and hammocks are slung in the trees – all perfectly positioned for sunset. There's an official Sunset Party on Sunday evenings – a family-friendly event with live music and fire dancers. Closes seasonally September to November.

Getting There & Away

All buses begin and end at Ginger Café, 100m south of Cuesta Arriba hostel, but you can flag the bus down anywhere along the road in Santa Teresa. At Frank's Place, the buses turn left and head inland toward Cóbano.

A direct bus to San José via the Paquera ferry departs at 7:30am and 3:30pm (US$13, six hours). Local buses to Cóbano (US$2, 45 minutes) depart at 7am and noon.

Tropical Tours (2640 1900, WhatsApp 8890 9197; www.tropicaltourshuttles.com), with its main office right next to Frank's Place, offers reliable shuttle service around the peninsula and as far as Liberia and the Nicaragua border.

Montezuma

Montezuma is an endearing beach town that demands you abandon the car to stroll, swim and (if you can stroll a little further) surf. The warm and wild ocean and that remnant, ever-audible jungle have helped this rocky nook cultivate an inviting, boho vibe. Typical tourist offerings such as canopy tours do a brisk trade here, but you'll also bump up against Montezuma's internationally inflected, artsy-rootsy beach culture in yoga classes, volunteer corps, veggie-friendly dining rooms and neo-Rastas hawking handcrafted jewelry and uplifting herbs. No wonder locals lovingly call this town 'Montefuma.'

It's not perfect. The accommodations are not great value, and the places to eat can be that way too (though there are some absolute gems). But in this barefoot *pueblo,* which unfurls along several kilometers of rugged coastline, you're never far from the rhythm and sound of the sea, and that is a beautiful thing.

Sights

★Montezuma Waterfalls WATERFALL

(parking US$2) A 40-minute river hike leads to a waterfall with a delicious swimming hole. Further along, a second set of falls offers a good 10m leap into deep water. Reach the 'diving platform' from the trail: do not try to scale the slippery rocks! Daring souls can test their Tarzan skills on the rope that swings over a third set. A lot of travelers enjoy these thrills but a few of them have died, so do it at your own risk.

To get to the parking area, head south from town and you'll see it just past Hotel La Cascada; once parked, take the trail to the right just after the bridge. You'll want proper hiking footwear. There are official rangers/guards (in official vests/hats) who work the trail and can offer the best advice, free of charge, on the safest routes to take, particularly during rainy season. Families with children or elderly members may want to enter via **Sun Trails** (Montezuma Waterfall Canopy Tour; Map p585; 2642-0808; www.montezumatraveladventures.com; tours from US$45; 9am, 1pm & 3pm), which has easy access but charges US$4 parking.

Playa Montezuma BEACH

(Map p585) The best beach close to town is just to the north, where the sand is powdery and sheltered from big swells. This is your glorious sun-soaked crash pad. The water's shade of teal is immediately nourishing, the temperature is perfect and fish are abundant. At the north end of the beach, look for the trail that leads to a cove known as **Piedra Colorada**. A small waterfall forms a freshwater pool, which is a perfect swimming spot.

Reserva Natural Absoluta Cabo Blanco NATURE RESERVE

(2642-0093; adult/child US$12/2; 8am-4pm Wed-Sun) Costa Rica's oldest protected wilderness area covers 12 sq km at the tip of

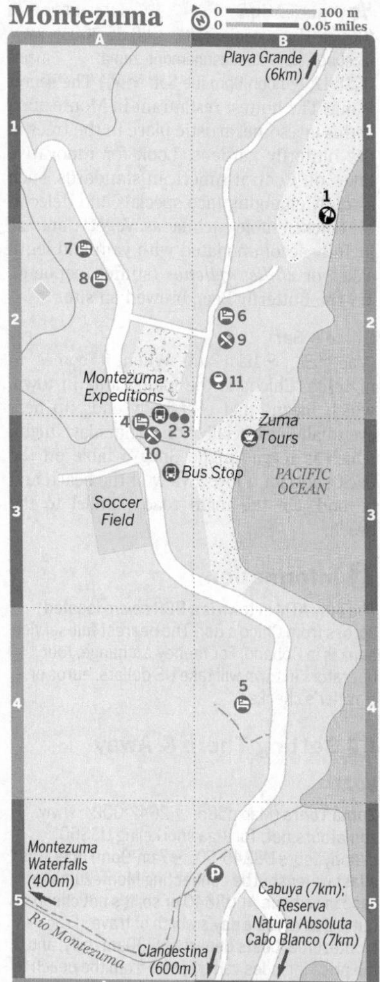

Montezuma

Sights

1 Playa Montezuma B1

Activities, Courses & Tours

Montezuma Yoga .... (see 5)
2 Sun Trails A3
3 Zuma Tours A3

Sleeping

4 Downtown Montezuma Hostel A3
5 Hotel Los Mangos B4
6 Hotel Pargo Feliz B2
7 Luna Llena A2
8 Luz en el Cielo A2

Eating

9 Orgánico B2
10 Soda El Balcón del Mar A3

Drinking & Nightlife

11 Chico's Bar B2

the Península de Nicoya. The unique park is covered by evergreen forests, bisected by a hiking trail and flanked by empty white-sand beaches and offshore islands. Follow the **Sendero Sueco** (Swedish Trail), which leads 4.5km down to a magnificent, jungle-backed beach at the tip of the peninsula. Note that the reserve is closed on Monday and Tuesday.

Sleeping

★Luz en el Cielo — HOSTEL, B&B $

(Map p585; ☎2642-0030; www.luzenelcielo.com; dm US$23-25, cabinas US$85-95, house US$125-145; P) In the heart of the jungle but two minutes from town, this homey hostel and B&B is an inviting retreat. Crowded dorm rooms are super-clean with sturdy wood furniture and lockers, while the 'luxury' dorms are more spacious, with private balconies and en suite bathrooms. The treetop *cabinas* are also wonderful, as are the amazing breakfasts from **Organico** (Map p585; ☎2642-1322; www.organicocostarica.com; mains US$8-12; 8am-10pm;), enticing hammocks and super-friendly staff.

Two new fully furnished houses with kitchens have been added to the lineup here: Casa Azul and Casa en el Cielo.

Luna Llena — HOSTEL $

(Map p585; ☎2642-0390; www.lunallenahotel.com; dm US$15, s/d US$55/65, without bathroom US$28/38; P) On the northern edge of town on a hilltop overlooking the bay, this budget option is absolutely delightful. The rooms are simple but stylish, colorful and clean; most have balconies. There is one massive kitchen, a BBQ grill and a breezy communal lounge with rattan chair-swings and stunning ocean views. Wildlife abounds in the surrounding trees.

Hotel Los Mangos — HOTEL $

(Map p585; ☎2642-0076; www.hotellosmangos.com; r with/without bathroom US$75/35, bungalows US$90; P) Scattered across mango-dotted gardens, this whimsical hotel has plain, painted-wood rooms in the main building and attractive (though dark) octagonal bungalows offering more privacy. Monkeys populate the mango trees and **yoga classes** (Map p585; ☎8704-1632, 2642-1311; www.montezumayoga.com; per person US$14; ⏲8:30am Mon-Fri, 6pm Tue, Wed, Sat & Sun) are held in the gorgeous, ocean-view yoga pavilion, next to a pool with an accompanying Jacuzzi. On the road south of town on the way to the waterfall.

Downtown

Montezuma Hostel HOSTEL $
(Map p585; ☎8516-6921; www.dtmontezuma.com; dm US$14, d with/without bathroom US$45/35; 📶) This funky little two-story hostel has art on all the walls, a clean communal kitchen and plenty of hammocks for your swinging pleasure. Rates all include all-you-can drink coffee and make-your-own pancakes for breakfast. The rooms – four-bed dorms and private doubles – are nothing special, but guests love the fun, friendly vibe. Quiet time after 11pm is strictly enforced.

Hotel Pargo Feliz CABINA $
(Map p585; ☎2642-0064; d US$35-50; 📶) You can't beat the location of the 'happy snapper's' beachfront *cabinas* in the heart of Montezuma. Rooms are simple, clean and fan-cooled. The communal balcony and garden terrace have relaxing hammocks with sea views, and at night the surf will lull you to sleep.

Eating & Drinking

Soda El Balcón del Mar SEAFOOD $$
(Map p585; www.facebook.com/sodaelbalcondelmar; mains US$8-12; ⏲7am-midnight) Hang out below the Tico-themed red-white-and-blue Chinese lanterns on the balcony overlooking the beach, watch flocks of pelicans drift by and kiss the afternoon goodbye. Lip-smacking appetizers include mussels and clams, and you can get a whole-fish catch of the day if that's your thing. Located across from the taxi stand.

★ **Clandestina** LATIN AMERICAN $$
(Cocina Hispanoamericana; ☎8315-8003; www.facebook.com/clandestinamontezuma; mains US$8-12; ⏲noon-9pm Tue-Sat; 📶🌿) The secret is out. The hottest restaurant in Montezuma is this awesome, artistic place in the trees at the butterfly gardens. Look for innovative takes on Central American standards, such as daily changing taco specials and delectable chicken mole enchiladas. Vegetarians are joyfully accommodated with yam and lentil cakes or *chilles rellenos* (stuffed peppers). Try the Butterfly Beer, brewed on-site.

Chico's Bar BAR
(Map p585; ⏲11am-2am) When it comes to nightlife, Chico's is the main game in town, which means that everybody ends up here eventually, especially on Thursday night, which is reggae night. Snag a table on the back patio for a lovely view of the beach and beyond. On the main road parallel to the beach.

ℹ Information

The only ATM in town is a BCR *cajero* located across from Chico's Bar. The nearest full-service bank is in Cóbano. For money exchange, tour operators in town will take US dollars, euros or traveler's checks.

ℹ Getting There & Away

BOAT

Zuma Tours (Map p585; ☎2642-0024; www.zumatours.net; Tortuga snorkeling US$60, canopy tours US$45-50; ⏲7am-9pm) operates a fast water shuttle connecting Montezuma to Jacó in an hour. At US$40 or so, it's not cheap, but it'll save you a day's worth of travel. From Montezuma, boats depart at 8:30am daily, and the price includes van transfer from the beach to the Jacó bus terminal. From Jacó, the departure to Montezuma is at 11am. During the high season, it may run an additional shuttle, departing Montezuma at 1:30pm and departing Jacó at 3pm. Book in advance from any tour operator. Also, dress appropriately; you will get wet.

BUSES FROM MONTEZUMA

DESTINATION	PRICE (US$)	DURATION	DEPARTURES
Cabo Blanco, via Cabuya	1.50	45min	8 daily, 5:30am-8pm
Cóbano	2	1hr	8:15am, 10:15am, 12:15pm, 4:15pm
Paquera, via Cóbano	3	2hr	3:45am, 6am, 10am, noon, 2pm, 4pm
San José	14	5hr	7:30am, 3:30pm

BUS

Buses depart Montezuma from the **sandy lot** (Map p585) on the beach, across from the soccer field. Buy tickets directly from the driver. To get to Mal País and Santa Teresa, go to Cóbano and change buses. The Paquera bus can drop you at the entrance to Refugio Nacional de Vida Silvestre Curú.

Montezuma Expeditions (Map p585; ☎2430-6541; www.montezumaexpeditions.com; US$40-70) and Tropical Tours (p584) operate daily private shuttles to San José, La Fortuna, Monteverde, Jacó, Manuel Antonio, Dominical, Tamarindo, Sámara and Liberia.

CENTRAL PACIFIC COAST

Stretching from the rough-and-ready port of Puntarenas to the tiny town of Uvita, the central Pacific coast is home to wet and dry tropical forests, sun-drenched beaches and a healthy dose of wildlife. On shore, national parks protect endangered squirrel monkeys and scarlet macaws, while offshore waters nurture migrating whales and pods of dolphins.

With so much biodiversity packed into a small geographic area, it's no wonder the region is often thought of as Costa Rica in miniature. Given its close proximity to San José, and its well-developed system of paved roads, this part of the country is a favorite weekend getaway for domestic and international travelers.

While threats of unregulated growth are real, particularly with a new $3.5 billion international airport approved for construction in Orotina, it's also important to see the bigger picture: namely the stunning nature that first put the central Pacific coast on the map.

Puntarenas

POP 34,100

The 'Pearl of the Pacific' is a battered port city at the tip of a sandy peninsula (8km long but only 100m to 600m wide). Lively and hot, this provincial capital served as a major coffee port during the 19th century. During the dry season, Tico vacationers pack the beaches. Otherwise it's the home of rowdy dockworkers and sailors alongside elderly women who scrub their sidewalks and keep the bougainvilleas blooming. Most travelers come here just to catch the ferry to the Nicoya peninsula.

Getting There & Away

Car and passenger ferries bound for Paquera and Playa Naranjo depart several times a day from the **northwestern dock** (Av 3, btwn Calles 31 & 33). If you are driving and will be taking the car ferry, arrive at the dock early to get in line. The vehicle section tends to fill up quickly and you may not make it on. In addition, make sure that you have purchased your ticket from the walk-up ticket window before driving onto the ferry. You will not be admitted onto the boat if you don't already have a ticket.

Schedules change seasonally and can be affected by inclement weather. Check with the ferry office by the dock for any changes. Many of the hotels in town also have up-to-date schedules posted.

Coonatramar (☎2661-1069; www.coonatramar.com; adult/child/bike/car US$2/1.10/4/18) has daily departures to Playa Naranjo (for transfer to Nicoya and points west) at 6:30am, 10am, 2:30pm and 7pm.

Naviera Tambor (☎2661-2084; www.navieratambor.com; adult/child/bike/car US$1.60/1/4.40/23) has daily departures to Paquera (for transfer to Montezuma and Mal País) at 5am, 9am, 11am, 2pm, 5pm and 8:30pm.

BUS

Buses for San José depart from the large navy-blue building on the north corner of Calle 2 and Paseo de los Turistas. Book your ticket ahead of time on holidays and weekends. Buses for other destinations leave from across the street, on the beach side of the Paseo.

BUSES FROM PUNTARENAS

DESTINATION	COST (US$)	DURATION	FREQUENCY
Jacó	2.10	1½hr	6:50am, 8:50am, 2:20pm, 4pm, 6:30pm
Quepos	4.40	3hr	12 daily, 4:30am-3:30pm
San José (via San Ramon)	4.70	2½hr	hourly 4am-9pm
Monteverde	2.70	3hr	8am, 1:15pm, 1:30pm, 2:15pm

DON'T MISS

CROCODILE BRIDGE

If you're driving from Puntarenas or San José, pull over by the Río Tárcoles bridge, also known as Crocodile Bridge. It's a top tourist attraction in the area, as the sandbanks below regularly feature a couple dozen massive, basking crocodiles. They're visible year-round, but the best time for seeing them is during low tide in the dry season.

Parque Nacional Carara

Situated at the mouth of the Río Tárcoles, this 52-sq-km **park** (US$10; ⏲7am-4pm Dec-Apr, 8am-4pm May-Nov) is only 50km southeast of Puntarenas by road or about 90km west of San José via the Orotina highway. Straddling the transition between the dry forests of Costa Rica's northwest and the sodden rainforests of the southern Pacific lowlands, this national park is a biological melting pot of the two. Acacias intermingle with strangler figs, and cacti with deciduous kapok trees, creating heterogeneity of habitats with a blend of wildlife to match, including the scarlet macaw and Costa Rica's largest crocodiles.

The park's four trails can easily be explored in half a day; come early to maximize wildlife sightings.

Information

Carara ranger station (⏲7am-4pm Dec-Apr, 8am-4pm May-Nov) Info on the park and the possibility of hiring guides; 3km south of Río Tárcoles.

Getting There & Away

Any bus traveling between Puntarenas and Jacó can leave you at the park entrance. You can also catch buses headed north or south in front of Restaurante Los Cocodrilos. This may be a bit problematic on weekends, when buses are full, so go midweek if you are relying on a bus ride. If you're driving, the entrance to Carara is right on the Costanera and is clearly marked.

Jacó

POP 9500

Few places in Costa Rica generate such divergent opinions as Jacó. Partying surfers, North American retirees and international developers laud it for its devil-may-care atmosphere, bustling streets and booming real-estate opportunities. Observant ecotourists, marginalized Ticos and loyalists of the 'old Costa Rica' absolutely despise the place for the *exact* same reasons.

Jacó was the first town on the central Pacific coast to explode with tourist development and it remains a major draw for backpackers, surfers, snowbirds and city-weary *josefinos* (inhabitants of San José). Although working-class Tico neighborhoods are nearby, open-air trinket shops and tour operators line the tacky main drag which, at night, is given over to a safe but somewhat seedy mix of binge-drinking students, surfers and scantily clad ladies of negotiable affection.

While Jacó's lackadaisical charm is not for everyone, the surfing is excellent, and the restaurants and bars are great, particularly those lining classy Jacó Walk.

Activities & Tours

Although the rainy season is considered best for Pacific-coast surfing, Jacó is blessed with consistent year-round breaks. Even though more advanced surfers head further south to Playa Hermosa, the waves at Jacó are strong, steady and a lot of fun for intermediate surfers. Jacó is also a great place to learn to surf or start a surf trip as many places offer lessons and it's easy to buy and sell boards here.

If you're looking to rent a board for the day, shop around as the better places will do 24 hours for US$15 to US$20.

Tortuga Surf Camp SURFING

(☎2463-3348; www.tortugasurfcamp.com; 2hr private surfing lesson incl equipment from US$50; ⏲8am-5pm) Regardless of your age or ability, this is one of the top places in Jacó to learn to surf or improve your technique. Michael and his crew are very patient and encouraging. Lessons should be booked at least 24 hours in advance.

Mt Miros HIKING

A worthwhile pastime that few tourists are aware of is following the trail up Mt Miros, which winds through primary and secondary rainforest and offers spectacular views of Jacó and Playa Hermosa. The viewpoint is several kilometers uphill. Note that the trailhead is unmarked, so ask a local to point it out to you.

Costa Rica Waterfall Tours ADVENTURE
(☎2643-1834; www.costaricawaterfalltours.com; Av Pastor Díaz; tours US$79-149; ⏲9am-5pm) This experienced, safety-conscious operator arranges some of the most adrenaline-charged excursions in town, from tamer waterfall rappelling to extreme canyoneering and cliff jumping.

Kayak Jacó KAYAKING
(☎2643-1233; www.kayakjaco.com; tours with/without transport from $90/65; ⏲7:30am-8pm) This reliable, responsible company facilitates kayaking and sea-canoeing trips that include snorkeling excursions to tropical islands in a wide variety of customized day and multiday trips. Though it does have a presence at Playa Agujas, 250m east of the beach, it's best to phone or email in advance.

Discovery Horseback Tours HORSEBACK RIDING
(☎8838-7550; www.horseridecostarica.com; rides from US$85) Nearby beach and rainforest rides are available through this highly recommended outfit, run by an expat couple who offer an extremely high level of service and professionalism and who clearly take excellent care of their horses.

Sleeping

★Room 2 Board Hostel & Surf School HOSTEL $
(☎2643-4949, USA 323-315-0012; www.room2board.com; dm/r from US$20/79; P❄@📶🏊) Now *this* is a hostel. On the newer side, spacious and professionally run, it has a buzzy on-site cafe, dedicated staff who arrange tours and surfing lessons, and various configurations of rooms spread over three floors. Roof-terrace hammocks catch the breeze, dorms come with excellent mattresses, solar-heated rain showers and lockers, and there are yoga classes and movie screenings.

Buddha House GUESTHOUSE $
(☎2643-3615; www.hostelbuddhahouse.com; Av Pastor Díaz; dm from US$12, r with fan & without bathroom from US$25, with air-con & without bathroom from US$40, with bathroom & air-con from US$50; P❄📶🏊) Bold colors and modern art create an artistic atmosphere at this 'boutique hostel,' where the best private rooms are spacious suites. Communal areas include a breezy patio, a spotless kitchen and even a small pool, and the staff are lovely. What's less lovely is the noise: the hostel is next to a bar that parties late into the night.

Hotel de Haan HOSTEL $
(☎8879-3332, 2643-1795; www.facebook.com/hoteldehaancr/; Calle Bohío; dm/r from US$12/35, casita without bathroom $28; P@📶🏊) This lively outpost is popular with backpackers and surfers on a budget. Basic private rooms have hot-water bathrooms and are tidy but dark. The open-air kitchen overlooks the pool area, and is a great place to meet and hang out with fellow travelers, which some guests do late into the night.

Hotel Perico Azul HOTEL $$
(☎2643-1341; www.hotelpericoazuljaco.com; r/studio US$60/75; P❄📶🏊) Tucked away off a quiet side street, this small hotel is difficult to fault. The rooms and apartments are light and spotless, with bright splashes of color, there's a small pool to relax around, staff go out of their way to make you feel welcome, and owner Mike runs the recommended Tortuga Surf Camp; surfing packages can be arranged.

Eating & Drinking

★Side Street Bistro FUSION $
(☎2643-2724; www.hermosapalmscr.com/side-street-bistro; Jacó Walk; sandwiches US$10-14; ⏲11am-4pm Mon-Sat, from 10am Sun) Recently relocated to the fabulous new Jacó Walk, this place bills itself as a food truck *sin ruedas* (without wheels). The small, often-changing menu includes creative sandwiches with roasted portobello mushrooms, tuna steak and coffee-and-cacao-rubbed tenderloin. Wash them down with local booze from next door's PuddleFish (p590), Jacó's first craft brewery. Brunch highlights include chicken and waffles and the breakfast burrito.

★Graffiti INTERNATIONAL $$
(☎2643-1708; www.facebook.com/graffiticr/; Jacó Walk; tapas $9-14, mains US$10-31; ⏲5-10pm; 📶🖉) With shiny new digs in Jacó Walk, this long-standing favorite has upped its aesthetic appeal while retaining what first made it great: creative dishes prepared with fresh, local ingredients. Tried-and-true favorites include cacao-and-coffee-encrusted filet mignon and a macadamia- or pretzel-encrusted daily catch. Save room for cheesecake and wash it all down with a yummy cocktail (cucumber-basil martini is our fave).

PUNTARENAS–PENINSULA FERRIES

All transportation is geared to the arrival and departure of the Puntarenas ferry. If either the bus or the ferry is running late, the other will wait.

From Paquera

The **Ferry Naviera Tambor** (☎2661-2084; www.navieratambor.com; adult/child/bicycle/motorcycle/car US$1.65/1/4/7/23) leaves daily at 5:30am, 9am, 11am, 2pm, 5pm and 8pm. The trip to Puntarenas takes about an hour. Buy a ticket at the window, reboard your car and then drive on to the ferry; you can't buy a ticket on board. Show up at least an hour early on holidays and busy weekends. The terminal contains a *soda* where you can grab a bite while waiting for the boat.

Buses meet arriving passengers at the ferry terminal and take them to Paquera, Tambor and Montezuma. They can be crowded, so try to get off the ferry fast to secure a seat. Most travelers take the bus from the terminal directly to Montezuma (US$3, two hours). Many taxi drivers will tell you the bus won't come, but this isn't true. There are no northbound buses.

Getting several travelers together to share a taxi to Montezuma (or wherever) is a good option since the ride will take half as long as the bus. A taxi to Montezuma is about US$12 per person, and to Mal País it's about US$20 – provided you have a full car.

From Playa Naranjo

The **Coonatramar ferry** (☎2661-1069; www.coonatramar.com; adult/child/bicycle/motorcycle/car US$2/1/4/6/18) to Puntarenas departs daily at 8am, 12:30pm, 4:30pm and 8:30pm, and can accommodate both cars and passengers. The trip takes 1½ hours. If traveling by car, get out and buy a ticket at the window, get back in your car and then drive on to the ferry. You cannot buy a ticket on board. Show up at least an hour early on holidays and busy weekends, as you'll be competing with a whole lot of other drivers to make it on.

Buses meet the arriving ferry and take passengers on to Jicaral, for travel on to the more northerly parts of the peninsula. If you're headed to Montezuma or Mal País, take the other ferry from Puntarenas to Paquera.

★**PuddleFish Brewery** CRAFT BEER
(☎2643-1659; www.puddlefishbrewery.com; ⊙10am-11pm Tue-Sun) From the same culinary gurus who brought Graffiti (p589) and Side Street Bistro (p589) to Jacó, this new microbrewery stationed in the glitzy Jacó Walk is the city's first. On tap are several of PuddleFish's own brews, including Punky Monkey and Lights Out Chocolate Coffee Stout, and the craft cocktails (ie the jalapeño ginger margarita) are outstanding. Live music Thursday and Saturday.

Monkey Bar CLUB
(☎8329-2304; Av Pastor Díaz; ⊙9pm-2:30am Tue-Sun) Attracting a young crowd of locals and visitors, Monkey Bar pumps with good times, reggaetón and pheromones. There's also a big VIP lounge in the back, with bottle service and oftentimes a special DJ.

Information

Jacó is the epicenter of Costa Rica's prostitution scene. Travelers who wish to explore this dark corner of Costa Rican nightlife should consider the health and safety risks and negative social impacts.

Locals warn against walking alone on the beach at night, as there have been several muggings.

Getting There & Away

BOAT

Zuma Tours (Map p585; ☎2642-0024, 2642-0050; www.zumatours.net) Runs speedboat transfers from Jacó to Montezuma (adult/child US$40/30, one hour), with shuttle pick-up in Jacó between 10am and 10:30am, and 11am boat departures from Herradura. From Montezuma boats depart at 8:30am. It's also possible to get dropped off in Mal País and Santa Teresa (adult/child US$50/40).

BUS

Gray Line, Easy Ride and Monkey Ride run shared shuttles from Jacó to popular destinations, including Granada, Nicaragua.

Buses originate in Puntarenas or Quepos, so consult your lodgings about the latest schedule and get to the stop early.

Puntarenas US$2.70, 1½ hours, 12 daily between 6am and 7:30pm.

Quepos US$2.70, 1½ hours, 12 daily between 6am and 7pm.

San José US$5.50, 2½ hours, eight daily between 6am and 7pm.

Quepos

POP 21,950

Just 7km from the entrance to Manuel Antonio, the small, busy town of Quepos serves as the gateway to the national park, as well as a convenient port of call for travelers in need of goods and services. Although the Manuel Antonio area was rapidly and irreversibly transformed following the ecotourism boom, Quepos has largely retained an authentic Tico feel.

While many visitors to the Manuel Antonio area prefer to stay outside Quepos, accommodations in town are generally very good value, and there's a decent restaurant scene that belies the town's small size. Quepos is also gridded with easy-to-walk streets, which provide the opportunity to interact with the friendly locals.

Activities

★Paddle 9 ADVENTURE

(Map p594; ☎2777-7436; www.paddle9sup.com; tours US$65-165) These newer kids on the block are a passionate, safety-conscious team who've introduced SUP (stand-up paddleboarding) to Quepos and who delight in showing visitors around the Pacific coast. Apart from the two-hour mangrove or ocean paddleboarding tours, the most popular outing is a eight-hour journey involving paddleboarding, lunch at a tilapia fish farm and swimming in various waterfalls. You can add $30 to any tour to make it private.

Oceans Unlimited DIVING

(Map p594; ☎2519-9544; www.scubadivingcostarica.com; 2-tank dive US$109) This shop takes its diving very seriously, and runs most of its excursions out to Isla Larga and Isla del Caño, which are south in Bahía Drake (connected via a two-hour bus trip). It also has a range of specialized PADI certifications, and regular environmental-awareness projects that make it stand out from the pack.

Unique Tours ADVENTURE

(☎8844-0900, 2777-1119; www.costaricauniquetours.com) This established local operator organizes entertaining rafting tours of the Río Savegre, ocean and mangrove kayaking outings and more. But what makes it unique is that it's the only operator to offer a trip to a hidden, remote hot spring, as well as coastal hikes to Parque Nacional Manuel Antonio. Prices vary depending on group size.

H2O Adventures ADVENTURE

(Ríos Tropicales; Map p594; ☎2777-4092; www.h2ocr.com) The venerable Costa Rican rafting company Ríos Tropicales has a hugely popular franchise in Quepos called H2O Adventures, which organizes rafting outings on the Naranjo, El Chorro and Savegre rivers, as well as kayaking and tubing outings. Rates start at US$75 for Class II through IV rapids.

Sleeping

★Villas Jacquelina GUESTHOUSE $

(Map p594; ☎8345-1516; www.villasjacquelina.com; Calle 2; r US$35-70; P ❄ 📶 ☒) By far the best budget option in town, this large, rambling building offers various configurations of rooms, the newest and most popular of which is a 3rd-story, open-air terrace called the 'Birds Nest.' The place is run by the indomitable Steve, a transplant with energy to spare and tons of local knowledge, who can help arrange tours.

Pura Vida Hostel HOSTEL $

(Map p594; ☎2777-7775; https://hostelpuravidama.com; incl breakfast dm US$10-15, r per person US$12.50-17.50; ❄ @ 📶) From the rainbow-hued facade to the interior murals, this place is nothing if not colorful. The rooms have tropical-colored walls, bright linens, tile floors and lockers. Big, shared balconies overlook the jungle-covered hills, where you're likely to spot squirrel monkeys passing through. It's on the southern edge of town on the road to Manuel Antonio.

Hotel Papa's Papalotes HOTEL $

(Map p594; ☎2777-3774; www.papaspapalotes.com; Av 2; dm $13, s with/without air-con US$50/35, d with/without air-con US$60/45; ❄ 📶) A decent budget choice in central Quepos, with private rooms that are a better bargain than at some nearby hostels. The decor won't make your social-media posts, but the place is clean and secure. If you opt for fan-only, you'll be woken up by the dawn chorus of traffic passing along the street; pack earplugs.

Eating & Drinking

★Marisquería Jiuberths SEAFOOD $
(Map p594; ☎2777-1292; mains from US$7; ⏰11am-10pm) Run by a hardworking fisherman's family, this institution with brightly tiled floors serves the best seafood in town, yet is practically unknown to visitors because it's tucked away. Whether you have the catch of the day or the satisfying fish soup, the portions are generous and the service attentive. Follow unpaved Calle 2 out of town. Cash only.

★Brooklyn Bakery BAKERY $
(Map p594; www.facebook.com/TheBrooklynBakeryCR; Av 3; bagels US$1.50, mains US$5-8; ⏰6am-3pm Mon-Sat; 📶✍) Real New York–style bagels and lox (a real rarity in Costa Rica)! Rye bread! Iced coffee! This adorable little bakery bakes its fresh wares every morning, as well as serving light bites and amazing salads throughout the day and specials at lunchtime, such as delicious Italian meatball sandwiches.

Soda Come Bien CAFETERIA $
(Map p594; ☎2777-2550; Av 1, Mercado Central; mains US$3.50-8; ⏰6am-5pm Mon-Sat, to 11am Sun) The daily rotation of delicious cafeteria options might include fish in tomato sauce, *olla de carne* (beef soup with rice) or chicken soup, but everything is fresh, the women behind the counter are friendly and the burly portions are a dream come true for hungry shoestringers. Or pick up a fresh *empanada* before or after a long bus ride.

Farmers Market MARKET $
(Map p594; Calle 4; ⏰4pm Fri-noon Sat) Self-caterers should check out the farmers market near the waterfront, where you can buy directly from farmers, fisherfolk, bakers and other food producers.

★Z Gastro Bar FUSION $$
(Map p594; ☎2777-6948; www.zgastrobar.com; Marina Pez Vela; mains US$15-25; ⏰7am-10pm; 🅿📶) Bright, open to the breeze from all sides and with colorful cushions strewn on its comfy couches, this is a terrific spot for lingering with a coffee and dessert, or over a meal of dorado *ceviche* in coconut milk, an octopus burger or delicious homemade pasta with mussels. The arty presentation matches the terrific flavors and the service is excellent. The sister restaurant **Z Poolside Bistro** is located next to Byblos Hotel.

★Gabriella's SEAFOOD $$$
(Map p594; ☎2519-9300; www.gabriellassteakhouse.com; Marina Pez Vela; mains US$25-35; ⏰4-10pm; 🅿❄📶) A contender for the region's best restaurant, Gabriella's does many things well. The veranda catches the sunset and the service is attentive, but the food is the real star, with a great emphasis on fresh fish and mouthwatering steak. We're particularly big fans of the seared tuna with chipotle sauce and the spicy sausage and shrimp pasta. In a word: terrific.

Café Milagro CAFE
(Map p594; ☎2777-1707; http://elpatiodecafemilagro.com; Calle 4; ⏰7am-9pm Mon-Sat) Café Milagro sources its coffee beans from all over Costa Rica and produces a variety of estate, single-origin and blended roasts to suit any coffee fiend's palate, with 1% of its profits going to environmental causes via international nonprofit 1% for the Planet. Live music nightly; plenty of vegan and veggie options on the dinner menu.

Cuban Republik Disco Lounge CLUB
(Map p594; ☎8345-9922; www.facebook.com/cubanrepublik.quepos; cover charge Fri & Sat US$2-4; ⏰10pm-2:30am Thu-Sat) Cuban Republik hosts the most reliable party in central Quepos, and it has various drinks specials. The DJs get loud late into the night and women

BUSES FROM QUEPOS

DESTINATION	COST (US$)	DURATION (HR)	FREQUENCY
Jacó	3	1½	12 daily, 4:30am-6pm
Puntarenas	5	3	12 daily, 4:30am-5:30pm
San Isidro de El General, via Dominical	5	3	5am, 11:30am, 3:30pm, 8pm
San José	7	3½	6 direct daily, 4am-5pm
Uvita, via Dominical	4	2	6am, 9:30am, 2:30pm, 5:30pm

get in free before midnight on Friday night. It's a nice, mixed Tico and gringo scene.

Getting There & Away

Scheduled private shuttles, operated by Gray Line, Easy Ride and Monkey Ride, run between Quepos/Manuel Antonio and popular destinations such as Jacó (US$35), Monteverde (US$59), Puerto Jiménez (US$79), San José (US$50) and Uvita (US$35).

All buses arrive at and depart from the busy, chaotic main **terminal** (Map p594) in the center of town. If you're coming and going in the high season, buy tickets for San José in advance at the **Tracopa ticket office** (2777-0263; 6am-6pm) at the bus terminal; *colectivo* (shared taxi) fares to San José are slightly cheaper and take two hours longer.

Manuel Antonio

As you travel the road between Quepos and Parque Nacional Manuel Antonio, the din from roaring buses, packs of tourists and locals hunting foreign dollars becomes increasingly loud, reaching its somewhat chaotic climax at Manuel Antonio village. Hordes descend on this tiny oceanside village at the entrance to the country's most visited national park. Don't show up all bright-eyed and bushy-tailed, expecting deserted beaches and untouched tropical paradise. Higher primates tend to be the most frequently sighted species, especially during the congested dry season, when tour groups arrive en masse.

But come here in low season or on a Monday (when the park is closed), and you'll find a tranquil little village with waves sedately lapping at the white sand. And when troops of monkeys climb down from the forest canopy to the tropical sands, you can get up close and personal with some marvelous wildlife.

Sights & Activities

★Parque Nacional Manuel Antonio NATIONAL PARK
(Map p594; 2777-8551; park entrance US$16; 7am-3:30pm Tue-Sun) Featuring lush jungle, picture-perfect beaches and craggy headlands, this tiny park brims with wildlife (and oftentimes, visiting humans). As you wander its lovely trails, you'll catch a glimpse of dangling sloths, squawking toucans and playful monkeys, and stumble on breathtaking views of the sea and nearby islands. To beat the crowds and maximize wildlife sightings, arrive early.

Swimming

There are four beautiful beaches within the park and one just outside the park entrance. The beaches are often numbered – most people call Playa Espadilla (outside the park) '1st beach,' Playa Espadilla Sur '2nd beach,' Playa Manuel Antonio '3rd beach,' Playa Puerto Escondido '4th beach' and Playa Playitas '5th beach.' Some people begin counting at Espadilla Sur, which is the first beach in the park, so it can be a bit confusing trying to figure out which beach people may be talking about. Regardless, they're all equally pristine and provide sunbathing opportunities; check conditions with the rangers to see which ones are safe for swimming.

Hiking

Parque Manuel Antonio has an official road, **Sendero El Perezoso** (Map p594), that's paved and wheelchair-accessible and connects the entrance to the network of short trails. None of them are strenuous, and all are well marked and heavily traversed, though there are some quiet corners near the ends of the trails. Off-trail hiking is not permitted. A new boardwalk stretching from the ranger station to Playa Espadilla Sur called Caminata Mai was completed at the end of 2017.

Sleeping

Vista Serena Hostel HOSTEL $
(Map p594; 2777-5162; www.vistaserena.com; dm US$11-18, bungalows with/without air-con US$60/50; P@) Perched scenically on a quiet hillside, this memorable hostel allows backpackers to enjoy spectacular ocean sunsets from a hammock-filled terrace and strum the communal guitar. Accommodations range from spartan econo-dorms to plusher dorms to bungalows for those who want a bit more privacy. The super-friendly owner Sonia and her staff are commendable for their efforts in assisting countless travelers.

Hostel Plinio and Bed & Breakfast HOSTEL $
(Map p594; 2777-6123; dm/d from US$14/60;) Attuned to backpacker needs, Hostel Plinio ticks most boxes: a convenient location near Quepos, a large pool and ample common areas with hammocks and

Manuel Antonio Area

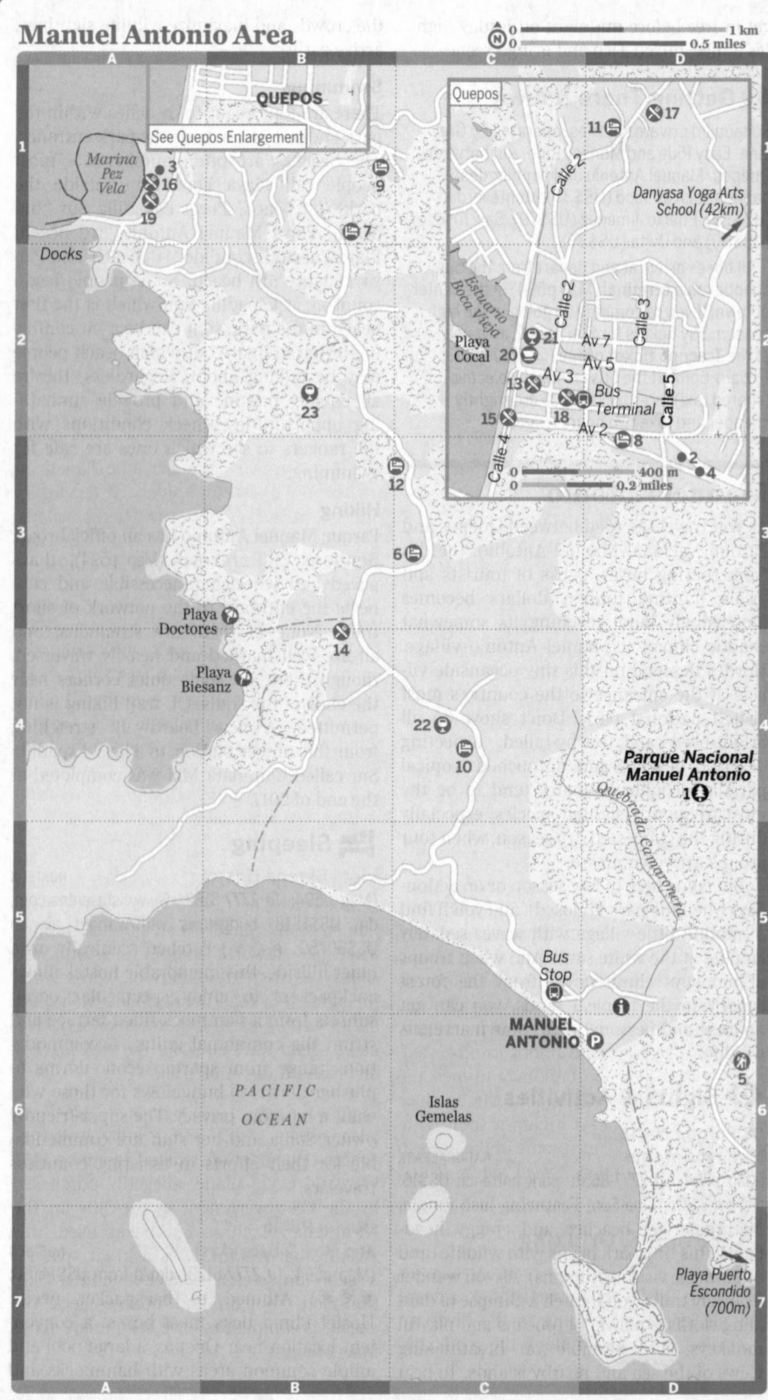

0 1 km
0 0.5 miles
QUEPOS
See Quepos Enlargement
Marina Pez Vela
Docks
Quepos
Calle 2
Danyasa Yoga Arts School (42km)
Estuario Boca Vieja
Calle 3
Playa Cocal
Av 7
Av 5
Av 3
Bus Terminal
Calle 5
Av 2
Calle 4
0 400 m
0 0.2 miles
Playa Doctores
Playa Biesanz
Parque Nacional Manuel Antonio
Quebrada Camaronera
Bus Stop
MANUEL ANTONIO
PACIFIC OCEAN
Islas Gemelas
Playa Puerto Escondido (700m)

Manuel Antonio Area

Top Sights
1 Parque Nacional Manuel Antonio........D4

Activities, Courses & Tours
2 H2O Adventures........D3
3 Oceans Unlimited........A1
4 Paddle 9........D3
5 Sendero El Perezoso........D6

Sleeping
6 Backpackers Manuel Antonio........C3
7 Hostel Plinio and Bed & Breakfast........B1
8 Hotel Papa's Papalotes........D3
9 Pura Vida Hostel........B1
10 Selina Manuel Antonio........C4
11 Villas Jacquelina........D1
12 Vista Serena Hostel........C3

Eating
13 Brooklyn Bakery........C2
14 Falafel Bar........B4
15 Farmers Market........C2
16 Gabriella's........A1
17 Marisquería Jiuberths........D1
Sancho's........(see 6)
18 Soda Come Bien........C2
19 Z Gastro Bar........A1

Drinking & Nightlife
20 Café Milagro........C2
21 Cuban Republik Disco Lounge........C2
22 El Avión........C4
23 Ronny's Place........B2

sofas for socializing, an efficient tour desk and superior doubles with jungle views for couples wanting more privacy. The drawbacks? The roadside location means some rooms are noisy, and the wi-fi doesn't reach everywhere.

Backpackers Manuel Antonio HOSTEL $
(Map p594; ☎2777-2507; dm/d incl breakfast from US$16/39; P ❄ @ 📶 🏊) This locally owned hostel has a very sociable vibe and a good location – relatively near the entrance of the park and walking distance from a good grocery store. The dorms are clean and secure (if small), and there's a grill and pool out back for socializing. Larger rooms, with a bunk and double bed, are good for groups of friends.

★Selina Manuel Antonio HOSTEL $$
(Map p594; www.selina.com/manuel-antonio/; dm US$20-25, r US$99-159; 🏊) Part of the Selina empire, which includes dozens of hostels recently opened across Central America, this one is already a legend. The dorms and private rooms are scattered among rainforested cliffs in elegant white buildings livened up with rotating art exhibits, and the bar has become the area's best nightlife spot, with frequent live music from some of the hottest local talent. Two pools. Sweet views. Killer breakfast buffet.

Eating & Drinking

Falafel Bar MEDITERRANEAN $
(Map p594; ☎2777-4135; mains US$5-9; ⊙noon-8pm Tue-Sun; 📶 ✍) Adding to the diversity of cuisine to be found along the road, this falafel spot dishes up authentic Israeli favorites. You'll also find plenty of vegetarian options, including couscous, fresh salads, stuffed grape leaves, fab fruit smoothies and even french fries for the picky little ones.

Sancho's MEXICAN $
(Map p594; ☎2777-0340; tacos from US$3; ⊙11:30am-10pm; 📶) A great view from the open-air terrace, potent house margaritas, excellent fish tacos and humongous *chile verde* (green chili) burritos are just some of the draws at this friendly expat-run joint. A place to knock back a few beers with friends in a convivial, chilled-out atmosphere, rather than woo your date.

Ronny's Place BAR
(Map p594; ☎2777-5120; www.ronnysplace.com; ⊙noon-9pm) The insane views of two pristine bays and jungle on all sides at Ronny's Place make it worth a detour for a drink and a tasty meal. While plenty of places along this stretch of road boast similar views, the off-the-beaten-path location makes it feel like a secret find. Look for the well-marked dirt road off the main drag.

El Avión BAR
(Map p594; ☎2777-3378; http://elavion.net; ⊙noon-11pm; 📶) Constructed around a 1954 Fairchild C-123 plane, allegedly purchased by the US government in the '80s for the Nicaraguan Contras but never used, this striking bar-restaurant is a great spot for a beer and stellar sunset-watching. Skip the food, though, and double-check the check, as complaints have been made about inaccuracies.

Information

The park **ticket office** (Map p594; ☎2777-6208; www.coopealianza.fi.cr; park entrance US$16; ⏰7am-3:30pm) is in Manuel Antonio village, a few hundred meters before the park entrance. The ranger station is just before Playa Manuel Antonio.

Getting There & Away

The **bus stop** (Map p594) in Manuel Antonio is at the end of the road into the village that runs along the beach. Buses depart Manuel Antonio beach direct for San José (US$9, 3½ hours) nine times daily between 4am and 5pm. Buy tickets well in advance at the Quepos bus terminal (p593).

Buses for destinations other than San José leave from the main terminal in Quepos.

Local buses (US$0.55, 20 minutes, every 30 minutes) and shared taxis connect Manuel Antonio village with Quepos.

Dominical

For as long as anybody could remember (which wasn't very long in Dominical), this was a lazy little town that drew a motley crew of surfers, backpackers and affable do-nothings, a place where a traveler could wander the dusty roads, surfboard tucked under an arm, balancing the day's activities between wave riding and hammock hang time.

Those days aren't entirely gone, but in 2015 a bunch of paver stones laid along the beach became the town's first real road. And as an increasing population of expats and gringos began to hunker down, some more sophisticated (though decidedly ecofriendly) businesses began to sprout. Now the sheer volume of cars, bicycles and pedestrians on the main street, particularly around the time of neighboring Uvita's hippie festival Envision (p598) and in the high season, is staggering. Rainier months remain as languidly 'old Costa Rica' as ever.

Sights & Activities

Dominical owes its fame to its seriously sick point and beach breaks, though surf conditions here are variable. This is a great opportunity to learn surfing in the white-water beach breaks, but beware of getting in too deep, as you can really get trashed out here if you don't know what you're doing. If you're just getting started, stay in the white water or make for nearby Playa Dominicalito, which is a bit tamer.

★Cataratas Nauyaca WATERFALL
(☎2787-0541/2; www.cataratasnauyaca.com; horseback tour US$70, pickup tour US$28, hike admission US$8; ⏰7am-5pm Mon-Sat, 8am-4pm Sun) This center, owned and operated by a Costa Rican family, is home to the coast's most impressive waterfalls, which cascade through a protected reserve of both primary and secondary forest. The family runs horseback-riding tours and tours by pickup truck to the falls (reservations required; Dominical pick-up available), where visitors can swim in the inviting natural pools.

★Alturas Wildlife Sanctuary NATURE RESERVE
(☎2200-5440; www.alturaswildlifesanctuary.org; minimum donation adult/child under 12yr US$25/15; ⏰tours 9am, 11am, 1pm & 3pm Tue-Sun) Around 1.5km east and uphill from Dominical, this wildlife sanctuary takes in injured and orphaned animals as well as illegal pets. Its mission is to rehabilitate those that can be and reintroduce them to the wild, and look after those that cannot. During the 60- to 90-minute tour you're introduced to its residents: a macaw missing an eye, monkeys that were caged since infancy, Bubba the famous coati and more. Entertaining, educational and a terrific cause.

★Sunset Surf SURFING
(☎8917-3143; www.sunsetsurfdominical.com; Mavi Surf Hotel; all-inclusive packages per week from US$1575; ⏰8am-4:30pm) Operated by Dylan Park, who grew up surfing the waves of Hawaii and Costa Rica, Sunset offers a variety of packages (including one for women only, and day lessons). It has a three-to-one student-instructor ratio and Park is an excellent teacher. Organic, all-natural sunblock is provided and 1% of proceeds go toward 'the planet.'

Dominical Surf Adventures RAFTING, SURFING
(☎2787-0431; www.dominicalsurfadventures.com; ⏰8am-5pm Mon-Sat, 9am-3pm Sun) A bit of an adventurer's one-stop shop: visitors can book white-water rafting, kayaking, snorkeling and dive trips, as well as surf lessons (from US$50), from an office on the main drag. Rafting trips start at US$90 (for runs on the Class II and III Guabo) and include a more challenging run on the Río Coto Brus' Class IV rapids.

Danyasa Yoga Arts School YOGA
(☎2787-0229; www.danyasa.com; classes incl mat US$16; ⊙shop 9:30am-8pm) This lovely Dominical yoga studio offers a variety of classes for all levels, including unique dance-yoga-flow hybrid styles and even ecstatic moon dance. The studio also serves as a center for retreats of all kinds.

Sleeping

Tropical Sands Dominical Eco Inn HOTEL $
(☎2787-0200; www.tropicalsandsdominical.com; d with/without air-con US$70/50; P❄☎) A lovely, secure hotel option hidden among lush foliage on the southern end of town, this place offers newly updated rooms with tile floors, wide-plank ceilings and small porches strung with hammocks. The grounds are beautiful and the expat owners (who speak Spanish, French and English) lovingly maintain them. It's also just steps from the beach.

Cool Vibes Hostel HOSTEL $
(☎8353-6428; www.hosteldominical.com; dm/r from US$13/38; P@☎≋) On the road at the southern end of town, this two-story sanctuary features a relaxing lounge, communal kitchen and attractive (but occasionally malfunctioning) plunge pool lined with potted plants. Tile-floored rooms are spacious and clean, with solid beds and bamboo furniture. Cash only; air-con costs more.

★**Danyasa Yoga Retreat** GUESTHOUSE $$
(☎2787-0229; www.danyasa.com; s/d/ste US$52/83/98; ❄☎≋) To visualize Danyasa, imagine eight refurbished cargo containers set amid tranquil greenery, each turned into a snug room or grander suite, with shared outdoor bamboo showers and a guest kitchen. Now imagine water features in the shape of Buddha's head, a relaxing new pool, yoga and dance classes designed to unleash your Inner Goddess and align chakras, and you're there.

Eating & Drinking

★**Cafe Mono Congo** CAFE $
(www.cafemonocongo.com; mains US$4-9; ⊙6:30am-7pm; ☎) Perch on a swing at the bar or at a riverside table to enjoy the best espresso in town, hands down. This open-air cafe also dishes up tasty, simple breakfasts like *gallo pinto* and *huevos rancheros* and (largely veggie) lunches, using organic local produce. Find it at the junction of the road into town and the main drag – couldn't be simpler.

Café de Ensueños CAFE $
(meals US$5-9; ⊙7:30am-8pm) Run by a lovely local family, this cafe is tucked away at the end of the southern spur road. Organic coffee drinks, fresh juices and hearty breakfasts are served alfresco under a covered terrace – an excellent spot for a quiet morning. Extra hungry? Go for the gut-busting Special Breakfast or the Pancake Tropical, which comes with eggs, bacon and fruit.

El Pescado Loco SEAFOOD $
(mains US$8-9; ⊙11:45am-7:30pm) This little open-air shack has only a handful of menu items, but when it comes to fish tacos with chipotle sauce and chunky guacamole, well, a taco doesn't get much better than this. The onion rings and fish and chips are nothing to sneeze at, either. Our only quibble: how about real cutlery instead of disposable?

Del Mar Taco Shop TACOS $
(☎8428-9050; tacos US$4; ⊙11:30am-9pm) On the approach to the beach, an expat cooks up some of the Pacific coast's best tacos in this casual surfer hangout. We prefer the fish tacos to the shrimp, which can vary in size. Also delicious are the daily Hawaiian BBQ specials and chunky burritos, and the guacamole is superb. On Taco Tuesday (April to November) tacos cost just US$2.

★**Fuego Brew Co.** CRAFT BEER
(☎8992-9559; www.fuegobrew.com; craft beer US$4-6; ⊙11:30am-10:30pm) Glowing electric purple from the center of Dominical, this sleek establishment is the town's first craft brewery and a place to sip *guanábana*-flavored Hefeweizen all day long. The bartenders are super-nice and the bar snacks are tasty, especially the seared tuna. Upstairs is the glistening hardwood bar and restaurant; downstairs is a seven-barrel brewing system and tasting room.

Information

Waves, currents and riptides in Dominical are very strong, and there have been drownings in the past. Watch for red flags (which mark riptides), follow the instructions of posted signs and swim at beaches that are patrolled by lifeguards. If you're smart, the beach is no problem, but people do die here every year.

Dominical attracts a heavy-duty party crowd, which in turn has led to a burgeoning drug problem.

BUSES FROM DOMINICAL

DESTINATION	COST (US$)	DURATION	FREQUENCY (DAILY)
Palmar	2	1½hr	4:45am, 8am, 11am, 12:30pm, 4pm
Quepos	5.75	1hr	5:30am, 8:30am, 11:30am, 1pm, 5pm
San José	10.25	4½hr	5:30am, 1pm
Uvita	1	20min	4:45am, 7:30am, 10:30am, 12:30pm, 4pm, 5:30pm

Dominical Information Center (☎2787-0454; www.dominicalinformation.com; ⊙9:30am-5pm) On the main strip, near the entrance to Dominical, this tourist info center has useful maps of town and bus timetables for the entire region. Bus-ticket, shuttle and tour booking services available.

Getting There & Away

Gray Line, Easy Ride and Monkey Ride offer private and shared shuttle services to popular destinations such as Jacó, San José, Monteverde, Tamarindo and Sierpe; Easy Ride has direct services to Granada, Nicaragua.

Buses pick up and drop off passengers along the main road in Dominical.

Uvita

Just 17km south of Dominical, this sweet little village consists of a few dirt roads lined with farms, guesthouses and tiny shops; a cluster of strip malls by the main Costanera Sur entrance; and a scattering of hotels in the jungle-covered hills above. With its gentle pace of life, it should give you a good idea of what the central Pacific coast was like before the tourist boom. Uvita's main attraction is **Parque Nacional Marino Ballena** (☎2743-8141; US$6; ⊙7am-4pm), a pristine marine reserve famous for its migrating pods of humpback whales and its virtually abandoned wilderness beaches. There are also good waterfalls nearby and once a year it hosts the country's biggest hippie-fest, the **Envision Festival** (www.envisionfestival.com; ⊙late Feb).

Held a short distance from the main entrance to Uvita, the **farmers market** (☎8680-9752; ⊙8am-1pm Sat) is a good place to mingle with locals and longtime expats, and purchase locally grown fruit and vegetables, honey and home-cooked foods.

Uvita is a perfect base for exploring Costanera Sur, which is home to some truly spectacular beaches, as well as an exhilarating natural water slide in the shape of **Cascada Verde** (US$2; ⊙8am-4pm).

Sleeping

★**Cascada Verde** HOSTEL $
(☎2743-8191, 8422-6504; www.cascadaverde.eu; dm/s/d from US$11/22/34; P@🛜) If you're looking for a quiet retreat in the jungle, this hostel run by a young expat couple is for you. About 2km uphill from Uvita, it features jaw-dropping jungle views from the dining terrace, a large communal kitchen, plenty of indoor and outdoor spaces for relaxing, appealingly designed rooms with bamboo partitions, and a waterfall a short walk away.

Flutterby House HOSTEL $
(☎2743-8221, 8341-1730; www.flutterbyhouse.com; campsite US$10, dm US$14-18, d US$40-120; P@🛜) Is it possible to fall in love with a hostel? If so, the ramshackle collection of colorful *Swiss Family Robinson*–style tree houses and dorms has beguiled us. The place is run by a pair of expat sisters, and the clientele here tends to be of the barefoot, surfing variety. The bar is a social hub.

Tucan Hotel HOSTEL $
(☎2743-8140; www.tucanhotel.com; campsite/hammock/dm US$12/12/15, d from US$33; P❄@🛜) Located 100m inland from the main highway, this cheapie is popular with international travelers of all ages. The rooms are arranged around a semi-open communal area, and there are also simple tents and hammocks, as well as a house in the trees. Bonuses include a shared kitchen, daily movies at 4pm, an Italian restaurant and a convivial atmosphere.

Getting There & Away

Most buses depart from the sheltered bus stops on the Costanera in the main village.

Dominical US$1, 30 minutes, nine daily between 4:45am and 5:30pm.

Quepos US$4, two hours, departs 5:30am, 11:40am, 1pm and 4pm.

San José US$9.20, 3½ hours, departs 5:30am, 11:30am, 1pm and 4pm.

Private shuttle companies – Grayline, Easy Ride and Monkey Ride – offer pricier transfers from Uvita to Dominical, San José, Quepos, Jacó, Puerto Jiménez and other popular destinations.

SOUTHERN COSTA RICA & PENÍNSULA DE OSA

From the chilly heights of Cerro Chirripó (3820m) to the steamy coastal jungles of the Península de Osa, this sector of Costa Rica encompasses some of the country's least-explored and least-developed land. Vast tracts of wilderness remain untouched in Parque Internacional La Amistad, and the country's most visible indigenous groups – the Bribrí, Cabécar, Boruc and Ngöbe – maintain traditional ways of living in their remote territories.

Quetzal sightings around San Gerardo de Dota are frequent, and scarlet-macaw appearances are the norm along the coast. Monkeys, sloths and coatis roam the region's abundant parks and reserves, and in Parque Nacional Corcovado there's also the rare chance to spy on slumbering tapir. Meanwhile, the rugged coasts of the Golfo Dulce and Península de Osa captivate travelers with abandoned wilderness beaches, world-class surf and opportunities for rugged exploration. This is the land for intrepid travelers yearning for something truly wild.

San Isidro de El General

Although it's a place where few travelers choose to linger, San Isidro de El General is the fastest-growing urban area outside the capital and a sprawling, utilitarian market town at the crossroads between some of Costa Rica's prime destinations.

'El General' (often referred to as Pérez Zeledón, the name of the municipality) is the region's largest population center and major transportation hub. If you're traveling to the southern Pacific beaches or Chirripó, a brief stop is inevitable. Some accommodations options just outside the town environs are worthy destinations in their own right.

Sleeping & Eating

Hotel Chirripó HOTEL $

(2771-0529; Av 2, btwn Calles Central & 1; s/d US$40/31, without bathroom US$17/24; P ❄ 📶) Let's put it bluntly: if you're traveling through town, weary and cash-poor, this is *the* choice. Popular with discerning budget travelers, this centrally located hotel is a two-minute stroll from the bus station and filled with bare, whitewashed rooms that are barren but utterly dirt- and grime-free.

Hotel Los Crestones HOTEL $$

(2770-1500, 2770-1200; www.hotelloscrestones.com; cnr Calle Central & Av 14; s/d with air-con US$50/60, without air-con US$40/50; P ❄ 📶 🏊) This sharp motor court is decked with blooming hedges and climbing vines outside – indeed a welcome sight to the road-weary traveler. Inside, functional rooms feature modern furnishings and fixtures, which are made all the better by the attentive staff who keep this place running efficiently. There's also a cute restaurant.

★ **Urban Farm Cafe** INTERNATIONAL $

(2771-2442; Calle Central; mains US$5-7; 7am-7pm Mon-Fri, to 4pm Sat; 📶 🌱) With its 'from farm to table' motto, this delightful cafe single-handedly pushes San Isidro's dining scene up a big notch. Breakfast options range from 'Hawaiian-style' macadamia pancakes with banana to veggie omelets and falafel, while its lunchtime wraps and salads are just overflowing with fresh vegetables. Wash it down with a delectable fruit smoothie.

La Casa del Marisco SEAFOOD $

(8366-1880, 2772-2862; Calle Central; mains US$6-12; 10:30am-10pm Mon-Sat, to 6pm Sun) Since this unpretentious seafood spot is usually slammed at lunchtime, it's best to come during off hours for its several daily varieties of *ceviche,* fresh fish or shrimp prepared as you like it (plus pastas, burgers, salads and soups). The crowd of local clientele not-so-subtly hints at the choice sustenance served here.

Getting There & Away

In San Isidro the **local bus terminal** (known as Mercado) is on Av 6 and serves nearby villages. The bus to San Gerardo de Rivas (for Parque Nacional Chirripó; US$4, 1½ hours) departs from the local terminal five times daily from 5:45am.

Península de Osa & Golfo Dulce

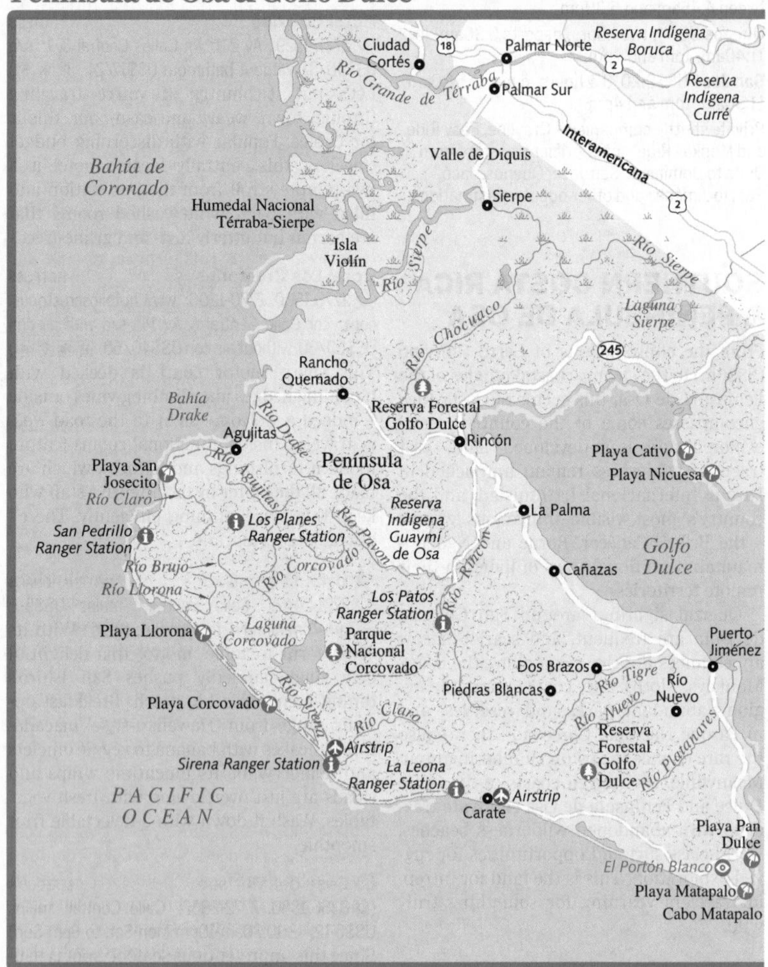

You will find **Terminal Tracopa** (☎2771-0468) on the Interamericana, just southwest of Av Central, and **Terminal MUSOC** (☎2771-0414), which only serves San José, just beside Kafe de la Casa. If heading for Paso Canoas, Golfito or Palmar Norte, try to catch a bus that originates from San Isidro, or risk standing room only.

Transportes Blanco (☎2771-4744) is on the side street west of the Interamericana.

San Gerardo de Rivas

If you have plans to climb Chirripó, you're in the right place – the tiny, tranquil, spread-out town of San Gerardo de Rivas is at the doorstep of the national park. This is a place to get supplies, a good night's rest and a hot shower before and after the trek.

With a new online reservation system, hiking permits recently became much easier to obtain. For those who don't have the time or energy to summit Chirripó, there are also lovely, less difficult hikes in private nature reserves, and rural tourism aplenty, from the local **trout farm** (☎2742-5054; ⏱9am-6pm Sat & Sun; & by appointment) to local cheese- and chocolate-makers in nearby Canaán. San Gerardo's bird-filled alpine scenery certainly makes it a beautiful place to linger.

The road to San Gerardo de Rivas winds its way 22km up the valley of the Río Chirripó from San Isidro.

Sights

★Cloudbridge Nature Reserve — NATURE RESERVE

(☎USA 917-494-5408; www.cloudbridge.org; admission by donation, tours US$10-30; ⏲6am-6pm) About 2km past the trailhead to Cerro Chirripó you will find the entrance to the mystical, magical Cloudbridge Nature Reserve. Covering 283 hectares on the side of Cerro Chirripó, this private reserve is an ongoing reforestation and preservation project founded by Genevieve Giddy and her late husband Ian. A network of trails traverses the property, which is easy to explore independently. Even if you don't get far past the entrance, you'll find two waterfalls, including the magnificent Catarata Pacifica.

Talamanca Reserve — NATURE RESERVE

(☎2742-5080; www.talamancareserve.com) With over 1600 hectares of primary and secondary cloud forest, this private reserve has numerous hiking trails, the longest being a seven-hour trek, and another leading to its 11 waterfalls. Talamanca is doing its best to promote itself as an alternative to Parque Nacional Chirripó, and nonguests are welcome to hike its trails for a day fee of US$25. All-terrain vehicle (ATV) tours are available both to guests and nonguests.

Sleeping

★Casa Mariposa — HOSTEL $

(☎2742-5037; www.hotelcasamariposa.net; dm US$22, d US$40-60; P@) Just 50m from the park entrance, this adorable hostel is built into the side of the mountain and is characterized by the warmth and knowledge of owners John and Jill. Traveler-oriented benefits – warm clothes to borrow for the hike, laundry service, assistance with booking the Chirripó lodge and tips on alternative activities in the area – make it ideal.

Casa Hostel Chirripó — HOSTEL $

(☎2742-5020, 8814-8876; www.facebook.com/Hostel-Casa-Chirripó-417397658422067; dm US$15, r with/without bathroom US$40/35; 📶) Near the soccer field, this colorful newer hostel gives guests a space to cook and socialize, and post-hike provides cozy rooms and dorms to lay down their weary heads. Taxis to the trailhead cost US$10, which can be split among groups. They can also organize tours to Chirripó.

Hotel Uran — HOSTEL $

(☎2742-5003; www.hoteluran.com; s/d US$36/57, without bathroom US$20/40; P📶) Just 70m below the trailhead, these no-nonsense budget digs are a longtime mecca for hikers heading to/from Chirripó. Budget-friendly rooms are fine for a restful snooze, while the on-site restaurant and laundry facilities cater to the shoestring set. Note that it's possible to buy beer here (the *pulpería* in town doesn't sell alcohol).

Casa de los Celtas B&B **$$**
(☎8707-2921, 2770-3524; www.casaceltas.com; s/d US$55/70; P 📶) Overlooking 1.6 hectares of native greenery and brightened by Sheelagh's orchid collection, this delightful B&B is run by two retired expat travelers, whose genuine warmth and knowledge of the area greatly enhances your stay. Choose between a twin room or a compact, self-contained cottage and feast on Sheelagh's gourmet cooking (two-course dinner US$18). Extensive breakfasts feature plenty of fresh fruit.

ℹ Information

By the soccer field, **Consorcio Aguas Eternas** (☎2742-5097, 2742-5200; infochirriposervicios@gmail.com; ⌚8am-5pm Mon-Sat, from 9am Sun) is the office responsible for the Crestones Base Lodge bookings, as well as other services including meals, porters and equipment rental. You need to reserve your lodgings via phone or email (have your park permit code from the park ranger's office ready). You also need to check in here the day before your hike.

The Chirripó **ranger station** (Sinac; ☎905-244-7747, USA 506-2742-5348; ⌚8am-noon & 1-4:30pm) is 1km below the soccer field at the entrance to San Gerardo de Rivas. If you've made reservations at Crestones Base Lodge and to hike up Cerro Chirripó, you must stop by the day before to confirm your permit. If you haven't booked your park permit in advance, there's a very slim chance of next-day availability.

ℹ Getting There & Away

Arriving via public transportation requires a connection through San Isidro. Buses to San Isidro (US$2, 1½ hours) depart from the soccer field six times daily (three daily on Sunday) between 5:15am and 6:45pm.

Palmar

At the intersection of the country's two major highways, this crossroads town serves as a gateway to the Península de Osa and Golfo Dulce. This functional banana-growing settlement makes a convenient base for exploring the Sierp area if you have a particular interest in pre-Columbian stone spheres, which the area is newly famous for; it was declared a World Heritage Site by Unesco in 2014. The **Festival de la Luz** in December is worth stopping for.

BUSES FROM SAN ISIDRO DE EL GENERAL

From Terminal Tracopa

DESTINATION	COST (US$)	DURATION (HR)	FREQUENCY (DAILY)
Golfito	8	4	10am
Neily	7	4	4:45am, 7am, 12:30pm, 3pm
Palmar Norte	10	2½	5am, 7am, 8:30am, 10am, 1pm, 2:30pm, 6pm
Paso Canoas	9	4½	8am, 10:30am, 4pm, 6:30pm, 9:30pm
San José	6	3	hourly
San Vito	6.50	3½	5:30am, 9am, 11am, 2pm, 7pm (connections in Neily)

From Transportes Blanco

DESTINATION	COST (US$)	DURATION (HR)	FREQUENCY (DAILY)
Dominical	3	1½	8am, 9am, 11:30am, 3:30pm, 4pm
Puerto Jiménez (via Palmar Norte)	9.60	5	6:30am, 11am, 3pm
Quepos	4.90	2½	8am, 11:30am, 3:30pm
Uvita	3.60	2hr	5am, 9am, 12:45pm, 4pm

Palmar is actually split in two – to get from Palmar Norte to Palmar Sur, take the Interamericana southbound over the Río Grande de Térraba bridge, then take the first right. Most facilities are in Palmar Norte, clustered around the intersection of the Carretera Interamericana and the Costanera Sur; if you're heading to Bahía Drake via Sierpe, this is your last chance to hit an ATM. Palmar Sur is home to the airstrip and a little park with an excellent example of a stone sphere.

Getting There & Away

Buses to San José and San Isidro stop on the east side of the Interamericana. Other buses leave from in front of the Pirola's Pizza and Seafood restaurant or the Tracopa window across the street. Buses to Sierpe depart from in front of the Gollo store.

Sierpe

This sleepy village on the Río Sierpe is the gateway to Bahía Drake, and if you've made a reservation with any of the jungle lodges further down the coast, you will be picked up here by boat. Beyond its function as a transit point, there is little reason to spend any more time here than necessary, though it's well worth taking a peek at one of the celebrated pre-Columbian stone spheres in the main square. If you're visiting the excellent **Sitio Arqueológico Finca 6** (2100-6000; finca6@museocostarica.go.cr; 4km north of Sierpe; US$6; 8am-4pm Tue-Sun) near Sierpe, it's worth stopping here for lunch. Mangrove cruises can also be arranged here.

Information

La Perla del Sur (2788-1082; info@perladelsur.net; 6am-10pm; wi-fi) This info center and open-air restaurant next to the boat dock is the hub of Sierpe – arrange your long-term parking (US$6 per night), book a tour and take advantage of the free wi-fi before catching your boat to Drake.

Getting There & Away

Scheduled flights (Sansa) and charters fly into Palmar Sur, 14km north of Sierpe. If you are heading to Bahía Drake, most upmarket lodges will arrange the boat transfer. Should things go awry or if you're traveling independently, there's no shortage of water taxis milling about – be prepared to negotiate a fair price. Regularly scheduled *colectivo* (shared) boats depart Sierpe for Drake at 11:30am (US$15) and 4:30pm (US$20).

Buses to Palmar Norte (US$0.70, 40 minutes) depart from in front of Pulpería Fenix at 5:30am, 8:30am, 9am, 10:30am, 1:30pm, 4pm and 6pm. A shared taxi to Palmar costs about US$10 per person.

Bahía Drake

POP 1000

One of Costa Rica's most isolated destinations, Bahía Drake *(drah-kay)* is a veritable Lost World, bordered by Parque Nacional Corcovado to the south. In the rainforest canopy, howler monkeys greet the rising sun with their haunting bellows, while pairs of macaws soar between the treetops, filling the air with their cacophonous squawking. Offshore in the bay, pods of migrating dolphins glide through turquoise waters near the beautiful Isla del Caño marine reserve.

BUSES FROM PALMAR

DESTINATION	COST (US$)	DURATION (HR)	FREQUENCY
Dominical	2	1½	8:20am, 1:20pm, 3:45pm
Golfito	3.20	1½	11:20am, 12:30pm
Neily	3.20	1½	7 daily, 5:10am-6pm
Paso Canoas	3.80	2	6 daily, 10:30am-8:30pm
Puerto Jiminez	6.00	4	3 daily, 9:30am, 1:15pm, 5:30pm
San Isidro	6.36	2½	8:30am, noon, 2:45pm, 5pm, 6:15pm
San José	11	5½	16-19 daily, 4:45am-6:30pm
Sierpe	0.70	40min	7 daily, 5am-5:15pm

One of the reasons why Bahía Drake is brimming with wildlife is that it remains largely cut off from the rest of the country. Life is centered on the sedate village of **Agujitas**, the area's transport hub, which attracts increasing numbers of backpackers and nature lovers with inexpensive digs and plenty of snorkeling, diving and wildlife-watching opportunities. The more remote corners of Bahía Drake are home to some of Costa Rica's best (and priciest) wilderness lodges.

Activities & Tours

The 17km trail connecting Agujitas to San Pedrillo ranger station is an excellent day hike. Along the way are gorgeous beaches, the possibility of a canoe tour with **Río Claro Tours** (☎8450-7198; 2/4hr tour per person US$25/40), and wildlife to be seen. You can also get a tour operator to drop you by boat at a point of your choosing and walk back to Agujitas.

About 20km west of Agujitas, **Isla del Caño** (www.sinac.go.cr/ES/ac/acosa/Paginas/IsladelCaño.aspx; adult/child US$15/5, diving charge US$4) is considered the best place for snorkeling in this area. Lodges offer day trips to the island (from US$80 per person), usually including the park fee, snorkeling equipment and lunch on Playa San Josecito. The clarity of the ocean and the variety of the fish fluctuate according to water and weather conditions: it's worth inquiring before booking.

Along the coast between Agujitas and Corcovado, **Playa San Josecito** and **Playa Caletas** attract many tropical fish, while **Playa Cocalito**, a small, pretty beach near Agujitas, is pleasant for swimming and sunbathing.

★ **Pacheco Tours** WILDLIFE
(☎8906-2002; www.pachecotours.com) Very competent all-rounder organizing snorkeling tours to Isla del Caño, day trips to Corcovado, daylong tours combining jungle trekking with waterfall swimming (The Floating Tour, US$65), and whale-watching excursions.

Corcovado Info Center WILDLIFE
(☎2775-0916, 8846-4734; www.corcovadoinfocenter.com; whale-watching/Corcovado day tours US$110/90) Leading tours into Corcovado and Isla del Caño, all guides with this outfit are local, bilingual and ICT-certified. They're at the beach end of the main road in Agujitas.

Drake Divers DIVING
(☎2775-1818; www.drakediverscr.com; ⏲7am-7pm) This outfit specializes in diving at Isla del Caño, charging US$135/185 for two-/three-tank dives. Snorkelers are welcome to come along (US$80). The equipment is not the newest and the boat is not a purpose-built diving boat, but the divemasters are experienced.

Sleeping

★ **Martina's Place** GUESTHOUSE $
(☎8720-0801; www.puravidadrakebay.com; dm/s/d from US$14/18/40; 📶) With a few fan-cooled dorms and rooms with air-con, this budget spot provides access to a clean, thoroughly equipped communal kitchen and is a friendly and economical place to lay your head in the middle of Agujitas. It's also an excellent spot to meet other travelers, tap into Martina's wealth of Corcovado intel and arrange a variety of local tours.

Drake Bay Backpackers HOSTEL $
(☎2775-0726, 8981-5519; www.drakebaybackpackers.com; campsite per person US$6, dm/r from US$15/40; P❄📶) This excellent nonprofit, off-the-beaten-track hostel is a boon for budget travelers wanting to connect with the local community. Competitively priced local tours can be arranged, and there's a nice hangout area and a BBQ patio. It's in the village of El Progreso, near the airstrip, straight after the river crossing.

★ **Finca Maresia** BUNGALOW $$
(☎8888-1625, 2775-0279; www.fincamaresia.com; Camino a Los Planes; incl breakfast s US$35-85, d US$45-100) The globe-trotting owners have created this absolute gem of a *finca* hotel that stretches across a series of hills. Budget travelers are drawn by the excellent value-to-price ratio and superb wildlife-watching opportunities. All rooms and the open-air communal area are exposed to an audio track of jungle sounds, and manager Juan is a phenomenal host.

Casita Corcovado B&B $$
(☎2775-0627, 8996-8987; www.casitacorcovado.com; r incl breakfast from US$85; ⊖❄📶) Jamie and Craig's lovely little ocean-facing home has three rooms, all sharing a bathroom and with comfortable orthopedic beds. Guests have access to two breezy patios and plenty of hammocks, with the amenities of the village at the doorstep, but it's the warmth and helpfulness of your hosts that sets this

DON'T MISS

CLIMBING CERRO CHIRRIPÓ

While much of the Cordillera de Talamanca is difficult to access, Costa Rica's highest peak, 3820m **Cerro Chirripó** (park fee per day US$18), is the focus of popular two-day ascents from San Gerardo de Rivas.

Most hikers go up to **Crestones Base Lodge** (☎2742-5097; www.chirripo.org/hospedaje/; dm US$35; 🛜), the only accommodations in the park, with room for up to 52 people in dorm-style bunks, and summit at sunrise the following day.

Information

It is essential that you stop at the ranger station (p602) in San Gerardo de Rivas at least one day before you intend to climb Chirripó to confirm your park permit (bring your reservation and proof of payment). After you've done that, you have to confirm your Crestones Base Lodge reservation at the consortium office (p602). You can also make arrangements at the ranger station to hire a porter (a fixed fee of US$100 for up to 15kg of luggage), though it's now less necessary than ever. Since Crestones offers meals and includes bedding in the accommodations price, you can travel light, without cooking gear or a sleeping bag.

Getting There & Away

Travelers connect to the trails via the mountain village of San Gerardo de Rivas, which is also home to the ranger station. From opposite the ranger station, in front of Cabinas El Bosque, there is free transportation to the trailhead at 5am. Also, several hotels offer early-morning trailhead transportation for their guests.

place apart. Delicious, home-cooked meals are also available.

Getting There & Away

All of the hotels offer boat transfers between Sierpe and Bahía Drake with prior arrangement. Most hotels in Drake have beach landings, so wear appropriate footwear.

If you have not made advance arrangements with your lodge for a pick-up, two *colectivo* boats depart daily from Sierpe at 11:30am and 4:30pm, and from Bahía Drake back to Sierpe at 7:15am (US$15) and 2:30pm (US$20).

A bus to La Palma (where you can connect to a bus to Puerto Jiménez) picks passengers up along the beach road and in front of the supermarkets at around 8am and 1:30pm (US$10, two hours). The return journey from La Palma is at 11am and 4:30pm. Double-check departure times locally.

Puerto Jiménez

POP 1800

Sliced in half by the swampy, overgrown Quebrada Cacao, and flanked on one side by the emerald waters of the Golfo Dulce, the vaguely Wild West outpost of Puerto Jiménez is shared by local residents and wildlife. While walking through the dusty streets of Jiménez (as it's known to locals), it's not unusual to spot scarlet macaws roosting on the soccer field, or white-faced capuchins traversing the treetops along the main street.

On the edge of Parque Nacional Corcovado, Jiménez is the preferred jumping-off point for travelers heading to the famed Sirena Ranger Station, and a great place to organize an expedition, stock up on supplies, eat a hot meal and get a good night's rest before hitting the trails.

Despite the region's largest and most diverse offering of hotels, restaurants and other tourist services, this town at its core is a close-knit Tico community.

Tours

★**Osa Wild** TOURS

(☎2735-5848, 8376-1152, 8709-1083; www.osawildtravel.com; tours from US$30, 1-day Corcovado tour US$85; ⏰8am-noon & 2-7pm Mon-Fri, 9am-noon & 1-4pm Sat & Sun) Osa Wild is *the* way to connect with Corcovado park and Osa. It's just what the area so desperately needed: a resource for travelers to connect with community-oriented initiatives that go to the heart of the real Osa through homestays, farm tours and sustainable cultural exchanges. It also offers more typical stuff like kayaking tours and guided trips through Corcovado.

Osa Aventura ADVENTURE
(8372-6135, 2735-5670; www.osaaventura.com) Run by Mike Boston, a biologist with a real passion for nature, Osa Aventura aims to introduce travelers to the beauty of rainforest life and to raise awareness of the need to preserve Corcovado's unique environment. Adventures vary from three-day treks through Corcovado to a tour that focuses on Golfo Dulce's rural communities. Custom tours also available.

Surcos Tours TOURS
(8603-2387, 2237-4189; www.surcostours.com) A trio of excellent guides make Surcos the best company tours into Osa that focus on wildlife and birdwatching. Tours vary from day hikes in Corcovado and Matapalo to multiday experiences in Corcovado and specialized birding tours. Arrangements for tours are made through its website.

Sleeping

Cabinas Back Packer GUESTHOUSE $
(2735-5181; s/d without bathroom with air-con US$30/40, without air-con US$15/30;) One of the better budget digs, it's squeaky clean, relatively quiet as it's a couple of blocks from the main street, and comes with a front garden strung with hammocks. Rooms share clean bathrooms and there are bicycles for guest use. There's even a brightly tiled kitchen, available for a US$5 fee.

Lunas Hostel HOSTEL $
(2735-6007; www.lunashostelpuertojimenezcr.com; dm/d without bathroom US$12/14;) A backpacker haven presided over by friendly and helpful owner Alex, who's been a guardian angel to more than one traveler in distress. While the fan-cooled dorms and rooms are can't-swing-a-cat size, the handmade furniture and excellent mattresses are a boon. Shared bathrooms only. Alex can arrange Corcovado tours, though there have been mixed reports about the guide he works with.

Cabinas Marcelina HOTEL $
(2735-5007; www.jimenezhotels.com/cabinasmarcelina; r with/without air-con US$42/38; P) Marcelina's place is a long-standing favorite among budget travelers looking for a peaceful night's sleep. The concrete building is painted salmon pink and is surrounded by blooming trees, lending it a homey atmosphere. Rooms have modern furniture, fluffy towels and tile bathrooms. The owner is largely AWOL, though, so this is not the place to book excursions.

★**Cabinas Jiménez** CABINA $$
(2735-5090; www.cabinasjimenez.com; s/d from US$45/60, cabinas US$80-120; P) Cabinas Jiménez is hands down the nicest place to stay in Jiménez proper. Rooms come with fridges and jungle scenes painted on the walls, and poolside rooms come with chill-out patios. Pricier *cabinas* have kitchenettes and fantastic views of the lagoon. Bikes and kayaks are free for guests' use, and the bilingual staff are friendly and helpful.

Eating

★**Restaurante Monka** COSTA RICAN $
(2735-5051; mains US$5-7; 6am-8pm;) Bright and airy and the best breakfast spot in town, Monka does excellent cold coffee drinks and smoothies, and has extensive breakfast platters, from American-style (involving bacon and pancakes) to Mexican-style huevos rancheros. The rest of the day you can fill up on good, inexpensive *casados*. Several breakfast options and *casados* are vegetarian.

Los Delfines COSTA RICAN $
(2735-5083; meals US$6-14; 10am-10pm) At the end of the beach road that passes the waterfront walk, Los Delfines is the perfect toes-in-the-sand spot for a late *gallo pinto* breakfast or a beer and delish *ceviche* after sunning on the crescent of beach just beyond.

BUSES FROM PUERTO JIMÉNEZ

DESTINATION	COST (US$)	DURATION (HR)	FREQUENCY (DAILY)
Neily	4.60	3	5:30am, 2pm
La Palma	2.60	1	at least hourly
San Isidro de El General	10	5½	1pm
San José	13	8	5am, 9am

Restaurant Carolina COSTA RICAN $
(☎2735-5185; dishes US$3-8; ⊙6am-10pm; 📶) This local favorite on the main drag still attracts its share of expats, nature guides, tourists and locals. Expect Tico standards, fresh-fruit drinks, extensive breakfasts, good coffee and cold beers that go down pretty easily on a hot day.

Shopping

★ Jagua Arts & Crafts ARTS & CRAFTS
(☎2735-5267; ⊙7am-3pm Mon-Sat) A terrific, well-stocked crafts shop, featuring local art and jewelry, a wonderful collection of high-quality, colorful Boruca masks and black-and-ocher Guaitil pottery, as well as woven goods by the Emberá and Wounaan people. Kuna weavings technically belong across the border in Panama, but they make excellent gifts.

Information

The **police** and **post office** (☎2735-5045; ⊙8am-noon & 1-5pm Mon-Fri) can be found near the soccer field.

Área de Conservación Osa (ACOSA; Osa Conservation Area Headquarters; ☎2735-5036; Corcovado park fee per person per day US$15; ⊙8am-4pm Mon-Fri) Information about Parque Nacional Corcovado, Isla del Caño, Parque Nacional Marino Ballena and Golfito parks and reserves.

Banco Nacional (☎2735-5020; ⊙8:30am-3:45pm Mon-Fri) Has an ATM.

BCR (Banco de Costa Rica; ☎2735-5260; ⊙9am-4pm Mon-Fri) Across from the church; it also has an ATM.

Getting There & Away

Several fast **ferries** (☎8632-8672, 2735-5095) travel to Golfito (US$6, 30 minutes), departing at 6am, 8:45am, 11:30am, 2pm and 4pm daily. Double-check current schedules, as they change often and without notice.

Most buses arrive at the blue **terminal** (☎2735-5189) behind the green paint store on the west side of town.

The *colectivo* (shared truck taxi) runs daily to Cabo Matapalo (1½ hours, US$5) and Carate (2½ hours, US$9) on the southern tip of the national park. **Departures** (☎8832-8680) are from Soda Deya at 6am and 1:30pm, returning at 8:30am and 4pm.

Parque Nacional Corcovado

This national park takes up 40% of the Península de Osa and is the last great original tract of tropical rainforest in Pacific Central America. The bastion of biological diversity is home to *half* of Costa Rica's species, including the largest population of scarlet macaws, and countless other endangered species, including Baird's tapir, the giant anteater and the world's largest bird of prey, the harpy eagle.

Corcovado's amazing biodiversity, as well as the park's demanding, multiday hiking trails, have long attracted a devoted stream of visitors who descend from Bahía Drake and Puerto Jiménez to see the wildlife and experience a bona fide jungle adventure.

Activities

There are three main trails in the park that are open to visitors, as well as shorter trails around the ranger stations. Trails are primitive and the hiking is hot, humid and insect-ridden, but the challenge of the trek and the interaction with wildlife at Corcovado are thrilling. Carry plenty of food, water and insect repellent.

One trail traverses the park from Los Patos to Sirena, then exits the park at La Leona (or vice versa). This allows hikers to begin and end their journey in or near Puerto Jiménez, offering easy access to La Leona and Los Patos.

The most popular trail, however, is still **La Leona to Sirena**, with an additional trail section running parallel to the beach trail for those who don't want to expose themselves to the relentless sun. The toughest day trek is from La Tarde to Sirena via Los Patos – a whopping 30km.

An **El Tigre trail loop** has been added that starts in Dos Brazos and dips into the park but doesn't join up with the rest of the trail network; you still have to pay the full park fee to hike it, though.

Hiking is best in the dry season (from December to April), when there is still regular rain but all of the trails are open. It remains muddy, but you won't sink quite as deep.

Tours

All visitors to Corcovado must be accompanied by an ICT-certified guide. Besides their intimate knowledge of the trails, local guides are amazingly informed about flora and fauna, including the best places to spot various species. Most guides also carry telescopes, allowing for up-close views of wildlife.

Guides are most often hired through the Área de Conservación Osa park office (p607) in Puerto Jiménez, or through hotels and tour operators. Two recommended local offices are the super-reliable, locally run Osa Wild (p605) in Puerto Jiménez and Corcovado Info Center (p604) in Bahía Drake. Prices vary considerably depending on the season, availability, size of your party and type of expedition you want to arrange. In any case, you will need to negotiate a price that includes park fees, meals and transportation.

Sleeping & Eating

Camping costs US$6 per person per day at the **San Pedrillo** and **La Leona** ranger stations, but is no longer allowed elsewhere in the park. Facilities include potable water and latrines. Remember to bring a flashlight or a headlamp, as the campgrounds are dark at night.

Note that all visitors are required to pack out all of their trash.

Sirena Ranger Station (dm US$30) serves large meals (US$20 to US$25 per meal) by advance reservation only and there are no cooking facilities. All other ranger stations have drinking water, but you have to bring your own provisions.

Nearby, in Dos Brazos, is a semi-sustainable rustic farmhouse in the midst of 25 hectares of rainforest. At **Bolita Rainforest Hostel** (8549-9898; www.bolita.org; dm/cabinas US$12/30) there's no electricity, so you'll be up with the howler monkeys and eating dinner by candlelight. Rooms come with mosquito nets and there are 15km of walking trails (and waterfalls) to explore. The office in the village provides walking directions.

Information

Information and maps are available at the office of Área de Conservación Osa (p607) in Puerto Jiménez, where you also have to pay your park entry fee of US$15 per day.

Park headquarters are at Sirena ranger station on the coast in the middle of the park. Other ranger stations are located on the park boundaries: San Pedrillo station is in the northwest corner on the coast; La Leona station is in the southeast corner on the coast (near the village of Carate); there's a new ranger station in Dos Brazos village; and the rebuilt Los Patos ranger station is actually just outside the park boundary, closest to La Tarde.

Getting There & Away

FROM BAHÍA DRAKE

From Bahía Drake, you can walk the coastal trail that leads to San Pedrillo station (about seven hours from Agujitas). Many lodges and tour companies run day tours here, with a boat ride to San Pedrillo (30 minutes to an hour, depending on the departure point) or Sirena (one to 1½ hours). You can make camping reservations at San Pedrillo or Sirena stations.

FROM CARATE

In the southeast, the closest point of access is Carate, from where La Leona station is a one-hour, 3.5km hike west along the beach.

Carate is accessible from Puerto Jiménez via a poorly maintained 45km dirt road. This journey is an adventure in itself, and often allows for some good wildlife-spotting along the way. A 4WD *colectivo* travels this route twice daily for US$9, departing Puerto Jiménez for Carate at 6am and 1:30pm, returning at 8:30am and 3:30pm. Otherwise you can hire a 4WD taxi for around US$80.

FROM LA PALMA

From the north, the closest point of access is the town of La Palma, from where you can catch a bus or taxi south to Puerto Jiménez or north to San José. It's 14km from La Palma to the ranger station at Los Patos.

Golfito

POP 7900

With a long and sordid history, spread-out Golfito is a rough-around-the-edges port that stretches out along the Golfo Dulce. The town was built on bananas – the United Fruit Company moved its regional headquarters here in the '30s. In the 1980s, declining markets, rising taxes, worker unrest and banana diseases forced the company's departure.

In an attempt to boost the region's economy, the federal government built the duty-free Zona Americana in Golfito. The surreal shopping mall **Depósito Libre** (8am-4:30pm Wed & Thu, to 6pm Fri & Sat, 7am-3:30pm Sun) attracts Ticos and expats from around the country, who descend on the otherwise decaying town for 24-hour shopping sprees. There other attractions, such as hiking or horseback riding in a wildlife refuge or kayaking to nearby mangrove forests and islands, but Golfito is largely a transportation hub for hikers heading to Corcovado, surfers heading to Pavones and sportfishers.

Getting There & Away

Fast ferries travel to Puerto Jiménez from the **Muellecito** (US$6, 30 minutes), departing at 7am, 10am, 11:30am, 1pm, 3pm and 5pm daily. This schedule is subject to change, so it's best to check for current times at the dock; in any event, show up early to ensure a spot.

Most buses stop at the depot opposite the small park in the southern part of town. Tracopa buses depart from the **stop** (2775-0365) across from the fire station.

Pavones

POP 2750

Pavones is a legendary destination for surfers the world over. As this is Costa Rica's southernmost point, you'll need to work hard to get down here. However, the journey is an adventure in its own right, especially since the best months for surfing coincide with the rainy season.

The village remains relatively off the beaten path, and though both foreigners and Ticos are transforming Pavones from its days as a relative backwater, Pavones' few streets are still unpaved, the pace of life is slow and the overall atmosphere is tranquil and New Agey.

Activities

Pavones is one of Costa Rica's most famous surf breaks and home to the world's second-longest left. Conditions are best with a southern swell, usually during the rainy season from April to October, but the rest of the year the waves are ideal for beginners. **Sea Kings Surf Shop** (2776-2015; www.seakingssurfshop.com; 9am-5pm Mon-Sat) has boards for rent and arranges surfing lessons.

Sleeping & Eating

★Rancho Burica LODGE $

(2776-2223; www.ranchoburica.com; dm US$15, s/d US$40/70, without bathroom US$25/45; P) This legendary Dutch-run outpost is literally the end of the road in Punta Banco, and it's where surfers gather to socialize in the evenings. Rooms are cooled with fans, and hammocks are interspersed around the property, which has convivial common areas, a restaurant and a trail to a romantic jungle lookout. Meals are family-style; guests aren't allowed to cook.

Clientele mainly includes surfers, but those interested in relaxation, wildlife and yoga will also land well here, as there's a newly constructed yoga deck and lots of rare birds flitting around. The owners are also involved in a community turtle conservation project.

Cabinas & Café de la Suerte GUESTHOUSE $

(2776-2388; r/house US$75/100;) Run by a friendly surfer couple (who also run the vegetarian restaurant on the premises), this colorful three-room guesthouse is just 50m from the beach and comes with a hammock-hung terrace shared by the upstairs rooms, and a secluded garden corner for the downstairs one. Rooms have fridges. From the supermarket crossroads, follow the beach road to the left.

Yoga Farm LODGE $$

(www.yogafarmcostarica.org; dm/r/cabin incl meals & yoga US$43/50/65) This tranquil retreat has simple rooms and dorms, three vegetarian meals prepared with ingredients from the organic garden, and daily yoga classes in an open-air studio overlooking the ocean. It's an uphill 15-minute walk from road's end at Rancho Burica: take the uphill road and go through the first gate on the left. No wi-fi or phones; rejuvenation is key.

BUSES FROM GOLFITO

DESTINATION	COST (US$)	DURATION (HR)	FREQUENCY (DAILY)
Neily	3	1½	every 30min 6am-7pm
Pavones	4	2½	10am, 3pm
San José, via San Isidro de El General and the Costanera (Tracopa)	15	7	5am, 1:30pm (2pm Sun)
Zancudo	4	3	10am, 3pm

Lanzas de Fuego Surf & Adventure Lodge LODGE $$
(☎2776-2014, 8634-0739; www.lanzasdefuego.com; per person US$45; ❄📶) Run by cheerful South African owner Rainy, this hillside lodge organizes multiday surfing, birding and sportfishing packages, with its own boat to whisk surfers to the best hot spots. It's an intimate, friendly place, with three cabins to accommodate eight guests, a huge thatched-roofed hangout space and a restaurant serving wholesome Tico meals. Cross the bridge and carry on until the signpost.

Information

We cannot stress this enough: Pavones has no bank or gas station, so make sure you have plenty of money and gas prior to arrival. Very few places accept credit cards and the nearest ATM and gas station are in Laurel, an hour's drive away.

Getting There & Away

Two daily buses go to Golfito (US$3.80, two hours). The first leaves at 5:15am, departing from the end of the road in Punta Banco and stopping by the two supermarkets. The second leaves at 12:30pm from the school. You can also pick up the early bus in Pavones; check locally for the current bus stops.

Paso Canoas

The main port of entry between Costa Rica and Panama is hectic, slightly seedy and completely devoid of charm. Fortunately, the border crossing itself is straightforward. As you might imagine, most travelers leave Paso Canoas with little more than a passing glance at their passport stamp.

If leaving Costa Rica, you'll be charged an exit tax of $8 here ($7 for the actual exit tax, plus $1 'commission' because you didn't pay through a national bank before you arrived at the border). You'll pay this tax at a window across from the **Migración & Aduana office** (☎2732-2804, 2732-2801, 2732-2150; ⏱6am-10pm).

BCR (Banco de Costa Rica; ☎2732-2613; ⏱9am-4pm Mon-Sat, 9am-1pm Sun) has an ATM near the Migración & Aduana office. Street vendors' rates for converting excess colones into dollars are not great. Colones are accepted at the border, but are difficult to get rid of further into Panama.

The **Autoridad de Turismo de Panamá** (☎507-526-7000; ⏱8am-4pm), in the Panamanian immigration post, has basic information on travel to Panama.

Getting There & Away

Tracopa buses leave for San José (US$14, 7½ hours) at 4am, 8am, 8:30am, 9am, 1pm, 4:30pm and 4:40pm. The **Tracopa bus terminal** (☎2732-2119; ⏱7am-4pm), a window really, is north of the border post, on the east side of the main road. Sunday-afternoon buses are full of weekend shoppers, so buy tickets as early as possible. Buses for Neily (US$0.70, 30 minutes) leave from the **Terminal de Buses Transgolfo** at least once an hour from 5am to 6:30pm. Taxis to Neily cost about US$10.

Just across the border, buses run to David, the nearest city in Panama, from where there are onward connections to Panama City and elsewhere.

UNDERSTAND COSTA RICA

Costa Rica Today

On April 1, 2018, Costa Rica elected a new president, Carlos Alvarado Quesada, of the center-left Citizen Action Party (PAC). Although polls predicted the runoff would be a close one, it wasn't. Alvarado – a 38-year-old novelist, musician and former cabinet minister – won more than 60% of the vote, defeating right-wing former TV anchor and evangelical preacher Fabricio Alvarado Munoz of the National Restoration Party. The decisive victory was celebrated by progressives and proponents of gay rights. Key challenges the new president faces include an escalating murder rate and a widening national deficit.

Alvarado succeeded former president Luis Guillermo Solís, also a member of PAC. Solís was Costa Rica's first president in half a century not to come from the two-party system, under which the social-democratic National Liberation Party and the center-right Social Christian Unity Party took turns holding power.

History

Like other Central American countries, Costa Rica's history remains a loose sketch during the reign of its pre-Columbian tribes, and European 'discovery' of the New

World was followed by the subjugation and evangelization of Costa Rica's indigenous peoples. But in the mid-20th century, Costa Rica radically departed from the standard Central American playbook by abolishing its army, diversifying its economy and brokering peace in the region, paving the way for today's stable and environmentally friendly nation.

Lost World

About 500 years ago, on the eve of European discovery, as many as 400,000 people lived in today's Costa Rica. The Central Valley hosted roughly 20 small tribes, organized into chiefdoms, with a *cacique* (chief) leading a hierarchical society that included shaman, warriors, workers and slaves. To the east, the fierce Caribs dominated the Atlantic coastal lowlands. Adept at seafaring, they provided a conduit of trade with the South American mainland.

Heirs of Columbus

On his fourth and final voyage to the New World in 1502, Christopher Columbus was forced to drop anchor near today's Puerto Limón after a hurricane damaged his ship. Waiting for repairs, Columbus ventured into the verdant terrain and exchanged gifts with welcoming natives. He returned from this encounter claiming to have seen 'more gold in two days than in four years in Spain.'

To the disappointment of his conquistador heirs, the region did not abound with gold and the locals were not so affable. The pestilent swamps, volcano-topped mountains and oppressive jungles made Columbus' paradise seem more like hell for new colonies. Scarce in mineral wealth and indigenous laborers, the Spanish eventually came to regard the region as the poorest and most miserable in all the Americas. It was not until the 1560s that a Spanish colony was established at Cartago.

Central Valley Sunday

Costa Rica's colonial path diverged from the typical Spanish pattern in that a powerful landholding elite and slave-based economy never gained prominence. Instead, modest-sized villages of small-holders developed in the interior Central Valley in what became known as a 'rural democracy.' Costa Ricans grew corn, beans and plantains for subsistence, and produced sugar, cacao and tobacco for sale. As the 18th century closed, the population topped 50,000.

As Spanish settlement expanded, the indigenous population plummeted. While disease was the main source of death, the Spanish exploited native labor relentlessly. Outside the valley, several tribes managed to prolong their survival under forest cover, staging occasional raids, but eventually they were defeated by military campaigns.

A Sovereign Struggle

In 1821 the Americas wriggled free of Spain's imperial grip. An independent Costa Rica took shape under Juan Mora Fernandez, the first head of state (1824–33). In 1824 the Nicoya-Guanacaste province seceded from Nicaragua and joined its more easygoing southern neighbor, defining the territorial borders.

As one empire receded, another rose. In the 19th century, the USA was in an expansive mood and Spanish America looked vulnerable. In 1856 the soldier of fortune William Walker landed in Nicaragua intending to conquer Central America, establish slavery and construct an interoceanic canal. When Walker marched on Costa Rica, he faced a hastily mobilized volunteer army of 9000 civilians. They stopped the Yankee mercenaries at Santa Rosa, chasing them back into Nicaragua.

Coffee Rica

The introduction of the caffeinated red bean transformed the impoverished nation into the wealthiest in the region. When an export market emerged, the government promoted coffee to farmers by providing free saplings. By the end of the 19th century, more than one-third of the Central Valley was dedicated to coffee cultivation, and coffee accounted for more than 90% of all exports.

An elite group of coffee barons monopolized the processing, marketing and financing of the coffee economy, but they lacked the land and labor to monopolize the crop. As such, the coffee economy in Costa Rica created a wide network of high-end traders and small-scale growers (unlike in the rest of Central America, where a narrow elite controlled large estates, worked by tenant laborers). Today Costa Rica has an estimated 130,000 coffee farms.

Banana Boom

The coffee trade unintentionally gave rise to Costa Rica's next export boom – bananas. Getting coffee out to world markets necessitated a rail link from the central highlands to the coast. In 1871 the government contracted the building of the railroad to Minor Keith, nephew of an American railroad tycoon.

The project was a disaster. Malaria and accidents forced a constant replenishing of workers. The government defaulted on funding and construction costs soared over budget. In 1890 the line was finally completed, and running at a loss.

Bananas were first grown along the railroad tracks as a cheap food source for workers. Desperate to recoup his investment, Keith shipped some to New Orleans. Consumers went bananas. *Fincas* (plantations) replaced lowland forests and bananas surpassed coffee as Costa Rica's most lucrative export by the early 20th century.

Joining with another American importer, Keith founded the infamous United Fruit Company, soon the largest employer in Central America. Known as *el pulpo* (the octopus) to locals, United Fruit owned huge swaths of lush lowlands, much of the transportation and communication infrastructure, and bunches of bureaucrats. A wave of migrant laborers arrived from Jamaica, changing the country's ethnic complexion and provoking racial tensions. Although Costa Rica became the world's leading banana exporter, the profits shipped out along with the bananas.

In 1913 a banana blight known as 'Panama disease' shut down many Caribbean plantations and the industry relocated to the Pacific. Eventually United Fruit lost its banana monopoly.

Birth of a Nation

Early Costa Rican politics followed the Central American pattern of violence and dictatorship. Presidents were more often removed at gunpoint than by the ballot box. Although Costa Rica began to implement more equitable policies in the early 20th century, disenfranchised groups resorted to protest politics, forcing the resignation of at least one president.

In the 1940s tension mounted as activists continued to champion the rights of the working class and the poor. Civil war broke out after disputed elections in 1948. Led by coffee grower and utopian democrat José Figueres Ferrer, armed workers battled military forces, and Nicaraguan and US forces joined in the fray. Peace was restored in under two months at the cost of 2000 deaths.

Figueres became head of a temporary junta government. His 1949 constitution granted full citizenship and voting rights to women, blacks, indigenous groups and Chinese minorities. His copious decrees taxed the wealthy, nationalized banks and built a modern welfare state. Most extraordinarily, Figueres abolished the military, calling it a threat to democracy. These actions became the foundation for Costa Rica's unique and unarmed democracy.

The Contra Conflict

The sovereignty of the small nations of Central America was limited by their northern neighbor, as the USA was hostile toward leftist politics. During the 1970s radical socialists forced the military regimes of Guatemala, El Salvador and Nicaragua onto the defensive. When they toppled the American-backed Somoza dictatorship in Nicaragua in 1979, President Ronald Reagan decided to intervene. The Cold War arrived in the hot tropics.

Under intense US pressure, politically moderate Costa Rica was reluctantly dragged in. The Contras set up camp in Costa Rica, from where they staged guerrilla raids and built a secret jungle airstrip to fly in weapons and supplies.

The war polarized Costa Rica. Conservatives pushed to re-establish the military and join the anticommunist crusade. On the opposing side, in May 1984 over 20,000 demonstrators marched through San José to give peace a chance. The debate peaked with the 1986 presidential election. The victor was 44-year-old Oscar Arias Sánchez, an intellectual reformer in the mold of Figueres.

Once in office, Arias affirmed his commitment to a negotiated resolution and reasserted Costa Rican national independence. He vowed to uphold neutrality and kick out the Contras. Soon, the US ambassador quit his post and a public ceremony had Costa Rican schoolchildren planting trees on the secret CIA airfield. Most notably, Arias became the driving force in uniting Central America around a peace plan, which ended the Nicaraguan war. In 1987 he was awarded the Nobel Peace Prize.

PURA VIDA

Pura vida – pure life – is more than just a slogan that rolls off the tongues of Ticos and emblazons souvenirs. In the laid-back tone in which it is constantly uttered, the phrase is a bona fide mantra for the Costa Rican way of life. Perhaps the essence of the pure life is something better lived than explained, but hearing '*pura vida*' again and again while traveling across this beautiful country – as a greeting, a stand-in for goodbye, 'cool,' and an acknowledgement of thanks – makes it evident that the concept lives deep within the DNA of this country.

The living seems particularly pure when Costa Rica is compared with its Central American neighbors such as Nicaragua and Honduras; there's little poverty, illiteracy or political tumult, the country is crowded with ecological jewels, and the standard of living is high. What's more, Costa Rica has flourished without an army for the past 60 years. The sum of the parts is a country that's an oasis of calm in a corner of the world that has been continuously degraded by warfare. And though the Costa Rican people are justifiably proud hosts, a compliment to the country is likely to be met simply with a warm smile and an enigmatic two-word reply: *pura vida*.

Paradise Found

Five hundred years after the early conquistadors cursed it, the dense rainforest revealed a hidden wealth: ecotourism.

After a crash in coffee prices in the 1970s, an unusual alliance was formed between big business and environmentalists. If wealth could not be sustained through the country's exports, then what about imports – of tourists? Costa Rica embarked on a green revolution. By 1995 there were more than 125 government-protected sites. Success encouraged private landholders to build reserves as well.

Tourism now outweighs both agriculture and industry as the biggest slice of the economy. The success of the 'green revolution' has created a new concern, namely the need for sustainable tourism. The increasing number of visitors to Costa Rica has led to more hotels, more transportation and more infrastructure upgrades. This tourist-driven encroachment inevitably places stress on the fragile ecosystem that people are flocking to see.

Culture

People

Most Costa Ricans are mestizo, having a mix of Spanish and indigenous and/or African roots (though the majority of Ticos consider themselves to be white). Indigenous groups comprise only 1% of the population. These groups include the Bribrí and Cabécar, the Brunka, the Guaymí and the Maleku.

Less than 3% of the population is black, concentrated on the Caribbean coast. Tracing its ancestry to Jamaican immigrants who were brought to build railroads in the 19th century, this population speaks Mecatelyu: a creole of English, Spanish and Jamaican English.

Chinese (1% of the population) also first arrived to work on the railroads and since then have had regular waves of immigration. Taiwanese immigration has been particularly strong.

Lifestyle

With the lack of war, long life expectancy and a relatively sturdy economy, Costa Rica enjoys the highest standard of living in Central America. Indeed, Costa Rica often tops lists of the 'happiest' places in the world.

Significantly, life expectancy in Costa Rica is almost the same as in the USA, thanks to a comprehensive socialized health-care system and proper sanitation systems.

Still, the divide between rich and poor is broad. The middle and upper classes largely reside in San José and other major cities. For the vast majority of *campesinos* (farmers) and *indígenas* (people of indigenous origin), life is harder, poverty levels are higher and standards of living are lower. This is especially true along the Caribbean coast, where the descendants of Jamaican immigrants have long suffered from a lack of attention by the federal government.

As in the rest of the world, globalization is having a dramatic effect on Costa Ricans, who are increasingly mobile, international and intertwined in the global economy.

ENDANGERED SPECIES

The number-one threat to most of Costa Rica's endangered species is habitat destruction, followed by hunting and trapping.

➡ The legendary resplendent quetzal – topping every naturalist's must-see list – approaches extinction as its home forests are felled.

➡ A booming pet trade has extirpated the population of large, squawky scarlet macaws.

➡ Sea turtles have suffered from the destruction of beaches, which directly affects their ability to reproduce, as well as from hunting and the harvesting of eggs.

Landscape

Despite its diminutive size – at 51,000 sq km it is slightly smaller than the USA's West Virginia – Costa Rica's land is an explosion of technicolor, topographical contrasts. On one coast are the breezy skies and big waves of the Pacific. Only 119km away lie the muggy and languid shores of the Caribbean. In between there are active volcanoes, alpine peaks and crisp high-elevation forest. Few places on earth can compare with this little country's spectacular interaction of natural, geological and climatic forces.

The national-park system protects 35 national parks, covering 11% of the country. Scores of other protected zones include wetlands and mangroves, in addition to a slew of privately owned and operated reserves. Authorities claim that one-third of the country is under conservation. Unfortunately, some of this land is still at risk – partly because the government lacks the funds and infrastructure to enforce its protection policies.

Wildlife

Animals

Poison arrow frogs, giant tarantulas and spider monkeys inhabit our imagination of the tropics. In reality, few places live up to our wild expectations – but Costa Rica does. Considered the world nucleus of wildlife diversity, it has over 615 species per 10,000 sq km. (Compare that to the USA's 104 species.)

Birders have recorded over 850 avian species in Costa Rica. Some 200-plus species of migrating birds come from as far away as Alaska and Australia, so it's not unusual to see your backyard birds feeding alongside trogons and toucans. Because many birds in Costa Rica have restricted ranges, you are guaranteed to find different species everywhere you travel.

Visitors will almost certainly see one of Costa Rica's four types of monkey or two types of sloth, but there are an additional 230 types of mammal awaiting the patient observer. More exotic sightings might include the amazing four-eyed opossum or silky anteater, the elusive tapir or the sly jaguarundi.

Plants

Costa Rica's floral biodiversity is staggering: close to 12,000 species of vascular plants have been described in Costa Rica, and the list gets longer each year. Orchids alone account for about 1400 species.

The diversity of habitats that created this many species is a wonder – one day you're canoeing in a muggy mangrove swamp, and the next day squinting through bone-chilling fog to see orchids in a montane cloud forest. While the country's beaches are beautiful, travelers would be remiss to visit Costa Rica without seeing some of its distinctive plant communities, including rainforests, mangrove swamps, cloud forests and dry forests.

SURVIVAL GUIDE

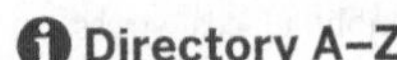

Directory A–Z

ACCESSIBLE TRAVEL

Independent travel in Costa Rica is difficult for anyone with mobility constraints. Although Costa Rica has an equal-opportunity law, the law applies only to new or newly remodeled businesses and is loosely enforced. Therefore, very few hotels and restaurants have features specifically suited to wheelchair use. Many don't have ramps, and room or bathroom doors are rarely wide enough to accommodate a wheelchair.

Streets and sidewalks are potholed and poorly paved, making wheelchair use frustrating at best. Public buses don't have provisions to carry wheelchairs, and most national parks and outdoor tourist attractions don't have trails suited to wheelchair use. Notable exceptions include Parque Nacional Volcán Poás (p536) – closed at the time of research due to volcanic activity – and the **Rainforest Adventures aerial tram** (☎2257-5961, USA 1-866-759-8726; www.rainforestadventure.com; adult/student & child tram US$65/33, combo tram/zipline tour US$90/65; ⏰7:30am-2pm; 👪).

Download Lonely Planet's free Accessible Travel guide from http://lptravel.to/Accessible Travel.

ACCOMMODATIONS

Accommodations come at every price and comfort level: from luxurious ecolodges and sparkling all-inclusive resorts and backpacker palaces to spartan rooms with little more than a bed and four cinder-block walls. The variety and number of rooms on offer means that advance booking is not usually mandatory, although it's recommended during holiday weeks (Christmas, New Year and Easter).

The term *cabina* (cabin) is a catch-all that can define a wide range of prices and amenities – from very rustic to very expensive. In general, dorm beds cost between US$12 and US$15, and a budget double costs up to US$40. High-season (December to April) prices are quoted in this book. Many lodges lower their prices during the 'green' season (May to November). Expect to pay a premium during Christmas, New Year and Easter week (Semana Santa). Prices are inclusive of tax and given in US dollars, which is the preferred currency for listing rates in Costa Rica.

Most destinations have at least one campground, which usually includes toilets and cold showers. Campsites are available at many national parks as well; take insect repellent, food and supplies. Camping prices are generally per person, per night.

If you're traveling in from another part of Central America, you'll notice that prices in Costa Rica are much higher than in the rest of the region.

CHILDREN

Although Costa Rica is in the heart of Central America, it's a relatively easy place for family travel, making pre-departure planning more similar to that required for North America or Europe than, say, Honduras.

- Hydration is particularly crucial in this tropical climate, especially for children who aren't used to the heat and humidity; fortunately, Costa Rica's tap water is safe everywhere (except for the rare exception, usually in remote areas).
- If you're traveling with an infant or small child, stock up on formula, baby food and snacks before heading to remote areas, where shops are few and far between.
- Many restaurants offers kids' menus, but these tend to be international rather than Costa Rican.
- Children under the age of 12 receive a discount of up to 25% on domestic flights, while on some carriers children under two fly free (provided they sit on a parent's lap).
- Children aged three and up pay full fare with most bus companies.
- Car seats for infants are not always available at car-rental agencies, so bring your own or make sure you double (or triple) check with the agency in advance.

CUSTOMS REGULATIONS

Travelers over the age of 18 are allowed to enter the country with 5L of wine or spirits and 500g of processed tobacco (400 cigarettes or 50 cigars). Pornography and illicit drugs are prohibited.

EMBASSIES & CONSULATES

Australia and New Zealand do not have consular representation in Costa Rica; their closest embassies are in Mexico City. Most countries are represented in San José. Mornings are the best time to go to embassies and consulates.

Canadian Embassy (☎2242-4400; www.costarica.gc.ca; Oficentro Ejecutivo La Sabana, 3rd fl, Edificio 5, Sabana Sur; ⏰7:30am-4pm Mon-Thu, to 1pm Fri) Behind La Contraloría.

Dutch Embassy (☎2296-1490; www.nederlandwereldwijd.nl/landen/costa-rica; Oficentro La Sabana, Edificio 3, 3rd fl, Sabana Sur; ⏰7:30am-4:30pm Mon-Thu, to 12:30pm Fri)

French Embassy (☎2234-4167; www.ambafrance-cr.org; Av 22, Curridabat; ⏰7:30am-12:30pm Mon-Fri) On the A022, off the D022 (a smaller road off Rte 2, the road to Curridabat).

German Embassy (☎2290-9091; www.san-jose.diplo.de; 8th fl, Edificio Torre Sabana, Sabana Norte; ⏰8am-noon Mon-Fri) Northwest of Parque Metropolitano La Sabana.

Guatemalan Embassy (☎2220-1297, 2291-6172; www.minex.gob.gt; Calle 64, Sabana Sur; ⏰9am-1pm Mon-Fri) Southwest Parque Metropolitano La Sabana.

Honduran Embassy (☎2231-1642; www.embajadahonduras.co.cr; Blvr Rohrmoser; ⏰9am-noon & 1:30-4pm Mon-Fri)

Israeli Embassy (☎2221-6444; 11th fl, Edificio Colón, Paseo Colón, btwn Calles 38 & 40; ⏰9am-noon Mon-Fri)

Italian Embassy (☎2224-6574, 2224-1082; www.ambsanjose.esteri.it; Calle 43, Los Yoses; ⏰9am-noon Mon-Fri) Between Avs 2 and 8.

Mexican Embassy (☎2257-0633; https://embamex.sre.gob.mx/costarica/; Av 7, btwn Calles 13 & 15; ⏰8am-5pm Mon-Fri) Northwest of Parque National.

SLEEPING PRICE RANGES

The following price ranges refer to a standard double room with bathroom in high season. Unless otherwise stated, a combined tourism and sales tax of 13% is included in the price.

$ less than US$50

$$ US$50–100

$$$ more than US$100

Nicaraguan Embassy (☎2233-8001, 2221-2884; Av Central 2540, btwn Calles 25 & 27; ⏰9am-5pm Mon & Wed-Fri) On the corner of 25A, in Carmen (San José).

Panamanian Embassy (☎2281-2442; www.facebook.com/EmbajadadePanamaenCostaRica/; cnr Av 10 & Calle 69, Barrio La Granja; ⏰9am-2pm Mon-Fri) A block north of Parque El Retiro in San Pedro (San José).

Spanish Embassy (☎2222-5745, 2222-1933; www.exteriores.gob.es; Calle 32, btwn Paseo Colón & Av 2; ⏰8am-3pm Mon-Fri)

Swiss Embassy (☎2221-4829; www.eda.admin.ch/sanjose; 10th fl, Edificio Centro Colón, Paseo Colón, btwn Calles 38 & 40; ⏰9am-noon Mon-Fri)

UK Embassy (☎2258-2025; www.gov.uk/government/world/organisations/british-embassy-in-costa-rica; 11th fl, Edificio Centro Colón, Paseo Colón, btwn Calles 38 & 40; ⏰8am-noon & 12:15-4pm Mon-Thu, 8am-1pm Fri)

US Embassy (☎2519-2000; https://cr.usembassy.gov; cnr Av Central & Calle 120; ⏰8am-noon & 1-4pm Mon-Fri) Opposite Centro Comercial del Oeste in Pavas (San José).

FOOD

The most popular eating establishment in Costa Rica is the *soda*. These are small, informal lunch counters dishing up a few daily *casados* (set meals). Other popular cheapies include the omnipresent fried- and rotisserie-chicken stands.

A regular *restaurante* is usually higher on the price scale and has slightly more atmosphere. Many *restaurantes* serve *casados*, while the fancier places refer to the set lunch as the *almuerzo ejecutivo* (literally 'executive lunch').

For something smaller, *pastelerías* and *panaderías* are shops that sell pastries and bread, while many bars serve *bocas* (snack-sized portions of main meals).

LGBTIQ+ TRAVELERS

In Costa Rica the situation facing gay and lesbian travelers is better than in most Central American countries, and some areas of the country – particularly Quepos and Parque Nacional Manuel Antonio – have been gay vacation destinations for two decades. Homosexual acts are legal, and in 2015 Costa Rica became the first country in Central America to recognize gay relationships. Still, most Costa Ricans are tolerant of homosexuality only at a 'don't ask, don't tell' level. Same-sex couples are unlikely to be the subject of harassment, though public displays of affection might attract unwanted attention.

The undisputed gay and lesbian capital of Costa Rica is Manuel Antonio; while there, you can pick up an issue of *Playita* (www.gaymanuelantonio.com/playita-magazine.html). The Spanish-language magazine *Gente 10* (www.gente10.com) is available at gay bars in San José.

Agua Buena Human Rights Association (☎2280-3548; www.aguabuena.org) This noteworthy nonprofit organization has campaigned steadily for fairness in medical treatment for people living with HIV/AIDS in Costa Rica.

Center of Investigation & Promotion of Human Rights in Central America (CIPAC; ☎2280-7821; www.cipacdh.org) The leading gay activist organization in Costa Rica.

Toto Tours (☎800-565-1241, USA 773-274-8686; www.tototours.com) Gay-travel specialist that organizes regular trips to Costa Rica, among other destinations.

MAPS

Unfortunately, detailed maps are hard to come by in Costa Rica, so it's best to purchase one online before your trip.

➡ The excellent, water-resistant 1:350,000 *Costa Rica Adventure Map* published by National Geographic also has an inset map of San José. Available online or in various book and gift shops in San José.

➡ Another quality option is the 1:330,000 *Costa Rica* sheet produced by International Travel Map, which is waterproof and includes a San José inset.

➡ The **Fundación Neotrópica** (☎2253-2130; www.neotropica.org) publishes a 1:500,000 map showing national parks and other protected areas; it's available online and in San José bookstores.

➡ The Instituto Costarricense de Turismo (ICT; Costa Rican Tourism Board) publishes a 1:700,000 *Costa Rica* map with a 1:12,500 *Central San José* map on the reverse; it's free at the ICT office in San José.

➡ Maptak (www.maptak.com) has maps of Costa Rica's seven provinces and their capitals.

➡ Few national-park offices or ranger stations have maps for hikers.

➡ The **Instituto Geográfico Nacional** (IGN; ☎2202-0777; 215, Zapote; ⏰8:30am-3:30pm Mon-Fri) in San José has topographical maps available for purchase.

➡ Incafo formerly published the *Mapa-Guía de la Naturaleza Costa Rica*, an atlas that included 1:200,000 topographical sheets, as well as English and Spanish descriptions of Costa Rica's natural areas. Used copies can be purchased online.

MONEY

US dollars accepted almost everywhere and dispensed from most ATMs; carry colones for small towns, bus fares and rural shops. Credit cards generally accepted.

➡ The Costa Rican currency is the colón (plural colones), named after Cristóbal Colón (Christopher Columbus).

➡ Bills come in 1000-, 2000-, 5000-, 10,000-, 20,000- and 50,000-colón notes, while coins come in denominations of five, 10, 20, 25, 50, 100 and 500 colones.

➡ Paying for things in US dollars is common, and at times is encouraged, since the currency is viewed as being more stable than the colón.

➡ In US-dollar transactions the change will usually be given in colones.

➡ Newer US dollars are preferred throughout Costa Rica; if your note has a rip in it, it may not be accepted.

➡ When paying in US dollars at a local restaurant, bar or shop the exchange rate can be unfavorable.

Tipping

Guides Tip US$5 to US$15 per person per day. Tip the tour driver about half of what you tip the guide.

Hotels Tip the bellhop/porter US$1 to US$5 per service and the housekeeper US$1 to US$2 per day in top-end hotels; less in budget places.

Restaurants Your bill will usually include a 10% service charge. If not, you might leave a small tip.

Taxis Tip only if some special service is provided.

OPENING HOURS

The following are high-season opening hours; hours will generally shorten in the shoulder and low seasons. Generally, sights, activities and restaurants are open daily.

Banks 9am–4pm Monday to Friday, sometimes 9am to noon Saturday

Bars and clubs 8pm–2am

Government offices 8am–5pm Monday to Friday; often closed between 11:30am and 1:30pm

Restaurants 7am–9pm; upscale places may open only for dinner, and in remote areas even the small *sodas* (inexpensive eateries) might open only at specific meal times

Shops 8am–6pm Monday to Saturday

PUBLIC HOLIDAYS

Días feriados (national holidays) are taken seriously in Costa Rica. Banks, public offices and many stores close. During these times, public transport is tight and hotels are heavily booked. Many festivals coincide with public holidays.

New Year's Day January 1

Semana Santa Holy Week; March or April. The Thursday and Friday before Easter Sunday is the official holiday, though most businesses shut down for the whole week. From Thursday to Sunday bars are closed and alcohol sales are prohibited; on Thursday and Friday buses stop running.

Día de Juan Santamaría April 11. Honors the national hero who died fighting William Walker in 1856; major events are held in Alajuela, his hometown.

Labor Day May 1

Día de la Madre Mother's Day; August 15. Coincides with the annual Catholic Feast of the Assumption.

Independence Day September 15

Día de la Raza Columbus Day; October 12.

Christmas Day December 25. Christmas Eve is also an unofficial holiday.

Last week in December The week between Christmas and New Year is an unofficial holiday; businesses close and beach hotels are crowded.

SAFE TRAVEL

Costa Rica is a largely safe country, but petty crime (bag snatchings, car break-ins etc) is common and muggings do occur, so it's important to be vigilant.

➡ Many of Costa Rica's dangers are nature related: riptides, earthquakes and volcanic eruptions are among them.

➡ Predatory and venomous wildlife can also pose a threat, so a wildlife guide is essential if trekking in the jungle.

TELEPHONE

➡ Cell (mobile) service now covers most of the country and nearly all of the country that is accessible to tourists.

EATING PRICE RANGES

The following price ranges refer to a standard meal. Unless otherwise stated, tax is included in the price.

$ less than US$10

$$ US$10–15

$$$ more than US$15

➡ Public phones are found all over Costa Rica, and chip or Colibrí phone cards are available in 1000-, 2000- and 3000-colón denominations.

➡ Chip cards are inserted into the phone and scanned. Colibrí cards (more common) require you to dial a toll-free number (199) and enter an access code. Instructions are provided in English or Spanish.

➡ The cheapest international calls from Costa Rica are direct-dialed using a phone card. To make international calls, dial '00' followed by the country code and number.

➡ Pay phones cannot receive international calls.

➡ To call Costa Rica from abroad, use the country code (506) before the eight-digit number.

➡ Due to the widespread popularity of voice-over IP services such as Skype, and more reliable ethernet connections, traveling with a smartphone or tablet can be the cheapest and easiest way to call internationally.

Cell Phones

➡ 3G and 4G systems are available, but those compatible with US plans require expensive international roaming.

➡ Prepaid SIM cards are cheap and widely available.

➡ See https://opensignal.com/networks for coverage details for each of the four cellular providers (Claro, Kolbi, Movistar, TuYo).

TOILETS

➡ Public restrooms are rare, but most restaurants and cafes will let you use their facilities, sometimes for a small charge – never more than 500 colones.

➡ Bus terminals and other major public buildings usually have toilets, also at a charge.

➡ Don't flush your toilet paper. Costa Rican plumbing is often poor and has very low pressure.

➡ Dispose of toilet paper in the rubbish bin inside the bathroom.

TOURIST INFORMATION

The government-run tourism board, the ICT (www.ict.go.cr/es), has an office in the capital; English is spoken. The ICT can provide you with free maps, a master bus schedule, information on road conditions in the hinterlands, and a helpful brochure with up-to-date emergency numbers for every region.

VISAS

Passport-carrying nationals of the following countries are allowed 90 days' stay with no visa: Argentina, Australia, Canada, Chile, Iceland, Ireland, Israel, Japan, Mexico, New Zealand, Panama, South Africa, USA and most Western European countries.

Most other visitors require a visa from a Costa Rican embassy or consulate.

For the latest info on visas, check the websites of the ICT (www.ict.go.cr/en) or the Costa Rican Embassy (www.costarica-embassy.org).

Visa Extensions

➡ Extending your stay beyond the authorized 30 or 90 days is time-consuming; it's easier to leave the country for 72 hours and then re-enter.

➡ Extensions can be handled by **migración offices** (☎ Juan Santamaria International Airport 2299-8001, Puerto Limón 2798-2097, Puntarenas 2661-1445, San José 2299-8100; www.migracion.go.cr).

➡ Requirements for extensions change, so allow several working days.

VOLUNTEERING

Costa Rica offers a huge number of volunteer opportunities. Word of mouth is a powerful influence on future participants, so the majority of programs in Costa Rica are very conscientious about pleasing their volunteers. Almost all placements require a commitment of two weeks or more.

Lonely Planet does not vouch for any organization that we do not work with directly, and we strongly recommend travelers always investigate a volunteer opportunity themselves to assess the standards and suitability of the project.

Forestry Management

Cloudbridge Nature Reserve (www.cloudbridge.org) Trail building, construction, tree planting and projects monitoring the recovery of the cloud forest are offered to volunteers, who pay for their own housing with a local family. Preference is given to biology students, but all enthusiastic volunteers can apply.

Fundación Corcovado (www.corcovadofoundation.org) An impressive network of people and organizations committed to preserving Parque Nacional Corcovado.

Monteverde Institute (www.monteverde-institute.org) A nonprofit educational institute offering training in tropical biology, conservation and sustainable development.

Tropical Science Center (www.cct.or.cr) This long-standing NGO offers volunteer placement at Reserva Biológica Bosque Nuboso Monteverde. Projects can include trail maintenance and conservation work.

Organic Farming

Finca La Flor de Paraíso (www.fincalaflor.org) Offers programs in a variety of disciplines from animal husbandry to medicinal-herb cultivation.

Punta Mona (www.puntamona.org) An organic farm and retreat center that focuses on organic permaculture and sustainable living.

Rancho Margot (www.ranchomargot.com) This self-proclaimed life-skills university offers a natural education emphasizing organic farming and animal husbandry.

Reserva Biológica Dúrika (www.durika.org) A sustainable community on an 85-sq-km biological reserve.

WWOOF Costa Rica (www.wwoofcostarica.org) This loose network of farms is part of the large international network of Willing Workers on Organic Farms (WWOOF). Placements are incredibly varied. WWOOF Mexico, Costa Rica, Guatemala and Belize have a joint US$33 membership, which gives potential volunteers access to all placement listings.

Wildlife Conservation

Be aware that conservationists in Costa Rica occasionally face harassment or worse from local poachers and that police are pretty ineffectual in following up incidents.

Asociación Salvemos las Tortugas de Parismina (ASTOP, Save the Turtles of Parismina; ☎2798-2220; www.parisminaturtles.org; homestays per night incl 3 meals & patrols US$40, without meals $20, registration fee US$50; ⏲by arrangement Mar-Sep) Helps to protect turtles and their eggs, and improve quality of life for villagers in this tiny community.

Earthwatch (www.earthwatch.org) This broadly recognized international volunteer organization works in sea-turtle conservation in Costa Rica.

Las Pumas (www.centrorescatelaspumas.org) A feline-conservation program that takes care of confiscated wild cats, both big and small.

Reserva Playa Tortuga (www.reservaplayatortuga.org) Assists with olive-ridley-turtle conservation efforts near Ojochal.

Sea Turtle Conservancy (www.conserveturtles.org) From March to October, this Tortuguero organization hosts 'eco-volunteer adventures' working with sea turtles and birds.

Getting There & Away

AIR

Aeropuerto Internacional Juan Santamaría (p529) International flights arrive here, 17km northwest of San José, in the town of Alajuela.

Aeropuerto Internacional Daniel Oduber Quirós (p570) This airport in Liberia also receives international flights from the USA, the Americas and Canada. It serves a number of American and Canadian airlines and some charters from London, as well as regional flights from Panama and Nicaragua.

Avianca (part of the Central American airline consortium Grupo TACA; www.avianca.com). The Colombian-owned airline is regarded as the national airline of Costa Rica and flies to the USA and Latin America, including Cuba.

BORDER CROSSINGS

Costa Rica shares land borders with Nicaragua and Panama. There is no fee for travelers to enter Costa Rica, but visas may be required for certain nationalities.

Nicaragua

A land border crossing opened in 2015 linking **Los Chiles to Las Tablillas**. A bridge crosses the Río San Juan just north of the Nicaraguan border.

- The Los Chiles–Las Tablillas border crossing is open from 8am to 4pm daily (☎2471-1233).
- Hourly buses connect Los Chiles and Las Tablillas (US$1, 15 minutes). There are also direct buses from San José and Ciudad Quesada (San Carlos).
- A Costa Rican land exit fee of US$7 is payable at immigration by credit or debit card only (no cash).
- After walking across the border, you'll go through Nicaraguan immigration. The entrance fee is US$12, payable in US dollars or cordobas.
- After exiting immigration, you can catch a boat up the river or hop on a bus or a *colectivo* (shared transport) to San Carlos (roughly US$2.50, 30 minutes).
- It's also still possible to cross this border by boat, which is a slower but more pleasant way of doing it. There is no scheduled service; boats depart Los Chiles when there's sufficient demand. Fares are approximately US$10 to US$15 per person, but if you have time constraints it may be possible to pay more and leave more quickly. You'll avoid the Costa Rican land exit fee, but you'll still have to pay US$12 to enter Nicaragua.
- If you are entering Costa Rica from Nicaragua, there are three lines in Nicaragua: one for payment (go there first and pay the US$3 municipal tax/exit tax), one for entrance, and one for exiting the country.

Situated on the Interamericana, **Sapoá–Peñas Blancas** is a heavily trafficked border station between Nicaragua and Costa Rica.

- The Sapoá–Peñas Blancas border crossing is open from 6am to 10pm (☎2677-0230).
- This is the only official border between Nicaragua and Costa Rica that you can drive across.
- Waiting times at this border can be several hours. Plan on at least an hour's wait.
- You'll pay a US$7 Costa Rican land exit tax to cross the border (via credit/debit card) and

then US$2 municipal tax (in dollars; colones are not accepted – bring some cash in small bills with you).

➡ After walking a few hundred meters, you will also pay US$7 to enter Nicaragua. Keep your passport handy but stowed safely away – officials from both countries may ask to see it.

➡ After you cross you can catch a Nicaraguan bus or taxi for the 30-minute ride to Rivas (bus fares are approximately US$1), the key transit point for other Nicaraguan destinations. You can also take a taxi to San Juan del Sur (US$25, 30 minutes). A new road to this Nicaraguan beach town was being paved at the time of research.

➡ Theoretically, if you stay for 90 days in Costa Rica, you're supposed to stay in Nicaragua three days before returning to Costa Rica, but in practice many foreigners (expats who live in Costa Rica but do not yet have residence) stay only three hours. Coming back into Costa Rica, you'll pay a US$3 municipal tax/exit tax. Costa Rican officials may query you about how long you plan to stay and base your visa (60 or 90 days) on this information. Importantly, you should have a return ticket home or out of Costa Rica, dated within 90 days.

➡ **Tica Bus** (☎2296-9788, Nicaragua 2298-5500, Panama 314-6385; www.ticabus.com), **Nica Bus** (☎2221-2679, Nicaragua 2222-2276; www.nicabus.com.ni) and TransNica (p530) all have daily buses that serve points north and south. Regular buses depart Peñas Blancas, on the Costa Rican side, for La Cruz, Liberia and San José.

➡ Note that Peñas Blancas is only a border post, not a town, so there is nowhere to stay.

Panama

Note that Panamanian time is one hour ahead of Costa Rican time.

At the time of writing, entry to Panama required proof of US$500 (per person), proof of onward travel from Panama (including a bus ticket from Panama back to Costa Rica, if you're not flying out of Panama) and a passport valid for at least six months. If you don't have an onward plane ticket yet, buy a refundable one originating in Panama, print the itinerary and then cancel the ticket.

The Carretera Interamericana (Pan-American Hwy) at **Paso Canoas** (☎2732-2150) is by far the most frequently used entry and exit point with Panama, and it's open 6am to 10pm Monday to Friday, and to 8pm on weekends.

➡ The border crossing in either direction is at times chaotic and slow.

➡ Get an exit stamp from Costa Rica at the immigration office before entering Panama; do the same on the Panamanian side when entering Costa Rica.

➡ There is no charge for entering Costa Rica. Entry to Panama costs US$1.

➡ The departure tax in Costa Rica is US$7, but you will be charged US$8 at the border because the company that handles the transaction takes a US$1 commission. You pay this through the window of a storage container across the highway from the Costa Rica Migration office. Panama has no departure tax.

➡ Northbound buses usually stop running at 6pm. Travelers without a private vehicle should arrive during the day.

➡ Those with a private vehicle are likely to encounter long lines.

➡ Tica Bus travels from Panama City to San José (US$42 to US$58, 15 hours) daily and Tracopa (www.tracopacr.com) has a route from San José to David (US$21), both crossing this border post. In David, Tracopa has one bus daily from the main terminal to San José (nine hours). In David you'll also find frequent buses to the border at Paso Canoas.

Situated on the Caribbean coast, **Guabito–Sixaola** (☎2754-2044) is a fairly tranquil and hassle-free border crossing open between 7am and 5pm.

➡ If you're coming from Bocas del Toro in Panama, you'll first have to take the frequent boat to Almirante (around US$2), then a public bus or shuttle to Changuinola (roughly 40 minutes), from where you can take a quick taxi to the border or to the bus station (roughly US$5).

➡ One daily bus travels between Changuinola and San José at 10am (approximately US$16, eight hours). Otherwise you can walk over the border and catch one of the hourly buses that go up the coast from Sixaola.

Río Sereno–San Vito (☎2784-0130) is a rarely used crossing in the Cordillera de Talamanca. The border is open 8am to 4pm on the Costa Rican side and 9am to 5pm on the Panamanian side. The small village of Río Sereno on the Panamanian side has a hotel and a place to eat; there are no facilities on the Costa Rican side.

DEPARTURE TAX

➡ There is a US$29 departure tax on all international outbound flights, payable in dollars or colones, though most carriers now include it in the ticket price.

➡ There is a US$7 land exit fee payable at immigration posts at land border crossings.

- Regular buses depart Concepción and David in Panama for Río Sereno. Local buses (around US$1.60, 40 minutes, six daily) and taxis (about US$30) go from the border to San Vito.
- For travelers departing Costa Rica, there is a US$7 exit tax, plus a US$1 admin fee, payable at a kiosk at the border crossing.

Getting Around

AIR

- Costa Rica's domestic airlines are Nature Air and Sansa. Sansa is linked with Grupo TACA.
- Both airlines fly small passenger planes, and you're allocated a baggage allowance of no more than 12kg.
- Space is limited and demand is high in the dry season, so reserve and pay for tickets in advance.
- In Costa Rica schedules change constantly and delays are frequent because of inclement weather. You should not arrange a domestic flight that makes a tight connection with an international flight.
- Domestic flights (excepting charter flights) originate and terminate at San José.

BICYCLE

With an increasingly large network of paved secondary roads and heightened awareness of cyclists, Costa Rica is emerging as one of Central America's most comfortable cycle-touring destinations. That said, many roads are narrow, potholed and winding and there are no designated cycle lanes, so there's an element of risk involved.

Mountain bikes and beach cruisers can be rented in towns with a significant tourist presence for US$10 to US$20 per day. A few companies organize bike tours around Costa Rica.

BOAT

In Costa Rica there are some regular coastal services and safety standards are generally good.

- The Coonatramar Ferry (p590) links the port of Puntarenas with Playa Naranjo four times daily. The Ferry Naviera Tambor (p590) travels between Puntarenas and Paquera every two hours, for a bus connection to Montezuma.
- Zuma Tours (p590) runs a daily water taxi between Montezuma and Jacó.
- On the Golfo Dulce a daily passenger ferry links Golfito with Puerto Jiménez on the Península de Osa. On the other side of the Península de Osa, water taxis connect Bahía Drake with Sierpe.
- On the Caribbean coast there is a bus and boat service that runs several times a day linking Cariari and Tortuguero via La Pavona.

> **ONWARD TICKETS**
>
> - Officially, travelers are required to have a ticket out of Costa Rica before they are allowed to enter. This is rarely and erratically enforced.
> - Those arriving overland with no onward ticket can purchase one from international bus companies in Managua (Nicaragua) and Panama City (Panama).

- Boats ply the canals that run along the coast from Moín to Tortuguero, although no regular service exists.

BUS

Local Bus

- Local buses are a cheap and reliable way of getting around Costa Rica. Fares range from less than US$1 to around US$20.
- San José is the transportation center for the country, though there is no central terminal. Bus offices are scattered around the city: some large bus companies have big terminals that sell tickets in advance, while others have little more than a stop – sometimes unmarked.
- Buses can be very crowded but don't usually pass up passengers on account of being too full. Note that there are usually no buses from Thursday to Saturday before Easter Sunday.
- There are two types of bus: *directo* and *colectivo*. The *directo* buses should go from one destination to the next with few stops; the *colectivos* make more stops and are very slow going.
- Trips longer than four hours usually include a rest stop as buses do not have toilets.
- Space is limited on board, so if you have to check luggage be watchful. Theft from overhead racks is rampant, though it's much less common than in other Central American countries.
- Bus schedules fluctuate wildly, so always confirm the time when you buy your ticket. If you are catching a bus that picks you up somewhere along a road, get to the roadside early.
- For information on departures from San José, see www.visitcostarica.com/en/costa-rica/bus-itinerary for a reasonably up-to-date copy of the master schedule, or check www.thebusschedule.com/cr for route planning. Another useful site for planning point-to-point bus trips is www.yoviajocr.com, which has a phone app as well.

Shuttle Bus

The tourist-van shuttle services (aka gringo buses) are a pricier alternative to the standard intercity buses. Shuttles are provided by **Gray Line** (☎2220-2126, USA 800-719-3905; www.graylinecostarica.com), **Easy Ride** (☎8812-4012, USA 703-879-2284; www.easyridecostarica.com), **Monkey Ride** (☎2787-0454; www.monkeyridecr.com), **Tropical Tours** (☎2640-1900; www.tropicaltourshuttles.com) and **Interbus** (☎6050-6500, 4100-0888; www.interbusonline.com).

- All five companies run overland transportation from San José to the most popular destinations, as well as directly between other destinations (see the websites for the comprehensive list).
- These services will pick you up at your hotel, and reservations can be made online or through local travel agencies and hotel owners.
- Popular destinations include Quepos, Monteverde/Santa Elena, Manuel Antonio, Jacó, Dominical, Uvita, Puerto Jiménez, Arenal, Montezuma and Mal País.
- Easy Ride offers international services directly from Jacó, Tamarindo and Liberia to Granada and Managua in Nicaragua and from Monteverde to Managua.

CAR & MOTORCYCLE

- Foreign drivers in Costa Rica are required to have a valid driver's license from their home country. Many places will also accept an International Driving Permit (IDP), issued by the automobile association in your country of origin. After 90 days, however, you will need to get a Costa Rican driver's license.
- Gasoline (petrol) and diesel are widely available, and 24-hour service stations are along the Interamericana. At the time of research, fuel prices averaged just over US$1 per liter.
- In more remote areas, fuel will be more expensive and might be sold at the neighborhood *pulpería* (corner store).
- Spare parts may be hard to find, especially for vehicles with sophisticated electronics and emissions-control systems.

TAXI

Taxis are considered a form of public transportation in remote areas. They can be hired by the hour, half-day or full day, or you can arrange a flat fee for a trip. Meters are not used on long trips, so arrange the fare ahead of time. Fares can fluctuate due to worse-than-expected road conditions and bad weather in tough-to-reach places.

Panama

POP 4.1 MILLION

Includes ➡

Best Places to Eat

- Cerro Brujo (p666)
- Lo Que Hay (p637)
- Pipa's Beach Restaurant (p650)
- Donde José (p637)

Best Places to Stay

- Dolphin Bay Hideaway (p679)
- Hotel Bocas del Toro (p672)
- Bambuda Castle (p662)
- Villa Távida Lodge (p650)

Why Go?

In Panama, nature is all about discovery. Explore the ruins of Spanish forts on the Caribbean coast or paddle deep into indigenous territories in a dugout canoe. Wildlife is everywhere in abundance: resplendent quetzals on the highland trail, screeching howler monkeys outside your cabin or a breaching whale that turns a ferry ride into an adrenaline-filled event.

Adventure tourism means zipping through rainforest canopies, rafting thundering white water or trekking to sublime cloud-forest vistas. On the coast, you can explore the wonders of the marine world while diving with whale sharks in the Pacific, snorkeling the rainbow reefs of Bocas del Toro or setting sail in the indigenous territory of Guna Yala, where virgin isles sport nary a footprint. Meanwhile surfers will be psyched to have world-class breaks all to themselves.

Add to this the cultural riches of Panama City, and you have one of Latin America's most captivating destinations.

When to Go

Panama City

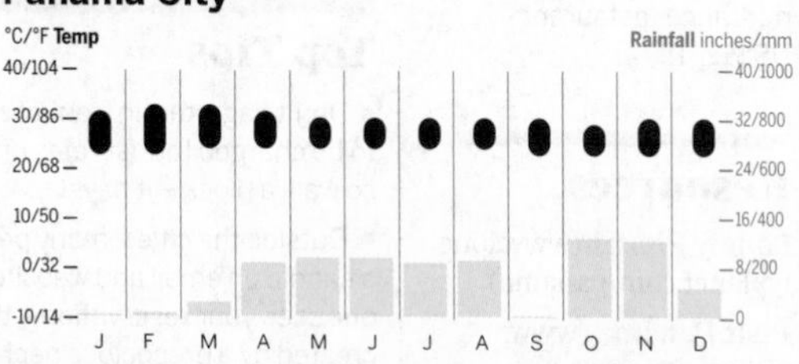

Dec–Apr
High season on the Pacific coast is also the dry season. Best time to hike or dive.

Jul
Rainy season, but relatively dry on the Caribbean. Low-season rates.

Aug–Oct
Migrating humpback whales in the Pacific. Shoulder season in Bocas.

FAST FACTS

Currency US dollar (balboa; $)

Visas Visas are generally not required for stays of up to 90 days.

Money ATMs are readily available except in the most isolated places.

Capital Panama City

Emergency Police ☎104

Languages Spanish, English

Exchange Rates

Australia	A$1	US$0.71
Canada	C$1	US$0.76
Euro zone	€1	US$1.14
Japan	¥100	US$0.90
New Zealand	NZ$1	US$0.68
UK	£1	US$1.33

Daily Costs

- Dorm bed: US$18; double room at a midrange hotel: US$60–130
- *Comida corriente* (set meal): US$7; meal in a midrange restaurant: US$12–18

Resources

Lonely Planet (www.lonelyplanet.com/panama)

Visit Panama (www.visitpanama.com)

Casco Viejo (www.cascoviejo.org)

Panama Today (www.panamatoday.com)

Entering the Country

There are three border crossings between Costa Rica and Panama. Most travelers cross at Paso Canoas (gateway: David). Note that Panama is always one hour ahead of Costa Rica.

TWO-WEEK ITINERARY

Start your Panama travels by imbibing the rush of **Panama City**. Visit **Panamá Viejo**, destroyed in a massive pirate raid, pedal along **Cinta Costera**, the coastal beltway, and day trip to nearby **Miraflores Locks** to witness mammoth ships squeezing through the canal. At nearby **Parque Nacional Soberanía** you can climb a canopy tower to search for toucans and sloths, or you can kayak **Lago Gatún** alongside howler monkeys and sunbathing crocodiles. Next, fly to **Bocas del Toro** for four days of chill Caribbean vibes. Snorkel the aquamarine waters and explore **Isla Colón** by quad bike. Alternatively, escape to **Isla Bastimentos**, with thatched resorts and jungle lodges. For a dose of culture, take a chocolate tour on the mainland or visit indigenous groups on other islands with a community tourism initiative.

Got a second week? Head over the continental divide to highland **Boquete** to explore coffee farms and cloud forests before hitting the great beaches of the **Pacific coast** and circling back to the capital.

Essential Food & Drink

Sancocho The *sine qua non* chicken soup of Panama.

Patacones Fried plantains, eaten everywhere by everyone.

Chicheme A favorite nonalcoholic drink made from milk, mashed corn, cinnamon and vanilla.

Seco The nation's favorite tipple, packing quite a punch at 35% alcohol content.

Top Tips

- Don't flag a taxi in front of a high-end hotel if you don't want to be charged tourist rates off the bat; taxis aren't metered, so walk a block – it pays!
- Outside the cities, many perfectly good lodgings don't have a handle on email and websites. Don't get frustrated if no one sees your reservation – the hotel email might have been created by a precocious nephew who never checks it. If you have even basic Spanish, call ahead.
- Panamanians are used to foreigners dissing local idiosyncrasies – like drivers not using signals, or crowds that can't form lines. But, instead, ask *why* it is the way it is and you'll have a lively conversation.

PANAMA CITY

POP 880,700 / ELEV 6FT

The most cosmopolitan capital in Central America, Panama City is both vibrant metropolis and gateway to tropical escapes. Many worlds coexist here. Welcoming both east and west, Panama is a regional hub of trade and immigration. The resulting cultural cocktail forges a refreshing 'anything goes' attitude that's more dynamic and fluid than in neighboring countries.

Unflinchingly urban, the capital rides the rails of chaos, with traffic jams, wayward taxis and casinos stacked between chic clubs and construction sites. A center of international banking and trade, the sultry skyline of shimmering glass and steel towers is reminiscent of Miami. In contrast, the colonial peninsula of Casco Viejo has become a hip neighborhood where cobblestones link boutique hotels with rooftop bars, and crumbled ruins with pirate lore.

Escape is never far away. Day-trip to sandy beaches (Pacific or Caribbean), admire the canal, or explore lush rainforests of howler monkeys, toucans and sloths.

Sights

Casco Viejo

Following the destruction of the old city by Captain Henry Morgan in 1671, the Spanish moved their city 8km southwest to a rocky peninsula at the foot of Cerro Ancón. The new location was easier to defend as the reefs prevented ships from approaching the city except at high tide. The new city was also easy to defend, as a massive wall surrounded it, which is how Casco Viejo (Old Compound) got its name.

In 1904, when construction began on the Panama Canal, all of Panama City existed where Casco Viejo stands today. However, as population growth and urban expansion pushed the boundaries of Panama City further east, the city's elite abandoned Casco Viejo and the neighborhood rapidly deteriorated into a slum.

Today Casco Viejo's crumbling facades have been mostly replaced by immaculate renovations. Declared a Unesco World Heritage Site in 2003, the area is getting international recognition. The newly restored architecture gives a sense of how magnificent the neighborhood must have looked in past years. Some developers, committed to mitigating the effects of gentrification here, are creating one affordable unit for each high-end one constructed, and working on interesting local cultural initiatives. Yet the consensus is that most of the neighborhood's former occupants have already been relegated to the periphery.

Plaza de la Independencia PLAZA

(Map p636) In this plaza, in the heart of Casco Viejo, Panama declared its independence from Colombia on November 3, 1903.

Iglesia de San José CHURCH

(Map p636; Av A) This Casco Viejo church protects the famous Altar de Oro (Golden Altar), the sole relic salvaged after privateer Henry Morgan sacked Panamá Viejo.

According to local legend, when word came of Morgan's impending attack, a priest attempted to disguise the altar by painting it black. The priest told Morgan that the famous altar had been stolen by another pirate, and even convinced Morgan to donate handsomely for its replacement. Morgan is said to have told the priest, 'I don't know why, but I think you are more of a pirate than I am.' Whatever the truth, the baroque altar was later moved from the old city to the present site.

Teatro Nacional THEATER

(Map p636; ☎501-4107; www.inac.gob.pa/teatros/73-teatro-nacional; Av B) Built in 1907, the interior of this ornate Casco Viejo theater has been completely restored. It boasts red and gold decorations, a once-magnificent ceiling mural by Roberto Lewis (one of Panama's finest painters) and an impressive crystal chandelier. Performances are still held here. For information visit the office at the side of the building.

Plaza de Francia PLAZA

(Map p636) At the tip of the southern point of Casco Viejo, this beautiful plaza pays homage to the French role in the construction of the canal. Its large stone tablets and statues are dedicated to the memory of the 22,000 workers who died trying to create the canal.

Paseo las Bóvedas WATERFRONT

(Map p636) This esplanade runs along the top of the sea wall built by the Spanish to protect the city. From here, you can see the Puente de las Américas arching over the waterway and the ships lining up to enter the canal.

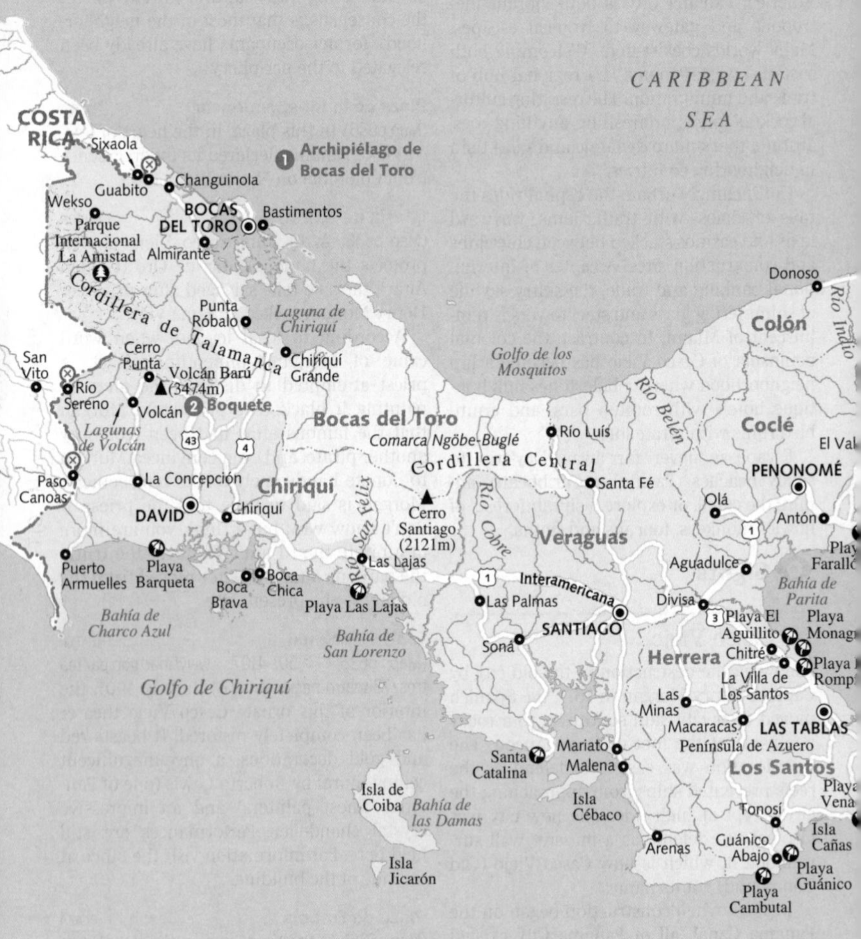

Panama Highlights

❶ Archipiélago de Bocas del Toro (p668) Whiling the days away sipping coconuts and snorkeling at laid-back resorts.

❷ Boquete (p660) Fueling up for highland adventures with local mountain-grown coffee in the town of eternal spring.

❸ Panama City (p625) Spending the day admiring the faded glory of the old city, Casco Viejo, then reveling till sunrise on Calle Uruguay.

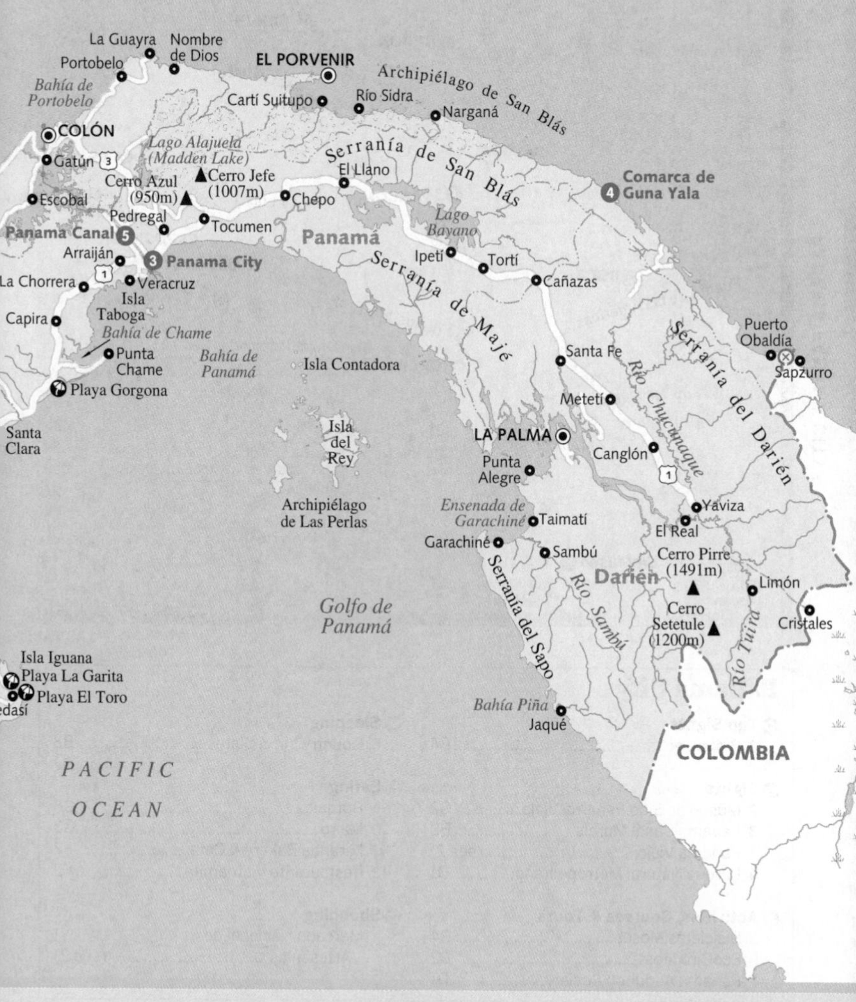

4 Comarca de Guna Yala (p685) Cruising white-sand cays, swimming in clear waters and soaking up sunrise on a sailboat.

5 Panama Canal (p643) Laying eyes on this awe-inspiring engineering marvel in the midst of an expansion.

Panama City

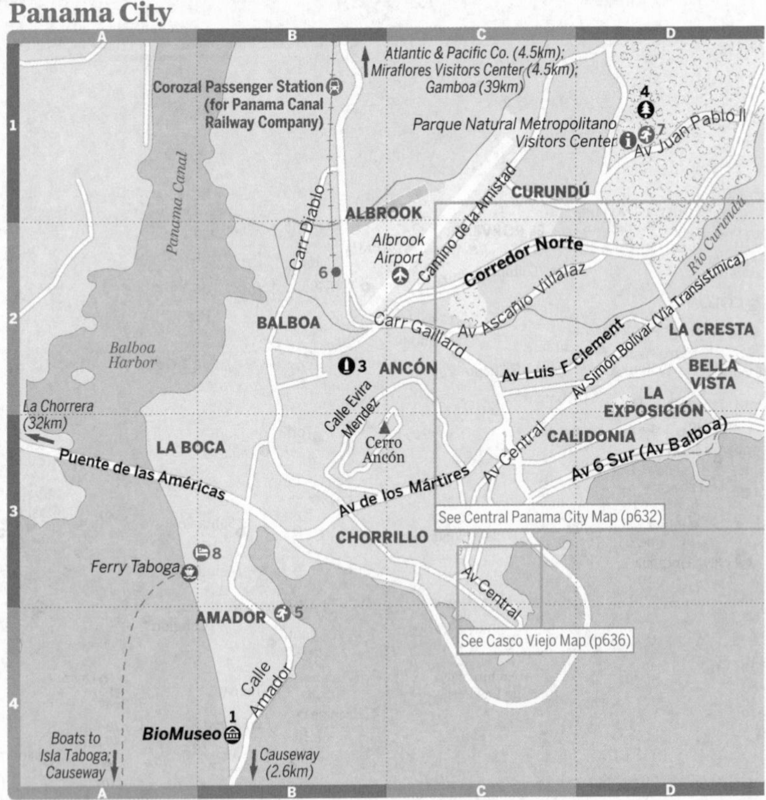

Panama City

Top Sights
1 BioMuseo B4

Sights
2 Museo de Sitio Panamá Viejo G2
3 Panama Canal Murals B2
Panamá Viejo .... (see 2)
4 Parque Natural Metropolitano D1

Activities, Courses & Tours
5 Bicicletas Moses B4
6 EcoCircuitos B2
7 Panama Audubon Society D1

Sleeping
8 Country Inn & Suites B3

Eating
9 Botanica G3
10 Maito G3
11 Miranda Bakery & Cafe F2
12 Restaurante Vietnamita F2

Shopping
Mercado Nacional de Artesanías .... (see 2)

Museo del Canal Interoceánico MUSEUM
(Panama Canal Museum; Map p636; 211-1649; www.museodelcanal.com; Calle 6a Oeste; adult/child US$10/5; 9am-5pm Tue-Sun) This impressive museum is housed in a beautifully restored building that once served as the headquarters for the original French canal company. The Panama Canal Museum (as it's more commonly known) presents excellent exhibits on the famous waterway, framed in their historical and political context. Signs are in Spanish, but English-speaking guides and audio guides (US$5) are available.

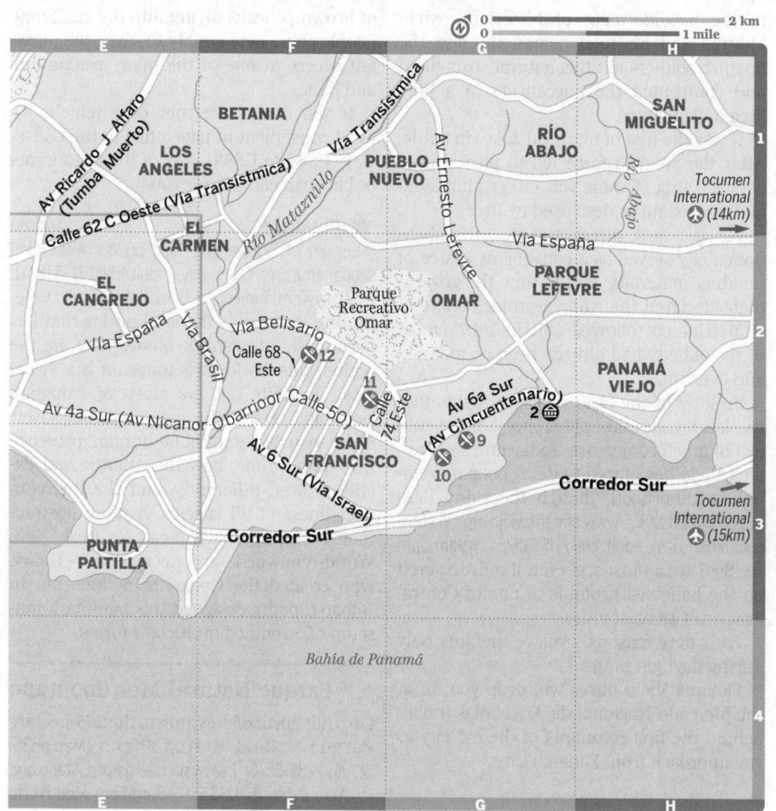

Palacio de las Garzas HISTORIC BUILDING

(Presidential Palace; Map p636; Av Alfaro) The Palacio de las Garzas is named after the great *garzas blancas* (white herons) that reside here. The president of Panama lives on the upper floor.

Museo de Arte Religioso Colonial MUSEUM

(Museum of Colonial Religious Art; Map p636; ☎519-9915; www.inac.gob.pa/museos; cnr Av A & Calle 3a Este; US$1; ⏰8am-4pm Mon-Fri) Housed beside the ruins of the Iglesia y Convento de Santo Domingo, the Museo de Arte Religioso Colonial has a collection of colonial-era religious artifacts, some dating from the 16th century.

Just inside the ruins' doorway, the Arco Chato is a long arch that stood here unsupported for centuries. It even played a part in the selection of Panama over Nicaragua as the site for the canal, since its survival was taken as proof that the area was not subject to earthquakes. It collapsed in 2003 but has since been rebuilt.

Panama Viejo

Founded on August 15, 1519, by Spanish conquistador Pedro Arias de Ávila, the city of Panamá was the first European settlement along the Pacific. For the next 150 years it profited mainly from Spain's famed bullion pipeline, which ran from Peru's gold and silver mines to Europe via Panamá. Because of the amount of wealth that passed through the city, the Spaniards kept many soldiers here, and their presence kept the buccaneers away.

In 1671, 1200 pirates led by Captain Henry Morgan ascended the Río Chagres and proceeded overland to Panamá. Although the city was not fortified, it was protected on three sides by the sea and marshes, and on the land side was a causeway with a bridge to allow tidal water to pass underneath. But to the bewilderment of historians, when Morgan and his men neared the city, the Spanish soldiers left this natural stronghold and confronted the buccaneers in a hilly area outside town.

It was the first of many mistakes in battle. After the Spanish force fell to pieces nearly everything of value was either plundered and divvied up or destroyed by fire.

For the next three centuries, the abandoned city served as a convenient source of building materials. By the time the government declared the ruins a protected site in 1976 (Unesco followed suit in 1997), most of the old city had already been dismantled and overrun.

So little of the original city remains that its size, layout and appearance are the subject of much conjecture. Today much of Panamá Viejo lies buried under a poor residential neighborhood, though the **ruins** (Map p628; ☎226-8915; www.panamaviejo.org; Vía Cincuentenario s/n; adult/child US$15/5; ⏲9am-5pm Tue-Sun) are a must-see, even if only to stand on the hallowed grounds of one of Central America's greatest cities.

For safety reasons, explore the area only during daylight hours.

Panamá Viejo buses will drop you off at the Mercado Nacional de Artesanías (p639) behind the first remnants of the old city as you approach from Panama City.

Museo de Sitio Panamá Viejo MUSEUM

(Map p628; ☎226-8915; www.panamaviejo.org; Av 6 Sur,; incl with park entry fee; ⏲8:30am-4:30pm Tue-Sun) In the original settlement of Panamá Viejo, this museum traces the history from pre-colonial times to colonial life. There's an impressive scale model of Panamá Viejo prior to 1671 as well as religious art, and exhibits on old maps and on pirate history. An optional extra is climbing **Mirador de la Torre**, the lookout tower; children under eight are not allowed.

Causeway

At the Pacific entrance to the Panama Canal, a 2km palm tree–lined *calzada* (causeway) connects the four small islands of Naos, Culebra, Perico and Flamenco to the mainland. The Causeway is popular in the early morning and late afternoon, when residents walk, jog, skate and cycle its narrow length.

The Causeway also offers sweeping views of the skyline and the old city, with flocks of brown pelicans diving into the sea. Some people come here simply to savor the pleasant breeze at one of the many restaurants and bars.

If you don't have your own vehicle, it's most convenient to take a taxi to the Causeway (US$4 to US$8). Any of the restaurants or bars can call one for you.

★**BioMuseo** MUSEUM

(Museum of Biodiversity; Map p628; www.biomuseopanama.org; Causeway; adult/child US$18/11; ⏲10am-4pm Tue-Fri, to 5pm Sat & Sun) Celebrating Panama as the land bridge that has permitted astonishing biodiversity in the region, this world-class museum is a visual feast. Exhibits tell the story of Panama's rich biodiversity through engaging, oversized visuals, examining human presence throughout time, how the Atlantic and Pacific evolved differently, and the interconnectedness of all species. A more abstract than literal approach creates a fresh view. World-renowned architect Frank Gehry, who created the Guggenheim Museum in Bilbao (Spain), designed this landmark museum of crumpled multicolor forms.

Parque Natural Metropolitano

On a hill north of downtown, the 265-hectare **Parque Natural Metropolitano** (Map p628; ☎info 232-5516; www.parquemetropolitano.org; Av Juan Pablo II; US$5; ⏲8am-5pm Mon-Fri, to 1pm Sat) protects vast expanses of tropical semideciduous forest within the city limits. It serves as an incredible wilderness escape from the trappings of the capital. Two main **walking trails**, the Nature Trail and the Tití Monkey Trail, join to form one long loop, with a 150m-high *mirador* (lookout) offering panoramic views of Panama City, the bay and the canal, all the way to the Miraflores Locks.

Mammals in the park include *tití* monkeys, anteaters, sloths and white-tailed deer, while reptiles include iguanas, turtles and tortoises. More than 250 bird species have been spotted here. Fish and shrimp inhabit the Río Curundú along the eastern side of the park.

The park was the site of an important battle during the US invasion to oust Noriega. Also of historical significance, concrete structures just past the park entrance were used during WWII as a testing and assembly plant for aircraft engines.

The park is bordered to the west and north by Camino de la Amistad and to the south and east by Corredor Norte; Av Juan Pablo II runs right through the park.

Pick up a pamphlet for a self-guided tour in Spanish and English at the **visitors center** (Map p628; ☎232-5516; www.parquemetropolitano.org; ⊙8am-4:30pm Mon-Fri, to 1pm Sat), 40m north of the park entrance.

Other Neighborhoods

★Museo de Arte Contemporáneo MUSEUM
(Map p632; ☎262-8012; www.macpanama.org; Av de los Mártires, Ancón; adult/child US$5/3; ⊙10am-5pm Tue-Sun, to 8pm Thu) This wonderful privately owned museum features the best collection of Panamanian art anywhere, an excellent collection of works on paper by Latin American artists, and the occasional temporary exhibition by a foreign or national artist.

Panama Canal Murals PUBLIC ART
(Map p628; Balboa; ⊙7:30am-4:15pm Mon-Fri) FREE The story of the monumental effort to build the Panama Canal is powerfully depicted in murals by notable artist William B Van Ingen of New York. The murals are mounted in the rotunda of the Panama Canal Administration Building. The paintings have the distinction of being the largest group of murals by an American artist on display outside the USA.

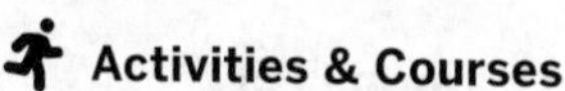

Activities & Courses

Panama Audubon Society OUTDOORS
(Map p628; ☎232-5977; www.audubonpanama.org; Parque Natural Metropolitano visitors center) Organises birding walks and monthly meetings with interesting speakers at the Parque Natural Metropolitano visitors center. It's a good opportunity to get to know some Panamanian birdwatchers and to learn more about tropical bird species. Both English and Spanish are spoken.

Casco Antiguo Spanish School LANGUAGE
(Map p636; ☎228-3258; www.cascospanish.com; Av A s/n; 1-week 20hr intensive US$250; ⊙7am-7pm Mon-Fri, 8am-noon Sat) This recommended Spanish school sits in the heart of Casco Viejo. Group lessons have only four students and private classes are available with excellent instructors. Also offers accommodations and activities.

Tours

Panama Road Trips TOURS
(☎6800-7727; www.panamaroadtrips.com; tours from US$25) This small enterprise runs affordable day trips to Portobelo or an Emberá village in addition to popular canal and city tours. Also works with interesting rural tourism options throughout Panama.

Barefoot Panama TOURS
(Map p636; ☎211-3700; www.barefootpanama.com; cnr Av A & Calle 7; city tour per person US$90;

THE JAZZ SOLUTION

Once a down-and-out section of the city with crumbling architecture and serious poverty, Casco Viejo is coming into a new chapter. Making a strong push toward revitalization, the neighborhood is home to dozens of new restaurants, cafes, shops and renovated historical buildings. In the midst of this architectural revival, another less tangible one struggles to take place: that of the Panamanian music community.

Jazz great and native Panamanian Danilo Perez returned here to the musical conservatory where he learned his first notes to establish **Fundación Danilo Perez** (Map p636; ☎211-0272; www.facebook.com/FundacionDaniloPerez; 1069 Av A, Casco Viejo), a musical foundation that has generated over US$1 million in youth scholarships. It also sponsors the Panama Jazz Festival (p634), a wildly popular citywide event featuring artists from all over the world.

Perez believes the discipline of music helps to create leaders and good citizens who can address the problems of society. Youth are chosen from inner-city Panama and all parts of the country, including Colón and the Comarca de Guna Yala. Some grants take students as far as the Berklee College of Music and the New England Conservatory. Many come back to the music conservatory to teach others and complete the cycle of community participation.

The foundation in Casco Viejo also houses a library and music museum and is open to the public (admission is free).

Central Panama City

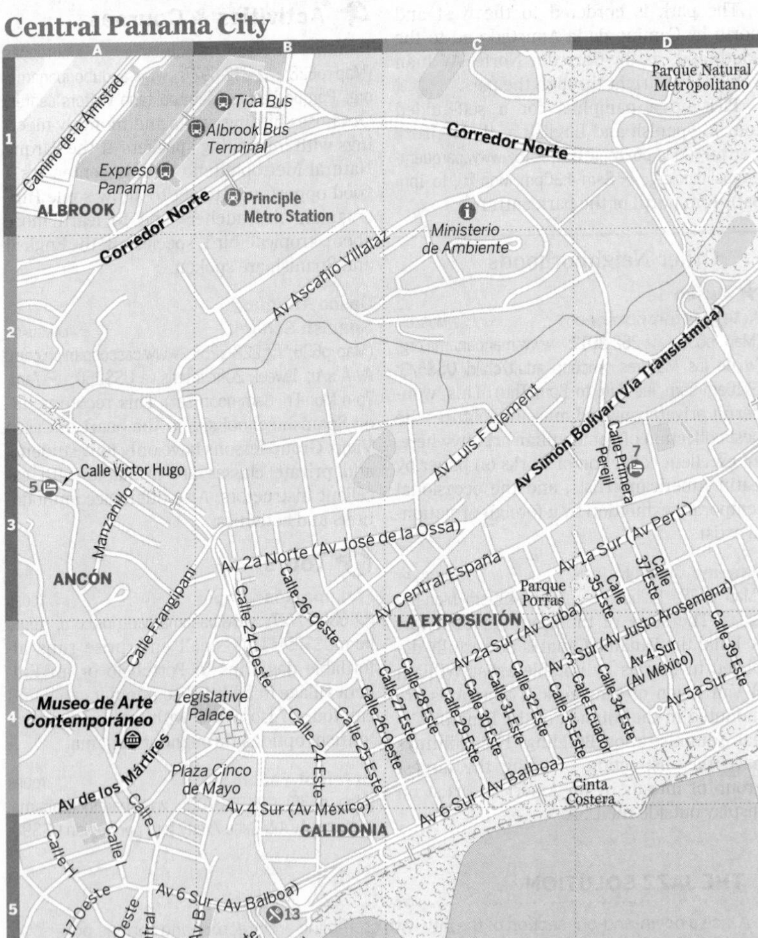

Central Panama City

Top Sights
1 Museo de Arte Contemporáneo A4

Activities, Courses & Tours
2 Ancon Expeditions F3

Sleeping
3 Baru Lodge H1
4 Bristol Panama F3
5 Dos Palmitos A3
6 El Machico G4
7 Mamallena D3
8 Riande Granada Hotel G2
9 Saba Hotel G2
10 W Hotel F3

Eating
11 Avatar G2
12 Hikaru G4
13 Mercado de Mariscos B5
14 Ozone Cafe F4

Drinking & Nightlife
15 La Rana Dorada G1

Entertainment
16 Restaurante-Bar Tinajas F3

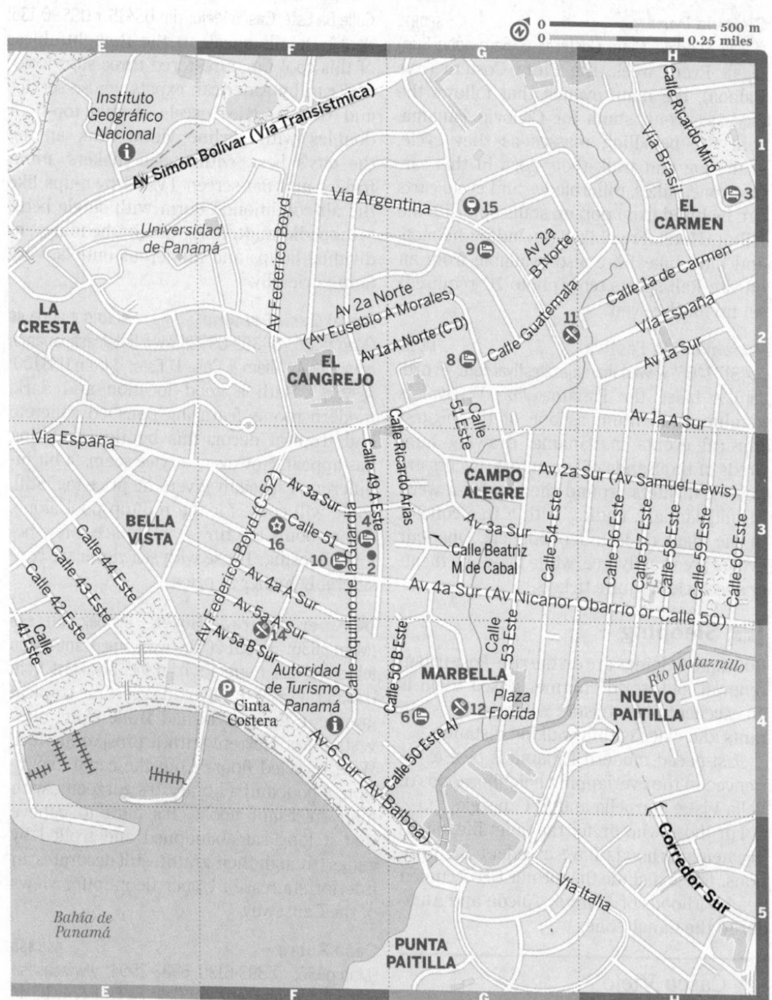

9:30am-6:30pm) Prompt and professional, this American-run agency based in Casco Viejo does a great tour of Panama City that takes in everything from the history to the flora and fauna. They offer 14 different tours, including day trips to San Lorenzo and Gamboa, with visits to a Wounaan indigenous village, and trips throughout the country.

Ancon Expeditions TOURS

(Map p632; 269-9415; www.anconexpeditions.com; Edificio Dorado, 2nd fl, Calle 49a Este, El Cangrejo; 9am-5pm Mon-Fri, to 1pm Sat) A pioneer in Panamanian tour operations, Ancon Expeditions offers city and nationwide tours as well as regularly scheduled canal transits. Try to book in advance as this is one of the company's most popular offerings.

Festivals & Events

Carnaval CULTURAL

(Feb/Mar) Carnaval in Panama City is celebrated with merriment and wild abandon in the days preceding Ash Wednesday, between February and March. From Saturday until the following Tuesday, work is put away and masks, costumes and confetti come out, and for 96 hours almost anything goes.

Ciclovía Panama SPORTS
(Cycle Sunday; Cinta Costera; ⌚6am-noon Sun) FREE Every week, the Cinta Costera (Ave Balboa), the main avenue that follows the city's seafront, shuts for Ciclovía Panama. Join the pedalling masses as they cycle, skate, jog and walk their dogs in this car-free zone. Bikes, rollerblades and cyclo carts can be hired from pop-up stalls opposite the Hilton Hotel. Free bikes (including helmets and kids' bikes) are also available from an on-site Rali sports tent (photo ID required) set up for the event.

Panama Jazz Festival MUSIC
(☎317-1466; www.panamajazzfestival.com; ⌚mid-Jan) A blast, the Panama Jazz Festival is gaining momentum as one of the biggest musical events in Panama, drawing hundreds of thousands of spectators. Events are held in theaters around the city for a week in mid-January, ending with a free concert in the Plaza de la Independencia. Open-air events are usually free, while big-draw theater spectacles require tickets.

Sleeping

Boutique lodgings are on the rise. Post-urban renewal, old-world charmer Casco Viejo is an excellent place to stay, with many restaurants and cafes within walking distance.

Fast-paced modern Panama is best experienced in the overlapping neighborhoods of Bella Vista, Marbella and El Cangrejo.

For those who prefer the quiet life, outlying neighborhoods have excellent B&B options. These include the former US-occupied neighborhoods of Albrook, Ancón and Amador in the Canal Zone.

Casco Viejo

Luna's Castle HOSTEL $
(Map p636; ☎262-1540; www.lunascastlehostel.com; Calle 9a Este; dm/d/tr incl breakfast US$16/37/55; ❄@📶) Housed in a creaky, colonial mansion, Luna's masterfully blends Spanish-colonial architecture with funky, laid-back backpacker vibes and great service. Cavernous dorms feature curtained bunks and air-conditioning. Perks include hammocks, house guitars, free bikes and laundry service. It has long been an iconic meeting point for budget travelers.

★Magnolia Inn INN $$
(Map p636; ☎202-0872, USA 1-786-375-9633; www.magnoliapanama.com; cnr Calle Boquete & Calle 8a Este, Casco Viejo; dm US$15, r US$90-135; ❄📶) Details speak to the thoughtfulness of this cool inn, a restored three-story colonial run by American expats whose service and travel advice excels. Ample top-floor doubles with skyline views rank among the city's best, with coffee makers, mini-fridges and flat-screen TVs. Grown-ups like the air-conditioned dorm with single beds, orthopedic mattresses, quality bedding, individual lamps and numerous outlets. Very family-friendly.

Hotel Casa Panama BOUTIQUE HOTEL $$
(Map p636; ☎303-0992; www.hotelcasapanama.com; cnr Av Alfaro & Calle 11 Este; d from US$100; ❄📶🏊) With a good location and dark, modern rooms featuring polished concrete and tropical decor, this boutique offering has appeal. However, service seems a bit indifferent, especially given the price tag. Still, some will come for the rooftop pool alone. Some rooms are tiny – ask to see a few before choosing. Those with sea views are considerably higher in price.

★American Trade Hotel HISTORIC HOTEL $$$
(Map p636; ☎831-2051; www.americantradehotel.com; Plaza Herrera s/n; d incl breakfast from US$350; P❄📶🏊) Evoking old-time tropical grandeur, the refurbished Trade Hotel reinvests Plaza Herrera with a prosperous feel. With recycled floors from the canal expansion, a pool and a library, it's gorgeous, with many pleasant nooks. It's hard to believe that it long sat abandoned and trolled by gangs (though their graffiti still decorates an interior staircase). Upper floors offer views of the Causeway.

Casa Sucre B&B $$$
(Map p636; ☎393-6130, 6982-2504; www.casasucreboutiquehotel.com; cnr Calle 8a Este & Av B; d/apt incl breakfast US$140/150; ❄📶) Set in an 1873 convent, this American-run B&B features plush lodgings amid family heirlooms and period furniture. The setting is serene, with a wraparound balcony overlooking the action of Casco Viejo. Watch for the friendly ghost rumored to dwell on the entrance staircase. There's also a downstairs cafe with great coffee, run by California natives Alyce and Rich.

Calidonia & Bella Vista

Mamallena HOSTEL $
(Map p632; ☎393-6611, 6676-6163; www.mamallena.com; Calle Primera Perejil, Calidonia; dm/d incl

breakfast US$13/33;) On a residential street that's somehow survived the wrecking ball, this small, homey hostel nails the mark on service. Amenities include 24-hour desk service, pancake breakfasts, a guest kitchen and DVD library. High-ceilinged dorms have air-con at night and the cute motel-style doubles offer considerable privacy. The on-site travel agency offers sailing to San Blas and popular day trips.

Saba Hotel HOTEL $$
(Map p632; 201-6100; www.thesabahotel.com; Vía Argentina s/n, Bella Vista; s/d US$48/60;) Modern and cheerful, the Saba is great value in Bella Vista. With lots of glass and bamboo, there's a sustainable theme that's probably more stylish than substantial. Amenities like iPod docks and flat-screen TVs are appreciated. Under new administration, service is attentive.

Bristol Panama HOTEL $$$
(Map p632; 265-7844; www.thebristol.com; Calle Aquilino de la Guardia, Bella Vista; d incl breakfast from US$270;) The elegant Bristol features oriental carpets, flamboyant orchids and precious woods, and that's just the lobby. Rooms are refined and lovely. No more do-not-disturb tags here: heat sensors determine if rooms are occupied. Other five-star amenities include a spa, 24-hour butler service and free cell-phone loan. The restaurant is run by an award-winning Panamanian chef.

W Hotel LUXURY HOTEL $$$
(Map p632; 309-7500; www.starwoodhotels.com/whotels; cnr Calle 50 & Calle Aquilino de la Guardia, Bella Vista; d/ste US$200/400;) Opened in 2018, this 203-room downtown high rise takes inspiration from the Panama Canal and the country's diverse cultures. Not your parents' luxury hotel, it's playful-modern, with colorful shipping containers, chairs upholstered in Congo dress 'rags' patterns and wall displays of woven hats. Bright rooms feature floor-to-ceiling windows and floating beds rimmed with LED lighting underneath. Staff aim to please.

El Cangrejo & San Francisco

El Machico HOSTEL $
(Map p632; 203-9430, 6473-5905; www.elmachicohostel.com; Calle 47 Este 2, Marbella; dm/d US$16/50;) In a suburban two-story, this stylish and popular Italian-run hostel indulges your inner kid with projected movies in the swimming pool, a PlayStation and foldable bikes for rent (US$10 per day). Also offers cheap tours, including to San Blas. Dorms sleep six to 12 people with blessed air-conditioning that runs at night. Doubles are relatively bare for the price tag.

Baru Lodge B&B $$
(Map p632; 393-2340; www.barulodge.com; Calle 2a Norte H-7, El Carmen; s/d incl breakfast US$70/80;) Tasteful and cordial, this inn sits on a residential street central to the action. Rooms are sleek and modern, with subdued colors and soft lighting. The English-speaking owner makes guests right at home. Cable TV, fast wi-fi and air purifiers are among the perks. Continental breakfasts are served on a garden patio with wicker seating.

Riande Granada Hotel DESIGN HOTEL $$
(Map p632; 204-4444, 291-9000; http://riandehoteles.com; Av Eusebio A Morales, El Cangrejo; d US$90;) With a chic look and feel, good-value Riande is popular with the millennial crowd. Spare and modern, it's clad in dripping foliage and a curtain of cascading water. There's a reputable restaurant and beer garden with an enormous wooden lounge deck around the outdoor pool. Rooms feature minifridges and flat-screen TVs.

Canal Zone

Dos Palmitos B&B $$
(Map p632; 6051-4723; www.panamabedandbreakfast.com; Calle Victor Hugo 0532B, Cerro Ancón; s/d incl breakfast US$80/85;) If your attraction to Panama is more about wildlife than wild life, check out this tucked-away French B&B. There are just four rooms, decorated with retro posters and vintage newsclips and featuring immaculate wooden floors, king-size beds and wicker furniture. The backyard terrace offers birdwatching and abundant breakfasts featuring homemade bread and fresh juice. Also offers transportation and tours.

Country Inn & Suites HOTEL $$
(Map p628; 211-4500; www.countryinns.com/panamacanalpan; cnr Avs Amador & Pelicano, Amador; d US$100;) They say there are only two lodgings overlooking the canal: one is the prison that once held Noriega, the other is this chain hotel. Though reminiscent of a retirement community in Panama City, Florida, it's well run and good value, with causeway access and a huge swimming pool. Rooms boast private balconies overlooking the Puente de las Américas.

Casco Viejo

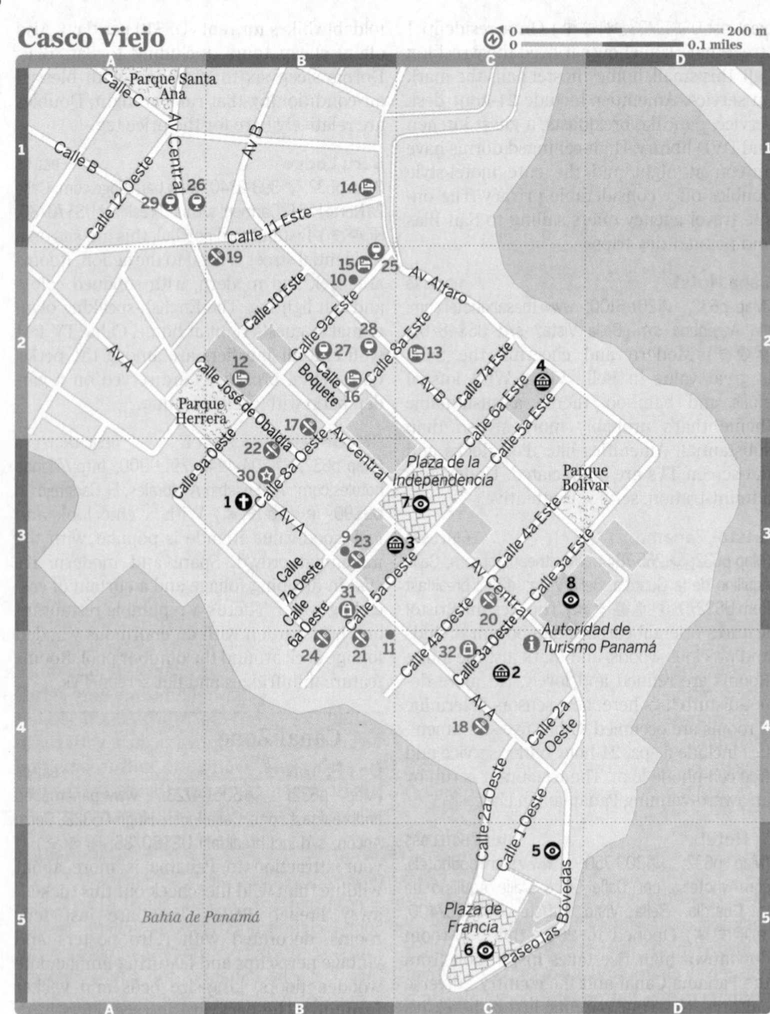

Eating

Casco Viejo

★Granclement GELATO $

(Map p636; www.granclement.com; Av Central; gelato US$3.50-5; ⊙12:30pm-9pm Mon-Fri, to 10pm Sat, 10am-8pm Sun) Pure pleasure defines these intense tropical-fruit gelatos and rich, creamy flavors such as orange-chocolate, coffee and ginger. A few scoops of these fussy French creations will sweeten a leisurely stroll through the Casco.

★Mercado de Mariscos MARKET $

(Map p632; ☎506-5741; Av Balboa; mains US$3-14; ⊙6am-5pm) Get your seafood fix above a bustling fish market. Come early, as service at peak time is painfully slow. Gems include whole fried fish and cavernous bowls of 'Get Up Lazarus' soup (a sure hangover cure). Outside, stands ladle out delicious US$3 plastic cups of *ceviche,* including classic concoctions, Mediterranean style (with olives) and curry.

★Super Gourmet DELI $

(Map p636; ☎212-3487; www.supergourmetcascoviejo.com; Av A; mains US$3-9; ⊙8am-5pm

Casco Viejo

Sights

1 Iglesia de San José B3
2 Museo de Arte Religioso Colonial C4
3 Museo del Canal Interoceánico C3
4 Palacio de las Garzas C2
5 Paseo las Bóvedas C5
6 Plaza de Francia C5
7 Plaza de la Independencia C3
8 Teatro Nacional C3

Activities, Courses & Tours

9 Barefoot Panama B3
10 Cacique Cruiser B2
11 Casco Antiguo Spanish School B4

Sleeping

12 American Trade Hotel B2
13 Casa Sucre C2
14 Hotel Casa Panama B1
15 Luna's Castle B2
16 Magnolia Inn B2

Eating

17 Barrio Pizza B2
18 Caffe Per Due C4
19 Donde José B2
20 Granclement C3
21 Lo Que Hay B4
22 Ochoymedio B3
23 Super Gourmet B3
24 Tropical Chocolate Cafe B4

Drinking & Nightlife

25 Bar Relic B2
26 Casa Jaguar A1
27 La Rana Dorada B2
28 Tántalo Bar B2
29 The Stranger's Club A1

Entertainment

30 Fundación Danilo Perez B3
Teatro Nacional .... (see 8)

Shopping

31 Casa Latina B3
32 Karavan C4

Mon-Sat, 10am-4pm Sun;) With the cheeriest staff around, Super Gourmet is a favorite of both locals and travelers. Stop by the air-conditioned cafe for traditional soups, fresh tropical juices or a baguette deli sandwich done American style. For breakfast, eggs on English muffins with cheese, bacon or vegetables or *arepas* (savory corn cakes) with an espresso drink hit the spot.

Tropical Chocolate Cafe CAFE $

(Map p636; 388-6843; www.facebook.com/tropicalchocolatecafe; Calle 6; bonbons US$2-10; 10am-7pm; ; Mercado de Mariscos) With red velvet chairs and lush tropical-themed wallpaper, this button-cute chocolate shop and cafe serves beautifully adorned natural bonbons: 100% Panamanian chocolate meets local pineapple, chili and cilantro. Coinciding with Sunday brunch, the cafe hosts story time for children at 10am and chocolate tastings by reservation (US$30 per person, two participants).

Barrio Pizza PIZZA $

(Map p636; 393-4444; www.barriopizza.com; Av Central s/n; mains US$8-13; 11am-11pm;) Happiness is blistering wood-fired pizza cooked to order and topped with truffle oil, roasted eggplant or meatballs. The simple menu also has Caesar salads, wine and beer. Come early for a seat.

Caffe Per Due ITALIAN $

(Map p636; 228-0547; Av A; mains US$5-12; 9am-10pm Tue-Sun;) Our pick for a quick bite, this never-fail Italian-run eatery serves scrumptious thin-crust pizzas. Check out the award-winning pizza bianca, with roasted garlic, brie, truffle oil, mushrooms and sun-dried tomatoes. For privacy, try the tiny brick courtyard with a couple of tables.

★ **Lo Que Hay** PANAMANIAN $$

(Map p636; Calle 5 Oeste s/n; mains US$12-20; noon-3pm & 6:30-10pm Thu-Sat, 11am-4:30pm Sun) Neighborhood *fondas* (cheap restaurants) serve cheap Panamanian classics, but this one – by Panama's top chef – delivers a massive twist. Sexy rice *(concolón)* has a crust of crisp perfection, served with smoked tomatoes or fragrant clams. There's also tender whole fish, yucca tostadas with carpaccio and mango kimchee served as streetside *encurtido*. It's overpacked, not air-conditioned and good fun. End with a massive *raspado* (shaved ice flavored with fruit).

★ **Donde José** PANAMANIAN $$$

(Map p636; 262-1682; www.dondejose.com; Av Central s/n; 8-course meal US$80, chef bar US$90; 7pm & 9:30pm seatings Tue-Sat) Elevating humble Panamanian staples to haute cuisine, this 16-seat eatery is Panama's hottest reservation. Chef Jose prepares *ñandu* beans (native black beans), crisp, tender pork and *ñame* (an indigenous tuber) in playful, revelatory fashion. Servers have an intimate, casual rapport through a cascade of eight courses. Reservations are best made months in advance. Drinks are extra.

★Ochoymedio FUSION $$$
(Map p636; ☎209-4185; www.ochoymediopanama.com; Calle José de Obaldía, btwn Calles 8 & 9; ⏲7-11pm Mon-Sun) Under hanging vines and fairy lights, this gastronomical garden by Michelin-starred chef Andres Madrigal is romance incarnate. Start with a tropical-style lychee *ceviche*. Keep it fresh and light with an arugula salad or spicy langostino yakitori. Opt for a table in the inner courtyard and kick-start your evening with an excellent cocktail named for a Beatles song. Service is great.

El Cangrejo & San Francisco

Miranda Bakery & Cafe CAFE $
(Map p628; ☎226-4014; www.facebook.com/mirandabakery; cnr Calle 75 Este & Calle Andres Mojíca, San Francisco; mains US$10-14; ⏲9am-6:45pm Mon-Fri, to 5pm Sat) This wonderful homestyle bakery and cafe gets packed with locals hungry for sourdough, fresh bagels and amazing fat burgers with crispy french fries, homemade hot sauce optional. There's also a velvety lava cake worth trying, plus good espresso and artisanal beer. The baked goods run out before noon.

Restaurante Vietnamita VIETNAMESE $
(Map p628; ☎394-6923; Casa 7a, Calle 68 Este, San Francisco; mains US$7-9; ⏲11am-10pm) Fragrant *pho* (broth with noodles) with brisket, garlicky sea bass with gangalal, and barbecued pork over rice noodles are some of the mouthwatering specialties at this authentic eatery with friendly owners from Hanoi. A cold beer or avocado smoothie and you're all set.

★Hikaru JAPANESE $$
(Map p632; ☎203-5087; www.hikaru.restaurant; Calle 50 Este Alley, Marbella; mains US$10-16; ⏲noon-2:30pm & 6-11pm Mon-Sat) For authentic Japanese food prepared by a Tokyo chef, this unassuming alleyside restaurant is pay dirt. While Hikaru serves good sushi and sashimi, you would be amiss not to sample the ramen noodles, prepared in a complex, buttery broth, or *takoyaki* (melt-in-your-mouth octopus fritters). Start with a cold Sapporo beer and some edamame in rock salt. Reservations recommended for dinner.

Botanica CAFE $$
(Map p628; ☎270-1111; http://botanicapanama.com; 6 Calle Esther Neira de Calvo, San Francisco; mains US$14-19; ⏲noon-10:30pm Tue-Sat, to 9pm Sun; 🖉) 🌿 An Instagram darling, this clean-style eatery from Mario Castrellon caters to gourmet tastes on a budget. Think bubbly pizza topped with lobster or manchego cheese and greens, tropical salads from the house garden and more. Tries to source quality ingredients from regional providers. Indoor and outdoor seating and delivery.

Avatar INDIAN $$
(Map p632; ☎393-9006; www.avatarindiancuisine.com; cnr Vías Argentina & España, El Cangrejo; mains US$9-16; ⏲11am-11pm) Serving rich kormas, fragrant rice and complex curries in a swanky piano bar, Canadian-run Avatar is sheer delight for spice enthusiasts. Southern Indian cuisine is the house specialty, though if you want it really hot you will have to insist. On weekdays, lunch is 25% off.

★Maito PANAMANIAN $$$
(Map p628; ☎391-4657; www.maitopanama.com; Av 3m Sur, San Francisco; mains US$16-25; ⏲noon-10:30pm Mon-Sat) 🌿 With style and pedigree, Maito toys with the classics, folding in everyday Caribbean, Latin and Chinese influences. While results are mixed, it's still worthwhile. Start with a watermelon Waldorf salad. Ribs glazed in passion fruit are tender but lack the crispness of the duck chow mein. Seafood risotto in squid ink proves divine. There's garden seating and impeccable service.

Bella Vista

Ozone Cafe INTERNATIONAL $$
(Map p632; ☎214-9616; www.ozonecafepanama.com; Calle Uruguay; mains US$10-22; ⏲noon-3pm & 6-10pm) Packed with worker bees at midday, Ozone is a local fixture serving enormous, fragrant portions of good food from 110 countries. There are even kosher and halal options. It's too bad the ambience is wanting – the dark location was once a garage. It's also hard to find – look closely for the sign.

Drinking & Nightlife

Bars and clubs open and close with alarming frequency in Panama City, though generally speaking, nightlife is sophisticated and fairly pricey. The well-to-do denizens of the capital love a good scene, so it's worth scrubbing up and donning some nice threads. Remember to bring ID. Most clubs have a cover charge of US$10 to US$25.

Big areas for nightlife include Casco Viejo, San Francisco and Bella Vista's Calle Uruguay. The current boom in craft beer has people hitting small breweries.

La Rana Dorada MICROBREWERY
(Map p636; ☎392-0660; www.laranadorada.com; cnr Calle 9 & Calle Boquete, Casco Viejo; ⌚noon-12:30am Sun-Wed, to 3am Thu-Sat) Replete with brass fixtures and polished wood bars, this gorgeous low-lit brewpub serves its own award-winning small craft beers, alongside tasty thin-crust pizzas or bratwursts (mains US$3 to US$9). After-work happy hour is just catching on, but it goes gangbusters here in indoor and outdoor spaces. A second location is on **Vía Argentina** (Map p632; ☎269-2989; Vía Argentina 20, El Cangrejo; ⌚noon-2am).

Casa Jaguar CLUB
(Map p636; ☎6866-8483; http://casajaguarpanama.com; Av Central s/n; ⌚8pm-2am Tue-Thu, to 4am Fri & Sat) Don your stilettos and glitter for a night out at the Casco's hottest club, located on the 2nd floor next to Teatro Amador. There's no hurry, though, as things don't heat up until late at night, with dedicated reggaetón and electronica rooms in addition to smaller nooks and crannies. Check the website for theme nights.

The Stranger's Club COCKTAIL BAR
(Map p636; ☎282-0064; www.facebook.com/strangersclubpanama; Av Central s/n; ⌚6pm-2am Mon-Wed, to 4am Thu-Sat, noon-4pm & 6pm-midnight Sun) For a buzzy scene of 20- to 40-somethings, duck into this dimly lit cocktail bar. The Consuelo, a revelation of muddled cucumber, gin and elderflower liqueur, is worth the trip in itself.

Tántalo Bar COCKTAIL BAR
(Map p636; http://tantalohotel.com/roofbar; cnr Calle 8a Este & Av B, Casco Viejo; cover US$5-10; ⌚rooftop deck 5pm-2am) Though it serves casual lunches, this ultra-hip cafe-bar is best known for sunset happy hours on its rooftop deck. Pair your cocktail with fusion-style tapas. Cover is charged after 10pm, but to get a spot on the tiny roof deck, show up around 7pm. Wednesday is salsa night.

Bar Relic BAR
(Map p636; www.relicbar.com; Calle 9a Este, Casco Viejo; ⌚9pm-2am Tue-Sat) Wildly popular with travelers and hip young Panamanians, this cavernous hostel bar is a hit. Service is friendly and patrons easily mingle in the ample courtyard with shared picnic tables. Not only are you partying outside (a rarity in Panama City) but you're also next to the historical wall of the city.

☆ Entertainment

Restaurante-Bar Tinajas DANCE
(Map p632; ☎263-7890; Av 3a A Sur, Bella Vista; entry US$5; ⌚noon-10:30pm Mon-Sat) A good opportunity to see traditional Panamanian folk dancing, this dinner show is a classic. Sure it's touristy, but it's nicely done just the same. Shows are held Wednesday to Saturday at 9pm with a US$12 minimum per person for drinks and food. Reservations recommended.

Teatro Nacional THEATER
(Map p636; ☎262-3525; Av B, Casco Viejo) Casco Viejo's lovely 19th-century playhouse stages ballet, concerts and plays.

Shopping

★Karavan ART
(Map p636; ☎228-7177; www.karavan-gallery.com; Calle 3a Oeste, Casco Viejo; ⌚10am-6pm Mon-Sat, 11am-3:30pm Sun) An excellent place to find original Guna embroidery with modern designs and Congo art from Portobelo, Karavan commissions local artists, works closely to develop new talent and recovers endangered culture and arts through nonprofit Fundación Mua Mua. Artisans work on-site.

Casa Latina ARTS & CRAFTS
(Map p636; ☎228-9828; cnr Av A & Calle 5, Casco Viejo; ⌚10am-7pm) Colorful Casa Latina has a large selection of beautiful handicrafts, ranging from the affordable to a Panama hat on sale for US$2500! Some of the items on collectors' lists include the detailed animal masks made by the Embera people and the handmade baskets created by women of the Waunaan communities.

Mercado Nacional de Artesanías MARKET
(National Artisans Market; Map p628; Panamá Viejo; ⌚9am-4pm Mon-Sat, to 1pm Sun) A great place to shop for memorable souvenirs.

Orientation

Panama City stretches about 20km along the Pacific coast, from the Panama Canal at its western end to the ruins of Panamá Viejo to the east.

Near the canal are Albrook airport, the Causeway and the wealthy Balboa and Ancón suburbs, first built for US canal and military workers. The colonial part of the city, Casco Viejo, juts into the sea on the southwestern side of town. In the south, the Causeway has numerous restaurants, bars and fine vantage points on the edge of the ocean.

Av Central is the main drag that runs through Casco Viejo. At a fork further east, the avenue becomes Av Central España; the section that traverses the El Cangrejo business and financial district is called Vía España. The other part of the fork becomes Av Simón Bolívar and, finally, Vía Transístmica as it heads out of town and across the isthmus toward Colón.

Information

DANGERS & ANNOYANCES

- Generally speaking, the tip of Casco Viejo southeast of Calle 12 Este and Calle 13 Este is safe for tourists and patrolled by police officers. Inland (north of Parque Herrera and Parque Santa Ana), there are high-density slums.
- Other high-crime areas to avoid include Curundú, Chorrillo, Santa Ana, San Miguelito and Río Abajo.
- Calle Uruguay, a clubbing hub, attracts opportunists. Don't take your full wallet out at night and avoid too-friendly strangers, specifically women, who are known to grope for wallets.
- Taxis generally allow unrelated passengers to share the cab, but robberies do occasionally occur. It's best to avoid taxis that already have a passenger. If you speak Spanish, you can offer a slightly higher fare to keep your taxi to yourself. Evaluate any taxi you hail before getting in (check for door handles and taxi licensing numbers). It's very common for taxi drivers to refuse fares to destinations simply for their own convenience.
- There are occasional reports of robbery near the ruins of Panamá Viejo – don't go after sunset, and always keep an eye out.
- When walking the streets of Panama City, be aware that drivers do not yield to pedestrians. Sometimes it's best to approach intersections like Panamanians – look both ways, then run like hell.

MEDICAL SERVICES

Medical care in Panama, especially in Panama City, is of a high standard.

Centro Médico Paitilla (☎265-8800; http://centromedicopaitilla.com; cnr Calle 53 Este & Av Balboa, Paitilla; ⏲24hr) This medical center has well-trained physicians who speak both Spanish and English.

Centro Metropolitano de Salud (☎512-9100; www.minsa.gob.pa/region-de-salud/region-metropolitana-de-salud; Calle Principal 237, Los Ríos; ⏲8am-noon & 1-3pm Mon-Fri) Offers yellow-fever vaccinations with international certificate (required for travel to Colombia if returning) for a minimal charge. Located in the Canal Zone.

MONEY

ATMs are abundant throughout the city. The Banco Nacional de Panamá counter at Tocumen International Airport is one of the few places in Panama City that exchanges foreign currency.

Panacambios (☎223-1800; ground fl, Plaza Regency Bldg, Vía España, El Cangrejo; ⏲8am-5pm Mon-Fri) buys and sells international currencies.

TOURIST INFORMATION

Autoridad de Turismo Panamá (Panama Tourism Authority) offices give out free maps. The usefulness of a given office depends on the employees; few speak English.

Autoridad de Turismo Panamá (ATP; Map p632; ☎526-7000; www.visitpanama.com; 29th fl, Edificio Bisca, cnr Av Balboa & Aquilino de la Guardia, Bella Vista; ⏲8:30am-3pm Mon-Fri) Panama's tourism bureau is headquartered in a highrise next to the Hilton hotel. There's also an ATP booth in **Casco Viejo** (Map p636; ☎211-3365; www.atp.gob.pa; Av Central s/n; ⏲8:30am-4pm).

Ministero de Ambiente (p689) Formerly known as ANAM, the Ministry of the Environment can occasionally provide maps and information on national parks. However, it is not set up to provide much assistance to tourists.

Getting There & Away

AIR

International flights arrive at and depart from **Tocumen International Airport** (PTY; Panama City; ☎238-2700; www.tocumenpanama.aero; Av Domingo Díaz; ⏲24hr), 35km northeast of the city center. It's in the process of undergoing a major expansion that should expand offerings considerably. Domestic flights and a few international flights depart from **Albrook Airport** (Aeropuerto Marcos A Gelabert; Map p628; ☎501-9272; Av Canfield, Albrook) in the former Albrook Air Force Station near the canal.

Air Panama (☎316-9000; www.airpanama.com; Albrook Airport) covers domestic routes and has its own travel agency. International carrier **Copa Airlines** (☎217-2672; www.copaair.com; Av Central s/n, Casco Viejo; ⏲8am-6pm Mon-Fri, 9am-1pm Sat) now flies to domestic destinations as well.

Flights within Panama are inexpensive and short – few are longer than an hour. However, if

GETTING INTO TOWN

Tocumen International Airport Located 33km northeast of the city center. The cheapest way to get into the city is to exit the terminal, cross the street (to the bus shelter) and catch a bus to the city. The 10-minute walk might seem longer with luggage. Taxis (around US$30) can be hired at the Transportes Turísticos desk at the airport exit; they're much faster than the bus.

Albrook Airport North of Cerro Ancón; handles domestic flights. A taxi ride to downtown should cost between US$5 and US$8.

Albrook Bus Terminal All long-distance buses arrive here; from here there are connections throughout the city. Routes are displayed in the front window; fares are US$0.35. After dark, take a taxi (US$3 to US$7) to your destination.

traveling to Darién Province, Isla Contadora or the Comarca de Guna Yala, it's quite possible that the plane may make multiple stops. Prices vary according to season and availability.

BOAT

There are regular ferries to Islas Taboga and Contadora, leaving from Panama City's Causeway and the Balboa Yacht Club.

Barcos Calypso (☎314-1730; Balboa Yacht Club, Amador Causeway; round trip adult/child US$15/10.50) Departures to Isla Taboga at 8:30am weekdays, plus 3pm Friday, and at 8am, 10:30am and 4pm weekends.

Ferry Taboga (Roka-Nk; Map p628; ☎6892-4844, 391-6605; https://rokapanama.com/ferry; Balboa Yacht Club, Causeway; adult/child round trip US$20/14) Daily service to Isla Taboga from Balboa Yacht Club at 8:30am, 10am and 3:45pm.

Sea Las Perlas (☎391-1424; www.sealasperlas.com; Brisas de Amador, Perico Island Causeway; adult/child one way US$49/39) This catamaran ferry service departs for Isla Contadora daily at 7:30am, returning at 3:30pm. The journey takes one hour and 40 minutes.

Taboga Express (☎6234-8989; www.tabogaexpress.com; Brisas de Amador, Isla Perico; round trip adult/child US$20/14) This catamaran is your fastest option to Taboga (30 minutes one way). Departs daily from Isla Perico on the Causeway at 8am, 9:30am, 11am, 3pm and 4:30pm. There are four returns daily.

BUS

Albrook Bus Terminal (Gran Terminal; Map p632; ☎303-3030; www.grantnt.com; Albrook; ⏲24hr), near Albrook Airport, is a convenient and modern one-stop location for most buses leaving Panama City. The terminal includes a food court, banks, shops, a sports bar, a storage room, bathrooms and showers. A mall, complete with supermarket and cinema, is located next door.

Both **Expreso Panama** (Map p632; ☎314-6837; www.expresopanama.com; Albrook Bus Terminal, Office 13-14) and **Tica Bus** (Map p632; ☎314-6385; www.ticabus.com; Albrook Bus Terminal, Stand 32) serve San José (Costa Rica); see their websites for hours.

Canal Zone buses depart from the Albrook terminal for Balboa and Clayton, Miraflores Locks, and Gamboa, leaving every 45 minutes. Those going to Clayton and intermediary stops are run by Metrobus.

CAR

Rental rates start at US$22 per day for the most economical cars, including unlimited kilometers. Insurance is considerably extra.

Tolls are your responsibility and carry heavy fines if unpaid. Make sure your dashboard toll sticker has credit before using it: use the ID number to refill the account in any supermarket.

Budget (☎263-8777; www.budgetpanama.com; Tocumen International Airport; ⏲24hr)

Hertz (☎301-2696; www.hertzpanama.com.pa; Tocumen International Airport; ⏲24hr)

National (☎275-7222; www.nationalpanama.com; Tocumen International Airport; ⏲24hr)

TRAIN

The **Panama Canal Railway Company** (PCRC; ☎317-6070; www.panarail.com; Carretera Gaillard, Corozal; one way adult/child US$25/15) operates a glass-domed train that takes passengers on a lovely ride from Panama City to Colón on weekdays, departing at 7:15am and returning at 5:15pm. The train follows the canal, at times engulfed by dense vine-strewn jungle. If you want to relive the heyday of luxury train travel for an hour or two, this is definitely the way to do it.

Note that Panama City's terminus is actually located in the town of Corozal, a 15-minute cab ride from the capital.

Getting Around

BICYCLE

You can rent bicycles in some hostels and at the Causeway. **Bicicletas Moses** (Map p628; ☎211-2718; Amador Causeway; per hour from US$4;

⌚9am-7pm) operates a booth with mountain bikes, tandems, bicycle carts and kids' bikes for rent.

BUS

Panama City has almost finished phasing out its *diablos rojos* (red devils) for modern, safe, air-conditioned Metrobus buses.

Most local buses are on the Metrobus system with designated bus stops. Rides cost between US$0.35 and $1.35, with the higher cost for *corredor* (highway) routes. Cash is not accepted.

Passengers must buy a Rapi-Pass (http://tarjetametrobus.com; US$2) at a special kiosk in Albrook Bus Terminal or at designated locations (such as supermarkets or main bus stops, all listed on the website). If you don't have one, try offering another passenger reimbursement for swiping their card. It also deducts the terminal tax at Albrook.

Buses run along the three major west–east routes: Av Central–Vía España, Av Balboa–Vía Israel and Av Simón Bolívar–Vía Transístmica. The Av Central–Vía España streets are one way going west for much of the route; eastbound buses use Av Perú and Av 4 Sur – these buses will take you into the banking district of El Cangrejo. Buses also run along Av Ricardo J Alfaro (known as Tumba Muerto).

Metrobuses stop at official bus stops and Albrook Bus Terminal near Albrook Airport.

From Albrook Bus Terminal, airport buses (US$1.25, one to 1½ hours) marked 'Tocumen Corredor' depart every 15 minutes to Tocumen airport.

METRO

Panama City's mostly underground transportation system is known as **El Metro** (☎504-7200; www.elmetrodepanama.com; fare US$0.35-1.35; ⌚5am-11pm Mon-Fri, to 10pm Sat, 7am-10pm Sun). Línea 1 runs west–east from Albrook and then north to San Isidro. There are plans for Línea 2 between Av Cincuentenario until the district of Chepo, with links to Tocumen Airport, and Línea 3 between Albrook and the City of Knowledge. The main terminal is across from Albrook Bus Terminal. Fares are paid with the same swipe card used for the Metrobus system.

TAXI

Taxis are plentiful but problematic. Some drivers do not travel (or even know) the whole city, so don't be surprised if they leave you standing on the sidewalk upon hearing your destination.

Taxis are not metered, but there is a list of standard fares that drivers are supposed to charge, measured by zones. One zone runs a

BUSES FROM PANAMA CITY

DESTINATION	COST (US$)	DURATION (HR)	FREQUENCY (DAILY)
Aguadulce	6.35	3	33
Antón	5	2	every 20min
Cañita	3	2½	11
Chame	2.60	1¼	37
Changuinola	29	10	8pm
Chitré	10	4	hourly
Colón	3.50	2	every 20min
David	15-19	7-8	15
El Copé	6	4	9
El Valle	4.25	2½	hourly
Las Tablas	10	4½	hourly
Macaracas	10	5	5
Paso Canoas	17-22	8	5
Penonomé	5.25	2½	48
Pesé	9.65	4½	6
San Carlos	3.25	1½	25
San José (Costa Rica)	40	16	1
Santiago	9	4	20
Soná	10	6	6
Villa de Los Santos	9	4	18
Yaviza	16	6-8	8

minimum of US$3; Canal Zone destinations run up to US$15. An average ride, crossing a couple of zones, would cost US$4 to US$6, and more for additional passengers, holidays or if it's late night. Always agree on a fare before you get into the cab, or better yet, ask your hotel to estimate the fare to your destination and then simply hand the driver the money upon arriving. Taxis can also be rented by the hour.

Watch out for unmarked large-model US cars serving hotels as cabs. Their prices are up to four times that of regular street taxis.

America Libre (☎800-8294)

Radio Taxi America (☎221-1932)

Taxi Unico Cooperativa (☎221-8258)

RIDE SHARING

Companies like Uber and Cabify offer an alternative solution to taking a taxi. They are cheaper and more convenient in off-peak hours. Note that Tocumen International Airport does not allow them to give curbside service.

AROUND PANAMA CITY

No visit to Panama City would be complete without taking a day trip to its famous waterway – just remember that the Canal Zone is much, much more than just the canal. The rainforest surrounding the canal is easily accessed and one of the best places to view a variety of Central American wildlife.

Panama Canal

One of the world's greatest marvels, the Panama Canal stretches 80km from Panama City on the Pacific side to Colón on the Atlantic side. Around 14,500 vessels pass through each year, and ships worldwide have traditionally been built with the dimensions of the canal's original locks (330m long and 33.5m wide) in mind.

The canal has three sets of double locks: Miraflores and Pedro Miguel on the Pacific side and Gatún on the Atlantic. A 10-year expansion completed in 2016 added two three-chambered locks, allowing the passage of super-sized 'neoPanamax' ships: Cocoli on the Pacific and Agua Clara on the Atlantic. Between the locks, ships pass through a huge artificial lake, Lago Gatún, created by the Gatún Dam across the Río Chagres, and the Culebra Cut, a 12.7km trough through the mountains. With each ship's passage, a staggering 197 million liters of fresh water are released into the ocean.

Sights

Miraflores Visitors Center MUSEUM

(☎276-8617; http://visitcanaldepanama.com/en/centro-de-visitantes-de-miraflores; adult/child US$15/10; ⌚8am-6pm) The easiest way to visit the Panama Canal is to head to the Miraflores Visitors Center, just outside Panama City. This modern center features a four-floor interactive museum that looks at the canal's history, operations, expansion and ecology, an instructive 15-minute film and several viewing platforms, including the main one on the 4th floor with panoramic views of canal transits (the best times are from 9am to 11am and from 3pm to 5pm when transits are more frequent).

There is a direct bus to the Miraflores Visitors Center from the Albrook Bus Terminal (p641) in Panama City, but it is infrequent. Otherwise take a Paraíso or Gamboa bus from the terminal. These pass along the canal-side highway to Gamboa and will let you off at the 'Miraflores Locks' sign (US$0.35) on the highway, 12km from the city center. It's about a 15-minute walk along the main road to the locks from the sign. You can also take a taxi; drivers will typically wait 30 minutes at the locks and then drive you back to the capital. Expect to pay no more than US$30 round trip, but agree on the price beforehand.

Pedro Miguel Locks CANAL

FREE North past the Miraflores Locks, the Pedro Miguel Locks can be seen from the highway to Gamboa. One hundred meters beyond the locks there's a parking strip from where onlookers can watch ships transit the canal.

Tours

★ **Yala Tours** ADVENTURE

(☎232-0215, 6641-6676; www.yalatourspanama.com) This small Swiss-run operation provides specialized trips throughout Panama, including day trips to Gamboa and the Canal Zone. A highlight is kayaking Río Chagres and Lago Gatún (US$160) while watching canal ships mow through. Also offers a canal-boat tour in Lago Gatún, wildlife-watching and hiking in Parque Nacional Soberanía (US$70), and cultural visits to an Emberá village.

Manakin Adventures Panama TOURS

(☎6384-4466, 908-9621; www.manakinadventures.com; canal/islands tour per person from

Panama Canal

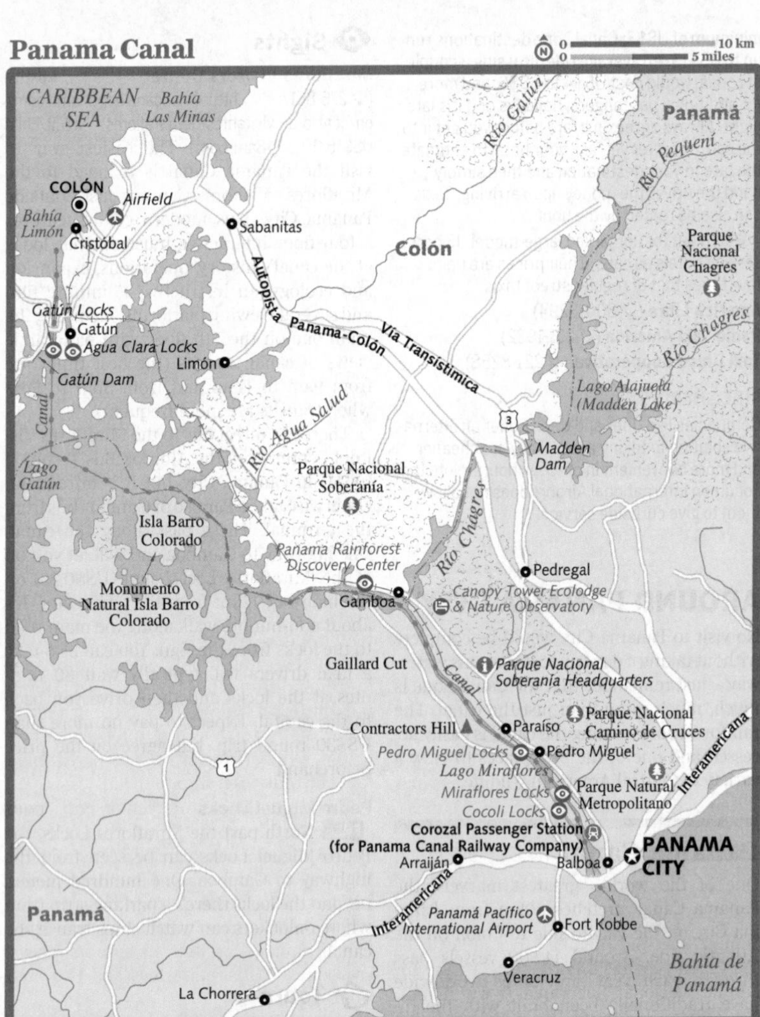

PANAMA PANAMA CANAL

US$60/70) This highly recommended agency knows the Panama Canal better than most and leads half-day tours to the Miraflores Visitors Center (p643) and Canal Zone. Nature lovers will want to join the boating trip on Lago Gatún to watch container ships in transit, stopping off at one of the lake's islands to meet and feed a colony of Geoffroy's tamarin monkeys.

Canal & Bay Tours BOATING
(☎6677-1576, 209-2002; www.canalandbaytours.com; partial/full transit adult US$150/195, child US$95/105) Offers partial canal transits (4½ hours), which pass through the Pedro Miguel (p643) and Miraflores (p643) locks every Saturday morning at 8:30am from the Amador ferry pier. On the first Saturday of every month, full transits (10 hours) run from Balboa on the Pacific Coast to Cristóbal on the Caribbean coast, passing all three sets of locks. They depart at 7:30am.

Sleeping & Eating

Jungle Land Panama HOUSEBOAT $$$
(☎6113-3143, 213-1172; www.junglelandpanama.com; s/d all-inclusive US$250/400) This overnight houseboat offers the novelty of a jungle retreat with canal ships passing by. Captain Carl hosts guests on a charming wooden

three-story houseboat on Lago Gatún, from where fishing, kayaking, stand-up paddleboarding and nocturnal safaris are at your fingertips. Day trips also available. Leaves from the boat dock in Gamboa.

Atlantic & Pacific Co. PANAMANIAN **$$$**
(☎232-3120; www.atlanticpacificrestaurant.com; Miraflores Visitors Center, 2nd fl; lunch buffet US$55, mains US$16-38; ⌚11:30am-4:30pm daily, 6-11pm Tue-Sat; ❄) This upscale restaurant is worthy of the canal, though prices do reflect the exclusive setting. Serving New Panamanian cuisine and using local produce, it provides distinctive choices, and plenty of them, at the sumptuous lunch buffet. Seafood is a highlight, as well as rich Panamanian coffee and desserts. Ask for balcony seating and watch boats pass the locks.

Around the Canal

The Canal Zone is home to a number of impressive attractions, especially if you're into wildlife-watching, hiking and birding. On a day trip from Panama City, you could visit the Miraflores Locks and finish at the Parque Nacional Soberanía and the Panama Rainforest Discovery Center. With prior arrangements, you could also take an organized tour of Isla Barro Colorado, one of the world's most famous tropical research stations, or visit an Emberá or Wounaan indigenous village on the shores of the Río Chagres.

Parque Nacional Soberanía

Some 27km from Panama City and just over the Colón provincial border, the 195-sq-km Parque Nacional Soberanía (www.miambiente.gob.pa) is one of the most accessible tropical rainforests in Panama. It extends much of the way across the isthmus, from Limón on Lago Gatún to just north of Paraíso, and boasts hiking trails that brim with a remarkable variety of wildlife.

Leaflets and information about the park, including a brochure for self-guided walks along the nature trail, are available from park headquarters near Gamboa. You can immerse yourself in the rainforest by overnighting in the ecologically minded **Canopy Tower Ecolodge** (☎Panama City 264-5720; www.canopytower.com/canopy-tower; per person incl meals US$199-320; Ⓟ) 🍃.

From Panama City take any Gamboa-bound bus from Albrook Bus Terminal (p641) (US$0.65) between 7am and 7pm, or a taxi (US$20 to US$30). If arriving by taxi, have the driver wait for you while you register at park headquarters and then take you to the trailheads, as they are quite far from the entrance station and office.

Panama Rainforest Discovery Center

Geared toward ecotourism and environmental education, this is an excellent **facility** (☎314-9386, 6588-0697; www.pipelineroad.org; adult/child US$30/5, night walk US$30; ⌚6am-4pm) 🍃 for birdwatchers and nature-lovers. Since you are probably here to watch wildlife, it's worth making an effort to roll out of bed early – 6am to 8am are the best times. With advance reservations, groups can set up special night tours.

A 32m-high observation tower (172 steps) made of recycled material from the canal is great for spotting blue cotinga and toucans; during premium hours, just 25 visitors are admitted at one time to minimize the impact on wildlife. The sustainably built visitors center provides information and has 15 species of hummingbirds (of Panama's 57) feeding nearby. A new sloth-rescue center offers sanctuary to these shy creatures and prepares them for reintroduction into the wild.

Guides at the visitors center and tower can point out wildlife. Currently, a 1.2km circuit of two forest trails offers options that range from easy to difficult. Lake-side you can view aquatic birds such as wattled jacanas, least grebes, herons and snail kites. Other animals around include monkeys, crocodiles, coatis, butterflies and two- and three-toed sloths.

Contact the center if you'd like to participate in bird migration counts. These are run by the **Fundación Avifauna Eugene Eisenmann** (☎306-3133; www.avifauna.org.pa), a nonprofit organization with the mission to protect Panama's bird fauna and rainforest habitat. Within the center, scientific research includes studies of migratory birds, green macaws and raptors as well as investigations into carbon capture.

There's no bus access to the park. It's best to book a taxi, rent a car or go with an organized tour. The center is 2km from the entrance to Pipeline Rd. Pass the town of Gamboa, at the end of Gaillard Rd, and follow the signs.

Monumento Natural Isla Barro Colorado

This lush island in the middle of Lago Gatún is the most intensively studied area in the neotropics. Formed by the damming of the Río Chagres and the creation of the lake, in 1923 Isla Barro Colorado became one of the first biological reserves in the New World. Home to 1316 recorded plant species, including 500 tree species, 381 bird species and 120 mammal species, the island also contains a 59km network of marked and protected trails. It is managed by the Smithsonian Tropical Research Institute (STRI), which administers a world-renowned research facility on the island. Isla Barro Colorado is open to a limited number of visitors on guided tours only.

Isla Barro Colorado Tour ECOTOUR
(www.stri.org; tour per adult/student incl lunch US$100/70; 7am-4pm Tue, Wed & Fri, 8am-3pm Sat & Sun) Once restricted to scientists, this 15-sq-km tropical research island is now open to a limited number of visitors on guided tours. The trip includes a boat ride down an attractive part of the canal, from Gamboa across the lake to the island. Hikes are demanding and last two to three hours. Reservations essential; book as far in advance as possible.

Isla Taboga

A tropical island with just one road and no traffic, Isla Taboga is a pleasant escape from the rush of Panama City, only 20km offshore. With the addition of some decent restaurants and boutique lodgings in the town of San Pedro and plenty of activities, it's growing as a destination. Named the 'Island of Flowers,' it is covered with sweet-smelling blossoms much of the year. First settled by the Spanish in 1515, the quaint village is also home to the western hemisphere's second-oldest church. While there are better beaches elsewhere, this quick, almost Caribbean getaway is a salve for city living.

Sights & Activities

Fine sand beaches lie in either direction from the ferry dock. Walk north (right) from the pier to **Playa Restinga** and south (left) along the island's narrow main road to San Pedro and the more urban **Playa Honda**. After a fork, a high road leads to the church and a simple square. Further down the road, a pretty 307m-tall public garden displays the statue of the island's patron, the Virgen del Carmen; nearby is the supposed home of 16th-century conquistador Francisco Pizzaro, who led the expedition that conquered the Inca Empire. The road meanders a total of 5.2km, ending at the old US military installation and bunker atop the island's highest point, **Cerro Vigía**.

Refugio de Vida Silvestre Islas Taboga y Urabá WILDLIFE RESERVE
This 258-hectare wildlife reserve was established in 1984 to protect a key avian habitat. Taboga and nearby Urabá are home to one of the world's largest breeding colonies of brown pelicans, with up to 10,000 here at any one time. The reserve covers about a third of Taboga as well as the entire island of Urabá, just off Taboga's southeast coast. May is the height of nesting season, but pelicans can be seen from January to April.

Festivals & Events

Festival de la Virgen del Carmen FIESTA
(Jul 16) The island's patron, the Virgen del Carmen, is honored with a seafaring procession each year on July 16. Seemingly everyone then participates in games, fire-eating and/or dancing on the beach.

Día de San Pedro FIESTA
(Jun 29) This holiday marks the founding of the town of San Pedro in 1524.

Sleeping & Eating

★ **Vereda Tropical Hotel** HOTEL $$
(250-2154; www.hotelveredatropical.com; d with fan/air-con incl breakfast US$65/80;) Atop a hill with commanding views, this pretty hotel charms with tropical tones, Mexican-style mosaic tiles, rod-iron railings and a caged parrot. Choose room 4 for its superb sea views. The dining patio (mains US$9 to US$18) also has sweeping views and music serenading from the speakers, but service can be a little slow.

Cerrito Tropical B&B $$
(6489-0074, 390-8999; www.cerritotropicalpanama.com; d incl breakfast US$80, 2-person apt US$130;) This smart Canadian- and Dutch-owned B&B occupies a quiet spot atop a steep road. The three ground-floor rooms are stylish but small; go instead for one of the three apartments with one or two

bedrooms, kitchens and terrace with sea views. Management can arrange tours such as fishing, hiking and whale-watching.

★ **London's Pier Bar & Grill** SEAFOOD $$
(☎6456-0484; www.facebook.com/londonPBG; mains US$7-16; ⏲8am-5pm Mon-Fri, to 9pm Sat & Sun) Our favorite new place for a bite and a sip, this English-owned seafront bar-restaurant with balcony seating serves excellent *ceviche, cazuela de mariscos* (seafood casserole) and cocktails. On Fridays, there's fish and chips for just US$8. Expect a very warm welcome.

Information

For more information, visit the excellent English-language site www.taboga.panamanow.com, which is kept fairly up to date.

Getting There & Away

The scenic boat trip to Isla Taboga is part of the island's attraction. Ferries land at **Muelle de Taboga** (Taboga Pier), the pier near the northern end of the island. Schedules can change, so check online for updates. Note that the police check ferry passengers for drugs upon arrival. Make sure you bring your passport with you.

Barcos Calypso (☎314-1730; www.facebook.com/BarcosCalypso; one way/round-trip adult US$9/15, child US$6/10.50) ferries depart from Isla Naos on the Amador Causeway in Panama City. The easiest way to reach the dock is by taxi (US$7). Trips take 45 minutes and depart Panama City at the following times:

DAY	TIME
Mon-Thu	8:30am
Fri	8:30am, 3pm
Sat & Sun	8am, 10:30am, 4pm

Round-trip ferries from Isla Taboga:

DAY	TIME
Mon-Thu	4:30pm
Fri	9:30am, 4:30pm
Sat & Sun	9am, 3pm, 5pm

The faster **Taboga Express** (☎6234-8989, 6261-1740; www.tabogaexpress.com; one way/round trip adult US$10/20, child US$7/14; 📶) catamaran makes the journey to and from the island in just 30 minutes. It leaves daily from the Brisas de Amador pier on Isla Perico on the Amador Causeway in Panama City at 8am, 9:30am, 11am and 3pm, with an additional departure at 4:30pm at the weekend. It returns from Isla Taboga at 8:45am, 10:15am, 2:30pm and 4pm, with an extra sailing at 5pm on Saturday and Sunday.

Archipiélago de las Perlas

Named for the large black-lipped pearl oysters once abundant in its waters, the Archipiélago de las Perlas comprises 39 islands and more than 100 unnamed (and mostly uninhabited) islets, each surrounded by postcard-worthy white-sand beaches and turquoise waters. Home to the palatial mansions of the rich and powerful, Isla Contadora is the best known island (though Isla del Rey is by far the largest). Popular US TV show *Survivor* filmed three seasons (2003–05) on several islands in the chain and versions in other languages continue to film here.

Visitors mostly head to four islands: Isla Contadora, the most accessible, developed and touristed; Isla San José, the site of an exclusive resort; and neighboring Islas Casaya and Casayeta, frequented by shoppers in search of pearls. Uninhabited islets offer ample opportunity for independent exploration, especially if you have a sense of adventure and the help of a local guide.

Activities

Whale Watching Panama WILDLIFE
(☎6758-7600; www.whalewatchingpanama.com; day trip adult/child US$160/130; ⏲Jul-Oct) To see humpback whales and dolphin pods in the Islas de Las Perlas, these day and multiday trips are led by expert biologist guides. Some trips have a spiritual focus (ie animal communication or shamanic whale-watching with yoga). The company adheres to international guidelines for whale-watching.

Coral Dreams DIVING
(☎6536-1776; www.coral-dreams.com; 2-tank dive US$120, snorkeling US$50; ⏲9am-5pm) This small PADI-certified outfit with experienced instructors is up the hill from Contadora Airport next to the **Welcome Center** (☎250-4081, 6278-0587; www.contadorapanama.com; boat tours per hour US$40, golf cart rentals per hour/day US$25/75; ⏲8am-5pm), but it doesn't always keep to its posted hours. Snorkeling tours go to Isla Mogo). It also runs whale-watching trips (July to October; US$60) with a hydrophone to hear whale calls, and rents out snorkel equipment.

Sleeping

★Gerald's B&B B&B $$

(☎6588-1046, 250-4159; www.island-contadora.com; d incl breakfast US$96-108; ❄📶🏊) With a good location near the ferry landing and an easy walk to Playa de las Suecas, Gerald's is central, clean and comfortable, with consistently good service. The nine rooms may lack views, but are large, modern and well equipped, with flat-screen TVs and air-con. The roof terrace with pool is delightful.

★Mar y Oro HOTEL $$

(Hotel Playa Cacique; ☎6349-0528, 202-7426; www.facebook.com/maryorohotel; Playa Cacique; d garden/sea view incl breakfast from US$95/120, ste US$160; ❄📶) Overlooking lovely Playa Cacique, this delightful property caters for romantic escapes. If you want to be right on the beach, it's your best option. The 14 rooms – half with sea views – and suites have flat-screen TVs, lock boxes and mini-fridges; suites feature full kitchens. The stunning Bella Vista suite offers just that from its own large terrace.

Getting There & Away

Most visitors initially travel to Isla Contadora, which is served by **Air Panama** (☎316-9000; www.airpanama.com) and **Sea Las Perlas** (☎391-1424, 209-4010; www.sealasperlas.com; adult/child one way US$49/39, round trip US$90/70) ferry service from Panama City.

PACIFIC COAST & HIGHLANDS

Between Chiriquí Province and Panama City, the regions of Coclé, Veraguas and Península de Azuero have long been overshadowed by the flash of the capital, the coolness of the highlands and the lure of the Caribbean. But for Panama's heart and soul, this may be the best place to look.

Dominated by agriculture, these are friendly provinces of laid-back colonial towns, farms and hillside villages. Founded by the Spanish four centuries ago, traditions live on in original colonial architecture, dazzling festivals and exquisite handicrafts.

Highlights include Santa Catalina, one of the best surf destinations in Central America, and the scenic mountain towns of Santa Fé and El Valle. The Pedasí coast is an up-and-coming destination for off-the-beaten-track beaches and surf.

El Valle

POP 7600

Officially known as El Valle de Antón, this picturesque town is nestled in the crater of a huge extinct volcano, and ringed by verdant forests and jagged peaks. El Valle is a popular weekend getaway for urban dwellers in need of fresh air and scenery and is also a retirement community for foreigners, with some 200 resident expats from more than 40 countries. With an extensive network of trails, this is a superb place for walking, hiking or horseback riding. Nearby forests offer excellent birdwatching, and the valleys of El Valle are home to an impressive set of waterfalls and natural pools.

Sights & Activities

Butterfly Haven WILDLIFE RESERVE

(Mariposario; ☎6062-3131; www.butterflyhavenpanama.com; adult/child US$5/1.50; ⏲9:30am-4pm) One of El Valle's top attractions allows you to walk among up to 250 butterflies as they flutter by in a screened 'flight house.' Learn more about these ephemeral creatures, which live for just a couple of weeks maximum, through a 15-minute video, life-cycle exhibits and a rearing lab, where you'll see lepidoptera in various stages of development.

Chorro El Macho WATERFALL

(Male Waterfall; adult/child US$5/2.50; ⏲8am-5pm) The most famous waterfall in the El Valle region is 35m-high Chorro El Macho, one of four cascades located about 2km north of town; it's a 15-minute walk from the road and the entrance to the **Canopy Adventure** (☎264-5720, 6613-7220; www.canopytower.com/canopy-adventure; canopy rides 1/4 lines US$20/75; ⏲8am-4pm) tour. Below the falls you'll find a natural swimming pool (US$2.50) surrounded by rainforest. There is also a series of short hiking trails that wend their way into the surrounding jungle.

Aprovaca GARDENS

(☎983-6472; www.aprovaca.com; adult/child US$2/1; ⏲8:30am-4:30pm) For the largest selection of *orquídeas* (orchids) in the region, visit this idyllic, not-for-profit garden east of the center, run by the local association of orchid producers. Volunteers work to maintain the lovely flowers inside the greenhouse and the grounds, and they welcome visitors to show off the more than 100 species of orchids cultivated here. Orchids

WORTH A TRIP

MAMALLENA ECOLODGE

At this mellow **ecolodge** (☎6673-0752, 6379-8267; http://mamallenaecolodge.com; Camino a la Laguna; dm/d without bathroom US$11/39, 2-person cabins with/without bathroom US$55/44, all incl breakfast;) on a sprawling 174-hectare farm, the seven rooms and eight-bed dorm are in a comfortable chalet and riverfront cabins in a stunning highland setting. You can hike the area and swim in a pleasing river pool. Guests can cook for themselves or sign up for good-value communal dinners.

Mamallena Ecolodge is a 1½-hour drive from Panama City and 30 minutes from El Valle in Coclé Province via a direct new road obviating the need to return to the Interamericana. From Panama City, coordinate a transfer or bus to Coronado where you can catch the La Laguna *colectivo* (US$3, 45 minutes), which will drop you off at the lodge.

are temperamental bloomers; check out the display room near the entrance to see what's flowering at the moment.

Pozos Termales El Valle HOT SPRINGS
(☎6621-3846; Calle Los Pozos; adult/child US$4/2; 8am-4:30pm) This thermal bath complex features three pools of varying temperatures – up to 38ºC, or 100.4°F – the waters of which have alleged curative properties. Post-soak, you can have a massage or apply healing mud to your skin from buckets. The baths are a 10-minute walk southwest of the center at the end of Calle Los Pozos, near Río Antón.

Sleeping & Eating

Bodhi Hostel HOSTEL $
(☎6429-4143; http://bodhihostels.com; Av Central; dm/d incl breakfast US$15/40;) Looking a bit worn around the edges but still voted tops in Panama, this central hostel counts six private rooms with shared showers, and a massive, bright and airy dorm with 27 beds in triple-deck bunks. Dorms are curtained and have lockers; the artwork is by volunteers. The Buddha theme, bafflingly prevalent in Panama, is present here.

★**Cabañas Potosí** CABIN $$
(☎6946-6148, 983-6181; www.elvallepotosi.com; Calle La Reforma 84; campsites with/without tent US$20/10, d & tr US$59-69;) A very welcoming place and good for a peaceful sleep, American-owned Cabañas Potosí is situated about 1km southwest of the town center. The parklike grounds provide lovely views of the peaks that ring the valley, including La India Dormida (The Sleeping Indian). Four concrete cabins for three people each have two beds and a fridge; more expensive rooms have attached kitchen and TV.

★**Park Eden** B&B $$
(☎983-6167, 6695-6190; www.parkeden.com; Calle Espave 7; d/ste incl breakfast from US$100/140, 4-person house US$260;) A beautiful country retreat run by a North American-trained Panamanian designer and his Ecuadorian wife, this gorgeous property has two rooms and two suites, plus a two-story house with living room and kitchen. Decor is a bit Laura Ashley, with lots of powder blue, lace doilies and quilting, but the friendly couple and their gardens are simply a delight.

Golden Frog Inn INN $$
(☎6565-8307, 983-6117; www.goldenfroginn.com; d/ste incl breakfast from US$90/135;) Attentive and relaxing, this deluxe Canadian-Panamanian–owned lodge with 11 very different rooms and suites is the perfect place to laze after a long day of play. Start with the swimming pool and migrate to the open-air living spaces and library. The expansive grounds include orchids and fruit trees; adjoining trails mean you can hike from right out the door.

★**Don Quijote** SPANISH $
(☎6095-0124, 983-6210; www.facebook.com/LosGabirros; Calle El Hato 1; mains US$8-12; 8am-9pm Tue-Sun) This 'spit' (ie grill) restaurant is a local favorite and noted for well-prepared Spanish dishes like *pulpo a la gallega* (octopus grilled with paprika), paella and the unusual *migas:* herbed breadcrumbs often served with ribs. The Quijote is a simple affair, almost like a *fonda,* with an incongruous little fountain in the center adding a dash of color. There's a warm welcome.

★**La Casa de Lourdes** INTERNATIONAL $$$
(☎6114-0117, 983-6450; www.lacasadelourdes.com; mains US$12-30; noon-3:30pm & 7-9pm) The creation of renowned Panamanian chef Lourdes Fábrega de Ward, this place has a

WORTH A TRIP

VILLA TÁVIDA LODGE

Villa Távida Lodge (☎6485-0505, 838-6114; www.villatavida.com; Chiguirí Arriba; campsite with/without tent US$25/15, d incl breakfast US$125-175, ste incl breakfast US$175-220; P ❄ 🛜 ≋) sits within the Reserva Privada Távida atop a summit surrounded by gardens, green valleys and shrouded peaks. Rooms are well equipped and the lodge restaurant provides quality dining using fresh produce from local organic gardens, with seating both inside and out. Places to relax include a hammock terrace with great views where you'll want to laze away the hours; walks on marked trails are available right out the door. There's a swimming hole under Cascada Távida, so bring your suit; and there's also a full-service spa.

By public transport, head to Penonomé (with frequent connections to both Panama City and David), then transfer to an hourly Chiguirí Arriba–bound bus.

nationwide reputation and an elegant setting around a garden patio in a lovely country villa (p649). And the menu? Sea bass Thai curry, blackened chicken in a tamarind sauce and desserts from both sides of 'the pond': sticky toffee pudding and pecan pie.

Information

ATP Office (☎983-6474; cocle@atp.gob.pa; Av Central; ⏲9:30am-5:30pm Wed-Sun) This small information kiosk next to the handicrafts market is among the most helpful in Panama. Can help with information on bicycle rentals and local guides too.

Getting There & Away

To leave El Valle, hop aboard a bus traveling east along Av Central; on average, buses depart every 30 minutes. Final destinations are marked on the windshield of the bus. If your next destination isn't posted, catch a bus going in the same direction and transfer.

To reach El Valle from the Interamericana, disembark from any bus at San Carlos, about 3km east of Las Uvas, the turning for El Valle. Minibuses collect passengers at the station here and travel to El Valle (US$1.50, 35 minutes, every half-hour). Last departure is 4pm weekdays and 7pm at weekends. From Panama City the trip to El Valle takes just over two hours (US$4.50).

Farallón & Playa Blanca

The village of Farallón (Spanish for 'cliff'), about 3km southwest of the Santa Clara turnoff, lies on a picture-perfect stretch of powder-white sand called Playa Blanca (White Beach), one of the most beautiful beaches on the Pacific coast. The main part of Playa Blanca is another 3km further on near the sprawling gated community of Buenaventura.

Sleeping & Eating

★**Togo Bed & Breakfast** B&B $$

(☎6804-2551, 993-3393; www.togopanama.com; d incl breakfast US$99-110, with kitchenette US$110-132; P ❄ 🛜) The perfect seaside destination, Togo occupies a renovated beach house and outbuildings where recycled materials are used to create a sleek and stylish design. The four rooms – one with kitchenette – are spacious and airy, with cool pebble-tile bathrooms, gorgeous original artworks and private terraces. The centerpiece is the lush garden, a controlled jungle strewn with hammocks.

★**Pipa's Beach Restaurant** SEAFOOD $$

(☎6252-8430, 6844-0373; http://pipasbeach.com; mains US$10-25; ⏲10am-6pm daily Nov-Apr, closed Tue May-Oct) Love, love, love this mostly outdoor bar and restaurant right by the beach and serving seafood with gourmet touches (such as Thai mussels and crab claws in three sauces). One of the delights of dining here is enjoying a cold beer or tropical cocktail while looking out to sea, feet buried in the sand and sometimes washed by the surf.

Getting There & Away

Buses traveling along the Interamericana generally drop you off at the Farallón exit ramp; it's a 2km walk to the center or you might be lucky and find a taxi waiting. An easier way to catch a cab is to be let off at the Santa Clara turnoff, where there are usually taxis waiting.

Chitré

POP 58,400

One of Panama's oldest settlements, the city of Chitré is hardly geared up for travelers, but it's an agreeable stop on the way to the peninsula's famed beaches. The capital of Herrera Province, it's the largest city on the Península de Azuero and the region's cultural and historic capital.

Sleeping & Eating

Hotel Rex HOTEL $
(☎996-2408, 996-4310; www.facebook.com/Hotel-Rex-Chitre-Panama-121877944544889; Calle Melitón Martín s/n; d/tr/q US$44/66/75;) With a prime location on Parque Union and decent **dining** (☎996-4310; mains US$7-15; 7:15am-10:30pm) downstairs, Rex is a solid choice. Its 33 clean tiled rooms have brick walls, cable TV, fresh towels and water thermoses. Ask for a room on the 2nd floor where there's a large communal veranda overlooking the cathedral and pretty main square.

★**Mare Bonita** FUSION $$
(☎6200-0124; www.facebook.com/pages/Restaurante-Mare-Bonita/372368832954808; Via Circunvalación; mains US$10-15; noon-10pm) A recent migrant from Pedasí (its loss), this tapas bar and restaurant is considered by many to be the best restaurant in Chitré and it certainly is the most inventive. The Madrid-trained chef keeps the menu in a state of flux, offering teriyaki chicken and Thai-style pork one week, gourmet hamburgers and fried fish *ceviche* the next.

★**Salsa y Carbon** PARRILLA $$
(☎996-6022; www.salsaycarbon.com; cnr Calles Julio Botello & Francisco Corro; mains US$8-15; 11am-10pm) This open-air Colombian BBQ house grills some of the best steak and ribs in the region. Meat and chicken are exceptionally tender and served with salad and *arepas* (maize flatbread). The covered outside seating catches cool breezes and is a delight on a warm evening. It's opposite Rico Cedeño Stadium and is always heaving.

Getting There & Away

Chitré is a center for regional bus transportation. Buses arrive and depart from **Terminal de Transportes de Herrera** (☎996-6426; Via Circunvalación), 1km south of downtown, just off the Vía Circunvalación. The terminal has a 24-hour restaurant. To get there, **Radio Taxi** (☎996-4442) charges less than US$2. The 'Terminal' bus (US$0.30) leaves from the intersection of Calle Aminta Burgos de Amado and Av Herrera.

Tuasa (☎996-2661) and **Transportes Inazun** (☎996-4177) buses head to Panama City (US$9.05, four hours, every 40 minutes from 6am to 6pm).

To get to David (US$9.50), take a bus to Santiago (US$3.25, every half-hour) and then catch a *directo* (direct bus). These *directos* leave from the gas station at the intersection of the Interamericana and the Carretera Nacional.

Pedasí

POP 2410

Unpretentious and laid-back, Pedasí's streets are lined with tiled colonials and leafy spaces. For years this sleepy retreat came to life only at festival times, but outsiders are discovering the big appeal of small-town life and relatively unspoiled beaches.

Sights & Activities

Snorkeling and diving around nearby islands, which are surrounded by large coral reefs, are major attractions. Sport fishers can land wahoo, tuna, mahi-mahi, amberjack and Pacific mackerel. For guided trips (from about US$200 for two passengers), ask at **Pedasí Sports Club** (☎6749-4308, 995-2894; www.pedasisportsclub.com; Av Central; 7:30am-9pm) or **Pedasí Nature Paradise Tours** (☎452-4560, 6823-8304; www.pedasiparadise.com/tours; Av Central; 8am-5pm).

Isla Cañas WILDLIFE RESERVE
Isla Cañas is one of a handful of places that olive ridley sea turtles nest in high numbers (the others are two beaches on the Pacific side of Costa Rica and two beaches in Orissa on the Bay of Bengal in India). Endangered species including the hawksbill, loggerhead sea, leatherback and green turtle nest here too. The turtles nest from July through early November, though peak months are usually September and October.

Refugio de Vida Silvestre Isla Iguana WILDLIFE RESERVE
(US$10) This 53-hectare reserve is centered on a deserted island ringed by corals. The water is shallow enough for snorkeling and, as elsewhere in the Pacific, the reef fish here are enormous. You can get here by boat (US$70) in 40 minutes from Playa El Arenal, a beach 3km northeast of Pedasí's gas station. Stick to the beaten paths on the island as unexploded ordnance is occasionally discovered here (the US Navy used the island for target practice during WWII).

Sleeping

★Casa Lajagua B&B $$

(☎6303-3848, 995-2912; www.casalajagua.com; d US$77-99, 4-person ste US$129-149; P❄☎≋) Set in beautiful leafy grounds away from the hubbub of Av Central, this welcoming place feels more like a resort than the chilled B&B it is. Six individually designed rooms and a suite with orthopedic mattresses and super-strong showers face a huge pool; hammocks swing everywhere, and breakfasts are massive.

★Casa de Campo B&B $$

(☎995-2733, 6780-5280; www.casacampopedasi.com; Av Central s/n; d incl breakfast US$99; ❄☎≋) Far and away the nicest place to stay in Pedasí, this hospitable and quite chic B&B screams getaway. The seven rooms are named and themed; our favorite is Marina, which has a king-sized bed and measures a full 380 sq meters. The main-street location is deceptive: out back there's a pool and lovely landscaped grounds with thatched *ranchos* and hammocks.

La Rosa de los Vientos B&B $$

(☎6530-4939, 6778-0627; www.bedandbreakfastpedasi.com; Via Playa Toro; d/tr/q incl breakfast US$65/80/90; P☎) With the feel of a rural hacienda, this lovely red-tile Spanish colonial just up from the beach has three smart rooms with colorful weavings, antique tiles and ocean views. It's designed to be ecofriendly, so there is no air-con, but fans do the trick. Multilingual owners Isabelle and Robert offer warm hospitality.

Eating

Fonda Mama Fefa PANAMANIAN $

(Calle Los Estudiantes; set meals US$3; ⏲5am-2pm Mon-Sat) Matriarch of Creole cooking, Mama Fefa usually runs out of lunch by noon (though you can linger longer). Cheap and cheerful, these huge *comidas típicas* (regional specialties) include meat or fish, rice, salad and a drink. Devotees share the space at a few outdoor tables. Follow the side street opposite the landmark supermarket for two blocks. It's on the right.

★Segreto ITALIAN $$

(☎6822-7575; www.facebook.com/pages/Segreto/581448718627827; Av Central; mains US$10-14; ⏲6-9pm Mon-Sat) Pedasí's best (some might stop there) Italian restaurant is set in what feels like a glassed-in conservatory. There are more complex *secondi* (main courses) with usually three meat and three fish dishes, but most come for the delectable pasta dishes. Host Mirko is welcoming and helpful.

Restaurante Smiley's AMERICAN $$

(☎6510-9652, 995-2863; www.facebook.com/smileys.restaurante; Av Central; mains US$10-16.50; ⏲noon-late Tue-Sun) Catering largely to expats, this friendly bar-restaurant serves up grilled fish, ribs and deli sandwiches (US$5 to US$7.50), including minced BBQ pork. There's also good live music on Tuesday and Friday nights, sports on the tube, and an extensive drinks menu to match. The daily lunch special is a snip at US$4.

Information

The **ATP** (☎995-2339; azuero@atp.gob.pa; ⏲8am-4pm Mon-Sat) office lies one block past the main road in the north of town. It has a list of boat contacts for Refugio de Vida Silvestre Isla Iguana and Isla Cañas.

Banco Nacional de Panama (☎995-2257; Av Central; ⏲8am-3pm Mon-Fri, 9am-noon Sat) in the center has an ATM. It's one of two in town on Av Central.

Getting There & Away

Buses to Las Tablas leave every hour between 6am and 4pm (US$2.40, one hour) from the **bus stop** next to the El Pueblo supermarket. Buses to Playa Venao (US$2.20, 30 minutes) leave at 7am, noon and 2pm. Buses to Cañas (US$2.40, 45 minutes) depart at 7am and noon.

Sunset Coast

The Sunset Coast is the name given to the west side of Península de Azuero facing the Gulfo de Montijo and Pacific Ocean. The sobriquet is accurate for it is the only place in Panama from which you can watch the sun go down from a beach.

Here you'll find long, sandy beaches virtually empty of holiday-makers, excellent surfing and the chance to see three species of turtles hatching. There are nature walks in the mangroves and Parque Nacional Cerro Hoya is just down the road.

The gateway to the Sunset Coast is Santiago, about 60km north of Mariato. Other important settlements include Malena and Torio, 11km and 15km south of Mariato respectively.

DON'T MISS

LAS FIESTAS DE AZUERO

Famous throughout Panama, the traditional festivals of Azuero were created around customs from early Spanish settlers. This is a side of Panama that few foreigners ever get to see. While you may lose a day from a *seco* (alcoholic drink made from sugarcane) hangover, taking part in the wilder side of the peninsula is more than worth the suffering. Some of the best-known festivals include the following:

Carnaval The four days before Ash Wednesday in Chitré, Parita and especially Las Tablas

Semana Santa March/April in Pesé and La Villa de Los Santos

Feria Internacional de Azuero Late April/early May in La Villa de Los Santos

Fiesta de Corpus Christi Forty days after Easter in La Villa de Los Santos

Fiesta de San Juan Bautista June 24 in Chitré

Patronales de San Pablo & San Pedro June 29 in La Arena

Feria de la Mejorana Late September in Guararé

Fiesta de la Fundación de Chitré October 19 in Chitré

El Grito de La Villa November 10 in La Villa de Los Santos

Fiestas Patronales de Santa Catalina November 25 in Pedasí

Activities & Tours

Malena Beach Conservation Association WILDLIFE WATCHING
(Asociación Conservacionista de Playa Malena; ☎6865-8908; Playa Malena; donation US$15) Volunteers of the Malena Beach Conservation Association work toward the preservation of three species of turtles. Chairperson Ana González and her community volunteers take visitors on turtle watches; peak season for laying and hatching is September through November. The organization also offers accommodations, horseback riding, boat tours, whale-watching and nature walks.

Centro AAPEQ WILDLIFE WATCHING
(☎6491-9365, 6389-5249; www.playamataoscura.blogspot.cl; Rusia de Quebro; ⊙hours vary) This association based near Morillo focuses its attention on the conservation of turtles and reforestation of the Mata Oscura mangrove. For a small fee, the affable couple in charge can take you on a tour through the mangroves or through the forest up to a waterfall, where you can see strawberry poison dart frogs. Kayaks are available as well.

Morillo Beach Eco Resort ADVENTURE SPORTS
(☎6017-0965; www.morrillobeachresort.com; Playa Morillo; tours from US$45; ⊙hours vary) While big plans are in the works here for a coastal lodge and farm-to-table Mexican restaurant, for now this up-and-coming Colorado-owned enterprise offers stand-up paddleboarding tours in the mangroves, visits to nearby Parque Nacional Cerro Hoya, surf lessons, snorkeling on Isla Cebaco and cultural tours. Its base sits tucked against the mangroves, with prolific wildlife including resident endangered Azuero howler monkeys.

Sleeping

Heliconia Bed & Breakfast B&B $$
(☎6676-0220; www.hotelheliconiapanama.com; Palmilla; s/d incl breakfast US$55/85; P ❄ ☜ ≋) The Sunset Coast's anchor tenant, Heliconia Bed & Breakfast in Palmilla, on the main road just north of Malena, is an excellent retreat thoughtfully crafted by two extremely knowledgeable Dutch biologists, who also offer recommended area tours. Heliconia has three smart rooms set within 8 hectares of botanical gardens, a lovely lounge and terrace, and an above-ground pool.

★**Punta Duarte Garden Inn** INN $$$
(☎6152-7817, 6645-4635; www.puntaduarte.com; Punta Duarte; r incl breakfast US$85-148; ❄ ☜ ≋) Brimming with style, this lovely inn offers a peaceful and inspired beach retreat. Off a wraparound veranda, there's five elegant, ample rooms with ocean views, playful styles and cool, original artwork. Some baths feature double showers and there's a Jacuzzi and pool on property. The German host Gabrielle provides a warm welcome. Meals are also available (US$8 to US$25).

WORTH A TRIP

ISLA DE COIBA

With the exception of Ecuador's Galápagos Islands and Isla de Coco in Costa Rica, few destinations off the Pacific coast of the Americas are as exotic as the **Parque Nacional Coiba** (998-0615; www.coibanationalpark.com; US$20) covering the 503-sq-km Isla de Coiba. Although just 20km offshore in the Golfo de Chiriquí, Coiba is a veritable lost world of pristine ecosystems and unique fauna.

Isolated for the past century due to its status as a notorious penal colony, Coiba offers travelers the chance to hike through primary rainforest and snorkel and dive in a marine park with increasingly rare wildlife. However, with virtually no tourist infrastructure in place, you're going to have to plan hard (and pay top dollar) to really see it up close. For diving trips, get in touch with **Dive Base Coiba** (6948-2240, 6662-4539; www.divebasecoiba.com; Pixvae; by appointment), the best in the business. For immersive multiday adventures, **Tanager Ecotours** (6676-0220, 6679-5504; www.tanagertourism.com; 3-day all-inclusive per person US$750;) offers hiking, snorkeling and wildlife watching.

Coiba was declared a national park in 1991, and in 2005 Unesco made it a World Heritage Site.

★ **Camino del Sol Ecolodge** LODGE $$$
(6810-7122; www.caminodelsol.com.pa; Punta Duarte; d/bungalow incl breakfast US$155/220;) In a 35-hectare preserve, this very private lodge showcases fine modern design with drop-dead Pacific views and plenty of attitude. The proud owner from St Tropez is architect, host and cocktail-maker. Glass bungalows and large rooms feature king-sized four-poster beds, oceanfront terraces and futuristic Italian furnishings. There's also a delicious infinity pool and a long trail to the water.

Getting There & Away

Up to 10 buses a day link Santiago with Torio (US$5, 1½ hours), via Mariato, between 6am and 5pm. The buses at noon and 2pm carry on as far as Rusia de Quebra, where Centro AAPEQ (p653) is located.

Playa Venao

POP 2500

A long, protected beach, Playa Venao – officially Venado but pronounced and spelled as 'Venao' – recently transformed from a wild beach to a 'go to' destination. Surfers lay the first claim to its waters; waves are consistent and break in both directions.

Sleeping & Eating

Eco Venao LODGE $
(6634-4550, 832-0530; www.ecovenao.com; campsite per person US$6, dm/d without bathroom US$11/35, 2-person cabins US$40, 6-person houses US$160;) On the north side of the main road, North American–owned Eco Venao offers a cool mountain ambience. Perfect for surfers and adventurers, its excellent options range from campsites and hostel dorms to beachside *cabañas* (cabins). The lush 140-hectare property means mini-adventures are close at hand, from howler-monkey visits and a playground to a short waterfall hike.

★ **El Sitio Hotel** HOTEL $$
(6223-6688, 832-1010; www.elsitiohotel.com; d US$99-109, ste US$129-195, apt US$215;) El Sitio's best feature is its location right on Playa Venao; 'You Are Where You Surf' is its motto. But even if you don't surf, the 16 splendid rooms, suites and apartments at this hotel partially built from recycled shipping containers will delight. Choose one of four suites with private sea-facing balconies or the fab new 'lighthouse' sleeping four.

★ **Panga** PANAMANIAN $$
(6787-2146; www.facebook.com/restaurantepanga; mains US$10-18; noon-3pm Fri-Sun, 6:30-10pm Wed-Sun) When chef Andres Morataya left award-winning Manolo Caracol and the hubbub of Panama City for Playa Venao, he opened this most inventive restaurant. The idea is to use products often discarded – deep-fried snapper gills, anyone? – or to prepare them in unique ways as in 'Prawns that Want to be Pork' cooked in a sauce usually served with suckling pig.

El Sitio Restaurant INTERNATIONAL $$
(832-1010, 6223-6688; mains US$10-22; 7am-9:30pm) This is an excellent choice for sunset dining or just drinks on Playa Venao.

Open-air El Sitio offers sesame-crusted tuna and a host of Asian-inspired dishes such as pad thai noodles with octopus, Thai crepes and chicken curry. A dedicated pastry chef prepares lovely desserts like tamarillo sorbet pavlova and chocolate lava cake.

Getting There & Away

The Playa Venao turnoff is 33km southwest of Pedasí, 2km past the turn for **Resort La Playita** (997-6727, 6615-3898; www.playitaresort.com; d/q US$120/150; P ❄ 📶). The Cañas–Tablas bus (US$3.60) passes by about 7am, while Cañas–Pedasí (US$2.20) comes at about 10am. West-bound buses pass by at 1pm or so. Confirm exact times with your hotel. You can also take a taxi from Pedasí (about US$25).

Santa Catalina

POP 300

Among Central America's top surf spots, Santa Catalina has right and left breaks comparable to Oahu's Sunset Beach on a good day. Enjoy it while it's still somewhat remote, undeveloped and home to some seriously wicked surf. Most non-surfers discover the area as the main springboard for day and overnight trips to Isla de Coiba and its national park, where there's outstanding scuba diving and snorkeling.

Activities

Dream Diving DIVING

(6765-0631; www.dreamdivingpanama.com; 8am-4:30pm) This excellent dive shop just at the turnoff to the beach is run by a very eco-minded Colombian and offers snorkeling trips to Coiba and two- and three-tank dives.

Surf & Shake SURFING

(6555-4375; www.surfandshake.com; 9am-6pm) On the road to the beach, just 150m in from the main street, Surf & Shake rents out boards and sells leashes, boards and surfwear, as well as tasty fruit shakes. Run by a German surfer, it's also a good spot for surf info.

Sleeping

Oasis Surf Camp CABIN $

(6670-5636, 6588-7077; www.oasissurfcamp.com; Playa Estero; camping with/without tent per person US$12/7, dm US$15, d with fan/air-con US$45/55, ste from US$135; P ❄ 📶) This Italian-owned surf camp is a classic, and its beachfront setting is one of the best. Bright, colorful cabins overlooking the black-sand beach have hot showers and ample hammocks. The suite is a two-bedroom wooden house with wicker furniture, a kitchen and great balcony views. It's on Playa Estero, just past a river guests must wade across to reach camp.

★ Deseo Bamboo CABIN $$

(6788-7891, 6951-6671; www.facebook.com/deseobambooecolodge; dm US$18, d/tr cabin US$69/84; P 📶) The crazy dream of a Neapolitan football player, these octagonal thatched huts are a tropical masterpiece. Bamboo huts feature traditional two-tier roofs that offer good ventilation. Rooms, including an attractive dorm, are spare but lovely. There's a congenial atmosphere, plus a yoga deck and a sushi bar, with weekly live music and events such as salsa dancing and movie nights.

★ La Buena Vida CABIN $$

(6572-0664; www.labuenavidahotel.com; 2-person villa US$66-88, 4-person studio US$110; P ❄ 📶) These lovely villas spill down a leafy hillside along the main road. Each is themed and decorated with colorful mosaics and tiles crafted by the American owners. With great service, they have ironed out every little detail here, from local tips to fast internet and quality lunchboxes for tours. There are popular yoga classes on a sprawling deck and professional massages.

Eating

La Buena Vida AMERICAN $

(6635-1895, 6572-0664; www.labuenavida.biz; mains from US$7; 6:30am-2pm;) If you're hitting the water early, this will be the first spot open for a bite and espresso fix. Great options include breakfast burritos and Greek scrambles with feta, olives, tomatoes and eggs. This funky tiled cafe perched above the main street also sells fresh fruit drinks and a lunchtime selection of salads, power bowls and wraps. Vegan friendly.

★ Chillinguito SEAFOOD $$

(6687-2992; mains US$8-15; 5-9pm Tue-Sat) This thatched restaurant does seafood in slightly different, scrumptious preparations. Try the shrimp in garlic sauce with crunchy sautéed vegetables, abundant green salads or fried clam *ceviche* with yucca. There's also fresh fruit drinks, organic kombucha and cocktails. Its signature drink, Tropical Dream, combines gin with frosty watermelon and mint. Service is slow – par for the course in Catalina.

★El Encuentro SEAFOOD $$
(☎6377-8909; mains US$12-14; ⏰6:30-11pm) At a converted gas pump, Deivis' popular no-nonsense *ceviche* stand does superb versions of the citrus-cured seafood on a nest of shoestring fries. The squid version is to die for. There's also a vegetarian option and rum drinks. It's a two-man show with every plate made to order, so plunk down at an outdoor table and enjoy the personal attention.

Getting There & Away

To reach Santa Catalina from Panama City, take a bus to Santiago, then another to Soná where buses leave for Santa Catalina (US$5, 1½ hours) at 5:30am, 8:40am, 11:20am, 1:30pm, 3:30pm and 4:45pm. Sunday services vary. If you miss the bus, hire a taxi from Soná to Santa Catalina (from US$45). Direct Panama City–Soná buses run every two hours.

From Santa Catalina, seven buses serve Soná daily, leaving at 6:15am, 7am, 8am, 10:45am, 1:30pm, 3:30pm and 6pm. In Santa Catalina, the bus stops at the intersection with the beach road. If you're staying outside the town center, most lodgings are a 1km walk on mostly flat but unshaded terrain. Note that there are never taxis in town, unless, of course, someone is arriving from Soná.

For direct shuttle service to Boquete (four hours), use **Hello Travel! Panama** (☎757-7004; www.hellotravelpanama.com; one way US$35). These air-conditioned minivans are a good time-saving way to get around Panama without dealing with confusing transfers. You can also go to Las Lajas, Horconcito or David. Departs at noon daily with pick-up on the main road or your hotel. Reserve online.

Santa Fé

POP 3050

Santa Fé has fresh, clean air and bucolic surroundings, yet it sees relatively few foreign visitors. With the lush mountainsides, waterfalls, mountain streams and accessible swimming spots of Santa Fé National Park on the town's doorstep, it's a great destination for hikers, birdwatchers and those simply wanting to soak up the beauty of the highlands.

This tiny mountain town 53km north of Santiago lies in the shadow of the continental divide. At an altitude of 500m, Sante Fé is cooler than the lowlands, and much of the surrounding forest is as it was when the Spanish founded the town in 1557. From here, a rough road to the Caribbean coast is under construction, which will eventually bring access to some of Panama's most remote outposts.

Sights & Activities

Río Bulaba RIVER
There's a lovely swimming hole on this river about a 20-minute walk from town. Head northeast along the road past the Coffee Mountain Inn on the way to El Pantino. The swimming hole is about 600m from there.

Here a local named William rents out inner tubes (US$8) and life jackets, which allow you to float idly down the river; it eventually merges with Río Santa Maria. He can also arrange a taxi return.

Cerro Tute MOUNTAIN
With excellent open views of the valley, Cerro Tute is home to the area's famed bird life and features a cliff blasted with up-currents that seem to prevent anyone falling off. An extensive trail network winds through primary and secondary rainforest. It's a few kilometers south of town on the western side of the Santiago–Santa Fé road; count on five hours there and back.

Chon & María Farm Tour TOUR
(☎6525-4832; half-day tour per person US$10; 👪) To see an organic farm up close, visit with Chon and María, hospitable *campesino* (farmer) hosts happy to show you around their small-scale operation. You can also check out their orchids and sample María's homemade cooking (lunch included). Though they only speak Spanish, this lovely couple finds a way to communicate with non-Spanish-speaking visitors that makes the trip worthwhile.

Sleeping & Eating

Hostal La Qhia GUESTHOUSE $
(☎6814-2650; www.panamamountainhouse.com; dm US$12, s/d without bathroom US$35/45, bungalow/cabin US$40/130; P 📶) Surrounded by lush gardens and hammocks, this bamboo-and-stone chalet makes a great base camp for mountain adventures around Santa Fé. There's excellent maps and detailed notes about the area's attractions. Snug rooms feature crisp bedding, while those upstairs are complete charmers. Dorms with six beds and a room with private bathroom occupy a small concrete addition with an outdoor kitchen.

★**Hotel Anachoreo** HOTEL $$
(☎6911-4848; www.anachoreo.com; s/d incl breakfast US$55/66; P) Hugging the hillside with panoramic views, this small inn steals your heart with its hammocks strung along fragrant garden beds, warm hospitality and breakfasts that might be the finest in Panama. Ample, high-ceilinged rooms have beds clad in netting, and delightful bathroom mosaics. The vibe is utterly tranquil. Guests can use a shared outdoor kitchen. Offers tours on hiking trails.

Restaurante Hermanos Pineda PANAMANIAN $
(☎954-0777; mains US$4-8; ⌚7am-9pm) This welcoming, family-run place just up from the town center serves better food than the plain-Jane menu would have you believe, including worthwhile fish and seafood served with *patacones,* rice or fries. There's also pizza (US$5 to US$12) and burgers. The large veranda overlooking the main road is a plus, as is the wall-sized map of the national park.

★**Anachoreo Restaurant** CAMBODIAN $$
(☎6911-4848; www.anachoreo.com; mains US$10-14; ⌚5:30-9pm Wed-Sun) This intimate eatery at the hotel of the same name ranks among the finest eating this side of Panama City. The Cambodian owner-chef is a wonderful cook and delightful presence. Don't miss the Cambodian chicken curry, her famous spring rolls and the exotic 'Fish Amok' wrapped in banana leaves and steamed in ginger and fresh lemongrass.

ℹ Getting There & Away

Buses from Santa Fé to Santiago (US$3, 1½ hours) depart from the **bus station** every 30 minutes from 4am to 6pm, stopping at the more central **bus stop** en route. Note that if you are trying to reach the surf town of Santa Catalina in one day, you must leave Santa Fé by 9am to make all the bus connections in time.

The road to the Caribbean coast is planned for completion in 2020. At the time of writing there was a rough section that's drivable with a 4WD.

CHIRIQUÍ PROVINCE

POP 451,230 / ELEV SEA LEVEL TO 3474M

Chiriquí claims to have it all: Panama's tallest mountains, longest rivers and most fertile valleys. The province is also home to spectacular highland rainforests and the most productive agricultural and cattle-ranching regions in the country. As a result, *los chiricanos* (natives of Chiriquí) take a particular pride in their province and wave the provincial flag – in every sense – at the slightest opportunity.

It's also a land of immense beauty. On the coast, the pristine Golfo de Chiriquí boasts long sandy beaches and a rich diversity of marine life. The mist-covered mountains near the town of Boquete, a favorite of North American and European retirees, is a good base for adventures such as white-water rafting and hiking the flanks of Panama's highest point, Volcán Barú (3474m). Boquete is also the center of Panama's coffee industry, which means that a potent cup of shade-grown arabica is never more than a cafe away.

David

POP 144,860

Although it feels more like an overgrown country town, David is Panama's second-largest city and the capital of Chiriquí Province. It's more a center of agricultural industry than a cultural hub; you will be disappointed if you have museums, clubs and fine dining in mind. Yet with foreign capital flowing into Chiriquí, David is rapidly gaining wealth and importance, and is poised to boom.

Halfway between Panama City and San José (Costa Rica), David is an important transportation hub.

Sleeping & Eating

★**Bambu Hostel** HOSTEL $
(☎730-2961; www.bambuhostel.com; Calle de la Virgencita; dm US$11-13, d with/without bathroom US$35/30; P) This great chilled-out house is the creation of a friendly musician and former Brooklynite. There's air-conditioned dorms, decent private rooms and a thatched 'jungle house' on stilts out back, with beds draped in mosquito nets. You might see a coati roaming the sprawling garden, which has a swimming pool, a cheap beer bar and the requisite hammocks.

Hotel Ciudad de David BUSINESS HOTEL $$
(☎774-3333; www.hotelciudaddedavid.com; cnr Calle D Norte & Av 2 Este; d/ste incl breakfast from US$75/106; P@) David's flashiest hotel, the sleek 'City of David' has 103 tastefully furnished rooms with wooden floors,

minibars and fully wired desks. Rooms 303 and 304 look onto the fabulous amoeba-shaped swimming pool; suite 305 has a balcony as well. There's a sauna, a fully equipped gym and a stylish bar-restaurant called – what else? – Stylo.

Pho Palace VIETNAMESE $
(☎6352-3000; Calle F Sur s/n; mains US$6-12; ⏰9am-10pm) A find for the area, this immaculate restaurant with screens, ambient lighting and flower arrangements serves authentic Hanoi cuisine. Big bowls of pho (noodle soup) and sweet-and-sour fish, plus more mainstream options like pineapple chicken and spring rolls. It's all well prepared, though service can be slow.

Café Rincón Libanés MIDDLE EASTERN $$
(☎730-3911, 774-2700; Calle F Sur; mains US$8-18; ⏰11am-11:30pm) This fairly authentic Lebanese restaurant southwest of downtown provides a welcome relief from a steady diet of rice and beans. Homemade hummus, tabbouleh, baba ghanoush and lamb kofta (meatballs) will make you wonder if you're in the Middle East. Try the homemade pink lemonade.

Information

The **ATP Office** (☎775-2839; chiriqui@atp.gob.pa; Calle Central; ⏰8:30am-4:30pm Mon-Fri) has information on David and Chiriquí Province.

The Ministerio de Ambiente (p667) provides tourist information and advice, and camping permits for national parks. It's 4.5km south of David's center.

The central branch of **Banco Nacional de Panamá** (☎774-6400; Calle B Norte; ⏰8am-3pm Mon-Fri, 9am-noon Sat) has an ATM and faces Parque de Cervantes.

Chiriquí Hospital (☎777-8814; www.hospitalchiriqui.com; cnr Calle Central & Av 3 Oeste) is one of the best hospitals in the country.

Getting There & Away

AIR

David's airport, Aeropuerto Enrique Malek (p741), is about 5km south of the center. There are no buses to the airport; take a taxi (US$5).

Air Panama (☎721-0841; www.flyairpanama.com; Aeropuerto Enrique Malek) and **Copa Airlines** (☎217-2672; www.copaair.com; Aeropuerto Enrique Malek) have daily 45-minute flights to and from Panama City, from US$90 one way. Air Panama also flies between David and Bocas del Toro town.

BUS

The Interamericana does not go through David but skirts around its western and northern sides. The David **bus terminal** (Av del Estudiante) is about 500m northeast of Parque de Cervantes. Most buses begin service around 6am.

Tracopa (☎775-0585; www.tracopacr.com) has direct buses between David and San José, Costa Rica (US$28, seven hours), from Monday through Friday at 7:30am and 3pm from the David bus terminal.

Golfo de Chiriquí

The gem of the Chiriquí lowlands is the Golfo de Chiriquí, home to the **Parque**

BUSES FROM DAVID

DESTINATION	FARE (US$)	DURATION	FREQUENCY (DAILY)
Boquete	1.75	1hr	every 20min to 9:30pm
Caldera	2.40	45min	hourly to 7:30pm
Cerro Punta	3.50	2¼hr	every 20min to 6pm
Changuinola	9.70	4½hr	half-hourly to 6:30pm
Guadalupe	3.50	2½hr	every 20min to 6pm
Horconcitos	2	45min	11am & 5pm
Las Lajas	5	1½hr	4
Panama City	18	7-8hr	every 45min 6:45am to 8pm
Paso Canoas	2.10	50min	every 15min to 9:30pm
Puerto Armuelles	4	2½hr	every 15min to 9pm
Río Sereno	5.10	2½hr	every 30min to 5pm
Santiago	9	3hr	hourly to 9pm
Volcán	3	1½hr	every 20min to 8pm

Nacional Marino Golfo de Chiriquí, a national marine park with an area of just over 147 sq km, protecting 25 islands, 19 coral reefs and abundant wildlife. The marine park also protects the 30-sq-km **Isla Boca Brava**, a lovely little island with hiking trails and beautiful outer beaches. It's home to howler monkeys, several types of nesting sea turtles and 280 recorded bird species. It is reached from the mainland village of Boca Chica. Resorts in the area offer a range of tours.

Visitors can surf, kayak the calm interior waters, snorkel, watch wildlife under the rainforest canopy or fish for big game.

Sleeping

★**Bocas del Mar** RESORT **$$$**
(☎6395-8757; www.bocasdelmar.com; Boca Chica; ste/superior incl breakfast US$295/379; P❄📶🏊) This elegant Belgian-owned resort on the mainland has 20 brilliant-white ultramodern bungalows that offer the ultimate in comfort. Amenities range from two infinity pools and massage services to suites with private hot tubs. Rooms have handmade furniture, lovely artwork and windows with smoky glass. A full menu of excursions includes horse riding, kayaking, and fishing and snorkeling tours. Excellent restaurant and service.

Cala Mia Boutique Resort RESORT **$$$**
(☎851-0025, 6972-6954, USA 1-210-390-4259; www.calamiaresort.com; Isla Boca Brava, Boca Chica; ste incl breakfast US$189-239; ❄📶🏊) Cala Mia on Isla Boca Brava offers luxurious ocean-front tranquility. Some 11 thatched bungalows have ample living spaces, handcrafted local furniture and their own deck with hammock. Two beaches – one with a bar – are just a stroll away, and a massage spa occupies its own islet, reached via suspension bridge. Organic three-course meals are served around a big community table.

Getting There & Away

To reach Boca Chica from David, take any of the frequent Interamericana buses heading east to the Horconcitos turnoff (US$2, one hour). From there a van (US$3, 50 minutes) leaves four to five times daily for Boca Chica. At the Boca Chica dock, hire a water taxi (US$4 per person) to take you 200m to the Isla Boca Brava dock at Hotel Boca Brava. If you drive your own vehicle, you can safely leave it near the village dock.

Playa Las Lajas

POP 1520

One of the longest beaches in Panama, 12km-long palm-fringed Playa Las Lajas seems to stretch forever. The beach gathers serious crowds at weekends, but during the week it often lies empty, so you can savor the glorious expanse all by yourself.

Ngöbe-Buglé (indigenous group from Panama; also know as the Guaymís) people sell handicrafts in a wooden-walled structure 500m west of the turnoff to Playa Las Lajas, 76km east of David.

Sleeping

Nahual Eco Hostel HOSTEL **$**
(Hospedaje Ecológico Nahual; ☎6620-6431; www.nahualpanama.com; dm US$10, s/d with bathroom US$30/40, without bathroom US$15/25; P📶) With *ranchos* (small house-like buildings) and attractive cabins, this fun, Italian-run place is the best bargain lodging in Las Lajas. It sits across the road from the beach in a leafy garden and is 100% chemical free. There are six rooms, including a dorm, and an open-air guest kitchen. The mostly vegan cafe serves organic food, homemade pasta and fish.

Las Lajas Beach Resort RESORT **$$**
(☎6790-1972; www.laslajasbeachresort.com; Playa Las Lajas; d/ste US$99/132; P❄📶🏊) A lovely destination on the beach, with 14 impeccable, ample and cheery rooms and great service. We love the indigenous designs on the bedspreads and murals on the walls; room 12 features portraits of Panamanian greats. Guests can float in the pool or ocean, rent body boards (US$6) or use the on-site agency, **Cocaleca** (☎6240-2705; www.cocalecatours.com; Las Lajas Beach Resort; ⏲hours vary), for great tours further afield.

Getting There & Away

From David, the Las Lajas turnoff is 76km east on the Interamericana. The town of Las Lajas is 3km south of the Interamericana and the beach a further 9km south.

To reach Las Lajas, take any bus from David (US$5, 90 minutes). You can take a taxi (US$5) to the beach from town.

Boquete

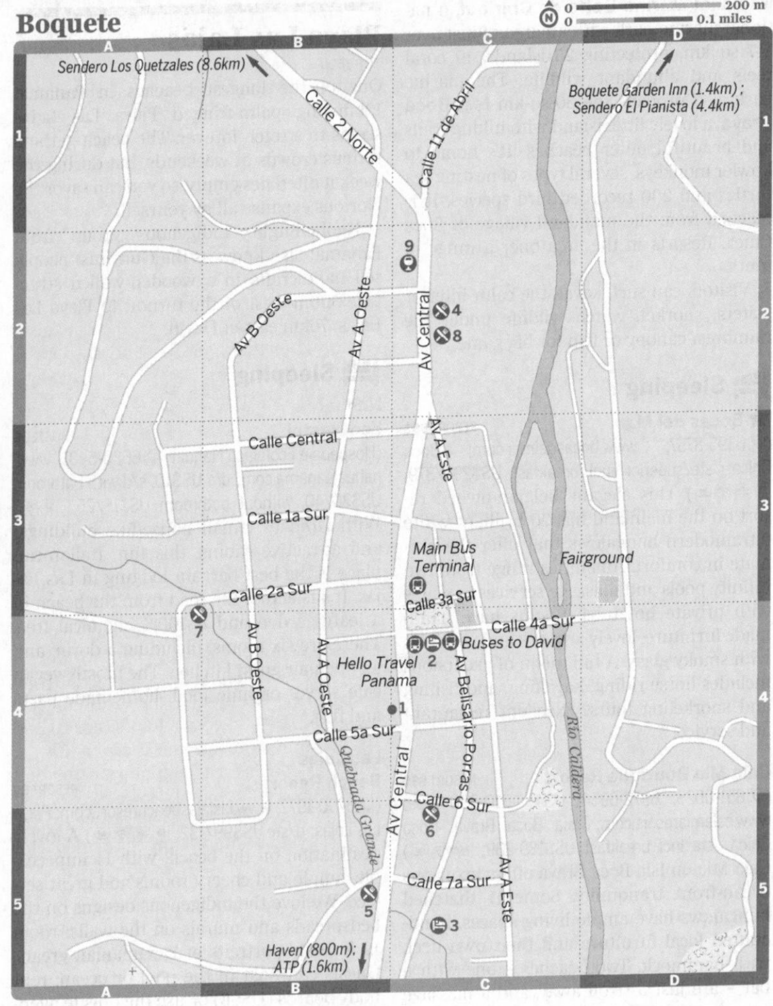

Boquete

POP 19,000

Boquete is known for its cool, fresh climate and pristine natural surroundings. Flowers, coffee, vegetables and citrus fruits flourish in its rich soil, and the friendliness of the locals seems to rub off on everyone who passes through. Boquete gained a deluge of expats after the American Association for Retired Persons (AARP) named it a top retirement spot. Until you see the gated communities and sprawling estates dotting the hillsides up close, though, you'd be hard-pressed to see what the fuss is about.

The surrounds, however, are another matter. Boquete is one of the country's top destinations for outdoor-lovers. It's a hub for hiking, climbing, rafting, visiting coffee farms, soaking in hot springs, studying Spanish or canopy touring. And, of course, there's nothing quite like a cup of locally grown coffee.

Activities

Hiking

With its breathtaking vistas of mist-covered hills and nearby forests, Boquete is one of the most idyllic regions for hiking and walking. Several good paved roads lead out of

Boquete

town into the surrounding hills, passing coffee farms, fields, gardens and virgin forest.

Trails are mostly poorly marked, and seasonally affected by floods and landslides, which can change the routes. In the past there have also been security issues. For these reasons it's really best to hire local guides to explore the trails.

Although many visitors will be content with picturesque strolls along the river, the more ambitious can climb Volcán Barú (p664). There are several entrances to the Parque Nacional Volcán Barú, but the most accessible trail starts near Boquete.

It's possible to access the Sendero Los Quetzales (p665) from Boquete, though the trail is uphill from here; you'll have an easier time if you start hiking from Cerro Punta above Volcán. Landslides have affected the trail in the past. Ask locals about conditions before heading out.

Finca Lérida HIKING
(trail fee US$12) For a relaxed hike without orientation issues, this coffee farm with its adjoining forest is an excellent option. For the entrance fee you also get a trail map and water. At 5000ft, it's a significant jump in altitude above Boquete, so dress for cooler weather. You can also do a guided hike (US$55 for two to three hours).

Sendero El Pianista HIKING
(Pianist Trail) This day-hike wends its way through dairy land and into humid cloud forest. You need to wade across a small river after 200m, but then it's a steady, leisurely incline for 2km before you start to climb a steeper, narrow path. Using a guide is highly recommended.

The path leads deep into the forest, but you can turn back at any time. To access the trailhead from Boquete, head north on the right bank of the river and cross over two bridges. Immediately before the third bridge, about 4km out of town, a track leads off to the left between a couple of buildings. The trail is not especially difficult, but it isn't always well maintained. In April 2014 two Dutch nationals died while hiking here, though the cause of their deaths remains a mystery. Don't go alone and always let the people at your hostel or hotel know your plans.

Rafting

Adventure seekers shouldn't miss the excellent white-water rafting that's within a 1½-hour drive of Boquete. Ríos Chiriquí and Chiriquí Viejo both flow from the fertile hills of Volcán Barú, and are flanked by forest for much of their lengths. In some places, waterfalls can be seen at the edges of the rivers, and both rivers pass through narrow canyons with awesome, sheer rock walls.

The Río Chiriquí is most often run from May to December, while the Chiriquí Viejo is run the rest of the year. Rapids are III and III-plus, and tours last four to five hours.

When booking a trip, inquire if the outfitter uses a safety kayak for descents and if guides are certified in swift-water rescue. These should be minimum requirements for a safe trip.

Boquete Outdoor Adventures ADVENTURE
(Map p660; ☎6630-1453, 720-2284; www.boqueteoutdooradventures.com; Plaza Los Establos, Av Central; ⏰8am-7:30pm) This highly recommended outfitter run by veteran outdoorsman Jim Omer offers quality rafting trips (US$65 to US$75) and tailored vacations that are ideal for families. Also offers cloud-forest hiking (US$35) and snorkeling by the coastal islands (US$75). Guides are bilingual and the company uses local service providers. Excellent source of information.

Tours & Courses

Coffee Adventures Tours BIRDWATCHING
(☎720-3852, 6634-4698; www.coffeeadventures.net; half-day tours per 2 people US$65) Dutch naturalist guides Terry and Hans are locally renowned as great birding and nature

guides. They also offer hiking in the cloud forest, including Sendero Los Quetzales (US$175 per person) and visits to indigenous communities. They have lodgings in three lovely cottages in dense forest 3km southwest of the town center.

Boquete Tree Trek ADVENTURE
(Map p660; ☎720-1635; www.boquetetreetrek.com; Plaza Los Establos, Av Central; canopy tours US$65; ⏰tours 8am, 10:30am & 1pm) Travelers love this four-hour canopy tour with 12 ziplines, 12 platforms and a rappel in secondary forest. Tours depart daily at 8am and 1pm. The lines pick up some serious speed, so you might want to consider going heavy on the handbrake. Its newest feature is a hanging bridge walk (US$30) crossing six bridges. Includes transportation from the center.

Habla Ya Language Center LANGUAGE
(Map p660; ☎730-8344; www.hablayapanama.com; Plaza Los Establos, Av Central; ⏰8am-6pm Mon-Fri, 9am-noon Sun) Habla Ya offers both group and private Spanish lessons. A week of group lessons (20 hours) starts at US$275. The language school is also well connected to local businesses, so students can take advantage of discounts on everything from accommodations to tours and participate in volunteer projects.

Festivals & Events

Feria de las Flores y del Café FERIA
(http://feriadeboquete.com; fairgrounds; ⏰Jan) The town's annual Flower & Coffee Fair is held for 10 days each January. While there's coffee in the name, it's strangely missing from exhibits, though you will find plenty of rum and children's carnival rides. Book accommodations well ahead.

Boquete Jazz & Blues Festival MUSIC
(www.boquetejazzandbluesfestival.com; fairgrounds; ⏰Feb) Local and international talent converges on Boquete for four days in February for the biggest annual music event in Chiriquí Province.

Feria de las Orquídeas FERIA
(fairgrounds; ⏰Apr) Showing more than 150 varieties, the orchid fair is held for 10 days every April. It's not all flowers: sundown brings rock concerts and dancing.

Sleeping

Pensión Topas GUESTHOUSE $
(Map p660; ☎720-1005; www.pensiontopas.com; Av Belisario Porras; s/d with bathroom US$29/42, without bathroom US$16/28; P 📶 🏊) Built around a small organic garden, this blue-and-orange lodging run by an eccentric German features Tintin murals, a collection of a half-dozen motorbikes and eight tidy rooms. A shady outdoor patio provides ample shared space, and perks include a shared kitchen, a swimming pool and cable TV. The best rooms are on the 2nd floor of the outbuilding with a balcony.

Mamallena Boquete Hostel HOSTEL $
(Map p660; ☎730-8342, 6723-2014; www.mamallenaboquete.com; Av Central; dm US$14, d with/without bathroom US$38/33; P 📶) Facing the central plaza, this turquoise ex-boardinghouse is backpacker central, complete with kitchen, laundry and free pancake breakfasts. For its huge capacity, it feels rather cozy. Three eight-bed dorms boast orthopedic mattresses, while 13 of the 16 private rooms have their own bathrooms. There's a sheltered patio area with grill. Service-oriented, it runs tours and shuttles to Bocas and Santa Catalina.

★ **Bambuda Castle** HOSTEL $$
(☎6873-8386; www.bambuda.net/boquete; El Santuario, Los Naranjos; dm US$14-16, d US$69-79; 📶 🏊) Once upon a time, a Dutchman built this castle to pay homage to his beloved. Now it's a surreal fun center with an indoor swimming pool and Jacuzzi, on-site bar and gardens overlooking the hills. There's three dorm rooms, but the most sought-after lodgings are fiberglass hobbit holes out back, though budding Rapunzels could opt for the two-story tower.

★ **Haven** BOUTIQUE HOTEL $$
(☎730-9345, 6491-5578; www.hotelboquete.com; Av A Oeste; d standard US$90-130, d deluxe US$110-150, ste US$150-200; P ❄ 📶 🏊) This sleekly designed hotel and spa provides a very chic retreat. British-owned, it has eight rooms with cool space-saving designs, set amid verdant gardens. Water features, river stones and palms set the scene for relaxation. Amenities include a full gym and spa with sauna, yoga, steam room, an indoor pool, a natural health center and a Jacuzzi. Professional and service-oriented.

WORTH A TRIP

LOST & FOUND HOSTEL

High in the cloud forest, this wondrous **backpacker community** (☎6432-8182; www.thelostandfoundhostel.com; Valle de la Mina; dm/d/tr without bathroom US$15/35/50; @ 📶) is accessed via a short and steep hike that is rewarded with mountain panoramas. There are four dorms (with eight to 16 bunks) and basic private rooms. Shared bathroom stalls are numerous and well maintained. The Canadian owners have plotted every detail, from fun treasure hunts to coffee tours and a viewing tower.

The kitchen is stocked with basic provisions for sale, and you can also order tasty homestyle meals. There's a mini-pub, a lounge and a movie room loft, set well away from sleepers.

Activities are varied and well priced, and as many as three excursions depart each day. There's an eight-hour maze of trails through La Fortuna Forest Reserve that go as high as 2200m. Hikers can visit an impressive waterfall and visit an indigenous community. You can also tour the trails on horseback (US$40) and visit a local coffee producer (US$25).

Given the isolation, it's necessary to call or email reservations 24 hours in advance. To get here take the bus from David (US$4, one hour) and ask to be dropped off at Km 42 near the large Lost & Found billboard. Follow the trail to the right of the provisions shop upward for about 20 minutes. You can also take a bus from Bocas del Toro Province, starting in Changuinola or Almirante (around US$7).

Tinamou Cottage Jungle Lodge COTTAGE $$
(☎6634-4698, 720-3852; www.coffeeadventures.net; d incl breakfast US$119-149) If you'd like to get away from it all but still be within striking distance of the town and its amenities, choose these lovely cottages on 9 hectares of dense forest, 3km southwest of Boquete. It's owned by Dutch naturalists who are well-known birding guides. Cottages are quite luxurious, with one or two bedrooms and kitchens, and breakfast comes in a basket.

Boquete Garden Inn INN $$
(☎720-2376; www.boquetegardeninn.com; Palo Alto; d incl breakfast US$99-135; P 📶) On the edge of the Río Palo Alto, this garden inn with a dozen rooms in six red-mud cottages is run by a welcoming Briton. The grounds overflow with blossoming tropical flowerbeds, and birds abound (95 species spotted). Rooms – there are five types – with canopy beds are lovely and modern. Service stands out.

Eating & Drinking

Café de Punto Encuentro CAFE $
(Olga's; Map p660; ☎720-2123; Calle 6 Sur; mains US$3-7; ⏰7am-1pm) In a converted carport and garden, this family-run eatery is a find. All guests are *mi amor* (my love) to the affectionate Olga, who cooks breakfast like nobody's business. The menu ranges from pancakes and bacon to Panamanian breakfasts (US$7) with bottomless cups of coffee. Expect to wait, but for this quality of home-cooked food, you won't mind.

APizza PIZZA $
(Map p660; ☎720-2358; www.apizzapanama.com; Av Central s/n; mains US$6-10; ⏰3-10pm Tue-Fri, from noon Sat & Sun) Crisp, thin-crust Neapolitan pies are the simple stars of this casual eatery. They're made from local mozzarella, San Marzano tomatoes and flour imported from the home country. Local Italians say it's the best in town, and who are we to argue? Also has soups and gluten-free options.

★ **Retrogusto** ITALIAN $$
(Map p660; ☎720-2933; www.ilretrogusto.com; Av Central s/n; mains US$7-19; ⏰5:30-10pm Tue-Sat, 11:30am-3pm & 5:30-9:30pm Sun) At this new Italian farm-to-table restaurant, it's a struggle not to order everything on the menu – it all looks and smells so good. But you can't go astray starting with stuffed mushrooms or an exuberant salad. Hormone-free beef, homemade pastas and bubbly artisanal pizzas with sourdough crust are all hits. Watch the action in the open kitchen. Service is attentive.

★ **Boquete Fish House** SEAFOOD $$
(Map p660; ☎6918-7111, 6521-2120; www.facebook.com/BoqueteFishHouseRestaurant; Av Central; mains from US$16; ⏰noon-8pm Mon-Sat; 🌶) One of our favorite places in Boquete

for great seafood is this fish house along the Quebrada Grande. It offers sea bass prepared in eight different ways – from the delightful version that's steamed and wrapped in lettuce leaves to good ol' fish and chips. There are wonderful veggie sides as well as meat and vegetarian choices.

★Colibri INTERNATIONAL **$$$**
(Map p660; ☎6379-1300; Calle 2a Sur; mains US$12-28; ⊙noon-9pm Tue-Sat, 11am-1pm Sun) Run by a warm Italian couple from Padua, this farm-to-table restaurant serves up fresh and delicious meals. The menu items are a real fusion between local and international, with gorgeous beef salad with passion fruit dressing, lobster from Boca Chica and local goat's cheese ice cream. There's also a good wine list and limoncello to cap the night.

Boquete Brewing Company MICROBREWERY
(Map p660; ☎6494-4992; www.boquetebrewingcompany.com; Av Central; ⊙3-10pm Tue, Wed & Sun, to midnight Thu-Sat) With craft-beer bars all the rage in Panama these days, Boquete's contribution is more than hipster-friendly, with an outdoor patio with a food truck serving great pub grub. There's eight beers and two hard ciders on tap at any given time, and they range from the sublime (hard lemonade) to the ridiculous (watermelon ale). Cheers!

ℹ Information

About 1.5km south of Boquete on the road to David, the large **ATP** (☎720-4060; chiriqui@atp.gob.pa; Hwy 43; ⊙9:30am-5:30pm) office sits atop a bluff overlooking town. Here you can pick up maps and obtain information on area attractions. There's a coffee shop on the ground floor and an exhibition upstairs detailing the history of the region (in Spanish only).

Try **Centro Medico San Juan Bautista** (☎720-1881; Calle 2 Norte) for medical care.

Banco Nacional de Panama (☎720-1328; Av Central; ⊙8am-3pm Mon-Fri, 9am-noon Sat) and **Global Bank** (☎720-2329; Av Central; ⊙8am-3pm Mon-Fri, 9am-noon Sat) both have an ATM.

ℹ Getting There & Away

The **main bus terminal** (Map p660) is on the main road near the main plaza. Buses to David (US$1.75, one hour) depart from the **south side of Boquete's main plaza** (Map p660) every 30 minutes from 5am to 6:30pm. From David they run from 6am to 9:30pm. Hourly buses run to the town of Caldera (US$2, 45 minutes).

Hello Travel Panama (Map p660; www.hellotravelpanama.com; Mamallena Hostel) has shuttle vans linking Boquete with Bocas del Toro (US$30 including boat, four hours), stopping at the Lost & Found Hostel (p663), and Santa Catalina (US$35, five hours). You can also link to Puerto Viejo, Costa Rica (eight hours).

Parque Nacional Volcán Barú

This 143-sq-km national park is home to Volcán Barú, Panama's only volcano and the dominant geographical feature of Chiriquí Province. Volcán Barú is no longer active, but it apparently once was, and counts not one but seven craters. At 3474m its summit, the highest point in Panama, affords views of both the Pacific and Caribbean coasts when clear.

The national park is also home to the Sendero Los Quetzales, one of the most scenic treks in the entire country. As its name implies, the trail is one of the best places in Central America to spot the rare resplendent quetzal, especially during the dry season (from February to May). However, even if the Maya bird of paradise fails to show, the park is home to more than 250 bird species as well as pumas, tapirs and the agouti paca, a large spotted rodent also called *conejo pintado* (painted rabbit).

Activities

Volcán Barú HIKING
Climbing Volcán Barú is a goal of many visitors seeking views from the summit of both the Pacific and the Caribbean coasts. It might not be worth it in poor weather, as the going is strenuous and rough, and there is little to see in cloud cover. You can enter the national park on the eastern (Boquete) and western (Volcán) sides of the volcano.

The eastern summit access from Boquete is the easier, but it involves a strenuous uphill hike along a 13.5km road that goes from the park entrance – about 8km northwest of the center of town – to the summit. The road is paved to the ranger station and several kilometers beyond. If you drive or taxi as far up as possible and then walk the rest of the way, it takes about five or six hours to reach the summit from the park gate; walking from town would take another two or three hours each way.

We recommended you hike at night, starting at 11pm or midnight and arriving at dawn to see the sunrise. But for this you'll need to hire a guide and be prepared for the cold. Another option is to spend the night. Camping will also allow you to be at the top during the morning, when the views are best.

The western access is just outside the town of Volcán, on the road to Cerro Punta. From this side, the views of the volcano are far more dynamic. The rugged 16.5km-long road into the park (requiring a 4WD vehicle) goes only a short way off the main road to the foot of the volcano. The view of the summit and the nearby peaks from this entrance are impressive, and there's a lovely loop trail that winds through secondary and virgin forest. The ascent takes 10 to 12 hours.

★**Sendero Los Quetzales** HIKING
(trail fee US$3) One of Panama's most beautiful trails runs between Cerro Punta and Boquete, crisscrossing Río Caldera. You can hike from either direction, but west to east offers more downhill: the town of Cerro Punta is almost 1000m higher than Boquete. The 8km route takes between four and six hours. Getting to and from the trailhead takes another couple of hours either side (about 23km in total). A guide is recommended.

A 4WD taxi can take you to the trailhead on the Cerro Punta side for about US$35 per person; a *colectivo* (shared taxi) will cost US$6. Taxi drivers know the area as Respingo. Road conditions may be very poor due to landslides. The trail is approximately 10km from Cerro Punta, first by paved road (6km) and later dirt (3.5km). When you exit the trail, it's another 8km along the road to Boquete, though you may be able to catch a taxi along the road. In total, the hike is about 23km, so plan accordingly if you intend to walk the length of the trail.

Buses run from David to Cerro Punta (US$3.50, 2¼ hours); last departure is 6pm. Consider leaving your luggage at one of the hotels in David to save yourself the hassle of backtracking. Take only the bare essentials with you on the walk, and a little cash for a good meal and/or lodging when you arrive in Boquete.

Be aware that conditions can change any time, especially after heavy rain. There's talk that hiking the trail with a guide may become a requirement – in recent times many travelers have gotten lost on this stretch and resources for rescue are practically nonexistent.

Sleeping

Parque Nacional Volcán Barú Camping CAMPGROUND $
(campsites US$5) Camping is possible in the park and on the trail to the summit from the Boquete side, along the Sendero Los Quetzales at a picnic spot called Mirador La Roca or at the ranger station at the entrance to the Sendero Los Quetzales on the Cerro Punta side.

Information

The best time to visit is during the dry season, especially early in the morning when wildlife is most active.

Be advised that overnight temperatures can drop below freezing, and it may be windy and cold during the day, particularly in the morning. Dress accordingly and bring a flashlight (torch).

Getting There & Away

The trailhead leading to the summit of Volcán Barú is best accessed from the town of Boquete, while the Sendero Los Quetzales is best approached from Cerro Punta. A taxi will cost US$35 and US$30 respectively.

Volcán

POP 12,720

Clinging to the southwest flank of towering Volcán Barú, Volcán has a pleasant feel and serves as a good base for eating and sleeping and as a springboard for excursions. If you want to see what Boquete was like back when it was just another town in the Chiriquí highlands, this may be the perfect stop for you.

Sights & Activities

Área Silvestre Protegida Lagunas de Volcán NATIONAL PARK
Some 4km west of Volcán, this protected area encompasses the highest lake system (1240m) in Panama. The two picturesque lakes swell in the rainy season, with lush, virgin forest at their edges and Volcán Barú in the background. Surrounding woodlands are excellent sites for birdwatching.

To get to the lakes from downtown Volcán, turn west onto Calle El Valle and follow the signs. Buses don't run here, but you can take a taxi from Volcán for about US$6.

Arte Cruz WORKSHOP
(☎6503-1128, 6622-1502; www.facebook.com/artecruzpanama/; ⏰8:30am-noon & 1:30-5:30pm

Tue-Fri, from 9am Sat & Sun) FREE On the west side of Hwy 41, some 3.5km south of Volcán, you'll spot this workshop where master carver and artist José de la Cruz González makes and sells exquisite signs, sculptures and furniture in mahogany and other woods, as well as impressive etchings on crystal and glass. José trained in fine arts in Italy and Honduras, and his work has been commissioned by buyers worldwide. Visitors are treated to his entertaining demonstrations.

Janson Coffee Farm TOURS

(☎6867-3884; www.jansoncoffeefarm.com; ⊙9am-3pm) Tours of this very productive coffee farm, located about 3km west of Volcán on the way to the lakes, range from a one-hour overview (US$10) to a 2½-hour all-in tour (US$35) that includes tasting expensive geisha coffee and touring the estate. Other activities include birdwatching and fishing tours, and horseback riding in dry season (December to February).

Sleeping & Eating

★Mount Totumas Cloud Forest CABIN $$

(☎6963-5069; www.mounttotumas.com; r US$110-180, cabin US$130-180; @📶) This 162-hectare ecolodge lies 20km northwest of Volcán. At 1900m it's among the highest in Panama, and the cloud forest bordering Parque Internacional La Amistad is a nature-lover's dream. Nine trails over 50km lead to waterfalls and hot springs. Choose from a stylish main lodge, a trailside treehouse or cabins with full kitchens. All have hammock decks with views.

The cabins are off the grid, so hot water, electricity and internet comes via a microhydroplant. Guests can sign up for guided hikes to the top of Mt Totumas (2630m) and into La Amistad park. Transportation is available from Volcán (US$60 one way), located 70 minutes away by a rough road, or from Boquete and David (US$100). Otherwise guests will need a high-clearance 4WD. Services are more limited September to October.

★Cerro Brujo MEDITERRANEAN $$

(☎6669-9196; Brisas del Norte; mains US$9-18; ⊙1-3pm & 6-9pm Tue-Sun) A gourmet restaurant in a funky country house with garden seating. The chalkboard menu offers just three or four daily options. Gregarious owner-chef Patti Miranda's mouthwatering creations use organic and local ingredients only. Offerings might include a spectacular salad from the garden, a lamb stew to die for, mahi-mahi coated in sesame seeds and, for dessert, *tomate de palo* sorbet.

Getting There & Away

Hwy 41, linking Volcán with La Concepción to the south, forks in the center of town: one arrow points left toward Río Sereno, on the Costa Rican border (35km); the other points right toward Cerro Punta (16km), the western entrance to the Sendero Los Quetzales.

Buses to David (US$3, 1½ hours) depart every 15 minutes from 5am to 7:30pm from the station next to the municipal market, 100m northeast of the police station on the road to Cerro Punta. There are also pickup-truck taxis parked by the Delta gasoline station near the Río Sereno–Cerro Punta fork in the road.

Cerro Punta

POP 7750

Lying at 800m, this tranquil highland town is reminiscent of an alpine village. Here the region takes on an almost European look, with meticulously tended vegetable plots and chalet-like houses with steep-pitched roofs. It's unsurprising to learn that a Swiss colony was founded here many decades ago and the hamlet just south is called Nueva Suiza (New Switzerland).

Visitors come to Cerro Punta primarily during the dry season (from mid-December to April) to access the two nearby national parks: Volcán Barú and La Amistad. The town itself makes a charming stop, however, especially since the area is known for its succulent strawberries, available for much of the year at roadside stands.

Sleeping & Eating

Hotel Cerro Punta HOTEL $

(☎6546-7334, 771-2020; www.hotelcerropunta.com; r US$37; P📶) This friendly hotel on the main road offers a row of 10 concrete rooms that accommodate three people. They are a bit tired and beaten up, but they overlook a grassy backyard, and the hot showers will be the last you'll see for a while if you're on your way to Volcán Barú or La Amistad national parks. Decent and good-value in-house restaurant.

Getting There & Away

Buses run from David to Cerro Punta (US$3.50, 2¼ hours, every 20 minutes), stopping at Volcán and Bambito along the way, and carrying on to Guadalupe. If you're coming from Costa Rica, catch this bus at the turnoff from the Interamericana at La Concepción.

If you're driving, the main road continues through Cerro Punta and ends at Guadalupe, 3km further on. Another road takes off to the left heading for the Las Nubes entrance to Parque Internacional La Amistad, just under 7km to the northwest.

Parque Internacional La Amistad (Las Nubes)

The 4000-sq-km **Parque Internacional La Amistad** (International Friendship Park; campsites US$10; ⌚8am-4pm), a favorite of hikers and naturalists alike, covers portions of both Chiriquí and Bocas del Toro Provinces. Although the lion's share of the park lies in the latter, the Chiriquí side, with its entrance at Las Nubes, is more accessible.

Most of the park is inaccessible terrain high up in the Talamanca mountains. It's worth making the trek, though, as the park is home to a recorded 90 mammal species and all six cat species. More than 450 bird species have also been recorded here, including quetzals and harpy eagles.

Sleeping

Las Nubes Ranger Station CABIN $
(☎775-3163, 774-6671; Las Nubes; dm US$15) This basic ranger station has a dormitory cabin with bunk beds. Due to its popularity among international school groups, reservations are advisable. Guests have kitchen access; stock up on provisions in Cerro Punta. Bring your own bedding; a mosquito net is a good idea. To reserve, call **Ministerio de Ambiente** (☎774-6671; Av Red Gray; ⌚8am-4pm Mon-Fri) in David or visit the Co-op Restaurant at the park entrance.

Information

Enter via the Las Nubes park office, 6km northwest of Cerro Punta. Camping permits (US$10 per person) are payable at the Las Nubes ranger station.

If you plan to spend much time at Las Nubes, be sure to bring a jacket or sweater. At 2280m above sea level, this area of the park has a cool climate; temperatures are usually around 75°F (24°C) in the daytime, but can drop as low as 38°F (3°C) at night.

Getting There & Away

The Las Nubes entrance is about 6km northwest from Cerro Punta; a sign on the main road in Cerro Punta marks the turnoff. A taxi should cost US$10.

BOCAS DEL TORO PROVINCE

POP 156,480 / ELEV SEA LEVEL TO 3336M

With its Caribbean islands dotting a shock of blue waters, Bocas del Toro is all that's tropical. This is Panama's principal tourist draw and it will no doubt provide some of your most memorable experiences. The archipelago consists of six densely forested islands, scores of uninhabited islets and the Parque Nacional Marino Isla Bastimentos, Panama's oldest marine park.

The longtime base of the Chiquita Banana company, the mainland boasts the Parque Internacional La Amistad, shared with Costa Rica. It's also home to diverse wildlife such as the elusive jaguar, traditional Ngöbe-Buglé settlements, and the Naso, one of few remaining American tribes with its own monarch.

Most visitors come for a hefty dose of sun and surf. Few are disappointed with the Bocas cocktail of water, fun and thatched luxury, but there's a lot more to what might be Panama's most beautiful corner.

Isla Colón

POP 9000

The archipelago's most developed island is home to the provincial capital of Bocas del Toro. From the mid-1990s, foreign investors flooded the island, creating hotels, restaurants and condos while infrastructure for water, trash and sewage lagged far behind. Today the island, which runs on diesel, struggles to find a balance between satisfying development and serving community needs.

Note that the town, the archipelago and the province all share the name Bocas del Toro. To avoid confusion, we refer to the provincial capital as Bocas town or simply Bocas.

Activities

Boat Tours

The most popular tours in the area are all-day snorkeling trips, which are perfect for nondivers who want a taste of the area's

Archipiélago de Bocas del Toro

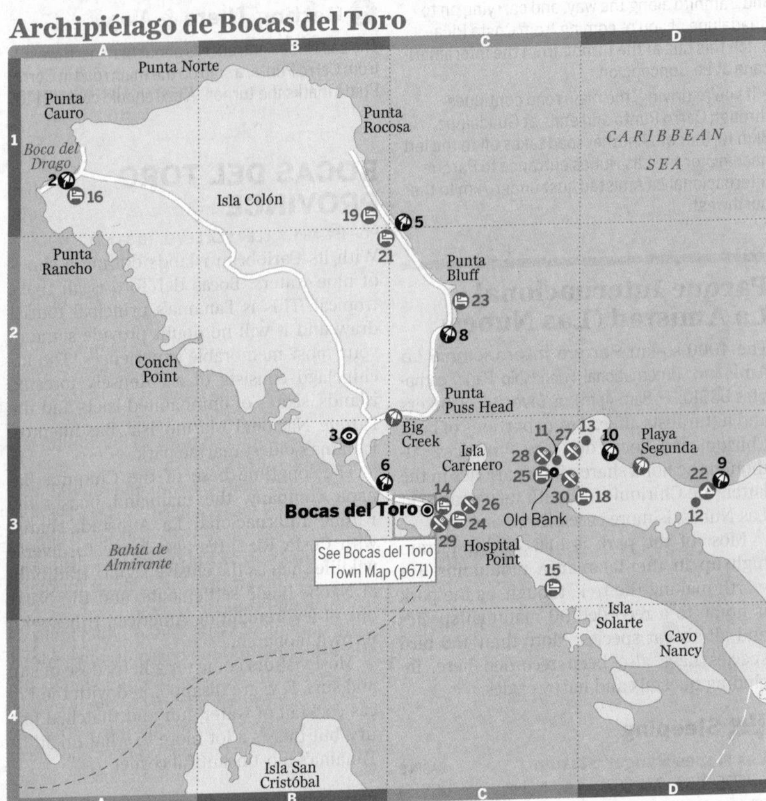

Archipiélago de Bocas del Toro

Top Sights

1 Parque Nacional Marino Isla Bastimentos ... E4

Sights

2 Boca del Drago ... A1
3 Finca Los Monos Botanical Garden ... B3
4 Nivida Bat Cave ... E3
5 Playa Bluff ... C1
6 Playa El Istmito ... B3
7 Playa Larga ... E4
8 Playa Punch ... C2
9 Red Frog Beach ... D3
10 Wizard Beach ... D3

Activities, Courses & Tours

11 Bastimentos Alive ... C3
12 Bastimentos Sky Zipline Canopy Tour ... D3
Scuba 6 Ecodiving ... (see 25)
13 Up in the Hill ... D3

Sleeping

14 Aqua Lounge ... C3
15 Bambuda Lodge ... C3
16 Cabañas Estefany ... A1
17 Casa Cayuco ... F4
18 Eclypse del Mar ... D3
19 Island Plantation ... B1
20 La Loma ... E4
21 Oasis Bluff Beach ... B2
22 Palmar Tent Lodge ... D3
23 Tesoro Escondido ... C2
24 Tierra Verde ... C3
25 Tío Tom's Guesthouse ... C3

Eating

26 Bibi's on the Beach ... C3
27 Coco Hill ... C3
28 Firefly Restaurant ... C3
29 Leaf Eaters Cafe ... C3
30 Sea Monkey ... C3

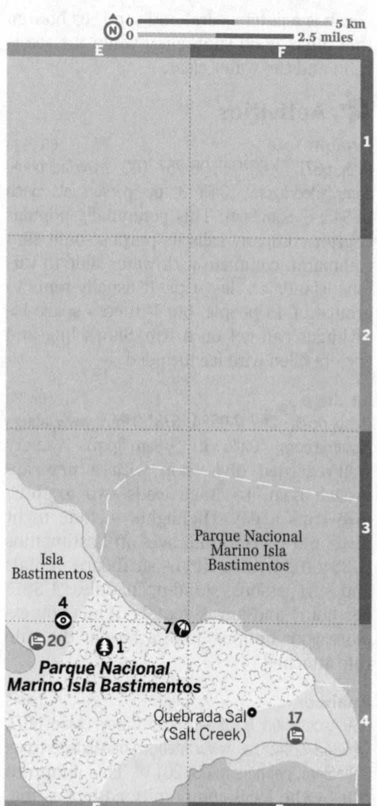

rich marine life. A typical tour costs US$25 per person, and goes to Dolphin Bay, Cayo Crawl, Red Frog Beach (p676) (US$5 entry) and Hospital Point.

A trip to the distant Cayos Zapatillas costs US$35, and includes lunch, beach time and a jungle hike on Cayo Zapatilla Sur.

Many 'tours' are really little more than boat transportation to a pretty spot. If you have your own snorkel gear (or if you rent it), you can also charter motor boats. Agree on a price before you go.

Diving & Snorkeling

Although experienced divers accustomed to crystal-clear Caribbean diving may be disappointed with the archipelago – nearly 40 rivers discharging silt into the seas around the archipelago reduce visibility dramatically – it still has much to offer. The islands' emerald-green waters are home to the usual assortment of tropical species and with a little luck you might see barracudas, stingrays, dolphins and nurse sharks. The better sites include **Dark Wood Reef**, northwest of Bastimentos; **Hospital Point**, a 15m wall off Cayo Nancy; and the base of the buoy near **Punta Juan**, north of Isla Cristóbal.

A two-tank dive will cost around US$85; there are also dive certification courses. A number of reliable suppliers offer good-value snorkeling and diving trips out of Bocas.

Surfing

Beginner surfers looking for a bit of reef experience should check out **Playa Punch** (Map p668), which offers a good mix of lefts and rights. Although it can get heavy when big, Punch generally offers some of the kindest waves around.

Just past Punch en route to Playa Bluff is a popular reef break known as **Dumpers**. This left break can get up to 3m and should only by ridden by experienced surfers; wiping out on the reef here is dangerous. There is also an inner break known as **Inner Dumps**, which also breaks left but is more forgiving than its outer mate.

Be careful walking out on the reefs as they are sharp and full of sea urchins – don't go barefoot. If you wipe out and get cut up, be sure to properly disinfect your wounds. Be aware that seawater in the Caribbean does not help the healing process; the warm water temperature means the ocean is full of live bacteria.

The island's most infamous surf spot is Playa Bluff (p670), which throws out powerful barreling waves that break in shallow water along the beach and have a reputation for snapping boards (and occasionally bones). The waves close quickly, but the tubes here are truly awesome, especially when the swells are strong.

Cycling

Whether you're heading along the paved road to Boca del Drago or taking a dirt track to Playa Bluff, a bike can seriously increase your mobility. Note that the bike ride to Boca del Drago from Boca town is taxing; if you're unsure of your fitness level, head for Punta Bluff instead. Bikes are available from some hostels as well as from Ixa's Bike World (p670) and **Bocas Bicis** (Map p671; Av E; per hr/day US$3/12; ⏲9am-7pm) in Boca town. **Flying Pirates** (Map p671; ☎6689-5050; www.flyingpiratesbocas.com; cnr Calle 3 & Av C; half/full day US$110/140; ⏲9am-7pm) rents out ATVs/quad bikes.

Hiking

If you're looking to seriously get off the beaten path, there is a network of undeveloped hiking trails that fans out across Isla Colón. One of the more popular hikes starts at the end of the coastal road in Mimbi Timbi to the northeast and carries on west along the coast to Boca del Drago. You will need about six hours of daylight to complete the hike, and you must carry in all your water. The trail winds past caves, caverns and plenty of vine-entangled jungle. A bike will help speed things up a bit, though you'll be carrying it part of the way, especially if it's been raining recently.

Kayaking

Sea kayaking is a great way to travel between islands. You will need to be wary of boat traffic, though, and the occasional swell. Some dive shops and hostels rent kayaks.

Bocas del Toro Town

Colorful and full of Caribbean-style clapboard houses, Bocas del Toro (better known simply as Bocas town) was built by the United Fruit Company in the early 20th century. Today it is a relaxed community of West Indians, Latinos and resident gringos, with a friendly atmosphere that is contagious. It's an easy place to adapt to and even easier to linger in.

Bocas serves as a convenient base for exploring the archipelago; *taxis marinos* (water taxis) can whisk you away to remote beaches and snorkeling sites for just a few dollars. The real allure here, though, is simply to be able to slow down and soak up the Caribbean vibes.

Sights

Playa Bluff BEACH

(Map p668) This lovely beach is pounded by intense waves. Though you wouldn't want to get into the water here without a board, the soft, yellow sand and palm-fringed shores are pristine. The beach is 8km from Bocas town, alongside the road after you round Punta Bluff. It serves as a nesting area for sea turtles from May to September.

Boca del Drago BEACH

(Dragon's Mouth; Map p668) Boca del Drago, in the northwest of Isla Colón, is one of the best beaches on the island, though the surf can be rough at times. Just offshore from the beach is a patchy coral-and-sand sea bottom that offers good snorkeling when the sea is calm and the water clear.

Activities

Dragon Tours BOATING

(Map p671; ☎6879-5506, 757-7010; www.facebook.com/Jadedragon9; Calle 3; per person incl lunch US$45; ⏰9am-5pm) This perennially popular charter company sails its purpose-built 19m catamaran complete with water slide to various islands on day trips. It usually rents to groups of 45 people, but if there's space individuals can get on a trip. Snorkeling and coolers filled with ice included.

La Buga DIVING

(Map p671; ☎757-9534, 6781-0755; www.labugapanama.com; Calle 3; ⏰8am-8pm) A very well-regarded dive shop with a new approach boat, La Buga leads two to three dive trips a day. Highlights include night dives and visits to the caves off Bastimentos (US$100). It also offers surfboard rentals and surf lessons, stand-up paddles (US$15 per hour) and kayak rentals. While you explore your options, grab a bite at the cute cafe attached.

Anaboca TOURS

(La Asociación Natural Bocas Carey; Map p671; ☎6843-7244; www.anaboca.bocasdeltoro.org; Calle 3era; per person US$20) This nonprofit run by the local community addresses marine-turtle conservation. In season (April to August), certified guides offer nighttime tours to groups of eight or fewer to view turtle hatching on Playa Bluff. You can also arrange overnight community stays, a good idea if you are there to watch hatching in the wee hours.

Bocas Surf School SURFING

(Map p671; ☎757-9057, 6852-5291; www.bocassurfschool.com; cnr Av H & Calle 5; half-/full-day courses US$59/89) This well-regarded school, conveniently located next to a small hostel, caters to beginner surfers with daily classes at 8:30am and 2:30pm. It also rents out boards for US$15 per day.

Ixa's Bike World CYCLING

(Map p671; Av H; bikes per hr US$3, fat bikes per 24hr US$15; ⏰8am-6pm Mon-Sat) Repairs and rents out a wide selection of bicycles from a hole-in-the-wall workshop at the northern end of town, with mountain bikes to take on Boca del Drago.

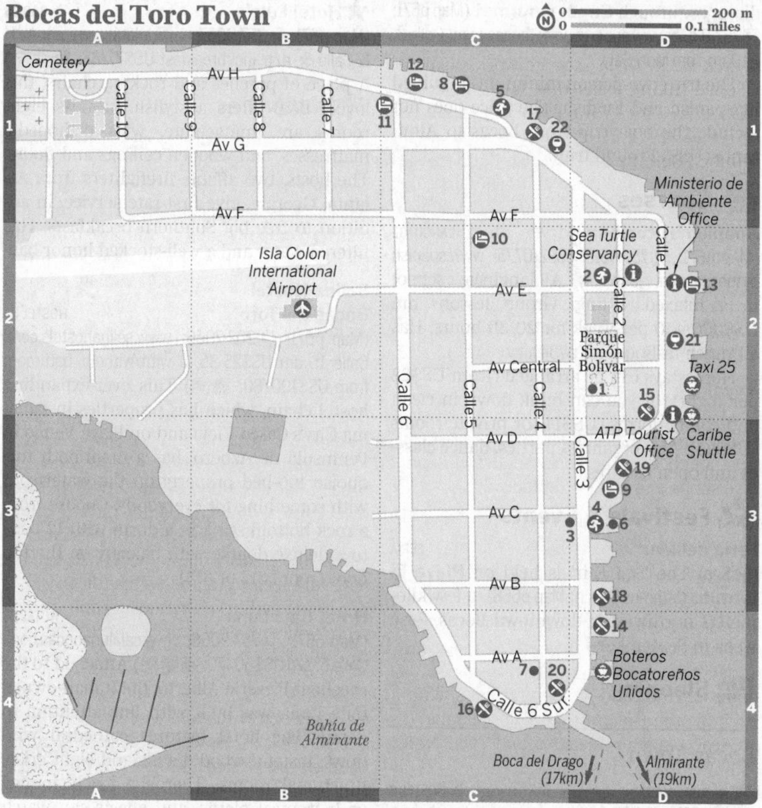

Bocas del Toro Town

Activities, Courses & Tours
- 1 Anaboca ... D2
- 2 Bocas Bicis ... D2
- Bocas Surf School ... (see 8)
- 3 Dragon Tours ... D3
- 4 Flying Pirates ... D3
- 5 Ixa's Bike World ... C1
- 6 La Buga ... D3
- 7 Spanish by the Sea ... C4

Sleeping
- 8 Bocas Surf School & Hotel ... C1
- 9 Hotel Bocas del Toro ... D3
- 10 Hotel Cala Luna ... C2
- 11 Hotel Lula's ... C1
- 12 Mamallena ... C1
- 13 Selina Hostel Bocas del Toro ... D2

Eating
- 14 Azul Restaurant ... D4
- 15 Cafe del Mar ... D2
- 16 El Último Refugio ... C4
- 17 La Casbah ... C1
- 18 Om Café ... D3
- Pizzeria Alberto ... (see 10)
- 19 Raw ... D3
- 20 Super Gourmet ... C4

Drinking & Nightlife
- 21 Barco Hundido ... D2
- 22 Bookstore Bar ... C1
- Selina Bar ... (see 13)

Oreba Chocolate Tour TOURS
(☎6649-1457; www.oreba.bocasdeltoro.org; Río Oeste Arriba, mainland; per person US$35) This guided tour leaves Bocas and takes you around an organic chocolate farm, run by the indigenous Ngöbe-Buglé community, on the mainland near Almirante. Tour the farm, see tree sloths, sample chocolate – classified as some of the highest-grade cacao in the world – and enjoy a traditional lunch. Book

direct or through **Super Gourmet** (Map p671; ☎757-9357; www.supergourmetbocas.com; Calle 3; ⏲9am-7pm Mon-Sat).

The trip (two-person minimum) is guided in Spanish and English. The price does not include the boat trip from Bocas to Almirante (US$12 round trip).

Courses

Spanish by the Sea LANGUAGE
(Map p671; ☎757-9518, 6592-0775; www.spanishbythesea.com; Calle 4) A language school in a relaxed setting. Group lessons are US$360/450 per week for 20/30 hours. Has a branch in Boquete (p734).

Homestays can be arranged (from US$22 per night), or you can bunk down in clean and comfy dorms (US$14) or private rooms (US$24). Also organizes parties, dance classes and open lectures.

Festivals & Events

Feria del Mar FERIA
(⏲Sep) The 'Sea Fair' is held on **Playa El Istmito** (Isthmus Beach; Map p668), a few kilometers northwest of downtown Bocas, for a week in September.

Sleeping

Bocas Town

★**Mamallena** HOSTEL $
(Map p671; ☎760-9934; www.mamallenabocas.com/bocas-del-toro; Av H; dm US$18, d US$45-60, q US$90; ❄📶) Our favorite hostel in Bocas town is this stylish new over-the-water option with tropical prints, palms and a wraparound bar with a pool table on the ocean deck. Big enough to meet folks but not industrial sized, it has regular happy-hour events and kayaking right off the dock (US$20 all day). The 14 rooms are all air-conditioned, some with balcony.

Bocas Surf School & Hotel HOSTEL $
(Map p671; ☎757-9057, 6852-5291; http://bocassurfschool.com; cnr Av H & Calle 5; dm/d without bathroom US$20/50; ❄📶) It's not every day that your hostel has its own swim-off dock. This super-cute cottage at a celebrated surf school (p670) offers 10 solid bunks in two rooms, and two doubles – the one on the 1st floor is quite posh. There's a communal kitchen and a good food truck parked on-site. Nonsurfers can rent kayaks.

★**Hotel Lula's** B&B $$
(Map p671; ☎757-9057; www.lulabb.com; cnr Av H & Calle 6; d/tr incl breakfast US$77/88; ❄@📶) A place of porches and rocking chairs, this lovely B&B offers a stylish stay. Its eight rooms are immaculate, with orthopedic mattresses, and wooden ceilings and floors. The hosts, two affable firefighters from Atlanta, Georgia, give first-rate service, in addition to free big Southern breakfasts. Has filtered water and a well-stocked honor bar.

Selina Hostel Bocas del Toro HOSTEL $$
(Map p671; ☎202-7966; www.selinahostels.com; Calle 1; dm US$25-35, d with/without bathroom from US$100/80; @📶) This ever-expanding hostel chain, which has properties in Panama City's Casco Viejo and on Playa Venao in Península de Azuero, has a mammoth turquoise 196-bed property on the waterfront with something for everybody. Choose from a rock-bottom bunk in a dorm with 12 beds to a deluxe double with balcony on the top floor (room 312 or 313).

Hotel Cala Luna HOTEL $$
(Map p671; ☎757-9066; www.calalunabocas.com; Calle 5; s/d US$60/70; ❄@📶) Attached to the excellent Pizzeria Alberto, the Italian-owned Cala Luna was built with fine attention to detail. The hotel features cathedral windows, tasteful wood details and eight crisp, functional rooms. There's a lovely lounge with tropical plants, and guests can watch planes coming in for a landing 30m above their heads from the rooftop lookouts.

★**Hotel Bocas del Toro** INN $$$
(Map p671; ☎757-9018; www.hotelbocasdeltoro.com; Calle 2; d incl breakfast US$129-299; ❄@📶) Our favorite place to stay in Bocas town, this three-story waterfront inn has 11 spacious all-hardwood rooms with firm beds, luxurious linens and a warm decor; some have seafront balconies. Perks include concierge service and amenities such as Silico Creek coffee produced by a Ngöbe-Buglé community. There's a fun streetside bar and an excellent waterfront restaurant serving Panamanian classics.

Around the Island

Cabañas Estefany CABIN $
(Map p668; ☎6956-4525; www.facebook.com/cabinasturisticasestefany; Boca del Drago; dm/d US$15/44, 7-person cabin US$100; 📶) Though a far cry from luxury, this 11-room complex is

one of the few budget beach lodgings on Isla Colón. Its brightly painted wooden *cabañas* are bare-bones and bathrooms have cold-water showers. Secure a room with a fan as it can get quite buggy. The rooms on the 1st floor have balconies and ocean views.

Tesoro Escondido CABIN $
(Map p668; ☎6711-9594; www.tesoroescondido.info; Playa Paunch; d/tr from US$50/60, 2-/3-/4-person cabins US$95/120/135) Exuding a very homespun charm, this colorful seafront lodge with eight rooms, three thatched cottages and a suite works its magic. Mosaic tables and recycled-bottle construction in the showers lend a bohemian air; the hammock-strewn upstairs balcony is a treat; and rooms 7 and 8, accessed by a stepped tree trunk, are awesome.

Oasis Bluff Beach B&B $$
(Map p668; ☎WhatsApp 1-479-381-0096; www.oasisbluffbeach.com; Playa Bluff; d incl breakfast US$120;) This airy, modern and tasteful off-the-grid home is a wonderful British-run B&B. It's on a sprawling green lawn facing the water, with a long wraparound porch on the 2nd story. Guests can order excellent meals too. It's 20 minutes from Bocas town.

★ **Island Plantation** BOUTIQUE HOTEL $$$
(Map p668; ☎6612-7798; www.islandplantationbocas.com; Playa Bluff; d/ste US$160/224;) Reminiscent of an intimate resort in Bali, this boutique property has seven lovely rooms with private open-air showers in the garden, king-size four-poster beds, mosquito nets and hardwood balconies. The stunner is a two-bedroom suite featuring an enormous hardwood veranda. Guests can dine on the beach for lunch; there's a clay oven for excellent pizzas. Warm welcome, great service.

Eating

Cafe del Mar CAFE $
(Map p671; ☎6212-8712; Calle 1; dishes US$6-9; 8am-10pm Tue-Sun;) For all-natural wraps, sandwiches and burgers served with homemade hot sauce, duck into this tiny eatery. There's also all-day breakfast, smoothies and juices, including a watermelon ginger cooler that's to die for. Preservatives are banned, and vegetarian choices are legion. Eat in or take-out. Great coffee too.

Pizzeria Alberto PIZZA $
(Map p671; ☎757-9066; Calle 5; pizzas US$8-14; 5-10pm Fri-Wed) Sardinian-run Alberto's is a favorite local haunt, where pizza with toppings such as artichokes, olives and Gorgonzola satisfies big appetites.

Raw ASIAN $$
(Map p671; ☎6938-8473; www.facebook.com/RawFusionBocas; Calle 1 s/n; mains US$12-15; 3-10pm Tue-Sun) It's just a little plank restaurant on the water, but the Asian-fusion offerings are spot on. Sake accompanies fresh tofu spring rolls and amazing tuna tapas. The salads are wonderful, and service is friendly and attentive. At night candles are lit and the full bar, specializing in original martinis (from US$7) and cocktails, starts humming.

★ **Om Café** INDIAN $$
(Map p671; ☎6127-0671; http://omcafebocas.com; Calle 3; mains US$9-19; 4-10pm Mon-Fri year-round, plus Sat Dec-Apr;) When you smell gorgeous aromas spilling out onto the sidewalk, you're at this welcoming Indian cafe serving classic curries, korma and thalis. Service can be slow, so pass the wait with an original cocktail, such as the Tipsy Turban (US$6), a dizzy mix of passion fruit or lime juice, rum and sugar. Good selection of vegetarian dishes.

La Casbah MEDITERRANEAN $$
(Map p671; ☎6477-4727; Av H; menu US$14, mains US$13-16; 6-10pm Tue-Sat) Locals and travelers love this Mediterranean restaurant

DON'T MISS

MONKEY GARDEN

One of the joys of visiting Bocas is touring the **Finca Los Monos Botanical Garden** (Map p668; ☎757-9461, 6729-9943; www.bocasdeltorobotanicalgarden.com; garden/birdwatching tours US$15/25; garden tours 1pm Mon & 8:30am Fri, birdwatching tours 6:30am & 5pm on request) a couple of kilometers northwest of the center. Painstakingly carved out of 10 hectares of secondary rainforest over almost two decades, it contains hundreds of species of local and imported trees and ornamental plants, and is teeming with wildlife. Co-owner and guide Lin Gillingham will point out howler and white-faced capuchin monkeys, sloths and various bird species. Tours, on Fridays and Mondays, must be booked in advance; garden tours depart regularly while birding tours are on demand.

WORTH A TRIP

BAMBUDA LODGE

Run by two Calgary friends focused on fun and service, this destination **hostel** (Map p668; ☎6962-4644, 6765-4755; www.bambuda.net; Isla Solarte; dm US$18, d US$69-99, d without bathroom US$59, d bungalows US$89, incl breakfast;) is set up in lush rainforest with fruit trees and trails, overlooking a coral reef. The attractive all-wood complex features a gorgeous swimming pool and an adrenaline-stoking 60m-long water slide plunging from hillside reception into the ocean. Water taxis provide transfers (US$5) from Bocas.

Bambuda counts two fan-cooled dorms with 10 beds each and private rooms that include quite deluxe jungle bungalows. The open-air bar and dining room serves set meals (US$8 to US$12). If they're in season, there's mango, star fruit and custard apples for the picking, while 10km of trails fan out in several directions. Nonguests can get a pass (US$8) to use the facilities. There's snorkeling equipment as well kayaks and canoes sometimes available.

serving up gazpacho, goat's cheese salad, and seafood and meat dishes such as tabbouleh couscous salad with chicken. The fish of the day comes in cream or white-wine sauce, and there's a nice veggie plate for noncarnivores.

Azul Restaurant FUSION $$

(Map p671; ☎6531-5916; www.facebook.com/azulrestaurantbocas; Calle 3era s/n, 2nd fl; set menus US$20; 6-10pm Tue-Sun;) Come to Azul for excellent-value gourmet dining set on a lovely 2nd-floor balcony (there's also seating inside). There's no menu, just the option of a vegetarian or non-vegetarian (though heavy on seafood) set meal with six courses (including two desserts). Options range from sesame mango tuna tartare to beetroot carpaccio and squid-ink risotto. Impeccable service.

★**El Último Refugio** CARIBBEAN $$$

(Map p671; ☎6726-9851; www.ultimorefugio.com; Calle 6 Sur; mains US$14-20; 6-10pm Mon-Sat) A favorite splurge of Bocas locals, this mellow North American–run place on the edge of the sea does date night right. Caribbean and seafood dishes include red curry calamari and miso-crusted grouper on the chalkboard. Service is friendly and the tranquil location makes it a great spot for a quiet, romantic dinner. Reserve ahead.

Drinking & Nightlife

Selina Bar CLUB

(Map p671; ☎202-7966; www.selinahostels.com; Calle 1; 7pm-midnight Sun-Thu, to 2am Fri & Sat) The bar at this landmark hostel is open daily, with happy hour between 7pm and 8pm, but most people make it here between 10pm and 2am on a Friday, when all the stops are pulled out and it's party time.

Barco Hundido BAR

(Map p671; Calle 1; 8pm-midnight) At some point you'll probably find yourself at this open-air bar, affectionately known as the 'Wreck Deck' after the sunken banana boat that rests in the clear Caribbean waters in front. A short boardwalk extends from the bar to an island seating area that includes swings; perfect for stargazing.

Bookstore Bar BAR

(Map p671; ☎6452-5905; Calle 2; noon-1am Mon-Sat, 5pm-12:30am Sun) Just what its name suggests: this cavernous spot sells both books and drinks, though most seem more interested in the latter. It's the best spot for live music in Bocas, with rock, salsa and punk on Tuesday and Saturday. Run by a couple of affable North Americans, it's a mecca for gringos at the start (and sometimes at the end) of an evening.

Information

ATP Tourist Office (Autoridad de Turismo Panama; Map p671; ☎757-9642; bocasdeltoro@atp.gob.pa; Calle 1; 9am-4pm Mon-Fri) In a large government building next to the police station on the eastern waterfront.

Banco Nacional de Panamá (☎758-3850; cnr Calle 4 & Av E; 8am-3pm Mon-Fri, 9am-2pm Sat) Exchanges traveler's checks and has a 24-hour ATM.

Bocas del Toro Hospital (☎757-9201; Av G; 24hr) The island's only hospital and has a 24-hour emergency room. A new Taiwan-funded facility is under construction to the northwest.

Ministerio de Ambiente Office (Map p671; ☎758-6822, 757-9442; Calle 1; 9am-5pm

Mon-Fri) Can answer questions about national parks or other protected areas.

Sea Turtle Conservancy (Map p671; ☎757-9186; www.conserveturtles.org; Calle 2; ⏲9am-5pm Mon-Fri) The world's oldest sea-turtle research and conservation organization has an information office in Bocas town.

DANGERS & ANNOYANCES

- Unlike in most other places in Panama, tap water is not safe to drink in the archipelago unless it is filtered. Bocas town has a water-treatment plant, but locals say the tap water is not to be trusted. It's certainly fine for brushing your teeth, but for drinking purchase bottled water or purify your own.
- The surf can be dangerous and there are frequent riptides – use caution when going out into the waves.
- The archipelago is generally a conservative place and local law bans men (and women) from walking the streets shirtless. Even if you are on your way to the beach, wear a shirt or you might be sent back to your hotel by the police.
- No matter what age you are, you will almost certainly be offered drugs for sale while walking the streets of downtown Bocas. Do not even think about it: Panama takes its drug laws very seriously indeed.

Getting There & Away

All arrivals must pay US$3 tourist tax when arriving at any port in Bocas del Toro.

Air Panama (☎757-9841; www.airpanama.com) flies to Panama City (from US$123, one hour) twice daily, sometimes via Changuinola (US$63), as well as to David (US$85). Office at the **airport** (Map p671; ☎757-9208; Av E).

If you don't fly into Bocas you'll have to take a water taxi (US$6) from Almirante on the mainland. On the waterfront, **Taxi 25** (Map p671; ☎757-9071; www.facebook.com/bocastaxi25; ⏲6am-6pm) makes the half-hour trip between 6am and 6:30pm every 30 minutes.

Caribe Shuttle (Map p671; ☎757-7048; www.caribeshuttle.com; Calle 1) runs a combination boat-bus trip (US$33) to Puerto Viejo and Cahuita in Costa Rica three times daily. There's also an option to go on to San Jose (US$76). It provides a hotel pick-up, but you must reserve one day in advance.

Getting Around

A cross-island bus goes to Boca del Drago (US$2.50, one hour) and another goes to Playa Bluff (US$3) from Parque Simón Bolívar, with departures between 7am and 7pm. It doubles up as a school bus, so afternoon trips may be delayed.

To reach nearby islands, you can hire boaters operating motorized boats and canoes along the waterfront. As a general rule, you should always sort out the rate beforehand, and clarify if it is for one way or round-trip. Always pay on the return leg – this guarantees a pick-up – though most boaters will want some money up-front to buy petrol. Though rates vary, you will get a better deal if you speak Spanish, are with a group and arrange for a pick-up.

Boteros Bocatoreños Unidos (Map p671; ☎757-9760; Calle 3; ⏲6:30am-11pm) runs to destinations including Isla Carenero (US$2), Isla Bastimentos and Isla Solarte (US$5) and Red Frog Beach (US$8). Scheduled boats leave for Almirante (US$6, 20 minutes) every half-hour. Staff are trained in safe boating and sustainable-tourism practices.

Isla Carenero

POP 350

Slightly larger than a postage stamp, this tiny isle ringed by sand feels a notch more relaxed than the main island. It lies a few hundred meters southeast from Isla Colón and its close location makes it a go-to for a leisurely waterfront lunch or happy-hour action. Often overlooked, it takes its name from 'careening,' which in nautical talk means to lean a ship on one side for cleaning or repairing. In October 1502 Columbus' ships were careened and cleaned on this cay while the admiral recovered from a bellyache.

In recent times many hotels have been added, and nature isn't as wild here as it is on the more remote islands. Yet Carenero remains a nice alternative if you're seeking peace and quiet.

Sleeping & Eating

Aqua Lounge HOSTEL $

(Map p668; www.bocasaqualounge.info; dm/d without bathroom incl breakfast US$15/32;) Rough, rustic and grungy, this 12-room backpacker palace is a matchstick construction on the dock facing Bocas town. And guests just can't get enough – from the hugely popular US$1-a-bottle bar (open from 7am to midnight; party night is Friday) to the wraparound dock with swimming platform and swings.

Tierra Verde HOTEL $$

(Map p668; ☎757-9903; www.hoteltierraverde.com; s/d incl breakfast US$65/75, ste US$150-175;) This family-run three-story hotel sits back from the beach amid shady palms and flowers. Designed in a contemporary island style, there are six spacious all-wood rooms on two floors. The suite at the top allows in ample light. There's the option of airport pick-ups (US$10). Go for rooms 4 or 5 for ocean views.

★ Leaf Eaters Cafe VEGETARIAN $

(Map p668; ☎6675-1354; www.facebook.com/bocasleafeaters; dishes US$8-12; ⊙11am-5pm Mon-Sat; ✎) For excellent pescatarian, vegetarian and vegan lunches, head to this over-the-water restaurant on Isla Carenero. Start with a cool cucumber-mint-coconut-watermelon shake. Quirky and flavorful offerings include 'hippie bowls' (brown rice with vegetables and dressing), grilled fish sandwiches with caramelized onions, blackened fish tacos and scrumptious shiitake burgers. Cheery decor and friendly atmosphere.

Bibi's on the Beach SEAFOOD $$

(Map p668; ☎757-9137, 6981-2749; http://bocasbuccaneerresort.com/surfside-restaurant-and-bar; mains US$7-15; ⊙9am-9pm) With great atmosphere, this over-the-water restaurant and surf outfitter makes tasty soups, killer *ceviche (*citrus-cured seafood), whole lobsters (US$27) and lightly fried fish. The service couldn't be friendlier and the sea views (and cocktails) will keep you lingering. Happy hour coincides with sundown: 4pm to 7pm.

ℹ Getting There & Away

Isla Carenero is a quick and easy US$2 boat ride from the waterfront in Bocas town. Oddly there is no public pier. Water taxis dock at the small marina on the tip of the island. From here, there is a track that leads to the little town and continues across the island. Exercise caution on the track, as there can be aggressive dogs around.

Isla Bastimentos

POP 1950

Although it's just a 10-minute boat ride from the town of Bocas del Toro, Isla Bastimentos is like a different world. Some travelers say this is their favorite island in their favorite part of Panama. The northwest coast of the island is home to palm-fringed beaches that serve as nesting grounds for sea turtles, while most of the northern and southern coasts consists of mangrove islands and coral reefs that lie within the boundaries of the **Parque Nacional Marino Isla Bastimentos.**

The main settlement on Bastimentos is Old Bank. It has a prominent West Indian population whose origins are in the banana industry. The island is also home to the Ngöbe-Buglé village of Quebrada Sal (Salt Creek).

Sights

Wizard Beach BEACH

(Playa Primera; Map p668) The most beautiful beach on Isla Bastimentos is awash in powdery yellow sand and backed by thick vine-strewn jungle. It's connected to Old Bank via a wilderness path, which normally takes 20 minutes or so but can be virtually impassable after heavy rains. The path continues along the coast to Playa Segunda (Second Beach) and Red Frog Beach.

Red Frog Beach BEACH

(Map p668; US$5) Small but perfectly formed, Red Frog Beach is named after the *rana rojo* (strawberry poison-dart frog), an amphibian you're most unlikely to encounter here due to development, local kids trapping them to impress tourists, and a tidal wave of day-trippers in season. From Bocas town, water taxis (US$7) head to the public dock next to a small marina on the south side of the island, from where the beach is an easy 15-minute walk.

Playa Larga BEACH

(Long Beach; Map p668) This 6km-long beach on the southeast side of the island falls under the protection of the marine park. Hawksbill, leatherback and green sea turtles nest here from March to September. It's also good for surfing. To get here, you can follow the path past Red Frog Beach, but the best access is the one-hour walk with a guide from Salt Creek.

Nivida Bat Cave CAVE

(Bahía Honda; Map p668; US$5) One of Bastimentos' most fascinating natural wonders, Nivida is a massive cavern with swarms of nectar bats and a subterranean lake. The cave lies within the borders of the Parque Nacional Marino Isla Bastimentos and half the fun is getting here. But it's next to impossible to do it on your own. An organized tour from Old Bank costs US$45 per person.

The tour involves a 25-minute boat ride from Old Bank to the channel entrance. You'll then spend a similar amount of time gliding though mangroves and lush vegetation. From the dock it's then a half-hour hike to the cave. Wear sturdy shoes or boots; you will be provided with headlamps at the cave entrance.

Activities & Tours

★**Up in the Hill** TOURS

(Map p668; ☎6570-8277, 6607-8962; www.upinthehill.com; Old Bank; 2hr tour & tasting US$25) It's worth the hot 20-minute haul up to this organic farm at the highest point on Isla Bastimentos to see a wonderful permaculture project with chocolate groves and many exotic fruits. Linger at the wonderful cafe serving all-day breakfast, chocolate with coconut milk and delectable baked goods. There's also coffee from Boquete, golden milk with fresh turmeric, and homemade hibiscus tea.

Bastimentos Alive ADVENTURE

(Map p668; ☎6514-7961; www.bastimentosalive.com; Old Bank; trek incl lunch US$45; ⏰8am-8pm Mon-Sat) Led by Tom, a young Dutchman, this well-regarded tour operator leads daily treks through the jungle, with stops at Red Frog Beach (p676) and lunch on Polo Beach. It also offers full-day excursions to Cayo Zapatilla for snorkeling, with lunch. Tours to Nivida bat cave and Laguna de Bastimentos are in the works. Trips depart from the Bastimentos Alive office.

Bastimentos Sky Zipline Canopy Tour ADVENTURE

(Map p668; ☎836-5501, 6987-8661; http://redfrogbeach.com/bocas-del-toro-zipline; per person US$55; ⏰10am, 1pm & 3:30pm) Seven ziplines, a swaying sky bridge and a vertical rappel are highlights of this attraction, brought to you by a well-known Costa Rican zipline designer, in the hills just south of Red Frog Beach (p676). Tours last two hours.

Scuba 6 Ecodiving DIVING

(Map p668; ☎6722-5245; www.scuba6ecodiving.com; Old Bank; 2-tank dive $95; ⏰8am-8pm) A PADI five-star resort, this recommended scuba-diving agency makes it a priority to educate about the marine environment and operates with a Leave No Trace ethic. Instructors speak English, Spanish and French. With Blue and Green Fin certifications. The office is located in **Tío Tom's Guesthouse** (Map p668; ☎6951-6615; www.tiotomsguesthouse.com; dm US$25-30, 2-person bungalow US$35; 📶).

Sleeping

★**Palmar Tent Lodge** CAMPGROUND $$

(Map p668; ☎838-8552; www.palmartentlodge.com; Red Frog Beach; dm US$23, d/tr tents from US$90/110, 2-person bungalows from US$220) On the edge of the jungle and facing celebrated Red Frog Beach, Palmar has introduced glamping to Bocas del Toro to unanimous acclaim. Accommodations are in solar-powered circular tents for two to three, with all the comforts (including large lock boxes for valuables), wooden dorms, or a luxurious two-story thatched 'jungalow' for two. Guests 12 years and up.

The huge open-sided restaurant-bar is the place to be most nights (and days, come to think of it). The fun and well-informed owners, two mates from Washington, DC, offer a laundry list of tours and excursions and there are yoga classes (US$6) twice daily onsite. Water-taxi shuttles, included with your reservation, link the lodge with Bocas town twice a day. No internet.

Eclypse del Mar CABIN $$

(Map p668; ☎6611-4581; www.eclypsedemar.com; Old Bank; d US$110, 4-person bungalows incl breakfast US$250-300; ⏰Jul-May; 📶) These stylish over-the-water bungalows offer a charming retreat right on the fringe of Old Bank. Their boardwalks lead straight into a mangrove reserve where you can spy on sloths and caimans. Each wooden house features canopy beds, cheerful pillows and even a floor window with fish flitting by. The on-site cafe serves seafood and good pub grub.

★**Casa Cayuco** RESORT $$$

(Map p668; ☎USA 1-313-355-6692; www.casacayuco.com; southern Isla Bastimentos; s/d incl 3 meals

> **DON'T MISS**
>
> **GREEN ACRES**
>
> Amid verdant forested slopes, **Green Acres Chocolate Farm** (☎6716-4422; www.greenacreschocolatefarm.com; Cerro Bruja Peninsula; adult/child US$15/free; ⏰10am & 2pm Thu-Tue) is teeming with wildlife: hundreds of orchid species, green and black poison dart frogs, and golden silk orb-weaver spiders. It's also a great place to learn about sustainable chocolate production. A two-hour tour led by North American owner Robert will take you seamlessly from cacao pod to candy bar and leave no question unanswered. Reserve ahead.
>
> The 12-hectare farm and botanical gardens face Dolphin Bay but are actually on the mainland's Cerro Bruja peninsula; it's about a 30-minute boat ride from Bocas.

OFF THE BEATEN TRACK

ADVENTURES IN NASO COUNTRY

Part of a project spearheaded by an ex–Peace Corps volunteer and her Naso husband to offer the Naso people an alternative income, **Soposo Rainforest Adventures** (☎6875-8125; www.soposo.com; Soposo; day tour per person US$90, 2-/3-day package incl lodging, meals & tours US$140/275) offers accommodations in stilted thatched huts and traditional foods at three included meals. Visits include transport from Changuinola. Tours may include community visits, camping trips, birdwatching and manatee viewing.

& wine from US$235/305;) This beachfront retreat combines nature with modern conveniences. It's off-grid and jungle-chic, with sweeping views from lofty suites in the post-and-beam hardwood lodge, and jungle cabins by the water. Table d'hote meals (wine included) eaten on the dock are a big deal to the foodie owners from Detroit; lobsters and octopus come from nearby waters. There's also yoga retreats.

★La Loma LODGE $$$

(Map p668; ☎6592-5162, 6619-5364; www.thejunglelodge.com; western Isla Bastimentos; r per person incl 3 meals & activities US$120-130) Integrated into a 23-hectare rainforest and its community, this 'jungle lodge and chocolate farm' offers tasteful stays to consistently rave reviews. The location is hidden in mangroves, accessed by boat. A steep hill leads past a rushing creek to four sedate, ultra-private cabins with handcarved beds. Each has a propane-fuelled, rainwater-fed bathroom, a mosquito net and solar-powered energy system.

Eating

★Firefly Restaurant FUSION $$

(Map p668; ☎6524-4809; www.thefireflybocasdeltoro.com; Old Bank; mains US$8-15; 5pm-9pm Wed-Mon;) A clutch of open-air tables facing rough surf, this reservation-only restaurant is the perfect sunset date. An American chef cooks up local and organic ingredients in Thai and Caribbean preparations. Think sweet chili calamari, coconut gnocchi and seafood curries. The tapas menu allows you to sample a range of flavors.

Sea Monkey FUSION $$

(Map p668; ☎6693-9168; Old Bank; mains US$13-16; 8am-11am & 5pm-10pm Mon-Sat) In a simple over-the-water clapboard house, this breezy little restaurant churns out wonderful plates of Asian beer fish and local patuk greens with handmade cocktails (from US$5). Perfect for a sundowner. Moreover, the end-of-the-pier location provides a bit of peace and quiet in raucous Old Bank.

Coco Hill VEGETARIAN $$

(Map p668; ☎6826-6485; Old Bank; dishes US$7.50-16; 10am-10pm Wed-Mon;) Close to the island's highest point, Australian Michelle concocts some pretty exotic meatless dishes at her vegetarian, vegan and gluten-free restaurant and bar. Unfortunately it can be closed without warning and it's a long hike in. The blackboard menu changes daily. Cocktails are made with fresh fruit juices.

Information

In the past there have been reports of muggings on the trail between Old Bank and Red Frog Beach. After a rape and fatal attack in 2017, police have stepped up their presence in numbers and the area is considered safe. Still, travelers should not hike alone or go on any trail after dark. Carry only essentials such as a towel and water – never valuables.

Getting There & Away

A water taxi from Bocas to Old Bank costs US$5 and US$8 to the public dock for Red Frog Beach. From Old Bank to Isla Solarte it's US$5. You'll pay from US$10 to US$25 one way to locations further south on the island from Old Bank.

Isla San Cristóbal

POP 450

A half-hour away from Bocas town and you're in another world among the Ngöbe-Buglé indigenous community on Isla San Cristóbal. These subsistence farmers and fishers have a strong sense of their cultural identity, though they live mostly in difficult circumstances. There are some community tourism initiatives in their communities. To the south, Dolphin Bay is famous for sightings of dolphin pods. Beyond there is a lodging on another nearby island and a mainland restaurant accessed by boat.

Sleeping

★Dolphin Bay Hideaway LODGE $$$

(☎6886-4502; www.dolphinbayhideaway.com; Isla San Cristóbal; d incl 2 meals US$175-225;) Located amid mangroves and gorgeous gardens, this ecolodge has five rooms on two levels, with a big wooden deck, docks with hammocks and both a lily pond and a pool. Rooms are colorful and well appointed, with canopy beds, mosquito nets and large fans. Two cabins complete the picture. North Americans Brian and Amy are delightful hosts and offer tours.

There is snorkeling equipment available as well as kayaks, canoes and stand-up paddleboards. Meals are eaten communally in the lovely dining room on the top level. Transfer from Bocas town costs US$30 one way.

Finca Vela LODGE $$$

(☎6809-5534; www.fincavela.com; Isla Pastores; d incl breakfast & transfers US$190, extra guest $40;) This stylish ecolodge run by a French family lets you leave the world behind. There's snorkeling right off the dock, where there's also a shady hammock hut and restored *cayucos* (dugout canoes) for guest use. Well-designed cabins show minimalist elegance. Take a golf cart uphill to the restaurant with a daily menu of local products cooked up by the French chef.

It's five minutes by boat to Almirante, and 30 minutes to Bocas town. Contact via WhatsApp as there's no signal on-site.

Getting There & Away

Getting to Isla San Cristóbal from Bocas town is not cheap. A water taxi will cost upwards of US$30.

Almirante

POP 12,730

A clutch of stilted homes on the water, this unkempt village has seen better days, but it remains the springboard for the Archipiélago de Bocas del Toro, so is always busy.

A number of Chinese-owned supermarkets will help with supplies, but for a proper sit-down meal head for Bocas town.

Taxi 25 (p675) runs a water shuttle to Bocas town (US$6, 30 minutes); a taxi between the bus terminal and the dock should cost no more than US$1.

An air-conditioned bus to Changuinola (US$1.45) leaves every 15 minutes between 6am and 8pm and takes 45 minutes. Taxis to Changuinola (from US$20) can be bargained, particularly if you start your walk from the dock to the bus terminal.

Changuinola

POP 42,000

Headquarters of the Chiriquí Land Company, the company that produces Chiquita bananas, Changuinola is a hot and rather dusty town surrounded by a sea of banana plantations. Although there is little reason to spend any time here, overland travelers linking to Costa Rica will have to pass through.

Sleeping & Eating

Hotel Golden Sahara HOTEL $

(☎758-7908; hotelgolden_sahara@hotmail.com; Av 17 de Abril; s/d US$32/42;) This big family-run place has 28 rooms, but make sure to choose one in the back as those on the main street near the central bus station are noisy. Friendly place.

Restaurante Ebony CARIBBEAN $$

(☎6506-8402; Av 17 de Abril; mains US$10-16; noon-11pm) More expensive than your typical Changuinola restaurant, but loaded with atmosphere, this Afro-Caribbean restaurant at the southern end of the main street serves up creole dishes (shrimp with coconut, rice and peas, achee and salt fish). Carved birds and portraits of black icons Malcolm X, Bob Marley and US president Barack Obama adorn the walls.

DON'T MISS

WONDERS OF THE ARCHIPELAGO

Tired of the crowds? Find adventure by hiring a boat to try out these excursions:

Cayo Crawl Get lost in these mangrove-dotted channels – also called Coral Cay – near Isla Bastimentos.

Cayo Swan Spot red-billed tropic birds and white-crowned pigeons in this cay near Isla de Los Pájaros, north of Isla Colón.

Cayos Zapatillas Set out for the pristine white-sand beaches and virgin forests on these two uninhabited islands southeast of Isla Bastimentos.

Dolphin Bay Spot dolphins frolicking at this densely populated breeding ground south of Isla San Cristóbal.

Getting There & Away

Buses for Costa Rica leave from the terminal just south of the Delta gas station. Other buses depart from **Terminal Urraca** (758-8115) between 6am and 7pm.

COLÓN PROVINCE

POP 285,430 / ELEV SEA LEVEL TO 979M

Colón Province is much, much more than its run-down capital. Think pristine beaches and lowland rainforests, colonial splendor and the modern engineering marvel of the Panama Canal. Portobelo, with its growing music and art scene, shows the best of the vibrant culture of the Congos – descendants of African slaves who have preserved the legacy of their ancestors – while the train trip between Panama City and Colón remains one of the greatest rail journeys in the Americas.

Colón

POP 29,640

With its colonial grandeur in decay and its neighborhoods marginalized, Colón is the city that Panama forgot, in spite of vigorous encouragement to attract Caribbean cruise ships. Before 1869 the railroad connecting Panama City and Colón was the only rapid transit across the continental Western Hemisphere. A last wheeze of prosperity was heard during the construction of the Panama Canal.

On the city's edge, the Zona Libre de Colón (Colón Free Zone) was created in 1948. Generating some US$6.5 billion in annual commerce, little benefit seems to trickle down to local inhabitants. From up close, it's an island of materialism floating in a sea of unemployment and poverty.

Recent improvements in city safety are attributed to tighter gang control. There is also a much ballyhooed – but barely visible – urban restoration plan, kicked off in 2014. One major improvement: the Autopista Panamá–Colón is now a four-lane highway.

Sleeping & Eating

New Washington Hotel HISTORIC HOTEL $

(441-7133; www.newwashingtonhotel.com; Calle Iera, Paseo Washington; s/d US$49/50; P❄☜≋) Looking out to the Caribbean from the northern end of Colón, the New Washington offers a pentimento or two of the glorious hostelry that opened in 1913 – stucco work, chandeliers, an impressive marble staircase in the lobby. From the 124 rooms, choose one that faces the sea or the pretty front gardens. There's a large pool and a bar-restaurant.

Cafe Lebanese LEBANESE $$

(431-1066; Paseo Gorgas; dishes US$8-18; 11am-9pm) If Panamanian *ropa vieja* (spicy shredded beef) and *patacones* (fried plantains) are not floating your boat after a week or so, head for this friendly eatery in the port area for a fix of meze and *kofta* (Lebanese-style kebabs). The menu is in several languages, including Arabic; count on the authenticity of the dishes.

Information

Away from the cruise port on the eastern side of the city and the bustling Zona Libre, Colón can be unsafe. Violent crime rates have lowered, but visitors should exercise caution when walking

BUSES FROM CHANGUINOLA

DESTINATION	COST (US$)	DURATION (HR)	FREQUENCY (DAILY)
Almirante (with boat connections to Isla Colón)	1.45	¾	every 30min
Altos del Valle (Bosque Protector de Palo Seco)	7.25	2¼	every 30min
David	9.70	4¾	every 30min
El Silencio (Parque Internacional La Amistad)	1.25	½	every 20min
Guabito-Sixaola	1.25	½	every 30min
Las Tablas (Las Delicias)	2	1½	hourly
Panama City	29	12	7am
San José (Costa Rica)	16	6	10am

around, even during the day and in well-trafficked areas. Paseo de Washington, the renovated waterfront area to the north, should be safe to stroll along by day, however. Always travel by taxi at night.

Getting There & Away

BUS

From Panama City's Albrook Bus Terminal (p641), express and regular buses for Colón depart every 30 minutes.

Colón's **bus terminal** (Terminal de Buses; cnr Calle Terminal & Av Bolívar) serves towns throughout Colón Province.

If you are headed east of Colón from Panama City, these buses can be boarded at **Sabanitas**, the turnoff for Portobelo, thus avoiding a trip into Colón. Be aware that buses may be standing room only, particularly on weekends, and Sabanitas is a bottleneck where traffic moves at a snail's pace.

DESTINATION	COST (US$)	DURATION (HR)	FREQUENCY (DAILY)
Escobal (near Área Protegida San Lorenzo)	1.25	35min	hourly
Laguaira	3	2	half-hourly
Nombre de Dios	3.80	2½	hourly
Panama City	3.50	1-1½	half-hourly
Portobelo	1.60	1½	half-hourly

TRAIN

One of the best ways to fully appreciate the canal's expanse (and function) is to travel from Panama City to Colón via the resurrected **Panama Canal Railway** (317-6070; www.panarail.com; one way adult/child US$25/15; departure from Panama City 7:15am, return from Colón 5:15pm Mon-Fri). Note that the Panama City terminus is actually in the town of Corazal, a 10-minute drive from the Albrook Bus Terminal.

Getting Around

While in Colón, it's not a good idea to walk around most neighborhoods. Fortunately, taxis congregate at the bus terminal, train station and the Zona Libre, and fares across the city are usually under US$2.

A round-trip taxi for three to four passengers runs around US$60 to Fuerte San Lorenzo (p682) and about US$20 to the Agua Clara Visitors Center (p681), or US$30 if including the **Gatún Dam**. From the terminal, the bus to Costa Abajo (US$1) will drop you off a couple of kilometers from the visitors center and dam.

Around Colón

Agua Clara Visitors Center — VIEWPOINT

(276-8325; http://visitcanaldepanama.com/en/centro-de-visitantes-de-agua-clara; adult/child US$15/10; 8am-4pm) This observation center offers a panoramic view of the Panama Canal expansion, including the three-chambered Agua Clara Locks. Covered decks view Lago Gatún and the original Gatún Locks as well; there is also a theater with two videos in English, a cafe and gift shop. With no on-site museum, the focus here is really about getting a good look at the expansion. A short rainforest trail has sloths, howler monkeys and toucans.

Exhibits close at 4pm but visitors must enter by 3:15pm; a visit should take about one hour. To reach here from Colón, catch any bus to Costa Abajo and alight before crossing the canal. It's a 2.5km walk up the access road to your left. A taxi will cost about US$20, or US$30 if you want to include Gatún Dam.

Gatún Locks — CANAL

(US$5; 8am-4pm) The impressive Gatún Locks, 10km south of Colón, raise southbound ships 30m from Caribbean waters to Lago Gatún. Just the size of them is mind-boggling: three sets of double lock chambers stretch on for 3km. Each chamber could have accommodated the *Titanic* with room to spare. With the opening of the Agua Clara Visitors Center, the viewing stand opposite the control tower has unfortunately now been closed.

Workers poured a record-setting 1.82 million cu meters of concrete to construct the Gatún Locks. The concrete was brought from a giant mixing plant to the construction site by railroad cars that ran on a circular track. Huge buckets maneuvered by cranes carried the wet concrete from the railroad cars and poured it into enormous steel forms. Locomotives moved the forms into place. This protracted process continued virtually uninterrupted for four years until the locks were completed.

Once the ships pass through the locks, they travel 37km to the Pedro Miguel Locks, which lower southbound ships 9.3m to Lago Miraflores, a small body of water between two sets of Pacific locks. Ships are then lowered to sea level at the Miraflores Locks.

Área Protegida San Lorenzo NATURE RESERVE

(San Lorenzo Protected Area) Centered on the ruins of the crumbling Spanish colonial fortress of **Fuerte San Lorenzo** (Fort San Lorenzo; www.sanlorenzo.org.pa; 8am-4pm) FREE, the 120-sq-km San Lorenzo Protected Area includes the former US military base of Fort Sherman, as well as 12 different ecosystems including mangroves, marshlands, semi-deciduous forests and humid rainforest. It's a prime location for birdwatching, with some 436 species recorded.

Portobelo

POP 4600

This Caribbean fishing village is so laid-back and languorous, it's hard to imagine it was once the greatest Spanish port in Central America. Mules carried Peruvian gold and Oriental treasures to Panama City via the fortresses at Portobelo. Though English privateers destroyed them many times throughout their history, several of these atmospheric colonial fortresses still stand amid village homes.

Today Portobelo's residents scratch out a living by fishing, tending crops or raising livestock. Though economically depressed, Portobelo is experiencing something of a cultural revival, with renewed interest in Congo art, music (especially *punta,* better known abroad as reggaetón) and dancing. The town bursts to life every October 21 for the Festival del Cristo Negro (Black Christ Festival), one of the country's most vibrant and spiritual celebrations.

There are also nice nearby beaches, accessed by boat, and worthwhile diving and snorkeling.

Sights & Activities

Playa Blanca BEACH

A 20-minute, US$45 return boat ride from Portobelo will bring you to this lovely white-sand beach on a tranquil cove surrounded by dense wilderness. It boasts some of the least disturbed reefs between Colón and the Archipiélago de San Blas, and its sheltered waters offer better visibility than beaches closer to Portobelo. There's a colorful reef in the center of the cove near the beach, as well as a second reef that sits in deeper waters about 100m offshore.

Fuerte San Jerónimo FORT

Fuerte San Jerónimo, close to the center of Portobelo, was the largest fortress ever built to protect the bay. Some two dozen embrasures with 16 cannons face the mouth of the bay, some exactly where the Spanish troops left them in 1821, the year Panama declared its independence. Beyond the impressive gateway, there's the remains of the officers' quarters, barracks, guardroom and huge observation terrace over the water.

Mirador Perú VIEWPOINT

(Perú Lookout) Atop a hill overlooking much of the bay is a small but well-preserved watchtower called Mirador Perú, which was built at the same time as **Fuerte Santiago**. There are steps carved into the hillside to reach the lookout, and the views of the coastline from here are expansive.

Golden Frog Scuba DIVING

(6586-4838; www.goldenfrogscuba.com; 2-dive trip US$100; diving 9am-1:30pm) A PADI dive center run by English-speaking dive master Rey Sanchez at the **Coco Plum Eco Lodge** (448-2309, 448-2102; www.facebook.com/CocoPlumPanama; s/d/tr/q US$55/65/80/90; P ❄). Excursions are made from a comfortable catamaran.

Festivals & Events

Festival del Cristo Negro FIESTA

(Black Christ Festival; Oct 21) On October 21 annually, pilgrims from all over Panama arrive in Portobelo to participate in this festival, which honors a miraculous 1.5m-high statue of the Black Christ housed in the **Iglesia de San Felipe** (Church of St Philip). After sunset, the statue is paraded through the streets, while pilgrims bedecked in purple robes and crowns of thorns dance and drink until the wee hours.

Festival de Diablos y Congos CULTURAL

(Festival of Devils & Congos; Feb/Mar) The most intriguing local party is this festival of rebellion and ridicule that mocks the colonial Spaniards. Participants assume the role of escaped slaves and take 'captives.' It's held two weeks after Carnaval, marking the start of Lent.

Sleeping

★**La Morada de la Bruja** BOUTIQUE HOTEL $$

(The Witch's Abode; 6759-6987, 6008-6867; www.lamoradadelabrujaportobelo.com; r US$50-75, 4-person loft US$80, 2-bedroom house US$200-225; P ❄ ᯤ) This chill photographer's home has been adapted for guests but maintains a very personal touch. Three small apartments and two ample waterfront houses – all differently colored – sport artful decor and a grassy seafront perfect for lounging. The bright, open interiors showcase photography and local Congo art. We like Casa Turquesa facing the sea best.

Casa Congo B&B **$$**
(☎202-0880, 6672-6620; http://casacongo.fundacionbp.org/es/houses-2/casa-congo; d US$80-100;) Part of a foundation that supports local arts and culture, this attractive waterfront inn features three pleasant and bright rooms and an apartment decorated with Congo art. It also offers workshops with artists. It's mostly doubles with one apartment that accommodates four (US$20 per extra person).

Shopping

★**Galería de Arte Casa Congo** ART
(☎6672-6620; http://casacongo.fundacionbp.org/es/foundation/gallery; Casa Congo; ⊙9am-5pm Mon-Fri, to 8pm Sat, 8am-5pm Sun) A wonderful gallery with museum-quality pieces made mainly by Afro-Caribbean craftspeople and artists. Helpful displays explain the cultural background of the groups represented, including Congo and indigenous cultures. It's not all high end though – you will also find reasonably priced jewelry and souvenirs.

Information

The **ATP** (☎448-2200; ⊙8am-4pm) just off the main road may test your Spanish skills. Many of the employees only speak Spanish with varying degrees of helpfulness about Portobelo, Colón Province and/or Panama. You'll find better service and more useful information at the local gas station.

Getting There & Away

Buses to Portobelo (US$1.60, 1½ hours, every 30 minutes) depart from Colón's Terminal de Buses from 4am to 6pm. **Buses to Colón** from Portobelo leave from a bus stop on the main road through town.

If traveling to Portobelo from Panama City you can avoid Colón by alighting from the Colón bus at the Supermercado Rey in Sabanitas, 10km before Colón. From there catch the bus to Portobelo (US$1.40, 1¼ hours).

Isla Grande

POP 1050

Palm trees and white-sand beaches form the backdrop to this lovely little island, just 15km from Portobelo. A popular getaway for folk fleeing the urban grind of Panama City, Isla Grande is an ideal setting for snorkeling, scuba diving or simply soaking up the island's relaxed vibe. There are no roads, just a footpath along the island's southern coast, backed by pastel-colored cottages. Many of the people living here are of African descent eking out a living from fishing and growing coconuts – you'll get a taste of both when you sample the local cuisine.

PORTOBELO'S TOP FIVE ESCAPES

- Taking a water taxi to Puerto Francés for private swims and jungle hikes.
- Snorkeling around Spanish cannons encrusted in the coral landscape.
- Kayaking up the tranquil Río Claro.
- Watching a sunset from **Fuerte San Fernando**.
- Joining a Congo **dance workshop** (☎6693-5690; Calle Principal, Casa Artesanal; per person US$20; ⊙noon-2pm Fri, to 4pm Sat & Sun) and bopping to cool African rhythms.

Activities

This 5km-long, 1.5km-wide island has two trails: one that loops the shoreline and another slippery cross-island trail. The lovely beaches on the northern side of the island can be reached by boat or on foot.

Some fine snorkeling and dive sites are within a 10-minute boat ride of the island. For diving, contact a Portobelo-based operator, like Golden Frog Scuba. Diving is restricted to between April and December, when seas are calmer.

Boat taxis can also take you further afield to explore the mangroves east of Isla Grande or to go snorkeling off the coast of the nearby islets.

Festivals & Events

Isla Grande Carnaval CULTURAL
(⊙Feb-Mar) Isla Grande celebrates Carnaval in a rare way: women wear traditional *polleras* (festive dresses), while men wear ragged pants tied at the waist with old sea rope, and everyone dances to African-influenced Conga drums and song. There are also satirical songs about current events and a lot of joking in the Caribbean calypso tradition.

RESPONSIBLE TRAVEL IN GUNA YALA

When visiting the Comarca de Guna Yala, consider how your visit may affect the community. Tourism revenue can play a vital role in the development of the region, particularly if you are buying locally produced crafts or contracting the services of a Guna guide. However, Western interests have already caused irreversible damage to the region. Be aware of your surroundings and remain sensitive about your impact.

One look at the paradisiacal setting, the colorful flag and the distinctive Guna dress and you might feel transported into the pages of *National Geographic*. Don't snap that shutter just yet, though. If the Guna appear less than friendly – and they sometimes do – consider their predicament. When tourist boats arrive, the number of people on an already congested island can triple. Then, nearly two-thirds of the populace (the tourists) turn paparazzi on the other third (the Guna). It's an unsavory scene repeated again and again. To rein in the situation, the Guna usually charge fees for photographs taken of them as well as landing/visitation fees for each island. If you can't afford the photo fee or don't want to pay it, put your camera away and strike up a conversation instead.

Remain mindful of the way you dress. Guna men never go shirtless and Guna women dress conservatively, with their cleavage, their belly and most of their legs covered. Arriving in Guna villages in a bikini or shirtless might be interpreted as a sign of disrespect.

Trash is a huge problem on the more populous islands, and there is no effective plan for its management. For the Guna, the cost of removal to the mainland is too high, and there is no designated site or 'culture' of waste management, since all refuse was relatively innocuous until outside influence prevailed. You may see litter and piles of burning plastic. With no current solution to the issue, do what you can to pack out your own garbage, if necessary, and try to consume fresh products with minimal packaging – ie choose coconut water over soft drinks.

Sleeping

Macondo Hostel HOSTEL $

(☎6102-6262; www.facebook.com/Macondo-Hostel-Isla-Grande-1541624226094296; dm/d/q US$15/35/45; 📶) Follow the signposted path a block inland to this agreeable, breezy, two-story hostel set in a lush tropical garden. Five and eight bunks occupy two ample-sized dorms with fans. The three private rooms sleep two to four people. It's good value for budget travelers, with shady shared spaces and hammocks. It's relaxed but you'll be sure to party here too.

Hotel Sister Moon CABAÑAS $$

(☎6948-1990; www.hotelsistermoon.com; d/tr with fan US$87/102, d with air-con US$120, day pass US$20; ❄📶🏊) Your best choice for island lodging is this lovely clutch of 11 hillside cabins surrounded by swaying palms and crashing waves. With no beach, guests sunbathe on attractive waterfront decks and swim in the pool. Perks include private balconies with hammocks; cabins 1 and 2 dangle right over the water. The in-house El Fin del Mundo restaurant is excellent.

Eating & Drinking

El Fin del Mundo SEAFOOD $$$

(☎6948-1990; www.hotelsistermoon.com; mains US$15-22; ⏲8am-8pm Mon-Fri, to 10pm Sat & Sun) Sister Moon's bar-restaurant is built right over the water. The menu features the island's famous coconut-infused seafood alongside high-end cocktails.

Floating Rum Bar COCKTAIL BAR

(cocktails US$6; ⏲noon-late) Why nurse a cocktail by the sea when you can do the same *in* the sea? This floating bar is anchored off the footpath and accessible by complimentary *lancha* (small motorboat). There's BBQ food on offer and the bar boasts a Tarzan swing that will get you into the drink in no time.

El Bar de Pupy BAR

(☎6789-7433, 6503-7530; ⏲9am-9pm) This Rasta-reggae bar-restaurant, hosted by the eponymous local lad Pupy, reaches right into the sea. While the day (or evening) away, your feet planted in the sand, enjoying grilled chicken, octopus with onion and garlic, or fresh fish (mains US$12 to US$15). Great cocktails too.

Getting There & Away

Isla Grande is a 10-minute boat ride from Laguaira, a tiny coastal hamlet linked with Colón by frequent buses. Boats arrive at the Isla Grande dock just down from the Hotel Isla Grande.

Buses to Laguaira leave from the Colón bus terminal (US$3, 1½ hours). From Panama City, take a Colón-bound bus to Sabanitas and change buses next to the Supermercado Rey for Laguaira. Buses return from Laguaira at 8am, 9am and noon.

In Laguaira, boats at the dock go to the island (or beyond), departing when full from 8am to 7:30pm Monday to Friday, to 7pm on Saturday and to 5pm on Sunday. The trip costs US$5 per person; secure parking is US$6 per day.

COMARCA DE GUNA YALA

POP 44,230 / ELEV SEA LEVEL TO 1160M

With white sand and waving palms, the islands of the turquoise Archipiélago de San Blas of the Comarca de Guna Yala diminish no one's vision of paradise. This is home to the Guna people, the first indigenous group in Latin America to gain autonomy. Though they have had contact with Europeans since Columbus sailed these waters in 1502, clan identity and the traditional way of life remain paramount.

A decade ago the road to the port of Gardi (Cartí) was finished, making the region more accessible than ever. Still off the beaten track, this narrow, 373km-long strip on the Caribbean coast with 365 offshore islands stretches from the Golfo de San Blás to the Colombian border.

Community (ie populated) islands numbering four dozen are acre-sized cays packed with thatched huts, livestock and people. Visitors often prefer the more remote outer islands with fewer inhabitants. Some islands charge a landing/visitation fee.

History

Although the Guna people have lived in eastern Panama for at least two centuries, scholars fiercely debate their origins. Language similarities with people who once lived several hundred kilometers to the west would indicate that the Guna migrated eastward. However, oral tradition has it that the Guna migrated to the San Blás islands from Colombia after the 16th century, following a series of devastating encounters with other tribes armed with poison-dart blowguns.

Regardless of the origins of the Guna, who called themselves the Dule, scholars agree that life on the islands is relatively new for them. Historians at the end of the 18th century wrote that the only people who visited the San Blás islands at that time were pirates and the odd Spanish explorer. However, the Guna flourished on the archipelago due to the abundance of seafood. They supplemented this with food crops grown on the mainland, including rice, yams, yucca, plantains, bananas and pineapples.

Today there are more than 44,000 Guna living in the *comarca,* with three-quarters living on the islands and the rest on tribal land along the coast; about 6000 Guna live elsewhere in Panama and Colombia. So communal are the island-dwelling Guna that they inhabit only 48 of the 365 keys; the rest are mostly left to coconut trees, sea turtles and iguanas.

Activities & Tours

Most lodgings offer complete packages, where a fixed price gets you a room, three meals a day and boat rides to neighboring islands for swimming, snorkeling and lounging on the beach. If you seek community life, you can also arrange visits to more populated islands.

Before swimming off the shores of a heavily populated island, consider that all waste goes here – unfiltered in most cases.

Snorkeling is good in places, but many coral reefs are badly damaged. You can often rent snorkeling equipment from your hotel; serious snorkelers should bring their own gear.

Jaunts to hike the mainland jungles are arranged with a guide. Most travelers are content with simply soaking up the Caribbean sun.

Cacique Cruiser BOATING

(Map p636; ☎6111-4241; www.caciquecruiser.com; day trips US$150) A licensed and highly recommended tour agency specializing in daily trips and excursions to San Blás, from one to six days. Also offers trips between Panama and Colombia on highly rated boats. The company is a major contributor to the local economy and supporter of social and environmental programs.

Sleeping & Eating

Carefully selecting your accommodations on the islands is key, since their remoteness makes it difficult to change your mind.

Camping on an uninhabited island isn't wise, because you run the risk of encountering drug traffickers in the night and being eaten alive by *chitras* (sand flies). The Guna do not allow the Panamanian coast guard or US antidrug vessels to operate in the archipelago, so the uninhabited islands are occasionally used by Colombian traffickers running cocaine up the coast.

Since there are almost no restaurants, each lodging provides meals for guests. They are usually seafood based, with lobster available at an extra cost. Quality varies, as some of the fishing stocks have been depleted, but there is always rice and a healthy supply of fresh coconuts. Always ask before taking a coconut – they are among the region's main sources of income.

★Cabañas Demar Achu CABAÑAS **$$**
(☎6806-5976, 6959-0866; camping/cabin per person incl 3 meals, transfers & tour US$55/80) This clutch of pleasant cabins over huge grounds is one of the best deals around, with prices cut to US$25/45 for stays longer than one night (plus US$30 transfers). The 20 cabins are well spaced for privacy, and there are spacious concrete bathhouses, volleyball facilities and hammocks. Shady camping is also all-inclusive and well priced.

Isla Tortuguita Camping CAMPGROUND **$$**
(☎6030-3428, 6651-8858; www.sanblastourspanama.com; camping/cabin per person incl meals & transfers US$86/135) One way to fulfill your castaway fantasy is to camp on this tiny isle run by a single family. Only 30 guests at a time are allowed to camp under the palms here. Tents and cushions are provided, and meals are well prepared. Some new cabins stand right over the water. It's run by Blas Tejada of **Restaurant Chef Blas** (☎6651-8858, 3030-3428; www.sanblastourspanama.com; dishes US$5-15; ⏲7-11am, noon-3pm & 6-7pm).

Cabañas Casso CABAÑAS **$$**
(Coco Loco; ☎6807-2768, 6151-7379; www.facebook.com/pg/sanblasfrontera; dm/r per person incl 3 meals & transfers US$30/70) Our favorite new place on Isla Naranjo Chico – which is also known as 'Coco Loco' – is small, with just four brightly painted cabins (one used as a dormitory with seven beds) that are perfectly formed and as upbeat as you'll find in the archipelago. Step outside your lodgings and you're halfway in the water.

★Yandup Island Lodge CABIN **$$$**
(☎203-7762, 6682-9848; www.yandupisland.com; per person incl 3 meals & tours US$155-175) Accommodations at this lodge are simple but comprise 10 lovely octagonal thatched-roof cabins with cold-water bathrooms; a half-dozen of the cabins sit right over the water. Light comes from solar panels and water from the mainland. The island's grassy grounds, palm shade and small but powdery beach might be reason enough to just stay put.

Cabañas Naranjo Chico CABAÑAS **$$$**
(☎6686-7437, 6086-7716; www.sanblaskunayala.com; r/beach cabaña/stilt cabaña per person incl 3 meals, transfers & tours US$95/115/135) Six cabins provide quiet and a lovely swimming beach. Beach-side cabins have sand floors; newer cabins set on stilts over the water are the most expensive. All have solar power. The Del Valle family are prompt with response times for reservations, which is rare in these parts. Prices drop to US$75/95/115 on the second night.

ℹ Information

Flights in and out of the *comarca* are limited, so book as far in advance as possible. You should also reserve your hotels in advance, especially since all-in package deals are the norm here. There's no cash machine, so visit an ATM before reaching the islands. The closest one is at Chepo on the Interamericana, about 20km southwest of the El Llano turnoff.

From May through November temperatures are generally lower in the archipelago. When there's no breeze and the mercury rises, humidity sets in and life on the San Blás islands can cease to be paradisiacal. During January and February the trade winds arrive.

In the *comarca* it helps to have a good command of Spanish as few Guna outside the tourist centers speak English. In fact, many older Guna do not speak much Spanish. In more remote areas your guide or boat operator may have to do the talking for you. A few words of Guna will win you friends wherever you go.

The Guna are very particular about what *uagmala* (foreigners) do on their islands. As a result, tourists must register and pay a visitation fee (usually around US$3) on most islands. You're expected to pay regardless of whether you stay for a week or only a half-hour. On smaller, privately owned islands, you must seek out the owner, obtain permission to stay and pay a fee of around US$7 per person to camp.

Visitors are expected to pay to take photographs of the Guna people (around US$1 per

GUNA LIVING 101

Lodging considerations in the *comarca* are vastly different from those on the mainland. Here, a spot in a thatched hut with a sand floor with three meals can cost anywhere between US$35 in a dormitory and US$170 in a luxury lodge per night. So, what's the difference?

Often it has more to do with access, ambience and organization than anything else. Densely populated community islands are more likely to have budget options, but they will not live up to your image of a remote tropical paradise at all. Resort islands with lodges generally have a bigger price tag, but they may not offer many opportunities to interact with locals. When planning, consider why you're visiting and ask yourself the following questions:

Space Does the island have shade? Privacy? Are there pleasant areas to swim or do you have to take a boat to reach swimming and snorkeling sites?

Access Is the island too remote, requiring expensive transfers to do anything?

Hospitality Have other travelers had good experiences here?

Water Is it potable? Consider bringing a filter.

Bathrooms Are there modern installations or does the toilet sit at the end of a dock?

Safety Do excursion boats have recently inspected life vests and good motors?

Lodgings generally include three meals (but not drinks), one outing per day (eg snorkeling or a community visit) and sometimes transportation to or from the airport or Gardi (Cartí) port, but do confirm ahead. Visits to other Guna islands may cost extra. It is always wise to bring snacks, insect repellent, a first-aid kit and a flashlight. Rates are generally lower from April to November.

When booking, remember that internet access is not prevalent here and any cell-phone number is only good until that phone accidentally falls into the ocean. But approach your hosts with good humor and patience, and they will probably reciprocate in spades.

subject or photo). If you want to take someone's photo, ask their permission first. You may not be required to pay for a photograph taken of an artisan from whom you buy crafts, but it depends on the person. You must carry your passport to enter the region.

Getting There & Away

AIR

Air Panama (☎316-9000; www.airpanama.com) has daily flights to Uggubseni (Playón Chico) and Assudub (Achutupu). There are also flights to Ogobsucum (Ustupo) three times a week and to Puerto Obaldía daily except Saturday. All flights depart from Albrook Airport in Panama City and take 30 minutes to an hour. Ticket prices vary according to season and availability but average about US$80 one way.

Book as far in advance as possible, as demand far exceeds supply. Note that planes may stop at several islands in the archipelago, loading and unloading passengers or cargo before continuing on.

BOAT

Sailboats travel to Colombia via the archipelago, but they tend to board in Puerto Lindo or Portobelo on the Caribbean coast in Colón Province these days. Lodgings in Panama City have more information about these privately run trips.

More a tour and a holiday than mere transport, the popular **San Blas Adventures** (☎6032-8498; http://sanblasadventures.com; 4-day trip US$445) four-day service takes travelers between Gardi (Cartí) and Capurganá just over the border in Colombia, visiting inhabited and deserted islands, sleeping in hammocks under thatched lean-tos or in Guna communities, and swimming and snorkeling along the way. In fact, 90% of the time is spent off the boat and on islands. Fiberglass boats have twin outboard engines. It's a good alternative to avoid the two-day ocean crossing by sailboat, rough seas and cramped overnight quarters. See the website for useful planning details.

CAR

The El Llano–Gardi (Cartí) road is the only land route into the district. It connects the town of El Llano, on the Interamericana 72km east of Panama City, to the San Blás coastal hamlet and port of Gardi (Cartí).

It's best to take a shared 4WD with a powerful engine, a winch and good tires. Your Panama City hostel can easily arrange transportation, as can **Mola Nega Adventures** (☎6884-0262,

6098-1874; www.molanegadventures.com), **Kuna Yala Expeditions** (☎6530-4834, 6708-5254; eliasperezmartinez@yahoo.com) and driver **Germain Perez** (☎6734-3454; www.cartihomestaykunayala.blogspot.com).

DARIÉN PROVINCE

POP 55,753 / ELEV SEA LEVEL TO 2280M

One of world's richest biomes is the 5790-sq-km Parque Nacional Darién, where the primeval meets the present with scenery nearly unaltered from one million years ago. Even today in the Darién, the Emberá and Wounaan people maintain many of their traditional practices and retain generations-old knowledge of the rainforest. In a stroke of irony, much of the Darién has remained untouched because of its volatile reputation.

The road to Yaviza – the most accessible part of the province – has scenes of habitat destruction. Cruising the waterways and hiking trails are the only ways to explore the slow-paced interior of Darién and the Pacific coast, where Emberá, Wounaan and Afro-Panamanians coexist.

The region's issues are complex. Police and military checkpoints are not infrequent because of drug trafficking. The Darién is not for everyone, but with careful planning and the right destinations, it offers opportunities for intrepid travelers to discover something truly wild.

History

Living within the boundaries of the Darién, the group commonly known as the Chocóes emigrated from Colombia's Chocó region long ago. Anthropologists divide the indigenous people here into two groups – the Emberá and the Wounaan – though, language apart, the groups' cultural features are identical. Both groups prefer to be thought of as two separate peoples though.

Before the introduction of guns, the Emberá and Wounaan were experts with the *boroquera* (blowgun), using darts envenomed with lethal toxins from poisonous frogs and bullet ants. Many scholars believe these groups forced the Guna out of the Darién and into the Caribbean coastal area and islands they now inhabit.

The Emberá and Wounaan are known for their incredibly fine dugout canoes. Known as *piraguas,* they have shallow bottoms that are ideal for use in the dry season when rivers run low. The Panama Canal Authority has long employed Emberá and Wounaan craftspeople to make the *piraguas* used to reach the upper parts of the canal's watershed. At the same time, as late as the 1990s, the US Air Force solicited Emberá and Wounaan help with jungle living. Many of them trained US astronauts and pilots at Fort Sherman, near Colón, in tropical-wilderness survival.

Today the majority of the nearly 10,000 Emberá and Wounaan in Panama (another 6000 or so are in Colombia) live deep in the rainforests of the Darién, particularly along the Ríos Sambú, Jaqué, Chico, Tuquesa, Membrillo, Tuira, Yapé and Tucutí.

Tours

The Darién is the only part of Panama where a guide is necessary, and it is obligatory in the national park. You can hire Spanish-speaking guides locally for about US$25 to US$35 per day, but transportation costs will be very expensive. Tour operators can take care of all arrangements without a language barrier, teach you about the incredible local ecology, cook for you and humor you when you have blisters. Another option is to go with an independent naturalist guide.

★ Jungle Treks ADVENTURE
(☎6438-3130; www.jungletreks.com) Run by veteran naturalist guide Rick Morales, this recommended outfitter specializes in boutique, expedition-style travel for groups of six or more. Destinations include the interior and Pacific coast. Check the website for set dates. Custom trips have a three-day minimum. Native English.

Ancon Expeditions TOURS
(☎Panama City 269-9415; www.anconexpeditions.com) Ancon travels to its own private lodge in Punta Patiño on the Pacific coast and further afield. Special programs for birdwatchers and hikers are outstanding. Excellent English.

EcoCircuitos ADVENTURE
(Map p628; ☎315-1488; www.ecocircuitos.com; Albrook Plaza, 2nd fl, No 31, Ancón) A reputable, sustainable operator offering conventional tours to the Panama Canal and canal transits, tours of Parque Nacional Soberanía, birdwatching on Pipeline Rd and fun kayaking trips on Lago Gatún.

Information

Information on the Darién quickly goes out of date. Always seek updates, ideally from a guide who leads frequent trips to the area or lives there.

Note that in order to travel in the area you must write to **SENAFRONT** (Servicio Nacional de Fronteras; ☎ Panama City 527-1000; www.senafront.gob.pa; Las Cumbres; ⏰ 8am-4pm Mon-Fri) in Panama City ahead of time, in Spanish, with details of your itinerary and carry a half-dozen photocopies of the letter (and the same number of copies of your passport) with you as it will be examined at checkpoints. The office can also suggest local guides.

In Yaviza, the Sede Administrativa Parque Nacional Darién can provide some information on the park and potentially help you find guides (usually rangers with days off). Travelers must register here to visit the park and check in with the police before heading out into the jungle. There are also a half-dozen checkpoints along the road to Yaviza beginning at Chepo and at all ports.

Panama City's **Instituto Geográfico Nacional** (Tommy Guardia; Map p632; ☎ 236-2444; http://ignpanama.anati.gob.pa; La Cresta; ⏰ 8am-4pm Mon-Fri) sells topographical maps for some regions of the Darién.

DANGERS & ANNOYANCES

The greatest hazard in the Darién is the difficult environment. Trails, when they exist at all, are often poorly defined and are rarely marked. Many large rivers that form the backbone of the Darién transportation network create their own hazards. Any help at all, let alone medical assistance, is very far away. If you get lost, you are almost certainly done for. To minimize these risks, it's recommended that you explore the Darién either as part of an organized tour or with the help of a qualified guide.

Dengue and malaria are risks. Consult your doctor before you go about necessary medication, and cover up as much as possible, especially at dusk. Areas of the Parque Nacional Darién are prime territory for the deadly fer-de-lance snake. The chances of getting a snakebite are remote, but do be careful and always wear boots on treks. Although they don't carry Lyme disease, ticks are widespread. Bring tweezers and a few books of matches to ensure you're able to remove the entire tick if it's burrowed well into your skin.

In May 2017 the US State Department lifted its warning about visiting remote areas of the Darién off the Interamericana, including the entire Parque Nacional Darién. It does, however, continue to advise on security, choosing safe transportation, health issues and documentation.

KNOW BEFORE YOU GO

To visit the Parque Nacional Darién you must pay lodging fees before you go. Call the **Ministerio de Ambiente** (Map p632; ☎ 500-0855, 315-0855; www.miambiente.gob.pa; Calle Broberg 804, Cerro Ancón, Albrook; ⏰ 8am-4pm Mon-Fri) in Panama City for the direct-deposit account number for the 'Cuenta de Vida Silvestre' at BNP (Banco Nacional de Panamá). Visit any branch, but be sure to keep your receipt to show at the **Sede Administrativa Parque Nacional Darién** (☎ 299-4495; Interamericana, Ministerio de Ambiente Bldg; ⏰ 8am-4pm Mon-Fri) in Yaviza, where you must stop to register (note: it's open only on weekdays until 4pm). If you somehow forget, the closest BNP branch to Yaviza is in **Metetí** (Banco Nacional de Panamá; ☎ 299-6125; Interamericana s/n; ⏰ 8am-3pm Mon-Fri, 9am-noon Sat).

Although the no-go zones in the Darién are well removed from the traditional tourist destinations, their dangers cannot be underestimated. Drug traffickers who utilize these jungle routes don't appreciate encountering travelers. In the past, former Colombian guerrillas or runaways took refuge here. Missionaries and travelers alike have been kidnapped and killed in the southern area of the Darién.

The areas between Boca de Cupe and Colombia, the traditional path through the Darién Gap, remain particularly treacherous. As there's only minimal police or military presence here, you're on your own if trouble arises.

Despite all this, most parts of the Darién can be visited in total safety.

Getting There & Away

The Interamericana terminates 285km from Panama City in the frontier town of Yaviza, and the vast wilderness region of the Darién lies beyond. The highway starts again 150km further on in Colombia. This break between Central and South America is known as the Darién Gap – literally the end of the road.

There are buses every hour from Albrook Bus Terminal (p641) in Panama City to Yaviza (US$16, 4½ hours). Be sure to tell the bus driver your destination if getting off along the way.

Darién Province

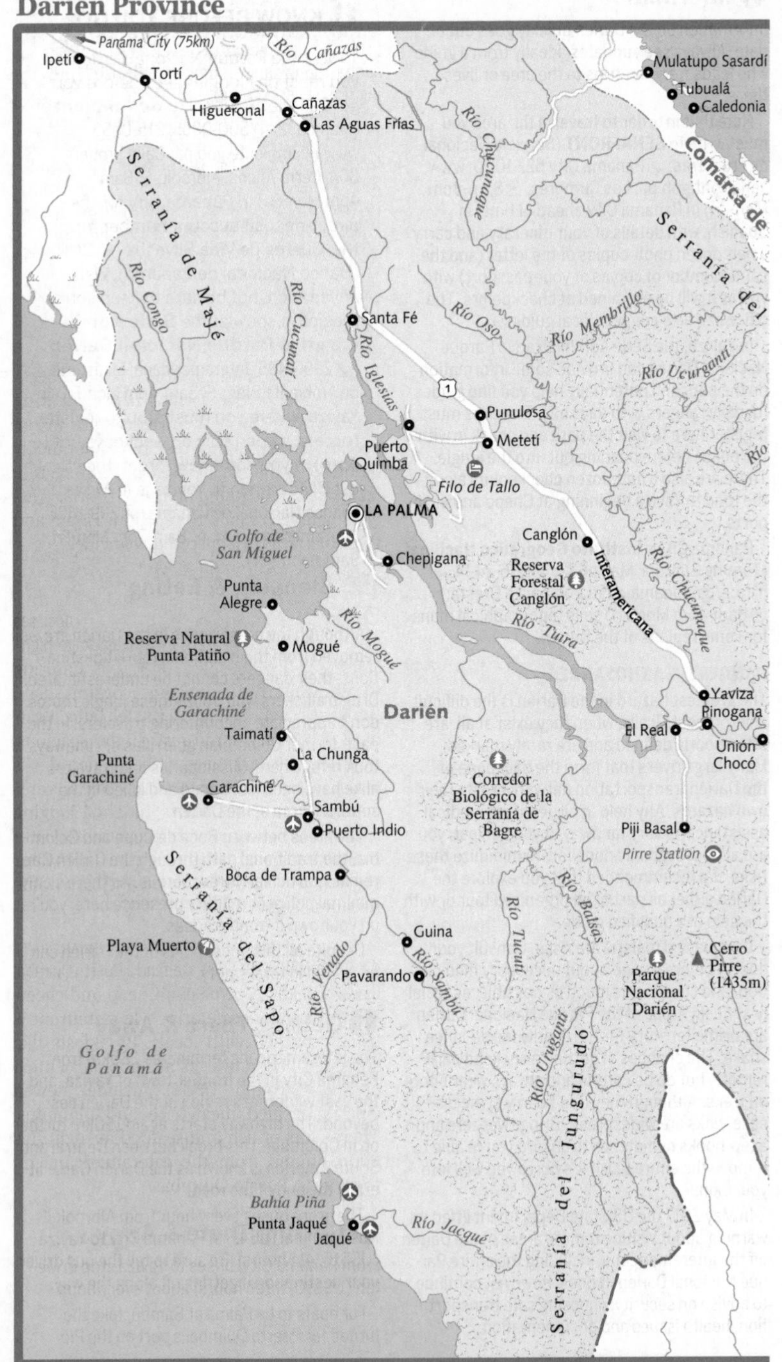

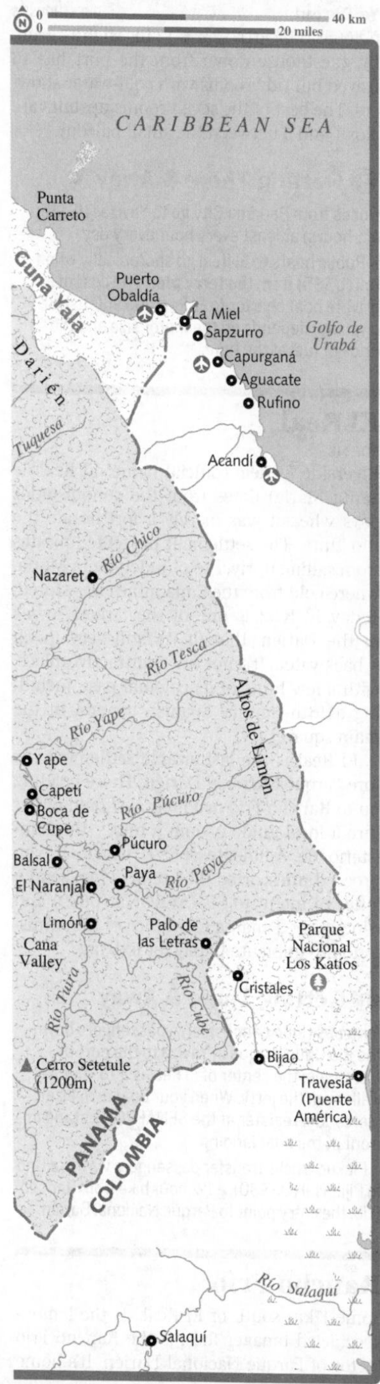

Getting Around

In the vast jungles of Darién Province, rivers are often the only means of travel, with *pangas* or *canoas* (long canoes; mostly motorized) providing the transportation.

Boats depart Puerto Quimba, near the Interamericana city of Metetí, for La Palma and from Yaviza for interior destinations such as El Real. In La Palma, you can hire motorized boats to Sambú. From El Real, travelers can access Pijibasal or Parque Nacional Darién via land transportation.

Metetí

POP 7980

Located 1km southeast of a police checkpoint, Metetí is the Darién's fastest-growing locality, with the best infrastructure in the region. The surroundings are being quickly deforested, though at least one interesting ecolodge can be found on the outskirts. Travelers generally come to reach La Palma and interior Darién via a scenic boat ride.

Sleeping & Eating

Canopy Camp LODGE $$$

(Panama City 264-5720; 7-night package high/low season US$3180/2125; P, wi-fi) Catering to serious birdwatchers, this ecocamp sits in the Reserva Hidrológica Filo del Tallo, a verdant secondary rainforest. Eight spacious, multiroom safari tents with wooden decks are outfitted with comfortable beds, screens, electricity and fans. Each thatched lodging is extremely private, with freestanding bathrooms equipped with open-air hot-water showers that bring the forest and its wildlife that much closer.

Restaurante Doña Lala PANAMANIAN $

(6722-8022, 299-6601; Camino a Puerto Quimba; mains US$9-12; 6am-9pm) Cheap and cheerful, this spotless cafeteria-style restaurant is usually packed with locals. Breakfasts like shredded beef and eggs are popular. Lunch options (around US$4) include stewed chicken, grilled meat, rice and plantains. There's lots of fish and seafood at night. It's 800m inland from the Interamericana on the way to Puerto Quimba.

Getting There & Away

From Panama City, buses to Yaviza stop in Metetí (US$10, three hours) about every hour.

For boats to La Palma or Sambú, take the turnoff for Puerto Quimba, a port on the Río

GETTING TO COLOMBIA

The Interamericana stops at the town of Yaviza and reappears 150km further on, far beyond the Colombian border. Overland crossings through the Darién Gap on foot are not recommended and are, in fact, illegal. The only way to reach South America is to fly directly to the city of your choice, to fly with Air Panama (p640) to Puerto Obaldía on Panama's Caribbean coast and cross over to Capurganá in Colombia, or to take a sailing excursion or a motorboat trip such as that offered by San Blas Adventures (p687).

Iglesias. A passenger pickup shuttles between Metetí and Puerto Quimba every 30 minutes from 6am until 9pm (US$2) or take a taxi (US$10). The 20km-long paved road between Metetí and Puerto Quimba is excellent.

From Puerto Quimba, boats to La Palma (US$3.50, 20 minutes) leave when full between 5:30am and 5pm. A one-way charter may also be an option. Passengers must register at the police checkpoint next to the ticket counter.

Boats seating up to 18 passengers also go to Sambú (US$22, 2¾ hours) daily.

Yaviza

POP 4400

Part bazaar and part bizarre, this concrete village is literally at the end of the road. Here the Interamericana grinds to a halt after 12,580km from Alaska, and beyond lies the famous **Darién Gap**, the no-man's-land between Panama and Colombia. Rough edged and misshapen, it's hardly a destination in its own right, but for travelers it's an essential check-in stop for entry to Parque Nacional Darién.

Sleeping

Hospedaje Sobia Kiru HOTEL $

(☎6150-5449, 299-4409; leticiapitti0311@gmail.com; d US$25; P ❄) A two-story turquoise house with 24 spick-and-span rooms and powerful air-conditioning, the 'Good Heart Inn' is on a side street running up from the port, next to the Cable Onda office. Manager Leticia Pitti Lewis extends a very warm welcome.

Ya Darien GUESTHOUSE $

(☎6653-0074; d US$25; ❄) This slightly grubby guesthouse down from the port has 16 frayed but tidy rooms with cold-water showers. The best of the seven rooms upstairs are Nos 1 and 5 between the small balcony.

Getting There & Away

Buses from Panama City go to Yaviza (US$16, 4½ hours) at least every hour every day.

Public boats to El Real go sporadically when full (US$5) from the **ferry pier**. The cost of a private boat charter to El Real (US$60 to US$90 one way) depends on the motor size and the price of fuel at the time.

El Real

POP 1185

Riverside El Real (official name: El Real de Santa María) dates from the conquistador days when it was merely a fort beside the Río Tuira. The settlement prevented pirates from sailing upriver to plunder Santa María, where gold from the Cana mines was stored. Today El Real is one of the largest towns in the Darién, though it's still very much a backwater. It's not an unattractive place, with a few hints of its colonial past, including a 16th-century Spanish cannon in the main square.

El Real is the last sizable settlement before Parque Nacional Darién. Those heading up to Rancho Frío or Pijibasal should either hire a local guide or join a tour – the Ministerio de Ambiente (p689) won't let you proceed unescorted. Before arriving, send a letter of intent to SENAFRONT (p689) and contact the Panama City office of the Ministerio de Ambiente to pay for lodging.

Getting There & Away

Piraguas (long canoes) ferry passengers down the Río Chucunaque in Yaviza to the port of Mercadeo; the center of El Real is a 15-minute walk from the jetty. When your boat arrives at Mercadeo, register at the SENAFRONT stand in front of the boat landing.

Pickup trucks transfer passengers via Pirre Uno to Pijibasal (US$30), a 1½-hour hike from Rancho Frío, the entry point to Parque Nacional Darién.

Rancho Frío

Some 17km south of El Real, as the lemon-spectacled tanager flies, is the Rancho Frío sector of Parque Nacional Darién. It's home to Station VIII (sometimes called Pirre Station, not to be confused with the station at the top of Cerro Pirre near Cana). Rare bird species here include the crimson-bellied woodpecker, the white-fronted nunbird and the striped woodhaunter. It's a riveting spot for birdwatchers.

The excellent trail network includes a two-day trek to Cerro Pirre ridge and a one-hour walk through jungle to some cascades; the Cascada del Río Perresénico is about a half-hour away on foot. Neither should be attempted without a guide as they are unmarked – if you get lost out here you're finished.

Visitors must write in Spanish to Panama City's SENAFRONT (p689) about their travel intentions in the Darién and carry photocopies of the letter and their passport with them; these may be examined at checkpoints.

Sleeping

Dormitory Lodge CABIN $

(per person US$15) At Rancho Frío (or Station VIII along the trail), this very basic two-story lodge has a total of 14 bunk beds accommodating 28 visitors. There's a small outdoor dining area beside a very basic but good-sized kitchen, a *bohio* (open-sided thatched shelter) with a few chairs and a number of flush toilets and cold-water showers.

You should pay the Ministerio de Ambiente (p689) in Panama City directly.

Getting There & Away

Rancho Frío is 17km from Mercadeo/El Real and can be reached by hiking (four hours), or a combination of boating and hiking or 4WD transportation (from US$30). It's a 1½-hour hike from Pijibasal. For those hiking, the trails offer minimal indications; it's imperative to go with a guide.

La Palma

POP 6000

The provincial capital of Darién Province, La Palma is a one-street town located where the wide Río Tuira meets the Golfo de San Miguel. Pastel-colored houses on stilts lord it over the muddy waterfront, a scene abuzz with commerce, bars and evangelist messages.

Most travelers pass through La Palma to take a boat ride to somewhere else, such as the nature reserve and lodge at Reserva Natural Punta Patiño or the Emberá village of Sambú up the muddy river of that name. If you have time, check out the ruins of 18th-century Spanish **Fuerte San Lorenzo**, five minutes away by boat (US$15).

Every facility of interest to travelers is located on Calle Principal, the main street, which is just over the boat pier. There's a bank, a hospital and a police station, as well as three hotels, bars, restaurants and provisions stores.

Sleeping & Eating

Pensión Tuira PENSION $

(299-6316; Calle Principal; d US$25-35;) Our favorite of the La Palma trio, this guesthouse has 18 so-so rooms, but the greatest attraction is the fabulous terrace with expansive views of the gulf. Room 13 just off the terrace is the best choice, though the smaller room 17 is also a decent option. Air-conditioning costs US$5 extra.

★**Lola Grill** PANAMANIAN $$

(6721-8632; Calle Principal; mains US$8-15; 7am-8pm Mon-Sat) A clean and cheerful cafe serving shrimp or fish *criollo*-style (with a flavorful sauce) in addition to grilled meats. Always a warm welcome. It's up a flight of steps from the main street.

Getting There & Away

Boats from Puerto Quimba (US$3.50, 20 minutes), the springboard for La Palma, leave when full, running between 5:30am and 5pm. Puerto Quimba has buses to Metetí, from where other buses head north for Panama City or south to Yaviza.

Chartering a private boat and guide will cost between US$120 and US$300 per day, gas included.

Reserva Natural Punta Patiño

On the southern shore of the Golfo de San Miguel, 25km from La Palma, is this private 263-sq-km **wildlife reserve** owned by ANCON and managed by the organization's for-profit arm, Ancon Expeditions. It contains species-rich primary and secondary forest and is one of the best places in the country to spot a harpy eagle, Panama's national bird. Even if the big bird proves elusive, there's a good chance of seeing everything from three-toed sloths and capybaras, the world's largest rodents, to pumas.

The only way to reach the reserve is by boat or plane. Landing on the tiny strip of ocean-side grass that's called a runway in these parts is definitely part of the experience.

Getting There & Away

The Ancon Expeditions (p688) tour includes the round-trip airfare between Panama City and **Punta Patiño Airport**, lodging, food and activities including a trip up the Río Mogué to the Emberá village of Mogué and a naturalist guided hike to a harpy eagle's nest.

Independent travelers can hire boats in La Palma to reach Punta Patiño for about US$450. Notify Ancon Expeditions in advance to reserve a cabin.

Sambú

POP 950

Riverside Sambú (sometimes appearing as Boca de Sábalo on maps) is an interesting stop, populated by Emberá, Wounaan, *interioranos* (or mestizos) and *cimarrones* (the ancestors of African slaves who escaped and settled in the jungle). Quite built up and populous by Darién standards, it makes a good springboard for visiting riverside indigenous communities further upstream and absorbing the slow jungle pace.

From Sambú, visitors can plan enjoyable trips across the Río Sábalo bridge to the twin village of **Puerto Indio** (with permission from the Emberá and Wounaan) and visit petroglyphs or mangrove forests. Another Emberá village worth visiting is **Bayamón** to the south. **Bocaca Verano** is a nearby lagoon with crocodiles and prolific birdlife.

Sleeping

Sambú Hause GUESTHOUSE $

(☎6672-9452; www.sambuhausedarienpanama.com; s/d US$10/20) Orthographically challenged Sambú Hause is an attractive yellow-and-turquoise thatched clapboard run by friendly Maria. Cozy but simple, it has two rooms with shared bathroom and one with its own facilities and air-conditioning. There's a lovely breezy terrace with BBQ. Cultural tours can be arranged here.

Getting There & Away

At the time of research, there were only charter flights flying in and out of **Sambú Airport**. A *panga* (small motorboat) from Puerto Quimba (US$22, 2¾ hours) goes to Sambú's **boat pier** daily at around 6am, making a brief stop in La Palma. It returns between 4pm and 4:30pm.

UNDERSTAND PANAMA

Panama Today

One of the world's largest transportation projects, the Panama Canal's US$17 billion expansion, completed in 2016, has doubled capacity and tripled traffic in the canal by digging deeper to accommodate bigger vessels and adding a third lane. Before the expansion, the canal hauled in US$2 billion annually.

As of early 2019, the Panama Canal expansion has reportedly exceeded expectations in both tonnage and traffic. Transit times have also decreased from three and a half hours to two and a half hours. The success of the wider locks have, according to Esteban G. Saenz, former vice president for transit business at the Panama Canal Authority, via *The American Journal of Transportation,* sparked discussions of a possible fourth lock.

Other upgrades include a new cruise port slated for the Amador Causeway in 2020 and the expansion of Tocumen International Airport, expected for the 2019 papal visit. And just like that, this little country of four million residents bets the farm and steps into the big league.

Although the canal has defined Panama for the last century, it's what lies just beyond this engineering marvel that could define the next 100 years. A third of the country is set aside as protected areas and national parks, and the country continues to promote ecotourism in hopes of replicating the success of its northern neighbor, Costa Rica.

History

The waistline of the Americas, Panama has played a strategic role in the history of the western hemisphere, from hosting the biological exchange of species to witnessing clashes between cultures. Once an overland trade route linking ancient Peru and Mexico, post–Colombian conquest Panama became the conduit for exported Inca treasures. Set amid two oceans, transit is a longtime theme here. As the Panama Railroad once brought prospectors to the California gold rush, the Panama Canal has become the roaring engine of global commerce.

Lost Panama

The coastlines and rainforests of Panama have been inhabited by humans for at least 10,000 years. Indigenous groups including the Guna, the Ngöbe-Buglé, the Emberá, the Wounaan, the Bribrí and the Naso were living on the isthmus prior to the Spanish arrival. However, the tragedy of Panama is that, despite its rich cultural history, there are virtually no physical remains of these great civilizations.

What is known about pre-Columbian Panama is that early inhabitants were part of an extensive trading zone that extended as far south as Peru and as far north as Mexico. Archaeologists have uncovered exquisite gold ornaments and unusual life-size stone statues of human figures as well as distinctive types of pottery and *metates* (stone platforms that were used for grinding corn).

Panama's first peoples lived beside both oceans and fished in mangrove swamps, estuaries and coral reefs. It seems only fitting that the country's name is derived from an indigenous word meaning 'abundance of fish.'

New World Order

In 1501 the 'discovery' of Panama by Spanish explorer Rodrigo de Bastidas marked the beginning of the age of conquest and colonization in the isthmus. However, it was his first mate, Vasco Núñez de Balboa, who earned lasting fame following his 'discovery' of the Pacific Ocean 12 years later.

On his fourth and final voyage to the New World in 1502, Christopher Columbus saw 'more gold in two days than in four years in Spain' in present-day Costa Rica. Although his attempts to establish a colony at the mouth of the Río Belén failed due to fierce local resistance, Columbus petitioned the Spanish Crown to have himself appointed as governor of Veraguas, the stretch of shoreline from Honduras to Panama.

Following Columbus' death in 1506, King Ferdinand appointed Diego de Nicuesa to settle the newly claimed land. These various attempts would miserably fail. Much to the disappointment of conquistadors, Panama was not rich in gold. Add tropical diseases, inhospitable terrain and less than welcoming natives, and it's easy to see why early Spanish colonies struggled and often failed.

In 1513 Balboa heard rumors about a large sea and a wealthy, gold-producing civilization across the mountains – likely the Inca Empire of Peru. Driven by ambition, Balboa scaled the continental divide and on September 26, 1513, became the first European to set eyes on the Pacific Ocean. He claimed the ocean and all the lands it touched for the king of Spain.

The Empire Expands

In 1519 a cruel and vindictive Spaniard named Pedro Arias de Ávila (called Pedrarias by contemporaries) founded the city of Panamá on the Pacific, near present-day Panama City. The governor ordered the beheading of Balboa in 1517 on a trumped-up charge of treason. He is also remembered for murderous attacks against the indigenous population, whom he roasted alive or fed to dogs.

Pedrarias nonetheless established Panamá as an important Spanish settlement, a commercial center and a base for further explorations, including the conquest of Peru. From Panamá, vast riches of Peruvian gold and Oriental spices were transported across the isthmus by foot. This famous trade route, known as the Sendero Las Cruces (Las Cruces Trail), can still be walked.

As the Spaniards grew plump on the wealth of plundered civilizations, the world began to notice the prospering colony, especially the English privateers lurking in coastal waters. In 1573 Sir Francis Drake destroyed the Nombre de Dios settlement and set sail for England with a galleon laden with Spanish gold.

The Spanish responded by building large stone fortresses at San Lorenzo and Portobelo. Still, Welsh buccaneer Sir Henry Morgan overpowered Fuerte San Lorenzo and sailed up the Río Chagres in 1671. After crossing the isthmus, Morgan destroyed the city of Panamá, burning it to the ground to return to the Caribbean coast with 200 mules loaded with Spanish loot.

The Spanish rebuilt the city a few years later on a cape several kilometers west of its original site. The ruins of the old settlement, now known as Panamá Viejo, and the colonial city of Casco Viejo are within the city limits of the present-day metropolis.

British privateering continued. After Admiral Edward Vernon destroyed the fortress of Portobelo in 1739, the Spanish abandoned the Panamanian crossing in favor of sailing the long way around Cape Horn to the west coast of South America.

The Empire Ends

Spain's costly Peninsular War with France from 1808 to 1814 – and the political turmoil, unrest and power vacuums that the conflict caused – led Spain to lose all its colonial possessions in the first third of the 19th century.

Panama gained independence from Spanish rule in 1821 and immediately joined Gran Colombia, a confederation of Colombia, Bolivia, Ecuador, Peru and Venezuela – a united Latin American nation that had long been the dream of Simón Bolívar. However, internal disputes led to the formal abolition of Gran Colombia in 1831, though fledgling Panama retained its status as a province of Colombia.

Birth of a Nation

Panama's future forever changed when world powers caught on that the isthmus was the narrowest point between the Atlantic and Pacific Oceans. In 1846 Colombia signed a treaty permitting the USA to construct a railway across the isthmus, granting free transit and the right to protect the railway with military force. At the height of the California gold rush in 1849, tens of thousands traveled from the USA's east coast to the west coast via Panama in order to avoid hostile tribes in the central states. Colombia and Panama grew wealthy from the railway, and the first talks of a canal across Central America began to surface.

The idea of a canal across the isthmus was first raised in 1524 when King Charles V of Spain ordered a survey to determine the feasibility of a waterway. Later, Emperor Napoleon III of France also considered the idea. Finally, in 1878, French builder Ferdinand de Lesseps, basking in the glory of the recently constructed Suez canal, was contracted by Colombia to build the canal, bringing his crew to Panama in 1881. Much like Napoleon, Lesseps severely underestimated the task, and over 22,000 workers died from yellow fever and malaria in less than a decade. In 1889 insurmountable construction problems and financial mismanagement drove the company bankrupt.

The USA saw the French failure as a business opportunity. In 1903 Philippe Bunau-Varilla, one of Lesseps' chief engineers, agreed to sell concessions to the USA, though the Colombian government refused. Bunau-Varilla approached the US government to back Panama if it declared independence from Colombia.

On November 3, 1903, a revolutionary junta declared Panama independent, and the US government immediately recognized its sovereignty – the first of a series of American interventions. Although Colombia sent troops by sea to try to regain control, US battleships prevented them from reaching land. Colombia only recognized Panama as a legitimately separate nation in 1921, when the US compensated Colombia with US$25 million.

The USA & the Canal

Following independence, Bunau-Varilla was appointed Panamanian ambassador to the USA and his first act in office paved the way for future American interventions in the region. Hoping to profit from the sale of the canal concessions to the USA, Bunau-Varilla arrived in Washington, DC, before Panama could assemble a delegation. On November 18, Bunau-Varilla and US Secretary of State John Hay signed the Hay–Bunau-Varilla Treaty, which gave the USA far more than had been offered in the original treaty. In addition to owning concessions to the canal, the USA was also granted 'sovereign rights in perpetuity over the Canal Zone,' an area extending 8km on either side of the canal, and a broad right of intervention in Panamanian affairs.

Despite opposition from the tardy Panamanian delegation as well as lingering questions about the treaty's legality, the treaty was ratified, ushering in an era of friction between the USA and Panama. Construction began again on the canal in 1904, and despite disease, landslides and harsh weather, the world's greatest engineering marvel was completed in only a decade. The first ship sailed through the canal on August 15, 1914.

In the years following the completion of the canal, the US military repeatedly intervened in the country's political affairs. In response to growing Panamanian disenchantment with these interventions, the Hay–Bunau-Varilla Treaty was replaced in 1936 by the Hull–Alfaro Treaty. The USA relinquished its rights to use its troops outside the Canal Zone and to seize land for canal purposes, and the annual sum paid to Panama for use of the Canal Zone was raised. However, increased sovereignty was not enough to stem the growing tide of Panamanian opposition to US occupation. Anti-US sentiment reached boiling point in

1964 during a student protest that left 27 Panamanians dead and 500 injured. Today the event is commemorated as Día de Los Mártires (National Martyrs' Day).

As US influence waned, the Panamanian army grew more powerful. In 1968 the Guardia Nacional deposed the elected president and took control of the government. Soon after, the constitution was suspended, the national assembly was dissolved and the press was censored, while the Guardia's General Omar Torrijos emerged as the new leader. Torrijos' record is spotty. Though he plunged the country into debt as a result of a massive public-works program, Torrijos was successful in pressuring US President Jimmy Carter into ceding control of the canal to Panama. The Torrijos–Carter Treaty guaranteed full Panamanian control of the canal as of December 31, 1999, as well as a complete withdrawal of US military forces.

The Rise & Fall of Noriega

Still feeling triumphant from the recently signed treaty, Panama was unprepared for the sudden death of Torrijos in a plane crash in 1981. Two years later, Colonel Manuel Antonio Noriega seized the Guardia Nacional, promoted himself to general and made himself the de facto ruler of Panama. Noriega, a former head of Panama's secret police, a former CIA operative and a graduate of the School of the Americas, quickly began to consolidate his power. He enlarged the Guardia Nacional, significantly expanded its authority and renamed it the Panama Defense Forces. He also created a paramilitary 'Dignity Battalion' in every city, town and village, its members armed and ready to inform on any of their neighbors showing less than complete loyalty to the Noriega regime.

Things went from bad to worse in early 1987 when Noriega was publicly accused of involvement in drug trafficking with Colombian drug cartels, murdering his opponents and rigging elections. Many Panamanians demanded Noriega's dismissal, protesting with general strikes and street demonstrations that resulted in violent clashes with the Panama Defense Forces. In February 1988, Panamanian President Eric Arturo Delvalle attempted to dismiss Noriega, but was forced to flee Panama. Noriega subsequently appointed a president more sympathetic to his cause.

Noriega's regime became an international embarrassment. In March 1988 the USA imposed economic sanctions against Panama, ending a preferential trade agreement, freezing Panamanian assets in US banks and refusing to pay canal fees. A few days after the sanctions were imposed, an unsuccessful military coup prompted Noriega to step up violent repression of his critics. After Noriega's candidate lost the presidential election in May 1989, the general declared the election null and void. Meanwhile, Guillermo Endara, the winning candidate, and his two vice-presidential running mates were badly beaten by Noriega's thugs, with the entire bloody scene captured by a TV crew and broadcasted internationally. A second failed coup in October 1989 was followed by even more repressive measures.

On December 15, 1989, Noriega's legislature declared him president, and his first official act of office was to declare war on the USA. The following day an unarmed US marine dressed in civilian clothes was killed by Panamanian soldiers while leaving a restaurant in Panama City.

The US reaction was swift and unrelenting. In the first hour of December 20, 1989, Panama City was attacked by aircraft, tanks and 26,000 US troops. The invasion, intended to bring Noriega to justice and create a democracy better suited to US interests, left more than 2000 civilians dead, tens of thousands homeless and destroyed entire tracts of Panama City.

On Christmas Day, Noriega sought asylum in the Vatican embassy. US forces surrounded the embassy and pressured the Vatican to release him. They bombarded the embassy with blaring rock music. Mobs of angry Panamanians surrounded the embassy, calling for Noriega to be ousted.

After 10 days of psychological warfare, the Vatican embassy persuaded Noriega to give himself up by threatening to cancel his asylum. Noriega surrendered to US forces on January 3, and was flown to Miami where he was convicted of conspiracy to manufacture and distribute cocaine.

After his US prison sentence ended in 2007 he was extradited to Paris in April 2010. A retrial found Noriega guilty and sentenced him to seven years in prison, but he was conditionally released to serve 20 years in Panama, starting in December 2011. In March 2017 he was diagnosed with a brain tumor. He died in May of the same year, following complications after surgery.

Modern Struggles

After Noriega's forced removal, Guillermo Endara, the legitimate winner of the 1989 election, was sworn in as president, and Panama attempted to put itself back together. The country's image and economy were in a shambles, and its capital had suffered damage not only from the invasion itself but also from the widespread looting that followed. Corruption scandals and internal fighting were rampant during the Endara administration. There was 19% unemployment and a lack of connection with the country's significant poor population, as the administration was peopled by wealthy businessmen. By the time Endara was voted out of office in 1994, his approval ratings were in single digits.

In the 1994 election, the fairest in recent Panamanian history, Ernesto Pérez Balladares became president. Under his direction, the Panamanian government implemented a program of privatization that focused on infrastructure improvements, health care and education. Although Pérez Balladares allocated unprecedented levels of funding, he was viewed as corrupt. In the spring of 1999, voters rejected his attempt to change constitutional limits barring a president from serving two consecutive terms.

In 1999 Mireya Moscoso – the widow of popular former president Arnulfo Arias, head of the conservative Arnulfista Party (PA) – took office and became Panama's first female leader. Moscoso's ambitious plans for reform were not realized. As Panama celebrated its centenary in 2003, unemployment rose to 18%. Moscoso was accused of wasteful spending – as parts of the country went without food, she paid US$10 million to bring the Miss Universe pageant to Panama. She was also accused of looking the other way during Colombian military incursions into the Darién. She left office in 2004 after failing to fulfill a single campaign promise.

Moscoso was followed by Martín Torrijos, a member of the Revolutionary Democratic Party (PRD) and the son of former leader Omar Torrijos. Although there has been much debate regarding the successes and failures of his administration, he did implement a number of fiscal reforms, including an overhaul of the nation's social-security system. His proposal to expand the Panama Canal was overwhelmingly approved in a national referendum on October 22, 2006.

Current Climate

On May 3, 2009, Panama bucked the Latin American leftist trend by electing conservative supermarket magnate Ricardo Martinelli president. Part of the conservative Democratic Change (CD) party, Martinelli was a pro-business choice who created an investment boom by slashing trade barriers and red tape. During his tenure, ambitious public projects like Central America's first subway system became the order of the day and Panama's 8% growth rate sparkled as the best in Latin America.

Eventually the honeymoon ended and the success story turned part pulp fiction, part political thriller. Martinell's former vice president and dark-horse opposition leader Juan Carlos Varela was elected president in 2014 on promises to play by the book and implement constitutional checks and balances. Martinelli faced charges of corruption in a US$45 million program to feed poor schoolchildren. There was also a wire-tapping scandal involving political foes. Remember those colossal infrastructure projects? Some US$1.2 billion of contracts have come under scrutiny and some project directors with government contracts have been arrested. Martinelli fled to Miami via private jet to a luxury condo that was made famous in the film *Scarface*. US marshals arrested him on June 12, 2017, putting into a Miami Federal Detention Center. He was extradited to Panama in June 2018 to face wire-tapping charges.

Adding to Panama's woes, an anonymous source leaked over 11.5 million documents from the Panamanian law form Mossack Fonseca in 2015. Known as the Panama Papers, they detailed financial information of worldwide leaders and public figures revealing corruption on a colossal scale. Mossack Fonseca had created shell companies that helped international entities and individuals evade of international sanctions, commit fraud and evade taxes. Though the law firm shut down in 2018, the fallout from the papers still continues.

Culture

The National Psyche

Panamanian identity is in many ways elusive. Perhaps it's only natural given the many years that Panama has been the object of another country's meddling. From the US-backed independence of 1903 to the strong-armed removal of Noriega in 1989 – with half-a-dozen other interventions in between – the USA has left a strong legacy in the country.

Nearly every Panamanian has a relative or at least an acquaintance living in the USA, and parts of the country seem swept up in mall fever, with architectural inspiration straight out of North America. Panamanians (or at least the ones who can afford to) deck themselves out in US clothes, buy US-made cars and take their fashion tips straight from Madison Ave.

Others are quite reticent to embrace the culture from the north. Indigenous groups like the Emberá and Guna struggle to keep their traditions alive as more and more of their youth are lured into the Western lifestyles of the city. On the Península de Azuero, where there is a rich Spanish cultural heritage exemplified by traditional festivals, dress and customs, villagers raise the same concerns about the future of their youth.

Given the clash between old and new, it's surprising the country isn't suffering from a serious case of cognitive dissonance. However, the exceptionally tolerant Panamanian character weathers many contradictions – the old and the new, the grave disparity between rich and poor, and the stunning natural environment and its rapid destruction.

Much of the famous Panamanian tolerance begins in the family, which is the cornerstone of society and plays a role in nearly every aspect of a person's life. Whether among Guna sisters or Panama City's elite, everyone looks after each other. Favors are graciously accepted, promptly returned and never forgotten.

This mutual concern extends from the family into the community, and at times the whole country can seem like one giant extended community. In the political arena, the same names appear time and again, as nepotism is the norm rather than the exception. Unfortunately, this goes hand-in-hand with Panama's most persistent problem: corruption.

Panamanians view their leaders' fiscal and moral transgressions with disgust, and they are far from being in the dark about issues. Yet they accept things with patience and an almost fatalistic attitude. Outsiders sometimes view this as a kind of passivity, but it's all just another aspect of the complicated Panamanian psyche.

Lifestyle

In spite of the skyscrapers and gleaming restaurants lining the wealthier districts of Panama City, nearly a third of the country's population lives in poverty. Furthermore, almost a quarter of a million Panamanians struggle just to satisfy their basic dietary needs. The poorest tend to live in the least populated provinces: Darién, Bocas del Toro, Veraguas, Los Santos and Colón. There is also substantial poverty in the slums of Panama City, where an estimated 20% of the urban population lives. Countrywide, 9% of the population lives in *barriados* (squatter) settlements.

For *campesinos* (farmers), life is hard. A subsistence farmer in the interior might earn as little as US$8 per day, far below the national average of US$11,500 per capita. In the Emberá and Wounaan villages of Darién, traditional living patterns persist much as they have for hundreds of years. Thatched hut communities survive on subsistence agriculture, hunting, fishing and pastoralism. The life expectancy in these frontier villages is about 10 years below the national average. The majority of the Emberá and Wounaan communities lack access to clean water and basic sanitation.

The middle and upper class largely reside in and around Panama City with a level of comfort similar to their counterparts in Europe and the USA. They live in large homes or apartments, have a maid, a car or two, and for the lucky few a second home on the beach or in the mountains. Cell phones are de rigueur. Vacations are often enjoyed in Europe or the USA. Most middle-class adults can speak some English and their children usually attend English-speaking schools.

People

The majority of Panamanians (65%) are *mestizo,* which is generally a mix of indigenous and Spanish descent. In truth, many non-black immigrants are also thrown into this category, including a sizable Chinese population – some people estimate that as much as 10% of the population is of Chinese ancestry. There are several other large groups: about 9% of Panamanians are of African descent, 7% of European descent, 7% of mixed African and Spanish descent, and

12% are indigenous. Generally, black Panamanians are mostly descendants of English-speaking West Indians, such as Jamaicans and Trinidadians, who were originally brought to Panama as laborers.

Of the several dozen native tribes that inhabited Panama when the Spanish arrived, few remain. The Guna live on islands along the Caribbean coast in the autonomous region of the Comarca de Guna Yala. Considered the most politically organized, they regularly send representatives to the national legislature. The Emberá and Wounaan inhabit the eastern Panamá province and the Darién; Panama's largest tribe, the Ngöbe-Buglé live in the provinces of Chiriquí, Veraguas and Bocas del Toro. The Teribe inhabit Bocas del Toro Province, while the Bribrí are found along the Talamanca Reserve. Despite modernizing influences, each of Panama's indigenous groups maintains its own language and culture.

Religion

Religion in Panama can best be observed by walking the streets of the capital. Among the scores of Catholic churches, you'll find breezy Anglican churches filled with worshippers from the West Indies, synagogues, mosques, a shiny Greek Orthodox church, an impressive Hindu temple and a surreal Baha'i House of Worship (the headquarters for Latin America).

Freedom of religion is constitutionally guaranteed in Panama, although the preeminence of Roman Catholicism is also officially recognized, with 85% of the population describing themselves as Catholic. Schoolchildren have the option to study theology, though it is not compulsory. Protestant denominations largely account for the remaining 15% of the population; although a recognizable population of Muslims and Baha'i also exists, and approximately 3000 Jews (many of them recent immigrants from Israel), 24,000 Buddhists and 9000 Hindus also live in Panama.

The various indigenous tribes of Panama have their own belief systems, although these are fading quickly due to the influence of Christian missionaries. As in other parts of Latin America, the evangelical movement is spreading like wildfire.

Although Catholics are the majority, only about 20% of them attend church regularly. The religious orders aren't particularly strong in Panama either – only about 25% of Catholic clergy are Panamanian, while the rest are foreign missionaries.

Arts

Panama's all-embracing music scene includes salsa, Latin and American jazz, traditional music from the central provinces, reggae, reggaetón and Latin, British and American rock and roll. Their biggest export is world-renowned salsa singer Rubén Blades, who even ran for president in 1994, finishing third. The jazz composer and pianist Danilo Pérez is widely acclaimed by critics, while Los Rabanes produces classic Panamanian rock. Heavy on the accordion, Panamanian folk music (called *típico*), is well represented by Dorindo Cárdenas, the late Victorio Vergara (whose band lives on as Nenito Vargas y los Plumas Negras) and the popular brother-sister pair of Samy and Sandra Sandoval. These days reggaetón (also known as *punta*) permeates all social levels in Panama. Key artists include Danger Man, who died in gang violence; balladeer Eddie Lover; and the artist known as Flex, who has also been very successful in Mexico.

Several of Panama's best novels were written mid-20th century. *El Ahogado* (The Drowned Man), a 1937 novel by Tristán Solarte, blends elements of the detective, gothic and psychological genres with a famous local myth. *El Desván* (In the Garret), a 1954 novel by Ramón H Jurado, explores the emotional limits of the human condition. *Gamboa Road Gang*, by Joaquín Beleño, is about the political and social events surrounding the Panama Canal. Today's notable authors include poet and novelist Giovanna Benedetti, historical novelist Gloria Guardia and folk novelist Rosa María Britton.

North American novelist Cristina Henríquez, who is half-Panamanian, offers insight into Panamanian identity from a sometimes displaced point of view. Her 2010 novel *The World in Half* was followed in 2014 by *The Book of Unknown Americans*, a love story that weaves in the experiences of diverse Latin immigrants to the USA.

The first prominent figure on Panama's art scene, French-trained Roberto Lewis (1874–1949) painted allegorical images in public buildings; look for those in the Palacio de las Garzas in Panama City. In 1913 Lewis became the director of Panama's first art academy, where he and his successor, Humberto Ivaldi (1909–47), educated a generation of artists. Among the school's students were Juan Manuel Cedeño and Isaac Benítez, and mid-20th-century painters Alfredo Sinclair, Guillermo Trujillo and Eudoro Silvera. More recent artists of note include Olga Sinclair and Brooke Alfaro.

Sports

Owing to the legacy of US occupation, baseball is the national pastime. Although Panama has no professional teams, amateur leagues play in stadiums throughout the country. In the US major leagues, Mariano Rivera, the record-setting pitcher for the New York Yankees, is a national hero. The batting champ Rod Carew, another Panamanian star, was inducted into the Hall of Fame in 1991. Former NY Yankee Roberto Kelly is also fondly remembered.

Boxing is another popular spectator sport, and a source of local pride since Panama City native Roberto Durán won the world championship lightweight title in 1972. A legend, he went on to become the world champion in each of the welterweight (1980), light middleweight (1983) and super middleweight (1989) categories. Currently, Panama also has three reigning world boxing champions.

Panama's first Olympic gold came in 2008 when Irving Saladino won the long jump in Beijing.

Landscape & Wildlife

The Land

Panama is both the narrowest and the southernmost country in Central America. The long S-shaped isthmus borders Costa Rica in the west and Colombia in the east. Its northern Caribbean coastline measures 1160km, compared to a 1690km Pacific coastline in the south, and its total land area is 78,056 sq km.

Panama is just 50km wide at its leanest point, yet it separates two great oceans. The Panama Canal, which is about 80km long, effectively divides the country into eastern and western regions. Panama's two mountain ranges run along its spine in both the east and the west. Volcán Barú is the country's highest point and only volcano.

Like all of the Central American countries, Panama has large, flat coastal lowlands with huge banana plantations. There are about 480 rivers in Panama and 1518 islands near its shores. The two main island groups are the San Blás and Bocas del Toro archipelagos on the Caribbean side, but most of the islands are on the Pacific side. Even the Panama Canal has islands, including Isla Barro Colorado, which has a world-famous tropical-rainforest research station.

Wildlife

Panama's position as a narrow land bridge between two huge continents has given it a remarkable variety of plant and animal life. Species migrating between the continents have gathered in Panama, which means that it's possible to see South American armadillos, anteaters and sloths alongside North American tapirs, jaguars and deer. With its wide variety of native and migratory species, Panama is one of the world's best places for birdwatchers.

Panama has more than 978 recorded bird species and more than 10,000 plant species, in addition to 125 animal species found only here. The country's 105 rare and endangered species include scarlet macaws, harpy eagles (the national bird of Panama), golden frogs, jaguars and various species of sea turtle. Panama is one of the best places to see a quetzal. Five species of sea turtle can be seen here, while among the primates there are capuchins, tamarins, and squirrel, spider and howler monkeys.

Tropical rainforest is the dominant vegetation in the canal area, along the Caribbean coast and in most of the eastern half of the country. The Parque Nacional Darién protects much of Panama's largest tropical rainforest region. Other vegetation zones include Pacific coast grasslands, highland mountain forest, cloud forest on the highest peaks and mangrove forest on both coasts.

National Parks & Protected Areas

Panama has 16 national parks and more than two dozen officially protected areas. About a third of Panama is set aside for conservation, while about 40% of land remains covered by forest. Panama also has more land set aside for habitat protection than any other Central American country, and its forests contain the greatest number of species of all New World countries north

NATIONAL PARKS & RESERVES

A few highlights include the following:

Parque Internacional La Amistad (p667) Home to several indigenous groups, pristine rainforest and abundant wildlife.

Parque Nacional Darién (p689) Unesco World Heritage Site with 5760 sq km of world-class wildlife-rich rainforest.

Parque Nacional Isla de Coiba (p654) Includes the 493-sq-km Isla de Coiba, regarded by scientists as a biodiversity hot spot.

Parque Nacional Marino Golfo de Chiriquí (p658) Protects 25 islands and numerous coral reefs.

Parque Nacional Marino Isla Bastimentos (p676) An important nature reserve for many species of Caribbean wildlife, including sea turtles.

Parque Nacional Soberanía (p645) A birdwatcher's paradise in lush rainforest.

Parque Nacional Volcán Barú (p664) Surrounds Panama's only volcano and highest peak, 3475m Volcán Barú.

Parque Natural Metropolitano (p630) Tropical semi-deciduous forest within the city limits.

of Colombia. Yet all of these statistics do not account for the fact that protected lands are, in fact, often poorly protected.

In many of the national parks and protected areas, mestizo and indigenous villages are scattered about. In some scenarios, these communities help protect and maintain parks and wildlife. Headquartered in Panama City, the Ministerio de Ambiente (www.miambiente.gob.pa), Panama's Ministry of the Environment, runs the nation's parks. All national parks, apart from Parque Nacional Coiba, are free to enter. Permits to camp or stay at a ranger station (US$5 to US$10) can generally be obtained at park entrances.

Environmental Issues

Unfortunately, deforestation is one of the country's gravest environmental problems. Additionally, with Panama's national parks grossly understaffed, illegal hunting, settling and logging take place even inside parks.

Another major concern is mining. Roughly 26% of Panama is mined or under mining concessions, bringing concerns of contaminated water sources, and the destruction of forest and human habitats. In spite of objections by prominent environmental groups, the government has approved and expedited large-scale mining projects, most notably a US$6.2 billion project – an investment greater than the initial expansion of the Panama Canal – to extract gold and copper.

A major victory for community interests was the 2012 passing of law 415, which prohibits extraction in indigenous territories and requires their approval for hydroelectric projects. The change came after a shutdown of Ngöbe-Buglé community protests in February 2012 left two protesters dead.

SURVIVAL GUIDE

Directory A–Z

ACCESSIBLE TRAVEL

Panama is not wheelchair friendly, though high-end hotels provide some accessible rooms. There are parking spaces for people with mobility issues and some oversized bathroom stalls. Outside the capital, adequate infrastructure is lacking.

Download Lonely Planet's free Accessible Travel guides from http://lptravel.to/AccessibleTravel.

ACCOMMODATIONS

Book accommodations two to six months ahead for Semana Santa ('Holy Week'; the week preceding Easter), the November festivals and the week between Christmas and New Year. Most lodgings require reservations in high season.

Hotels In abundance in the midrange and high-end categories.

B&Bs A midrange phenomenon most common in the capital as well as Boquete and Bocas del Toro.

Hostels Cheap and spreading in Panama, ranging from quiet budget digs to party central.

Lodges From rustic to high end, found mostly in the highlands.

CUSTOMS REGULATIONS

You may bring up to 10 cartons of cigarettes and five bottles of liquor into Panama tax free. If you try to leave Panama with products made from endangered species – such as jaguar teeth, ocelot skin and turtle shell – you'll face a steep fine and possible jail time.

EMBASSIES & CONSULATES

More than 50 countries have *embajadas* (embassies) or *consulados* (consulates) in Panama City. With the exception of those of the USA and France, most embassies are located in the Marbella district of Panama City.

Ireland, Australia and New Zealand have no embassies or consulates in Panama. In all three cases, refer to the relevant nation's legation in Mexico.

Canadian Embassy (☎294-2500; www.canadainternational.gc.ca/panama; Piso 11, Tower A, Torre de las Americas, Punta Pacifica; ⏰8:30am-1pm Mon-Fri)

Colombian Embassy (☎392-5893; http://panama.consulado.gov.co; 1st fl, Condominio Posada del Rey, Vía Italia, Punta Paitilla; ⏰7:30am-1:30pm Mon-Fri)

Costa Rican Embassy (☎6521-4665, 264-2980; www.embajadacostaricaenpanama.com; 30th fl, Edificio Bisca, cnr Aquilino de la Guardia & Av Balboa, Bella Vista; ⏰9am-1pm Mon-Fri)

Costa Rican Consulate (☎774-1923; www.embajadacostaricaenpanama.com; Calle B Norte & Av Primera, Torre del Banco Universal No 304; ⏰9am-1pm Mon-Fri)

Dutch Consulate (☎280-6650; www.paisesbajosmundial.nl/paises/panama; No 23, 23rd fl, Tower 1000, Calle Hanono Missri, Punta Paitilla; ⏰9am-12pm Mon-Fri)

French Embassy (☎211-6200; www.ambafrance-pa.org; Plaza de Francia, Las Bóvedas, Casco Viejo; ⏰8:30am-11:30am Mon-Fri)

German Embassy (☎263-7733; www.panama.diplo.de; Piso PH, World Trade Center, Calle 53 Este, Marbella; ⏰9am-noon Mon-Fri)

UK Embassy (☎297-6550; www.gov.uk/government/world/panama; 4th fl, Humbolt Tower, Calle 53 Este, Marbella; ⏰7:30am-4:30pm Mon-Thu, to 12:30pm Fri)

US Embassy (☎317-5000; https://pa.usembassy.gov/; Av Demetrio Basillo Lakas 783, Clayton; ⏰8am-5:30pm Mon-Thu, to noon Fri)

FOOD

Except in very top-end restaurants in Panama City and at a few in the provinces, it's usually not necessary to book eating options in advance.

Mercados Produce markets, usually with food stalls attached, sell fruit in abundance but vegetables less so.

Panaderías For something light, head for a 'bakery' or *pastelería* (pastry shop) for a pastry and coffee.

Cafeterías Budget, often self-service restaurants that serve simple meals usually till late in urban areas.

Fondas Small, often family-run restaurants serving *comida corriente*, an inexpensive set meal.

Restaurantes Restaurants range from simple setups dishing out regional specialties to swanky affairs.

INTERNET ACCESS

Public wi-fi access is increasingly common in bus terminals, plazas, libraries and restaurants. Hotels and hostels in more tourist-oriented areas have wi-fi and some computer terminals for use; the Guna Yala and Darién regions are generally exceptions. If desperate, visit the local school – it's often possible to pick up a signal outside.

LEGAL MATTERS

You are legally required to carry identification at all times. This should be an ID with a photograph, preferably a passport. Although this may seem like an inconvenience, police officers reserve the right to request documentation from tourists at all times, and several readers have been forced to spend the night in prison for failure to produce proper ID.

It is illegal for women and men to walk around topless, even if you are on your way to the beach. This rule is strictly enforced in Bocas del Toro town on Isla Colón, and you can expect to be stopped on the streets by police officers if you don't cover up. You are never allowed to enter government buildings dressed in shorts.

In Panama you are presumed guilty until found innocent. If you are accused of a serious crime, you will be taken to jail, where you will likely spend several months before your case goes before a judge. Some simple but valuable advice: stay away from people who commit crimes. For example, you can expect to go to jail if discovered in a car found to contain illegal drugs, even if they aren't yours.

In Panama penalties for possession of even small amounts of illegal drugs are much stricter than in Europe, the USA and Australia. Defendants often spend years in prison before they are brought to trial and, if convicted (as is usually

SLEEPING PRICE RANGES

The following price ranges refer to a double room with bathroom in high season. Unless otherwise stated, tax is included in the price.

$ less than US$60

$$ US$60–130

$$$ more than US$130

the case), can expect sentences of several more years. Most lawyers won't accept drug cases because the outcome is certain: conviction.

If you are jailed, your embassy will offer only limited assistance. This may include a visit from an embassy staff member to make sure your human rights have not been violated, letting your family know where you are and putting you in contact with a lawyer (whom you must pay for yourself). Embassy officials will not bail you out.

LGBTIQ+ TRAVELERS

Panamanians are more out than ever, though this openness is much more prevalent in Panama City than anywhere else. You will probably meet more openly gay locals here than in other parts of Central America, though the culture is generally discreet.

Gay unions are still not legal here, but many think this may change relatively soon. According to locals, discrimination is more prevalent against lesbians than gay men.

MAPS

Outside of Panama City, maps are hard to come by.

Canada-based **International Travel Maps** (☎ Canada 604-273-1400; www.itmb.com; 12300 Bridgeport Road, Richmond, BC, Canada V6V 1J5) publishes an excellent 1:300,000 color map of Panama (US$11.95) showing the geographical features, cities, towns, national parks, airports and roads of Panama. Maps are available for purchase online.

At Instituto Geográfico Nacional (p689) in Panama City, you can buy topographical maps of selected cities and regions. Various free tourist publications distributed in Panama also have maps, though hiking maps are rarely available at national-park ranger stations.

MONEY

Panama uses the US dollar as its currency. The official name for it is the balboa, but it's exactly the same bill. People use the terms *dólar* and balboa interchangeably.

Panamanian coins are of the same value, size and metal as US ones, though both are used interchangeably. Coins include one, five, 10, 25 and 50 *centavos* – 100 *centavos* equal one balboa (dollar). Most businesses won't break US$50 and US$100 bills, and those that do may require you to present your passport.

ATMs

Throughout Panama, ATMs are readily available, except in the Darién, on Islas Contadora and Tobago and in the Archipiélago de San Blas. Look for the red 'Sistema Clave' sign. Generally speaking, ATMs accept cards on most networks (Plus, Cirrus, MasterCard, Visa, Amex), though a charge is usually levied depending on your issuing bank. The amount that can be withdrawn at one time varies from bank to bank, though it is usually US$500 maximum.

There are several places where it's essential to show up with cash. Among tourist destinations, the following places have no banks, and it's a long way to the nearest ATM: Santa Catalina, Santa Fé and Isla de Coiba in Veraguas; Isla Contadora and Isla Tobago in Panamá Province; Isla Grande and Portobelo in Colón; and most of the Darién.

Bargaining

It's OK but not all that common to bargain at markets and street stalls, but educate yourself first by asking around to get an idea of the pricing of different items, particularly handmade goods, and the specific factors that contribute to the quality. Rather than intensive negotiations, just ask for a *descuento* (discount).

Credit Cards

Although they are widely accepted at travel agencies, upscale hotels and many restaurants, credit cards can present difficulties elsewhere. It is always advisable to carry enough cash to get you to the next bank or ATM.

Always find out if your hotel or restaurant accepts credit in advance to avoid unpleasant surprises.

If charging a big-ticket item, it's best to check in with your bank in advance. Most cards charge a fee (between 3% and 10%) for international use.

Tipping

Restaurants Tipping should be 10%, but check to see if it's included in the bill.

Taxis Tipping is optional, but you can round up a dollar or two, especially at night.

Guides It is customary to tip US$7 to US$10 per person for day tours; tip on the high end for naturalist guides.

OPENING HOURS

Opening hours vary throughout the year. The following are high-season hours.

Banks 8am–3pm Monday to Friday, 9am–noon Saturday

Bars and clubs Bars from 9pm; clubs 11pm–3am or 4am

Government offices 8am–4pm Monday to Friday

Malls and shops 10am–9pm or 10pm

Offices 8am–noon and 1:30–5pm Monday to Friday

Restaurants 7–10am, noon–3pm and 6–10pm (later in Panama City); often closed Sunday

Supermarkets 8am–9pm; some open 24 hours

PUBLIC HOLIDAYS

New Year's Day (Año Nuevo) January 1

Martyrs' Day (Día de los Mártires) January 9

Good Friday (Viernes Santo) March/April

Labor Day (Día del Trabajo) May 1

Founding of Old Panama (Aniversario de Panamá La Vieja; Panama City only) August 15

Independence Day (Día de la Independencia) November 3

First Call for Independence (Primer Grito de la Independencia) November 10

Independence from Spain (Independencia de Panamá de España) November 28

Mothers' Day (Día de la Madre) December 8

Christmas Day (Día de la Navidad) December 25

SAFE TRAVEL

- Crime is a problem in parts of Panama City, though the city's better districts are safer than in many other capitals.
- The city of Colón has a high rate of street crime, so consult hotel staff on areas to avoid.
- When traveling in Darién Province, always register with SENAFRONT (border control) before traveling and go with a guide.
- There have been cases of drug trafficking on boats traveling the Caribbean from Colombia north to Panama.

Hiking Safety

Though it's tropical, Panama's weather runs the gamut from hot to cold, and hiking is not always easy here. Always ask local outfitters or rangers about trail conditions before heading out, and ensure you go adequately prepared. Carry plenty of water, even on short journeys, and always bring food, matches and adequate clothing – jungles *do* get quite a bit colder at night, particularly at higher elevations.

Hikers have been known to get lost in rainforests, even seemingly user-friendly ones such as Parque Nacional Volcán Barú and the Sendero Los Quetzales. Landslides, storms and vegetation growth can make trails difficult to follow. In some cases, even access roads can deteriorate enough for transport to leave you a few kilometers before your intended drop-off point. This is just the reality of the jungle, and there is no official rescue organization to help you here. If you are heading out without a guide, make your plans known at your hotel or hostel and tell them the number of days you expect to be gone.

Never walk in unmarked rainforest; if there's no trail going in, you can assume that there won't be one when you decide to turn around and come back out. Always plan your transportation in advance – know where and when the last bus will pass your terminus, or arrange for a taxi pick-up with a responsible, recommended transporter.

Police

Police corruption is not as big a problem in Panama as it is in some other Latin American countries. However, it's not unheard of for a police officer to stop a motorist for no obvious reason, invent a violation, and levy a fine to be paid on the spot. Showing confusion will sometimes fluster the officer into letting you go, though don't expect much leniency if the police are traveling in pairs. If there has been a violation, suggest you go to the police station to pay.

Some cities in Panama have tourist police – a division created to deal specifically with travelers. Identifiable by armbands on their uniform, officers in this division may be more helpful but it is unlikely.

Swimming Safety

Unfortunately, drownings occur every year in Panamanian waters, about 80% of them caused by riptides – strong currents that pull the swimmer out to sea. They can occur even in waist-deep water. The best advice: ask about conditions before entering the water. If it's dangerous, don't tempt the ocean.

TELEPHONE

Panama's country code is 507. To call Panama from abroad, dial the international access code (usually 00 but 011 in the USA) then 507 (Panama's country code) and the seven-digit (landline) or eight-digit (cell/mobile) Panamanian telephone number. There are no local area codes in Panama.

Pay phones have been replaced with internet calling services. If you are traveling for an

EATING PRICES RANGES

The following price ranges refer to a meal.

$ less than US$12

$$ US$12–18

$$$ more than US$18

extended period, it may be useful to get a SIM card (US$5) if you have an unlocked cell phone. Otherwise, kiosks in malls and most *chinitos* (Chinese-run convenience stores) sell pay-per-use phones from US$20, and many come with minutes loaded. Having a phone can be invaluable for last-minute reservations or directions, especially since some lodgings are unresponsive to emails.

TOURIST INFORMATION

Autoridad de Turismo Panamá (p640) is the national tourism agency. Outside the flagship Panama City office, ATP runs offices in Bocas del Toro, Boquete, David, Paso Canoas, Portobelo, Santiago, El Valle and Pedasí. There are smaller information counters in both Tocumen International Airport (p741) and Albrook domestic airport (p640).

ATP has a few useful maps and brochures but often has a problem keeping enough in stock for distribution to tourists. Most offices are staffed with people who speak only Spanish. A few employees really try to help, but the majority are just passing the time. As a general rule, you will get more useful information if you have specific questions.

VISAS

Visitors from most European countries as well as the USA, Canada, Australia, New Zealand and South Africa get a 90-day stamp in their passport upon entering Panama.

After 90 days, visas can be extended at *migración* (immigration) offices. Travelers entering Panama overland will probably be asked to show an onward ticket and potentially proof of sufficient funds (US$500) or a credit card.

Citizens from certain other countries will need to obtain a visa, available at Panamanian embassies or consulates. Contact the one nearest you or call Migración y Naturalización in Panama City.

VOLUNTEERING

Volunteering opportunities are few in Panama, so potential volunteers should look for programs run by reputable, well-known NGOs such as the **Grupo de Conservación de Tortugas de Jaqué** (Colegio de la Tierra; ☎264-6266, 6047-2373; www.colegiodelatierra.org) in Darién. Many of the expat-run hostels employ volunteers on a casual basis in exchange for room and board.

THE TRANSPANAMA TRAIL

This cross-country circuit (www.transpanama.org) runs from the border of Costa Rica toward Panama City, but you can hike any three-day stretch for a good taste of Panama's rugged backcountry. More information is available on the website, where you can also download GPS tracks for free.

Getting There & Away

Panama is well served by a number of airlines. It can be reached overland from Costa Rica by bus and Colombia by boat. Flights, cars and tours can be booked online at lonelyplanet.com/bookings.

AIR

At present Panama has three active commercial international airports:

- Tocumen International Airport (p741) (Panama City)
- Aeropuerto Enrique Malek (p741) (David)
- **Panamá Pacífico International Airport** (Panama City) Located 12km southwest of Panama City. Viva Air Colombia airline began using this small airport, the former US Howard Air Force Base, in 2014.

LAND

There are three border crossings between Costa Rica and Panama. Most travelers cross at Paso Canoas (gateway: David). Note that Panama is always one hour ahead of Costa Rica.

To enter Panama from Costa Rica, you'll need a passport and an onward ticket. Some nationalities may require a visa.

You can also be asked for an onward ticket if you are entering Costa Rica. If you do not possess one, it is acceptable to buy a return bus ticket back to Panama.

Border Crossings

At all three border crossings, you can take a local bus up to the border on either side, cross over, board another local bus and continue on your way. Be aware that the last buses leave the border crossings at Guabito and Río Sereno at 7pm and 5pm respectively; the last bus leaves Paso Canoas for Panama City at 9:30pm.

Two companies, Expreso Panama (p641) and Tica Bus (p641), operate daily *directo* (direct) buses between San José (Costa Rica) and Panama City, departing from Albrook Bus Terminal (p641). Both recommend making reservations a few days in advance.

The most heavily trafficked border crossing to/from Costa Rica is at **Paso Canoas** (open 7am to 7pm, Panama time), 55km northwest of David on the Interamericana. Some tips:

- The best place to spend the night before crossing is David.
- Ensure that you have both entry and exit stamps in your passport.

- Allow one to 1½ hours for the formalities on both sides. Buses from David depart frequently for the border (US$2.10, 50 minutes, every 15 minutes) from 4am until 9:30pm.
- On the Costa Rican side, you can catch regular buses to San José or other parts of the country.
- From David, there are also taxis to Paso Canoas (US$35).

The Caribbean border post at **Guabito/Sixaola** (open 8am to 5pm, Panama time), 15km northwest of Changuinola, sees less traffic than Paso Canoas on the Pacific side, though most travelers find it hassle-free.

- Buses from Changuinola depart frequently for the border (US$1.25, 30 minutes, every half-hour) from 5:30am to 7pm.
- On the Costa Rican side of the border, you can catch regular buses on to Puerto Limón and San José, as well as regional destinations.

The least-used crossing into Costa Rica is the border post at **Río Sereno** (open 8am to 5pm Monday to Saturday, to 3pm Sunday, Panama time), located 40km northwest of Volcán.

- Buses to the border depart from David and travel via La Concepción, Volcán and Santa Clara (US$5.10, 2½ hours, every half-hour till 5pm).
- On the Costa Rican side of the border, you can take a 15-minute bus or taxi ride to San Vito, where you can catch buses to regional destinations.

SEA

It's possible to cross to Colombia by sea, which makes for a very enjoyable passage. Expensive multiday sailboat voyages depart from Colón Province, while most motorboat trips depart from Cartí in the Comarca de Guna Yala.

Getting Around

AIR

Panama's domestic destinations are served by Air Panama (p640) and Copa Airlines (p640). Domestic flights depart Panama City from Albrook Airport (p640). Located near the Costa Rican border, David's Aeropuerto Enrique Malek (p741) frequently handles flights to and from San José.

Book ahead in high season, when demand for flights to destinations like Bocas and the Comarca de Guna Yala exceeds availability.

BICYCLE

If you can get over the heat, you can cycle through Panama easily enough, with lodgings within a day's ride away. Cycling within larger Panamanian cities – particularly Panama City – is not for the faint of heart. Roads tend to be narrow, and people drive aggressively. Also, frequent rains reduce motorists' visibility and tire grip.

The best places for cyclists in Panama City are the coastal routes of the Cinta Costera (a dedicated bike lane from downtown and around Casco Viejo) and the Causeway. Weekend cyclist groups often go out to Gamboa via a shady but narrow road.

Outside the cities, Panama's Interamericana boasts the best quality in Central America, although sections have an extremely narrow shoulder. Roads in many of the provinces (especially in Veraguas and Colón) are in poor shape – plan accordingly and bring lots of spare parts.

> **SPEAK PANAMEÑO**
>
> You can express your appreciation with *chévere* ('cool'), *buena leche* is 'good luck', *una pinta* means 'a beer', while *vaina* just means 'thing.'

BOAT

Boats are the chief means of transportation in several areas of Panama, particularly in Darién Province, the Archipiélago de Las Perlas, and the San Blás and Bocas del Toro island chains.

From Panama City, there are regular ferries from the Causeway to Isla Taboga and Isla Contadora. Panama City is also the jumping-off point for partial and full Panama Canal transits.

If you're planning an excursion to Isla de Coiba and the national marine park, the best way to reach the island is through an organized boat tour. Local fishers also ply the waters off the coast of Veraguas, though this is a riskier proposition as the seas can get really rough.

The tourist mecca of Bocas del Toro town on Isla Colón is accessible from Almirante by frequent water taxis.

Colombian and Guna merchant boats carry cargo and passengers along the San Blás coast between Colón and Puerto Obaldía, stopping at up to 48 of the islands to load and unload passengers and cargo. However, these boats are often dangerously overloaded. Taking passage on a sailboat, or the four-day motorboat service to Colombia, is a wiser option.

Since there aren't many roads in the eastern part of Darién Province, boat travel is often the only way to get from one town to another, especially during the rainy season. The boat of choice here is the *piragua* (long canoe), carved from the trunk of a giant ceiba tree. The shallow hulls of these boats allow them to ride the many rivers that comprise the traditional transportation network of eastern Panama. Many are motorized.

BUS

You can take a bus to just about any community in Panama that is accessible by road. Some of the buses are full-size Mercedes Benzes equipped with air-con, movie screens and reclining seats. These top-of-the-line buses generally cruise long stretches of highway.

Most common are small Toyota Coaster buses, affectionately called *chivas*. Use these to visit towns on the Península de Azuero and along the Interamericana.

Panama City has just about finished phasing out its *diablos rojos* (red devils) for modern, safe, air-conditioned buses on the Metrobus system. Riders can obtain swipe cards at Albrook Bus Terminal or main bus stops. Official bus stops are used, and the transportation is air-conditioned.

CAR & MOTORCYLE

Due to the low cost and ready availability of buses and taxis, it isn't necessary to rent a vehicle in Panama unless you intend to go off the beaten track. Some beach areas have notoriously poor roads. There are car-rental agencies in major cities such as Panama City and David. Many also operate out of Tocumen International Airport.

HITCHHIKING

Hitching is not common at all in Panama; most people travel by bus, and visitors would do best to follow suit. In any case, hitching is never entirely safe in any country and we don't recommend it. Travelers who hitch should understand that they are taking a small but potentially serious risk.

TAXI

Taxis are cheap and plentiful, though not all drivers have a good grasp of locations.

Some tips:

- Before even getting into a taxi, state your destination and settle on a fare. Panamanian taxis don't have meters, but there are standard fares between Panama City's neighborhoods.
- Get informed. Ask the staff at your accommodations for typical rates between city sectors; these usually go up after dark.
- Taxis can be scarce late at night and around the holidays. At these times, it's best to call for a radio taxi.
- More expensive 'sedan' taxis operate from upscale hotels. They charge double what you'd pay a hailed cab.
- Consider using Uber; it's reliable, cheap, and the drivers are helpful and friendly.

TRAIN

The country's only rail line is the historic Panama Railroad, which runs from Panama City to Colón. The Panama Canal Railway (p681) offers daily passenger service on a fully operational vintage train. Aimed at tourists looking to relive the heyday of luxury rail travel, the hour-long ride runs parallel to the canal and at times traverses thick jungle and rainforest.

Understand Central America

Central America Today

The outlook for Central America depends on where one is standing. In the region's southern stretches, the future looks bright, with mostly stable politics and expanding economic opportunities in tourism and transportation. Things look bleaker in the Northern Triangle (Guatemala, Honduras and El Salvador), where many citizens struggle to break out of an interminable cycle of violence and poverty. And in the deeply troubled core of the isthmus – Nicaragua – a bloody crackdown on anti-government protestors has the country on edge.

Best in Print

A Mayan Life (Gaspar Pedro Gonzáles; 1995) First published novel by a Maya author and an excellent study of rural Guatemalan life.

The Country Under My Skin (Gioconda Belli; 2003) An enthralling autobiography detailing the Nicaraguan poet's involvement in the revolution.

Getting to Know the General (Graham Greene; 1984) Portrait of a Panamanian general by his longtime friend.

The True History of the Conquest of New Spain (Bernal Díaz de Castillo; 1568) Eyewitness account of Cortés' 1519 expedition to Mexico.

Best on Film

Ixcanul (2015) Multi-award-winning film about a young Kaqchiquel girl's coming of age in Guatemala.

Mosquito Coast (1986) Harrison Ford and family search for a simpler life in Central America.

Curse of the Xtabai (2012) Belizeans are quite proud of this feature-length horror film, the first to be 100% filmed and produced in Belize.

King of the Jungle (in production) The story of John McAfee, eccentric inventor of McAfee Virus Scan and murder suspect in Belize, as played by Johnny Depp.

Power & Politics

Democracies in Central America are often fragile, but transfers of power in the region's most stable nation are smooth. On April 1, 2018, Costa Rica elected President Carlos Alvarado Quesada, a 38-year-old novelist, musician and former cabinet minister from the center-left Citizen Action Party. The decisive victory was particularly sweet for proponents of gay rights and for Afro-Caribbeans, who were delighted to see economist Epsy Campbell Barr become Central America's first female vice president of African descent.

In stark contrast, Nicaragua has devolved into civil unrest that's left hundreds of people dead, mostly due to moves by the country's long-time leader, Daniel Ortega, who took the presidency for the second time in 2006. In 2018 Ortega attempted to overhaul the social security system and reduce pension benefits, prompting clashes between hundreds of unarmed protesters and the police and pro-government militaries, who used live bullets. Though Ortega rescinded the social security cut, the political crisis endured, with protesters demanding that the government be held accountable.

In Honduras, a similarly undemocratic shift in term limits led to the controversial reelection of Juan Orlando Hernández of the National Party of Honduras in late 2017. Protests broke out decrying the results as fraudulent, with 17 people killed, and although international observers called for a new election, it didn't happen. Honduras isn't alone in this matter: perceived (and actual) corruption from the political elite remains rampant across Central America and Mexico, breeding distrust and resentment.

Poverty & Violence

Up and down the isthmus, millions of people continue to face extreme poverty and soaring crime rates.

Even the most prosperous nations (Costa Rica and Panama) have poverty rates above 20%, with a wide disparity between the richest and poorest citizens. Other countries are faring much worse, with some 59% of the population living below the poverty line in Guatemala and 61% in Honduras. Unemployment and income inequality are ongoing challenges throughout Central America.

Meanwhile, crime continues to plague poverty-stricken barrios and rural villages, especially in Guatemala, El Salvador and Honduras. The latter two countries have frequently topped the list of nations with the highest homicide rates, though Honduras has shown improvement. Government corruption, gang violence and drug-cartel activity pose overwhelming challenges for citizens of these countries – the only escape often involves a perilous attempt at emigration to the USA.

US Relations

Throughout the 20th century, the USA meddled in Central American politics, helping oust democratically elected leaders and prop up military dictators aligned with US interests. The resulting civil wars and genocides sent waves of refugees to the USA, where anti-immigration policies landed some on the streets or in prisons. These places became breeding grounds for gangs such as Mara Salvatrucha (MS-13), with the USA deporting members to El Salvador. Today the gangsters continue to wreak havoc in their homeland, deriving financial support from the drug trade, which is in turn fueled by North America's enormous appetite for illegal narcotics.

Although US president Donald Trump's campaign promise to build a wall between Mexico and the USA has so far failed to gain traction in Congress, in 2018 his administration began enforcing a 'zero tolerance' policy toward those who crossed into the USA illegally. The government directed officials to separate asylum-seeking and illegal immigrant families, and to hold the adults and children in different detention facilities. A public outcry reversed the rule, but not before an estimated 2300 families were separated.

Keeping the 'Eco' in Ecotourism

Much of Central America has embraced tourism as a promise of prosperity that offers employment, investment and an endless stream of cold hard cash. It's the number-one industry in both Costa Rica and Belize, and plays a smaller but increasingly significant role in Nicaragua, Honduras and Panama.

The challenge of balancing the demands of the tourist sector with its environmental impacts is an old story in Costa Rica, where debates rage around paving roads, building on beaches and chopping down trees. Once-remote destinations such as Monteverde will see major boosts in visitors as their main access routes get paved in coming years, challenging

AREA: **521,875 SQ KM**

POPULATION: **48,361,00**

GDP (IN US$): **PANAMA 61.8 BILLION; NICARAGUA 13.8 BILLION**

UNEMPLOYMENT RATE: **COSTA RICA 10.2%; GUATEMALA 2.3%**

if Central America were 100 people

58 would be mestizo
20 would be Caucasian
16 would be indigenous
4 would be Afro-Caribbean
2 would be other

Belief Systems

(% of population)

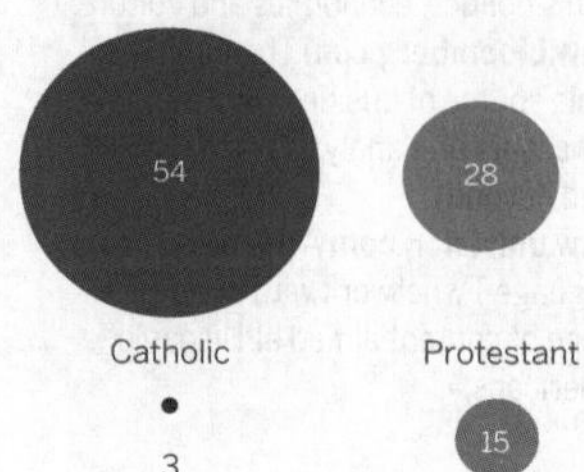

population per sq km

Central America | North America | Europe

≈ 25 people

Best in Music

Rubén Blades The Panamanian salsa icon and ex-presidential candidate; check out his collaboration with Calle 13.

Café Tacvba A Mexican rock band with modern beats.

Gaby Moreno Singer-songwriter from Guatemala with a lush Latin sound.

Sonido Gallo Negro Get entranced by this percussive, psychedelic Mexican *cumbia* band.

Rodrigo y Gabriela Fast, rhythmic acoustic guitarists who made their name busking in Europe.

Aurelio Martínez Albums *Garífuna Soul* and *Laru Beya* received rave reviews all over the world.

Best in Media

www.ticotimes.net The Tico Times is Central America's oldest and most popular English-language news source, and is based in San José, Costa Rica.

www.elfaro.net A reputable, digital journalism outlet run out of San Salvador, with Spanish-language coverage of corruption, organized crime, inequality, migration and culture.

www.latinamericanpost.com The LatinAmerican Post covers the region's politics, economics and culture.

www.bloomberg.com The most reliable source of business and market news, data and analysis on the region (and beyond).

www.univision.com A Spanish-language TV network with a wide range of content aimed at Hispanic Americans.

their off-the-beaten-track grandeur. In Belize, Norwegian Cruise Line has developed an island near Placencia, exposing the region (home to the world's second-largest coral reef system) to increased cruise-ship traffic and other environmental impacts.

At the same time, the benefits are indisputable. Tourism provides millions of jobs, as well as a solid customer base for small-business owners. Landowners have a financial incentive to preserve forests, while farmers can supplement their income through rural tourism. Indigenous communities have also capitalized on tourism by selling artisanal craftwork and promoting music and dance, creating an impetus for governments to recognize these local cultures.

Canals: Bigger & Deeper

The Panama Canal has long been one of the region's biggest success stories, fueling one of the fastest-growing economies in Latin America. Then in 2016, the canal got even bigger. One of the world's largest transportation projects, the US$5.4 billion expansion has doubled the waterway's capacity and tripled traffic in the canal by adding a third lane and digging deeper to accommodate bigger vessels. Today millions of containers traverse it each year.

The widened canal will likely prove a boon for Panama's economy, but detractors fear that the project, coupled with other large-scale development (including a massive expansion of Tocumen International Airport), have shackled the nation with debt. Another less pressing concern is Nicaragua's proposed rival canal, a US$50 billion waterway meant to connect the Atlantic and the Pacific. As of late 2018, construction had stalled due to insufficient funds and fierce opposition to the project.

Environmental Activists

Latin America is now recognized as the world's most dangerous region for environmental activists, with staggering numbers of people killed each year for protecting forests, rivers and other patches of the Earth from business and government exploitation. In 2016, 14 conservationists were slain in Honduras, including prominent indigenous leader and Goldman environmental prizewinner Berta Cáceres.

More recently, though, there have been some favorable developments. The number of killings in Honduras dropped in 2017, and the following year, Honduran authorities arrested a former military intelligence officer for plotting the killing of Cáceres. Two days after the arrest, 24 representatives from Latin American and Caribbean nations met in Costa Rica and signed 'the Escazú Accord,' a legally binding pact to create a safe environment for activists while investigating and punishing perpetrators.

History

In the pre-Columbian era, the mighty Maya empire stretched across the Central American isthmus. After this heyday, the region's inhabitants endured conquistadors and colonialism, brutal civil wars and bloody coups. More recently, the seven spirited nations have aimed to overcome this legacy of violence and establish peace and prosperity in their corner of the planet – though with decidedly mixed results.

Empires & Nations

Meet the Maya

The Maya were one of Mesoamerica's greatest pre-Columbian civilizations and for centuries their territory extended from southern Mexico to Nicaragua, and from Honduras to El Salvador. Their most noteworthy achievements included a perfected hieroglyphic writing system, precise astronomy and advanced mathematics, and they designed and built grandiose stone temples and palaces.

The Maya endured for nearly three millennia, reaching their apex between AD 250 and 900 and particularly thriving in the high plains of Guatemala and the lowlands of Belize and the Yúcatan. In the 16th century, European conquistadors invaded from across the ocean, vanquishing the region and transforming Central America.

Read about the Maya

Ancient Maya
(Robert J Sharer; 2006)

Breaking the Maya Code
(Michael D Coe; 1992)

Blood of Kings
(Linda Schele & Mary Ellen Miller; 1986)

Meet the Conquistadors

When Columbus explored the verdant Central American isthmus in 1502, he encountered gold-accessorized natives and excitedly believed that he had found a paradise of vast riches. Two decades later, Spanish conquistadors trained their sights on Central America, in search of the fabled El Dorado.

The first permanent Spanish settlement in Central America was erected in Panama (present-day Darién) in 1510. It served as base for the Pizarro brothers, conquistadors from the Extremadura area of Spain, who trooped south to assault the Incas; and for Vasco Núñez de Balboa, who ventured west to gaze on the Pacific. Panama was also the launch site for Gil González Dávila, who sailed north to Nicaragua, where he

TIMELINE

1100 BC

Proto-Maya settlements begin to appear in the Copán Valley in Guatemala. By 1000 BC settlements on the Pacific coast show early signs of developing a hierarchical society.

3114 BC

The Maya creation story says that the world was created on August 13 of this year, which corresponds to the first date on the Maya Long Count Calendar.

AD 250–1000

The Classic period of the Maya civilization is characterized by the construction of cities and temples and other artistic and intellectual achievements. The population reaches around 400,000.

betrayed the *cacique* (tribal leader) Nicarao and beheaded his rival conquistador, Francisco Hernández de Córdoba.

Another Extremaduran, Pedro de Alvarado, crossed the Atlantic in 1510, and his ferocity placed him second in command on the legendary march of Hernán Cortés against the Aztecs. Rumors of a jade kingdom to the south led Alvarado on a four-year campaign across Central America, slashing through the jungle and cutting down its native inhabitants. He never found the kingdom, but became military governor of Guatemala, which he tyrannized for 15 years. In his final battle against desperate natives, Alvarado's horse rolled over and killed him.

Joyce Kelly's *An Archaeological Guide to Northern Central America* (1996) offers the best descriptions of the Maya sites of Belize, Guatemala and Mexico.

Spanish Rule

By the middle of the 16th century, the days of vainglorious conquistadors had passed, and the Spanish Crown now imposed imperial bureaucracy. Alvarado's fiefdom was reorganized into the Kingdom of Guatemala, under the Viceroy of New Spain. For most of the next 300 years, this included present-day states of Central America and Mexico's Chiapas. The capital was located in Santiago (now Antigua) in southwest Guatemala. Meanwhile, present-day Panama was also under Spanish rule, but part of the Viceroyalty of Peru, with its capital in Lima.

The Crown's hold was not complete, however. In northeast Honduras (present-day Belize), upstart British squatters built a haven for pirates, smugglers and poachers, who withstood all of the king's eviction efforts.

Independence in the Americas

In 1821 the Americas wriggled free of Imperial Spain's grip. Mexico declared independence for itself, as well as for Central America. The Central American colonies then declared independence from Mexico and, with an empire up for grabs, the region descended into conflict.

The newly liberated colonies considered their fate: stay together in a United States of Central America or go their separate national ways? At first, they came up with something in between – the Central American Federation (CAF) – but it could neither field an army nor collect taxes. Accustomed to being in charge, Guatemala attempted to dominate the CAF, thus hastening the federation's demise. One by one, the constituent parts became independent nation-states.

Douglas Preston's *The Lost City of the Monkey God* (2017) is a fascinating read that details new archaeological finds in the Moskitia.

Gods & Monsters

Maya Mysticism

In the world of the Maya, even the king listened to the high priest. Priests provided counsel, managed the seasonal calendar, kept records of the kingdom, educated noble sons and planned religious feasts. Why were the priests so influential? Because they could talk to the gods – and there

1000–1600

During the Postclassic period, the Maya civilization continues to develop. Highlands Maya organize into competing kingdoms, establishing language and cultural groupings that survive today.

c 13th century

Ruthlessly organized Toltec-Maya migrants from southeast Mexico establish kingdoms in Guatemala.

1502

Christopher Columbus sails down the Caribbean coastline looking for a sailing route to the Pacific Ocean. The journey results in the first recorded contact between indigenous inhabitants and Europeans.

1510

The first permanent Spanish settlement in Central America is established in Panama (present-day Darién), becoming a base for several well-known conquistadors from the Extremadura area of Spain.

were a *lot* of gods to talk to. More than 250, in fact: gods for life, death, rain, thunder, east, west, fighting, loving, hunting, fishing, mountains, rivers, heroes, demons, medicine, corn and even chocolate. They inhabited the three realms of the Maya: the twinkling heavens above, all things living and earthly, and the ominous multi-level underworld.

High atop El Castillo, the 30m-tall centerpiece temple at Chichén Itzá, Maya priests paid homage to Kukulkan, the plumed serpent-god protector of the Itzá chiefdom. During the equinox, the late afternoon sun created an eerie effect in light and shadow of a slithering feathery snake descending the steps of the temple. This was the moment for making sacrificial offerings, perhaps of blood drawn from a nobleman's tongue or penis, and asking for divine favor.

Catholicism

When the Europeans arrived, they brought their own supernatural conduits. In the ensuing clash of divine powers, the Maya gods were obliterated. Henceforth, there could be only one deity in Central America: the Catholic god. An advance guard of Jesuits, Franciscans and Dominicans penetrated the heathen wilds, established religious outposts and suppressed 'false' idols. Bishop Diego de Landa, converter-in-chief, confiscated all sacred texts – which contained the accumulated knowledge of the Maya culture – and burned them to ash. Local temples and ritual sites were ransacked, abandoned and reclaimed by the dense rainforest. In their place rose new, baroque-style monuments in the lush mountain valleys, proclaiming the victory of the new god.

As with the Maya, Spain's conquering chiefs and high priests shared a vision of power and reverence while enjoying lives of privilege and status. The Catholic Church long monopolized religious conviction in Central America, serving as a complement to political power.

Evangelical Protestantism

Today a new contest for Central American souls is under way, as Evangelical Protestantism woos worshipers away from Catholicism. The region's first born-again political leader was Guatemala's General Efraín Ríos Montt (also known for his killing sprees against indigenous peoples). In Guatemala, Honduras, El Salvador and Belize, Protestants now comprise a near-majority of the population. Media-savvy ministers and North American missionaries hasten the conversion rate.

Maya pyramids and Catholic cathedrals have made room for Protestant mega-churches, such as the Friends of Israel Bible Baptist Tabernacle in San Salvador, which draws around 50,000 churchgoers each Sunday. In gang-controlled areas around El Salvador, joining an Evangelical church has become an escape route for countless former members.

Impressive Cathedrals

Iglesia Merced *(Antigua, Guatemala)*

Basílica de Nuestra Señora de Los Ángeles *(Cartago, Costa Rica)*

Catedral de León *(León, Nicaragua)*

Iglesia La Merced *(Granada, Nicaragua)*

1540
The Spanish establish the Kingdom of Guatemala, which includes most of Central America: Costa Rica, Nicaragua, Honduras, El Salvador, Guatemala and the Mexican state of Chiapas.

1638
British Baymen 'settle' Belize when former pirate Peter Wallace lays the foundations for a new port at the mouth of the Belize River, on the site of today's Belize City.

1821
Central America becomes independent from Spain and briefly joins the Mexican Empire, and then the United Provinces of Central America. Most of the nations celebrate this achievement yearly on September 15.

1847
Spanish, mestizo and Maya peoples engage in the War of the Castes on the Yucatán Peninsula. The violence sends streams of refugees into Belize.

Paradise & Plunder

New World Economy

The pre-Columbian economy rested on agriculture and trade. The Maya built terraced fields in the steep mountains, raised platforms in the swampy lowlands, and slashed and burned the thick forests. They grew corn, tubers, beans, squash and peppers. They tamed the wild fruits of the forest: papaya, mango, banana and cacao. They fished the rivers and lakes with nets – and with cormorants on a leash – and they hunted down tasty forest creatures such as peccary, deer and monkey. But the tropical terrain made grand-scale agriculture impractical, and the region was notably lacking in precious metals.

The Spanish were undeterred, and instead harnessed the region's main economic resource – people. The Crown authorized the creation of feudal-style agricultural estates, the notorious *economienda,* whereby powerful colonial overlords exploited an indigenous labor force. They produced New World luxuries for Old World aristocrats – indigo from El Salvador, cacao from Guatemala, tobacco from Chiapas. The *economienda* system, however, did not take hold in Costa Rica, the poorest region of colonial Central America, where private family farms prevailed over corporate feudal estates.

The coffee-processing cooperative Coopedota, located in Costa Rica's Valley of the Saints, launched the world's first officially certified carbon-neutral coffee.

Coffee Rica

In 1843 the merchant vessel HMS *Monarch* arrived in London from Puerto Limón carrying bulging sacks of roasted red beans. The riches that Costa Rica had long promised had finally been uncovered, as the volcanic soil and moist climate of the Central Valley highlands proved ideal for coffee cultivation. The drink's quick fix made it popular with working-class consumers in the industrializing north. Thousands of coffee saplings were quickly planted along shady hillsides in Guatemala, Nicaragua and Honduras. The Central American coffee boom was on.

Costa Rica went from the most impoverished to the wealthiest country in the region. The aroma of riches lured a wave of enterprising German immigrants to Central America. Across the region, powerful cliques of coffee barons reaped the rewards from the caffeine craze.

Banana Boom

In Costa Rica, getting coffee out to world markets required rail links from the central highlands to the coast. Meanwhile, the California gold rush prompted a Panamanian rail link between the Atlantic and Pacific. US companies undertook the railroad construction projects, both of which were disastrous due to malaria and yellow fever. Local recruits

1853–56

Tennessee-born William Walker attempts to conquer Central America. His Yankee mercenaries are defeated during a march on Costa Rica, and the self-declared president of Nicaragua is executed by a Honduran firing squad.

1903–14

With the support of the USA, Panama declares itself independent from Colombia, and canal concessions are granted to the USA. The Panama Canal is completed a decade later.

1946

The US Army's School of the Americas, which trained some of the worst human-rights abusers in Latin America, is founded in Panama. Four decades later the school relocates to Fort Benning, Georgia.

1948

In an unprecedented move, Costa Rica's President José Figueres abolishes the country's army and redirects military spending toward education and healthcare, ushering in an era of peace.

gave way to US convicts, to Chinese indentured servants, and to freed Jamaican slaves.

In Costa Rica, bananas were planted along the tracks as a cheap food source for the workers. As an experiment, would-be railroad tycoon Minor Cooper Keith shipped a few bananas to New Orleans, and he struck gold – or rather, yellow. Northern consumers went crazy for the elongated finger fruit.

By the 1900s, bananas had replaced coffee as the region's most lucrative export. The United Fruit Company converted much of Central America into a corporate fiefdom, controlling transportation, communication, postal service, labor markets and export markets – as well as more than a few politicians.

The **Panama Railroad** (www.panamarailroad.org) website contains photographs, historical information and fascinating travelogues about the area, including one written by Mark Twain in 1868.

Ecotourism

In the 1980s, following a downturn in world coffee prices, an unusual alliance was formed between economic developers and environmental conservationists. If exports alone could not sustain the economy, then what about imports…of tourists?

Costa Rica led the region in launching a green revolution, establishing some 125 national parks, forest preserves and wildlife reserves. Its neighbors followed the trend, and Indiana Jones enthusiasts were soon clambering around ancient temples in the Yucatán and Guatemala. Birders flocked to Panama to glimpse nearly 1000 species of feathered fauna, and the Belize Barrier Reef was recognized as a Unesco World Heritage Site.

With ecotourism, the rainforest and the reef were essentially paying for themselves, making it financially beneficial to take care of them. Tourism brought hundreds of millions of US dollars to the economy, becoming one of the region's main sources of foreign currency. Moreover, tourism profits stayed in the countries, boosting standards of living.

A SAINT FOR THE PEOPLE

In the late 20th century, a wave of 'liberation theology' washed over the region, setting populist priests against rapacious dictators. Subversive clerics were feared by the ruling class, which mobilized its coercive agents to quell the criticism. The most notorious episode in this conflict was the assassination of the Archbishop of San Salvador, Oscar A Romero, who was gunned down while saying Mass in 1980.

The heinous crime made Romero a martyr: the UN marked his death date, March 24, as the Day of Truth and Dignity for Victims of Human Rights Atrocities, and the Vatican bestowed sainthood on the bishop in 2015.

1960–90

US-backed military dictators rule much of the region. Crackdowns on impoverished and indigenous peoples lead to the formation of active left-wing guerrilla groups in Guatemala, El Salvador, Honduras and Nicaragua.

1972

Jacques Cousteau visits the Great Blue Hole, bringing unprecedented publicity to the small nation of Belize and boosting its popularity as a destination for divers and snorkelers.

1980s

After coffee prices plummet, Costa Rica makes up for the losses in exports with a brand new form of import business. Ecotourism is born.

1981

After years of anti-colonial and pro-independence political movements, Belize (which was called British Honduras until 1973) receives formal international recognition of its independence from Great Britain.

Dictatorship & Democracy

A Democratic Oasis

After independence, politics in Central America usually featured a few elite families competing for control of state patronage, through shifting alliances of army officers and coffee barons. Presidents were more often removed at gunpoint than by the ballot box. Across the region – and particularly in Costa Rica, El Salvador, Honduras and Guatemala – the polarized left and right fought for power through coups and electoral fraud.

In Costa Rica, the unsustainable situation came to a head in 1948, when economic and ethnic tensions spiraled into civil war. Armed workers battled military forces, and Nicaraguan and US forces joined the fray. Peace was restored two months – and 2000 deaths – later. Out of the chaos came a coffee grower and utopian democrat, José Figueres Ferrer, who became the unlikely leader of a temporary junta government. He taxed the wealthy, nationalized the banks and built a modern welfare state. His 1949 constitution granted voting rights to women, as well as full citizenship to black, Indian and Chinese minorities. Most extraordinarily, Figueres abolished the military, calling it a threat to democracy. His transformative regime became the foundation for Costa Rica's uniquely unarmed democracy.

Central America's longest civil war was fought in Guatemala, lasting 36 long years. By the time it ended in 1996, 200,000 citizens had been killed.

Cold War in the Hot Tropics

In 1823 the USA challenged European colonialism by claiming hegemony over the Western Hemisphere with the Monroe Doctrine. By the mid-20th century, the USA was routinely acting to constrain the autonomy of Central America's nation-states, seeking to influence political choices, economic development and foreign policies. After all, it's a direct drive down the US Army–constructed Pan-American Hwy.

In the 1950s Guatemala's democratically elected president, Jacobo Arbenz Guzmán, vowed to nationalize the vast unused landholdings of the United Fruit Company (offering as compensation the property value declared on its tax returns). Democracy be damned: United Fruit appealed to its friends in Washington; in 1954 a CIA-orchestrated coup forced President Arbenz from office. His successor, Colonel Castillo Armas, was hailed as an anti-communist hero, treated to a ticker-tape parade in New York City and honored with a Doctor of Law degree from Columbia University. Three years later, Armas was gunned down in the presidential palace; soon after United Fruit's confiscated lands were finally returned.

Armas was succeeded by a series of military presidents. More support came from the US government – in the form of money and counterinsurgency training. Violence became a staple of political life, land reforms were reversed, voting was made dependent on literacy (disenfranchising

1979–87

Guerrilla groups known as the Sandinistas overthrow the dictatorial Somoza regime in Nicaragua. The US-backed Contras launch a counter-revolution, ushering in an era of civil war that polarizes the region.

1980–92

After years of strife, El Salvador descends into all-out civil war between a US-backed military and various guerrilla groups. After 12 years of fighting and some 75,000 deaths, a compromise is finally reached.

1987

Costa Rican president Oscar Arias Sánchez wins the Nobel Peace Prize for his work on the Central American peace accords, which bring about greater political freedom throughout the region.

1989

The USA invades Panama and ousts dictator Manuel Noriega, who is indicted in the USA on drug-trafficking and money-laundering charges. He is found guilty and sentenced to 40 years in prison.

around 75% of the population), the secret police force was revived and military repression was common. In 1960 left-wing guerrilla groups began to form, and the Guatemalan civil war was on.

Gradually, guerrilla warfare spread. By the 1970s, radical socialists had forced military oligarchies around the region onto the defensive. In Nicaragua, the rebellious Sandinistas toppled the American-backed Somoza dictatorship. Alarmed by the Sandinistas' Soviet and Cuban ties, the USA decided it was time to intervene. The organizational details of the counter-revolution were delegated to junior officer Oliver North, who secretly aided and abetted the Contra rebels to incite civil war in Nicaragua.

The conflict polarized the region. When civil war erupted in El Salvador after the assassination of Archbishop Romero, the US pumped huge sums into the moribund military, effectively prolonging that conflict as well. Throughout the 1980s, government-sponsored death squads decimated villages, while guerrilla groups did their best to undermine elections and stifle the economy. Meanwhile, Honduras became a base for the US-sponsored covert war in Nicaragua.

The young president of Costa Rica, Oscar Arias Sánchez, was the driving force in uniting Central America around a peace plan, which finally ended the Nicaraguan war. For his efforts, Arias became the first Central American to be awarded a Nobel Peace Prize. Within a few years, peace treaties were also signed in El Salvador and Guatemala.

From Colonialism to Neocolonialism

While civil wars raged around the region, two countries remained relatively peaceful, albeit under the control of greater powers.

In Belize, it was not the Spanish but rather the British who took hold, logging the forests, growing fruit and sugarcane, and dubbing the colony 'British Honduras.' While an independence movement gathered force throughout the second half of the 20th century, full independence was put off until a nagging security matter was resolved: namely, the Guatemalan constitution explicitly included Belize as part of its territorial reach. Only British troops at the border stopped the larger country from following through on that.

It was not until 1981 that Belize was at last declared an independent nation-state within the British Commonwealth. Even Guatemala recognized Belize as a sovereign nation in 1991, although to this day it maintains its territorial claim on 53% of Belize's land. In a 2018 referendum, Guatemalans voted in favor of taking the issue to the International Court of Justice; Belize is set to hold a similar referendum on April 10, 2019.

Meanwhile, at the southern end of the isthmus, Panama was still a province of Colombia at the start of the 20th century. When a military junta declared Panama independent, the USA government immediately

The US Army's School of the Americas, originally based in Panama, trained some of the worst human-rights abusers in Latin America – including Manuel Noriega. For information on the school's history visit www.soaw.org.

1991

Guatemala recognizes Belize as a sovereign, independent state, but tensions continue, and Guatemala still refuses to relinquish its territorial claim over parts of Belize.

1996

Peace accords are signed in Guatemala, bringing to an end the 36-year civil war, in which an estimated 200,000 people died.

1999

The USA ends nearly a century of occupation of Panama by closing all of its military bases and rescinding control of the canal.

2012

Despite end-of-the-world predictions from non-Maya people, Baktun 13 ends without major incidents and a new Great Cycle of the Maya Long Count calendar begins.

recognized the sovereignty of the new country – backing it up with battleships when Colombia tried to regain control. In return, Panama granted the US concession to the canal, as well as a broad right of intervention into Panamanian affairs.

In the years following the completion of the canal, Panamanians became increasingly disenchanted with US intervention and occupation. As the northern giant gradually ceded its rights, the Panamanian military grew more powerful. When Manuel Noriega came to power in the 1980s, he expanded the military and brutally crushed all dissent; drug trafficking, election rigging and murder all played a role in his regime. The USA finally intervened in 1989, invading Panama City and arresting Noriega. A decade later the USA rescinded control of the canal and withdrew all troops, finally leaving Panama to negotiate its own uncertain future.

Guatemala's Volcán de Fuego erupted on June 3, 2018, leveling several villages, coffee farms and a golf resort within 20km of the colonial gem Antigua. More than 300 people were killed or reported missing and 2800 were left homeless. The eruption was the volcano's most powerful since 1974.

Imperfect Democracy

Today a new era of democratization has unfolded, as both right-wing and left-wing dictatorships have stepped aside to allow contested elections. Here's one auspicious sign of the times: a former Salvadoran guerrilla organization managed to transition to mainstream politics, even fielding a successful presidential candidate.

The systems are not perfect, however. In 2009 democratically elected Honduran president Manuel Zelaya was ousted by the military (on orders from the Supreme Court), and more recently, an unexpected and incredibly narrow electoral victory by President Juan Orlando Hernández sparked allegations of fraud and deadly protests. A contentious 2015 Supreme Court ruling paved the way for Hernández to be elected for a consecutive term, an event Honduras hadn't seen since military rule four decades prior.

In 2014 the Nicaraguan Congress made a similarly controversial decision to abolish term limits – just in time for President Daniel Ortega to run for his third consecutive term. He was reelected in 2016 and, after he announced plans to cut welfare benefits, violent protests erupted across the nation in 2018. Hundreds of people were killed, ostensibly by paramilitary groups. As of early 2019, with the situation still volatile, President Ortega was refusing to step down.

2017

In a Costa Rican election widely seen as a referendum on gay rights, progressive Carlos Alvarado Quesada, a novelist and political scientist, defeats Fabricio Alvarado Munoz, a right-wing journalist and evangelical preacher.

2017–18

The Trump administration employs a zero-tolerance immigration policy that separates thousands of families along the Mexico border. Public outrage results in a policy reversal, but reunification of families often proves difficult.

2018

Guatemala's Volcán de Fuego erupts, burying nearby villages in lava, killing hundreds of people and covering roads and crops with ash and debris. It is the country's most severe eruption in 45 years.

2018

NIcaragua descends into chaos after President Daniel Ortega announces an unpopular welfare proposal. Even after Ortega cancels the overhaul, protests continue and hundreds of people are killed.

People & Society

At the crossroads of continents, Central America has been influenced not only by its North and South American neighbors, but even more so by its European colonizers and African immigrants. With populations descended from these four corners – as well as prominent indigenous groups – the region's culture is a rich and fascinating blend. Family life remains sacred throughout the isthmus, but the disparity between urban and rural lifestyles is growing.

The Peoples of Central America

Central America may appear homogeneous at first glance, but this mostly Latin American region is a patchwork of European-, Amerindian- and African-descended groups – most of which have intermixed with each other. Some 78% of the regional population are in fact mestizo (Spanish-Amerindian mix) or Caucasian (European). Most of the remaining population is made up of dozens of distinct indigenous groups, from the once-mighty Maya to the barely-surviving Maleku. A small but significant percentage descends from African slaves and immigrant workers.

Mestizo

Mestizos are people of mixed Spanish and indigenous Amerindian descent. They are the largest ethnic group in Central America, comprising about 58% of the regional population; they're also the largest ethnic group in every Central American country except Costa Rica. (El Salvador has the region's highest percentage of mestizos, at 86%.) Even Belize – which was not settled by the Spanish – has a large

THE FIRST MESTIZOS

In 1511 the Spanish ship *Valdivia* was wrecked at sea when a reef ripped through its hull. About 15 survivors drifted for several days before making it to shore in northern Belize, where they were promptly apprehended by anxious Maya. Just to be on the safe side, the locals sent 10 of the Spaniards to the gods and kept five for themselves.

One of the captives was conquistador Gonzalo Guerrero, a skilled warrior – and apparently not a bad diplomat, either. Guerrero managed to win his freedom and a position of status with the Maya chief at Chetumal. He became a tribal consultant on military matters and married the chief's daughter; their three children are considered the first mestizos (mixed-race Spanish and indigenous people) in the New World.

Eight years later, Hernán Cortés arrived in the Yucatán and summoned Guerrero to serve him in his campaign of conquest. But Guerrero had 'gone native,' with facial tattoos and body piercings. He turned down the offer, saying instead that he was a captain of the Maya. Cortés moved on in his search for gold and glory, while Guerrero organized Maya defenses in the wars that followed. It would take the Spanish more than 20 years to finally defeat the Maya of Yucatán and Belize.

and growing mestizo population, due to the influx of refugees from neighboring countries.

While not uniform, the mestizo culture defines the region, which is predominantly Catholic and Spanish-speaking.

Caucasian

Costa Rica has an unusually high percentage of Caucasians – 66% – due to limited intermingling between Spanish farmers and indigenous groups. Europeans descended on Costa Rica throughout the 19th century and lately there's been an influx of North American retirees.

Approximately 20% of the Central American population is Caucasian – mostly of Spanish origin, descending from conquistadors and colonists who settled here, beginning in the 16th century.

Guatemala, Nicaragua and Panama all have smaller but still significant Caucasian populations – 12% to 18% – mostly descended from Spanish settlers. In the late 19th and early 20th centuries, the government of Nicaragua gave away land to German and French immigrants who were willing to cultivate it, which contributed to its 17% Caucasian population.

In the 20th century Central America became a refuge for alternative thinkers seeking a peaceful place to live according to beliefs that were unwelcome in North America. Belize has a small but visible population of Mennonites (of German/Dutch descent), who settled here in the 1950s and 1960s in an attempt to preserve their traditional way of life and strict moral code. A few years later, a group of Quakers fled the USA to avoid conscription into the military; they settled in Monteverde, Costa Rica, eventually founding the famous cloud-forest reserve.

Indigenous

The Maya are the most famous and populous indigenous group in Central America, but there are dozens of lesser-known Amerindian groups. These native peoples make up 16% of the overall regional population.

Maya

The Maya are the largest indigenous group in Central America, with an estimated population of seven million. From 2000 BC to AD 1500, the Maya civilization spanned the northern part of Central America, building great cities, undertaking elaborate rituals and engaging in violent warfare. Contemporary Maya culture does not bear much resemblance to its ancient counterpart, but it does retain some unique remnants of the heritage, including traditional clothing, religious practices and – most significantly – language. Throughout Central America, there are some 32 distinct linguistic groups that comprise the modern-day Maya population.

Historically, the K'iche' people were responsible for the *Popol Vuh*, a 16th-century account of ancient Maya society and culture that has been one of the most important sources for scholars.

K'iche'

The largest Maya linguistic group, the K'iche' people number around 1.6 million, constituting some 11% of the population in Guatemala. They live in El Quiché and the surrounding highlands. The K'iche' got some international attention when their spokesperson, Rigoberta Menchú, won the Nobel Peace Prize in 1992.

Yucatec

The Yucatec Maya are found in the Mexican states of Yucatán, Campeche and Quintana Roo. In the 1840s, the Caste War of the Yucatán sent streams of refugees into Belize, resulting in significant Yucatec Maya populations in Corozal and Cayo as well. It is estimated that there are about 1.2 million people who currently speak the Yucatec Maya language.

Q'eqchi'

The Q'eqchi' people (Kekchí, in Belize) number just under one million. They are geographically dispersed, but there are concentrations in Alta and Baja Verapez, Guatemala, and in Toledo, Belize.

Ch'orti'

The Ch'orti' people reside mostly in southern Guatemala and northwestern Honduras, with a total population of about 51,000. The Ch'orti' language – still spoken by some in Guatemala – is related to the inscriptions found on the ruins at Copán.

Afro Central American

From their earliest arrivals in the New World, the Spanish brought African slaves to trade and to work. In the 19th century, many other peoples of African descent arrived from Jamaica and other parts of the Antilles. African laborers, both immigrants and slaves, played a crucial role in the development of the region – felling forests, building railroads and dredging canals. Today their descendants make up about 4% of the Central American population, and they are concentrated mainly on the Caribbean coast.

The largest concentration of Maya people is in Guatemala, where they represent nearly 40% of the population. There are also significant populations in Mexico, Belize, Honduras and El Salvador.

Creole

Creoles are mixed-race people who are the descendants of African slaves and European baymen, loggers and colonists. There are significant Creole populations in Belize (called Kriol, 25%) and Nicaragua (9%), most of whom are descendants of escaped or shipwrecked slaves. Racially mixed and proud of it, Creoles speak a fascinating and unique version of English: it sounds familiar at first, but it is not easily intelligible to a speaker of standard English.

In the 1780s, after much conflict, the Spanish and the British reached an agreement allowing Brits to cut logwood and mahogany in Belize. In return, Britain agreed to abandon the Mosquito Coast of Nicaragua. Thousands of settlers – many of African descent – migrated to Belize to work in the labor-intensive logging industry. After several generations of mixing with the loggers and other colonists, the Kriols became the most populous ethnic group in Belize.

Afro-Panamanians & Afro-Costa Ricans

In the second half of the 19th century, both Costa Rica and Panama undertook railroad construction projects to facilitate the transportation of produce and people. In Panama the goal was to move people across the isthmus and on to California during the gold rush. In Costa Rica the goal was to transport coffee from the dense interior to Puerto Limón, so it could be shipped out to the world. In both cases, construction laborers were recruited from around the Antilles (especially Jamaica).

Many of these Afro-descended laborers stayed on to work on the banana plantations that sprang up alongside the railroads. Because the plantations were US-owned, the workers had little contact with local Spanish-speaking populations, so they retained their customs and language. Today some 8% of the population in Costa Rica has African

OTHER INDIGENOUS GROUPS

In pre-Columbian Central America, the southern part of the region was inhabited by many distinct indigenous groups that were unrelated to the Maya. Dozens of them endure to this day, although they all face challenges in preserving their culture, language and identity in this era of increasing global uniformity. These are some of the most prominent groups:

Ngöbe-Buglé Panama's largest indigenous group is the Ngöbe-Buglé (no-bay boo-glay), who number around 156,000 and occupy a *comarca* (autonomous region) that spans the Chiriquí, Veraguas and Bocas del Toro Provinces.

Lenca The Lenca inhabit southwestern Honduras and eastern El Salvador, with population estimates ranging from 137,000 to 300,000.

Miskito The Miskito hail from the remote coastal areas of Honduras and Nicaragua, especially around the Río Coco. There is no reliable population total, but estimates range from 50,000 to 200,000.

Guna Perhaps the most well-known Panamanian indigenous group, due to their distinctive dress, is the Guna, who inhabit the Archipiélago de San Blas and run their native lands as a *comarca*. With a large degree of sovereignty, the 50,000 or so Guna are fiercely protective of their independence.

Emberá and Wounaan In Panama, the Emberá and Wounaan inhabit the jungle of the eastern Panamá Province and the Darién. Although the groups are distinct, the difference is more linguistic than cultural.

Bribrí and Cabécar The Bribrí group lives in the Talamanca region of Costa Rica, isolated from mainstream Tico culture. Estimates of the Bribrí population range from 12,000 up to 35,000. The Cabécar are still more isolated, living high up in the Cordillera de Talamanca. Their language is distinct from Bribrí, but they share similar architecture, weapons and spiritual beliefs.

Mayangna The Mayangna (sometimes called the Sumo) traditionally inhabited the area along the Mosquito Coast in Nicaragua and Honduras, frequently coming into conflict with the Miskito people who also lived there. Their total population is around 10,000.

Tolupan The Tolupanes (also called Jicaque or Xicaque) live in small communities in Honduras, with a total population around 10,000.

Pech Traditionally inhabiting the forested areas of northeastern Honduras, the Pech peoples struggle to hang on to their culture. This indigenous group – now estimated at around 3800 people – has suffered from the destruction of the rainforest and the influx of mestizo farmers into their hunting grounds.

Brunka Some 2600 Brunka (or Boruca) people occupy the indigenous reserve in southern Costa Rica, practicing traditional agriculture and making handicrafts for sale. The Brunka are best known for the annual Fiesta de Los Diablitos, a three-day event that symbolizes their struggle with the Spanish.

Rama The Rama are an indigenous group that lives along the Caribbean Coast in Nicaragua, mostly on Rama Cay. With a population of around 2000, the Rama live off subsistence agriculture, fishing and hunting.

Naso In Panama, the Naso (Teribe) inhabit mainland Bocas del Toro and are largely confined to the Panamanian side of the bi-national Parque Internacional La Amistad. Their traditional villages are rapidly disappearing throughout the region and only a few thousand Naso remain.

Maleku Near the town of San Rafael, Costa Rica, the Guatuso Indigenous Reservation is home to about 600 Maleku people. This tiny indigenous population is ironically one of the country's most visible, as they often perform ceremonies for tourists in nearby La Fortuna.

roots. Descended mainly from Jamaican workers, they are concentrated on the Caribbean Coast and most speak an English dialect.

In the early 20th century the French commenced construction of the Panama Canal and continued to import labor, bringing thousands of workers from the French Antilles. Some scholars estimate that around 20,000 Afro-Antilleans remained in Panama after the completion of the canal. Nowadays, Afro-Panamanians make up about 9.2% of the population.

Garifuna

In the 17th century, shipwrecked African slaves washed ashore on the Caribbean island of St Vincent. They hooked up with the indigenous population of Caribs and Arawaks and formed a whole new ethnicity, now known as the Garifuna (plural Garinagu). When St Vincent changed hands, the Garinagu were deported and shuffled around to various islands; their population dwindled until a small group finally arrived on the Honduran coast. From here, these people of mixed Native American and African heritage began to spread along the Caribbean coast of Central America.

Currently there are significant populations of Garifuna peoples in Honduras, Belize and Guatemala, with smaller numbers in Nicaragua. Many still speak the Garifuna language, which is a combination of Arawak and African languages. While the Garinagu make up a small percentage of the population (6% in Belize and 1% in Honduras) their cultural influence is disproportionately large. They have a strong sense of community and ritual, in which drumming and dancing play important roles. In 2001 Unesco declared Garifuna language, dance and music to be a 'Masterpiece of the Oral and Intangible Heritage of Humanity' – one of the first recipients of this honor, which is the cultural equivalent of the World Heritage list.

Central American Lifestyles

In Central America, the contrast between urban and rural lifestyles is pretty stark, with gaping disparities in opportunity, education and income. For better or for worse, some things such as family and church remain constant – though *which* church may be a subject for debate these days.

Family

The family unit in Central America remains the nucleus of life. Extended families often live near each other and socialize together. Those with relatives in positions of power – nominal or otherwise – don't hesitate to turn to them for support. Favors are graciously accepted, promptly returned and never forgotten. Despite modernizing influences – education, cable TV, contact with foreign travelers, time spent abroad – traditional family ties remain strong at all levels of society. Old-fashioned gender roles are strong too, although this is changing in Costa Rica, Nicaragua and Panama.

Despite their closeness, many families have at least one member who has emigrated to the USA to work. Remittances from abroad are a major source of income for families across the region.

Religion

Religion continues to be a major force in the lives of Central Americans, though the once staunchly Catholic region is changing. Ever since the arrival of the Spanish – and with them missionaries, priests and papal decrees – Central America has been dominated by Catholics. Today more than half of the region's population practices Catholicism.

But the 20th century brought a new set of missionaries – this time evangelical Protestants from North America – commonly known as *evangelicos*. The fiery services and paradisaical promises have particular appeal among the rural poor. Nearly a third of the region's population has been wooed into joining the faith.

Urban vs Rural

Central America is characterized by a vast chasm in levels of healthcare, education, wealth and modernity. These differences often line up along the urban–rural divide. In capital cities, well-heeled residents drive high-end cars, own vacation properties and travel overseas. Meanwhile, just an hour's drive away, an indigenous family might paddle a dugout canoe and practice subsistence agriculture.

The region's countryside has seen waves of outgoing migration, as the sons and daughters of farmers seek better lives in the cities.

Even in the region's most prosperous countries (Costa Rica and Panama), around 20% of the population lives below the poverty line. In the poorest countries (Guatemala and Honduras), the number is more than 50%. The vast majority of the destitute live in rural areas, many representing indigenous groups. Across the region, the rural poor have significantly lower standards of living, fewer opportunities for education and less-than-adequate healthcare.

The middle and upper classes reside mainly in urban areas, especially in capital cities, where they enjoy a lifestyle that is similar to their counterparts in North America or Europe.

Arts & Culture

You probably didn't come to Central America for high culture: art museums and symphony halls are thin on the ground. To discover the richness of Central America's arts, you have to look in unexpected places – gritty dance clubs and dark alleys, rural villages and women's cooperatives. In Central America, anyone and everyone is an artist, or a musician, or a poet. Art is all around you, so keep your eyes open.

Street Art

Throughout Central America and Mexico, the art scene is vibrant and visible, as some of the most poignant contemporary work takes the form of street art – murals and mosaics that grace decrepit buildings and brighten city streets. Often these paintings record historic events and raise awareness of social issues, a tradition that dates from a time when a large percentage of the population was illiterate. Interestingly, street art is most vibrant in war-torn countries such as El Salvador, Guatemala and Nicaragua.

In El Salvador, the best examples are in Perquín, La Palma and Suchitoto, as well as in the capital and the villages along the Ruta de las Flores. In 1997 national icon Fernando Llort created a colorful, folkloric ceramic-tile mural entitled *Harmonia de Mi Pueblo*. A tribute to persevering Salvadorans and a celebration of peace, the artwork was mounted on the facade of the Catedral Metropolitana in San Salvador. Artists and residents were shocked and outraged when the local archbishop had the mural removed in 2012, without consulting the government or the artist.

Paintings cover the walls in many Nicaraguan cities, especially the Sandinista strongholds of León and Estelí. The latter is home to a new movement of *muralistas,* who use more recognizable graffiti techniques to deliver their social commentary.

Urban Maeztro is the pseudonym of a Honduran street artist who makes provocative, overtly political work, decrying the violence that pervades Tegucigalpa.

The most famous Guatemalan artist is Efraín Recinos, whose murals grace the National Music Conservatory. He's also a celebrated architect and sculptor. Not exactly a street artist, Recinos was awarded Guatemala's highest honor, the Order of the Quetzal, in 1999.

In Cozumel, Mexico, a recent project involving dozens of large murals in the town center is calling attention to marine issues such as shark finning, overfishing, coastal development, climate change and coral reef conservation.

Poetry

In Central America, peasants can be poets, and poets can be politicians. Poetry is beloved throughout the region, especially in the countries that have seen the most violence and poverty – always good inspiration for verse.

Guatemala's first great literary figure was poet and Jesuit priest Rafael Landivar, whose collection of poetry was published in 1781. The literary spokesperson of the Guatemala people is Miguel Ángel Asturias (1899–1974). His masterpiece novel, *Men of Maize,* won the Nobel Prize for Literature in 1967, but before that he was a poet-diplomat and an outspoken political commentator.

INDIGENOUS ARTS & CRAFTS

Souvenir hunters will be delighted by the wealth of handicrafts and folk art that is available in Central America, much of it produced by indigenous groups in the region.

Especially in the highlands of Guatemala, the Maya weave festive, colorful clothing and textiles. The *huipil* (a women's tunic) is often a true work of art – a multicolored web of stylized animal, human, plant and mythological shapes. Many women still use the pre-Hispanic backstrap loom to make these creations.

Panama's indigenous groups produce high-quality woodcarvings, textiles, ceramics, masks and other handicrafts. The Emberá and Wounaan are renowned for their woven baskets, some of which are highly decorated with bright colors and natural motifs, made from the nahuala bush and chunga palm. The Guna are known for their *molas* (the embroidered panels used by women in their traditional dress). Ocú and Penonomé people produce superior panama hats.

In Costa Rica, indigenous crafts include intricately carved and painted masks made by the Boruca, as well as handwoven bags and linens and colorful Chorotega pottery.

In Nicaragua, any *campesino* (farmer) can tell you who the greatest poet in history is: Rubén Darío, voice of the nation and founder of the *modernismo* literary movement. Nicaragua is also home to the peculiar cultural archetype of 'warrior poets,' folks who choose to use both the pen and the sword. The best-known example is Gioconda Belli, who was working undercover with the Sandinistas when she won the prestigious Casa de las Américas international poetry prize.

Music

At the intersection of Latin beats and Caribbean cool, there is the *música* of Central America. You'll hear calypso, reggae, soca and salsa around the region, but you'll also discover lesser-known, uniquely Central American musical genres that incorporate the best of the more mainstream styles.

Salvadoran poet Roque Dalton was exiled for his radical politics – and eventually executed for allegedly playing double agent. His notable works include *Taberna y Otros Lugares* (1969), a political vision in verse.

The marimba is a percussion instrument that resembles a xylophone, except it's made of wood and so produces a mellower sound. The instrument is usually played by three men; there's a carnival-like quality to its sound and compositions. Marimba music is used during Maya religious ceremonies, and it's considered the national instrument in Guatemala. But it's also popular in Costa Rica and Nicaragua, where musicians have updated marimba folk with a rocky *cumbia* (Colombian dance tunes) beat.

Musicians and linguists speculate that the name *punta,* a traditional Garifuna drumming and dance style, comes from the word *bunda,* which means 'buttocks' in many West African languages. The word derivation is not certain, but it is apt. Played at celebrations, this music inspires Garifuna peoples everywhere to get up and shake their *bunda.*

In the 1970s, Belizean musician Pen Cayetano traveled around Central America and came to the realization that Garifuna traditions were in danger of withering away. He wanted to inspire young people to embrace their own culture, so he invented a cool and contemporary genre by adding electric guitar to traditional *punta* rhythms – and *punta* rock was born. Since the 1980s, *punta* rock has become popular across the region (and across ethnic groups), especially in Belize and Honduras.

Once the music of the urban poor in Panama, reggaetón nowadays permeates all countries and social strata in Central America (and beyond). Taking cues from hip-hop, especially the rap-like vocals, this unique genre also incorporates musical influences from Jamaican dancehall, Trinidadian soca and Puerto Rican salsa. Reggaetón is wildly popular across the region, especially in Panama, Costa Rica and Guatemala.

Survival Guide

Directory A–Z

Accessible Travel

Central America generally isn't well equipped for those with disabilities: services such as specially equipped phones, toilets or anything in braille are rare to the point of nonexistence. Expensive international hotels are more likely to cater to guests with disabilities than cheap hotels; air travel or pre-arranged transportation will be more feasible than most local buses; and off-the-beaten-track destinations will be less accessible than well-developed ones.

Belize and Costa Rica are better equipped for travelers with mobility issues than other Central American countries (due in part to the many elderly travelers who arrive on cruise ships). In both countries, it's possible to find hotels and attractions that can accommodate wheelchairs, especially in the most popular tourist spots. Some of Costa Rica's national parks are also wheelchair-accessible, including Parque Nacional Volcán Poás and Parque Nacional Carara.

Accommodations

The cost of accommodations varies from country to country. Nicaragua, Honduras, El Salvador and Guatemala are the cheaper countries, while Mexico, Belize, Panama and Costa Rica (and many beach destinations) are more expensive. Features such as a private bathroom, hot water and air-con will drive up the price.

Reservations are necessary in tourist areas during peak season, particularly during Semana Santa (Holy Week, preceding Easter) and the week between Christmas and New Year, when locals are also traveling around the region.

Prices do change; use prices listed by Lonely Planet as a gauge only.

BOOK YOUR STAY ONLINE

For more accommodations reviews by Lonely Planet authors, check out http://lonelyplanet.com/hotels/. You'll find independent reviews, as well as recommendations on the best places to stay. Best of all, you can book online.

Children

Central America is a safe and exciting destination for families with children. Beaches on two coastlines, wildlife-rich forests and endless opportunities for adventure are guaranteed to thrill kids of all ages.

➡ Be sure children are up to date on all routine immunizations. Some recommended vaccines may not be approved for children, so be careful they do not drink tap water or consume any questionable food.

➡ For more ideas about family travel, see Lonely Planet's *Travel with Children*.

Customs Regulations

All visitors leaving and entering a Central American country go through customs. Be prepared for bag checks at both airports and land borders. Most are just a quick gaze-and-poke, more of a formality than a search – but not always. Be polite to officials at all times.

Discount Cards

A member card from **Hostelling International** (HI; www.hihostels.com) isn't terribly useful in Central America, except in Mexico and Costa Rica, where some hostels offer minimal discounts to cardholders. Those going on to South America, however, may want to invest in the membership, as the card is more commonly accepted there.

Carriers of the **International Student Identity Card** (ISIC; www.isic.org) can get very good discounts on travel insurance, as well as discounted air tickets.

Electricity

Most cmmon are plug types A or B (as is used in the USA). In Belize you may come across type G plugs. Voltage varies between 110v and 220v.

Embassies & Consulates

As a visitor in a Central American country, it's important to realize what your own country's embassy can and can't do. Generally speaking, your embassy will not help much if you're even remotely at fault in a situation – remember that you are bound by the laws of the country you are in. Your embassy will not be sympathetic if you end up in jail after committing a crime locally, even if such actions are legal in your own country.

In an emergency, you may get some assistance in obtaining a new passport, contacting family members or contacting a lawyer.

Food & Drink

Reservations for eating here are practically unheard of, except at high-end restaurants in the biggest tourist centers.

Street food Urban areas throughout Central America have cheap street food, served from *carritos* (carts) or food trucks. Options vary by country, but may include tacos, *pupusas* (grilled cornmeal with cheese or bean filling) or *churrasco* (BBQ meat) with rice and beans.

Comedores A simple diner serving set meals – almost every town has one. Also known as *sodas* in Costa Rica.

Restaurantes A more formal dining experience than the *comedor*, with a wider menu and probably a selection of wines and beers.

Health

The most critical health concern in Central America is mosquito-borne illnesses (p732), including malaria, dengue and the Zika virus. Take precautions to prevent mosquito bites: strong insect repellent with DEET is essential. At the time of writing, pregnant women were advised against traveling to Central America due to the outbreak of the Zika virus.

There are no required vaccinations (p733) for Central America, except if you are coming from a yellow-fever-infected country in Africa or South America – then you must have a yellow fever vaccine. Among others recommended are typhoid, rabies and hepatitis A and B. Visit your doctor well ahead of your trip, since most vaccines don't produce immunity until at least two weeks after they're given. Ask your doctor for an International Certificate of Vaccination (aka 'the yellow booklet'), which will list all the vaccinations you've received. This is mandatory for countries that require proof of yellow-fever vaccination.

Several prescription medications are available for the prevention of malaria. One of these may be recommended, depending where exactly you are traveling in Central America. Consult your doctor well before departure.

Most insurance providers do not cover overseas expenses, so it's strongly recommended to purchase a traveler's insurance policy that includes health coverage.

Before You Go

HEALTH INSURANCE

Find out in advance if your insurance plan will make payments directly to providers or reimburse you later for overseas health expenditure. If the latter, be sure to collect receipts.

If your travel insurance (p732) does not cover you for medical expenses abroad, consider buying supplemental insurance. Check lonelyplanet.com/travel-insurance for more information.

RESOURCES

It's usually a good idea to consult the health sections of your government's travel

TRAVEL WITH CHILDREN

- Do not expect all the amenities that are available at home, as you're unlikely to find conveniences such as high chairs in restaurants, cribs at hotels, or changing tables in public toilets.
- Many car rental agencies offer child seats (for a fee), but they must be reserved in advance and quality is not guaranteed.
- Formula, diapers (nappies) and other baby necessities are widely available in grocery stores.
- Discreet public breastfeeding is common, though less so in urban areas.

advice website (p737) before departure. Other resources:

World Health Organization (www.who.int/ith) Publishes a superb book called *International Travel and Health,* which is revised annually and available on its website at no cost. The website lists updated risks and worldwide vaccination certificate requirements.

MD Travel Health (www.mdtravelhealth.com) Provides complete travel health recommendations for every country, updated daily.

In Central America

AVAILABILITY & COST OF HEALTHCARE

Good medical care is available in most of the region's capital cities, but options are limited elsewhere. In general, private hospitals are more reliable than public facilities, which may experience significant shortages of equipment and supplies.

Many doctors and hospitals expect payment in cash, regardless of whether you have travel health insurance. If you develop a life-threatening medical problem, you'll probably want to be evacuated to a country with state-of-the-art medical care. Since this may cost tens of thousands of dollars, take out travel insurance (p731) that covers medical expenses before your trip.

US travelers can find a list of recommended doctors abroad and emergency evacuation details on the website of the **US State Department** (http://travel.state.gov). Click on International Travel, then Before You Go, then Your Health Abroad.

Many pharmacies are well supplied, but important medications may not be consistently available. Be sure to bring along adequate supplies of all prescription drugs.

INSECT-BORNE DISEASES

All travelers are advised to take precautions against insect-borne diseases, including malaria, chikungunya, dengue and Zika. Many of these illnesses cannot be prevented with vaccines or medication, so the most effective prevention is to avoid bug bites:

- Use an insect repellent that contains 20% or more DEET.
- Treat clothing, bedding and camping gear with permethrin, which binds tightly to clothing.
- Cover exposed skin with long sleeves, pants and hats.
- Sleep in places with screened windows or use a bed net.

TAP WATER

Tap water is not safe to drink in many parts of Central America. Vigorous boiling for one minute is the most effective means of water purification. At altitudes greater than 2000m (6500ft), boil for three minutes.

Another option is to disinfect water with iodine pills. Instructions are usually enclosed and should be carefully followed. Alternatively you can add 2% tincture of iodine to 1L of water (five drops to clear water, 10 drops to cloudy water) and let it stand for 30 minutes. If the water is cold, longer times may be required. The taste of iodinated water may be improved by adding vitamin C (ascorbic acid). Iodinated water should not be consumed for more than a few weeks. Pregnant women, those with a history of thyroid disease and those allergic to iodine should not drink iodinated water.

A number of water filters are on the market. Those with smaller pores (reverse osmosis filters) provide the broadest protection, but they are relatively large and also readily plugged by debris. Those that have somewhat larger pores (microstrainer filters) are ineffective against viruses, although they do remove other organisms. Manufacturers' instructions must be carefully followed.

Insurance

A travel insurance policy covering theft, loss, accidents and illness is highly recommended. Some policies compensate travelers for misrouted or lost luggage. Also check that the coverage includes worst-case scenarios: ambulances, evacuations or an emergency flight home. Some policies specifically exclude 'dangerous activities,' which can include scuba diving, motorcycling or even trekking. Be sure to read the small print.

There is a wide variety of policies available. Policies handled by student-travel organizations usually offer good value. If a policy offers lower and higher medical-expense options, the low-expenses policy should be OK for Central America –

medical costs are not nearly as high here as elsewhere.

If you are robbed (p737) and need to make a claim, you must report the loss or theft to local police within 24 hours. Make a list of stolen items and their value. At the police station, you need to complete a *denuncia* (statement), a copy of which is given to you for your insurance claim.

Worldwide travel insurance is available at www.lonelyplanet.com/travel-insurance. You can buy, extend and claim online anytime – even if you're already on the road.

Internet Access

Internet access is widely available. Wi-fi is available at all but the most basic accommodations, as well as at some cafes and restaurants. Many hostels also have computers for guest use.

Internet cafes are less prevalent than they used to be; rates range from US$0.50 per hour in cities and touristy destinations to US$6 in remote areas.

Either Alt + 64 or Alt-G + 2 is the command to get the @ symbol on Spanish-language keyboards.

Language Courses

Spanish-language courses are available in many Central American cities, including the following:

Mexico San Cristóbal de las Casas (Map p90; ☎967-678-40-69; www.institutojovel.com; Madero 45; individual/group classes per week from US$215/140, homestay per week from US$140), Playa del Carmen (Map p66; ☎984-803-33-88; www.ihrivieramaya.com; Calle 14 Norte 141; per week US$230)

Guatemala Antigua (Map p124; ☎7832-1422; www.spanishschoolplfm.com; 6a Av Norte 43), Quetzaltenango (Map p158; ☎7763-1061; www.plqe.org; 5a Calle 2-40, Zona 1)

El Salvador Suchitoto (☎2327-2366, 7230-7812; www.pajaroflor.com; 4a Calle Poniente 22)

Honduras Copán Ruinas (Map p380; ☎2651-4360; www.guacamaya.com; Calle de las Gradas, off Av Copán)

Nicaragua Granada (Map p444; ☎7779-0209; www.facebook.com/nicaraguamiaschool; Calle El Caimito, alcaldía, 3½ c E; 1 week all-inclusive per person US$280), León (☎8183-7389; www.leonspanishschool.org; La Casa de Cultura, Iglesia de la Merced, 2c O; 20hr course with/without homestay US$250/150), Managua (☎2270-2339; www.vivaspanishschool.com;

RECOMMENDED VACCINATIONS

VACCINE	RECOMMENDED FOR	DOSAGE	SIDE EFFECTS
chicken pox	travelers who've never had chicken pox	2 doses; 1 month apart	fever, mild case of chicken pox
hepatitis A	all travelers	1 dose before trip; booster 6-12 months later	soreness at injection site, headaches, body aches
hepatitis B	long-term travelers in close contact with the local population	3 doses over 6-month period	soreness at injection site, low-grade fever
measles	travelers born after 1956 who've had only 1 measles vaccination	1 dose	fever, rash, joint pains, allergic reactions
rabies	travelers who may have contact with animals and may not have access to medical care	3 doses over 3- to 4-week period	soreness at injection site, headaches, body aches
tetanus-diphtheria	all travelers who haven't had a booster within 10 years	1 dose lasts 10 years	soreness at injection site
typhoid fever	all travelers	1 dose 2 weeks before travel; booster 2 years later	abdominal pain, nausea, rash
yellow fever	required for travelers arriving from a yellow-fever-infected area in Africa or South America	1 dose lasts 10 years	headaches, body aches; severe reactions are rare

Metrocentro, 5c E, del Edificio Banco Produzcamos, 2c S; lessons per hour US$10; ⌚8am-5pm Mon-Fri), San Juan del Sur (☎2568-2142; www.spanishcornerschool.com; Royal Chateau Hotel, 1c N; classes per 1/10/20hr US$10/85/135; ⌚8am-10pm)

Costa Rica Heredia (CPI; ☎2265-6306, USA 1-877-373-3116; www.cpi-edu.com; private lessons from US$30, 20hr group tuition from US$460, 1-week homestay from US$200), Monteverde (CPI; Map p564; ☎2265-6306; www.cpi-edu.com; Cerro Plano; weeklong classes from US$460; ⌚8am-5pm), San José (Map p525; ☎2280-1685, USA 866-230-6361; www.spanishandmore.com; Calle Ronda, Barrio Dent), Tamarindo (Map p578; ☎2653-2673; www.coastalspanish.com; per week from US$365), Playa Sámara (☎2656-3000; www.interculturacostarica.com; courses per week with/without homestay US$470/315)

Panama Bocas del Toro (Map p671; ☎757-9518, 6592-0775; www.spanishbythesea.com; Calle 4), Boquete (☎720-3456; www.spanishatlocations.com; Entrada a Palmira), Panama City (Map p636; ☎228-3258; www.cascospanish.com; Av A s/n; 1-week 20hr intensive US$250; ⌚7am-7pm Mon-Fri, 8am-noon Sat)

Legal Matters

It is advisable (and sometimes required) to carry a passport or photo ID at all times.

Costa Rica, Guatemala and Honduras have dedicated tourist police working in the big cities. In some countries the police force has a reputation for corruption, and from time to time you may be stopped and hassled or asked for a bribe. Law enforcement is generally professional, visible and effective, though. Throughout the region, police checkpoints and vehicle searches are not uncommon.

Marijuana and cocaine are illegal everywhere in the region and penalties are severe. Reforms to drug laws in Mexico stipulate that first-time offenders are not punished for possession of a small amount of drugs for personal use. Still, it's inadvisable to carry any amount of drugs, and if you are caught you may be shaken down for a bribe. Allowable amounts are strictly enforced, and offenders will generally be arrested and prosecuted.

In many countries, you are presumed guilty until found innocent. If you are accused of a serious crime, you will be taken to jail. In this case, your embassy will offer only limited assistance. This may include a visit from an embassy staff member to make sure your human rights have not been violated, contacting your family and putting you in touch with a lawyer (whom you must pay yourself).

LGBTIQ+ Travelers

Central America can be an unwelcoming place for LGBTIQ+ travelers, but there are some bright spots. Same-sex marriage was legalized in Mexico in 2009 and in Costa Rica in 2013. The current president of Costa Rica, Carlos Alvarado Quesada, has been unusually vocal in his support for gay rights.

Advocacy groups in other Central American countries are eager to follow suit. Consensual gay sex has also been decriminalized all around the region. That said, official and unofficial harassment is possible anywhere in Central America. In general, public displays of affection will not be tolerated and gay men (and possibly women) could find themselves the target of verbal or physical abuse. Discretion is definitely the rule in Central America, especially in the countryside. Lesbians are generally less maligned than gay men, so women traveling together should encounter few, if any, problems.

Where to Go

There is usually at least one gay bar in big cities. The following are some of the more public gay and lesbian scenes:

Mexico The biggest and best gay scene in the region is at the bars and clubs in Cancún (p51) and Playa del Carmen (p64).

Guatemala Travelers will find a small and subdued gay scene in both Antigua (p120) and Guatemala City (p108).

El Salvador The charming mountain town of San Vicente (p330) is a popular gay destination.

Nicaragua Travelers will find a few gay-specific bars in Managua (p431).

Costa Rica There are thriving scenes in San José (p518) and Manuel Antonio (p593).

Panama Bars come and go, but the gay scene in Panama City (p625) is surprisingly limited. The normally discreet population is more open during **Carnaval** (⌚Feb/Mar) festivities, which usually feature a gay float in the parade.

Maps

The best map of the region is the fold-up color 1:1,100,000 *Central America Travel Reference Map* (US$13), produced by **International Travel Maps & Books** (www.itmb.ca) in Canada.

ITMB also publishes separate maps covering each of the Central American countries and various regions of Mexico, as well as several maps of South America.

Money

ATMs

➡ Bring an ATM (or debit) card. ATMs are available in most cities and large towns and are almost always the most convenient, reliable, secure and economical way of getting cash. Many ATMs are connected to the MasterCard/Cirrus or Visa/Plus networks.

- The exchange rate from ATMs is usually as good as (if not better than) that at any bank or legal money changer.
- Notify your bank of your travel plans so international transactions are not rejected.

Cash

It's a good idea to always have a small amount of US dollars handy – enough to get a room, a meal and a taxi, at least – because they can be exchanged or even spent practically anywhere. It's particularly useful when crossing the border or when an ATM isn't available. Central American currencies don't always fly in the next country; plan ahead before you head to remote areas and take more than enough cash.

Getting change for bigger notes in local currency is a daily concern. Notes worth even US$20 can sometimes be difficult to change.

Credit & Debit Cards

- American Express, Visa and MasterCard are the most widely accepted credit cards in Central America.
- Some card companies charge a fee (from 2% to 10%) for international transactions.
- Some banks issue cash advances on major credit cards.
- Although credit cards are widely accepted, it is not always economical to use them. In Costa Rica, for example, many hotels offer a discount for cash payment.

Exchanging Money

If you insist on still using traveler's checks, or you've got foreign cash to convert, you can handle this at a bank or a *casa de cambio* (currency exchange office). Rates between the two are usually similar, but in general *casas de cambio* are quicker, less bureaucratic and open longer or on weekends. Street money changers, who may or may not be legal, will handle only cash.

Sometimes you can also change money unofficially at hotels or in shops that sell imported goods (electronics dealers are an obvious choice). Compare exchange rates and commission fees first; big cities tend to offer better rates.

Don't accept even slightly torn notes, as most locals won't when you try to use them.

Black Market

The *mercado negro* (black market) – also known as *mercado paralelo* (parallel market) – is generally limited to money changers at borders, who may or may not be legal. They are known to slip in torn bills or to shortchange on occasion, though they accept local currencies that banks elsewhere sometimes don't take. Such unofficial exchange rates for the US dollar can be lower than official bank rates.

PHOTOGRAPHY

- Always ask before photographing individuals, particularly indigenous people.
- Paying people for a portrait is a personal decision; in most cases, subjects will tell you straight off the going rate for a photo.
- Some tourist sites charge an additional fee for video cameras or cameras.
- Don't photograph military installations or personnel; it may be illegal in some areas.
- In churches, photography or the use of flashes is often prohibited.

Opening Hours

Standard opening hours can be found in the Directory section of each individual country.

Post

International postal rates can be quite expensive. Generally, important mail and parcels should be sent by registered or certified service; otherwise they may go missing. Sending parcels can be awkward, as often a customs officer must inspect the contents before a postal clerk can accept them, so don't seal them until the packages have been inspected. The place for posting parcels overseas is sometimes different from the main post office.

UPS, FedEx, DHL and other shipping and private courier services are available in some countries, providing an efficient but expensive alternative.

Public Holidays

New Year's Day January 1 (region-wide)

Martyrs' Day January 9 (Panama)

Baron Bliss Day March 9 (Belize)

Good Friday March or April (region-wide)

Holy Saturday March or April (region-wide)

Easter Monday March or April (region-wide)

Juan Santamaría Day April 11 (Costa Rica)

Day of the Americas April 14 (Honduras)

Labor Day May 1 (region-wide)

Sovereign's Day May 24 (Belize)

Mothers' Day May 30 (Nicaragua)

Army Day June 30 (Guatemala)

Feast of San Salvador August 6 (El Salvador)

Mothers' Day August 15 (Costa Rica)

Assumption Day August 15 (Guatemala)

Founding of Old Panama August 15 (Panama City only)

National Day September 10 (Belize)

Battle of San Jacinto September 14 (Nicaragua)

Independence Day September 15 (Costa Rica, El Salvador, Guatemala, Honduras, Nicaragua)

Independence Day September 21 (Belize)

Francisco Morazán Day October 3 (Honduras)

Columbus Day October 12 (Belize, Costa Rica, Honduras)

Revolution Day (Día de la Revolución) October 20 (Guatemala)

Army Day October 21 (Honduras)

All Souls Day November 2 (El Salvador, Guatemala, Nicaragua)

Independence Day November 3 (Panama)

First Call for Independence November 10 (Panama)

Garifuna Settlement Day November 19 (Belize)

Independence from Spain November 28 (Panama)

Immaculate Conception December 8 (Nicaragua)

Mothers' Day December 8 (Panama)

Christmas Day December 25 (region-wide)

Safe Travel

➡ Parts of Honduras, El Salvador and Guatemala are plagued by high crime rates and gang activity. Visitors are rarely affected, but some have been victims of grab-and-run theft, assault, rape, carjacking and murder.

➡ Capital cities tend to have the highest rates of crime.

➡ Many sexual assaults occur on isolated beaches.

➡ Avoid night buses (with the possible exception of Mexico and Panama), as highway robberies often happen at night.

➡ Avoid drug use entirely.

➡ Seek out updates from other travelers, tourist offices, police, guesthouse owners and Lonely Planet's Thorn Tree (www.lonelyplanet.com/thorntree).

Darién Province

Certain parts of Darién Province (p688), on the Panama–Colombia border, are restricted. Travel requires special permission from Servicios Nacional de Fronteras (SeNaFront) in Panama City.

Drugs

Marijuana and cocaine are available in many places, but are illegal everywhere in the region and penalties are severe. Recent reforms to drug laws in Mexico stipulate that first-time offenders are not punished for possession of a small amount of drugs for personal use, but that doesn't mean the cops won't shake you down for a bribe.

➡ Avoid any conversation with someone who offers you drugs.

➡ If you are in an area where drug trafficking is prevalent, ignore it and do not show any interest, since drugs are sometimes used to set up travelers for blackmail and bribery.

➡ Legal concerns aside, purchasing recreational drugs supports groups that engage in human trafficking and child prostitution, and contributes to violence and political unrest throughout the region.

Natural Hazards

Central America is prone to a wide variety of natural disasters, including earthquakes, hurricanes, floods and volcanic eruptions. General information about natural-disaster preparedness is available from the **US Federal Emergency Management Agency** (www.fema.gov).

Nicaragua

In April 2018 political clashes between anti-government supporters and Nicaraguan president Daniel Ortega led to violence and death across the country. Consult your government's travel advisory service before considering travel.

Police & Military

Corruption is a serious problem among Latin American police, who are generally poorly paid and poorly supervised. In many countries, they are not reluctant to plant drugs on unsuspecting travelers or enforce minor regulations to the letter in the hope of extracting *coimas* (bribes).

➡ If you are stopped by someone claiming to be a plainclothes policeman, never get into a vehicle with them. Don't give them any documents or show them any money and don't take them to your hotel. If the officer appears to be the real thing, insist on going to a police station on foot.

➡ Military checkpoints are frequent in places such as Panama's Darién Province, El Salvador, Guatemala and Mexico, and are there as a way to combat drug trafficking.

➡ In police stations, English-speaking interpreters are a rarity. Some cities have a tourist police service that may be more helpful.

Robbery & Theft

Thefts do happen, particularly in larger cities and transit points such as bus stations.

Most is of the pickpocket or grab-and-run variety. To protect yourself:

➡ Be wary of offers of food, drinks, sweets or cigarettes from strangers on buses, trains or in bars, as they could be laced with sedatives.

➡ Don't use a smartphone or laptop in public places, as it may attract the attention of thieves.

➡ Keep most of your money in a safe place and only carry pocket change (or whatever you can afford to lose) for daily use.

➡ Purses or bags can be slashed or grabbed. Use a cheap, nondescript bag for walking around cities.

➡ Be wary of anyone pointing out a spilled substance (mustard, dog feces) on your clothes. It's a classic pickpocketing ploy: one thief helps to clean the victims, the other robs them.

➡ Avoid night buses.

➡ It's worth splurging on taxis after dark, particularly in cities. Don't wander alone down empty city streets or in isolated areas.

➡ When possible, keep valuables sealed in a signed envelope in a hotel safe.

➡ Keep doors and windows locked.

➡ Don't camp overnight on beaches or in the countryside unless you can be sure it's safe.

➡ Get local safety news from guesthouse owners, tourist offices and other travelers.

➡ Don't resist a robbery. Many thieves are armed.

If you are the victim of a robbery, go to the police to report the theft and to get a police statement to present to your insurance company. Say '*Quiero poner una acta de un robo*' (I want to report a robbery). You may have to write up the report yourself, then present it for an official stamp and signature.

GOVERNMENT TRAVEL ADVICE

The following government websites offer travel advisories and information on current hot spots.

Australian Department of Foreign Affairs (www.smarttraveller.gov.au)

Canadian Department of Foreign Affairs (www.travel.gc.ca)

Foreign Office of the Federal Republic of Germany (www.auswaertiges-amt.de/en)

Japanese Ministry of Foreign Affairs (www.mofa.go.jp)

Netherlands Ministry of Foreign Affairs (www.government.nl/ministries/ministry-of-foreign-affairs)

New Zealand Foreign Affairs & Trade (www.safetravel.govt.nz)

UK Foreign & Commonwealth Office (www.fco.gov.uk/travel)

US Department of State (www.travel.state.gov)

Photocopies or photos of original passports, visas and air tickets and careful records of credit card numbers are invaluable during replacement procedures. Replacement passport applications are usually referred to the home country, so it helps to have someone back home with a copy of your passport details.

Swimming Safely

Hundreds of people drown each year at Central America's beaches. Of these, the vast majority of fatalities are caused by riptides. Rips occurs when two currents that move parallel to the shore meet, causing the opposing waters to choose the path of least resistance, which is the path out to sea. They can be present even in waist-deep water. The best advice: ask about conditions before entering the water. If it's dangerous, don't tempt the ocean. Some tips:

➡ If you are caught in a rip, stay calm and swim parallel to the shore to get out of it – rip currents dissipate quickly.

➡ Contrary to popular belief, a rip will not pull you down and hold you under the water. A rip simply carries floating objects, including people, out beyond the zone of breaking waves.

➡ When the current dissipates, swim back in at a 45-degree angle to the shore to avoid being caught by the rip current again.

➡ Do not try to swim directly back in, as you would be swimming against the rip and would only exhaust yourself.

➡ If you feel a rip while you are wading, try to come back in sideways, thus offering less body surface to the current. If you cannot make headway, walk parallel to the beach until you get out of the rip.

Smoking

Smoking regulations vary widely from country to country. In Belize and Nicaragua, there are few restrictions, and smoking in bars and restaurants is generally permitted. In Costa Rica and Panama, it is banned in enclosed spaces, as well as outdoor public places. The other countries' laws are

VIVA EL CA-4!

Guatemala, Honduras, El Salvador and Nicaragua's 'CA-4 Border Control' agreement allows free travel for up to 90 days within this sub-region for citizens of the four countries and many foreign nationals (including residents of the USA, Canada, the UK and Australia).

On paper, at least, you should only have to pay a tourist fee once to enter these four countries. Yet border patrols may also charge you a few dollars for 'paperwork'; if they insist, you won't have much alternative but to pay.

somewhere in between, but generally ban smoking in enclosed public areas.

Telephone

Internet cafes with net-to-phone (VOIP) service provide the cheapest way to make international calls, with rates varying between US$0.10 and US$0.50 per minute to the USA and Europe.

From traditional landlines, the most economical way of calling abroad is using phone cards purchased at kiosks or corner stores. You can also try direct-dial lines, accessed via special numbers and billed to an account at home. It is sometimes cheaper to make a collect or credit-card call to Europe or North America than to pay for the call where you are.

Many towns and cities have a telephone office with phone booths for local and international calls. Rates can be high. Avoid credit-card phones in Mexico and the black 'press button' phones in Guatemala, which charge extortionate rates.

Cell Phones

Cell phones are widely used. You can purchase a local cell phone in a kiosk for as little as US$20, or a prepaid SIM card for around US$5 (the cell phone you use it with must be GSM-compatible and SIM-unlocked).

Toilets

The toilets of Central America are fine; it's just the plumbing that has issues. Nowhere in the region should you deposit toilet paper or anything else in the toilet unless a sign specifies that it's OK to do so. Wastebaskets are generally provided.

Some public toilets have attendants who charge a small fee (US$0.10 or so) and provide paper. It's a good idea to keep a spare roll of toilet paper handy while traveling.

Tourist Information

Travelers will find a tourist office in the capital city of each country; some countries have them in outlying towns as well. If you're a student, look for student travel agencies in the capital cities of Costa Rica and Panama and in Cancún, Mexico.

Check www.visitcentroamerica.com, which has standard tourist-board coverage of all countries.

Visas

At present citizens of the USA, EU, Canada, Australia, New Zealand and many other nations can arrive in all Central American countries (including Mexico) without arranging a visa beforehand. Check ahead from your country before planning your trip, as this may change.

Many countries charge an entry or tourist fee upon arrival – from US$5 to US$20.

Note that, if you need a visa for a certain country and arrive at a land border without one, you will probably have to return to the nearest town that has a consulate and obtain a visa. Airlines will not normally let you board a plane to a country for which you don't have the necessary visa. Also, a visa in itself may not guarantee entry: in rare cases, you may still be turned back at the border if you don't have sufficient funds (p738) for your visit or an onward or return ticket (p741).

Sufficient Funds & Onward Tickets

Having your passport checked is a routine procedure upon arrival in a country, but some officials may ask about your financial resources, either verbally or on the application form. If you lack 'sufficient funds' for your proposed visit, officials may limit the length of your stay. (US$500 per month for your planned stay is generally considered sufficient; traveler's checks, and sometimes a credit card, should qualify toward the total amount.)

Several Central American countries require you to have an onward ticket (p741) leaving the country.

Visa Extensions

Once you are inside a country, you can always apply for a visa extension at the country's immigration office (*migración*). There's usually a limit to how many extensions you can receive; if you leave the country and reenter, your time starts over again.

Volunteering

Voluntourism allows travelers to learn more about a place

they visit and – ideally – 'give back' to the host community.

Some international organizations make arrangements for volunteers, which can be an expensive endeavor. You can also find local volunteer opportunities once in the country (although advance arrangements are still recommended). Be aware that most volunteer opportunities require a minimum time commitment; volunteers also usually pay a fixed fee to cover room and board.

On offer are programs to teach English, pick up trash, work on farms, construct homes, maintain trails, monitor turtle-nesting beaches, care for rescue animals and assist at medical clinics. Volunteer opportunities are often in isolated locations, and may involve long hours and grueling work. But the work can also be tremendously rewarding.

Lonely Planet strongly encourages those considering volunteering to do research and make informed, responsible choices.

International Volunteer Organizations

Some of these international organizations offer the chance to get college credit or take Spanish classes as a part of the volunteer opportunity.

Lonely Planet does not vouch for these organizations and strongly recommends travelers always investigate a volunteer opportunity themselves to assess the standards and suitability of the project.

Amigos de las Américas (www.amigosinternational.org) Youth-oriented summer programs range from working in a national park to helping with community development in Costa Rica and Panama.

Habitat for Humanity (www.habitat.org) Help with home construction, clean air and water projects or community development.

Idealist (www.idealist.org) A forum for advertising volunteering opportunities, internships and jobs around the world.

International Volunteer Programs Association (www.volunteerinternational.org) Does not run its own programs, but partners with other associations to recruit volunteers and ensure a rewarding experience.

ResponsibleTravel (www.responsibletravel.com) UK-based, ecofriendly tour operator with many volunteer trips.

STA Travel (www.statravel.com) A worldwide student-travel agent that offers trips with a volunteering element.

Transitions Abroad (www.transitionsabroad.com) Has numerous volunteer links; look on its website under Central America.

Women Travelers

Women traveling solo through Central America typically find that popular perceptions overestimate the dangers they face. The biggest adjustment is getting used to the vocal male population, many of whom hoot, hiss and whistle. Ignore this behavior and most of the time you will be simply left alone.

Of course, women should take all the normal precautions they would in any new territory or big city. Dress according to local norms to avoid unwanted attention (often this means avoiding shorts). Talk to locals to find out which areas may be dangerous. Certain bars and soccer games tend to be testosterone-fueled territory where a woman's presence will invite attention.

Locals, particularly families, will often go out of their way to help a single female traveler. Keep in mind, though, that it's more typical for Latin American women to socialize with other women, and women in Central America's more conservative societies rarely have male friends – so befriending someone's husband can attract resentment. Socializing with men here in general is a little unusual – it's probable that they will think you want more than friendship.

In the case of sexual assault, contact your embassy and see a doctor.

Work

According to law you must have a permit to work in Central America. In practice, people may get paid under the table or through some bureaucratic loophole, if they can find suitable work. Many travelers work short-term jobs (through the aforementioned loophole) for subsistence wages in restaurants, hostels or bars geared to international travelers. Before taking such a job, consider volunteering instead, as many of these jobs could just as well be performed by locals.

Teaching English is another option, though bear in mind that wages do not match international standards. Big cities offer the best possibilities for schools or private tutoring. Many schools will require Teaching English as a Foreign Language (TEFL) teaching certificates.

Some international organizations publish job opportunities.

Transportation

GETTING THERE & AWAY

Most visitors reach Central America by air or overland from Mexico. Flights, cars and tours can be booked online at lonelyplanet.com/bookings.

Entering the Region

Make sure your passport is valid for at least six months past your arrival date and has plenty of blank pages for stamp-happy officials. Always keep it with you while traveling between destinations.

Air

All Central American countries have international airports. Other than flights from South America, most arriving flights go via US gateways (particularly Houston, Miami or New York's JFK) or Mexico City.

International Airports

MEXICO

Aeropuerto Internacional de Cancún (CUN; Cancún; ☎998-848-72-00; www.asur.com.mx; Hwy 307 Km 22)

GUATEMALA

Aeropuerto Internacional La Aurora (GUA; Guatemala City; Map p114; ☎2260-6257)

Aeropuerto Internacional Mundo Maya (FRS: Flores)

BELIZE

Philip Goldson International Airport (BZE;Belize City; ☎225-2045; www.pgiabelize.com)

EL SALVADOR

Monseñor Óscar Arnulfo Romero International Airport (SAL; San Salvador; ☎2349-9455; www.elsalvadorinternational.com)

HONDURAS

Aeropuerto Internacional Ramón Villeda Morales (SAP; San Pedro Sula; ☎6689-3261)

Aeropuerto Internacional Toncontín (TGU; Tegucigalpa; ☎2234-0106; www.interairports.hn; CA-5)

Aeropuerto Juan Ramón Galvez (RTB; Roatán; ☎2445-1880)

NICARAGUA

Managua International Airport (MGA; Managua; www.eaai.com.ni; Carretera Norte Km 11)

COSTA RICA

Aeropuerto Internacional Juan Santamaría (SJO; San José; ☎2437-2400; www.fly2sanjose.com)

CLIMATE CHANGE & TRAVEL

Every form of transport that relies on carbon-based fuel generates CO_2, the main cause of human-induced climate change. Modern travel is dependent on airplanes, which might use less fuel per kilometer per person than most cars but travel much greater distances. The altitude at which aircraft emit gases (including CO_2) and particles also contributes to their climate change impact. Many websites offer 'carbon calculators' that allow people to estimate the carbon emissions generated by their journey and, for those who wish to do so, to offset the impact of the greenhouse gases emitted with contributions to portfolios of climate-friendly initiatives throughout the world. Lonely Planet offsets the carbon footprint of all staff and author travel.

Aeropuerto Internacional Daniel Oduber Quirós (LIR; Liberia; www.liberiacostaricaairport.net)

PANAMA

Tocumen International Airport (PTY; Panama City; ☎238-2700; www.tocumenpanama.aero; Av Domingo Díaz; ⌚24hr)

Aeropuerto Enrique Malek (DAV; David; ☎721-1072)

Departure Tax

All seven Central American countries levy departure taxes on air passengers, ranging from US$29 to US$40, although they are usually included in the price of the ticket.

Tickets

Central America's slender isthmus shape makes 'open-jaw' tickets – flying into one place (say Cancún or Guatemala City) and out from another (eg Panama City) – an attractive option, and the good news is that it's often not much more expensive than a round-trip ticket. If you're flexible on where you start and end, shop around: discount fares come and go.

You might think going to a hub city, such as San Salvador on Avianca, would save money, but sometimes it's *more* expensive. The reason – in the confusing world of airline ticket pricing – is that airlines are trying to compete with more direct options. Again, shop around.

High-season rates (generally July and August, Christmas to New Year, and around Semana Santa) can be considerably more expensive.

Student travel agencies such as **STA Travel** (www.statravel.com) offer student discounts for those under 26.

If you're flying from Europe or Australia, the chances are you can get a free stopover in a US gateway city such as Los Angeles or Miami.

ONWARD-TICKET REQUIREMENTS

If you're planning on flying into one country and back from another, note that immigration officials may require proof of onward or continuing travel. The restriction mainly ensures that nonresidents don't stay long-term without permission.

Showing 'continuing travel' to another country (say, a flight home) and explaining how you'll get there is almost always enough. Most travelers are never asked. It's still a good idea to ask the airlines, as they can be fined for bringing in a passenger without proper documentation. Also, it may be worth showing a print-out of a 'bus reservation' for leaving the country.

This requirement also may pop up at land borders. Crossing into Costa Rica, for instance, it's sometimes necessary to purchase a bus ticket at the border leaving Costa Rica – even if you don't plan to use it. For private cars entering, no onward ticket is required but proper documentation for the vehicle is needed.

ROUND-THE-WORLD TICKETS

Round-the-world (RTW) tickets are an option, as all Central American countries (and Mexico) are served by the largest provider, Star Alliance.

FROM SOUTH AMERICA

Avianca (Colombia; www.avianca.com) and **Copa Airlines** (Panama; www.copaair.com) connect Central American cities to Argentina, Bolivia, Brazil, Chile, Colombia, Ecuador and Peru.

If you're planning to visit both Central America and South America on a trip, note that some airlines allow a free stopover in Central America. Panama City is often the cheapest link to and from South America, especially Colombia, Ecuador and Venezuela (unsurprisingly, given their distance from Panama).

Note that many South American countries require onward air tickets upon arrival.

Land

From Mexico

BUS

It's possible to take a bus from the US or Canada into Mexico and directly into Central America. The three most convenient land borders between Mexico and Central America:

- The Chetumal–Corozal (Belize) border in Quintana Roo (Yucatán Peninsula).
- The Ciudad Cuauhtémoc–La Mesilla (Guatemala) border.
- The Ciudad Hidalgo–Ciudad Tecún Umán (Guatemala) border in Chiapas state (about 38km south of Tapachula).

CAR & MOTORCYCLE

Most people driving to Central America do so from the US (or Canada). Buying a car in the region (including Mexico) is very complicated: you're better off bringing a car (with all the ownership papers) from North America.

Prior to departure, purchase liability insurance that is valid in Mexico, such as **Oscar Padilla Mexican Insurance** (☎North America 800-466-7227; www.mexicaninsurance.com). Make sure you bring your documentation, as you'll have to show it at the border. Mandatory insurance is for sale at the border as you enter Belize, Nicaragua, Costa Rica and Panama.

Insurance is not required in El Salvador, Guatemala or Honduras.

Drive the Americas (www.drivetheamericas.com) is an excellent resource, with trip planning tips, vehicle recommendations, vehicle sales, road-tripper profiles and active forums for asking and answering questions.

A few other pre-trip considerations:

- You will need a valid driver's license from your home country.
- Unleaded gas (petrol) is now available throughout Central America.
- Make sure that your car's shock absorbers and suspension are in good shape for the bumpy roads.
- A spare fuel filter – and other spare parts – could be invaluable.
- Check with a national tourist board or consulate for any changes to the rules on bringing a car into Mexico, or Central America, before showing up in your vehicle.

From South America

There are no road connections between South America and Central America (via Panama). Instability in the Panama–Colombia border region, plus the difficulty of travel, have essentially made the trip over the Darién Gap an impossibility. All visitors to the Darién must register with the police.

Sea

Unless you're a yachtie or on a cruise ship, options for boat travel heading to/from the region are limited. The most popular route is taking a (shared) chartered sailboat between the Archipiélago de San Blas, Panama and Cartagena in Colombia (US$550 per person). The five-day trip usually includes a few days on the islands and two days' transit to/from Colombia. There is also a shorter route to/from the border town of La Miel, Colombia and nearby Sapzurro, Colombia (US$400 per person). For more information about the journey, contact the following.

Blue Sailing (☎Cartagena 57-5-668-6485, USA 203-660-8644; www.bluesailing.net) This company keeps the schedule for more than a dozen boats that sail between Colombia and Panama. Look online to see photos of the boats, to learn about the captains and to book the trips.

Sail Colombia Panama (☎Colombia 57-312-214-4844; www.sailcolombiapanama.com) Does sailing trips to Colombia out of Puerto Lindo, Portobelo and El Porvenir, with an option for a (pricier) private cabin.

Casa Viena (☎Cartagena 57-320-538-3619; www.casaviena.com) A Cartagena hostel that helps with boat trips to Panama.

Sailing Koala (☎Cartagena 57-322-516-3359; www.sailingkoala.com) A recommended sailing operation.

Mamallena Tours (☎Panama 507-6676-6163; www.mamallena.com) This tour company – based at the hostels of the same name in Panama City and Cartagena – organizes sailing trips between the two countries, via San Blas.

Note that cargo boats are a risky business; smuggling is common on the Colón–Cartagena cargo route.

GETTING AROUND

Buses are the cheapest and most accessible way to get around, particularly along the Pan-American Hwy (also called the Panamericana or Interamericana), which runs through all the countries except Belize.

Air

Many flights connect the region, run by international carriers as well as the national airlines. Some smaller domestic airlines provide services too. Occasionally it will be necessary to change planes in the carrier's hub city (eg a Managua–Panama City flight may change planes up north in San Salvador).

Cost is an obstacle. Despite relatively short distances, individual one-way and round-trip tickets within Central America (whether bought abroad or within the region) can be expensive.

- Flights can sometimes be overbooked; reconfirm your ticket before arriving at the airport.
- Airfares can vary wildly – depending on the length of stay, time of year and special promotions – so treat high-season fares as a rough gauge only in identifying potential routes.
- Note that San Salvador and San José are the most popular hubs. Occasionally a promotional return flight may be even cheaper than a one-way fare.
- Worthwhile domestic flights include Managua to Nicaragua's Corn Islands (about US$165 return), which saves a two-day bus/boat trip each way. Flights within Panama and Costa Rica can also be cheap.

Bicycle

Long-distance cycling in the region can be dangerous, as few drivers are accustomed to sharing narrow streets in cities, or often-shoulderless two-lane highways, with bicycles. That said, cycling is on an upswing, with mountain rides and coffee-plantation tours (including guide and bike) available all over Central America.

You can rent bicycles in several cities and traveler hangouts, such as San Cristóbal de Las Casas (Mexico), Flores (Guatemala), Granada (Nicaragua), La Fortuna (Costa Rica) and Panama City. There are many mountain-bike tours available (notably in cooler locales such as Guatemala's highlands and San Cristóbal de Las Casas). Consider the seasons if you're planning to cycle a lot. The dry season (roughly December to April) should spare you from getting soaked.

If you're planning to cycle across borders, keep a document proving your ownership of the bike handy for immigration officials.

Check out **El Pedalero** (www.elpedalero.com) to read cyclist Gareth Collingwood's adventures and tips on cycling around Latin America.

Boat

Traveling by boat is a common way to get around the region, including several border crossings:

- Travelers between Palenque, Mexico, and Flores, Guatemala, cross the Río Usumacinta near Frontera Corozal, Mexico, and Bethel, Guatemala.
- There is a regular water taxi between Punta Gorda, Belize, and Puerto Barrios (and sometimes Lívingston), Guatemala.
- A newer weekly boat services make trips between Placencia, Belize, and Puerto Cortes, Honduras, and Belize City and Puerto Cortes (via Dangriga, Belize).
- There's a river border crossing between San Carlos, Nicaragua, and Los Chiles, Costa Rica, though nowadays most folks use the new bridge at Las Tablillas.

Key domestic water journeys include the ride down the Río Dulce in Guatemala, or down the Río Escondidas to Bluefields, Nicaragua, and then out to the Corn Islands in the Caribbean.

Other Caribbean islands reached by boat include the Bay Islands in Honduras; Caye Caulker and Ambergris Caye in Belize; and Cozumel and Isla Mujeres in Mexico. And of course, the Panama Canal is one of the world's most important waterways, connecting the Caribbean and the Pacific.

Bus

Some of the most memorable moments of your trip will come from bus rides. Bus service is well developed throughout the region, though not always comfortable. While some buses are air-conditioned with reserved seats that may recline, many others are colorfully repainted former US school buses (aka 'chicken buses'), with a liberal policy toward lugging merchandise (though it's unlikely you'll have to share your seat with a chicken).

Avoid night buses throughout the region (with the possible exception of Mexico and Panama), as these have been popular targets for highway robbers.

First-class and some 2nd-class buses depart on scheduled times from a *terminal de autobuses* (long-distance bus station); others leave from parking-lot bus terminals once they are full (these stop to collect more passengers all along the way – so you're likely to be able to get a lift from the highway if need be). Be aware that many cities have more than one bus station. Bus companies can have their own terminals as well. Departure frequency varies.

Luggage may be stored in a lower compartment or piled on the roof of the bus. Keep an eye on your luggage if you can, particularly on the easily accessible racks in a packed bus. Always keep your valuables tucked away on your person. Watch out for pickpockets on crowded buses and in bus stations.

In some places, travel agents run private shuttle services (mostly vans with air-con) to popular destinations. They're more comfortable and more expensive than public buses.

Colectivos & Minibuses

Connecting hub towns with smaller ones on short-haul trips is an array of minibuses

BUS DURATIONS

Remember that bus connections and border-crossing formalities can add extra time to the trip.

ORIGIN	DESTINATION	DURATION (HR)
Cancún, Mexico	Belize City	9-10
Flores, Guatemala	Guatemala City	8-10
Guatemala City	Copán Ruinas, Honduras	5
Managua, Nicaragua	San José, Costa Rica	9
San Cristóbal de Las Casas, Mexico	Antigua, Guatemala	11
San José, Costa Rica	Panama City	14
San Salvador, El Salvador	Tegucigalpa, Honduras	8
Tegucigalpa, Honduras	Managua, Nicaragua	8

TIPS FOR BORDER CROSSINGS

Going from one of Central America's seven countries (or Mexico) into another can be a frenetic, confusing experience. But with a little planning it's usually a breeze (make that a *slo-o-ow* breeze). Some considerations:

➡ Before you leave one country for another, read up on your destination's entry requirements.

➡ Don't leave a country without getting your passport stamped at that country's immigration office. Occasionally, agents are not vigilant so be on the lookout.

➡ Crossings often require changing buses at the border, walking a few hundred meters across, or catching a *colectivo* (shared taxi or minibus taxi) to the nearest bus station. Not all of the borders are open 24 hours, but bus schedules tend to match opening hours.

➡ Money changers linger around nearly all borders; rates can be fair but some changers try to shortchange, so count carefully.

(called *rapidito* in Honduras, *chiva* in Panama, and *colectivo* in Costa Rica and Mexico). When available, these are cheaper than 1st-class buses and run frequently. The catch: they also make frequent stops and the driver rarely considers them full.

Car & Motorcycle

A drive through Central America will likely offer an amazing trip, but it's unlikely to save you money. In addition to fees, there's paperwork, tolls, parking concerns and other red tape. Border crossings are a particular hassle. You'll also need to be prepared to stop for passport checks at military checkpoints. Also, highway robberies aren't unknown, so avoid driving at night.

Driver's Licenses

To drive in Central America, you must have a valid driver's license from your home country or an International Driving Permit (IDP), which is issued by automobile associations worldwide.

Be prepared for police checkpoints – always stop and have your papers handy.

Rental

Central America is relatively easy to explore by private vehicle. This option would be more popular if it weren't for the cost (rental, insurance and fuel). Rentals range from about US$15 per day in Nicaragua to US$55 per day in Belize, but 4WD vehicles are more expensive (generally US$30 to US$80). If your goal in renting a car is to reach some otherwise unreachable areas (such as isolated beaches south of Tulum in Mexico and around Costa Rica's Península de Nicoya), it's worth paying for a 4WD: paved roads only go so far.

➡ At the time of research, the price of gas ranged from about US$0.87 (in Panama) to US$2.99 (in Belize) per liter.

➡ In many cases it's cheaper to arrange (even same-day) rentals with major car-rental agencies on their websites.

➡ To rent a car, you'll need a passport and a driver's license.

➡ Some agencies rent to those 21 and over; others to only those 25 and over.

➡ All of Central America drives on the right-hand side of the road.

➡ Rented cars are usually not allowed to leave the country – though Budget, for example, allows travel from Guatemala to Mexico, Honduras and El Salvador, with some restrictions.

➡ Scooters and bigger motorcycles are available in some places, the latter usually costing about the same price as a compact car.

Rental Insurance

Mandatory insurance is a huge add-on to the cost of car rental in most Central American countries, and your insurance policy back home is not accepted here. The (usually) mandatory Collision Damage Waiver (CDW) can double your daily rate, while many companies will give a hard sell for more expensive comprehensive insurance. If your credit card provides insurance on car rentals, be sure to bring the documentation to prove it; in most cases, you'll still have to pay for the CDW.

Hitchhiking

Hitchhiking (*tomando un jalón* – literally 'taking a hitch') is never entirely safe in any country in the world, and Lonely Planet does not recommend it. However, it is common in parts of Central America. Travelers who hitchhike should understand that they are taking a small but potentially serious risk. If you do get a ride, it is polite to offer to pay gas money, even though the driver may turn it down.

Language

Latin American Spanish is the language of choice for travelers in all of Central America except for Belize (where English is the official language, but both Spanish and a local Creole are also widely spoken). Maya and Náhuatl are the most common of a number of indigenous languages spoken throughout the region.

Latin American Spanish pronunciation is easy, as most sounds are also found in English. Note that kh is a throaty sound (like the 'ch' in the Scottish *loch*), v and b are similar to the English 'b' but softer (between a 'v' and a 'b'), and r is strongly rolled. There are some variations in spoken Spanish across Central America, the most notable being the pronunciation of the letters *ll* and *y*. In our pronunciation guides they are represented with y because they are pronounced as the 'y' in 'yes' in most of Central America. In some parts of the region, though, you may hear them pronounced like the 'lli' in 'million'. If you read our colored pronunciation guides as if they were English, you'll be understood. The stressed syllables are indicated with italics in our pronunciation guides.

Where both polite and informal options are given in this section, they are indicated by the abbreviations 'pol' and 'inf'. The masculine and feminine forms are indicated with 'm' and 'f' respectively.

> **WANT MORE?**
>
> For in-depth language information and handy phrases, check out Lonely Planet's *Latin American Spanish Phrasebook*, *Mexican Spanish Phrasebook* and *Costa Rican Spanish Phrasebook*. You'll find them at **shop.lonelyplanet.com**, or you can buy Lonely Planet's iPhone phrasebooks at the Apple App Store.

BASICS

Hello.	*Hola.*	o·la
Goodbye.	*Adiós.*	a·*dyos*
How are you?	*¿Qué tal?*	ke tal
Fine, thanks.	*Bien, gracias.*	byen *gra*·syas
Excuse me.	*Perdón.*	per·*don*
Sorry.	*Lo siento.*	lo *syen*·to
Please.	*Por favor.*	por fa·*vor*
Thank you.	*Gracias.*	*gra*·syas
You are welcome.	*De nada.*	de *na*·da
Yes.	*Sí.*	see
No.	*No.*	no

My name is ...
Me llamo ... me *ya*·mo ...

What's your name?
¿Cómo se llama usted? ko·mo se *ya*·ma oo·*ste* (pol)
¿Cómo te llamas? ko·mo te *ya*·mas (inf)

Do you speak English?
¿Habla inglés? a·bla een·*gles* (pol)
¿Hablas inglés? a·blas een·*gles* (inf)

I don't understand.
Yo no entiendo. yo no en·*tyen*·do

ACCOMMODATIONS

I'd like a single/double room.
Quisiera una habitación individual/doble. kee·*sye*·ra *oo*·na a·bee·ta·*syon* een·dee·vee·*dwal*/*do*·ble

How much is it per night/person?
¿Cuánto cuesta por noche/persona? *kwan*·to *kwes*·ta por *no*·che/per·*so*·na

Does it include breakfast?
¿Incluye el desayuno? een·*kloo*·ye el de·sa·*yoo*·no

air-con	*aire acondicionado*	ai·re a·kon·dee·syo·*na*·do
bathroom	*baño*	*ba*·nyo
bed	*cama*	*ka*·ma
campsite	*terreno de cámping*	te·re·no de *kam*·peeng
guesthouse	*pensión*	pen·*syon*
hotel	*hotel*	o·*tel*
youth hostel	*albergue juvenil*	al·*ber*·ge khoo·ve·*neel*
window	*ventana*	ven·*ta*·na

DIRECTIONS

Where is ...?
¿Dónde está ...? — don·de es·*ta* ...

What's the address?
¿Cuál es la dirección? — kwal es la dee·rek·*syon*

Could you please write it down?
¿Puede escribirlo, por favor? — *pwe*·de es·kree·*beer*·lo por fa·*vor*

Can you show me (on the map)?
¿Me lo puede indicar (en el mapa)? — me lo *pwe*·de een·dee·*kar* (en el *ma*·pa)

at the corner	*en la esquina*	en la es·*kee*·na
at the traffic lights	*en el semáforo*	en el se·*ma*·fo·ro
behind ...	*detrás de ...*	de·*tras* de ...
in front of ...	*enfrente de ...*	en·*fren*·te de ...
left	*izquierda*	ees·*kyer*·da
next to ...	*al lado de ...*	al *la*·do de ...
opposite ...	*frente a ...*	*fren*·te a ...
right	*derecha*	de·*re*·cha
straight ahead	*todo recto*	*to*·do *rek*·to

EATING & DRINKING

Can I see the menu, please?
¿Puedo ver el menú, por favor? — *pwe*·do ver el me·*noo* por fa·*vor*

What would you recommend?
¿Qué recomienda? — ke re·ko·*myen*·da

Do you have vegetarian food?
¿Tienen comida vegetariana? — *tye*·nen ko·*mee*·da ve·khe·ta·*rya*·na

I don't eat (red meat).
No como (carne roja). — no *ko*·mo (*kar*·ne *ro*·kha)

That was delicious!
¡Estaba buenísimo! — es·*ta*·ba bwe·*nee*·see·mo

Cheers!
¡Salud! — sa·*loo*

The bill, please.
La cuenta, por favor. — la *kwen*·ta por fa·*vor*

KEY PATTERNS

To get by in Spanish, mix and match these simple patterns with words of your choice:

When's (the next flight)?
¿Cuándo sale (el próximo vuelo)? — *kwan*·do *sa*·le (el *prok*·see·mo *vwe*·lo)

Where's (the station)?
¿Dónde está (la estación)? — *don*·de es·*ta* (la es·ta·*syon*)

Where can I (buy a ticket)?
¿Dónde puedo (comprar un billete)? — *don*·de *pwe*·do (kom·*prar* oon bee·*ye*·te)

Do you have (a map)?
¿Tiene (un mapa)? — *tye*·ne (oon *ma*·pa)

Is there (a toilet)?
¿Hay (servicios)? — ai (ser·*vee*·syos)

I'd like (a coffee).
Quisiera (un café). — kee·*sye*·ra (oon ka·*fe*)

I'd like (to hire a car).
Quisiera (alquilar un coche). — kee·*sye*·ra (al·kee·*lar* oon *ko*·che)

Can I (enter)?
¿Se puede (entrar)? — se *pwe*·de (en·*trar*)

Could you please (help me)?
¿Puede (ayudarme), por favor? — *pwe*·de (a·yoo·*dar*·me) por fa·*vor*

Do I have to (get a visa)?
¿Necesito (obtener un visado)? — ne·se·*see*·to (ob·te·*ner* oon vee·*sa*·do)

I'd like a table for ...	*Quisiera una mesa para ...*	kee·*sye*·ra *oo*·na *me*·sa *pa*·ra ...
(eight) o'clock	*las (ocho)*	las (*o*·cho)
(two) people	*(dos) personas*	(dos) per·*so*·nas

Key Words

appetisers	*aperitivos*	a·pe·ree·*tee*·vos
bottle	*botella*	bo·*te*·ya
bowl	*bol*	bol
breakfast	*desayuno*	de·sa·*yoo*·no
children's menu	*menú infantil*	me·*noo* een·fan·*teel*
(too) cold	*(muy) frío*	(mooy) *free*·o
dinner	*cena*	*se*·na
food	*comida*	ko·*mee*·da

fork	*tenedor*	te·ne·*dor*
glass	*vaso*	*va*·so
hot (warm)	*caliente*	kal·*yen*·te
knife	*cuchillo*	koo·*chee*·yo
lunch	*comida*	ko·*mee*·da
main course	*segundo plato*	se·*goon*·do *pla*·to
plate	*plato*	*pla*·to
restaurant	*restaurante*	res·tow·*ran*·te
spoon	*cuchara*	koo·*cha*·ra
with	*con*	kon
without	*sin*	seen

Meat & Fish

beef	*carne de vaca*	*kar*·ne de *va*·ka
chicken	*pollo*	*po*·yo
duck	*pato*	*pa*·to
lamb	*cordero*	kor·*de*·ro
lobster	*langosta*	lan·*gos*·ta
pork	*cerdo*	*ser*·do
shrimps	*camarones*	ka·ma·*ro*·nes
tuna	*atún*	a·*toon*
turkey	*pavo*	*pa*·vo
veal	*ternera*	ter·*ne*·ra

Fruit & Vegetables

apple	*manzana*	man·*sa*·na
apricot	*albaricoque*	al·ba·ree·*ko*·ke
artichoke	*alcachofa*	al·ka·*cho*·fa
asparagus	*espárragos*	es·*pa*·ra·gos
banana	*plátano*	*pla*·ta·no
beans	*judías*	khoo·*dee*·as
beetroot	*remolacha*	re·mo·*la*·cha
cabbage	*col*	kol
carrot	*zanahoria*	sa·na·*o*·rya
celery	*apio*	*a*·pyo
cherry	*cereza*	se·*re*·sa
corn	*maíz*	ma·*ees*
cucumber	*pepino*	pe·*pee*·no
grape	*uvas*	*oo*·vas
lemon	*limón*	lee·*mon*
lentils	*lentejas*	len·*te*·khas
lettuce	*lechuga*	le·*choo*·ga
mushroom	*champiñón*	cham·pee·*nyon*
nuts	*nueces*	*nwe*·ses
onion	*cebolla*	se·*bo*·ya
orange	*naranja*	na·*ran*·kha
peach	*melocotón*	me·lo·ko·*ton*
peas	*guisantes*	gee·*san*·tes
pepper (bell)	*pimiento*	pee·*myen*·to
pineapple	*piña*	*pee*·nya
plum	*ciruela*	seer·*we*·la
potato	*patata*	pa·*ta*·ta
pumpkin	*calabaza*	ka·la·*ba*·sa
spinach	*espinacas*	es·pee·*na*·kas
strawberry	*fresa*	*fre*·sa
tomato	*tomate*	to·*ma*·te
watermelon	*sandía*	san·*dee*·a

Other

bread	*pan*	pan
butter	*mantequilla*	man·te·*kee*·ya
cheese	*queso*	*ke*·so
egg	*huevo*	*we*·vo
honey	*miel*	myel
jam	*mermelada*	mer·me·*la*·da
oil	*aceite*	a·*sey*·te
pasta	*pasta*	*pas*·ta
pepper	*pimienta*	pee·*myen*·ta
rice	*arroz*	a·*ros*
salt	*sal*	sal
sugar	*azúcar*	a·*soo*·kar
vinegar	*vinagre*	vee·*na*·gre

Drinks

beer	*cerveza*	ser·*ve*·sa
coffee	*café*	ka·*fe*
(orange) juice	*zumo (de naranja)*	*soo*·mo (de na·*ran*·kha)
milk	*leche*	*le*·che
red wine	*vino tinto*	*vee*·no *teen*·to
tea	*té*	te
(mineral) water	*agua (mineral)*	*a*·gwa (mee·ne·*ral*)
white wine	*vino blanco*	*vee*·no *blan*·ko

SIGNS

Abierto	Open
Cerrado	Closed
Entrada	Entrance
Hombres/Varones	Men
Mujeres/Damas	Women
Prohibido	Prohibited
Salida	Exit
Servicios/Baños	Toilets

EMERGENCIES

Help!	*¡Socorro!*	so·*ko*·ro
Go away!	*¡Vete!*	*ve*·te

Call ...!	*¡Llame a ...!*	*ya*·me a ...
a doctor	*un médico*	oon *me*·dee·ko
the police	*la policía*	la po·lee·*see*·a

I'm lost.
Estoy perdido/a. — es·*toy* per·*dee*·do/a (m/f)

Where are the toilets?
¿Dónde están los baños? — *don*·de es·*tan* los *ba*·nyos

I'm ill.
Estoy enfermo/a. — es·*toy* en·*fer*·mo/a (m/f)

I'm allergic to (antibiotics).
Soy alérgico/a a (los antibióticos). — soy a·*ler*·khee·ko/a a (los an·tee·*byo*·tee·kos) (m/f)

SHOPPING & SERVICES

What time does it open/close?
¿A qué hora abre/cierra? — a ke *o*·ra *ab*·re/*sye*·ra

I'd like to buy ...
Quisiera comprar ... — kee·*sye*·ra kom·*prar* ...

I'm just looking.
Sólo estoy mirando. — *so*·lo es·*toy* mee·*ran*·do

Can I look at it?
¿Puedo verlo? — *pwe*·do *ver*·lo

I don't like it.
No me gusta. — no me *goos*·ta

How much is it?
¿Cuánto cuesta? — *kwan*·to *kwes*·ta

That's too expensive.
Es muy caro. — es mooy *ka*·ro

Can you lower the price?
¿Podría bajar un poco el precio? — po·*dree*·a ba·*khar* oon *po*·ko el *pre*·syo

There's a mistake in the bill.
Hay un error en la cuenta. — ai oon e·*ror* en la *kwen*·ta

QUESTION WORDS

How?	*¿Cómo?*	*ko*·mo
What?	*¿Qué?*	ke
When?	*¿Cuándo?*	*kwan*·do
Where?	*¿Dónde?*	*don*·de
Which?	*¿Cuál?* (sg) *¿Cuáles?* (pl)	kwal *kwa*·les
Who?	*¿Quién?*	kyen
Why?	*¿Por qué?*	por ke

ATM	*cajero automático*	ka·*khe*·ro ow·to·*ma*·tee·ko
market	*mercado*	mer·*ka*·do
post office	*correos*	ko·*re*·os
tourist office	*oficina de turismo*	o·fee·*see*·na de too·*rees*·mo

TIME & DATES

What time is it?
¿Qué hora es? — ke *o*·ra es

It's (10) o'clock.
Son (las diez). — son (las dyes)

It's half past (one).
Es (la una) y media. — es (la *oo*·na) ee *me*·dya

morning	*mañana*	ma·*nya*·na
afternoon	*tarde*	*tar*·de
evening	*noche*	*no*·che
yesterday	*ayer*	a·*yer*
today	*hoy*	oy
tomorrow	*mañana*	ma·*nya*·na

Monday	*lunes*	*loo*·nes
Tuesday	*martes*	*mar*·tes
Wednesday	*miércoles*	*myer*·ko·les
Thursday	*jueves*	*khwe*·ves
Friday	*viernes*	*vyer*·nes
Saturday	*sábado*	*sa*·ba·do
Sunday	*domingo*	do·*meen*·go

January	*enero*	e·*ne*·ro
February	*febrero*	fe·*bre*·ro
March	*marzo*	*mar*·so
April	*abril*	a·*breel*
May	*mayo*	*ma*·yo
June	*junio*	*khoon*·yo
July	*julio*	*khool*·yo
August	*agosto*	a·*gos*·to
September	*septiembre*	sep·*tyem*·bre
October	*octubre*	ok·*too*·bre
November	*noviembre*	no·*vyem*·bre
December	*diciembre*	dee·*syem*·bre

TRANSPORTATION

boat	*barco*	*bar*·ko
bus	*autobús*	ow·to·*boos*
plane	*avión*	a·*vyon*
train	*tren*	tren
first	*primero*	pree·*me*·ro
last	*último*	*ool*·tee·mo

NUMBERS

1	*uno*	oo·no
2	*dos*	dos
3	*tres*	tres
4	*cuatro*	*kwa*·tro
5	*cinco*	*seen*·ko
6	*seis*	seys
7	*siete*	*sye*·te
8	*ocho*	*o*·cho
9	*nueve*	*nwe*·ve
10	*diez*	dyes
20	*veinte*	*veyn*·te
30	*treinta*	*treyn*·ta
40	*cuarenta*	kwa·*ren*·ta
50	*cincuenta*	seen·*kwen*·ta
60	*sesenta*	se·*sen*·ta
70	*setenta*	se·*ten*·ta
80	*ochenta*	o·*chen*·ta
90	*noventa*	no·*ven*·ta
100	*cien*	syen
1000	*mil*	meel

next	*próximo*	*prok*·see·mo
airport	*aeropuerto*	a·e·ro·*pwer*·to
aisle seat	*asiento de pasillo*	a·*syen*·to de pa·*see*·yo
bus stop	*parada de autobuses*	pa·*ra*·da de ow·to·*boo*·ses
cancelled	*cancelado*	kan·se·*la*·do
delayed	*retrasado*	re·tra·*sa*·do
ticket office	*taquilla*	ta·*kee*·ya
timetable	*horario*	o·*ra*·ryo
train station	*estación de trenes*	es·ta·*syon* de *tre*·nes
window seat	*asiento junto a la ventana*	a·*syen*·to *khoon*·to a la ven·*ta*·na

A ... ticket, please.	*Un billete de ..., por favor.*	oon bee·*ye*·te de ... por fa·*vor*
1st-class	*primera clase*	pree·*me*·ra *kla*·se
2nd-class	*segunda clase*	se·*goon*·da *kla*·se
one-way	*ida*	*ee*·da
return	*ida y vuelta*	*ee*·da ee *vwel*·ta

What time does it arrive/leave?
¿A qué hora llega/sale? a ke *o*·ra *ye*·ga/*sa*·le

Does it stop at ...?
¿Para en ...? pa·ra en ...

Which stop is this?
¿Cuál es esta parada? kwal es *es*·ta pa·*ra*·da

Could you tell me when we get to ...?
¿Puede avisarme cuando lleguemos a ...? *pwe*·de a·vee·*sar*·me *kwan*·do ye·*ge*·mos a ...

I want to get off here.
Quiero bajarme aquí. *kye*·ro ba·*khar*·me a·*kee*

How much is it (to the airport)?
¿Cuánto cuesta ir (al aeropuerto)? *kwan*·to *kwes*·ta eer (al a·e·ro·*pwer*·to)

Please take me to (this address).
Por favor, lléveme a (esta dirección). por fa·*vor* *ye*·ve·me a (*es*·ta dee·rek·*syon*)

Driving & Cycling

I'd like to hire a ...	*Quisiera alquilar ...*	kee·*sye*·ra al·kee·*lar* ...
4WD	*un todo-terreno*	oon to·do·te·*re*·no
bicycle	*una bicicleta*	oo·na bee·see·*kle*·ta
car	*un coche*	oon *ko*·che
motorcycle	*una moto*	oo·na *mo*·to

child seat	*asiento de seguridad para niños*	a·*syen*·to de se·goo·ree·*da* *pa*·ra *nee*·nyos
diesel	*petróleo*	pet·*ro*·le·o
helmet	*casco*	*kas*·ko
mechanic	*mecánico*	me·*ka*·nee·ko
petrol/gas	*gasolina*	ga·so·*lee*·na
service station	*gasolinera*	ga·so·lee·*ne*·ra
truck	*camion*	ka·*myon*

Is this the road to ...?
¿Se va a ... por esta carretera? se va a ... por *es*·ta ka·re·*te*·ra

Can I park here?
¿Puedo aparcar aquí? *pwe*·do a·par·*kar* a·*kee*

The car has broken down.
El coche se ha averiado. el *ko*·che se a a·ve·*rya*·do

I had an accident.
He tenido un accidente. e te·*nee*·do oon ak·see·*den*·te

I've run out of petrol/gas.
Me he quedado sin gasolina. me e ke·*da*·do seen ga·so·*lee*·na

I have a flat tyre.
Se me pinchó una rueda. se me peen·*cho* *oo*·na *rwe*·da

GLOSSARY

alcaldía – mayor's office
apartado – post-office box
artesanía – handicraft
Av – abbreviation for avenida (avenue)
ayuntamiento – municipal government

bahía – bay
bajareque – traditional wall construction, where a core of stones is held in place by poles of bamboo or other wood then covered with stucco or mud
balneario – public beach or swimming area
barrio – district; neighborhood
Black Caribs – see *Garífuna*

caballeros – literally 'horsemen,' but corresponds to the English 'gentlemen'; look for the term on bathroom doors
cabaña – cabin or bungalow
cabina – see *cabaña;* also a loose term for cheap lodging in Costa Rica (in some cases it refers to cabins or bungalows, in others it refers merely to an economical hotel room)
cajero automático – automated teller machine (ATM)
calle – street
callejón – alley; small, narrow or very short street
calzada – causeway
camión – truck; bus
camioneta – pick-up truck
campesino – farmer
Carretera Interamericana – Interamerican Hwy, or Inter-americana (also referred to as the Pan-American Hwy, or Pan-americana); the nearly continuous highway running from Alaska to Chile (it breaks at the Darién Gap in Panama)
casa de cambio – currency exchange office
casa de huéspedes – guesthouse
cascada – waterfall
catedral – cathedral
cay – small island of sand or coral fragments; also caye, cayo
cayuco – dugout canoe
cenote – large, natural limestone cave used for water storage or ceremonial purposes
cerro – hill
cerveza – beer
Chac – Maya rain god; his likeness appears on many ruins
chac-mool – Maya sacrificial stone sculpture
chamarra – thick, heavy woolen blanket (Guatemala)
chapín – citizen of Guatemala; Guatemalan
chicken bus – former US school bus used for public transportation
cine – movie theater
ciudad – city
cofradía – Maya religious brotherhood, particularly in highland Guatemala
colectivo – shared taxi or minibus that picks up and drops off passengers along its route
colón – national currency of Costa Rica
comedor – basic and cheap eatery, usually with a limited menu
conquistador – any of the Spanish explorer-conquerors of Latin America
Contras – counterrevolutionary military groups fighting against the Sandinista government in Nicaragua throughout the 1980s
cordillera – mountain range
córdoba – national currency of Nicaragua
corte – piece of material 7m to 10m long that is used as a wraparound skirt
costa – coast
criollo – Creole; born in Latin America of Spanish parentage; on the Caribbean coast it refers to someone of mixed African and European descent; see also *mestizo* and *ladino*
cuadra – city block
cueva – cave

damas – ladies; the usual sign on bathroom doors

edificio – building
entrada – entrance
expreso – express bus

faja – waist sash that binds garments and holds what would otherwise be put in pockets
finca – farm; plantation; ranch
fritanga – sidewalk BBQ, widely seen in Nicaragua
fuerte – fort

Garífuna – descendants of West African slaves and Carib Indians, brought to the Caribbean coast of Central America in the late 18th century from the island of St Vincent; also referred to as *Black Caribs*
Garinagu – see *Garífuna*
gibnut – small, brown-spotted rodent similar to a guinea pig; also called *paca*
golfo – gulf
gringo/a – mildly pejorative term used in Latin America to describe male/female foreigners, particularly those from North America; often applied to any visitor of European heritage
gruta – cave

hacienda – agricultural estate or plantation; treasury, as in Departamento de Hacienda (Treasury Department)
hospedaje – guesthouse
huipil – long, woven, white sleeveless tunic with intricate, colorful embroidery (Maya regions)

iglesia – church
indígena – indigenous
Interamericana – see *Carretera Interamericana*
invierno – winter; Central America's wet season, which extends roughly from April through mid-December
isla – island
IVA – *impuesto al valor agregado;* value-added tax

ladino – person of mixed indigenous and European parentage, often used to describe a *mestizo* who speaks Spanish; see also *mestizo* and *criollo*

lago – lake

laguna – lagoon; lake

lancha – small motorboat

lempira – national currency of Honduras

malecón – waterfront promenade

mar – sea

marimba – xylophonelike instrument

mercado – market

Mesoamerica – a geographical region extending from central Mexico to northwestern Costa Rica

mestizo – person of mixed ancestry, usually Spanish and indigenous; see also *criollo* and *ladino*

metate – flat stone on which corn/maize is ground

migración – immigration; immigration office

milpa – cornfield

mirador – lookout

mola – colorful hand-stitched appliqué textile made by Kuna women

muelle – pier

municipalidad – town hall

museo – museum

Navidad – Christmas

oficina de correos – post office

ordinario – slow bus

paca – see *gibnut*

PADI – Professional Association of Diving Instructors

palacio de gobierno – building housing the executive offices of a state or regional government

palacio municipal – city hall; seat of the corporation or municipal government

palapa – thatched, palm-leaf-roofed shelter with open sides

Panamericana – see *Carretera Interamericana*

panga – small motorboat

parada – bus stop

parque – park; sometimes also used to describe a plaza

parque nacional – national park

peña – folkloric club; evening of music, song and dance

pensión – guesthouse

petén – island

playa – beach

pozo – spring

propina – tip; gratuity

pueblo – small town or village

puente – bridge

puerta – gate; door

puerto – port; harbor

pulpería – corner store; minimart

punta – point; traditional Garífuna dance involving much hip movement

quebrada – ravine; brook

quetzal – national currency of Guatemala, named after the tropical bird

rancho – thatched-roof restaurant

río – river

Ruta Maya – Maya Route, describing travels to the Maya sites of Mexico, Guatemala and Belize (chiefly), but also El Salvador and Honduras

s/n – sin número (without number); used in addresses

sacbé (pl **sacbeob**) – ceremonial limestone avenue or path between Maya cities

salida – exit

santo – saint

Semana Santa – Holy Week, the week preceding Easter

sendero – path or trail

sierra – mountain range; saw

stela, stelae – standing stone monument of the ancient Maya, usually carved

supermercado – supermarket; anything from a corner store to a large, Western-style supermarket

templo – temple; church

terminal de autobus – bus terminal

Tico/a – male/female inhabitant of Costa Rica

tienda – small shop

típica – see *típico*

típico – typical or characteristic of a region, particularly used to describe food; also a form of Panamanian folkloric music

traje – traditional handmade clothing

turicentro – literally 'tourist center'; outdoor recreation center with swimming facilities, restaurants and camping (El Salvador)

venado – deer; venison

verano – summer; Central America's dry season, roughly from mid-December to April

volcán – volcano

Zapatistas – members of the left-wing group Ejército Zapatista de Liberación Nacional (EZLN), fighting for indigenous rights in Chiapas, Mexico

FOOD & DRINK GLOSSARY

aguardiente – clear, potent liquor made from sugarcane; also referred to as *caña*

aguas de frutas – fruit-flavored water drink

batido – milkshake made with fresh fruit and milk or water

bocas – savory side dishes or appetizers

bolitas de carne – snack of mildly spicy meatballs

cafetería – informal restaurant with waiter service

cafetín – small *cafetería*

caña – see *aguardiente*

carne ahumada – smoked, dried (jerked) meat

ceviche – raw seafood marinated in lemon or lime juice, garlic and seasonings

chicha – heavily sweetened, fresh fruit drinks

chicharrón – pork crackling

cocina – literally 'kitchen'; small, basic restaurant, or cookshop, usually found in or near municipal markets

comedor – cheap, basic eatery, usually with a limited menu

comida a la vista – meal served buffet- or cafeteria-style

comida corriente or corrida; casado – set meal of rice, beans, plantains and a piece of meat or fish

comida típica – typical local-style meal or food

empanada – turnover stuffed with meat or cheese, baked or fried, sometimes with fruit filling as a dessert.

fritanga – sidewalk BBQ, widely seen in Nicaragua

gallo pinto – common meal of mixed rice and beans

garnaches – fried corn tortillas, served open faced or wrapped, with chicken, fish or beef, shredded cabbage and sometimes cheese

gaseosa – soft drink

guacamole – a dip of mashed or chopped avocados

guaro – local firewater made with sugarcane (Costa Rica)

horchata – sweet rice milk drink with cinnamon

huevos fritos/revueltos – fried/scrambled eggs

licuado – fresh fruit drink, blended with milk or water

menú del día – fixed-price meal of several courses

mondongo – tripe soup

pan de coco – coconut bread

panadería – bakery

patacones – fried green plantains cut in thin pieces, salted, pressed and then fried

plato del día – plate (or meal) of the day

pico de gallo – fresh salsa

pipa – coconut water, served straight from the husk

plátano maduro – ripe plantains baked or broiled with butter, brown sugar and cinnamon; served hot

plato típico – meal typical or characteristic of a place or region

pupusa – cornmeal pocket filled with cheese or refried beans, or a mixture of both (El Salvador)

raspados – shaved ice flavored with fruit juice

refresco – soda, or soft drink; in Costa Rica a drink made with local fruits

rellenitos – refried black beans in mashed plantain dumplings

ropa vieja – literally 'old clothes'; spicy shredded beef

rotisería – restaurant selling roast meats

salbutes – see *garnaches*

sancocho – a spicy stew usually made with chicken

seco – alcoholic drink made from sugarcane

soda – place that serves a counter lunch; soda or soft drink (Panama)

tamales – spiced ground corn with chicken or pork, boiled in banana leaves

tapado – rich Garífuna stew made from fish, shrimp, shellfish, coconut milk and plantain, spiced with coriander

tortilla de maíz – a fried cornmeal cake in Panama

vegetariano/a – male/female vegetarian

Behind the Scenes

SEND US YOUR FEEDBACK

We love to hear from travelers – your comments keep us on our toes and help make our books better. Our well-traveled team reads every word on what you loved or loathed about this book. Although we cannot reply individually to your submissions, we always guarantee that your feedback goes straight to the appropriate authors, in time for the next edition. Each person who sends us information is thanked in the next edition – the most useful submissions are rewarded with a selection of digital PDF chapters.

Visit **lonelyplanet.com/contact** to submit your updates and suggestions or to ask for help. Our award-winning website also features inspirational travel stories, news and discussions.

Note: We may edit, reproduce and incorporate your comments in Lonely Planet products such as guidebooks, websites and digital products, so let us know if you don't want your comments reproduced or your name acknowledged. For a copy of our privacy policy visit lonelyplanet.com/privacy.

OUR READERS

Many thanks to the travelers who used the last edition and wrote to us with helpful hints, useful advice and interesting anecdotes:

Alyne Francis, Antje Schoenborn, Bill Maryon, Brittany Lee Garcia, Gitte Taasti Jensen, Joe Tilley, Jon Wisloff, Jurriaan Witteman, Mark Van Laarschot, Marty Carey, Maximilian Cornelius, Melanie LaVita, Michael Weber, Nick Bel, Nicola Metcalfe, Payson Sheets, Ruben Swieringa, Saskia Boer, Selime Demirci, Shane McCarthy, Tobias Hammer.

WRITER THANKS

Ashley Harrell

Thanks to editor Alicia Johnson and co-author Paul Harding for being lovely to work with; Stacey Auch for the best road trip ever; David Roth for becoming a scuba diver; Richard Harrell for braving the Blue Hole; Ronni Harrell for letting Dad visit; Kat Marin for the good company and the help; Tacogirl for the invites and the floaties (sorry!); Kelly Samuels for the cookies and the good times; and Joanne Edwards for being a riot and pleasure to know.

Isabel Albiston

Thanks to the many Salvadorans who helped me on my travels. Your friendliness, patience and willingness to chat are greatly appreciated. My thanks in particular to Andrea Rivas, Elena Rivera, Tommie Jackson-Smith, Mauricio Herrera, Manolo Gomez, William, Roberto Moran, Rafael Rivas, Walter Segura, Carlos, Katy Hooper, Ian Louden, Tom Dukeson, Emma Englen, Nathaniel Perlow, Dave Mendez, Marbel Membreño, David Crowley and Francisco Mejia.

Ray Bartlett

Thanks first and always to my family and amazing friends for letting me go on these adventures and still remembering me when I get back. To the incredible Alicia Johnson, for the editorial wisdom and speedy answers when I needed them. To all people I met or who helped along the way, especially Virginia, Mereja, Nathalie, Valerie, Peggy, Marlon, Ismael, Jane, Kelsey, Stuart, Rachna, Flor, and so many others. Thanks so much. Can't wait to be back again soon.

Celeste Brash

Thanks to Honduras for helping me make some amazing friends on this trip. Especially to Howard, David Sedat and Anna Kaminski in Copan; Frony, Grethel and Angel in the mountains; Oto, Josue, Regina, Camille and the tourist office in Tegus; Bobby for all over the country; Jennifer, Patrice and Vania in Roatan; Jorge Salverri, Junior, Julia and boyfriend in Moskitia; John Depuis in La Ceiba and Frank in SPS. You are all amazing!

Paul Clammer

Muchas gracias to Valeria Ayerdi in Xela for friendship and advice on everything important, and to Natalia Pedermo Ayerdi – the coolest David Bowie fan in Guatemala. On the lake, thanks to Deedle and Dave Ratcliffe for the reassuring pots of tea. In Xela, cheers to Bryan Seibel, Mark Peacock and Josh Wood. In El Paredón to Sonal Amin of La Choza Chula, and in Antigua to Sunny Flores. In the Cuchumatanes, I could have had no better guide than Carlos Tucuxlopez – *gracias.* At Lonely Planet, thanks to Alicia Johnson, not least for the understanding when I was moving house (and country). Finally, thanks and love above all to Robyn, no matter which continent we end up on.

Steve Fallon

Muchísimas gracias to the folk who offered assistance, ideas and/or hospitality along the way, including fellow traveler/guide Juan José Calvache in the Darién; Reggie & Cherie Flagg in Panama City; and the boys on the boats in the San Blás islands: Adam Riley, Fabio Carino and Brett Dickey. *Y a mi querido Panamá – ¡el país que unió las dos mitades del mundo!* (And to my dear Panama – the country that united the world's two halves!) As always, my share is dedicated to my now spouse, Michael Rothschild.

Paul Harding

It was a pleasure to meet many wonderful people on my travels in Belize. Thanks for chats and advice to (among others) Deborah in Corozal, Jo and Caz in Punta Gorda and Daniel in San Ignacio. Thanks at Lonely Planet to Alicia Johnson and to my co-writer Ashley Harrell. Most of all thanks and hugs to Hannah and Layla at home for their patience and love.

John Hecht

Very special thanks to Jesus Navarrete, Ursula Reischl, Chicken Willy, Destination Editor Sarah Stocking, co-author Ray Bartlett and to all the *Quintanarroenses* for their generous support and the good times. As always, my heartfelt gratitude to Lau for taking care of the kitties and everything else.

Anna Kaminski

Huge thanks to Alicia Johnson for entrusting me with half of this beguiling country, and to everyone who has helped me along the way. In particular: Claudio in Managua; Brian in Ometepe; Jorge and Kristin in Granada; Helio in San Juan de Oriente; Catalina in Las Peñitas; John in León; plus Brett and Carol in San Juan del Sur and Granada for the company and research input.

Brian Kluepfel

Thank you to Paula Paz, my constant companion through good times and bad. To ace editor Alicia Johnson and wonderful Lonely Planet folks including Neill 'King of Malahide' Coen, Cheree Broughton, and the entire author support network. In Costa Rica, thanks to Wilfredo 'El Pollo' – a great birder and nicer person; Pippa of Bijagua; Carole of La Cruz; and Sonia Escalante, queen of La Fortuna; and the Tico bus system. Also, to anyone who answered their phones, Whatsapp chat, emails, or in some way helped me out.

Tom Masters

I was accompanied on a big chunk of my travels through Nicaragua by the imperturbable Rosemary Masters, who didn't allow civil strife to keep her away. Huge thanks also to Claudio Perez Cruz, Juana Boyd, Henry Soriano, Alex Egerton, Anna Kaminski, Salvador & Mina Acosta, Guillermo González Prado, Darling Rayo, Romain at Lighthouse, Teresa Mariscal, Leopoldo Flores Lovo and the various staff at *Hola Nicaragua*, Hotel Los Arcos in Estelí, Maria's B&B in Matagalpa and Hotel Casa Royale in Bluefields.

Carolyn McCarthy

Many thanks go out to the Bethels for accompanying me on part of my journey, and for Daniel and Marta for providing some much needed refuge. I am also grateful to Rick Morales, Beatriz Schmidt, Annie Young and Carla Rankin for sharing their insights and contacts. Many others provided assistance in the form of homemade hot sauce, police intervention and karaoke. Lastly, my thanks to the isthmus for offering up one more great, sparkling adventure. *Hasta la próxima.*

ACKNOWLEDGEMENTS

Climate map data adapted from Peel MC, Finlayson BL & McMahon TA (2007) 'Updated World Map of the Köppen-Geiger Climate Classification'; *Hydrology and Earth System Sciences*, 11, 1633–44.

Chichén Itzá illustrations pp62–3 and Tikal pp208–9 by Michael Weldon.

Cover photograph: Jungle river crossing, Uspantán region, Guatemala, Tolo Balaguer/Alamy ©

THIS BOOK

This 10th edition of Lonely Planet's *Central America* guidebook was researched and written by Ashley Harrell, Isabel Albiston, Ray Bartlett, Celeste Brash, Paul Clammer, Steve Fallon, Paul Harding, John Hecht, Anna Kaminski, Brian Kluepfel, Tom Masters and Carolyn McCarthy. Bridget Gleeson and Regis St Louis curated the Nicaragua and Panama chapters respectively.

This guidebook was produced by the following:

Destination Editors Alicia Johnson, Sarah Stocking

Senior Product Editor Saralinda Turner

Product Editor Rachel Rawling

Regional Senior Cartographer Corey Hutchison

Senior Cartographer Alison Lyall

Book Designer Jessica Rose

Assisting Editors James Bainbridge, Judith Bamber, Michelle Bennett, Katie Connolly, Samantha Cook, Peter Cruttenden, Andrea Dobbin, Emma Gibbs, Carly Hall, Gabrielle Innes, Lou McGregor, Alison Morris, Lauren O'Connell, Christopher Pitts, Ross Taylor, Fionnuala Twomey, Simon Williamson

Cover Researcher Brendan Dempsey-Spencer

Thanks to Hannah Cartmel, Grace Dobell, Bailey Freeman, Martine Power, Kirsten Rawlings, Vicky Smith

Index

Map Pages **000**
Photo Pages **000**

Map Pages **000**
Photo Pages **000**

Map Pages **000**
Photo Pages **000**

Map Pages **000**
Photo Pages **000**

Map Legend

Sights

- Beach
- Bird Sanctuary
- Buddhist
- Castle/Palace
- Christian
- Confucian
- Hindu
- Islamic
- Jain
- Jewish
- Monument
- Museum/Gallery/Historic Building
- Ruin
- Shinto
- Sikh
- Taoist
- Winery/Vineyard
- Zoo/Wildlife Sanctuary
- Other Sight

Activities, Courses & Tours

- Bodysurfing
- Diving
- Canoeing/Kayaking
- Course/Tour
- Sento Hot Baths/Onsen
- Skiing
- Snorkeling
- Surfing
- Swimming/Pool
- Walking
- Windsurfing
- Other Activity

Sleeping

- Sleeping
- Camping
- Hut/Shelter

Eating

- Eating

Drinking & Nightlife

- Drinking & Nightlife
- Cafe

Entertainment

- Entertainment

Shopping

- Shopping

Information

- Bank
- Embassy/Consulate
- Hospital/Medical
- Internet
- Police
- Post Office
- Telephone
- Toilet
- Tourist Information
- Other Information

Geographic

- Beach
- Gate
- Hut/Shelter
- Lighthouse
- Lookout
- Mountain/Volcano
- Oasis
- Park
- Pass
- Picnic Area
- Waterfall

Population

- Capital (National)
- Capital (State/Province)
- City/Large Town
- Town/Village

Transport

- Airport
- Border crossing
- Bus
- Cable car/Funicular
- Cycling
- Ferry
- Metro station
- Monorail
- Parking
- Petrol station
- Subway/Subte station
- Taxi
- Train station/Railway
- Tram
- Underground station
- Other Transport

Routes

- Tollway
- Freeway
- Primary
- Secondary
- Tertiary
- Lane
- Unsealed road
- Road under construction
- Plaza/Mall
- Steps
- Tunnel
- Pedestrian overpass
- Walking Tour
- Walking Tour detour
- Path/Walking Trail

Boundaries

- International
- State/Province
- Disputed
- Regional/Suburb
- Marine Park
- Cliff
- Wall

Hydrography

- River, Creek
- Intermittent River
- Canal
- Water
- Dry/Salt/Intermittent Lake
- Reef

Areas

- Airport/Runway
- Beach/Desert
- Cemetery (Christian)
- Cemetery (Other)
- Glacier
- Mudflat
- Park/Forest
- Sight (Building)
- Sportsground
- Swamp/Mangrove

Note: Not all symbols displayed above appear on the maps in this book

Tom Masters

Nicaragua Dreaming since he could walk of going to the most obscure places on earth, Tom has always had a taste for the unknown. This has led to a writing career that has taken him all over the world, including North Korea, the Arctic, Congo and Siberia. Despite a childhood spent in the English countryside, as an adult Tom has always called London, Paris and Berlin home. He currently lives in Berlin and can be found online at www.tommasters.net.

Carolyn McCarthy

Panama Carolyn McCarthy specializes in travel, culture and adventure in the Americas. She has written for *National Geographic, Outside, BBC Magazine, Sierra Magazine, Boston Globe* and other publications. A former Fulbright fellow and Banff Mountain Grant recipient, she has documented life in the most remote corners of Latin America. Carolyn has contributed to more than 40 guidebooks and anthologies for Lonely Planet, including Colorado, USA, Argentina, Chile, Trekking in the Patagonian Andes, Panama, Peru and USA National Parks guides. For more information, visit www.carolynmccarthy.org or follow her Instagram travels @mccarthyoffmap.

Regis St Louis

Regis grew up in a small town in the American Midwest – the kind of place that fuels big dreams of travel – and he developed an early fascination with foreign dialects and world cultures. He spent his formative years learning Russian and a handful of Romance languages, which served him well on journeys across much of the globe. Regis has contributed to more than 50 Lonely Planet titles, covering destinations across six continents. His travels have taken him from the mountains of Kamchatka to remote island villages in Melanesia, and to many grand urban landscapes. When not on the road, he lives in New Orleans. Follow him on www.instagram.com/regisstlouis. Regis contributed to the Panama chapter.